William Tolar

Proceedings in the case of the United States against Duncan G. McRae

William Tolar

Proceedings in the case of the United States against Duncan G. McRae

ISBN/EAN: 9783337143244

Printed in Europe, USA, Canada, Australia, Japan

Cover: Foto ©Andreas Hilbeck / pixelio.de

More available books at **www.hansebooks.com**

MILITARY COMMISSION.

PROCEEDINGS

IN THE

CASE OF THE

UNITED STATES

AGAINST

DUNCAN G. McRAE, WILLIAM J. TOLAR, DAVID WATKINS,
SAMUEL PHILLIPS AND THOMAS POWERS, FOR THE
MURDER OF ARCHIBALD BEEBEE AT FAYETTE-
VILLE, NORTH CAROLINA, ON THE 11TH
DAY OF FEBRUARY, 1867,

TOGETHER WITH THE

ARGUMENT OF ED. GRAHAM HAYWOOD,

SPECIAL JUDGE ADVOCATE,

IN REPLY TO THE

SEVERAL ARGUMENTS OF THE COUNSEL FOR THE DEFENCE.

COLONEL J. V BOMFORD, U. S. A., President of Commission.
MAJOR ROBERT AVERY, U. S. A., Judge Advocate.

Reported by Chas. Flowers and Chas. P. Young, Phonographic Reporters,
No. 119 West St., New York.

PUBLISHED FOR
ROBERT AVERY, U. S. A., Judge Advocate,
RALEIGH, N. C.

1867.

INDEX.

PROCEEDINGS

OF A

MILITARY COMMISSION,

CONVENED AND HELD AT RALEIGH, N. C., BY VIRTUE OF THE FOLLOWING

ORDER, VIZ:

HEADQUARTERS SECOND MILITARY DISTRICT.
CHARLESTON, S. C., JUNE 18TH, 1867.
SPECIAL ORDERS,
No. 75..

[Extract.]

* * * * * * *

II. A Military Commission is hereby appointed to meet at Raleigh, N. C., at 10. A. M., on the 24th of June inst., or as soon thereafter as practicable, for the trial of such prisoners as may be properly brought before it:

DETAIL FOR THE COMMISSION:

1. Colonel J. V. Bomford, 8th Infantry.
2. Bvt. Lieut. Col. Thos. P. Johnston, Capt. A. Q. M., U. S. V.
3. Capt. P. H. Remington, 8th Infantry.
4. 2d Lieut. C. E. Hargous, 40th Infantry.
5. 2d Lieut. Louis E. Granger, 40th Infantry.

Bvt. Maj. Gen. R. Avery, Major V. R. C., Judge Advocate.

The commission will sit without regard to hours.

* * * * * * *

By Command of
MAJOR GENERAL D. E. SICKLES:
J. W. CLOUS,
Capt. 38th U. S. Infantry,
A. D. C. and A. A. A. G.

Official:
J. W. CLOUS, Capt. 38th Infantry,
A. D. C. and A. A. A. G.

———

RALEIGH, N. C., July 22d, 1867.

The Commission met pursuant to the above order.

Present: Colonel J. V. BOMFORD,
8th Infantry,
Bvt. Lieut. Col. THOS. P. JOHNSTON,
Capt. A. Q. M. U. S. V.
Capt P. H. REMINGTON,
8th Infantry.
2d Lieut. C. E. HARGOUS,
40th Infantry.
2d Lieut. LOUIS E. GRANGER,
40th Infantry.
Bvt. Maj. Gen. R. AVERY,
Major V. R. C. Judge Advocate.

The Judge Advocate stated that he had been mustered out of his volunteer rank, and that his rank would hereafter appear of record, as 1st Lieut. 44th Infantry U. S. A.

The Judge Advocate then read the following extract from an official letter, addressed to the Judge Advocate, dated, Headquarters Second Military District Charleston S. C. 21st June 1867.

* * * * *

The Maj. General directs that you employ Ed. Graham Haywood to assist you in the prosecution of these cases * * * * *.

Which letter was signed.
J. W. CLOUS,
Capt. 38 Infantry, A. A. A. G.

Whereupon ED. GRAHAM HAYWOOD, Esq., Attorney and Counsellor at Law, was introduced as Counsel to assist the Judge Advocate in the prosecution. The Commission then proceeded to the trial of William J. Tolar, Duncan G. McRae, Thomas Powers, Samuel Phillips and David Watkins, otherwise called Monk Julia, all citizens of Cumberland County, in the State of North Carolina, who being called into the court, and having heard the order read, convening the Commission, were asked if they had any objection to any member named therein, to which they replied in the negative.

The members of the Commission were then severally, duly sworn by the Judge Advocate, and the Judge Advocate was then duly sworn by the President of the Commission, all of which oaths were administered in the presence of the accused, and Chas. Flowers was duly sworn by the Judge Advocate as Recorder of the Commission.

The accused here asked leave to introduce as their Counsel, Samuel F. Phillips and Richard Battle Esqrs. of Raleigh N. C. Thomas C. Fuller and James McRae, Esq., of Fayetteville, and Robert Strange Esq., of Wilmington N. C.

All Attorneys and Counsellors at Law which request was granted by the Commission, and they were duly introduced as Counsel for all the accused.

The Counsel for the accused, hereupon presented the following plea to the jurisdiction of the Commission.

UNITED STATES OF AMERICA,
District of North Carolina.

Duncan G. McRae, William J. Tolar, David Watkins, Samuel Phillips and Thomas Powers Defendants, Ats. of the United States of America Plaintiffs,

And the said Defendants in their own proper persons come in and defend the wrong, and pray judgement of the charge and specification, on the part of the prosecution, because they say that the crime with which they stand charged, was committed in the County of Cumberland, in the State of North Carolina, and that the Superior Court of Law for Said County, has full and complete jurisdiction of the said crime, charged against them; and because they say that this Court has not jurisdiction of the said crime. Whereupon they pray judgement whether the Court will further take cognizance of the said charge and specification &c.

The Commission was then cleared for deliveration, and after some time so spent was reopened, and the Judge Advocate announced that the Commission overruled the plea to its jurisdiction in this case.

The accused were then arraigned on the following charge and specification:

CHARGES AND SPECIFICATIONS PREFERRED AGAINST WILLIAM J. TOLAR, DUNCAN G. McRAE, THOMAS POWERS, SAMUEL PHILLIPS AND DAVID WATKINS, OTHERWISE CALLED MONK JULIA, ALL CITIZENS OF CUMBERLAND COUNTY IN THE STATE OF NORTH CAROLINA.

CHARGE—MURDER.

Specification:—In this that William J. Tolar, late of the County of Cumberland, in the State of North Carolina, Duncan G. McRae, late of the same place, Thomas Powers late of the same place, Samuel Phillips late of the same place and David Watkins, otherwise called Monk Julia, late of the same place, on the eleventh day of February in the year of our Lord one thousand eight hundred and sixty seven, at, and in the County of Cumberland aforesaid, in and upon one Archibald Beebee, a person of color otherwise called Archibald Warden, otherwise called Archy Beebee otherwise called Archy Warden, feloniously, wilfully, and of their malice aforethought did make an assault.

And that the said William J. Tolar, a, certain pistol, then and there charged with gunpowder and one leaden bullet, which said pistol, the said William J. Tolar, in his right hand then and there, had and held, then and there did discharge and shoot off, to, against, and upon the said Archibald Beebee otherwise called Archibald Warden, otherwise called Archy Beebee otherwise called Archy Warden, and the said William J. Tolar, with the leaden bullet aforesaid, out of the pistol aforesaid, then and there, by force of, the gunpowder aforesaid, by the said William J. Tolar, discharged and shot off as aforesaid, then and there did strike, penetrate, and wound the said Archibald Beebee, otherwise called Archibald Warden otherwise called Archy Warden otherwise called Archy Beebee, in and upon the left side of the head, of him, the said Archibald Beebee, otherwise called Archibald Warden, otherwise called Archy Beebee, otherwise called Archy Warden, near the back of the head of him the said Archibald Beebee, otherwise called Archibald Warden, otherwise called Archy Beebee, otherwise called Archy Warden, near the left ear of him the said Archibald Beebee, otherwise called Archibald Warden, otherwise called Archy Beebee, otherwise called Archy Warden, giving to him the said Archibald Beebee, otherwise called Archibald Warden, otherwise called Archy Beebee, otherwise called Archy Warden, then and there with the leaden bullet aforesaid, discharged and shot out of the pistol aforesaid by the force of the gunpowder aforesaid by the said William J. Tolar in and upon the left side of the head of him, the said Archibald Beebee, otherwise called Archibald Warden, otherwise called Archy Beebee, otherwise called Archy Warden, near the said back of the head of him the said Archibald Beebee, otherwise called Archy Beebee, otherwise called Archy Warden, near the

left ear of him, the said Archibald Beebee, otherwise called Archibald Warden, otherwise called Archy Beebee, otherwise called Archy Warden, one mortal wound of the depth of five inches, and of the breadth of half an inch, of which said mortal wound he the said Archibald Beebee, otherwise called Archibald Warden, otherwise called Archy Beebee, otherwise called Archy Warden, then and there instantly died.

And that the said Duncan G. McRae, Thomas Powers, Samuel Phillips, and David Watkins, otherwise called Monk Julia, then and there feloniously, wilfully, and of their malice aforethought, were present, aiding, abetting, comforting, assisting and maintaining the said William J. Tolar, in the felony and murder aforesaid, in manner and form aforesaid, to do and commit; and so that the said William J. Tolar, Duncan G. McRae, Thomas Powers, Samuel Phillips, and David Watkins, otherwise called Monk Julia, him the said Archibald Beebee, otherwise called Archibald Warden, otherwise called Archy Beebee, otherwise called Archy Warden, in the manner and by the means aforesaid, feloniously, wilfully, and of their malice aforethought, did kill and murder against the peace and dignity of the State of North Carolina, and of the United States of America.

All this at the Town of Fayetteville, in the County of Cumberland, in the State of North Carolina, on or about the eleventh day of February in the year of our Lord, one thousand eight hundred and sixty-seven.

ROBT. AVERY.
Maj. V. R. C. Bvt. Maj. Gen'l. Vol's.
Insp. B. R. F. & A. L. N. C.
Judge Advocate G. C. M.

Raleigh, N. C., May 21, 1867.

The charge and specification were then read aloud by the Judge Advocate.

The Judge Advocate then addressing the accused, said: You, William J. Tolar, Duncan G. McRae, Thomas Powers, Samuel Phillips and David Watkins, otherwise called Monk Julia, have heard the charge and specification preferred against you, how say you—Guilty, or not guilty? To which the accused, William J. Tolar, Duncan G. McRae, Thomas Powers, Samuel Phillips and David Watkins, otherwise called Monk Julia, pleaded as follows:

To the specification—not guilty.
To the charge—not guilty.

The Counsel for the accused, offered the following request, on behalf of Duncan G. McRae, one of the accused, viz:—That his case be severed, and he be put upon a separate trial, for the offence of which he is charged.

The Judge Advocate said: I object to the severance of this case from the others, for two reasons. 1st. That it is in the election of the Commonwealth to try him separately, if it so chooses, but that it will be a great expense to the government, and an unnecessary prolongation of this trial; and, secondly, that the crime was in the nature of a conspiracy, that the parties are jointly guilty, and that it would be necessary for a proper protection of the interests of the Government, that these cases should be tried together. There has been no cause shown why it should be done. The Court has heard no reasons given.

The Counsel for the accused then gave the following reasons:

May it please the Court:—The case in behalf of Mr. McRae is unconnected with a large portion of the case now before the Court. He was the examining magistrate, before whom the deceased had been brought for the purpose of investigating the offence with which he was charged. We understand that he was, and remained sitting at the place, occupied by him during that investigation; that he was not in the crowd or about the crowd. A great deal of the testimony that will be heard before the Court, involving these other persons, as we understand does not touch him at all; and we therefore thought it a case that appealed strongly to the discrimination of the Court, for allowing him to be judged without that sort of connection and complication with the case that may be made out against the others. We think it goes to complicate Mr. McRae unnecessarily, with the case that may be made out against these other parties. On that account it is a matter that appeals very strongly to the discrimination of the Court, to let him be heard alone. He was committing magistrate, he sat where he was sitting during the trial, when the homicide was committed; he is not charged on the ground that he was in the crowd at all, and he wishes, in favor of his life, and the serious charge that is brought against him, that he may be tried upon the facts as they appear against him alone, and not be mingled up, as he thinks he must be, by having his case heard at the same time, with the accusations against these other persons.

The Counsel for the Prosecution then offered the following remarks:

The Government of the United States, through its officials, has preferred a charge against these men jointly. The general practice in the Courts of law is for the Court not to allow a severance, where the prosecuting officer for the Government insists upon it that it is not necessary.—There are some very rare cases where, in spite of the opposition of the Government official, the Court will allow a severance, but the cases are very rare indeed. One instance suggests itself to my mind, and is a strong case, where the defence say that to defend one of their clients they will have to convict the others. That is a strong ground for a severance, and the Court, we think, will not hear to a severance, except it be for some such strong reason as that.

There was an important case which came before the Supreme Court of the United States, which I recall. The case I refer to was that of Marchant and Colson in the Supreme Court of the United States in the year 1827. Judge Strong gave the opinion —"Where two or more persons are jointly charged in the same indictment for a capital offence, they have not a right to be tried separately, without the consent of the prosecutor."

It has been stated by the gentleman who represents Mr. McRae in this case, that he was the committing magistrate, and occupied his seat until the perpetration of the murder. That remains to be proved, for it is alleged, by a part of the witnesses, that Mr. McRae left his seat, went out in the balcony in front of the house, and by his voice exhorted the crowd who were going on with the murderous deed.

If Mr. McRae's position be such as the Counsel have stated, he is not guilty at all, and I can't see any serious evil that can happen to him; why he cannot make his defense as completely if he be not guilty at all, in a joint trial, as if he were tried by himself. The complication does not involve him unless he made himself a party to what the others committed, and if he did make himself a party to what these virtual participators in the offence were guilty of, then it is necessary to prove their innocence in order to prove his. It seems to me to be one of those cases where the interest of the Govern-

ment demands that all of these parties be tried together. Therefore we insist upon it.

The objection of the Judge Advocate to the severance of the case of Duncan G. McRae was sustained by the Commission.

The Commission being ready to proceed with the examination of witnesses:

MATTHEW N. LEARY, jr., a witness for the prosecution, having been first duly sworn, testified as follows:

Examined by the Counsel for the prosecution. Q. What is your name? A. Matthew N. Leary, jr. Q. Where do you reside? A. In Fayetteville. Q. What is your occupation in Fayetteville? A. Saddle and harness maker was previous to the war. Since the war I have added to that a small grocery in the same building. A. Have you been a free man all your life? A. All my life, sir. Q. Where did you reside in the beginning of the year 1867? A. In Fayetteville. Q. Did you know one Archy Beebee there? A. I did sir, by sight. I knew him when I saw him. Q. Where is he now? A. Dead. Q. When was he killed? A. On the 11th of February. Q. What day of the week? A. Monday afternoon. Q. Where was he killed? At or near the South east corner of the market house. Q. Can you describe the market house in the town of Fayetteville so as to make the Court understand the locality? A. The market stands about the centre of the town, a street running each way. Q. There are four streets that terminate at the market house? A. Four streets, North, South, East and West, with an arch that passes right through from one side to the other. Q. An arch opening to each street? A. Yes sir, to each street. Q. What is the name of the street that runs West from the market house? A. Hay street. Q. What is the street that runs East? A. Person street. Q. What is the street that runs South? A. Gillespie street. Q. And North? A. Green street. Q. Those four streets terminate in the market house? A. Yes, sir. Q. And an arch opens upon each? A. Yes, sir. Q. You say this man was killed at what corner of the market house? A. At or near the South-east corner. Q. The South-east corner. A. Yes, sir. Q. What was the first time that day that you saw Archy Beebee? A. The first time I saw him was when the Sheriff and perhaps the Deputy were bringing him out. Q. Out of where? A. Out of the arch. Q. Which arch? A. The east arch. Q. How came you there? What did you come to the market house, for? A. I suppose curiosity took me there? Q. What excited your curiosity? A. This boy had been charged with an attempt of committing a rape, and notice was given that a hearing or trial would come off that afternoon. I suppose curiosity carried me to go and look at it. Q. You went up to hear something of the trial? A. Yes, sir. Q. The boy, when you got there, was coming out of the arch? A. No sir. When I first saw him I had been there some ten or twenty minutes before he come down the arch. The notice was given, or I heard some one say he was coming, when I noticed him. Q. You are certain you had been there ten or twenty minutes before he came down the arch? A. Yes Sir. Q. How far were you standing from the arch? A. When he came. Q. Yes? A. I suppose about 10 or 12 feet. Q. Square in front of it? A. I was standing to one side, rather facing the arch, between the arch and the corner. Q. Was the arch nearer touching you to the left or right? A. The arch. I was in the centre. Q. Were you nearer to the left hand or right hand? A. Perhaps nearer the right hand side. Q. Ten or twelve feet in front, towards the right hand side a little? A. Yes Sir. Q This ten or twenty minutes that you speak of, were you standing at the same spot? A. About the same spot. Q Did you see any of the prisoners at the bar? A. Yes Sir. Q. At the market house before Bebee made his appearance? A. I saw one of them. Q. Which one? A. Tolar. Q. You saw Mr. Tolar there before you saw Bebee? A. Yes Sir, Q. Did you see any of the others? A. I don't recollect distinctly. Q. What was Mr. Tolar doing when you saw him? A. He was standing upon the pavement near the arch on the east side of the market house. Q Was he saying or doing anything? A. Nothing at all that I could see sir. Q. How many men were gathered at the market house, during these ten or twenty minutes that you were standing there, before Beebee made his appearance? A. There was a good large crowd, I suppose between one and two hundred. Q. Was the crowd increasing or growing less while you stayed there? A. Increasing Sir. Q. Was there any disturbance, or noise or threats, or anything of the sort? A. Nothing that I heard, Q. The crowd was quiet was it? A. Yes Sir. Q Was Mr. Tolar standing alone, or was some one near him? A There were a good many standing around there, I don't recollect who. Q Do you recollect who was standing nearest him? A. No Sir Q Did you see any persons there with arms that day? A. I did Sir, Q During the ten or twenty minutes you were there before you saw Bebee? A. No sir. I did not Q You saw none there with arms? A. No Sir I did not. I saw no arms there. Q You say there was a crowd of a hundred or more? A Perhaps between one and two hundred persons. It might have been more. Q. Did it vary at different times; sometimes more and sometimes less? A. They seemed to be gathering. Q Never growing less? A. No Sir. I don't suppose it did Q Finally you saw Beebee make his appearance at the east end of the market house, in charge of Mr. Wemyss and Mr. Hardie? A. Yes Sir. Q. What occurred then? A. There was a rush made at that time in the rear and at the left side. Q. By whom? A. By the parties standing there, I could not designate who they were, it seemed to be the crowd that was gathered there. Q Was there any cry? A. There was a cry from the Sheriff, saying—I don't recollect whether it was " quit " or "don't men," It was either "quit" or don't men." Q. Did you hear any other exclamations? A. None at all Sir. Q Did you see Mr. Tolar in the crowd at that time? I did not Sir. Q. Did you see any of these other prisoners? A. I don't recollect seeing them. Q. Do you know these prisoners personally, all of them? A. Yes Sir. Q. What happened then? A. They passed on, to or near the south east corner of the market house, and when they made a rush this man Be bee seemed to fall, or go down, and as he rose, or in attempting to rise, a pistol was fired. Q. Did you see the pistol fired? A. I did Sir, Q. Did you see it distinctly? A. I did Sir, Q. Did you see who held it? A. I Did Sir Q. Who fired it? A. Mr. Tolar. Q. Have you any doubt about it? A. None in the least. Q Were you standing on the pavement out side of the market house? A. Yes Sir. Q You say he stumbled, and partly or wholly the prisoner fell? A. He appeared to go down Sir, Q And as he rose, you say, he was fired upon? A. Yes Sir. Q You saw the pistol in the hand of Mr. Tolar. A. Yes Sir. Q. Did you see the negro fall, Beebee? Yes Sir. Q. And when the shot was fired was the back of his head or front of his face towards it? A. Tolar was standing rather behind in t e rear, to the left, Q. Did you see the man Beebee after he fell? A. No

Sir, I did'nt just then; after that I went off, I went out to my establishment, and afterwards I came back and saw him. Q Did you see what became of Mr. Tolar after he fired the pistol? A. Mr. Tolar went, as well as I can recollect in towards the arch on the east side of the market house. Q. Was that immediately after he fired? A. Immediately afterwards. Q At that time did you see any of these other prisoners at the bar? A I don't recollect seeing them Sir. Q. Did you hear any other exclamations or outcries, from any portion of the crowd? A That evening? Q. Yes Sir. A. I did not Sir. Q From the position which you occupied could you see the windows of the Town Hall over the market house? A. I cannot say, as to that Sir; I might possibly have seen them. Q Is there any porch or balcony outside? A. There is a balcony on the outside, perhaps that might have cut off the sight. Q There is a balcony on the outside? A. Yes Sir. Q. On which end of the market house? A. On the east and west end. Q. Did you look into that balcony at all that day? A. No Sir. Q. Can you say whether any one was in or was not in it? A. I cannot Sir, Q. How close were you to Mr Tolar when he fired the pistol? A. I may perhaps have been between three and five feet. Q Nearer than you are to me? A. Yes Sir Q. As near as you are to the gentleman next to you? A. No Sir, he was perhaps further off than that, about as near as the second gentleman. (about four feet.) Q. You were that close to Mr. Tolar when you saw the pistol fired? A Yes Sir Q What did he do with the pistol after it was fired? A. I did'nt notice. Q. Were you alarmed? A I was somewhat alarmed at it Sir, in fact I turned off immediately afterwards and went down to my establishment. I did'nt remain there in the crowd.

Cross examined by the Counsel for the accused.

Q What did you say your business was? A Saddle and Harness making is my trade, but in addition to that I have added a grocery: I carry on a small grocery business in the same building. Q. How far is your establishment from the market house. A. I suppose it may be perhaps about two hundred yards, I wont say positive. Q Two hundred yards from the southeastern side? A. From East side, sir. Q On what street are you? A On the South side of Person street. Q. You say as soon as the affair took place you went down to your establishment? A. I went down to my establishment. Q. How long was it after that before you saw Beebee? A. Perhaps it may have been half an hour, sir; I would not say positive, between a quarter and a half an hour. Q Did I understand you to say you don't know whether you could or could not have seen the upper windows of the market house from where you were standing? A. You did, sir. Q You did'nt see anybody on the balcony? A. I did not. sir. Q. You heard no cry in the crowd at the time Beebee was shot? A. None but what was made by the Sheriff, sir. Q. You heard nobody say anything in the crowd but what was said by Sheriff Hardie? A. That was all I heard, sir, Q. You say you did'nt see Mr. Phillips there? A. I don't recollect seeing him there. Q Or Monk? A. I don't recollect. Q. Or Tolar? A. I saw Mr. Tolar. Q Mr. Powers? A. I don't recollect seeing him. Mr. Tolar, you say, you were from three to five feet from? A Between three and five feet, I would not say positive what the distance was. Q. How far was it from where you were standing to where Beebee fell? A. It may have been, perhaps ten or twelve feet, I could not say positive how far. Q. It could not have been as much as twenty feet? A. O, no! I don't know whether it could have been ten. Q. How near did you say Tolar was to Beebee when he shot? A. Well, I suppose Tolar must have been the same distance that he was from me, about. Q From three to five feet? A. Yes, sir, three to six or somewhere near that. Q. Were you standing on the sidewalk or on the street? A. On the street, sir. Q Is the side walk raised? A. Yes, sir. Q. How much? A. Well, I can't say how much, about eight or ten inches, I suppose. Q Were there any persons between you and Beebee at the time he was shot? A. There was Mr. Tolar a little to the left, between me and Beebee. Q Was there any other person in the crowd between you and Beebee at the time he was shot? A. There may possibly have been. Q Did you have a clear view of Beebee? A. I could see nothing when he raised up but his head. Q. Could you see him when he fell? A. I saw him go down, I could not see him after he fell. Q. What prevented you from seeing him after he went down? A. There was, perhaps, persons in front—the crowd moving. Q. Enough of persons to prevent you from seeing him? A I could see him when he was standing up. Q I understand you to say that as he stood you saw him distinctly? A. Yes, sir, that is, I could see the upper portion of his body. Q. From the shoulders up? A. Yes, sir. Q. How tall a man was Beebee? A. Well, I can't say how tall he was, perhaps he may have been a man of my height. Q You were very well acquainted with him, were you not? A I knew him by sight. Q Was he a drayman in your town? A. I think he was said to have been, sir. Q. You had seen him on the street frequently? A. Yes, sir. Q Was he particularly tall? A. Well, I can't say that he was. Q. A man of ordinary height? A. He may have been a man six feet high, or five feet ten, or five feet eight or ten, something like that. Q. Was he a taller man than the Sheriff? A. Well. I can't say that he was. Q Did the Sheriff have hold of him? A. I think he did. Q. Did you observe how they appeared as they stood together? A I think the Sheriff was on the left hand side of Beebee. Q On the left side? A. As well as I can recollect, sir Q You say that when the deceased fell down he fell for some reason, you don't know what? A. Yes, sir, he appeared to fall. Q. As he fell you did not see him? A No, sir. Q You saw him as he stood up—there were quite a number of persons between you and him, were there not? A. I don't know that there was, there must have been some persons. Q. Enough to prevent you from seeing him? A. Yes, sir, when he went down. Q. There were a number of persons between you, could not see any part excepting his head and shoulders when he stood up? A. Well, I could see his body down some distance. Q How far down did he go when he fell? A. I don't know, I could not say how far down he went, sir. Q But when he went down you did'nt see him? No, sir, I did'nt see him. Q. Don't your recollection serve you now that there was quite a number of persons between you and him when he fell? A. There were some persons standing between us I don't know how many. Q And you think you were ten or twelve feet from him? A. Yes, sir. Q. You say there were one or two hundred persons and the crowd was gathering? A. Yes, sir. Q Were they all white persons, or all colored, or mixed—the greater part of the crowd consisted of what color? A. I can't say as to that. Q A large crowd there of both colors? A. Yes, sir. Q. You went there out of curiosity? A. Yes, sir. Q. You heard that they had Beebee up, and I understood you to say they found him guilty? A. No, sir. Q You were there ten or twenty minutes before he came out? I suppose about that time. Q And during that time this mixed crowd was gathering, you say, and when Beebee come down stairs Captain

Tolar was standing by the arch? A No, sir, I did'nt say about the time he came down, I said when I went there, not at the time he came down —when I got there, or shortly after I saw Captain Tolar standing there. Q. And when Beebee came down did you see him at all? A. See Tolar? I did'nt see him till I saw him with a pistol, sir. Q. Did you see who they were in the crowd that rushed at Bebee when he came down, when the Sheriff said "don't" or something of the kind? A I did'nt see who they were, sir. Q. Were they white men or colored men rushed at him? A. It was white men. Q. You saw them? A. Yes, sir. Q You did'nt see any colored men? A. I saw no colored men, Q. What white men? A. I could not say who the men was. Q Did nt you know the crowd? A. I did nt, sir; that is I might have known them if it had been on any other occasion Q. Were they citizens of Fayetteville? A. I guess they generally were, sir. Q. You keep a grocery there; you are also a saddler; pretty well acquainted with them in the town? A, Yes, sir, very well. Q. Raised there? A. Yes, sir. Q. You say you don't recall any man's face that was there, except Mr. Tolar's? A. I don't recall any sir. Q. How long after this affair were you examined about it first? A. Soon after which affair. Q. How soon after Bebee was killed were you first examined about it? A. This is the first examination. Q. You have never been before the Government? A. No sir. Q. You have never been sworn before? A. No sir. Q. Did you ever talk about it to any officers before this? A. I don't recollect speaking to any of the officers sir, I spoke to my father about it, that evening perhaps, and to my brother, and some others in the shop. Q The reason why I asked you was to see why it is that you didn't recollect any other face that was there. If your attention was called to the transaction shortly after. I suppose you might have recollected some faces besides that of Captain Tolar. I asked you whether you were examined before any official authority of State or Government, shortly after that, you were not, you say? A. Not at all. Q. And you say you have no means of recalling any other face that was there? A. I can't recall any face that was there except Captain Tolar's. Q. Do you recollect any colored persons that were there? A. Well I recollect one, by the name of Simmons, Robert Simmons. Q. Any body else? A. Well, I can't say that I do. Q. Were you not considerably frightened? A. Well, I was right smart excited. Q. Were you not excited when the crowd made the rush? A. That was the time. Q. You became very much excited when the crowd made the rush? A. Well I became flushed over it a little, because I hadn't expected anything of the kind to occur. Q. Did the crowd rush at him angrily? A. Yes sir. Q. White men did? A. They were white sir. Q. He said nothing? A. I didn't hear anything sir. Q. You saw but one pistol? A. That was all sir. Q That was in Captain Tolar's hand? A. Yes, sir. Q. Was Captain Tolar standing on the side walk? A. No sir, he was in the street, standing outside of the side walk. Q. And the Sheriff was between him and the prisoner, that is between him and Beebee—Sheriff Hardie? A. The Sheriff was on the left of Beebee. Q. And Tolar was in the street? A. Tolar was in the rear rather to the left. Q. Tolar was in the rear, and rather to the left? A. Yes, sir. Q. And you saw him fire? A. Yes, sir. Q. Did you see him draw the pistol? A. I did, sir. Q. What kind of a pistol? A. It looked to me, like what they call one of these repeaters. Q. What kind of a repeater? A. Well I can't say: it was a pistol about a foot long, I suppose it was sir, it might have been a little longer. Q. What they call a

Navy revolver. A. Something of that kind. Q. You think it was a Navy revolver. A. I can't say for certain. Q. You are not sufficiently familiar with these weapons to say whether it was a Navy revolver or not? A. No, sir. Q. But it was a weapon about a foot long? A. Yes, sir. Q. Did any body take hold of Beebee that you saw, except the Sheriff? A. Well, I can't say. Q. Was there any guard there except the Sheriff? any body in whose charge Beebee was except the Sheriff? A. He came out between the Sheriff and Mr. Wemyss. Q You don't know anything more about it than that? A. No, sir. Q. Did I understand y u to say that Tolar was rather to your left, between you and the prisoner, was he exactly between you and the prisoner? A. He was rather to my left, at the time the pistol fired he was, sir. Q Tolar was in the street? A. Yes, sir. Q. This man Beebee was on the side walk? A. Yes, sir. Q. And it was just as the man rose Tolar shot him? A. Yes, sir, just as his head came up in the attempt to rise, a pistol fired. And thereupon Tolar went in under the arch? A. He went either in or towards the arch, sir. Q. That is, he went a little back? A. Yes sir, he turned back. Q. What time did you leave? A. I left directly after that. Q. Just then? A. Yes, sir. Q. Did you walk? A. Yes, sir. Q. You didn't run? A. No, sir. Q. You walked away? A. Yes, sir. Q. I understand you to say, that during the ten or twenty minutes you were there, before B ebee appeared, there was no talking? A. No, sir. Q. Nothing said by anybody? A. No, sir. Q. You said nothing yourself? A. No, sir. Q. Just stood there watching, out of curiosity to see what would be done? A. Yes, sir. Q. How long did they have Beebee up there before they brought him down? A. I don't r-collect, sir. Q. You had'nt seen him before that day? A. No. sir. Q. Was there any outcry made there to rescue Beebee from the Sheriff, by anybody, to take him away out of the custody of the Sheriff? A. Nothing more than I might judge from that rush, sir. Q. Any attempt on the part of colored persons there? A. None at all, sir. Q. No attempt at all? A. Nothing of the kind that I saw.

Examination resumed by the Counsel for the prosecution.

Q. Mr. Leary, when Mr. Tolar fired the pistol, did he say anything? A. I did'nt hear him say anything. I don't recollect anything being said. Q. Did he make any movement? Did you see him move at the time? A. He turned back from where he was standing. Q. The Counsel for the prisoners has asked you whether you heard anything said, while you were there the ten or twenty minutes which you mentioned? A. Nobody said a word. Q. Do you mean there was no talking? A. There may have been some talking, Q. No talking connected with this affair? A. That is what I supposed he meant.

The Counsel for the accused——That is what I meant.

Q. This crowd you speak of—were they inside of the market house? A. I can't say as to that sir. Q. Did you see whether there was any ins de of the Market house. A. I don't recoll ct seeing them Q. Was there any crowd at the west end of the market nouse? A I can't say sir; I did'nt notice sir; I was not around there.

JOHN ARMSTRONG, a witness for the prosecution, having been first duly sworn, testified as follows:

Questioned by the Counsel for the prosecution.

Q. What is your name witness? A. John Armstrong is my name sir. Q. Where do you live? A. In Fayetteville. Q. How long have you lived there sir? A. I have been living there sometime.

I was raised within ten miles of Fayetteville. At one time I was in Alabama a while. Q. Have you been living in Fayetteville for several years? A. Yes, sir. Q. Were you there at the commencement of this year? A. Yes, sir. Q. Were you a free man before the war? A. No sir. Q. What was y ur occupation at the beginning of this year ? A. I was was running on the railroad. Q. What railroad? A. Western. Q Did you know Archy Bebee? A. Yes, sir. Q. When did you see him last? A. I saw him the evening before they took him from the market house, after he was killed ; I never went to his burying. Q When did you last see him alive? A. On the 11th of Febuary, I think it was; in the afternoon. Q. The 11th of Fet ruary this year? A. Yes, sir. Q. What time in the afternoon was it? A. I could not say—it was somewhere about three o'clock, sir ; after three o'clock. Q. Do you remember what day of the week it was? A It was on Monday even ng. Q. On Monday evening, the 11th of February, af- ter three o'clock you saw him alive? A. Yes, sir. Q Where was it you saw him? A. When they carried him up stairs in the mar et, and I saw him when they fetched him down. Q. Where is the guard house; what street is it on? A. I am not able to tell you sir. Q· What direction does it run from the market house? A. Coming from Campbellton bridge, it is on the left. Q. Does the street run north or south? A. It runs south. Q. This guard house is on a street that runs south from the market house? A. Yes, sir. Q. On which side of the street is it, as you go from the market house? A. On the left hand side as you come down sir. Q. How many doors is it along that street fi om the market house ? A. I am not able to say. Q. Did'nt you say it was on the street that runs s uth from the market house? A. Yes, sir. Q. Which end of the block is it nearest to, the market end or the other end? A. The other end. Q. Nearest the southern end of the block, on the left hand side of the way? A. Yes, sir. Q. Did you see Becbee when the was brought out of the Guard House? A. Yes, sir. Q How came you there that day? A. On my way from dinner, Ned B ebee— Q. You must not tell what he said ; you were at dinner, and in con- sequence of something you heard, some conversa- tion that occurred there, you w nt to the market house? A. Yes, sir. Q. D d you notice any ex- citement or not? A. Yes, sir. Q. You had come down wh t street to go to the market house? A. Hay street. Q. Hay street, is that the street that runs west from the market house? A. Yes, sir. Q. You were coming down that street that runs w st from the market house, after 3 o'clock in the afternoon; did you hear or notice anything un- usual? A. I saw a good ma y passing, and I saw some young boys had pistols. I was coming down the street, paying very little attention to them, but I saw there was a great excitement on the street. Q. You saw several young boys with pistols on Hay street? A. Yes, sir. Q. And you noticed an excitement among the gentlemen, what sort of an excitement? A. There was a sort of a crowd, more than I generally saw. Q. What did you see, anything except the crowd? A. No, sir. Q. Any greater crowd in the street than usual? A. Yes, sir, a great deal more than I had been given to see. Q. You say you noticed more per- sons than usual, and several boys with pistols? A. Yes, sir. Q. Did you see any men with pis- tols? A. Yes, sir. Q. Who did you see? A. I saw none until I got to the market house, I saw two boys have a pistol in the street. Q. You saw no pistols till you got to the market house, except these two boys? A. No, sir, one was Mr. Lind- ley's son, and one Mr. Blake's. A. Do you know

came out of the door or afterwards? Before Q How was he brought down? A Sheriff Hardie, after the ladies passed down was the first person that came through the door? Q Wait a moment During the time that you were standing about the market house, when this crowd was underneath there, did you see any body with weapons? A Yes Sir. Q Who? A' I saw Mr Ed Powers have a pistol. Q Was he in the crowd? A He was under the market house, Q Ho was one of the men who whispered to Captain Tolar? A Yes Sir, he whispered to Captain Lolar? Q Where did he have that pistol? A He had it in his belt Sir, Q What sort of a pistol was it? I cannot tell Did you see any one else with a pistol? I saw Mr Sam Phillips, he came down from towards his store and had a small pistol in his hand, When was that before Beebee came down stairs? Yes Sir, Before he came down stairs you saw Mr Sam Phillips have a pistol in his hand? Yes Sir, a small pistol, Where- was he? He was standing in the street, Was he talking to any one? He was not saying nothing to no one at all, You saw Hall and Ed Powers and Sam Phillips with pistols? Yes Sir, Was Sam Phillips with these others? No Sir, not at all, He was outside of the market house? Yes Sir, Did you see any one else with pistols or weapons of any sort? Yes sir, I saw Tom Powers with a knife. What sort ot a knife? About as long as my hand. The knife was about ten inches long, was it? I suppose it was. Did you see any one else with weapons? I saw Mr Monk Julia have a knife. Monk had a knife? Yes Sir, When you saw Powers with a knife. was it open or shut? It was open. Was it in his hand? Yes Sir, Was that during the time when you were standing near the arch ot the market house, and Beebee was up stairs? Yes Sir, Was it during the time that this whispering was going on? Yes Sir. At the same time, did Monk have his knife, at the same time, a Yes Sir, You say Sheriff Hardie was the first one that appeared in front of the prisoner? Yes Sir, Who came next? Sheriff Hardie came and stood on the steps, and then went back, and then Mr Faircloth came out and stood on the steps; and the next thing I saw was Mr Wemyss and Archy, and I am not able to say which side Mr Hornrine came down, but he 'was in company with them, You say first Sheriff Hardie came out, and then Hardie went back, then the prisoner appeared? Sheriff Hardie appeared right before the prisoner, and Mr Wemyss. he had him fastered by the thumb, On the right hand of Beebee, or the left? On his right, Who else was there? Hornrine, Did you see whether he had the prisoner? I dont know that he had hold of him at all, I think Mr Faircloth reached back and got him by one arm, Which arm was it? His left arm. Q What occurred then? A As they got down the steps ———. Q. How many steps is it from the door down to the noor? A I am not able to say how many steps it is, I never counted them. Q Can't you come somewhere near it? A I would not wish to tell anything I don't know. Q Was it a hundred? A No, sir. Q It was not a hundred? A No, sir. Q Was it fifty? A I am not able to say sir. Q Can't you say whether it was fifty or not? *No, sir. Q Don't you know there were not fifty steps? A There might be, I never counted them, I like to tell that I know. Q Don't you know there was not fitty? A No, Sir. Q The witness seems to think that it is improper for him to testify about the number of steps unless he has counted them. That is not so at all; it makes no difference whether there are ten or five or a dozen; so that we can get some sort of an opinion. You don't preten! to say how many steps there were then? A. No, sir. Q Down the steps

they came; what happened then? did anything happen before they got to the bottom of the steps? A No. sir, about the time they got off the steps Mr. Monk Julia ran up with his knife. Q Did he say anything? A Yes, he said, "Give me up that negro, I intend to have him." Q Monk Julia said that, "give me up that negro, I intend to have him?" A Yes sir, and he struck at the prisoner; and then Mr. Tom Powers come up and as they neared the arch he rushed up, and grabbed the prisoner with his left hand, in the collar, and cut at him with his knife. Q Did he say anything? A He said "I remand the prisoner." Q Do you know whether he said, "demand," or "remand?" A He said "I remand this prisoner." Q He grabbed at him with one hand and cut at him with the other? Yes, sir. That was Thomas Powers? Yes, sir. Did he and Monk Julia rush up almost at the same time, or at the same time? I didn't see Monk Julia at that time; they shoved him off. He was the first man that struck? Yes, sir. What did he say? He said, "I intends to have the prisoner." Did he have his knife? Yes sir, and some one pulled him off. Who was it? I am not able to say. In the meantime in the arch stood Tom Powers? Yes, sir. And came back to the steps, and stood at the foot of the stairs, and he demanded the prisoner, or remanded the prisoner? Yes sir. And struck at him with his knife? Yes, sir. And the Sheriff did what? Shoved him off and said "it is my prisoner," and Mr. Powers said, "it is my prisoner, and I be damned if I don't intend to have him, give him up." Mr. Powers said, "he is my prisoner, and I be damned if I don't intend to have him?" Yes, sir. He wanted the Sheriff to give him up and the Sheriff told him he would not, and he shoved him back again? Yes, sir. Well, what happened then? Captain Tolar come shoving in, this way (with his hands before him as if parting the crowd.) What become of the prisoner at this time? When Mr. Powers cut at him the second time he fell. Mr. Powers cut at him the second time? was that inside of the market house? Outside, in the street. It was outside of the market? Yes, sir. Powers was just ou side of the arch? Yes sir, right at the edge of the arch. How many steps did Beebee go from the arch before he fell? I don't suppose he got more than one or two steps before he fell. Then Powers was standing right at the arch, was Beebee moving along all the while, towards the guard house? Yes, sir. Q And Mr. Powers, made a second move to cut him again, after he got out of the arch? A Yes, sir. Q He made the first move just as he turned the arch? A Yes, sir. Q And he made the second attempt after he got out? A. Yes, sir. Q Did you see Monk Julia at that time? A No sir, I didn't see him at that time. Q What happened then? did you hear any outcry in the crowd at all? A Yes, I heard some man say "shoot, shoot, shoot the damned son of a bitch, or he will get clear!" Q How many voices did you hear say that? A I heard one. Q Did you hear more than one? A There might have been different voices. Q How many times was it repeated? A I heard the word once or twice "shoot! shoot!" Q Was there any other outcry in the crowd that you heard? A No sir. I don't know that there was. Q Was the crowd pressing Be-bee all the while? A Yes, sir. Q How far were you from the point where the prisoner was first assaulted with a knife? A I suppose I was not more than ten feet, sir. Q In front of the East end of the market house? A Yes sir. After Powers made this second attempt with his knife, what occurred? Captain Tolar, he came up, and shoved the crowd back, or aside, and he sort of stepped back, right opposite me, and he had on a large shawl. Did he say anything as he came forward? No sir; he only waved his hands back. You are certain he didn't say anything? If he did I didn't hear him. He come forward, pressing his way through the crowd, did he? Yes sir. Did he use his hands before him? Yes sir. He shoved the gentleman aside by both hands? Yes sir, and as they got up right opposite me, he drawed a pistol. Did he have to take his hands back and draw the pistol? Yes sir. You say he had a shawl on; was it thrown over both shoulders? Yes sir. Did he draw his pistol from under his shawl? Yes sir, from under his shawl, and then he throwed his left hand on some one's shoulder. Who did he place his hands upon? I am not able to say. Was he a gentleman in front of him? Yes, sir. He just throwed his left hand that way (representing) and drawed his pistol from under his shawl, and held it up, I reckon, near a minute, till he got it right, and shot him. Did you see Captain Tolar shoot Beebee? I did, sir. Have you any doubt about it? No sir, I have no doubt about it; I saw him with all my eyes. You saw him? Yes sir. That day? Yes sir. Was there any other pistol fired there that day? No sir, I never heard nary other. And you say Captain Tolar made his way through the crowd, and drew this pistol from under his shawl? Yes sir. Put his left hand upon a man's shoulder, who was in front of him, and extending the pistol, fired? Yes sir. Did Beebee fall? Yes sir. Was his face towards Captain Tolar? His back was turned toward him. What did Captain Tolar do then? I said to him "There, Captain, you have killed that poor man." You said "There Captain, you have killed that poor man?" Yes sir. You spoke to him? Yes sir. Is that the man? Yes sir. You spoke to him and told him he had killed that man? Yes sir, and he aimed to conceal the pistol under his arm, where he had taken it from; he made a flirt, and he throwd his shawl in my face, and when I got the shawl out of my face I saw the pistol pass out of the crowd. Who did you see it in the hands of? I saw Ed Powers and Sam Hall have it. The shawl was flirted in your face and as soon as you could see, you noticed what? I saw the pistol was not in Tolar's hands, and Ed Powers had one. Was it the same one? I am not able to say it was the same pistol. Did it look like the same pistol? Yes, sir. Who did Ed Powers pass it to? Sam Hall. Did you see who he passed it to? Mr. Lutterloh's son, Ralph. Was it going further from the prisoner Tolar, all the time? Yes, sir, it was going from Mr. Tolar all the time. Did you see who Ralph Lutterloh passed it to? No, sir, I did'nt pay any attention; the crowd was very thick. Did you see any of these other prisoners about that time? a After the firing of the pistol? Yes. I saw Mr. Sam Phillips. Well what was he doing? He had a pistol in his hand. The one you first saw him with? Yes, sir. How close was he standing to Tolar? When he fired he was on my left, and Mr. Tolar was on my right. You were between them? Yes, sir. Sam Phillips had a pistol, on your left? Yes, sir. How close was he to the deceased man Beebee? He was some distance from him, sir. How far? a I reckon about ten or twelve feet. Was he further from him than Tolar was? Yes, sir.

Tolar was nearer to the deceased man than Phillips? I dont suppose Tolar was more than two steps from the deceased. What was Phillips doing with this pistol; did you see him before or after Tolar fired? Both before and after. Immediately after, and immediately before? Yes, sir. What was he doing with the pistol? He was not doing anything with it; he had it laying in his hand, and held his hand shut up on it. Did he have it in both hands? In one hand, laying in the other, and his hand was shut up on it. Did he say anything? No, sir, I never heard him speak to no one. Phillips you say said nothing? No, sir, I never heard him say a word. Do you mean he did'nt say anything to any one? He may, sir, but I did'nt hear him. He said nothing that you heard? No, sir. After this what became of Tolar? Captain Tolar walked back, stood a little while, and then went off. In what direction? Under the arch. Under the arch at the East end of the market house? Yes, sir. Did he disappear in that arch then? Yes, sir, he went through, the arch, and went and stood up at Mr. Hinsdale's shop. Where is Mr. Hinsdale's shop? It is West from the market house. You go out of the West end of the market house to go to it? Yes, sir. Is it on the left or right as you go out? On the left. Is it the first house on the corner? Yes, sir. It is the first house on the corner, on your left as you go out at the Western arch? Yes, sir. Did you see him go any further? I saw him start with one of the Boons; I dont know which one it was; I know it was one of the Boons. Did you see what became of Tom Powers? No, sir, I did'nt see him after Sheriff Hardie thrust him back. Did you see anything of what became of Monk Julia? Yes, sir. Did you see him after the prisoner fell at all? Yes, sir. What happened then? He made an attempt to get at him. He said he wanted to cut off his head to carry it down to Campbelton with him. He said he wanted to cut off his head to carry it down to Campbelton with him? Yes, sir. Was the deceased dead at that time? I reckon he was dead. How long after he was shot? As soon as the prisoner fell he made his way to him. Did he have any knife? Yes, sir. What happened to him? They kept him off. Who kept him off? One of the policemen struck him with his stick, and then Mr. Jim Nixon grabbed him and jerked him back, and he said, "You don't do it; you don't do any such a damned thing!" and he took him and carried him off down the street. Did you see what became of Mr. Phillips? No, sir; I never paid any attention to what became of Mr. Phillips. From the point where you stood the greater part of the time you were there that day, could you see the balcony at the east end of the market house? Yes, sir. Did you see any on it? I saw two gentlemen standing out there, but it is more than I am able to say whether it was after the prisoner was killed or not. How long was it between the time the prisoner appeared at the door at the head of the steps, and the time he was killed? I don't suppose it could have been more than one or two minutes. It was very quick work, was it? Yes, sir. You don't know exactly when it was, but sometime during the time that you were around the market house, you saw some one on that balcony? Yes, sir. Do you know who it was? No, sir; I did'nt pay any attention. Do you know whether they were white or black? They were white. Was that the first time you had looked up there that day? It it more than I am able to say. But you remember there were two gentlemen up there during that time? I might have looked up and I might not. You don't remember that your attention was attracted to that balcony at all that day? No, sir. But sometime during that day you saw two gentlemen in it? Yes, sir. You could see it from the point where you stood? Yes, sir. At the point where you stood all the time? Yes, sir. You say you did look into that balcony at sometime while you were there? Yes, sir. What induced you to looked there? What called your attention to it? I am not able to say I don't know whether it was before or after Beebee was shot. It is uncertain? Yes. sir. I am uncertain whether it was just before or directly after. Did you see Mr. M. N. Leary Jr. in the crowd that day? I saw Leary behind me, after Tolar killed Archy. You saw him there that day? Yes, sir. Was he standing near you? He was 'some distance behind me. I don't know how nigh he had been to me.

Cr ss examined, by the Counsel for the accused.

Did I understand you, that you were standing in about the same place all the time you were there? I only moved about to let gentlemen pass me, sir. You stood at one place all the time, except so far as going backwards and forwards as some one was passing? Yes. sir. And you stood at a place where you could see up in the Balcony all the time? Yes, sir. At no time, while you were there, were you at a point in the street from which you could not see in the balcony? No sir, And when Captain Tolar killed Archy, I understand you to say that Leary was standing some distance behind you? I said after he killed him, I looked around and Leary was standing some distance behind me. How long was it alter? I am not able to say. Did you see Leary any other time? No sir; not that I remember. How long did you stay there after Bebee was killed? I stayed there until sunset sir. What time in the evening was it he was killed? It was something after three o'clock, I am not able to say. When the three o'clock bell rang I was at the depot, and started for the market house. At three o'clock you were at the depot. How far is that from the market house? It is not more than two hundred yards. At what time was it you saw Bebee come out of the guard house? I cannot say what time of day it was, but it was after three o'clock. Did you go from the market house down to the guard house, or did you stop at the market house? I stopped right about the middle way of the arch, out there on the pavement. Is the guard house between the market house and the depot? No sir; it is on a different street. You stopped at the market house when you came from the depot? Yes, sir. Did I understand you to say in the first of your examination, that you saw Archy at the guard house? Well I saw him when he come out of the guard house. You saw him at a distance? Yes, sir Coming up from the guard house? Yes, sir. You say that something passed between you; some conversation? No sir; that was Ned. Be.bee. You had no conversation with the prisoners? No sir. Where did you see Ned. Beebee? First he came to my house, sir. Is your house between the market house and the depot? It is on the other side of the depot, from the market house. Did you do any business at the depot in passing along? Yes sir. How long were you at the depot? I don't know when the three o'clock bell rang; I started for the market uouse from the depot. Do you know whether Ed. Bebee is any relation to this other

Beebee? He may be, but I don't know it Did you speak to Archy at the market house? No sir. You saw Mr. Wemyss and the Sheriff with him when he came from the guard house? Yes, sir. And several police? Yes, sir — Was there any crowd at the market house then? Yes, sir How long did you get to the market house before the prisoner came up? When I got to the market house, and had got around it, they were coming out of the guard house How far from the market house to the guard house? It is just at the end of the block. Is it a hundred yards! It may be a hundred yards, and it may be more Might it be two hundred yards? No sir, it is not two hundred yards. Is it less than a hundred? I am not able to say. Can you guess within fifty yards? I am not able to say—I have never measured it You can't come within fifty yards? I don't know sir, I know i. is not two hundred yards. When you got to the market house you say Beebee was coming out of the guard house? Yes, sir. When did Miss Massey come up? She came up after the prisoner went up stairs. How long after? I am not able to say. It was a very sh rt time, sir. Where did she come from, which direction? I never paid any attention. Did you see which way the horses heads were turned? Towards the guard house. Which street is the guard house on? I don't know, sir. Which way do you live from the market house? I live West, sir. And the depot is which direction? It is West. Which direction is the guard house? South from the market. Bebee came up then with the guard, and they carried him up to the room where he was examined? Yes, sir. These steps that run up stairs in the market house, upon which side of the arch are they? In under the arch, and goes up on the right side of the arch. How many arches in the market house fronting East? I never paid any attention. There are three, are there not, at the East end, one large and two small ones? I would think there were four at each end running under. I never paid particular attention. Don't you know how many arches at the East end, big and little? I think there is two. Which side of the market house is it that the steps run up to the town hall where they were examining Bebee? As you are coming under the arch from the East it is to your right hand. en. How broad is the market house at the East end? I am not able to say, sir. As much as 40 feet? I am not able to say. As much as a hundred? I can't tell you anything about it. After you have entered the larger arch, how many pairs of stairs run up to the town hall? There is only one pair of steps. How many steps make the stairs? I don't know, sir. How high is the first story of the market house? I never measured it. Twenty feet? I don't know, sir. Fifty feet? I don't know, sir. You don't know whether it is fifty feet? No, sir. You stood about ten or twelve feet from the front of the market house? Yes, sir. How far were you from the side walk running along in front of the market house? Sometimes I would not be more than five feet, and sometimes nearer. And you say you were ten or twelve feet from the market house, did you measure that distance? No sir, I just give a guess. How could you attempt that when you could not guess the height of the first story? I guessed it as near as I could, I don't tell you exactly. If you were standing ten or twelve feet from the front of the market house how far were you from the stairs that run up to the town hall? The steps are some distance under the arch, how far I am not able to

y. You did nt measure the front of the market house? No, sir, I never measured it. You are unable to tell us how far you were from th, stairs running up to the town hall? Yes, sir. Can you tell how high the balcony is? No sir. You say a couple of gentlemen stood there sometime during the day? Sometime while the crowd was around the market, I won't say whether it was before Archy was shot or not. How long were you standing in the street from the time you went there to the time Archy was shot? I might have been there from three quarters of an hour, to a hour, I am not able to say exactly. And during that time you saw a couple of gentlemen in the balcony? Yes sir. Do you recollect what kind of clothes they had on? No sir, I just threw my eyes upon them. You don't recollect what kind of hats? No sir. Do you recollect their faces? No sir. Do you recollect the color of their faces? White men. What was the color of their coats? I dont know sir. You recollect nothing but the color of their faces? No sir. And that color was white? Yes sir, they were white gentlemen. I didnt pay any attention to who they were. Do I understand you to give an opinion as to how long they were up stairs trying Beehee? No sir I dont give you to understand how long they were. It may have been an hour, but I don't think it was. And you say when you were up there you saw a good deal of whispering in the crowd? Yes sir. Did you whisper any? No sir, what I said I spoke out. You spoke out what you had to say? Yes sir. How far were you standing from Tolar when Ed. Powers went up to him and whispered to him? I dont know exactly how far I was from him. Where was Tolar standing when Powers whispered to him? He was standing under the arch, leaning against where they hang beef up. How far was he under the market house? The steps were on my left and Captain Tolar was right in front of me. He was on the left hand side of the market house? He was under the market house. At the left hand part, was he not? Yes sir. Was there much of a crowd there? Yes sir. Some of them talking were they not? Some were and some were not. Some of them laughing? Some of them. And you say, among this crowd some talking, some laughing, all moving about; some one went up and whispered to Mr. Tolar? Yes sir, he didn't speak out. He went pretty close to Tolar, and Tolar leaned down to hear what he had to say? Yes, sir, I would consider that whispering. Were not they talking so that anybody by them could have told what they were saying? One that was standing by them might have heard, but I didn't. If you come to me in a crowd of men, and I was taller than you, I would have to hold my head down to hear what you said; that was the way he did I suppose, was it not? They were very close together, and I would consider it whispering. Just as a small man and a tall man would do in a crowd. I would consider it whispering, I would speak out. How did you know they said anything to one another? Mr. Powers went to Captain Tolar, and I could see them whispering. You say there was a large crowd there; what induced you to notice them? I was noticing the men who had the pistols. Did Powers have a pistol? Yes, sir. And Hall? Yes, sir. You were noticing them? Yes, sir. Because they had pistols you observed them? Yes sir. You observed Powers when he went to Tolar? Yes, sir. How far did he have to go? I don't know, it was a very short

distance. Was Hall under the market house? Yes sir. On which side of the market house was he? He was behind Mr. Tolar. How far was he from Tolar? I am not able to tell you, sir. q Give some idea; as far as from you to me? No sir; not that far. As from you to either of those other gentlemen? He may have been. There was some gentlemen standing between Mr. Hall and Mr. Tolar, after Mr. Powers had left him. And when Powers had spoken to Tolar he went to Hall? Yes sir. Were they pretty much of the same size, Hall and Powers? Powers is a little tallest I think. Was Hall any further from you than Tolar? who was furtherest from you? It was about the same distance, only Mr. Tolar was right in front of me. But I would consider it the same distance. And you say they whispered together? I saw Mr. Powers come to Captain Tolar and whisper to him. You could not hear what was said? No sir. And there was a noise all the time? Yes sir. Were you far enough out in the street to see the windows of the Town Hall from where you were standing. No sir, I could not see the windows. You saw up in the balcony? Yes sir. After Powers spoke to Hall, then Hall went and spoke to Tolar? Yes sir. They whispered or spoke just like Mr. Powers did? Yes sir, and then Mr. Hall went back to Mr. Lutterloh. They were all talking together? Yes Sir, Did I understand you to say that if any body had been standing there, they could not have heard what they said? I don't state how loud they spoke. You say you just saw them going up and speaking to one another? Yes Sir, And you say it was whispering because you did'nt hear any thing of it? But in what tone they spoke to one another you can't say. If I were to talk to this gentleman at the distance I am from him, and you did not hear me, would you call it whispering? If he were to lean his head over close to you, I would call it whi-pering. If you wanted to speak out you would not hold your head close to him, Did this carriage stay there while the trial was going on? Yes Sir. The carriage stayed there until the ladies came down stairs, Which end of the market house was the carriage? The east end. Was the carriage between you and the market house? No Sir, I was between the carriage and the market house. The carriage did'nt stop right at the side walk? No Sir, It did'nt drive up to the side walk? No Sir, Just stopped in the middle of the street, and the ladies got out, and De Vaun handed them up stairs? Yes Sir, After they had been up there some hour or so, you say the first thing you saw was Hardie came down with Faircloth, out of the room? Mr De Vaun was the first man that came down, after these ladies went up, and a colored man by the name of Dennis McKeever went up right behind the ladies, I am talking about coming down. Who was the first man that came out of the room? a Mr. De Vaun. Where did he go? He stood on the steps and helped the ladies out. They came out first? No, sir, Mr. De Vaun came out first. And when the ladies came down he helped them in the carriage? Yes, sir. And a man named Maultsby called De Vaun, and they went around behind the carriage? Yes, sir. The carriage was between them and the market house? Yes, sir. Was any body standing on the other side of the carriage? I did'nt see any one. The driver was standing holding the reins when Mr. De Vaun helped the ladies in. How far was the carriage from you? About ten feet; Mr. Maultsby came up, and they walked around the carriage and whispered together; When Mr. De Vaun went back up stairs, and Mr. Maultsby went round on my left, and jumped upon that bench and waved his hand and said, "look out boys." What bench was it he jumped on? On bench under the arch, sir, to your left hand. Not on the same side of the arch that the stairs run up? Yes, sir, the same side. On your left? Yes, sir. And he stood there by the foot of the stairs and waved his hand and said, "boys look out?" No, sir, he got up on a bench where they lay watermellons. Had you seen Maultsby before, during the day? Yes, sir. What was he doing? He came to the carriage and said, "I am mighty sorry for Archy; He will never go away alive." I did'nt ask you anything he said; it was improper to say that. I just wanted you to say what he had been doing during the day. I did'not see him before he come to the market house. After he did what you have described what occurred then? Immediately Monk Julia said, "boys you follow me." Where was Mr. Tolar then? Mr. Tolar was standing back where he was when Mr. Powers was whispering to him. Does Maultsby live in Fayetteville? Yes, sir. Is he there now? I cant tell, sir. When did you see him last? On the 5th day of July. He is there? He was then. Monk Julia said, "boys follow me?" Yes, sir. What did he do? He just stood around where this lady always has her little stand, near the steps, and Mr. Powers went under there Did he have the knife in his hand? Yes, sir. How long a knife was it? I did'nt pay much attention to his knife, for he was further off than Powers was. How long was that before Bebee came down? It was but a very few minutes after Mr. Maultsby spoke the word before Sheriff Hardie came and stood on the steps, and then went back and Mr. Faircloth come and stood on the steps, and I looked around and Archy was on the steps, and Mr. Wemyss and he came down with Sheriff Hardie in front. As they got off the steps then Monk struck at h m, did he? Yes, sir. Struck at him with his knife? Yes, sir. And the Sheriff knocked him down? No, sir, he shoved him away. All this while there was a large crowd on the side walk? No, sir, they were giving way then to let them pass with the prisoner. There was a large crowd on the street? Yes, sir. All the while? Yes, sir. Between you and the market house? [No, sir, I kept my position, for I wanted to see. Was there a crowd between you and the Market House? No sir, not then. Did the crowd give way and get behind you? No sir; they just strung themselves along, and I stood and tried to get nearer. Did you get on the side walk? No sir. And just then, after Monk Julia disappeared, the Sheriff came out of the arch, and as he turned the arch Powers said something, and struck at Beebee with his knife? He struck at him, I am not able to say whether he struck him or not. What did he say? He said, "I remand the prisoner he is mine, give him up"! and the Sheriff said, "he is my prisoner," and pushed him off? Yes sir. And then they started off to the guard house with him, and you say Archy fell? Yes sir, and as he was about to rise Captain Tolar shot him. When did Tolar come out of the Market House? During the time Powers made his efforts at Archy, I saw Captain Tolar coming through the crowd, pushing them aside. That was the second time that Powers struck? Yes sir. Had Tolar anything in his hands? No sir. Had he a shawl on? Yes sir. Had he it on the whole day? I am not able to say

sir. Was it a cold day? No sir. The 11th of February—It was not a cold day? No sir. When you saw him coming out he was shoving the crowd one side; saying anything? No sir, he never spoke a word that I heard. Which side of Beebee was he? Behind Beebee, coming up behind him. When you saw him was he nearer the Market House than Beebee was? Beebee might have been a little nearer the arch Captain Tolar never got off the pavement. They were coming in what direction? They were coming south sh. Did you see Tolar draw his pistol? I saw him draw it from under his shawl; and he laid his left hand upon a gentlemans shoulder, and raised the pistol, and his hand trembled; and he shot: and I said, " there Captain you have killed that poor man," and he never spoke to me, but just drawed his lip up. I understand you to say he came out shoving the crowd on both sides, making his way through the crowd? Yes sir. And now you say there was no body on his left? I was on his left. You were out in the street, he didn't shove you? I just stepped back, and still stood on his left. You were not on the sidewalk at all? The crowd occupied the whole of the sidewalk, and he come pretty close on the edge of the sidewalk, sir. Were you three feet from the edge of the side walk? I might have been three feet. Didn't I understand you to say that he came shoving his way through the crowd? Yes sir. But then you say that there were no persons on his left hand at all? I was on his left hand when he fired the pistol. You were the only one? There might have been more behind me, I didn't pay attention. There was nobody between you and Tolar? No sir, none between me and Captain Tolar. How far were you from Tolar? I was near enough when he threw back his shawl for it to fall in my face. He was on the side walk and you were in the street, three feet from the side walk? I got right up to him then. You walked up to the sidewalk then? Yes sir.— Did you get on the sidewalk? No sir.— Which side of the sidewalk was the Sheriff? He was next the Market house. q The Sheriff had Beebee by his left hand? No sir, Mr. Wemyss had him. The Sheriff didn't have him at all? No sir. The Sheriff was walking on the Market side? Yes sir. And the prisoner was on the outside of the sidewalk? He was on the sidewalk? He was outside from the market? Yes sir. And Mr. Wemyss, where was he? Mr. Wemyss was on his right. Wemyss was next the street? No sir, next the market house. Was the Sheriff behind? Right in front. Which side was Beebee of the Sheriff? Bebee was on the Sheriff's left, going in the guard house. But the Sheriff didn't have hold of him. No sir. I am talking about Sheriff Hardie. You say the Sheriff was on the left hand of Bebee? No sir; I said he was on the right. Where was Wemyss? Wemyss was on the right. Wemyss was next the street? Wemyss was next the market house, sir. As you come out the of East end of the market house and turn South, you say Wemyss was on the market house side of Beebee? Yes sir. And that the Sheriff was too? Yes sir. Was the Sheriff behind Mr. Wemyss or before him? Just before him, sir. Then Beebee was between you and the Sheriff? Yes sir. Sheriff Hardie was over beyond you from Beebee? Yes sir. Sheriff Hardie was over beyond Bebee from Tolar? Yes sir. Bebee was between Tolar and the Sheriff? Yes sir. That is so; you recollect that? Yes sir. You

recollect the Sheriff walking before Wemyss?
Yes sir. He had him tied, Wemyss had?
He had him tied by one finger. And Tolar
came behind Beebee? Yes sir. And shot him
behind? Yes sir. And you were standing
so near Tolar that you could say, "there Captain, you have shot that poor man!" and thereupon he said nothing except drawing in his
breath and rather fixing his lips, sir."
Yes, sir. At the time he fired he threw his
shawl off of himself? No, sir, he was trying
to conceal the pistol when he threw the shawl in
my face. And when you threw it back he did'nt
have any pistol? No, sir, and I saw a pistol
pass out of the crowd. When the shawl got
out of your face the pistol or one that looked like
it was in the hands of who? Mr. Eddie Powers.
He was standing how far? He was very
close to Mr. Tolar—there may have been a gentleman or two between them, but it was very close.
I think when you were first examined you
said Tolar threw the shawl off upon somebody
before that? No, sir. It was not thrown except when it was thrown into your face? That
is the only time it was thrown off. Did he
throw it off of both shoulders? No, sir, only
his left shoulder. The shawl did fall off of
him entirely? No, sir, just off of his arm.
He was putting his pistol up the last thing, you
say, before the shawl fell into your face? Yes,
sir. And when the shawl got out of your face,
whether the pistol was put up or not you don't
know? No, sir. But you did see a pistol like
it pass through the crowd? Yes, sir. It
passed to Lutterloh? Yes, sir. Did Ed.
Powers give it to Lutterloh? Ed. Powers gave
it to Hall and Hall to Lutterloh. How long was
that afterwards? It was as quick as I could
see. Tolar did'nt attempt to pass it away until
after the shawl fell into your face? I don't
know whether he passed it at all or not. You
don't say it was the same pistol? No, sir.
The last you saw of Tolar he was trying to put
his pistol, was he a little vexed, by his movements?
He looked like as if he was very scared, sir.
Like how? As if he was scared—as if he
was frightened. Frightened at what he had
done perhaps? Yes, sir. Was he frightened
before that? He did'nt look frightened until
I spoke to him. You scared him I suppose?
I don't know whether I did or not, I suppose
he was scared at what he had done. With regard to Mr. Phillips, you saw Mr. Phillips come
up the street? I saw Mr. Phillips, sir, and I saw
him standing out by himself with a small pisto
in his hands, I am not able to say whether it was
cocked or not. Did he say anything? No,
sir. I never heard him speak to no one. Did he
stand in the same place after the pistol was fired?
He walked down around to the foot of the
market. Did he say anything then? I never
heard him speak to no one. Was the pistol
still in his hand? He had the pistol when I saw
him again standing there, but I don't know what
he done with it. I want to know more particularly how Sheriff Hardie and Beebee and Wemyss
were at the time Beebee was shot by Tolar, as you
say. Do I understand you, Wemyss had the prisoner under charge? Yes, sir. On Wemyss'
left he was standing to the right of Archy Beebee?
Yes, sir. And the Sheriff in front o Wemyss? Yes, sir. And Beebee between Tolar
and the Sheriff? Yes, sir. And between
you and Sheriff Hardie? Who? Archy Beebee? Yes, sir, Did you have any pistol
there that day? No, sir, I did not. I had one
and I thought I would carry it but I did'nt.
Questioned by the Court:
You say you heard some one say shoot, did

the voice appear to come from the crowd below
or from above? I did'nt pay no attention
which way the voice come. I was engaged look-
ng at the crowd and I did'nt know which way the
voice come.

Re-direct examination:
There is one thing you spoke of, you said Mr.
Maultsby, mark you, I don't ask you to tell
me what Mr. Maultsby said, but you spoke
of his having said something about Archy
now what time was this said? After Mr.
De Vaun, helped the ladies out of the carriage. Where was he standing? He
was walking under the market. Now I understand you to say that after that young lady and
her mother had got there. Mr. Maultsby was
walking through the crowd into the market house,
and that while in that place he made use of that
speech? Yes, sir.
The counsel for the prosecution.
The witness says that just after Mrs. Massey and
her daughter came, and they were assisted out of
the carriage by De Vaun, Mr. Maultsby, the same
man that held up his hand as a signal; that
Maultsby moved up the centre of the market house,
making use of the expression alluded to by the
witness in the cross examination. We wish to use
that expression as evidence, and if you have no
objection we will ask the question.
The counsel for the accused objected.
The court; you will please state your objections.
The counsel for the prosecution—I wish the court
to fully understand the case. This man has stated
that just after Miss Massy and her mother got
to the market house, a man by the name of De
Vaun, helped them up stairs. That after they
had gone up stairs Maultsby, the same man
who threw up his hand and said, "now boys."
This man Maultsby, started forward, walking
through the crowd into the market house, and
made use of the expression with regard to the
prisoner, while he was up stairs. Now we ask for
that expression; we say it is an act and a declaration accompanying the commission of the crime
that makes it evidence.
The counsel for the accused remarked:
May it please the Court: De Vaun in this case is
one of the peace officers in the charge, of prisoners, acting in behalf of justice there. I think I
may submit to the Court that there is nothing here,
that has appeared in this case, to implicate De
Vaun. The mere fact that a Constable, a business
man about town, in the course of his business, interrupted by another citizen to have some talk
with him. is no evidence to implicate him in an
offence of this sort. I submit the fact to the
Court that Maultsby or any body else, interrupting a peace office who is not on duty, and having some
conversation with him, is no evidence that he was
talking for some wrong purpose. Nothing is more
usual than where a peace officer has been confined
upon duty, that some citizen has some private
business with him, and goes up and carries him
off to have some talk about it, nothing has occurred in the rise of this affair to implicate De Vaun
at all. So far as this investigation has gone, so
far as these able gentlemen, who represent the
United States can see, De Vaun ought not even to
be tried; he is perfectly clear. And I might say
the same of Mr. Maultsby. So far as these gentlemen are concerned there is nothing requiring
his arrest; nothing in the way of justice, nothing
in the way of their duties to the State or the
United States that requires them to bring Maultsby before this Court, for the purpose of trying
him, for any thing that has occurred there. So

far as this trial goes Maultsby is considered a perfectly innocent man.

But something that he says in private, unheard by these men upon trial, is to be put in here for the jeoparding their lives; a man, I say, named Maultsby, whose connection with this affair is so slight that the prosecuting Attorney and Judge Advocate do not care to bring him up here from Fayetteville—has said something to one of these witnesses unheard by these persons, that is to go to jeopard and take away their lives. That is the whole case. Maultsby goes and talks to De Vaun a peace officer in the discharge of his duty; talks with him about any of the ten thousand subjects that interest men of business, or otherwise; and then goes up to this witness and makes a declaration to him, and then goes off and says something that b· inuendo may or may not mean something; but whether it means little or much, the gentlemen here think it amounts to nothing requiring him to come here and defend himself, and yet that man, by having spoken to a witness, occupies such a situation, as to his words, as to jeopard these lives. He is not part nor party in this matter. For that you have the character of the gentlemen who are carrying on the prosecution; for having looked through it, they say he is not to be prosecuted. Upon what grounds, then are the words of this man to be taken as evidence in the prosecution? They are not in the same boat; and until some common design is brought to my view, I cannot see how the language made use of by one should be taken as evidence against the other, What Maultsby said in the presence of the men may go for what it is worth, His standing on a bench and saying what he did, will be the subject of observation after a while in the court; but in the mean while that other words, private words, whispered perhaps, according to the expression of the witness unheard by these men, that such evidence is to be brought in here on such a trial—I object.

The Counsel for the prosecution then spoke as follows:

May it please the Court. It seems to me that by this time, taking this as a *prima facie* case, and nothing appearing on the other side, one thing, at least must be satisfactorily made out to this court; and that is, that there was a combination of persons in Fayetteville, that day, concerned in taking the life of Archy Bebee; that it was not the outburst of the moment, but there had been a previous combination and arrangement between certain parties, then and there concerned in the immediate act, by which, the life of this man was taken away, For what is the evidence as to that thing? De Vaun, a constable, comes down the steps; Maultsby, a man who has been in this crowd a portion of the time, goes and has a whisper d conversation with him. Immediately upon De Vaun's disappearing up the steps again, and just before this unfortunate prisoner, who met his death then and there, that day makes his appearance, Maultsby leaps up on a bench to make himself conspicuous, so that his co-conspirators could see him and says "look out!" Look out for what? for what immediately followed, the appearance of this man Beebee, who by concert, then and there was murdered.

How does the Counsel assume that the United States does not see fit to prosecute Maultsby? Upon what ground pray can the defence say, because he is not included in this particular prosecution, that Maultsby himself may not be called upon to answer for this offence? It is not necessary, certainly, to put them all in the same charge and specification; but it is a bare assumpti n upon the part of the defence, to say that Maultsby is

not to be tried as a co-conspirator in this combination which we say exists. But not only is the fact that Maultsby had a whispered conversation with De Vaun before the Court; but this Court must see that the principal participator in this act, Capt. Tolar was in whispered conversation with many individuals that day. The crowd was gathering! More than one individual was concerned, as is already proved, nothing appearing to the contrary. Tom Powers and Monk Julia did make an assault upon the prisoner, all tending to a common purpose, which culminated in the shot that was fired by Tolar.

Now all that the law requires before evidence of this character, that I propose to introduce, can be introduced is this, that the court shall be satisfied that the prosecution have made out a *prima facie* case of combination; that there shall be enough of evidence to make it probable that there was a combination between certain parties, certain men of Fayetteville, and that Maultsby was a party to this combination; for the law is explicit and clear, as laid down in Wharton's Criminal Law, Section 702, that in a case of conspiracy, or any other crime perpetrated by several persons, "When once the conspiracy or combination is established," and I insist upon it, but that we have established it here, "The act or declaration of one conspirator or accomplice in its prosecution is considered the act or declaration of all, and is evidence against all. Not only is the act or declaration of one of the conspirators evidence against the others, but his act or declaration is evidence against the others, though the man be not on trial at the time who made the declaration."

The principle is this, that when men unlawfully combine together, the declaration of any one of them in the prosecution of the crime is evidence against all, and what stronger evidence is it possible for a court of justice to have before it, of a combination than is here shown before this Court. In the learned remarks of Judge McLean, in a case that was before him in one of the United Statest Courts. V. McLean, page 601,—a gentleman of great legal attainments, and of great experience in questions of this sort—he tells Courts of Justice that they are not to expect that the facts of a conspiracy or agreement to commit a crime will be found out and proved by direct evidence, for it is impossible to do that unless one of the conspirators turns States' evidence, and proves it for us, but we must prove such facts and circumstances surrounding and accompanying the final execution of the offence, as will induce the Court to see *prima facie* there was a combination. The conspiracy is rarely, if ever, proved by positive testimony. When a crime of magnitude is to be perpetrated by a combination of individuals, they do not act openly, but covertly and secretly. The purpose formed is known to none, except those who enter into it, unless one of the original conspirators betray the rest, and give evidence against them. The only possibility in ninety-nine cases out of a hundred, of proving the conspiracy, is by such circumstantial testimony.

What is the testimony in this case?

Mr. Maultsby was there on the ground; this is the first circumstance; he was the man who was seen in conversation with De Vaun, the person who assisted the ladies in the carriage. The court will notice that De Vaun had just come from up stairs, where the prisoner was confined. It is a logical conclusion from the consequences to say that De Vaun was asked at that time, if the prisoner was to come down.

That Maultsby, finding he was to be brought down, immediately turned and sprung upon that bench, where his co-conspirators could see him, and said "look out boys." And this was responded to by these very prisoners at the bar, they thereby making him their agent for that purpose; and the fact of Maultsby, being a conspirator with these persons, is reason sufficient for having his conversation, which the witness has alluded to, go in as evidence against them.

There are many cases, in the books but it is too clear almost for argument. If the Court thinks that we have by *prima facie* evidence established—that is if we have made a strong case, to show—that Maultsby was concerned in this transaction, then his declaration, so inadvertently called out, or not called out at all, but leaked out, in the examination, his declaration is evidence.

The law also admits the declaration of a third party, made in the presence of a party who is accused of an offence. His own declaration is evidence against him; the declaration of a third party is evidence against him if made in his presence. Cases have occurred where declarations of third parties, in the presence of the defendant, although he was drunk, have been admitted, it being the province of the Court to decide how far he was so drunk that he did not know what that declaration meant.

But the main ground that we rest this point upon, is that the United States have established a conspiracy against certain parties to slaughter this boy, Beebee, as he came from that trial. We have made out the *prima facie* case, that these prisoners at the bar, I mean the prisoners Tolar, Watkins and Powers,—the case not being so clear as to Phillips—were concerned in this conspiracy—a case in which not only they are concerned, but Maultsby is shown to have been concerned with them, and although he is not charged here, he is as much their agent as if he were included in this indictment. I am sorry to detain you so long; I submit the question to the decision of the Court. The Court was then cleared for deliberation, and after some time so spent, was re-opened; and the Judge Advocate announced that the Court over-ruled the objection to the admissibility of the question.

Re-direct examination by the counsel for the prosecution.

I understand you to say that just after Miss Massey and her mother went up stairs, after De-Vaun had helped them out of the carriage, Mr. Maultsby walked through the crowd into the market house? Yes, sir. What did he say? "I am sorry for Archy—he will never go back alive." How far were you from him? I was right at him when he spoke the words. Did he speak loud? Yes, sir. Is that all he said? Yes, sir. What were the exact remarks? "I am sorry for Archy, for he will never go back from here alive."

Re-cross examination by the Counsel for the accused:

Was that after the carriage had driven away? No, sir. Where was the carriage? It was standing where it first stopped, sir. It was after the ladies went up stairs? Yes, sir. Did he speak these words to you? No, sir, he just spoke the words. That was first you had seen of him? No, sir, I saw Maultsby before the carriage came. Did he talk to De Vaun when the carriage came first? No, sir, I did'nt see him. He did'nt speak in particular to any one the expression you refer to? No, sir, but just spoke to the crowd. Was that before Archy had gone up stairs? Yes, sir. Who was standing near Maultsby? I was very close to him myself. There were several standing around. He did'nt come up with the carriage? No, sir, he was there when the carriage came.

On motion, the Commission adjourned to meet on Tuesday, the 23d inst., at 11 o'clock, A. M.

RALEIGH, N. C., July 23d, 1867.

The Commission met pursuant to adjournment. Present, all the members of the Commission, the Judge Advocate, the Counsel for the prosecution, the accused and their Counsel.

A portion of yesterday's proceedings were read. The Recorder, having been unable to complete the record of yesterday's proceedings, on motion the Commission adjourned, to meet on Wednesday, the 24th inst., at 11 o'clock, A. M.

RALEIGH, N. C., July 24th 1867, 10 A. M.

The Commission met pursuant to adjournment. Present, all the members of the Commission, the Judge Advocate, the Counsel for the prosecution and the accused and their Counsel.

The Judge Advocate then continued the reading of the proceedings of the Commission on the 21st instant.

Witness, John Armstrong made the following corrections in his testimony—in answer to the question on page 88, line 15, in place of "Yes sir" he wished to insert. "At the time the outcries of shoot the damn son of a bitch," occurred it was that I looked up into the balcony."

In answer to the question on page 89, line 4 he wished to insert the following, in place of "No, sir," "Yes sir." I recollect very well when the word came to shoot the damned son of a bitch, I throwed my eyes up and saw two gentlemen standing up there. But I took my eyes down, attracted by the movement of Mr. Tolar, coming through the crowd, and I throwed my eyes on him and kept my eyes on him."

The proceedings of the 22nd and 23rd having been read were approved.

On motion, the Commission was cleared for deliberation, and after some time spent the doors were re-opened.

The Judge Advocate stated that the prosecution proposed to enter a *nolle prosequi* in the case of Defendant Samuel Phillips.

The Commission was cleared for deliberation, and after some time spent, the doors were re-opened, and the Judge Advocate announced that the motion of the Judge Advocate to enter a nolle prosequi in the case of defendant Samuel Phillips had been sustained by the Commission.

The Commission then proceeded with the trial of William J. Tolar, Duncan G. McRae, Thos. Powers and David Watkins, otherwise called Monk Julia.

LOUIS SMITH, a witness for the prosecution, having been first duly sworn, testified as follows:

Examined by the Council for the prosecution:—
What is your name? Louis Smith.— Where do you live? Fayetteville, How long have you lived there? I was born there; near twenty-one years ago, sir. What is your occupation there? I am doing no particular work, stayed with William Baker for five or six years. Have you been staying with him since the war? No, sir, I stayed some time in Virginia, running on the line of steamers from Franklin to Edenton. Were you living in Fayetteville at the beginning of this year? Yes, sir. Do you know Archy Beebee? I do sir; or I did. What has become of him? He is shot now sir. Did you see him shot? I did sir. Where was he shot, at what town? Fayetteville. What part of the town? At the market house.— Were you present? I was, sir. Do you remember what month it was? February, I think.

Do you remember the day of the mouth? No, sir. Do you remember the day of the week? Monday, sir. In the afternoon or morning? Afternoon, sir. How came you at the market house that day? He was an associate of mine, and I heard the trial was going on, and I went down to hear it. What time did you go to the market house? I don't know exactly what time, I don't think I was there over fifteen or twenty minutes before Beebee came down. He was up-stairs when you got there? Yes, sir. And you think you were there fifteen or twenty minutes before he came down? Yes, sir. Where were you standing? On the south east side of the market house. On the side walk or in the street? On the side walk. Under the market house or outside? I was at different places during the time I was there. Were you under the market house at all, sir? Yes, sir. Were you walking about? Yes, sir. While Beebee was up-stairs did you see any of these prisoners at the bar? I did, sir. Who did you see? I saw Tom Powers for one. Any one else? I seen Monk Elder. What is his other name? We always call him Monk Julia. Did you see any of the others? No, sir. Was there any crowd at the market house when you first got there? Yes, sir, a right smart crowd. How many do you suppose? There might have been 30, or more; 50, perhaps. Was the crowd larger when you went away? Yes, sir. Between t ie time the deceased man, Beebee, was killed, and the time you first went there, did the crowd grow larger or smaller? It growed larger. Constantly grew larger? Yes, sir. You say you saw the defendant Powers and the defendant Monk Julia, during the fifteen or twenty minutes you were there, while Beebee was up-stairs? Yes, sir. What were they doing? They were walking about. Did you hear them say anything? No, sir. Nothing to attract your attention? No, sir. Did you notice any body doing or saying anything that attracted your attention during that time? . No, sir. Was there any cause of alarm? . No, sir. Was the crowd quiet? Yes, sir, it seemed to be quiet; there was a good deal of talking and whispering around, There was a good deal of whispering? Yes, sir. W o did you see whisper? I never paid any atten'i:n who it was Can you say or can't you? I can't say. You can't pretend to say, but you noticed some whispering? Yes, sir. What was the first thing that attracted your attention, as being unusual? After they started down with Archy? Who started down with Archy? Mr. Wemyss and the Sheriff I think had him. Did any one come out of the door, down the market house steps before Archy came down? Yes, sir. Who was it? There were two ladies, and I don't know whether any gentleman or not. If I am not mistaken Mr. Israel Bauns. Is his name Vaun or Baun? I don't know, but I think it is Baun. You think he came down with them? Yes, sir. What became of those lad es? They got in the carriage. Where was that carriage? At the eastern end of the market house. How far was it from the arch,— how many steps? I suppose four or five. How many steps across the pavement in front of the market house? I don't know, sir. How many yards? I am not acquainted much with yards. Can't you show us by something here how wide it is? I guess it is as wide as from me to Major Johnson, may be not quite so wide. Was the carriage on the side walk? No, sir. How far was it from the edge of the side walk? Well, may be it was four or five steps, Did these ladies go to that carriage and get in? Yes

Sir. What became of the carriage? It drove off down the street, Sir. Was that before you saw Archy at all? Yes Sir, You say when they came down—speaking of Archy,—who was with him? Mr Wemyss was with him, Which side of him? On the right side, I think, Any one else? Mr Hardie was with him; but I think Mr Hardie was on the left, or right in front ot Mr Wemyss, I cannot exactly remember but I know they were both with him, Did you see any one else with him? No Sir, I didn't pay any attention, Was any body else with him? There was a'ri h' smart crowd,—some five or six, You don't know who they were? No Sir. What happened as he came down? After he stopped off the steps I saw Mr Powers make toward him, and he said, ''demand the prisoner!'' and Mr Elder followed him with a knife, and made a cut at him, and was shoved off by some one, Who was it said ''demand the prisoner?'' Mr Thomas Powers. Have you any doubt about it? Not a bit, What did Sheriff Hardie reply? I didn't hear him say any thing, Sir, Where did Mr Powers come from, how far did he have to walk to get up to make that demand? He was standing on a bench, on the left hand side as you come down the steps; he was standing inside of the bench, Did he move? Yes, Sir, he made a step or two. He made use of this expression? Yes, Sir, Did you see him do any thing? No sir, the crowd rushed up pretty strong and I got back a little further, Where were you standing? I was standing on the side walk, In front of the arch? Yes Sir, just on the outside of the arch, Right square in front of the middle of the arch? A little towards the left corner as you go out of the arch, On the pavement? Yes, Sir, What did you say you saw Elder or Monk doing? He cut at him with a knife? He had a knife? Yes, sir, Did you see any other knives or weapons? I never saw any other knife, What happened then; after Powers made this demand, and Elder rushed up with a kni'e,—what happened then? The Policemen seemed to be beating them pretty strong with their clubs; and just as he was coming from under the arch, Monk made at him again, with his knife, and Mr. Nixon shoved him off. What is Mr. Nixon's first name? Jim Nixor. That was jus. as Beebee got outside of the arch? Yes, sir. What had become of Mr. Tom Powers? I didn't see him at that time at all, sir, I don't know where he was. What happened next? After he cleared from under the market the crowd all rushed up towards him again, and I heard a ''shoot him!'' ''shoot him!'' and I stepped off the side walk right close along side of him, and I seen Mr. Tolar rushing through the crowd, and he ran over and said ''Clear away gentlemen,'' and he ran right over and fired, and then I moved a step or two forward and saw Mr, Phillips come up with a pistol in his hand, but the man was shot then. Some one asked him if it was him who shot, and he said no, he did'nt get a chance. How close were you to Mr Tolar when he fired the pistol? I was not very far from him. Could you put your hand on him? Yes, sir, by reaching over. Was he to the left of you or the right? Mostly in front of me. Did you see any pistol in Mr. Tolar's hand? Yes, sir, when he shot it. What became of it? I don't know, sir, I saw him carry his hand down by his side. Who was standing nearest him when he fired? Ed. Powers was tanding he hind him, Samuel Hall was close by, and Mr. Lutterloh's son and a young man named George Ha'l was not very far off. What is Mr Lutterloh's son's name? Ralph. And a young man by the name of George Hall? Yes, sir. Didn't you mention Sam Hall?

Yes. sir.   Are they brothers?   No, sir
Is George Hall a grown man?   Yes sir, a
young man, grown up.   Which is Mr. Tolar?
That gentlem an with the specks on.   Is be
the man you saw fire the pistol?   He is the
man.   What became of him after be fired the
pistol?   He turned around, and I don't remember whether he went under the market
house or not, but the next time I saw him he was
going into Mr. Hinsdale's store.   Where is Mr.
Hinsdale's store?   On the opposite corner.
After you go out of the west end of the market
house?   Yes, sir.   On Hay street?   Yes,
sir.   What else did you see there that day, any
thing?   No sir—yes I heard Monk say after he
was shot, "let me cut his damned throat."
What was he doing when he said that?   Mr.
Nixon had hold of him and asked him "what in
the hell he wanted to kill a dead nigger for," and
took him off one side.   What was Monk doing when Mr. Nixon was holding him off, was he
struggling?   No sir, he didn't seem to be.
Did he have any weapon?   He had a knife in
his hand.   Did you see any one with weapons
that day, beside the weapons you have spoken
of?   No sir.   What was the last you saw of Tolar after he fired the pistol?   Captain Wells asked me who fired the pistol, and I told him Tolar did it, and he asked me where he was, and I
pointed him out to him, over on Hinsdale's corner.   That was the last I saw of him.   Did
you see any weapon about him the last time you
saw him?   No sir.   Did you notice any of
the witnesses there in the crowd?   I saw Sam
Toomer.   Anybody else?   John Armstrong.
Anybody else?   I saw Robert Simmons—
I didn't see any of the other witnesses.   After the man was shot, I saw Lerry and
Mrs. Elliot.   Did you see any of these
defendants in that crowd that day?   None
but Mr. Kelter and Mr. Powers.   I only noticed
them particularly.   From where you were standing, could you see the balcony that goes out from
over the market house?   Yes, sir.   Was any
one on it?   I never noticed it at all.   You
mean that there was no one on it?   I did'nt see
any one.   I did'nt look up there.   Could you
have seen them from where you were, if you had
looked?   If I had looked, I could.   You spoke
of some shouts that were made—what were those
shouts?   'Shoot him!' "shoot him!!"   How
many times did you hear that?   Once or twice,
How many voices did you hear?   I could not
say.   Was it several or a single one or in two or
three or four?   I hardly think it was more than
two or three times.   Do you think it was said by
the same person?   I don't know, sir.   But you
heard that exclamation two or three times?   Yes,
sir.   Did you see what became of the deceased
after the pistol was fired?   Yes, sir; I saw him
fall.   Did you see him after he had fallen?   Not
for some time afterwards.   How long afterwards?   I guess about twenty or twenty-five
minutes.   Was he dead the?   Yes, sir.   You
spoke of Monk Julia or David Watkins having made an attempt to cut the deceased man
with his knife before he got outside of the
arch?   Yes, sir.   What became of Monk after
that?   He came round and stepped a step or
two back; and just as they turned to go out of
the arch he made another cut at him.   What became of Mouk then?   He got off of the sidewalk
and went around to the steps at the corner of the
market.   Where was the prisoner then?   He
was between the arch and the corner.   How close
was Monk to the prisoner as he stood there?   Five
or six feet, may be further off.   Did he stand
still?   No sir.   They were trying to get him on

—trying to get on with Beebee—but the crowd
was rushing up so they could not move much.—
What was Mouk trying to do?   He was trying
to cut him.   What did he do?   Well he was
cutting with his knife to (illustrating).   How
many could you count, do you suppose, from the
time the man Beebee came out of the door on the
steps until he was shot?   How many men could
I count?   How many in number?   I don't
know sir.   Was it as long as you could count a
hundred?   Yes, sir.   Could you count more?
I don't know sir.   I want to know whether it
was quickly done, or whether it took several minutes.   Yes, sir—from seven to ten minutes I
should think.   How long do you suppose you
have been examined now?   About ten or fi teen
minutes I suppose.   Do you think it was as long
as that?   Yes, sir   Where was the Sheriff
when Beebee was shot?   To the right of him.
D d you notice any of those other five or six officers
that came down the steps with him?   Yes, sir
I saw Mr Hornrird and Mr. McGuire.   Had they
their clubs?   Yes, sir.   Did they endeavor to
protect the prisoner?   Yes sir, it seemed as if
they tried to protect him.   When Archy was
shot, was that the first time you saw him fall that
day?   No, sir.   He had a comfort around his
nec ; and in the struggle, some one had him in the
comfort—and he went out of sight, he and Mr.
Wemiss both, and he raised up and straightened
himself back, and was shot.   Who was it had
him by the comfort?   I don't know, sir.   Was
he up fairly on his feet?   Yes, sir, right straight
up, straining his neck back.   And then he was
shot?   Yes sir.

Cross examination by the Counsel for the accused.

You say you went down to the market house
about three o'clock that cay?   No, sir, I did'nt
say what time it was   What time was it?   I
do not know, sir.   Where cid you go from?   I
went from Jim Bowman's house.   Where is that?
Right above where Mr. John Hall's store is.
How far is that from the market house?   I
never measured it.   Five hundred yards?   Yes
sir, and more too.   What time do you think it
was when you got there?   I don't know exactly.   You say you went down to hear the trial?
Yes, sir, I heard Archy's trial was coming off——
Trial for what?   For committing a rape on
a woman.   What woman?   William Massey's daughter.   When you got there did you
see Beebee come from the guard house?—
No sir.   Where was Beebee when you first
got there?   He was up in the market house.
How long was it after you got there before Beebee
came down?   It was not long.   Quarter of an
hou—half an hour?   It was not half an hour.
B tween a quarter and a half an hour?   Yes,
sir, it was some fifteen or twenty minutes.   Where
were you standing during the time you were waiting there?   I was not standing in any particular place.   About what place?   I was first
under the market house, and then out.   When
you were under the market house were you near
the eastern arch?   Yes, sir.   When Beebee
was brought down the steps where were you
standing?   I was standing between the eastern
arch and a bench.   How far off from the steps?
I don't know, sir—five or six steps.   How near
were you to the bench?   I was not more than a
step or two.   You mean Becky Ben's bench?
Yes. sir.   Which is on the left as you come down
the steps of the market house?   Yes, sir.   You
come down the steps of the market house, and you
pass through Becky's stall, and as you do that
you pass near the bench you have been speaking
of?   Yes, sir.   You were a step or two off

from the bench? Yes, sir. How long had you been there before the prisoner was brought down? I went there just as he started down. And before he got down? I was there from the time he was coming from the door down to the foot of the stern. Had you been standing at the bench for some minutes before Beeb e was brought down? A very short time. How many minutes? It was no minutes; it was not more than a minute. You were not there more than a minute? No, sir. Well, before you went up there near the bench, for five minutes or so, where were you standing? About five minutes before I went there I was outside of the market house, when the ladies got out of the carriage. Could you see at that time every thing that happened under the market house? No, sir, I could not while I had my back turned toward the market house. You did have your back turned? As the ladies got into the carriage I had my back turned. Then you turned and came back into the market house, and took your stand near that bench? I passed near it, but I was not stand ing near it for five minutes before he came down. I want to see if you can remember for how many minutes you were standing near that bench before the prisoner was brought down stairs—? Not more than a minute. Did you see Maultsby there that day? Yes, sir, after the prisoner was shot. Did you see him before the prisoner was shot? If I did I don't remember. Did you hear anything from him? I did not, sir. Did you see him about the bench before the pri oner was shot? I did not. Didn't you see him on the bench just as the prisoner was being brought down? No, sir. Did'nt you hear him say something there from that bench just as the priso ner was being brought down stairs? No, sir. If Maultsby had been upon that bench at the time the prisoner was brought down stairs, could you have seen him? If I had turned I could. If Maultsby had jumped upon that bench, and had called out, "Th re he comes, boys!" in a loud tone of voice just as the prisoner was being brought down stair, could you have heard him? Yes, sir Did you see, or did you hear any thing of that sort? No, sir. Do you know Maultsby well? Yes, sir. Isn't he a tall man? Yes, sir. And you say that while you know Maultsby, and know him well, while you were standing there near that bench, at the time the prisoner was brought down, that you did'nt see him jump upon that bench, and hear him ex claim, " here he comes, boys!"? No, sir, I don't recollect to have seen him at all until after the prisoner was shot. Now, when the prisoner came down stairs, who came first?—you say Miss Massey came down? Yes, sir. Who came with her? I am not sure whether Israel Baun was with her or not. Any other lady with her? Yes, sir, her mother was with her. It was the young lady that Beebee was charged with having at tempted to ravish, and her m ther, that came down stairs? Yes, sir. How long did they come down before the prisoner was brought down? About four or five minutes. Did you look at Miss Massey when she came down? I did, the best I could get a chance to look. Did you look at her neck and her face? She had a veil on her face. Did you look at her neck? Yes, sir. I could see the back of her neck. Did you see any mark upon her neck? I saw a scratch. Was the blood flowing from it? It looked red. How long was the scratch? I don't know, sir. Was it a quarter of an inch or an inch? I guess it was about an inch. On what part of her neck was the scratch? On the right side. Well, in about four or five minutes after she pass-

ed down you say, the prisoner was brought down? Yes, sir. Who came down with Beebee, Mr. Wemyss and Mr. Hardie did you say? Yes, sir Did Mr. Hardie have hold of the prisoner? I could not say positive, whether he did or not. Did you notice whether he was in front of him or in the rear? Mr. Hardie—to the best of my re membrance, Mr. Hardie was on the left, when they first started down the steps And Mr. Wemyss on the right? Yes, sir. Did you see any other members of the town guard there with them? I never noticed them. Did you notice Mr. Bond there with them? I noticed Mr. Bond being with them after they got outside of the market house. But on the steps? No, sir. Did you notice Mr. Faircloth with them? No, sir. Well you say when they got down to the front of the steps, there it was, that Monk Julia rushed upon the prisoner with his knife? Mr. Powers made the first rush. Before they got off the steps? No, sir, after they got off the steps. Was that when they got into Becky Ben's stall? Yes, sir. Where did Monk rush from? From near that bench. Was he inside of the stall at the time? Yes sir, inside of the stall. He rushed at him with his knife? Mr. Powers made the first rush. Did you see Powers have a knife in his hand at that time? No, sir I never saw any knife in his hand. Powers just ran up and said, " I demand the prisoner?" Yes sir—I didn't notice his hands. What reply did Mr Hardie make? I never noticed any at all. Did you see Mr. Hardie at that time? Yes, sir. You saw Mr. Hardie at that time? Yes, sir. What do you think was Mr. Hardie's position, at the time Powers rushed at the prisoner? I think he had got sort of front of him. He was on the right hand; Mr. Wemyss—he was on the left? I didn't notice anybody in particular. Did Mr. Hardie have hold of him at that time? No sir, I don't think he did. They then came out of Becky Ben's stall, and when they got nearly out of the arch you say, then somebody else rushed at Beebee again? I saw Monk Julia rush at him again. Did you see anything in his hand? I saw him have his knife in his hand. What prevented Monk from getting at him, at the time he rushed upon him? The first time, I could not see. The second time what prevented him? The second time he rushed, Mr. Nixon prevented him. Did you see the police use their clubs there, and beat the crowd back? I saw them use their clubs pretty considerable. When you lost sight of Archy as you say, when he and Mr. Wemyss went down, do you know what Mr. Hardie's position was? During the time he went down, and after Monk Julia made the second attempt at him, Mr. Hardie changed his position and got right in front of Mr. Wemyss. Mr. Wemyss was on the prisoner's right hand? Yes, sir. Now, at the time the pri oner raised up—after the time he got up after you saw him go down, where was Mr. Hardie then? In front of Mr. Wemyss. Which way was Beebee's face looking? Looking down towards the South street. The street running South? He was fronting that way. How far was he off from the outer edge of the pavement? He was not very far. Well, how far; give some idea? The crowd was very thick before him, I could not see how far. Was he a foot? Yes, sir it was over a foot. Then when he raised up and when he was fired upon, was he nearer the centre or was he nearer the outer edge of the pavement,—the prisoner Beebee? I think he was near the edge How far do you think he was from the edge of the pavement when the shot was fired? I could not see for the crowd. You ay he was near the edge of the pavement. Yes, sir. And you think that Mr Wemyss was on his right hand, and that Mr. Hardie was in front of Mr. Wemyss? Yes, sir. You saw Mr. Hardie then? Yes, sir. And you swear that at that time Mr. Hardie was in front of Mr. Wemyss? Yes, sir. Was he directly in front of Mr. Wemyss? Yes, sir. That would throw him to the right of Mr. Beebee? Yes, sir. So that was Mr. Hardie's position? Yes, sir. To the front of Wemyss, or to the front and right of the prisoner? Yes, sir, he was further in front of the prisoner than Mr. Wemyss? You are not mistaken about that? No, sir, I am not mistaken. No danger for you to be mistaken? No, sir, not a bit of it. Well then you say you saw the pistol fired? I did, sir. And you say that Tolar shot him; where was Tolar standing? He was standing in the rear of the prisoner. How far were you from Tolar at the time he shot? I was not very far from him. How far would you think? As far as from here to Captain Reming ton I should think. Was Tolar on the pavement? Yes, sir. Was he near the edge of the pavement, or was he near the centre of the pavement? He was not far from the edge of the pavement. Which was nearer, taking a line right back; which was nearer the edge of the pavement, the prisoner, Beebee, or Captain Tolar;—suppose you had truck a straight line from where Beebee was standing, to where Tolar was standing, would that straight line have gone to the right or left of Tolar? It would have gone to the right. How much? I don't know sir. If you think how far the prisoner was, and how far Tolar was from the edge of the pavement, you can answer my question? I didn't go to look to see how far he was standing from the edge of the pavement? But you are sure Tolar was upon the pavement? Yes, sir. You have no doubt about that? No How far was Tolar off from the deceased—from Beebee? About as far as from here to colonel Bomford. About how many men were between Captain Tolar and the prisoner at that time? I dont know, sir. Were there a good many? No, sir. Was there one man? I think there was one man, I saw him put his hand upon one man's shoulder—his left hand. There was not a great many men? No, sir. So you think then the space was clear? Yes, sir, the space was clear from the prisoner's shoulders up to his head, between him and Captain Tolar at that time. What was between Tolar and the lower part of his body? some men leaned to one side. And Tolar when he fired was as far from the prisoner as you are from Colonel Bomford? Yes, sir, almost that distance. Did you see Tolar draw the pistol? Yes, sir. Where did he draw it from? Right from down to his left side. Did he have on a belt? I didn't see any belt. He had on a brown shawl. And he drew it from under the shawl? Yes sir. What sort of a pistol was it? I looked like a navy repeater. How long was it? It looked like about a foot long. You saw him draw it? Yes, sir. Did you see him cock it. No, sir. Did you see him present it? I did, sir. How long an aim did he take? But a very little aim before he fired. Did you see the smoke? Yes, sir. You saw the smoke arise from Tolar's pistol? Yes, sir. Did you see John Armstrong there? I did, sir. Where was John standing at the time Tolar fired? John was standing near Mr. Tolar—I think right at the side of him. Which side? He was on the left hand side. Was John Armstrong on the pavement? Yes, sir. So Tolar was standing on the pavement, and John was standing on the pavement to his left hand side? Yes, sir. How far was John off from Tolar at that time? I

didn't take much notice, he didn't seem to be standing very far. There could not another man have got between them. Was John near the edge of the pavement? He was on the pavement, John was on the pavement; and Tolar was to his right? Yes sir. And you think there was space for another man between them? No, sir, I don't think there was. You noticed Tolar's shawl? Yes, sir. Did you notice anything peculiar about his shawl? No, sir. Didn't you notice that his shawl was off his arm? I never paid any attention to its being off his arm. Did you see him after he fired? Yes, sir Did you have your eyes fixed on him after he fired? Yes, sir. From the time he fired till he turned off? No, sir, not all the time. Did—you notice just before he turned off, did you notice that his shawl was off his arm? No, sir, I didn't notice. Did you see him throw his shawl back? I don't know that I did. You didn't see that? No, sir. You say that after Tolar fired he went back up to Mr. Hinsdale's? He stood where he was standing for a minute or two. And then went back to Mr. Hinsdale's? Yes, sir. I was talking to some one, and when I saw him again he was going between the market house and Mr. Hinsdale's store. You don't know whether he went through the market house or around it? No, sir. When he got up to Mr. Hinsdale's store, did you see him then? Yes, sir. Did he stand out in front of the store, or did he go into the store? He went into the door frouting on Hay street. Tolar went into the door frouting on Hay street? Yes, sir, and then he passed around and took his stand in the door frouting east. That store of Hinsdale's is a corner store? Yes, sir. And has two doors near each other? Yes, sir. One frouting upon Hay street and the other toward the market house? Yes, sir. And Tolar went into the Hay street door and passed around and took his stand in the door which was frouting East? Yes, sir. How long did he remain there? I could not say, sir. At the time that Tolar fired the pistol, and before he turned off, you were there near him? Yes, sir, I kept my same position except stepped back a little. Now when Tolar turned off after shooting the man, did any body say anything to him? I didn't hear any one. Did you see any body turn round, and say to him, "there Captain, you have killed that poor man"? No, sir, I don't think I did. If that remark had been made in a moderate tone of voice, were you near enough to have heard it? I don't know as I could hear it distinctly, almost every one around was talking. You were near him at that time? Yes, sir. And you heard no such remark as that? No, sir. And you are certain that you did'nt see him then, throw back his shawl as he turned round? No, sir, he moved his shoulders just a little. He just shrugged up his shoulders? Yes, sir. You did'nt see him throw his shawl back? No, sir. What did Tolar do with his pistol? I don't know what became of it. You didn't see whether he returned it to the place where he put it from? I don't think he did, after he fired the pistol he moved his arm back, and the crowd all closed right up. How many people do you think were there at that time—about the time he was shot? I don't know, sir. Was there a large crowd? Yes, sir, a pretty good crowd. Both white and black? Yes, sir. You have no idea as to the number—75, 100, 200? I dont know, sir. Were there as many as 50? Yes, sir, more than 50. As many as a hundred? I could not say and be justified, sir. Were there about as many blacks as whites? I am not able to say. Did you go there armed on that occasion? No, sir, I was not expecting any such a thing to occur. You carried no arms with you at all? No, sir. You didn't have a pistol? I did not. But you just went down there because you heard Archy was to be tried, and you wanted to see how it was? Yes, sir. I understood you to say in your direct examination, that you saw Mr. Phillips come up? Yes, sir. Where did he come from; which direction? He came from behind me. When did he go up to Captain Tolar? I never saw him near Captain Tolar; he was on the outside of the side walk. And you say he had a pistol in his hands? Yes, sir. What sort of a pistol was it? It was a small pistol, one of those small four barrelled pistols. Which hand did he have it in? He had one hand hold of the breech, and the barrel was laying in his other hand. What did he say? Somebody asked him, "Sam, was that you shot," and he turned and said, "no, I didn't get a chance to shoot." Did you see him make any effort to shoot? No, sir. Did you see him pressing into the crowd? No, sir. You didn't see him present the pistol at all? No, sir. Did you see the pistol distinctly that Phillips had in his hands? I saw it what I could. Now I ask you if you saw that pistol with sufficient distinctness to say whether it was a navy revolver? It was not a navy revolver. You are certain of that? Yes, sir, if it was, it was smaller than any one I ever saw before. That was all you heard Mr. Phillips say,—that he didn't shoot, because he didn't get a chance? He said he didn't get a chance to shoot.

Re-direct examination by the Counsel for the prosecution:

You were asked by the gentleman that has just examined you whether, when you were standing inside of the market house, near Beeky's bench, you could have seen anybody who jumped up on it and shouted to the crowd, "look out boys!" I could have seen it if I looked. You mean to swear that no such a thing happened? No, sir, I don't know whether it did or not. I didn't see it When you saw Mr. Tolar, after he fired the pistol do you mean to swear, or not, that he didn't throw his shawl off his shoulder? No, sir, I didn't see him do it. Do you know whether he did or not? I don't. You didn't notice him make any such a movement? No, sir. Where did you say that John Armstrong was standing about the time Tolar shot? He was standing near him. How high is the pavement from the earth below? It is not more than about six inches. Did you say he was standing on the pavement? Yes, sir. How do you know? I was on the ground and they were the other side of me. You are quite sure he was standing on the pavement? Yes, sir, I think he was on the pavement And you are sure the Sheriff was standing in front of Mr Wemyss when Archy fell? Yes, sir. Was the Sheriff nearer the wall of the market house than Beebee was? Yes, sir. The Sheriff and Mr. Wemyss then had the market house wall on their right? Yes, sir. And Beebee on the left? Yes sir. Was the Sheriff in a line with Beebee and Tolar or not? I don't hardly think he was, sir. The pistol shot fired by Tolar, in your opinion, did not range with the Sheriff? No, sir.

On motion, the Commission adjourned, to meet on Thursday, the 25th instant at 10 o'clock, A. M.

RALEIGH, N. C., July 25th, 1867.

The Commission met pursuant to adjournment.

Present, all the members of the Commission,

the Judge Advocate, the Counsel for the prosecution, the accused, and their Counsel.

The proceedings of yesterday were then read and the following corrections were made in witness Louis Smith's testimony:

Add to answer of witness, line 11, page 162. (Pamphlet, page 18, second column, line 29 from top) "grasp by the comfort in front of the th oat." Line 15, page 177, (Pamphlet, page 20, first column line 32) amend the question to read:— " running back parallel with the east front of the market house," and strike out the words," to where Tolar was standing," line 15, same page.

Yesterday's proceedings were then read and approved

Dr W C McDuffin, a witness for the prosecution, having been first duly sworn, testified as follows: Examined by the Counsel for the prosecution: What is your name? W. C. Duffie. Where do you reside? In Fayetteville. How long have you been living there? About fifteen years. What is your occupation? Physician sir. You are a practitioner of medicine? Yes, sir. Did you know Archy Beebee? No, sir, not personally Did you know him by sight? No. sir. Were you in Fayetteville on the 11th of February last? Yes, sir. Were you called upon to examine a person who was wounded that day? Yes, sir, I examined a colored man who was said to be Archy Beebee. Where were you when you were called upon? I was between the market house and Hinsdale's drug store, on the West side of the market house. Is that Hinsdale's drug store at the corner of Hay street? Yes, sir. You were there when called? Yes, sir, I was called by the Sheriff. What is the name of the Sheriff? Hardie. Did you go? I did, sir,—I went and examined the wound. What did you find was the condition of the boy? Dying, sir, he was insensible, and upon examination I found a bullet hole in the back of his head on the left side about two inches from his ear about upon a line with the top of his ear. How far did the bullet penetrate? It did not go out, sir it went into the brain. I probed it but a short distance, he died during the time I was examining him—he did not breathe more than two or three times while I was examining the wound. Was that wound the cause of his death? Yes, sir. He had no other injury upon him; I examined the body; no other injury than the bullet hole in the head. Did you find the bullet at all? No sir. How far did you insert the probe? Not far, probably two inches, it was all soft in the brain, I suppose it had probably lodged against the skull on the opposite side. It didn't have momentum enough to go through. Did you see any of these prisoners at the bar, there that day? I don't recollect that I did. I simply examined the wound, and the Sheriff spoke of calling a jury of inquest or something, and I went off. There was a large number of persons there. Did you hear any pistol shoot? I heard it from where I was standing. Were you at Hinsdale's store when you heard the pistol? Yes sir. Had you been at the market house at all that day? I suppose I had several times, passing backwards and forwards; my office is in market square. What time of day was it when you were called? It was about four o'clock in the afternoon. What time was it when you heard the pistol shoot? It was immediately before that. Had you noticed any crowd at the market house? I don't think I had, prior to that time I was aware of the trial going on. Did I understand you to say there was nothing unusual in the crowd that attracted your attention that day? No sir, not before the time of the occurrence.

Do you know anything further of the deceased at all? No sir. Is there any light at all you can throw upon the subject? No sir; I cannot say that I know of anything; the first I knew of it was the excitement at the time of the firing of the pistol, and I still didn't go up until the Sheriff saw me standing there, and he called me and I went, and he asked me to examine the man. You did so? Yes sir. Could you tell what the calibre of the bullet was? Well, sir, it was not a very large bullet; I could insert my little finger in it up to the nail; I suppose about the size of an ordinary repeater, the bullet of an ordinary repeater.

Cross examination, by the Counsel for the accused:

I understand you to say that you didn't observe any unusual crowd there that day? No sir, I think not, before the occurrence. Nor did you observe anything unusual, of any sort, about the market house? No sir, I didn't observe anything. That you had been at the market house several times during the course of the day? Yes sir, I presume I had; I don't recollect now, because I am in practice constantly, and would be out of town all day sometimes; I don't know whether I was out of town that day or not. Hinsdale's place is on the West side? Yes sir. Your office is on which side of the market house? North-east. You say the ball had made an opening that you could put your little finger in, up to your nail? Yes sir. That was all? Yes sir. It was through the skull bone, of course? Yes sir. A smooth hole apparently without any fracture further than the size of the bullet. And the ball hadn't pierced the skull on the other side? I did not discover it sir, it was not visible. You didn't see any of the prisoners there that day? I don't recollect seeing any one in particular; there were officers there, and a good many people, black and white. How much of a crowd do you suppose? I don't know sir, a hundred probably. All colors, sir? Yes, sir, of every description. More of one than another color? I don't know; perhaps more white persons than black. How long before that had you been at the market house? Well I was between those during times several times; I don't know that I was in the market house before. Were you past the market house while Beebe was being tried? Yes sir. I think I passed the west end of the market house, from Mr. Smith's Drug store to Mr. Hinsdale's; I passed ordinarily by the market house of course. The west side? Yes, sir, this occurrence took place on the east side of the market house, and if there had been a large crowd there I don't know that I could have seen it unless it had been very large. How long is the market house from east to west? I don't know, sir eighty or one hundred feet I suppose. I believe it is square. You speak of this pistol that was used, as one of ordinary size—an ordinary repeater? Well that is my idea of it, that is what I think it was. What is your idea of an ordinary repeater? The five shooter as they are called; I have been accustomed to seeing them a good deal, I suppose the ball was about that size—that is as near as I can Judge. About what size pistol would it be? Well, from ten inches to a foot in length I suppose. Would it be a navy revolver? I think they are longer sir, carry a larger ball than that. It could not be such a one? I don't think the ball was as large, sir,

Re-direct examination, by the Counsel for the prosecution:

Are you very familiar with arms? No, sir. Can you pronounce with certainty upon the calibre of a gun or pistol from the bullet? I dont think I can.

ROBERT W HARDIE, a witness for the prosecution, having been first duly sworn, testified as follows:

Examined by the Counsel for the prosecution, What is your name? Robert W. Hardie, sir. Where do you reside? In Fayetteville, North Carolina. What is your occupation? Sheriff of Cumberland county, sir. Are you acquainted with Archy Beebee? I was sir. When did you see him last alive? On the 11th of February Give an account of all that happened that day from the time you first saw him in the day, until you last saw him? At 3 o'clock—within a few minutes of 3 o'clock, upon the 11th of February, in accordance with my orders, I went to the guard house in Fayetteville. I had no jail, my jail having been burned. I went to the guard house or started to the guard house. I had ordered the Town police to meet me there precisely at 3 o'clock, and I got about seventy five yards from the guard house, when I saw them at the door. I gave them a sign, and they went in and brought Archy Beebee out. Who are the town police you speak of that were there? My Deputy, a man by the name of Wemyss, Bond, the town Constable; Sam Fairclotth, the chief of the night police; George Hornrind, a man by the name of Brown, Daniel McGuire; and I am not certain as to the other, I think he was sick. What occurred then? They came out; I went in front of them, to the Magistrates' room which is in the town hall, over the market. How far is the guard house from the market house? Between three fifty and four hundred feet. Was there any disturbance in your passage from the guard house to the market house? [No sir, there was some crowd I passed through the crowd at the head of the prisoner. We went up into the market house. You say there was some crowd? Yes, sir. How many in that crowd do you suppose? I suppose there were 30 or 40. Did you notice any one in the crowd? No, sir, I just walked right through them. Can't you mention a single individual in that crowd? I don't think I could, sir. I didn't pay attention to any individual sir. Is it impossible to name a single man who was in that crowd? I don't recollect a single individual that was there. I passed right through the crowd. Was there anything said to you? Not a word. Anything said to the prisoner? Not a word, sir. We passed through the crowd, and went up stairs in the market house. Who went up with you, sir? All the police. I was in front of the prisoner, the others behind the prisoner, Mr Wemyss and Mr. Faircloth having ag hold of the prisoner and the others behind them, and I immediately in front of the prisoner. When we got there Duncan G. McRae asked——. We don't want to hear what any one said. Who did you find in the town hall? I found Duncan G. McRae, James W. Strange, Joseph Arey, John W. Lett, French Strange, the County Solicitor, Thomas H. Massey, I think was all at that time. You think those were all that time? Yes, sir. What happened after you got up stairs? I then went after W. H. Horn, Counsel for the prisoner, and then at the request of Archy Beebee, I went after Dennis Hogans, his uncle; but first let me say Miss Massey and her mother were there. Were they in the room when you went up with the prisoner? Either then or after I returned from after Captain Horn, I cannot tell which; I think when I returned from Captain Horn. How long were you absent? But a very few minutes, sir. Captain Horn's office was not more than a hundred yards. How far did you have to go for Dennis Hogans? It occupied some little time to find him ; he was not far off ; he was in the market house, and I had to go to the upper end to find him. Which do you all the upper end ? The west end. Did you notice whether the crowd was larger or smaller when you went down stairs ? I seemed to be about the same. Did you notice any disturbance ? Not a particle. Who did you find up stairs when you returned ? I found Miss Massey and her mother. Were any persons gone ? They were all there that I left there, and an old woman by the name of Dely Stewart, a colored woman, and an old man by the name of Matthew Morgan. What was the object of that meeting ? The object of that meeting was a preliminary examination for an assault. You must not tell what he did ; it was a preliminary examination for some offence that was alleged against him ? Yes, sir. Did the examination take place up stairs ? Yes, sir. Who was the presiding magistrate ? Duncan G. McRae Did any one assist him ? Yes sir, Joseph Arey, James W. Strange and John W Lett. I want you as nearly as you can, to describe accurately the position of the parties in that room while this examination was going on, and give a description of the room ;—what is the size of the room ? I don't know that I can do that exactly ; the room is probably 30 or 40 feet square. How many win dows in each end, the east to begin with. Two and a door. Does the door open to the stairs ? No sir, it opens to the main building. The building is a two story building. There are wings east and west, one story. This door leads out to the top of the wing. The top of the wing is like a floor inclined enough to allow water to run off. How wide is the roof ? It is about 25 feet, I should say. Is there any railing or molding or anything around it ? There is a balustrade around it two and a half feet high, probably. As I understand you there are two windows and a door that open on that ? Yes, sir. Was that door opened or closed ? I presume it was closed; it was a cold day. You can't say ? No sir, I didn't notice it. The north and south side, are there any windows on them ? Yes sir, four on each side. On the west end ? The west end has a door and window exactly corresponding with the east end. One door and one window ? One door and two windows. The balcony is nothing but the roof of the first story ? Yes, sir. And it is about 25 feet wide ? Yes, sir. The inside of this room is how many feet square ? I suppose 30 or 40 feet. Is there any subdivision of the floor up there ? All in one room sir. Where the steps come up from the market house, how are you facing when you come through the door, north, south, east, or west ? When you go up and get to the head of the stairs, you would be facing north. When you open the door and enter the room you would be facing north ? Yes sir. Taking the east front of that room, how far towards the middle of the east front does that door fall ? It is right in the center. You land there, about the center of the east end of the room ? Yes, sir When you came back and enter-d at that door where was Major McRae sit ting ? He was sitting at his table, upon the west end of the room sir. Is that table in the middle of the west end ? It is near the stove, sir. Where is the stove ? In the north west corner,— no—it is in the south west corner. The stove is in the southwest corner, and this table is near the stove ? Yes, sir. Was he sitting behind the table, near the stove. Where was the prisoner Beebee seated that day ? There was—I don't know what it was built for—but it makes a seat,— something like a bench or a double bench, one facing one way, and one another. Beebee was

sitting there. Was he facing the committing magistrate ? The committing magistrate was to his right sir. It was a sort of an armed settee ? No sir, just like two benches put together without backs. Major McRae was seated you say at that table.—was any one seated there with him ? The others were seated around him. Who was ? James W. Strange, Mr. Arey and Mr Lett;—they were sitting around as near the stove as they could and be comfortable. How long did the examination last after you went up the second time ? I suppose it lasted something like half an hour, sir. Were you ordered to take the prisoner back ? Yes, sir. Did you feel any apprehension about his safety ? I did not, sir. You had no reason to apprehend danger ? No, sir I believed I had sufficient force to protect the prisoner and prevent a rescue Do you believe now if you had had sufficient force you could have protected him ? No sir; I could not guard against the pistol shot, sir. Who went out of the door first to go down stairs ? Miss Massey and her mother, and Mr. Bond, I think went with them. Israel Bond ? Yes sir, the town constable. Did they go out together ?— Yes sir, he went to accompany them to the carriage. They went out together. Did you go out at that time ? No, sir. They left you there ? Yes, sir. Did they leave all the others there ? Yes, sir. How long after they had gone out before some one else left the room ? I think I was next No one else had left before you left ? N t that I noticed. Who left with you ? The prisoner was ordered in my custody. I started with him. Mr. Wemyss was on his right side; Mr. Bond had returned before I started. How long was his absence ? Not more than a minute or two; just time to walk down apparently and come back. Mr. Wemyss was on his right side; Mr. Faircloth upon his left ; I was immediately in front, and the other police were in the rear. I came down stairs in that position. Describe those position again. Mr. Wemyss on his right with his thumb fastened by a twitch, Mr. Faircloth locked arm with him on the left; I was in front, and the balance of the police were behind him. We came down stairs in that way, and when we got down, I saw there was some crowd, and I said ' Gentlemen make way !" Before you got down stairs did you notice any crowd ? No, sir, I could not see. Are there not two flights of stairs.—a pair of stairs, a landing and then another pair ? Yes. sir, but you can't see from that landing. After you go out of the door on the landing, how many steps is it down to the floor of the market house ? You go down some seven or eight steps and turn. There is a door right there, where there was a policeman stationed ; and then there are three or four rickety steps further down to the floor. When you got to the bottom of that last step, on the floor of the market house, which way were you facing ? East, sir. How many steps would it take you, from the bottom of the steps, to come plumb against the wall of the market house, in a straight line ? It is probably four steps ; twelve or fourteen feet. When you opened that door could you see the crowd ? One step, and I could As soon as you stepped through the door ? Yes sir, then I could. Was the crowd any larger than when you went up stairs ? I think not sir. Did you pause a moment when you got on that step ? I didn't pause there, I went on to the floor of the market,—a brick floor. You didn't pause till you got to the brick floor ? No sir, when I got there I noticed the others were not following me as close as I desired, and I turned around and asked them what was the matter, and in a moment they came up. You started down the stairs, you and that party? I was just a step ahead of them. When you got to the first landing you were together? Yes, sir. But you noticed when you got on the floor of the market house that they had paused on the first landing? Yes, sir. That was the first time that you had noticed it? Yes, sir. Did you notice any reason for the panic? No, sir. You didn't see anything? No, sir. Do you know now what caused it? I do not sir. Did the prisoner in your presence show any unwillingness to come out of that door? Not in my presence Did he manifest any trepidation in facing the crowd? He was much alarm d up stairs—at least I judged so from his looks. Was there any outcry in that crowd? Not a word up to that moment. You told the officers to come on? Yes, sir. They did come on? Yes, sir. What happened then? To get out of the market house on to the pavement, to start for the guard house, we have to go under an arch on the eastern side. They were close behind me, Wemyss and the prisoner, as I described them : I heard some one say. "Damn him, give him up, I demand him" The party was hid from me on account of the brick wall of this arch : I instantly turned and saw a hand, apparently trying to catch t e prisoner. Of course as an officer, your attention was attracted when you heard some one demand your prisoner?—Yes, sir. You instantly turned? I did, sir. And as you turned you saw this hand? Yes, sir. Whose hand was it, Mr. Hardie? I would not say as a fixed fact, the best impression that I had, it was Mr. Powers'. Have you a decided impression? Yes, sir, a decided impression, though I don't know the fact How soon did you see Mr. Powers after you had caught his hand? Immediately I caught him and pushed him off. Did you look in that direction? My attention, my whole attention—was turned to the boy. I said "stand back, the prisoner is in my custody and I will protect him." I said "men use your clubs." I saw another hand from behind him. Mr. Bond instantly caught him, whoever it was. Do you know who it was? I do not, sir. Have you any decided impression? No, I have not You heard the voice that cried out "we demand the prisoner? Yes, sir. Did you know that voice? I think it was Mr. Powers. You know him well? I am not very well acquainted with him. Mr. Hardie, it is a painful duty for you to testify in this case? No, sir, I am here to tell the truth, the whole truth, and nothing but the truth, and I am going to do it. You say you are familiar with Power's voice? I am tolerably so, but it was not his voice so much, it was the appearance of the man, being pox-marked, that attracted my attention. Did you notice the pox-marks? Yes I noticed the pox-marks when I caught him, en the side of the face. You think you recognized his voice? I thought it was his, I would not be positive about his voice. I am not sufficiently familiar with his voice to speak of that positively. The chief ground upon which you based your opinion was the fact of his being pox-marked? Yes, sir. Do you see the man here? Yes, sir. You didn't see who made the second attack. No, sir, I saw Mr. Bond got him. I think he went down with him ; and at that moment there was an attack in front. Do you know who it was. I think it was Monk. I heard very distinctly the blow. The blow struck at the prisoner? At the man who made the attack on him in front. You think it was Monk—did you see him? I think I saw him. You thought you saw him—is that your impression now? Yes.

sir. Is it a decided impression? Yes, sir. Did he have any weapon? I did not see any, sir. Did you see any weapons in the hand of any one? I did not, sir. Had you seen, from the time you left the door on the steps, to the time we are speaking of now, any newspapers? No, sir. not up to that time? As I now understand it, y u have got about to the point where you turned out of the arch? Yes, sir. Where were you then? On the pavement, just turning. They had made a circle around us, and I then started. Was the crowd pressing on you? My o der to use the clubs had relieved the press a little. We then started facing south The walk seemed to be apparently clear. Was that the direction toward the guard house? Yes, sir, due south. Had you got outside of the point where the market house reaches to ? No, sir, we never got to the corner of the market ; we got four or five steps when Beebee made a tremendous effort to escape, and from some cause they all came down together, Wemyss, the prisoner, and Faircloth. What do you mean by a tremendous effort to escape ? What was he doing? He used all h s strength, jumped, jerked and bounded to get away. Did he say anything? Not a word that I heard. He seemed to be very much alarmed. Was the crowd noisy or still? There was not much noise. There were exclamations of "Give him up ! Give him up!" "I demand him!" I saw no great outburst. Do you know how many times you heard that cry ? I think I heard it twice, sir. Well, sir, he made this bound or effort to escape. Were you afraid he would get away? I was a raid he would get away, and I was fearful they would kill him. If he got away I was fearful, after the effort that had been made, that they would kill him. Was he trying to escape from you or the crowd? He was trying to escape from the officers; what his object was, of course I could not tell. It was during the midst of this uproar around him? Yes, sir. How many times had he been assaulted ; how many rushes had been made at him ? It was all in one rush. There were three that I knew of certain, who rushed at him. How long was it—how many moments from the time that you got to the foot of the steps to the time when he made this effort to escape; I want to know whether it was all simultaneous. It was as quick as could be done. Mr. Hardie, did you see any fire-arms in the crowd that day, up to that time? I did not, sir. Did you see any knife fall in the crowd? I did not see it, I heard it:—I heard a metal fall. Was that the time this effort happened, or afterwards? Immediately before, sir. Immediately before that you heard a strike corresponding to the clash of a knife? Yes, sir, and I distinctly heard the striking of a club, and I heard a man say, "damn it, they have broke my arm, I believe." You heard the striking of a club, the man's exclamation, and the fall of a knife? Yes, sir. Where is that knife? I never saw it, sir. Who picked it up that day. I dont know, I only know from hearsay, sir. Have you never seen it since? I never have, sir. Did you see it that day, sir? No, sir, I saw no weapons in the hands of any one, sir. You only know from hearsay, what has become of the knife; do you know from hearsay what has become of it? I only heard —— Don't tell me; I merely wanted to know whether you have an y knowledge where it can be found? No, sir. What happened after this effort of Beebee to escape? When they all fell, I was fearful he would escape; I stepped down and caught him by the back of the collar,; they all raised up together. He had a struggle and a fall, and the constable and officers went down with him? Yes, sir. Did you notice whether he had on any comforter that day? He had something round his neck. Did you have him by that? No, sir, I had him behind the neck. Did any one have him in front at that time? No, sir. Were you standing behind him? I was standing behind him, sir. You raised him up, did you? I stooped down to assist to raise him, and as he got up straight, a pistol or a gun was fired, from immediately behind him, as I supposed; the ball passed through my hair, and entered his head just over my knuckles. Did he fall instantly? He didn't fall, he sank. Make any outcry? No, sir, only a groan. Did he die immediately? There was a gentleman passing not far off, I hollored to him to run to Mr. Hinsdale's, and a physician there, Dr. McDuffie, heard my voice, and came immediately; I said, "Doctor can any thing be done to him;" he asked me for some water, I turned around to the stand of a woman by the name of Becky Jenkins, and asked her for some water, I handed it to Dr McDuffie; at that moment I saw Dr. Hague go by; I called him; he came in, and they both said he would die in a minute. Did he die from the pistol shot? I suppose so. He received no other wound that you are aware of? No, sir. Did you see who shot that pistol? I did not, sir; it was fired behind me. You are confident? Yes, sir. Can you describe the relative positions of the prisoner and Mr. Wemyss, at the time the pistol was fired? The prisoner was facing due south, on the pavement, Mr. Wemyss was upon his right hand, Mr. Faircloth was upon his left; I was behind him; I say behind him, I dont know that it was exactly behind him, I may have been covering Mr. Wemyss partly; partly behind the prisoner and partly behind Wemyss. What was your reason for thinking the bullet passed through your hair? It produced a sensation that I have never experienced before, I supposed I was shot, and put my hand to my head to see if I was shot; it produced a burning about my ear. Was any hair cut? There was short hair there, I could pull it out. Could you see where the bullet had cut a lock away? No sir, I could only judge from the short hair coming out. Have you ever been under fire in battle? No sir. Have you ever had a pistol shot at you that you are aware of? No sir. Have you ever had a pistol fired very close to your ear? I have never had a pistol, I have had a gun fired immediately at my ear. Did it produce the same sensation? No sir. Did you look around to see where the noise came from? I did not sir, not for an instant. It was an instant before I looked round, and I saw one or two persons coming to me, or I supposed they were coming to me. How far was the prisoner from the edge of the market house when he was shot? The sidewalk I suppose to be about eight feet wide sir; I suppose he was five feet from the market house wall. About three feet from the edge of the sidewalk? Yes, sir. And I understand you, nearly at the corner? Very near the corner. The bullet came from his rear? Yes, sir. And struck him just behind the left ear? Yes sir, within two inches of his left ear, sir. Which way was his face turned, due south? I think it was; in fact I know it was. Did you look around in the direction the shot seemed to come from? Yes sir. Who did you see? I didn't look all the way round, I only saw Mr. Phillips making his way through the crowd; and my attention was immediately attracted by a noise in front, and I looked around and saw Mr. James

L. Nixon, just at that moment catch Monk, and after a good deal of shuffling carry him off. Was Mr. Phillips the only person you saw that you recognized? He was the only one, it was only an instant, I just turned my head, my attention was attracted in front of me. Phillips was the only person? The only one I remember. You have thought of it well? Yes sir. I noticed him from the fact of his coming through the crowd —making his way up there through the crowd. There is no doubt that the pistol was shot at] that time? None in the world. The man was killed, and fell at that time? No doubt about that sir. You don't know who shot it? I do not, sir. You didn't see any one with weapons at that time? I did not, sir. Did you see any of these prisoners at the bar about that time? I only saw Monk in front of me, Nixon taking him off. Had you seen Captain Tolar that day at all? No, sir. Did you see many after the firing? I saw a great many come up, to where Beebee was. Did you see Captain Tolar then? I never saw Captain Tolar.

Cross examination by the Counsel for the accused.

Mr. Hardie, when you brought the prisoner from the guard house, you say there was a crowd about the market house? Yes, sir. Where was that crowd collected, out on the pavement or under the market house? Most of them were under the market house. Was the crowd so large as to attract your attention particularly? I had often seen them there larger. Do you know whether it is usual for crowds to collect there as long as that, when trials are going on of any interest, in the market house? I have often seen it, sir. You have often seen it? Yes sir. Did I understand you to say that that crowd appeared to be quiet and orderly? Perfectly so, sir. There was nothing in the demeanor of the crowd that aroused or excited your suspicions? None in the least. You went up into the market house—and I will see whether I understand you—you went up into the market house, entering by the eastern arch? Yes sir. What is the distance from the main eastern arch, to the foot of the stairs, leading up into the Court room? Well sir, I suppose it is ten or twelve feet. As the stairs rise from the floor or pavement of the market house, in what direction do they first run? As they go up they run due west. How many steps do they run west before they make a turn? About five sir. After you have gone up those five steps, and before you have made a turn, is the door there? Yes sir. That is the door? Yes sir. You then make a turn, in what direction would the steps run, after you make that turn? North sir. Due north? Due north sir. Do the stairs run up close beside the eastern wall? Yes sir. And when you enter the room up stairs, from the stair steps, you are close beside the eastern wall, and near that door which opens out upon what you call a balcony? Yes sir, you are right at it. That is upon your right hand as you go to the head of the stairs? Yes sir. Is that door which opens out upon the balcony, on a level with the floor of the Court room? No sir, you go up about two steps. Where did I understand you to say the table was that was used by the justice? The table was at the west end near the stove, the stove is in the south west corner of the Court room. And the table is near the west end? Yes, sir. What is the distance between the west side of the table, and the western wall of the market house, or what was the distance on that day? Well sir, I suppose six or eight feet. Was Mr. McRae and his associate justices on the East side, or the West side of the table? They were on the west side. So that they were between the table and the western wall, of the market house? Yes, sir. The distance being about six or seven feet? Yes, sir. Was Major McRae sitting down when you got there? Yes, sir, he was sitting at the table. Did he remain sitting during the whole time you were there? Yes, sir, taking down the evidence. I understood you to say there were no persons there present except the prisoner, the witnesses, the justices, yourself and the members of the police force, the counsel for the accused, the county solicitor, and uncle of the prisoner, Dennis Hogans, and the grand father of the young lady upon whom the assault is said to have been made. I since recollect Robert Mitchell was there, who married an aunt of Miss Massey. And then I understand you to say when you first got up there, that neither Mr. Horn, the Counsel for the accused, nor Dennis Hogans, protector of the accused were there.—You went down first for Mr. Horn? Yes, sir. When you went down did you leave Mr. McRae still sitting in the position that he occupied when you went up? Yes, sir. What was he doing when you went up? He was writing. When you went down with Mr. Hardie, after Mr. Horn, did the crowd appear to have grown during the time, or was it about the same size? About the same I think. Had the crowd maintained its position? They were spread out pretty much over the market house. They were spread generally out, I understand you to say? Yes sir. Did you notice anything unusual in the crowd at that time? No sir. No whispering? No sir. Was there any apparent excitement among the crowd at that time? Nothing that I saw. How long were you gone when you went after Captain Horn? I was gone three or four minutes. When you returned on your way back did the crowd appear to be any larger? No sir. Did there then appear to be any excitement? Nothing that I saw, sir. When you went back up into the market house did Mr. Horn go up with you? I think he did, sir. What was Mr. McRae doing then? He was at the table, sir. And in his chair? Yes sir. Busy with his papers? Yes, sir. How long did you remain there, until you went down after Dennis Hogans? Only a moment. When you left there that time did you leave McRae still in his place writing? Yes sir. When you got down that time did you notice any difference in the crowd, from what you observed on the former occasions? No sir, I did not. How long were you there amongst the crowd looking for Dennis Hogans? I walked through and asked a colored man where he was, and he told me he was at the North-end of the market house, I walked there directly and looked and finally saw him and called him. Did he go up with you? He went up with me. When you returned from the crowd at that time was it any larger? No sir. Was there any difference in the state of feeling prevailing in the crowd? None sir. When you got back into the court room that time, where was Mr. McRae? He was sitting in the same position. How long did that investigation last? I suppose about half an hour. During the time that that investigation was going on, did Mr. McRae occupy the same position? Yes sir. He never left his seat? No sir. I understand you to say when you started down, the order of procession was, yourself in front, the prisoner next, attended on the right by Mr. Wemyss, who had a thumb twitch around his right thumb; that Faircloth,

a member of the town police, had his right arm locked in the left arm of the deceased, that the town constable and the other members of the police force that you have stated, were immediately behind, all around with their clubs? Yes sir. That you got down to the landing, and there was a policeman stationed at the door? Yes, sir. That you had the door opened, and you went out in front—the same order of procession? Yes, sir. And you noticed nothing unusual until you had got upon the bottom step, or upon the floor of the market? I didn't see any thing unusual until I was coming out of the arch. You got to the floor of the market, and then thought the party was not following you as closely as they should follow you, and you looked back and saw them, where? They were just in the inside of the door. Were they then visible to the crowd below? No, sir. How far were you, Mr. Hardie, from a bench that runs on the left of that stall known as Becky Ben's stall? I could reach it. I ask you if at that time any one leaped upon that bench? No, sir. Did you hear an exclamation of "Come on, boys," or anything like it? I heard nothing of that sort. Could anything of that kind have occurred, a man leaping upon that bench and exclaiming "come on, boys," in a tone of voice loud enough to be heard by the crowd, without you hearing it? I don't think there could. Don't you feel certain it could not? Yes, sir. I think I understand you to say that directly afterwards the party with the prisoner came down, you still continued in front of them? Yes, sir. That you passed on until the prisoner had got nearly out of the eastern arch and upon the pavement; that at that time you were being obstructed by the brick wall, a hand was thrown out to grasp the prisoner? My attention was attracted by the exclamation. Just give me that exclamation, if you please, precisely as it was.—The exclamation was, "Damn him, give him up ; I demand him." Not " We demand?" I think it was "I;" I will not be positive about that. "I demand him?" Yes, sir. Well, was it about this same time that a hand was thrust out to grab him, the prisoner? As I turned, then I saw the hand and caught it. Did you see the man's face at that time? I saw it as I turned. Was there anything in that hand ? I didn't see anything in the hand. You saw no knife? No, sir. It seemed to be a grab at the deceased? That is what I supposed it was at the time. I understand you to say, Mr. Hardie, that it is your best impression that that was Mr. Powers? Yes, my best impression. Did I understand you to say that impression was produced upon your mind merely by the fact of his having a pox-marked face? It was a pox marked face, and I think I knew Mr. Powers. Is there any room for your being mistaken as to that? I must say that my best impression is that it was Mr. Powers. And that impression was made upon you mainly by the fact that the man had a pox-marked face? Yes sir, and my knowledge of him. Probably but few persons in my county, I am less acquainted with than Mr. Powers. I have seen him but rarely, and never had any official connection with him in any way. You said something about the voice, are you sufficiently well acquainted with the voice to designate him by it? No sir, I don't think I am. Then the voice made no impression upon you? It made a slight impression; and it went only in a measure to confirm me in the view that I had, that it was Mr. Powers. From the casual glance, and the fact of his being pox marked that made an impression upon you that it was Mr. Powers? Yes sir, I don't swear positive. It is my best impression, it was Mr. Powers. You say first a grab, with an expression, "I demand him," then you ordered the police to beat them back, with their clubs, which they did, at once? Yes, sir. And then at that instant another grab was made? Yes sir, and I thought Mr. Bond and the person came down together, though I don't know, they appeared to go down. Bond was ordered to use his club, and I have no doubt he did it. And then a third grab you say was made? Yes sir, in front of him. I simply saw a man. Who do you think it was? I think it was Monk? Did you see anything in his hands? No, sir. Are you certain that was Monk? No sir; my best impression was that it was Monk. Why did you think so? From his size and his appearance. I only saw him between the shoulders of the party. I understand you to say that you don't swear it was Monk? No, sir; only my best impression; not as a positive fact. About that time you say the crowd had been beaten back? Yes, sir. It gave way so as to leave an open space before the prisoner, and the party conducting him to the guard house? Yes, sir. Do you remember whether there was any body at all in the front of the prisoner and the party conducting him to the guard house? At that time I don't think there was, sir. When I got straight I looked across the street to Colonel Draughon's store. The door was open, and his nephew, who was acting as clerk, was standing in the door, and I thought if I could get in there with him he would be safe. I was then very much alarmed for the safety of the prisoner. About that time then the struggle you described occurred? Yes, sir. Up to that time, I understand you to say, you were still in front? Up to the time the first demand was made I was in front; when I caught his hand I then got in the rear, because there was a crowd much larger there. So at the time you first caught the hand which you thought was the hand of Mr. Powers, up to that time you had been in front? Then you shifted your position and got in the rear? Yes, sir; they passed around me. Then this struggle occurred between the prisoner and Mr. Wemyss and Mr. Faircloth, and they all three went down together? Yes, sir. You think when they went down together the prisoner was about five feet from the eastern wall of the market house, and about three feet from the outer edge of the pavement? Yes, sir. After they had fallen, I understand you to say that you reached down, and with your hand you caught him in the back of the neck, through the collar of the coat and shirt? The collar of his coat; I don't recollect about his shirt, I know I had him by his jacket—a blue jacket—no, a gray jacket. And you assisted in lifting him up, and had got him to an upright position before he was shot? Yes, sir, standing straight up. What was the height of the prisoner as compared with your own height? He was about six feet tall—fully six feet. Is the pavement at that part of it elevated above the surrounding country? Yes, sir. And he raised right up? Yes, sir. You still retained your hold on the collar? Yes, sir. At that time you think you were directly behind the prisoner, or it anything a little to the right? Yes, sir, probably a little to the right, covering him and Mr. Wemyss probably. I suppose that one half of my body was opposite to his body, and, one half covering Mr. Wemyss, for Wemyss was close to him. Have you any doubt but what you were in that position? I have none whatever—that was the position that I occupied. About the time you got him straight you heard the report of a firearm of some kind? Yes, sir. And you thought you were shot yourself?

Yes, sir. That you put up your hand and you felt something like a bullet pass there? I felt a stinging sensation. And you put up your hand and you found that your hair had been cut? I put my hand up to see if there was any blood, and then I felt the hair. I could pull out the short hair. Did you find anything on the back of your neck? Some gentleman passed back of me and remarked— Stop! you must not say what he remarked. I put my hand up and it was a little black. You found your hand was a little colored, and this color came off of your neck? Yes, sir. What was that black produced by? I supposed it was from powder. Have you any doubt about that? I was satisfied at the time, that it was the smoke of powder. And that was back of your neck under your ear? Yes, sir. I understand you to say sir, that you looked back, after the pistol was fired? I turned my head, it was an instant before I was satisfied I was not shot. Were there a great many men directly behind you, when you looked back? I didn't look all the way back, I didn't get my head around, before my attention was attracted in front. In that casual glance you gave behind, could you tell whether there were many men in your rear? I could not sir. Did you turn to the left or the right? To the left sir. Could you tell whether there were many men to your left and rear? There was some crowd standing there. Mr. Phillips was making an effort to get to me. Were they near you? They were from three to five feet off. Were there many of them? A dozen or fifteen probably. Were they standing still? They seemed to be perfectly stock still. It seemed to me that everything was over in an instant. Did you notice whether they were white men or black men? They were both. And the only man you recognized was Mr. Phillips? Yes, sir, it was only a glance for an instant, and immediately my attention was called back to the front. And Phillips was parting the crowd to get to where you were? Yes, sir. I think I understood you to say you didn't see a pistol in the hands of any body that day? I did not sir. And you didn't see any weapons in the hands of any body? No, sir. What knowledge have you of fire arms? I have always been very fond of sporting. What knowledge have you of small fire-arms—pistols? Very little indeed, sir; I have no knowledge of fire-arms except shot guns. I think I understood you to say it was a very cold day? Yes, sir. Mr. Hardie, what was that man Beebee being tried for, at the market house?

The Counsel for the prosecution objected to the question.

The Counsel for the accused said:

I think we are entitled to it in this view—If there had been a trial for a small misdemeanor the crowd would not naturally gather. There was a large crowd—we say they gathered under a natural impulse of curiosity, which impulse grew out of the fact that it was a grave offense, and not only a grave offense but a trial of a sort that would excite the curiosity and cause the gathering of a large crowd of people.

The Counsel for the prosecution replied:

The Government objects to any such question being asked, as totally irrelevant and impertinent to this issue. There is but a single fact here to be investigated, and that is whether Archy Beebee came to his death by the hands of these defendants, who are charged with either killing him or being there present, aiding and abetting. We say it is irrelevant for what Beebee was arrested, or for what offense he had been committed, because the Counsel cannot pretend to justify their clients f they committed this act upon the deceased, upon the ground that he had been guilty of any offense whatsoever. He might have burned the Capitol, he might have ravished a thousand wo men, he might be the veriest scoundrel that ever disgraced the earth, and yet, he is entitled to the protection of the law, until he be tried by the law.

It can have no possible relevency to this issue, and its tendency, if it have any weight at all, must be to mislead and prejudice the minds of this Court, and surely the Court can see that the offense that Archy Beebee committed upon that occasion, for which he was arrested and placed upon a preliminary examination, cannot be any justification to the men that killed him,—it cannot even be a palliation for their crime.

The offense that he committed cannot possibly mitigate that crime from murder to manslaughter, and the only possible object with which evidence of that character can be introduced into such aCourt as this,must be either to affect the feelings or prejudices of by-standers, or to act upon the feelings of this Court, and to mislead them from the performance of their duty,—not that it will have that effect, but we are all mortals,subject to imperfection; and its tendency is that way. And therefore it is, that the law excludes Courts from hearing it, unless they see fit to call it out themselves, upon their own examination.

In behalf of the Government yesterday I allowed the simple statement to come out—what this boy was committed for. I knew it was improper at the time; but I determined to give the prisoners, in the painful position in which they stand, as much benefit as could be gained, by the Court having the knowledge of what the allegation was against Beebee. It came out yesterday, and further than that, the Government is not willing to go; nor did the prisoners have a right to insist that we should go that far. We submit the question to the decision of the Court.

The Counsel for the accused said:

The principles laid down by Colonel Haywood on behalf of the Government, we admit as sound principles of law. Admitting those principles of law however; we submit to the Court, that, without any wish to take any benefit, from the bystanders opinion—and we have nothing whatever to say about there being any bystanders here—and without the least intention to prejudice the Court; we think it a material point, among the many points surrounding this case, to show why that crowd, had gathered there; that they had gathered, not under any design of resisting the laws, but under an impulse of natural curiosity, whether or not, in some possible line of defence, that may not be material, I hope the Court will not easily decide. We think it will be material.

The Commission was then cleared for deliberation, and after some time so spent the doors were re-opened, and the Judge Advocate announced that the Commission sustained the objection of the prosecution, as to the admission of the question.

Cross examination resumed, by the Counsel for the accused.

Mr. HARDIE, you spoke of the nervousness of the prisoner up stairs? Yes, sir. Was that the first time you had noticed any trepidation in the prisoner; after he got up stairs? I didn't notice the prisoner particularly before. Did I understand you to say, sir, that up to that time no demonstration of violence had been made by any parties, towards the prisoner, either in his sight or in his hearing? Not that I saw nor heard, sir. Was that trepidation greater during the investigation or after it.

close? I didn't see any change from his general appearance he seemed to be nervous and alarmed. Re-direct examination, by the Counsel for the prosecution:

One question I omitted to ask in the examination, which does not come properly in the cross examination.

I proposed to ask whether there was any relationship between Thomas Powers and Miss Massey, within your knowledge? There is. What is it? Mr. Powers is her uncle,—so represented to be. I understand you to say in the cross examination, that after you had got to the foot of the steps in front of the prisoner, the prisoner being then on the first landing, you didn't see any one jump up on Becky Ben's bench, and waive their hand? I did not sir. Did you see any one stand on there at all? I think there was a colored boy standing on there, sir. I think his name was Louis. Do you know his other name? He used to belong to Mrs. Smith, I don't know what he goes by. Have you seen him here as a witness? I have seen him here in Raleigh. Louis Smith? Yes, sir, I think it was Louis Smith. He was standing on Becky Ben's bench? Yes, sir. Didn't I ask you if you recognized any one in the crowd as you came off the steps and you said you did not? I did not then : I had passed the steps and I recollect seeing some one over me and I looked up and I think it was Louis Smith I saw. Is he the only person you recognized in the whole crowd? He was the only one. Why was your attention so distracted that you did not see more in the crowd? My attention was centered on the prisoner, I had no other thought or feeling than simply the prisoner. You were walking in front of the prisoner:—your attention was absorbed with him. Yes, sir. You noticed no other person in the crowd? No, sir. You think if any one had leaped up on that bench you would have noticed them? Yes, sir. And your attention was so absorbed that you can't recollect a face that was in that crowd ? I don't recollect a face at all, sir. Did I understand you to say you meant with certainty to declare that the exclamation was "I demand the prisoner," or "we demand the prisoner." No, sir, I can't say which it was for certain. My impression is it was "I demand the prisoner." But your mind is in a state of uncertainty? Yes, sir. Was it a right hand that you caught hold of when you seized that man? I think it was a left. Did you see his right hand? No, sir. You saw no knife in his hand?— No, sir. Which hand did you have in the back of this man's neck? I think it was the left, sir. I understood you in the previous examination to say the right—? I think you must be mistaken. I stooped down and caught him, I had my right hand to use. It was your left hand? Yes, I think it was, sir. Did you have that hand on his collar till he was shot? Yes sir. You never let go? I did not, sir.

Questioned by the Commission :

You say the last time you saw Archy Beebee was on the 11th of February—February of what year? 1867. Had you any reason to believe there would be an attempt made by the crowd upon the prisoner, that day? I had none, whatever. Then why did you order the attendance of the town police? Mr. Wemyss, one of my assistants, came to me that morning and told me about.the arrest of Archy. I was then in my office. I was there till 10 o'clock, and I went over, (my office is probably ¾ths of a mile from the market house,) Mr. Wemyss came to me and remarked "There is more indignation about this affair of yesterday than I have seen in this community for a long time, and I fear there will be trouble." "Wemyss, have you heard any threats?" "I have heard none, but the excitement is so great, I fear there will be some difficulty." "If you think so, I will attend the trial myself," I said "and I will have the police force there with me." I told him to summon the police, and afterwards I saw the Captain himself, and ordered him to meet me at the guard house at 3 o'clock. When you heard the shot and turned round, might not Tolar have been behind you, and you not have seen him? Yes, sir. When you heard the knife fall upon the pavement, as you have stated you did in one part of your testimony, who picked it up? I don't know, sir. Who did you hear had picked up the knife? Monk. Who told you who picked up that knife? I don't recollect that, sir. Have you heard what disposition has since been made of that knife? I never heard. Have you heard any one assert that they kept possession of that knife, or had seen the knife since that time? I never heard. In whose hands was it when you last heard? Monk's.

The Commission then adjourned to meet on Friday, the 26th inst., at 11 o'clock, A. M.

RALEIGH, N. C., July 26, 1867, 10 A. M.

The Commission met pursuant to adjournment. Present, all the members of the Commission, the Judge Advocate, the counsel for the prosecution, all the accused and their Counsel.

Yesterday's proceedings were then read and approved.

SAM TOOMER, a witness for the prosecution, having been first duly sworn, testified as follows:

Examined by the Counsel for the prosecution.

What is your name? Sam Toomer, sir. Where do you live? In Fayetteville at present. Where did you live at the beginning of this year? Fayetteville. What was your occupation there at that time? Driving a dray, sir. How long had you been driving a dray in Fayetteville? Over a year. I don't know exacty how long. Did you know Archy Beebee? Yes, sir. What has become him? Well, sir, I suppose he is dead now. When was the last time you saw him alive? The last time I saw him alive was sometime in February. I don't know exactly what day. It was February of what year? This year, sir. Do you remember what day of the week it was? No, sir, I am not certain. Where did you see him then alive, in what part of the town? He was on a dray, sir, with me. Is that the last time you saw him? No, sir. The last time I saw him he was standing on the opposite corner of the market house. In what town? Fayetteville. How came you at the market house that day? I just come and saw a great collection there in the afternoon, and I heard there was going to be a trial there. Did you go on your dray, or walk there? I come down on my dray, sir. What time of day was it when you got there? It was after 3 o'clock as well as I can recollect. Which end of the market house did you stop your dray at? On the south side. Did you remain on the dray or get off? I got off, sir. Where did you go then? I stayed on that same side a little while, I don't know how long exactly. Where did you move to next? I came around to the east side of the market house? Did you go inside of the market house to get to the east side, or go around? I went around, sir. When you got there was there a crowd there? Yes, sir. How many people do you suppose? There might have been fifty, or seventy-five or one hundred probably;

a right good crowd. Were they white and colored? Yes, sir, both. Where was the prisoner Beebee at the time you had got to the market house? Up In the market house, sir. When you got there? Yes, sir. How long were you there before he came down the steps of the market house? I might have been there a half an hour before he came down the steps. You went around to the east end of the market house, did you go inside or stay outside on the pavement? I stayed outside. On the payement or off the pavement? Off the pavement. Were you in front of the middle arch? I was just opposite the middle arch, just a little to the lower edge of the middle arch, not far from a little China tree that stood on the edge of the pavement. You stood a little towards the south of the arch? Yes, sir. Off the pavement, near a little China tree that stood on the edge of the pavement? Yes, sir. Did you keep that same position, or did you move about? I didn't move about much. How long were you standing in that position now, before Beebee was brought down stairs? I might have been standing in that position five or ten minutes probably. Where had you been before; I understood you to say you were there about half an hour before he came down? I come from the south end round to the east. Did you go at once from the south end to this position? Yes, sir. Did you notice any of these prisoners about the bar, that day before Beebee came down stairs? I don't know that I saw any of these men, without it was Monk Julia. Did you see him? Yes, sir. What was he doing. Walking about there under the market house, on the pavement. You don't remember seeing any of the others? Not that I recollect. Was Monk doing or saying any thing? Nothing that I noticed. Did you notice whether he had any pistol, or any weapon? Not at that time, sir. Was there any thing unusual in his appearance at all? No, sir. This crowd that you speak of, was it under the market, or outside or both? Both under and outside. Did you notice any thing unusual in the crowd during the 30 minutes that you were there? No, sir. Notice any whispering? No, sir. Were you alarmed in any way? No, sir, not up to that time. There was nothing unusual to attract your attention that you knew of? No, sir, not that I knew of. Did you see John Armstrong there that day? Yes, sir, I saw him after the man got shot, sir. I mean during the time you were standing there, before the man Beebee came down stairs? Yes, sir, I recollect seeing him. Where was he standing when you saw him? On the south end where I come to. Did you see him again before Beebee came down stairs? Yes, sir, he was knocking about there. Did you notice him any where else before Beebee came down stairs? Yes, sir. Where was he standing the next time you saw him, before Beebee came down? He was around to the east end just after I got there. Where was he standing, on your right or left? He was standing to my right. On the pavement or off the pavement? Off the pavement. Near the edge or far from it? He was about the middle when I saw him. Was that after you had taken your position near the china tree you speak of? Yes, sir. Did you see any other of your companions or any other persons that you recognized in that crowd, that you have seen about here during the last few days? Not that I know of, sir. Did you see Louis Smith? I didn't see him at that time. Before Beebee came down stairs did you see him? Not that I paid any attention sir. You can't remember any other that you noticed in that crowd? No, sir. And there was nothing that attracted your attention at all? No, sir. What was the first thing that attracted your attention? The first thing that I sort of noticed, sir, was when the prisoner was coming down stairs, as he got to the foot of the steps. When he came out of the market house who was with him? Mr. Wemyss had hold of him for one, that I noticed. Which side was Wemyss on? On the right side as well as I can recollect, and the Sheriff on his left. Did you see any one else with the prisoner? Not that I noticed sir. Were those the only two persons that you noticed with the prisoner? The only two that I noticed. You say no one else was with him, or not? I would not swear positive either one way or the other; I don't say for certain whether there was any body else with him or not. There was a crowd around there at the foot of the steps, and there probably might have been some one else with him, but I never noticed any particular person. In coming down the steps did any thing happen before Beebee got to the bottom of the steps? Not that I noticed sir. Did you hear any out-cry? Not before he got to the foot of the steps. When he got to the foot of the steps I saw this man Monk, just after he got to the foot of the steps go to him as if he wanted to cut him, and that time Mr. Wemyss shoved him off. What did he want to cut him with? He had a knife. Did he strike? Yes, sir, it seems as if he struck at him. Did he move towards him quietly? No, sir. Was it a rush or not? It was a rush with him, at that time. He rushed at him with his knife? Yes, sir. And struck, did he? Yes, sir. What else did you notice? He was shoved off at that time, and they made out then, from under the market house, and as he got to the arch again, just as he was coming out from under the arch, he made another strike at him. Monk? Yes, sir, Monk; and he was shoved off again, and he turned toward the prisoner, the way he was going on the pavement, as he was coming on down, and as he got very near against the opposite corner he made another strike. Was he in front or behind as he made that last strike? He was more to the left hand of the prisoner, sort of behind him. That was the third strike? Yes, sir. Did you see him strike him again? No, sir. From the time the prisoner was passing from the foot of the steps to this point, where you have got him now, near the corner of the market house, did any body else interfere with him? Nobody that I saw. Did you hear anybody use any exclamation? As he got to the foot of the steps, some one said, "charge boys!" but I don't know who it was. You heard that expression? Yes, sir. Did you hear any other expression? Not that I noticed at present time. Try and recollect and see if you did or did not? Not that I recollect at that time. You don't recollect hearing any other expression between the time the prisoner got to the foot of the steps and the time he got to the corner of the market house? No sir, not that I recollect, there might have been some other words passed. During that time you have just spoken of did you see any of these prisoners at the bar in the crowd, except Monk? Not that I noticed sir. What happened next? As he got to the opposite corner then I noticed Capt. Tolar coming out the same way that I come. Coming out of where? From under the market house. Out from the East arch? Yes, sir, the same way that I come, and he just pushed the men aside from each side, and I saw him after he got his pistol to a certain height and he raised it a little higher, and shot him. Do you know Capt. Tolar? Yes, sir. Do you see him in this room? Yes, sir. Point him out. Yonder he is sir, with green specks on. You saw that man hit his pistol and fire? Yes, sir. Did Beebee fall? Yes, sir. Did you know Capt. Tolar before that time? I didn't know his name. I knew the man. Have you any doubt about that being the man? None in the world. You are certain? Yes, sir, certain. How was the man you say fired the pistol dressed? As well as I can recollect he had on a kind of a yellow shawl. He had on a shawl? Yes, sir. Where did he draw that pistol from? I never noticed where he drawed it from, I noticed it after he got it to a certain height. Did you hear whether he said anything? I didn't hear. How close was he to Beebee when he was shot? Inside of five feet, I don't know exactly the distance. Was he standing on the pavement or off the pavement? He was standing on the pavement. Was he near the edge of the pavement or near the middle. He was nearer the edge than the middle. Who was the nearest man you saw to him? There was some one or two men that was between him and the prisoner when he shot the pistol, which leaned their heads on one side. Do you know who they were? No, sir, I do not. Did you notice any one else near him on his right hand—near Tolar? John Armstrong was on his left hand as well as I can recollect. Was John then standing on the pavement or off the pavement? When I saw him he was standing off the pavement. That was when the pistol was fired? Yes, sir. When the pistol was fired did you notice whether the Sheriff was standing behind Beebee? He was standing more to the right of the prisoner, in front of Mr. Wemyss, both of them were sort of to the right of the prisoner. And he was in front of Mr. Wemyss? Yes, sir. Where was Mr. Wemyss standing? He had hold of the prisoner on his right hand. Was he exactly in a line with the prisoner? As well as I can recollect. On a line with him on his right? Yes, sir. Well, now, where were you standing at that moment with respect to them? Drawing a straight line from Mr. Wemyss by the prisoner would it strike you? No, not a straight line. You were a little in front of the group? Yes, sir. And a little to the left? Yes, sir. A line running from the prisoner straight along the market house would have passed on your right? Yes, sir. As Tolar was standing, a line drawn from him running in the direction of the prisoner straight down the market house, would that have gone to the right too? Just a little. Was Mr. Tolar behind or in front of the prisoner when he fired? Behind him, sir. Did you notice the prisoner fall during that time or stumble? He seemed to stumble. Was that before the pistol was shot? Just before, and when he raised up again some one put his hand in the collar around his neck. I don't know who it was—and he sort of throwed his head back, and at that time he was shot. Did you see Beebee after he was shot? I saw him as he commenced falling, sir. Up to that time had you seen any of these other prisoners beside Monk and Tolar." Not that I noticed, sir. Who were the nearest men standing about Tolar, at the time he fired? John Armstrong was on his left? Yes, sir. Did you notice anybody else? No, sir. At the time that pistol was shot, was the crowd any smaller than it was when you first got there? No, sir. Was it any larger? It might have been larger. What became of Mr. Tolar after he fired that pistol? He stood there for a moment, and he turned right off and went under the market house; I noticed him after he went under and then he went out of my sight. Did you notice what he did with the pistol after he fired? You did not see whether he had any pistol in his hands when he went under the market? He didn't have any pistol in the hand, he shot the pistol, he turned his right hand to me. And he had no pistol in it? No sir. Did you see any one else that was concerned in this affair? I saw Mr. Phillips just after Captain Tolar shot the man; he had a pistol in his hands. What was he doing with the pistol? He was standing with it in his hands; he looked as if he was cocking it or uncocking it. What sort of a pistol was it? It seemed to be a very small pistol, as well as I can recollect, sir, about a four-barrelled pistol it looked to me like. Did he say anything? Not that I heard him, sir. This is all you know about this affair that you think will be of use here? Yes, sir. Did you see any other persons there with arms there that day? I did not, sir, not that I can recollect.

Cross examination, by the Counsel for the accused:

How long have you been living in Fayetteville? I have been living there two years, sir. What was your condition before the war? Slave, sir. Who did you belong to before the war? I belonged to Mr. Frederick Davis, of Chatham county. And you have been living in Fayetteville two years? Yes, sir. In what part of Chatham county was Mr. Davis living? About a mile from the court house in Pittsboro', sort of east from the court house. Have you been driving a dray ever since you went to Fayetteville? Not ever since I have been there, no sir. What were you doing there before you commenced driving a dray? I waited on Griffith's and Kinsons's, in the store they have up in the hotel row. You say you went down that day upon your dray? Yes, sir. Where from? Mr. Lutterloh's store. And you got there about half an hour before the prisoner was brought down from the market house? Yes, sir. When you were going from the south side of the market house round to the east side, how did you get there? I went around, sir. There was a crowd standing on the corner, and I went around that crowd and come into the market house. Did you pass on the pavement or off the pavement? Off the pavement. You say when you got around to the east side of the market house, you took your stand just a little below the main arch and off the pavement and near a small china tree. Yes sir, it was just about the south end of the main arch. From the position you occupied there, near that china tree, could you see all of Becky Ben's stall, and the benches which were about there;— the foot of the stairs leading down from over the market house? I could see the foot of the stairs, sir. How could you see that, through the main arch or through the small arch? Through the small arch. Looking through that small arch, could you see that bench, which was on the left of Becky Ben's stall,—left going down from the market house? No, sir, not where I was standing. Was the crowd there collected under and around the market house, during that day, larger than you are in the habit of seeing there? Yes, sir. You say nothing occurred in the crowd to attract your attention? No, sir. Not before the man came down? Nothing that I thought of. You saw nobody cut at him at all except Monk? No sir. Were you looking at the prisoner all the time, from the time he got down

the steps, until he got out of the arch? No, sir, I could not see him exactly all the time,—as he got against the arch, inside of it, I could not see him until he got out. And you say nobody rushed at him, and no body cut at him, with the exception of Monk? No, sir. And you say Monk rushed at him and cut at him three times? Yes sir. You spoke something about the prisoner making a stumble just before he was shot.— Yes, sir. Do you know whether that was a stumble or whether it was an attempt to get away from the guard? I don't know, it seemed as if he stumbled;—I don't know what it was, sir. Then when he rose up you say Mr. Wemyss was on his right hand;—how far was Mr. Wemyss from the eastern wall of the market house, at the time the prisoner rose up? He was not very far from it,—I don't exactly know the distance. Say about how many feet was Sam? It might have been one foot, or a foot and a half, or two feet. And standing immediately on his left was the prisoner, Archy Beebee? Yes, sir. Close to him? Close to him. Close up against him? No, not close up against him but close to him. And Hardie was in front of Wemyss? Yes, sir. You are certain of that? Yes sir. At that time, you say you saw Captain Tolar come out of the market house; was that the first time, that day you had noticed Captain Tolar? Yes, sir, it was. That was the first time you noticed him? Yes, sir. And just about that time, when they had got the prisoner up after he had stumbled, you say you saw Capt. Tolar coming out of the east end of the market house thrusting the crowd aside? Yes, sir. That was the first time you saw Tolar that day? Well sir, I might have seen him before, about the market house, but I don't know that I did; I didn't pay any attention to him. Now at the time Tolar was thrusting the crowd aside as you described, did he have any weapons in his hand? Not that I noticed sir. Did you notice to see whether he had any weapons in his hands or not? No, sir. Did Tolar make any halt until he got up and presented the pistol to Beebee's head? did he make any halt from the time he cleared the market house until he presented the pistol. He was not going exactly in a rush, only moving the men out of the way; I didn't see him make a halt. So you say he didn't make a halt, b t was advancing slowly, pushing the men away as he advanced? Yes, sir. And he went straight down the pavement, until he got up within five feet of Beebee? Yes, sir, and raised his pistol. That you didn't see where he drew it from? No, sir. When he got it on a level he elevated it a little and fired? Yes, sir. I saw it after he raised it a certain height and he raised it a little higher from that. What sort of a pistol was it? It seemed to me like a dark looking pistol. Not a white looking one? No, sir. Well about what size was it? About as long as my hand. Which was the longest pistol, the pistol that Tolar had or the pistol you saw in Sam Phillips' hands? As well as I noticed, the pistol Tolar had was the longest. A little the longest? Yes, sir. You think Tolar's pistol was about as long as your hand. Yes sir? Now pay attention to this question Sam—suppose a line had been struck from Archy Beebee's feet, straight back upon the pavement, parallel with the eastern wall of the market house, would that line have passed to the right or left of Tolar, at the time he fired? That line, sir, would just come a little to his right? Just a little to his right? Yes, sir, it would have struck him on his right. So that Tolar was about the center of the pavement? Yes, sir, he was between the center and the edge. Nearer the center, or nearer the edge? I don't know exactly, whether he was nigher to the center or the edge. What is your impression? He might have been nigher the edge than the center. How far off from Tolar were you at that time? I was between ten and twelve feet from him, sir. And to his front and left? Yes, sir, his left hand side was to me when he shot the pistol. So that you were to the left of Tolar rather than in front? Yes, sir. How many persons were between Tolar and the deceased man Beebee at the time the pistol was fired? Well, sir, there were two that I noticed which leant their heads to one side when the pistol shot. And only two? Yes, sir. Do you know who they were? I do not, sir. Were they white men, or black men? I never noticed, sir; I was looking at the pistol. Why did they lean their heads; did Tolar say anything to them? Not that I heard of. Did he touch either of them? He touched the hindmost man, as well as I can recollect. With his left hand or right hand? Left hand. At the time of the shooting, you say you noticed John Armstrong? Yes, sir. How far was he off from Tolar? He might have been a foot and a half, or two feet, not further I am certain, and if anything he was nigher. Did you say Armstrong was on the pavement or off? He was just at the edge of the pavement, off of the pavement. On the pavement or off? Off. You spoke of Tolar's shawl, did you notice anything peculiar about the shawl? No, sir, no more than I commonly would about a gentleman's shawl. Did he have the shawl pinned? Yes, sir, it was fastened in front. So that it could not fall off? Yes, sir. And so that it could not be thrown off? It seems to me it was fastened in front. Didn't it fall off? No, sir, it didn't fall off. I saw some of it turned back on his right shoulder, but it did not fall off. You say then, the edge of the shawl, though it was fastened in front, one edge seemed to fall over his right shoulder? Yes, sir. How did he get the edge of the shawl back? I don't know, he got it there; he shoved it back I suppose with his elbow; it was just turned back a little. Didn't you see him take his hand and throw it back? No, sir, I did not. Would you have seen that, if it had occurred? No, sir, I don't think that I would have seen it, if it had occurred; because I didn't notice him particularly before he was raising his pistol. I am speaking about after he fired the pistol? After he fired the pistol the shawl came back to its place again. See if you can recollect this; after he fired the pistol, didn't you see him throw his shawl back with his hand? No, sir. You didn't see him? No, sir, I didn't. Were you not looking at him then? Yes, sir. How happened it that you didn't see him do that? I didn't see him; he might have done it. What is your impression—that he did reach out and throw it back after he fired the pistol, or that he did not? My impression is that I don't know whether he throwed it back after he fired the pistol or not, but he must have throwed it back before, because the wrong side of the shawl was laying back a little. So that your impression is that he threw it back before, and not after he fired the pistol. Yes, sir. You say you saw nobody else there with arms, on that occasion, except Sam Phillips? And Mr. Tolar and Monk. What did you say Mr. Phillips was doing? He was standing just after Tolar shot the pistol. How far from Tolar? · He was a little further off than I was at the time I noticed him. And to Tolar's left? Yes, sir. Did you hear anybody make any remarks to Phillips

at that time? No, sir. Were you near enough to have heard a man make a remark, if he had made one in a moderate tone of voice? Well, sir, I might if I had been noticing it, but they were speaking around in the crowd;—so many different voices that probably I might not have noticed it. You say you could not tell whether Phillips was cocking or uncocking his pistol? I could not, sir. Did you notice whether he had his thumb on the cock? I did not examine him close enough for that, but he had the pistol in his hands. Did you notice whether that was a four barrelled pistol? It looked like a small four barrelled pistol sir. You saw it? Yes, sir, I saw it was a pistol. And you think you cannot be mistaken about the size? I may be mistaken a little about the size. I will ask you the question—whether it was not a navy revolver, a foot or fifteen inches long? I don't think it was that long, I know it was not that long. Was it as long as my hand? Yes, sir, it was as long as your hand. Was it longer? Not to my recollection. I wish you to be certain about that? I cannot, because the view I got of it would not enable me to give the exact length. You saw him make no attempt to use it? None in the world. How far was Mr. Phillips from Beebee, at the time the shot was fired? I didn't see him then. Do you know how many men were between Phillips and Tolar at the time the pistol was fired? I do not, sir. Were there any men between them then? There might have been, but I never noticed Phillips at that time. How many persons were there between you and Tolar at the time of the firing? Well there was nobody between me and Mr. Tolar, exactly, but they were standing both sides. I could see him plainly, there was a lane running through there between us. There was a lane there for you to see through? Yes, sir, there were some on the side walk which was standing very close by me, but I could see the best part of him at the time he fired. And after the firing Tolar went back under the market house? Yes, sir. And then you lost sight of him and don't know what became of him? No, sir, I do not.

The Judge Advocate asked permission to employ an additional clerk, at a compensation not to exceed $5 per day. He said that he had already employed one clerk and one stenographer, but that they were unable to complete more than sixty pages per day of testimony; and that the employment of one additional clerk, such a one as he had had recommended to him, would enable him to take one hundred pages of testimony per diem; that the economy of this course must be evident to the Commission.

The permission asked by the Judge Advocate was granted by the Commission, and an additional clerk will be employed at a compensation of $5 per day, from this date.

On motion, the Commission adjourned to meet on Saturday, the 27th inst., at 11 o'clock A, M.

RALEIGH, N. C., July 27, 1867, 10 A. M.

The Commission met pursuant to adjournment.

Present, all the members of the Commission, the Judge Advocate, the Counsel for the prosecution, all the accused and their counsel.

The proceedings of yesterday were read by the Judge Advocate. The following corrections were made in witness Sam Toomer's testimony:

On page 283, line 10, the witness wished to insert the following, "At that time some one cried, 'command the prisoner.'"

On page 289, line 19, (printed p. 30, col. 2, line 64, Records) insert, "grasping the comfort in front of the throat, just under the chin."

On page 308 and 309 (printed Record, p. 32, col. 2, line 13) make the question read, "Did you notice whether that was a four-barrelled pistol in the hands of Mr. Phillips?" The proceedings of yesterday having been read, were then approved.

JAMES L. NIXON, a witness for the prosecution, having been first duly sworn, testified as follows:

Examined by the Counsel for the prosecution. What is your name? James L. Nixon. Where do you reside? Fayetteville. What is your business there, sir? I keep a grocery. Where did you reside at the beginning of this year? Fayetteville. Did you know Archy Beebee? No, sir, I don't think I did. Did you know him when you saw him? I had seen him a heap of times but I didn't know him when I did see him. Did you ever see a man called Archy Beebee? I saw him many a time, I didn't know his name was Archy Beebee when I saw him. When was the last time you saw this man who was called Archy Beebee? I saw him on Monday. What month? I don't recollect. What year? This year. Was it cold weather or warm? It was pretty cold weather, sir. In the winter time? Yes, sir, I think it was. The last time you saw him was a Monday evening in cold weather sometime this year? Yes, sir. Where did you see him then, sir? At the market house in Fayetteville. How came you at the market house that day? I went to hear the trial that was going up there. Was Archy Beebee the man who was on trial? Yes, sir. You went up there out of curiosity? Yes, sir. What time of day was it when you got there? I think it was after half past two o'clock when I got there. Did you see Archy Beebee when you first got there? He was going up the steps as I went up I think. Up the steps that go to the town hall up stairs? Yes, sir. What do they call the room over the market house? The town hall I believe. Who was going up stairs with him? The guard. Who were they? I forget who went up with him. Do you know any one person who went up with him? I don't remember. Was any person with him? Yes, sir. Where were you standing as he went up stairs? I was standing right on the pavement of the market house. Which end of the market house? The east end. Were you inside or outside of the market house? Just about under it, right on the pavement. Is there an arch in front of the market house? Yes, sir. Were you in that arch? Under it. Were you under the middle or one end? To one side. Which side? The north side. You were standing under the north end of the arch? Yes, sir. Looking towards the steps? Yes, I was looking at them going up the steps. How long did you stay there? About two hours I guess, or an hour and a half. Did you change your position? Walked about there backwards and forwards. Did you walk inside of the market house? Yes, sir. Walk outside? Yes, sir. Did you go away from that east end? Yes, sir, I went through the market house, I don't know that I went out of it, I went all about in the market house? How long do you think Archy Beebee was up stairs, from the time you saw him go through the door on the stairs? About three quarters of an hour, I guess, or hour. You didn't leave there until after he had come down stairs? No, sir. During the three quarters of an hour that Archy Beebee was up stairs, what passed in the crowd, if anything? Well, there was a big crowd, and they were going to have a trial. How many do you suppose were in that crowd? I reckon a hundred around about there, or more, or may be not that many, a good big crowd. Did you see any of these prisoners at the bar in that crowd? I saw one.—two. Who? Thomas Powers and Daniel Watkins. What other name does Daniel Watkins go by? That is his proper name; they call him Monk. Any name besides Monk? "Monk Julia"—his mother's name was Julia. Is that the man, (pointing). Yes sir. Did you see Thomas Powers in the crowd? Yes, sir. Do you see him here? Yes, sir. Point him out. (Witness does so.) These two men—were they under the market house or outside? Under the market house. Where was Tom Powers? He was upon a stall, just as you go up stairs. Becky Ben's stall? Yes, sir. He was standing on it? Yes, sir. What was he doing there? He was looking towards the stair steps. Did you notice any thing peculiar about his appearance? No, sir. Did he turn to look at you at all? No, sir, I don't think he did. Did he turn to look around the crowd? I don't think he did. His eyes were fixed on the stair steps? Yes, sir, looking towards the stair steps. What was Monk Julia doing? He was going around among the crowd. What was he saying? He was saying that a man that would do that ought not to have a trial at all. Anything further? No, sir, that was about the substance. Was that the substance of all he said? Yes, sir. Was that repeated once or several times? It might have been several times;—I remember it once. Did he say it to any one in particular? He was talking about, but not to any one in particular. Was he proclaiming it generally in the crowd? Just talking. In a loud tone of voice? About as loud as I am talking now. What other persons did you notice in that crowd under the market house that you recognized that day? There were several people there, but I can't remember who, half the town it looked to me, like, was there. Can't you remember any persons? Yes, Mr. Leggett was there. What is Mr. Leggett's first name? I don't know, sir. Who else did you see there? Mr. Powers. What Powers? Edward. Edward Powers was there? Yes, sir. Did you see any one else there? Mr. Ralph Lutterloh. Any one else? No, sir, I don't remember any other names. You didn't see Capt. Tolar there at that time? I don't remember seeing him inside of the market house. Did you see him anywhere else while the negro was up stairs? No, Sir, I might have seen him but I don't remember. The only persons that you remember having seen now, that you can name are Monk, Tom Powers, Leggett, Ed Powers, and Lutterloh? Yes, sir. Think well and study whether you can remember any one else? Yes, sir, Jim Andrews, the fellow that went with me. Any one else that you can remember seeing in the crowd? Mr. Bond I think was there. While the negro was up stairs? Mr. Bond I saw, I think, while the negro was up stairs. These men that you speak of, you told what Monk was doing, and you told what Tom Powers was doing, what were the other men that you spoke of doing? They were talking about the case. Were they talking with one another, or any one else. With one another I thought. Were they together? Yes, sir, these three were; there were more around them. These men Leggett, Lutterloh, Ed.

Powers, and Monk you say were standing together? Yes, sir. What were they saying? They two made the same remark that Monk made; that it was not right that he be tried, that he ought to be killed without a trial. Was that all? That he ought to be killed,—any negro that had committed such an act ought not to have a trial at all. Was that all that they said? I believe that was all. Who was the first person you saw coming through the door on the stairs? Coming down? Yes, from the town hall? If I am not mistaken the Sheriff started first. Did you see this young lady upon whom it was charged that Beebee had attempted to commit a rape? Yes, sir, I was there when she got out of the carriage. When did she come down? About as nigh as I can guess ten or fifteen minutes before the prisoner come down. Do you mean the Sheriff came out before this young lady? No, Sir. I understood you to say the Sheriff was the first person you saw come through the door? I thought you were talking about when the negro was brought down. Who came first after Beebee was taken up? Some officers were going in and coming out during the trial. Who did you see go in and come out? I can't tell, some I supposed who had business up there. Who was the first person you noticed come through that door that you remember? I don't think I can tell you. Who was the second? I can't tell you, I know when the lady come down. Did you see her come through the door? Yes, sir. Who was with her? Another lady—an old lady. Any one else? I think Mr. Bond was with her, I know he helped her in the carriage. Is his name Israel Bond? Yes, sir. He helped her in the carriage? Yes, sir. What became of him after he helped her in the carriage? I don't know, sir. Did you see any one else go to the carriage? No, sir, as soon as they drove off I never looked any more. While it was standing there? No, sir. You swear that no one else did go to the carriage? No, sir, I will swear I didn't see anybody go to it. Were you standing in the arch when the carriage drove off? I was standing right at the arch. You don't know what become of Bond? No, sir. Could you see the stair steps when you were standing in the arch? Yes, sir. Did Bond go up those stairs again? I can't say sir, he might have went. You remember that he did go? I do not. Do you remember that he did not? No, sir. Do you remember any one who went up stairs at that time? I can't say who did. I saw some. During the time between the lady came down stairs and the time Beebee came down? Yes, sir. Was it Israel Bond? I can't say, sir. Don't you know him? I know him, but I was not noticing him at the time. You were noticing enough to see some one go up? Some one went up, I supposed it was some one connected with the trial. Couldn't you tell who it was? I can't recollect. Didn't you notice? I might have noticed, but I have forgotten now. Have you any impression who it was? No, sir, none at all. But you have an impression that some one went up? Yes, sir. As the prisoner and guard came down stairs, the prisoner came first? Yes, sir. Who was along with the prisoner? I think Mr. Wemyss. Where was he? On the left of the prisoner. You know your right hand from your left. Yes, sir. Was he on the side toward the market house? I am certain he was on my right, the left of the prisoner. Who else did you see there with the prisoner? I think Mr. Faircloth.

Was he on the right or left of the prisoner? I think he was a little before him. You think the Sheriff was before him, and Faircloth was before him, and Mr. Wemyss was on his left? Yes, sir. Did you see any other officers? McGuire might have been there. I might have been there—do you mean to say, you think he was there? I think there were more guards there, and it might have been McGuire. Do you know who they were? I know the guard, but I dont know who were there; I know Mr. Wemyss was there, and Mr. Faircloth, and the Sheriff, and there were three guards. But you don't know who? No, sir. Well what happened? They came on down the steps and there was a rush made, as if they wanted to see him,—about ten or twelve. You think they wanted to see him? Like they wanted to get up to him, like men would, trying to see any body, or any thing strange. How many men ran up in that way? About fifteen or twenty I reckon, may be more. Did that rush alarm you at all? Yes, sir. I heard a man demand the prisoner. Was that at the same time that this rush was made that you heard this demand for the prisoner? Yes, sir. What did the Sheriff reply? I don't recollect what the Sheriff said. You heard the voice that said those words,—"I demand the prisoner?" Yes, sir. What words did he use in demanding the prisoner? "Demand the prisoner," or "give me the prisoner." Do you think those were the words, or may they have been slightly varied? They might have been slightly varied. That is my impression. Had you ever heard the voice before, that uttered those words, "I demand the prisoner?" I think I have. Did you recognize it at the time? I thought I did, sir. Whose voice was it? Tom Power's. Did you think it was him? I think to the best of my belief it was him. Did you see him in the crowd at that time? No, sir. I started off just as the prisoner was demanded. You turned to go off then? Yes, sir. How far did you move? I moved from the arch to the corner of the market, next to Fishblates. When that rush was made did you see any other of these prisoners at the bar in the crowd? No, sir. I don't think I did. But you saw a rush made by how many men? Fifteen or twenty. Can you name any one of them? I don't think I can. Did you see Monk about that time? I saw him before that time. After the prisoner had come out of the door? No, sir. You moved off to the north-east corner of the market house? To the north corner. The corner can't be the north corner to my understanding of it. I would call it north. Where the east face and the north face of the market house meet, you were standing? Yes, sir. That is what I mean by the north east corner. That is where you went to when that rush was made? Yes, sir. Did you look back? Yes, sir; I saw a scuffle in the crowd. Did you see anybody in that scuffle? I saw a whole lot. Did you see Monk at that time? No, sir. Did you see anybody you recognized? No, sir, I don't remember I did; I saw the guard was hitting with their sticks, and they sort of backed off, the crowd did, and they got out in the street where there was more, and made a general rush. On whom? Towards the guard. Then there was a little scuffling and the pistol fired. Did you see the pistol fired? No, sir. Did you see the pistol flash? I saw the smoke. Did you hear the report? Yes, sir. Did you see the man Beebee at the moment the pistol fired? I think I did, sir It looked like he had been throwed down, and he was rising; I didn't think he was perfectly straight, and he never got straight. Where was Sheriff Hardie standing at the time the pistol was fired? I don't know, sir. Could you see Mr. Wemyss? Not until I got up there. You can't say where Wemyss was standing? No, sir. Could you say where the prisoner was standing as he rose? Yes, sir. He was standing at or near the south corner, next to Mr. Draughon's store. On the pavement? Yes, sir. Had he got outside of the point to which the market house reaches? No, sir. Had he got past that little arch? I think he was about where it ends, he was lying there when I went around afterwards. And that is the point you saw him when the pistol was fired? Yes, sir. Where did the smoke of that pistol come from? It looked like it was between me and Archy. Did it come in front of Archy? I don't know whether it was to his back or face. Was Archy's face towards you? His head was sort of towards the market. Was it turned over his shoulder? Sort of raised up, that wey, (representing.) What did you do after the pistol was fired? The crowd gave way, and I went up there. Did you walk across the pavement or around it? I walked off of it. Did you look near that point where you saw the smoke, and see anybody you recognized, I mean immediately after the pistol was fired? I saw a crowd standing there. Did you see Tolar there that day at all? After the thing was done. How long afterwards? I don't know, two or three minutes. Where was he standing? Standing off, outside of the crowd. Where? Off from the market house, five or ten steps, off from the pavement. Was he in front of the arch? I don't exactly know about that, I can't say. How far was he from Archy, or the point where Archy was lying? I reckon fifteen feet, or twenty perhaps. Who was standing near him? I don't remember, sir. You saw the Sheriff, what was he doing? He was brushing his hair back that way, with his left hand. I asked him if he was shot, and he said no, but he thought he was. Who else did you see there then? I saw Dr. McDuffie, and another Doctor. I forget, whether it was Black, or McSwain. Have you told all you know about this thing. All I can recollect, sir. I want to call your attention again to who was inside of the market house while the negro was up stairs, while you were standing in that arch? John Maultsby was in there for one, and Jim Jones, I forgot just now and remember since. Who else? I can't designate anybody else that I know that I can remember. I didn't tell you about Monk and the knife afterwards. Let us hear what that is? After he was shot, and about dead Monk was coming up with his knife. Was that the first time you saw Monk with a knife that day? Yes, sir, the only weapon I saw that day. What was he doing then? He said he was going to cut his throat, or something like that, and I caught him and kept him off. I understood you to say within two or three minutes after the shot was fired you saw Mr. Tolar standing some twenty feet off the pavement? Ten or fifteen or twenty. He was not on the pavement? No, sir. Not in the market house? Not at that time. But he was standing on the ground off the pavement, some 10 or 15 or 20 feet from the place where the man fell? Yes, sir.

The Counsel for the accused declined to Cross examine the witness.

The Counsel for the prosecution addressing the Commission, said:—

"I submit, if the Court pleases, under the circumstances of this case, that I have a right to put a leading question to this witness. The witness has stated the circumstances of this case differently to me before coming upon the stand, in a very material point; and I want to put a searching inquiry upon that point to him. I want to ask the witness if he has not said to me, since he has been here, previous to this morning, that Captain Tolar was standing under the market house, at the time these several other gentlemen were standing there, that he alludes to; and that he participated in conversation with them from time to time.

The Counsel for the accused:—

We leave the matter entirely to the Court. The Court knows the general rule, that leading questions shall not be put to a party's own witness — We however make no objection, if the Court sees proper to allow it.

The Counsel for the prosecution:—

I will state to the Court that State cases differ in that respect from all others, that when a State produces a witness, it has a right to impeach him if it sees fit; a witness may make a statement, and then when brought upon the stand may contradict himself. The rule is that a State may impeach its own witness, may at least assist in refreshing his memory. All I want to do is to call the witnesse's attention to the fact whether he has stated that Tolar was standing within the market house at the time that Leggett, Lutterloh, Ed. Powers, Maultsby and others he describes; if he has not also stated that he participated in the conversation that then took place.

The Commission was cleared for deliberation, and after some time so spent, the doors were reopened, and the Judge Advocate announced that the Commission decided to admit the question asked by the Counsel for the prosecution.

Direct Examination, by the Counsel for the prosecution, resumed.

Mr. Nixon, I want you to refresh your memory now. Didn't you, state to the Judge Advocate and myself, day before yesterday, or yesterday, in this little room, when we were talking over this matter, that Tolar was inside of the market house, at the time you speak of, and you were standing in the arch of the market house at the same time that Leggett, Ed. Powers and Maultsby were inside there? I forget. Do you remember whether you made that statement to us? I forget whether I did or not. What do you think about it now? was he or was he not there? I think he was. Have you any doubt about it? I don't think I have now, that the first time I saw him was under the market house. Didn't you recollect that, just now when I asked you first? No, sir, or else I would have told you.

On motion the Commission adjourned to meet on Monday, July 29, 1867, at 10 A. M.

RALEIGH, N. C. July 19, 1867, 10 oclock A. M.

The Commission met pursuant to adjournment. Present all the members of the Commission, the Judge Advocate, the Counsel for the prosecution, all the accused and their Counsel.

Yesterdays proceedings were then read and approved.

ELIZA ANN ELLIOTT, a witness for the prosecution, having been first duly sworn testified as follows.

Examined by the Counsel for the prosecution. What is your name? Eliza Ann Elliott. Where do you reside? I live in Fayetteville, N. C. What is your business there? Making and selling ready made clothing. Do you remember the day Archy Beebee was killed in Fayetteville? I do sir. What day was it? Monday. Do you remember what month it was? It was in February. Were you at the market house when he was killed? Yes, sir, I was. What time was it? I believe it was Monday evening. I dont know exactly what hour. What time that day did you go to the market house? I went after I eat my breakfast; I went down to sell some things. Did you go back home that day? No, sir. I never went back home at all, until about sunset. Were you about the market house all that while? Yes, sir. Is that your usual habit when you are selling articles? Yes, sir. Did you see Archy when he was brought out of the guard house? Yes, sir. Where were you standing at that time? At the corner of the market house. Which corner? Towards the guard house. Were you on the pavement or off? On the pavement, right at the corner of the market house. That is the south east corner—did you see Archy when he was brought out of the guard house? Yes, sir. Who was with him? There was two men with him, old man Wemyss, and I never took notice who the other was. Were they all? There were some others, but I didn't notice who. Did you notice whether they were officers? Some of them were policemen, I think. Did you know them? Sam Faircloth was behind, I think. Which side was Wemyss on, before he went up-stairs? I think he was on the left side. You think Wemyss was on the left side? Yes, sir. Didn't you remember that Wemyss had a twitch on his hand? He had a sore place on his hand. That he had something he was leading Archy by? He had something in his hand, but I never took notice. Was Wemyss towards you or on the other side? He was on the side that I stood on. Who else did you see along with him? This town constable Bond, was along. Did he have hold ot the prisoner? Well I wou't say whether it was him or one of the policemen. I won't say for certain. Did you notice Sheriff Hardie, there at all? I saw Sheriff Hardie that day several times. Did you see him when the prisoner was brought up to the market house? I won't say, for I never noticed when they come from the guard house with him. Are you certain that Wemyss was there? Yes, sir, I really think Mr. Wemyss was along. And you can't say any one else who was in the crowd, as I understand you, there were several in it? I never took any notice. You know there were several persons, but you don't know who? No, sir, I didn't take any notice. Was there any noise or shouting in the crowd as he came through. No, sir, there was not much said. What was the size of the crowd at that time; how many men do you suppose were standing in that crowd when Archy came to go up-stairs? A good many. Give some idea—how many do you suppose there were? I don't know, sir, a right smart crowd. A hundred? Well, I won't say, without I knowed; if I knowed I would tell, a good many come up after. There was a right smart crowd? Yes, sir. And you saw a good many come up after he went up-stairs? Yes, sir. Where did you move to after Archy went up-stairs? I went about under the market house, and out from under the market house How long was Archy up-stairs? Sometime, I can't say exactly how long. I don't expect you to tell to a minute but give some sort of an estimate. I reckon an hour or such a matter. During that time you were moving about under the market house and outside of the

market house? Yes, sir. This crowd you speak of, that was considerable when you got there and continued to grow while the negro was up stairs, where was it, inside of the market house or outside? A good many under the market house and some outside? How often did you go inside of the market house while the negro was up stairs. I never taken any notice, I was just walking about there and talking. Were you under there several times? Two or three times backwards and forwards. Who did you see under the market house at that time? Well, I seed several I was acquainted with, there was the two Mr. Hall's was under there. What were their names? Wilbren Hall and Samuel [Hall, Ed. Powers and Tom Powers was there, and Mr. Tolar, and several that I knew. There was Ashley Peoples and Dave Oliphant, John Maultsby—I can't tell, there was several. You saw Captain Tolar under the arch at that time and you saw Tom Powers? Yes, sir. Did you see Monk there that time? I saw this little Monk Jule, called Monk Watkins. Well, now, you say you were under the market two or three times, did you see them about the market house every time you went under there? I didn't notice every time—only I saw them under sometimes and outside some. Did you see Capt. Tolar sometimes underneath and sometimes out? Yes, sir. What were these men doing that you saw there? They were saying the nigger ought to be killed. Who said that? Tom Powers said it, and Dave Oliphant said it, and Ed. Powers—I can't tell who all. Were they talking together to one another? Yes, sir. They said it was a damned shame to have any lady served as that one was. Was Mr. Tolar taking any part in the conversation? He was talking as well as the rest. Was that underneath the market house or outside? I heard some talking under the market house and some outside. Was that all the conversation you heard? This little Monk Jule had his knife open, and said he was going to cut his throat, and cut his head off and stick it upon a stake or something—he was always going on with some of his foolishness anyhow. Was that all these other persons said—'but he ought to be killed? Yes, sir, that was all they said before he came down stairs. Did you see any weapons? Yes, sir, I seed weapons. I mean while Archy Beebee was up stairs. I seed some one or two. Who did you see have weapons. I saw this Tom Powers have a weapon. What sort of weapon? It was one of these sharpshooters—navy-shooters they call them. Had he it in his hand? No, in his bosom, here. Who else did you see have one? I saw this one armed Sikes have one and hand it to Tolar. Was that before the negro came down stairs? Yes, sir. Where was Captain Tolar standing when Sikes handed him the pistol? Betwixt Phi'. Taylor's store and the market house. In the street? Yes, sir. And you saw him when he handed him his pistol? Yes, sir. What did Tolar do after Sikes handed him this pistol? He was standing about there. Didn't he move away? No, sir. How long was that before Beebee came down stairs. that you saw that pistol handed to Tolar? It was not very long; I can't tell you how many minutes. Was it half an hour? I can't tell exactly? Was it a short time or long time? It was not very long? Had he been up stairs half the time he stayed up there? Yes, sir. Was it more than half the time? Well, I can't tell you; I never took no notice how long he was up there. Did you see Miss Massey that day? Yes, sir. And her mother? Yes, sir. Did you see them when they came down tairs? Yes, sir. Where was Captain Tolar when these ladies came down stairs? I saw him after they came down stairs. I saw him out from the pavement, out from under the market house. Was he standing near the same point he was when Sykes handed him the pistol? Not exactly; nearer where the negro was shot. Further south? Yes, sir. When Miss Massey and her mother came down, had Archy come[down stairs? No, sir; they came down first. Who helped them into the carriage? did any one? Yes, sir; there was a gentleman, but I didn't notice who it was. What became of them after they got to the carriage? They went down to Mr. Taylor's I guess. How many men helped them into the carriage? I didn't notice how many. Were there more than one? There were several. I never noticed who helped them in, or how many. You think there was certainly one man? Of course there was one helped them in. Don't you know whether there were more than one went up to the carriage to speak to them? I never noticed, for this girl was crying, and the girl didn't have much talk to no one. I want to know whether you noticed one person, or more than one person help this lady in the carriage? I never took any notice how many helped them in. Did you say there was one? I didn't say; I said there was one I noticed—some helped her in. There were some standing there, but I didn't notice who. Where were you standing when this lady got into the carriage? I was standing from under the market house, opposite a little tree, sort of off the pavement from under the market house. Off the pavement near a little tree? Yes, sir. You mean that row of little trees that runs in front of the pavement? Yes, sir. How many of them? do you remember? I never took any notice; some two or three. I want to know which one it was you were standing near? The one nearest the corner. Towards the guard house? Yes, sir. That was the time the ladies got into the carriage. How long after the ladies got into the carriage before Archy came down stairs? It was a mighty little time. Did you keep in the place where you were standing? Yes, sir. Until Archy Beebee came down stairs? Yes, sir. Could you see the steps where you were standing? Yes, sir. Could you see Beebee come down? I saw him part way, and when they commenced to turn down there were so many I didn't see him. When he got most down to the ground I could not see him. You could see him at the top of the steps? Yes, sir. Who was with Archy when he came outside of the door on the steps? Old man Wemyss and Sheriff Hardie, I didn't notice who the others were. Which came out of the door first? Sheriff Hardie came out first. Was he before or behind, on the right or left side of the prisoner? I think he was on the right side of the prisoner. You think the Sheriff came out first on the right of the prisoner? Yes, sir. Where did Wemyss come? They were both together. Wemyss on the right too? Well, you see Wemyss was on one side; and he on the other when they went to come down. And you saw no one else that you could speak of? No, sir; I was just standing, looking to see what they were going to do—— Did Archy say anything? I heard him say "O Lord, don't carry me there!" Did you hear anything said in reply? Sheriff Hardie said he was there. Was that all? Yes, sir. What happened next? The next I saw, was when they came out on the pavement there. When they went around the arch you lost sight of them, for a few moments? Yes, sir. I lost sight of them because there was so many standing in there, From the time they got to the foot of the step, until they appeared around the arch you lost sight of Archy? Yes, sir; I saw him once as he came through the arch, I saw him—— You lost sight of him from the time he come to the foot of the steps until he turned round the arch? I saw him a little before he got to the arch, and lost sight of him as he went down to the foot of the steps, and when he come to turn, I saw him. Just before he got to the arch? Yes, sir. Did you hear any exclamations or shouts in the crowd at that time? Yes, sir; I heard them holler out "shoot him! shoot him!" "kill the damn son of a bitch" Who did you hear holler that? I heard Tom Powers and Samuel Hall and Captain Toler. Where was Captain Tolar when you heard him shout? He was right before me. He had come from where you saw him last? Yes, sir; he was right before me, some three or four feet from me. You were standing near that little tree? Yes, sir. And Captain Tolar was before you—which way were you facing? Just like I am to you. Which way were you facing,—towards the guard house? Yes, sir—down towards the guard house. The way he turned to go; I heard what they threatened and I was looking to see. And your face was towards the guard house? Yes, sir. And you were standing near that tree, and Captain Tolar was in front of you? Yes, sir. He was in front of you when he made this exclamation "shoot him?" Did you hear anybody else cry out "shoot him?" Yes, sir; up on the pavement of he market house, I heard some one cry out shoot him. Who did you hear cry out? I took it to be McRae's voice, and I looked and saw McRae on the top of the market house, and some other gentleman with him, somewhat favored Captain Horn. That was at the time these others were shouting "kill him!"? Yes, sir. Before the shot was fired? Yes, sir; that was before the shot was fired. What do you mean by looking up on the pavement? I call the pavement on the top of the market house; there is a place out there—a porch or something. Do you know Major McKae well? Yes, sir; I have been acquainted with him for about fifteen years, off and on. Have you seen much of him during the last few years? Yes, sir; I have seen him every day, sometimes two or three times a day. Did you have any talk with him? O, yes, I have talked to the old man several times. Do you know his voice? Yes, sir. I understand you to say when you heard that shout, you thought it was McRae's voice? Yes, sir. Was that before you saw him on the top of the house? Yes, sir. You thought it was his voice before you looked up? Yes, sir. And then you looked up and saw him standing in this balcony? Yes, sir. Have you any doubt about that? No, sir, I think it was him. Where was he standing in that balcony? He was standing about the middle of it. Had he his hat on? No, sir, he was bare headed. And you think Capt. Horn was with him? Yes, sir. Was his mouth open? Well, I didn't notice about his mouth being open, only he hollered out "shoot him," and I took it to be him, and he was like the rest of them. How do you mean? Some was laughing and talking—he always has on a smiling look—almost always laughing. Do you remember the expression of his face;—did it strike you? Well, I don't know, I took it to be him, and I looked up. I want you to be very particular about this—have you any doubt, whether it was oim? Well, I can just tell you, I took it to be him; I only flashed my eyes up and down. You took it to be him from his voice, and you took it to be him when you looked at him? Yes, sir. You have known him for fifteen years, and you have known him well for the last two or three years? I have seen him almost every day. You were still standing near that little tree? Yes, sir, I was watching to see what was going on. Now Mrs. Elliott, I understood you to say just now, that you were looking down towards the guard house? Yes, sir, I was looking the way he went—I was only watching him How did you flash your eyes up with your head turned the other way? I can turn up my eyes, this way. A sort of side view? Yes sir. What happened then immediately after this shouting that you speak of? They hollered out clear the way. Who was "they"? It was Tom Powers and Captain Tolar and some more of them;—I never noticed, but they were right before me. Was Tom Powers before you too? He was off sort of one side of Captain Tolar. Which side? The left side. Did you see Sam Phillips there in the crowd? Not at that time. You were standing near that little tree off the sidewalk. Yes, sir, And Captain Tolar was standing right in front of you? Yes, sir. Now, I want you to take this pencil and show us on this chart where those people were standing? (Witness points out where Tolar and Archy Beebee were standing) Was Beebee standing there when the pistol was fired? Yes, sir. Who fired the pistol? Capt. Tolar.—he flung back his shawl, just so, and presented it. And you say Tom Powers was standing near his left? Yes, sir. Did you see any one else near him, that you can name? Tom Powers was there, Ed Powers was there. Where was E.d. Powers standing? On the left side of him. Where was Tom Powers? Sort of 'hind Ed. Powers. Did you notice Monk at that time? He had his knife open. I mean the moment before the shouting took place? He was right in the crowd with his knife open. You saw him then? Yes, sir Where was he standing at that moment? I won't say for certain where he was standing when the pistol was fired;—when the pistol was fired Monk rushed up to cut his throat, and cut old man W mys' hand That was just after the niggar fell. You say you saw the man who fired the pistol? Yes, sir. And it was Tolar? Yes, sir. How close was he to the negro when he fired, do you suppose? He was pretty close to him. Was the pistol barrel touching the negro's head? Not exactly, a little bit off. The muzzle was a short distance from his head? Yes, sir A foot do you suppose? I can't tell. Can you form any idea? It was about so from this gentleman, (about a foot.) What did Tolar do with the pistol after he fired? He gave it to Ed. Powers, and Ed. handed it to some one else, and it passed on out of the crowd—Captain Tolar flung it one side to Ed. Powers. Do you mean he threw it down? No, sir, he flung it down to his right side, and Ed. Powers took it and gave it a fling and it went out of the company. I understood you to say Ed. Powers was standing on Tolar's left hand? I meant to say Tolar was standing on the left hand of Powers, was what I meant. You say now Ed. Powers was standing on the right of Tolar? Yes, sir; he was. It was Tolar on the left side of Powers. Was Tom Powers on his left hand or right? On his left. And Ed. Powers was on the other side? Yes, sir. And you saw Ed. Powers take the pistol? Yes, sir; he gave it a sling and Ed. Powers took it and gave it a sling. Which did he sling it to? I never noticed, he gave it a sling and by that time you see it was gone, it went out of the company. You never saw it afterwards? No, sir. Did you see Major McRae any more that day? Yes, sir; Major McRae came down stairs. What did he have to say? He came down stairs, and said he suppo

ed the negro was shot, he supposed they killed him. Was that all? All I heard him say. Did he come up and look at the negro? Yes, sir; in under where he was shot down, and Jim Nixon had taken this Monk Julia and carried him out of the company. I went under the market house, and Mr. McRae came down, I guess he went to look at him. You don't know? I won't say, he went that way. You were under the market house when McRae came downstairs? Yes, sir. And it was as he came through the market house you heard him say that? Yes, sir. Who was he talking to? He said it to the crowd, I never noticed. What became of Tolar after he fired the pistol? He passed it to Ed. Powers, and went up the street, up towards Hay Mound Hill, and after a while he came back. As soon as he fired the pistol he left the crowd? Yes, sir.— And went up Hay street? Yes, sir. How far up did you see him go? I saw him go up some distance he went right straight up. Hay street is the street that runs west from the market house? I believe that is what they call it. Is there anything further that you know about this matter? Did you see anybody standing on Becky Ben's stall that day at any time? I think so. At what time? I saw John Maultsby stand up there. What time? Well it was a little while before this negro was brought down stairs. And I heard John Maltsby say "they are coming! look out boys!" You saw Maultsby on that stall? He was standing up on a bench there. Which bench? Becky Ben's What was he doing? He was only looking. Did he say anything? When he went to come down stairs, he hollered "look out, boys, they are coming!" and he went from under the market house, and went out where I told you where he was before they came down. Did you see any body stand up by him? There was a good many, some on the benches and some down, I never noticed particularly who was with him. Do you think any body else was standing on that bench? There was some several boys—little youngsters. Were there any men? I won't say for certain, I tell you just what I know. You think there were several boys there? Yes, sir. Do you know any of them Well, there were some colored boys and some white boys. Can you name any of them? You see I knows a good many boys but I never knows their names. I see you, and I know you are Lawyer Haywood but I don't know your name. Can you tell me the last names of any of them? Whose sons were they? They were colored boys mostly and I wont say who they were. You can't say who was there? No, sir. During the whole time you were there you said you saw Tom Powers with a pistol, and you saw Sikes give it to him? Yes, sir. Did you see anybody else with a pistol or a knife? I saw Monk with a knife. Anybody with a pistol besides? Well, I won't say say for certain whether I did or not.

Cross examination by the Counsel for the accused:

Your name is Eliza Elliott? Yes, sir. What is the name of your husband? George Elliott. How long has it been since you married George Elliott? I have been married to him two years this coming September. What was your name before you married Geo Elliott? I have had two or three names. The name just before you married George Elliott? Eliza Taylor. What was your husbands name when your name was Taylor? His name was Robert Taylor—Lieut. Taylor- he was a yankee. What has become of him? He died of typhoid fever, in Alexandria, Va. When did he die? This July two years ago. And you were married in the September afterwards? Yes, sir. When did you marry Taylor? I met him when the army come through Fayetteville. Gen. Sherman's army? They called it Sherman's army. How long had you been acquainted with Taylor before you married him? He come through and I married him and went right home with him. Had you been acquainted with him one day before you married him? Of course I was acquainted with him one day. Were you acquainted two days? I was married the third day I saw him, if that is what you want to know. How long did you live with him after marrying him. Two months. What was your name before you married Lieut. Taylor? Kennedy. Your husband's name? Thomas Kennedy. When did he die? He was killed in Maryland, the "rebs" killed him in Maryland. When did the rebs kill him? When they were fighting in Maryland. What was your name before you married Kennedy? I was a Mason. Was that your maiden name? That is what they say. You had never been married before you married Kennedy? No, sir, I was married to Tom Kennedy when I was twelve years and three months old. Where did you live at the time you were the wife of Kennedy? I lived in Fayetteville part of the time and part of the time up country. In what county up the country? In Cumberland, and part of the time in Harnett. What were you doing during the war? I was making clothes to sell. Did you spend any time during the war in Raleigh? Yes, sir, I came here to work when they gave out sewing—made soldiers clothes. When you were here in Raleigh did you make the acquaintance of a colored man by the name of William Edwards, a baker? William Edwards, I went there and boug t some vict als, you know, cakes and one thi g or other, that was all the acquaintance I made with him. That was during the time when the war was going on? Yes, sir that was so. Since you have been up here as a witness have you seen that man William Edwards? I saw him t'other day, one Sunday that I was walking, and he was standing opposite the jail. Since you have b en up here have you got William Edwards to write letters for you? I didn't know he could write. Have you got him to write any letters for you since you have been here this time? No, sir. You swear that you have not got Wil liam Edwards to write you any letters? Not that I know of; there was some man that wrote some letters. I don't know whether it was William Edwards. I was not acquainted with Wil liam Edwards, only just like I walk to your offi e, and buy cakes and go on. I was not a quainted with the nigger. I had no use for the nigger. The question I ask you is, whether William Edwards, the colored man, the baker in this place, that you knew here during the war, whether you have got him to write any letters for you since you have been here this time? I got a colored man to write a letter to my husband. Was that colored man William Edwards? That is what they said. I didn't know he was till he wrote the letter. Was that a pox-marked man? Yes, sir, he had b ad the small pox. And they said his name was William Edwards? Yes, sir; but I didn't know his name when I bought cakes at his place. He was the same man? He said he was. I don't know what his name is. Mrs. Elliott, I will ask you this question—pay attention, if you please, and answer it properly. I will ask you whether, at the time you went to get William Edwards to write that letter for you, on that Sunday, and in the city of Raleigh, you knew nothing about this matter in the world? I only said this: they asked me several times about it; I said when I was called to testify

on it I would tell what I had seen and heard. I ask you again whether you did not tell him so? No, I didn't tell him no such a thing. I didn't tell no one I didn't know nothing about it. I will ask you the question whether you did not, at the store of Edward Powers, in the town of Fayetteville, tell Edward Powers that they told many lies with regard to what your testimony would be on the occasion; that you knew nothing about the matter at all? I didn't tell Ed. Powers no such tale as that, neither. I will ask you whether you did not, in that conversation, remark to Ed. Powers, that "that they have said that I would testify that you passed the pistol, but it is a lie. I have never said anything of that sort?" I told him I hadn't said nothing then about it, but when come to be sworn about it I would tell all I seen, or heard and knew. I said I hadn't done it. I didn't say I was not going to. He had a chill, on him, as he was scared to death, for fear I had said something. I ask you the question whether when you came from Fayetteville to this place, and the stage was stopped at James McGuffin's, in the County of Cumberland, and you didn't then and there tell Dr. McDuffie that you knew nothing about this matter; that McRae had nothing to do with it and that they had re; orted lies with regard to what you said about it? I can tell you just what I said: I said there had been a good many lies told about this case, and I should only tell what I knowed, and seen, and heard. I said I didn't want to be in it, but they summoned me, and I would tell all I seed and heard. Then you say you didn't have that conversation with Dr. McDuffie at that place? I told Doctor that there had been a good deal said about it. Mrs. Elliott, where do you say you were standing when the prisoner came down the market house steps? I was standing out from under the market house, opposite a little tree. I will then ask you this question, were you not at that time, when the prisoner was brought down out of the market house, were you not at that time under the market house, and in Becky Ben's stall or Becky Jenkins' stall? No, sir, I just told you where I stood. After the negro, Archy Beebee, was shot, didn't you turn round and say to Becky Ben or Becky Jenkins—you know her? I reckon I do know her, she has been cooking and one thing or other about there a good while. I ask you, whether you did not, directly after the negro was shot, say "By God, I am going out and see who shot him." No, I didn't say, by God I was going out to see who shot him. I didn't say any such word as that; as I turned from him when they shot him I met Rachael Lord, a colored woman. She was standing behind me and I said, did you see who shot? Rachael said she didn't know him, I seed it, but I didn't know who it was. I told her it was Capt. Tolar done it. That is what I told Rachael Lord. I ask you whether you did not come back under the market house after you had gone out that time, and say, to Becky Ben, "I could not find out who shot him, I could not find out anything about it?" I can tell you what Becky Ben said, Becky Ben said "don't you tell nothing about it, have nothing at all to do with it." I said it ain't nothing to me nohow, that is just what I told her, I didn't shoot the nigger, and it was none of my folks done it. You said you didn't tell Becky Ben that you knew nothing about it? No, sir, I haint never denied who done it. You say you were not under the market house at the time the negro was shot, or at the time he was brought down stairs? No. You were out of the market house? Sort of off the pavement, and near the little tree I told you. Who was on your right hand at the time you was standing there, just as the negro was brought out? I was not noticing who, I was only noticing to see who was going to kill the nigger. You didn't know who was upon your right hand? I was not taking any notice.—I was only watching them to see who killed him. Who was upon your left hand? Well, I never noticed who was. Who was at your back? Do you reckon I could see behind me and before me? Who was in front? Capt. Tolar was in front of me. Centrally in front? He was when he shot this man. How many steps was Capt. Tolar in front of you? He was about three or four feet. Did I understand you to say Ed. Powers was at Capt. Tolar's right? Ed. Powers was at the right side of Capt. Tolar. How far was Ed. Powers from Capt. Tolar? He was close at him, I told you.—near enough to take the pistol. Who was on Capt. Tolar's left hand? This Tom Powers was sort of off to his left. Who was in front of Capt. Tolar? This Archy Beebee and Sheriff Hardie and old man Weinyss was in front of him, and I cant tell who all, for I could not see everybody, I only tell who I see. How far was Capt Tolar off of the pavement? He was but a mighty few steps. How many steps? I never counted. I see'd he was not very far. How many steps do you think he was? I don't think any thing about it. How many steps do you think he was now, off from the pavement? I never taken any notice, he was not far from it. I ask you whether there was any body upon Capt. Tolar's left band at that time? There was a good many there, but I was not noticing to see ev ery body that was around there. Can you name one man that was on Tolar's left at that time— any one man? Thomas Powers was close to his left. Was Tom Powers directly on Capt. Tolars left? I never taken any notice how many steps, he was not far from Tolar. Was Louis Smith on Tolar's left hand? Louis Smith and several black men stood right close around him. Do you recollect any of these black ones' names? Yes, I can tell you several. Name some of them? John Armstrong, Bob Simmons, Louis Smith, Sam Toomer, Matthew Leary, and one of the Jenkins's was standing there. That was Tom, was it not? I think that was what they call him, he was a thick, fat fellow. They were all on Captain Tolar's left hand? They were all standing there in a bunch, they were looking to see who killed him. Which seemed to be nearest to Captain Tolar, John Armstrong? John Armstrong was near him, he was near enough to tell him, "Captain Tolar you have shot that poor negro." You heard that? Yes, sir, he spoke it right there in the company. Well then, John Armstrong was nearest to Captain Tolar, on his left hand? He was close, I won't say which was the nearest, I saw him there very near him. How near was Matthew Leary to John Armstrong? Well I won't say, I saw them in a bunch together, they were all looking as well as the rest. All in a bunch together? Some were in a bunch. Where did Captain Tolar draw the pistol from? I can't tell, he took and flung his shawl back, so, and presented the pistol to the negro's head and shot him down. Did he draw the pistol from his left side, or right side? I told you I don't know which side. When you first saw the pistol in Tolar's hand, was he raising it, in this way, or was he bringing it down, in this way? He flirted the shawl, and presented the pistol right to the black man's head. In flirting up his shawl, do you mean that the muzzle of his pistol, at any time went up so, (representing.) He flung it up so, (representing.) And then drew it down, and presented it? Yes, sir. Do you

know what sort of a pistol it was? They call it a navy pistol. How long? I never measured it, I only tell what I know. How long had Tolar been standing there, at your front, as you say? I never taken any notice, how long he had been there. Don't you remember you saw Captain Tolar come rushing up, pushing the crowd aside, and as soon as he ran up to him, he shot him? Captain Tolar was standing, as I told you; when he said, "clear the way" he flung his shawl back so, and presented the pistol right to his head and shot him, and I saw it. He had been standing still then for some time, had he? He was standing in front of me sometime. You say you have known Mr. McRae off and on, for fifteen years? I have been acquainted with him ever since I was first married to Thomas Kennedy. What do you mean by off and on, sometimes you know him, and sometimes you don't? Suppose now I see you here, and maybe next year or next month I see you again, That is what I mean, if you want to know. Well, you say you heard a number of persons cry out "shoot him"? Yes, sir; there was some voices cried out shoot him. And you say one of these persons was Tom Powers? Yes, sir. Who were the others? Tom Powers, Ed Powers and Capt. Tolar. I can't tell you, there was several; I can't tell all. How did it happen that you were so particular in noticing these persons cry out 'kill him," Tom Powers and Captain Tolar and Ed. Powers? Because my eyes seed it. It was not because you knew their voices? Of course I knew their voices; I was near neighbor to Capt. Tolar sometime. Did you know Ed. Powers' voice? I have been acquainted with him long enough. Did you know Tom Powers' voice? Well I don't know Tom Powers' voice as good as I did the others, but I know his voice. You saw their mouths open? I saw them speak, you know. Then you heard—how many voices upon that balcony that you called the pavement? I heard them say "shoot him!" and I looked up— flashed my eyes up. How many voices were there? I heard two voices up there. I heard two say "shoot him!" "shoot him!" I took it to be McRae and this Lawyer Horn. Is that the gentleman there? (pointing) It favors him. And you thought you heard both of these two voices? I can tell you just how it was. I heard a voice upon the market house and took it to be McRae's voice. I looked up and I saw McRae and another man, and I took it to be Lawyer Horn. You have heard McRae's voice often enough to know it when he speaks? Did you know Horn's voice? I was not much acquainted with him. I never talked to him as much as I have to Mr. McRae. Just answer the question, whether these two voices were the voices of McRae and Horn? It was just one man spoke, it was not two different voices. The same person spoke out "shoot him!" "shoot him!"? Yes, sir.— And you swear positive, without doubt, that when you looked up there, one of these persons was Duncan G, McRae? It imitated him so near, I believe it was him. Have you any doubt about it? I just tell you all I know about it. How far were you from him—as far as from here to the gallery up there? Well I don't know how many feet high the market house is. I was standing on the pavement and I cut my eyes up and he was standing on that place. You say you were about opposite the middle of the balcony? I was standing outside of the market house. off the pavement. off opposite that tree. How far were you off from the market house? Well I was off—you know how wide the pavement is; I was a step or two from the pavement. How much of McRae's body did you see? I saw from the middle up. What prevented you from seeing the balance of his body? I didn't take pains to look. Then you just cut your eyes up and cut them down again? Of course I did to see who it was shot him. And you saw it? I did. You saw Capt. Tolar after he had shot him throw his arm down to his side and Tom. Powers got the pistol? He did, he took it out of Tolar's hand? And passed it back? Yes, sir. How far did Tolar go up Hay street? I don't know, I saw him going up, I never noticed how far he went up. Which side of Hay street did he go up? He went by Hinsdale's store. How far up the street did you see him? I don't know how many yards or how long;—you know I said I saw him go a right smart way up the street. About whose store did you see him last? I never noticed what store he had got to. Had he got as far up as the hotel? He was as far up as the hotel or above it. Did he make any stop after coming out of the market house? He never made no stop—after awhile he come back. You are certain he didn't stop at Hinsdale s? Well, I seed him before Hinsdale's. Don't you know how he stopped at Hinsdale's store for a long time? Well, he went into Hinsdale's, but I won't say whether he went in before he went up Hay Mount or afterwards. Mrs. Elliott you don't seem to understand me I want to know when Tolar went out of the market house whether he made any halt at Hinsdale s store. I seed him when he shot this man and flung the pistol around and wheeled and went right off and went right out through the market house. At that time did he make any stop at Hinsdale's store? I wont say whether he made any stop or not, I was talking to Rachel Lord. How long was it after you saw him come out of the market house before you saw him go up Hay street? I don't know how many minutes. Was it a very short time? It was not very long. Was it an hour? I might say it was a half an hour? Do you know whether it was more? It might not have been a half an hour.

Re-direct examination by the Counsel for the prosecution:

Mrs. Elliott, I understand you to say that the two exclamations "shoot him" "shoot him," were not from two different men? No, sir, there was just one person's voice. One person exclaimed this? Yes, sir. You thought that voice was Major McRae's? Yes, sir. You have been asked about the conversation you had with Ed. Powers. Yes, sir. What did I understand you to say that conversation was? You see I was passing by Ed. Powers' store and he called me in his store and asked me "had I said anything about him having a pistol or being in that crowd," I said, "I have said nothing about it yet." Hadn't you said anything about it then? No, and he was like one that had ager on him;—he had the trembles so bad for fear I had told it. What was the just of the conversation, if anything? He said he did not think I would tell that on him. What did you tell him? I told him I hadn't said anything about it because I hadn't. You had not at that time? I had not at that time—you know I wouldn't have said anything about it if I had not been sworn and requested to tell what I knew that went on. You do not like to tell anything about him now? You know I had to tell the truth. I understood you to say in the cross examination that Tolar was standing still for a minute or two before he fired that pistol? Yes, sir. That he did not rush through the crowd parting them right and left? I did not see him rush through the crowd. He was standing still a minute or two?

Yes, sir. A longer time than a minute or two? I don't know—I won't say—I never taken any notice and I don't know whether he was standing still at all—I saw him when he flung the pistol back—I turned my head up when the cry came "shoot him, shoot him." I do not know what he may have done when I had my eye on him. I want to know if Tolar was standing still when he fired that pistol? Yes, sir. How long had he been standing still before he fired—do you suppose, as long as you can count five? I can't tell exactly how long he was standing still when I cut my eye off him, and when I looked back he was standing still. How long had you been noticing him before the shot was fired? I had been watching him right smart. Had he been standing still at that position any length or time or not? He was standing still when I saw him draw the pistol. For a minute or two before he fired that pistol? I saw him there about the same position all the time; I won't say how many minutes. It was more than a second? I guess it was. Do you know exactly where Tolar was standing when the negro man came down stairs? He was standing off from under the market house. Not under the market house? No I don't think he was—I seed him about the time the negro turned from under the market house—I saw Capt. Tolar in the company there. Where? Well, opposite me up towards the tree. As the negro turned the arch? Yes, sir. And he did not change his position until he fired? I did not see that he did; but then I won't say, because in such a place as that everybody is frightened—I can't say exactly.

Hereupon the Commission had a recess of ten minutes, after the expiration of which time the Commission was called to order and proceeded with the examination of witnesses.

JAMES W. STRANGE, a witness for the prosecution after having been first duly sworn, testified as follows:

Examined by Counsel for the prosecution.

Were you one of the Justices that presided at the preliminary examination of Archy Beebee, on the day he was killed? I was, sir. We wish you to state to the Court, sir, the position which Major McRae occupied in that room, at the time Archy Beebee left the room to go down stairs; where he was seated in the room? Well, sir, that table being east, Major McRae was sitting in the center of it. On the west side of the table? Yes, sir. That table was sitting in the southwest corner of the room? Yes, sir. And pretty near the wall? Yes, sir. I understand you to say, that Major McRae was seated in the middle of that table at the time Archy Beebee left the room? Yes, sir. How long did he retain his position there? We set there after he went down until after the pistol was fired. You are absolutely confident? As positive as I am sitting in this chair. Did you retain your seat? We all retained our seats until after the pistol was fired. Who do you mean by we all? The entire Court. Who were they? Major McRae, Mr. Arey, Mr. Lett and myself. And you all retained your seats until that pistol was fired? Yes, sir. Did you leave the hall then? Yes, sir. Did any one leave the room and go out in the balcony in the east end of the hall before you left the room? Not that I am aware of; some one said, he was shot; I do not know whether he went out to see or not. You heard the rumor that the negro was shot? Yes, sir.

Cross examination by the Counsel for the accused:

Are you acquainted with the general character of Mrs. Elliott?

Counsel for the prosecution objected.

We wish to have some understanding about the mode in which this examination is to be conducted.

Counsel for the accused:

I would state to the counsel, that it will save the trouble of calling Mr. Strange as a witness in the defence.

Counsel for the prosecution :

We admit that the character of the woman is not to be sustained.

Counsel for the accused:

Then we have not a question to ask the man.

JOSEPH AREY, a witness for the prosecution after having been first duly sworn, testified as follows : What is your name? Joseph Arey. Were you a magistrate of Cumberland county in the winter of 1866 and 1867? I was, sir. Were you presiding at the preliminary examination that took place in the case of Archy Beebee? Upon the invitation of Major McRae who was the presiding magistrate, I was invited to assist him on the examination. You were present there? Yes, sir, present and assisted. Will you state to the court the position that Mr. McRae occupied in the hall from the time that Archy Beebee left the hall until the time the pistol was fired ? He was sitting at the table. Did he leave that seat at all? No, sir ; I do not think he stirred; I am pretty certain he did not. Are you absolutely certain he did not? I am certain. You heard the pistol fired ; you were sitting at the same table? Yes, sir. Who else was sitting at the table? Mr. Strange, Mr. Lett and myself; I forget what other one there was ; three of us—Strange, Lett and myself were assisting. And I understand you to say you are absolutely certain? I am confident That Major McRae did not leave that seat until after the pistol was fired? He did not; I am confident. Did you leave it after the pistol was fired? Soon after the pistol was fired a person came and said "he is dead." Soon after that I went down, and during my stay he never left the seat. During the time you were in the room he never left the seat? At one time, I was a little bothered about this, but upon reflection, I have no doubt that he never left his seat during my stay there. You did not leave the room until after the pistol was fired, and until some one had come in the room and stated that Archy was dead? I did not leave it in some little time after that.

Counsel for the accused declined to cross examine the witness.

HENRY W. HORN, a witness for the prosecution after having been first duly sworn testified as follows :

What is your name? Henry W. Horn. What is your profession? Lawyer. Were you, Archy Beebee's Counsel on the day that his preliminary examination took place? I was, sir. Were you in the town hall at the time Archy was carried out of the hall? I was there at the time he went out ; not when he was carried in. Did you remain there until you heard a pistol fired below? I did sir. Can you state the position that Major McRae occupied in that room at that time? He was sitting in the south west corner of the hall with the table between him and the door through which Archy had to go ; he was writing the proceedings of the trial, taking the testimony down. He was writing? Yes, sir. Do I understand you to say he was engaged in writing until the pistol was fired? During the time it was necessary to write up the papers, after the trial. Did he leave his seat till after the pistol was fired? He did not, sir. Did any one leave the room before you heard the

pistol fired? No one that I recollect, sir, except when the Sheriff went down with the prisoner, and the posse that was with him. Did you notice whether the door that opened on the balcony on the east end was opened, or not? I do not think it was locked, because I went out myself immediately after the pistol was fired, on the balcony. Did any one pass through there from the hall after the pistol was fired? Were you standing in a position where it was in your view? I was sitting where I could see the door all the time. I cannot; say positive, but my impression is that no one went out. You say you went out immediately after the pistol fired;' did any one come out with you? No one with me, sir. You are confident that there was no one with you? Yes, sir. Did you find any one on the balcony when you went out?' No, sir Was it you that reported the negro was dead? I came back and mentioned the negro was shot. Did you say anything from that balcony? Not a word. I was not there a second scarcely. Was Major McRae in the room when you returned, occupying the same spot? Yes, sir. Did you leave him in the room when you left there? I was with him, I think, when he went down. It was some minutes after the firing before we came down ; it is my impression we came down [together, but I am not sure about that. I know that several of us came down together. You are sure that he did not leave the room before the pistol fired? No, sir.

Counsel for the accused declined to cross-examine the witness.

The Judge Advocate asked the permission of the Commission to enter a *Nolle Prosequi* in the case of Duncan G. McRae. The Commission was cleared for deliberation, and after some time so spent, the doors were again opened. and the Judge Advocate announced that the Commission had granted the permission asked by the Judge Advocate to enter a *Nolle Prosequi* in the case of Defendant Duncan G. McRae, and he was thereupon discharged.

On motion, the Commission adjourned to meet on Tuesday, 30th inst., at 11 o'clock A. M.

RALEIGH, N. C., July 30, 1867, 11 A. M.

The Commission met pursuant to adjournment. Present, all the members of the Commission, the Judge Advocate, the counsel for the prosecution, all the accused and their Counsel.

The reading of the testimony taken yesterday was waived, no objection being made thereto.

The Judge Advocate asked the Commission for a compulsory process against witnesses William Porter, Duncan McLean, William H. Carpenter, James Kendricks and Owen Moore, several days having elapsed since the date on which they were summoned to appear.

The Commission was cleared for deliberation, and after some time so spent, the doors were reopened and the Judge Advocate announced that the Commission had granted the compulsory process asked for, in the cases of William Porter, Duncan McLean, W. H. Carpenter, Jas. Kendricks and Owen Moore.

CALVIN HUNTER, a witness for the prosecution, after having been first duly sworn, testified as follows :

Examined by the Counsel for the prosecution : What is your name? Calvin Hunter. Where do you live? Fayetteville. Did you live there at the beginning of this year? Yes, sir. How long had you been living there? I left here when Gov. Holmes did. And went to Fayetteville? Yes, sir. You have been living there ever since? Yes, sir, with the exception of seven months and a half when I went to Richmond, Va., in the time of the war. Do you remember the day Archy Beebee was killed? I do, sir. What is your business in Fayetteville? Boat carpenter. Do you work at your trade? Yes, sir, daily. You say you knew Archy Beebee? I knew him. When did you see him last alive? On the 11th of February, in the morning—no, in the afternoon a little, he was carried by the officers up to the market house from the guard house. Hsaw came you to be at the the market house that day? what time did you go up? I went up town soon in the morning and my wife told me— You must not tell what any one said to you. You went up early in the morning? I did, sir. Were you up town all day? I was until the time I saw Archy killed. Where did you go to first? I went to William Jordan's. Where did you go from there? I went up to Mr. Hinsdale's corner. Did you remain there sometime? About three quarters of an hour, to the best of my knowledge. Were you standing there when Archy was brought out of the guard house? I was not. Where were you standing when Archy was brought out of the guard house? Betwixt Mr. Draughon's corner and the market house. Where does Draughon's store stand? Upon the southeast corner of the market house. Do you have to pass by Draughon's store to go to the guard house from the market house? Yes, sir, when you go from the Main street When you go from the market house to the guard house you pass by Draughon's store? Yes, sir. You were standing there when Archy was brought out of the guard house? I was in the street. Not on the side walk? No, sir, I was not. Did you see Archy brought out of the guard house? I saw him brought out. Who was with him? Mr. Wemyes and Faircloth, and some behind, but I didn't notice who they were. Was there any crowd at the market house at that time. Just standing about talking a few, I didn't see much of a crowd. Not when Archy was brought out of the guard house? No, sir, I didn't see much of a crowd. Was he brought by you? Passed me, I was sort of to his left as he was going to the market house. He was brought right by you where you were standing? Yes, sir. What became of him? He was carried up into the market house. Where did you move to after he went up-stairs? I moved up on the pavement near a woman, that sells cakes, by the name of Becky Jenkins. Inside of the market house? No, sir, on the outside. There is a shelving there, and old hooks, and I leaned against them. On the east tront? On the south side there, the stall shows towards Mr. Draughon's. Were you looking into the market house? I was not when Archy come in; after he went up stairs and was out of my sight, I was looking to the people standing there. But where was your face turned, were you looking inside of the market house? Yes, sir. Did any crowd gather there while Archy was up stairs? One or two come about, but they didn't make any thick crowd at that time. How many men do you suppose inside of the market house, while Archy was up stairs? There might have been four or five or six, seated on a bench, and some standing. You don't think there were more than four or five? I don't think there was. How long was Archy up stairs? I can't tell how long he was up there. You can't come somewhere near it? No, sir, I cannot, to be accurate. What time of day was it when he was carried up stairs? Archy was carried there, it my memory serves me right—it was in the afternoon, because I had left

there about 10 o'clock, and bought me a pair of pantaloons, and they told me to come to dinner then. You think it was after dinner? I knew it was. Didn't you think at first it was in the forenoon? I did, the day was short—but I think it was in the afternoon. Did you notice any crowd outside of the market house, while Archy was up stairs? Not until after the trial. Not till after he came down? No, sir. You say you cannot tell how long he was up stairs? did you notice who was standing inside of the market house, those five or six minutes you speak of? I did, not, sir. Did you notice anybody standing around there at that time? I saw a young man called Monk Jule. Do you see him here? Yonder he is, sir, over yonder. You saw that man there? Yes, sir, I did. What was he doing? He had a knife out, cutting a stick. Inside of the market house? In the middle aisle of the market house. Was he saying anything? I didn't hear him, I didn't hear any conversation by any body. Did you notice anybody doing anything? Nothing at all. Just standing about? Yes, sir, any more than talking as usual. Who did you see standing and talking? I saw John Maultsby for one. Where was he standing? He was standing near Mr. Tompkins stall, just under the north of the market house. Did you notice any one else that you can recollect? No, sir. Did you see Miss Massey that day? Yes, sir, I did. Where were you standing when she came down? I was standing outside in front of Becky's stall, outside of the market house, towards Mr. Draughon's. She had a veil on. It was her and another lady. Did you say she came down before Archy was brought down or afterwards? Before Archy sir.

The witness here points out upon the "plan of the market house" the position he occupied while the young lady came down stairs; on the south side near the east corner.

What became of Miss Massey when she came down stairs? She goes right down the street like as if she was going to liberty point. Did she walk down? No, sir, she went in a vehicle. She got in the carriage first? Yes, sir. Who helped her in the carriage, did anybody? Yes, sir. Who? A gentleman by the name of Mr. Vaun, the town coustable. Did any one else assist her in getting in the carriage? There was another gentleman, but I disremember who he was. You think there were only two? There was only two, to the best of my knowledge. That is your recollection? Yes, sir, only two. How long after that carriage had driven off, before you saw Archy come out of this door on the stairs. I suppose betwixt eight or ten or fifteen minutes. Between eight and fifteen min utes? I think so. When he came out of the door who came first? There were some boys up on the bench before me, and I could just see their heads, and I could not tell who came first. Who were those boys? I didn't know them, little white boys—I could not see them till they got down on the second step. Who was on that step? Mr. Wemyss and Archy. Any body else? Faircloth was a little to the right of Mr. Wemysss, coming down, after he got so that I could see them. Where was Wemyss standing with regard to Archy? Mr. Wemyss was standing upon the right of Archy and I saw, when I peered through, I saw he had a twitch around his thumb, and a little stick, to take hold of. Did you see Sheriff Hardie at all at that time? I did. Where was he? He was right in front of Mr. Wemyss, and as they got, to the best of my knowledge, about five or six feet from off the steps. Before they turned out of the market house? Yes, sir. There was a rush made, like, and I heard Mr. Hardie say "you don't do it," and "stand off" and the crowd commenced to rush up, and begin to push me sort of back out of the way; and I run around. To which side? To the eastern side of the market house. Where did you stand then? I stood near the center of the market house, about ten feet from under the piazza of the market house. You stood off of the pavement? Yes, Sir. When this rush took place you run around, and got to the front of the market house? I did. Did you see who Hardie was talking to when he said what he did? I understood it to be Mr. Tom Powers. Did you see him at that time? I did. What was he doing? He was in the crowd; and I saw two knives, and I could not tell who had the knives when the push was made to Monk Julia, and he ran out of the crowd, as if he wanted to get another chance, and I stepped off again and said, "come away Sandy," and they scuffled then and got around to the point of the market house. Who is Sandy? Sandy McLean, is a man that lives in Fayetteville. Was he there with you that day? He was, sir. Did you hear Powers say anything? I took it to be his voice demanded the prisoner. Do you know his voice? I should think I would, but there being so many, I would not swear. You saw him in the crowd? I did; he was pressing forward. What position was he in; were his hands extended—did he have any weapons? I didn't see any weapons. You didn't see him have any weapons? I did not, sir. What was he doing with his hands? He appeared like he was trying to get to Archy. Was he grabbling at him? Trying to get in where he was. After they turned the corner of the market house, what happened then? After they turned the corner of the market house, the crowd commenced to get thick, and somebody flung his hand up so, and said, "clear the way," and give me a shove, and shoved me out from a view of the prisoner, and before I recovered, the pistol fired, and I could not tell who done it. You saw the pistol? I saw the pistol over the crowd—over their shoulders. You were pushed aside and your vision turned from towards the pistol? Yes, sir, and before I recovered, the pistol was fired. Did you see where the smoke came from? Of course I saw the smoke. Where was the smoke, near the point where you had seen the pistol? Near about the place. You heard the report and saw the smoke? Yes, sir. Did you notice who was standing near that point? I did not, sir. Did you notice Archy after the pistol fired? I didn't until I could get up to him, he was down then. Where must the man have been standing, that had the pistol? He was standing right in front of me. Was he on the pavement or off? On the pavement, near the edge of the market house. You think he was standing on the pavement, in front of you, near the edge? Yes, sir. You judge that from what you saw of the pistol, the arm that held it? Yes, sir. You could not pretend to identify him? I could not, upon oath. Did you see Archy immediately after that? I did in a few minutes. Was he alive or dead? He was near about dead, they said he was not quite dead. Where was his wound? Right in the left side of his head, right behind his ear, his blood was running out on the pavement. Did you see Captain Tolar that day, at all? I saw Mr. Tolar. What time? I saw him about the time the pistol fired. Where was he standing then? He was coming out of the

crowd, and turning the corner of the pier, where they come out of the market house. He went out of the crowd and went to Mr. Hinsdales. Through the market house? He went in at the east end of the market house, and right out of the west. And went to Mr. Hinsdale's store? Yes, sir. Did you see him after that? I didn't. Where was the point where you first saw Mr. Tolar—how far from the arch? Well, I suppose about five or six feet when I first saw him. Was it anywhere near the spot where you had seen the pistol before? No, sir, because he had moved, the pistol was about a yard from where I saw Mr. Tolar afterwards. it was about that close, (representing about a yard.) It was six or eight feet from the point where you saw the pistol? It was about three or four feet, to the best of my knowledge. Did he say anything? I didn't hear him. How was he dressed? He had a gray shawl,—and for pants and coat, I didn't take notice, because he had a shawl on. Did you see Ed. Powers there that day. I did sir. Where was he when you saw him? He was near the pier where Mr. Tolar went up to. On the pavement? Yes Sir. Did you notice any one else in the crowd near Mr. Tolar? I saw Mr. Samuel Phillips, he was near right in front of me. Between you and the point where the pistol was fired? Yes, sir. How near were you to Sam. Phillips? After the pistol fired he moved—I suppose he was about six feet from me. How far were you from the place where you saw the pistol? I think I was from five to six feet. Was Phillips between you and that point? Yes, sir, off to my left like. I thought you said he was in front? He war in front of me, a little to the left. Was he between you and the point you saw the pistol? Not directly, sir. Did you see him have any weapons? I did not, sir. Is that all you know about this subject? That is all I know, sir.

Cross examination by the counsel for the accused:

Calvin, how old are you? I asked Major Holmes a few days before I come here, and he told me, that I was fifty-five years of age or fifty-six. When was it, that you went off with Gov. Holmes? I can't tell indeed to save my life. You went off, you are sure, with Gov. Holmes? I did. How old were you at the time? I dont know. sir. Were you a man grown? No, sir. Sixteen or seventeen years? I could not tell to save my life. Were you a small boy? I was a boy. A small boy or a large one? I have ro particular size to give you, I know I was a boy. You went up town, you say, on the morning that Archy Beebee was killed? Yes, sir You went to Mr. Jordan's? I did, sir. What did Mr. Jordan keep? He kept a store in front and a bar room back. Did you go into the front, and then go back into the bar room? I did do it, sir. How many drinks did you take that day? I took only one at Jordan's in the morning. Did you take any more? I did not, sir. About what time was it when you went up to Jordan's? It was a little after sunrise. When was it you took the drink? Directly after going there—in about ten minutes, I suppose. And you took no other liquor that day? No, sir. You are given to drink pretty freely? I do when I feel like it, in cold weather. That was a pretty cold day? It was not so very cold, but I felt like it, and I took some that morning. Now Calvin, how long had you been up town—you say you got there about sunrise—how long had you been up town before Archy Beebee was brought out of the guard house? I didn't have any watch, and I didn't notice the time. I will ask you the question, whether you have said all along in talking about this matter—whether you have not all along said that it was before twelve o'clock that Archy Beebee was brought up to the market house? Well, tho pantaloons corrected me. Answer my question—have not you all along from that time, the 11th of February, up to to day—havn't you always said, in conversation about this matter, that it was before twelve o'clock? I told them it had slipped my brains. Have you said that, or not? I have said it because I was not correct exactly then. When did you find out it was not correct? I found it out the other day. I sent for my pantaloons, and I received a few lines from my wife, and I had a piece of paper there, and I told my wife to look on that piece of paper and see what day that paper was made out—it was a due bill. I ask you, Calvin, if you ever found out that it was after twelve o'clock that Beebee was brought there till you came up here as a witness in this case, yes or no. I always like to be correct, sir; I don't like to speak too fast, I might have said that, not having the correct time. I understand you to say you never did find out until after you got up here in Raleigh. I found it out by my paper; if I was wrong I had a right to be put right again. Did you find that out before you got to Raleigh, or after you got to Raleigh? After I got to Raleigh, of course. I ask you if you ever found out that it was not before twelve o'clock until you had talked with the other witnesses? I never talked with them about the matter—every man kept his evidence to himself. You were sworn about this matter once before, were you not? I was sir, before the Bureau there. Were you not sworn before the coroners inquest? I was. I ask you if you did not state at that time, when you were before the coroners jury, that you did not see anything like a pistol on that occasion? No sir, I didn't tell them so. Didn't you tell them you didn't know anything about it? They would not have summoned me the second time if they heard me say that. Just answer my question? I told them I didn't know who it was that shot the pistol. Didn't you swear before the coroner's jury that you didn't know anything about the shooting? No sir, I did not, I said I see the pistol. You spoke just now about some persons being up on a bench, about the time Archy came down—do you mean the bench that runs along the south-front of the market house? Yes, sir, right where Becky Jenkins' sells—the outside bench. Not the inside bench? No sir, where they lay beef on. And you say there were some boys on that bench? Yes, sir. Three or four boys? Yes, sir, And they were the persons who called out, "watch out, here he comes?" The boys said they were coming. And it was the boys on the bench outside of the market house, and not anybody or that bench in the market house? No say, sir, I heard nobody in there said so. You say when Miss Massey and her mother came down, they went to this vehicle. Where was this vehicle? It was standing on the eastern side of the market house? On the pavement? No, sir. In the street near the pavement? No, sir. How far from the pavement? I suppose some twenty feet. You say you saw there, Mr. Bond? Mr. Vaun. Did you see anybody else there? There was a gentleman, but I didn't notice who it was. Was that Mr. Phil. Taylor? It might have been him—one went right in front of the lady. See if you can recollect whether or not you saw Mr. Phil. Taylor and Mr. David Cashwell there? I don't think I did notice them. Did you notice anything unusual at the carriage? No sir, nothing at all. Nothing that attracted your attention? No, sir. When the carriage drove off you didn't see which way it went? I did, sir. Which way did it go? It went right down the main street. Right down Person street? Right down the street from the market house. How far down that street did you see it go? The last time I saw it, it was near Mr. Wesley Letts' alley. You noticed the carriage until it got down that far, did you? Yes, sir. That is a hundred yards from the market house? Yes, sir. Did you watch the carriage until it got a hundred yards? I did from first till last. I knew it was the carriage, for there was no other in eight. You spoke about seeing Capt. Tolar; are you sure Capt. Tolar had on a shawl? He did. Did you notice the shawl particularly? Not particularly. Are you certain that it was a gray shawl—was not it a black shawl? No, sir. Was it a gray shawl? It was a kind of gray; but it was not so light as some shawls, a dim gray and a black streak around the border. Was it what they call a dark gray or a light gray shawl? A little darker than a common gray. It was what you would call an iron gray? An iron gray is pretty light. It was darker than an iron gray? A little bit. You are sure it was gray? I know it was gray, or something to that effect. I didn't put my hand on it to examine it. You saw Sam. Phillips there? I did see him. How far was he from Tolar? When I got beside Tolar, it appeared as if it was some three feet. He was standing in front of me, a little more to one side. Was Phillips to Tolar's right hand or left? He was to his left. Three feet from him? Yes, sir. What did you hear Phillips say on that occasion? I never heard him say a word sir. Were you looking at Phillips? Just a moment or so. I paid no strict attention to him. Do you swear, before this Court, that this pistol you saw was not in the hands of Phillips? I do not swear it. I ask you if the pistol you saw raised in that way was not just about the point in the crowd that Samuel Phillips was standing? Yes. sir; it was. I ask you if Phillips did not have on a gray shawl? I didn't see him, he didn't have on no shawl then. You are certain of it? Not when he was standing before me. Well, while you were there about the market house, did you see any conversation take place between Ed. Powers and Tolar? I did not, sir. Did you see them more than once that day—Ed. Powers or Capt. Tolar? No, sir. When Archy was brought down from the market house, did you see any body on that bench, which was on the left hand side of Becky Ben's stall as you go up stairs, on the inside? No, sir; I did not. You saw nobody there? I did not. You speak of having seen John Maultsby? I did. What was John doing? He was standing on the pavement when I saw him. Where? Near that bench, right at the end, as you come from up stairs, before Archy came down. Did you see him about the time Archy came down? No, sir; he had got out of my sight. Then he was not near that bench at the time Archy came down? Not that I saw. And after the shooting you say you saw Capt. Tolar some distance off from where you had noticed the pistol? Yes, sir. And you saw Sam Phillips just about the same place? A little off to the left of me but just in front. And that Tolar turned and went through the eastern arch of the market house, and out of the western arch, and went up to Mr. Hinsdale's store? Yes, sir; he went through the arch. Now Calvin, let us get positions. When you moved around on the east side of the market house, were you on the pavement or off the pavement? I had moved. I mean the time that Archy was shot—were you then on the pavement? I was off the pavement sir. How many feet off from the pavement? Right at the edge of the pavement. Were you nearly opposite the main arch? No sir; a little down to the South, to the corner of the market house. Were you nearer opposite the small arch? About opposite the small arch. About the middle of the small arch? Not that far down. Near about the upper portion of the small arch? Yes, sir. Well then you say Tolar was standing on the pavement? He was not standing at all when I saw him. What was he doing? He was in the act of going out; the pistol had fired. So that you didn't see Tolar at all until after the pistol had fired? I didn't see him. I will ask you the question whether it is not your impression that Tolar was not the man that shot the pistol that day? That is not for me to say sir. I just want your impression, from what you saw, and not from what you heard? After the pistol fired he was not near where the pistol was, because he had moved, and even if he had not moved I could not tell anything about it. That is out of my reach. Then you have no impression about it? No, sir, it was an excitement, and so I will leave the subject. You will leave the subject? Yes, sir. How far was Sam Phillips off from Archy Beebce at the time the pistol was fired? I suppose he was about some six or seven feet, there was a crowd betwixt him and there. How far was Phillips off from you at the time the pistol was fired? He was about some three feet from me—off to my left—but nearly in front like. Was there anybody between Phillips and Beebee at the time the pistol was fired? There was several heads. Did you see these heads dodge out of the way? I did not particular. Did not particular? No, sir; I did not. Were there more people standing between where Tolar was seen by you, directly after the pistol was fired, were there more people standing between that place and Beebe or were there more people between Phillips and Beebee? There was more between Tolar and Beebee than there was between Phillips and Beebee. They came in as though they were shoved in. How long do you think it was between the time you were shoved aside and the time you recovered yourself? I recovered in a second. Did you then look right at Captain Tolar? I did. Did you see any pistol in his hands at that time? I did not. Who was standing near Capt. Tolar at that time? There was several. On Tolar's left hand? I could not tell. Anybody that you knew. No, sir; any more than Sam Phillips and other heads, I did not notice. Did you see anything of John Armstrong there? I did. Was he standing near Capt. Tolar at that time? Not when I saw him, that was before the shooting. I mean after the pistol was fired? I didn't see John then until I heard his mouth under the market house. When the man shot, you didn't see John Armstrong any where near Tolar, but you heard him talking under the market house—you heard his mouth? Yes, sir. You mean Armstrong was under the market house? Yes, sir; I heard his jawing there. I didn't know what he was jawing about. After the pistol was fired did you see whether Tolar's shawl had fallen off of him? I did not. Did you see him throw his shawl back? I did not. Did he do anything of the sort? Not that I know of. And you were looking at him? I was not looking particular at Mr. Tolar. I think I understood you to say that while you were standing on the outside of the market house, about the time that

Archy came down stairs, you could see all of that bench on the inside? I could not while the boys were upon it. I mean the bench inside? Well I don't think I could see all of it. Re-direct Examination, by the Counsel for the prosecution. I understand you to say it has been your impression until very lately that this killing took place before twelve o'clock? I did, but I had made a mistake, on account of my not paying attention. That was your impression until very lately? Until I corrected myself. You are satisfied now that you were wrong? Yes, sir, I was wrong. Counsel for the accused. I forgot to ask a question in the cross examination, which I will ask now with your permission. Counsel for the prosecution did not object. Cross examination resumed by the Counsel for the accused. What time of day was it, now, as you recollect it, that Archy was brought to the market house? Betwixt two and three o'clock. Re-direct examination resumed, by the Counsel for the prosecution. I understand you to say you were examined before the Coroner's jury? I was sir. Did you give the same statement there you do now? I did as far as the pistol was concerned. You did as far as the firing of the pistol was concerned? Yes, sir. They only asked me did I see who shot, and I told them I did not. That was the only question they asked you? Yes, sir. Were you alarmed that day? I was a little, at the firing of the pistol. Were you on the day of that examination? No, sir, I was not particularly. You were simply asked that one question, if you knew who fired the pistol? Yes, sir. And you were put aside? Yes, sir. What was it that these boys cried out when Archy was coming down stairs? "There they come" How many of these boys said that? There was three or four of them. Did they cry out loud? Just ordinary. I can't understand clearly where you were standing when this pistol was fired—at the time you saw the pistol you got a shove? Yes, sir. How far were you shoved? I was just shoved up against another man and I staggered. You didn't alter your position? I did not. When you recovered you were near the same place? Yes, sir. Where were you standing, on the ground off the pavement? I was off the pavement. Near the edge of the pavement? Yes, sir, opposite the upper end of the small arch at the eastern side of the market. Were you past the pier that connects the arches? About the far edge of the pier, I was standing near there. Were you facing the market house. No, sir, I was looking right at the guard following up Archy. You were turned a little towards the south? I turned my face towards the south watching Archy. How far was that pistol from you when you were in that position? Three or four feet. In front of you? Yes, sir. In a line between you and Archy? Not directly in a line. Was it more to the right of the line or to the left? It was more to the right. Where was Phillips standing when you saw him? He was sort of to my front and left? The pistol was to the right of the line from you to Archy and Phillips was to the left of the line from you to Archy? Yes, sir. If Phillips had been standing where you saw him stand could that pistol have been in his hand as you saw it? It looked as if the pistol had been fired from that position it would have killed Mr. Hardie. You saw the pistol? I did when it went up. Do you know whether it was in Phillips' hand or over Phillips' head? It was not. Was it in the direction where you saw Phillips standing? It was to my right, Phillips stood more to my left. Phillips was to your left, and this pistol was to your right? Yes, sir. How far was Phillips from the point where you saw the pistol? It might have been three or four feet. You speak of having heard Armstrong's mouth under the market house? I did, sir. When was that? That was after Archy was shot down a second or so—a minute I mean. It was not at the time the pistol was fired? No, sir. Was it before or after you saw Tolar? It was after. Mr. Tolar was gone when you heard that voice? Yes, sir. Tolar had appeared and departed before you heard John's voice? He had departed, but I didn't see him appear. You had to see him before he departed? I did. I heard John directly afterwards. How much of a crowd was there there when the pistol fired—how many men do you suppose? As soon as ever Archy come down I looked and it was just like a parcel of bees. How many men do you suppose there was in that crowd? I suppose there was some forty or fifty more or less, I am not prepared to tell you. There was a considerable crowd? There was a right smart crowd. How many men were there between the point you saw the pistol and and where you were standing? There were several, as many as could get in it seemed to me. Was the crowd packed in as tight as they could be? They were as many as could get in it seemed—there was enough. Didn't I understand you to say that just as you received this shove you heard some one say "clear the way"?—? I did—I didn't know who it was. It was the rush of the crowd—when the cry of clear the way was given that shoved you aside? The pistol went up then I got a shove, and just as he got the pistol up over his head they said clear the way and gave me a shove, and before I recognised the pistol was fired. How far was it from the spot where you first saw Tolar, to the spot where you saw the pistol? From where I first spied Mr. Tolar I suppose it was three or four feet.. He was in motion when you first saw him. Yes, sir. He was not standing still? No, sir He was going out of the crowd and going into the market house? Yes, sir, he was going out from the crowd. How many people were there between the point where you saw the pistol and Beebee? how far was Beebee from the point where you saw the pistol? He was about three feet. How many people were between the point where you saw that pistol and Beebee? Well, they stood in such a way I could not see. Less than three feet was the point where you saw the pistol, from Archy's head? Yes, sir. Now, when was it when you saw Phillips? I saw Phillips before the pistol fired? And how far was he from Beebee? He was there about four or five or six feet. He was further from Beebee than the point where you saw the pistol was from Beebee? They were not the same direction? Yes, sir, he was further. And they were not the same points at all? No, sir. And Phillips was further from Beebee than the point where you saw the pistol? Yes, sir. I understand you to say Phillips was closer to Beebee than Tolar was after the pistol was fired? No, sir, because when I saw Mr. Tolar he was going away,—no, Mr. Phillips was further off, because Tolar had just left about four feet. After he had moved off four feet Tolar was closer to Beebee than Phillips was? I suppose he was.

ROBERT SIMMONS, a witness for the prosecu-

tion after having been first duly sworn, testified as follows: What is your name? Robert Simmons. Where do you live? In Fayetteville, sir. What is your occupation there? I keep a grocery there. Was that your occupation at the beginning of the year? Yes, sir. Did you know Archy Beebee? Yes, sir. When did you see him last alive? I saw him alive last about the 11th of last February. Morning or afternoon? It was afternoon, sir. Where did you see him? what town and near what part of the town? He was at the market house. At the market house, where? In Fayetteville. How came you at the market house that day? what time did you go there? I disremember the time I went there exactly, but I think it was between one and two o'clock. Did you have any business that carried you up there? I heard there was going to be a trial, and I thought I would go and listen to it. What part of the market house did you go to? The south end of the market house. You went under the market house, sir? Yes, sir. When you got there was Beebee up stairs ¿ No, sir. Did you see him when he was brought into the markethouse? Yes, sir. Were you standing under the market house when he was brought up to be carried up stairs? I think I was standing under the market house when he was carried up stairs. Who went up stairs with him? Mr. Wemyss, I think, and Mr. Faircloth. I think there were some other persons, I didn't pay much attention. Was there anybody else beside Mr. Wemyss and Mr. Faircloth. Did you see Sheriff Hardie? I did not see him, I disremember, because I was not studying at that time. You know there were more than two? Yes, sir. You do not remember who they were? No, sir. How many people were in the market house when he went up stairs? I don't know how many there was—a good many. What was the size of the crowd? It was a pretty large crowd. How many? I don't know how many. Can't you make some sort of an estimate? Not rightly, from the market inside appeared several, off toward the east corner it was. There was a considerable crowd in the east end? Yes, sir, and some outside on the pavements like. You were standing underneath? Yes, sir. Where were you standing? Near the middle. On the north or south side? I was standing near the center of the market house, towards the east leaning on the bench. What bench was that? That was Beckie Jenkins' bench—talking to Beckie and Tom Powers. About the time they carried him up? Yes, sir. How long was he up there? Well, I disremember sir, may be it was half an hour or perhaps an hour. You cannot say with any certainty about the time? No, sir, it might have been shorter than half an hour. What were you and Powers talking about? Well, in the first place we were talking about this case that was on hand and what a bad thing it was—and I told Mr. Powers that I did not know anything about the young lady nor about who done it—it did not concern me at all: but I knew one thing, her father was a friend of mine he done me a great favor one time. What did he have to say about it? He never said much, only said it was a shame or something of that sort, I disremember the words he said now. How long did you stand there? I never stood there very long after they carried him up, I walked out on the side walk. Did you leave Powers standing by Becky Ben's stall? I disremember whether he did or not. Did you notice anybody else under neath the market house, besides Powers—anybody you can name. There was persons there but I did not pay any attention to them. Did not you see anybody's face that you can remember? I don't think I could. Did you see Capt. Tolar at that time? No, sir. Did you see Monk Julia there? No, sir. You can't recollect any face at that time except Tom Powers? No, sir. Then shortly after Archy went up stairs you went out of the market house? Yes, sir. At the east front? Yes, sir. Where did you go then? I stayed out on the pavement like? Did you remain on the pavement until Archy came down stairs? I walking about from one place to another, I was about that pavement all the time. Did you see or hear anything that attracted your attention while you were standing out there? No, sir. Can you tell any one who was in the crowd that you noticed then? Yes, sir, I can tell some. Who did you see then? I saw Capt. Tolar, he was not in much of a crowd, he was standing by himself. Was he underneath the market house when you first saw him? He was standing toward the north corner, near close up to the pillar like. When was the next time you saw him? I never saw him no more at all. Did you see him before Archy came down stairs? Not that I recollect. Did you notice any one else out there? Yes, sir; I noticed several. Name some that you can recollect? I saw Mr. Ed. Powers stand out there; Sam Hall, Mr. Lutterloh, Henry Sikes; I don't know who all else I saw. These men—Ed. Powers and Lutterloh, Sikes and Hall—were they standing together or apart; did you notice them conversing? They were just walking about; perhaps like other persons. I understand you that Tolar was standing by himself? He was, when I first saw him, sir. Where you were standing; could you see the steps that Archy came down? Yes sir. Did you see him when he was brought out of the door? Yes sir. Did anything happen in the court that attracted your attention before he was brought out of the door? Nothing in particular; though when the Ladies came down, Mr. Bond held the horses off for them; and he started back to go up stairs and Mr. Maultsby said "Israel be sure to attend to what I told you when you get up stairs" and he says "I will," I don't know how far he got up the stairs before Maultsby went inside of the stall where Becky sells, and there was some young boys and he told them to get out of the way; I thought he was making room for the prisoner and I never noticed particular. You say after Bond helped the ladies and was going back, Maultsby met him and had the conversation you just related? Yes, sir. What became of Bond,—did he get up in the market house? I don't know whether he got up or not. Maultsby went into Becky Ben's stall and told those lads to get out of the way; what did he say to them? He told them to clear the way. Were they in the way of the prisoner going down? They were sitting around; some on the steps and some on the benches, you know. The prisoner came down directly after Maultsby did this? Yes, sir. You are not certain whether Bond got up stairs? I am not certain. Did you see the prisoner when he came out of the door? Yes, sir. Who was with him,—who came out first? I am not able to say who came out first; I noticed the prisoner, there was a great rush up to the place that he was; a parcel of men there. You could not tell the position they occupied in the group around him? No, sir. You noticed there was a group going down stairs, and Archy was in it, and about that time there was a rush? Yes,

sir, that was before Archy had come down stairs; he was almost to the lower step, when I first saw him. He was near the foot of the steps when you saw him? Yes sir; then Calvin Johnson said to me, "look out! look at the knives, they are going to kill that fellow;" and I saw a great crowd of men rush up to the steps where he was coming down. What happened then? I heard the sheriff then holler, men go back or beat back or nomething of that sort; I know he said something to that effect, and the crowd seemed to be going back a little. Did you hear any exclamations? any body say any thing beside the sheriff? No, sir. Did you see any of these prisoners at that time? Yes, sir, some of them. Who did you see? I saw Mr. Powers and Mr. Monk Julius. Did you see Capt. Tolar at that time? I did not see him at that time. You saw Powers and Monk Julia in the crowd near the prisoner, there at the foot of the steps? Yes, sir. Did you see any weapons at that time in the hands of any one? I saw Mr. Powers have a knife, and I saw Monk Julia have a knife. What sort of a knife did Mr. Powers have? It looked like a small knife. What kind of a knife had Monk? It was a small knife. What do you call a small knife; how long a blade had the knife that Powers had? I think it was three or four inches in length, perhaps. The blade or the knife? The blade; it was two and a half or four inches; something like that. What happened next? They did not get to the prisoner at that time; the Sheriff and his men seemed to beat them back and the Sheriff come on out with the prisoner and the men, and several turned around the arch; the rush was made on them again and they went on near to the south corner of the market. Did you see anybody that was engaged in that second rush? I saw several that were engaged in it; I don't recollect them all. Name such as you do recollect? I recollect Mr. Powers being in it, and Monk Julia. Which Powers? Thomas Powers. Any one else that you recollect? Mr. Sikes was in it. Did you see any one else in the crowd? Mr. Maultsby was in the crowd. John Maultsby? Yes, sir, but I never saw him do anything. He was in the crowd that was rushing on them? Yes, sir. Mr. Maultsby was not trying to get out of the crowd? Not that I saw, sir. Mr. Henry Sikes? No, sir, it did not appear like they were trying to get out; they were with the crowd. They made part of the crowd? Yes, sir. They were right in the crowd. Yes, sir. What happened then that you saw? Just before they got to the corner they rushed on to the Sheriff again and he told his men to beat back; some person says, "go ahead Monk," and then some persons said, "shoot him," "shoot him," or something of that sort; I saw Captain Tolar walk up and come around on this way, like on my right, and reached right over and shot. He passed your right did he? No, sir, he did not pass my right; he come right up to my right, like. Where were you standing at the moment you saw Captain Tolar; on the pavement or off? I was standing off the pavement. Were you in front of the big arch? I was on the south of the big arch. Were you further south? Yes, sir. How far were you standing from the edge of the pavement? I don't know exactly; I might have been standing three or four or five feet. A step or two? Yes, sir. You were standing further round than the big arch; do you remember the little arch that is there, there are three arches in front of the market house? There are four vacancies that front south. I am talking about fronting east? East, I mean to say. Are you certain that there are four? Yes, sir, here is a corner, and here is another arch, and there is two over this side again, just the same; there is one on each side of the big arch. I mean the opening: I don't mean the pillars, you saw three openings, the big arch and two little arches? Yes, sir. And you were standing off the pavement a step or two facing which way? Facing the market house. You were standing near the south corner? Nearly in front of the south corner. The prisoner was near the south corner, and now that was the time you saw Mr. Tolar—where did he come from? It looked to me like when the rush was made from the crowd, I would not have seen him as soon as I did, but some one shoved against me and I cast my eyes back upon him, and he came from the north where he was standing. He passed you on the right? He did not pass me; he walked right up against me like. Could you have touched him with your hands? I don't think I could touch him. Where was he standing, on the pavement or off? I don't exactly know whether he was on the pavement or off; I know he was pretty close to the edge of the pavement. How far was he from Archy? He was not far from him; it looked as if the muzzle of the pistol was some two feet, or something like that from his head. You know Captain Tolar? I know him very well. You knew him before that? Yes, sir. Are you certain he is the man that fired that pistol? I am certain. What sort of pistol was it? It was a large Navy pistol. You saw him level it and fire? Yes, sir. Did you see what became of Archy after the firing? Archy fell. Did you see what became of Captain Tolar after the firing, and what became of the pistol? I did not see what he did with the pistol; I turned right off and went to Mr. Davis's. Mr. Davis, and Captain Green and Mr. Dodd were standing there. It sort of frightened me, and I said——. Don't tell your conversation. He turned and went off? Yes, sir. You did not see what became of Captain Tolar? When I got to Mr. Davis's Mr. Tolar had turned around; his back was turned towards the arch, and he was standing talking to some gentlemen. Did you notice how long he stayed there? No, sir. Was he standing there the last time you saw him that evening? Yes, sir. Who was standing nearest him when he fired the pistol? I disremember, sir. Can't you tell any one? I don't know. Did you see John Armstrong that evening at the time Tolar fired the pistol? Yes, sir, he was standing a little to my right. Between you and Tolar? Yes, sir. He was standing nearer to Tolar than you? Yes, sir. Did you see Sam Phillips that evening? Yes, sir. About the time the pistol was fired? Yes, sir. Where was he standing? If my memory serves me right, he was there near the arch when I first saw him. I think it was about the time the word was said, "shoot him." I cast my eyes that way, and I saw Mr. Phillips with his pistol in his hand, like if he was cocking it, but he never raised it any higher. That was about the time the pistol was fired? Yes sir. Your impression was he was near the arch of the market house? Yes, sir. My memory may have slipped, but I think he was near the arch; he says he was not, but I think he was. Your opinion is that he was. Yes, sir. That he was next the arch, and that he was there about the time the pistol was fired? In such an excitement it may be my memory slipped, but I think he was standing there. Did you see him fire that pistol he had in his hand that day? No, sir. Did you look at the pistol at all? did you examine it that day? No, sir; but I know he

did not fire it. You are certain that it was not his pistol that went off in the crowd? It was not his pistol. Was he standing near enough to Tolar to put his arm under his cloak and fire, as if it was Tolar fired? No, sir; there was no arm under the cloak. Could not Phillips have put his hand underneath, and made it look as if it was Tolar? Not from where I saw him, sir. You say you can't say who was near Tolar? No, sir, I don't recollect. Was anybody between him and Beebee when he fired the pistol? Yes, sir. How many persons do you think? There were some, I don't know how many. Did you see Beebee fall that day before he was shot? Yes, sir. Mr. Beebee looked over like he was cutting at him, and Beebee dodged and sort of went down. Did Powers have any knife in his hand? Yes, sir; and Monk he was running around like he was trying to cut, but he never got a chance; he was not nigh enough to reach there. Beebee got up again before he was shot, or was he shot while he was down? It seemed like the Sheriff and Mr. Wemyss or some of them raised him up, as soon as he was raised up he was shot. Where was Sheriff Hardie standing when Archy was shot? I don't know exactly his position, only I know he was right there with the prisoner. Do you know whether he was behind him or before him or on the right or left of him? I don't know whether he was behind him or before him; I think he was a little to the right of him. In front of him or behind? It look to me like he was in front of him to the right. That was your impression? Yes, sir. I understand you to say you are somewhat uncertain as to whether he was close to him? I am uncertain as to the position, it looked to me as if he was close to him. Did you see Wemyss? Yes, sir. Do you know where he was standing? No, sir; I don't exactly know where he was standing only I know I saw him have hold of the prisoner; he had one of these thumb screws. I want to ask you particularly about Phillips. When he had that pistol; he had it up high, holding it to take a sight? He had it down in this direction, in his right hand, laying in his left, (representing.) Did you see him elevate it at all? No, sir. Did you notice who he was talking to? No, sir; for I turned right off.

Cross examination by the Counsel for the accused.

How long have you known Captain Tolar? I have known him for eighteen months or two years. Did you ever have a difficulty with him about a buggy? No, sir; I never had any difficulty I bought a buggy at Mr. Cook's sale that he claimed, and I paid him for it. Paid Tolar for it? I think I paid him for it or settled it through him and Mr. Cook. You were very angry with Captain Tolar about that matter? No, sir. Did not talk to him in an angry manner about it? No, sir; he said it was his father-in-law's buggy, and I told Mr. Cook he sold me a buggy that belonged to another man. I think I paid Mr. Tolar for it; I know it was settled between us, and I did not lose my money nor he his. You did not give up the buggy until Tolar brought witnesses to prove it? No, sir; I think I went with Mr. Tolar to Mr. Cook; I am not certain. Did not you refuse to show Tolar the buggy when he came to claim it? He came and said Thomas Drake said I had his bugy, and I told him if I had it of course he ought to have it. Did not you refuse to show it to him? I did not show it to him until I found out it was his. You did not have any angry conversation with him on that occasion? No, sir; only I told him if it was his buggy of course he ought to have it. Have you been very active aoout this matter against Capt. Tolar in Fayetteville? No, sir; I have not.— Hav'nt you been persuading colored men not to stand by Captain Tolar or not to take his part in this matter; hav'nt you been persuading John Merrick not to have anything to do with Tolar; not to assist him or his family in any way? No, sir. You are certain you have not? Yes, sir; I swear it. When did you tell this story about Tolar shooting this man first? The day he done it How did it happen that you were not before the coroner's inquest about this matter? Because they never sent for me sir; I did not make myself smart enough to tell I knew any thing about it until General Avery was up there, some persons told him I knew it, and he sent for me. Now let me see—when the young ladies were up stairs, Miss Massey and her mother, before they came down where were you standing? I was standing outside on the pavement. Did you see them come down? Yes, sir; they come right by me. Where did they go after passing you? They got in a rockaway and went down the street.— Who helped them in the rockaway? Mr. Bond I think, and Mr. Mitchell and Mr. Powers. Was there any body else beside Mr. Bond and Mr. Mitchell? Mr. Powers, Which Powers? Thomas. Was there any body else? There might have been. Did you see Phil. Taylor or David Cashwell? They might have been there. I might have been there but was not;—were they there or not. They might have been there:—I don't know whether they were or not. Who was driving that rockaway? A black man. What is his name? I don't know, sir. Did you know him? No, sir. Where did he drive it after these ladies got into it. He went down the street and I think he turned around the corner by Mr. McGriffin's. You think he went down Person street? I know he went down that street. Not down Gillepsie street towards Robert Mitchel's store? Not at that time. You feel confident of that? Yes, sir. You say when Bond turned off Maultsby said what you have told? Mr. Bond after helping the ladies in the carriage turned around and started up to the market house and Mr. Maultsby said, Israel don't forget to attend to that business I told you; he said, I will. Mr. Bond started up as if he was going up stairs. How long was it aft-r Bond went up before Archy Beebee was brought down? It was not any time hardly. When Archy Beebee first appeared coming down the stairs where were you standing? I was standing out on the sidewalk like. Standing still on the sidewalk? Yes, sir. Did you have a good view of him? Yes, sir. Could you see the foot of the stairs and those benches around Becky Ben's stall? When he got down low enough to see I was not looking exactly at him, then, I was looking off in the street;—Caivin Johnson touched me and said look at the knives and then I got back off of the sidewalk. At the time Archy came down so that you could first see him could you then see the crowd that was around Becky Ben's stall and the benches that were about Becky Ben's stall? At what time? At the time that Archy Beebee was first seen by you coming down the steps. If I had been looking at him I could. When you were looking through the main arch and looking to the top of the steps where Beebee first appeared would not that bench—that bench standing on the left hand side of Becky Ben's stall—would not that bench be directly in the line that you were looking? Out towards the market house. You don t understand about the bench—it is the bench on the left hand side.

(The witness explains his position and that of the bench on the left hand side.)

See if I understand you; standing where you were at the time Beebee made his first appearance coming down the steps and looking at him, that bench which runs along by Becky Ben's stall you could see? Do you mean the inside bench? Yes; you could see that? Yes, sir; I could see that bench. Was not that bench directly in a line with your eye when you were looking from your position towards the upper part of the market house steps? Looking through the market house westward the bench stands west and East; the steps of course, was more south; I looked right between the end of the bench and the pillar of course, in looking through to the steps. Could you see the bench? Of course there was nothing between me and the bench. Now at that time when the prisoner Beebee had got to the steps of the market house did anybody jump up on that bench? Well; if he did I did not see it to notice it. But that bench was directly in your eye and you saw no body jump upon it? It was directly in my eye and I saw the bench and steps, but whether any person jumped upon it—it is always a custom for young men to jump up on the bench. But you saw nothing on that occasion? No, sir. Did you know John Maultsby? Yes, sir. Did you see him jump up on the bench? If he did I did not notice. Did you hear him say anything at that time? Not that I know. Did you see him anywhere at that time? He was in the crowd with the other men. Standing on the floor of the market house? Yes, sir. You are certain of that? Yes, sir, I am certain, he went in there. You are certain he was standing there? There was not much standing to do; they went right in and out; he may have been on the bench and may not. I understand you to say you saw Maultsby at that time? I saw him go in with the crowd. Was he on the bench or not? He was not on the bench; he was under the market house, and went in between the arch and the bench. You saw him rush up towards the stairs? Yes, sir. You saw Beebee coming down the stairs? Yes, sir. He rushed up with the crowd inside of Becky Ben's stall? Yes, sir. Then he was upon the floor of the market house? When he went in he was. You mean he might have jumped on the bench as Beebee was coming down, but you feel certain that he did not jump on the bench when Beebee started down, is that your testimony? No sir, I did not say that; he had been in there before that; he might have jumped on the bench, I don't pretend to say. Now, when you saw Beebee coming down stairs, who was in front of him, anybody? Well, sir, I could not tell particular, because they were low down; I had my eyes cast off towards the street; about that time I cast my eyes there. It appears to me they were near on the lower step, and I could not recognize who was in front of him or who were behind him. Now, at that time, did you see anything of Capt. Tolar? Not at that time. How many rushes were made at Beebee before he cleared the arch of the market house? It did not appear to me ike there was more than one grand rush, then. Did you see anything of Tolar in that rush—that is, the first rush I am speaking of, before he cleared the arch, I mean before he got out on the pavement? I never saw but one that looked like a grand rush; Becky's stall was nearly filled with men, you see. Then they got Beebee out on the pavement? Yes, sir. Who was in front of him? I don't know who was in front of him. Did you notice the Sheriff at that time? I noticed the Sheriff was with him. Did you notice whether Sheriff Hardie was in front of him or behind him? I can't say for certain whether he was in front or behind, only I know he was pretty close to the prisoner. At that time how far were you off from the pavement? Perhaps three or four or five feet, I was not very far. Were you opposite the center of that main arch, or were you nearer towards the north of the main arch? I was at the south part of this pillar that leads to the little arch. You were north of the pillar then, of the small arch? Yes, sir. And about four or six feet off from the pavement? Somewhere's along there. Now, who was on your left hand side at that time? I don't recollect, sir. Who was immediately on your right hand side at that time? Well, I don't recollect who was exactly on my right hand side; Calvin Hunter had just left me to go further off. Where was John Armstrong? He was a little further off, I know, because he spoke to me as soon as it was done. What did he say? He said ain't that a damned shame. So he was close on your right? Yes, sir, he was close on my right; I think another man was in between me and John like. How far were you off from Archy Beebee, at the time he was shot? Well, I was not very far from him, perhaps four or five feet—something like that. He had passed me like, he was down towards the lower pillar. You say that Beebee fell down or sunk down in some way,—when he was raised up did you see him? Yes, sir. Did you see who was with him at that time? I saw the Sheriff and policemen. You think the Sheriff was a little to his right and front. I don't know exactly the Sheriff's position, only I know he was pretty near him. Did the Sheriff have hold of him? It looked to me like he had hold of him, sir. What part did he have hold of—his hand, or arm, or body? I don't think there was many men who was able to tell—he was so close to him, it looked to me like he had hold of him, but I don't known where. Did he have him about the neck? He might have had him about the neck—of course I never seed—for I didn't pay any attention. As the Sheriff was standing in front of him—was the Sheriff's head turned towards Beebee, or was it turned down towards the guard house? It looks reasonable that it would be turned towards the guard house. Then it was turned towards the guard house, and not towards the prisoner. He might have turned his face around. Then you say as soon as Beebee was got up you saw the pistol shot fired? Yes, sir. You say this pistol was in the hands of Mr. Tolar? It was. Where did Tolar get the pistol? I don't know sir. When he came rushing up, did you see the pistol in his hands? When I saw Capt. Tolar, somebody shoved me, and then Capt· Tolar threw up his hand. Did he have a pistol in his hand then? It was all at once, just as soon as I was shoved I cast my eyes:—of course he must have had the pistol in his hand. Did he raise the pistol up and fire at once? Yes, sir. Did he take any aim? He raised the pistol up slowly. Did you see him cock it? I didn't see him cock it, I saw him fire it plain. As soon as Tolar fired, what did he do then? He turned right around, and sort of stopped there, and then he whirled around. Did he turn from his left or right? It appeared to me like he turned to his right. Do you know whether he turned to his left or right? I don't know for certain about it, sir. Did you see him have on a shawl? Yes, sir, What kind of a shawl? It looked to me like a sort of grayish shawl. Did he throw his shawl off from his shoulders? I never noticed about that, sir. Do you recollect seeing him, as soon as he shot, dirt the shawl back with his right hand. He

might have done it, but if he did, I didn't know it, sir;—as soon as he fired the pistol, my attention was called to the prisoner. I want to know whether you saw Capt. Tolar turn off. at all either to the right hand or to the left, before you started toward Davis's corner? Yes, sir. Did you hear any remark made to Tolar, by any one; or did you hear Tolar make any remark at that time? No, sir. Now let us see about the position of Mr. Phillips, did you say Captain Tolar was on the pavement or off at the time of the shooting? I did not say whether he was on or off, but I know he was pretty close to the edge. Was Beebee on or off? He was on it. Near the centre or near the edge? I think he was near the centre, sir. Where did you say Sam Phillips was standing? When my attention was drawed to Mr. Phillips, I saw him about the time the alarm was given to shoot; it looked as if he was across from me next to the pillar. Next to the market house? Yes, sir. He was to Tolar's right? He was, if I am not mistaken. Was he directly to his right or to his right and front? To his right and front. Then Phillips was nearer to Beebee than Tolar was? When I saw him, but he was on the other side like. And you say when you first saw Phillips, that he had the pistol in his hand; the breach in his right hand, and the barrel in his left hand, as if he were cocking it; was that before or after the shot was fired? It was about the time this man was shot; but he said it was not. He has been talking about it to you has he? He asked me if I said he had the pistol, and I told him, I thought so. You and he have been talking about it several times? No, sir; he asked me what I was going to say about his having a pistol, and I told him, I was going to say he had it in his hand at the time Beebee was shot;—he said he took it out to protect the sheriff? That was what Phillips told you. Yes, sir—to protect the sheriff. To protect him after the pistol was fired? When did Phillips tell you that; before he got out of jail? No, sir—the next day after the shooting was done; Mr. Phillips came to me, and told me, "Simmons, we are trying to get up all the colored men who knows anything about this, to go up to the Bureau and be sworn" and I said you had your pistol in your hand; you would have shot him, I expect; and he said I did not intend to do it; I told him I did not want anything to do with it, and I told him, it looks as if you wanted to get me to have something to do with it. Have you had any talk with Phillips about the matter in Raleigh since you have been up here? No, sir—not in particular, In general? No, sir—I have had no talk with him any more than I would to any other man. Witness, I ask you the question; if Sam Phillips since he has been here, and since he has been released from jail, has not been to you and talked over with you that part of his testimony that related to his having a pistol? Not in particular, sir. Has not he done it all? Of course he was talking the same way he was the first time, after this shooting was done. I am speaking about since Phillips has been here in Raleigh, and since I have been in Raleigh? I say he has only made the same remarks that he did that day. Has not he done that several times? No, sir, not several times. Two or three times? He might have made it once; if he made it twice I don't recollect it; he said Louis Smith made a mistake, and me and Louis was present, and he told me he thought I had made a mistake—he said "you told me I had had the pistol before this fellow was killed; I says well; I say so yet; I say you did. What kind of a pistol was that, that Sam Phillips had in his hand? It looked as if he had the upper part of it in his hand; it looked like one of these small navy pistols. Was it as long as the pistol Tolar had? No, sir. It did not carry as large a ball? It might have carried as large a ball, but it was a shorter pistol. About an ordinary sized one? An ordinary repeater; I think they call them navy repeaters. But you say it was a smaller pistol than the one Tolar had? Tolar's was a sort that cavalry carries. And Phillips was a smaller size? Yes, sir. How long was Tolars pistol? I don't know the length of one of those pistols. Do you think it was fifteen or twenty inches in length? No, sir, it might have been a foot in length; I have never measured one. What I want to know is, how much longer do you think the pistol Tolar had, was than the pistol Phillips had? I can't tell exactly the length. A difference of four inches in length? There might have been a difference of two inches or something like that; maybe four inches. Were you armed on that occasion? No, sir, I was not armed. Did you have no arms at all? No, sir. What were your declarations there that day, about taking the prisoner Beebee away from the Sheriff; what did you declare that you would do if you could get a sufficient crowd to help you, about taking Beebee away from the Sheriff? Nothing. You say you said nothing about that? No, sir. Either before or after the occurrance? No, sir, neither before or afterwards. What did you say about it? After he was killed, I said, it ought to have been done according to law. What else? I said, if the law said "hang him," take him out in the woods and hang him, and not kill him in the street. That is all you said about it? That is all I said about it; of course I had no right to say anything about it, and I did not. And you say after you ran across to Mr. Davis's you did not see anything of Mr. Tolar? I did not say that. What did you say? I saw Captain Tolar standing with his back turned towards the small pillar, and talking to a crowd of gentlemen, apparently. How long did Tolar stand there? I do not know, sir, how long. How long did you see him there, three or four minutes? He did not stay there three or four minutes. How long; a minute or two? He might have stayed there a minute. And while you were there, both in the position where you were, and while you were at Davis's, Tolar was standing there with his back to the market house? Yes, sir, when this shooting was done he sort of turned around, and as I turned off, he turned off, and when I got to Mr. Davis's he had got to the pillar looking northwards like talking to some gentlemen. You think he stayed there as long as a minute or two? Yes, sir. Which pillar do you mean? The one between the large arch and small one. Looking north? Yes, sir.

Re-direct examination by the Counsel for the prosecution.

I understand you to say there were some men between Tolar when he fired the shot, and the prisoner who was shot down? Yes, sir. Do you know who those were? No, sir, more than they were some fellows. Did you notice any men bending their heads out of the way of the pistol? No, sir, as soon as he was raised up the pistol was just reached over their heads. The pistol was high enough to reach over their heads? Yes, sir, he was pretty tall. Do you know who it was Tolar was talking with when you went over to Davis's corner? I saw Ed. Powers and Mr. Lutterloh. They were talking with him? Yes, sir. They were in the group after the firing of the pistol? Yes, sir, a whole crowd. I don't

know how many. You saw in that crowd Ed. Powers and Mr. Lutterloh. Yes, sir. Do you remember seeing anybody else that you could name? No, sir, for I never noticed them particularly at that time. I had got down to Mr. Davis's, and I didn't know but what there might be some other shooting, and I rushed off farther. I understand you to say that Phillips saw you the day after this transaction took place? Yes, sir; he was on the jury; he come to me and asked me if I would go up, and he said the Bureau wants to get all the evidence it can, and I want you to go up. I said, "Well, the Bureau have not sent for me, and I don't love to get in your scrapes." I says, "you were there; you saw it; you had your pistol, and I expect you would have shot him; and he said, no, I had it out to protect the Sheriff." I said that "there had been some threats made, if any colored man knows it he would be killed any way." Did Phillips ask you to swear to a lie? No, sir. You say the conversation he has had with you since he has been here is pretty much the same as he said to you then? Yes, sir. Your opinion is still what it has always been, that he had the pistol out at the time the other man fired? Yes, sir. He has not asked you to alter your testimony? No, sir, he only told me I was mistaken. Who was the first person that you made your statement to about this business? —I don't mean an official statement but who did you talk to about it? Mr. Davis and Captain Green and Mr. Dodd. You were not examined before the Coroners inquest? No, sir. When was the first time that you were examined on oath about this matter? It was when the General was down at Fayetteville. Did he send for you? Yes, sir.

On motion, the Commission adjourned to meet on Wednesday July 31, at 11 o'clock A. M.

The Commission met pursuant to adjournment. Present all the members of the Commission, the Judge Advocate, the Counsel for the prosecution, all the accused and their Counsel.

The proceedings of yesterday were then read.

The following question and answer were inserted in witness, Calvin Hunters testimony, on page 419.

Have not you been known by the name of Calvin Johnson? Yes, sir, when I was a slave.

Yesterdays proceedings, having been read were then approved.

JESSE REYNOLDS, a witness for the prosecution, having been first duly sworn, testified as follows:

Examined by the Counsel for the prosecution. What is your name? Jesse Reynolds. Where do you live? Fayetteville? How old are you? I am twenty two years old. Were you in Fayetteville the day Archy Beebee was killed? Yes, sir. At the market house that day? Yes, sir. What time of day did you go to the market house? About one o'clock may be, or a little sooner, or later. Were you there when Archy was brought out of the guard house? Yes, sir. Where were you standing when he was brought up to the market house from the guard house? I was standing at the east corner. Were you on the front face of the market house, or on the south face? On the south face. Was the prisoner brought by you? Yes, sir. Did you stand there until he was carried up stairs? I stood there till he passed me and I ran around and got up on the east bench. The bench in the little arch? Yes, sir. You stood on that bench? Yes, sir, until he went up stairs.

Where did you go after he went up stair? I went around in the big arch; and walked about there. Did you go inside of the big arch? A little piece. While he was up stairs? Yes, sir. Who did you see in the market house? I seen Mr. Tolar, and Mr. Maultsby. What Maultsby? John Maultsby, and Mr. Powers. What Powers? Tom Powers, and I seen Mr, Nixon. What is his name? James Nixon. Any one else? Well, sir. I seen several around there. Did you see Monk Julia? Yes, sir. Any one else that you can name? I believe that is all I took any notice of. Was there much of a crowd in the market house? There was a pretty big crowd. How many people? A hundred or over. In the east front? All around by the steps. Inside do you mean? Yes, sir, and outside too. These men that you mention as having seen inside of the market house, Tolar, Tom Powers, Monk Julia and John Maultsby, where were they standing? They were standing up there together. Were they in the same group? They and several more were standing together. What part of the market house were they standing in? Under a big arch, on the right hand side as you go in. Was there a bench there? Yes, sir. A bench that was from the pillar or the right hand side? Yes, sir. Did you notice whether they were conversing together, or saying anything? I did not take any notice of it. They were talking there. Did you hear Maultsby say anything while the negro was up stairs? I heard him say to another man with him—who was that man? I don't know his name, a stranger to me. What sort of a man was he? He was a tall man, with red whiskers, and sort of red hair. Had you seen him about there before? I saw him that day. Mr. Maultsby was talking to him? Yes, sir. What was he saying? He was talking about this Archy; and I heard Mr. Maultsby say, "if he was not guilty, he was Archy's friend, but if he was, he was in for it as well as the rest." That if he was not guilty he was Archy's friend, but if he was he was in for it? Yes, sir. Were you standing there when the lady came down stairs? Yes, sir. Were you standing outside or inside? Outside, and opposite the big arch. Were you close by it? Yes, sir. Which side, right or left? The left side as you go down towards Liberty Point. When the lady came down stairs what happened? She went in the buggy, her and her mother, and she called Mr. Powers to her. Which Powers? Tom Powers—and Mr. Powers come back and said his sister. Who asked him what she said? Monk asked Mr. Powers what she said, Mr. Powers told him his sister did not want him to have anything to do with the case, and Monk said, "you can do as you please, if it was me, as you, I would have something to do with it." That was the substance of the conversation? Yes, sir. This young lady and her mother called Tom Powers to them, he went and when he came back Monk asked him what they said, and he said they didn't want him to have anything to do with it? Yes, sir. And Monk told him if it was him he would have something to do with it? Yes, sir, he said, "if it was me as it was you, I would have something to do with it. Is Tom Powers any kin to Miss Massey? I believe Mrs. Massey is Tom's sister. Did Monk say if it was his kin folks? It meant the same thing, if it was me, as it was you, I would have something to do with the case. How long was that before the negro came down stairs? He came down in a few minutes after that occurred. Could you see

the steps as they came down? Yes, sir. What happened as he bame down? He went round the corner to start to the guard house, and Mr. Powers took hold of him. How? By his arm. With which hand, do you remember? I can't tell—of his right arm I believe. He took hold of the negro's right arm? Yes, sir. Which hand did Mr. Powers use? I disremember—but he took hold of him. You think he put his hand upon him? He put his hand upon his arm and Mr. Wemyss I think shoved him off. What did he do then? He went up in the crowd. In what crowd? Where the policemen was. How do you mean he went up? After they shoved him off once he went up again. He walked very slowly or ran up? Not very slow or fast, a common gait. You didn't think he was trying to make his way into the crowd? I don't know whether he was or not, I can't tell about that. Did he give way to everybody else? he didn't press into the crowd? I didn't see him press in but he went up towards the crowd. What was Monk doing all that time? Monk run up the same time. What happened then? Well, sir, they started on to the guard house with the prisoner, the officers did, and when he got to the corner the pistol was fired and he fell. Where were you standing when Archy fell? I was standing right behind him—right by the edge of the big arch. The arch nearest to Archy? Yes, sir. When the pistol was fired? Yes, sir. Who fired the pistol? I don't know, sir. I ask you in the presence of God, who sees your heart,—who fired that pistol? I say I don't know, sir. What hindered you from seeing? Well, sir, I had my eyes on the prisoner as I told you before. Your eyes were on the prisoner? Yes. sir. Did you see the prisoner? Yes, sir. Was he on your right or left hand? He was sort of on my right arm—(touching his left arm). Is that your right? I mean on my left. Did you see the smoke of the pistol? No, sir. How far was the pistol from you, from the sound? I could not tell exactly by the noise of it. What is your impression? I reckon he was as far as here to that window or further (about fifteen feet). You think it was as far as from you to that window? It might be further and may be not. I can't tell. Did you see Capt. Tolar in the crowd? The last I saw of him was when he was standing under the market house.

Cross examination by the Counsel for the accused:

What is your business? Any kind of laboring work. You say when Maultsby came back he sat down on a bench with some other man and said to him, "If Archy is not guilty I am his friend." No. sir, I didn't say that—he said if Archy was not guilty that he was his friend,—is what I said;—" but if Archy is guilty he is in for it."

The Counsel for the prosecution did not think the prisoner understood the question.

The Counsel for the accused would ask it again.

Cross examination resumed by the Counsel for the accused:

When Maultsby came down and sat down upon that bench he made this remark: "If Archy was not guilty I am his friend?" Yes, sir. But if he is guilty he is in for it? Yes, sir. Referring to the trial that was going on up above?

The Counsel for the prosecution:

That is a question of opinion. The witness does not know positively that he referred to the trial.

The Counsel for the accused:

If there is any objection to the question I will leave it out.

The Counsel for the prosecution objected to the question.

The Counsel for the accused:

Let it be struck out, sir.

The question was stricken out.

Cross examination, resumed by the Counsel for the accused:

Did you see Maultsby do anything that day? No, sir, I didn't see him do anything at all. Did you see him jump up upon that bench, which runs by Becky Ben's stall, about the time the prisoner was brought down stairs? No, sir. About that time can you swear whether Maultsby did or did not jump up upon that bench, running by Becky Ben's stall? Well, I can't swear it, he may have done it, but I never seen him. If he did it you didn't see him? No, sir. At the time the prisoner was being brought down, could you see any person who jumped up on Becky Ben's stall? I didn't see anybody jump up there, it was only boys and young fellows up when they come down. Was Maultsby among the crowd up there? No, sir. Did you see him anywhere? I saw him under the market house, talking to that man. Was he sitting there talking to that man at the time the prisoner was brought down stairs? I don't know. I understand you to say that Tom Powers went up and put his hand upon the prisoner Beebee? Yes, sir, put his hand upon his arm. Did he put his hand upon his arm gently? Just laid his hand upon his arm like, only he grabbed hold of him. You are certain he did grab him by the arm? Yes, sir. Did he keep his hand upon the prisoner's arm until they shoved him off? Yes, sir. How long before they shoved him off did he have his hand there? They shoved him off immediately. Which hand did he put upon his arm,—his right hand or left? I didn't notice about that. See if you can remember from the position? I tell you I never took any notice which hand it was, but he put it upon his arm. Was there any knife in that hand? Not that I saw, sir. No knife in it? No, sir, not that I seen. You were looking at him? Yes, sir. And you saw no knife? I saw no knife. Did Monk have any knife? Yes, sir. Which hand did he have it in? His left hand, I believe. I think I understand you to say when Powers went up to the crowd that he did not rush up, but he just walked up in an ordinary gait? Just walked up and put his hand upon him. How far did say you were off from the prisoner at the time he was shot? I may have been ten feet, or a little further, about that distance ten or twelve feet. Were there many persons between you and Beebee at the time he was shot? There was right smart. Did you see anything of Sam Phillips there that day? Yes, sir. At the time Beebee was shot, did you see Sam Phillips? No, sir; I seen him after he was shot. Where was Phillips? He was standing off towards Mr. Davis' store. To the left of you? Yes, sir; not exactly towards the store, but sort of down the street. How long was it after Beebee was shot before you saw Sam Phillips? It may have been five minutes, or such a matter, or a little longer. How near was he at that time to the place where Archy Beebee was shot? May be as far as that window—(about 20 feet.) Did he have any thing in his hand? Yes, sir. What did he have? A pistol. How did he have it? He had it in his left hand working it with his right; looked as if he was rubbing the dust off of it. Rubbing the dust or smoke, could you tell?

No, sir; he was rubbing something off of it. What sort of pistol was that Mr. Phillips had? It was a six-shooter, I think. How long was it? I suppose about that long ,(representing by his hand.) That is about ten inches? Yes, sir. You think it was about ten inches? Yes, sir. How far was Phillips off when you saw him fire, or ten minutes after the pistol was fired—how far was Phillips from the place where you saw the smoke? I didn't see the smoke. Didn't you see the smoke of the pistol when it was fired? No, sir. Could you state what part of the crowd the pistol was fired from, from the sound of the report? No, sir, I could not. So you don't know where the person was who fired the pistol? He was standing off on my left, but I don't exactly know the spot, how far nor how nigh. Did you see a pistol in the hands of any body else, except Phillips, that day? No, sir. Did you hear Phillips make any remarks about shooting the negro that day? I went up to him and asked him what he meant by that, and he allowed there was going to be a fray there. What else? That was all he said. That was directly after the firing? May be five or ten minutes, or a little longer. The man was dead and the crowd begin to get a little thinner. And you saw nothing of Captain Tolar at the time the pistol was fired? No, sir. Do you know Tolar? Yes, sir. Did you know him before that time? Yes, sir. Was he one of the people that was standing in front of you, between you and the prisoner? No, sir. He was not? If he was I didn't see him. You last saw Tolar, you say, under the market house? Yes, sir. Before the pistol was fired? Yes, sir. Did you see him there directly after the pistol was fired? That was the last time I saw him that day. You didn't see him but once that day? That was the last time I seen him before the pistol was fired. Did you see him after the pistol was fired? A day or two afterwards, I think. But the same day? No, sir.

Re-direct examination by the Counsel for the prosecution:

Witness, I want you to state exactly in your own words, what it was you heard Maultsby say to that gentleman with the red beard? He said, "If Archy was not guilty that he was his friend, and if he was guilty he was in for it," some kind of way he brung it out. Didn't you say to me that he said he would see them out? No, sir; he said he was "in for it." Did he say "he was in for it," or "I am in for it?" He said "I" of course.— That is the way I understood you; you understood at that time, Mr. Maultsby to mean, that he himself, Maultsby, was in for it? He said those very words. He said "it the darkie was not guilty, he was his friend, but if he was guilty, he was in for it." Just put yourself in the place of Maultsby, and repeat the same words he used. Now consider yourself Maultsby, and say what Maultsby did? I don't want to put myself in the place he was, but he said this "If Archy was not guilty I was his friend, but if he was guilty I was in for it.' What did you say Mr. Phillips was doing with the pistol when you saw him? He was fingering about the revolver. The lower part of the pistol? Yes, sir; the part next to his hand. What was he doing? I didn't notice. Was he rubbing it, sort of jlike he was scratching the rust off with his thumb nail. How long did you say that was after the firing? Maybe five minutes. Did you say the crowd was thinning out? Yes, sir; they began to thin out. Did you hear Powers say anything? I didn't hear him. Did you hear anybody demand the prisoner? No, sir.

Henry Hagans, a witness for the prosecution, after being first duly sworn, testified as follows:—

Examined by the Counsel for the prosecution. Where did you live at the beginning of this year? In Fayetteville. What is your business there? Shoemaker. Whose shop did you work in, the first part of this year? I worked with Mr. Henry Sykes. Is that the one armed man? Yes, sir. Did you know Archy Beebee? Yes, sir. Were you in Fayetteville the day he was killed? Yes, sir. What day was it? I think it was the 12th of February. Was it in the morning or afternoon? Afternoon. About what time? A little after three o'clock. Were you at the market house? Yes, sir. What time did you get up there? I got up there about five minutes past three o'clock, I think. Was there a clock in that market house? Yes, sir. Does it keep time? Yes, sir. Was Archy up stairs? Yes, sir. Where did you go to stand when you first went there? I sat down under one of those little arches; the one towards the river, rather inclined to Mr. Fishblate's store. That is on the east front. On the north front (on the plan of the market house the witness pointed out his position as on the east front, but on the corner toward Mr. Fishblate's, looking down towards the river.) How long were you seated in that small arch? About ten minutes I guess. Where did you go when you moved from that point? In front of the arch towards Mr. Draughons. Did you stand there? Yes, sir. Any length of time? Yes, sir; I stayed there till after the pistol was fired; I don't know exactly what time. Were you on the pavement? I was off the pavement. Did you move before Archy came down stairs? I moved to that place as Archy was coming down stairs. I never moved until after the lady come down stairs. You were sitting in that small arch until the lady came down stairs? Yes, sir. Did any one go with the lady to the carriage? Yes, sir; Mr. Bond, the constable. Any body else? Her mother. Any one else? Not that I saw, sir. Did you go inside of the market house at all? No, sir. Did you see who was in the market house while the lady was up-stairs? No, sir. Did you see any of these prisoners in the crowd there that day while Archy was up-stairs? Only one, sir. Who was that? Monk Julia. Who else did you notice in the crowd, if any one? No one but the man I was working for, Mr. Sykes, and Armstrong and Simmons. You noticed Mr. Sykes there? Yes, sir. Where was he? Well, sir, he was standing on the pavement right in front of the central arch? Was that before the lady come down stairs? Yes, sir. Did you see the inside of the market house at all? Up-stairs? No, inside of the lower part of the market house, through the big arch? I did not notice in particular. You did not lock in there? No, not in particular. You did not go in at all? No, sir; I mean to say I did not look in the market house before the boy came down stairs; I did not mean after he came. Could you see the stairs from where you stood, when the boy was coming down? Yes, sir. Did you see him coming down stairs? I did, sir. Who was with him? I think it was Sheriff Hardie and Mr. Wemyss. Any one else? If there were I did not notice; I think there were some policemen, but I did not notice particularly which ones. Did you see him from that time until the time he got outside? No, sir, he was a little between the central arch and the little arch. The pillar got between you? Yes, sir. What happened when he got down stairs? The first thing I saw was the crowd rushing to him   Who was

in the crowd; any body you can identify? I saw Mr. Sykes and Mr. Powers. Which Powers? Mr. Thomas Powers. Any one else? Not as I could discern. Did you see Monk Julia? I saw Monk, too. Any one else? Not at that time. Had you seen Mr. Tolar up to that time? I did not. What happened in the crowd that rushed up to him; did you hear anything said? Yes, sir, there was a word said. What word? It was either "I demand the prisoner," or "gentlemen he is mine." Some expression of that character? Yes, sir. Who used that? Thomas Powers. Did you see him when he spoke? Yes, sir. Do you know him well? I did not. What happened in the crowd that rushed up to him; did you hear anything said? Yes, sir, there was a word said. What word? It was either "I demand the prisoner," or "gentlemen he is mine." Some expression of that character? Yes, sir. Who used that? Thomas Powers. Did you see him when he spoke? Yes, sir. Do you know him well? I did not. No doubt but that he is the man who spoke those words? No, sir. Did he seize the prisoner? He was in the act of seizing him. Did he get hold of him? No, sir, the crowd kept rushing until he vanished from me. At that time what was Monk Julia doing? I do not know what Monk was doing at that time. Did you see any weapons in the hands of any one at that time? I do not know, sir. What happened next? The next that happened, I heard some one say "shoot him, shoot him," and I looked and I saw a pistol and I saw a man that had the pistol. Where was he standing? He was standing near the edge of the side walk. On the pavement or off? On the edge of the pavement. Was he opposite the small arch or the big one? He was nearer to the little arch than he was to the central arch; I do not think he was standing opposite the little arch, but he was nearer to it than the central arch. Which way was his face? His face was sort of towards the corner of the market house. How was that man dressed that had the pistol? I did not notice in particular; he had on a shawl. What kind of a shawl? A long citizens shawl; a sort of greyish color. Did you know the man? Yes, sir. Who was it? Captain Tolar. Did you know him before? Yes, sir, I saw him there selling beef in the market house. You saw him with the pistol in his hand? Yes, sir. You saw him when he fired? Yes, sir. Did you see Archy when he fell? I saw him when he sunk in the Sheriffs hand. What became of Captain Tolar when he fired? I could not exactly tell; just as he fired the pistol, it either went in his pocket or through under his left arm, and he flirted the shawl off, and turned, and I never saw him any more. Didn't you see him any more that day? I did not sir. Who was standing nearest to him that you saw? John Armstrong was the nearest man that I saw, that I could call by name. How near was the man? I could not tell exactly how near; but he was close enough to throw the shawl on John Armstrong. Did you see it fall on him? Yes, sir. Who else did you notice near him? I could not call any name. Did you see Ed. Powers or Maultsby or Sam. Hall? I did not. Did you hear anybody hurrah for the man that did it, or any thing of that sort? I heard a man out in the street ask whether he was shot, and some one answered, yes; and he took off his hat and said hurrah, and some other expression, but I could not tell what it was. Who was that man? Jonathan Hollingsworth. Did he use any name when he made that hurrah? not that I can recollect. How long was that after the man was shot? It was about two minutes I guess. Did you see Mr. Phillips there that day? I did sir, I saw him before the thing occurred but not afterwards. Did he have a pistol when you saw him? I did not see it sir. What weapons did you see there that day? who did you see with a weapon? I never saw but the pistol and the knife. Who had the knife? Monk Julia. Do you know whether Sykes had a weapon that day? He had a weapon. How do you know? He showed it to me after he came back to the shop. You were staying at the same shop? I was working for him at that time.

Cross examination, by the Counsel for the accused.

Where do you live now? I am living here at present, sir. When did you leave Fayetteville to come here? I left Fayetteville Tuesday morning a week ago. Had you been subpœnaed as a witness before you came here? I was not sir. Have you been since coming here? I suppose so. Have you had any talk with any of these witnesses from Fayetteville about this matter since they came up here? No, sir, not any talk in particular. Haven't you had repeated conversations with Sam Phillips since you have been here? No, sir, not concerning this case. Witness, I ask you on your oath if you have not stated this matter to Sam Phillips, and he has dragged it out of you since he has been here? Dragged out which sir? This statement that you have made here—answer the question, don't be afraid—how do you answer it sir? You say has not he got it out of me? I ask you upon your oath, here in the presence of God—I ask you if Samuel Phillips has not been at your shop pumping you about this matter? He has been to my shop, sir. Before you were summoned as a witness in this case? Yes, sir, he was. And he pumped you about this matter? He asked me a few questions about it sir. Didn't Phillips refresh your memory about it, and didn't Phillips tell you what to say? No, sir, he did not. How many times did Phillips come to your shop! He never come to my shop but once. When was that. It was last Saturday. Had you told anybody you knew about this matter before that? No one, but Robert Simmons in Fayettevill, and Louis Smith. Now just go on and tell the Court what that conversation was between you and Phillips last Saturday—what did Phillips say to you, when he first come there? First his business with me was to mend his boots —then—. Don't hesitate tell the truth? I want to tell the truth of course, that is the reason why I am studying. I think the first was sir—I can't exactly tell what was the first. Did he commence the conversation with you about this matter, or did you commence it? I don't think it occurred between either of us, the first commencement. Now just remember this—I ask you if Phillips did not go to your shop, and shortly after the conversation commenced say to you—Hagans, I am looking up witnesses to prove that Tolar shot this man Beebee? No, sir, he did not actually. Then state what he did tell you? Mr. Nixon and Mr. Phillips came to my shop, and was talking concerning this matter. They asked me I think was not I at the market house that day. Who asked you? I think Mr. Phillips asked me. Very well? I am not positive whether it was Phillips or not. I told him I was. He asked me did I see the pistol when it was shot. I told him, I did. Mr. Nixon asked me did I know who done it. I told him I did. He asked me who. I told him Capt. Tolar. You swear you told Nixon on that occasion? Yes, sir. I told him there in my shop, or in the shop I worked in. What did Phillips tell you then? I think that Phillips asked me about Sykes next. He began to talk about Mr. Sykes, and I spoke of Mr. Sykes laughing and going on; that he was close enough when the pistol was fired to hear the

whistle of the ball by his car. How many conversations have you had with Phillips about the matter since that day? None, sir. I mean how many conversations have you had with Phillips since that time, upon Tolar's shooting the negro on that occasion? I have not had any conversation, sir, since that, with Mr. Phillips. Neither at his boarding house or elsewhere? No, sir. No other conversation upon that subject at all with him? No, sir, only the day I was to report to General Avery, sir. Did you have any conversation with Phillips on that day? I did not have any conversation, but he was the man that came and told me General Avery wished to see me. He was the man that came to you? Yes, sir. That is the only conversation you have had with him since? Yes, sir. What did you say in that conversation? I says, you haven't reported me, have you? and he didn't give me any answer. He told me to go to General Avery's office at five o'clock in the afternoon. Did you see Captain Tolar at the market house that day, at all, until just after the time the pistol was fired? I did not, sir. Did you see John Maultsby there? I saw him there, but it was after the pistol fired that I saw him. You saw nothing of him before? I did not, sir, to be positive about it. At the time you say Powers went up to the prisoner, before he cleared the arch, what did you say was his expression? It was either "I demand" or "gentlemen, he is mine," I can't say which for certain. Was it certainly one or the other? I can't say whether it was or not, but the definitions of the words, was that. Either "I or mine?" Yes, sir. Was it not we? I don't think it was. You think it was "I demand the prisoner," or "he is is mine?" Yes, sir. You feel sure that he did not say "we demand the prisoner," or "he is ours?" No, sir, I don't think he said that. At the time the prisoner was shot, you were still sitting there in that small arch? No, sir. Where were you then? I was nearly between the little arch and the centre arch. Between the little southern east end arch and the large main arch, do you mean? Yes, sir. Were you on the pavement or off? I was off. How far were you off? I don't know for certain. How far do you suppose? It might have been three or four feet. How far was Archy Beebee from you at the time he was shot? He was about the center of the side walk, and about six or seven feet from me. Did you see anything of a scuffle just before he was shot? Nothing only a rush right up in the crowd. Did you see Beebee fall or sink down just before he was shot? I did not, sir. Were you looking at him? I was, sir. See if you can't remember just before he was shot that he had a scuffle with the guard and they all sank down together, did not you see that? I did not, sir. But that took place, did it not—you saw everything there that took place? I did not know whether it did or not, because I did not see it. At the time Beebee was shot was he standing straight up or was he in a stooping posture? I don't know, sir, whether he was or not, I could not exactly say. Which way was his face turned? Towards the guard house, sir. Did you see Sheriff Hardie at that time? I did, sir. Where was he? He was with the prisoner. What side was he on? He was on the side between the market house and him, sir. Was anybody between Hardie and the prisoner? Not that I saw, sir. Was there any one else on the prisoners right hand side. I did not notice. Did Sheriff Hardie have hold of him? If he did not have hold of him, he was mighty close to him, I did not see his hands then. Was there room between Sheriff Hardie and the prisoner's right for anybody to have been between them? I don't think there was, sir Can't you be certain about these things, you saw it all? I can't, there was so much excitement I could not be exactly positive about everything that occurred. Who else was about the prisoner at that time : who else had hold of him, anybody? I don't know, sir, whether there was or not. Did you see Fairclouth there? Not at that time. Did you see anything of Wemyss about the prisoner? I did not, sir. So the only person that you saw that had anything to do with the prisoner was Sheriff Hardie? Yes, sir. And Hardie was close to him on the right hand side? Yes, sir. Where did Tolar come from when he came there to shoot the man? I don't know, sir, the crowd rushed all up together, I could not see where he came from. Was he standing still or was he pressing forward? At the time I saw him he was sort of leaning over in the act of shooting the boy. Were his feet upon the pavement or was he walking or rushing up at that time. I think he was still pretty much—was sort of akimbo like. Was that the first you saw of Tolar? Yes, sir; first the cry was " shoot him ! shoot him " ! Who said that ? I don't know, sir ;—and after that, I looked, and saw the pistol, and I looked and saw who had it. At that time, how far was Tolar off from Beebee ? Well, sir, I don't suppose he was much further than I could point a pistol to that desk, (about four feet.) How many persons were between Tolar and Beebee? As far as I can say, there was one. Who was that? I don't know; his back was to me. Was he a white man, or colored man? He was a white man. Do you know whether that was Sam Phillips or not ? I do not, sir. Did you see where Tolar got the pistol from ? No, sir,—I did not, I just saw him raise it up and fire it. Was the muzzle elevated or was it level? It was not exactly straight out;—it was a little down from the level. He was leaning over, pointing down? Yes, sir Was Beebee straight or was he bent at that time? I could not exactly say, whether he was bent or not. Did you see Tolar fire the pistol ? Yes, sir. Did you see the smoke come from it ? Yes, sir. And you say, you then saw him return it? He tried to return it under his left arm. Don't you know he threw the pistol down to his right side ? No, sir; he threw it either under his left arm, or passed it into his left pocket. You swear he did not throw it down to his right side ? Yes, sir. What became of the pistol after that? I don't know sir, I did not see it any more. Did you see whether Tolar concealed it about his person : did he slip it inside of his vest? I say he either concealed it, or passed it through under his left arm. You say John Armstrong was standing there? Yes, sir. Which side ? On the left side. Was there anybody between Armstrong and Tolar ? I did not think there was. And Tolar threw his shawl back and hit Armstrong in his face? On the right shoulder it struck Armstrong, it might have his face too. Which way was Armstrong's face ?The market was in front of him. He was facing towards Tolar ? No, sir ; Tolar was standing to his left side. Now how did it happen that you noticed John Armstrong so particularly that day, what attracted your attention to Armstrong? Because he was so near the prisoner I could not help seeing him and the prisoner at the same time. How far was Armstrong off from the prisoner? He was not very far; I could not tell the exact distance from him to the prisoner, but he was close

enough to flirt his shawl on him, Who do you mean by the prisoner ? I mean Captain Tolar. I mean Beebee, I ask you why it was you come to notice Armstrong that day ? The reason was, he was so close to Captain Tolar ; I was noticing him and I could not help from noticing Armstrong at the same time. Was there anybody else around Captain Tolar, either to his front, to his left or behind him ? There was a good many around about him. Was there any person as near to him on any side as Armstrong was ? I suppose there was, sir. Tell us who they were? I don't know sir, who they were. So you know Armstrong was there ? Yes, sir. And there were other persons just as near, and you don't know who they were? No, sir; I don't know who they were, I am very well acquainted with Armstrong sir, and the reason I noticed him in particular, he was between me and Captain Tolar, and of course if I looked at Captain Tolar I was looking at Armstrong the same time. Do you know Ed. Powers? I do sir. Was he close there? If he was I did not see him. Do you know Sam. Hall? I do sir. Was he close there? I did not see him sir. Do you know Mr. J. G. Leggett? Not personally. Do you know Ralph Lutterloh? Yes, sir. Was he close there? I did not see him. So Armstrong is the only one you remember seeing at that time? I saw a good many, but I didn't know them. How far did you say you were from Tolar at the time the pistol was fired? I never said how far. How far do you say now? I don't know exactly but I guess I was about—— As far as to Lieut. Hargous? I suppose I was not more than about four feet or so from him. About four feet ? I guess so. Were you immediately to Tolar's left or to his front and left, or to his rear and left? I was somewhat to his rear and left. And Armstrong was between you and Tolar? Yes, sir; he was in front of me and Tolar, to the left of Mr. Tolar and I was in the rear, to the left of Mr. Tolar. Was Armstrong immediately on a line directly to Tolar's left or was he to the front and left of Tolar? He was not on the line, of course. A little to the rear and left ? A little bit, sir. And you were still further in the rear of Tolar than Armstrong ? Yes, sir. Was that while you were four feet off from Tolar ? Yes, sir. You were about three feet in his rear, is that it ? More than that sir. So you were more than four feet ? You said three feet ; I said more than three feet.

Re-direct examination, by the Counsel for the prosecution.

When was the conversation you had with Mr. Phillips? It was last Saturday. Who was present beside Mr. Phillips ? Mr. Nixon was present ; it was between us three. Did you say you had any conversation with him since? No, sir. Had you mentioned this matter to any one before you came up here ? Yes, sir. Who was it? Mr. Robert Simmons and Mr. Louis Smith.

On motion, the Commission adjourned to meet on Thursday, August 1st, at 11 o'clock, A. M.

RALEIGH, N. C., Aug. 1st, 1867, 11 A. M.

The Commission met pursuant to adjournment. Present, all the members of the Commission, the Judge Advocate, the Counsel for the prosecution, all the accused and their Counsel.

Yesterday's proceedings were then read and approved.

JAMES KENDRICKS, a witness for the prosecution, having been first duly sworn, testified as follows:

Examined by the Counsel for the prosecution.

What is your name? James Kendricks. Where did you live at the beginning of this year? I was living in Edgecombe County. Where were you living at the time Archy Beebee was killed? Fayetteville. What was your occupation there at that time? I am a printer by trade, but I was not doing anything then; I was out of employment. Do you remember what day Archy Beebee was killed? I remember the day of the week, sir. What day was it? Monday. Do you remember what day of the month it was? No sir; I did not know until I saw it in the "Sentinel." You don't know of your own knowledge? No, sir. Was it this year? Yes, sir. It was a Monday in this year? What time did you go to Fayetteville? In January, sir. What time did you leave there? I left there about a month ago, or a little over. It was during the time you were at Fayetteville? Yes, sir Where was Archy killed, what part of the town? At the market house. Were you present? Yes, sir. What time did you go to the market house that day? I don't know what time of day it was, I got there before the prisoner was brought to the market house, and remained there until he was killed? Were you at the market house before the prisoner was brought out of the guard house? Yes, sir. Did you see him when he was brought up to the market house? Yes, sir. Where were you standing when he was brought to the market house? I don't know the position exactly, when he was brought up, I was standing out on the side walk, some where; I don't know exactly where. On which front of the market house? The east side of the market house. You can't fix your location? Not with certainty. Did Archy Beebee pass by you as he was brought up? Yes, sir. Do you remember what officers were with him? Yes, sir. Sheriff Hardie, and Wemyss, and Faircloth, and McGuire, and Horneinde, I think. Did you go up-stairs where the trial took place? No, sir. I attempted to go up, but they allowed no one but those interested. Where did you go to then? After he had gone up-stairs I remained about at different places, out-side and inside. Inside do I understand you also? Yes, sir. Under the market house and outside, moving about? Yes, sir. How long was Archy up-stairs. Well, sir, he was up there a good while; I don't know how long. As much as an hour? I don't know hardly how long. You have no idea how long he was up there? No, sir. While he was up there was there any crowd about the market house? Yes, sir, there was a right smart crowd about there. Were they outside or inside? Scattered about, both under and outside. Tell me who you noticed in that crowd that you knew, while Archy was up-stairs, that were standing under the market house? I noticed several young men there. I noticed Mr. Tolar and Tom Powers, and Mr. Watkins, or Monk Julia, and several others, I don't know exactly who. See if you can recollect? I saw John Maultsby. During the time the negro was up-stairs? I think it was, I am not positive, I saw a great many. May I don't remember who they were. Do I understand you to say you saw Tolar, and Tom Powers, and Monk Julia there while the negro was up stairs? Yes, sir. Where was Captain Tolar standing? In different places. Did you see him at any place during that time? I guess he was like the most of them, he was moving about from place to place, but I saw him under the market, at one time, I think he was seated on a bench, under the market. On which bench? A bench that runs under the market, on your right as you come out of the arch. What was he doing or saying; did you hear or see him do any thing? I don't know that I heard him say anything particular. I heard him make a remark, when the prisoner came down stairs, but I don't remember any remark while the prisoner was up-stairs. Did you hear Tom Powers say anything, or Monk Julia? No, sir. Did you hear any remarks in that crowd where you were standing? No, sir. Was there any excitement in the crowd? They seemed to be right smartly excited. How was it indicated;—this excitement? They seemed to be right smartly enraged, about the way the negro acted towards the lady. What manifestation of this rage was there? They said he ought to be punished; I never heard any one, that I remember, make any threats of violence. Who came down stairs first? The ladies came down stairs first. Miss Massey and her mother? Yes sir; I think accompanied by Mr. Bond. The Town constable? Yes, sir. Who went with them to the carriage? Mr. Powers, I think went with them. Was he conversing with them, as he went to the carriage? I think he was. Do you know what he said? No sir. What became of Mr. Powers after he went to the carriage? I don't know, sir—he came back in the crowd, I guess. I don't want you to guess—did you see him in the crowd afterwards? Yes, sir. Did you notice whether the carriage drove off before Archy came down? Yes, sir. Where were you standing, when you first saw Archy? I was standing right under the market house. Under it? Inside of the arch. The main arch? Yes, sir. On which side—the right or left as you enter? I don't know, sir, that I was on either side. I might have been near the centre, just inside of the arch, I would not fix any location for certain. I understood you to say you heard Captain Tolar say something when the negro came down stairs? That was when he was on the steps; I heard Captain Tolar remark to some one, I don't know who it was, that he "hoped he would not have to shoot; but if he did, it would be a good shot," or something to that effect:—that was the first threat, and the only one, I heard made. You heard Captain Tolar say words to that effect? Yes, sir. That he hoped he would not have to shoot, and if he did, it would be a good shot." Something to that effect, I won't say the exact words. Did you see any weapons at that time, or had you seen any up to that time? No, sir, the first I saw in Captain Tolar's hand, about the time —— We have not come to that part of the narrative. You had not seen any up to that time? I did not see any, sir. Did any one approach the negro or do anything to him before he got down stairs? No, sir. Do you remember who was with him as he come down the stairs? The officers that I mentioned, were with him. You think all those were with him? Yes, sir. Do you remember who came out of the door first, of these officers? No, sir, don't—I don't know but what Mr. Bond was standing at the door—him or the Sheriff, one of them, was standing at the door, I think to prevent any one from going up, and as they came down they might have come out first. You can't speak with certainty? No, sir. When was the first assault made upon the negro?—I understand you to say that Tolar made this speech as the negro was on the steps? Yes, sir. After he had cleared the door? Yes, sir, and as the prisoner come out, and turned to go around the arch I heard Mr. Powers demand him, "Give me this man," or something to that effect." Did you see Powers at that time? Yes, sir. What was he doing with his hands? He put his hands on his coat collar. You mean he just laid it there or grasped it? Well, I don't know whether he grabbed at it or just put his hand on his collar; I know he went up and told them to give the man up to him, or words to that effect. Did you see Monk at that time? No, sir. What was the reply of the Sheriff? The reply of the Sheriff was, he should not do it, and said something about his being an officer, or something, I did not understand what the words were. What happened then? Then a general scuffle ensued, and I saw no more of it until I went around outside. Was Powers pushed off? I think he was. You say Powers laid his hand on his collar, and demanded the prisoner, and the Sheriff refused to give him up; there was a general scuffle, and you lost sight of the individuals? Yes, sir. And then you changed your position? Yes, sir, I went around outside, of the pavement. You ran out of the Arch, or walked out? I don't know whether I ran or walked. Did you move rapidly or slowly? I don't remember sir. Did you move around the crowd or through? On the outer edge. You did not get completely out of the crowd? No, sir. But around the outer edge, where it was thinner? Yes, sir, around the outer edge. It was hard to get out of the crowd. Where were you standing when you stopped, after making that motion? Just outside of the pavement. You were standing off of the pavement? Yes, sir. How far from the pavement? A step or two I reckon. Which way were you facing? I was facing towards the crowd sir, I was right east from the market. Where was the prisoner? He was right out on the pavement. What direction from you? Sort of south west. How far do you suppose you were from the prisoner? Well sir, I can't say, perhaps as far as from here to that post (about twenty feet.) You think you were as far as that pillar? I was moving about through the crowd in general, they pushed on down, and as they pushed I kept up with the crowd. At the moment the pistol was fired where were you standing? Nearly opposite the small arch, the one furthest south, on the east front of the market house, and a step or two from the pavement. Did you see the man who fired the pistol? Yes, sir. See him distinctly? Yes, sir. Who was it? Mr. Tolar. W. J. Tolar? The one they call Capt. Tolar. Is this the man, (pointing)? Yes, sir. Where was he standing from you when you saw him fire the pistol? He was near me. Could you have laid your hand on him? I think I could sir. Was he to your right or left? I disremember whether he was to my right or left. Was he in front or behind? He was one side of me, I think he was to my left, when I was facing towards the negro, sort of to my left and front like. You think he was to your front or left and front, facing the negro? Yes, sir. He was further south than you? A little further. Was he on the pavement or off? He was off. How far do you think from the pavement. A step or two off the pavement I reckon. I think at least he was in reach of me, and I don't think I could have been more than a step or two off the pavement. Did you see him distinctly? Yes, sir. Describe how he fired, what position he was in? The only thing I saw about it, I saw him have the pistol in his hand, and leaning over the crowd and firing. He held it in his right hand? Yes, sir, as soon as he had done it I throwed my eyes on the Sheriff and prisoner. Did you see the prisoner fall? Yes, sir. You lost sight of

Tolar then? Yes, sir. Did you notice what sort of a pistol it was? It looked like a Colt's navy repeater—I never saw the pistol before or since. Was there any one between you and Capt. Tolar? I don't know, sir, whether there was or not. What became of Mr. Tolar after he fired the pistol, when was the next time you saw him? The next time I saw him he was standing up against a pillar in the market. The pillar south of the large arch do you mean? Yes, sir. Between the small arch and large arch. Yes, sir. With his back towards it? Yes, sir. How many minutes was that after he fired? A very short time, I don't know how many minutes.— Did you see who was standing near him when he fired? No, sir. Did you see anything of Monk in the crowd, or Tom Powers? I did not see anything of either until after the negro was shot. After I saw Mr. Powers when he demanded the prisoner, I never saw either of them, that I know of, until the negro was shot. Did you see them afterwards? I saw Monk afterwards. What was he doing? He was running around with his knife open, towards the negro, and Nixon grabbed hold of him, and told him to behave himself, or something like that. Did you see any one else in the crowd, besides those you have mentioned? No, sir. Do you remember seeing anything of Ed. Powers? No, sir. Of Sam Hall? No, sir. Of Ralph Lutterloh? You mean after he was shot? Just afterwards? Yes I think I remember seeing Powers after he was shot, but I don't think I remember seeing any one else. What was he doing? I don't remember his doing anything in particular. You remember he was there? I saw him there in the crowd. I don't remember seeing Hall or Lutterloh.

Cross examination, by the Counsel for the accused.

Mr. Kendricks, when were you subpœnaed as a witness in this case? I received it Saturday last. It was dated further back. Give us the date of it? It was perhaps the 24th, I was summoned to be here on the 27th. You got it Saturday? Yes, sir; about twelve o'clock. Just tell to the Court, what relationship exists between you and Samuel Phillips? He is my uncle. How does that come about, did he marry your mother's sister or did your father marry his sister. My father married his sister. Who did you tell what you knew about this matter before you were summoned? I recollect two persons for certain that I told about it, and the third I am not certain that was immediately after the thing occurred. I told Mr. Maultsby about it. Which Maultsby? Old John Maultsby, as we call him, John Maultsby, Sr. and I think I told Russell, who is his partner—A. B. Russel—and I told Jno McCoy about it. That was the same day the shooting was done. You feel sure you told John Maultsby senior and McCoy? I am pretty positive about these two, and I think I told Archy Russel. You told them the same story you have told here to-day? Yes, sir. Certain of it? Yes, sir. Haven't you had conversations with your uncle Samuel at all about this matter?

The Counsel for the prosecution, wished to ask a question he had omitted in the direct examination.

The Counsel for the accused did not object.

Direct Examination resumed, by the Counsel for the prosecution.

I understood you to say when I was talking with you, that you heard some exclamation in the crowd, as to who did it, at the time it was done? I did. Who was the person you heard make that exclamation? George H Kingsworth.— What did u say? He called out two or three times, after the pistol was fired; "Capt. Tolar shot him?"

Cross-examination resumed, by the Counsel for the accused.

You have talked this matter over several times with your uncle Sammy? I have talked to him with regard to it. You have talked a good deal in regard to it since you have been here together? In regard to the feelings in Fayetteville? No! in regard to what your evidence would be, here to day? No, sir. You have not told him what you were going to swear here to day? No, sir. Have not compared notes with him at all? No, sir. You say when you first got there, you saw a considerable crowd about the market house? Yes, sir. Did you see any thing unusual about the crowd? No, sir, I can't say that I did. How long had you been there before you saw Captain Tolar? Well, I don't know, sir; I saw him several times in the crowd. Did you notice anything unusual in his appearance? I did not. Didn't you know that Captain Tolar's business lay about the market house almost altogether? I knew he was a butcher. Don't you know that is Captain Tolar's usual place of transacting business, under the market house in Fayetteville? I know he is a butcher; I did not know the man more than I knew him when I saw him. Now you say Tolar was sitting down on a bench when Beebee started down stairs? No, sir; I did not say he was sitting there, I don't know the exact position of Tolar, when Beebee started down stairs; at one time he was there. Where was Tolar when Beebee started down stairs and you heard this remarkable declaration from him? He was standing under the arch to the best of my belief. Inside of the main eastern arch? Yes, sir. Who was near him? I don't know that I can name one that was near him. Was there anybody near him? Yes, sir; they were all around about there. Were you nearer to him than anybody else? I don't know that I was. Were there any other persons nearer than you at that time? They might have been nearer; I did not remember any one that was nearer, or any one that was as near, but they were all around. Was that crowd around Tolar, at that time, composed entirely of whites, or was it a mixed crowd? I am unable to say; I guess it was a mixed crowd. How many persons do you think there were around him at that time? I did not have any idea. About how many, twenty-five, thirty, forty, fifty? Twenty-five, perhaps, near him within a few feet of him. You are all acquainted in Fayetteville. Yes, sir. Been living there all your life? Yes, sir. Were they citizens or were they strangers? Pretty generally I would say they were citizens. And you cannot name a single man around him? No, sir, I did not pay any attention to any one around him at that time. I ask you if there were not men in that crowd around Captain Tolar, men that you had known much longer than you had known Captain Tolar? Not that I noticed of; I notice none in the crowd around him, particular. There might have been men there that I knew all my life. You have not known Tolar a great while, have you? No, sir. Did you have any speaking acquaintance with him at all? I have spoken to him, I have never been introduced to him. Did you have your attention attracted to him, particularly, before he made that remarkable declaration? No, sir. It was the remark that attracted your attention to Tolar? Yes, sir. Did you hear any other remarks made in the crowd? I did not, that I remember of. The crowd was entirely still? No, sir, I said they were pretty much excited. But you heard no other remarks that you remember? I heard no threats before the negro came down stairs, or after, beside Tolar's. You heard Tolar say what? give us his exact language. I heard him say—"I hope I won't have to shoot, but if I do, it will be a good shot," or something to that effect. Was that said in a whisper. No, sir. Was it said out in a loud tone of voice? He just remarked it loud enough for me to hear, and loud enough for others to hear, if they had been listening; he just spoke it out perhaps not as loud as I am talking now. Mr. Kendricks, I will ask you if there was any one man in that crowd that did hear that, except you? I don't know, sir. Have you ever heard any other man say he heard it? I have not. Have you ever heard of any man who said he heard it? I have not. Well, you say that the negro was brought down, and then you shifted your position from the market house back off of the pavement? Yes, sir. About opposite the upper part of the eastern arch? Not the upper part; just about right of the main arch, but to the east, and fronting the main arch like. I would not say whether I was directly opposite the main arch or pillar, but I was somewhere near directly opposite the arch. You were out on Person street, opposite the main arch? Yes, sir. Was it about the time you got your position there that you saw Tom Powers lay his hand on the prisoner? No, sir; it was before that; that was when I was under the market when he first came down stairs. Are you sure that Powers put his hand on the prisoner? I am sure he put his hand at his coat, but whether he grabbed it I am not able to say. Are you sure it touched the prisoner? I could not swear positive. I believe he took hold of him. By which hand? The left hand I believe. Did he have anything in his left hand? Nothing that I saw. Anything in his right hand? Nothing that I saw. Did you see whether he had or not? I did not look to see; I saw nothing. Did you see Monk have any knife before the prisoner got out of the arch? I don't remember seeing him until the negro was shot, after he came down stairs. So you got the position you described, and there you took your stand? No, sir, I did not take any stand, I was moving about as the crowd moved. The prisoner was shot when he got down near the south east corner of the market house? Yes, sir. And he was on the pavement at the time he was shot? Yes, sir. What part of the pavement was he on, nearer the market house, nearer the center or nearer the outer edge of the pavement? I judged he was nearer the outer edge of the pavement. Who was with him? The officers. What officers were with him? Mr. Hardie, and Mr. Wemyss, and McGuire and Faircloth, were all in attendance. What side of the prisoner was Wemyss on? Wemyss was on his right side. Right or left? On his right, next to the market. Where was Faircloth? Well, sir, I don't know exactly the position, Faircloth and Hornbine, as near as I can recollect were in his rear, right behind. I am speaking of the very time the pistol was fired; were you looking at the prisoner then? As soon as the pistol fired I looked at the prisoner, just as soon as the pistol was shot my first attention was to see the effect of it. Where was Hardie at that time? He had his hand in the man's collar. Was Hardie in his front, to his right and front, or in his rear? It appeared to me he was on his right rear, but I am not positive. It seemed to me, he was just to his rear, with his right hand upon his collar, it might have been his left hand. Did he have him by the collar? I think he did, I won't swear positive; he had him in the collar behind, I think. While you were standing there you saw Captain Tolar raise the pistol—Where did Tolar come from? I don't know; he was in the crowd as I was: about first in one place and then in another. Did you see him draw the pistol? The first I saw, I saw him lean over and put the pistol out, and then I noticed him until the pistol fired, and after the pistol fired I turned to look at the Sheriff and the prisoner. How far was Tolar off from the prisoner Beebee at the time he fired upon him? I don't know; not far off, though. Was he fifty feet or fifty yards, or five feet, or what distance? Five feet perhaps. He was five feet? He was that much any way. But he was at least that? Yes, sir. How many persons were between Tolar and the prisoner? I don't know how many. Say how many you think? I have no idea how many there were. As many as three? Oh! yes, as many as three. As many as five? As many as five. As many as ten? I don't know sir, how many there was, there was several. You think there was as many as between five and ten, immediately between Tolar and the deceased? Yes, sir; not right directly in a line between him and the prisoner, but they were scattered about between him, as it were, and the prisoner. Just name one of those men? I can't name one of them. Not one? Not one that I know of. Were they black men or white men? There might have been both. Might have been both? Yes, sir. How far were you from Tolar at the time of the firing of the pistol? At the time the pistol fired I was very near Mr. Tolar. I don't know but what I could have put my hand on him. You were on Tolar's left? No, sir, I think I was on Tolar's right; he was on my left—I am not positive as to that, as I said awhile ago; I think he was to my left. I understand your face was looking towards the guard house? Towards the prisoner, yes sir. Was he on your right hand, or left hand? I said I thought he was on my left and right. Left and right? I mean left and front, a little further south than I was but still to my left hand. Then you were three or four steps off from the pavement, and how far off from the pavement was Tolar? I did not say I was three or four steps. Well, how far off was Tolar? He might have been three steps: I was off a step or two and I could have reached him. You think then Tolar was from seven to nine feet off from the pavement? No, sir: I dont think he was that far. Well, how far. He might have been four or five feet, may be more. At least four or five fe t? I guess he was and perhaps more—I know I was a step or two off the pavement and I was right near him; I don't swear that positively, because I might have stepped it in a step. Was there anybody between you and Tolar? I don't know sir, whether there was or not. Don't you know whether there was anybody between you and Tolar? I don't remember; I just saw the pistol and I never noticed any one else at all, until the pistol fired. Was there any body to Tolar's left; immediately—at that particular time, on his left? I expect there was ; the crowd was all around him. Just name one man who was immediately on Tolar's left. I can't name one, sir, I just said I had my eyes on Tolar at that time because I saw him lean over with a pistol, and whether there was any body between him and me, I don't know. Then I understand you to say at that time you cannot name a man who was to Tolar's front, to his right, to his left, or to his rear? Not at that particular time, because I was noticing nothing but the weapon in his hand. And of the men there all around him you cannot tell whether they were white or colored? They were both in the crowd, I said. Did you see your uncle Sammy Phillips have a pistol there that day? I did. Just describe to the Court if you please where your uncle Sammy was standing about the time this shooting occurred? It was not far off from where I was—I don't know exactly the position he was in. I ask you, if, at the time that shooting occurred, your uncle Sam. Phillips was not nearer to the prisoner Beebee than Capt. Tolar was? I can't say positive in regard to that; I remember very distinctly seeing him have a pistol. Just answer the question whether at the time this shooting occurred, your uncle Sammy Phillips was not nearer the prisoner than Captain Tolar? I don't know that he was—I don't know that he was not: he was off the pavement, outside the pavement, in the crowd—I don't know the particular location, how far he was from the prisoner. Was he to your left and front or to your right and front, or immediately on your front? I think he was on my left and front—he was to the left of me and perhaps to the front. Do you swear that he was nearer to the prisoner, or that he was not nearer? I say I don't know; I would not swear either way. What was your uncle Sammy doing with that pistol? He had it in his hand; he said afterwards he had it for the protection of the Sheriff. I don't want to know what he said afterwards,—— He was not doing anything with it; only had it in his hand, that I saw. Witness, after this thing occurred—after this shooting was over, your uncle Sam showed you his pistol, didn't he? He did. What did he show you his pistol for? I don't know; he made the remark, "some one would have to suffer for this thing," he said he had his pistol out but for the intention of assisting the Sheriff, if it was necessary." How long after the shooting, before he showed you his pistol? It was a few minutes; he showed it to me at the store. How far is it from the market house down to his store; fifty or seventy-five yards? Yes, sir. When you got down there at the store, I ask you if your uncle Sam did not call your attention particularly to the fact of his having a pistol; Did not he say "look at it, my pistol has not been shot; there is going to be some trouble; I want you to examine and see that my pistol has not been shot?" There was nothing of the sort said, he just put it down there, and said "there is my pistol." I ask you the question whether that pistol which your uncle Sammy took so much pains to show you—whether that pistol was a large pistol or a small one? It was a large pistol; what they call a navy repeater sir; I think it was a Remmington patent. How large was it? A large size. The largest size of Remmington's patent? I don't know that it was the largest size, but it was a good sized pistol; it was maybe a foot long or over, or very near it. Was it as long as the pistol that Tolar had? It was longer I think. I never saw Mr. Tolar's since, but judging from just seeing, I should judge Phillips was the larger pistol. He did not show you the little four barrelled pistol that he had about him? No, sir, I never saw any four barrelled pistol. He did not show you the ordinary sized repeater that he had about him? No, sir. He just put out this long navy pistol, and laid it down, and called your attention to the fact, that as there was going to be trouble, that pistol had not been fired? Yes, sir; it was a large sized Remington's six shooter that I examined. When had you seen Tolar before that day? I do not remember. Had you seen him before in a week? I don't know. Had you seen him before in a month? I don't know sir. Are you sure you ever saw him before that day? I would not swear that I had.

Re-direct examination, by the Counsel for the prosecution.

Did you understand the last question or two that was asked—do you mean to say you had never seen Captain Tolar before you saw him fire that pistol? I said I would not swear whether I had seen him before or not. Have you any doubt about it being the man that sits there now?—None whatever; I have seen him very frequently since and talked to him since. And that is the man whether you knew him well before or not? Yes, sir. Sam Phillips is your maternal uncle as I understand? Yes, sir. He is your mother's brother? Yes, sir. Why haven't you talked with him about your evidence since you have been here? Well! sir, because I told you when I gave in my evidence, that I would not do it. You promised me you would not do it? I promised that upon my word and honor I would not. You kept that promise? Yes, sir. You speak of having mentioned who it was fired that pistol the very day it occurred, and you said, among others, you told it to old John Maultsby? Yes, sir. What did John Maultsby say to you when you told him? He told me not to say anything about it. He told you to keep your peace upon that subject? Yes, sir. I understand you to say you had talked it over with your uncle at that time? I don't know that I did—I don't think I did. Your best impression is that you did not? Yes, sir. When you say you gave the same evidence—you told the same story that you did here to-day, do you mean you stated all the particulars with the same fullness that you have on this examination?—No, sir; I just simply told Mr. Maultsby who done the shooting. 'It was in a sentence or two? Yes, sir. And he advised you to hold your peace? Yes, sir; he might have asked me who shot, and I told him, and he told me to say no more about it. As I understand you, when you saw that pistol elevated and ready to fire, your whole attention was absorbed by it, so that at that moment you cannot exactly tell who was near it, and that as soon as it did fire your attention was immediately attracted to the point to which it was directed, the negro? Yes, sir. When did you first see Sam Phillips, was it during the time the pistol was elevated, or after? I think it was immediately after. I won't be positive whether that was immediately after or before; it was very near the same time. You can't say whether it was immediately after or before? No, sir. Did you see any pistol in his hand at that time? Yes. sir. Was it the same pistol you saw in his hand that you saw afterwards? I would not swear it was the same pistol; it was a pistol of the same general character. There was no mark on it that I knowed that I could swear to its being the same pistol. What did you do after this negro was shot—did you go up to look at him? Yes sir. Did you and Sam Phillips leave the crowd together? I don't know that we went together. I walked down to his store in his company. You and he walked together from the market house? Not particularly right together. Was he in your presence? Yes, sir. So that you could see him and the pistol, or unload it or clean it? I think I could have seen him done either if he had done so. Could you have seen him? I think

I could. He was in your sight pretty much? Yes, sir. How soon did you leave the market house after the shooting? A few minutes; as soon as he shot I went up and saw he was killed. You left in a minute or two? Not that soon. How long do you think? In such times as that I would not like to swear positively; I don't know how long it was from the time he was shot, but it was short. Where did you join the company of Mr. Phillips? I saw him walking along, and I walked over and went on down in his company over near Taylor's corner, and we walked on down to his store. Did you see his pistol before he left the crowd, besides the glance you had at it? No, sir. Did you examine it when you got to the store? I looked at it. Did you see whether it was loaded? Yes, sir. Were all the barrels loaded? Yes, sir. When you saw the pistol in your uncle's hand just after the firing, what was he doing with it; how was he holding it? I don't know exactly how he was holding it. Was it elevated as if about to shoot? He had it out in his hand. Was it pointed up. I don't know how it was pointed exactly. I want to know whether it was presented or not? I don't know whether it was presented, or whether he just had it in his hand. I would not swear whether it was up or down. You saw him with this large pistol in his hand just about that time? Yes, sir. Did you see any smoke come from the pistol barrel, or smoke from the tube? No, sir. Did it strike you at the moment that he might have been the man that fired the pistol? No. sir. You saw the man who fired the pistol? I did. How many pistols were shot? Only one. You saw that fired? Yes, sir. It is impossible for you to be mistaken about it? It is, sir. And you have entertained that opinion from the moment it took place until now? Yes, sir.

WILLIAM H. CARPENTER, a witness for the prosecution, after having been first duly sworn, testified as follows:

Examined by the Counsel for the prosecution. What is your name? William H. Carpenter. Do you remember the day Archy Beebee was killed? Yes, sir. Where were you living then? I was living at Mr. Brandt's cotton factory. In Fayetteville? Yes, sir. Were you working there? Yes, sir. Were you near the market house at the time he was killed? I had been up at the ware-house baling yarn and was returning; I had got through and started back to the mill, just as he come out to go to the guard house. Did you go through the market house? Yes, sir, I came out of the east end and turned around towards where Mr. Davis' store is, and I heard a pistol fired, and I looked around and I saw William Tolar coming around, and he put a pistol under his clothes, down by his right side. Was that after the firing? Yes, sir, the firing of the gun made me turn around, and I saw him pass betwixt me and the out edge of the crowd. The gun went off, and that attracted your attention? Yes, sir. You passed through the market house from the west end to the east end? Yes, sir. You went around the crowd? Yes, sir. You went through the big arch? Yes, sir, and stayed there in front of the little arch, and while I was standing there, the pistol went off. You turned and looked in the direction you saw Tolar coming? Yes, sir, he passed before my eyes and I saw his hands, and he put the pistol away. What did he do then? He turned and went around and stood against a bench. Outside of the arch? Yes, sir. Did you go off then? I went down to the mill.

Cross examination by the Counsel for the accused:

You say you were living with Mr. Brandt. Yes, sir, I worked at his factory. Are you at work there now? I am when I am home, sir. The day the shooting took place you had been at work at the ware house that day baling yarn. You came up to the west end of the market house, and passed immediately through? Yes, sir. Was there any crowd in the market house, then? The crowd was about going around—they were going around with the man. Did you stop at all? I did not stop until the firing struck my attention. You were walking through slowly? I was walking slowly. Slowly, or your moderate gait? Just an ordinary gait. When you got into the west end of the market house, did you see Beebee? I did not. Where was he? He was in the crowd. They were going out when you came to the west end? Yes, sir. Just as you got to the west end, they were going out of the east end? No; I was near about half way of the market house when they were coming down the steps. You did not see Beebee? I never noticed him, sir. Was there a large crowd in the market house then? There was right smart around about there. How long is the market house? I don't know, sir. When you got to the east end where was Beebee? He was right back of that corner, as you turn around to the south betwixt the big arch and the little arch. When you turned the arch, did you look in the direction of Beebee? No, sir; I kept right on towards Mr. Davis's; the way I had to go to the factory. Where were you standing when the pistol fired? About five steps from the big arch. Were you on the ground? Yes, sir. Did you hear anything said whatever? No, sir; I just came up. And as you looked around, you say you saw Captain Tolar? I saw him pass before me; he had the pistol in his right hand, in the action of putting it away. He was walking? Yes, sir. That was immediately after the firing? As quick as I could turn around. You had your eyes on Davis's corner? I was going that course, and when the pistol fired I turned my head around. Tolar was walking away? Yes, sir. On which side of you was he; the right or left? He was right before me. His right side was to you? Yes, sir. He had turned and was walking from Beebee? He was walking from the crowd like. He had his back towards the prisoner? His left side as nigh as I can recollect. He was walking towards the north was he? Going around him then rds the west, towards the little arch. Which little arch? The little arch south of the big arch. Did you see Beebee? I saw him afterwards. Where was he lying? About the south corner of the market house on the side walk. When you saw Captain Tolar, he was walking towards the small arch that is south of the large arch? Yes, sir. He had his right side towards you? Yes, sir; when I saw him he was putting away the pistol. Was anybody around him then? I don't think there was; nobody that I noticed. Any body near him? I don't know sir; whether there were or not. Did Tolar put the pistol in a pocket? I can't know; I just saw as he raised up his coat or whatever he had on, he was in the act of putting it away. He had on a shawl, hadn't he? I never noticed. You say you know him very well? Yes, sir; I have seen him sell beef under there very frequently. That is all you saw—you did not see who fired? No, sir. But you did see Captain Tolar with the pistol? Yes, sir. Did you see Mr. Phillips? I did not sir.

Did you see any other pistol there? That is all the one I saw. Did you see the smoke of the pistol? I never noticed for that sir; it sort of scared me a little. The firing frightened you? Yes, sir. How near was Tolar to you? I suppose as nigh to me as that table. About twelve or fifteen feet? About that distance; about some ten or fifteen feet. How far was he from Beebee? Well; I should think—I don't know exactly how far. About how far? I can't come at the distance. Can't you come within ten feet of it? I suppose I might come within ten feet of it; I dont know how thick the crowd was; he was outside of the crowd. A large crowd there? A hundred and more I reckon. White and black? All together.

Re-direct examination by the Counsel for the prosecution.

Did you notice what sort of a pistol that was? I could not tell; it was a repeater of some kind; I could not tell what it was.

DUNCAN N. McLEAN, a witness for the prosecution having been first duly sworn testified as follows;

Examination by the Counsel for the prosecution.

What is your name? Duncan N. McLean. What is your profession or pursuit? I am a school teacher by profession. Where do you reside sir? In Fayetteville. Are you a licensed minister of the Gospel, sir? No, sir. Were you in Fayetteville at the time Archy Beebee was killed? I was there when a negro was killed; I don t know his name. Were you there the day the negro was killed, that was taken up upon the charge of an assault upon Miss Massey with an attempt to commit rape? Yes, sir. Did you know his name was Archy Beebee? I never heard it until I saw it in the paper. There havn't been other negroes killed in Fayetteville have there; this is the only one you know of? Yes, sir; I think it is. You were in Fayetteville at the time? Yes, sir. Where were you at the time that pistol was fired? I was at Mr. Newberry's, sir. That is Mr. Newberry's store on Person street? Yes, sir. How many stores down from the market house? It is two stores. On the left hand side of the way? It is the second store on the left hand side of the way. You were in that store at the time of this firing? Yes, sir. Where were you standing in the store? I was standing at the window. Did you see the pistol fired? No, sir. How did you know it was fired? I heard the report, and I saw the smoke, and if I am not mistaken I saw the blaze. Then you did see it fired? I did not see the pistol, but I saw the smoke. You saw the act of firing? I did not see the pistol; I heard it and saw the smoke, and if I am not mistaken I saw the blaze. But did not see the pistol fired? No, sir. Who fired that pistol? I don't know sir. Didn't you see the man that fired it? I might have seen him in the course of time, but I did not see him at the time he fired it. You did not? No sir. Had you been in the crowd before, that day? Yes, sir, you there before the pistol was fired? Yes, sir. What did you go there for? I went there, thinking I should hear some of the trial. Did you attempt to go up stairs to hear the trial? I w nt near the stairs; I was told I could not go up. How long were you there? Probably about five minutes. Who was there when you were there? I don't know sir. Not a soul? Yes, sir, there was a good many there. Not a soul that you knew? There was a great many persons there that I knew—but it has been some time, and I don't remember who was. Haven't you memory enough to recall a single face? I have a very good memory. Have you attempted to exert it? No sir. Haven't you refrained from exerting it? No sir. Exert it now and see if you can recall a single face in that crowd, when you were there five minutes? I don't remember a single person—it I had been called on a short time afterwards, I might have remembered. You went in that crowd and remained in it five minutes, but you can't remember a soul that was there? I cannot. Then you left the crowd? Yes, sir. Did you go back after the pistol was fired? Yes, sir. Were you in the crowd again? Yes, sir. Immediately after the pistol fired? I went up to look at the negro. Was that directly after the pistol was fired? Yes, sir. Who was there then? I don't remember. Was any person? I saw a great many persons, but I don't remember any particular person that I saw directly after, except sheriff Hardie and Wemyss and Dr. Foulkes. I want to know whether you recognized any faces at that time? No other faces but those three. They were your acquaintances and neighbors; it was not a crowd of strangers that had come to the town for the purpose of sacking it? No, sir; I knew them probably at the time. But you can't recall a single face? I don't remember a single face that I saw. Is this all you know about this affair? I think it is, sir.

The Counsel for the accused declined to cross examine the witness.

On motion the Commission adjourned to meet on Friday, August 2d, at 11 o'clock, A. M.

RALEIGH, N. C., Aug. 2, 1867, 11 A. M.
The Commission met pursuant to adjournment. Present all the members of the Commission, the Judge Advocate, the Counsel for the prosecution, all the accused and their Counsel.

The reading of the testimony taken yesterday, was waived, there being no objection thereto.

Yesterday's proceedings were then read and approved.

WILLIAM. R. PORTER, a witness for the prosecution, having been first duly sworn, testified as follows:

Examined by the Counsel for the Prosecution: What is your name? William R. Porter. What is your age? Sixteen years the 22d of next September. Did you live in Fayetteville last February? I did, sir. Were you present at the market house when Archy Beebee was killed? I was, sir. How came you there at that time? I had been out hunting in the morning, and seeing a crowd there I went, np. While you were out hunting did you see any of these prisoners at the bar? I saw Monk Julia in the morning. Did you have any conversation with him about the charges against Archy Beebee? I did not have any conversation with him; he told me about this, me and George Hollingsworth. What did Monk have to say at that time? He said, "Archy had got into a difficulty, and if it was proved against him it would go very hard with him." You had been hunting, and came up to the market house where there was a crowd? I did, sir. Was Archy Beebee up stairs at the time you reached the crowd? He was. How long after you got there before he came down? About fifteen minutes. Where were you standing before he came down? I was standing at a tree right in the centre of the arch. Did you remain there until he came down? I did, sir. Who did you see in the crowd that you recognized, before the negro came down, any of those prisoners at the bar? I saw Tom Powers and Monk Julia. Did you see Captain Tola

before the negro came down? I did not. Do you know Captain Tolar? I do, sir. Did you know him at that time? Yes, sir. You know him well? Yes, sir. Did you see John Maultsby or Ed. Powers? I have no recollection of seeing either one. Or Sam. Hall? No, sir. Henry Sikes? No, sir. Well, did you see the negro on the stairs when he was coming down? I did, sir. Do you remember who was in charge of him? The Sheriff and police. Can you name them? I know two of them, Mr Wemyss and Faircloth. Did you notice who came down first? I did not sir. Did you notice which side Mr. Wemyss was on? I don't recollect, sir. You saw him in a group of officers; you can't pretend to locate them? No, sir. But Hardie and Wemyss and Faircloth were in that group? Yes, sir. Was any assault made on him before he reached the bottom of the steps? I did not see anything of the kind. Was any assault made on him before he got out side of the market house? I did not see any. What was the first thing you saw in the way of an assault? Just as he turned the corner, the crowd rushed at him; some person, I don't know who, demanded the prisoner;—the sheriff refused to give him up and just at that time the crowd rushed, and I turned my head, and I saw Captain Tolar standing there with a navy repeater, or a large Colt's repeater, in his hands; I saw him in a shooting position, and I watched him, and I saw the smoke of the pistol, and I heard the pistol fire, and I saw the man fall. Who fired the pistol? Captain Tolar. Was he on your right or left? He was on my left. He was further left than you? He was. There was a confused rush? There was. You looked to your side? I did, sir. To your left and front was it? Yes, sir. There you saw Captain Tolar in a shooting position? He was. Was he stooping at all? He was. Slightly bent? Yes, sir, slightly bent. How close was he to the prisoner Beebee? About five feet, as near as I can come at it. Was he standing on the pavement or off? About two feet and a half or three feet to my left. You saw the negro fall? I did, sir. Did you see what became of Captain Tolar? I did not, sir. Did you see him afterwards before he left the crowd? I did not, sir. Did you see any thing of Monk Julia afterwards? I don't have any recollection of seeing him. Do you remember seeing Tom Powers? I saw him before the thing occurred, but not afterwards. How long did you remain after he shot? I remained until the body was sent home. Did you mention to any one that day that you had seen this thing? I told my father that evening. What advice did he give to you? He told me not to say anything about it. And you have accordingly held your peace since then? I have, sir. Did you hear any exclamation in the crowd when the shooting took place? No, sir. None that I can recollect? Nothing to my recollection. Did you see any weapons in the crowd that day? I saw Monk and Tom Powers have a knife. What sort of a knife had Monk? I suppose it was a pocket knife; he was whittling a stick before the thing occurred. Before the negro came down? Yes, sir. When was the time you saw Tom Powers have a knife? Before the negro came down. Was it open? It was, sir. Do you remember which hand he held the knife in? I do not, sir. Was it before the man came down stairs,—immediately before? Yes, sir. I was only there fifteen minutes before the man came down stairs. How long before the man came down that you saw Tom Powers with this knife? Ten minutes, I suppose. I was there about five minutes before I saw Tolar at all. You spoke of having heard some one demand the prisoner—do you know what words were used? He said "I demand the prisoner." Could you speak with certainty whether it was "I demand,"or not—don't you recollect the exact words? was it not "we demand?" I don't recollect whether it was "we" or "I." I recollect it was "demand the prisoner." Do you know whose voice that was? I do not, sir. Did you see from whence it came? I did not, sir.

Cross Examination by the Counsel for the accused:

When were you subpoenaed as a witness for this case? The 29th, sir. The 29th ot July? Yes, sir. Where was the man you call Monk, the time you speak of having met you hunting that day? He was down in Camelton. Do you remember what day of the month it was? I did not; I knew it was in February, I don't know what day of the month it was. Do you remember what day of the week it was? I think it was on Monday, sir, I am not certain—yes, sir, it was on Monday. You say that Monk told you that this man Beebee had been accused of an attempt to commit a rape upon Miss Massey, and that if it was proved, it would go hard with him? Yes, sir. You heard no threats of violence towards the prisoner? No, sir. That was all he said? That was everything he told me. I think. you stated you were not there when the prisoner was carried up into the market house? I was not. sir. That you got there about fifteen minutes before he was brought down? I did, sir. And you took your stand out from the main arch and about two or three feet from the pavement? About two and a half or three feet I think. Did you move about any, or did you keep your position all the time? I stood right there. Stood still? I did sir, Perfectly still? Till the crowd rushed, and they pushed me forward, and I got back to the same place. I think you say you saw nothing of the rushes made at the prisoner, which were made at him, until he had passed out of the market house? Nothing. Did you see the prisoner at the time he was shot? No. sir. I saw Captain Tolar, at the time the pistol fired; I saw the man fall. And Capt. Tolar was on which hand? On my left. To your front or to your rear? On my left and front. How far was Capt. Tolar off from you? About two and a half or three feet. That would carry him from five or six feet off from the pavement? No, sir, I was standing at the tree that is nearly at the edge of the pavement, Capt. Tolar was about two and a half or three feet from me. Then how far was Capt. Tolar off from the edge of the pavement? About two and a half or three feet. He was not further than that? No, sir. I was standing at the edge of the pavement and Capt. Tolar was two and a half or three feet to my left and front. Did you see him when he came there? I did not sir. What was he doing when you first saw him? He was in a position to shoot. Stationary? He was sir. Was not rushing forward? He was not sir, Were there no persons between Capt. Tolar and the prisoner? There was some. How many? I dont know sir; there was both black and white. A good many were there? Yes, sir. Approximate it, say how many—ten, fifteen, twenty? I suppose there were ten, may be more. How many feet was Capt. Tolar from the prisoner at the time? About five feet. And there were as many as ten persons between him and the prisoner? Yes, Sir, I can't say whether there were that many. Were those persons who were between Capt. Tolar and the prisoner, still. or were

they moving about? They were moving about Did you see where Tolar drew the pistol from? I did not sir, when I first saw him he had the pistol in his hand. When you first saw him in what position did he have the pistol? was he presenting it? He was presenting it towards the prisoner. How long after you first saw him was it before you heard the report of the pistol? It might have been a minute, I kept my eyes on him. Do you think it was a minute? It might have been, or it might have been less, It was very short I know. What is your impression about it; that it was a minute, more or less? It was a minute, more or less. And during that time Tolar stood there with the pistol presented? He did sir, moving it about to get a chance to fire. Those persons who were in front of Tolar, between Tolar, and the prisoner did they lean aside to the right or left? They were moving backwards and forwards. You saw no leaning aside of these persons in front of Tolar? I did not, sir; I saw Tolar moving the pistol to get a place to shoot. Did that occur, or did it not, that the persons in front of Tolar leaned forward, to the right or ieft? No, sir. It did not occur? No, sir. Mr. Porter, who was standing on the left of Captain Tolar? I do not know, sir. Who was standing in front of Captain Tolar? There were some persons between him and the prisoner; I don't know who they were. Who was standing on the right of Capt. Tolar except yourself? There were some colored men, I do not know who they were. Can't you name one of them? I cannot. I did not know them. Who was standing in the rear of Capt. Tolar? There were men, I do not know who they were. I ask you if you can give the name of a single man in that crowd, who was anywhere about Captain Tolar at that time? I cannot say sir. Why was your attention attracted to Captain Tolar? When the crowd rushed, I turned around and saw Captain Tolar with a pistol in his hand; and I kept my eyes on him. And that was the only reason why your attention was attracted to him because he had a pistol? Yes, sir. Did you see anybody else have a pistol? I did not sir. Either before or after the occurrence? I did not sir. You say you turned yourself, which way were you looking before you turned? I was looking at the prisoner. What caused you to turn so as to look to your right hand upon Capt. Tolar? Capt. Tolar was to my left. What caused you to turn to your left? Nothing, only the crowd and the rush. How far was Tolar from you? Two and a half or three feet. Did Tolar make any remark? I did not hear him sir, I was there but a short time before the thing occurred. I mean immediately before the shooting, did Tolar make any remark? I did not hear him make any remark. Did you see Tolar push the crowd off from him, right and left? I did not sir. Did you hear him say "stand back," or anything of that sort? I did not. Were you near enough to have heard him? Yes, sir. Were you near enough to have seen him push the crowd back if he had? I was sir. Can you state positively whether he did or did not? He did not. Mr. Porter, I understand you to say that you saw the flash, and heard the report. I did sir. Do you swear positive, without any doubt, that it was Tolar that fired the pistol there that day? I do sir. You swear that? I do sir. Were you excited. No, sir; I was perfectly cool. And Tolar shot him? He did sir. And nobody else shot him? No sir. And you can't be mistaken about it? No, sir; I cannot. What did he do after he shot him?

I don't recollect; I went closer to the prisoner to see the man. How long was it after that pistol was fired before you moved up towards the prisoner? It might have been two or three minutes or five minutes. That two or three or five minutes, what was Tolar doing? I did not see Tolar any more, I took my eyes off of him, as soon as he fired. You didn't look at him any more? No, more. You don't know what he did with the pistol? No, sir. You don't know which way he went? I do not know sir. • And all you know about this affair is the single isolated circumstance that Tolar shot? He did sir. And that is all you know? Yes, sir. Mr. Porter, was there anybody between you and Captain Tolar? There might have been two or three colored men. You don't know their names? I do not sir. Do you know John Armstrong? I do not, sir. Have you never seen him? If I did I did not know him. Did you see the prisoner just about the time he was shot? No, sir, I was looking at Captain Tolar when the pistol fired. And when you turned your eyes on the prisoner was he then standing erect or was he sinking? He was falling back. Who were nearest him at that time? The police, I believe, sir. Do you know Hardie, the Sheriff of Cumberland county? I do, sir. Was Hardie about him? He was, sir. Where was Hardie? He was to his right and front. He was to the prisoner's right and front? Yes, sir. Ain't you mistaken about that? No, sir. Can you swear to that positive? I do, sir. Did he have hold of him? I do not recollect; I did not see him have hold of him. What is your best impression,—that he did or did not? I think he did. Where do you think he had him? I cannot say, sir; he may have had him by the collar. You mean the collar around the neck? Yes, sir. If he had him by the collar did he have him in front, or at the side? The prisoner was to the rear; Sheriff Hardie was to his right and front. And you think he had his left hand where? Either on his shoulder or his collar, I cannot say which. And if in his collar it was about the front part of his neck? A little to the right of the front. But whether he had him at all you do not undertake to say? No, sir, if he had him, he had him either on his shoulder or collar. I saw the left hand extended towards the prisoner. There was such a crowd you could not tell whether he had hold of him or not. Was not there a great deal of noise, and a great deal of confusion? I do not recollect much noise, but the crowd was excited. Were they not moving about rapidly in every direction? They were, sir, moving towards the prisoner. Both in front of Tolar, and between the prisoner, and in every other direction? Yes, sir. It was almost impossible to tell anything that was done there that day, wasn't it Mr. Porter? If you were looking right at a man and saw him do anything, it was not. You could only see that which you were looking at directly at the time; you could only tell about that? That is all sir.

Re-direct examination, by the Counsel for the prosecution.

Mr. Porter, speaking of these persons you say, to the number of about ten who were standing between Tolar and Beebee when Tolar fired, do you mean they were standing in a straight row, one behind another? No, sir, they were not standing in a straight row. They were standing to his right and left? Yes sir; to his right and left. You mean the cluster of men that

were there about him, would amount in your opinion to about ten? Yes, sir. You don't pretend to identify the number? No, sir, I cannot. You don't mean as I understand you, that Tolar was far enough off from Beebee for ten men to have stood back to breast, between Tolar and Beebee? No, sir. The Counsel for the defence has asked you if certain men leaned arise. You say there was no man that did lean aside? There did not, so far as I saw. What I want to know is, if you did swear that it did not happen, or if you did not see it happen? I did not see it happen. I understand you to say that the time you saw the man with the pistol in the act of firing, your attention was absorbed by it? It was. And you stopped aside when Tolar fired this pistol—you say you did not see anything of that sort? No, sir. Did I understand you to say your attention was entirely absorbed by the man with the pistol? you kept your eye on that man—thinking something terrible was going to happen—until the pistol was fired? I did sir. The Counsel has asked you whether Tolar, in coming through the crowd, to get his position to fire, pushed them right and left, and said "make way gentlemen," or something to that effect? I did not hear anything of the kind. The first time you saw Tolar was when he was in the act of shooting, presenting the pistol? Yes, sir. You don't know where he came from? No, sir. You don't know how he got there? No, sir. The first time you saw him that day, was when the pistol was presented? It was. You think you would have heard this exclamation, if it had been made? I would. Do you swear positive that it did not take place? I did not hear it. Did you see what Tolar did with the pistol, after he fired? I did not sir. Your attention then was directly turned to the prisoner? Yes, sir; I went towards the prisoner. The crowd was thick, and it was slow getting there; every person wanted to see. Was your attention deeply absorbed by Tolar, when you saw him about to fire that pistol? It was sir. Do you think it possible that some one in the crowd may have made use of the exclamation, without you hearing it? I did not hear any one — But when your attention was attracted to the pistol, was it possible that some one may have said something that escaped your attention? I could not say. But you heard nothing said? I did not sir.

BRYANT BURKETT, a witness for the prosecution, having been first duly sworn, testified as follows:

Examined by the Counsel for the prosecution.
What is your name? Bryant Burkett. Did you live in Fayetteville at the beginning of the year? Yes, sir. What is your business there? Stilling turpentine for Mr. Fishbebate. Did you know Archy Beebee? Yes, sir. Were you present when he was killed? Yes, sir. Where did it occur? At the southeast corner of the market. In what town, sir. Fayetteville. What time of day do you think it was? In the afternoon, I don't know what time. What time did you go up to the market house? I was there nearly all day. I was there before they brought Archy out of the guard house. Where were you standing when Archy came up from the guard house? I was standing about the north east corner. On the pavement? Yes, sir. Who was with Archy when he came down from the guard house—in charge of him? I don't know who all; there wat some police; Mr. Bond was along, the town constable, and Mr. Faircloth, the policemen, and I don't recollect whether Sheriff Hardie was along

at the time? You recollect Mr. Bond and Mr. Faircloth? Yes, sir. Were there others? There were some, but I don't recollect who they were. Did you notice any disturbance in the crowd before Archy Beebee went up stairs? No, sir. How many persons were there when Archy went up stairs? There was a large number, a hundred I guess there was before Archy went up. Were there more when he came down, or fewer? There was more. Did the crowd grow continually? Yes, sir. You noticed no disturbance in the crowd before Archy went up at all? No, sir. You saw him go up? Yes, sir. Did these officers go up with him? Yes, sir. How long did he stay up stairs? I don't know exactly, it was something like an hour; it might have been more. While he was up stairs where were you standing? I remained there a short time, and then stepped over to Mr. Fishblate's store, the northeast corner, and I stayed there about five minutes, and then I went back there. I walked about the center of the market house, and then came on through the big arch and I walked then out sorter in front of the big arch, and I remained pretty much there until he came down. When you came back from Mr. Fishblate's store which arch did you go through? The northern arch. And came through the market and stood about a little, and then passed in front of the east arch? Yes, sir. Off the pavement or on? Off the pavement. How far off the pavement? About three or four feet. In coming through the market house at that time did you notice who was in the market house? No, sir. Can you mention any one who was in there? No, sir, I don't recollect seeing any one, only Mr. Powers, I recollect seeing him there. Tom Powers? Yes, sir. Where was he when you saw him? He was standing sorter at the big arch where the steps come down from up stairs. Do you mean on the side of the big arch towards the steps? Yes, sir. Inside? Yes, sir. Inside of the big arch towards the steps? Yes, sir. Did you see any one standing near him? No, sir, I did not, no particular one. Did you see anything peculiar about him? No, sir. He was standing there? Yes, sir. Which way was he facing, towards the steps or arch? Towards the arch. Was he looking towards the arch? Yes, sir. Did you see any one on Becky Ben's bench? No, sir, I did not. Was Tom Powers the only one of these prisoners at the bar you saw there that day, before Archy came down? Yes, sir, he is the only one that I knew. You saw neither Monk nor Captain Tolar? I saw Monk when they were coming down with the prisoner. That was the first time you saw Monk? Yes, sir. You noticed no one in the crowd before? No sir. Did you hear any exclamations or threats in the crowd from any quarter? No, sir, none whatever, until they came down with the prisoner. Who came down first—Miss Massey and her mother, or the prisoner? Miss Massey and her mother. Who came down with them? Mr. Bond and Mr. Powers went with them to the carrige. Did he see them as they passed through the market house, or did they call him to them after they got into the carriage? I don't know how Mr. Powers went; Mr. Bond went with them. When was it you noticed Mr. Powers talking to them? He was at the carriage. You don't know whether he went with them, or was called there? No, sir. Did you see any one else go to the carriage? No, sir. Did Mr. Powers have any conversation with the ladies at the carriage? Yes, sir, I think he was talking with them. Do you know what was being said? Did you hear him say what was being

said? No, sir. Did the carriage then drive off, or not? Yes, sir. Where did Tom Powers go when the carriage drove off? I don't know sir. I didn't see him then any more. You lost sight of him? Yes, sir. You were standing still in the same place, about in front of the arch? Yes, sir. How far from the pavement? About three or four feet, I reckon. When Archy came down stairs, could you see the stairs? Yes, sir. Was it while he was still on the stairs? No, sir; he was down. After he got down an assault was made by whom? Monk was cutting at him when I saw him. While Archy was still in the market house? Yes, sir; he was just clearing the arch. Did you see any one else? No, sir; I saw a good many others around, but I don't know who they were. Can't you name any of them? No, sir, only the men who had him in charge. Did you hear any voices or any exclamations, or any demands at that time?— Yes, sir; I think I heard voices to demand him. Did you know the voices? No, sir; I did not. You heard a voice demanding him? Yes, sir. What were the words used, can you tell? I think they said "We demand the prisoner," or some how that way. Are you confident that was the expression used? I think it was—I am not sure. Was the prisoner given up to them? No sir. You don't know who it was made this demand? No, sir. Did you see any one with weapons at that time? I only see one weapon, the one that Monk had. Was that the only weapon you saw that day, at that time? I saw a pistol —— That was later was it not? Yes, sir. Was the pistol you subsequently saw, and Monk's knife, the only weapons you saw? Yes, sir. What happened after Archy turned the arch and came down? Well, I saw a pistol when it fired off. Which way did Archy move when he came down? He moved around to the right, as soon as he cleared the arch. Going towards the guard house? Yes, sir. The officers still with him? Yes, sir. Did the crowd retreat and leave them, quietly? No, sir. Were they pressing on them all the time? Yes, sir. In this pressure he worked his way out, facing the right towards the guard house? Yes, sir; the men that were in charge of him were carrying him out. How far did he get on the pavement before this pistol was shot? He never got but a few steps, sir, he was very near the corner of the pavement when he was shot. The south east corner of the pavement, do you mean? Yes, sir; the south east corner. He was very near there when he was shot? Yes, sir; first I saw a pistol and then I saw it fired. You saw a pistol, and then you saw it fired? Yes, sir. Who had the pistol? I don't know, for certain, who it was, had it. Why do you say for certain? I can't say, because I was low down, off of the pavement, and whoever shot it, was up on it. When you said you could not say for certain who had it, I thought you might have some reason for a decided opinion? No, sir, I don't know. You saw the pistol elevated above the crowd, and saw it fired? Yes, sir. Did you see the prisoner Beebee, fall? Yes, sir. You don't know whose hand held that pistol? No, sir. Where were you standing at the moment the pistol fired? I was standing pretty near the same place I was all the time, about the center of the arch, three or four feet from the pavement. Was the pistol fired to the right or left of you? It was rather to the right of me, pretty near to the front, and rather to the right; nearly front the way I was facing; I was facing towards the arch. Was your right side towards the arch, looking towards Archy? Yes, sir. And this pistol was to your right and front? Yes, sir. How far did it appear to be from you? It was about the distance I am from you now, (about ten feet.) Was the man who fired it on the pavement or off? He was on. Did you see Captain Tolar shortly after the pistol was fired? Yes, sir. Where was he? He was leaning against the wall, near the side of the big arch. Was that the first you saw of him? Yes, sir. He was standing against the wall near the big arch? Yes, sir. What was he doing? He was standing; I could not tell what he was doing. Did you see anything of Monk after the pistol was fired? No, sir. Anything of Tom Powers? No, sir. Did you see anything in the crowd that day, of Sam Hall, or Ed. Powers? No, sir. Or John Hollingsworth? No, sir. Did you see anything of Henry Sykes? No, sir. John Maultsby? No, sir. You did not see any of them that day? No, sir. Did you see Tolar when he left the market house? No, sir. Did you see the prisoner after he was shot? Yes, sir. How long did you remain in the crowd before you went away? After the firing I went off very soon; not over five minutes anyhow. Did you hear any exclamation in the crowd at the time of firing, or shortly afterwards? Yes, sir, I heard two or three voices; a couple anyhow, "there now, Mr. Tolar has shot Archy," but who it was, I don't know. Was that immediately after the firing? Yes, sir. You heard where you stood, two or three voices; certainly two saying, "there now, Mr. Tolar has shot Archy?" Yes, sir. Both of the two voices, did they seem to be in the same spot, or the same voices, or were they different voices? One was to the right, sort of behind me and the other was right to my right. You are certain of hearing two voices. I think you spoke with us certainty of hearing a third one? I am uncertain. Where did you think that third voice was? If there was a third voice it was pretty near my right. Were these voices the same voices or different voices? Different voices apparently. From different persons? Yes, sir. Was that expression used loud enough for many persons to hear it? I suppose it was. As loud as I am talking to you now? Yes, sir. Is that all you know of this matter? Yes, sir; that is all I know, sir. You have had no talk with Captain Tolar about it since? No, sir; I have not spoken to Captain Tolar since. Nor with Tom Powers? No, sir, Nor with Monk Julia? No, sir; I have not. Have you talked with any of these men who were under arrest, about this affair? No, sir; I never did.

Cross examination by the Counsel for the accused.

Mr. Burkhead, at the time they were turning out of the arch with the prisoner Beebee and that exclamation about demanding the prisoner was made, are you certain whether it was "I demand the prisoner" or "we demand the prisoner?" It seems to me he said "I demand the prisoner," but it may have been "we demand the prisoner." What is your best impression about it? I really cannot say. What is your best impression? I understand you to say you are not certain what is your best impression; wasn't it "I demand the prisoner?" Yes, sir; it seems that was it. That was your best impression? Yes, sir. Mr. Burkhead, you say that at the time the pistol was shot, you were about opposite the center of the eastern arch? Yes, sir. And about three or four feet from the pavement? Yes, sir. That the pistol shot was fired by one person who was standing on the pavement?

Yes, sir. Have you any doubt about that? No, sir. You are absolutely certain that this pistol shot was fired by the man who was on the pavement? Yes, sir. No doubt about it? No doubt sir. From what you saw of the flash and smoke, and from what you heard of the report was the man who fired the pistol, near to the edge or near to the center of the pavement? Nearer to the edge. So he was upon the pavement or nearer the edge of the pavement? Yes, sir. How far off was the man who fired the pistol from you? Well; he was about the distance from me to Lieutenant Hargous (eight or ten feet.) How many persons were between you and the man who fired the pistol? I don't know, sir; there was a thick body of people there. Did you know any of them? No, sir. Not one? Well; I don't know no one for certain. How far did you say the man was who fired the pistol from Beebee? Well; I don't think he was but a short distance. How many feet? I suppose he might have been three or four feet. Was he directly in Beebee's rear? Yes sir; I think he was. Suppose a line had been drawn from Beebee's feet at the time he was shot along the pavement, and parallel with the east front of the market house, would that line have passed right or left of the man who fired the pistol? It would pass more to the right. How much more to the right? Not but little. Wouldn't it have struck his right foot? I really don't know, sir. What is your best impression? whether it would have passed far to his right or right against his right? I think it would come right up to his right. Right up to his right? Yes, sir. So that the man who fired the pistol was very nearly centrally to the rear of Beebee, the prisoner. Yes, sir. How many persons were between the man who fired the pistol and Beebee? A good many, I don't know, sir; I could not tell. Were there a good many? Yes, sir, I think there was a good many. Were they standing still or were the moving backwards and forwards in confusion? They were moving backwards and forwards. Were they leaning over to one side or the other? I don't know sir. I didn't see that. You saw nothing of it? No, sir. Is it your best impression that anything of that sort occurred? I don't think it did. You could not see any thing of the man who fired the pistol at all, could you? Yes, sir, I saw the hand. The hand was all you could see? I could see the pistol; that was as much as I could see, and the hand. His hand and pistol were all you could see? Yes sir. Did you see anything of Sam. Phillips that day? No, sir. Neither before or after the firing? No sir, only at his store, as I passed through the arch I saw him; I didn't see him at the market house. You say that shortly after the firing you heard several voices in the crowd exclaim, "there, Captain Tolar has shot Archy?" Yes, sir. I ask you if you did not hear other voices exclaim that other persons had shot him? No, sir, I did not. Didn't you hear some voices in the crowd cry out that, "no-armed Williamson has shot him"? No, sir. Were there no other cries? I didn't hear them; there might have been. Did you say, sir, that these voices which cried out that "Tolar has shot Archy," came from about the place where Tolar was? One was pretty much about the place, and the other was off to the left of the place where Tolar was. What do you mean by the place; where Tolar stood then or afterwards? Where I saw him afterwards. But where you saw him afterwards was not the place from which the pistol shot proceeded? No, sir. How far was it from the place where the pistol shot proceeded? It was five steps I suppose. To the right or rear? It was to the rear. So that the voices you heard to your right saying "there Tolar has shot Archy," were five steps towards the rear of the place where the pistol was fired? Yes, sir. Now, the other voice you heard, where was that? It was sort of back to my right. That was further than you were? Yes, sir. Fifteen or twenty feet, wasn't it? Ten or twelve. The crowd was thick wasn't it, between those voices and the place where the pistol shot was fired? It was very thick, but not as thick as that towards the place where Archy was. The crowd was thicker from the direction where that voice was, than it was between you and the place where the pistol shot fired? Yes, sir; that is what I am trying to tell, the first voice that I heard in front of me to my right, the crowd was thicker than it was back in the rear. Was that voice to the rear, to the front, to the right, or to the left of where the pistol shot was fired? It was to the rear. And there the crowd was very thick? Yes, sir. I understand you to say you noticed nothing unusual in the crowd at all before the prisoner was brought down stairs? Yes, sir. You know Captain Tolar well? Yes. sir. Do you know whether his business is about the market house a great deal? Yes, sir. Don't you know that is his usual place of doing business? Yes, sir. I ask you sir, whether you know or do not know that whenever a trial of any importance is going on up stairs in the market house, that the crowd generally collect there under the market house and around the eastern arch? I never saw a crowd collect there unless they were on business. Have you ever been there to many trials? I never was there but to one in my life. Then you don't know any thing about it? No, sir. When was the first time you ever told about this matter? I have never told any one at all about it, until I came here to General Avery, yesterday. How did it happen that you were summoned as a witness? I don't know, sir. You don't know who had you summoned as a witness? No, sir. You told nobody about it; from the time of the occurrence, till you came up here and told General Avery about it? No, sir.

Re-direct Examination, by the Counsel for the prosecution:

I want to understand about these voices; how long was it after the pistol fired that you heard these voices? It was but a very short time. As long as you could count fifty? No, sir. You don't think you could have counted fifty before you heard the voices? No, sir. The one that was nearest the point where the pistol fired. was that the voice you heard first or last, or did you hear both voices about the same time? About the same time. Now where was the voice that was nearest you, as well as you could locate it; where did it appear to come from? I think the voice that was the nearest to me was the one that was in front of me. In front of you and to your right? Yes, sir. On the pavement? Yes sir. Was it near the spot where you had heard the pistol fired? Yes, sir. How near to that spot do you suppose it was? Four or five steps I think. Do you mean four or five feet, or steps? Four or five feet, I mean. Where do you think the other was? To the rear, sort of to my right. How far was that from where the pistol was fired? Ten or twelve feet.

JAMES DOUGLAS, a witness for the prosecution, having been duly sworn, testified as follows:

Examined by the Counsel for the prosecution: What is your name? James Douglas, sir.

Were you living in Fayetteville at the beginning of this year? Yes, sir. Do you remember the time Archy Beebee was killed? Yes, sir. Do you remember what day of the month? No, sir. Remember the season—whether it was cold or warm? I suppose it has been about four or five months ago. Since Christmas? Yes, sir. Do you remember what day of the week it was? Yes, sir, it was on Monday evening? Had the sun set? No, sir. Monday afternoon? Yes, sir. What time did you go up to the market house—what time of the day? I went up to the market house—well, I was there off and on all day; my business was around there. What is your business? I am cooking at Mr. Fishblate's, near the market. And you were off and on at the market all day? Yes, sir. Were you at the market when Archy Beebee was brought out of the guard house? Yes, sir. Where were you standing at that time? On the south side of the market house. Near the east corner? Yes, sir. Near the south east corner on the south side? Yes, sir. Is there an arch that opens in front of where you were standing, to the stairs steps? Yes, sir, a large arch opens there. I am talking about the small arch? Yes, sir; there is a small arch opening just over a bench. I am speaking of another arch a narrow arch that is not used as a thoroughfare at all; that is not as large as the open arch; is there such an arch as that on the South side? Yes, sir. You were standing near that point? I was standing about the edge of the pavement on the south side. I want to know how far east you were standing—how far from the front of the market house? I was standing just around the corner. Was Archy Beebee brought by you? Yes, sir. Who had him in charge? Mr. Wemyss I think was on the right hand side of him, and Mr. Faircloth on the left. Did you notice any one else in charge of him? Sheriff Hardie leading the way, I think. Any other officers in the group? I think Mr. Bond, the town constable was along. Did you notice any others? A man by the name of Mr. McGuire, another police. All these officers carried him up stairs? Yes, sir. Did you go up stairs? No, sir. Did you attempt to go? I did not attempt to go exactly, for I heard the order given that no body was allowed, only witnesses; I was standing on the south side, and I looked over the bench, at the prisoner when he was carried up stairs. Does that bench run right across the little arch? Yes, sir. And you say you looked at the prisoner when the prisoner was carried up? Yes sir. What was the reason you did not go up? The order was given that nobody was allowed, only witnesses; and I did not go up. How long did Archy stay up stairs? I reckon they kept him up there nearly an hour and a half. Where were you, during the time he was up stairs? About the market house. How long did you stay at that point on the south side of the market house? I left there shortly afterwards. Did you notice any thing that happened in the crowd before you left that point? No, sir. Nothing at all? No, sir, I went around on the eastern side of the market, and seen a man walking up and down whittling a stick. Who was that? Monk Julia. Was he inside or outside? Outside, sir. Walking outside? No, sir. Where were you standing then, when you saw him? I was standing just in front of the eastern side of the market house. Were you on the pavement or off? I was off. Could you see any one else who was inside of the market house, at that time? I saw a good many persons. Can you name any of them? I saw Mr. Tolar, he was walking up and down. What Tolar? William James Tolar. Do you see the man here? Yes, sir, there he sits, (witness points.) You saw him in the market house? Yes, sir. And you had seen Monk? Yes, sir. Who else did you see? I saw a good many persons; but I particularly took notice of those two walking, and the rest seemed to be standing still. Could you tell any one who was in there? No, sir, I don't know that I could. Was Tom Powers there? I did not see him that I know of. Did you see Tom Powers there? No, sir. Sam Hall? No, sir. Ralph Lutterloh? No, sir. John Maultsby? No, sir, I don't recollect seeing him. John Hollingsworth? Yes, sir, I saw him. Was he inside or out? He was standing on the southeast corner, sir. Was that before you went around the east end? Yes, sir. He was standing on the southeast corner? Yes, sir. Who was with him? He was with no one particularly—he was looking at a paper that was pasted up on the market—seemed to be reading it. Did he seem to have any conversation with any one? Not particularly, he was just standing about there. Did you see Henry Sykes there? No, sir, not that I recollect. And you did not see John Maultsby? I don't think I saw him. Where were you standing when the lady came down stairs? Just in front of that eastern arch. Did you notice anything at all before the lady came down stairs that attracted your attention in the crowd—or anybody in the crowd—hear any threats of violence or anything of that sort? No, sir. You were standing out in front of that east arch, just off the pavement when the lady came down stairs? Yes, sir. Who was with her— How many ladies were there? I think there were two. An old lady and a young lady? Yes, sir. And Mr. Bond was with them? Yes, sir. Was any one else with them? I don't think there was. Where did they go? They went out and got into a carriage. Did any one speak to them then? No, sir, I did not see any one. Did you say no one did? I did not see any one. You were not particularly noticing them? No, sir. You cannot say any one went to the carriage but Mr. Bond? No, sir. Did you see the carriage drive off? Yes, sir, I believe I did. Which way did it go? I think it went right around the corner, it came out rather north. On the north face of the market house? Yes, sir. Do you know where it went then? No, sir, I did not look after it. What did you notice next that attracted your attention? Mr. Bond passed by me and went up stairs. He came back from the ladies? Yes, sir. And went up stairs? Yes, sir. And shortly after that, they brought the prisoner down, and you saw him as he was going down? Yes, sir. Who was in charge of him? Mr. Wemyss and Mr. Faircloth. Was Sheriff Hardie there? I think he was in front of the prisoner. And you saw Mr. Wemyss and Faircolth? Yes, sir. Which side of the prisoner was Wemyss? He was on the right hand side of the prisoner. Where was Faircloth? On the left hand side, sir. Was any assault made on the prisoner as he came down stairs? Not until he got down on the floor. What happened then. I heard some one demand the prisoner. Who was it? I don't know who it was. You heard a voice demand the prisoner? Yes, sir. What did he say? He said, "I demand this prisoner." What did the Sheriff say? I don't know sir—I could not tell what he said. Did he say anything? I don't know that he did: he may have said some-

thing: I could not tell hardly who spoke or who did not. Did the confusion begin with that demand for the prisoner? Yes, sir. They were pressing on towards the prisoner? Yes, sir. Did you see anybody in that crowd that was pressing on? Yes, sir: when I heard the word, "I demand the prisoner" I looked over in the crowd and I saw a man by the name of Monk have a knife in his right hand over the prisoners shoulder—he seemed to be cutting at his body, but whether he cut him or not, I could not say. Did you hear anything said by any one at that time? No, sir, not particularly. Did you see any weapons at that time? No, sir. What happened after that; was he the only man you noticed in the crowd who was pressing on? Yes, sir, at that time; I think some body there pushed him or dragged him away, some way or other; then they went around on the eastern side of the market house. To go toward the guard house? Yes, sir, and they got about half way between the right hand corner of that arch and the corner of the market house. Mr. Wemyss I think fell with the negro, he was down on the bricks and the prisoner was right down on him at the same time, and Mr. Faircloth was on one of his knees on the left hand side of the prisoner. There seemed to be a general tumble? Yes, sir, and every body rushed then, to see what was the matter, and I among the rest, sir. Where did you rush to then? I rushed up towards the prisoner. Did you go up on the pavement? No, sir. You rushed towards the prisoner, on the ground, outside of the pavement? Yes, sir. How close did you get to him? I reckon I could have touched him in about two steps. Did you go on the pavement at all? No, sir. He was close to the edge of the pavement, was he? About midway. You got close to the edge of the pavement? Yes, sir. You think you got close enough to the prisoner to put your hand on him? I think I could. What occurred then? After they fell down— Did the prisoner fall before the rush was made, or afterwards? Before the rush was made; that is before I rushed to see what was going on. Did any body else rush when you rushed? There was a number of people rushed up. What I want to know is this, whether the crowd ceased to press on, and then went back, or whether they were pressing on the prisoner all the while? I think it was pressing on the prisoner all the while. That was your impression? Yes, sir. And then when they were down you made this rush forward through the crowd and got close enough to the prisoner to have laid your hand on him? Yes, sir. Well, how did the prisoner get up, and what happened? He raised up, and when he went to raise up I think Sheriff Hardie grasped his comforter that he had around his neck. Do you mean that he grasped with both hands? I think he did. Both hands in front? Yes, sir. That left the Sheriff just in front of the prisoner? Yes, sir; when the prisoner threw his head back I suppose he was trying to get loose from the Sheriff when the prisoner rose and threw his head back, Mr. Tolar stepped up and laid his hand on my right shoulder, and I gave way to him on the right, and he raised this pistol from under his shawl and held it right to the man's head; you may say, about six inches from his head and fired. Which hand was it he laid on you? His left hand on my right shoulder. And then fired the pistol right in front of you? Yes, sir. Did you have your eyes fixed on his face? I don't know that I did particularly. Did you see the man who held the pistol? Yes, sir. You know him now; point him out. (Witness does so.) Was that the man that had the pistol? Yes, sir. He fired it in your sight? Yes, sir. Did you see Archy fall? Yes, sir. How many men were between you and the prisoner—the prisoner Archy I mean? I don't know how many; I don't think there was any body between me and the prisoner. Mr. Faircloth was on his knees, I think,§ at the time. What was the position that Mr. Tolar was in when he fired; was he leaning over or stooping? I don't think he was leaning over; I think he just threw his hand up and threw back his shawl—it slipped off of his right shoulder, and he threw his hand back to catch his shawl. Did you see what he did with his pistol? No, sir; he then wheeled off and went out towards the opening of the market house, and I stepped back about five or six feet from where I was standing at that time. Who did you see there? I saw Mr. Phillips coming through the left of the crowd with a pistol held in his hand. After this pistol was fired you turned off five or six steps to your left? No, sir; I stepped right back. And you met Phillips coming up from your left? Yes, sir; I didn't meet him, he came right up towards me; he had a pistol in his hand. What sort of a pistol was it? I suppose it was a repeater of some kind. How long was it? It was about a foot or eighteen inches long. It was a large long pistol? Yes, sir. Was it smoking? I did not notice whether it was or not. Did you notice any sign of his having shot. Did you hear any other pistol that day? No, sir, I only heard one that day. Who fired that day? Mr. Tolar. You cannot be mistaken about it? No, sir, I don't think I can. When you met Phillips, what was said? Well, he walked up towards me with a pistol in his hand, and I asked him, if he thought that was right, and he said "no, he didn't," and he said "who was it," and I wheeled around to point out Mr. Tolar, and he was out of my view. Did you hear any exclamation at all in the crowd at that time? Well, I heard some one say "anybody who knew too much about it would fare the same way." "Anybody who knew too much about this business would fare the same way?" Yes, sir, that was about the substance of it, and then Mr. Phillips said to me, "if I was you I would not have anything to say about it, for I am afraid to talk about it myself," and I wheeled off and left the crowd. You met Mr. Phillips with a pistol? He came up to me. And you said "Mr. Phillips, is that right," and he says "no, Jim, it is not?" Yes, sir. And he then asked "who did it," and you turned around to point out the man?" Yes, sir. And he was out of your sight, and some voice in the crowd announced, "if any body knew too much"——or in other words, that it was safe for men to keep silent? Yes, sir. And Phillips advised you to keep quiet, and said he was afraid to talk himself? Did you part with him, then? Yes, sir, I left them. When Phillips asked "who did it" you turned around to point him out who did it? Yes, sir, I called his name at the same time I went to point him. Did you see who was standing near Tolar when he fired? No, sir, I did not. You don't remember who was standing behind him or on either side of him? No, sir Did you see anything after the man was shot, of Monk Julia? Yes, sir. What was he doing? He made a rush at the prisoner again with his knife, and Mr Nixon grasped him around his body and kept him off. What did Monk say, when he was after the prisoner? I don't know what he said exactly; he rushed at the prisoner with his knife in his hand. Did you see any other weapons besides Monks knife, and Captain Tolar's pistol? Yes, sir; John Hollingsworth had a pistol, a belt and I think a knife. What was he doing when you saw him with them? He was standing at the South side of the market house reading an advertisement. Was he talking to anyone else, or any one standing with him? No, sir. Did you see or hear him take any part in the matter at all? No, sir; I did not see him, or hear him make any threats at all. Did you see him afterwards, that day? I don't know whether I did. I mean before the man was shot or just afterwards? No, sir; I don't think I did; he had on a blue jacket, and he was about the only one that had on a blue jacket; and I would have noticed him if I had seen him. Did you see any one else take any part in this affair, except these persons you have mentioned? No sir. Did you see Ed. Powers there that day? No, sir. Sam Hall? No, sir. Ralph Lutterloh? No. sir; not that I recollect, sir. John Maultsby? Not that I recollect, sir. You have told all that you know about it to the best of your belief? Yes, sir.

Cross examination by the Counsel for the accused:

Your name is James Douglass? Yes, sir. Otherwise called James Hawley? Yes, sir. Lived in Fayetteville all your life? Yes, sir. Formerly a slave of Mrs. Elisa Hawley? Yes, sir. That is who you are? That is who I am, sir. Jim, who came down the market house stairs just before the prisoner was brought down? Mr. Bond came down there, sir; I don't recollect whether he was first to come down or not; he is the only one I recollect. Did he come down before Miss Massey and her mother? He came down with them. Who came down next? I could not say who came down next. He went back up stairs. See if you recollect whether anybody came down between Bond, Miss Massey and her mother, and the party in charge of the prisoner—did anybody come down between those? I don't recollect. Do you recollect whether any witness who were up there came down between them? I don't recollect for I did not know who the witnesses were. How large a crowd was there under the market house that day? Well, sir, I could not say the number, but I reckon there was a crowd of about forty or fifty, may be, met there first and the crowd got larger and larger. Is it any unusual thing to see a large crowd about there when an important trial is going on up stairs? I don't know that it is. There was nothing in the crowd there that attracted your attention particularly was there, before the prisoner was brought down? No, sir, nothing attracted my attention particularly. Nothing occurred to attract your attention particularly? Only I saw a man walking up and down with a knife in his hand whittling a stick. Is that unusual? No, sir. How came that to attract your attention? It did not attract my attention any more than anything else, only it was connected with the man who appeared to take part in the mischief, sir. Then the crowd was quite orderly? Yes, sir, it seemed to be. Were most of them sitting down? Yes, sir, there were some sitting down and some standing up. And out of that crowd of forty or fifty the only persons that you noticed before the prisoner came down stairs, that you can recollect, was Monk, who was walking up and down whittling a stick, and Captain Tolar? Yes sir. How came you to remember Captain

Tolar? Well, sir. he was about the largest man that was there, and the only man that had his shawl on—I could see him walking up and down midway of the market house. Was he doing anything? No, sir. Was he saying anything? No, sir, not that I could see. You could see him do nothing and hear him say nothing? No, sir, I didn't see him do anything or hear him say anything. You say when Archy came down stairs that you think Sheriff Hardie was in front? Yes, sir. And Wemyss on the right hand? Yes, sir. And Faircloth on the left? Yes sir. And other members of the police force behind him? No, sir, I didn't say that—I don't know whether there were any others or not, I don't recollect seeing any others—I just merely seen the men that had hold of him. They came on that way then, until they had about cleared the eastern arch of the market-house? No, sir. They just got outside of it, between two benches, where Becky sells her cakes, and so on. Then they had cleared the arch? No, sir. They had not cleared the market-house? No, sir. They were under the market-house. And it was then you heard some one say, "I demand the prisoner"? Yes, sir. Are you sure of that— Can't you be mistaken about that? No, sir. Don't you know he said, "we demand the prisoner"? No, sir. You know he said "I demand the prisoner"? You swear he said "I demand the prisoner"? You swear that? I don't swear that. Do you think that is what he said? I am not positive about that, but he said something to that effect. Do you know who that was? No, sir. About that time you saw Monk reach over with his knife in his hand, after he heard the demand for the prisoner? Yes, sir. Was Monk the only person that you saw rush upon him? He was the only man that I saw that had any weapons at that time. Did you see any more weapons in the hands of anybody at all just before the prisoner was shot? No, sir. I don't think I did. Then they carried the prisoner down to near the south-east corner of the market-house, the sheriff being still in front, Mr. Wemyss upon his right hand and Mr. Faircloth upon his left? They carried him down between the corner of the eastern opening and the south-east corner of the market house. That was near the south east corner of the market house. Yes, sir! When they got there you say that the struggle took place? Yes, sir; I think Mr. Wemyss fell. And the prisoner and Faircloth all went down together? Yes, sir. Just at that time, I understand you to say you rushed up from the position you occupied, and got up near that south east corner of the market house but off the pavement, and so near the prisoner that by reaching out your hand you could have touched him. No, sir; I don't say I could have touched him then; I suppose I might have touched him by taking a step. How far were you off at that time from the edge of the pavement? There was a tree that stands just off the edge of the pavement, and I was standing against that tree. The last tree? There was two trees, right in the eastern part of the market house with boxes around them and one without, and I was standing right near that tree without a box. How long were you standing at that place after you got there before the pistol shot was fired? When the rush was made they all rushed together, it was only a short time. At that time you say, while standing there, the man went down and he was raised up, and when he rose up Mr. Wemyss, was on the right hand and the Sheriff was in the prisoners front? I

was not confident, but I think it was Sheriff Hardie grasped his comforter. You think he had it in both hands? I think he did. Are you certain the Sheriff had hold of him at all? I am not; some one had him. Are you certain you saw Sheriff Hardie at that time at all? I could not say for certain, whether it was him or not, but the man grasped his comfort, sir, and held him. You are certain that some one in front grasped the comforter with both hands and held him up? No, sir ; he was pulling him down, it seemed to me like. Did he grasp that portion around his neck with his hands? About the ends of the comforter with both hands I think, and when he grasped the ends of the comforter the prisoner threw his head backward. Just at that time I understand you to say, a man came up and with his left hand upon your shoulder, sort of turned you back? Yes, sir: I gave way to him. Was he upon the pavement; or off? He was not on the pavement he was off. I thought he was standing off the pavement. Was there any body between you and him? I could not say whether there was or not. Mr. Faircloth I think was between you and him? I mean right on the right; the man rushed upon your right; was there any body between you and the man on your right? No, sir, no body; I think I was looking over Calvin Hunter's shoulder. Which one of Calvin Hunter's shoulders? His right shoulder. So Calvin Hunter was to the front of you? Yes, sir, he was rather to the left of me; he was not exactly in front of me, he was to my left hand. So there was no body between you, immediately on your right, and the man who pushed you aside and fired the pistol? Not that I know of. Do you know whether it is so or not? There might have been some one there, and I never took any notice of him. Was the man close up against you? Yes, sir. That is my question; whether there was any man between you, immediately on your right, and the man who fired the pistol? There was not any man between me and the man who fired the pistol. What did he say when he rushed up? I don't know that he said anything at all. Did he say anything? I don't believe he did. Didn't you hear that man say, "make way, give way?" No, sir, I did not hear that; I would not have known the man was there at all if he hadn't pushed me out one side, and as I felt him pull me I gave way on the right. When that man rushed up and pushed you, that attracted your attention, and you then looked right at him? No, sir, I turned around a little to the right, and as I turned, I saw the hand come up, and the man shot him. Did he have the pistol leveled when you first saw it? No, sir, I saw it when it went up; his hand was raised up over his right side. So he had his hand over his right side and presented the pistol and fired? Yes, sir. And at that time he was standing straight. I reckon he was standing straight, I couldn't say whether he was standing up there either straight or crooked. Was the pistol cocked or was it a self-cocker? I could not say that. Did you see his finger on the trigger? Not particular. Did you see the smoke from the muzzle? I don't know that I saw the smoke, I smelt the powder. Did you see the smoke from the tube? I didn't notice about it. So you noticed no smoke? I saw him when he fired the pistol and he turned around and left. Did you see the fire escape from the muzzle. Yes, sir. And you saw no smoke from the muzzle or tube? I never noticed about the smoke particular. And you swear that that man shot the pistol? Yes, sir. Well, as soon as he fired the pistol, then what did he do? He wheeled around and made that motion with his shawl; his shawl slipped off of his right shoulder. Did he make that after he wheeled around or before? He made it as soon as he fired the pistol. So the shawl slipped off of his right shoulder? Yes, sir. Did not the shawl slip off his right shoulder? was the shawl fastened? I don't know sir, whether it was or not. What sort of a shawl was it? It was a gray kind of a shawl; I call it a drab-colored shawl. You would not call it a gray shawl? Not exactly. Was it as gray as your coat? No, sir. And you are sure no part of the shawl slipped off from his left shoulder? That was all that was holding the shawl at that time; it was off of the right and hanging on the left. Don't you know that as soon as he fired the pistol he took that shawl and threw it around him; did not he catch it with his hand? No, sir; I don't think he did; he fired the pistol, and as soon as he fired the pistol he made this movement with his arm, catching at the right hand corner of the shawl. Did he get it back on his shoulder? I don't know; that was the movement he was making. Did that shawl strike you? No, sir. Which way did the shawl fall when he threw it back, to the front, the right or to the left? As soon as he fired the pistol he turned around and made that movement with his shawl, with his pistol in his hand. Did the end of the shawl fall to the right or front? I could not see whether it did or not. So Calvin Johnson was the only man you saw about the man who fired the pistol? He was about the only one that I recollect of. Do you remember John Armstrong? I know him. Did you see John Armstrong there? I saw him about there. Did you see him at that time? I could not say. Don't you know John Armstrong was standing between you and the man who fired the pistol? No, sir; I don't know it. Was not he standing there? I could not say, sir; I could not say whether he was or not. Did not you know? No, sir; I do not. You have just sworn there was not room enough for anybody to be between you and Capt. Tolar, and now I ask you whether John Maultsby was standing there or not? Between me and Captain Tolar I think it was impossible for any man to have got. Then you swear he was not standing there? I won't swear. But you say it was impossible for any man to be there. I think it was. What sort of a pistol was it? It was a long pistol—I don't know the name of it, I reckon you would call it a repeater—a pretty heavy pistol. What did he do with it after he fired it? I don't know what he done with it. Did he throw the pistol to his left side or to his right side? He brought it around to his right side. Did he put it back in the right side of his person? I did not see him put it there. Were you looking at him as he turned around? As soon as the pistol fired I turned immediately, and Mr Tolar turned, and he made that motion with his pistol. Now, Jim, just at the time that Captain Tolar fired the pistol, did anybody stand right near him, and right near you on his left side, or anybody make any remark to him? Not that I heard, sir. Didn't you hear a man standing there, say, "there, Captain, you have shot that poor negro? I don't know, sir, whether he did or not; I could not say, sir. I come here to state what I know myself. You are sure you did not hear that remark? I am not so sure; I might have heard it, and at the same time never taken any notice of it, sir. You can't recollect that you heard that remark? No, sir. And you were right near him? Yes, sir. Well now.

at the time Tolar turned back did you see Sam. Hall near him? No, sir. Did you see Ed. Powers near him? No, sir. Did you see anybody near him, that you remember. No, sir, not in particular. At the time Tolar fired that pistol, was there anybody standing between him and the prisoner Beebee? Not that I know of, Mr. Faircloth was on his knees I think—if anybody was between him and the prisoner he was the only man. So you say Tolar was on the inner circle—that there was nobody between him and the prisoner, and that he put the pistol within an inch or two of his head? No, sir, I said about six inches from his head. And there was nobody between Tolar and the prisoner at the time he fired? Not that I know of sir, except it was Mr. Faircloth, and he was down on one of his knees at that time. You profess to have seen all these things? I don't profess to see a man between me and the prisoner. You could have seen the man between you and the prisoner? I could have seen one if I had looked and if there had been one there. You say you don't know what became of Tolar after tha? He turned right off and went through the crowd. Who have you talked this matter over with before you come here? I don't know that I have talked it over with anybody particular. Have you talked it over with Mr. Fishblate since he went back from Raleigh? I don't know but what I did. I think you say you live with Mr. Fishblate? Yes, sir. As soon Mr. Fishblate went back from Raleigh you and he talked this matter all over. No, sir, we did not talk it all over. You talked over most of it? No, sir, he was sick at the time I was summoned here, and he asked me what I knew about it, and I told him I knew the man that killed him, and that is all the satisfaction I gave him. Are you certain that you saw that carriage with Miss Massey and her mother go off that day? Yes, sir. Are you certain you saw them get into that carriage at all? I did not look after the ladies when they brought them down. You did not see them get into it at all? No, sir. Then you don't know who helped them in? No, sir, I don't. And you don't know which way the carriage drove? No, sir, I don't. But you think the horses heads were turned towards Mr. Fishblates? Yes, sir. Can't you say whether that carriage drove down towards Liberty street? No, sir. Can't you say whether it did drive there? No, sir. Can you say it drove down Gillespie street or towards Robert Mitchell's? I could not say that either, I heard it when it moved off. Were you excited on that occasion? I don't know that I was before the pistol was fired—I think I grew a little excited, I don't know anything about it; of course I did not feel any more excited than I would have been at any other time. Were you armed that day? No, sir. Had you no arms about you at all? No, sir.

Re-direct examination by the Counsel for the prosecution:

I want to understand your position a little at the time this pistol fired—I understand you to say that you were at a point where, by reaching over, you could have brushed the prisoner? Yes, sir. You were standing there near that little unboxed tree and he was about the middle of the wide walk and about the middle of the arch? Yes, sir. And the man who fired the pistol laid his hand on your right shoulder and pulled you around? Yes, sir. And you think you were so close to Captain Tolar that no one could possibly have been between you? I don't think any man could have been between us, sir. You saw the flash from this pistol—you don't remember having een the smoke? No, sir. Was any other pistol fired that day? No, sir. When you saw Mr. Phillips just after the firing of this pistol, how was he dressed? He had on his ordinary clothes. Did he have on a shawl? I disremember whether he had or not? I don't think he had. Your impression is that he did not? Yes, sir, he had his pistol laying on his hand, that drew my attention more than anything else.

A motion was then made to adjourn until Thursday, August 6th, at 11 A. M.

The Judge Advocate objected to the adjournment:

"The expense of this trial is about a hundred dollars daily, and there is no reason why this case should not go on without delay. There are witnesses enough yet for the prosecution, who are here awaiting examination, to occupy the time of the Commission at least four days. Of course the Commission has it in its power to adjourn as long as it pleases, but I ask it in justice to these prisoners who are confined, and in behalf of other prisoners, who cannot be tried until this trial closes, that the Commission throw nothing in the way of completing these trials at the earliest possible day."

The motion to adjourn till Tuesday, August 6, was amended, and a motion was made to adjourn till Monday, August 5th, at 11 o'clock A. M., which was carried, the vote standing:

For adjournment:
Brevet Lieutenant Colonel THOS. P. JOHNSON, Captain A. Q. M., U. S. V; Second Lieutenant G. E. HARGOUS, 40th Infantry; Second Lieutenant LOUIS E. GRANGER, 40th Infantry.

Against adjournment:
Colonel J. V. BOMFORD, 8th Infantry; Captain P. H. REMINGTON, 8th Infantry.

Whereupon the Commission adjourned to meet on Monday, August 5th, at 11 A. M.

RALEIGH, N. C., Aug., 5th. 1867, 11 A. M., The Commission met pursuant to adjournment. Present all the Commission, the Judge Advocate, the Counsel for the prosecution, all the Accused and their Counsel.

The reading of the testimony taken on Friday, August 2d, was waived, there being no objection thereto.

Friday's proceedings were then read.

It was moved that the whole of the record referring to the adjournment be expunged, which motion was carried.

The proceedings of Friday, the 2d inst., having been read were then approved:

JAMES McNEILL, a Witness for the prosecution, having been first duly sworn, testified as follows:

Examined by the Counsel for the prosecution.

What is your name? James McNeill. Where do you live? Fayetteville. Were you living there at the beginning of this year? Yes, sir; have lived there all my life. Were you living there the day Archy Beebee was killed? Yes, sir. What is your business in Fayetteville? Cabinet maker. Were you at the market house the day Archy was killed? Yes, sir, I was. What other name had Archy Beebee, besides Beebee? I don't know, I always called him Archy Warden, he always belonged to Mr Warden. Were you at the market house when he was killed? No, sir; I was not. Were you there before? Yes, sir, And afterwards? Yes, sir. What time did you get there first that day? I was coming from dinner; I think it was betwixt two and three o'clock when I first came down. I went to dinner at one o'clock. When you got there, was Archy up stairs in the Court

room? No, sir. He had not come from the Guard House? No, sir. Where were you standing when he was brought from the Guard House? I was standing in the middle of the street, sir. At which end of the market house? The end towards Cambeltown bridge, the east end. Opposite the big arch? Yes, sir. At the east end of the market house? Yes, sir. In Person street? Yes, sir. Did you see Archy when he was brought up? Yes, sir. Who was with him? I don't recollect any one except Mr. Wemyss? Was nobody else with him? Yes, sir. What became of Archy when he got there? He went up stairs. Did you attempt to go up stairs? No, sir. Where did you move to after he went up stairs? I kept walking around there from one place to another. How long was he up stairs? He was up there some considerable time. An hour? I don't know, sir, I guess probably about that time. Was there any crowd there while he was up stairs? Yes, sir, a very large crowd. How many persons? I don't recollect, there was a good many, though. As many as a hundred? I would not like to say for certain. Did it grow any larger or less while you were there? Some came after I was there. Did you go under the market house at all? No, sir. Did you notice anybody in the crowd, any of these prisoners at the bar, or any one else before he came down, while Archy was up-stairs? Yes, sir. Who did you see there? I saw Captain Tolar, and Mr. Powers, and Mr. Mouk? Tom Powers do you mean? Yes, sir. Did you notice any one else in the crowd, in conversation with them? Not that I recollect. Were you standing out there when Miss Massey came down stairs? Yes, sir. Who was with her. Mr. Bond, I think, the town constable. Where were you standing when she came down stairs? Right in front of the arch, out in the street. Where was the carriage? It was out to the right of the arch, towards Mr. Taylor's store. Was it in the middle of the street? It was a few paces from the pavement. Out side of the crowd? Yes, sir. How near were you to the carriage? I guess I was about as near as I am to you, (about 8 feet.) How near were you to the carriage when the ladies got in? About as far as to those two gentlemen, (about 12 or 15 feet.) Did any one else go to the carriage besides Mr. Bond, to speak to the ladies? Mr. P. Taylor went to the carriage and spoke to the old lady, and I think he spoke to the young lady. Did you see any one else? Well, I don't recollect. I recollect personally seeing him there—and Mr. Powers, after Mr. Taylor stepped off, this young lady's mother called him there. Were you near enough to hear what was said? I overheard them say, after he started away, she says to him, "Tom, don't you have anything to do with it—you go home," and he was crying at that time. He was weeping at the time? Yes, sir. What did he say in reply? He shook his head. Which way? Like he said he would not have anything to do with it. Then at that time I said to him, "Mr. Powers is that young lady a relation of yours," he says "yes, she is my niece," I says to him then, "the times have changed so much during the war, and since the war, I don't know those who I used to know," and by that time Captain Tolar came up, and touched him on the shoulder, and they stepped off together. Where did Tolar come from? I do not know, sir, he was to the left of me when he came up. Where were you facing? I was facing towards where the carriage was standing.

Did he come from further out in the street, or towards the market house? From towards the market house, I think. Were you facing Mr. Powers when you were talking to him? Yes, sir. Which shoulder did Captain Tolar touch? I don't recollect. What occurred then? They walked up towards the market house, and I walked on behind them a few steps, and I heard Captain Tolar say to Mr. Powers, "when he comes"—(I saw the young man standing up at the door,) Mr. Tolar says. "when he comes down you grab him, and break the ice, and that will be all you will have to do,"—something like that. Was that all Captain Tolar said? I think it was, sir, if I mistake not. "You grab him and break the ice, and that is all you have to do?" Yes, sir, and I turned my back and ran as hard as I could towards Mr. McFoxe's store. Captain Tolar came up and touched Mr. Powers on the shoulder, and you followed them up? Yes, sir. And you heard him say what? He says "as he comes down you grab him and break the ice, and that will be all you will have to do." You think those are the exact words? I think so, as well as I can recollect. It has been so long I may have forgotten the exact words—but I think they are. It alarmed you, what was said, sufficiently to make you run away? Yes, sir. Did you see any weapons in the crowd? I only saw one, that was a pocket knife which Monk Julia had before the man came down, whittling a stick, but I did not know what he was going to do with it. You then ran off after this conversation? Yes, sir. Where were you when the pistol fired? I was at Mr. McFoxe's store. Was that in sight of the market house? Yes, sir. How far from the market house—fifty yards? I don't think it was quite fifty. As far as across this room from corner to corner? Yes, sir; about that distance. You heard the pistol? Yes, sir. Did you go back? Yes, sir. What did you see when you went back? I saw this man laying there, Dr. McDuffie was attending him, and Mr. Wenyes was trying to make the crowd scatter, so that they could get air to him, and Mr. James Strange was there. He was coming from where the prisoner was, and he was saying it was a pity they shot him down that way. And after that some strange gentleman—I never saw him before—he was saying something and Mr. Eddie Powers said that he thought it was nothing but what was right. Did you see any weapon upon Mr. Eddie Powers at that lime—or anything peculiar in his appearance? No, sir; I saw no weapon. He looked very pale. And he said it was perfectly right? Yes, sir. That was just after Mr. Strange had been denouncing it as improper? Yes, sir.

Cross examination, by the Counsel for the accused.

Your name is McNeill? Yes, sir. What family did you formerly live with? Mr. Duncan McNeill. Any relation to George McNeill? None that I know of, sir. You came there between two and three o'clock? Yes, sir; I was there about that time. I understood you to say you stood opposite the arch as Beebee was coming down stairs, or as the ladies were coming down stairs? As the ladies were coming down stairs. About the middle of the street? A few paces off from the arch. How wide is the street there? I don't know sir, a right good sized street.— Seventy-five feet? No, sir; I think not. You were not at the middle of the street? I was standing in the arch, in the street a few paces from the arch. You were nearer the market house than the middle of the street? Yes, sir. You were standing how far do you suppose from the market house? About as far as from me to you

sir. About fifteen feet from the market house? Yes, sir. Were you further from the market house than the carriage? The carriage was right behind me, sir; rather to my right, going into the arch. And you say you were about as far from the carriage as from me to you? No, sir, I did not. How far were you? I never took any particular notice. I understand you to say, in answer to the government, that you were about as far as from you to us, from the carriage? I said when Mr. Powers was talking to me. Did you move? Not till Mr. Powers went up and said something to the ladies; then I stepped back. Which way? From the carriage. How near to the carriage were you at the time the ladies got in? Well, I was not any distance, scarcely. As soon as Mr. Powers walked up to speak to the ladies, you walked back? I stepped back a pace or two. But you heard what the old lady said? Yes, sir. And she said to Mr. Powers as he walked away, "Tom, don't you have anything to do with it." Mr. Powers went to the carriage and he started to step off, and she called him back, and she whispered to him, as well as I can understand, it was "Tom, don't you have any thing to do with it, you go home." You swear that she said that and you heard her say it? Yes, sir. That was the second time she called him? The first time he went himself. And then he moved off and she called him back, and she said that to him? Yes, sir. And he shook his head as if he agreed not to have anything to do with it? Yes, sir. Then as he walked off Mr. Tolar met him and talked to him? No, sir, I spoke to himself, first. And you asked whether the young lady was not akin to him, and he stopped and talked to you? Yes, sir. Which direction was Powers making then from you? He walked right up towards the market. And he met Tolar? No, sir, Tolar came up during the time he was talking to me. Did you hear Tolar say anything to him? He came up and touched Mr. Powers, and after they come up towards the market I heard him say, "Tom as he comes down you grab him and break the ice, and that will be all you have to do," and at that time I turned my back and ran. How far was he from you when he said that? They were right before me; I was walking along behind them. You walked on up towards the market house? Yes, sir. How far did you walk with them? Some two or three steps. You heard nothing else said? No, sir. You heard nothing else of the conversation between the old lady and Tom Powers, than what you have told? No, sir. You say you got there about three o'clock? Yes, sir. And you stood about the middle of the street for some time? When I first went there I was standing a good ways in the street fronting the arch. And you waited till Archy went up stairs? Yes, sir. Did not walk under the market house at all? No, sir. And you stood there all the while Archy was up stairs? I was walking around about there. And you say you saw there Monk and Tom Powers and Capt. Tolar? Yes, sir. You saw a number of other people? Yes, sir. You don't recollect who? No, sir. And then you recollect who? No, sir. And then you your stand opposite the Arch about the time the ladies came down? Yes, sir. When did you first give in your testimony about this matter? When I went around to the shop, I told one of the boys, and I have not told any one since, as I recollect. because I did not want anything to do with it. You have not mentioned it from that time to this? Not that I recollect. You have not been called upon to tell what the old lady said to

Tom Powers from that time to this? Only as I spoke it to the General as I came up. You have not told what Tolar said to Powers from that time to this? No, sir. This is the first time you have had occasion to recall the words? Yes, sir. And you swear to them according to your best recollection? Yes, sir. Are you positive that those are the words they used? Yes, sir. You have no doubt about it at all? To the best of my knowledge, it is. You have no doubt about it? No, sir.

Re-direct examination, by the Counsel for the prosecution.

Did you see any one have any conversation with Mr Bond as he went to the carriage? No, sir.

Questioned by the Commission:

When Capt. Tolar touched Tom Powers on the shoulder, and said to Powers "you grab him as he comes down and break the ice, and that is all you will have to do," did Capt Tolar say anything else, that he himself or anyone else would do anything afterwards? No, sir; I did not hear him say anything, because soon as I heard that word I ran right away. Did he use any such expression as "and we will put him through?" Yes, sir; I think he did; I forgot that, sir.

Re-direct examination resumed, by the Counsel for the prosecution.

Now state the conversation again, the whole of it, as it occurred? Mr. Tolar says to Mr. Powers: "You grab him as he comes down and break the ice, and we will put him through," that is the words. Are you certain that that expression was used? Yes, sir: that was the expression. You said just now you had never stated this conversation before; you mean to no one before? I said to no one except you and Gen. Avery. Was that conversation the same as you stated to us, with that addition of "we'll put him through?" Yes, sir. Are you confident that expression was used? Yes, sir.

The Counsel for the prosecution said he had no objection to having the witness cross examined on that point.

Re-cross examination, by the Counsel for the accused.

How came it you did not mention that just now? I forgot it, it was the first time I was ever in a crowd and I got excited. Didn't you tell General Avery that "you grab him, and we'll put him through?" Yes, sir. But you forgot it a little while ago, haven't you forgot anything else? I think not. You have told everything now? I think so. When did you come up here? I came up here Thursday. Have you been talking to any one about this matter as the trial went on? No, sir. The only persons you have spoken to about it since February are General Avery and Colonel Haywood? Yes, sir. You have not told another soul since? Not that I recollect, sir.

PHILLIP PICKETT, a witness for the prosecution, having been first duly sworn, testified as follows:

Examined by the Counsel for the prosecution.

What is your name? Phillip Pickett. Do you live in Fayetteville? Yes, sir. Have you lived there all this year? Yes, sir. Did you know Archy Warden or Archy Beebee? Yes, sir. Which name did he go by? Both sir. When did you see him alive last? I don't know sir exactly. Do you remember what day of the week it was? I saw him Monday. Do you know what month? No, sir. It was since Christmas, wasn't it? Yes, sir. Were you at the market house when he was carried up stairs? No, sir. You got there while he was up stairs? Yes, sir. What time of the day was it when you got there? I don't know exactly the hour.

After dinner or before dinner? After dinner. Was the sun set? No, sir. When you got there he was up stairs? Yes, sir. Where did you go when you first got to the market house? I stood at the south east corner of the market house. On the east face? My face was directly west. Which wall would your elbow touch,—your right elbow? It would touch the east corner. Then you were a little outside of the market house? Yes, sir. The market house was right west of you? When you were looking west, you could see right straight ahead? Yes, sir. Were you looking in the direction of Haymount? Yes, sir. Could you see up Hay street? Yes, sir. Was any crowd there? No, sir, I saw no crowd at the time. Mr. Tolar was standing, and Monk and a young man by the name of John Hollingsworth, and I think Dr. McDuffie was standing there talking,—I am not certain about Dr. McDuffie,—and John Hollingsworth had a pistol, and he had on a blue jacket, and his pants tucked in his boots. He had a pistol where? On his right side. Where every one could see it? Yes, sir. Did you see any arms on these other men? No, sir. Where were these gentlemen standing? At the south arch. Was there any crowd at that time inside of the market house and the east end? Not that I know of; I was not looking that way. There was no noise there? No, sir. You say these gentlemen stood about the south arch of the market house? Yes, sir. They were talking together, were they? Yes, sir. Did you hear what they were saying? No, sir. What occurred next? I walked further down to the east arch, and stood there with a boy by the name of Andrew Haynard, who lives in town now; we both stood there talking a long while, when Mr. Bond came down stairs with this young lady. Before Mr. Bond came down stairs, did you notice any crowd inside of the market house? No, sir, only I noticed Mr. Powers setting on the bench where Becky Ben keeps her victuals. Which Powers? Tom Powers. Was he the only person in the market house? No, sir, a good many persons were around there, but I didn't notice who they were. Did you see anything more of Captain Tolar and Monk, and John Hollingsworth after you had seen them inside the arch? No, sir, they were walking about the market; they walked through the south arch into the market. You saw them after you got into the east arch; you saw them go back through the south arch? They just walked right through. Did they go out of the market house? Not that I know of. Where did they walk through to? They were just walking about. Did they walk down towards the east arch? Not that I know of. Were they together when they were walking about? No, sir, not after they were standing talking. They were not connected in any way? No, sir. Well, did you hear any conversation pass between Captain Tolar and any one of so I did not, sir. You say you saw Tom Powers seated on Becky Ben's bench? Yes, sir. Was that after you had seen Tolar at the south arch? Yes, sir. When you first came around to the eastern arch? Yes, sir. Where were you standing when that young lady came down stairs with her mother. Just on the outside of the pavement at the east arch. Just off the pavement? Yes, sir. Opposite the east arch? Yes, sir. Well, what happened then? Mr. Bond came down with the lady and went to the carriage and helped her in, and Mr. John Maultsby said he would go and see if they found him guilty. Stop one moment, was that the first time you saw John Maultsby that day? Yes, sir. Where was he standing when he said he would go and see whether they found him guilty? At the south east corner, Where did he go? He went to the carriage. Who did he talk to when he got there? Mr. Bond. Did you hear what he said to Mr. Bond? He asked whether he was found guilty, and he said "yes," and he came down to the south-east corner, where Mr. Jones was standing, and Mr. Jones asked him how it was, and he said he was found guilty. You heard all this said? Yes, sir. What became of Maultsby then? He walked up towards the north east corner, and I don't know where he went to. Did you see him pass the main arch? Yes, sir. He moved towards the north east corner? Yes, sir. The last you saw of him, he was near the North east corner? Yes sir. What happened then? Mr. Jim Jones, before he walked up, he said "John, mention that other thing." Was that just after he told him the negro man was found guilty? Yes, sir. What else did he say? That was all the remarks I heard; "John mention that other thing." I thought you said, he said "John don't forget it? No, sir. What did John say? He said he would and walked off then to the north east corner, and then Mr. Jim Jones walked around south and sat down on a bench. One of those benches that runs across the little arch? Yes, sir. On the outside? Yes, sir. What happened next? After a while they came down with Archy. How long was it after this conversation, that Archy came down? About fifteen minutes. Where were you standing when Archy came down? At the same place, sir, On the pavement? Yes, sir; about the middle of the arch; they came down with him, and just as they neared the arch and started down on the pavement to the guard house— Did you see any thing happen in the market house before he got out side? I did not; some one rushed at him, and some said "kill the damned rascal," and I saw Mr. Monk commence to cut at him with a knife. You heard what exclamation? "Kill the damned rascal," You did not see who made that rush? No, sir. You saw nobody in the crowd but Monk with a knife? Not right close to him. Did you see anybody further off with a knife? No, sir; he made at him to cut him, and Jim Nixon ran at him and pulled him off and told him to go away; and by that time they were scuffling and got down on the pavement. Who got down? The sheriff and Mr. Wemyss had hold of him; they all went down: Archy went down, and Mr Wemyss got down on the top of him like; just about this time they got straight Mr. Tolar stepped up and shot him. Did you see Mr. Tolar? Yes, sir. That was the first time you had seen him since you saw him in the market house? Yes, sir. Where did he come from? I don't know, sir. Were you standing in the same place in the street in front of the arch? Yes, sir—I wasn't in front of the arch exactly,—had moved a little further down. Tolar, you say, stepped forward and shot him? Yes, sir. How far was Captain Tolar from you when he shot? Not more than four or five feet. How far was Archy from you? He was about three or four feet. You were closer to Archy than to Captain Tolar? I was, sir. Were you in front of the main arch of the market house? No, sir, I moved down a little. You moved down as the crowd moved down? Yes, sir. Where was Archy, on the pavement or off? On the pavement. Were you on the pavement or off? Off the pavement. You were about four feet from him you say? Not

more than that. Was he near the edge of the pavement? About the middle. You were near the edge? Yes, sir. Captain Tolar was to your right or left when he fired? To my right, sir. You say he was about five feet from you? He may have been about that. Was anybody between you and him? There was. Who was it? I don't recollect. Was there anybody between him and Beebee? Yes, sir. Can you tell who they were? I could not. What sort of a pis ol was that Captain Tolar had? I could not say. Could you say anything about the size of it? No, sir, I could not because he fired right over some one's shoulder—it hid it. Can you tell whether it was a large pistol or a small one? It looked like a medium sized pistol. Did you see the pistol? I got a glimpse of it. Are you certain whose hand it was? Yes, sir. How was Captain Tolar dressed that day? That I could not say; I think, though, that he was dressed in a dark gray suit but I would not say positive. Did he have on an overcoat? No, sir, I think he had on a shawl. Are you certain about the shawl? I am not certain about the shawl; he had on a shawl or blanket. He was the man who fired the pistol? Yes, sir. Did you see the pistol when it went off? Yes, sir. And the smoke and flash? Yes, sir. You heard the report? Yes, sir. How close was the muzzle of the pistol to Archy's head? It was a right good piece off; it was not right at his head. Tolar, you say, was nearly five feet from him. I could not say exactly. Was Tolar standing on the pavement or off? That I could not say because the people were between me and Mr. Tolar. Was he standing pretty near the edge? I think he was, sir. You could only judge of the distance from seeing the head and shoulders? Yes, sir. But you are certain it was his hand that held the pistol? I am, sir. And you were looking at it the moment he fired? Yes, sir. What position was Captain Tolar in when he fired? I don't know exactly. Did he fire with his left hand? No, sir, I don't think he did; he fired with his right hand. Was he standing very erect or leaning over the crowd—did he point it through the crowd or over the crowd? Over the crowd. Did you see Sheriff Hardie at the time he was shot? Yes, sir. Where was he standing? I think he was on the right hand side. In front or behind? At the side of him. Did you see Wemyss? Yes, sir. Where was he standing? He had hold of him on the left side I think, one was on one side and one on the other side anyhow. They were on different sides? Yes, sir. Did you see Archy fall? Yes, sir. Did you see what became of Tolar after he fired? I don't know sir. Where did he go after he fired? I don't know sir; when he fired he wheeled and ran the pistol under his shawl. Which side? On his left side I think. You didn't see where he moved to? I did not. Did you go up to the man who was wounded? I was standing right there. You did not have to go far? No, sir. Did you see what became of Tolar afterwards? I did not sir. Did you see who was nearest to Tolar when he fired? No, sir. Did you see anything of Edward Powers? I did not see him in that crowd; I saw him there before this thing happened. Did you see Ralph Lutterloh? Yes, sir. Did you see anything of Henry Sykes there that day? No, sir. Did you see anything of Mr. Leggett there that day? I know one Mr. Leggett. but I didn't see him anywhere about there sir. Did you see Sam Hall that day? I did sir. Was that before the shot? Yes, sir.

Where was he when you saw him? He was knocking about the market. Inside or out? Inside and out, too. Did you see him have any conversation with any of these prisoners. I did not, sir.

Cross examination by the Counsel for the accused.

Phillip Pickett is your name? Yes, sir. How long have you lived in Fayetteville? All my life sir. You know Dr. McDuffie? I do sir. You know him very well, don't you? Yes, sir. How far were you from that knot of men,—Hollingsworth, Tolar and the rest of them? I was not more than twenty-five feet. Any body between you and them? There was not, sir. Who did you say they were? I saw Mr. Tolar and Mr Monk, and I won't say whether the other was Dr. McDuffie or not. Why ain't you certain? Because it has been such a long time I disremember. How do you know it was Tolar? I know it; I can recollect it was Tolar. How can you forget it was Dr. McDuffie? I don't know sir; it has been so long. I want to know how you came to forget Mr. McDuffie and not to forget Tolar? I can't say; I know for certain it was him and Monk and John Hollingsworth, but the others I forget who it was. You recollect John Hollingsworth very well? Yes, sir. And Monk very well? Yes, sir. And you recollect Tolar very well? Yes, sir. And Dr. McDuffie you know as well as any one; and you don't recollect whether it was he or not? No, sir. You can't give any reason why you don't recollect? I give this reason; it has been so long I forget whether it was him or not. That same reason would cause you to forget the others too? No, but I don't forget the others. How came you to recollect either and not the other? Because I can recollect the rest, and I think the other was Dr. McDuffie. You don't know why you don't recollect him? I only give the reason that it was so long. Were you standing there with your elbow at the east corner of the market house looking west? Yes, sir. And you were twenty-five feet from the men? About that. And you saw them all and you say one of them had a pistol?— Yes, sir. You don't forget that? No, sir. You don't forget that one had his pantaloons in his boots? No, sir. And you don't forget one had blue pantaloons on? I said a bluejacket. You don't forget that? No, sir. But you do forget who the fourth man was? I don't exactly forget, it sort of slipped my memory. Then you walked from the east corner to the arch? Yes, sir. The main arch on the cast side? Yes, sir. And you walked in, or did you not? I did not, sir. Where did you go to? On the outside of the pavement, just off the pavement. How far were you from the arch? Not more than six feet, anyhow. Six feet from the pavement? From the arch. Were you off the pavement? Yes, sir. How wide is the pavement? It is not more than about five feet. And you were about one foot from the pavement? I might have been about that, I would not say for certain. And you stood there when Miss Massey came down? Yes, sir. And she went to the carriage with Mr. Boud? Yes, sir. Who did you say went to the carriage then? Mr. Maultsby. Didn't Tom Powers go to the carriage? I did not notice. How far from the carriage were you? Not very far, sir. Was it a mile? Not more than about twenty feet. Were you looking at the carriage? I was, sir. You say you did not see Tom Powers go there? I did not notice him. You saw Maultsby go? I did, sir. And he said he would ask whether they found Beebee guilty or not? Yes, sir. And he went, and you heard the conversation with Boud; heard him ask him whether he was guilty or not, and Bond said he was, and then he came back? Yes, sir. And you were standing, looking where you were; did you move away? No, sir. You were six feet from the arch? About that, sir. Was the man named Jones standing by the arch? No, sir; he was standing down by the corner. Which corner? The south east corner. Did Maultsby go down to the south east corner? Yes, sir. Is Jones a white man? Yes, sir. He went to the south east corner and Jones asked him whether they found him guilty? Yes, sir. And he walked up on the pavement to the north east corner? On the outside of the pavement? Where was Jones standing? On the outside of the pavement. Maultsby went down after talking to Bond, to the south east corner, off the pavement, and then he walked along the street up towards the north east corner? Yes, sir. And you heard Jones say what? "Mention that other thing." And what did John Maultsby say? He said he would. You did not hear anything more said; what that other thing was? No, sir. Maultsby went up to the north east corner? Yes, sir. You saw him pass the big arch? Yes, sir. What became of him? I don't know. How long was that before Archy came down? About fifteen minutes, sir. How long was it between the time Miss Massey came down and Archy came down? About fifteen minutes. No time had passed between the time Miss Massey had come down and Jones and Maultsby had this talk? That was about the same time. Did you see Archy as he was on the stairs coming down? Yes, sir. And you saw him when he come on the floor inside of the market house? Yes, sir. Did anybody go up to him? Not that I know of, sir. You saw him? I did, sir. If anybody went up to him you could have seen them? I think I could, but I didn't see any one. You were standing there with your eyes fixed on Archy? Yes, sir. And you saw nobody do anything to Archy, until they turned the corner. I did not, sir. Then you heard some body say, "kill him?" Yes, sir. And Monk ran up with a knife? Yes, sir. Did you see Tom. Powers then? I did not, sir. Did you see Tom. Powers after they passed the arch and came out? No, sir. You were still standing in front of the arch? I was, sir. Did you see Captain Tolar until he came up and shot him? Only when I saw him talking. Had you seen him from the time you saw him talking until he came up and shot him? I saw him walking through the market house. Did you see him passing out back of you in the street while you were standing there? I did not notice him. At the time, Massey was sitting in the carriage? I did not notice him. Did you notice Tom. Powers? I did not sir. You were standing at the place all the while? I was, sir. If they had passed through the arch to the carriage by you, how near would they pass? They could have passed within ten feet of me, sir. Was your face in that direction or the other direction? My face was directly west, sir. No body could have gone out of the arch without passing under your eye? No, sir. You did not see Tolar or Powers go out? I don't recollect. You did not see Powers go the carriage? No sir. You saw Powers walking about under the market house? No sir; I saw Ed. Powers. Did you see Tom. Powers? He was sitting down on Becky Ben's seat. Was that the only place you saw him that day? Yes sir, to my recollection. After Archy came down did you move? I moved down, yes sir; I moved down between the corner and the arch. Between the corner and the little arch, or the large arch —— there is a little arch there, is there not? There is a bench runs across that. Were you opposite that. I was not exactly opposite it, I was about the pillar. Which pillar? The brick pillar. The pillar between the little arch and the big arch? Yes, sir. You stood how near the pavement? I was just off of it. Where did Tolar come from? I don't know, sir, when I saw him he was coming up in the crowd, sir. You say you was standing opposite the pillar, between the big arch and the little arch, and just off the pavement? Yes, sir. And you were nearer Beebee than you were to Tolar? I was, sir. Tolar was some five feet from you? I think he was probably some four feet; about that, sir. · And Tolar, when he shot, did not make the crowd give way or shoot over? I did not notice, the crowd was moving continually. But when he held up the pistol, he held it over the crowd? He did, sir. Did you say how near the pistol came to Beebee? I did not, sir. Beebee had just fallen before that? Yes, sir. And gotten up? Yes, sir. And you say Sheriff Hardie was on the right hand? No, sir, I didn't say; I said I thought he was. Which side was Wemyss on? I don't know, sir; one was on one side and the other on the other side. Were they close up to the prisoner? Yes, sir. Both of them had hold of him? Yes, sir. Had hold of him by the arm? I think as well as I can recollect, Mr. Wemyss had a little string hold of his thumb. You think Mr. Wemyss had hold of him by his thumb? Yes, sir. Where did Sheriff Hardie have hold of him? I don't know whether Mr. Hardie had hold of him with a string or not. Did you see Faircloth? I did, sir. Where was he? I don't recollect whether he was behind or before. Was Hornrinde there? I did not notice him, sir. You say you were just off of the pavement? I did, sir. The pavement was about five feet broad, and you were about five feet from Tolar? Along about that, sir. And Tolar was to your right? He was. And you were opposite the pillar, between the little and large arch? Yes, sir. Was Tolar near the edge of the pavement? I could not say, because of the crowd. You can't say whether he was off of the pavement? No, sir. You don't know whether he was off or on? No, sir. Supposing he had been off of the pavement, he would have been behind you would he not? No, sir. Was there room for a man to stand between you and the pavement? He was further down than I was. You were standing looking right at the market house? Yes, sir. And Beebee was between you and the market house? Yes, sir. Then Beebee was opposite the pillar between the big arch and the little arch? Yes, sir. Then Tolar was opposite the big arch wasn't he? In that direction. What did Tolar say when he came up? I did not hear him say anything. Did you hear anybody say anything at that time? I heard nobody, only Mr. Hardie and Wemyss telling the people to stand back. You say Tolar fired with his right hand? I think he did. He ran the pistol under his left side after he shot? Yes, sir. He had the pistol in his right hand then? Yes, sir. I understand you to say you saw Powers on the bench? That is the only time I remember seeing him sir.

Re-direct examination, by the Counsel for the prosecution:
Did you hear Captain Tolar say anything after he fired? I did not, sir. Did you hear any one say anything? I heard some one say he gloried in his spunk. Was that all you heard? That is all I heard. You remember hearing some one say he gloried in his spunk? Yes, sir. Whose spunk? They didn't call any names. Did they say "his spunk?" They said they gloried in the man's spunk that fired the pistol. That was all the remark he made? Yes, sir. You did not hear anything about its being a good shot? Yes, sir; I think some one said it was a very good shot. Who was that? I do not know sir.

On motion the Commission adjourned, to meet on Tuesday the 6th inst., at 11 A. M.

RALEIGH, N. C., August 6th, 1867, 11 A. M.

The Commission met pursuant to adjournment.

PRESENT.

Col. J. V. Bomford, 8th Infantry.
Brevet Lieut. Col. Thomas P. Johnson, Capt. A. Q. M. U. S. V.
2nd Lieut. C. E. Hargous, 40th Infantry.
2nd Lieut. Louis E, Granger 4th Infantry.
1st Lieut. R. Avery, 44th Infantry, Judge Advocate.

The Counsel for the prosecution; all the accused, and their Counsel.

ABSENT.

Capt. P. H. Remington, 8th Infantry.

The Judge Advocate read the following telegram :—

" HEADQUARTERS, 2nd Military District,
CHARLESTON, S. C., August 5, 1867,
It is expected that your Commission will sit daily, and that its session will commence as early, and continue as late as may be requisite for the promptest practicable dispatch of all business in readiness. Make daily reports of length of Session and causes of adjournment.
By command of General SICKLES
J. W. Clous.
Capt. A. A. A. G."

The Judge Advocate stated that the absence of Capt. Remington, was occasioned by sickness, whereupon, on motion, the Commission adjourned to meet on Wednesday, the 7th inst., at 11 o'clock A. M.

RALEIGH, N. C. Aug. 7, 1867, 11 A. M.

The Commission met pursuant to adjournment. Present.—All the members of the Commission, the Judge Advocate, the Counsel for the prosecution, all the accused and their Counsel.

The reading of the testimony taken on Monday the 5th instant was waived, there being no objection thereto.

The proceedings of Monday and Tuesday, the 5th and 6th insts., were then read and approved.

THOMAS JENKINS, a witness for the prosecution having been first duly sworn, testified as follows,

Examined by the Counsel for the prosecution .
What is your name? Thomas Jenkins. Where do you live? Fayetteville What is your business there? Carpenter, sir. How long have been living there? All my life. Did you know Archy Beebee? I did, sir. What name did he go by beside Beebee? Warden, sir. You remember the day he was killed. Not exactly, sir, it was sometime in February, sir. Do you remember what day of the week it was? Not exactly. Were you at the market house that day? Yes, sir. What time of day did

you go to the market house? Directly after breakfast, betwixt eight and nine o'clock. Were you there all day? Yes, sir. Did you see Archy when he was brought out of the guard house? Yes, sir. Where were you standing? I was standing near the corner? The south corner? The south corner. On the south face? On the east face, sir, between the south and east, so that I could look up and down the street both ways. Who came up from the guard house with Archy? Mr. Faircloth and Mr. Wemyss. Anybody else? Well, there was a good many others along with him but they were about all that had hold of him. Did you see him go up stairs? Yes, sir. Did you go up stairs? No, sir. Did you try? No, sir. How long was Archy up stairs? As nigh as I can recollect I don't think he was up there more than an hour. Was there any crowd there? Yes, sir, a good many people there. How many do you suppose? Not less than between one hundred and fifty and two hundred. Did the crowd grow larger while Archy was up stairs or less? No, sir, it remained about the same. Was any crowd in the market house? There was some in the market house. Any outside? Yes, sir. Which end of the market house was the crowd? The crowd appeared to be at the east end, sir. Who did you notice in that crowd that you knew while Archy was up stairs? I seed Mr. Phillips and Mr. Maultsby. Mention their first names? Sam. Phillips and John Maultsby, and Samuel Hall and Eddie Powers and Mr. Bond. Did you see him there while Archy was stairs? Yes, sir. He did not go up stairs with Archy? I don't know whether he went up or not—I saw him while he was up stairs. Did you see any of these prisoners? Yes, sir, I seed Mr. Tolar standing right at a bench inside of the market house. Which bench? A bench where Becky Ben sells. Did you see anything of Tom Powers or Monk? I don't know Tom Powers. Did you see Monk? Yes, sir. Did you see anything of Henry Sykes? I don't think I did. What was Mr. Tolar doing? He was standing leaning against the bench, with the shawl on him, sir. Where were those men, you speak of seeing? They were round about the market house, out and in, talking to one another. Who were they talking to? First to one and then to another; sometime they would be talking to Mr. Tolar and then again Monk would be talking to some of them and Mr. Maultsby would be talking to some of them; and Mr. Hall would be doing the same. Did you see any weapons in anybody's possession while Archy was up stairs? No, sir. Who was the first person that came down stairs? The first person that came down, that I seed was the lady and her mother. Any one with them? Mr Bond was with them; he come down and he:ped them in the carriage, then took hold of the horse, and held him off and the man drove them off. Did any one else speak to the ladies? Mr. Bob Mitchell, and Mr. Phil Taylor? Any one else? I don't exactly recollect whether there was or not; I don't recollect as I saw any one else. Did any one else go there? A good many were round about there; but I don't recollect exactly, to my remembrance who all did go to the carriage. When Archy came down stairs what happened—who was with him? Mr. Wemyss and Mr. Faircloth was at the time he came down. Which side was Wemyss on? On his right hand side. Mr. Faircloth was on the other side? Yes, sir. Where was sheriff Hardie? If I recollect the sheriff was right before him. What happened then? As he came out of where he was coming down the steps, I seed Monk make one or two wipes at him with his knife. That was before he got down the steps? Yes, sir. Did Monk say anything? He was cursing and going on mightily at that time. What was he saying? He was saying he wanted to cut the damned son of a bitch to pieces, and then at that time some persons pushed him off—and one of them pushed him out of the way, and they went on out to the big arch, and they turned down towards the guard house. You say Monk made at him while he was on the steps. Yes, sir. Did nothing else happen before he got into the big arch? Nothing else, except some one pushed him one side. They got out of the market house before any one else assaulted him? Yes, sir, and after they got through the arch to turn down towards the guard house, it appeared like some persons pushed against him, or said something to him, but I did not bear what they said, and it seemed like they were crowded up so, it appeared like some of them had fell down some way or other. Were you facing them? Yes, sir, right in front of Beebee, and then just as he raised up, Mr. Phillips was standing there against the market, between the market and the walk near the arch, and Mr. Tolar stepped up, and just as he raised up he shot him, right in the back part of his head. Do you know Mr. Tolar? Yes. sir; I know him when I see him. Did you know him then when you saw him? Yes, sir. What sort of a pistol did he use? I do not know exactly; it was a sort of a reddish pistol. What size was it? I don't know, sir; it appeared like it was seven or eight inches long, or something like that. Did you see the flash of the pistol? Yes, sir. The smoke? Yes. sir. Was it in Tolar's hand when you saw the flash and smoke? Yes, sir. Which hand? His right hand. How was Tolar dressed? He had on a pair of gray pantaloons, and a shawl over him, sir; I don't know what sort of a coat he had on. Do you know what sort of a hat he had on? I don't recollect exactly what sort of a hat. How close was he to Beebee when he fired? He was between four and five feet, sir. Was anybody between Tolar and Beebee when he fired? Mr. Phillips was to the right-hand of him. Did you see any of these other men that you spoke of, as talking, about the market house at that time? I saw them at the left hand. Who did you see? I saw John Maultsby. Anybody else? Mr. Nixon. Jim Nixon? Yes, sir. Any one else? No one else, but Monk at that time sir. Do you mean that Jim Nixon was at the left hand of Tolar, when he fired? Yes, sir. How close to him? Between five and six feet. Nobody between him and Tolar? Yes sir, there was some four or five right in a bunch together. How close was Maultsby to Tolar? Maultsby appeared to be about four feet from him. Anybody between him and Tolar? Well, not particularly, the crowd was standing near him. Can you say who was the nearest man to Mr. Tolar when he fired the pistol? The nearest man when he fired the pistol was Mr. Sam. Phillips. He was on the right hand? Yes, sir. Who was the nearest man on the left? John Maultsby, I think. Were there any colored men near him? I seed Simmons stand around there—Bob. Simmons. Was he pretty close to him? Yes, sir, he was in ten feet of him. Did you see any one else nearer him? There were several colored men. Chess. Gilmore was there. How close was he to him. About five feet sir. Any one else? That is all I recollect, particularly, there were others but I don't recollect who they were. There were other people there? Yes, sir. White men, or colored men? Both, sir. The crowd was pressing close together was it? Yes, sir. Did you see Archy Beebee fall, after the pistol was fired? Yes, sir. Did you see what became of Tolar after he fired? Yes, sir, he turned, and it appeared as if he either went under the arch, or to the north corner of the market house, and then the crowd got between us, and I lost sight of him. Did you see what he did with the pistol? No, sir, I did not, his hand dropped down and I did not see what became of it.

Cross examination by the Counsel for the accused:

What did you say the size of the crowd was that day Tom? It appeared to be, as near as I can guess, between one hundred and fifty and two hundred people. Both black and white? Yes, sir. Were there more blacks, or whites? I think there was more white people than colored. About what proportion of the crowd was blacks; one third, or one quarter? I reckon there were nearly fifty colored men. While Beebee was up stairs in the market house, did you notice anything unusual about the crowd? No, sir, nothing more than common; more than people just talking to one another. When you say you saw Captain Tolar, and Sam. Hall, and Ed. Powers, and others, talking under the market house, who were they talking to; or how were they talking? They were just talking like common,—talking no secret talk that I know of. Not whispering? No, sir; not in particular. Did you see any of them talking to other people? Yes, sir, I saw them talk to other people besides one another. So they were walking about, and talking, generally like all other persons? Yes, sir, Nothing unusual about that talking? Nothing that I heard, sir. You say when Beebee was brought down, that Wemyss was on his right hand? Yes, sir. And when he got down to the door, Faircloth, who was guarding the door, took hold of him on the left? Yes, sir. Did I understand you to say that Monk cut at him with his knife, while he was upon the stair steps? Yes, sir, before he got outside, sir. How many steps was Beebee off from the floor of the market when you first saw Monk cut at him with his knife? Well, he was some two steps, sir. When Monk cut at him did he get up on the steps? He was standing on the ground, and made the wipe at him as he was coming down. Was Monk to one side of the steps, or was he in front of the steps? He was one side. Which side? The left side of Beebee as he come down stairs, inside of Becky Ben's stall. You swear that Monk cut at him there? Yes, sir. Are you certain that was Monk? Yes, sir. You know him well? Yes, sir. And it was Monk and nobody else? Yes, siree. Did any one else cut at him after he got outside of the arch? Nobody that I seed. Did not you see everything that took place? As far as I seed I never saw any one else cut at him but Monk. How many times did you see Monk cut at him? I think seed him cut at him twice. Was Beebee on the steps when he cut at him both times? The fixamine he was; he had just got down on the What step, and he cut at him again, and then here one pushed him off. Did you see nobody cut it Bebee at all after he left the steps? No, sir. Then they carried Bebee out of the main eastern arch of the market house, and which way did they turn? Right down towards the guard house. Now, Tom, where were you standing at that time? I was standing right at the corner next to Mr.

Draughon's store. Were you on the pavement or off? Right on the top of the pavement. Were you nearer to the market house or nearer the edge of the pavement? I was nearer the market house—near the center of the pavement. How far down the pavement had Beebee got before he fell? About three feet from the corner, sir. How far was he off from you then? He was about four or five feet from me, sir. Were you immediately in front of him, or was he to your right? I was near even with the corner, sort of a little to one side. In front of him? Not exactly on the walk before him. A little to one side? Yes, sir. When he fell was there anybody between you and him? Mr. Wemyss was between me and him, and Mr. Faircloth was on the other side. Who helped him up? Mr. Wemyss had hold of him, sir, and as he went down on the right hand side Mr. Wemyss held on to him, and eased him down. Did you see anything of the Sheriff? Yes, sir, Sheriff Hardie was right before him, sir, sort of to the left hand. Certain of that, Tom? Yes, sir. That Hardie was to Beebee's front and left? Yes, sir, when he fell. Hardie was off towards the edge of the pavement? Yes, sir. Did Hardie have hold of him? No, sir, I don't think he did, no person had hold of him but Mr. Faircloth and Mr. Wemyss. You are certain Hardie did not have hold of him? No, sir, I don't think he had hold of him. How far off from Beebee was Hardie? I reckon he was between tween two and three feet, sir. So Hardie was two or three feet to Beebees front and left? Yes, sir. Near the edge of the pavement? Yes, sir. And did not have hold of him at all? No, sir. What did Beebee have around his neck that day, anything? I don't recollect what he had around the neck. Did he have anything around his neck? I do not know, sir, whether he had or not. Just now you said when he rose the nearest person you saw to Beebee was Sam Phillips? Yes, sir. The Counsel for the prosecution said he did not think the witness said that before—that Sam Phillips was the nearest person to Beebee; he does not understand the question.

The Counsel for the accused; I will ask the question again.

Cross-examination resumed:—

Which way were you looking at the time Beebee raised up? Towards Mr. Fishblate's store. Now who was the nearest man, except Mr. Wemyss, and Faircloth, and Hardie, who was the nearest man to Beebee at the time he was raised up? I think it was John Maultsby, sir. Looking as you were, north, which side of Beebee was he on? He was on the left hand side of him, sir. He was to the left of Beebee? Yes, sir. Do you mean your left or Beebee's left? Beebee's left. Was he on the pavement or off? He was on the out edge of the pavement. Was he on the pavement? Yes, sir, right on the edge of it. Who was the next nearest man that you saw? After he was killed? No, what man was next nearest to Beebee—you say Maultsby was nearest, at the time he was shot, what man was next nearest? I don't recollect more than Faircloth and Wemyss. I am not talking about them? The next nearest one was Mr. Phillips. Sam Phillips? Yes, sir. How far off from Beebee was Sam Phillips? He appeared to be about three feet, as nigh as I can recollect. Was he to Beebee's right, or was he to Beebee's left? He was to Beebee's right. Beebee, looking south, Phillips would have been to his right and rear? Yes, sir, next to the wall. How far was Phillips from the wall

Not more than six or eight inches, sir. Phillips was on the pavement? Yes, sir. You are not mistaken about that? No, sir, I am certain about it, for I was looking right at him. And you can't be mistaken? No, sir. What did Phillips have in his hand? I never seen him have anything in his hand, sir. Did he have anything or did he not? I never seen him have anything in the world, in his hand. Did he have anything in his hand that day? Not that I seed, sir. Neither before the shooting, at the time of the shooting nor after the shooting? No, sir: not that I know of. I ask you the question Tom, if at that time when Beebee was shot, Sam Phillips did not have a pistol in his hand? No, sir; I never seed him have nary one. I ask you if directly after he was shot, Sam Phillips have a pistol in his hand? I never seed him have a pistol all day. Where did you place Capt. Tolar, was he on the pavement or off? He was right on the pavement, sir. Was he nearer to the market house or nearer the outer edge of the pavement? Between the market house and the outer edge of the pavement. Was he on a straight line, back of Beebee? Yes, sir. So that if a line had been drawn from Beebee's feet, back parallel with the east front of the market house, that would have struck right between Tolar's feet? Yes, sir. You looked at it well? Yes, sir, You can't be mistaken? No, sir. Where did Tolar get that pistol from? I do not know, sir. Did you see him draw it? When I seed it, it was in his hands. How did he have it when you saw it; was it level? When I first saw it, it was right level, pointed right to Beebee. Are you sure that was a pistol Tolar had? Yes, sir. It was certainly a pistol? Yes, sir. What did you say was the length of it, Tom? As nigh as I can guess at it, it appeared between seven and eight inches. You saw it? Yes, sir. Do you not know that that pistol was twelve inches long? I don't know that it was sir. You are a carpenter?—Yes, sir. You are in the habit of judging of lengths and distances by your eye? Yes, sir. I ask you if you don't know that that pistol was twelve or fifteen inches long? No, sir. Was it or was it not that long? Well, as nigh as I can recollect, to the best of my judgement, I think it was between seven and eight inches, as nigh as I can come to it by guess. Won't you say it was twelve or fifteen inches long? It didn't appear to me like it was that long. Was it a single barrelled pistol? It was a single barrel what I seed him have. Was it what they call a revolver? Just a single-barrelled pistol as far as I seed it, sir. Could you tell whether it was a single barrelled pistol or a repeater? I could not tell, sir, because it was done so quick I did not examine it. Who were nearest the prisoner: were they white men or black men—that line of men that was pressing on? They were white and black altogether. Can you tell no other white men who were near, except John Maultsby, Sam. Phillips and Captain Tolar? Not that I can remember—there was others but I can't remember who they were. You say then John Maultsby was the nearest to Tolar, on his left hand side? Yes, sir. Are you certain of that? Yes, sir. How far was he off from Tolar, on the left hand side? It appeared as if he was between two and very nigh three feet, not over three feet at the outside. And nobody between him and Tolar? No, sir, not at time. What colored men did you say you saw about there? I seed Bob. Simmons there. Any other colored man? Chess Gilmore. Any other? I did not, particularly—I can't recollect who they were. How many persons did you say were between Tolar and Beebee when he fired? There was no persons between Tolar and Beebee at the time he fired. Nobody at all? No, sir. A clear, open space? Yes, sir. How far off from Beebee's head was the pistol at the time he fired? Well, I reckon it was between two and three feet, sir. As far as that? I reckon it was about as far as that from his head. And there was nobody between them? No, sir. Did you see Tolar when he came there? Yes, sir. How did he come? He just come right around through the crowd, with his shawl on him. Did you hear Tolar, when he came into the crowd, say, "make way, gentlemen"? No, sir; I never heard him say so. Didn't you see him push the crowd right and left? No, sir; I never seed it. Tom, I ask you the question, if there were not at least two men between Tolar and Beebee, and those men leaned, one to the right hand and the other to the left hand to let him get a fair shot? No, sir. As soon as Tolar shot, you say he just brought the pistol down to his right side? Yes, sir. Didn't he bring it to his left side? No, sir; he had it in his right hand all the time. Then he didn't put the pistol back under the shawl? No, sir. Did you see the pistol when he turned around? No, sir. How was Tolar's shawl fastened around him; was it pinned? I don't know whether it was fastened or not. Did it fall off? No, sir. Did any portion of it fall off? Not that I seed, sir. When he raised his arm to fire the pistol, didn't the corner of the shawl, which would have laid across his right arm—didn't that fall off? If it did I didn't see it. Do you know whether it did or not? It was on him all the time. When Tolar turned around to leave the crowd, did he turn to his right or left? He turned right around to his left. Turned to his left? Yes, sir. That brought his face down towards Camelton bridge? Towards Liberty Point. You are sure he turned around that way? Yes, sir. Don't you recollect when he turned around, that you saw him gather up his shawl and throw it back on him? No, sir; he did not; he just turned right around and walked right off. And made no motion with his shawl at all? No, sir. Didn't you see him throw his shawl in some face, as he turned around? When he turned around, the shawl was on him; it might have been pinned, and it might not, but I am certain it did not fall off while I saw it. Now, see if you can't remember, when Tolar turned round, that he threw his shawl into the man's face who was standing next to him on his left? No, sir. Is that so, or not? I can't remember that falling off at all. How do you say about it?—yes, or no—did he do it, or did he not—did he throw the shawl in the man's face, or did he not? He did not, sir. Did you see anything of John Armstrong there that day? No, sir; I didn't see him there that day at all; he might have been there. Do you know him? Yes, sir: I know him well; I have known him ever since the war—not before. Now, Tom, do you swear that John Armstrong is not the man that was standing close by Tolar's left, instead of John Maultsby? I am certain it was not the man, sir. Do you swear that when Tolar turned around he did not throw his shawl in John Armstrong's face, immediately on his Yes, sir. You swear to that? Yes, sir. care you swear John Armstrong was not close by lar? If he was I did not know him. If I seed him that day I did not know him; I was not much acquainted with him, no how—I didn't know much about him. Didn't you tell me you had known him ever since the close of the war? I have seen him, but I never was acquainted with him much. You knew him when you saw him? I knew him when I saw him, but I didn't know his name. Don't you know his name now? I know what people call him. That man who is called John Armstrong—did you see Capt. Tolar throw his shawl into his face that day? No, sir, I did not. Didn't he do it? No, sir, he did not. Are you certain of that? I am certain he did not do it. Didn't you see him throw one end of it in Armstrong's face? No, sir. He didn't do that? No, sir. What was the color of this shawl? It was a kind of grey looking shawl? You took notice of it enough to tell the color? Yes, sir. You say that Tolar turned round and went towards the market house? Yes, sir. Which way did he go after he passed through the market house? I dont't know, sir, I lost sight of him after that. The crowd got so thick I lost sight of him. I was looking at Beebee lying there at that time. Did Tolar stop at all after he turned off? I never seed him stop at all. Did you see whether he stopped at all? No, sir, he didn't stop at all. If he stopped, he stopped on the other side of the market house. Didn't you see him stop near the pillar of the arch? No, sir, he never stopped half a minute. Did he stop there at all? No, sir, he never stopped there at all. You are certain of that? Yes, sir.

Questioned by the Commission :
When you saw Tolar, and the others that you mentioned, talking under the market house, and before Beebee came down stairs, could you hear them talking? No, sir, I never heard what they said. Could you hear the sound of their voices? No, sir.

Edward Brown, a witness for the prosecution, having been first duly sworn, testified as follows:
Examined by the Counsel for the prosecution.
What is your name? Edward Brown. Has any one talked to you about your testimony since you were at my office? No, sir. None at all? Some of them asked me what I come here for and I told them I was subpoenaed here as a witness. Who asked you that? Some of the witnesses. Who were they? Some men that came last week, Mr. James McNeill for one. Who else? Mr. Nixon. What did Mr. Nixon ask you? He asked me what brought me here. What else did he ask you? He asked me how his brother was coming on. Is that all? That was about all. I don't ask you if it was about all, I asked you if it was all? That is all he asked me. How long were you with Mr. Nixon? It was at dinner; we sat down in the back part of Mr. Parker's Hotel after dinner. How long were you sitting there? Some fifteen or twenty minutes. Did you talk about this trial? No, sir. It was not mentioned? No, sir.

The Counsel for the prosecution said he would tender the witness to the Counsel for the accused, preferring not to examine him.
The Counsel for the accused declined to examine him.

CHELS GILMORE, a witness for the prosecution, having been duly sworn, testified as follows:
Examined by the Counsel for the prosecution.
What is your name? Chels Gilmore. Where do you live? Fayetteville. What is your business there? Boating, pretty much. When did you reach Raleigh? This morning, sir. Did you know Archy Beebee? Yes sir; me and him worked together. What names did he go by? Generally went by Archy War-

den—Mr. Warden used to own him. Do you remember what time he was killed? I don't recollect what day of the month, but I recollect he was killed on Monday? What time of the year was it? I ain't got no recollection of that, sir. Since Christmas? Yes, sir. Where was he killed? At the market house. What town? Fayetteville. Were you there? Yes, sir. Were you there when he was brought out of the guard house? When I got there he was up stairs. How long were you there before Archy came down stairs? I reckon an hour. Where were you standing? On the south side of the market house, as you go to the guard house, standing back near a little tree, near the corner, twixt the corner and the wall. Were you on the pavement? Yes, sir. Which way were you facing? Towards the market house. On the south face near the corner, facing towards the market house? Yes, sir. Who was standing there with you? There was this Jim Douglass pretty close by me. Did you see any one else that you knew? I saw more, but I can't recollect them all. Did you see Tom Jenkins? Yes, sir; and Calvin Johnson was there, and this McNeill fellow was there. Was there any crowd at the market house? There was about a hundred men there that day. Where were they standing; in front of the market house? Yes, sir. Outside too? Some were outside. Which end of the market house? The south end. Which street does the south end front on? I was standing on the south corner of the market house. You say this crowd was at the south end? Yes, sir. What street runs into the south end of the market house? It is called Mollit street. Which street runs down towards Liberty Point? That is Front street. That is the side they were standing on? Yes, sir. Was this crowd around the same end of the market house that they came out of? Yes, sir. You think it was the south end? Yes, sir. Was it the end towards the river. Yes, sir. Were you standing where you could see inside of the market house? Yes, sir. In looking in, which arch did you look through? One of the little arches. Was it the little arch right by the steps, that you looked through? Yes, sir. Who did you see in that crowd that you knew that day? Mr. Maultsby was there, and Mr. Phillips. What Maultsby? John. What Phillips? Sam. Who else? I saw Mr. Tolar there; I saw Sam Hall. Who else. I saw Mr. Ralph Lutterloh and I saw Mr. Sykes there. Did you see Mr. Tom Powers there? Yes, sir; I saw him there. Did you see anything of Monk? Yes, sir, I saw Monk; I saw Mr. Nixon—Mr. Nixon knocked Monk off. I am talking now about while Archy was up stairs—I understand you to say you saw Sam Hall, Ralph Lutterloh and Mr. Sykes, Tolar and Tom Powers? Yes, sir. Did you see anything of Monk? Yes, sir; he was there. Did you see Maultsby there? I saw him there. Where were these men standing when you saw them? They were all standing under the market house; all collected together. I mean all those men that you named? Some were under the market house and some on the pavement. Were they standing together? They were pretty thick. Were those men all together or scattered through the crowd? Scattered through the crowd. What were they doing? Standing up and talking. Where was Mr. Tolar standing? He was standing in the crowd with them. What part of the crowd? He was standing next to the pavement. Do you remember all these things you are telling me? Yes, sir. You remember the positions of these men? Yes, sir. Mr. Tolar was standing next the pavement, you say? Yes, sir. In the arch? Yes, sir. In the big arch? Yes, sir. That was while Archy was up stairs? Yes, sir. You mean he was standing underneath the market house, on the outside? Standing under the shed part. Do you mean to say he was standing right in the opening of the arch? Yes, sir. Did you see any weapons in the hands of any one? No, sir. Not while Archy was up stairs? No, sir. Did you see Miss Massey and her mother when they came down stairs? Yes, sir. Who came with them? Mr. Vaun. Any one else? Not that I know of; I disremember; Mr. Maultsby stood talking to them after they got into the carriage. Did Mr. Bond leave the carriage before Mr. Maultsby went up to them? No, sir, he did not. Did any one else go to the carriage and talk to the ladies? No, sir. You say you didn't see any one else go to the carriage? No, sir. What became of Bond when the carriage drove off? He went back up stairs, I believe sir: for the prisoner had not come down yet. I understood you to say that no one else went to the carriage to speak to these ladies but Bond and Maultsby? No, sir I didn't see any one else go there. Did you see anybody else go there? Not positively; but I didn't notice any body. Are you certain you didn't notice any body? I am certain. You say Mr. Bond went up stairs? Yes, sir. What became of Maultsby? He stepped out of the crowd; I could not see him; he went back under the market house. Did he go right straight from the carriage, under the market house? Yes, sir. Did you hear any noise from any quarter at that time, before Archy came down? No, sir. You didn't hear a word or threat? No, sir. Did you see any weapons? No, sir. Was the crowd pretty still and quiet? Very quiet, sir. Were they walking about much, or standing still? Stirring about, talking pretty low to one another. And you saw Archy, as he came out of the door coming down the steps? Yes, sir. Who was with him? Mr. Wemyss had him. Who else was with him? I believe Mr. Faircloth—I don't know what man it was behind him. You say Mr. Wemyss was on which side? On the left side. On Archy's left side? Yes, sir. You say he was on his left side? Yes, sir, he had hold of his left hand—he had a string on his thumb, leading him down. Wemyss had a string on his hand and was standing on his left side? Yes, sir. Where was Faircloth? He was walking along behind him I think. Did you see Sheriff Hardie there? I don't recollect seeing him at all—he might have been there. Did you see any other officers around. No sir, I don't recollect seeing any others but them two. Do you say there were any other officers? Not that I know of—I just tell what I saw. I want you to tell me whether you saw any more officers? I don't recollect. If there had been any there could you have seen them? I might have seen them and not noticed them. You don't remember noticing the Sheriff? No, sir. You don't remember then, any other officers? I just noticed those that were walking with the prisoner as he came down the steps. You can't say whether there were any others or not? I can't say, sir. What became of the prisoner Beebee when they started to go out to turn the corner—what became of him before they turned the corner? They turned down the steps, and when they turned the corner to go to the carriage— Do you mean when they were coming out of the stall, or when they coming out of the arch? Coming out of the stall. Well, what happened? Some one says "shoot him," and some one says

"cut him," and some one says "knock him down," and they made at him, and the officers at them with their clubs. Who were these people? They were so thick I could not tell. You can't tell any man who was in that rush? No, sir, they was the same as a bunch of bees. But there is a difference between bees and men, because men are bigger, and they are not so much alike? But it is a hard matter to tell, as thick as they were. You say you can't tell a single soul who was in that rush? No, sir, I know some one said "rally up boys," but I can't tell who it was. You heard the expressions, "rally up boys," "cut him," "knock him down," "shoot him?" Yes, sir. And you can't tell who used them? No, sir. And you don't know who was in that crowd? No, sir. Very well, what happened then? They run up, and they were knocking at him, and were cutting at him with the sticks. You mean some one was knocking at him with the sticks? Yes, sir, I could not see him, but they were cutting at him, and the officers was knocking them off. Who had the sticks; the men who were after Archy or the men who were protecting him? The men who were protecting him; the prisoner tried to keep his head under the officer's arms, trying to keep them from hitting him; the officers were knocking at them; the officer fell right back on the pavement, and the prisoner fell on his stomach; the officer was walking backward to keep off the crowd. The officer was walking backward keeping off the crowd with his stick? Yes, sir. What were the crowd trying to do? They must have been trying to kill him. Did you see any weapons? No, sir. Did you see any knives? No, sir. Did you see any pistol then? Yes, sir. At that time? Yes, sir. Before Archy fell, who had the pistol? Mr. Phillips had the pistol. Was he in the crowd? Yes, sir. Was he pressing on with the others? I saw him standing up with his pistol in his hand. You recognized one man in the crowd then? Yes, sir. That was Sam Phillips? Yes, sir. And you recognized nobody else who was in that crowd? No, sir. How came you to recognize him? I was standing pretty close to him. You told me just now you could not tell me a single man who was in that crowd? I had not started that, yet. Just at this point you recognized one man in the crowd? Yes sir. You can't tell me of any body else who was in that crowd that was pressing on the prisoner at the time he fell down? Well, they were mixed up, and I could not tell any one of them. Just take your time about it? Well, Mr. Sykes, and Mr. Lutterloh's son, and Mr. Sam Hall, and a fellow by the name of Tom, I can't call his name now. You say at the time you saw Mr. Phillips you saw these other men; repeat those names again. Sam. Hall, Mr. Sykes, and Mr. Lutterloh's son; they were all three all there; and Monk Julia. You did not see Tom Powers? No, sir. You did not see Mr. Tolar? Yes, sir, I saw Mr. Tolar and Sam. Phillips both. Did you say you saw Tom Powers? No, sir. Do you know him? No, sir. You don't know whether you saw him or not? No, sir, I am not acquainted with him. Now did I understand you to say you saw all these men that you have now spoken of, before Archy Beebee fell down the first time? Yes, sir. After they turned the arch of the market house and were going out? Yes, sir. Where were you standing at that moment? I was standing at this little tree on the pavement. Under the row of trees that run along the edge of the pavement? No, sir, there was but one little green tree there then, they have set out some since this happened. How near is that to the exact corner of the street? It is a little way betwixt the two arches. (Witness is shown a chart of the market house, and represents his position as being on the pavement with his back against the tree, in front of the big arch.) You were standing there when Archy fell? Yes, sir. Did you stand there until Archy was shot? Yes, sir. What happened after Archy fell down? The officer got on his hat. Wait a moment; what kind of a pistol did Phillips have? I could not see much of it, but I saw it in his hand. Was it a big pistol? It was. Was it painted sky blue? I think it was; I ain't certain; I can't tell. You think it was painted sky blue? It might have been, a good many is. That is a common color for pistols? Yes sir, it is a common color. You can't tell whether it was a big one or a little one. No, sir, because I didn't see it at all. Can't you see anything around here that is the same color as that pistol? If a man has anything in his hand holding it in his hand, you cannot tell how large and how much of it is behind his hand. But you can tell what color it is? I can't recollect whether it was a white barrel or blue barrel. You mean a bright shining barrel or a blue one? Yes, sir. You can't say how big that pistol was? No, sir. Which part did you see, the barrel or the stock? The muzzle. How long was the muzzle that you saw? (Represents about the length of his finger from the second joint.) Was that all of the barrel? I cannot tell. You just saw the end of the muzzle of the pistol in his hand? Yes, sir. How was he holding it? (Represents in his right hand the palm of his hand down and at his right side.) Was he cocking it? No, sir. What was he doing? He was looking at the crowd. Was he rushing on with the crowd? No, sir, he was standing right still. The rest of these men were pressing on the prisoner? Yes, sir. After Archy got up you saw him put on his hat; what sort of a hat was that? I don't know, sir, what sort of a hat it was, that fell off when he fell down. Did he have on a different hat after he got up than before he fell? No, sir. What happened after the officer put his hat on? He stood up and said, "gentlemen I want you to stand back; I had orders to carry the prisoner to the guard house," says he "I am going to carry him." Who was that officer? Mr. Wemyss, and in the meantime he was standing up and talking and shaking his stick at them, and after he put his hat on, Mr. Tolar pushed Jim Douglass to one side and he came in pretty close and he put his right hand under his shawl, and he walked up right to the row of men that was standing next to the prisoner, and he came up behind him with his shawl on, and drew his hand right this way, (witness represents Tolar holding the pistol in his right hand presented toward Bebce,) and the shawl sort of dragged off of his shoulder, and he turned and walked right up to the market house. Did you know Mr. Tolar? Yes, sir. Was he the man that fired the pistol? Yes, sir; Sam. Phillips never fired the pistol. Didn't you see Sam. Phillips fire the pistol? No, sir. Do you know Captain Tolar? Yes, sir. You know him well? Yes, sir. How close were you to him when he fired? About two steps from him. Where did he come from when he come up there and put in his pistol and fired it? He come along up from the crowd; from the market house. Did he come out near you? Yes, sir. Did he pass in front of you? Yes, sir. Further down south than you? Yes, sir. Was

he standing off the pavement or on the pavement? About the middle of the pavement, sir. And you saw him put his hand on Jim. Douglass, and pull him out of the way? Yes, sir. Did he walk through the crowd slowly or rapidly? Pretty slowly. Did he say anything? Never said a word. You say he didn't, or you didn't hear him? I didn't hear him. What did he do with the pistol after he fired? Stuck it under his shawl on his left side and walked off. It ain't possible for you to be mistaken about these things? No, sir; I was looking at the man with my natural eyes; I ain't going to tell any more than I know; I didn't come here to tell lies. Have you talked to Sam. Phillips since you have been here, at all? No, sir; I never seed him. You just got here this morning? Yes, sir; I ain't seed none of them that come from Fayetteville. Did you see any colored men standing close to Tolar when he fired? Yes, sir. Who were they? Jim McNeill was there, and Jim Douglass, and Calvin Johnson, and this here John Armstrong, Did you see him? Yes, sir; soon after the pistol was fired I saw him. Where was he standing when saw you him? He was coming nigher to see the prisoner; I don't know how long he had been there. What became of Phillips after you saw him with his pistol in his hand? He walked up toward the crowd and I never saw him any more until I saw him at his store. You saw him just about the time Archy fell first? Yes, sir; I did. And you never saw him afterwards until after the whole skirmish was over? No, sir. The pistol that you saw him have, and the pistol that you saw Tolar have,—were there the only pistols that you saw that day? They were the only ones. You have told me what colored men were standing nearest to Captain Tolar; now, what white men were standing close about him, in front of him, to the right of him, or left, or behind? I told you a little while ago who were rushing on him. Were they still pressing on him when he fired? No, sir; every man was standing right still. The rush had stopped had it. Yes, sir; the rush had stopped after he fell down. You mean that these young men that you spoke of before were all standing about there? They were all standing about there, sir. Who was the nearest man to Tolar that you saw about there? I can't say, because they were all mixed up so; one might be here now, and directly another and again the same man again. I want to know what set of men there were grouped that were so close to Tolar? I could not tell, sir. I want you to tell me who you saw at the same time you saw Tolar shoot, near him, what white men? I was busy looking at the prisoner; it frightened me and I can't re collect. Didn't you tell me that just before the prisoner fell you saw in this rush upon him, Sam Hall, Ralph Lutterloh and John Maultsby? They were all there and they all rushed together, and I could not tell who were who. I ask you if you didn't tell me in the previous part of this examination that when the rush was made on the prisoner, you saw in the rush Sam Hall, John Maultsby and certain other persons that you named? I said there was Sam Hall and Sykes and Ralph Lutterloh; I told you they were there. Did you name any others? I believe not. Do you remember any others now? No, sir. Now you say they were there just before the prisoner fell down, do you? Yes, sir. Were they in that crowd that was rushing on to the prisoner? They were all together. Were they in the party? Yes, sir. How close were they to the prisoner when you saw him? About three feet. The whole crowd do you mean? Yes, sir.

What became of the men that were concerned in it; they turned and ran down Person street didn't they? They stood right still. They stood right in their tracks as though they were petrified? Yes, sir, remained standing right still. Did you see whether they were standing still there after the pistol was fired? After the pistol fired, every body poured up to see. and I could not tell whether they did it or not. Did you see where Archy Beebee was shot: did you go up to him? Yes, sir. Did you see any thing of Monk after he was shot? I saw Monk and Mr. Nixon, when he was shot. Did you see anything of him after he was shot? I saw Monk try to cut him, and Mr. Nixon fling him off. What did Monk say? He said, "I want to cut his damned thoat." Did he go very close to him? Yes, sir. Did he have any weapons? I could not tell whether he had a knife out or not; I saw Mr. Nixon fired it. Now you say, after Tolar fired he returned his pistol under his arm? Yes. sir. He fired it with his right hand, did he? Yes, sir. And he put it under the left arm. Yes, sir. How was Tolar dressed that day? I didn't notice, he had his shawl on. Did you notice what sort of a hat he had on? A black hat, I don't know what sort. You didn't notice what sort of clothes? No, sir. Did you see anything about the shawl falling off of his shoulder? The shawl sort of dropped down as he put out his pistol and fired. Do you mean that it dropped off when he pulled his pistol out, and fired? After he fired. Which shoulder did it drop off of? Off the left one. When he put his pistol back, was it? Yes, sir. What did he do? He sort of flung it up on his shoulder. Are you sure he put that pistol in there? Yes, sir, I was looking at him with my natural eyes, I was there within two steps of him. Do you wear spectacles? No, sir. Don't you usually look with your naked eyes? Yes, sir. I thought, perhaps you sometimes wore glasses? No, sir. This shawl fell off of his shoulder? Yes, sir. What makes you think he put the pistol up there? I saw him when he come up; he didn't look like he had anything, and he put his hand under his shawl—I didn't know what he was going to do until the pistol was fired and he slipped it back. Did you see him take his hand out? Yes, sir. After he had put the pistol in? Yes, sir, if there had been two pistols, or three, fired I could not have told who shot him, but there was not—there was not but one pistol fired and everybody was standing right still when he was firing. There was not but one pistol? No, sir. You say you were standing with your back against that tree—didn't the crowd push you away from from the tree? No, sir. Did it push against you? Yes, sir, but I never moved. Did you have any weapons that day? No sir, after he was shot I said I wished I hadn't been there amongst it. Did you hear anybody cry out, in the crowd saying, he had shot him, or anything of that sort? I never heard anybody say he shot him, without it was Jim Douglass—. Wait a moment—you hadn't any right to tell what any body has told you since; I want to know whether any body cried out in the crowd while Tolar was still in the crowd? No, sir. You didn't hear any body say Captain Tolar shot him, or any thing of that sort? I heard it a few minutes after that, but not at the time. Had Captain Tolar gone away? Yes, sir. Was it after he turned off? I heard it a few minutes after he was gone. You say you do not know Tom Powers. No, sir.

Cross examination by the Counsel, for the prosecution.

Chels, you have been fireman on a steamboat for a long time? Yes, sir. You were blown up once? Yes, sir. You say you were standing just opposite the main arch, against that tree? Yes, sir. How large a crowd did you say there was there that day? I reckon about a hundred. Were they all white or mixed? Mixed up. More white than black? More white ones than black. You saw Beebee when he came down? Yes, sir. And Mr. Wemyss was upon his left hand? Yes, sir. Is that what you say? Yes, sir. You are certain of that, Chels, that Mr. Wemyss was on his left hand? I think he was—I won't say for certain When they came down the steps, was Mr. Wemyss nearer to the Market house, or was he nearer down towards the wall? He came down on the right hand side. Whose right hand side, yours or Beebee's? Beebee's right hand side. And how came he to manage to have that thumb twitch around Beebee's left thumb, if Wemyss was on Beebee's right hand? I didn't say he had it around his left thumb. You say now he had it on his right thumb? He was on his right side; of course he had it on his right thumb? So he had that string on Beebee's right thumb? Yes, sir ; he had his club in his right hand. (witness explains, standing by the Counsel for the prosecution, his position in reference to Mr. Wemyss. Mr. Wemyss being on the right hand side, and Beebee on the left.) Which side was Faircloth on? He came walking along down sort of behind him.— Now, after they got down to the floor of the market house then which side was Wemyss on; when they came down the stall? They came like as if they came down the steps. Where was Faircloth walking? Right behind him. Did Faircloth have hold of him? No, sir; I didn't see him hold of him then. Now, Chels, did he have hold of him or not? Well, he may have had hold of him, but he was coming down pretty close behind him; I could not tell—he may have had his hand hold of him and may not; there was a parcel of men before him and Mr. Wemyss had him, and I could not tell whether Faircloth had or not. Where was Hardie, the Sheriff, at the guard house or Phil. Taylor's corner? I don't recollect of seeing him at all; Hardie wasn't there with the rest. You know one way or the other; was he there or not? I never recollect seeing him there. What do you swear; that he was there or that he was not there? I can't answer that question. You say before Archy came down that Bond came down? Yes, sir. And Bond you say. gallanted the ladies out to the carriage? Yes, sir. Where was that carriage standing? It was standing as you go from the river, right in front of the market house. How far was that carriage from you? About as far as from me to that table. (About twenty-five feet.) Who was driving that carriage? A colored man, but I didn't know him. Did you look at him? I didn't notice him; I sort of noticed the lady—where she was scratched on the neck there—I never noticed the black man. How long did Mr. Bond stay at the carriage after the ladies were helped in? I saw him standing talking to them; I could not hear what they said; then he wheeled right off and went back up stairs. Was anybody else at the carriage during the time that Bond was standing there talking with them? I don't know, sir; Mr. Maultsby's son went there and talked with him Did Maultsby's son go before Bond left or after? He left directly after Mr. Bond left. He was there while Bond was there? Yes, sir. Which left first?—Bond or Maultsby? Mr. Bond came away first. Did anybody else go to the carriage? I didn't see anybody else. Did anybody go or not? I didn't see them. You saw nobody else around the carriage at all? No, sir. Who held the horses off? I don't know —I didn't notice them then. Which way did the carriage go? It went down the street. Down towards Mr. Mitchell's, or down towards Liberty Point, or over towards the guard-house, or where? It turned right down the street, and I heard them coming down the steps; I was trying to see whether they come down with the prisoner, and I never noticed which way it went. Where was the prisoner when you first saw him? Coming down the steps. Was anything done to the prisoner at all until after he cleared the market house,—until after he got out from under the arch, —did anybody do anything to him? No, sir— at the time the prisoner came down,—you know there was a stall there,—about the time he got to the corner of the brick wall they rushed on him, and the officers were knocking at them, and that is the time he fell down. Nobody made a rush at him until he got just under the arch upon the pavement? Yes, sir, just as he was coming out some one said "rally up, boys." And, at that time, Beebee was right under the arch going out? Yes, sir. Then the crowd rushed upon him? Yes, sir. As soon as they did, Beebee fell? Yes, sir. How far was Beebee off from the arch at the time he fell? About the middle of the pavement. Just opposite the big arch? Yes, sir. You were standing there, you say, opposite the big arch, and Beebee fell just opposite you? Yes, sir. And opposite the big arch? Yes, sir. That was where Beebee fell? Yes, sir. And as soon as they drew him up, who put the hat on his head? The officer fell down on his back and the prisoner on top of him; the officer picked up his hat; I don't recollect, I think the prisoner, though, when he was shot, was bareheaded; I don't know whether his hat was on the pavement or not, but I saw the officer pick up his. What officer was that? That was Mr. Wemyss. And you saw nothing of the Sheriff? No, sir— when he was shot, nobody had hold of him but Wemyss. Just as soon as he got up from that fall he was shot? Yes, sir. He was shot opposite the centre of the main large arch? Yes, sir. He was right opposite to you? He was, sir. Then you say at that time the crowd was rushing upon him? No, sir; when he was shot every man was standing still. Now, while that crowd was rushing on him, before he was shot, I ask you if Mr. Sam. Hall rushed upon him? I said he was there; I could not tell whether he was rushing or not. I ask you if Mr. Ralph Lutterloh rushed upon him? They were all there; I could not tell who was rushing. You saw the crowd rush, and, although you name these persons, Sam. Hall, Ed. Powers, Ralph Lutterloh and others, you don't undertake to swear and you do not wish the Court to understand you to swear, that they rushed upon him? No, sir, I do not, I would not want to tell any more than I know, sir. I could not tell whether they were rushing upon him—they were mixed in such a manner. Now, Chels, recollect, take your time and think about it, did you see Mr. Hall and Ralph Lutterloh and Ed. Powers and Sykes—did you see them after Beebee came down—I mean after Beebee got down? Yes, sir. You are certain you saw them? Yes, sir. You kept your position against the tree, with your face looking into the market house? Yes, sir. Tolar, you say, came out of the market house? Yes, sir. Out of that east arch? When I saw him he was coming right along the pavement amongst the crowd, with his hand under his shawl? Which side of Tolar was James Douglass on at the time Tolar shoved him? He was next to the market house? Jeems was right on his right hand side? Yes, sir, I was on Tolar's left hand side. And Tolar shoved Jeems off? Yes, sir, like anybody wanting to get through. Now, Chels, at that time you say, when Tolar was coming up and shoved Jeems off, he had his right hand under his shawl? Yes, sir. Which hand did he shove Jeems off with? He shoved him off with the left hand. Did he take his left hand and push him off towards the right side? Yes, sir. And that pushed Jeems almost up against the market house? Yes, sir. He put his hand on Jeems' arm and pushed him off? Yes, sir.

(Witness illustrates the position of Tolar and Douglass—Tolar on the right of Douglass coming through the crowd and placing his left hand on Douglass' elbow pushing him to the right.)

You and Jeems have been talking about it since that time? No, sir, we did not talk about it since the day of the frolic,—I mean the day it occurred. You and Jeems had a talk about it? No, sir. No talk at all about it? No, sir. You say Tolar came up, and had his right hand under his shawl? Yes, sir. You saw that? Yes, sir. You saw him draw the pistol out? Yes, sir. At the time he drew the pistol out, how high did he have it—as high as his eye? I cannot tell. Don't you know Tolar was stooping down to shoot? No, sir. Was he standing up straight? Sort of leaning a little. Did you see the smoke from the pistol? I saw the smoke, because I was in two steps of him. There was but one pistol fired and I was in two steps of him, and if I could not see the smoke, I haint got no eyes. What sort of a pistol was that Tolar fired; was that a white pistol, or a sky blue pistol? I could not tell. Do you know whether it was a green pistol? I could not tell. You can't tell what sort of a pistol it was? He shot it so quick, I could not tell. How large a pistol was it? I could not tell. Was it as long as my arm? No, sir, if it had been that long everybody would have seen it. Was it as long as my hand? I cannot tell. What is your best impression about it? that it was a long pistol or a short one? I don't want to say, unless I can give some idea. You won't say whether it was a long pistol or a short pistol? No, sir. You are sure it was a pistol? Yes, sir. Was it a single barrel pistol, or was it a revolving pistol? I could not tell that. If I could tell that, I could tell what sort it was. Tolar shot him, and when he shot him or when he drew the pistol to shoot him the shawl fell off of his shoulder? Yes, sir. And he put his pistol back under his left side? Yes, sir. Did he slip it inside of his vest, or just under his shawl? I could not tell, when a man has a shawl on, you could not tell whether he put it under his vest or not. Don't you know that as soon as he fired the pistol he just brought it down to his right side? No, sir, he did not. You swear he did not? I will swear till I drop dead he did not. How far was Tolar from Beebee at the time he fired? About four steps from him. Was Tolar directly behind him? Yes, sir. I mean when Beebee was shot, was he in the center of the pavement, or nearer the market house? About the center of the pavement. When Tolar was he in the center of the pavement? Yes, sir. How far were you off from Tolar at the time he shot? About two steps from him, sir. On his left? Yes, sir. Anybody between you and Tolar? There was some one standing there, I was busy watching him, I did not notice who he was. Was he a white man? Yes, sir. You are certain it was a white man? Yes, sir. Don't you know it was a colored man? No, sir. Don't you know it was a mulatto man? No, sir, it was a white man. Do you know John Armstrong? Yes, sir. Don't you know that was John Armstrong? No, sir, I can tell a white man's face from John Armstrong's. It was not John at all? No, sir. You say you saw Sam. Phillips with a pistol? Yes, sir. Was he on the pavement or off? On the pavement, about five steps from where Mr. Tolar shot, I looked around after he shot and saw him standing there. You saw him with a pistol before Beebee was shot? Yes, sir, I saw him have it in his hand before that. When you first saw him have it in his hand was he nearer to Beebee than Tolar was, or was he further off? He was away back behind Mr. Tolar. Was there a good thick crowd between you and Sam? Not such a big crowd but what I could see him. You say Sam Phillips did not shoot? No, sir, he didn't. You are certain? I would swear till I hung dead by the neck, that Sam Phillips did not fire the pistol, sir. How happened it you spoke up so quick, and said you knew Sam Phillips did not shoot him? I didn't say that. When the Counsel for the prosecution examined you, I understood you to say you knew Sam Phillips did not shoot him, how came you to say that? Because if I am looking at you, and see another man do a thing, and you don't do it—and that is the reason I say he didn't do it. Who has been talking to you since you have come up here about your testimony? I come right from home to-day, and nobody has been talking to me. Not before you come here? No, sir. I mean before you started from home; who has been talking with you and fixing your testimony? Nobody at all, sir. Haven't you talked to anybody about this matter since the shooting occurred? No, sir, not a soul. Never mentioned it to anybody? No, sir. You never told anybody before that you saw Captain Tolar shoot the man? Yes, sir. Who did you tell? John Martin. Which John? Little John. How long since you told John about it? I told him when it was first done, on Tuesday I went to the boat, and he said "nobody can't tell who shot him," and I said "Mr. Tolar shot him;" I told Mr. Dodd so too. And you told little John Martin? Yes, sir, and I told Mr. Dodd so, no longer than last week. As soon as Tolar shot the pistol, he turned around and flirted his shawl up,—didn't you see him take the end of his shawl, that was hanging over the right shoulder and throw it back on his shoulder? No, sir. Don't you know that when Tolar turned round, after firing the pistol, that he threw the right end of his shawl into the face of the man, that was standing on his left hand? No, sir. Didn't you see him throw the right end of the shawl into John Armstrong's face when he turned off? I didn't see that. Didn't he do it? I don't say, because I don't know. Didn't he throw the end of the shawl into the face of the nearest man to him, when he turned off? No, sir; because the shawl was not flirted at all, the shawl was hanging over the left arm when he shot, and the end of it didn't get off; and he first threw it right back. Where did Tolar go? He went like he was going to walk around the corner, and I never saw him no more. So Tolar turned and went towards the market house? Yes, sir. He didn't go through the market house? No sir. But he

did make to go around the corner? Yes sir. That is the north east corner? Up towards Mr. Fishblate's store. And you saw Tolar, as soon as he fired, turn around and go toward the north east corner of the market house? Yes, sir. And you swear he didn't go through the market house? Yes, sir. Don't you know, Chels, that when he turned off he went right straight through the market house, through that big arch? No, sir. He didn't do that? No, sir. You swear to that? Yes, sir.

Re-direct Examination by the Counsel for the prosecution:

Do you ever drink anything? Hardly ever. You haven't taken anything to drink to day? No, sir; I hardly ever drink; I have been a fireman some fifteen years, and I have a heap of responsibility on myself, and I never drink; I have not drunk to day, nor for a week, nor for a week before that. Do you say Beebee fell in front of the arch? Yes, sir. You say he fell right in front of the big arch? Yes, sir. He was right at your feet when he fell? Yes, sir, he was within two steps of me when he was shot. Mr. Wemyss and the officers did not let him fall they just let him down. Anybody who knows where the tree is I was standing by will know I was close. The tree is about the middle of the arch? Yes, sir. After Archy fell was he on your right hand or left hand? On my right hand. And you were standing near that little tree in front of the arch? Yes, sir. The main arch? Yes, sir. You say you have not talked to anybody about this business? No, sir. Except your telling Mr. Dodd that you knew who it was—did'n't you have a talk with the Judge Advocate this morning? Yes, sir. You didn't mention that? No, sir. You have had a talk about what your testimony would be since you have been here, then, haven't you? No, sir, not before I gave it in here to you. I mean before you came here? I talked to that man. (The Judge Advocate.) Did you ever hear that Sam. Phillips was suspected of having shot this pistol, before you come in here to-day? No, sir. Didn't you ever hear anybody say they were trying to put it off on Sam. Phillips? Yes, sir, I heard Mr. Dodd said so. I want to know, generally, whether you have ever heard it; I don't want to know who told you, but have you heard from any quarter that they were trying to put it on Sam. Phillips? No, sir. Did the gentleman who was examining you here this morning, say anything about Sam. Phillips? He asked me who all were there, and I told him what names I could recollect. I ask you if he said anything about Sam Phillips? I told him Phillips was there. Did he ask you if Phillips fired the pistol? I told who was there, and he axed me who fired the pistol? I don't know what he axed me about that time, but he axed me who were there, and I told him all who were, as nigh as I could recollect. What I want to know is, why, when I was examining you first, why you said so quickly "you know Sam. Phillips did not do it," what was it set your mind that way. Because I saw he didn't do it and everybody was standing still. You didn't see him do it—now why didn't you say I know Mr. Hardie didn't do it? I seed him with my own eyes. Why did you select one particular man out, and say you knew he didn't do it; did you have any reason? I ain't got a bit of reason for that—all what I wanted to do, was to tell what a man done and what another man did not: I was only just naming the men what had pistols, and the one that shot. Was there any blood that came out of Archy's head after he was shot?

any stain on the pavement? No, sir, I did not see any. Any marks that showed the spot where he fell? He didn't fall, because he was laid down. His head was on the ground wasn't it? Well, I didn't see any sign of blood at all, I didn't go close enough to him. And you say, that place where he was laid down was right in front of the main arch? Yes, sir. And a man coming right out of the inside of it, would have trod on him? No, sir, it wasn't in the real middle. (The witness explains on the chart where he laid, and stating the position as in front of the little arch and not in the main arch.) Was it in front of the small arch that the boy fell? Yes, sir. Which tree was it you were standing by? By the little tree in front of the little arch. Have you ever had any accidents happen to you in blowing up, or anything of that sort? Yes, sir. Did it affect your mind so that you can't remember as well as you could? I got a right smart jar; I can't recollect all these things exactly. When did that blowing up take place? I forgot now what time; it was some considerable time; I can't recollect now. Have you been blown up more than once? Only once.

On motion the Commission adjourned to meet on Thursday, the 8th inst., at 11 o'clock, A. M.

RALEIGH, N. C. Aug. 8, 1867, 11 A. M.

The Commission met pursuant to adjournment.

Present.—All the members of the Commission, the Judge Advocate, the Counsel for the prosecution, all the accused and their Counsel.

The reading of the testimony taken yesterday, was waived, there being no objection thereto.

Yesterday's proceedings were then read and approved.

SIMON BECKTON, a witness for the prosecution, having been first duly sworn, testified as follows:

Examined by the Counsel for the prosecution.

What is your name? Simon Beckton. Do you live in Fayetteville? Yes, sir; just the other side of Fayetteville, across the bridge.— What is your business? I am farming. Did you know Archy Beebee? Yes, sir. Were you in town the day he was killed? Yes, sir. What time did you go down that day? It was pretty early in the morning. How long did you stay in town? I stayed there till about five o'clock. Where was Beebee killed? At the market house. Were you there at the time? Yes, sir. What time did you get to the market house? I got to the market house early in the morning. Did you stay there all day? Yes, sir. You were there when Archy was brought out of the guard house? Yes, sir. Where were you standing when Archy was brought out of the guard house? I was standing right facing the market house, the east side. In front of the big arch or one of the little arches? The big arch. On the pavement or off? Off the pavement, on the ground. How far from the pavement do you think? Not over eight or ten feet. Who came with Archy from the guard house? Mr. Wemyss had hold of him, and there were some more behind him. Do you know Mr. Wemyss? Yes, sir. You knew him before that? Yes, sir. How long have you been living about Fayetteville? About twelve or fifteen years. Was Archy brought by you to be carried up stairs? Yes, sir. He was brought along the pavement was he? Yes, sir. Did the officers go up stairs? Yes, sir; Mr. Wemyss did, and Mr. Vaun went up. Do you know what became of the rest of the officers? No, sir. Do you know whether they went up or not? I don't know. How long was Archy up stairs? He was up some time. Can't you

form some idea? No, sir. During the time Archy was up stairs were you standing in the same place? Yes, sir. Were you standing about the same place all the time? Yes, sir; all the time he was up stairs. You were not moving about? No, sir. Did you see any carriage while Archy was up stairs? Yes, sir. How far was that carriage from you? I could not tell the exact distance. It was not very far.— Was it as far as from you to those nearest gentlemen? (about four feet.) I could not say for certain, I was looking at them, but could not tell exact. Was the carriage before you or behind you? It was behind me. Was it in front of the market house? Yes, sir. How far was the carriage from the side walk? I could not tell. It was behind you? Yes, sir.— You say you were then three or four feet off the side walk? Yes, sir. The carriage was behind you? Yes, sir. And you can't give me any idea how far it was from you? No, sir. I don't expect you to tell me the exact distance but I want you to give me a notion. Could you hear anybody who was talking at the carriage—were you near enough for that? I saw Mr. Vann go to the carriage. I want to know if you could hear anybody talking as loud as I am now? Yes, I could hear them of course. Could you have heard what they said? Yes, sir, if they had talked loud. Was there any crowd there? Yes, sir. How many men do you suppose? I could not tell. A big crowd? Yes, sir. Did you see anybody in that crowd you knew? Yes, sir. Tell me who? I saw John Maultsby, for one, Mr. Leggett, Tom Powers, and I saw Sam Hall, Ralph Lutterloh, and Monk Jule. Did you see Henry Sykes there? Yes, sir. Did you see Capt. Tolar there? Yes, sir. While the boy was up stairs? Yes, sir. Did you see Capt. Tolar up there? I saw him directly after I got up there in the morning. Did you get there early enough in the morning to see what people were doing about the market house—had they stopped selling there—the butchers under the market? I think there was beef under there. Did Capt. Tolar sell beef that morning? No, sir, I never saw him sell any. You saw him when you first got up there, early, but you never saw him sell beef that day? No, sir. Do you remember whether you saw him while Archy was up stairs? I disremember whether I saw him while he was up stairs or not. You saw these others while Archy was up stairs, and you saw Capt. Tolar, early in the morning, when you first got there, and he was not selling beef? Yes, sir. What time in the morning did you get there? It was pretty early, the sun was not high. Was the sun an hour high? I think it is likely it was. Was it two hours? I could not say, it was mighty early in the morning. You say the people were still selling in the market house, and I understand you to say there was beef still there? Yes, sir.

(Counsel for the accused stated that the bell rung at seven and a half o'clock in the morning.)

Direct examination resumed:

Did the bell ring after you got there? I think it rung after I got there. How long after you got there? I did not take any account of it. You think the bell rung after you got there? Yes, sir. What were these men doing that you saw about there, while Archy was up stairs? I saw them walking about there and talking. Nothing uncommon about it? No, sir. Did you hear any threats? I did not, sir. Did you see any weapons? Yes, sir. While Archy was up stairs? Yes, sir, I saw Tom Powers with a pistol. Did he have it in his hand? He had it in a belt. Where was Tom Powers when you saw him with the pistol? He was walking around among the crowd there. Did you see any other weapons? No, sir. Did you see these ladies come down stairs, Miss Massey and her mother? Yes, sir. Which came down first, Archy or the ladies. The ladies came down first. Who came down with them? I saw Mr. Vaun come down with them, and he went to the carriage with them, and helped them in. Did they pass by you to go to the carriage? Yes, sir, not very far from me. Could you have put your hand on them? No, sir; not exactly. They passed pretty close to you? Yes, sir. How close? I could not see, but I think about four or five feet. The ladies got into the carriage did they? Yes, sir. What happened then; did any one go to the carriage? I think so; yes, sir; I saw Mr. Vaun, standing there, and talking with them, and I saw Mr. Maultsby go there and talk with them. Did you see any one else? No, sir. Do you not recollect any one else? No, sir. Think of it, and see if you can recollect any one else. Mr Powers I think went to the carriage to them. Which Powers? Tom Powers. Are you certain about that? There was so many I could not exactly tell who it was. Is that your best impression; do you swear to it, as a fact? I don't exactly swear as he was one, but I think he was one. You don't swear to it positively? No, sir. Did you hear anything that was said by the ladies, or by those standing talking with them? No, sir. You heard nothing of the conversation? No, sir. Didn't I understand you to say you were near enough to the carriage to hear? I said I didn't hear anything, but if they had been talking loud enough, I could have heard it. You did not hear the ladies say any thing to anybody? No, sir; only I see the motion of their mouths talking in the carriage, to Mr. Maultsby, and Mr. Vaun. Mr. Maultsby and; Mr. Vaun are the only ones you are positive of going to the carriage? Yes, sir. What became of Mr. Maultsby—where did he go when he left the carriage? He went back to the market house. Did he go into the market house or can't you say that? He went back to the market house; I saw him when he turned off from the carriage. Do you know whether he went in, or remained in the crowd in front? He went in the crowd in front of it. And then you lost sight of him? Yes, sir. What became of the carriage? The carriage went off after they had done their talking. Did the carriage go off before Archy came down stairs? Yes, sir. What became of Mr. Vann? He went back under the market house. Did you see whether he went up stairs or not? I didn't notice. How long was it after the carriage went, before Archy came down? I could not exactly say how long it was. Did you notice Mr. Powers with this pistol that you spoke of, before the carriage drove off? I noticed it before they brought Archy out of the guard house. You don't say you saw him with a pistol while Archy was up stairs? No, sir. You saw Mr. Powers with that pistol early in the morning? Yes, sir; when the crowd began to gather around the market. Were you there when the crowd began to gather? Yes, sir. Who were the first men that gathered? I didn't notice about that. Who were among the first? I don't know, sir. The crowd was just about the size it usually is at the market house? No, sir, it was bigger. You told me you saw Mr. Tom Powers early in the morning—what I want

to know is, whether he was there before the crowd gathered, or after the crowd had partially gathered, or whether he was among a part of the crowd that gathered first? Well, sir, he was there in the morning when I got there. Were there many there then? There was some few. Were there more than usual at the market house No, sir. And Tom Powers was there with a pistol? Yes, sir. Was Captain Tolar there at the same time? No, sir; it was not then that I saw Capt. Tolar. When did you see Capt. Tolar? He came there afterwards. He came there shortly after you got there? If you don't know don't try to guess at it. If you can't distinguish the time say so. I don't exactly know what time he come, but I saw him there in the morning. Now, these other men that you have named—Sam. Hall and John Maultsby and Ralph Lutterloh, and Sykes, and Leggett—did you see them there early in the morning? No, sir; they came there after they carried the man up stairs. You saw them at that time? Yes, sir. Did you see Mr. Powers at that time? Yes, sir; he was there. Did you see him there? Yes, sir. Did you see Mr. Tolar there at that time or not? Yes, sir. Didn't you tell me, when I first examined you on that point, that you saw Capt. Tolar there early in the morning? I said when I first went up I saw him, and when they brought him down out of the market house? I mean when he was up stairs? Yes, sir; he was there then. You saw him there while the man was up stairs? Yes, sir. Where were you standing when Archy started down stairs? Right in front of the market? Under the market? No, sir. In the same place you spoke of? Not many steps from there. You were standing some eight or ten feet from the pavement, in front of the big arch? Yes, sir. Did you see Archy when he came out of the door to come down? Yes, sir. Who was with him? Mr. Wemyss had hold of him. Which side was Wemyss on? On his left side, he had Archy on his left. He was on Archy's right? He had his left hand hold of Archy. That would put him on his right wouldn't it? Yes, sir. Did you see any body else in charge of the prisoner? No, sir; I didn't see any one else. Was there any body else along with Mr. Wemyss to help him in carrying this prisoner to the guard house? I never saw any one else, only I saw when they came down stairs all pitched on him. Did you notice who was with him besides Wemyss? I saw Mr. Wemyss have hold of him, and there was some one else behind him, and I did not notice whether they had hold of him or not. There were some other men on the steps at the same time? Yes, sir. Was there any man in front of Archy? No, sir; I didn't see any one else. Did you know Sheriff Hardie? Yes, sir. Did you see him that day? I never saw him until after the man was shot, What was the first thing that attracted your attention, in the way of an attack upon the prisoner? When they brought him down they hollered "shoot him! shoot him!" Was that while he was on the steps? No, sir he had got down on the ground. He was down to the bottom of the steps, when you heard a great many say "shoot him! shoot him!"? Yes, sir. Now after this cry of "shoot him!" what was done; did any body do anything to him? They come around the corner of the market, and turned around to the guard house; and I saw Tolar—— While he was still in the market house, did any body else do anything to him, or attempt to do anything to him? I didn't see, except they pitched at him, when he came down stairs. You didn't see any assault made while Archy was still in the market house? I didn't see, except when the crowd made at him, and Mr. Wemyss says "stand back.," When was that, before Archy turned the arch to go down to the guard house? Yes, sir. You heard Mr. Wemyss say "stand back" before that? Yes, sir. Who was he saying "stand back" to? Mr. Maultsby, and all them I called their names over. All that you mentioned before? Yes, sir; and a good many more. What were they doing? They were making at him, Were they the persons who were shouting "shoot him?" I noticed some was crying shoot him, but I don't know who they were. You saw Tom Powers with a weapon early in the morning—now during the time the rush was made on him, did you see any weapons then in the hands of any one? No, sir. Did they do any thing to Archy then? They were around him, I don't know whether he was hit or not. You saw no weapons? No, sir. Then I understand you Archy turned the arch to go down to the guard house? Yes, sir. Did these men you speak of press on him? They sort of hollered as he turned the corner. What happened then? Mr. Tolar fired the pistol. Did he fire as soon as he got out of the market house? Yes, sir, about two steps around the corner, going towards the guard house. Do you mean this man was shot after he got outside of the market house? He was about one or two steps from the corner, I think. You think he was shot after he had got two steps from the big arch? Yes, sir, You say you saw the man who shot him? Yes, sir. Who was it? Tolar. What Tolar. Capt. Tolar. William J. Tolar? I don't know how he spells his name. Is this the man? Yes, sir; that is the man with the green specks on. Where was Captain Tolar standing when he shot him? I disremember whether he was standing on the pavement or on the ground, but he was standing sort of right behind Archy, when Archy was turning to the guard house. Was he pretty close to the edge of the pavement? Yes, sir. He was close to the edge of the pavement, either on or off? Yes, sir. And he was facing towards Archy, was he? Yes, sir. How far was he from Archy? I don't think he was more than two steps, if that. Did you see him when he came up to the point where he fired from? No, sir, he was standing there when I saw him. You didn't see where he came from? No, sir. Did you see the pistol fired? Yes, sir. Hear it? Yes, sir. Did you see the smoke? Yes, sir. Did you hear any other pistol fired that day? No sir; I never heard but one pistol. That was the pistol you saw fired? Yes, sir. Did you see the flash? I could not say, I saw the smoke. Were your eyes on the man when he fired? Yes, sir. Which hand did he hold it in? His right hand; it was under his shawl and he drawed it out from his left side, and held it out towards Beebee's head I see him standing there with his hand under his shawl. Did you see him standing there before he shot? Yes, sir. Did you see him standing so when Archy was on the stairs? At the time Archy was coming down stairs, I saw him stand with the pistol under his shawl or coat. You are certain about that? Yes, sir. Do you remember that distinctly? Yes, sir. Did he draw the pistol in the same spot he fired? Yes, sir. He didn't move his feet. No, sir. He returned the pistol did he? I saw him return it in his coat. He put it back in the same place he got it from? Yes, sir. Did you see him put his hand up, to put it back? Yes, sir. What did he have on? He had on a shawl.

Did he put it under the shawl? I don't know whether he put it under the shawl, or the coat. Did you see his hand go under? Yes, sir. You saw it come out with the pistol, and as soon as he fired, you saw him put it back? Yes, sir, and he wheeled and went off. Did you see him draw his hand out again? No, sir. Where was Tolar standing at the time you saw him with his hand in his breast, while Archy was coming down, when this rush was made on him? He was standing out side, I don't know whether he was on the pavement or ground. Was he standing close to the market house? No, sir, not close to the market house. He was some distance off from the market house? Yes, sir. Was he near the same spot where you afterwards saw him fire the pistol? Yes, sir. He was not exactly at the same spot? I don't know, sir, about that. When Capt. Tolar fired the pistol you say he was standing just off the pavement or just on it, you can't say which—but near the edge? Yes, sir. Was he in front of the big arch, or the pillar, or the little arch? I don't think he was exactly in the center of the big arch, but I think he was a little back. He was opposite the arch, and towards the left hand side, as you were looking into the market house? I think to the right. You were looking into the market house, were you on the right or left of him? He was at my right. Was there anybody between Capt. Tolar and Beebee, when he fired? John Armstrong was not far from him. Was he in front of him? I think he was a little behind him, a little to his right. Draw the picture in your mind as you saw it, and tell us who you saw near him? Jim Douglass, I think was close to him. Was he standing before him, or behind him, to the right or left of him? Jim Douglass was facing him, I think, standing with his back against the bench of the market house. John was a little behind, to his right, and Jim Douglass was just before John? Yes, sir. Who else did you see about there, close about him? I disremember who else, but a good many people. Did you see any white men about him? Yes, sir, a good many of them, but I could not call their names. When Tolar returned the pistol, as you said, which way did he go? He turned and went around the corner of the market towards the north. Did you see him turn the north corner? Yes, sir. You are certain he did not go through the market? Yes, sir. You saw him when he went round that north corner of the market? Yes, sir. What became of him then, did you see him any more? No, sir. Did you go up and look at Archy? Yes, sir. Was he dead? I saw him fetch three gapes. And then he was dead? Yes, sir. Did you see anybody standing around there? Anybody else attempt to get at him? After he fell, I saw Monk run up to cut his throat. How do you know he was going to cut his throat? I saw him with his knife in his hand. He might have been going to cut his leg? I saw him running up with his knife in his hand. That is the reason you think he was going to cut his throat? Yes, sir. You didn't hear him say anything? Mr. Nixon stepped up and said, Monk, you don't do so, pushed him off the pavement. You didn't hear Monk say anything? I heard him cussing, but I didn't understand what he was saying. Did you go off and leave the body lying there? I stayed there about an hour afterwards, or half an hour. Did you see any of these men about there after Beebee was shot, that you have spoken of, Tom Powers, Sam Hall, Leggett, Lutterloh, or any of those? No, sir. Didn't see them? No, sir. The last time you saw them was when this rush was made? Yes, sir. Just as Archy got to the foot of the stairs? Yes, sir. That was the last you saw of them, when this rush was made? Yes, sir. Did you learn or see anything more about this difficulty? No, sir, I saw them rearing about there, and talking one to another. When was that? After he was shot. Did you hear anybody make any exclamations or say who did it at the time the pistol was shot or immediately afterwards? I heard John Armstrong say as soon as it was done—there was a good many of them said they saw who did it? Was it said so that the crowd could hear it? No, sir, not so that all the crowd could hear it. You heard a good many say immediately afterwards that they saw who did it. Yes, sir. Was that before Tolar left the crowd? That was after he was gone. And one of those you say was John Armstrong? Yes, sir. Who else? I heard Jim. Douglass say so. Anybody else? I heard Jim. McNeill say so. That day, then and there? Yes, sir.

Cross examination by the Counsel for the accused:

Simon who did you belong to formerly? The first man I belonged to was Fred Beckton, in Jones County. Did you ever belong to Jim Beckton, who lived over at Mary's Garden? Yes, sir.

The Counsel for the accused asked for a suspension of the examination, until they had retired for the purpose of having a consultation; which request was granted.

At the close of the consultation the Counsel for the accused announced that they they declined to cross examine the witness.

PATRICK EVANS, a witness for the prosecution, having been first duly sworn, testified as follows:

Examined by the Counsel for the prosecution: What is your name? Patrick Evans. Where do you live? Fayetteville. Were you living there at the beginning of this year? Yes, sir. Did you know Archy Beebee? Yes, sir. What day was he killed? He was killed on a Monday; I think it was about the 12th or 13th of February. Were you at the market house when he was killed? Yes, sir. What time did you go there that day? I don't recollect what time it was I got there—about the time he come up stairs. Who was with him? I don't recollect, sir, the crowd that had him. There were some officers? Yes, sir. You don't recollect who they were? No, sir. Did he go up stairs? Yes, sir. How long was he up there? I suppose he was up there more than a half an hour. Where were you standing while Archy was up stairs? I was not in front of the market house, and under a portion of it. Were you under the market house first or in front first? I was in front first, and then I was under the market house when they fetched him down. Did you see the ladies when they come down? Yes, sir. Was that before Archy come down? Yes, sir. Where were you standing when they came down? I was standing out in front. You didn't go underneath until they came down? No, sir, I might have gone under but I was not in front while they came down. You saw the ladies while they came down? Yes, sir. Did they pass you when they went to the carriage? Yes, sir. How far was the carriage from you? I went close to the carriage; I wanted to see the lady. You had some curiosity to see the lady? Yes, sir, I wanted to see the lady, and I sort of walked along as they

did and kept a little in front of them. Who went with the ladies to the carriage? I don't recollect that; I didn't notice to see who was with them. Did you notice whether anybody went to the carriage that they got in? Yes sir. Several persons? Yes, sir; it was right smart around the carriage. Do you remember who they were? I do not, sir. What became of the carriage? It drove off towards home, or where she was living. What became of the gentlemen who were around it talking to her? They all turned off and scattered about there, sir; I don't know what became of them. Nor who they were? No, sir. Did you see any of these prisoners at the bar in the crowd that day while Archy was up stairs? I don't recollect. Either Captain Tolar, or Monk, or Tom Powers? I saw Monk; I didn't see any of the rest of them. You saw him there while the ladies were up stairs? Yes, sir; he was there. What was he doing? He was standing about there. Saying anything? No sir. Doing anything? No, sir. Was the crowd quiet, or were there any signs of excitement? Yes, sir; they all seemed to be tearing about and going on pretty smart; there was a good deal of talking about there. What marks of excitement were there? They were all talking and standing about, and moving from one place to another. Were these the only marks of excitement? Yes, sir; it seemed very like a hive of bees. You didn't notice the expression of their faces, nor hear any threats? No, sir; for I was not thinking of it. The excitement—was it intense enough to excite you? No, sir. After the ladies went away in the carriage, did you go under the market house? Yes, sir. You stood under there until Archy came down? Yes, sir. How long was it after the ladies left before Archy came down? I don't know, sir, exactly, it was not very long. Was it a quarter of an hour? I don't think it was—five or ten minutes I suppose. Who did you see under the market house at that time? I don't recollect seeing any one but Monk, and I saw Mr. James Atkinson. Any one else that you can remember at that time? Mr. Phillips came up about that time. Was he under the market house? Yes, sir. You saw him, and Jim Atkinson, and Monk? Yes. sir; they was about all I recollect. You didn't see Captain Tolar, nor Tom Powers? No, sir. Did you see Archy when he started down stairs? Yes, sir. You were standing back under the market house? Yes, sir. So that the steps he came down were to your right and front? Yes, You were standing about the middle of the market were you? Not so far back as the middle. Could you see Archy when he was coming down stairs? Yes, sir. Who was with him? I can't say. Was there any one with him? Yes, sir; the guard was with him. You can't say who? No, sir. You know the town officers of Fayetteville pretty well? Yes, sir. Can't you remember? I can't recollect; I was not noticing them; I was only noticing him. Was anything done to him before he got to the foot of the steps? No, sir; I saw nothing done until he got off the steps. What did you see then? After he got down off the steps, I think he was on the floor before a rush was made, and I heard some of them say "this is my prisoner." The crowd that was inside or outside? All. There was a general rush, and you heard the exclamation, "it is our prisoner"? Yes sir. Are you certain it was, not "it is my prisoner"? That was another remark made, "this is my prisoner." You heard both? Yes, sir; and of course then the rush continued until they got out from under the market house.

What was in that rush ; did you see any weapons? I saw no weapons in the rush at that time, but just before the voices, I saw Monk with a knife in his hand. Was he saying anything? No, sir; I didn't hear him say a word. Did you hear the sheriff say anything? No, sir. Did you see any signs of clubs? Yes sir; their clubs were up beating the crowd back. You were still under the market house? Yes, sir. Did you follow the crowd out? Yes sir. I kept as close as I could get while it was such a rush; a man was a little sort of dubious in getting up close. What happened then? The same remarks were made, "kill him"; that was hollered pretty loud all the time until they turned the arch and as they did, they hollered "shoot him? That was the first you heard "shoot him," after they turned the arch? Yes, sir. They seemed to have changed the method of killing him? Yes, sir; the guard kept them off and they didn't get hold of him. As he got to the foot of the stairs, there was a general rush made? Yes, sir. You heard the exclamations that were made in several directions from several voices "kill him," "kill him."? Yes, sir. And you heard the exclamations "he is our prisoner" and "he is my prisoner."? Yes, sir. That continued until he turned outside of the market house? Yes, sir. And before the exclamation commenced "shoot him."? Yes, sir. Was that from very numerous voices? Yes, sir. Could you see any who were shouting that? No, sir; he was rearing and pitching; of course they were all striking at him, and in fact there was a good deal of noise; about the time they turned he had fallen, and as he arose, that pistol fired. Did you see him when the pistol fired? I was looking at him, and Mr. Phillips both, when the pistol fired; Was he in the same line of the voices with Mr. Tolar? Sam was a little off from him. What was your reason for looking at Sam Phillips? At the first time I saw him with a pistol in his hand. And you kept your eyes on him? Yes, sir; for I thought he was going to do something. You had your eyes on him when the pistol was fired? Yes, sir. Who fired the pistol? I can't say sir. Your eyes were on Phillips when the pistol was fired? Pretty much on the prisoner, but I was looking at Phillips. You saw him distinctly when you heard the report? Yes, sir. And he was not firing the pistol? No, sir. You don't know who fired it? I don't know sir. Did you see Captain Tolar in the crowd? I didn't sir, until after when the remark was made to get back, and it was then I suppose that Captain Tolar killed him. Was that immediately after it happened? Yes, sir. Was it in a loud tone of voice? I heard it, and any body around there could hear it, and I remarked to some of them "where is he" and I looked up and saw him towards Mr. Hinsdale's store. Were these expressions used at all, till after he got up to Mr. Hinsdale's? I think Simm was remarked to me, "yonder he goes now." Did you hear this from several quarters? Yes, sir; saying Captain Tolar killed him. How long was it after you heard the explosion of the pistol? As soon as the crowd got back a little, that expression was used. That was the general talk in the crowd? Yes, sir; it was not more than half a minute before the remarks were made. Was Captain Tolar in the crowd when these remarks were made? I don't know sir, whether he was or not. Do you think it was half a minute after you heard the pistol shot that you heard these remarks? No, sir; I only said it was half a minute by the time he was up about Mr. Hinsdale's. You heard the report of the pistol and immediately heard the remarks? Yes, sir. As soon as the pistol was discharged you heard from several voices that Captain Tolar had done it? Yes, sir. That prevaded the crowd? Yes, sir; and then some one told me that he was going up toward Mr. Hinsdale's and I looked at him, and it appeared to be the same shawl, I didn't see his face. That man you saw when they pointed him out to you, was Captain Tolar? It looked to be; his back was to me. You know him don't you? Yes, sir. You think there is no doubt about its being the same man? No, sir. How long was it between the time Archy got to the foot of the steps and the time that the pistol was fired? It was just as long as he could get to the place. Do you suppose you could have counted fifty, between the time he got to the foot of the steps, and the time he was shot? I don't know sir, it was but a short time. As soon as the man could have walked around there? Yes, sir. And I understand you to say it was a short time between the time he got to the foot of the steps and the firing of the pistol? Yes. sir. Did the officers seem to be trying to do their duty? Yes, sir; I think they done their duty, they tried to do every thing to keep them off. Did you see any pistols besides the pistol you saw in the possession of Phillips? No, sir. Have you tried to recollect? Yes, sir; but I don't recollect any others. Can you tell me who you saw in the crowd immediatly after the shooting? I don't know sir; I dont recollect decidedly, of course there was a good many about there. Can't you remember any colored men that you spoke to? Yes, sir; there was a good deal of colored men ; I can remember some of them. Who did you see? There was Simmons and Tucker and a good many others. Did you see John Armstrong? Yes, sir. You know John? Yes, sir. Did you see him there immediately after the thing occurred? Yes, sir. Did you see Calvin Johnson? Yes, sir. Did you see Jim Douglass? I do not recollect sir. Did you see James McNeill there? I don't recollect of seeing him.

Cross-examination, by the Counsel for the accused.

When was the subpoena served on you to come up here? Last Saturday. What is your business in Fayetteville? I am keeping a little grocery. Keep a shop do you? Yes, sir. What is Sam. Phillips' business in Fayetteville? He is a merchant there, sir. He is keeping a shop too? Yes, sir. How far is your shop from Phillip's shop? It is some one hundred yards and may be two hundred. On the same side of the street? Yes, sir. Are you often about the market house? Well not very—I am generally there in the morning. In going from your place to the market house you pass right by Phillip's store? Sometimes I do: sometimes I go on the other side: just as often on one side as the other. And in passing back you generally pass by Phillips' store? Often times I do. Don't you generally pass that way by Phillips store as many as two or three times a day ? Yes, sir. Going and returning from your place of business? Some days more and some days probably not that much. You pretty generally stop there when you pass? No, sir, I don't. You call in sometimes? Sometimes I may want to buy tobacco or something I have not got and I go in, but not more than, and not often, as to any other store. You and Sam know each other pretty well? Yes, sir. Have known each other for a long time? Yes, sir, some eight or nine years. Ever had any difficulty with him? Not but once; that wasn't any thing great, sir. You were on good terms? Yes, sir. Friendly terms? Yes, sir. You

and Sam, talked this matter over I suppose?
No, sir, he has never had anything to say to me
about it.   Never said anything to you about it
at all?   No sir.   Neither before you were
summoned, or since?   No, sir, I have never
spoken to him since.   You say you were there
that day when Archy was shot?   Yes, sir.
You saw Archy come down?   Yes, sir.
Where were you standing?   I was standing
right at the end betwixt a bench, (there, like.)
You were inside the market house?   Yes, sir.
At the time he came down the steps?   Yes,
sir.   Did you see pretty nearly every thing that
occurred while they were bringing him down
stairs?   I don't know sir, about it—I was mostly noticing him.   Who did you see with him,
Patrick?   I could not tell you to save my life
who had him in charge.   Do you know whether
Mr. Wemyss was along with him?   I don't
know sir.   You know him?   I do, sir.   Was
Faircloth?   I don't know, sir.   You know
him?   Yes, sir.   Do you know whether Mr.
Hardie was along with him?   I don't.   You
know Hardie well?   I do, sir.   You can't
name one man that was along with him that
day?   I didn't notice them—I didn't charge
my memory with it; I only noticed Archy,
I wanted to look at him and he was the only one
that I noticed; in fact I didn't think it was going
to be anything of that sort at that time.   How
long did you say it was that the ladies came down
before Archy came down?   I would say some
five minutes, more or less.   Did anybody else
come down the steps between the times that
Miss Massey and her mother came down and the
time that Archy came down?   I don't recollect.
Did anybody come down after Archy came down?
After he came down of course I was noticing
him all the time and I would not have seen them.
I ask you to give me the name of a single man
that was in that crowd, white or colored, at the
time Beebee came down the steps?   I could
not tell, sir, I told you once I did not recollect.
You can't tell the name of a single one?   No,
sir.   Did you shift your position after Beebee
came down—did you take any other position
after he came down?   Of course I followed up
as they moved, I kept up along close by.   You
didn't move your position from the end of Becky's
stall until after the prisoner had passed by you?
Of course I come right in as they came down the
steps.   And you hadn't moved your position at
all, until after the rush commenced?   Yes, sir.
Then you were in the rush as well as anybody
else.   Of course, I was behind them like.
You were pressing in to see what was to be seen?
Certainly, I was trying to see what was to be seen.
And you were just as much in the rush to see
what was done as anybody else was?   Of course
—I was not as near as the others were—I was
standing back of them.   But you were rushing
up to see what was to be done?   Of course, I
was.   Just like the others?   No, sir, I was
not as near as they were.   Now, Patrick, did
you see anything done at Beebee at all while he
was in the market house?   I saw them all, it
looked like to be catching at him.   Just name
one man that you saw at that time catching at
him or trying to get hold of him.   I told you
before I could not—that it was a general rush,
and Mr. Wemyss and all them were knocking
them off?   You remember Mr. Wemyss was
with him, then?   No, sir, I seed the guard was
there.   You said Mr. Wemyss—do you remember he was there?   No, sir, I don't recollect—
it was only the guard that was in charge of him,
I don't recollect which ones.   You say of
course—why do you say of course?   It is only

a word, I reckon, that I have got in the habit of
using.   You don't mean anything by that—it is
just a common word?   Yes, sir.   Was Mr.
Hardie with him at that time?   I don't know,
sir.   And while you say that you saw him from
the time that he started down the steps or came
to the landing up to the top of the steps until he
got out of the market house—during that whole
time you can't name one single man who was
about him—you can't give the name of a single
man who was in that crowd?   No, sir.   And
you were looking closely?   I was looking at him
as closely as I could look.   And you saw him
all the time?   No, sir, not all the time, because
sometimes there was so many around him, and I
could not see him.   Did you see him at the
time this grabbing occurred?   Very often he
was up higher than their heads.   How did he
get up?   I don't know, sir, jumping up, I suppose.   Don't suppose?   He was jumping.
And then from the time he was coming from the
steps of the market he was jumping up higher
than the heads of the men?   Sometimes.
How many times.   I could not say, sir.
Did he jump up as many as five or
six times?   I don't believe he did.   Did he
jump up as much as two or three times?   I
think he did; as many as twice.   How high did
he jump from the pavement?   I don't know, sir.
I only saw he was higher than the others; his
head was about a foot and a half higher than
theirs.   You saw him when under the market
house, jumping up as high as a foot and a half
above their heads?   I didn't say under the market house.   I am speaking about under the
market house?   I didn't see him jumping high
under the market house.   Did you see him all
the time he was under the market house.   Not
all the time.   Did you see him at the time these
men were rushing at him, under the market house?
Yes, sir; I saw them when they all rushed at him,
Didn't you look to see who one of these men were
who were grabbing at him?   I didn't.   How
many grabs did you see made at him?   I can't
tell you.   Do you think there were a dozen or
fifteen?   I could not say   You saw some
grabs made at him?   I saw them all rushing at
him.   And you didn't see the men who grabbed
at him?   No, sir.   In these grabbs that were
made, did you see any knife?   No, sir.   Did
you see any pistol?   Only the pistol Mr. Phillips
had in his hand?   Was Phillips in the market
house?   Yes, sir.   Did you see him with a
pistol under the market house?   Yes, sir,   So
you saw Phillips before the negro came out of the
market house?   Yes, sir.   What place under
the market house was Phillips when you first saw
him with a pistol?   He was coming from me,
just come under the arch.   He was coming in the
eastern arch?   Yes sir.   Coming up towards
the crowd?   Yes, sir.   Where was Archy then,
when you first saw Phillips?   I don't think he
had come down the steps   So you saw Phillips
come up with a pistol before you saw Archy come
down the steps?   I think it was.   Be certain about
it; either before or after, just as you please.   That
is what I want to do: I want to tell you just as it is.
Well, tell it,—was it before or after Archy came
down, that you first saw Phillips with a pistol?
It was before he came down.   How far did
Phillips come from?   I was standing back
when I told you, and he was there at the arch.
How many feet was it?   I don't know, sir.
About how many?—three, or three hundred?   I
can't say, because he was standing at the arch,
and I was back in the market.   It was a short
distance?   Yes, sir.   How did Phillips have
the pistol?   Just had it down in his hand.   In

his right hand? Yes, sir. Holding it by the stock? Yes, sir. With the hand down his right leg? Yes, sir. What sort of a pistol was it? From what I could see of it, it looked to be a good sized pistol, about a six shooter. How long was it? It was a good long pistol. How many inches? I could not pretend to say; it was about as long as my hand. How many inches is that? I don't want to say how many inches, I don't know. Was it six inches long? It might have been six inches long. Was it eight inches long? I don't know, sir, I could not say. Was it ten inches long? No, sir, I don't think it was ten. Then you say it was between six and eight inches long? Yes, sir. You say it was a six-shooter? Yes, sir. I said it looked to be one. What reason have you for thinking it was a six-shooter, and not a five-shooter? Because it was just about that size. How was it mounted; was it steel mounted? I don't know, sir, he had most of it in his hand; I only saw the barrel. And that was before Beebee came down stairs? Yes, sir. Well, then, Beebee came down stairs and the crowd rushed on him, you say? Yes, sir. And the crowd passed you before you left your position under the stall? Yes, sir, a little. So that you got behind the crowd? A little, sir. Where were you at the time the man was shot? I was pretty much against the pillar. Against the main southern pillar? Yes, sir. The large southern pillar, of the main eastern arch? Yes, sir. And you were pretty much against that? Yes, sir. On the pavement? Yes, sir. Which way was your face fronting? My face was fronting pretty much east. Towards Liberty Point? Yes, sir; more towards Mr. Davis's, rather than Liberty Point. And that was the way your face was fronting? Yes, sir. You are sure you were nearly against the pillar of the market house? Yes, sir. Well, now, at the time Beebee was shot, where was he? He was right on the pavement; he tell a little further down than from the big arch; he fell near the center of the little arch. So you think he was standing near the center of the little south-east arch? Something not far from that, sir. Was he nearer the lower pillar of the small southern arch? Yes, sir. How far were you off from Beebee at the time he was shot? I wasn't farther than to that table, (about six feet.) Were you near enough to have touched him? I don't think I could have touched him, sir. About six feet? I don't know whether it was six feet there or not. It was about that distance? I don't suppose it was quite six feet. Between four and six feet? It was more than four feet. Was Beebee about the center of the pavement? No, sir; to re, I think to the edge than to the center. How far do you think Beebee was off from the eastern edge of the pavement? I could not say. Did you see him about that time at all? Yes, sir. And he was nearer to the eastern edge of the pavement than the center? I think he was; I would not be positive about that. Did you see him fall then, just before the pistol fired? Yes, sir, I didn't exactly see him fall, but they all went down pretty much together. Then you saw him raise up? Yes, sir. Now, when they raised up together, who was with Beebee? I don't know, sir. Was there any man there that you knew at the time they raised up? No, sir. Was Sheriff Hardie anywhere about? I can't tell you. Was Mr. Wemyss? I can't tell. Faircloth? I can't tell. Can't you tell a man? I don't recollect at that time. When Beebee rose up after they fell, was there a man in the crowd that you could tell? There was but one in the crowd that I could tell, and that was Mr. Phillips. Where was Mr. Phillips at that time? He was a little to my right. Nearer to the market house than you? Of course he was nearer; he was standing betwixt me and Mr. Davis like. Was he on the pavement or off? I don't know, sir; I think he was on. Was he very near the edge if he was on? Yes, sir. How far was Phillips from Beebee at that time? I could not decidedly say how far. Which way from Beebee was he—on a line with you? Yes, sir; he was pretty much on a line with me—he was a little in front of me. Then Phillips, if he was on a line with you, and near the edge of the pavement, he was nearer to Beebee than you? He was about as close, I suppose. He was about three or four feet? He may have been a little further than that. May have been how many feet? I can't tell you how many; he wasn't very far off. Could Phillips have reached out his hand and touched him? I don't think he could. By bending over? I don't know about that. He was there on his right hand? Yes, sir. What was he doing with his left hand? I don't know, sir. He had the pistol then? Yes, sir. Was it the same pistol he had before? It looked like it. A small six or eight inch pistol? Yes, sir. It was about the some pistol you think, he had before? Yes, sir. Did you see Phillips with a pistol after that time? After he was shot I saw him with a pistol. What was he doing with the pistol then? He held it up in front of me and he said "they have killed him" and he said "you all know my pistol didn't shoot him, for you can see it has not been fired." How loud did Phillips speak that? About an ordinary tone of voice. So directly after the shooting, Phillips, in an ordinary tone of voice, said, holding up his pistol, "they have killed him, but you all see I didn't kill him"? Yes, sir. How long was that after they killed him? It was pretty soon. Was Phillips standing at the same place he was when the man was killed? No, sir; he had moved. At the time Phillips raised that pistol and spoke those words, what man was there standing near him? I can't recollect —I know it was spoke in the crowd. How far were you at that time from Phillips? I was right close to him then. Were you near enough to put your hand out and touch him? I think I could. Was there a good many persons around him? Yes, sir; a good crowd around him. And you can't name a single man? I can't. Either black or white? No, sir. Did anybody look at his pistol, whether it was loaded? I just slightly noticed it. You didn't examine it; you just glanced your eye at it? Yes, sir, I just glanced my eye at it. At that glance could you tell whether it was a four or six-barrelled pistol? I didn't take notice enough to know how many times it shot, whether six or four. You could not tell anything about it then? No, sir. You say you don't know who shot him? No, sir; I could not tell who shot him. Did you see how far Phillips was from you at the time Beebee was shot? I don't know, sir, how far he was from me. He was about the edge of the pavement? I think he was somewheres about the edge of the pavement—I don't know, exactly, how far. You didn't see the pistol when it was shot? No, sir, I didn't. You didn't see the smoke? I saw the smoke, yes, sir. Where did the smoke rise from? Of course, when I looked up the smoke was right there, I could not tell where the smoke come from. I ask you, when you looked there after that pistol shot was fired if the smoke of it was not there close by Sam Phillips? No, sir, it 'was not. Say where it was? It was right about pretty much where the man fell. Was there any man nearer to him than Sam. Phillips at the time the pistol was fired, and at the time you saw the smoke? Yes, sir, there was a crowd nearer than he was. Can you name a man that was nearer? No, sir, I can't, I don't recollect any man, because I was not noticing. You spoke of having seen John Armstrong there? Yes, sir, but I didn't know you were asking me about that time. When did you see him? That was after he was dead and we all had moved off. Directly after he fell? Yes, sir, not very long. Where was John standing then? He was off of the pavement. How far off of the pavement was he? I don't know sir, because we all got off of the pavement, and were standing there talking, me and Armstrong, and Simmons and Tucker and some others. You were all standing in a group talking to each other? Yes, sir. How long after the man was shot? It was, of course, just as soon as he was shot, we all got back right off of the pavement. Just as soon as the pistol was fired you all got off of the pavement? As soon as we could, well, we stood and looked down on him a little, and then we all marched back pretty quick. Were you off of the pavement or were you on the pavement when you heard the voice say "Tolar has shot him?" I was on the pavement then. You hadn't got off at that time? No, sir. Now at that time when the voice said "Tolar shot him,' where was Tolar? I don't know sir, for I didn't see him, but just after that, as I got off of the pavement, some one remarked "yonder he goes" and I saw him going up the street. So at the time the voice said that, you don't know where Tolar was? No, sir. In a very short time, afterwards you saw Tolar about Hinsdale's? Yes, sir; they said that was him. Now from the time that elapsed, and from the distance Tolar had got, can you say whether Tolar heard that remark? I could not say. You don't swear that he was there and heard it? No, sir. Your impression is that he was not in that crowd? I would not say either way, because the remarks were made a short time before they said "yonder he goes." At the time you were forming that group, you and Armstrong and Simmons, where did Armstrong come from? I don't know sir where he come from, I could not say. These people who were in that crowd that day, were they strangers in the town of Fayetteville, or were they citizens of the town? I suppose they must have been the citizens of the town. I don't recollect seeing any particular stranger there. Were you not acquainted with a number of persons, who are spoken of as having been there—do you know Sam Hall? Yes, sir. Ralph Luterioh? Yes, sir. Ed. Fowers? Yes, sir. Leggett? Yes, sir. Watkins? Yes, sir. Phillips? Yes, sir. Tom Powers? Yes, sir. John Maultsby? Yes, sir. You are acquainted with all these men? I am sir. Acquainted with all of them well? Yes sir. And still you can't undertake to swear that any of these men were there? No, sir. I mean the time between when the prisoner was brought down and when he was shot? I can't swear for any more than I told you I saw, of course I can't go any further than that, And Phillips is the only one you have mentioned? And Monk. Between the time the boy Beebee was brought down the steps, and the time the pistol shot was fired, can you name any man who was in that crowd, with the exception of Sam Phillips and Monk? Before that I had seen Atkinson

Now you say there were several voices, cried out "Tolar shot him"! I ask you for the name of a single man who made that cry. I can't say sir,

Re-direct Examination by the Counsel for the prosecution:

Where was it you saw Jim Atkinson standing? In front of the Market house as I went up. When you went up after the ladies had gone away? No, sir; just as the prisoner was carried up. That was the time you saw him? Yes, sir; because I went by and spoke to him, that is the reason I remember. Did I understand you to say your eyes were on Phillips at the moment you heard the report of the pistol? Yes, sir. Did you see Phillip's pistol at that time? Yes, sir. You saw not only the man, but the pistol? Yes, sir. Did it go off at the time you heard the report? No sir. You swear positively it did not? Yes, sir. Was he in a position to fire? No, sir, How was he standing? He was standing with his face towards the prisoner, but his pistol was down. Was he in the crowd rushing forward? No, sir. Did he have his hand thrust out? No, sir. Was he standing still? Yes, sir. with his pistol in his right hand, down by his side? Yes, sir. It did not go off? No, sir. You saw him at the very instant the report reached your ears from the other pistol? Yes, sir. How long was it after this report and Beebee fell that Sam Phillips proposed to some one to examine his pistol? That was right straight off. As quick as the thing could be done? Yes, sir. One thing followed immediately after another without anything intervening? Yes, sir. What was it he said then? "They have killed him; here is my pistol; my pistol has never been fired." Did any one take it to examine it? Not that I know of. Do you remember whether they did or not? I don't remember. But he offered it, and any one was at liberty to take it? Yes, sir. It was the same pistol you saw in his hand in the previous part of the day? Yes, sir, I took it to be the same pistol. It resembled it in appearance? Yes, sir. When you talked about this man Beebee being higher than the heads of the crowd, do you mean that he was like a bird in the air—his whole body? No, sir, I mean his head, of course. His head was bounding like a man who was jumping? Yes, sir. And sometimes he was a foot or a foot and a half above the heads of the crowd? Yes, sir. Now the Counsel for the defense has asked you if you were not in that rush; how about that? No, sir; of course I was standing back, just to see whether they struck him or not, that was what I was looking for. Were you in the rush like those other men? No, sir. Was your position at all like theirs? No, sir. Were you pressing on like them? No, sir. You were on the outside edge of the crowd trying to see what was to be done? Yes, sir. But these other men were pressing on with vigor and exclamation, as I understand it? Yes, sir. You can't name who they were? No, sir. But it seemed to be generally participated in by the crowd? Yes, sir. You were asked about your intimacy with Mr. Phillips. Have you said anything to Mr. Phillips about what you were going to swear to? No, sir, he never asked me a word about it. Has he ever talked to you about it since you have been here? No, sir. I have not spoken a dozen words to him since I have been here; for he remarked to me that he wanted to ask me about his people, but he would not dare come nigh to me, because he knew it was not right for him to be talking to me. Was there any particular friendship between you and Mr. Phillips? No, sir. You said there had been some little difficulty between you at one time? A little, but that is all done away now. There was no particular friendship? No, sir. It was not the store, above all others, you trade at? No, sir. Does he keep the same sort of a store you do? Yes, sir, he may have more and different articles. You have no particular intercourse with him? No, sir, none at all. Where did you say Phillips was standing at the time your eyes were upon him, and the pistol was fired? He was standing pretty much in front of me. Was he to your right and front, or left and front? He was a little to the right and front. Was he any nearer to Beebe than you were? No, sir, he might have been as near. You think he was near the edge of the pavement? I think he was not far from it. In giving these lengths, and so on, I understand you to say you cannot speak with exactitude about it? No, sir. But these are the best impressions that you can give? Yes, sir.

On motion, the Commission adjourned to meet on Friday, the 9th inst., at 11 o'clock, A. M.

RALEIGH, N. C., Aug. 9th, 1867, 11 A. M.
The Commission met pursuant to adjournment.

Present: All the members of the Commission, the Judge Advocate, the Counsel for the prosecution, all the accused and their Counsel.

The reading of the testimony taken yesterday was waived, there being no objection thereto.

Yesterday's proceedings were then read and approved.

JOHN SHAW, a witness for the prosecution, having been first duly sworn, testified as follows:

Examined by the Counsel for the prosecution. What is your name? John Shaw. Where do you live? In Fayetteville. How long have you been living there? Two years. Were you living there when Archy Beebee was killed? Yes, sir. Were you at the market house that day? Yes, sir. Did you get there before Archy came out of the guard house? Yes, sir. How long were you there before Archy was brought out of the guard house? I was there some better than an hour. Where were you standing? I was standing on the guard house side when he was brung out. Which side is that? The South side. Were you standing near the south-east corner? Yes, sir. Between the big arch on the south, and the little arch on the south? Yes, sir. You saw Archy when he was brought out? Yes, sir. Did you stand there until he was carried up stairs? Yes, sir. Who brought him out of the guard house? Mr. Wemyss. Any one else? There was one or two more, but I didn't notice any one except Mr. Wemyss. You don't remember who they were? No, sir. Archy went up stairs? Yes, sir. How long was he up stairs? I could not exactly say point blank—he was up there I reckon as much as an hour or half an hour. Did you stand in that same place all the while Archy was up stairs? No, sir: I did not. Where did you move to? I moved to the east side of the market house. Did you go inside? No, sir. Did you stand on the pavement or off? I was standing with my foot on a post that was standing right on the side of the pavement. How long after Archy had gone up stairs, before you moved to that post? I will say half an hour. You moved to the post shortly before he come down? Yes, sir. Did you see any crowd at the market house, while you were standing on the south side, and before you moved to the post? Yes, sir; there

was a good many under the market house. And outside? A few. Which end of the market house were they mostly? About the centre of the market. Did you see any one there that you knew? Yes, sir. Who did you see? I saw Mr. Thomas Powers for one—I saw Monk for another, and I saw several more, Did you see Capt. Tolar there? No, sir; I didn't see him at that time. Did you see anything of Ed. Powers and Sam Hall? No, sir. John Maultsby? Yes, sir. Tell any one else you saw that you can remember? I believe that is all I can recollect now. You saw Tom Powers, and Monk and Maultsby there? Yes, sir. You don't remember seeing Ed. Powers and Hall? No, sir. What were these men doing when you saw them; what was each one of them doing? Mr. Maultsby was just walking about under the market house; Mr. Powers was talking to some others under there. You noticed nothing peculiar about their behaviour? No, sir. What was Monk doing? He was walking about. Did you see any weapons in the hands of any one? No, sir. No knives or pistols? No, sir. Did this crowd continue to grow larger, or did it grow smaller? I did not particularly notice. Then you moved to the corner and stood there with your foot on that post that you speak of? Yes, sir. What happened while you were standing there; did you see any person that you can name in the crowd, further than these three, before Archy came down? Yes, sir; I saw Mr. Bond's passing. Was that when he came down with the ladies. It was after he came down with the ladies? [Didn't you move around to the post till after the ladies came down? No, sir. Did you see the ladies come down the steps? I saw them when they were on the steps, but didn't see them get into the carriage. Who was with them on the steps? Mr. Bond. Did you see the carriage go off? Yes, sir. You did not see them get into the carriage? No, sir; it had had gone some distance before I noticed it. Were you standing at that post when Archy came down? Yes, sir. Did you see him? Yes, sir, I saw him. You saw the boy as he came down the steps? Yes, sir. Who was with him? Mr. Wemyss. Any one else? Mr. Hardie. Any one else? No, sir, that was all I can recollect. Do you mean to say there was no one else with him, or no one else that you noticed? No one that I noticed. Did you notice whether there were others there that you could name? Mr. Faircloth was there, but I could not tell whether he was with there or not. Which side of the prisoner did Mr. Wemyss come down on? On the right side of him. And where did Mr. Hardie come down? He come down to the left side of him. Certain of that? He was when he got on the ground, I didn't see him when he come down the steps. Didn't you see the boy, as he came down the steps? I saw him but I didn't see Mr. Hardie until he was at the foot of the steps. Then in passing from the steps to the big arch to turn out to go the guard house, that pillar would be between you and these men? Yes, sir. Did you see anything happen to him while he was in your sight? No, sir. You didn't see any assault made on him then? No, sir. Did you hear any noise or exclamations while he was inside? I heard some person say, I could not tell who, as he started away from the foot of the steps—I heard some person say "Rally, boys!" and by that time he was out of my sight. Was that all you heard? Yes, sir. Did the crowd move about much? They were stirring pretty thick. Did you see him when he was brought into the arch, to turn towards the guard house? No, sir, not till he got on the outside of the arch. Were you still standing with your foot on that post? Yes, sir. What happened then? I seed Monk with his knife in his hand, making at him, trying to cut him. How close was he to him? I reckon two or three feet of him. What kept him from cutting him? Mr. Wemyss; he had a string on his thumb, and had hold with his left hand, and he was knocking at him with his stick. You saw Monk then just after he got outside of the market house, trying to cut him with his knife within two or three feet of him? Yes, sir. And he was kept off by Mr. Wemyss? Yes, sir. What else did you see? I saw Mr. Tolar come up, he had on a gray shawl and gray pants. Now, stop one moment, there; where was Mr. Tolar when you first saw him? He was standing right against the pass-way, where the boy came down? In the arch? Yes, sir. Which end of the arch was he nearest to, the north end or the south end? The north end. You first saw him after Monk had made this cut at him with his knife? Yes, sir. Was he standing still when you saw him? Yes, sir. What did he do then? Then he walked up a step or two, on towards the boy, in the crowd. How did he get through the crowd? He just shoved along there. Did you see what he was doing with his hands? No, sir, I never noticed them till he got to where he stopped. Where did he make the final stop? He went across the pavement, out on the ground to this little tree in front of the small arch. He was standing on the ground? Yes, sir. Were you looking at him all the time? I was looking at him. You say he had on a gray shawl and pants? Yes, sir, and he had his right hand under his shawl, under his left arm, and when he got there, there was some person standing pretty much in front of him, and he shoved him out of the way, and drew his pistol and raised it, and shot. Which hand did he shove him with? The left hand, and he shoved him to his left side. How close was he to Beebe when he shot? He was not more than two, or three and a half feet. The muzzle of the pistol was not against Bebee's head when he fired? No, sir. How far do you suppose the muzzle was from his head? About two or two and a half feet. You saw the pistol in his hands? Yes, sir. What sort of a pistol was it? It was a large pistol. Do you suppose the barrel was as long as this pencil? Yes, sir, the pistol appeared to be eight or nine inches long. You mean including the handle and all? Yes, sir. What is your business at home? It has been working at turpentine. You have never worked at anything to require you to measure much? No, sir. It was a large pistol? Yes, sir. You saw it distinctly? Yes, sir. In Tolar's hand? Yes, sir. In his right hand? Yes, sir. Did you see it go off? Yes, sir, I saw the smoke and the flame too. And heard the report? Yes, sir. Did you see Archy fall? No, sir, the crowd rushed in so. I saw him as he was starting to fall, but didn't see him when he reached the ground. Did he begin to sink immediately after the pistol fired? Yes, sir. Where was Archy standing when he was shot, had he passed the little arch? No, sir, he was agin' the little arch. Was he near the edge of the pavement, or near the middle? Near the middle. He was near the middle of the pavement, about opposite the little arch? Yes, sir. How far were you from Tolar; from where you stood, how many steps would it have taken you to reach Tolar? About four steps. How many steps would it have taken you to reach

Archy? I could have stepped on Archy from the post. After he fell? Yes, sir. Did he change his position at all when he fell? He just fell right straight out. Did you see who was standing nearest to Tolar when he fired the pistol? No, sir, I did not. There were several around him, but to tell you positive who was standing right at him, I could not. How many men were between him and Archy, when he shot? No person at all. Mr. Sheriff Hardie was a little to his front To his right and front, or left and front? Right and front. Where was Wemyss? He was pretty much to the side of him. Which side? The side near the Market House. You say there was no one between Tolar and Archy? No, sir. Didn't I understand you to say he put out his left hand and pushed a man out of the way? I mean when the pistol fired. Just before the pistol fired there was some row? Yes sir. Who was that man he pushed away? I could not rightly tell you; I thought it was James Douglas. You have heard since that it was him, have you not? No, sir. Has no one told you since, that it was James Douglas? No, sir. Then, your impression at the time was, it was James Douglas? Yes, sir. You think so still? Yes, sir. You are not confident? No, sir. Did you see any one else near him, either colored or white, at the time he fired the pistol, or just before? No, sir. Did you see anything of Tom Powers, at all, after the negro got down stairs, out on the pavement? No, sir, I did not. Did you hear any exclamations, from any quarter, as to who had fired the pistol? No, sir. Did you hear any exclamations at all, after the negro had got outside, from the crowd, anything as to what they were going to do with him? When this rush was made, just before Mr. Tolar shot, I heard somebody say "shoot him! shoot him!" Did you hear that twice? Yes, sir. Did it seem to be the same man? Yes, sir. The same man repeated that twice? Yes, sir. Did you know who that was? No, sir, I did not. Did you see anything of Monk? I saw him after the boy was killed. What was he doing then? I saw him and Mr. Nixon together. What was Nixon doing to him? He was talking to him. What was Monk doing? He was standing up—trembling. Was he talking loud? No, sir. That is all you saw of him after the shooting? Yes, sir. Did you see anything of Maultsby, about the time of the shooting? No, sir. And you can't tell who was nearest to Tolar? No, sir. After Tolar had fired, what did he do with the pistol? I don't know, sir, it went down in the crowd, and I never saw it any more. Did you see what became of Tolar, himself? No, sir. You lost sight of him after he fired? Yes sir. Where was your attention directed to after he fired? I went to look at the boy. Did you have any arms there, that day? No, sir. Did you anticipate anything of this sort? No, sir. Were you any party to any agreement to go there and rescue him that day? No, sir. Were you any party to any agreement to go there to protect him that day? No, sir. Do you know of any such agreement, either to rescue or protect him? No, sir, I do not. Is that all you know of this business? Yes, sir.

Did you know Capt. Tolar before you saw him there that day? Yes, sir., How long have you known him? I have known him for a year or such a matter. You know him well? Yes, sir. There is no possibility of your being mistaken about the man? No, sir, I know him well. Who fired the other pistol that was fired there that day? There was but the one fired. That one you saw fired? Yes, sir. Did you see any one else with a pistol, or any arms there, at any time that day, except Monk with a knife? I saw Mr. Phillips have a pistol. Where did you see Mr. Phillips have that pistol? He had it at the Market, after the boy was killed. Did you see him with a pistol before the boy was killed? No, sir, I did not. Had you gone up to the boy and looked at him? Yes, sir. You had passed away from the boy when you saw Phillips? Yes, sir. How long did it take you to get up to him? It didn't take me any time. How long did you stand there looking at him? Not many minutes. Did you stand there until he was dead? Yes, sir, he was about dead. How often did he gasp after you got up to him? He gasped once or twice. Then you turned to go off you saw Phillips? Yes, sir. Where was he standing when you saw him? He was standing up towards the arch. Standing on the sidewalk? Yes, sir. You say he had a pistol? Yes, sir How far from the boy was he standing? Five or six steps from the boy. Back behind him? Yes, sir. In front of the big arch? Yes, sir. Was he right in front of the big arch? No, sir, right at the edge. The South edge? Yes, sir. How was he holding the pistol? Just down in his right hand, by his side. What sort of a pistol was it? It was a little, small pistol; just a common little pocket pistol; it looked like a four, or five, or a six shooter. Did you hear Mr. Phillips say anything? I did not, sir. See him do anything with the pistol? No, sir. Wasn't it that pistol that fired? No, sir, it was not. Did you see Tolar distinctly, when he fired? Yes, sir. Could you see all about it? Yes, sir, I could see him from his waist up. Now, I want to know it some man could not have poked his hand under his arm and fired the pistol, and you not have known whether it was Tolar or not? No, sir. It was a perfectly natural position for his arm? Yes, sir. Which pistol was the largest, the one Tolar fired, or the one Phillips had? Tolar's was a heap the largest pistol. How came you to notice that pistol that Phillips had? He had it in his hand, and I was walking off and I just glanced at it. You didn't examine it? No, sir, I did not. Did Tolar draw his pistol after he got his position near the edge of the pavement, or did he draw it while he was coming through the the crowd? He took about one step after he drawed the pistol. You say it was a large pistol? Yes, sir. Was it as large a pistol as you have ever seen? I could not tell certain about that. You can't say whether you have seen a larger one? No, sir. You have seen a smaller one? Yes, sir.

Cross examination by the Counsel for the accused:

Who did you belong to in former times? Maj.

Shaw. Major Angus Shaw? Yes, sir. You say you have been living in Fayetteville about two years? Yes, sir. While you were living there Colonel Conwin was there? Yes, sir. Living there when he was there with his regiment? Yes, sir. Colonel Curwin tied you up by the thumbs? No, sir; he did not. Were you not tied up by the thumbs by some of his officers there—the yankee officers? No, sir; I was not. I ask you, John, if you were not tied up by the thumbs for the charge of cattle stealing? No, sir; I wasn't. You are certain you were not? Yes, sir. What time did you go to the market house that day? Well, I went up there first in the morning, and then I went back home, and I went back there about ten o'clock. What time was it that Beebee was brought out of the guard house? I can't recollect firmly, but I think it was about two o'clock, or three; I wont be certain which. And you were there all the time until Beebee was brought out of the guard house? Yes, sir. Were you there all the time on the south-side of the market house, between the large southern arch and the small southern arch. I was until Beebee was brought down. How far were you from the south-east corner? I was sitting on that bench there, right opposite where Mr. Leonard's office used to be. Who was there during that time? There were several parties. Just say whether there was any body there that you recognised? Tom Munroe was one that was there that I remember. Any body else? William Smith. Are these colored persons? Yes, sir. Was Louis Smith there? I didn't see him at the time, that I recollect. Was Jonathan Hollingsworth about there? I didn't see him. Do you know him? Yes, sir. Was George Hollingsworth there? No, sir. Was Calvin Hunter about there? I saw him passing. Did you see him stop about there? No, sir, I don't recollect that he did. Did Calvin take a seat on that bench by you? He did not, sir. Did he take a seat on the bench next below you? I don't know, sir; I didn't see him that day. So you don't recollect whether Calvin Hunter took a seat there or not? No, sir. How long had you moved from that position around the south-east corner before Beebee was brought down? It was some time. About how many minutes, fifteen or twenty minutes? Yes, sir; fifteen or twenty minutes before he was brought down. Now, from that place where you took your stand, your foot upon that post, could you see the steps of the market house? Yes, sir, I could look right straight under there. Which arch did you look through to see the steps of the market house? Between the two arches. By the arch I mean the opening—which opening did you look through? I looked right between the small and the large arch. Between the small arch and the large arch is a pillar—did you look through the pillar? No, sir; there is no pillar. I think there is? I don't think there is, sir.

(Witness shows on the chart his position as looking through the large arch.)

So you were standing with your foot upon that post, at the south-eastern corner, and you looked through the large eastern arch? Yes, sir. You didn't look through the small arch? No, sir.

(Witness again shows his position on the chart, and this time says he was looking through the small arch on the south-east corner.)

You were standing with your foot on that post near the south-east corner of the market house? Yes, sir. Off the pavement? Yes, sir. And you looked through that small arch, which is nearest down towards the guard house, and upon the east front? Yes, sir. And you could see Archy from where you stood by the steps? Yes, sir. Which foot did you have on that post; do you recollect? I had my left foot on the post. And in that position you say you saw them coming down the market house steps with Beebee? Yes, sir. What part of the steps were they on when you first saw Beebee? They were on the lower portion, coming down next to the ground. How many steps off from the ground were they when you first saw him? I could not tell firmly, point blank. Just come near it? Two or three steps. And at that time who did you say was with him? Mr. Wemyss. While he was upon the steps? Yes, sir. Was anybody else with him but Mr. Wemyss? I could not tell you whether there was on the steps, or not; I never saw Mr. Hardie until after he got on the ground. Which side did you see Wemyss on? On his right hand side. Did Wemyss have hold of him? Yes, sir. How did he have him? In his left hand. Did he have him in the collar? No, sir. Did he have him by the comforter around his neck? No, sir? How did he have him? He had a string around his thumb. You didn't see whether Faircloth had hold of him or not? No, sir. Did you see Faircloth there at all? He was along behind Archy I think as well as I can recollect. Well now, at that time when you first saw him upon the steps; did you see any thing of Hardie, either upon the floor or upon the steps or any where else, when you first saw Beebee? I don't think I did, I think Mr. Hardie was up the steps farther. They got down upon the floor and then you saw Hardie? Yes, sir. Hardie came down afterwards? I don't know whether he came from up the steps or not; I could not tell you positively. Don't you remember that Wemyss had just got down on the floor of the market house, and as soon as he did Hardie came running down the steps right after him? No, sir; I could not say that, because I don't know firmly. You don't know whether that is so or not? No, sir. That is right, tell what you know; now after they had got down upon the floor, then you saw Hardie? Yes, sir. Now where was Hardie when you first saw him? He was walking by the side of him, What side? On his left side. Did he have hold of him? I can't say certain whether he had or not. Was he close to him? Yes, sir; he was close enough to have hold of him, but I could not say whether he had or not. Did you loose sight of them before they got out of Becky Ben's stall? Yes, sir. You lost sight of him directly after they cleared the steps? Yes, sir. When they got behind the pillar, how far did they come from the foot of the market house steps out towards the end of Becky Ben's stall; before you lost sight of them? They did not have to go a very long distance—just a few steps. As many as three or four steps? Yes, sir. Now during the time they were going those three or four steps from the foot of the steps or to where you lost sight of them, were you looking at them all the time? I looked at them as long as I could see them? Now during that time, while you were looking at them between the steps and the arch of the market house when they got so that the pillar shut out your view, did you see any thing unusual occur? Of Mr. Tolar? Any thing strange; any thing that was noticeable? No, sir; I did not. Then you saw no more of them until after they had turned around the corner of the main arch? No, sir. When they turned there, you were still standing with your feet on that post? Yes, sir. Now what was the first thing that attract-

ed your attention after they had turned that corner upon the pavement? I heard some persons say "rally." That was the first thing? Yes, sir. As soon as the party with Archy turned that corner then you heard some one say "rally"? They said it as they were turning the corner. Well then, what was the next thing? Well, I saw Mr. Tolar coming up, but did not notice of his having any weapons; I saw Monk have his knife. How far did Archy get down the pavement before he struggled; before he made a scuffle, or did he make no scuffle at all? I didn't notice his making any scuffle. Now, I want to know of you whether you were looking closely at Archy, from the time he turned that corner, until the time he was shot? No, sir, I was not looking at him all the time. Sometimes you were looking at him and sometimes looking at other people? No, sir, I was not; I was looking back towards Mr. Tolar after I heard them say to rally, upon him. How far had Archy got down the pavement before he was shot? He got right against the arch. Against which arch? Against the pillar. Which pillar? The little pillar. The pillar of the little arch? Yes, sir, right on the corner. Had he got down opposite you? Yes, sir, just about opposite me. And in the center of the pavement? Yes, sir. What do you mean by opposite you? If any one was to walk along and get against me in front, I would call that opposite. Which way were you looking at the time? I was looking up in Mr. Tolar's face, then. So you say Archy was in a straight line between that little post and the corner of the market house? I could not say who, he was directly straight, because I didn't notice particularly enough for that. What is your impressions, that he was a little further down or a little farther back than that? He was somewhere along against the arch. Just against the little post? I would not say for certain point blank. Was it before he got there or after he got there that you saw Tolar come up into the crowd? It was just before he got right against the arch. Could you see Tolar come through from the north portion of the large arch? Yes, sir. Up near the north pillar? Yes, sir. Tolar went right across the pavement? Yes, sir. Didn't make any halt at all? He did halt a little for the people. You saw Tolar come right across the pavement? He didn't come right straight across, he went cat-a-cornered. He went across the pavement and off the pavement? Yes, sir. At the time Tolar fired, how far was he from you? He was two or three or four steps. Was Tolar off the pavement or on? He was off. How far off? No distance to be mentioned. Are you certain he was off the pavement at all? Yes, sir, I am certain he was not standing on the pavement. And he was only two or three steps from you? Yes, sir. How did Tolar have his hands when you first saw him start? He had one hand under his shawl. What was he doing with his left hand? He was swinging his left hand. He had his right hand under his shawl? Yes, sir. That was a gray shawl? Yes, sir. Was the shawl pinned or fastened in any way? I could not say certain that it was, I don't know whether it was or not. Did you notice whether it was caught together or holding together up by his throat? I don't recollect. But you are certain he had his right hand under his shawl at his left side? Yes, sir. And he came right up—did he come running or walking? Walking. Walking fast or at a moderate gait? He just stepped up at a common gait. Until he got within three or four steps of Beebee?

Yes, sir. Was anybody between him and Beebee? When he was coming along, there was one man that I noticed being between them, that he pushed away. Did he push anybody else out of the way? I don't know that he did; I never saw him push out one person. And when he got up there he pushed that person out of the way? Yes, sir. That person was in front of him. Yes, sir. Right between where he stopped when he fired, and where Beebee was when he was shot? Yes, sir. Could you see that was Jim Douglas? Yes, sir. Which way was that person looking? I cannot tell exactly, I was not noticing the person, I was noticing him. But you had to notice the person; which way was that person looking? I don't know rightly; I could not say for certain which way the person was looking. Don't you know whether he was looking back at Tolar? I don't think he was; he might have been looking across the street. Tolar came up, with his left hand; he pushed him out of the way? Yes, sir. Where did he push him? Some where about his shoulder. Just shoved him one side? Yes, sir. Did you notice whether he turned him around or not? I did not, sir. Did you notice whether it was a smart push or a gentle push? I never noticed in particular. Which way did he push him: by his right, or to his left? As he walked up, he pushed him to his left. Now at that time you say Tolar drew the pistol? He didn't walk, I don't think, more than one step after he drew the pistol from under his shawl. So he drew the pistol, and then took another step forward? Yes, sir. And he brought the pistol up how? He threw the muzzle (witness represents throwing the muzzle first into the air, and then bringing it down to a level.) Was he standing straight at the time? No, sir. Was he leaning backward? No, sir, just leaning front a little. Was the pistol pointed straight, or was it pointed down a little? I could not tell. Was Beebee standing straight at that time? I don't know, sir. I wasn't noticing Beebee at the time. You had all your attention directed at Tolar? Yes, sir. Was there anybody between you and Tolar at that time? No, sir, there was not. So it was a clear open view? I could see him. Nothing to obstruct it at all? No, sir. No body between him and Mr. Tolar? I don't know that there was anybody between Tolar and Beebee, only the man he had pushed out of the way. And he wasn't between him then, was he? No, sir. Did you notice who was on Tolar's left hand at the time? No, sir, I did not. Where was James Douglass? I never noticed James Douglass; I thought it was him that Captain Tolar pushed out of the way. What became of him after he pushed him out of the way? Who ever it was he pushed, he stood there. Stood on Tolar's left? Yes, sir. So he was the only man near to Tolar on his left? Yes, sir. You are certain about that? Was there a crowd around Tolar, or was Tolar sort of outside the crowd? At the time he shot the man, all crowded up pretty much behind him. Behind him on the pavement, or off? Some were on, some off, and some were under the market. Well, was the crowd up near to Tolar, or was he in advance of the crowd? They were up near to him. How far off was the nearest one from him? I don't know, sir, rightly. Now, John, can you give us the name of a single man, just one, white or black, that was standing there in the crowd at the time the pistol was fired? Yes, sir. Just give it to us. Pat. Evans was one. Where was he standing? He was standing up against the arch. Which arch? The small arch, he had passed in and got up with his back against

the arch. Against which side of the arch, the south east side? Yes, sir. You are sure that he was down there? Yes, sir. You say he was standing there when the pistol fired? I could not tell you for certain. That is what I ask you for; how long before that did you see him standing there? It was after. How long afterwards? By the time I could get in to look at the boy I saw Pat. I repeat the question: can you give me the name of a single person, white or colored, that was standing there in that crowd at the time the pistol that was fired, except Tolar? Monk was there for one I am certain. Where was Monk at that time? He was in the crowd, but to tell you rightly where he was, I could not. You didn't see him at the time the pistol was fired? No, sir, not at that time, but I saw him so shortly afterwards that I knew he could not have got out of the crowd. You haven't told me the name of a single person who was about there at the time the pistol was fired? I told you Monk was there. Give me another if you think you have proved Monk was there. Robert Simmons was another. Now tell us where Robert was? He stood right out behind him, so that Robert was right there between the corner of the market house and Davis' corner? Some where along out in that quarter, sir. How far was Robert behind him? I could not tell you, sir. Was he two or three feet; could you have turned around and touched him? No, sir. Just point out something to show how far off he was from you. He was in speaking distance. That might be fifty yards; as far as the Judge Advocate? Further. As far as that pillar? I reckon he was, (about twenty-five feet.) Was Robert Simmons standing behind you and about twenty-five feet? Yes sir. And he was back of you? Yes, sir. Now tell us another one? I believe that is all that I can recollect, sir. You can recollect no one? No, sir. I don't mean to your front; either to your right, or to your left, or near; any where; another man that was in that crowd at that time? That is all I recollect, sir, now. Was Monk there, did you say? Yes, sir, he was there. And as for Simmons, you are certain he was there? Yes, sir, for I heard his voice. Because he was behind you, and you could see him? I didn't see him; I only heard his voice. What did he say? He was talking to some persons; I don't know rightly who. What did he say; one word he said? I don't recollect nary a word that he said, but I heard his voice behind me. Did you see John Armstrong there? I did not, sir, not till after he was killed. Where did you see him then? After I passed Mr. Phillips, I went over to the corner store, Mr. Taylor's store, and came back, and John Armstrong, Sam Toomer and several others were there. That was some time afterwards? Yes, sir. Did you see any thing of James McNeil there? No, sir, I don't recollect that I did. Did you see any thing of Calvin Hunter there at the time of the shooting? No, sir, I saw him just before the boy came down the steps, passing by there, but didn't see him after the boy was shot. I mean at the time the boy was shot, did you see him then? No, sir, I didn't. Did you see young Leary there? No, sir. Nor Sam Toomer? Not until afterward. You saw no person there at the time the shot was fired except those you have named? No, sir. Now, as soon as Tolar fired the pistol you saw the flash? Yes, sir. You saw the smoke? Yes, sir. You are certain it was that pistol that was fired? Yes, sir. Then what did he do? He went off from the crowd. Which way? I could not say, sir. What did he do with the pistol? I don't know, sir. Which way did he turn? He turned right straight around. Did he turn toward the market house, or the other way? I could not tell, sir; I didn't notice, but I noticed he was gone out of the crowd shortly afterwards. You didn't see what he did with the pistol? No, sir; when he fired, it went down into the crowd, and I didn't see it any more. Why was it your whole attention was drawn toward Mr. Tolar before he drew the pistol? Because I saw him have it in his hand under the shawl. You saw the pistol before he drew it? No, sir, I didn't. Was your attention attracted towards him merely because he had his hand under his shawl? Yes, sir, if a man was to have his hand under his shawl standing up in the crowd of course you would notice him, it would be a little more curious than any one else. How large a shawl was it? It was a good large shawl. Was there another man there in that crowd before Tolar drew his pistol that had a shawl on except Tolar? I never noticed any other one, sir. Was there no man there, that you noticed, that had a shawl on, or his hand under his shawl? No, sir. So that was the only reason why your attention was drawn to Tolar before he drew the pistol, because he had his hand under his shawl? Yes, sir. And there was no other reason? No, sir. Nothing in his manner? No, sir. Nothing in his coming up? No, sir. And no other reason in the world except that he had his hand under his shawl that attracted your attention? No, sir. Do you know Tolar? I have been knowing him for a year and better. Were there not other men in the crowd· that you had known as long as Tolar, and longer? Yes, sir; there was other men that I knew longer. And there was no other man in the crowd that you noticed at all, except Tolar? I just noticed several, but then I didn't pay any particular notice of any of them. You didn't take sufficient notice of them to remember them? No, sir. You say, shortly after the shooting; almost as soon as the firing was done, that you pressed up into the crowd to see the boy? Yes, sir. And he was lying then upon the pavement? Yes, sir. That you then made your way out of the crowd, and as soon as you did, you saw Sam. Phillips with a pistol in his hand? Yes, sir. Which hand did he have the pistol in? In his right hand. And his right hand was down by his right leg? Yes, sir. Was he doing anything with the pistol? . Not a thing. Was he saying anything about the pistol? No, sir. Did you hear him say a word to nobody. I did not, sir. Did you hear anybody say a word to him? No, sir; not at the time. He was just standing there with the pistol in his right hand? Yes, sir. You saw that pistol? I just looked at it as I walked by him—i didn't stop to notice it. Did you see it sufficiently well to be sure it was not a small pistol? Yes, sir. One of these small pocket pistols? Yes, sir. Looked like a four or five shooter? Yes, sir. You spoke just now of something about the length of it; was it five inches long? I guess so. How many inches do you think it was, five or six or seven; don't you think it was longer than seven? It might have been; I could not say it was any longer. Take eight inches; do you think it was longer than eight inches? I don't think it was. Can't you say nine inches? It might have been nine, but I don't think it was nine. Will you undertake to swear it was not nine inches long? No, sir; I would not. Will you swear it was not ten inches long? Yes, sir; I will swear it wasn't twelve inches l ong. Will you swear it wasn't ten inches long? I don't know, sir about that; I would not swear about it, of course.

But you are willing to swear it was not twelve inches long? Yes, sir. The whole pistol? Yes, sir. Do you remember how it was mounted whether it was brass or silver or steel mounted? No, sir; I didn't notice it particularly. Did you see Mr. Phillips hold it up? No, sir. You didn't hear him say "look at my pistol, it hasn't been shot off." ? No, sir. You heard nothing of it? No, sir. Where did Phillips go with the pistol after you saw him? I don't know where he went, sir. Where did you go after you saw the pistol in Phillip's hand? I went over to Mr. Taylor's store, and stopped there a few minutes, and come back to the market again; and I never saw Mr. Phillips any more after that.

Re-direct Examination by the Counsel for the prosecution?

You say you haven't been much accustomed to measuring? No, sir. How many inches do you think that tape is? It might be twenty-four (tape measures two feet eight inches.) Tell me how long do you think twelve inches is on that tape?

(Witness measures off eleven and three eighth inches.)

Show how long one inch is?

(Witness measures off one inch and a quarter.)

Counsel for the prosecution said : "I nearly wished to show how inaccurate witness' guesses were in reference to the length of pistols."

How long do you suppose the barrel of Mr. Phillips pistol was by this tape ?

(Witness measures off five and one fourth inches.)

How long was the stock?

(Witness measures off four and three-eighth inches, making the total length of the pistol about nine and a half inches)

Did you see Phillips' pistol well? I just had one look at it. And your opinion is formed from that? Yes, sir. You think Tolar's pistol was bigger than that? Yes, sir; it was a larger pistol than that. The Counsel for defence has asked you who you saw at the time Tolar fired the pistol; did you see any body at the very moment the pistol was fired? Nobody except him. Your eyes were fixed upon him at the time? Yes, sir. It is impossible for you to say that you saw anybody else at that moment? Yes, sir. You saw a man about firing a pistol, and you looked at him until the pistol fired? Yes sir. Didn't you think the pistol was about to fire, when you saw it pointed out? Yes, sir. Didn't you think it was about to fire at Archy? Yes, sir. Were you alarmed at the moment? Yes, sir, it sort of frightened me. It shocked you? Yes, sir. Your attention was drawn by that ? Yes, sir. You saw nobody else at that time ? No, sir. Immediately afterwards and immediately before, you had seen some men ? Yes, sir. At this instant, you could not see anybody else? No, sir. Now, did you see Tolar's pistol better than you saw Phillips' pistol? Yes, sir, I did ? You saw it better ? Yes, sir. You say that was a big pistol ? Yes, sir. How long do you think that was on the tape ? (Witness measures off sixteen inches.) You swore positively just now that Phillip's pistol was not twelve inches long? No, sir, I didn't swear that. I said I thought I could swear it was not, but I didn't do it. I understood you to say so. No, sir, I didn't; I said I would not be willing to swear either way. I understand you will swear to no length ? No, sir. That you make an estimate about it; you have a strong opinion, but as to swearing positively, you can't do it ? No, sir. You have been asked what attracted your attention to Tolar more than anybody else ? You said because he had his hand in his breast; did he have his hand in his breast when you first saw him? Yes, sir. And you think that was what attracted your attention to him? Yes, sir. Was the crowd pretty noisy at the time you first saw Tolar? Had you heard this expression, "rally, boys"? No, sir. Did you see Tolar first, or hear somebody say "rally, boys"? I saw Mr. Tolar before I heard that expression. And he had his hand in his breast then? Yes, sir. Are you certain about that, which you heard first? Yes, sir, I didn't particularly notice him as much then as I did after hearing the word. I saw him come walking up. You saw him, and immediately or shortly afterwards you heard the word rally? Shortly afterwards. Then you saw him more? Yes, sir. Did you expect any mischief from him when you saw him moving? No, sir. I could not tell much about it. You were beginning to be suspicious that something was going to happen? Yes, sir, by seeing Monk with his knife trying to cut at him. You say Tolar was in the crowd with his right hand in his breast; you saw Monk make at this man and cut with his knife; you saw the man with his knife in his breast, moving through the crowd towards the prisoner? Yes, sir. And that attracted your attention you say? Yes, sir. And after this circumstance, you looked at him until he had fired? Yes, sir. Didn't you look at Monk when you saw him making at him with a knife? No, sir. Didn't that attract your attention, too? I didn't notice him at all, he was pushed back. Where did you say Pat Evans was? Standing against the wall. Just after you had gone up, and looked at the prisoner? Yes, sir. Against the wall of the market house or the arch? The arch. Which arch do you mean, the small arch at the corner? Yes, sir. In the opening? No, sir, he was standing with his back against the brick wall. My meaning of the arch is the opening in the wall that you go through, he was not standing in the opening? No, sir. Against the bricks between the little and big opening? Against the little opening. Which side was he on, the side that is nearest to the big opening? No, sir. The side next to the corner? Yes, sir. You say Pat Evans was standing there when you saw him? Yes, sir. That was after the pistol was fired, and the man was down? Yes, sir. You said Bob Simmons was standing about twenty five feet from you? Yes, sir. He was behind you? Yes, sir. Did you see him before or after you went up to the dead body? I saw him when I went to the dead body. Was he standing out there when you saw him? I heard him speak to some person. So your opinion was from the sound of his voice, or did you see him? No, sir. You didn't see him? No, sir, not until afterwards. You heard a voice that you thought was his, and you think it was twenty-five feet off? Yes, sir. I understand you to say you didn't see him at all? I never saw him till after. You saw him after Beebee was shot? Yes, sir. Where was he standing when you saw him? He was standing looking at the boy. But you had heard his voice before? Yes, sir. Almost at the time of the shooting? Yes, sir. You say you didn't see Armstrong there, for how long after the shooting? I saw him in a short while afterwards. Had you walked away? I had walked around the street and back. Let me see if I understand you: after this pistol was fired you immediately pursued your way in the crowd and saw the dead man? Yes, sir. You turned off and went out of the crowd, and went across the street? Yes, sir. Did you go all the way across to the next pave-

ment? Yes, sir. Where did you go to across the pavement? To Mr. Taylor's. Didn't you say you had seen Tom Monroe and William Smith that day? Yes, sir. What time? Before Beebee come down. Were you taken up by Colonel Curwin for any offense, or by any of his troops? No, sir. You were not even taken up? No, sir. Nor any charge against you that you ever heard of? No, sir, our folks had a false charge against me. How long ago was that? Year before last. Were you ever tried for that offense, I don't ask you what the charge was? No, sir. Have you ever been convicted at all? No, sir. The charge was a false one? Yes, sir.

The Counsel for the accused said he would like to cross-examine the witness on the subject just introduced.

The Counsel for the prosecution said the subject was not a new one, but one opened by the Counsel for the accused.

The Counsel for the accused said he desired to ask the witness, if the Court pleased, in reply to the questions asked by the prosecution, that he had been taken up by our people upon a false accusation. I desire to ask him whether he was punished; what that accusation was, and what the punishment.

The Commission granted the request of the Counsel for the accused to cross-examine the witness on that subject, but instructed the witness that he was at liberty to refuse to answer any question that would tend to criminate himself.

Re-cross-examination by the Counsel for the accused:

What was that charge upon which you were taken up? About some money between me and Mr. Bunn. How were you punished? They didn't punish me at all. That is the only time you have been taken up? Yes, sir.

Re-direct examination resumed, by the Counsel for the prosecution:

Were you ever tried at all? Yes, sir. Before whom? Mr. Robert Awel. He is a Justice of the Peace? Yes, sir. You were not subjected to any punishment at all? No, sir, he did say there was to have been some punishment put upon me, but then he said if I would pay it, it would be all right.

Re-cross examination resumed, by the Counsel for the accused:

He said if you paid it it would be all right? Yes, sir. And you did pay it? Yes, sir.

JOHN DALEY, a witness for the prosecution, having been first duly sworn, testified as follows:

Examined by the Counsel for the prosecution:

What is your name? John Daley. Do you go by any other name? No, sir. Are you ever called John Tyler? I have often been called John Tyler. Do you live in Fayetteville? • Yes, sir. What is your business? I am a sexton, sir. Did you bury Archy Beebee? Yes, sir. Who ordered you to bury him? The Sheriff sent for me, sir. How long did you bury him after he was killed? The next day, sir. Do you remember what day you buried him? On twelfth day of the month, sir. The Sheriff ordered you to do it? Yes, sir. Did the Sheriff pay you for it? He gave me three dollars a few days afterwards. Was it for that? He never said, he just gave me the money. What day was it the Sheriff gave you the three dollars? It was the eighteenth of the month, sir. Did you ever have any talk with Mr. Tolar, about it, or did he ever say anything to you about it? We met one day on the pavement. Was that after the Sheriff paid you? About a week, sir. Where was that, in the town of Fayetteville? Yes, sir. What part of the town? Down near the market, between Mr. Banks and Mr. Kyles. About a week after the Sheriff had given you the three dollars? Yes, sir. What occurred then? He said "Boy, did you bury that boy?" I said "Yes, sir." He said "I suppose I owe you something?" I never said anything, and he gave me two dollars. Was that all that passed between you? He asked me if that satisfied me. I said I was satisfied with what the Sheriff gave me. Is that all the conversation? That was all we had, sir.

Cross-examination by the Counsel, for the accused:

When were you summoned in this case? Last Monday. Who have you ever told about this matter before you were summoned? I don't recollect, sir; there were several people asked me about it. Before you were summoned? Yes, sir. Who had told you about this matter—name them. John Armstrong was one person, sir. When was that? He asked me some three or four weeks ago. After John got back from Raleigh, or before? It was before he come to Raleigh. He come up and asked you about it? Yes, sir. He was the first one? No, sir, he was not the first one. He was one? He was. Who was another? Robert Simmons asked me if I got pay for it. How long ago did Robert Simmons ask you about it? I don't know, sir; it was shortly afterwards. Before Simmons had returned from Raleigh? It was before he come to Raleigh. Who was another? She was a woman—I don't recollect her name—she lives around by Mrs. Welches. A white woman or a colored woman? A colored woman, sir. That was there? Yes, sir. Anybody else? Not that I can recollect. So you remember having told it to these three—John Armstrong, Robert Simmons, and a colored woman whose name you don't know? Yes, sir. Were you acquainted with Capt. Tolar before that time? I had saw him, sir; before then. Did you have any acquaintance with him? No, sir; not before that time. Tolar had never spoken to you about this matter, had he; before the time you speak of? No, sir; not about that matter. Had he ever spoken to you about any matter? Not that I can recollect. Was Tolar at the funeral? No, sir; if he was I didn't see him—I don't recollect seeing any white persons there. And you were brought up by the sheriff to bury him? Yes, sir. And the sheriff paid you three dollars? Yes, sir. What is your usual charge for burying the dead? Three dollars is the price for digging the grave. That is all you did? Yes, sir. And the sheriff paid you three dollars? Yes, sir. Did he ask you what the charge was? No, sir, he didn't ask me. The sheriff didn't tell you what he was paying you the three dollars for? No, sir. Don't you know it was for that service? I know he didn't owe me anything else. And you say a week afterwards Tolar met you, where? Between Banks' and Kyles, on the pavement that goes across there. Did he call you by name? No, sir, he just said "boy." Now give us the exact language of Tolar. "Boy did you bury that boy," says I "yes, sir." Was that the only boy you had buried? No, sir. During that week had you buried any? No, sir. How long was it after the burial of Archy, that Tolar met you? It was a week afterwards. It was a week after the sheriff paid you, you said? Yes, sir. So it was some ten or twelve days after you buried Archy? Yes, sir. Had you buried any others in those ten or twelve days? No, sir; on the day it was done I was digging a grave. You had buried boys before

that time? Yes, sir. And Tolar just come up to you and said: "Boy did you bury that boy?" Yes, sir. He didn't call the name of the boy? No, sir. He didn't say any thing about the name, and you told him you had buried him? Yes, sir. He didu't ask you the charge, or ask you whether you had been paid, or ask you any thing else; he just paid you the two dollars? Yes, sir, he paid me two dollars. Did he have the two dollars loose in his pocket, or did he get it out of the pocket where there was more money, or did he have to get it out of a pocket book? He got it out of a pocket book where there was some other money. Was it a two dollar bill? Yes, sir. So he took it out of his pocket book, and he had other bills there? Yes, sir. Did you see whether he had any one dollar bills? No, sir, I never noticed that. Did you see any other bills at all, but that two dollar bill? I noticed some five dollar bills there. Did you notice any other two dollar bills? No, sir. You never made any demand on him at all for pay? No, sir, I didn't know he had to give any to me. He then asked you if that satisfied you? Yes, sir. And you told him you were satisfied before? Yes, sir. Whose grave was that you dug the day you buried Beebee? A child of James McIntyres. Where did he live? He lived down in one of Mrs. Utley's houses. Where is Capt. Tolar? He is here. Point him out? There he is with specks on.

Re-direct examination by the Counsel for the prosecution:

How many times had you seen Capt. Tolar, in your life, before he paid you that two dollars? I could not tell, sir, I saw him numbers of times. And you knew that man who was called Capt. Tolar? I knew who was called Mr. Tolar. And that is the man who paid you the two dollars? Yes, sir. No sort of doubt about that? No, sir, that is the man. Did he have on his spectacles that day? I disrecollect whether he had on his specks or not. Mr. Fuller asked you if you didn't understand that that three dollars the Sheriff paid you, was paid you for burying the body? That is what I thought that day. Didn't you understand that the two dollars paid you by Tolar was for burying the same body? Yes, sir. Now, this child you were digging the grave of the day before, was it a boy child or a girl child? It was a boy child. How big a grave was it? The child was about three years old. And you say you didn't dig any other grave between the time you digged Beebee's grave, and the time you saw Capt. Tolar and he gave you the money? No, sir. No other grave? No, sir. Let me have that conversation again that you had that day with Capt. Tolar; you met him on this little side walk, and he said "Boy, did you bury that boy," is that it? Yes, sir. And you told him what? I told him I did. Then what did he say? I suppose I owe you something. What did you say? I never said "Yes, sir," and I never said "No, sir." Did he have his pocket book in his hand? No, sir. He took it out before he gave you the money? Yes, sir, and he gave me a two dollar bill, and asked me, "does that satisfy you," and I said, "I was satisfied with what the sheriff gave me,' and he said "Did the sheriff give you some?" and he walked on. Is that all? Yes, sir. So, I understand that he knew the sheriff had paid you; you were not trying to cheat him? No, sir, I didn't know anything about getting any from him. You saw him have other money in his purse? Yes, sir. Was there anything peculiar about this two dollar bill? Nothing, only one end of it was split, sir. You say you have told certain persons about this conversation you had with Tolar. Yes, sir. They asked me did I get paid for it. Did you get pay for burying Beebee, is that what they asked you? Yes, sir. What did you tell them? Yes. Did they ask you who paid you? Yes, sir. Robert Simmons asked me who paid me, and I told him the sheriff had given me some money, and Mr. Tolar had given me some money. Did you tell John Armstrong the same thing? Yes, sir. And this woman? Yes, sir. Do you remember you ever told it to others that you can recollect? I have told it to some persons else, but I don't recollect who. Have you ever told it to any white people that you remember? No, sir, not that I recollect. Do you remember having mentioned it to any white man at all? No, sir. There were some white gentlemen standing near at the time Bob Simmons axed me. Who were they? One was named Mr. Newel, but I don't know any more about the name than that. He was standing near when you told Simmons? Yes, sir. Do you know who had you summoned here? No, sir.

On motion, the Commission adjourned to meet on Saturday, the 10th inst., at 11 A. M.

RALEIGH, N. C., August 10, 1867—11 A. M.

The Commission met pursuant to adjournment.

Present: All the members of the Commission, the Judge Advocate, the Counsel for the prosecution, all the accused and their Counsel.

The reading of the testimony taken yesterday was waived, there being no objection thereto.

Yesterday's proceedings were then read and approved.

The Judge Advocate said: "I am requested by the Commission to state that the order for the summons of eighteen witnesses, the list of which I hold in my hand, to be summoned for the defence, will be granted, if the Counsel for the defence state that these witnesses are each and all of them necessary and material to the defence, and that list includes all the witnesses the defence now intends to summon; that should the defence hereafter require other witnesses, the Commission will require the defence to state what necessary and material fact it is intended to prove by the witnesses, which may be hereafter required."

The Counsel for the accused: "I will state to the Court that the witnesses, whose names are upon the list that the Judge Advocate holds in his hands, I am informed, and I believe are necessary and material, each and every one of them. The most of them I have seen myself, and I know they are necessary and material, and the others are furnished me by my associate Counsel, resident in the town of Fayetteville, and, upon his information, I state to the Court that I believe they are necessary and material.

They are all the witnesses that, at this time, we think will be required. It may be necessary, however, hereafter, to ask for the summoning of other witnesses, and if so we have no objection at all to set forth, in an affidavit, that they are material, and the grounds of their materiality."

The Commission thereupon ordered the issuing of the summons for the witnesses for the defence.

RACHEL LORD, a witness for the prosecution, having been first duly sworn, testified as follows:

Examined by the Counsel for the prosecution: What is your name? Rachel. Rachel what? Rachel Lord. Where have you been living for the last two or three years? In Fayetteville; I have lived there all my life. Did you see Archy Beebee the day he was killed? Yes, sir. What time did you go to the market house that day? About three o'clock, or half after, or such a matter. Did you go there before Archy was brough'

out of the guard house? He was up stairs when I got there. When you got there where did you go to; which end did you come up to first? I come up on Green street, and come up to the north corner, towards Mr. Fishblates'. That is the north east corner? Yes, sir. Did you stand there? I stood there a few minutes. Now while you were standing there, was you up stairs? Yes, sir. Did you see any crowd around the market house? Yes, sir. Much of a crowd? Yes, sir. How many people do you think were there? I don't know, sir. What is your opinion; do you think there were a hundred? Yes, I reckon so. Two hundred? I reckon there was, before it was done with. Was it larger before it was done with than it was when you first got there? Yes, sir; they kept gathering. How long did you stand about that north east corner? I don't know, sir. Five minutes? About half an hour, I reckon. Archy was up stairs all the time? Yes, sir. While you were standing there, did you see inside of the market house? Yes, sir. And outside along the pavement. Yes, sir. Did you see anybody there you knew? I don't know, sir; I don't recollect—it has been a right smart while; I saw Monk, and he is the only one I recollect. What made you notice Monk; what was he doing? He was cutting there with his knife, and I was afraid—that is what's the matter; and I stood there and looked on a few minutes. What was he doing with the knife? He was cutting. Cutting what? I don't know sir, what he was cutting. Was he whittling? Yes, sir. Was he saying anything? I hear him say he was going to cut a damned nigger's throat. That was while you were standing at the north east corner? Yes, sir. You are certain about that? Yes, sir. Did you notice anybody else in that crowd that you knew? I saw Sam. Hall and Ed. Powers skeeting about. While Archy was up stairs? Yes, sir. And you were standing at the corner? Yes, sir. What do you mean by skeeting about? I mean running around, and through the market house, and whispering to each other—I don't know what they were saying. You mean they were running about actively in the crowd? Yes, sir; gay and lively, all through the market house. Those were Ed. Powers and Sam. Hall? Yes, sir. Did you see any one else? I don't know, sir; I don't recollect who I did see. Think if you can recollect any body at all? No, sir. Have you thought about these things since you have been summoned? Yes, sir; I have studied about it. But in all your studying, you don't recollect but these persons? No, sir; I don't. Were you standing at that north east corner when Archy came down stairs? No, sir. How long had you moved away from there before he came down? I was standing there when he started down, I moved a little further back, so that I could see better. Just before he came down did you see these ladies that came down and went to the carriage? Yes, sir. Did you know them? No, sir, I knew their names. I saw Miss Massey. Did you see the carriage? I saw the carriage standing there when I went there. How far was it from you? About as far as that young gentleman (thirty feet.) Who went with the ladies to the carriage? I don't know, sir. Did you see anybody go with them? Yes, sir. You don't know who it was? No, sir. I saw Maultsby. Did he go with them to the carriage? No, sir, he went there after they got in. There was another man went with them, Mr. Vann, I reckon his name was. Don't you know? No, sir. What makes you think it was Mr. Vann? I heard some say that was his name, I would know the man if I was to see him, I knew his face. When was it you heard some one say that was his name? I don't know, sir, but I have heard several times that was his name. Since you came here? Yes, sir. You did see Maultsby go to the carriage, was that after the ladies got in? Yes, sir. What did he have to do? He went there and said something to them. Did he speak to the ladies or Mr. Vann? He was whispering to the ladies, I think. Did you see any one else go to the carriage? I don't recollect any one else. You don't know that any one else did go? No, sir. You saw the carriage drive off? Yes, sir. Did the boy come down after that? Yes, sir. Directly after? Yes, sir, pretty soon after. How long? About five minutes. As he started down you moved away? Yes, sir, I did. You moved away so as to get a better sight of him, as he came down the steps? Yes, sir. You moved further to the east front? Yes, sir. What happened then, what did you see that attracted your attention? I saw the crowd making a rush at Archy, and Archy told Mr. Hardie "Do, don't take me down stairs," and I turned my back and ran and hid behind a box at Mr. Taylor's. When was that rush made at him, that you speak of? That was just before he spoke. Was that rush made at him before he got down the stairs? Yes, sir, he seemed to be four or five steps from the floor, then. And it was then the rush was made, and you heard this exclamation of his, "Do don't take me down there?" Yes, sir. You say you ran then? Yes, sir. Where did you run to? I ran to Mr. Taylor's store, and hid behind a box in front of his store. How far off was that from the market house? About as far as from here to that corner (about forty feet) may be a little farther. You ran over to Mr. Taylor's and hid behind a good's box? Yes, sir. What happened then? I stayed down there until I heard some one cry out "shoot him," shoot him!" and I heard them say clear the way, and I expected I would see him relieved and go to the guard house, and then I saw that gentleman (Tolar) draw his arm up or his hand and shoot. You heard the cry "shoot him, shoot him," and you heard a cry of clear the way, and you thought he would get safe, and you unmasked and had a good look at him, and saw what was going on? Yes, sir. And you saw some gentleman shoot him? Yes, sir. Did you see the gentleman who shot him? Yes, sir, I saw from his shoulders up. I didn't know his name, I had seen his face often. You saw the pistol in this man's hand that you speak of? I saw him shoot, I could not tell what kind of a pistol it was. Could you tell whether it was a pistol at all? I am certain it was a pistol. You know it was not a gun? I am certain it was a pistol. You saw well enough to see it was a pistol, but what sort of a pistol you cannot say? No, sir. How was the man dressed who fired the pistol? It looked to me he had on a gray coat, but some of them said it was a shawl, I could not tell which it was. Your impression was what? I thought it was a coat, but it was a shawl. How do you know? Them that were near said so. What did you think? I thought it was a coat, but I didn't notice much; I was looking at the pistol and the aim. Your impression was that the man had on a gray coat? He had on a gray suit of some kind, I don't know what it was. Did you see any part of him besides his arm? From his shoulders up. Did you see what kind of a hat he had on? I don't recollect, I saw the man shoot for certain. Did you see what became of

the man after he shot? I never looked any more, I went right straight home. As soon as the pistol fired, you turned and left? Yes, sir. Have you ever seen that man since who fired the pistol? No, sir, I never seen him there since. I seen him pass out here once or twice. Do you see him in the court? I think that is him sitting right over there. Which one do you mean, can't you see anything peculiar about him that you can tell? It looks as if he had something the matter with his eye. With a moustache? Yes, sir. That is the man you think fired the pistol? Yes, sir. And you went off immediately after that? Yes, sir. Was his back to you when he fired? When he fired he was kind of sideways from me.

Cross-examination by the Counsel for the accused.

Rachel, where had you been up Green street, when you came down to the market house? I had been over to Mr. Anderson's store. Your sister Ann was along with you? I haven't got any sister Ann. What is your sister's name that was with you? I had no sister with me, my sisters were all at home. Who was with you? There was nobody with me in particular; there was some there, but they were not with me. I am talking about when you came from Mr. Anderson's to the market house. There was nobody with me. I come alone, I had a bundle. And you were alone? Yes, sir. You were not coming from a funeral that evening? No, sir, I was not. Have you any sisters at all? Yes, sir, I have. How many? I have got six. I don't want but one, have you got one that is living with Mr. John Davis? Yes, sir. What is her name? Her name is Fanny. She was living with him when I come up here. Now, Rachel, I will ask you if that sister Fanny was not with you that evening? No, sir. I will ask you if your sister Fanny did not tell you just before you came up here, that you knew nothing about this matter? No, she did not, and nobody else didn't tell me so. And you told your sister Fanny, "well, I don't know anything about it, but I can't get more at home than I can make up in Raleigh as a witness in this case"? No, sir. I didn't tell no such a thing. I never said a word of it to any one. There ain't three men nor women in town that knows I know anything about it. You say you didn't tell your sister Fanny? No, sir, I didn't tell nobody so. And you came and took your stand at that north-east corner,—were you standing on the pavement, or off? I was standing on the pavement right at the corner, right opposite Mr. Taylor's where there was a good's box. I am talking about when you first got there? I stood right at the corner then. Outside or inside? Outside. Were you close up against the corner? I was on the edge of the pavement. On the outer edge of the pavement? Yes, sir. So you were on the outer edge of the pavement, at the north east corner of the market house? Yes, sir. And you were there how long before Archy was brought down? I don't know, sir; about a half an hour, or a quarter, or such a matter; I don't recollect anything about the minutes and the hours, but I know I was there. You know you were there? Yes, sir. No doubt about that? No doubt about that—I am certain about that. Then before Archy came down, you say you saw Monk? Well I did. Monk was walking about with a knife in his hand? Yes, sir. Cutting a stick? I don't know what he was cutting—I didn't notice what he was cutting. He was cutting something? Yes, sir. Why was your attention attracted to Monk; haven't you often seen a man going about cutting a stick? Yes; but then I never hardly ever go to the market house and see such a crowd, and I noticed him because there was such a crowd. What was it that attracted your attention to Monk at that time? I heard Monk say he was going to 'cut a damned niggers' throat," or something to that amount. You heard him say that a half an hour before Archy came down stairs? I don't know how long before he came down. Who did he say that to? I don't know, sir. How far was he off from you? He passed by me about three feet, twice. And both times he said I am going to cut a damned nigger's throat? He didn't say it both times—he said that the first time; I don't know what he said the last time. Where was Monk then, outside the market house, or under? He was outside. You know Monk well? Yes, sir; I knew him well. How long had you been knowing Monk? I had been knowing Monk a good while. How come you to know Monk so well? I have seen him often enough—I stayed down at Camelton, a while, and Monk used to pass there pretty regularly two or three times a day; Monk was small when I first knew him—we used to play together. You say while you were standing there you saw Sam. Hall and Ed. Powers? Yes, sir. Where were they "skeeting about"? Outside and under through the market house, and all around it. You say they were gay and lively? Yes, sir. Laughing and talking? Yes, sir. Are you sure they were laughing and talking? Yes, sir; but I could not tell what they were saying. Did you hear them laugh any? Yes, sir. How long have you known Sam. Hall? I have known Sam. Hall from a small boy. How came you to know Sam. so well? I have played with Sam. when he was a small boy; I don't suppose he knows it now; but I haven't forgotten it. You haven't played with him since you have been grown? No, sir. And Ed Powers, do you know him? Yes, sir, we were all playmates together. And you know them well? Yes, sir. Did you see them have any knives or any weapons of any kind? No, sir. Was there anything that they did, or anything that they said that called your attention to them particularly? No, sir. Nothing at all? I didn't see it nor hear it. Well, you stayed out there awhile, and you saw them bring Archy down, and then you moved your position? Yes, sir. Where did you go then? I went right across to Mr. Taylor's store. I am speaking now of when you first moved your position, for the purpose of seeing Archy? I moved back a few steps from the pavement. When you got there you could see the steps pretty well? Yes, sir. Which arch did you see through, the big arch or the little arch? The big middle arch. So you moved off the pavement so that you could see up the steps? Yes, sir. You saw Archy as soon as he got down to the landing place? It looked to me like it was five steps or so from the floor. The crowd was so thick I could not see exactly. It was thick at the foot of the steps? Yes, sir. Archy was up there coming down the steps, and at that time the crowd was very thick at the foot of the steps. Inside of Becky Ben's stall? Yes, sir. Thick as they could be? Yes, sir, I don't think they could be any thicker. Working about considerably or standing still? Some of them were working and some standing still, some talking and some hollering, I don't know what they were not doing. When you first saw Archy, who was with him? Mr. Wemyss for one, and Mr. Hardie for another, and I don't know any other one that was in the crowd. Where was Mr. Wemyss? Mr. Wemyss was at the right of Archy, he looked to me as if he had

his hand in his collar; he might not, but it looked to me he had. He either had his hand in his collar or on his coat, either one or the other? Yes, sir. You could see that pretty plainly? Yes, sir. Had a good position to see through the main arch? Yes, sir. Which hand was it Mr. Wemyss had there on his collar? I don't know whether it was the right hand or left. Mr. Hardie, where was he? He was to the left. Did you notice whether he had his hand in his collar? It looked to me as if he had him by the back of his neck. You are certain Sheriff Hardie had hold of him by the back of his neck? I don't know exactly he might not. You know Mr. Wemyss pretty well? Yes, sir. You have been knowing the old gentleman a good deal? Yes, sir, I lived joining him eight months. And you know Mr. Hardie pretty well? Yes, sir. You have known him a long time? Yes, sir. And you are certain of course that they were both there? Yes, sir. You think Mr. Hardie had him in the collar in the back? Yes, sir, I think he had. Could you tell from where you were standing whether he had him inside of the collar or just hold by the coat? I don't know, I didn't look as close as that. Could you tell whether he had him by the coat, or just had his hand on the shoulder? I don't know, sir; I know he had him somewhere. Do you recollect which hand it was? No, sir. Idon't know that neither. About that time Archy saw the crowd out there, and he began to shrink back, and he said, "don't carry me down there"? He said, "Oh! do, don't take me down there." And he commenced jerking back? Yes, sir. Now refresh your recollection. Don't you recollect this, that Wemyss had him by the shoulder, and he jerked him forward? I recollect some one jerked him, but I didn't see who it was, You don't recollect whether it was Wemyss or Hardie? No. sir. It was one of them? Yes, sir. Well, they came on that way down stairs? Yes, sir. Poor fellow; they jerked him right down, although he didn't want to go down? I ran off when I heard him say that. I could not say whether they jerked him down or not. After he said that to Hardie, I turned and ran. You ran straight across to Mr. Phil. Taylor's store? Yes, sir. That is on the same corner. Yes, sir. And as soon as you ran there, you crouched down behind a good's box? Yes, sir. Was it next to the pavement, or next to the door? It was right agin two trees that are standing there. You kneeled down there, and that shut out your view completely from the market house? Yes, sir, I didn't see any bing at all while I was down there. I don't know what passed. How long had you been there before something else attracted your attention? I don't know, sir: it might have been about five or ten minutes, and not longer. Five or ten minutes? Yes, sir. Did anybody pass you, while you were there? I never raised up to see what was going on. Did you put your handkerchief over your head? No, sir, I had a bonnet on, and pulled it over my head, and put my head down against the box. You don't know whether anybody saw you kneeling down or not? No, sir, I don't know. And you kneeled down there a short time, and then something attracted your attention in the crowd; what was that? When I heard them say "shoot him, shoot him," I didn't raise right then, but when I heard them say, "clear the way," I raised up, and I thought I would see him get clear, and go to the market house. When you get up, you stood behind the box still? No, sir, I sort of moved out; I was following the crowd to the guard house, but he was shot and killed. Which way did you move? I moved right straight across up towards the market house. As if you were just going across the street? Yes, sir. So you could see? Yes, sir. Did you see who that was that cried out, "shoot him"? No, sir, I don't know who it was. When you looked over there, what was the first thing that occurred? The first thing I saw when I looked over there, I saw that gentleman (pointing to Tolar) throw his arm up. You didn't see Archy when you looked ed over there? I saw Archy's head, Archy was pretty tall. How far had Archy got when you saw him? I don't know, sir. Had he passed the arch? Yes, sir, he had passed the arch, and got agin a little tree; I think he was opposite the corner. The south-east corner? Yes, sir. Which way was his face turned? Towards the South. Towards the guard house? Yes, sir. How did you know it was Archy if you just saw the back of his head? I know Archy very well; I would know him any where if I could see him; I would know him if I could see him a quarter of a mile. What sort of a hat did he have on? I think he had on a black hat, a rough and ready hat. Don't you recollect it was a white rough and ready hat? No, sir. Don't you recollect it was a cap he had on? I don't recollect ever seeing him with a white hat or a cap on. Do you recollect that he had on any hat that day? I think he had on a hat, a black rough and ready hat, I think he had, but wont say for certain, because it has been a right good while since that, and I don't recollect all that I saw there. Who was with Archy at that time? Mr. Wemyss had hold of him then when he was shot. Mr. Hardie and Mr. Wemyss both had hold of him; I could not say who the rest were. Now, at that time, where did Mr. Wemyss have hold of him? Mr. Wemyss was on the right side. And Mr. Hardie on the left side? No, sir, I think they were both on one side. Mr. Hardie in front and Mr. Wemyss behind? It looked to me he was in front. Did you see Mr. Hardy at that time with his hand hold of Archy's comforter around Archy's neck? I didn't notice who it was had hold of Archy's comforter. You saw a hand on Archy's comforter? Yes, sir, I don't recollect who it was. It was either Mr. Hardie or Mr. Wemyss hand on Archy's comforter? I reckon it was, sir. He was in front? Yes, sir. Now, did he have him close up to the throat or did he have him by the ends of the comforter? He didn't have him by the ends of the comforter? I think they were tucked up. You could see it, you think the ends were tucked up? I think so, sir, it looked as it he had hold of the comforter right about his breast. I know you want to tell the truth about this matter, see if you can recollect whether it was Mr. Hardie or Mr. Wemyss that had him in front? I can't recollect; it aint no use to waste time to tell about it; it was one. It was one, but you don't recollect who it was? No, sir. About that time you say Archy had got almost down to the corner? He had got near about opposite the corner. And you were standing there not far from Phil. Taylor's store? Yes, sir, and Archy just had one foot off the pavement. Which foot? The left foot. Did he have on boots or shoes? I don't recollect; I didn't come to look that close. But don't you recollect that you saw him at that time with his boots outside of his pantaloons, can't you recollect that? I don't know, I didn't see whether he had boots or not; he may have been bare footed, for all I can recollect. He had his left foot off the pavement? Yes, sir. He was pretty near the edge of the pavement, wasn't he? Yes, sir. Well, at that time you say

somebody commenced to cry out "shoot him?" I said, "clear the way." Who was that? I don't know, sir. Was it the same man that shot him? I don't reckon it was. You don't know who it was? There was a big crowd there, and I was off a little ways; I don't know who was in the crowd; but I aint going to say it was this one or that one, or tother one, for I don't know. There were a good many people between you and that place, you say? Yes, sir. Where did this man come from who shot him? I didn't know, sir. Where did you see him? He was partly in the crowd. Was he on the pavement, or off the pavement? It looked to me as if he was on the pavement. Was he walking out, or was he standing still? It looked to me as if he was pulling back. You mean the man who shot was pulling back? It looked to me he was pulling back to shoot. How did he stand, with his shoulder thrown back? The crowd was so thick I could not exactly see. Don't you know he was leaning over towards him? I don't think he was. You think he throwed himself back? If he leaned over I don't think I could have seen him. You only saw a portion of him—from about his shoulders up? Yes, sir, if I hadn't been looking I would not have seen that much, there was such a crowd there. He ran up, or was he standing there leaning back? I don't know whether he ran or walked. Where did he get the pistol from, did you see that? No, sir. You didn't see him get the pistol out of his pocket? No, sir. You saw he just had the pistol up, and presenting it? I saw him throw his arm up twice. Which arm? I don't know which arm it was; I am not certain which arm it was. See if you can't recollect? No, sir, it ain't no use. You put yourself in the position you were in that day, on the man's left, and he upon your right; and you saw the pistol. You know you could not have seen his right arm? I don't know whether I could or not. Was it the man next to you? I don't know; I know it was his arm. You didn't notice which arm? I was noticing the pistol, and, of course, I saw the arm, but don't know which one. You say you don't know what sort of a pistol it was? No, sir, and I dont know. Now, at the time the man shot, that was the first time you had seen him? That was the first time I had noticed him. At the time he raised his arm to fire, which way was he looking? He was looking towards Archy. You didn't see his face, did you? No, sir, I just saw one side of him; if I hadn't known him before, I would not have known him that day, but I had seen him so often I knew the side of his face. The left side was presented to you? Yes, sir. Don't you know that at that time he was a long ways off the pavement? No, sir, I don't know it sir. Don't you know he was right at the edge of the pavement? I don't know how near he was to the edge of the pavement; I didn't notice anything but the pistol and the shooting. Now, see if you can't recollect? No, sir, I can't. This is something else, I want you to recollect now? No, sir. You cant recollect it? No, sir. That is strange, you cant recollect whether he was close up to the market house;

or whether he was about the middle of the pavement at the time? No, sir, I never looked close enough. Was he down toward Mr. Davis' store? I can't tell. You can't tell anything about it? No, sir. What did the man do after he shot? I saw the man throw his arm back; I don't know what he done with the pistol. Which arm was that he threw back? I saw him throw his arm back; I don't know which arm it was; I saw his arm up, and I saw it go back; I didn't see anything more of it, after that. Was that the arm nearest you, or the arm furthest off? I don't recollect. You don't recollect anything about that? No, sir, I don't say anything more than I know. Well, Rachel, who else did you see there that day? I don't know sir, I saw a great many. Did you see anything of Ed. Powers, or Sam. Hall, at that time? If I did, I don't recollect it now. See if you can't recollect something about it? No, sir, I can't. Didn't you see something of Monk at that time? After the shooting, I saw Mr. Nixon take hold of Monk and lead him down towards Mr. Taylor's store; he brushed up against me twice. That was the time he brushed against you it was not before the shooting? He brushed against me twice before, and twice after; I know he brushed me once before, and I think twice, and I know he brushed against me twice afterwards. Monk was brushing you pretty considerably that day? Yes, sir, he was. How came he to be brushing you so much that day? I don't know, sir, he went up against me; I don't know how often he did; I was standing close up to him. Was there any man who was in that crowd that day, whose name you can tell, except the names of Monk, or Sam. Hall, or Ed. Powers? No, sir. From first to last, you don't recollect seeing anybody else? I don't recollect who I did see; it has been a right good while. And you say directly after the shooting, that you started off and ran away? Yes, sir, I went right straight on towards home. Where do you live? I forget the name of the street. I live in the street down from the market house; I come out in the morning, and look at the market house to tell what time it is; I live in Mr. Webster's house; grandmother and I stay in the kitchen, and Mr. Webster stays in the rest of the house.

Re-direct examination, by the Counsel for the prosecution.

Rachel, do you say that Beebee had on a hat that day? I think he had, I don't exactly recollect, but I am pretty certain he had on a hat. Did you see that hat at the time the pistol went off? No, sir. Was his hat on his head when the pistol fired? I don't know, sir. I don't recollect exactly about that. When was it you saw his hat on his head? I saw it when he was coming down the steps. You say when he came down the steps, that hat he had on his head was a black hat? Yes, sir. Do you recollect seeing it on his head any more after that? I don't believe I did. You don't think you saw him with a hat on his head, except when he was on the stairs? No, sir. Now about that comforter, when did you see that? I saw that when he was coming down stairs, and I saw he had it on after he was shot. But at the time he was shot, could you see him well enough to see it? No, sir. So the conclusion you came to that he had it on when he was shot, was formed before and

after? Yes, sir. You could not see Archy very well at the moment he was shot? No, sir. Did you say there was a big crowd around him? Yes, sir. And you were some forty or fifty feet off? I reckon about that. And there was a crowd between you? Yes, sir. How did you see his left foot? Well, sir, when they said "clear the way," the crowd sort of thinned out, and I saw Archy make one step off. Are you certain you could tell Archy's foot, as he stepped off through the crowd? Yes, sir. You noticed him step off the pavement with his left foot? Yes, sir; he fell that way, too. It was likely his left foot was off when he fell, but I want to know whether you could see his left foot, whether you can state positively that Archy had his left foot off, at the time he was shot, and you could see him at that time? When they hallooed "clear the way," I could see him plain enough. I think you said the reason why you could see Archy so plain was because he was a tall man? Yes, sir, he was. You could have seen a short man, if you could see his foot on the ground? When they hollered "clear the way," I could. You think he fell with one foot off the pavement; do you think that foot was off the pavement before he fell? Yes, sir, I guess it must have been. That is your opinion, is it? Yes, sir. You say you haven't talked with anybody about this? No, sir, you can't find them people to tell you I talked with them. Were you ever examined on oath before? No sir. Who did you see in that crowd after Archy was shot that you knew? I don't know, sir. I don't recollect seeing anybody, then; I went on home. I had a bundle; and I came back again, but I don't recollect seeing anybody in the crowd, for I didn't stop long enough to see who I did know. The only persons you recollect seeing in that crowd the whole time you were there from first to last, were Sam Hall, Ed. Powers, Monk, and the gentleman who shot the pistol, and Archy and Mr. Wemyss and Mr. Hardie? Yes, sir, they are all I recollect. Did you see distinctly when Archy said "do, don't take me down there," that Mr. Wemyss jerked him forward? I said it looked to me like somebody did. You could see that he had hold of him? Yes, sir. Are you certain you saw Archy that day? Yes, sir, I saw him when he come down stairs.

The Judge Advocate stated to the Commission that there were no witnesses who could be examined at present. He had sent summonses as long ago as last week, for witnesses to appear the day before yesterday, but they had not yet appeared.

Whereupon, on motion, the Commission adjourned to meet on Monday, the 12th instant, at 11 A. M.

RALEIGH, N. C., Aug. 12th, 1867, 11 A. M.
The Commission met pursuant to adjournment.

Present: All the members of the Commission, the Judge Advocate, the Counsel for the prosecution, all the accused and their Counsel.

The reading of the testimony taken on Saturday the 10th inst., was waived, there being no objection thereto.

Yesterday's proceedings were then read and approved.

DAVID OLIPHANT, a witness for the prosecution, having been first duly sworn, testified as follows:

Examined by the Counsel for the prosecution.
What is your name? David Oliphant. Where do you live? In Fayetteville. You have been suffering with sickness for the last few days? Yes, sir. Feel unwell to-day? Yes, sir. What is the disease you are complain-

ing of? Chills and fever. Have you had any chills to day? No, sir. Have one yesterday? Yes, sir. Day before yesterday? Yes, sir. You live in Fayetteville? Yes, sir. Were you living there the day Archy Beebee was killed? Yes, sir. Remember what day of the week it was? I don't recollect. What time did you go up to the market house that day? I can't tell exactly. Was it before dinner or after? It was after dinner. Before sunset? Yes, sir. Had Archy been brought up from the guard house when you got up there. They were just bringing him from the guard house. Were you standing inside of the market house? Yes, sir. Could you see the door of the guard house, from where you were standing inside of the market house? Yes, sir. Who came up along with Archy from the guard house to the market house? I think Mr. Wemyss, Mr. Hornrinde, and Mr. Brown. Any one else? Not that I can recollect. Were there others with him that you can recollect? Mr. Faircloth, I think was with him. Was there any crowd at the market house when you got there? A pretty good crowd. How many do you suppose? I reckon about a hundred. When you first got there? Yes, sir. Where were they standing? Under the market house and some outside. Was Archy carried up stairs? Yes, sir. How long did he remain up there? About an hour, I reckon. Were you down under the market house all the while he was up stairs? Yes, sir. Sitting or standing? Both. Who did you see in the crowd that you knew, while Archy was up stairs? I saw Mr. Sam. Phillips and Mr. Tolar. Mr. J. W. Tolar? Yes, sir; and I saw Mr. Watkins and Mr. Powers. Which Powers? Tom Powers. Any one else? Mr. Leggett. Did you see Jim Nixon? Yes, sir. Did you see Ed. Powers or Sam. Hall or Ralph Lutterloh? I don't recollect seeing them. You saw Phillips and Tolar, and Tom Powers and Monk? Yes, sir. Where was Tolar standing while the negro was up stairs? He was standing right there at Becky Ben's stall. Who was standing near him? Mr. Leggett, was standing pretty near him. Were they conversing together? I think they were. Was he the nearest man to him to your best recollection? Yes, sir. Did you see any weapon about Mr. Tolar at that time? Well, I don't know for certain whether it was a pistol he had or not, but I think it was a pistol under his coat. You saw something under his coat? Yes, sir. Under which side? The left side. The protuberance was on the left side? Yes, sir. Where was Tom Powers? He was by an old white woman's stall, that sells cakes under the market house. What is her name? I don't know, sir, what her name is. Is it the opposite side of the market house from Becky Ben's? No, sir, on the same side. Did you remain there until Archy came down inside of the market house? Yes, sir. Did Mr. Tolar remain there until Archy came down? Yes, sir. How was it with the rest—with Tom Powers? He remained there too. He didn't go away at all? He went down the street before Beebee came down the stairs, and then he come back. How long was he absent? I can't tell how long it was, fifteen minutes, I suppose. He went away for a short time while Beebee was up stairs, and returned? Yes, sir. Did he return to the same place where he was before? Yes, sir. Did you see Monk while the man was up stairs? Yes, sir. What was he doing? He was not doing anything. Did you see him whittling? No, I didn't see him whittling. I saw him have a knife in his hand, I believe he was

trimming his finger nails. Did you hear him say anything? No, sir. Did you hear Tom Powers say anything while Archy was up stairs, about the offence he was charged with? I heard him say he thought it was a shame the way the young lady was treated. Is that about all? Yes, sir. Did you hear that while Archy was up stairs? Yes, sir. Did you hear Tolar say anything about it? I heard him say if that was let go on, it would go on again. Was that while Archy was up stairs? Yes, sir. Was he talking to any one in particular, or to the crowd? To the crowd, I believe, that was around there. Was there any excitement in that crowd, any expressions of anger or disgust at what had taken place? No, sir. Was the crowd perfectly quiet? Yes, sir. No talking about? They were talking first to one and then to another; I didn't know what they were talking about. What is Miss Massey's name? Sis Massey, they call her. Did you see her that day when she came down stairs? Yes, sir. Who was with her? Mr. Bond was with her. Did she come down before Archey? Yes, sir. Was her mother along? Yes, sir. What became of them when they came down stairs? They went to the carriage. Where was the carriage? Out in front of the market house. Some distance from the pavement? About ten or fifteen feet, I reckon. Did you go out of the market house when they went to the carriage? Yes, sir, I went out to the carriage, too. Mr. Bond you say handed the ladies into the carriage? Yes, sir. Did any one else go out there to speak to them? Mr. Owens went out there, believe. Ain't you certain about that? Yes, sir, I am certain. Did any one call for Mr. Powers, that you know of? I think his sister called for him. You were standing out there, how close were you to the carriage when Powers went up? I was not more than three feet, I reckon. He went up and spoke with his sister? Yes, sir. Did you hear any of the conversation? I heard Mrs. Massey to say for Tom not to have anything to do with it. Did you hear his reply? I don't think he said anything at all. Did you hear what Mr. Maultsby had to say? No, sir. Was he speaking to the ladies or Mr. Bond? To the ladies. Did you see him speak to Bond, at all? No, sir. Did you see any one else go to the carriage? Not that I can recollect. Did you see Phil. Taylor there? No, sir. Robert Mitchell? No, sir. What became of Mr. Powers when he left the carriage? He went back under the market house. Did you go under the market house at the same time? Yes, sir. Did you have anything to say to him? No, sir, he said, under the market house, that he thought it was a shame, the way the girl was treated. What became of Mr. Maultsby, after he came from the carriage? I can't tell, sir. Mr. Maultsby disappeared from your sight, then, and you didn't see him again until after this thing was done? No, sir. Were you near Mr. Powers when he came back under the market house? Yes, sir. Did he move any nearer to the steps than he was, before Archey came down? No, sir. He stayed at the same place? Yes, sir. How far was that from the foot of the steps? It was about ten feet I reckon. Was it on the same side of the market house? Yes, sir

Was he sitting down or standing up? Sitting down. Where was Mr. Tolar, in the same place still? He was leaning up against one of the pillars. At the east end? At the south end. Which street does the south end front down? I don't recollect now; it was towards Mr. Taylor's corner. Was it at the same end that Archey came out? No, sir, it was at the same end of the market, but he was not right at the same place. He was at the same end of the market house that Archey passed out? Yes, sir. He was standing there before Archey came down? Yes, sir. Do you mean he was standing against the side of the arch? Yes, sir. The right hand side as you go out? Yes, sir. Wasn't the right hand side of the arch the side nearest the steps? No, sir. Just think a moment, Mr. Oliphant, when you come down the steps ain't the right hand side of the arch the one nearest the steps? He was standing on the right hand side as you go in the market. Of the same arch that Archey went out of? Yes, sir. Was he standing there before Archey come down? Yes, sir. When did he move from Becky Ben's stall to that place, do you know? I don't recollect. You remember at one time he was at one place, and just before Archey came down he was at the other? Yes, sir. Where were you standing when Archey came down? I was standing right there by old Becky's stall. Did you see Monk about that time? Yes, sir. Was he there too? Yes, sir. Where was he? He was standing right there by old Becky's stall too. Pretty close to you? About ten feet from me, I reckon. Now, when Archey came down stairs, did you see him? Yes, sir. Who was with him? There was Mr. Wemwyss, and Mr. Hardy, and Mr. Horninde, I think. Was anything done to him before he got down stairs? No, sir, not that I know of. You heard no exclamations from the crowd? No, sir. Saw nobody make at him before he got down stairs? No, sir. As he was passing through Becky's stall, and come to where he came out, was anything done to him? Mr. Powers caught hold of him and told him he could not go any further. Was that just as he got to the arch? Yes, sir, just as he went to turn the corner. Where was Mr. Powers standing then? He was standing on the right of Beebee as he came down stairs. So that Beebee passed by his left hand? Yes, sir. And just as he got to the arch he touched him—laid his hands on him? Yes, sir. Do you mean he laid his hands on him roughly, or grabbed him, or jerked him? He just put his hands on him and told him he could go no further. That was what you heard him say, that he could go no further? Yes, sir. Did you see Monk then? Yes, sir. What was he doing? He had his knife in his hand. Was he pretty close to Mr. Powers? He was about three or four feet from Mr. Powers. What happened after Powers put his hand on the prisoner Beebee? They pushed Mr. Powers off. Who pushed him off? Mr. Wemwyss, or some of them that had hold of the darkey,

Sheriff Hardy or some of them. At the time Mr. Powers laid his hands upon the prisoner Beebee, Monk had his knife out, within four feet of him, and Powers was pushed off, and you say Tolar was standing at the same place? Yes, sir. He hadn't moved from that place then? No, sir. Was there any rush made upon him, at all? A pretty good rush, I guess. That was at the same time that Powers made this grab? Yes, sir. Was Tolar in the rush? No, sir; I think he was not. Then they got the prisoner outside of the arch? Yes, sir. What happened then? Mr. Tolar walked around to about where the negro was. What became of Mr. Powers and Monk? I never seen Mr. Powers any more. Did you see him go away? No, sir. Was he in the crowd that pressed on? I think he was in the crowd, I could not say. Have you any reason for your opinion at all, except that you had seen him there just before? No, sir; I didn't see him pressing on with the crowd. You say Mr. Tolar moved around towards where the prisoner was? Yes, sir. Did you move out of the market house too? Yes, sir. Did Mr. Tolar keep moving or stop? He stopped. How close was he to Beebee when he stopped? About five or six feet from Beebee, or may be further. How close were you to Mr. Tolar when he stopped? I was about two or three feet I reckon— I was on the right of Tolar. Were you in front of him or to the rear, or square to his right? Square on his right. Where was Mr. Tolar standing at that time; on the pavement or off the pavement? Off the pavement. How far from the edge? Just off the edge, about three feet off the edge. And where was Beebee, was he on or off the pavement? On the pavement. What did Mr. Tolar do after he stood still? He pulled out his pistol. Where from? He got it some how or other. You don't know whether he drew his pistol, or whether it was handed to him then? No, sir. Did you see him with the pistol in his hand? Yes, sir. What did he do with it? He cocked it and fired it. He cocked it and fired it? Yes, sir. You saw him level it? Yes, sir. You saw it discharged? Yes, sir. You saw the smoke and the flash? Yes, sir. You heard the report? Yes, sir. Was it directed towards Beebee? Yes, sir. Did Beebee fall afterwards? Yes, sir. What did Tolar do with the pistol? I can't tell you what he done with it after he fired; I think he put it under his coat; he threw his shawl back and I think he put it under his shawl some how or other; I don't know how he got it under though. What was that about throwing his shawl? He threw his shawl back over his left shoulder, and the pistol, I think, went under his shawl, and he walked up under the market house and leaned against the pillar that he leaned against before he came out. He leaned against the pillar on the same side that Archy had come by? No, sir, on the other side. You say that after he had fired this pistol he drew back his arm, and threw his shawl on his left shoulder? Yes, sir. Did you see him move his hand any where else about his person? No, sir. You didn't see him dispose of the pistol at all? No, sir. Did you see him pass his hand under his coat behind? Yes, sir, I think he did. Was that after he had thrown his shawl up? Yes, sir. Did you see whether there was any pistol in his hand when he passed it back? No, sir. He went and stood by that pillar after that? Yes, sir. Did you hear any exclamations in the crowd?

No, sir. Did you hear any exclamations in the crowd just as Archy come out of the arch? Nothing more than they said it was a shame. Did you hear any body in the crowd crying out any thing? I heard them cry out "shoot him," and I started and ran away, and went up to where the bell rope was, and then turned around and came back. That was an instantaneous movement? Yes, sir. As I understand you, after Powers failed to grab him, and then was driven off, there was an exclamation to shoot him? Yes, sir. Upon hearing that, you ran back towards the bell rope, and instantly thought you would go and see what was to be done, and turned back and came up to Mr. Tolar? Yes, sir. Did you see Archy fall down that day before he was shot? I saw him fall before he was shot. You saw that? Yes, sir. And as he raised up he was shot? Immediately afterwards. I supposed he was trying to get loose from the guard. That was your impression? Yes, sir. Did you see anybody with knives that day except Monk? No, sir. Any one with pistols? Nobody but Jonathan Hollingsworth, and he was a guard, and that was the reason he had a pistol. He was a guard at the time a guard of what? He was guarding the bridge at the time I believe. What makes you believe that? He had been guarding it. I don't know whether he was guarding it that day, he said he was. You are not at liberty to say what he said—do you know of your own knowledge, that he was guarding it that day? No, sir. How far is the bridge from the market house? About a mile. They don't put out their guards as far as that; do you think they do? I should not think they would. You saw Hollingsworth with a pistol, when was that, before Archy came down stairs? No, sir. Did you see Maultsby any more after you saw him at the carriage? No, sir. Did you hear any one in the crowd say who it was that fired, before Capt. Tolar went away? No, sir. I heard some one say a little boy hollered out that Capt. Tolar shot him. While Capt. Tolar was there? Capt. Tolar was leaning up against that brick pillar. Was it loud enough for him to hear it? I should think it was. What was the expression? Some of them said a little boy hollered out "Capt. Tolar shot him." Anything else? No, sir. Did any body stop the boy? Some one slapped him down they said. As I understand you, Capt. Tolar hadn't left the crowd? No, sir. Did you see what became of Capt. Tolar afterwards? When he was standing up against that brick pillar I started to go under the market house, and Mr. Tolar went over to Mr. Hiesdale's store. Were you going to speak to him? I thought I would speak to him, and he went off. How close were you to Mr. Tolar when he fired? I can't tell exactly how close; it was about four feet I reckon. From two to four feet, or. if anything, was it more than four feet? It was not more than four feet. Was there any one between you and him? No, sir. Were there persons behind you and before you? There was people behind me. Was there any one between you and the prisoner Beebee? There was plenty of them on the pavement before me. None between you and the edge of the pavement? No, sir. Was there any one between Tolar and Archy when he fired? O, yes, there was right smart between them. Several persons? Yes, sir. Did you notice who they were? No, sir, I never noticed. Do you know a man in Fayetteville by the name of John A. Smith? No, sir. You say there were persons between them, but you don't know who they were? Do you know John Armstrong? Yes, sir. Did you

see him there that day? No, sir, I never seen him at all, he might have been behind Mr. Tolar. You didn't see him? No, sir. Who did you see nearest to Tolar at the time he fired the pistol? I never took any particular notice, because I was excited. Somewhat alarmed were you? Yes, sir. Did you see the pistol that Tolar fired with? Yes, sir. What sized pistol was it? I can't tell you exactly, it was about so long, (16 inches by measure.) Do you know what sort of a pistol it was, Colt's, or Remington's, or couldn't you tell? I think it was a Colt's repeater. A Colt's repeater of large size? Yes, sir. Did you see any thing of Monk after the pistol was fired? Yes, sir. What was he doing? He started to go to the nigger and Jim Nixon caught hold of him and carried him off, down the street, and told him there was no use coming around there with his knife, the nigger was dead. Was he saying any thing when he started towards him? Not that I heard. Did he have any weapon in his hand? He had a knife in his hand. How close did he get to the negro? Not very close, before Jim Nixon caught him. Did he get within five feet of him? Yes, sir; I reckon he did. You say you saw Sam Phillips there that day? Yes, sir. Did you see him standing near Tolar when he fired? No sir. What time was it when you saw Sam. Phillips; before the negro came down stairs? Yes, sir. Did you see him afterwards at all? Not until that evening in his store. Did he have any weapon when you saw him? I think it was a pistol he had in his coat. You saw something in his hands? No, sir. You are under the impression he had a pistol under his coat? Yes, sir. You didn't see what sort of a pistol? No, sir, I am pretty certain he had a pistol, though. You judge simply from what you heard or from what you saw. From what I saw. From the appearance of his hand in his breast? Yes, sir. And the swell in his clothing? Yes, sir. Do you know William Porter? Yes, sir. Did you see him there that day? No, sir. Do you know James Kendricks? Yes, sir. Did you see see him there that day? No, sir.

Cross-examination by the Counsel for the accused:

When were you summoned as a witness in this case? Friday, sir. Got up here yesterday? Yes, sir. After this firing was all over, the shooting of the negro, you say you went down to Mr. Phillips' store? In the evening. Did you find Mr. Phillips at the store? Yes, sir. Did you go down with him? He had gone down before; I never went there till about dark. He showed you his pistol when you got there? No, sir, he didn't show me his pistol. What did he say about the pistol? He never said a word about his pistol. What did he say about the affair? He didn't say anything about it at all. How many conversations have you had with Sam. about this matter? I have not had any conversations with him about it. I mean from the day the thing occurred up to the present time; how many conversations have you had with Sam. Phillips? I have not had any conversations with Sam Phillips at all about it. You have never spoken to him on the subject? I have never spoken to him about it all. Hasn't he spoken to you about it? No, sir. You say he has not? No, sir. And you have had no conversation with him whatever? No, sir. What time did you get to the market house that day? I cant exactly tell what time it was; it was just before they brought Beebee up from the guard house. Where did you go from? I went from Bill Clark's bar room. How many drinks had you taken that day? I had taken one. Hadn't you taken more than one drink that day? No, sir; I had not. Where did you take that? I took it at Bill Clarks. And you took no other drink that day? Not until after the fellow was shot, then I went down and took another drink with Nixon and Monk. What did you go to the market house for, that day? I just went up there because I wanted to. Were you armed? No, sir; I didn't even have a pocket knife, much less a pistol. You had no arms at all No, sir. You just went up there to see what was going on? Yes, sir. Did you see Beebee when he left the guard house door? Yes, sir. You say at that time there were Mr. Wemyss and Mr. Brown and Mr. Faircloth? I think they were the town guard that was with him. Was there anybody else with him that you can recollect; was Hardy with him coming up from there or not? I don't know whether Hardy was with him then or not. Did you see him all the way from the guard house until he went up stairs? Yes, sir. You can't recollect any other persons who were with him? No sir. Was there a crowd with him? There were some four or five with him. You know Sheriff Hardie well, do you? Yes, sir. You don't know whether he was with him or not at the time? I don't recollect. You say you stood about there all the time Beebee was up stairs? Yes, sir. Till he was brought down? Yes, sir. How large did you say the crowd was? I said there was about a hundred or very near it. Was there anything unusual in that crowd from the time Beebee went up stairs, un til he come down? No, sir; nothing that attracted my attention. Nothing unusual in the crowd? No, sir. Hear any threats made by anybody? Nothing more than what I just told to that gentleman. Nothing more than that one or two persons said it was a shame that she should have been treated so? Yes, sir. And that is the only thing you heard, that was of a threatening character? Yes, sir. Where did you say Tom Powers was standing? He was standing on the left of Beebee as he come down stairs. While Beebee was up stairs when you first saw Tom Powers he was sitting on a bench up there, in what part of the market? About midway of the market; it was just this side of where the bell rope was. He was sitting there on a bench? Yes, sir. What was he doing, anything? No, sir. Did you see him do anything, or did you hear him say anything, until Beebee was brought down? No, sir. Did he keep that position until Beebee came down? He got up just as Beebee came down stairs. How long before Beebee came down stairs was it you saw Capt. Tolar? It was half an hour, I reckon. Did you see him when he came there? Yes, sir. Where did he come from? The upper part of the market somewhere. You didn't see him enter the market? No, sir. You just saw him come from the upper end of the market? Yes, sir. And he came down and took his stand against that northern pillar of the main eastern arch? Yes, sir. Did he stand with his face to the pillar, or with his side? He was standing with his side to the pillar. Which side was he leaning up against the pillar? His left side. His left side was leaning against that northern pillar of the eastern arch? Yes, sir. Which way was his face? Towards the river. Was any body with him? No, sir. He was

standing there alone? Yes, sir. Did you see any body with him at all, before Archy came down? I saw Mr. Leggett with him. Did you see any body else there with him? I saw Mr. Phillips there with him. You saw Leggett and Sam Phillips with him? Sam Phillips was standing there; I don't know whether he was talking to him or not. Don't have Sam talking; you saw Leggett and him talking, though? Yes, sir. Did you hear what they were talking about? No, sir. Do you mean to say they talked in whispers? No, sir. Just talked in an ordinary conversational tone? Yes, sir. And you didn't hear what they were talking about? No, sir You said something about your thinking Tolar had a pistol? Yes, sir. What reason have you for thinking that that was a pistol? From what I could see, and where he had his hands, I thought it was a pistol; I won't be certain. Did you see the stock of it? I saw something like it. Do you know whether it was the stock of a pistol, or whether it was a watch? It was not a watch. How did it look? It looked to me like a piece of wood, of some description. Where was it? It was in his breast pocket, under his coat on the left side. Inside of the coat, or outside? On the inside of the coat. What did he have around his shoulders, anything? He had a shawl around his shoulders. Was the shawl fastened? I won't be certain whether it was fastened at the top or not. Don't you recollect whether it was pinned up, or whether it was loose, could you see under the shawl? Yes, sir, you could see under the shawl if you were close to him; I think it was loose. You could see something you thought was wood? Yes, sir. Do I understand you to swear positively that that was a pistol? No, sir, I don't swear positive; it was my belief that it was a pistol. Then you saw him standing there, and he had something, and you don't know what that something was? No, sir, I don't know what that something was. Was he doing anything? No, sir. Doing nothing? No, sir. Standing there still? Yes, sir. When the boy was brought down stairs, where did I understand you to say you were standing, just as he got to that portion of the stairs when you could first see him, where were you? I was standing there at old Becky Tyler's stall. How far were you off from the stair steps? I was not very far; it was right opposite to old Becky's stall, and just as soon as they commenced bringing him down stairs, I went across to old Becky's stall, and Mr. Powers was standing inside there. Now, at the time Beebee was so nearly down the steps that you could see—at the time you first saw him, who was with him? I can't say for certain; I know Sheriff Hardie and Wemyss were with him, and Mr. Faircloth. Where was Wemyss? Wemyss had a string around the fellows finger. Which finger, his front or little finger? It was his thumb. Which thumb, on his right hand or left? I never noticed whether it was his right hand or left. Which side of him was Wemyss? He was on the right side, I think. So he had the string around the prisoner's right thumb? Yes, sir. Where was Hardie? He had him in the back of the neck, somewhere,

That was up stairs when they were just coming down? He had him by the back of the neck when he went to turn the market house I am talking about when you first saw him coming down the steps; did Hardie have him at all? I never noticed. Do you know whether he had him at all? I don't know whether he had hold of him. Do you know whether Hardie was about him? Yes, sir. Which side was Hardie on? He was right behind him, as well as I could see. You saw every thing about it, didn't you? Yes, sir. That is the way they came down stairs: Wemvyss on the right hand side with a twitch around his right thumb, and Hardie behind him? Yes, sir. Who came down to the floor first, Wemyiss, or Beebee, or Hardie? I think Mr. Wemyss and Faircloth and the boy got down first. And then Hardie came down? Yes, sir, he was close behind them. How long was it after the boy came down before Hardie came down? It didn't lack anything at all, he just got down right behind them. Didn't Hardie come down before them? He did not. You are certain he came down behind them? I am certain he did. They got down on the floor of the market and then Hardie stepped down behind them? Yes, sir. And you saw them? Yes, sir. Now, at the time the boy appeared on the steps of the market house, did you see John Maultsby? No, sir, I never saw John at that time. Who did you see on that bench by Becky Ben's stall, at the time the boy was brought down? I saw Bob Simmons for one. Was he sitting down? He had his knee on that bench. Looking which way? He was talking to old Becky, I believe. You understand the bench, I mean. It is that bench which runs to the left of Becky Ben's stall, as you come down through the stall; just as you get in Becky Ben's stall there is a bench to the left, it is that bench I am speaking of. Did you say he was on that bench at that time? It was a bench on the left hand side as you go in the market house, I am speaking of. I mean the one on the left hand side as you come down the steps. No, sir, I never seen anybody there. Do you know John Maultsby, well? Yes, sir. I will ask you if you don't know as a fact, that at the time Beebee was seen first coming down the steps that Maultsby jumped up on that bench? I never seen him, sir. Did he do it, or did he not? If he done it I never saw him. I ask you if you don't know that in addition to jumping up on a bench, Maultsby raised his hand when he jumped up on that bench, and said "watch out, boys?" It he done it I never saw him. Could that have occurred there, Maultsby's jumping up on the bench and crying out those words in an ordinary tone of voice, could that have occurred without you seeing it?

Counsel for the prosecution objected to the question.

Counsel for the accused—I will ask the question:

Could you not see everything upon that bench? I didn't notice that bench and I didn't see it. You saw nothing of it at all? No, sir. You didn't see John Maultsby at all? No, sir. From the position you occupied over there by Betsy Tyler's, looking at anybody coming down those steps, could you not have seen a man who jumped up upon that bench? I never seen any man jump up upon the bench. Wouldn't you have looked right over the bench from the position you occupied, would not your line of sight have been right over that bench? I was noticing up the stairs, I didn't notice who was on the bench

at all. Could you have seen up the stair steps at that time without seeing right over that bench, was not that directly in your line of vision? Which bench do you mean?—that one towards Draughon's. The one Becky keeps her cakes on? I never seen him. Wouldn't you have seen him looking the way you were, up the stairs? It looks like I would have seen him if he had done it? What is your impression, that it was done or was not? I don't think he done it? You saw nothing of it? I did not, sir. How long was it before Beebee came down, that Miss Massey and her mother came down. It was about ten or fifteen minutes I reckon. Did anybody come down the steps, between the times that Miss Massey and her mother came down, and the time that Beebee came down? Not that I recollect, sir. You say Miss Massey came down, and her mother, and Mr. Bond took them out to the carriage? Yes, sir, I think it was Mr. Bond. And you went out to the carriage at the same time? Yes, sir. What did you go for? I just went out there because I wanted to. I just went out to see what was going on. You went out to see what was going on? Yes, sir. What I went out there for, some of them said her throat was scratched, and I wanted to see if it was. That is what you went out for? Yes, sir. Who was in the carriage at the time you got out there? There was a black man there, but I don't know who it was. Then Miss Massey and her mother got into the carriage and drove off. I suppose they went down to Mr. Hollingsworth's, I don't know. How long had they been out there before Tom Powers was called up? They hadn't been there no time hardly. You are certain Mrs. Massey called out Tom Powers. He went out on his own accord. I understand you to say Miss Massey called him out there? Miss Massey spoke to him. Tom was not very far from the carriage when she spoke to him, and then Tom went up to the carriage, she did not call him from under the market house I know. And Tom said nothing to her? She told Tom not to have anything to do with it. Was that all that passed between them? That was all I heard. Tom went to the carriage and Mrs Massey told him not to have anything to do with it? Yes, sir. You didn't hear Beebee's name mentioned? No, sir, that was all I heard. Where did Tom go to after he left the carriage? He went back under the market house. What part of the market house did he go to? He went right up there by old Becky's stall. Did he go up near the steps? No, sir. He didn't go near the steps? He didn't go inside of Becky's stall at all. Did he go in under the market house at all at that time? Yes, sir, he leaned up against the pillar. Where were you at that time? I was standing right there by old Becky's stall. You had shifted from old Betsy Tyler's stall? Yes, sir. The boy hadn't come down stairs then. Directly after Tom Powers came back from the carriage, where were you? I was standing by old Betsy Tyler's. Tom went right ahead of me, on one side of the market, and I went on the other, over to old Betsy's stall. Where did Tom take his stand when he came back from the carriage? He was standing right there at old Becky's stall, and he moved and went on the inside there at that pillar. Did he lean against the pillar? I think so. You mean the pillar that separates the main arch from the Southern arch? Yes, sir. Which way was he looking? Towards the north. Did he continue to look north until Beebee was brought down? Yes, sir. Tom didn't change his position when he first came on the floor of the market? He changed his position to stand up straight. He didn't leave that place until Beebee was brought up to where he was? No, sir. You are certain Tom staid there until the sheriff and the officers brought Beebee around to go out of the stall? Yes, sir. You can't be mistaken about that? No, sir. You say when they brought the prisoner along there Tom put his hand upon him? Yes, sir. Which hand?. His right hand, from what I could see, from the way the fellow was coming it looked as if it was his right hand. What part of his person did he put his hand upon? Upon his coat. Did he grasp his coat, or just put his hand gently on him? I don't know whether he had his hands on or not. That was upon Beebee's right side? Yes, sir, and Mr. Wemyss or some of them pushed Tom off. You say Tom didn't grab him? He had hold of him some how or other. Did he grab him or just lay his hand upon him? If I should command a prisoner that way I would take hold of him. Did he command the prisoner? He told him he could not go any further. Did you hear him say that? Yes, sir. You are certain those are the words he used? They are the only words I heard him use. How did he say that, in an easy tone of voice; did he just take hold of him and say he could not go any further? Just about that way. You heard no other words but these used? No, sir. And, accompanying that, he laid his hands upon his coat? Yes, sir. Was it his right hand? I think it was, it looked to me like that. You are here to tell what you saw and not what you think? I could not tell exactly, but I think it was his right hand, I am not positive. Did he have any knife in his hand? I didn't see any knife, sir. At that time you say he was pushed back? Yes, sir. Who pushed him back? Mr. Wemyss or some of them in the crowd. What did he say when they pushed him back? He never said any thing at all, sir. How did he push him, gently or roughly? They just pushed him off. Did you see the guard use their clubs that day? I think Mr. Wemyss struck Monk. That was the only use you saw made of the clubs that whole day was it? Yes, sir. Now, I want to know at the time Powers had his hand up, as you say, and put it on the prisoner, where were you standing at that moment? I was standing at the end of old Becky Ben's stall. How far were you from Tom? About four or five feet? Do you feel very certain that these things occurred just as you have given them? Yes, sir. And Tom said what you have said he said? I think that is what he said: I know that is all I heard him say at that time. At that time did you see Capt. Tolar? I seen Capt. Tolar, he was leaning up against that pillar at the time Powers put his hand on him. Where was Tolar standing? He was standing at that brick pillar. How did he have his hand then? Under his coat. Was that his right hand? Yes sir. What was he doing with his left hand? He had his shawl in his left hand holding it over his right hand. Then they moved on with the prisoner: what occurred next? Capt. Tolar went around. How far had they got with the prisoner? That was when Tom grabbed hold of him. Then the crowd generally rushed upon him? Yes, sir. But Tolar was not in that rush? No, sir. Were you in it? No, sir. You were just standing still? I was standing still. You didn't go into that? No, sir, You feel pretty sure Tolar didn't go into it? I am sure he didn't go into that: if I had been into it myself I would not have seen Tolar. Then they carried

him through the arch and got him on the pavement, and out there what happened—when was the time you saw Monk rushing at him? That was when they were going around the end of the market house. What end? Around the arch where they come down. Then you saw Monk rush at him with a knife? Yes, sir. What sort of a knife was it? I can't tell. Which hand did he have it in? In his right hand. How far had they got with Beebee on to the pavement before he was shot? It was only about the corner. The corner of the market? Yes, sir: nearly about right on the corner under a little tree; he fell right there where there was a little post. At the time Beebee was shot did you see him? I seen Beebee when he poked up his head, and I saw him when he fell. You saw that? Yes, sir. Then where was Beebee; was he nearer to the market house, or nearer to the center of the pavement or nearer to the outer edge of the pavement? From what I could see he was near about right at the corner. Then he was very near the edge of the pavement? Yes, sir. Near the edge of the corner? Yes, sir. And you say that just before he got there you saw Tolar leave his position up there near the pillar where you have described him, and walked along across the pavement and off the pavement? Yes, sir. You are certain you saw him walk up? I did sir. Where were you standing then; on the pavement or off? I was on the pavement; as soon as I saw him go around, I went around too: and I saw him have his pistol in his hand, and he cocked it, and some of them hollered out, "shoot the damned son of a bitch," and he fired it. We will get to that directly: what was his position when he went across; the same that it was before, with his hand under his shawl? Yes, sir. Did he go around there in the rush? He appeared to walk tolerable fast to get around there. Was there anybody in his way before he got up near enough to shoot Beebee? There was right smart between him. I mean anybody he had to push out of the way? No, sir. Were you close to Tolar from the time he left that position by the pillar, until he got around to the place where he shot him? Tolar went right on ahead of me and I went behind him. What distance was there between you and Tolar at the time you were following him around. About three feet. Now during the time that Tolar was going around there to his position, did you see him push anybody out of the way? He had his left hand, and hushed them, and after that he told them to look out or something like that. Did he touch anybody when he did that way? I should think he touched some; I don't know how it was. I don't ask you for what you think; did you see him touch any body? There was two or three black men that I think he touched; I am certain he did. Name one of them? I can't tell for I don't know their names. Did you see him touch John Armstrong? No, sir. Did you see him touch Robert Simmons? No, sir. Did you see him touch Jim McNeill? No, sir. Did you see him touch James Douglass or James Hawley the yellow man that stays at Fishblates? No, sir. Did you see him touch Matthew Leary? No, sir. You know these men don't you? Yes, sir. You think Tolar touched some body as he went on, did you see him push any body out of the way? He pushed two or three out of the way. Did he push them out of the way to the right or left? To the left, sir. Now when Tolar got up where he took his stand to fire, then I understand that you were on his right? Yes, sir. How far were you then from the edge of the pavement? I was about two feet, I reckon, or three. How far was Tolar to your left? About three or four feet, sir. So that Tolar was seven or eight feet from the edge of the pavement at the time he fired? No, sir, he was n't that far. Count up; you say you were two or three feet from the edge of the pavement, and you were three or four feet from him. He could have been closer than eight feet to the pavement. How far was he? I think he was about six feet or seven may be. Won't you make it beyond seven? No, sir. At that time who was on Tolar's left? There was a whole crowd on Tolar's left; I could not tell who they were? Didn't you notice the man who was nearest on his left? No, sir, I never noticed any body at all only him; I saw them make the rush; saw the negro try to get away from them. At that time who was between you and Tolar? There wasn't anybody at all right between us. You were the nearest man? I was about the nearest to him; I stood off; I didn't go right up on him. Nobody between you at all? Nobody between us at all. Tolar you say had the pistol in his hand; you didn't see where it got it from? No, sir, I never seen where he got it from. And you saw him cock it? Yes, sir. How did he cock it; did he take it in both hands to cock it? I think he took it in both hands, I think he did. I will ask you whether he did or not? He had it in his left hand and took hold of the barrel with his right hand and cocked it with his thumb. How did he raise it up; did he throw it first in the air and bring it down to a level, or did he raise it to the level first? He just raised it up, and leveled and fired it. You saw that pistol? I did, sir. And you say it was a long pistol? Yes, sir, it was a tolerable long one. And you say you think it was a Colt's pistol? I think it was, I don't know one from another. Was it a round barrel, or was t what they call an eight sided barrel? I never took the pistol in my hand; I could not tell. Do you know whether it was a single-barrel pistol, or whether it was called a revolver or repeater? It didn't have but one barrel, but I think it was a six shooter from what I could see. You said just now that it was how long?

(Witness measures off sixteen inches on the tape.)

You are confident that was the length of it. About that long, I am not confident, but I think it was. Did I understand you to say that when Tolar went there, he said "I will shoot the damned son of a bitch."? I didn't hear him say that sir; I didn't think he cursed at all. Did I understand you to say he said anything? He never said anything, only for them to get out of the way, and some of them hollered out "shoot him," and he said then "get out of the way" and he took his left hand and pushed them. How many persons were between Tolar and Beebee at the time the pistol shot was fired? I could not tell you how many, a good many; there was some five or six I suppose. Were they standing still? They were standing still looking on. Do you know whether they were standing still or moving about? They were moving about, some of them. Then they were not standing still? Some of them were standing still and some moving. So there were as

many as five or six persons between him and Beebee, some standing still and some moving about? Yes, sir. All excited apparently? Yes, sir. Great confusion? Yes, sir. Did you see these men who were bending over in front of Tolar, leaning out of the way to the right and to the left? Some of them were leaning to the right that was in front of Tolar? Were any of them leaning to the left? They were all on each side trying to lean right and left to keep from getting shot I reckon. Still they were moving about? Some of them, were and some were not. Can you name a single person white or black who was in that crowd at the time the shot was fired? No, sir; for I was excited myself. I think you said you didn't see anything of Sam. Phillips there at that time? No, sir; not at that time. Did you see any other pistols in the crowd? I seen Jonathan Hollingsworth have a pistol, there. And with the exception of that and Tolar's pistol you saw no others? I think Mr. Phillips had a pistol, I won't be certain. That is what I am talking about; did you see it? I seen him place his hand under his coat—I am pretty certain I seen the stock of the pistol; I am not sure of it. You are pretty certain you saw the stock of the pistol? Yes, sir. Was that just at the time the negro was shot? It was just before they brought him down stairs; I never seen Sam. Phillips after that at all. You didn't see Phillips with the pistol in his hand at all? No, sir. As soon as the shooting occurred what did you say became of you? I went down to Clark's bar room. And took another drink? Yes, sir. Did you stay there long enough to see Phillips throw his pistol up to show it to the crowd after the shooting occurred? I never noticed whether he threw up his pistol or not. You never saw that? No, sir; I never saw his pistol only what I could see under his coat. You spoke just now of when Tolar shot, of his having put his pistol back; did you see where he put it? No, sir; I don't know whether he handed it to any body back of him or whether he kept it under his coat. Under the left side of his coat? Yes, sir; he threw his shawl back and I don't know what he did with it. How did he throw his shawl; from his right arm over his left? Yes, sir. Throwing it across the breast? Yes, sir. Did you see the shawl strike any body? No, sir. Did you notice whether there was any body near enough on the left at that time to have been struck by the shawl? There was a good many on the left right close to him. Did you see anybody at that time on his left that you knew? No, sir, I was not taking notice who was around him, I was just looking on to see what I could see, that was all I cared for. Did Tolar leave there before you left or did you leave first? I went and stood off against that pillar, and I went up to where he was. How did he go there? He walked back there of course. Did he turn with his face towards the market house or off from the pavement? With his face towards the market house. Did he turn to his right? I can't exactly tell how he turned, but any how he went back to the market house. I want to know whether he turned to his right hand side wheeling to his right, or whether he turned wheeling to his left? I think he turned to his right. You think he made a right wheel? I think he did as well as I can say. Well that brought him nearer to you did it? Yes, sir, he went right by me, then he went up and took his stand against the same pillar of the market house, he had come from. Against the north pillar of the eastern arch? Yes, sir, and I started to go up towards him, and he went over towards Mr. Hinsdale's. (Witness represents on the chart Tolar's position as standing against the north east pillar of the main east arch.) Did he stand on the pavement or under the arch inside? Right under the arch. So it was against the face of the pillar that he took his stand? Yes, sir. How long did he stand there? He never stood there but a mighty little time, he went off. How long do you think it was? About three or four minutes, I reckon. Then he went over to Mr. Hinsdale's? Yes, sir. Which way did he go, around the market house? He went through through the market house as well as I could see. Did he stop anywhere before he got to Mr. Hinsdale's? I never seen him stop. Did he stop at Mr. Hinsdale's? Yes, sir. Which door did he go into? I never noticed him any more, I don't know which door he went in. You were saying something about hearing a little boy hollering out who shot him? I didn't hear the little boy, myself, I heard some one say that the little boy did do that. When did you hear that? Directly after it was done. Where was Mr. Tolar at the time the man spoke that? He was leaning up against that pillar. How far off from where the man was, what I want to know is, whether Tolar was near enough to have heard that remark. I don't know; I reckon he might have heard it. Was it made in a loud tone of voice? There were some men talking there, and said that the little boy hollered out that "Tolar shot him," and said that they had slapped the little boy down. I want to know if that was said loud enough to Tolar for him to have heard it? I don't know that he could have heard it, he may have heard it, I didn't hear it myself, and I was standing pretty close to Tolar myself. Witness, you don't seem to understand me, I understand you to say you didn't hear the little boy say who shot him? No, sir. You mean you heard a man in the crowd say that a little boy was slapped down? Yes, sir. Now I ask you if that man who said that he heard the little boy use that expression, if he was in such a position that when he said it Tolar could have heard it? No, sir, I don't think Mr. Tolar could have heard it. You don't think Tolar could have heard it? No, sir.

Re-direct examination by the Counsel for the prosecution. How came you to be summoned here, do you know? No, sir. You say you have never talked to Mr. Phillips about this business? No, sir. Have'nt you been very careful who you talked to? Yes, sir. Didn't you come here unwillingly to testify? Yes, sir; I did. It was very hard for you to have to tell it? Yes, sir. Didn't Colonel Cogswell see you before you came up here? Yes, sir. Did any of his officers ask you about this business? The Lieut. asked me. What did you tell him? I told him I didn't see who shot him. You have told that to several persons? Yes, sir: I have never told but to one man and that was Henry Sykes that I knew anything about it; I didn't think he had ever told it. You don't remember ever having told it but to one man? I don't recollect. Phillips has nothing to do with your testimony to day? No, sir. You said that Mr. Hardie came down stairs behind Beebee? I am certain he was right close behind him. That is your impression? He was close enough behind him, that when he got down stairs he grabbed him by the back of the coat. Is that the reason you think he came behind him? Yes, sir; and I saw him come down behind too.

Re-cross Examination by the Counsel for the accused.

So you frequently told others a different story? Yes, sir: I told them, because I never was put on oath. How many times have you told any body that you didn't know who shot him? I have told several that I didn't know who shot him, because I didn't want to come here.

ROBERT MITCHELL, a witness for the prosecution, having been first duly sworn testified as follows:

Examined by the Counsel for the prosecution. What is your name? Robert Mitchell. Where do you live? Fayetteville. What is your occupation there? Merchant. Were you a merchant there early in this year? Yes, sir. At the time Archy Beebee was killed? Yes, sir. Do you remember what day of the month it was he was killed? I do not sir. You remember the time? Yes, sir. Was it since last Christmas? I think it was sir. Did you see Archy when he was brought from the guard house? Yes, sir. Where were you standing at that time? I was in my store. What street is your store on? Gillespie street. On which side as you go from the market house? The west side of Gillespie St. That is the side opposite the guard house? Yes, sir. Could you see the door of the guard house? No, sir: I could not see the door; the guard house is rather back from the street and there is a little entrance that you go into. Could you see that entrance? Yes, sir. Did you see Archy when he came out of that entrance? I saw him the time he got in front of my store. He passed in front of your store on the opposite side of the street? Yes, sir. How long after he passed before you went to the market house? I could not say how long it was; it was after the ladies drove up to the market house; I then went up there, and Archy was up there; or the boy; I didn't know his name was Arch; I have heard since it was Archy Beebee; I went up stairs then. Was Archy up stairs when you got to the market house? Yes, sir. Are you a relation of Miss Massey that is, the young lady upon whom this violence was attempted? My wife is her aunt. Her father and your wife are sister and brother? Yes, sir. What is his name? William H. Massey. What is the young lady's name? Elvira Massey. You went over there for what purpose? I went there as a matter of protection to her, sir. As a matter of courtesy and protection? Yes, sir. Did you stay up stairs in the market house? I did, sir. I stayed there until the trial was over. Did you notice the crowd as you passed through it; was there many persons there? I didn't notice particularly; I saw a good many persons. Was it a larger crowd than is usually there? It was a pretty large crowd. Have you ever seen such a large crowd there upon the occasion of a trial? I don't know that I did. How long have you been living in Fayetteville? I have been living there all my life, pretty much; I have been living there regularly for the past fifteen or sixteen years. You were up stairs then, when Mrs. Massey and her daughter came down? Yes, sir. They came down before you came down? Yes, sir. How long before, a minute or two? It was a short time; not more than that. Who went down with them? Mr. Bond, the Constable, her mother and herself went down together about the time they started down, me and Mr. Massey, who is my father-in-law, went after them. The young lady's grand-father and yourself went down together? Yes, sir. Is Miss Elvira Massey's father living? No, sir. Who are her nearest male relatives, has she brothers? Yes, sir. Grown up? No, sir, no brothers grown up; a young man by the name of David Shepherd Massey, he is the next child to Miss Elvira. Is he grown? No, sir. I mean men; what men are her nearest male relatives, that you are aware of, living there? I reckon Mr. Tom Powers is. What sort of a relationship between her and Mr. Powers? He is a brother to her mother. He is Miss Elvira's uncle? Yes, sir. A maternal uncle? Yes, sir. Was there any relationship between Mr. Tolar and Miss Elvira? I am not certain whether there is or not; I have heard Mrs. Massey speak of being related to some Tolars, but whether it is Capt. Tolar's family, or another Tolar's family, that live down the river. I am not able to say. You are not certain about any relationship existing, or if it exists, you don't know what it is? No, sir. But you think you have heard your father-in-law say there is some between them and the Tolars? Yes, sir. I think his name was Needham Tolar; whether Capt. Tolar is any relation to them or not, I don't know. Do you know old John Maultsby? Yes, sir. You know young John? Yes, sir, I know both of them. What relationship exists between young John and Miss Elvira? Well, sir, I don't know what relationship exists between them; I know what they say is the relationship between John Maultsby's father's mother and my father-in-law, they were brother and sister; that is what I understood. John Maultsby's father's mother and Miss Elvira's grand-father were brother and sister? Yes, sir. That makes them second cousins; do you know whether there is any relationship between Sam Hall and Miss Elvira? None that I know of. Do you know whether the Lutterlohs are connected in any way? Not that I ever heard of. When you came down stairs, did you go to the carriage where the ladies were? I did, sir. Who was there, at the time? I think Mr. Bond was there, and I think Mr. Philip Taylor. Do you remember any one else coming up there while you were there? Probably Mr. Massey went with me, I won't say positive. You don't remember seeing any one else? No, sir. Did the carriage drive off before you left? Yes, sir. You saw no one else speak to them in the carriage that you recollect of except Mr. Philip Taylor, and you think it is possible that your father-in-law may have gone up with you? Yes, sir, they went to turn the horses off and the horses didn't appear to be willing to go and Mr. Bond or Mr. Taylor took hold of the horses; it is my impression it was one of them who took hold of them, and sort of lead them around; he started them off and they went down Person street. Did you leave immediately after

that? I did, sir; I went back to my store. Did you see Mr. Tolar, or any of these other gentlemen on trial here, at any time that day? I am not positive that I did; I think I saw Mr. Tolar in the market house sometime. Did you see Mr. Powers that day at all? I have no recollection of seeing him that I think of. Do you know Jonathan Hollingsworth? I don't know him, sir; I may know him if I could see him, but I never knew his name. Did you see Monk while you were in the crowd at all? I didn't see him until the matter was over with. You didn't see him during the time you were racing through the crowd to go to the carriage? No, sir. You didn't go up there until the carriage drove up with the ladies in it? No, sir. You went up with them, or immediately afterwards? I went up immediately afterwards. How long did the carriage remain there? I can't say exactly. As much as five minutes? I can't say; it was a short time. There was some conversation going on all the time? Yes, sir; but who they were I have no recollection of. You have no recollection of any other persons being there than you said? No, sir. The horse was led off, and you turned immediately and went towards your store? Yes, sir. How far had you gone before your attention was attracted back to the crowd? After the carriage left I went over to the store; I went around to the south end of the market and went to my store. You didn't go through the market? No, sir, I went around the south-east corner; I am not certain whether I went on the pavement or not, but I recollect very distinctly that when I got over very near my store, about a little tree that stands in front of Mr. Peter Johnson's, who is two doors above my store, I heard a crowd rushing and some persons hollering out "shoot him" "kill him," or something to that effect; I turned around, in the meantime I saw a crowd, a good many persons coming up towards the market house, and I heard a pistol fired; that was right at the south-east corner of the market; I heard a gun, or pistol, or something; I saw the smoke; I kept on to my store, I didn't go back at all until after the crowd dispersed. How long a time did it take you to walk from the market house to the point where you heard the pistol fired? I have no recollection of stopping; I might have stopped before I got there, but it didn't take me but a short time to go there. How many yards was it? I am going to tell it as close as I can; I suppose about seventy-five yards. Archy Beebee was going down stairs when you left the market house? No, sir. He wasn't on the stairs? No, sir. And by the time you had walked seventy-five yards you heard this rush? Yes, sir. You don't remember stopping anywhere? I don't remember to have stopped, though I might have done it. What is your impression, that you did not stop? I don't know whether I did or not. I am trying to fix the time that it took for this whole transaction. I can't say; my impression is probably I might have stopped, or I might not; I would not be positive about it. Do you remember stopping anywhere? I don't remember that I stopped anywhere after I left the carriage. Then by the time you had got seventy-five yards from that spot, you heard this rush, and heard the pistol fired? Yes, sir, when I turned around to look, I saw the sticks; it seemed the police appeared to be using them—at the south end of the market house, they appeared to be above their heads, and it was all done in a flash. Did these things happen in as quick succession as you are telling them? I would think they did. Could you have counted a hundred during the time you were looking at the crowd until after you saw the sticks? No sir. From the time your counsel until the pistol fired could you have counted a hundred? Just before the pistol fired I saw the sticks. I want to come to your estimates; you were out of the crowd and were cooler than any who were in it; how many could you have counted between the time you heard that first rush and the time the pistol was fired; between the beginning and the termination of the whole affair? Really, I can't say how much I could have counted; I might have counted a hundred, or two hundred, or probably could not have counted a hundred. It was very quick. was it? Yes, sir. A minute or two would embrace all? I can't say; I mean to tell you as nearly as I know; I would not say it would take a minute or half a minute; it may have taken more, but it was all done very quick. There was a rush at the market up stairs, as I understand, when he was coming down, and continued until he got around to the east end of the market and you heard the report of the pistol, and saw the smoke from it? Yes, sir. Did you notice what became of Phillman Taylor when he left the carriage? I did not, sir, I didn't pay any attention to any persons at all. Did you notice what became of your father-in law; did he go off with you? I don't think he went off with me; I will not be positive what became of him; I think he came down to my store afterwards; I will not be sure, but I left immediately and came out of the crowd. Do you know whether Phil. Taylor left there at all, or whether you left him in the crowd? I don't recollect; he keeps at the northeast corner of the market house; the carriage stopped nearly fronting his door, it might have been a little to the west of his store, but if it was it was very little; it was about the market square You don't recollect what became of him? No, sir.

Cross examination by the Counsel for the accused:

Mr. Mitchell, who was up stairs during the time of the trial, do you remember? Yes, sir. Just give us the names of all, if you please? Well, sir, there was Squire McRae, Joseph Arey, J. W. Strange, were the magistrates. And Lett? Now, I forget about Lett, I wont say for certain, about Lett, I recollect these three; Mr. Horn, who was the attorney; Mr. Massey, grand father of this young lady, Mrs. Massey and Miss Massey, Mr. James Dodd and myself, and an old colored woman. I don't know who she was, that was giving evidence, and a boy by the name of Morgan Dennis McKeever, and this boy that was shot, and Mr. Bond was up there occasionally; I don't know whether he stayed there all the time or not. Do you remember French Strange? No, sir. Do you remember Hardie, the sheriff? I think he was there. Wemyss? Well, he may have been there. Faircloth? I think Faircloth was down at the door. Brown? I don't recollect him being there. McGuire, member of the town guard? I guess they were down at the door, I don't remember them being up stairs; they may have been there, but I don't remember; there were but very few people there. The door was kept closed and only those who were immediately interested in the case were permitted to go up? Yes, sir, that is so, because when we went to the door and knocked they did not want to let us in, and as soon as they opened the door and found it was Mr. Massey and myself they asked if we could come up, and the magistrate said let all the relatives come up on both sides. Do you remember whether any body went down before you or not? Yes, sir, I remember Mr. Bond taking Miss Massey and her mother, and going down. Then the next to them was yourself and Mr.

Massey? I think we were next—may be Mr. Dodd went down before I did; I won't be positive about that, but I am satisfied that after Mrs. Massey went down with her daughter, Mr. Massey and I went immediately after; if there was anybody else went before that I have no recollection of it, though there may have been. You say you noticed nothing unusual about the crowd when you went down? I didn't notice the crowd much. When you got to the carriage who was there? I think Mr. Bond was there. At the time you got to the carriage had the ladies got seated? They were being seated; they had got in, or probably they were getting in. At that time the only persons you saw at the carriage was Mr. Bond and Mr. Philiman Taylor? That is all I recollect; there may have been others. Did you enter in conversation with the ladies? No, sir; Mrs. Massey remarked something or other about to say to Tom; what she said to me about it, I have no recollection. That was a remark addressed to you? I think it was; I can't say for certain. She remarked to you to see Tom, and what else you don't remember? I don't remember what the words were; the young lady was crying and I didn't wish to have anything to do with it. While you were there at the carriage was Tom. Powers there? I have no recollection of seeing Tom. Powers at all sir. While you were there at the carriage, see if you can't refresh your recollection; did you hear either Miss Massey or Mrs. Massey say Tom don't do it, or anything to that effect? No, sir; she remarked to me to see Tom; that she was afraid, as I think about it now, may be I am giving her statements wrong, but if it is, I don't want to be understood that I am going to tell it for the fact. If you don't know it is a fact you had better not tell it at all? She remarked to me to see Tom, for I am afraid he will do some harm; I wont say she ever said that but I took an inference that she wanted me to see Tom. And the carriage left before you turned away from it? Yes, sir; and after the carriage left I turned; I intended to have staid there with the young lady till the carriage went off as a matter of protection and respect. You say that William H. Massey, father to this young lady is not living? No, sir. How long has he been dead? Well, it has been five or six years; he died in 1872—I think in February or March. Mr. Mitchell, your store is close to the market house? My store, is, I reckon, you know pretty much where it is as well as I do. You are examined for the benefit of the court, who know nothing about it? Well, my store is, counting the corner store, the fourth store from the south-east corner of the market square; it would be about a hundred yards. You are frequently about the market house are you not? Yes, sir. Is it unusual to see Mr. Tolar at the market house? No sir; it wasn't unusual at that time. You know where his place of business was? Yes, sir. Where was it? It was in the market stall, on the south of the market. So his usual place of business was the market house? Yes, sir; that is the usual place where Mr. Mimms had his business. Don't you know that Capt. Tolar succeeded to Mr. Mimms in his business? Yes, sir; I have seen him selling beef there. Did you carry out that request of Mrs. Massey? No, sir; I didn't see Mr. Powers. Did you look for him at all? I turned at the time she spoke about Tom, but I didn't see him. You never told him the message she gave you? No, sir; I never told nothing to him at all.

Re-direct Examination by the Counsel for the Prosecution.

Are the people who sell beef in Fayetteville selling all day or only in the morning? It depends entirely on the business if they don't sell out in the morning they stay there till evening. Do the butchers keep their stalls there with beef on them all day? Some times when they don't sell out in the morning. Do you mean that W, J. Tolar was in the habit of being there all day with his beef at that time? I can't say about it; I know I have seen him there in the morning, and I have seen him there until after noon; I recollect seeing him there until noon but after noon I have no recollection of ever seeing him there. Is not it an unusual thing for the butcher's stall to be opened in the afternoon? There is no regularity in hours for the market; if a man takes beef in the market and sells it out before breakfast, all right; if he don't he just stays there all day or until late in the evening; now Mr. Bill Mitchell often stays there until sunset, and brings his beef he doesn't sell out, and leaves it with me. He lives in the country don't he? He lives out about a mile. Does Mr. Tolar live in the country? I think his slaughter pen is just out at the edge of the town; I think his residence is near about the edge of the town; it may be just in it; I am not positive, but I think it is just at the suburbs of the town. Did you see any beef there that day? I have no recollection about that at all, Do you have any reason to know that Capt. Tolar has ceased butchering there of late? He has ceased to butcher there. I am speaking of before he was arrested? He moved away from Fayetteville in the spring but what time he moved away I don't know, neither do I recollect how far back it was that he brought beef and sold it in the market house. I cant say positively that he has done it for the last six months and I won't say positive that he didn't do it. As I understand it you know at one time he was carrying on the business of butcher? Yes, sir. And whether he was at it at this time, you can't say, with certainty? No, sir; and I won't say he wasn't; I recollect he was doing it last winter for I bought beef at his stall. You say that as a general rule you have seen him there in the morning but not in the afternoon? I don't remember seeing him in the afternoon, that I recollect of. That was between three and four o'clock that the affair occurred, wasnt it? I think it was. You can't recollect exactly what Mrs. Massey said to you? I can't recollect what she said. My impression is she remarked to me to see Tom and talk to him, but, I won't be positive that is what she said. To comfort him do you mean; did you conceive any apprehension that he was going to attempt something at the time? Counsel for the accused objected to the question. Counsel for the prosecution. You can't state what she said? Not positively. Let it pass then. Question by the Commission. What was the sum and substance of the request made to you by Mrs. Massey relating to Tom? Well, sir, I can't answer with certainty further than just what I was going to tell you; my impression was that she was afraid Tom would kill the boy, it was my impression only. You can't pretend to state the words, but the impression left on your mind at the time was that she was apprehensive he was going to get into some diffi-

culty? Yes, sir, I can't say now; may be Mrs. Massey didn't ask me that, but she asked me to see Tom Powers and it made this impression upon my mind: my impression is that she was apprehensive that he would do some harm. You can't tell whether that was your impression at the time, or what she said, but whatever she said produced that impression on your mind at the time? I reckon it must have done it, I think so now. You think now that is the impression produced upon your mind at the time? Yes, sir.

Re-cross examination by the Counsel for the accused:

Was there anything said about doing any damage to the boy at all? None that I heard of except what I related that came from the sister of Mr. Powers.

On motion the Commission adjourned to meet on Tuesday, the 13th instant, at 11 o'clock, A. M.

RALEIGH, N. C., Aug. 13, 1867—11 A. M.

The Commission met pursuant to adjournment. Present, all the members of the Commission, the Judge Advocate, the Counsel for the prosecution, all the accused and their Counsel.

The reading of the testimony taken yesterday was waived, there being no objection thereto.

Yesterday's proceedings were then read and approved.

SAMUEL A. PHILLIPS, a witness for the prosecution, having been first duly sworn, testified as follows:

Examined by the Counsel for the prosecution. What is your name? Samuel A. Phillips. Did you reside in Fayetteville at the time Archy Bebee was killed? I did, sir. When was the first time that you heard Archy Bebee had attempted to commit a rape upon Miss Massey? It was on Monday morning, about nine o'clock, the eleventh of February. Before breakfast? No, sir, after breakfast. Where were you at the time? At my store. Do you remember who brought you the information? Archy Russell first told me, I think. Did you hear others speaking of it afterwards? Yes, sir. Is Miss Massey connected with you in any way? No, sir. Before Archy was brought out of the guard house, did you hear any persons speaking of this affair? I heard a good many say that he ought to be killed, or ought to be hung. Can you specify any persons that you heard speak that way? I don't know, sir, that I can any particular persons, a good many people talked of it during the day, and I don't recollect any particular persons that made the remark. You can't state any person? No, sir. Did you meet Tom Powers, or Capt. Tolar, or Monk Julia, at any time during that morning? No, sir, not during the morning, that I have any recollection of. Not before three o'clock in the afternoon? No, sir. Did you learn at that time or have you heard since, and before you came here, of any agreement, or combination between any men or set of men, for the purpose of bringing the prisoner, Archy Bebee, to justice? No, sir. You were never any party to any such agreement? No, sir. And never heard of any such agreement? No, sir. If it existed you know nothing of it? No, sir. Do you know what relationship, if any, exists between Mr. Tolar and Miss Elvira Massey? I have heard it said since this occurrence that they were some relation. Who by? It has been a street talk, I don't recollect any person. Did you ever hear it said by any members of his or her family? No, sir. You don't know anything about it of your own knowledge? No, sir, I do not. At what hour did you first go to the market house that day? About half past three in the afternoon. You hadn't been to the market house before that day? I think I might have been up there, I generally tend the market in the morning; I don't recollect whether I had been there that morning or not. If you were you don't recollect it now? No, sir. But you were up there about half past three in the evening. Yes, sir. Did any one go with you? Yes, sir. Who was it? I think Mr. Thornton walked up from my store with me. What Thornton? Jacob Thornton. Did you both go together into the crowd? When we got to the east end of the market house I think he stopped to talk to some person, and I walked on under the market house. How far is your store from the market house? About one hundred and twenty-five yards. What street is it on? Person street. Which side of the way, right or left? On the left as you go down towards the river. You came to the market with Jacob Thornton? Yes, sir. Was there any crowd at the market house, when you reached there? Yes, sir. What would you estimate the crowd at? I would suppose there were some fifty persons. Did you go underneath the market house, or stay outside? I went underneath. Did you have any weapon at that time with you? Yes, sir. Would you recognise that weapon if you saw it? Yes, sir. (A pistol is shown to the witness.) Is that the one? It was one of that kind and size. The same make and size? Yes, sir, a Remington. It was one like that, but you can't say for certain whether it was the same one or not? No, sir. Is there no mark about it by which you could recognize it? No, sir. It was admitted by the defence that that was the pistol.

Direct examination resumed, by the Counsel for the prosecution:

Your opinion is also that this is the same pistol? Yes, sir. You heard that when you first went up there that evening? Yes, sir. What was your reason for carrying that pistol? About ten o'clock in the day or perhaps a little later, Mr. Wemyss came down to my store, and was speaking of this affair, and said the trial came off at three o'clock, and during the time he stayed there he told me he would like me to be present, I told him I would do so. Mr. Wemyss is an officer? Yes, sir. Where did you carry the pistol about your person when you went up there? I had on an overcoat, I had no belt nor pocket to put in the sleeve of my overcoat, the left sleeve. Did you have it out at all, when you went up there? No, sir. Did you go underneath or did you stay out on the pavement? I went underneath. Did you go in at the east front? Yes, sir. Who did you see under there? or by the way was Archy Beebee up stairs when you got to the market house? I suppose so. You saw him come down afterwards? Yes, sir. And you didn't see him go up? No, sir. Your best impression was he was up stairs? Yes, sir. Who did you see in the crowd you knew? I saw Mr. Tom Powers and Mr. Henry Sykes? Any one else that you can name? Capt. Tolar, Edward Powers, Ralph Lutterloh. Was Sam Hall there at that time? Not at that time I think. Do you remember any one else? No, sir, I can't remember any other persons at that time. Were those gentlemen underneath the market house? Yes, sir. Did you have any conversation with any of them? I don't think I did at that time. Did you have no conversation with Mr. Tom Powers? Not at that time, sir. Nor with any of them that you remember? No, sir. Where was Capt. Tolar standing when you saw him? He was on the west side of the

market house, running north and south, rather to the west side of the main arch, standing near the stall he had formerly used for selling beef. Was he using that stall selling beef at the time you saw him? I don't think there was any beef there that evening. Did you ever see him there when he was selling beef? Yes, sir. Did he wear his ordinary clothes or a butcher's apron? I think he generally wore his ordinary clothes. You saw nothing of any beef there that day? I don't recollect seeing any. Did you see him sell any that evening? No, sir. Do you know whether he was engaged in the business of butcher at that time? I don't. Do you know whether he had been engaged in the business of butcher for sometime previous to that? He had before that. Do you know that he had ceased, or do you know nothing about it? I know nothing about it. He was standing on the west side of the southern arch? On the west side of the large main arch, running north and south. In the south-west corner of the market house? Yes, sir, rather on the south-west corner. What was he doing there? He appeared to be as I thought in conversation with those other men. Which others? Powers and Sutterloh. Ed. Powers or Tom? Ed. Powers. He seemed to be in conversation with Ed. Powers and Ralph Lutterloh? I took them to be in conversation. Were they standing together? Yes, sir. Was there any one else near them, or did the whole crowd stand off from them? They appeared to be in a group by themselves. A little off from the crowd? Yes. sir. There was a crowd there, as I understand you? Not much of a crowd there at that time. How many persons do you suppose were inside of the market house? I don't suppose there were more than twenty-five persons under the market, black and white. Did you notice how Capt. Tolar was dressed? I didn't notice any part of his dress except his shawl. You said you saw Tom Powers under the market at that time—where was he? He was sitting on a bench, just on the east side of the main arch. The east side? Yes, sir. He was one side of the arch, and Tolar the other, with those gentlemen? Yes, sir. What was he doing? They were sitting there. Was any one with him? Mr. Sykes I think was sitting with him. Did you see any one else sitting there with him? There were some three or four others, but I don't recollect who they were. Do you think you would recollect, if they were called to you? I don't know, sir. You recollect Mr. Sykes was sitting there? Yes, sir. Did you hear any part of the conversation between him and Mr. Sykes? I did not, sir, Did you hear any part of the conversation between Capt. Tolar and Ed Powers, and Ralph Lutterloh? No, sir. Can you say with certainty they were talking to each other? I can't say for certain. They were together as men in conversation? Yes, sir. You heard nothing that was said? No, sir, I did not. Did you see anything that made you apprehend any difficulty at that time? No, sir. Did you see any weapons about any one? No, sir. Did you see any protrusions about the men's clothing, as if they were armed, or anything that attracted your attention? No, sir. If it existed, it was not evident enough to attract your attention? No, sir. How long did you stay at the market house at that time? About ten minutes, perhaps, not that long; I went back down to my store again. Did you go from the east end of the market house? Yes, sir. You stayed there how long? About ten minutes, sir. How long did you remain at your store before you returned? I remained there but a very few minutes; I can't say exactly how long I remained there; I then walked back to the market house again; when I got to the market house the second time, I saw there was a great many more people than there was when I was there first. How many do you suppose there were in the crowd when you got back there? A hundred or more. Did you go inside of the market house then? Yes, sir, I went under the market house again pretty much the same way I did before; Mr. Powers and Sykes were sitting on the same bench where they were at first. Did you see Capt. Tolar? I saw him at that time; I think he was on the south side of the market house, out side of the market house on the pavement. Was any one with him? No, sir, no person with him at that time. You went into the market house, where did you go? I went to the centre of the market. Did you stand there, or speak, or converse with any one? I stood there for a minute or two, and then turned around to where Mr. Sykes and Mr. Powers were sitting, and I made some remark to Mr. Powers, asked him if he was Captain of that company, or something of that kind; I think that was the precise words, and he answered "No." Was there anything peculiar about Mr. Powers' appearance? He appeared to be very sad, like as if he was grieved. He was quiet, apparently? Yes, sir. Didn't relish your joke? No, sir. I want to know if anything struck you at the time about his appearance? The cause of my speaking to him in that way was, I saw the crowd had gathered there, and I knew that this girl was a relative of his, and I didn't know but there might be some trouble; that was the cause of my speaking that way to him. Did you have your weapon then? Yes, sir. Did you have it out? No, sir. Did you see any weapons at that time, before you left the market house; I mean while Archy was still up stairs, and before he came down? Yes, sir. Did you remain there that second time until Archy came down? No, sir. How long did you remain there? I remained there a few minutes and went back to my store. At that time, you say Tom Powers and Sykes were sitting at the same place you first saw them, and Tolar was on the pavement outside? Yes, sir. Did you see anything of Ed Powcas and Ralph Lutterloh at that time, before you left the market? Mr. Tolar walked back under the market, then I saw Ed Powers come up to him, meeting him like, under the market; they stopped there for a minute or so, and then I saw Mr. Lutterloh come up, and Sam Hall. Did these men have something to say to one another? I could not tell whether they were saying anything or not. When you left did you leave them standing there together? I did, sir. Did you see anything of John Maultsby there, at all? No, sir. See anything of Mr. Leggett? Yes, sir, I saw Mr. Leggett there the second time. Where was he standing? In the

group near Mr. Tolar and those other men. As I understand it, Mr. Tolar came back from the south end of the market and those others came together from some other direction? From the west end of the market. Did they all come up together? No, sir, I think not. They came up separately? I think they did. Did Leggett come up there too? Yes, sir, I didn't see Mr. Leggett when he came up, I cast my eyes away, and when I cast them back there again I saw him in the group; I didn't notice which way he came from. Then you went off again? Yes, sir. Did you see anything of Monk there, that second time? Yes, sir, as I was coming out the second time I saw Monk at the east end of the market, standing speaking to some person near the east arch. What was he doing? He was standing like as if he was having some talk with him. Now, I want to know if, during the short time you were there, you saw any weapons in the hands of any one? I saw Mr. Ed. Powers have a pistol, sir. Was it in his hand or in a belt? He had it under his clothes, like; I saw the end of it. Did you see any one else? I think that is the only one I saw at that time. Did you see any knives? Monk had a knife in his hand whittling. You went off down to your store again? Yes, sir. The first time you came up from your store, you say Jacob Thornton came with you? Yes, sir. Did any come up with you the second time. No, sir. Did any go back with you the first time? No, sir. Did any one go back with you the second time? No, sir. How long did you stay at home, sir? I just went down to the store and gave my little boy orders what to do, I told him to stay and keep the store open— that I would be back in a few minutes. Then you left? Yes, sir. And went back up to the market house? Yes, sir. When you got up there that time, where did you go, inside, or did you remain outside? I stopped at the entrance of the main eastern arch. Did you stop at the middle of it, or at one of the pillars? Nearer the north side of the arch. About at the entrance, near the north side of the arch? Yes, sir. Were you standing at that point when Mrs. Massey and her daughter, Elvira, came down? No, sir, I think I had moved out on the out side of the market when the ladies came down. How long were you there, from the third time you returned to the market house, until the time Archy came down stairs? The ladies came down in two or three minutes after I got to the market the third time; then I suppose it was some five minutes, or perhaps a little more before Archy came down. You stood a very short time at the entrance of the market house? Yes, sir. Where did you move to then, before the ladies came down? I moved off nearer the edge of the pavement at the east end of the market. Do you mean directly in front of the arch? Yes, sir. Between the arch and the carriage that was standing there for the ladies? Yes, sir. How far do you think you were standing from the pavement? I think I was standing on the edge of the pavement. How far behind you was this carriage? The carriage was some forty or fifty feet, perhaps more, or perhaps less, I can't be certain about the distance. You were standing there when the ladies came down? Yes, sir. Who came down with them? Mr. Bond. Any-one else, did you notice? I don't recollect any other person. Did they pass by you to go to the carriage? Yes, sir. This last time that you were back there, between the time you got there and the time the ladies passed to the carriage' did you see any weapons? Nothing more than the knives; Monk had a knife, and I saw one or two others have knives, whittling. Who were the others? I don't recollect the others, sir. You saw no pistols in the crowd? No, sir. You saw one or two others have knives whittling? Yes, sir. When these ladies passed out to the carriage did they pass right by you? Yes, sir. Did you have to get out of the way to let them pass? No, sir; I was standing rather on the north side of the arch. You were on their left as they passed you? Yes, sir. Did you look at the young lady? Yes, sir. Did you keep your eyes on them until they got to the carriage? No, sir. You just looked as they passed? Yes, sir. Did you keep your eyes towards the market house? Yes, sir, towards the steps. After these ladies went to the carriage did you see any one else go to the carriage? Yes, sir, I saw several go to the carriage, and then come back again towards the market. Who were they sir? I dont remember all of them, I saw Capt. Tolar for one, and Robt. Mitchell, I saw him coming from the carriage, I didn't see him go to the carriage. Did you see Capt. Tolar going to the carriage? Yes, sir. Did you see any one else? I saw Mr. David Cashwell at the carriage. Did you see what became of Capt. Tolar after he went to the carriage? I saw him come back to the market house. How long did he remain at the carriage? Not more than a minute or so. Did he go up to the carriage and come back? He walked up to the carriage and stopped like as if he was speaking to the ladies a moment or so, and the next I saw of him, he was coming back towards the market house. Did you notice where he went then? Yes, sir. Where did he go? He went under the end of the market. Did you see where he went inside of the market? No, sir. You lost sight of him? Yes, sir. You saw Capt. Tolar go to the carriage and come back, you saw Robert Mitchell go to the carriage, and you saw David Cashwell at the carriage? Yes, sir. Did you see any person conversing with Bond? No, sir. Did you see any other person go to the carriage? I think I saw other persons go to the carriage, but I don't recollect who they were. Did you see John Maultsby go to the carriage? I did not sir. Did you see Tom Powers go to the carriage? I am not certain about that, I could not say for certain whether Tom Powers went to the carriage or not. You could not say he did not? No, sir, and I could not say he did. You have a vague impression; you would not like to say one way or the other? Yes, sir. Those are all the persons you can remember at this time? Yes, sir. I am under the impression that I saw Mr. Phil. Taylor leave the carriage. Did you

see Tom Powers after you got back to the market house that third time at all? Yes, sir. Where was he then? He was near a bench there by Becky Ben's. Did you see him have any weapon then? No, sir, I did not. Did you see Monk at that time? No, sir, not at that time. Did you see Monk before Archy came down stairs, after you got back the third time? Yes, sir. What was he doing then? He was standing near this bench. How far was he from Mr. Powers? He was close to him. Do you mean there were none between them? No, sir, I don't mean that, I don't recollect whether there was any person between them or not. He was pretty close to him. Did you see anything, after you came back that time, of Ed Powers and Ralph Lutterloh? Yes, sir. Where were they? They were near the same place, standing right under the arch like. Did you say they were standing right under the arch? Under the market you know. A few steps within the arch you mean? Yes, sir. Near Becky Ben's stall? Yes, sir. You say you saw Tom Powers standing there, and Monk near him, and Ed Powers and Ralph Lutterloh standing in the same group, standing close enough to have any conversation do you mean? Two or three steps off, yes sir. Did you see Henry Sikes at that time? No, sir, I did not. Did you see Sam Hall then? I saw Sam Hall just before Beebee came down. Where was he then? He was in the same crowd. Ralph Lutterloh, and Ed Powers and Sam Hall, and Capt. Tolar and Mr. Leggett were close to each other? Yes, sir. Did you see any weapons in the possession of any of them at that time? No, sir. Did you have your pistol out then? No, sir. Did you draw it out at that time? No, sir. You hadn't drawn your pistol out, up to the time that Archy Beebee came down stairs? No, sir. Did you see any one come down stairs after Miss Massey and her mother came down, and before Archy did? Yes, sir. Who was it. Mr. Hornrinde. Was that immediately before Archy came down stairs? No, sir, it was some couple of minutes. He didn't form part of the same escort? No, sir. Do you remember seeing any one else come down? No, sir. You think Mr. Hornrinde came down after the ladies had come down, and before Archy did? I think he did. Just tell how the prisoner came down, who you saw with him, and all the circumstances connected with it? Mr. Hardie came down first, came down two or three steps and stopped on the steps, as if looking around to see what was going on—if anything was going on below, and then immediately after him came Mr. Wemyss— he had hold of Beebee by the right thumb, had a string on his right thumb—and Mr. Faircloth was on the other side. Was Wemyss on his right side? Yes, sir. And Faircloth on his left? Yes, sir. Did you see any one else in the group—any other officers? I don't recollect any other persons. Now Mr. Phillips, I want you to think well of the question I ask you, just before Archy came down, during that third visit that you made to the market house, did you hear any threat from any quarter at all? I don't know that I heard any particular threats, I saw a sign. What sign. I saw from the looks of the crowd that there was to be something or other done, but I could not tell what. What was the peculiarity in the looks of the crowd? The peculiarity in the looks of the crowd was, they were standing in groups here and there, under the market and outside. Does not a crowd usually gather there, when there is a trial up stairs? No, sir, not such a crowd as that. That was larger than I had ever seen at a trial. From the largeness of the crowd, and the way they were grouped about, you were apprehensive, that there was some difficulty about to occur? Yes, sir. You entertained that apprehension before Archy came down? Yes, sir. You say Hardie came down the stairs about two or three steps and he then looked around as if to see what was going on? Yes, sir. And Wemyss came out on the right of the prisoner, and Faircloth on the left; do you remember any other officers? I don't remember. You can't say whether there were or not? No, sir. Was anything done before Archy got down stairs that you saw? No, sir; I didn't see anything done. Were you standing in front of the large arch? Yes, sir. On the edge of the pavement? Near the edge of the pavement; I may have moved up nearer by this time. Were you on the pavement? Yes, sir. You moved up a little nearer towards the steps? I think I did. You say you saw no movement made on him while Archy was still up stairs? No, sir. When he first got to the bottom of the steps, did you see anything? When he got about the end of Becky Ben's, I saw there was a rush made at him like. Were there any shouts or exclamations at the time? Yes, sir; I heard a voice say, "I demand the prisoner." Did you hear any other shouts? I heard Sheriff Hardie speak and tell him, "he is my prisoner," and "stand back," or something to that effect. Did you hear any reply? I dont recollect of any reply—I heard several voices at that time. What were they saying? Demanding the prisoner. It was not a single voice that you heard demanding the prisoner? No, sir. It was more than one voice you heard when I first heard it, it was a single voice. Then when Sheriff Hardie replied you heard these numerous voices? Yes, sir. That was the general cry, we demand the prisoner? It appeared to be three or four voices. Was there any profanity used or simply, "we demand the prisoner"? I don't remember any other words. You say there was a rush made upon the prisoner? Yes, sir; the crowd appeared to move up. Do you mean the crowd closed in easily, or closed in with a rush? They closed in with a rush. Did you see who was in the front of that crowd, nearest the prisoner? I could not tell. Did you see any one lay hands on the prisoner, or attempt to grab him, at the time that rush was made? I saw a hand—I saw two or three hands attempt to catch him. Do you know who they belonged to? Mr. Tom. Powers was one; I don't know any other. Did you see anything of Monk at that time? Yes, sir; Monk was in the crowd. Do you remember seeing him? Yes, sir. Did he have his knife at that time? Yes, sir. Did you see any weapon in Mr. Powers hand? No, sir. Did you recognize any voice that cried out "we demand the prisoner"? I think the first voice was Tom Powers'. How long have you known him? A good while. Ten years? I think I have. Do you know his voice? Yes, sir. Have you met him frequently? Yes, sir. I could not swear positively it was his voice. It was my impression. Was it your impression then? Yes, sir. Did the police

succeed in keeping him away? They succeeded in pushing the crowd back, and moved on until they got just at the end of the arch to make a turn, and there was another rush made. Just as they were at the end of Becky Ben's bench this first rush was made; they succeeded in repelling that, and got as far as the arch—at the turn of the arch? Yes, sir. And then there was another rush? Yes, sir. Were there any exclamations made, or was the language kept up from the first, in the way of exclamations? There was a good deal of noise at that time, and some one or two voices crying out, "I demand the prisoner." The confusion was considerable about that time? Yes, sir. Had you your weapon out then? No, sir, just at that time the officers succeeded in pushing back the crowd, and then I moved around to my left. Did you move off of the pavement? Yes, sir. You moved to your left and rear? Yes, sir. In the second rush did you see any person who was concerned in it? No, sir, I could not tell who was in the second rush. Did you see any persons among the heads that you recognized? Yes, sir, I saw Mr. Tolar, Tom Powers, Mr. Leggett, and Mr. Ed. Powers. See anything of Lutterloh or Sam Hall at that time? At that moment I did not; immediately after that I discovered they were in a bunch there. Was that after you had moved, that you discovered that? Yes, sir. Did you move out there after this rush was made? Just after they had succeeded in repelling the second rush. Where did you move to after that time? did you get stationary after a few minutes? Yes, sir. Or did you keep moving? I moved to the place and made a little stop. Where was that place? It was off to the left. Facing what part of the market house? About the centre of the pillar between the two arches, as well as I can recollect. How many feet do you suppose it was from the pavement? I don't think it was more than one or two or three. You just moved a step or two? Yes, sir. That was about the time the second rush was repelled? Yes, sir, and then immediately they made another rush, and I saw the sticks of the policemen. I saw them using their clubs, and I saw them knock a knife out of some person's hand, or I took it to be a knife. Why do you say it was a knife? I saw knives at that time. Did you see several knives at that time? I saw three or four. Were they in men's hands? They appeared to be cutting at the prisoner. You saw several knives, that appeared to be cutting at him at that time? Some three or four, I can't say how many. Do you know who had knives? I do not, sir, except Mr. Powers and Monk, I know that they had knives. You know they were attempting to use them then? They were acting like as if they were trying to cut. Did you see what sort of a knife Monk had? No, sir. Did you see what sort of a knife Powers had? No, sir. You saw the police using their sticks? Yes, sir. Was the crowd crying out at that time, or was it still? They were making a good deal of noise. I don't recollect any certain words they were speaking at that time. They appeared to be using a good deal of profane swearing, "damned if he aint my prisoner," or something of that sort. There were three rushes you say? Yes, sir, at the time this third rush was made the prisoner appeared to stumble, or tried to jump or get away from the officers—either from the officers or from the knives, I can't say which—and he stumbled and went down, or went down from some cause or other; he had a stumble and a fall, and about the time they were raising him up— Did you see any one else fall with him? They appeared to fall on their hands. How many? I think Mr. Wemyss and Mr. Faircloth both went down with him, and if I am not mistaken I think Sheriff Hardie caught hold of him. Did he quite recover himself? They raised him up and just as they got him up he was shot. Had you moved from the position you last described? Yes, sir, I moved still further around to the left. You were keeping almost parallel with the prisoner? A little to his front, I think. Where was the point he was standing when he was shot, according to your recollection? I think he was immediately in front of the little arch, on the south east corner. About midway of it do you mean? I think so. Was he on he pavement or off? He was on the pavement. Near the edge or middle or near the market house? I think he was rather near the edge of the walk. Did you see Sheriff Hardie at the moment the pistol went off? Yes, sir. Where do you think he was standing? Rather in the rear of the prisoner, and had hold of him by the collar at the back of his coat. On which hand? A little to the right. Which hand did he have hold of his collar with? I could not say, I think it was the left hand, I can't say for certain. Did you see Wemyss about that time? Yes, sir. Where was he standing? He was standing to his left. Were you on trial when Sheriff Hardie was examined as a witness here? No, sir. You didn't hear his testimony? No, sir. You say Sheriff Hardie was standing in the rear of the prisoner, and a little to his right? That is my impression. And you think he had hold of his collar by the left hand? I think so. Wemyss was where? On the left of the prisoner it appears to me, I won't be certain about that. Did you see Faircloth at that time? No, sir, I don't recollect seeing Faircloth at that moment. When the negro went down they appeared to get decidedly twisted up, in some way, and I am not certain where Mr. Wemyss was, but I am pretty certain that Hardie had hold of the back of his coat, by the left hand. You can't speak with certainty about Wemyss? No, sir. But your best impression is, he was a little to his left? Yes, sir—I mean a little to his right, right in front of Hardie. Did you see the man who fired the pistol? I did, sir. How close was he to you? He was about six or seven feet. Was he to your right or left? He was to my right. On the pavement or off? I think he was just off the edge of the pavement. How far from Beebee? He was pretty close to him. As far as he was from you? No, sir. He was nearer to Beebee than he was to you? Yes, sir. How far was Beebee from you? Beebee was a little nearer to me than the man who fired the pistol, was. Who was the man who fired the pistol? W. J. Tolar. Did you see the pistol in his hand? I did, sir. See the flash? I did, sir. The smoke? Yes, sir. And heard the report? Yes, sir. Did you see the man fall immediately after he was shot? Yes, sir. When did you see that pistol first? The first time I saw it, it was immediately before Beebee was shot. As it was brought to the level? The first thing I noticed of Capt. Tolar particularly was his shawl on his left shoulder sort of flew up, and immediately after that I saw him level the pistol at Beebee. Do you know whether he drew that pistol from about his person? I do not, sir. Did you see any one hand him that pistol? No, sir. What sort of a pistol was it? I could not tell about the size of it; as well as I could tell in the crowd, it was a tolerable large sized pistol. Was it as large as this one, (the one presented in the Court as the pistol Phillips had?) I don't

think it was as large as that. Did you see it sufficiently well to describe what sort of a pistol it was? No, sir. Did you see what Tolar did with it after he fired? No, sir, I did not. Just after he fired your attention was attracted to him or to the negro? To the negro, sir: immediately after the pistol fired there was a rush made right up upon the negro, or where Sheriff Hardie was, and the officers and I thought they were going to attack the officers, that is what I thought at the time; I made my way around then on the south-side of the crowd like, making my way to the sheriff. Did you make your way to him? I got close to him before the crowd was backed off. Did you have any thing to say to him? No, sir, I did not speak to him at all. Did you notice any movement he made just after the firing? Yes, sir. What was it? I saw him put his hand up to the side of his face like; I thought at that moment that he was shot. Then did you move around to go towards him? Yes, sir. What time did you first draw your pistol? It was immediately after the pistol fired. Hadn't you it in your hands before? No, sir. You are certain about that? I don't think I had, I would not be positive about it. Was your pistol loaded? Yes, sir. Your impression is you did not draw it until the pistol fired? That is my impression. But you do not speak with absolute certainty about that? No, sir, I don't. Did you see what became of Capt. Tolar after he fired? I saw him turn around and go back through the crowd; the last time I saw him he was about the opening of the arch, the east of the market. Did you see who was standing near him when he fired? Yes, sir, I saw some standing near him. Who was the nearest person to him in your estimation? Mr. Edward Powers was the nearest one I think. Where was he standing? He was standing right immediately to his rear and right. Was there any person between him and Ed. Powers? I don't think there was, sir. Did you see who was standing in front of him? No, sir. Was there any person between him and Beebee when he fired? As well as I can recollect, sir, there was two men standing side and side like, and the pistol was fired between the heads of those two men, over their shoulders. Were they colored or white men? I think they were white men. Those that were nearest to him in front? Yes, sir. And you think Powers was the nearest man on his right and rear? Ed. Powers—Yes, sir. Who else did you see near about him? At that time I saw Mr. Leggett close by, and I saw Mr. Ralph Lutterloh. Were those men all together? Right in one company? They seemed to be in one company? Yes, sir. Did you say Leggett? Yes, sir. Who else? Ralph Lutterloh, Did you see Sam. Hall at all? I did'nt see Sam. Hall at that time. Did you see Sykes at all? Not at that time. Did you see the pistol any more after you saw it leveled and fired? Soon after the firing I saw a pistol in Mr. Ed. Powers' hand. How quick after the firing? It was perhaps a minute or so. Do you know how long a minute is? I think so. You think it was at least a minute? Yes, sir. As long as you could have counted one hundred and twenty? I think I could have counted a hundred and twenty. Was he standing by Tolar at the time you saw the pistol in his hand, or had Tolar moved? Tolar had moved a little. At that time did you see anything of John Armstrong? I did sir. How near was he standing to Tolar when the pistol fired? I don't know sir, how near Tolar he was; he was pretty close to him; he was between me and Tolar, rather in the rear of myself and Tolar but nearer to

Tolar than I was. You were only five or six feet off you think? Yes, sir. Was he nearer to you or Tolar? He was nearer to Tolar than he was to me. Did you see any one else that you recognized near about there, white or black? A man they call Calvin Johnson was to my rear, as I turned around, and a man by the name of Robt. Simmons. Did you hear any exclamations in the crowd just after this pistol was fired, as to who did it? Yes, sir. What was said? I heard some one say in the crowd that Captain Tolar shot him. Did you know who it was? No, sir. Did you hear it said more than once? I did not. Was Capt. Tolar in the crowd at the time? I don't think he was. Had he left the place altogether? I think he turned and walked off towards the end of the market. Did you see him go away from the end of the market? No sir. Could any one standing at the end of the market have heard this voice? Yes, sir. Loud enough for the crowd to hear? Yes, sir. If he was standing at the end of the market he could have heard it? Yes, sir. How long after he fired was it that you heard it? Immediately after. Before you saw the pistol in Ed. Powers hands? It was after that. What sort of a pistol was it you saw in Powers hands? It was a smaller pistol than the one I had, rather. Was it a larger sized pistol? I could not say whether it was a large Navy Repeater, or a small one, it was smaller than mine. Do you mean a half a size smaller? It was more than half a size. It was somewhat smaller than the one you had? Yes, sir. According to your best impression, which was the longer pistol, the one in the hands of Ed. Powers or the one in Tolar's hands? According to my impression they were about the same size. Are those the only pistols you saw in the crowd—your own, Captain Tolar's and the one you saw in the hands of Ed. Powers? That is all I saw. Did you have any other pistol with you that day, besides this one? I did not, sir. Had you any other pistol? Not at that time, I have one now. You had none at that time? No, sir. Do you know what has become of the pistol that Mr. Tolar used that day? I do not. Have you no reason for knowing? No, sir. Never heard him say? No, sir. Do you know what has become of the pistol that Ed. Powers had that day? No, sir. You spoke of having heard one exclamation in the crowd that Capt. Tolar did it, was that a single exclamation? It was a single exclamation at that time, after that I heard several use it. You know when Captain Tolar left the crowd? No, sir I do not; I know when he turned around and walked off after the negro was shot. You saw him go as far as the arch, did you see him enter the arch? No, sir. So far as you know he may have been standing there at that time? So far as I know. The last you saw of him he was at that point? Yes, sir. Still in motion? Yes, sir, he appeared to be coming towards the the north corner of the market house. That was the impression you had? Yes, sir. You said something just now about your attention being attracted just before the pistol fired, by his shawl—did you see any falling or movement of the shawl—after the firing? I don't recollect after the firing, when he went to turn around the shawl appeared to fall off one of his shoulders, like. You have no reason for knowing what he did with his pistol? No, sir. You could not assist us in tracing it all? No, sir. Have you any bullets that will fit this pistol? No, sir. Do you know what has become of the loads that were in it that day? No, sir, I wrote home for them to send the loads that were

drawed out of it. You say you didn't see Tolar when he went off, after he got opposite the end of the arch? I did not. Didn't see him any more that day? No, sir. Did you see anything of Monk after the shooting? I saw Monk immediately after he was shot, Monk was in the crowd that made a rush on him after he was shot down. He wanted to cut his throat. Did he say any thing of that sort? Yes, sir. Did he have his knife still? Yes, sir. Did you see how he got away? Mr. Nixon, I think, was the person that caught him, and told him he could not do no such of a damned thing. Did he go off a little then? He went off. Was he still talking? Yes, sir. What we call "ripping and rarring?" Yes, sir. Did you see Tom Powers after the shooting at all? I don't recollect seeing him after the shooting. Did you see any of these other men you have spoken of—do you know what became of Ed. Powers? No, sir. How was he holding the pistol, down by his side? Yes, sir. Was he talking to any one? No, sir, not that I know of. Did you see him when he went away from that point where he was holding the pistol? No, sir. I think you said you saw Lutterloh and Leggett? Yes, sir. Did you see what became of them? No, sir, I didn't. How long did you remain there before you went off? I remained there some five or ten minutes. Just after this shooting took place did you show your pistol to any one? Yes, sir, immediately after I had run around as I told you towards Sheriff Hardie I come back then and said "the negro has been shot, and I want you to look at this pistol and see that it has not been shot;" I held it up in my hand, there was some three or four looked at it. Did any take it in their hands and look at it? Yes, sir. Do you remember who it was? I can't remember who it was. Your pistol had not been fired at that time? No, sir, it had not. You swear most solemnly, in presence of Almighty God, that you did not fire that pistol? I swear most solemnly that I have not fired a pistol since then either; immediately after the firing of the pistol there was a loud voice in the crowd saying: "any one that divulges this thing shall share the same fate that the negro did." Was there any thing further that can throw any light on this matter? No, sir. You heard this voice immediately after the firing—that any one who divulged this matter would share the same fate? Yes, sir; there was one thing I left out: before the crowd came from under the market I heard a remark: "I hope I wont have to shoot him, but if I do I will make it a safe shot." Who was it made that remark? I can't tell. As Archy was coming down stairs? Yes, sir. You say you didn't recognize the voice? No, sir. You can't say whose voice that was? No, sir.

Cross examination by the Counsel for the accused:

How long have you been living in the town of Fayetteville? About twenty-two years. Were you acquainted with the late William H. Massey, the father of Miss Elvira Massey? Yes, sir. Where is he now, sir? Dead, sir. What was his business before the war? He was a constable. What was your business? Constable. You and Wm. H. Massey were both constables? Yes, sir. Were you friends? Yes, sir. Were you intimate friends? Yes, sir. Were there more intimate friends than either you or he had than you were to him and he was to you? Yes, sir, there were, though we were friendly. You were exceedingly friendly? Yes, sir. Are you the same Sam. Phillips which is in these charges, and was subsequently released from prison? I am, sir, I suppose so. Don't you know it is so? I think I do. Just an swer truly what you know. I know that I was arrested on the charges and imprisoned. Have you ever been sworn to this matter before? No, sir. You were never sworn? No, sir. In no manner, shape or form have you been sworn about this killing of Archy Beebee before? No. sir, except that I was on the jury of inquest. Then you were one of the Coroner's jury of inquest? I was, sir. Which assembled in the town of Fayetteville the next day after Archy was killed? The same day, sir. And the next day, too? Yes, sir. Had it session that afternoon, and then adjourned over to meet next morning? Yes, sir. Do you remember the hour it met the next morning? I don't recollect what hour it was. Before breakfast or after? I think it was after breakfast. Can you give the names of any persons who were present on that Coroner's jury? I can give some: S. H Fishblate, Thomas A. Hendricks, Thomas A. Owens, one of the Williams's, Arthur Williams, I think it was, James Harris, Silas Sheets—I don't recollect any other names. Who was the active man upon that jury in getting up testimony and examining witnesses? I don't know who you may call the active man; I should think it was the Coroner's duty to do that. I am not asking you for what you think; I ask you who was the most active man upon that jury? I don't know, sir. Was there a man more active than Samuel A. Phillips? I don't know, sir; I know that I was requested by Sheriff Hardie at dinner hours to get up all the testimony I could. Did you get up what you could? I did, sir. So you were an active man in getting up testimony? I got up those who were told me to get up; I done the best I could at that time. To get up such witnesses as were suggested to you by others, and such as suggested themselves to you? Yes, sir. Who summoned the witnesses before that Coroner's inquest? I don't recollect, sir, whether it was the Coroner, or the foreman of the jury. Do you recollect whether it was Fishblate? I do not. Or Phillips? It was not me. Or Mc-Duffie? I don't recollect. Or Haines? I don't know, sir. Or Thomas A. Hendricks? I don't recollect who it was. But you remember the jury had a session in the afternoon, and they adjourned till some time the next morning, and then had an adjourned session? Yes, sir I ask you to pay particular attention to this question: I ask you that if, during the forenoon of that second session, you didn't call Thomas A. Hendricks, a member of the jury, into your store in the town of Fayetteville, and then and there say to him these words, or words to this meaning: "Mr. Hendricks, if you are a friend of mine, you will not examine those witnesses closely to-day." I did no such a thing. At dinner hour I had conversation with Mr. Hendricks; I was pointed to Robert Simmons; I was told that Robert Simmons knew who killed the man. You swear positively, in the presence of your God, that you said no such thing? I did not, sir. Had the jury adjourned at that time? Yes, sir. I don't care about that conversation then: had you had any conversation with him at any time, similar to that, before the jury formed their verdict? No, sir, I never had before nor since. And you never had any conversation with him the substance of which I have given? I was going to tell you the conversation I did have. I don't care about that, I mean before the finding of the verdict? I did not. Mr. Phillips, you say you were sworn as a juror on that occasion? Yes, sir, I think I was; they usually swear jurors. Do you know the nature of the oath that you took on that occa-

sion? I do, sir. Let us have the substance of it, if you please? I can't recollect; the substance of it is, that you will well and truly enquire into the case before you. It was the usual oath that the Coroner administers? Yes, sir. You have been a constable; you are familiar with those things, and you think it was the usual oath? Yes, sir. Sam. Phillips did you sign the verdict of that Jury? I did, sir. I ask you now, sir: how you dared under the sanction of that oath to sign a verdict, that that man came to his death by a pistol shot in the hands of some man to the Jurors, unknown? I have two reasons for doing that; one reason is according to my recollection of the Jury inquest, that you have nothing to do with what you know yourself, and you are not compelled to divulge, but it is according to the evidence brought before you; my second reason is, that of hearing this threat that any persons that divulged anything of this kind, would share the same fate the negro had done, and I hadn't the boldness to come forward and tell it. You hadn't the boldness? No sir. Though you had sworn in the presence of Almighty God to do your duty, you swear here that you hadn't the boldness? I had not, sir. I will ask you if that jury did not, on that occasion find that the deceased man, Archy Beebee, came to his death by a pistol shot fired by the hands of some person, to the jury, unknown? I think that is the finding of the verdict. And that was the finding of Sam'l A. Phillips? Of course it was, I was in the jury. I understand, Mr. Phillips, that you say that this pistol (holding a pistol in his hand) was the pistol that you had with you that day, and this was the only pistol? I think that is the same pistol. You think this is the same pistol and the only one? Yes, sir; the only one. Who brought this pistol from the town of Fayetteville to the city of Raleigh? Mr. C. W. McCoy. Your brother-in-law? Yes, sir. Will you be so kind as to tell us how this pistol was charged? Yes, sir; it was charged with three large balls in three barrels, and the other three were loaded with buckshot. A single buckshot in three chambers? Two buckshot in each barrel, if I mistake not. Was there any patching about the buckshot? Yes, sir. Do you remember what kind of patching it was? It was Factory sheeting. It was Factory sheeting? Yes, sir. You say three of the cylinders were charged with two buckshot each? I think so, sir. Let us be particular about that. It was loaded with buckshot, I am certain; three barrels were loaded with buckshot; whether with single buckshot or two or three, I don't know; my impression is there was two buckshot, one immediately behind the other. You swear positively there was two in each one of the three? I won't swear positively; I will swear positively they were lead with buckshot. Do you swear positively that the patching which was around these buckshot was Factory sheeting? I swear that that was the kind of patching; it was provided they were the same loads in it that they were when I loaded it; they might have been reloaded. Three barrels you say were charged with balls and three were shot? Yes, sir. And you say there was packing around the three barrels that were charged with buckshot, and no patching around the balls? I think not. Mr. Phillips, had this pistol been discharged at all between that time and the time that you left Fayetteville? Yes, sir, one or two barrels. How many barrels? I dont recollect how many. See if you can recollect? It had been discharged; all the barrels except two I think. How long before you left Fayetteville were they discharged by you?

I cant recollect exactly how long; if you recollect yourself, there was a good many houses breaking into lately in Fayetteville, and it was at that time I shot off those barrels.   Well, sir; did you shoot off the buckshot loads?   They were all loaded with balls; with large balls up to that time. On the day that this shooting of Beebee occurred were all these cylinders loaded with large balls?   Yes, sir.   And the buckshot and the patching in the three barrels was put in there since then?   Yes, sir.   Then you only shot off three barrels and left three charged?   I don't recollect whether it was three or four. But you didn't discharge all of them?   I discharged some and reloaded with buckshot.   In what condition did you leave this pistol at the time you left Fayetteville, how many barrels were charged?   I can't say for certain.   Had any body shot it at all after you used it?   They didn't up to the time I left there.   I mean up to the time you left, how many of these barrels were loaded and how many were empty?   I don't know, sir; I would not pretend to swear. Were there any loaded?   Yes, sir.   Were there any of them empty?   My recollection is that there were some of them empty.   How many?   I don't recollect how many.   Your recollection fails you there?   Yes, sir.   You don't recollect how many were empty at all? No, sir.   Who emptied these barrels, who fired off the pistol?   I did it myself, sir.   How long was it before you left Fayetteville that you fired off any of them?   I don't recollect that. Was it a week?   I don't how long it was. Was it a month?   I don't know, sir.   Was it two months?   I don't how long it was. Can't you say whether it was a week or a month? I can say it was inside of six months.   It was since the killing of Beebe?   After all.   And after discharging them you didn't load them any more?   I didn't load them any more except those there I loaded with buckshot.   You didn't load any of the other cylinders?   I think not, sir.   Did you discharge the other three that were loaded with balls, or did you leave these balls in there?   I don't recollect whether I left these balls in or not; I recollect there was one of the balls that was in the pistol when I bought it, but I can't say for certain if more than one of the original ones.   Can you say that at the time you left Fayetteville, there were certainly three charges of buckshot in those cylinders and one ball in another cylinder.   Yes, sir. You can say certainly they were there when you left Fayetteville?   Yes, sir.   Were those old loads?   The charge of the ball was an old load, those that were loaded with buckshot, I loaded myself this spring.   I want to know whether you are certain that there was only one cylinder charged with ball?   I can't say for certain.   And you discharged them yourself? Yes, sir.   When you discharged the pistol at the last time before leaving Fayetteville, did you remove the cap from the nipple of the barrel that was discharged.   I don't think I removed any cap.   I am speaking of the cap from the pistol barrel, the barrel you fired? I dont think I did remove that.   Have you any recollection about that at all?   No, sir; no more than just this, that I hardly ever do remove the cap.   You have no recollection whether you removed the cap or whether you did not?   I have not sir.   What do you call this pistol?   I call it a Remington pistol.   What size do you call it?   I call it a Navy repeater; I don't know whether that is proper or not.   You dont call it an Army repeater?   I always called it a Navy repeater.   Now, sir, while we are upon

that subject, take this pistol and look at it and tell me how much shorter the pistol that Ed Powers had, was than this one?   I can't tell you that.   Come at it as near as you can.   I have done that; I think it was shorter.   Do you think it was a size smaller?   I can't tell; I didn,t measure them.   It it your impression that it was two sizes smaller?   I know it was smaller. Is this about the size of Tolar's pistol?   I think the size of that Tolar had was pretty much the same size of the one Powers had.   Then you say the pistol Tolar had was a smaller pistol than this?   Yes, sir.   Did you see it distinctly, the one Tolar had?   I saw it in his hand when it was levelled at the negro.   And you think it was not as large a pistol as this?   I dont think it was.   Do you know what name they call such a pistol as the one Tolar had?   No, sir; I don't.   You don't know whether it was a Remington pistol?   It was not if I understand the way the Remington pistols are made if they are made like that one it was not a Remington pistol.   Was it a Colt?   I don't know sir. Did it have a round barrel?   I will show you the difference; I think the cylinder of the pistol was marked; had no top piece on it like this one has.   You are sure it was'nt one of these patterns?   I am pretty confident it was'nt.   You say you went up to the market house first at the time Archy was up stairs?   Yes, sir.   How long did you stay there before he was brought down?   I don't know sir; it was about half past three when I went up first.   At that time you say you saw a crowd of thirty or forty or fifty people?   Perhaps fifty people.   Did you notice anything unusual in that crowd at that time?   No, sir; I did not.   I think you say you saw at that time Capt. Tolar standing to the north of the southern-most arch?   The first time I saw him he was standing at or near the bench where he sells beef.   That was to the west of the southern-most arch?   Yes, sir. Inside or outside?   Under the market.   Do you know whether Capt. Tolar kept a desk there? Not at that time.   Did you see him up about the desk or was he nearer down towards the end of the stall?   He was on the outside of the beef stall.   What was he doing then?   He appeared to be moving from towards the west end of the market.   Who else did you see and recognize on that occasion?   I saw Mr. Ed Powers, and Mr. Leggett and Ralph Lutterloh.   Did you leave them there when you went back?   I am under the impression I did, but I can't say for certain as to that.   You spoke of their talking together?   No, sir; I don't know whether they were talking or not.   You didn't see them talking?   They were in a group, close together. No other person around them?   No, sir.   Did you see anything of Maultsby at that time, or Tom Powers?   Yes, sir.   Anything of Monk I didn't see him the first time.   What was Tom Powers doing?   He was sitting on a bench : him and Henry Sykes together.   You said there were other persons there whose names you don't remember?   Yes, sir.   Do you know Jim Jones? Yes, sir.   Did you notice him sitting there? I don't think he was.   Did you have the pistol with you at that time?   Yes, sir.   You went down to your store and remained there a short time and returned, bringing the pistol back with you? Yes, sir. Was that pistol cocked? No, sir. Had the crowd increased any when you got back the second time? Yes, sir. How much larger was it than it was at first? It appeared to be twice as large. Did you notice these same persons there when you got back the second time? I noticed when I got back the second time they were in the same place; Mr. Powers and Sykes, I think, were in the same place. Where did you see Mr. Tolar? If I mistake not, he was on the south side of the market on the pavement. Any body with him? No, sir, I don't think there was any person with him at that time. Where were Hall and Ed Powers, and Lutterloh at that time? I didn't see them at that moment. Did you see them at all, before you left the market that second time? Yes, sir. Did they get with Tolar again? They were close to him. Where were they standing then? They appeared to be standing close by where they were at first; Tolar moved around from where he was on the pavement under the market house, slowly. Did you leave them standing there when you went off the second time? I think they were close by. I can't say for certain whether I left them right there or not; my attention was not entirely upon that group. How long was that when you went off the second time and left them standing, before Beebee was brought down stairs? I can't tell, sir, I went back down by the store and remained there a few minutes and then returned; I was at the market house after I returned, before he was brought down. Do you think it was ten minutes? Yes, sir. Do you think it was a quarter of an hour? I wouldn't be surprised if it was. Was it half an hour? I think not, sir. You are certain it was not half an hour? I don't think it was. When you come back the third and last time, where did you find them standing? Near Becky Ben's stall, all of them. Just name them over? I can't name every body; I know Captain Tolar was there, and Ralph Lutterloh, Ed. Powers, Leggett, Sam. Hall, if I recollect right, came up in a minute or so afterwards from towards the west end of the market. And they were all grouped together? They were all around pretty close there; were some twenty-five or thirty of them around there together. So at that time, though they were standing together, twenty or thirty made up the crowd? Yes, sir. Was Capt. Tolar standing there when you came up the third time? Yes, sir. How long had he been there before Mrs. Massey and her daughter were brought down? It was some four or five minutes, perhaps. At that time I understand you to say that you were standing a little off the pavement, opposite the center of the main eastern arch? Yes, sir. At the time they came down? Yes, sir, I think I was standing near the edge of the pavement. And the carriage, you think, was thirty or forty feet from you? Yes, sir. To your back? Not exactly to my back, nearly to my side; I was standing facing in towards the steps. Miss Massey and Mrs. Massey and Mr. Bond came down the steps and past out of Becky Ben's stall across the pavement, passing by you and went to the carriage? Yes, sir. Did you turn around and see them get into the carriage? I did not. How long was it after they had been to the carriage before Capt. Tolar went out to the carriage? I don't know exactly how long it was; it was a short time. Where did Tolar come from when he started to go to the carriage? I don't recollect that. You don't recollect whether he left that entrance to Becky Ben's stall and went there? No, sir. When did you see Tolar first go to the carriage? He was close to the carriage when I saw him first. On which side of the carriage did he go; the side which was next to the market house, or the side which was further down. There was not either side next to the market house; they were standing with the horses next to the market house; he went on the side towards Davis' store. Were the curtains of the carriage up? The front curtains were up, I think. Do you know whether the side curtains were raised or not? The side curtains in front I mean. You think the side curtains in front were up? That is my impression. There is no doubt but that Tolar went there? No, sir, You are very certain of that? I am. And you think he went on that side that is down towards Ichabod Davis'? I can't say for certain; I thought he went on that side. Did Tolar turn around and look into the carriage? He appeared to be speaking to the ladies Did you see him leaning inside of the carriage? I don't recollect whether I saw him leaning into the carriage or not, but I was under the impression he was speaking to the ladies. How long did Tolar stay there at the carriage? He didn't stay there but a very short time. How short? I can't tell exactly. Was it a minute? I don't know, sir, I think it was likely. Who was there at the carriage besides Tolar at that time? I don't recollect at that time, I recollect seeing David Cashwell at the carriage, and if I am not mistaken, I think I saw Philliman Taylor come from the carriage; I saw Robert Mitchell come from the carriage. At the time Tolar was at the carriage, you say you don't remember to have seen anybody else there at all? There were some persons there, but I don't recollect who they was. Was it a man or a woman? It was a man. Wa it a white man or colored man? I don't recollect that. Do you know how he was dressed? No, sir, I have no impression about it. I understand you now Mr. Phillips to swear that you have a distinct recollection, and that you can't be mistaken that Capt. Tolar did go to that carriage? I am confident that I saw him at the carriage, sir. When he came away from the carriage, where did he go? The next I saw of him he was under the market house. Did you see him when he came away from the carriage? I saw him under the edge of the market. Did you see him when he turned off from the carriage to go under the edge of the market? I don't think I did. And the next you saw of him he was under the edge of the market? Yes, sir. What edge? At the eastern end near the arch. What part of the arch? The south-east, nearest to the central part, I can't place him exactly, he was in the eastern end of the main arch running east and west. Was he up against the bricks? My impression is that he was nearer the north side. Do you remember whether he was leaning against the pillar or not? I don't know for certain. That I understand you to say was before Beebee was brought down stairs? Yes, sir, a very short time. How was Tolar standing at that time? I think he was standing on his feet; that is all the way I can tell. You think he was standing on his feet? Yes, sir, I should suppose he was. Perhaps he was standing on his head, did you see anything about his arms or hands? No, sir, nothing peculiar that I know of. Did you notice whether his hands were hanging down by his side? No, sir, I can't tell whether he had them in his pocket or hanging down. You didn't notice where his hands were ?   No, sir. Don't you remember seeing him have his hands under his shawl ?   No, sir, I don't.   Was there anything in Tolar's manner at that time that attracted your attention ?   No, sir, nothing peculiar that I know of.   Where were you standing then ; at the same position off the pavement ?   I think I was standing on the pavement at that time.   You think you had got on the pavement at that time ?   About the edge of the pavement. Opposite the center of the main arch ?   I think it was more to the north side of the arch.   You are very certain of that are you ?   I think it was nearer the north side than the south side. From the position you occupied then did you have a perfect view of Beebee and the party that was coming down stairs ?   Yes, sir.   From that position then did you go up towards the north portion of the eastern arch, and look towards those stair steps ?   Yes, sir.   Was that bench of Becky Ben's a cake bench as you call it directly in your line of sight ?   Yes, sir.   You were here in this room I think at the time John Armstrong was examined ?   Yes, sir, I was.   And you heard his testimony ?   Yes, sir.   I ask you, sir, if at that time when the boy was just being brought down stairs if any one jumped upon that bench of Becky Ben's and cried out, look out boys ?   I have no recollection of seeing anything of that kind, sir.   And it was directly in your line of sight ?   Yes, sir.   You saw nothing and heard nothing of that sort ? No, sir.   Do you know John Maultsby well ? Yes, sir.   Is he a tall or short man ?   He is a tall young man.   Did he jump upon that bench at that time, and make that exclamation ?   I have no recollection of that sir.   And you say Beebee came down the steps ; Mr. Wemyss on the right hand and Faircloth on the left and Hardie in front ?   I think Hardie came down in front.   I understand you to say you were not here on trial at the time Hardie was examined ? I don't know sir.   Have you read his testimony in the papers since that time ?   I forget whether I did or not—if it was in the paper I think I have read it.   So you put Mr. Hardie in front ? Yes, sir.   And you say when he got down near the foot, he took a survey of the crowd ?   When he got down a step or two, he stopped between the turn and the bottom of the steps.   Was there anything unusual in the crowd at that time? There was a great many people gathered right about Becky's bench.   I think I understand you to say in your direct examination that then you discovered signs of excitement ?   There was a great many gathered all around that bench ; of course that is the sign I saw.   That was the only sign that you saw ?   I can't say that, because another sign of excitement I saw, was some three or four men have knives whittling—they appeared to be waiting to see the prisoner come down.   Do you think a man is excited when he is whittling with his knife ?   Not every time—sometimes they are.   I ask you if that whittling with the knives attracted your attention as indicating an excitement in the crowd at that time? It did at that time.   To see three or four men whittling at sticks with those knives is a sign of excitement.   Under them circumstances ?   Yes, sir.   And the gathering of the crowd up towards the foot of the steps and the seeing of three or four men whittling with knives on the sticks were the signs of excitement you saw in the crowd ? Yes, sir ; and the natural appearance of the crowd that had gathered there at that certain point. When did you say the first rush was made upon the prisoner ?   It was made after they got off the steps before they got to the turn of the arch. And you then heard this crying out, "I demand

the prisoner "?   Yes, sir.   Are you certain those are the words "I demand the prisoner"? Yes, sir.   You can't be mistaken ?   That was my impression ; that those were the precise words. And you think a hand grasped at the prisoner ? Yes, sir ; I saw more than one hand.   The party then was thrown back, and they came along ont until they got near that southern portion of the Eastern arch before you saw the next rush made ?   Near the turn sir.   Where were you standing at the time ; had you shifted your position at all ?   I had moved a little to my left at that time.   That made you a little lower down ? A little lower down to the left.   Still off the pavement ?   Yes, sir ; some foot or two.   And that brought you down opposite the center of the main eastern arch ?   It brought me rather to the south.   Rather to the south than the center ?   Yes, sir.   There, you say, the second rush was made ?   Yes, sir.   Was Capt. Tolar in either of these rushes sir ?   I con't say for certain, that he was.   I ask you if at the time those other rushes were made you saw Capt. Tolar at all ?   I don't think I did.   You think you saw him at neither of those times ?   No, sir.   Did you see Ed Powers ?   I don't think I did.   Sam Hall ?   No, sir.   Ralph Lutterloh ?   No, sir ; I dont think I saw either of them in those rushes ; not to tell them from others.   Did you see Tom Powers in either of those rushes?   Yes, sir.   Which one ; the first or second ?   I saw him in the first and second. Did you see Monk in either of these rushes ?   I saw Monk in the second ; I did not see him in the first ; I noticed in the first rush that he was rather in the rear of the main rush, but was not in front of the rush.   Then Beebee was carried down to the point where he was shot ?   When the second rush was made I saw the police clubs used.   Up to that time you hadn't drawn your weapon at all ?   No, sir ; I think I hadn't though I cant say for certain that I hadn't.   Well sir ; how far had Beebee got down the pavement before he made this struggle that you speak of ? when Wemyss and he fell down on the pavement ?   It was immediately after turning the arch.   A step or two after turning the arch ?   Yes, sir. When he went down did you loose sight of him ? I lost sight of the entire party ; I could see the bulk below.   When he was raised up you say you think Wemyss was on his right hand ?   That is my impression : rather in front to the right ; Sheriff Hardie I think was rather in the rear to the right.   That would have taken Hardie rather nearer to the wall of the market house than Beebee was ?   Rather nearer.   How much nearer do you think Hardie was to the wall of the market house than Beebee ?   It was very little difference ; they were very close together ; he appeared to be helping to raise Archy up.   Are you certain at that time Hardie had him in his left hand in the back of the collar ?   I think he did.   You are certain it was back of the coat collar ?   I think it was.   Don't you know it was in front ?   I don't know.   Don't you know it was in front of the comfort around the throat ?   No, sir.   You know it was at the back ?   I don't say I know ; think it was at tho back.   Now at the time Beebee was shot where were you standing ?   I was standing off the pavement sir ; some two steps or so.   What do you mean by that; six feet? No, sir, it was not six feet, I reckon. About how many feet was it off the pavement? I can't say for certain how many it was; a short distance though, from the edge of the pavement. Was that opposite the lower small arch or opposite the main arch or where? My impression was it was very nearly opposite the center of the small arch. It was opposite the center of the small southern arch? I think it was very nearly opposite the center of the small arch. Now at the time Beebee was raised up, which way was his face turned? I think his face was rather to the corner of the market house. It was not down the pavement? I think it was rather turned in towards the corner of the market. Then you think instead of looking to the south west? I think he was rather looking south he was looking to the south-west. You are certain his face was not turned due south towards the guard house? I don't think it was turned due south. Did you have your pistol out at that time? Just immediately after he was shot. I mean just at the time he was shot? I don't think I did. How did you hold your pistol when you had it out? I held it by the hilt as other folks do. You held it down by your side? I don't recollect whether I had it up or down. Did you hold it in one hand or both? In one hand, sir. Don't you know you held it in two hands? No, sir, I don't know. Did you or did you not? I can't say sir. Did you cock it? I don't recollect about that, sir. Directly after the firing was over did you rub it? No, sir; I did not. Didn't you rub the smoke and dust off of the cylinder? I did not sir. You didn't rub it at all? I did not sir. Beebee was raised up and then you saw Capt. Tolar? Yes sir. You don't know where he got the pistol from? I am not certain where he got it from. Did you see him take it from any part of his person? It was my impression he took it from his left side under his shawl, by seeing his shawl move back and his hand come out with the pistol in it. You think the hand come out from under the shawl? I think it did. Did you see him cock his pistol? I don't recollect. You were looking at him close were you not? Yes, sir. About how many feet off? I can't say for certain; it was a short distance though. Did he throw the pistol up, to level, and fire, or did he throw it above the level and then draw it down? My impression is he took his hand from his left side, and put it right there between two men's heads. You say you saw it fired? I saw him fire. You saw the smoke? Yes, sir. From the muzzle? Yes, sir. From the tube? I can't say whether I saw it from the tube or not. You saw the flash? I did sir. And you swear that he shot that pistol? I swear it was in his hand. And that there was no other pistol fired that day? Not at that place. And you say at the time of the firing there were how many between Tolar and Beebee? I think there were two standing; one on one side and one on the other. And the pistol was fired over their shoulders between the two heads of the two persons? Yes, sir. Just name these persons, or either of them? I can't do it, sir. Were they colored or white persons? I think they were white. Did they lean aside to the right or left? I think

they leaned their heads off a little. Did Tolar say anything? I don't recollect hearing him make any remark at that time. I mean when he was going up, or just before he shot, did he make any remark at all? I didn't hear him make any remark. When he came up to that position did he come rushing? He didn't come rushing particularly; he came up through the crowd. Were you looking at him at that position? I was sir. Did you see all that he did? I don't know that I saw all that he did. You saw no rushing up there on Tolar's part? I saw him come up through the crowd. Did he part them to the right and left as he came up? He must have parted them; I didn't see him. I ask you for what you saw, did you see him lay his hand upon a single man as he came up? I don't recollect seeing him lay his hand upon any person. Either his right hand or his left hand? He may have done it; if he did I didn't notice it. Mr. Phillips, who was the man standing immediately upon his left at the time he had his pistol up there? To his front? I don't care where, so that you put him next to his left? I can't tell who was the man immediately to his left. Who was the man immediately to his left and front? I don't know, sir. Was John Armstrong the man? I can't recollect, sir. Did you see John Armstrong that day? Yes, sir. Did you see him there at that time? I saw him immediately after the negro was shot. Did you see him there at that time? I saw him immediately after the pistol fired. You havn't answered my question; did you see him there immediately at that time? I have no recollection of seeing him there immediately at that time. Did you see Jim McNeil there immediately at that time? No, sir. Jim Douglass? I saw him immediately after the firing, but just as the pistol was fired I didn't see him. How many men were between you and Capt Tolar? I can't tell, sir. Were there any? Yes, sir, I think there were. Were these black men or white men? I think there were some of both. Can you name one of them? No, sir, I can't. Can't you name one of those men? No, sir. Was there any person between you and Beebee at the time Beebee was shot? Not immediately between me and Beebee. A little to the front and right of you, or a little to the left and front of you? I think there were persons both side of me. Can you name one of them, either white or black? I can't. What became of Tolar after he fired the pistol? The last time I saw him he was opposite the mouth of the big arc.a. Which way did he turn; did he make a right wheel or a left wheel? I can't recollect about that. You say when he drew his pistol his shawl fell off of his left shoulder? I didn't say that. What did you say? I said I saw his shawl move back. Did you see anything about Tolar's shawl when he turned off? If I am not mistaken, I thought his shawl moved either on one shoulder or the other, and I forget which. What do you mean by moving? Sort of dropping down. It didn't drop off the shoulder? I don't think it dropped clear off at the shoulder. Did you see him throw the shawl as he turned around? I don't think he did. You saw nothing of it?

No, sir.   As he turned off to leave that position, did he go around the crowd or did he pass directly through it?   I think he passed directly through it.   Coming from his position directly through the crowd up to that main eastern arch of the market house?   That is my impression, sir.   Do you know a man, black or white, who was standing there near Tolar at the time he turned around?   Mr. Ed. Powers was standing close by him, when he shot.   I mean at the time he turned around to go back to that eastern arch?   I don't recollect that I can call a man, to swear positive to, at that moment.   That crowd which was there that day, was it composed of Laplanders and strangers, or was it composed of citizens of the town of Fayetteville?   Most of it was composed of citizens of the town, of course.   Are you not well acquainted with the citizens of the town?   Yes, sir.   And in all that crowd, at these different times I have asked you about, it is impossible for you to name one man?   It is impossible for any man to remember all the circumstances that took place in a crowd of that kind.   Now, when Capt. Tolar went back to that arch, did he stop there?   I don't know, sir.   Did you lose sight of him?   The last I saw of him I think he was right in front of the eastern end of the market; rather nearer the northern edge of the big arch.   On the pavement or off?   On the pavement.   Walking?   Yes, sir.   Which way?   Towards the north side of the arch.   Of the big arch?   Yes, sir.   Was it before Captain Tolar got out of the way or after, that you made the exhibition of your pistol, and called upon them to look at it?   I think it was after he moved off.   Where were you standing at the time you made that flourish with the pistol and called upon the bystanders to take notice of it?   I was standing at that time down nearer Draughon's corner.   About how far from the place where you were standing at the time of the firing?   I come three or four steps from where I was first standing.   And you called upon the crowd there to look at that pistol?   Yes, sir.   Why did you do that?   I did it because I knew that the crowd had seen me with a pistol; I didn't keep my pistol concealed at all; I wanted them to be certain I didn't fire it.   You did it for the purpose of furnishing proof that you hadn't fired it?   Yes, sir.   And you say there was a good many persons standing around you at that time?   Yes, sir.   Some of them took the pistol in their hands?   Yes, sir.   Now just name one of them that were standing about there?   I can name one that I saw standing up there.   Jim. Douglas was one.   Did he take it in his hands?   No, sir, I don't think he did.   Name one of them that had it in his hands to examine it?   I can't do it, sir.   And still you were exhibiting it there for the purpose of proving that you didn't fire it, yet you don't recollect a single man that had it in his hands?   No, sir, I don't.   Not one?   No, sir.   You were very particular about this matter, you spoke of it afterwards?   I spoke of it in my store.   Who did you speak of it to, sir.   I don't recollect all, there was some two or three persons in the store.   You can't name one of them—your nephew, Jim. Kendricks, was one; can't you name others?   I don't know even that he was one until I heard him say so.   Was Dave Oliphant there?   I don't recollect whether he was there or not.   You recollect what hour that afternoon you saw Dave Oliphant?   No, sir, I don't   Do you recollect having seen him at all that afternoon?   I don't recollect at all.   And you say you showed

your pistol the second time?   Yes, sir.   What remark did you make when you showed it that second time at your shop?   I don't recollect any remark I made.   I think though that I remarked the negro was killed, and that there would be trouble; I said I wanted them to see my pistol hadn't been fired.   Did anybody take hold of it and examine it?   I should think Kendricks took hold of it; I know it passed out of my hands; I think they were looking at it.   Didn't you say just now that you didn't know Kendrick was there at all till he told you so?   I say I forgot it entirely till he told me he was.   And now you say you think Kendrick had hold of it; it didn't leave your hands at that time?   Yes, sir, it left my hand.   You think Kendrick took it out of your hands?   I think he took it in his hands.   Did he examine it?   I suppose so; I don't know that he did, but I would suppose that he did.   How many persons did you say were at your shop then?   I don't know, sir.   How long was that after the killing had occurred.   It was only a very short time.   Put in minutes and hours?   I can't do it, sir.   Was it five minutes?   It was not as much as an hour.   And of those persons who were there in your shop that you were showing the pistol to, you don't recollect a single other person except your nephew, Jim Kendricks?   No, sir.   Not another one?   No, sir.   Are you well acquainted with Captain Tolar?   I have known him for some eighteen months, and perhaps a little longer than that; I am not certain as to the time I have known him.   Do you know him well?   I know him when I see him, I have no particular acquaintance with him.   Just now when you said you heard a voice saying, "I hate to shoot him, but if I do have it to do, I will make a safe shot,"—whose voice was that?   I don't know, sir.   Did you think at that time you had ever heard that voice before?   I don't know, sir, whether I did or not; I don't pretend to say who it was.   What time do you think that was, that you heard that voice?   It was immediately before Beebee was brought down the steps.   Did that voice proceed from the crowd?   Yes, sir, from the crowd on the inside about the bench.   In a loud tone of voice?   It wasn't very loud or very low; it was so that I could hear it very distinctly.   How many persons were between you and the voice?   I don't know, sir.   Were there any?   Yes, sir.   Were they black or white?   Black and white, all mixed up together.   Were there a good many or only a few between you and the voice?   Where the voice came from I can't tell; I knew the voice came from where the crowd was standing.   Can you tell one person who was closer to the place where the voice came from than you were?   Yes, sir; I can name Mr. Leggett.   And it was so spoken out that you could hear it?   Yes, sir.   As loudly as I am speaking now?   No, sir, I think not.   Did you see Sheriff Hardie summoned about this business before the coroner?   Yes, sir.   Was his testimony substantially the same as he gave in here?   I don't recollect, sir; whether it was or not.

Re-direct examination resumed by the Counsel for the prosecution:

I understand you to say you saw Ed. Powers standing to the right and rear of Capt. Tolar when he fired?   I did, sir.   I understand you to say that subsequent to that time you saw Ed. Powers with a pistol in his hand?   Yes, sir.   And immediately after the firing?   Yes, sir.   Was he standing in the same spot at both times?   I think he was, sir.   The Counsel for the defence has dwelt upon your statement that the time these rushes were made, you saw signs of excitement in the crowd? Yes, sir. You testified that there was an impression in your mind that the crowd was excited? Yes, sir, I had an impression. That was what you thought then? Yes, sir. You don't pretend to state what the reasons were you thought so? No, sir. Have you ever analysed your judgment to find why you come to your conclusion; have you ever thought over every reason that you had for it? Yes, sir. Well, sir, now tell me every reason you had for that opinion as if you were sitting down to state why you entertained that opinion? One reason was I had heard a great deal of talking around through the streets concerning this matter. You went there having heard this talk? Yes, sir. I understand you to say you saw these groups of men there? Yes, sir. You saw these men whittling with their knives? Yes, sir. You saw the crowd; the expression of their faces? I think so. At any rate you imbibed the impression that a difficulty was about to occur? Yes, sir. Mr. Phillips, did you have any conversation with Mr. Hendricks about this matter at all? Yes, sir. When was it? At dinner hour, when the coroner's inquest adjourned. Was it in connection with this affair? Yes, sir. Did you have any conversation beside this one at the dinner hour of the second day? No, sir. I call for that conversation.

The Counsel for the accused objected to the question.

Counsel for the prosecution:

I will state, if the Court please, the bearing of this question: The Counsel in the cross examination did as the law requires he should do. He proposed a question to the witness, whom he is assailing, with a view to contradict him hereafter; and in proposing that question he asked him if he had a certain conversation with Thomas A. Hendricks. His first question is carefully worded; he says: Did you, at a certain time—naming the time—have a conversation with Thomas A. Hendricks, of a certain character—stating it.— The witness says he had no such conversation; but he goes on to say he had a conversation at some other time. But, says the Counsel for the defence, stop! we don't want that. Then afterwards he asks a general question: if he had no conversation with Mr. Hendricks,—not confining it to the time and place first named,—if he had no conversation with Mr. Hendricks of the character stated.

I insist upon it, under these circumstances, the witness having had a conversation with Mr. Hendricks of some sort, he is entitled to state what it is. The aim of the Counsel is to bring Mr. Hendricks in, to prove that he did have a conversation of some kind with the witness, and I think it is due to the character of the witness, and due also to Mr. Hendricks, that a statement of the actual conversation, which this witness admits he had, should be made, so that Mr. Hendricks may have an opportunity of correcting himself,—if he be incorrect,—as to the time the conversation took place; that this witness may have an opportunity of showing what the conversation was that he had with Mr. Hendricks, and that this Court may be at liberty, when the two statements come before them, to decide what the actual conversation was.

In common fairness to this witness, he ought to be permitted to state what the conversation was which he had with Mr. Hendricks. He was about to explain; he was interrupted; and then a general question was asked him as to whether he had any conversation with Mr. Hendricks, at any time, of the character named.

If the Counsel had confined himself to the first inquiry as to time and place, circumstances and substance, then perhaps we would not have been entitled to call for this testimony; but when he goes on and asks if he, the witness, had no conversation with Hendricks of the character I have spoken of, then we insist upon it, the witness is at liberty to sustain himself by stating what conversation he had with Mr. Hendricks, and when it was. That is the ground upon which we ask the question."

Counsel for the accused:

"We object to the question for this reason: that the questions were, as the Counsel states, carefully worded, both of them, and that both the questions were restricted to a particular time. The first question asked the witness was: did you have any such conversation with Thomas A. Hendricks before the meeting of the coroner's jury at the adjourned session. The next question was: did you have a conversation of the substance that I have named with Thomas A. Hendricks before the finding of the coroner's inquest?"

The Counsel for the prosecution said the last question was not confined to any time.

The Counsel for the accused called for the reading, by the recorder, of his notes in reference to the questions under discussion.

The recorder then read from his notes as follows:

"Had you any conversation similar to that before the jury found their verdict? No, sir, I never had then or since. And you never have had any conversation with him, the substance of which I have given? I was going to tell the conversation I did have. I don't care about that, I mean before the final finding of the jury? I did not."

The Counsel for the prosecution said:

The second question read by the recorder is the one to which I referred, and I still maintain the position I have taken. Just see how this thing will work. The Counsel has made a general inquiry of this witness, and Mr. Hendricks, when he comes in here for the purpose of contradicting the witness, cannot be warned in any respect, while if we had this witness' statement as to the actual conversation which he admits that he had with Mr. Hendricks, we could then say are you certain it was at that time and place, and thus possibly reconcile the whole. By a contrary course, this witness will be placed in such a position, that if Mr. Hendricks should swear positively to a particular conversation, it is utterly out of our power again to contradict it, (for we cannot bring in evidence in reply,) and the only opportunity the witness has for explanation, is for him now to state what conversation he had with Mr. Hendricks, and when and where."

The Counsel for the accused:

"If the Court please: 'Hard cases are always the quicksands of the law.' The rule of evidence, as I understand it, as it is laid down in the books, and practiced in the courts everywhere, is just this, neither more nor less, that when a conversation is called for on one side, the other side is entitled to the whole conversation that occurred at that time, not any other conversation that occurred. Then the only enquiry for the Court is whether I did, in my cross examination, call for any conversation that was subsequent to the finding of the jury of inquest. The Counsel has had read from the records a question, which, standing alone and unqualified, might perhaps bear out his assertion."

The witness here stated that the conversation he had had with Mr. Hendricks took place before the final finding of the jury.

The Counsel for the accused said, "If that be

the case, then, of course, the Counsel is entitled to the conversation, because my question restricted it to that time.

Re-direct examination resumed by the Counsel for the prosecution.

I understand you to say you had some conversation with Thomas Hendricks at dinner time of the day after the murder was committed? Yes, sir. That your conversation took place before you signed the verdict before the coroner's inquest was closed? Yes, sir. Right in the midst of it? Yes, sir. You had an adjournment for dinner? Yes, sir, and then I had the conversation with Mr. Hendricks. Is Mr. Hendricks any relation of yours? No, sir. Are you friends? I don't know, sir, I know him. Was he a member of the jury, also? Yes, sir, I was told by the sheriff to get up some witnesses, as many as I could by the time the jury met again after dinner, and I heard Robert Simmons say on the evening before that he knew who shot the boy, and I went up there to Simmons to request him to come up to the market at three o'clock at the time the jury met. We don't want the conversation you had with him; did he refuse to come? Yes, sir. Don't state the ground of his refusal. I don't know how to explain my conversation with Mr. Hendricks then. It will explain itself; you saw Simmons before you saw Hendricks? Yes, sir. And he declined being a witness? Yes, sir, Mr. Hendricks passed my store before the meeting of the jury again, and I called him in, or he stepped in, rather, and I called him back to my desk; says I, "Mr. Hendricks, there are two ways of doing business—one is a right way, and the other is the wrong way; there is a way for the jury to go too far, and there is a way for them not to go far enough; and I think it is going most too far to take a man into his house, and close the door on him, to try to make him become a witness;" then I spoke concerning the conversation I had with Simmons; I told him I had been down to Simmons and heard him say yesterday evening who killed Archy; and he told me that he didn't know what everybody was running after him for; that it appeared to him they wanted to get him into a scrape; he told me you had him in the house and shut the door on him, and says he, "now I don't know anything at all about it, and if I did know, I don't want to know anything." That was what Simmons said, what you told Hendricks? Yes, sir, that is all the conversation that I have had with Thomas Hendricks to the best of my knowledge, I believe. You never had any conversation at all with him in which you told him anything of the character that the Counsel for the defence has asked you? No, sir. I understand you to say that you were a member of the coroner's inquest? I was. You were sworn a member of that inquest? Yes, sir. That your impression was then that your oath did not bind you to disclose? That was my impression; yes, sir. That your oath was to bind you upon the evidence? Yes, sir, I asked the coroner that question, whether the oath took, required a member of the coroner's inquest to disclose what was within their own knowledge; Mr. Blake was the coroner; I said, "suppose some man on this jury saw the shooting of this negro, and knows all about it," and he said "all they have got to do is to find the verdict according to the evidence brought before them." Yes, sir. That was your impression of it? Yes, sir. That was the explanation you had from the coroner? Yes, sir; and that, may it please the Court, is my understanding now.

Counsel for the accused:—It is a matter of argument.

Counsel for the prosecution:—Yes, sir, I mention to the Court that I don't think a man is bound by his oath to disclose, because he is a member of the Coroner's Inquest.

Re-direct examination by the Counsel for the prosecution resumed.

You hadn't the moral courage to oppose the popular feeling? No, sir, I hadn't. You thought it was not your duty to make the disclosure, and you didn't make it? No, sir. Did you conceive you were perjuring yourself at that time? No, sir, I didn't. It was not your understanding that you were required to disclose it? No, sir, it was not. About this pistol, where did you get it originally? I am not certain whether I bought it myself or got some other man to buy it, but it was bought from one of the 13th Pennsylvania cavalry. Was it loaded when you got it? Yes, sir. Were those loads in it the day you went up to the market house? Yes, sir. Did you have any fixed ammunition for it? No, sir. How long had you owned it before this affair took place? I bought it in June after the surrender. And you think that some of these same loads remained in it to the day you came here? Yes, sir; I am confident there was one of the same loads? Is it your impression that there were more than one? My impression is there was two, but I am not confident of but one. Was that pistol ever unloaded to your knowledge between the time you purchased it and the time you were on the ground, when Archy Beebee was shot? It had never been unloaded. And you say it was loaded with the bullets that fitted without patching, to the best of your knowledge? Yes, sir. There were no buckshot in it at that time? No, sir.

Re-cross examination by the Counsel for the accused:

Mr. Phillips, when you asked Mr. Blake, the coroner, with regard to your duties, who heard you ask him? No person at all, sir. Where was he? In my store, sir. In the front room or back room? It is all in one room. In the front part or back part? I don't recollect whereabouts in the store. Did you call him in there or did he come in there of his own accord? He came in of his own accord. Was that before the finding of the coroner's jury or afterwards? It was before, it was the dinner hour of the same day I had this conversation with Mr. Hendricks. The twelfth of February? Yes, sir.

The Judge Advocate stated that there was but one more witness to be examined for the prosecution, and he would not arrive until Thursday, and if the defence would be willing for the prosecution to introduce the witness as soon as he arrived, they would announce that the prosecution was formally closed.

The Counsel for the accused refused to accede to the proposition of the Judge Advocate with reference to the introduction of a witness for the prosecution, after the defence had opened their case.

The Judge Advocate then stated that there would be no witness to be examined to-morrow, under the circumstances, whereupon, on motion, the Commission adjourned, to meet on Thursday, the 15th, inst. at 11 o'clock A. M.

———

RALEIGH, N. C., Aug. 15, 1867, 11 A. M.

The Commission met pursuant to adjournment: Present all the members of the Commission, the

Judge Advocate, the Counsel for the prosecution, all the accused and their Counsel.

On page 1326 Witness SAMUEL A. PHILLIPS wished to make the following correction in his answer to the question, "you solemnly swear in the presence of Almighty God that you did not fire the pistol?" Witness; answer was "I swear most solemnly that I have not fired a pistol since then either." The meaning of that answer Mr. Phillips stated was that he did not fire the pistol at that time or at any other time during that day.

The reading of the testimony taken on Tuesday was then waived there being no objections thereto.

Tuesday's proceedings were then read and approved.

The Judge Advocate stated that there was no witness to duy to be examined.

On motion, the Commission adjourned to meet on Friday the 16th Inst. at 11 o'clock, A. M.

RALEIGH, N. C., Aug. 16th, 1867, 11 A. M.
The Commission met pursuant to adjournment.

Present: All the members of the Commission, the Judge Advocate, the Counsel for the prosecution, all the accused and their Counsel.

Yesterday's proceedings were then read and approved.

GEORGE W. SMITH, a witness for the prosecution was called.

Questioned by the Counsel for the prosecution.

What is your name? George W. Smith. Do you know what would become of you if you were to tell a lie? 'I would be punished hereafter. Do you know what would become of you if you were to swear to a lie in court? I would be put in prison. You know that when you are sworn you take an oath—you call upon God to witness—you call God down here to witness that you are telling the truth—that you will tell nothing but the truth, and that you will tell all the truth that you know—nothing but what you saw and heard yourself? Yes, sir. You understand that do you? Yes, sir.

The Judge Advocate asked the Commission if they were satisfied that the youth understood the nature of an oath.

The Commission had no objection to the witness being sworn,

GEO. W. SMITH, a witness for the prosecution, was then duly sworn, after which, he testified as follows:

Questioned by the Counsel for the prosecution.

What did you say your name was? Geo. W. Smith. Where do you live George? Down there in one of Mr. Mitchell's Houses. In what town? Fayetteville. How old are you? I will be thirteen to-morrow. Were you in Fayetteville the day Archy Beebee was killed? Yes, sir. Were you near the market house? Yes, sir; pretty nigh there—I was not no further than across the street. Where were you when you first saw Archy that day? I was right there by the market house, when they were carrying him up stairs. By whose store? J. B. Davis's store, When Archy was carried up stairs? No, sir; I was at the market house when he was carried up stairs, and as soon as they carried him up, I left. You were at the market house when he was carried up? Yes, sir. Then you went off to where? To J. B. Davis' store, and I was shooting marbles there with a boy—and I heard them cry out "clear the way"! The first thing you noticed afterwards—you heard

them say "clear the way;" what did you do then? The boy who was with me he says:— "let's go up there," and I said "no let's shoot on," and by and by we heard them say "kill him" and by and by the pistol went off, and I went on up there. You went up there when you heard the pistol? Yes, sir. But not before? No, sir. Did you go up just as soon as the pistol shot? Yes, sir. Did you go right into the crowd? Not right in the midst of the crowd, because he was laying about three feet from the side walk. Who did you see when you went up, that you knew? I saw Monk Julia, that was one I saw, and I saw Mr. McDonald, and I saw my brother and Jim Done. What is your brother's name? Rufus Smith. Did you see Captain Tolar there at all? No, sir; I never saw him. Did you say you went right up to Archy Beebee as soon as the pistol was fired? Yes, sir. And I saw Mr. Wemyss getting up, he fell when the negro was shot, I am told. You must now tell us what you were told, just what you saw; when you got there Archy was dead, and you found Mr. Wemyss getting up? Yes, sir. What was Monk Julia doing when you saw him? He was jawing and rearing, that was all I know about it. How near was he standing to Archy? About as close as I am to you (about eight feet.) You say he was rearing about there? Yes, sir, I had heard him say before they carried him up, if they brought him out he would be a dead man, if any one would join him he would lead the way. When was that? In the morning before Archy was brought. Where did you hear him say that? At the corner of the market house. Did Monk have a pistol when he was rearing and roaring about so? I never saw no pistol, sir. See no stick? No, sir. Any knife? I saw a knife in his hands. What was he saying? He said he ought to be dead, and he would cut his throat, he would, and if anybody would join him he would lead the way. He didn't say that after he was shot? He said that before, and he said it after he was shot. Did you hear anybody say anything in the crowd cry out who killed him? Yes, sir. When was that, when you first got in the crowd after the pistol fired? Yes, sir. Directly after. Yes, sir, as soon as the pistol fired I ran right up there, and they all hollered out, "Tolar, Tolar shot him." Did you hear several people say that? Yes, sir, I heard a heap of people say that, and I asked my brother who shot him, and my brother said Tolar. Your brother was in the crowd when you got up there? Yes, sir. You must not tell what anybody said—you heard several persons cry out Tolar shot him. Yes, sir. And that was right straight after the pistol was shot? Yes, sir.

Cross-examination by the Counsel for the accused:

You live in Fayetteville, George? Yes, sir. Lived there all your life? Yes, sir, I lived up on Hay Mount Hill till we moved down there. You were playing marbles that day? Yes, sir. Where? There are at J. B. Davis' corner. You didn't see Archy when he came out of the market house? No, sir, I was still shooting when they hallowed "clear the way." You were shooting yourself? Yes, sir. How many of you were playing? Only two of us. You kept on playing? Yes, sir, we played on until the time they shot the pistol? You heard them say "shoot, shoot?" Yes, sir, we heard them cry "just clear the way," and we heard them holler "shoot him, shoot him!" and then we heard him fire the pistol, and then we run up and saw Archy laying there, and we heard them all hollow out "Tolar." Did you see Captain Tolar? No, sir, I could not see him. You know him, don't you? No, sir, I never saw him before in my life. Was he in the crowd when you heard them say "Tolar?" I never saw him, sir, I know don't know anything about that, sir. Well, George, when they cried shoot him, it didn't scare you, did it? Yes, sir, it scared me a heap, that was the reason I did not go right up there. You would not go there when they said "shoot." No, sir. After they shot, you went there? Yes, sir. Did you go right straight there? Yes, sir. I went up there as soon as the pistol fired. Did you take up your marbles before you went? Yes, sir. How many marbles did you have down that day in the ring? One belonged to me and one to the other boy. Did you and he have any dispute about the marbles before you went? No, sir. You got yours, and he got his? He had mine. Did you make him give them up before you went? No, sir, he had won them. There was nothing further to be done about that, he had your marbles and his own, and you and he had no settlement to make about the marbles? No, sir. Did you hear them cry "Tolar, Tolar!" before you went over the street? Just as soon as I got across the street. You didn't hear Tolar's name mentioned at all after you got across the street? No, sir. How far from the edge of the pavement did you say Archy was lying when you got there? About eight feet. You mean in the street? Yes, sir. You know what you mean by the pavement. That brick wall. From the edge of the pavement you say he was lying about eight feet? · Yes, sir. Which way was his head—towards the wall, or towards the edge of the pavement? Towards the wall of the market house. How far was he lying from the corner of the pavement? I never noticed to see how far he lay from the corner. Did you notice whereabouts he was lying? Do you know the arches there, how many arches are there at that side of the market house, do you know? Them round places? Yes. Two or three on one side I believe. There are three? I never took no notice. You didn't notice how he was lying, whether he was lying in one of the arches or not? He was not lying in one of them. Was he lying with his head next to the arch, or next to the brick wall? Next to the brick wall. The wall towards the corner of the market house, or the wall that is between the two arches? The wall next to the corner. His head was lying, if I understand you now, next to the wall, at the corner of the market house? Yes, sir. You say that Mr. Wemyss was getting up after you got there? He was getting up when I was running across the street. Was there any crowd around Archy and Mr. Wemyss, when you got up there? Yes, sir, right smart of people. When did you first see Archy—how near did you have to get to him before you saw him? I had to get about as close as from here to you, (about twelve feet,) and I could just see through the men's legs. Then I ran up there, and I saw him then, when I got as close as I could. How long did you stay there? I stayed there about ten minutes, and then I went on home. My bucket was under the pump then getting some water. I went up there and stayed about ten minutes, and when I went back and found ma had been to the pump, and sat my bucket under there. Did you go up the street to get water? No, sir, I had been shooting there, and ma had brung the bucket there to me, and hallowed to me to come on, and I told her as soon as I got my marbles back I would, and she sot it under there and went on home. Was that after Archy was shot? That was before. Was

Archy dead when you got there? Yes, sir, he was dead; I saw him open his eyes and shut them. He was not dead then? Not exactly quite dead. He rolled his eyes back? Yes, sir. Was it after that or before you heard them say "Tolar shot him?" Just after the pistol fired, when I was running across the street. As you ran across the street? Yes, sir. When you got there Archy was not quite dead? No, sir. He rolled his eyes back once or twice? Yes, sir. And you saw Mr. Wemyss getting up then? Yes, sir, I saw him getting up. About the time you heard them cry Tolar you saw Mr. Wemyss get up? Yes, sir. Where abouts was Mr. Wemyss, just where Archy was shot? Yes, sir, Archy I believe was hitched to Mr. Wemyss thumb; he had hold of Archy's hand, or something that was around Archy's hand. Which hand, the right or left? I don't know, sir, which hand it was. You, think, George, he had hold of him when he got there? No, sir, he didn't have hold of him when I got there; when I was running across the street. When you saw Mr. Wemyss get up? Yes, sir. You think he had hold of him then? Yes, sir. Was there a large crowd around him when he was getting up? Yes, sir, a tolerable large crowd. Yet you could see? Yes, sir. You had no trouble in seeing? No, sir. Do you know Mr. McDuffie? Yes, sir, I have seen him at our house often. Was he there when you got there? I don't know, sir, he might have been at the further end of the crowd, I never saw him. You didn't see him at Archy when you got there? No, sir. Who did you see? I saw Monk Julia, and my brother, and Jim Done. You say you didn't see Dr. McDuffie there at all? No, sir, I never saw him. You don't recollect seeing him there that day? No, sir.

Re-direct examination by the Counsel for the prosecution.

George, when you stopped playing marbles you went right straight over to the crowd? Yes, sir, as soon as the pistol went off I started right off. Didn't you stop to pick up your marbles? Yes, sir. That was all you did? Yes, sir. As soon as the pistol fired, you picked up your marbles and went right over? Yes, sir. When was it you saw Mr. Wemyss, before you got over there? Yes, sir. You saw Mr. Wemyss get up? Yes, sir. How did you see, over the heads of the crowd? No, sir, through the legs. You were not so tall as some, and could see between their legs? Yes, sir. You saw him getting up before you got there? Yes, sir. When was it you heard this cry of "Tolar Tolar," before you saw Mr. Wemyss? I heard them hollow that just as I started across the street. What was it they said; the people were crying out how? "They hollowed "Tolar! Tolar shot him!" Did they just say Tolar's name, or Tolar shot him? Tolar shot him, was all they said. You don't know Mr. Tolar now? I saw him to-day when he was speaking to pa, and pa told me that was Mr. Tolar. That was the first time you ever knew him? Yes, sir. You didn't know him that day? No, sir. You would not have known him if you had seen him that day, would you? No, sir. You know Dr. McDuffie? Yes, sir. He comes to see people at your house when they are sick? Yes, sir. You didn't see him there that day, that you remember, at all? No, sir.

Rufus Smith, a witness for the prosecution, was called.

Questioned by the Counsel for the prosecution:

How old are you, Rufus? Ten years old. Do you go to school when you are at home? Yes, sir. Have you been to Sunday school? Yes, sir. You know what becomes of bad boys who tell lies? Yes, sir. What does the Sunday school teacher tell you about that? I would go to hell, sir. And do you know what will happen to you if you tell a lie when you are sworn; do you know it is worse than at any other time? Yes, sir.

It is a greater sin to tell a lie when you are sworn on the Bible than it is to tell a lie at any other time, because you get men into trouble by it.

Do you know what will be done to you if you swear to a lie here to-day? Yes, sir. What? Be put in jail. You will be punished in some way if we find it out; don't you think God will punish you hereafter? Yes, sir. You have been taught there is a God, havn't you? Yes, sir. And you know it is a sin to tell a lie? Yes, sir. And more of a sin to swear to a lie? Yes, sir.

The Commission was satisfied that the youth understood the nature of an oath; whereupon Rufus Smith, a witness for the prosecution, having first been duly sworn, testified as follows:

Questioned by the Counsel for the prosecution.

What is your name? Rufus Smith. Where do you reside, Rufus, in what town? In Fayetteville. Do you remember the day that Archy Beebee was killed? No, sir. Do you remember there was such a man as Archy Beebee killed in Fayetteville? Yes, sir. Were you in Fayetteville when it happened? Yes, sir. Were you at the market house that day? Yes, sir. When did you first see Archy that day? I seen him at the guard house. You saw him at the guard house? Yes, sir. Early in the morning? No, sir. When they were bringing him up to the market house? Yes, sir. Did you go along up to the guard house with him? No, sir. I was coming from dinner and I saw them take him out. Were you coming up towards the market house? Yes, sir, and when I got along by the guard house I saw them bringing him out. Did you go on then up to the market house? Yes, sir. Did Archy go up there too? Yes, sir. Were you up to the market house when Archy went up stairs? Yes, sir. Did you go up stairs too? No, sir. Did you try? I went to the steps, and they told me to go down. Where did you go, when Archy went up stairs? I was sitting on one of them benches. Which bench, were you sitting on? One of them benches close by old aunty Ben's. How long did you sit there, do you know? No, sir. Was there any body in the market house while you were sitting there? Yes, sir. How many people, do you recollect? A heap of them. Did you see anybody there you knew? Yes, sir. Who did you see, that you knew? Mr. McDonald and Jim Done, and a heap of people. Was there any body else, that you can tell us of that you knew? any other boys? No, sir. Were

you sitting still on that bench? Yes, sir. Did you stay on the bench until Archy came down? Yes, sir. You stayed there until Archy came out to come down? Yes, sir. Did you see the lady there that day, that Archy had been trying to do something wrong to? Yes, sir, I seen her, when she went up stairs. Did you see her when she came down? No, sir. You didn't see her when she came down? No, sir. How did she come there, did she walk, or come in the carriage? She come in a carriage, You saw her go up stairs? Yes, sir, her and her mother. You didn't see them come down? No, sir. You stayed on that bench until Archy came down? Yes, sir. Did you hear anybody talking in the market house, while Archy was up stairs? No, sir, I heard them talking but I could not get what they said. People were talking about, were they? Yes, sir. You don't remember what anybody said? No, sir. When Archy came down stairs did you see him come? Yes, sir. Were you still sitting on the bench, when he come down? When I found out he was coming down I went to where he was coming down. You went to the foot of the steps? Yes, sir. Who was with him? Mr. Wemyss. Anybody else? No, sir. No one else? No, sir. Wemyss the only man who was with him? Yes, sir, the only man I saw. Do you mean he is the only man who was with him that you knew, or that there were others there that you didn't know? He was the only man I saw, I don't know whether there was any more there or not, because I was only on one side of him. Did Mr. Wemyss have hold of Archy? Yes, sir. How did he have hold of him? He had hold of him some how. You don't know how? No, sir. Did anybody do anything to Archy while he was coming down the stairs, or after he got down? He got down and then the man shot him. Did the man shoot him inside of the market house? No, sir, right there on the pavement. Did you see anything done to him in the market house, while he was passing from the steps to go outside on the pavement? No, sir. You were in there were you? Yes, sir, Did you go out of the opening in front of the market house, when Archy went out? Yes, sir. The same time he was going out? Yes, sir. What happened after you went out there? The man shot him. Did you see the man who shot Archy? Yes, sir. Did you know who he was? Yes, sir. You saw him? Yes, sir. Do you see him in the court now? Yes, sir. Where is he? Yonder he is, with spectacles on. Is that the man? Yes, sir. Did he have the spectacles on that day? I don't know sir. What is the man's name? Mr. Tolar, they told me his name was. Who told you so? The people there did. Do you see anything about that man now, that you saw that day, that makes you know it is he? No, sir, George told me he had a little black spot on his face—George—no Rufey told me—Rufus—no George told me so. Did you see that little black spot on his face that day? No, sir, I never seed it. You must not tell what anybody told you—you must tell what you saw, you saw the man shoot the negro? Yes, sir. Did folks tell you there right then who it was? Yes, sir. Who did they say it was? Tolar. Was that just after the shooting? Yes, sir, the boys all told me it was Tolar. What became of the man that shot, after he fired the pistol? I don't know sir. You don't know where he went to? No, sir. Did you see what he did with the pistol? yes, sir, I thought he put it in his left sleeve. You think he put it in his sleeve after he fired it? Yes, sir. Didn't it scare you when the pistol went off? Yes, sir. Did you run away? No, sir, I stayed there a while, and then I went on back home. Did you see your brother George there that day? No, sir, he was not there, he was down shooting marbles, with another boy. Did you see him after the pistol was shot? Yes, sir. Where were you standing, when the pistol was shot? I was standing with my back towards my home. Were you standing on the same side of the market house that you came out of? No, sir. Which side of the market house were you standing on? On the side towards my home. Do you know what street your home is on? No, sir, pap told me in yonder, but I forgot. Is it the same street that the guard house is on? Yes, sir. You were standing on that side of the market house towards the market house? My back was towards my house, and my face towards the black man. Did you see him when he fell? Yes, sir. Did you go up and look at him? No, sir, I never went up to look at him; the men told me not to go there; and then I was about two feet from him, and I looked at him though; I seen him. Who told you not to go up to him? Mr. McDonald. What did he tell you not to go up to him for? He told me not to say anything about it. He told you not to say anything about it? Yes, sir. Did you say anything about it? No, sir, I said it all before he told me. What did you say? I told the people that Tolar shot him. You said that? Yes, sir. You were one of the people who were saying that in the crowd that day? No, sir. the boys all around there asked who shot him and I said Tolar. And then Mr. McDonald told you to say nothing about it? Yes, sir. Did you tell any body since? No, sir, no body except my mammy. And you saw the man when he fired the pistol? Yes, sir. What sort of a man was he, a short man or a tall man? A tall man, taller than pa.

Cross-examination by the Counsel for the accused:

Rufus, do you know me? No, sir. I live at Fayetteville with you; I want to talk with you a little about this matter, and don't get scared, no body is going to hurt you; where had you been that day before you went to the market house? I had been no where but home. You came from home up to the market house? Yes, sir. Do you know a good many people in Fayetteville, Rufus? I know some, but I don't know many; I know some boys. Do you know little Willie Porter? Yes, sir, and he told me it was Tolar; him and a whole heap more boys. Have you seen Willie lately? Yes, sir, I seen him a little while before I left home; I seen him

down there to the guard house, by them old barrels of white lime. Did he have a little talk with you? No, sir, he never had a talk with me. He told you he had been up here to Raleigh, did he? Yes, sir, he came to my house the morning before he come, and told me he was going; he said they sent after him, and said his dad wrote a letter telling not to let him go. So he came to see you the morning before he came off? Yes, sir. And then after he got back, you saw him up there about the lime barrels by the guard house.? Yes, sir. And you and Willie just talked this matter over; I suppose you told Willie what you knew about it, didn't you? No, sir, I told him one day that Tolar shot the man, and he said yes, and then he told me he was going to go to the trial; I told him not to tell nothing on me (crying). Since Willie got back from Raleigh, you and he had that talk out there by the old lime barrels, at the guard house, Willie told you what he had said up there in Raleigh, did he? He told me that Tolar done it. Did he tell you they brought him up in a nice place like this? No, sir, he never told me nothing about this. Did he tell you about any of these gentlemen that you would see here, dressed up in uniform? No, sir, he never told me nothing about them. Did he tell you about swearing, that you would have to swear to things when you came up here? No, sir, he never told me nothing about that. He just told you what he had said while he was up here? Yes, sir. Did he tell you you must tell the same tale that he told? No, sir, he never told me anything about that. Rufus, you say you knew Capt. Tolar that day? No, sir, I never knew him that day; the boys just told me it was him. When you saw him use the pistol you didn't know who he was? No, sir. Just now when you came up here in this room you didn't know him then till your father pointed him out to you? Yes, sir, I did know him; I knowed the man, and I asked pa if that was Tolar, and he told me yes; I knowed the man and showed pa the man and asked him if it was Tolar.

(Witness exhibits much agitation and retires for a few moments.)

Cross-examination resumed:

I believe you told me you didn't know Mr. Tolar that day? No, sir. Had you never seen him before that day, that you remember? I don't know, sir, whether I ever seen him or not. How long after that before you saw Mr. Tolar, to know him? To-day is the second time I ever seed him. To-day is the first time after the shooting that you saw Mr. Tolar, to know him? Yes, sir. When you were sitting over there, just before you went into that little room, you and your father and your little brother, George, you asked your father which one was Capt. Tolar? No, sir, I showed him that man and asked him if that was Tolar, and he told me it was. When these soldiers were bringing Capt. Tolar and the others up here, you and your father and your little brother, George, met them on the street, didn't you? Yes, sir. And your father shook hands with Capt. Tolar? I don't know whether he done that or not? He just spoke to him? I don't know whether he spoke to him or not. Was that the time your father told you it was Capt. Tolar. No. sir. How come you to ask your father, after you got up here it that was not Captain Tolar? I had seen the man and I asked pa if that was Tolar so that I could tell. Rufus, you think that Capt. Tolar didn't have spectacles on that day? I don't know, sir; whether he did or not—I never seed. That black speck under his eye, did you notice that, that day? No, sir; I never seed it—a boy asked me, who is that man, that shot him, and I said Tolar, and he said, "don't you see that black speck under his eye?" and I said no. That was what the boy told you? The boys all told me that. Rufus, were you standing in front of Capt. Tolar, or behind him, when he shot? I was not standing in front of him. You were standing behind him? No, sir. Which side of him were you standing? I was standing with my back towards my house. Were you out on the pavement? Yes, sir. That pavement where Archy fell? Yes, sir. And had your face down towards the guard house, and towards your mother's house? Yes, sir. Were you looking right at Archy when he was shot? Yes, sir. Were you close down by the corner of the market house? I was about two yards from the corner of it. How far was Capt. Tolar off from Archy when he shot him? About two yards I reckon. Was Archy between you and Capt. Tolar? No, sir. Were you nearer to Capt. Tolar, or near to Archy? I was a little bit closer to Archy. And you had your back down towards home? Yes, sir. (crying.) Rufus, did you see Capt. Tolar, when he came up to that place, where he was standing when he shot him? No sir. He was standing there when you first saw him? Yes, sir. Did you see where he got the pistol from? I don't know whether I seen it or not, I thought he took it out of his sleeve. Which sleeve, his right or left? His left I thought, I don't know whether it was or not; I dont know whether it was his right or left—I can't tell anybody elses, I can tell my own. You can't tell any one elses right hand? No, sir, not without they throw a brick, or something so that I can see. Did you notice whether Tolar had his pistol in his right hand or left? No, sir. Did you notice what sort of a pistol it was? No, sir. You don't know whether it was a small or large one? No, sir It was not a gun though? No, sir. About how near did Capt. Tolar put the pistol to Archy's head? I don't know, sir. How far was Capt. Tolar from Archy at the time he shot; as far as from you to me? Not as I know of. How far far do you think he was? About two yards. Can't you point to somebody that is sitting around you about the same distance from you? No, sir. Can't you point to some of them? No, sir. I don't want you to tell what you don't know'; I just want you to tell what you saw? I told you all I know about it. I know you have, you and I know all about it, but these gentlemen don't know, and you have to tell it to them. Rufus, can you show some gentleman here that is just about the same distance off from you as Captain Tolar was, at the time he shot him? No, sir. Do you think he was as far off as that gentleman? (about forty feet.) I think he was, but I don't know. Did you notice whether Captain Tolar was standing on the pavement or off, at the time he was shot? Never noticed whether he was off or on. You know that great big place they call an arch? No, sir, I don't know it. That

big opening—great big door? No, sir, I don't know it. (Witness is shown a drawing of the market house, but does not recognize it.) You can't tell whether Mr. Tolar was on the brick walk around the market house? No, sir, I reckon he was off. How many were there between you and Mr. Tolar? I don't know, sir. Were there any? I don't know, sir, whether there was any or not. If you had asked me the first time I might have told you something about it. Rufus, many men were there between Mr. Tolar and Archy—do you remember whether there were any? No, sir. Did you hear Captain Tolar say anything before he shot him? No, sir, I never heard him say a thing. Did you notice what he had on? No, sir. Did you notice whither he had on a cloak or anything around him? No, sir, the boys pointed me to his legs and face, and told me that was Tolar, and said he had on a shawl. What boys told you? Jim Done, and a heap of them. Did Willie Porter tell you that? No, sir. Was Jim Done there all the time with you? Yes, sir. Did he go there with you? No, sir, when I went up there he was up there. And you were with him all the time you were there till you went away? Yes, sir. What part of the market house did you and Jim Dave stay about—under the market? Yes, sir. So from the time you got there until you went away you and Jim Done stayed under the market house together? Yes, sir. Jim was with you all the time, was he not? Yes, sir. What were you and Jim doing, were you playing? We were just talking together. How big is Jim? About my size, but he is a little older though. He was eleven when I was nine. When you looked at Captain Tolar and saw him shoot, did you see his legs? No, sir, not when I seed him shoot. Did you see his face? No, sir. Did you see his hands? Yes, sir, I saw his hands. Do you know Mr. Sam Phillips in Fayetteville, that keeps store below the market house? Yes, sir. Could you tell at that time whether it was Mr. Tolar or Sam Phillips shot? Yes, sir, I saw it was Tolar, I never knowed whether it was Sam Phillips, I don't know whether he was up there. Did you see Archy after he was shot? Yes, sir, he was lying down there on the pavement. Did you hear anybody saying anything about him while he was lying on the pavement? I heard some negroes come up and say 'poor fellow, he is dead.' Were you standing pretty close to him then? Yes, sir. You didn't see what became of Capt. Tolar after Archy was shot? No, sir. So all you saw about it was you just looked there and saw Tolar raise up the pistol and shoot him? Yes, sir, I don't know any more. You don't know where he put the pistol? No, sir, but I thought he put it in his sleeve, but I don't know whether he did or not. Rufus, what McDonald was that? James. You mean the great big man that sells goods at auction? Yes, sir. You know Mr. McDonald pretty well? Yes, sir. You are certain you saw Mr. McDonald there? Yes, sir. What was Mr. McDonald doing? He told me not to take and tell anybody. You are certain that was Mr. McDonald are you? Yes, sir, he was with me. Did you notice how long Mr. McDonald had been there? You just saw him about the time of the shooting—you didn't see him before? No, sir. Was it before or after the shooting that you saw him? After. You didn't see him at all before the shooting? No, sir. I don't know whether I seed him or not; if I did, I didn't know it. How long after the shooting was it? I don't know any more about it. Was it a short, or long time? I can't tell!

the time of day, I don't know. Was it while you were there on the ground? No, sir. Where were you when he said this to you? I was standing on the pavement.

Re-direct examination by the Counsel for the prosecution.

You know Willie Porter? Yes, sir. After he had been up here to say what he had to say in this case, he went back to Fayetteville? Yes, sir. How many times have you seen him since he went back? Once. Did he come to see you? No, sir. Did he tell you what he had said when he was up here? No, sir. Did he tell you what he had said when he was up here? No, sir. At the time we are talking about now. did he say anything to you about Tolar's having shot him, was it then he told you that Tolar shot him, or directly after he was shot? He told me when he came to my house before he left. Did he tell you after he came back from here, and just before you came? No, sir. You didn't talk about it then? He went to see you after he went back from here? No, sir. Did he talk to you about what he had said up here? No, sir, I don't know no more about it. Have you seen Willie Porter since he was down here to Raleigh? Yes, sir. Where? I saw him at the guard house, near the old lime barrels. He told you he had been up here? Yes, sir. Did he tell you what he had said, when he had been here? No, sir. Right away after Beebee was shot, did anybody tell you who it was that shot him? Yes, sir. Did you ask who it was? Yes, sir. Did you see the man who shot him, and ask what that man's name was? Yes, sir. What did they tell you? They told me it was Toler. Did some of them then speak about a black spot under his eye? Yes, sir, Bud Sochamy and Jim Done told me that then.

JOHN H. SMITH, a witness for the prosecution, having been first duly sworn, testified as follows:

Questioned by the Counsel for the prosecution. What is your name? John H. Smith. Do you reside in Fayetteville? Yes, sir. Were you in that town the day Archy Beebee was killed? Yes, sir. Were you at the market house that day? No, sir. Where were you, sir? I stood on the east side of the store door,—Mr. Mitchell's door, on the south-east side. Was that at the time the shot was fired? Yes, sir, and before it. Were you standing there when Archy Beebee was brought up from the guard house? Yes, sir. What street is Mr. Mitchell's store on? On Gillespie street, sir. How many doors down from market square? Not more than four doors. Mr. Robert Mitchell's? Yes, sir. You were at his store door? Yes, sir. When Archy passed up? Yes, sir. And you were standing about there more or less, until he was brought down? Yes, sir. You didn't go up to the market house at all? No, sir, I never left the store. Did you notice any crowd at the market house that day? Yes, sir. Was the crowd larger or smaller than you have usually seen there? It was a good sized crowd, scattered all over the market house. Was it large enough to attract your attention, as an unusually large crowd? Yes, sir. How long have you been living in Fayetteville, Mr. Smith? Twenty one years sir. Do you usually see such a crowd as that at the market house, when a trial is going on up stairs? Not as large as it was that day. Was it larger than any you have ever seen there, under such circumstances? I don't know that it was, I have seen larger crowds. I mean under like circumstances of a trial? No, sir. It was un-

usually large was it for an investigation before a Justice? Yes, sir. It was not the ordinary crowd that was gathered there, when a trial was going on? No, sir, not at all. Could you see the steps that come down from the town hall up stairs from where you were standing? Yes, sir. Did you see Archy when he came down those steps? Yes, sir. Could you tell who was with him? I saw Mr. Wemyss, on one side, I could not tell who was on the other. Were you standing out in front of the store? No, sir, standing right by the door, on the door step. Did you see Archy from that time until the time he fell? Yes, sir. Could you see him when he was passing around the arch? No, sir, I saw him immediately he got around on the south side of the arch, on the corner. Could you see him in the market house, passing from the foot of the steps to the arch? No, sir. You lost sight of him then? Yes, sir. Was there any noise or disturbance loud enough to reach you, between the time that Archy got to the foot of the steps, and the time he come to the entrance of the market house turning out? Yes, sir, there was loud cries of "shoot him, kill him." At that time? Yes, sir. Was it in the time he passed from the foot of the steps to the time he turned out of the market house? Yes, sir. You could hear those loud cries of shoot him, kill him? Yes, sir. Was that shout a general shout? Several in the crowd. Was it one voice? It sounded to me like it was several. Could you recognize any voices? No, sir. Were those the only expressions you heard? They were all I heard at that time. How often were those repeated? Not more than two or three times. Each expression repeated two or three times? Yes, sir. By different voices did it appear, or by the same voice? I could not tell very well about it. I understood you to say you heard several voices? Yes, sir. It did not all seem to be the utterance of one man? No, sir. You didn't so understand it at the time? No, sir, I thought it proceeded from the crowd. You thought it was the outcry of the crowd? Yes, sir. When Archy came out side of the market house, you could see him? Yes, sir. Did you see anything then that happened? I saw him struggle. After the cries were made? Yes, sir, he seemed to be trying to get away from the guard, and in struggling he fell, and Mr. Wemyss went down with him. You saw that from where you stood? Yes, sir, and as he was trying to recover, I saw the pistol fired; but I could not tell who shot it, and I saw a man advancing, trying to crawl to him with a knife in his hand after he was shot. How do you mean, trying to crawl to him? On his hands and knees. Was that man between you and Archy? Yes sir. Who was that man? Monk Julia. You recognized him then, could you see whether he was armed at all? I saw he had a knife in his hand. He was crawling on his hands and knees? Yes, sir. Did he get into where the boy was? No, sir, somebody jerked him off. How long were these exclamations continued, I want to know whether these were continued up to the time of the appearance of the negro. They stopped immediately after the pistol fired. Were they continued from the time he made his appearance until that time? Yes, sir.

Cross Examination by the Counsel for the accused:

You say you were standing on the south-east corner of Robert Mitchell's store door? Yes, sir. What is the distance from that point of Robert Mitchell's store door up to the south-east corner of the market house? I dont know, sir; but I should suppose in a straight line from where I stood up to the corner of the market house where the prisoner was in custody of the guards it could not be more than eighty five or ninety yards—perhaps a hundred. Between eighty-five and a hundred yards? Yes, sir. You say you saw the prisoner when he was brought down stairs? Yes, sir, I could see right through the arch there. See him come down the steps through the small south east arch? Yes, sir Did you see his face? I saw him before, and I could see him then. You could distinguish him from any other negro, at that distance? I could not say it was exactly him, but I supposed it was him. It was the same man that you saw go up? I suppose so. You are not here to suppose—could you distinguish that mans features—could you swear positively that was Archy Beebee? Yes, sir, I will swear I saw him coming down stairs. And you will swear it was Wemyss on his right hand side? It appeared to be on his right hand side. Was it upon his right hand side or not? To the best of my recollection it was on the right hand side. That is not a matter of recollection, that is a matter of knowledge—was Wemyss or was he not, on his right hand side. He was on his right hand side. Did you see any body else with him. I saw Mr. Hardie in front of him. You could tell it was Hardie? Yes, sir. Coming down the steps? Yes, sir. Did you see any of them after they got upon the floor of the market house? I saw them after they turned the corner. After they turned the corner of the arch, you mean? After they turned the corner of the market house. What do you mean by the corner of the market house? I mean the corner after they come down the stair steps, of course; they had to go around the corner to take the wooden walk to go towards the guard house; I saw him after they turned around the corner to go towards the guard house. You mean the corner of the arch? I mean the corner of the market house. Now at the time you saw Wemyss standing on his right, who else did you see standing with Beebee? I could not tell who the others were, I saw Mr. Hardie plainly. Where was Mr. Hardie standing? He was in front of him. Directly in front? Yes, sir. Did he have hold of him? Not that I could tell. Did you see his hand reached out at all? I saw him fighting against the crowd. You say Hardie was in front of him; you mean Hardie was further to the south? Yes, sir. Beebee had his face towards the south? I could not tell about that, because he was struggling at the time. Do you say Hardie was further south than Beebee? Yes, sir. Could you see that distinctly? Yes, sir, very distinctly indeed. There could be no doubt about that? Not a bit, sir. Whether Hardie had hold of him or not, you say you can't tell? No, sir. And you saw Hardie's hand? I could see Hardie trying to fend off somebody with his arms. Which way were these persons coming that he was fending off? They were rushing in every direction. Did the crowd seem to be in much confusion? No, sir, it appeared to be running in every direction through to the place. Where did Beebee fall? He fell between the corner of the market house and the tree which is south of the market house. Did he fall near the corner of the pavement? I could not tell, sir. You saw the flash of the pistol? Yes, sir, And

where was that flash? The flash came from the north-east of the prisoner. From the flash was the person who fired the pistol off the pavement or on? I could not tell. Where did you see the flash? just descibe some point where the flash was. On the chart the witness says, the man must have stood who fired the pistol, almost exactly east from Archy, a little north east, if any thing. If the man had stood anywhere about that main eastern arch on the pavement, it would have been impossible for you to have seen the flash? I could not tell about that. If a man had been standing any where on the pavement opposite any portion or that smaller southern-most arch on the east front, could you have seen the flash? I think I could. And you feel sure that the man was standing to the east of the arch? A little to the north or east. Was there a large crowd about there at that time? Yes, sir, a very large crowd indeed. Did you hear the report of the pistol? Yes, sir. Very loud? Not more than an ordinary pistol shot. It was as loud as ordinary? Yes, sir. Fully as loud? Yes, sir. How long after you heard the report of the pistol before you saw that man on his hands and knees crawling about? Not more than two seconds. Where was that done? point it out on the diagram.

Witness points out the position due south of the arch.

He was coming from the south and going out north? Yes, sir. And he was upon his hands and knees? Yes, sir. And he had a knife in his hands? Yes, sir. And you saw the knife? Yes, sir, saw it plainly. Could you tell whether it was a knife that opened and shut? I could not tell; I could see it was a knife plain enough. Which hand did he hold the knife in? I could not tell. And you say that was Monk? Yes, sir. How do you know it? Because I had seen him often enough before to know who he was; I saw him when he was jerked up. You swear as to that positively that you saw it? Yes, sir. Did you see anybody else with weapons from that point? No sir. You saw no weapons at all? No, sir; I saw a great crowd rush with their arms raised, but what they had I could not tell. Did you go up there after the man had fallen? No, sir. When were you summoned as a witness in this case? Not until Wednesday evening of this week. When did you get here? I got here this morning. Who had you talked with about this matter before you came up here? Not a soul. Cobert Mitchell got home before you came up? Yes, sir. Did you have any conversation with him about it? None, except that he said they were going to send for one of my boys. No conversation with him or any one else about this matter of killing? No, sir, not a soul; the only conversation I had was with John Williams, the same man that stood in the door by the side of me the same time and saw the same thing I did.

The Judge Advocate announced that the prosecution in this case was now closed, and they were ready to hear from the defence.

Mr. Fuller, one of the Counsel for the accused, said he had no objection to the introduction of witnesses for the defence to-day; but Mr. Phillips, one of his associate counsel, who had been absent for some days, and just arrived this morning, would prefer not to go on until to-morrow.

The Judge Advocate said that the defence had been notified to be ready, and he saw no reason why there should be any time lost.

A motion for adjournment was then made, which was lost.

J. B. DAVIS, a witness for the defence, after having been first duly sworn, testified as follows:

Examined by the Council for the accused. What is your name? I. B. Davis. sh. Where do you reside? I live in Fayetteville. What is your occupation? I carry on a Tin business. At what point in Fayetteville do you conduct your business? On the south-east corner of the market square. Were you in Fayetteville at the time Archy Beebee, otherwise called Archy Warden was shot? I was, sir. Were you at any place near the market house that day? I was in my store. Look at this diagram, if you please, familiarize yourself with it, and then point out positions upon it?

Witness is shown a diagram of the market house, and points out the store marked J. B Davis as his place of business.

About what time of the day was it that Beebee was killed? About four o'clock. Where were you standing at that time? I was standing upon the north-west corner of the pavement around my store. About how far is that from the south-east corner of the pavement around the market house? About fifty or sixty feet in a direct line. Did you see Beebee when he was carried up stairs? I did not. Did you see him when he was brought down stairs? I saw him as he came down the stairs. Did you see him then continuously until he was killed? I lost sight of him when he went down the first time. Did you see him until he got out upon the pavement? There was an obstruction there that broke the view I had of him. Was that obstruction the pillar between the main arch and the southern arch? Yes, sir. After he got upon the pavement did you notice any thing unusual at all either in the crowd, in the appearance of Beebee, or did anything occur there to attract your attention? When the boy came around on the pavement, I saw as I supposed, a demand for him, by the position of the hands; I heard no remarks, he then came on down to about midway of the main pillar, between two arches: there he went down with his guard : afterwards I never saw him any more until he was dead. Where did he fall? He fell about the corner of the building on the pavement. About the corner? The south east corner. Was that where he fell? Yes, sir. Well, sir, where was your position at that time, had you changed it? I had not. Were you standing in that corner in front of your door? Not in front of my door, on the corner. How far were you at that time off from Beebee? I should say about fifty or sixty feet. Was there any body in that crowd at the time off the shooting that you noticed? I saw no one in the crowd at the time of the shooting near the boy that I knew, except Sheriff Hardie. Where was Sheriff Hardie? I could not tell the position that he occupied with the boy. Did you see the boy at all after he raised? I never saw the boy after he went down the first time. Were you looking in that direction at the time the pistol shot was fired? No, sir, my attention was directed to about the center of the main arch. What was there that attracted your attention; who was it that you saw there? Capt. Tolar drew my attention there. Just tell why your attention was attracted to Capt. Tolar? Capt. Tolar was standing about the center of the pavement, he being a large man and standing still while the most of the crowd was in motion, is why my attention was attracted to him. He was on the center of the pavement at what place? About the center of the main arch. What did you see him do? I saw him do nothing except standing still. Were you looking at him when the pistol shot was fired? I was, sir. Did Tolar fire that pistol shot? He didn't fire no shot. Have you any doubt about that Mr. Davis? None in

the world. You swear that you saw him at the time the pistol shot was fired? Yes, sir. And he fired no shot at all? No, sir. And at that time you say he was standing on the pavement about the center of the pavement and opposite the center of the main arch? Yes, sir. Did you hear the report of the pistol which was fired? I did. Did you see the smoke of the pistol? I did. From the sound of the report, and from the smoke that you saw, where was the person standing who fired the pistol? He was standing there on the ground off the pavement, he was very near the curb stone. Opposite what part of the arch? I should say he was a little to the right of the corner of the building. What do you mean "to the right?" The north-east portion of the building. Looking westward? Looking north from where the boy fell. Just describe it with regard to the arch; was he opposite the upper portion, the middle or where? He was about the left hand portion of the arch on the ground. And you say he was about the south east portion of the small southern arch? Yes, sir. And about a foot and a half off from the curb-stone? I could not tell the distance from the curb-stone. What is your best impression with regard to it? I should think a couple of feet from the curb-stone, but in the ground. Have you any doubt about that matter, Mr. Davis? I have none. And you heard the report? Yes, sir. Do you know who fired that pistol? I did not, sir. Do you know anything more about this matter? I do not. Are you acquainted with the general character of a freedman by the name of John Shaw?

Counsel for the prosecution objected to the question.

The Commission called for the reading of the question by the recorder; the recorder read the question "Are you acquainted with the general character of a freedman by the name of John Shaw?"

Counsel for the defence added the words "for truth" making the question to read "are you acquainted with the general character of a freedman by the name of John Shaw, for truth?"

Counsel for the prosecution withdrew his objection.

Direct examination resumed by the Counsel for the accused. What is your answer to that question? I think I am, sir. What is his character? It is bad. Do you know as a fact whether John Shaw has been tied up by the thumbs for stealing, by order of the military authorities in Fayetteville, within the last two years? I do. You know that to be a fact, sir. I tied him up myself. In what capacity were you acting at that time? Orderly Sergeant. Orderly Sergeant of what? Of the local police. Who was the Captain? Capt. Orrel, sir. And he was charged with cattle stealing? Yes, sir. And you were ordered to tie him up by the thumbs, and you executed the order? I did, sir.

Cross-examination by the Counsel for the prosecution:

What is your first name? Ichabod. How long have you been living in Fayetteville? Fifteen years, sir. Have you been in the same business during all that time time, that you are now? I have, sir; I served an apprentice-ship there. You say you were an orderly sergeant of the local police, you don't mean you belonged to the United States army? No, sir, I was orderly sergeant of the local police that was formed there by Colonel Curwin. What was the date of Archy Beebee's death? The 11th of February. At four o'clock in the afternoon?

About four, sir. At what time that day did you first see Capt Tolar? I don't think I saw him during that day until I saw him at the market house? What time did you first see him at the market house? I saw him there sometime between the hours of three and four. Where was Archy Beebee when you saw him there; had he gone up stairs, or was he still at the guard house when you first saw Capt. Tolar? He was up stairs. Where were you? I was standing on my corner. Where was Capt. Tolar? He was standing about the center of the pavement. Did he stand there until the shooting took place, in the center of the pavement? He was standing there until the shooting; the last I saw of him he was standing there. Was he standing there during the whole interval of time when you first saw him, and when the shooting was done? He was. How long an interval? I should think it was about five minutes. You saw him standing there five minutes before the shooting took place? Yes, sir. That was the first time you had seen him that day? Yes, sir. Did you see Archy Beebee when he was brought up from the guard house? I did not, sir. How do you know he was up stairs? I heard that he was. We are asking about your own knowledge? I don't know of my own knowledge that he was up stairs. You don't know where he was when you first saw Capt. Tolar standing there? Not of my personal knowledge. How long had you been standing there on the corner of the pavement when the pistol shot was fired that killed Archy Beebee? I should think I had been standing there probably about eight minutes, not exceeding ten. Where were you before you were standing there? I was in my store. All day? I might have been about the street some during the day. You came from your store to that point? Yes, sir. You came from your store and stood there about eight minutes until it was done? I should think so. Did you notice any extraordinary crowd at the market house that day? I should suppose there was forty or fifty. You have frequently seen as many there before on the occasion of a trial? Yes, sir. No excitement was there? There didn't seem to be. Everybody was calm and cool? Everybody was calm. Did you hear anything of the allegation that was made against this negro Beebee that he had attempted to commit a rape upon a white woman? I had heard it during the day. Did you know his trial was going on at that time? I did not, sir; I was busy in my store at the time. During the eight minutes that you were standing there, in this crowd of forty or fifty, which was about the ordinary crowd that gathers at the time of a trial, did you see anybody that you knew? I don't recollect recognizing any one except Capt. Tolar. He is the solitary soul you saw in that crowd that day? The only one I remember seeing. Did you see him from the first time that you were standing there at that point on the pavement until the pistol was fired? I did. Had your eyes on him all the while? I think I did. Never lost sight of him once? I don't think I lost sight of him once. You say you can't recollect a single person you saw in that crowd that day? I don't recollect any person, as I said, except Sheriff Hardie and Tolar. Was any one else in that crowd? Not that I recollect of. Didn't you notice Tom Powers that day? No, sir. Didn't you see Monk Julia. If I did, I don't recollect it. Didn't you see Ed. Powers that day? I did not. Didn't you see Sam. Hall? I did not. Didn't you see J. G. Leggett? I saw him after the shooting was over. Didn't you see him in that crowd? No, sir. You say there was a crowd of forty or fifty?

Yes, sir. Were they all black people? No, sir. Part colored? Yes, sir. What proportion were colored? I could not tell what proportion. Were they in part colored people? They were all mixed together. They were not strangers? No, sir. You saw no one you knew except this man Tolar? No, sir, I recollect no other person. You kept your eyes fixed on him intently for eight minutes? I should think I did. You were looking at him when the pistol was fired? I was looking at him when the pistol was fired. Did you see the negro when he was coming down on the steps? I did. Who was with him at that time? Sheriff Hardie and some police. Who were the police? Faircloth and McGuire, I think. Then you saw them in the crowd that day. I saw them on the steps. Didn't they go in the crowd? I didn't see them in the crowd. You didn't see Hardie in that crowd? I saw Hardie as he came around the corner. Did't see Wemyss in the crowd? I don't remember. The only thing you saw of these policemen was on the steps? I saw them when they came down the steps. Did you see them after they got immediately to the bottom of the steps? I could not see them. It was only while they were on the steps you saw them? Yes, sir. When did you loose sight of the prisoner? When my view was obstructed by the police. You lost sight of the prisoner after he got to the foot of the steps? I lost sight of the prisoner after he came down to the foot of the steps. And you didn't see him any more until he went down near the arch? I saw him when he went down near the arch. Didn't you see him when he turned out of the large arch? I could not see him when he turned. You could not see him when he came out of the main arch of the market house, on the pavement? No, sir. I mean when he turned out of the arch? I saw him then. Was any assault made on him then? I saw a lifted position of hands as if demanding him. Didn't you hear any sound? I could not tell. Was that crowd as still as death? I don't think it was. Didn't you hear any noise? I heard a rustling about the pavement as of the feet of the crowd. Nothing but the feet of the crowd? I heard nothing else. No word said? I heard nothing. Were your ears stopped, sir? No, sir. You say you heard no sound except the rustling of men's feet? I heard nothing of the kind. Nothing of what kind? Of the voice of any persons? I didn't ask you if you heard any voice; I asked you if you heard any noise? I heard no sound except the rustling of feet. That was the only sound that you heard at the time Archy came out of the arch? That was the only sound I heard that I recollect of. You said in your examination in chief that you saw, as you supposed a demand made manifest? I saw hands raised as I supposed in a demanding position, but heard no words. How many hands did you see? I saw two. Were they hands belonging to the same man? I think they were. That was the only thing you saw of any hands? That was the only thing I saw of hands. Didn't you see anything of a rush or pressure made upon the prisoner? I did not. Didn't you hear anything of the Sheriff's telling them to keep off—to stand back? I never heard it. Didn't you see anything of an attempt of the police to use their clubs there? No, sir. Did any such a thing happen? I could not tell of my knowledge, I was not in the crowd. But you pretend to have been so near that you can speak of seeing a particular man for eight minutes? I could not see the boy, as I said; the crowd was around the boy. You say you saw two hands? I did. What was the position of those hands? (Witness represents position of the man's hands. Both hands raised as nigh as his head, about two feet apart, with the palms from his face.) You saw a man standing in a crowd of moving men with his hands in that position? I did. And you construed that into the demand? That was my impression. You say there was no rush? I saw no rush. You saw no use of clubs? I saw none. You saw no effort of the crowd to get at the prisoner Beebee? I saw nothing except what I have told you, the demand as I supposed it to be. What became of Capt. Tolar after the firing of the pistol? I went into the store, and I don't know where he went. Didn't you look to see who fired the pistol? I did not see who fired the pistol. When the pistol fired, didn't you look in that direction? I turned my eyes in that direction. What became of Capt. Tolar then? When I looked around he was still standing there; immediately I turned and went to my store. How was he dressed? I could not tell about his dress more than he had on a shawl. Did you see what sort of a hat he had on? I don't remember. Did he have on his spectacles that day? I don't remember that. You remember nothing about him but his dress? None of his dress but his shawl. What was he doing? Standing still. With his his arms folded upon his breast, or hanging loose? I could not tell about that, sir. Was the crowd moving all about him? There seemed none moving in the rear of him; the crowd was moving in front. He was in the rear of the crowd? Yes, sir. Did you see that pistol that was fired that day? I did not, sir. All you saw was the smoke? That was all. You heard the report? Yes, sir. Have you ever talked to Capt. Tolar about this business? Never spoke with him upon this subject at all. Have you ever testified upon this matter, at all? No, sir. Ever told any one what your testimony would be? No one except the Counsel. When was that? That has been a month or more, I should think. You have never told any one before? I never had. Do you know how the Counsel found out what you would testify to? They found it out when I told them. How did you come to tell them? He asked me. Do you know how he come to ask you? Yes, sir, I told him I was standing on the corner. How came you to tell him that? We had a conversation about this thing; he was a Counsel for the prisoner and I told him of it. Did he come to you or did you go to him? He came to me. How did he know you were the proper person to come to? I don't know, only he knew that I was standing on the corner as I told him. How came you to tell him that? Because he was the Counsel for the defense and I wanted him to know it. Didn't you tell him you were going to swear Capt. Tolar didn't shoot the pistol? I did. Are you any relation to Capt. Tolar? I am not, sir. Are you a Mason? I

am. Is Captain Tolar a Mason? I think he is. Don't you know he is? I don't know with my personal knowledge more than I think I have seen him at the Lodge? Isn't that as good a person knowledge as you could have? About all I could get unless I had seen him made a Mason. Have you any special friendship for Capt. Tolar? None in the world. How long have you known him sir? Two years I suppose. Did you go over and see this boy after the shooting? I did. Who did you see there then? I don't remember who I saw. You must remember some one that you saw in the crowd? I don't know that I do. Don't remember a single person? There were several persons passing about to and from, just as I did. I simply wanted to know who was there; you certainly must recollect some one. I remember some that were there after the killing; I saw Mr. Blake there then. Let us know who was there after the killing? I remember seeing Mr. Blake there. What is Mr. Blake's first name? Isham. That was while the negro was lying there? It was some time after the killing. An hour? I should not think it was. The negro was still there? Yes, sir. How long do you suppose it was? It was a quarter of an hour or more after the crowd had somewhat dispersed; I paid no attention to who was there; I dont remember who was there. You don't remember who was there? I do not. Not a soul? Yes, sir: I told you I remembered Mr. Blake. Let us have some more? I don't remember who they were, as I didn't charge my memory with them. Can't you remember any others who were there? I don't at present. Will you try to recollect, sir? I don't remember who they were. Have you made an effort to recollect? Yes, sir; sort of refreshed my memory. Suppose you made a great effort? I don't remember sir. You say you didn't go over there till a quarter of an hour after the boy was shot? About a quarter of an hour. You went from the crowd back into your store? Yes, sir. You stood there fifteen minutes? I don't know that I stood there all the time. You didn't go away from the store? No, sir. You didn't go away from the store from the time you went from the corner into the store to the time you went over to see the negro? I might have been out around the door or on the pavement. You were not away from the immediate neighborhood of your store during that time? I don't think I was. Who else was there? My workmen. Who were they? A man by the name of Carter and one by the name of Mr. Webster. Anybody else there? Mr. Webster was in the store. Any one else that you remember seeing, during that fifteen minutes? No other person in the store, except a couple of black boys, and a couple of white apprentice boys. Give us their names? One of their names is Joseph Sochamy. He is a black boy? He is a white boy. What is the other? The black boy's name—by the way, they were not at the store; they were at the river putting a roof on a steam-boat, their names are George Grange and George Smith. The white ones were there? One was there. You stood there at the store and about the store fifteen minutes? Yes, sir. And you can't recollect any of these men, after exerting your memory to the utmost? I did not charge my memory. Now sir; perhaps if I give you some names you can tell me whether they were there or not. I don't think I can tell of my own knowledge; I stayed there but a few minutes; I went to look at the boy and looked at him, and went away. Don't you think you can tell me who was there if I named them? I could not tell of my own knowledge. Did you see Ed. Powers there? No, sir. Did you see J. G. Leggett? He passed me on my corner twice. When was that? Immediately after the killing he passed down from the market—he came from that direction, and went down to Mr. Burns' store; he and Mr. Burns went back to the market. And he came from the direction of the market house? Yes, sir. And went back again? Yes, sir. Did he have anything to say to you at the time he passed? No, sir, I didn't speak to him. Did you see Henry Sykes there? If I did, I don't recollect. Did you see Calph Lutterloh there? I did not, I don't remember seeing him there through the whole day. And this man Isham Blake is the solitary person? He is the only person that I remember, and I don't know that I would have remembered him, only he summoned me in the coroner's jury; but I didn't serve. Why didn't you serve? I was not drawn. You were summoned? Yes,sir, but did not serve. How many were summonned? Well, I didn't ask; I suppose the usual number which is twenty four; out of that they draw twelve. Did you ask to be summoned? I did not sir. Did you try to avoid it? I did. You say you know the general character of John Shaw for truth and veracity? I do. Who have you ever heard speak of his character for truth and veracity? I heard a number of persons speak of it. Give us one—now mark you—you are on your oath? I heard my brother speak of him. When? Some time ago. Since this man was murdered? No, sir. Before? Yes, sir. You heard your brother; what is his name? His name is John M. Davis. What did he say? I heard him say he would not believe him on oath. What was the occasion? It was in connection with this cattle stealing scrape. Who else have you ever heard say so? I don't remember any persons just now. Do you pretend to say that you know what the people in the neighborhood generally say of a man when you can't tell but what you own brother has said of his character? You said you knew his general character for veracity, and his general character for veracity is what the people generally say about him where he lives; that is now the question, do you know that? I don't know what his neighbors think of him; I don't know what is generally said of him by the community: if that is the question I don't. So I presumed at the time you gave the answer. I understood Mr. Fuller to ask the question to me directly. Mr. Fuller asked you the question which was required by the law; do you know the general character of so and so for truth, not what you thought of him. I didn't understand the question that way. Then you don't know whether he has got any reputation for truth in one way or another in his neighborhood? You don't know what people generally say about him; you and your brother don't think you would believe him on oath? I didn't say I would not. You don't think his character is good because your brother would not believe him? No, sir. That is your reason for thinking his character is bad, is it? My reason for thinking his character is bad, is that he was convicted of stealing, and was

hung up by the thumbs as a punishment. Now you give that as a reason for knowing his general character; that is the way you know the general character, is it? I understood the question directed personally to me; what I thought of his character. Do you say that what you think of a man's character always is his general character? No, sir, I understood the question personally to me, what I thought. But there is no misapprehension about the question, for attention was drawn to it at the time, and the Counsel was especially held down to the question which the law requires; do you know the general character of so and so, and you say you didn't understand that question. I did not, sir. You don't pretend to know his general character? Not what his neighbors say of him. That is his general character. I don't pretend to know. You don't know what the neighbors generally say? I do not, sir. You never heard it called in question except in the single instance? That is all that I remember. Now, sir, about this hanging up by the thumbs; was that a trial before the military authorities? It was a trial before Capt. Orrel. Wasn't it before a civil magistrate who was acting at that time as captain of the local police, wasn't he a civil magistrate? He was. Was this execution under military authority at all? It was, as I understood it; as he was acting as captain of the local police. This conviction that you speak of was before a civil magistrate? I think it was as he termed it a military court, or he was acting as a captain. When was that? It was the Spring of '66, soon after Col. Curwin left there. What was the charge against this negro? Cattle stealing, sir. He stole a drove I suppose? I don't know how many; cattle stealing was what I understood. Didn't you hear what it was alleged he stole? I did not, sir. Who told you? Capt. Orrel told me, it was in the order he gave me for the execution of the punishment. Where is the order? I don't know, sir. Was it a written order? Yes, sir. Have you got that order? I don't know whether I have or not. You undertook to tie a man up by the thumbs, execute the sentence of the law upon him, and have nothing to show for your authority for so doing? I had the order at the time, and may have it now; I don't know that I have. Then you don't know anything about his having stolen cattle? I know that was the charge against him. You know that was the charge against him; you were not present at the trial? No, sir. How did you know the charge? According to the order I had. You know you have an order telling you there was such a charge; you don't know what the charge was; you were not present at this trial? No, sir, I only saw the charge given to me on paper. That was in the charge was it, that was an order to hang the negro up by the thumbs"? That was an order. And that was set out the charge against him? Yes, sir. I ask you upon oath, do you remember that that set out any charge at all? It did set out a charge as cattle stealing. You swear positively that that order set out a charge, as well as the order for you to execute this punishment? I do. What has become of that order? I don't know, sir, I may have it, or I may not. Can you tell me where I would be likely to find it without your having to go after it? You could not find it without I was to go for it, and I don't know that I could produce it at all. This order was from who? Capt. Orrel. He was not the military commander of Fayetteville? No, sir. He was not in the United States service at all was he? No, sir. You didn't see Beebee when he was carried up to the market house that day? No, sir. You were out there about eight minutes before he was shot? I think so. Don't you know? Yes, sir. What did you go out there for? I went out of the door. What for? I could not tell; it was natural to walk out around my own door. You went and stood perfectly still? I was standing on the corner. Did nothing attract you out there? Not that I remember of. You just walked out by chance, and was attracted by Capt. Tolar, because he was a large man? And he was standing still. And the rest of the crowd was very boisterous? The crowd in front of him were moving around. Were they very boisterous? I should think not, sir: They made no exclamations, and no noises that you heard? Not that I heard. And yet the distinction between them and Capt. Tolar was so great that it distracted your attention from them entirely, although you knew the prisoner was in their midst at the moment and your whole attention was absorbed by him for eight minutes? My attention was fixed on Tolar. You never had your eyes off of him? I don't think I did. You said nothing to him? I did not. You interchanged no signs of intelligence? No, sir. And you solemnly swear that for eight minutes you stood on that corner, and looked at Captain Tolar? About that period of time. Without your attention being distracted by anything? Yes, sir. What was the first thing that drew your attention from him? The pistol shot. Then you looked off? I looked off. And you swear that the pistol shot fired while your eyes were resting on Tolar? It was. You swear most solemnly that he didnt shoot that pistol? I do swear most solemnly that he didn't. It is impossible for him to have shot that pistol? He could not have done it from where he was. Your reputation rests upon the fact of his having shot the pistol. I can't help it, sir. It is so? I think it does, but he didn't shoot that pistol that killed that negro. And you don't know who did shoot it? I do not, sir. You didn't see anybody with a pistol that day? I did not. You didn't see a pistol in that crowd that day? I did not. You didn't see anybody wearing a pistol? I did not. Nothing to attract your attention or to excite your suspicion that anything was going on that day? Nothing. Do you know any combination, or agreement between any men, or set of men to be instrumental in the killing of the negro? I never heard one word of it. Do you know it? I don't know sir. You never heard it? I did not. From Tolar? I never spoke with him on the subject in my life. Either before or after the killing? Neither before or since. Now sir, you say Capt. Tolar was the only man you saw in that crowd? The only man that I recollect except Sheriff Hardie. Was there no man in that crowd as tall as Capt. Tolar? That is a question I can't answer, I don't know—I don't know his height. Did you know Archy Beebee when you saw him? I did, I know him when I saw him coming down the steps. Was he a tall man or a short man? He was a medium sized man. What do you call a medium size? Five, eight; five, six, or something like that; he was about that height. Do you swear he was not six feet? No, sir. You think he was a medium height? I think so, sir. I understand that you lost sight of Beebee at the time he got to the foot of the stairs and you never saw him until he fell. I never saw him until he got around the arch, and went down. You saw him before he went down. Yes, sir, after he got around the arch I saw him. How far was Tolar from him at the time you saw him? Just as he turned the arch, I should think he was five or six feet. Standing where? Standing about the center of the arch. In the middle of the pavement? Yes, sir About the centre of the large arch about the middle of the pavement, as Archy Beebee

turned the arch, he was standing? Yes, sir. Then you saw Archy Beebee until he fell? I saw him go down. How far did he go from the arch before he fell? I should think a couple of feet— I could not tell the distance exactly. You saw him just then, and you saw him when he fell? I saw him go down. That was before he was shot? Yes, sir. You saw him go down; did you see him come up again? I did not. Then while you were looking at Archy Beebee, from the time he turned, until he fell—did you see Tolar then? I could see them both. And anybody else? I saw Sheriff Hardie? Did you see Beebee when he was shot? I did not. Did you see him when he fell? I did not. You didn't see him again until after he was shot? No, sir. You say that that crowd was quiet except the shuffling of feet? I said I heard no exclamation or any noise. If it had been made you would have heard it; you were close enough to hear it? I was about fifty feet from him. About the width of the street? Yes, sir. Any noise as a man's voice could be heard that distance; you could hear any voice that distance, couldn't you? Yes, sir. Any noise you could have heard then? Yes, sir. You think if there had been any noise you would have heard it? Yes, sir. And you didn't hear any noise; nothing to attract your attention? I didn't hear it, sir. You didn't hear any noise; there was no noise or confusion in the crowd to the best of your belief and recollection? There was no noise, as to confusion I could not tell, as I was not there. You could not tell; why? Because I was not in the crowd. You could not see the crowd; the crowd was in commotion? Yes, sir. The crowd being in commotion didn't attract your attention, but a single individual in it did, from his standing still as a statue? My attention was fixed on Captain Tolar.

Re-direct examination by the Counsel for the accused:

Mr. Davis, how far did I understand you to say Captain Tolar was from Beebee at the time the pistol shot was fired? I should say it was ten or twelve feet. Were there many persons between Beebee and Capt. Tolar at that time? I should say, sir, as well as I could judge, there was ten or a dozen. And I understand you to say they were in motion? Yes, sir. Moving about in every direction? Yes, sir. And Tolar stood there still? He was standing still.

Questioned by the Commission:

Did the crowd, in moving out of the arch at the time Beebee was brought out, pass between Tolar and the south side of the arch? They did, sir; they passed between him and the south side of the arch. Now how far was Mr. Tolar standing from the south side of the arch? I should think it was four or five feet. Didn't you say a few moments ago that it was three feet. I said, sir, if I remember right, that it was about two or three from where Beebee went down the first time. From the south side of the main arch didn't you say Captain Tolar was standing about three feet? I don't remember it, sir. You say this crowd passed between Tolar and south side of the arch? Yes, sir. And the crowd that were following him up? All the crowd didn't. Did any of them pass there? I suppose they did. Did they pass around the other side of Tolar? I saw more of them pass to the rear of him. You saw Tolar all the time while this crowd was passing? All the time.

On motion the Commission adjourned to meet Saturday, the 17th inst., at 11 o'clock, A. M.

RALEIGH, N. C., Aug. 17, 1867. 11 A. M.
The Commission met pursuant to adjournment.

Present, all the members of the Commission, the Judge Advocate, the Counsel for the prosecution, all the accused and their Counsel.

The reading of the testimony of George Smith, Rufus Smith and John X. Smith, taken yesterday, was waived, there being no objection thereto.

The testimony of J. B. Davis was then read.

Mr. Davis made the following corrections in his testimony:

On page 1495, line 15, he wished to substitute "South east corner," in place of "North east corner;" making the sentence to read, "a little to the right of the south east corner."

On page 1497, line 7, the witness said he did not understand the question to refer to neighborhood or general character; he supposed the question to be addressed to him personally, what he knew of his own knowledge.

On page 1526, he wished to substitute "1865," in place of "1866."

Yesterday's proceedings having been read, were then approved.

J. G. LEGGETT, a witness for the defense, having been first duly sworn, testified as follows:

Examined by the Counsel for the accused.

What is your name? J. G. Leggett. Where do you reside? In Fayetteville. How long have you been residing in Fayetteville? About fourteen months. Where were you residing before you came to Fayetteville? Near Washington, the eastern part of this State. What is your business in Fayetteville? Manufacturer of spirits of turpentine and rosin. Were you at the market house in Fayetteville, on the day that Archy Beebee was shot? Yes, sir. At what part of the market house did you enter? At the east end of the market house, where I went in at. Where was the deceased man, Beebee, at the time you entered the market house? I don't know, sir; I understood he was up stairs; I did not go up there at all. How long after you reached the market house was it before the deceased man, Beebee, was brought down? Well, sir, I think about ten or fifteen minutes. At what point of the market house did you stop, when you first went there? I think I stopped about six or eight feet from the main entrance; about eight feet I think. Of what main entrance? The east entrance. Did you stop inside of the market house or out side? On the inside of the market house. How long did you maintain your position about that place, inside the market house? I suppose, sir, I was there from between five and seven minutes; I didn't notice particularly. Who was with you while you were there? There was a number of gentlemen there; Mr. Ed Powers, Mr. Ralph Lutterloh, Capt. Tolar, and I think Mr. John Maultsby was there. Any one else? I think Mr. Samuel Hall was near the crowd where I stopped, and Mr. Sykes. What Sykes? I don't know his name, a one-armed man. Sam Hall and the one-armed Sykes? Yes, sir. Did all of them continue standing there as long as you remained in that position? They were there, I don't know that they occupied their position all the time, they were moving around there, more particularly Hall and Sykes, and Maultsby; they were oft to the west end, rather further off than where I was from the others. Rather towards the west end? Rather

towards the centre of the market, near the bell rope. Was that at the time of your arrival? Yes, sir. During the time you were there in the immediate company of Tolar, Ralph Lutterloh, Ed Powers and John Maultsby, did any conversation occurr between you and them or between any person of that number? Yes, sir; I went there mainly to see what was going on, and they were telling me what had taken place; it was something that I had not heard of. With reference to the trial of the man Beebee? Yes, sir. We don't call now for anything that was said in the crowd; was that conversation carried on in an ordinary tone of voice? Yes, sir. Did you see any whispering? I did not, sir, I saw no whispering at all. Could you state positively, whether there was any whispering between those parties at the time you were there or not? If there was I didn't see any. Was there anything about the manner or demeanor of any of those persons there that was calculated to excite suspicion, or to attract attention? I didn't see any sir. Did you remain in that position until Beebee was brought down? No sir, I had moved a little further towards the door, at the time he came down, or at least when the lady was brought down. Were you in that position at the time Mrs. Massey and her daughter came down the steps? Yes, sir, when they came down I moved a little towards the main entrance; I did not know them, I turned around and asked some person if that was the lady. Who accompanied them when they came down? I think Mr. Bond. The town Constable? I think he is; I don't know for certain. What became of Mrs. Massey and her daughter, did you see? They were carried to the carriage by Mr. Bond. Where was the carriage standing? The carriage was standing off in the street near the side walk. Off from what potion of the market house? I think it was standing off near the small arch. Which small arch? The arch towards the south corner. You think it was there? Yes, sir, I didn't notice particularly. Did you see Mrs. Massey and her daughter when they got into the carriage? I saw them get into the carriage, Mr. Bond helped them in. Did any person go from the crowd which was under the market house, or near the market house, to that carriage, while it was standing there? No, sir, I saw no one go to the carriage at all, except Mr. Bond. Did you see any person about the carriage at all, any male person except Mr. Bond? Yes, sir, I saw a colored man, who I supposed was the driver. Was he occupying the driver's seat? Yes, sir. Did you see any white man at all about the carriage? No, sir, I didn't see any particularly, only passing around, you know. Where were you standing sir, at the time the ladies and Mr. Bond came down and went to the carriage? I was standing about three feet, I suppose in five feet, of the main entrance. The east entrance? Yes, sir. And under the market house still? Yes, sir. Who was standing there with you at that time? Mr. Ed Powers, Ralph Lutterloh and Capt. Tolar, and I think Mr. Maultsby. Any body else? There was others that was off around as they generally are in a crowd. I ask you sir, whether Capt. Tolar went to that carriage at all? I dont think he did sir.

Did you notice whether he did or did not? No, sir, I don't think he went, if he had I would have seen him. You were standing with him? Yes, sir, I am certain he did not go. How long a time elapsed, between the ladies getting into the carriage, and the bringing of the man Beebee down stairs? I don't think it was more than five minutes. During that time, between the getting into the carriage, by the ladies, and the bringing down of Archy, were you occupying the same position you were in. Very near the same position. You didn't move out from under the market house? No, sir. Was Capt. Tolar with you? We were all there in a group. The same persons that you have named? Yes, sir, we hadn't come out from under the market house. When did you go out from under the market house? After the boy was brought down. Did you see the boy Beebee when he first made his appearance on the stair steps coming down? Yes, sir, I think he was very near the bottom of the steps when I first saw him. You didn't see him then, when he first made his appearance coming down the steps? No, sir, I think I first noticed him near the bottom. Who was then with him? I think Sheriff Hardie and Mr. Wemyss, and one or two police men, Mr. Faircloth I recognized, and I think there was two others. Do you recollect on which side of him Mr. Wemyss was? I think Mr. Wemyss was on his right sir, Do you remember where Sheriff Hardie was? I think he was in front. Do you remember who was on the prisoners left? I do not sir, there was one more policeman I think, that was along. Were you looking at the prisoner, from the time you have described, till he got to the floor of the market house? Yes, sir. From your position, looking at the prisoner, could you see that bench that runs to the east, or runs to the left of Becky Ben's stall, coming down the market house steps? Yes, sir, that is nearly in front of the stairway. At that time did any one jump up on that bench? No, sir, I didn't see any one jump up on the bench at all. At that time, when the prisoner was being brought down where was John Maultsby? He was off towards the bell rope I think, near the center. Who was with him sir? I think Mr. Sykes, and I believe that Mr. Hall was near there. You think at the time Maultsby was up near the center of the market house, about the bell rope, and with him were Mr. Sykes and Sam Hall—you mean the one armed man? Yes, sir. Any body else there with him, that you remember? There were others there, but I don't recollect who they were. Where is the bell rope? It is about the center of the market house, generally it is fastened to a post. And that is where Maultsby and Sam Hall and Sykes were, at the time the man was brought down stairs? They were near there when I saw them last. I ask you sir, whether you know it as a fact or do not, whether any one jumped up on that bench, at the time the prisoner was being brought down, called Becky Ben's cake bench, and made an exclamation of any sort? No, sir, I heard nothing of that, nor didn't see any one jump on the barrel. That brings them to the foot of the stairs; how large was the crowd at that time; I mean the crowd under the market house, and the crowd outside? Well, sir, I am not prepared to say; at that time under the market house there was not a great many persons:

I don't suppose over twenty-five; there might have been more. Outside do you know how many there were? No, sir, I don't; there was a considerable of a crowd there when I came up. Up to the time of the prisoner's getting to the floor of the market house was there any thing in the crowd that attracted your attention? Nothing at all, sir, only the prisoner; my attention was directed to him. Were there any manifestations of excitement in the crowd? None at all, sir, that I saw. What occurred next, sir? The prisoner come on round the stall there, and passed out between where we were standing and the side walk. When the prisoner got down to the floor of the market house, was your position at that time the same you have described? Yes, the same. Did you alter your position at all? I did not till the prisoner passed me. Did Tolar alter his position, or did he continue to stand there by you? We were all there, Mr. Powers, Mr. Tolar, and Mr. Lutterloh, we all walked out together from under the market. Any thing unusual occur to attract your attention before the prisoner got out of the market house? Nothing at all, sir. Then you walked out of the market house, where did you go then? I walked about the center of the pavement and stopped there. The centre of the pavement, where? The east end of the market house. Near the small arch, or where? About the center of the large arch; I reckon it was a little to the south of the center of the large arch. And these persons went out there with you? Yes, sir. What did you do when you got there? I stopped there; I saw signs there of a mob, and stopped. Did these that you have named stop there too? Yes, sir; then the prisoner Beebee was brought down. Which corner of the main arch did he turn? He turned the right corner, sir. Right corner going east? Yes, sir. In turning that corner did he pass you and Tolar and Ed. Powers upon his right or left? He passed to our right, sir; he passed just around the corner, and he was on the right. That threw you on the prisoner's left? Yes, sir. You say at that time you noticed some signs of excitement; just state what they were? As soon as I got out on the street, on the side walk, I saw a young man, I don't know who he was; I thought he was tight, you know, attempting to strike the prisoner; the sheriff then commenced trying to keep the crowd back, you know; that was the first that I saw, and they still continued going on. Who do you mean by they, the prisoner and the party with him? The prisoner and the men who had him in charge; Mr. Wemyss, I think, was on his right at the time. What was the next you saw? The next I saw they had got with the prisoner near the corner. Near which corner? The south-east corner. What occurred there? They rather halted there, and this young man was carried off, I think; I thought he was drunk, he was carried off by some person, I don't know who, but at least there was a large man come up and got hold of him, and about that time a pistol went off, I suppose it was a pistol, I saw the flash of a pistol, and I saw Mr. Wemyss and the prisoner fall. Did you notice whether the prisoner stumbled or went down before the pistol shot was fired? I don't know, sir, I don't remember. There was some exertions on the part of the prisoner, but there was a considerable crowd around. Now, at the time the pistol shot was fired, just at that time, did you see Tolar? Yes, sir, Capt. Tolar was to my right. Now, at the time the pistol shot was fired, where was Tolar standing? He was standing at the center of the side walk, and a little to the south side of the main arch. Was Tolar on the pavement? Yes, sir. Where were you standing at that time? I was standing a lit-tie in front—to his left, and a little in front nearer the center of the pavement than he was How much to his front were you? Very little, sir; Mr. Lutterloh was a little to my front and to my right, and Mr. Ed. Powers was a little in front of him and to my right; we all walked out there together. Was there anybody nearer to Tolar on the left than you were? I don't think, there was, sir. That was the position of yourself, of Tolar and of the balance of the party, at the instant the pistol was fired? Yes, sir, that was the position. Did Tolar fire that pistol? No, sir, he did not. Have you any doubt about that Mr. Leggett? None in the world, sir. You swear positively and directly that Tolar did not fire the pistol at that time? I do, sir. Was there more than one pistol shot fired? No, sir, there was not. Do you know, sir, who fired the pistol? I do not, sir, I did not see the pistol. I understand you to say that you saw the flash and saw the smoke? Yes, sir. Well, sir, at what point did you see the flash, and from what point did the smoke arise? From where I was standing it was at angle of almost forty degrees, off to my left. Left and rear, or left and front? Left and front. An angle of forty degrees with you or with the market house? With the market house—I mean the flashing was off directly to my left. How far was it from Tolar? I think it was about eight feet from me. Was it further from Tolar than from you? Yes, sir, he was to my right 'ten. How far was it from Tolar? It must have been at least nine feet. Could you tell from the flash and smoke whether the person who fired that pistol was off the pavement or on? He was off the pavement, sir. How far was that flash and smoke off from the deceased man Beebee? I thought it was about three feet, sir. At that time how far was Tolar from the deceased man Beebee? Well, sir, it must have been at least twelve feet—ten or twelve feet; I never measured the distance. Were there many persons between Tolar and Beebee? Yes, sir, I suppose there were about as many as could get on the sidewalk—about fifteen or twenty. Were there persons standing still? No, sir, they were in commotion. Did Tolar advance upon Beebee at all? No, sir, he did not. At the time the pistol was fired, was any remark made by any person to Tolar? I never heard any remark at all. Did you make any remark to Tolar? I asked him or Mr. Powers, I forgot which, I said "did you ever see anything like that?" and I turned off then immediately, and left the place. When you left the place did you leave Tolar standing there? I left him there. Where was Beebee at the time he was shot? He was near the corner of the pavement. Was he nearer the market house, or nearer the center of the pavement, or nearer the outer edge of the pavement? I think he was nearer the outer eastern edge of the pavement. So you turned off and left Tolar, and this party that you were with, standing just there? Yes, sir. Where did you go then? I went then over to Mr. Riley and Burns. How did you go? I went around the rear of the crowd, and struck the walk about half way from the market and Mr. Davis' corner. What Davis' corner? J. B. Davis. Did you see any thing of Davis then? I passed him on the corner. Where is that store of Burns and Riley, to which you went; is it further east than the store of Mr. Davis. Yes, sir. Did you go into the store? Yes, sir. How long did you remain there? Not over ten minutes. What became of you then? Major Burns and myself went back again. Major Burns, of the firm of Riley and Burns? Yes, sir,. Went back where? To where the prisoner was shot. Did you pass the

store of J. B. Davis, on your return? Yes, sir Did you see anything of him then? He was there still. Where was he? He was near the corner—I think he was a little on the walk. Near his own corner? Yes, sir. Did you go up to Beebee the deceased man. Major Burns and myself went up there, and looked at him. At that time did you see anything of Tolar? No, sir, I didn't see Captain Tolar any more that day. Is this all you know about this matter? That is all I know sir.

Cross Examination by the Counsel for the prosecution:

What is your first name? Jordan, sir. Where did you first hear of the attempt of the negro, Archy Beebee to commit violence upon the young lady, Miss Massey? I heard it on the day I reached the market house, the time I first got there. What time that day? I think it was between three and four o'clock. At the time you first went to the market house that day? Yes, sir. Do you swear that you have never heard of that matter in any shape form or way from any person at all until you went to the market house that day? I don't think I had sir; I think perhaps Mr. Henry McDonald mought have spoken to me in regard to it; I think perhaps he may have told me at his store. At what time were you at his store? I went to the market house direct from his store. Are you positively certain that you had never heard of that matter before you heard that from Mr. McDonald? I think that is the first of my hearing of it. Have you thought of it well? Yes, sir. And you swear positively, that you never heard of this matter to the best of your recollection until you got to the market house that day? I don't think I did, as I said before, I think perhaps Mr. Henry McDonald might have spoken to me about it. That was a few minutes before you got to the market house but before that, you swear positively you didn't hear of this? I don't think I had. Aint you certain about it? I think I am certain of it. Where were you on the Sunday previous, the tenth of February, sir? I was at the still yard pretty much all day. How far is the still yard from the market house? I think it must be a quarter of a mile. Down what street do you go to go there? Up Hay street. From the market house? Yes, sir. Do you go along that street to go to Mr. William B. Wright's residence? No, sir, I don't know where William B. Wright lives. Did you ever hear of the spot, the locality of the road where this alleged violence was attempted on that young woman? Not until that day. How far is that spot from your still yard? I don't know, it is, I reckon, a mile. Is it the same direction from the market house that the still yard is? No, sir. Suppose you started from the market house, what street would you take to go towards the locality of this first crime of Archy Beebee; the place where it was alleged that this act was committed? I would go across Eccles bridge. What street? I don't know the name of the street. How far is that point from the market house, weere it is alledged that this rape was attempted? I should suppose it is very nearly a mile, sir; I don't know, I never saw the place but once. When did you see that place? I saw it about a week ago, or two weeks ago, I should think it was. Is that the first time and only time you have seen it? Yes, sir. What was the object of your visit there? I was passing there, and Mr. Lett, I think, showed me the place. Suggested that you should go and see it? No, sir, we were traveling by it. You didn't go to inspect it? No, sir. You say that on the Sunday previous to the day when this alleged ravishing was attempted, you were at the still yard pretty much all day, were you there all day. I don't think I was. What part of the day did you leave there? I think I left there in the evening. About sun down? No, sir, about an hour by the sun. That was the tenth of February? Yes, sir. You had heard nothing of this transaction up to this time? No, sir, I went home from the still house to my supper. Which way did you go to supper? By a north course; it is east of north, I think. Did you hear any thing of this transaction? I heard nothing at all. You went home then? Yes, sir. Did you meet with any acquaintances on the way? No, sir. Meet with no one that you remember speaking to on the way? No, sir. Did you have no visitor at your house? No, sir. Did you stop and take dinner at home? Yes, sir. Was supper ready when you reached there? No, sir. You got home about sun down? Yes, sir. And you staid there until supper? Yes, sir, I remained there all night. You didn't leave the house that evening? No, sir. And you had no visitors there that evening? No, sir, none at all. You are confident that there was none. Yes, sir. And you heard nothing up to that time? I heard nothing up to that time. You stayed in the house all night. Yes, sir. What time did you leave next day? After breakfast. What time do you breakfast generally. About eight o'clock that season of the year. You didn't leave the house before breakfast? I didn't go to the still. When did you leave the house? About eight o'clock, to go to the still. Didn't you leave it before? I might have walked out in the yard. It was the first time you had left your own premises? Yes, sir. Had you had any visitors at your premises that morning? None at all. You heard nothing of this transaction at home? No, sir. When you left your house you went to the still? Yes, sir. Met no acquaintances by the way? No, sir; the first person that I remember being in conversation with that morning, was a man who I had bought out his cooper shop. He said nothing about this? No, sir. Is he the only man you remember meeting that morning? Yes, sir. Did you see him after you got to your still house or before? Before. What is his name? His name is Bryan Leggett; he lives in Robinson County. Is he any relation of yours? Yes, sir. What? He is about a third cousin, I suppose You had some business conversation with him? Yes, sir. And you then stayed, how long at the still house? I stayed there until about eleven o'clock; I then went around to the shop where I had bought out, and then went back home and got dinner. Where is the shop? On North St. How near is that to the market house? I don't recollect sir; I reckon it is prehaps not quite half a mile. From your still house you went to your shop? Yes, sir, You had just bought it out? Yes, sir; bought it out on Saturday. Did you meet any acquaintances on your way to that place? No, sir; up to that time I had very few acquaintances in the place, Did you meet any acquaintances at the cooper shop? No, sir. Did you have the keys to the shop? No, sir. Was it locked? No, sir; there was no key to the shop the shop was open. Were the men at work? No, sir; not at that time. You found the shop deserted? Yes, sir; he had left to go over the river. You left your stilling place at 11 o'clock and went to this cooper shop direct from the stilling place? Yes, sir, Where did you go from, there? I went back to the still. Had no conversation with any one on the way? No, sir.

How long did you remain there then? Until about half past eleven o'clock. You had no conversation with any one at the still? No, sir; I went home to dinner at half past twelve, and after I got my dinner I went by the still, and went on down town. You had seen no one, and had no idea that such a thing had transpired? I knew nothing of it. You went down town on business or pleasure? I went down on business; I went down to see, Mr. Reilly, and Burns, with regard to money matters; about Mr. Leggett for his timber. Were these acquaintances of yours before you went to Fayetteville? No, sir; we were both engaged in the same business at that time. Were they connected with you in any way? No, sir. You went with the purpose of making some money arrangements with them? Yes, sir. In going from your house, I think you said after dinner you didn't go back to your still? Yes, sir. In going from the still to see Messrs Reilly and Burns, who was the man you said you saw and spoke to on this subject? Mr. McDonald; I went immediately to his store first; I owed him for some turpentine that he had bought for me on Saturday. You went to Henry McDonalds as well as to Messrs Reilly and Burns on business? Yes, sir. Did you pass by Henry McDonalds in going to Reilly's and Burns; is that in your route? No, sir; not directly; I passed around Mr. Hinsdale's corner to my right to go to his place. What street were you going down when you turned to your right? Hay St. If you had gone directly straight ahead, you would have got to Reilly's and Burns'? Yes, sir. But before going there you turned to the right and went to McDonald's? Yes, sir. That was just before you went to the market house? Yes, sir. Then your first visit to Reilly and Burns' was made after this shooting took place? Yes, sir. But you say your object in going there was to see them on business. You can't say whether Mr. McDonald spoke to you or not of this matter? It appears to me he did; I think I asked him what all that crowd was doing over there, and I was in a hurry and it was getting late. Did you see Mr. McDonald in the market house in the crowd afterwards? I did not, sir. You went to McDonald and from there directly to the market house? Yes, sir, I got on the pavement, about at the south west corner. Then you went into the arch and walked in about eight feet, I understand you to say? Yes, sir. How long was it after you first got there before Archy was brought down stairs? About ten minutes. When you got there did you march right up the center of the market towards where the bell rope is? Yes, sir. There you encountered who? I found there Mr. Hall, Mr. Lutterloh, Mr. Powers, Capt. Tolar,.Mr. Maultsby, Mr. Sykes and a number of other gentlemen. When you first entered the market house, were Mr. Ed. Powers, Ralph Lutterloh and Capt. Tolar standing together? I think Capt. Tolar was standing off rather to the left. To the left as you went, sir? To the right of me as I went in. Was he standing or sitting? Standing. Nearer the center of the market house or nearer the wall? Nearer the wall on the right. And these other gentlemen were standing near him: Lutterloh and Powers were the nearest to him? Yes, sir. They were the nearest individuals to him that you saw? I think they were about as near as anybody that I noticed. Don't you know that they were nearer than any body else? They might have been as near as anybody else. Were they as near as men usu ally are in public place and conversing together. Yes, sir. Were they carrying on a conversation with one another? I didn't notice. Did you go up and speak with them and shake hands with them? I don't think I shook hands with them at all. Mr. Leggett, were any of these gentlemen armed? If they were, I didn't know it; I did not see any weapons at all. You saw no weapons then? No, sir. Do you know whether any one of those gentlemen was armed around you? I don't know, sir. Did you see any belts on any of them? No, sir. Did you see any protuberances about the breast, chest or back, where a man might wear a pistol? I don't think that I did. Nothing that attracted your attention? No, sir. Neither belt nor pistol? I saw neither. How was Capt. Tolar dressed that day? I think he had on a shawl, and a rather light suit if I am not mistaken. A grey suit? Yes, sir. Did he have on spectacles? I don't think he did. Do you remember whether he had on a cap or hat? A hat. What sort? I think it was rather an ordinary hat, something about the shape of this (a low, flat top crown and narrow brim.) A black hat? Yes, sir. And you saw no weapons up to that time in the hands of anybody? No, sir. Now, when you got to the market house at that time, how many were inside of the market house? I suppose there must have been twenty or twenty-five persons; or there might have been more or less. In going through and passing along the side walk and entering, did you see any groups outside? There was a number of persons at the east end. Were the people scattered all about out there? Yes, sir. How many men do you suppose there were on the outside? I should suppose there were between forty and fifty. Forty or fifty beside the twenty-five inside? No, sir, all together. Do you think there were more inside, or out? I think there was more inside. You will estimate them at the uttermost at twenty-five? Yes, sir. And outside you don't think there were as many? I don't think there was. And it was about the usual number of men standing there when nothing was going on? No, sir, not unless it was in holidays, or something of that sort. There were rather more than the ordinary crowd at the market house; was it more than the ordinary crowd upon public occasions? No, sir, I don't think there was more than I had seen on public occasions. You say after entering there, you stayed until Archy came down, about ten minutes? I should think about ten minutes. And that you stood there with Capt. Tolar until Archy came down? Near there, sir. Capt. Tolar didn't go out of your presence till the negro came down? No, sir. He was not on the outside of the pavement at all during these ten minutes? No. sir. He was not out during five minutes before the negro came down? No, sir. Nor within three minutes of the time the negro came down? No, sir. He was not out within one minute of the time the negro came down? No, sir. He was inside of the market house in your presence? Yes sir. You are certain about that? Yes, sir. And he didn't leave your presence? He didn't leave my presence. While you were standing there with these three gentlemen, Powers, Lutterloh and Tolar, you say you saw Sam Hall, Henry Sykes, and John Maultsby together? Yes, sir. They were standing near the center of the market house? Yes, sir. Near about where the bell rope hangs down in the center of the market house. Yes, sir. And you were not as far back as the center? I was nearer the front. How were you standing, with your face to the west? I was facing at the time to the west? And they were standing at that time to your left, and west and south of you? They were standing in front of me. How many

paces from you? I don't know sir, two or three steps I suppose—four probably. They were standing about in a line with you? Three or four steps back. Did these two groups of gentlemen get together at all? No, sir. When you walked out or when the prisoner came down what became of them? I dont know what became of them. When you last saw them were they standing at that point? Yes, sir. Did you see any of these gentlemen have weapons that day? I did not, sir. Did you see any marks of any weapons about them? I did not. Have you never heard any of this first group of gentlemen say you have mentioned, say since that he had a weapon that day? No sir. Have you heard Ed. Powers or Lutterloh or Tolar say so? No, sir. Have you heard Sam. Hall or Sykes, or Maultsby say since that day, that he had a pistol? No, sir. You neither saw any pistol that day, nor have heard these gentlemen say that they had a pistol or any weapon that day; I understand you swear that positively? Yes, sir. You have been in their society since? I have sir. While you were standing at the point you first went to, when you went into the market house, about eight feet from the entrance near the center, it was while you were standing there that Miss Massey and her mother came down stairs, was it? Yes, sir. Did you turn about to look at them? Yes, sir. Did you move nearer to the arch? Yes, sir, Nearer to the front? Yes, sir. How much nearer? I suppose a couple of paces. You faced about and moved a little to the right and front? Yes, sir, I faced to the left. You moved towards them? Yes, sir. Where did that bring your position? That made me about five or six feet from the main entrance. You were looking towards the foot of the stairs? Yes, sir. And followed them with your eyes as they passed out of the arch? Yes, sir. When you moved your position towards where they were going, what became of Ed. Powers, Ralph Lutterloh and Capt. Tolar? They were there. Were they following? Yes, sir, we all moved on towards the door. You moved together? Yes, sir. Was there any proposition that you should move together—anybody say let us go forward? None at all. It was an unpremeditated movement? Yes, sir. As these ladies came down you faced about and moved towards them? Yes, sir, rather towards them—there was a bench in front of us. Now sir, in moving towards them was Capt. Tolar behind you or before you? Mr. Tolar, I think, was rather behind me, sir. Did you see him then? Yes, sir, he was there as soon as they passed on. Did you see him while you were changing your position, while he was behind you? No, sir. But you know he was just behind you, and when you saw him again he was close to you? He was, when I saw him again. At the moment you were changing your position you lost sight of him? Yes, sir. In moving towards this new position you moved two or three steps? I think that we moved to about six paces from the main entrance. Capt. Tolar, you say, came behind you? Yes, sir. Where were Ed. Powers and Ralph Lutterloh? They were near me, I was in front of them at the time she came down. You stood in the front after you got to the stationary position the second time? Yes, sir. Did you see Tom Powers there that day? I don't know him, sir, if I saw him that day I did'nt know him. You don't recollect seeing that pox marked faced man, (pointing to Mr. Powers?) No, sir. Do you know Monk Julia? No, sir. That man passes by that name, on the left of these is the group, (pointing to Monk Julia,) did you see him that day? I don't know that I did; there was a man about his size, I don't know whether it was him or not. You didn't know him at the time, and you can't say whether this man was there or not? No sir, I could not. When the ladies came down stairs you and Capt. Tolar, and Ed. Powers and Ralph Lutterloh all stood still and let the ladies go out to the carriage? Yes, sir. Did you remain there until the negro came down stairs? Very near that point. How far did you move from it? We stood about there till the negro came down. You saw Miss Massey come out to the carriage? Yes sir. Do you know Mr. Bond? I know him by name. You knew the man that was with them that day was Mr. Bond? Yes, sir. Where did you say this carriage was standing? It was standing off nearly opposite the center of the arch, at the south end of the market. The south arch of the east face? Yes, sir. How far was it from the pavement? It was very near the pavement. You could have stepped from the pavement into the carriage? I think perhaps it was six feet, I didn't notice very particularly. Can't you say with certainty? I can't. Can't you say whether twelve feet? Yes, sir, I don't think it was as far as twelve feet. You think it was about six feet? I should think it was about six. Was the carriage there when you came? Yes, sir. Do you remember noticing it? I don't, but I think it was there. But you don't remember whether you saw it at that time? No, sir. When was the first time you remember seeing it, when the ladies went out? Yes, sir, that was the first time I noticed the carriage. How long did the carriage stand after the ladies went to get into it, before it moved off? It moved off very quick after they got in. As quick as it could be done? I don't know about that. You saw no friend of these ladies go to the carriage and talk to them? I saw no person go to the carriage except Mr. Bond. Then it went off as soon as the ladies got in? I think it did. You didn't see any body go to the carriage except Bond? That was all the male person I saw go to the carriage. Did you see any females? No, sir, except those that got into the carriage. Were your eyes fixed on the carriage all the time? No, sir. You don't pretend to say that others might not have gone to the carriage and you not have seen them? I don't think they did, but they might have. It is within the range of possibility? I dont think any went there. You don't think one or two, or three, or five or six persons in succession could possibly have gone there? No, sir, they could not; I don't think it is possible that one could have gone there without my seeing them. And you say Bond was the only person that went there? He was the only person, and he turned off from the carriage, and the last I saw of him he was passing toward the market house, and the carriage drove off immediately. Bond, when he turned and come back, where did he go to—up into the court room? I think so. Can't you speak with certainty about it? No, sir; I can't. Can't you say whether he went back in the court room? I think he did; I am not positive. I would like you to avoid the use of the word "think"; you may say I can't speak with certainty upon that point, but I don't want you to give your opinions by thinking—you can't say whether he went back or not? No, sir; I

can't. But you have a decided impression that he did go back? Yes, sir. Well now, when Bond was coming from the carriage to go back up the steps, did you see him all the time? No, sir. There were moments when you could not see him? Yes, sir. You are certain you saw him from the time he came down the steps till he left the carriage? Yes, sir. Did you see any one speak to Bond from the time he left the court room and come down stairs to the time he started back? Not that I recollect of. Do you recollect that any one did speak to him? The ladies spoke to him when he left them. Do you recollect that no male person spoke to him? Not that I recollect of. Did you see any male person speak to him? I can't say sir. Well now; while the ladies were at that carriage did Mr. Robert Mitchell go to say anything to them? I didn't see him. Did Mr. Phillimun Taylor go there to speak to him, or was he there at the carriage at all? I didn't see him go at all. Your impression is that he was not? That is my impression. You swear positively. If he went there I didn't see him. Did you see Mr. John Maultsby go up there to speak to these ladies? No, sir. Did you see him speak to Mr. Bond? No, sir. You don't think that Robert Mitchell spoke to the ladies, nor Phillimun Taylor, nor John Maultsby? If they did I didn't see them. You dont think either one of these persons spoke to Bond? If they did I didn't see them sir. You say you didn't know Tom Powers that day? No, sir. But you didn't see any person but Bond speak to the young lady in the carriage, and therefore Tom Powers could not? I didn't see any one speak to the ladies except Mr. Bond. Now, sir; while the ladies were getting into the carriage your eyes and attention, were absorbed by Capt. Tolar all the time : did you loose sight of him at any time while these ladies were getting into the carriage. I suppose I must, my attention was directed to them. Is it possible that Capt. Tolar may have left while you were standing looking at the ladies? Well, I don't think it is, sir. But your attention was not on him all the time? The ladies passed out very quickly, and drove off very quickly, and he was there when I looked around. It could not have been two minutes from the time the ladies came down before they went off, could it? It could not have been more than a minute. During that time your attention was distracted from Captain Tolar? Yes, sir. And you can't say you had your eyes on him, but when you looked back he was there? Yes, sir. Did you see any weapons then? I did not, sir. Capt. Tolar was not out of your immediate attention, then, except when you were changing your position from your first position to the second, and the time the ladies were getting in the carriage? No, sir, he was not. He occupied your attention then from the time you got there until the time Archy came down stairs? Yes, sir, he was in the crowd He didn't go out of the market house? No, sir. Do you swear positively he was not standing in the middle of that parement five minutes before Archy came down stairs? Yes, sir. Do you say he was not standing there for three minutes? Yes, sir. For one minute? Yes, sir. You were standing together when Archy started down stairs? Yes, sir. Mr. Leggett, did you have a pistol that day about your person? No, sir. Did you have any weapons about your person? No, sir, I didn't have a pocket knife. You had no weapons of any description? None at all, sir. We are approaching the point when Archy Beebee came down stairs and lost his life; did that crowd during that time grow any? Yes, sir, there was more persons about the time the boy was shot. In the ten minutes you were there the crowd had gathered? Yes, sir. How much? I think there must have been seventy five persons there. You think that from thirty to thirty-five persons had come up there within the ten minutes? Yes, sir. That these persons came inside or stood outside of the market house? They were standing outside. Did any of them come in? Some might have come in, but I didn't pay any particular attention to them. Then you saw the door open and Archy come down stairs? No, sir, I don't know about the door. You couldn't see that? No, sir. As Archy came down stairs, were you facing east or west, or south-east? I don't recollect, at that time I think I was looking rather west. Your back was rather towards the front of the entrance? Yes, sir. Was Capt. Tolar fronting you? Yes, sir. You were standing around in the same circle, and you had your back towards the east, and he had his back towards the west, and those other gentlemen were right and left of you? Yes, sir. When this negro came down stairs the first you saw of him he was pretty nearly down? About the bottom step, sir. Did you see Sheriff Hardie before you saw the negro? Yes, sir, Sheriff Hardy was in front. Did you see him come out first and look around? No, sir, I did not. Did you see him come down stairs first, and beckon to those coming after him? No, sir. Didn't he do that? If he did I didn't see him. Have you no impression about it? No, sir. The first recollection you have of seeing Hardie that you have, he was in front of the negro as he came down stairs? Yes, sir. Immediately in front? Yes, sir. And Wemyss was on his right? Yes, sir, there were three or four other policemen. Mr. Faircloth was one of them, the other two I don't that I know them. And they were on one side or the other of Archy as he came down the steps? Yes, sir. Did you notice whether Archy had on his hat or not? I don't recollect. Don't you recollect that he had his hat on as he came down the steps? I am of the impression that he had a hat on. Your impression is that his head was covered? Yes, sir. Did you notice how Mr. Wemyss had him tied? No, sir, I didn't. While he was coming down the steps, there was no noise you say? Nothing at all. No outcries? No, sir. No rushing? No, sir. No suppressed hum of indignation? None in the world. No voice or disturbance whatever; nothing that indicated a mob? No, sir. Was the crowd perfectly still? Not perfectly still; they were walking about and persons were talking. You heard the ordinary hum of conversation? Yes, sir. No rush? No, sir. No eagerness to see the prisoner? No, sir, none at all. They didn't gather and turn their faces and move towards the prisoner, as he came down, as a crowd usually does? The first move I saw was made when he passed around the end of the bench; there was of course some curiosity, nothing more than that. How was that manifested? The press on the outside to get up on the side walk. That was when the negro had passed out of the arch? Yes, sir, about the time he got to the corner. The first you noticed was after he came to the foot of the steps and got out of the arch? Yes, sir, that brought the window right in my view. Do you mean the small arch? Yes, sir. That brought the small arch on your right? Yes, sir. And then you faced about east? Yes, sir. And as the prisoner came from the foot of the steps to the main arch coming out, you noticed the crowd through the small arch? Yes, sir, and the crowd was

pressing up towards the market house. Did you see any man make a rush, or attempt to put hands upon the prisoner before he got to the entrance of the arch turning out? I did not, sir. Were you in the house at that time? I was. How far were you from the south corner of the main arch, as the negro turned around, when he come out? About six or seven feet. You saw no rush? No, sir. You saw no struggle of the policemen to hold the prisoner? No, sir. He had got outside on the pavement before you saw anything of that sort? That was the first I saw. You didn't hear any one demand the prisoner? No sir. You didn't hear any one use any expression of that character? No, sir, I didn't. You were standing inside of the market house, I understood until the negro got out? Just about the time he passed the corner. Do you mean by passing the corner that he passed the main arch? Yes, sir. You didn't move until he was in the main arch? Yes, sir, we moved on out about the center of the pavement? You moved about the center of the pavement? Yes, sir, Do you swear positively that before that time you had noticed no individual make any demonstration of hostility towards this negro, Archy Beebe? None in the world sir; I saw nothing at all that indicated a mob until after he got out. Nothing that indicated individual hostility? No, sir. It was like any other crowd and any other prisoner being brought out except that there was less curiosity manifested than usual until Archy got out side on the brick pavement? No, sir, no less curiosity than I have seen in such a crowd there, that was the largest crowd I had ever seen in Fayetteville, during any occasion of that sort before. But you say there was some curiosity manifested? Yes, sir. But that curiosity was entirely on the outside? No, sir, there was some under. Then the persons under the market house did turn towards the prisoner? They moved out on the pavement. Did they move on simultaneously with yourself and Ed. Powers, and Ralph Lutterloh, and Capt. Tolar? Yes, sir. Did you see Sam. Hall, Henry Sykes and John Maultsby in that movement? No, sir, I think they were going the other way. Why do you think they were going the other way? Because I didn't see them going out. You know that you and Ed. Powers and Ralph Lutterloh and Capt. Tolar moved out, and that crowd moved along with you, and that it was a simultaneous move of curiosity, as you say? Yes, sir, a movement of curiosity. Now, if I understand you, Beebee was in the arch when the crowd turned before you started to move out? He was just about the corner. You were behind him? Yes, sir. Were you immediately behind him? No, sir, we were off to his left. He had his back towards you, and you were to his left? Yes, sir. Up to that time Capt. Tolar hadn't been on the pavement? Not that I know of. Then you went out on the pavement? Yes, sir. You went into the rush that was made on the prisoner, didn't you? No, sir. Didn't you individually go out? We walked out there. There was some sort of a rush made on the prisoner? That was after we walked out there. I am talking about before you went out; the crowd moved on the prisoner? Some part of it, there was but one man that I saw. You didn't see any of the crowd in a state of agitation. Not until after the pistol was fired. How long was it from the time that Archy Beebee turned out of the arch to the time the pistol fired, was it a minute? Yes, sir. Was it two? No, sir. You don't suppose it was two? No, sir. And you say Captain Tolar didn't move out of the arch until Archy had got out? He moved out about the same time. He had been out two minutes before he was shot? No, sir. I want to know, just after you got out side with Capt. Tolar, Ed Powers and Ralph Lutterloh, whether you all stood perfectly still? I don't think we were perfectly still. Did you face south or north? South. Towards the prisoner? Yes, sir. Then did you stand still or more about? Stood still. You stood there till the pistol was fired? Yes, sir. And the others did? Yes, sir. And you were in front of Capt. Tolar, to his left? Yes, sir. And the others were a little to his front? They were to my right, a little to Capt. Tolar's front. How tall are you? I am six feet two inches. How tall is Capt. Tolar? I don't know, sir. What would you judge from his appearance? Six feet, I should suppose. You are a taller man than he? Yes, sir. And you were standing by him, and a little to his front? Yes, sir. And you were standing still? Yes, sir. Looking on? Yes, sir. And you say these other two gentlemen to his right and front were still? Yes, sir. How tall a man is Ed Powers? I don't know, sir. You have seen him; is he below the medium height, is he as tall as Capt. Tolar? No, sir. How much shorter, is he a very small man? He is a man, I suppose, weighing about a hundred and sixty pounds. About his height? I suppose he is about five feet eight or ten inches; I could not say for certain. He is not a small man? No, sir. How tall is Ralph Lutterloh? He is about the same sized man as Ed Powers. And you say you are six feet two inches, and you say Capt. Tolar is about six feet? Yes, sir. And you were standing still in that crowd that day, in the midst of the hottest excitement that there was, and you saw no action but upon the part of one man? No, sir, I saw nothing that indicated a mob. Did you see John Maultsby after you got out side of the arch at all? I don't recollect that I did. Do you recollect that you didn't? I don't think I saw him. Have you any impression about it? I have no impression of seeing him. Did you see Sam Hall or Henry Sykes out on the pavement after you got out there? No, sir. You have tried to recollect in connection with these things all that you can about it? Yes, sir. After Archy turned out of the arch and started down that pavement, and you got to the position where you could see, you are a tall man and could see very well in the crowd? Yes, sir. Did any body demand the prisoner? No, sir. Did you see any man strike at him with a knife? I saw a man strike at him, but I didn't see a knife. What sort of a man was he? He was a small man. Do you recognize the prisoner, Monk Julia, as the man? I don't recognize him. Was he a man about that size? About his size. Anything of that description? I could not say. You saw a small man, about his size, striking at him with no knife? If he had a knife I didn't see it; he was striking with his fist. That was just after Archy got out of the market house? No, sir, he had got at least six feet towards the south east corner. Now, between the time he was going that six feet, did you see any assault made on him? I saw nothing except the crowd was up very close, and the Sheriff was making them stand

back; that was all I saw. What was the Sheriff saying? I think, as well as I can recollect, he told them to stand back. Did you see his club? No, sir. Did you hear it strike? No, sir. Did you hear the noise of a knife striking out of any one's hands, and hear it fall on the pavement? No, sir. Didn't you see the policemen trying to keep the crowd back with their clubs, at the time the boy was shot? No, sir. You saw no struggle to keep the crowd back until the time he was shot? No, sir, only one, this man that I was telling you about. He was striking at him? Yes, sir. That was immediately before the shooting? It was a very few moments. Had the man stopped striking at him when you heard the shot? Yes, sir, I didn't see him; I think some body carried him off. Mr. Leggett, when did you first perceive that the crowd was making an assault upon the prisoner? After he had got out about six feet from the corner of the main arch. Until that time you had no idea of an assault? None in the world. Had no reason for thinking so? No, sir. Had never heard it? No, sir. Had never formed any part in any combination for the purpose of bringing him to punishment? No, sir. You swear it positively? Positively. And until the instant before he was shot, you had no idea, from the conduct of that crowd, that they intended to assail him? No, sir, I had not. Did you see Tom Powers there at all, that day? If I did, I didn't know him. Did you see any man you recognized as the man they called Tom Powers? I don't recollect that I did. Do you know John Jackson? No, sir. Who was standing nearest to you and Capt. Tolar, and Ralph Lutterloh and Ed Powers, in that crowd? At what point, sir? At the point when you were standing in the middle of the pavement, before the shooting took place. I don't recollect. Do you recollect seeing any one in the crowd at that time, that you knew? No, sir. Do you know Sam Phillips? Yes, sir. Did you see him there? No, sir. Don't you recollect seeing any one in that crowd you know, besides the gentlemen you have named? At present I do not. Up to that time you had seen no weapon in the possession of any one? I had not, sir. After this negro left the arch which way was your face turned? Turned eastward. After the negro came out side of the arch, and you took a stationary position in the centre of the pavement, which way did you look, towards the prisoner? Yes, sir. Were your eyes on Capt. Tolar, when they were turned toward the negro? No, sir, not immediately. He was a little to your right and rear? Yes, sir. Place me where Capt. Tolar was, relatively, so that we can exactly understand it.

(Witness places the Counsel to his right about two feet, and to his rear about one foot, as indicating the relative positions of Tolar and himself.)

And your attention was directed to the prisoner Beebee, from the time he left the arch until he was shot? Yes, sir. You say that from the time the negro left the arch until the time he was shot, you were looking towards him? Yes, sir. And the first assault you saw was this small man attempting to strike with a knife? No, sir, I didn't see a knife. An attempt to strike him? Yes, sir. You saw no weapons that day in the hands of any one? I did not, sir. Did you see the negro fall while you were looking at him? No, sir, I didn't see him fall they blundered or stumbled, or something. Did you see whether he fell down? I don't think he fell entirely down. You think he fell pretty nearly down and was recovered by the officers? Yes, sir. And it was after that, that the shot was fired? Yes, sir. About that time was it that this person struck at him? Yes, sir. When was the shot fired? He had took about one step after that in front—it might have been two steps. You say you had no weapon there that day? No, sir, no weapon at all sir. Where was the man standing who fired that shot? He was standing to my left and front. You were standing then a little to the south of the center of the main arch, in the middle of the pavement? Yes, sir. Your face towards the south, and this man was to your left and front? Yes, sir. Can you take this diagram and indicate to me the position you think that man occupied who fired that pistol—I want to know where a line drawn from him directly east and west, would have hit the market house, how far from the corner? Very near the corner. A foot? Not more than that. You think he was how far from the edge of the pavement? About five feet. Where did you see the smoke? About three feet from the prisoner. You say as I understand you now, after the prisoner came out of the arch, he moved two or three steps before anything was done? Yes, sir. Then about that time you saw him blunder, and this effort made to strike him by some one? Yes, sir. That he took one or two steps after that? One or more. One or more might embrace a hundred. I can't say sir, there was such a crowd. It was not instantly after he rose? No, sir. You think he took a step or two or three? It might have been I am not positive about that. Still going towards the guard house? The police and Sheriff were still pressing on towards the guard house. And he moved one or two or three steps after that? He moved near the corner. And then he was shot? Yes, sir. And the man who shot the pistol stood out about five feet from the edge of the pavement? It must have been about five feet sir. And a line drawn twelve inches from the corner of the market house or the east face, directly east and west would have struck the man who fired the pistol? Yes, sir. Was Archy on the pavement or off the pavement, when the pistol was fired? He fell on the pavement. Didn't I understand you to say you thought the man was about three feet from him, who shot? Where I saw the smoke was about three feet. And you think the man must have been about five feet? Yes, sir. Did you see Archy after he was shot? Yes, sir. Was he shot in the back of the head sir? I never saw the wound, I saw him about ten minutes after he was shot. You didn't see where the wound was? No, sir, Major Burns and myself went there and stood a very short time and passed off. When that pistol was fired Archy's back was towards the man who fired it? I can't say. You think he was going toward the guard house? Yes, sir. And the person who fired it was in the position

you described, but you can't say whether his back was towards the man who fired? No, sir, I cannot. Immediately after this affair, or before this affair, you heard nobody in the crowd cry out kill him? No, sir. You heard no body cry out " shoot him, shoot him"? No, sir. You heard neither of those? No, sir. No, curses? Yes, sir, this man who was striking was cursing. What was he saying? He was using profane words, but I don't recollect his expression. He was the only man you saw make any attempt at that time? Yes, sir. Did you see Capt. Tolar after the pistol fired? Yes, sir. Immediately? Yes, sir. You didn't see him when the pistol was fired? No, sir. Your eyes were towards the boy Beebee? Yes, sir. But immediately afterwards you turned and looked at him? At the time the pistol fired I turned around, and made a remark. And Capt. Tolar was standing there then? Yes, sir. How long did you stay? I moved off immediately. You just turned and said " did you ever hear anything like that," and turned right off? Yes, sir. But you are confident Capt. Tolar was there? I know he was. You saw him? I saw him. You saw him when you turned? Yes, sir. It was an instantaneous turning but you know that he was standing there, and the pistol was not fired from behind you? I know it was not. Didn't you feel a curiosity to find out who it was who fired the pistol? I wanted to get away from there. Why? Because I was afraid there was to be other shots, I didn't know who was shot, at the time I thought Mr. Wemyss was shot, he fell with Archy. Did any body in the crowd attempt to arrest the man who shot the pistol? No, sir. Didn't you turn your glance in that direction, where the pistol shot came from, and see who fired the pistol? I turned my eyes in that direction. Your glance was attracted by the shot? Yes, sir. Were you not more curious to see who fired the shot, than you were to see where the smoke was? No, sir, I was more anxious to get away than anything else. You left hurriedly? Yes, sir. You had but a momentary glance around, and then went away. Yes, sir, I turned around and said " did you ever see anything like that " and went off. You wanted to get out of the crowd? Yes, sir. You made this momentary speech and then moved off? Yes, sir. And you went directly by Ichabod B. Davi's store? Yes, sir. You went and got Mr. Burns, and you saw Mr. Davis standing on his corner? I went to Mr. Burns. Didn't he come back with you? Yes, sir, he asked me if I would not go back, I refused once, and he insisted; and we went back together. And you saw Mr. Davis on the corner, when you went back? Yes, sir. How many stores did you pass going down to Major Burns? I think there were three or four. Who else was out of their stores standing on the street? I don't recollect seeing any one, except Mr. Cook, and there was some one with Mr. Davis, I don't recollect who. Some one with Mr. Davis? Yes, sir, a man standing talking to him. Can't you say who it was? I don't recollect. Who else did you see besides Mr. Davis passing along the street? I don't recollect who else beside Mr. Davis, when we this back he was alone. Who else did you see isitate walk? I didn't notice any one in panate ar- How came you to notice him? He was ed, upon on the corner, and being well acquainted with him I noticed him, I don't think there was anybody else there. There was a pistol fired in the most public part of town, in front of three or four stores, and there was but one man standing out in the street? I don't recollect but him. How often have you compared notes with Mr. Davis upon that point. We never have compared at all. Didn't you compare notes with him last night? No, sir. Didn't you stand upon the corner of this street, in the City of Raleigh, in the presence of one of this Court, and have a conversation with him about this testimony? I might have conversed with him, but not comparing notes. Did you not know that Mr. Davis was going to swear that he was standing right at the corner, before his own store? Yes, sir. How long have you known it? I have known it three weeks, I reckon. Didn't you know he was going to swear that you passed him while he was standing on that corner? No, sir. Didn't you know that he was going to swear that you passed back by him when he was standing on that corner? I think I did. You knew he was going to swear to that before he came here? Yes, sir. And you recollect that one single man, and no other, that you passed along the whole of that passage, before three or four stores, in an excited time? He was the only man that I noticed in passing by. Now pray, sir, what was the character of your conversation with Mr. Davis with regard to his testimony? I don't recollect, sir. You were conversing about it? I don't know, sir, that there was any particular conversation on any particular point. Didn't he tell you what he had sworn to. I don't know but he did. Didn't he tell you a good part of what he had sworn. The most he told me was about the man he had hung up by the thumbs. He spoke of making some correction in his testimony on that point. Didn't he speak to you of any other part of his testimony? Yes, sir, about his location; I think that is about all. And you knew that before? I knew his position. He had told you he swore that you saw him there, that you passed by him while he was there? He told me, I think, he swore that I passed by him coming down. He told you that last night? · Yes, sir. Now I wish you would try and recollect some one else that you passed? I don't recollect; there is no doubt I passed others. Did you have any conversation with him then? I think I had, when I went up. Which do you call up? When I went up there to the market house with Mr. Burns, we had no conversation when I went down, except I think I told him there was some one killed. You had no further words? We might have had other conversation, I don't recollect. How long was it before you got back to the market house? Five minutes, perhaps, I don't recollect the time. You saw no weapons there that day? None at all. And you saw no excitement except the immediate attack? I saw but one pistol that day. I understood you to say you had seen no pistol? I said I didn't see a pistol in that crowd. Major Burns had one lying on his desk. Did he take it off or put it on? It was lying there. Right before him? No, sir. When you left the crowd to go down to Major Burns, did he go along with you from the crowd? No, sir, he was not there at all. You found him at his store when you went in? Yes, sir. Where was his pistol? It was lying on the desk. Was he sitting behind the desk? No, sir, he was behind the counter. Did you examine the pistol? No, sir. What became of it? An't know, sir. Do you know who put it there? No, Major Burns put it in his pocket when he feet, t. I talked more to him about the matter saw none else; we didn't stay but a very few close, as

moments where the boy was dead. You were perfectly sober that day, Mr. Leggett? Yes, sir. You are not in the habit of getting on a spree? No, sir. You know exactly what happened? Yes, sir. If you are not mistaken, it was not on account of being confused by liquor? No, sir, I am not mistaken. You were perfectly yourself that day? I was, sir. Can you name any other person who was in that crowd at any time that day, besides these you have named? I don't recollect that I can, I saw but very few colored persons there, I don't know that I can name any other person that I could call to mind just now. I understand when you first got there you found Tolar, and Ralph Lutterloh, and Ed. Powers with him? Yes, sir. They didn't go there with you? No, sir. You were with that group until you left? Yes, sir, it was about ten minutes I think I was in the group. You never saw John Maultsby, nor Henry Sykes, nor Sam Hall, after the first few moments, after you entered, when they were standing near the center of the market? No, sir, I never saw them any more that I can recollect of. You swear that you know of no combination, arrangement or agreement, of any sort, between any set of men to take off this negro? None in the world. I understand you to say you heard no outcry in that crowd that day at all, such as "kill him, shoot him." I did not hear anything of the sort at all. You didn't hear any cries at all, any excited cries, in any form, either from the police in resisting the press, or the crowd in pressing on him? Nothing more than the police keeping the crowd back. What did they say? They were just crying out, "stand back," and "get out of the way." Were the crowd crying out at all then? No, sir, I heard no cry. You were right in the crowd, if there had been any cry, you would have heard it? Yes, sir. You are not deaf? No, sir. Did you ever hear Mr. Davis was a little deaf in his left ear? No, sir. How long have you known him? About four months. You never heard him complaining of deafness? No, sir.

Re-direct examination by the Counsel for the accused.

Mr. Leggett, you were examined about this matter before the coroner's inquest, the day after the killing of Archy Beebee? Yes, sir. Was the testimony which you gave there with reference to your knowledge about the shooting, in substance the same that you have given here to-day?

The Counsel for the prosecution objected to the question.

The Counsel for the accused said he did not care to press it.

Re-direct examination resumed:

You have been asked the question whether you have not compared notes with Mr. Ichabod Davis about this matter, and I understood you to reply that you have talked over the matter with Mr. Davis. Yes, sir. Has any talk that you have had with Mr. Davis on this subject, changed or influenced your testimony in any degree? None at all, sir. How long a time do you think elapsed from your first moving out to the pavement to the shooting of the boy Archy? Not more than two minutes. How long a time do you think it was, from the time when he was brought down and reached the market house floor, until he was shot? As near as I could come to it, five minutes, I had no watch. You speak of this matter, dividing it off in distinct periods, do you mean to say the whole thing occurred as fast as the police carried him on, that it occurred almost as fast as a person could walk? That is about the way they moved. How long had you been acquainted with Capt. Tolar before this matter occurred? I can't say, sir, but a short time.

What was the nature of your acquaintance with
him, were you intimately acquainted? No, sir.
Cross-examination resumed by the Counsel for
the prosecution:
Are you a Mason? No, sir, I am not.
Re-direct examination resumed, by the Counsel for the accused:
It was then a mere passing acquaintance? Yes,
sir. Was your acquaintance in the town of Fayetteville at all extensive, at that time? No, sir.
You speak of having known or having seen particularly the young men, Sam Hall, Ed. Powers,
Ralph Lutterloh, Maultsby, &c., had you known
them long? I had known Maultsby perhaps longer than any of the rest, he had been hauling
rosin for me. Was there any reason why you
know those others better than the generality of
the citizens of the town of Fayetteville? Yes,
sir. What are those reasons? Mr. Powers was
about the second man I got acquainted with, being a merchant, not a great ways from my still.
Lutterloh was the same. Living right in the vicinity of Powers? Yes, sir. And Sam Hall?
He lived in the immediate vicinity. How far do
they live from your still? About two hundred
yards. In coming from your still up Hay street,
you have to pass the corner of the place where
young men resort? Yes, sir. So you got acquainted with them earlier than you did any one
else, in the town of Fayetteville? Yes, sir.
For that reason your attention was attracted to
them more particularly? Yes, sir.
On motion the Commission adjourned to meet
on Monday, August 19th, at 11 A. M.

RALEIGH, N. C., Aug. 19th, 1867, 11 A. M.
The Commission met pursuant to adjournment.
Present: All the members of the Commission,
the Judge Advocate, the Counsel for the prose-
cution, all the accused and their Counsel.
The testimony of Mr. J. G. Leggett, taken on
Saturday the 17th instant, was read.
On page 154, 1st column, the following question and answer were omitted, by the recorder.
Was he striking with his fist, by a blow straight
from the shoulder, or by a downward blow? By
a downward blow.
The proceedings of Saturday having been read,
with the above addition, were then approved.
Mr. Phillips, one of the Counsel for the accused
said:
"May it please the Court; before we proceed,
we wish to make a statement to the Court, and
receive such information as may be proper that
we should receive, with regard to the matter,
that took place here upon Saturday. At the close
of the examination of witness, Leggett, we understand that he was arrested, and has since been
held in close custody.
Now, professionally, we have no interest in
what questions there may be, between the United
States and Mr. Leggett, as an individual; what
breach of the law he may have committed, or
may be charged with committing, is a matter, I
say, in which, professionally, we are not interested; but we are interested in his character as a
witness, in the effect that the treatment of one
of the witnesses for the defence may have, upon
the others, still to be summoned for the defence.
That a witness for the defence, upon closing his
testimony; should be arrested and placed in custody, is of course well calculated to intimidate
the other witnesses for the defence. I feel assured that the United States desires that the prisoners here, shall have the benefit of the same sort
of trials that they would have in any court in the
country; and more than that, if I may be permitted to say so, I feel fully satisfied, by the

personal constitution of this court, that they are
personally desirous that these prisoners—what
ever their judgement may be, upon them, when
the case has been made out, shall have a fair trial,
a trial with which the community at large may
be satisfied I say that under these impressions
we wish to be assured, or wish to have some assurance conveyed that may effect, or remove
rather, the effect already produced upon our witnesses, by the manner in which this gentleman
has been treated. We wish to know why he has
been arrested, if it be compatible with the public
interest, and that he has not been arrested for any
purpose of weakening the cause of the defence of
the prisoners here upon trial."
The Judge Advocate said:
"On behalf of the Court: I wish to say, regarding the arrest of Mr. Leggett, that it is a
matter with which the court has no concern whatever. Mr. Leggett was arrested upon an order
from General Sickles, issued sometime since, and
held in my hands simply to allow Mr. Leggett to
give in his testimony before he was arrested."
Mr. Phillips:
"It has this peculiarity about it. We had other witnesses under subpoena here who were arrested; the order come for their arrest, and was carried out before they were placed upon the witness
stand. The manner in which Mr. Powers and
Lutterloh, and others were arrested, has not affected our testimony at all and we did not question
the transaction at all. Leggett, it seems, was ordered to be arrested at the same time. If he had
been arrested then, we would have had no cause
of complaint. But certainly if Powers and Lutterloh and the others had not been arrested, and if
each one of them, as be closed his testimony, had
been arrested, what would have been the effect
upon the rest of the witnesses, that were coming
upon the defence. It is the manner which has produced an injury to the defence. which an explanation may be able to retrieve."
The Judge Advocate:
"The gentleman has assumed what, he will pardon me for saying, he does not really know—that
the order for the arrest of Mr. Leggett was issued
at the same time the order was given for the arrest of Powers and Lutterloh. I don't know that
it behooves either the counsel for the prisoners, or
the Judge Advocate, or this Court, to censure
General Sickles for what he may choose to do in
this matter. I stated it was a matter with which
the Court had nothing to do, and I reiterate that
statement."
The Counsel for the prosecution remarked:
"May it please the Court, I think it is necessary to make a few remarks upon this matter, because I believe that I am more responsible than
any one else, for the fact of Mr. Leggett's arrest,
shortly after his testimony was taken. At the
commencement of this case, I found that several
witnesses, summoned by the defence, were, in our
opinion, implicated in the felony, alleged in the
charge; and suggested to the Judge Advocate that
as some of them were arrested, it would perhaps
be well not to arrest Mr. Leggett, until after his
testimony was given. The object of the suggestion
is evident; and it was to avoid even the appearance of terrifying or intimidating the witnesses.
But I must say—and in this assertion I am sure
my brethren of the bar, who appear for the defence, will sustain me,—that it is not unusual even
in a civil court, where a judge becomes satisfied
that a witness on the stand has perjured himself,
for him to order from the bench the immediate arrest of that witness, and there is no judge in this
State, nor out of this State, who would hesitate
for a single moment, to order the immediate arrest of a witness, if he became convinced, upon

such witness giving in his testimony, that he was himself implicated in the felony, then on trial.

This, however, was not the case with Mr. Leggett, for in reality his arrest had been ordered long before he was summoned as a witness, and had nothing to do with his evidence."

The Counsel for the accused:

"With regard to witnesses being arrested in civil courts. I think my brother Harwood will not say that he ever knew of a case in which a judge ordered the arrest of a man from the bench, while the jury was present trying a case. Judge Caldwell, one of our most eminent criminal judges, was so sensitive of the effect that any action of that sort would have upon the jury, that when he saw, as he thought, a case of notorious perjury before him, he whispered to the officer of the court, and told him to carry the witness, after he had left the stand, out into one of the jury rooms, and await the conclusion of the trial, in such a manner as it would not be seen by the jury. It is to the detriment, and it seems to me to the desparagement of all judgment, to arrest a man in the face of a jury."

The Commission was cleared for deliberation, and after some time so spent the doors were reopened, and the Judge Advocate said:

"I am desired by the Court to state that the witness, Jordan G. Legget, was arrested by an order from Gen. Sickles, for complicity in the murder of Archy Beebee, on the eleventh day of February, one thousand eight hundred and sixty-seven. That the Court knew nothing of his arrest till it had taken place; that the Court knows nothing of any contemplated arrest of any other party in connection with this affair."

Mr. Tolar, one of the defendants, stepped forward and swore to the following affidavit, to-wit:

MILITARY COMMISSION,
Raleigh, N. C., Aug. 19, '67.

STATE OF NORTH CAROLINA, }
COUNTY OF WAKE. }

United States }
   vs. }
William J. Tolar, }
Thomas Powers, }
David Watkins. }

William J Tolar makes oath that he is advised and believes that Dr. — Kirk, Surgeon of the Post of Fayetteville, North-Carolina, and Francis Kunstler, First Sergeant of Co. K 8 N. Y. Infantry, on duty at said Fayetteville, are material witnesses for him in this case.

That he expects to prove by said Dr. Kirk that in obedience to an order of his military superior he, (said Kirk,) about the — day of August, A. D., 1867, exhumed the body of Archy Beebee, alias Archy Warden, and upon examination of said body, extracted from the skull one certain leaden bullet, which said leaden bullet he (said Kirk) delivered to Francis Kunstler, first sergeant as aforesaid, and that he expects to prove by Francis Kunstler, first sergeant as aforesaid, that the said leaden bullet delivered to him a aforesaid, was brought by him, said Francis Kunstler, from Fayetteville aforesaid, and was by him, Francis Kunstler, said first sergeant, given into the hands of Robert Avery, 1st Lieut. 44th U. S. Infantry, the Judge Advocate of this Military Commission.

Sworn to and subscribed, this 19th day of Aug., A. D., 1867, before Robert Avery, 1st Lieut. 44th U. S. Infantry, and Judge Advocate Military Commission.

(Signed:)   W. J. TOLAR.

The Counsel for the accused:

"On that we ask the Court to order that the witnesses therein named, Surgeon Kirk, and first

sergeant Kunstler, be summoned by the Judge Advocate."

The Court ordered the witnesses to be summoned.

MRS. LUCY J. DAVIS, a witness for the defence, having been first duly sworn, testified as follows:

Examined by the Counsel for the accused.

What is your name? Lucy J. Davis. What is the name of your husband? Dr. James Davis. Where do you reside? In Fayetteville. How long have you resided in Fayetteville? About eight years. Were you in Fayetteville on the day Archy Beebee, or Archy Warden, was killed? Yes, sir. At the time Archy Beebee was killed where were you? At that window, (on the diagram the east window of the store marked "the store of R. O. and J. H. Ellis," facing north.) From that point did you see any thing of Archy Beebee? Yes, sir. Where was he at the time you first saw him? He was on the pavement, and about opposite the center of the southern arch, upon the east side. Did you see him at the time he was shot? Yes, sir. Where were you then? I was right at that window, (as above.) Was that window raised? Yes, sir. Were you looking out of it or leaning out? I was looking out of it. Your body was on the inside and you were looking out of it? Yes, sir. What do you take to be the distance from that window to the point where you saw Archy Beebee when he was shot? I should think it was a hundred feet. Did you have a distinct view of him? Yes, sir, I saw him plainly; I saw his features and all: I never saw him before. Did you know him at that time? No, sir. Who was he in the custody of? Mr. Hardie had him. Is your acquaintance very extensive in Fayetteville? Tolerably so. You then saw where he was standing at the time he was shot? Yes, sir. Point out his position at the very moment he was shot? As near as I could judge, about there. (About opposite the centre of the south east corner of the market house.) Was he on the pavement or off? He was on the pavement. Was he nearer to the market house wall, nearer the centre, or nearer the edge of the pavement? Nearer the edge, I should think. Did you see who shot him? No, sir, I didn't see who shot him; I didn't know the one who shot him Did you see the man who shot him? No, sir, I saw the smoke of the pistol. Where did the smoke arise, from what point? About there, (a point off the pavement about three feet, and to the left and a little to the rear of Beebee.) Was the smoke rather behind or rather in front of Beebee? A little to one side. A little to the left? Yes, sir. You say you didn't see the person who shot the pistol? No, sir. But you saw the smoke and it arose from that point? Yes, sir. Did you know Capt. Tolar at that time? Yes, sir. Where was he standing? About ten feet back from Beebee. On the pavement or off? On the pavement. Nearer to the centre than the out side? Yes, sir. So Capt. Tolar at that time was standing back upon the pavement, about ten feet from Beebee, and nearer the centre of the pavement than the outer edge of the pavement? Yes, sir. Have you any doubt about that ma'am? No, sir. You were not in that crowd at all? No, sir. Were you excited that day? No, sir. You were looking down upon the crowd? Yes, sir. And that Tolar was at the point you have stated? Yes, sir. You knew him well? Yes, sir. Is there any possibility about your being mistaken about his position? No, sir, there is no possibility. I think I understood you to say you had known Tolar before that day? Yes, sir. How long before had you known him? I saw him once about two years ago. And you know him then? Yes, sir. Was there any acquaintance existing between yourself and Capt. Tolar? None at all. Between your husband and Capt. Tolar? None at all. A mere passing acquaintance? Yes, sir.

Cross-examination by the Counsel for the prosecution:

Mrs. Davis, do you remember what hour of the day it was that Archy Beebee was killed? I should think about three o'clock as near as I can recollect. How long had you been standing at the window before he was killed? I put up the window when I heard the noise. I was sitting at the large window, I had been at the large window I reckon fifteen minutes. That is further from the market house than the small one? No, sir, it is nearer than the small one. You had been sitting at the large window about fifteen minutes? Yes, sir. And you went to the small window and raised it, when you heard a noise? Yes, sir. While you were sitting at this large window, what attracted your attention first to sit there for fifteen minutes? I had been in the room, and my husband wanted to go down stairs, and he asked me to stay there until he came back, and I was sitting at the window and I saw the carriage with Miss Massey and another lady in it, and I told him not to go down for they were coming to have some teeth extracted; and he said no, "that is that girl," and I said "do tell me all about it." Don't me the conversation, you were sitting there for fifteen minutes? Yes, sir. During the time you were sitting at that window the carriage came up, and Miss Massey and her mother got out? No, sir, they were going away. You saw them when they got into the carriage? No, sir, I saw them when they passed the window. You saw the carriage as it went off. Yes, sir. How long do you think it was, between the time that carriage went off and the time Archy was killed? Five or ten minutes, I don't think it was longer than that. Did you go to the small window immediately after the carriage went? I went as soon as I heard some one hallowing. How long was that after the carriage passed by? Very soon after, four or five minutes I guess. What was the exclamation you heard? The first I heard was "stop the nigger, he will get away," was the first I heard. Did you hear any other exclamation? I heard some one holler "shoot him!" as near as I can recollect. Did you hear that several times? I heard it twice, "Shoot him, shoot him?" Yes, sir. Did you hear any other exclamation? No other. When you got to that little window was the crowd in a good deal of commotion? No, sir, not a great deal. How many prsons do you think there were Mrs. Davis? I reckon about seventy-five or a hundred in all. I understand you to say you did not see Mrs. Massey and her daughter when they got into the carriage? No, sir. Were you looking at that time? No, sir, I didu't know anything about it then, I was sewing.—What was the first thing that attracted your attention to Capt. Tolar? I wanted to see who it was, and who it was about. Did you see Capt. Tolar before you saw the pistol shot? I saw him just about the time; You didn't see him

then, before? I saw him a little before, just as I put the window up, I saw Captain Tolar and one or two others. Did the pistol fire immediately after you saw Captain Tolar? Yes, sir. You say you were not alarmed? No, sir, I don't think I was alarmed. You were cool and self-possessed? Yes, sir. Did you close the window immediately after the firing of the pistol? I stood there some few minutes. Did you see what became of Capt. Tolar after the pistol fired? I didn't pay any more attention to him after that. Do you remember how he was dressed? I think he had on a gray suit. Do you remember whether he had on a gray shawl? Yes, sir, he had on a shawl thrown carelessly around him. And you saw him distinctly enough to see his features? Yes, sir. Could you see whether he had his spetacles on? I dont recollect. Did you notice whether he had on a hat? I think he had on a black hat. Tall crowned, low crowned hat or a crushed hat? It was not a very low one. Do you remember it with accuracy at all? I don't recollect very much about his hat. And you can't say with certainty to his spectacles? No sir Where was he standing when you saw him? In the center of the pavement about. Was he standing opposite the small arch, or opposite the large arch, or opposite the pillar between the two arches? Opposite the main arch I believe. You think he was standing about opposite the main arch? I think he was. About opposite the center of it, or can't you speak with that degree of particulaty about it? I think he was about the main arch. The arch is somewhere about twelve feet in width; I want to know what point of the arch he was opposite? I didn't pay much attention. You say he was about ten feet in the rear of Beebee, or where Beebee was when he was shot? Yes, sir, about ten feet, Will you just point out some object with in reach of you, that you estimate at ten feet now (Points out two objects as being ten feet apart, which measures thirteen feet.) Do you think it was about that distance they were apart? Yes, sir. You say you lost sight of Capt. Tolar immediately afterwards and didn't see what became of him? No, sir, I didn't see what became of him. You have been living in Fayetteville eight years, did you recognize any one in that crowd that you saw standing near Capt. Tolar. I recognized Mr. Maultsby, and Mr. Sykes was in the crowd—I recognized him. Was he standing near Capt. Tolar? Not very near—some three or four feet from him, Was he to the right or left? He was nearer to Beebee I think as near as I can recollect. How near was he to Beebee? I don't recollect how near Sykes was, but I recollect seeing him there, and I think he was nearer to Beebee than Tolar was. Where did you see Maultsby? I saw him standing in the crowd. Was he near Capt. Tolar? Some three or four feet from him. Do you know Mr. Leggett? Yes, sir. Did you see him? Yes, sir. Was he standing near Capt. Tolar? About three feet. In front or behind him? On the side of him, I believe. Exactly on the side? I can't tell exactly. Which was the nearest to you? I believe Capt. Tolar was the nearest to me. You think Leggett was a little to his rear then? Yes, sir. Did you see Ralph Lutterloh? No, sir. You know him? Yes sir. Did you see Ed. P. Powers; do you know him? No, sir. I don't know him. Was Capt. Tolar in the midst of the crowd or on the outside edge of it? He was rather on the edge of the crowd, Were there any persons behind him besides Mr. Leggett, further to the rear still? There might have been, I didn't notice. You think he was on the outside edge of crowd? Yes, sir, I think there was not a great many around there. Did you see any colored men standing around there, near Capt. Tolar, at that time? I saw some negroes there, but I did not notice who they were. Do you recollect they were near him? I don't recollect. When Archy Beebee was shot say you saw the smoke come from the pistol? Yes, sir. You didn't see the person who shot him? No, sir. Have you ever expressed any opinion that you could describe the person who shot him? I don't think I could. And would not know him if you were to see him? I might possibly. Could you describe what sort of a man he was. No, sir, I had an idea he was rather a little man, but I don't know whether it is correct or not. You saw the smoke and flash from the pistol distinctly? Yes, sir. Did you see Beebee fall? Yes, sir. What was the first thing that drew your eyes from Tolar? A pistol. The flash of the pistol? The smoke of the pistol. You heard it distinctly? Yes, sir. You think Beebee was on the pavement about opposite the south east corner of the market house? Yes, sir, Beebee was on the pavement. Near the edge? Yes, sir. Had he passed the little arch of the market house on the east end? I think he had. He was further south than that? Yes, sir. I think he was. And near the edge of the pavement? That is the point I think. This man who shot, the place where you saw the smoke, you think was east of him? Yes, sir. Do you mean directly east; suppose Beebee to have been facing south, was this man directly on his left, or south of his left, or to the north of his left? He was to the south of his left. A little further around than he was? Yes, sir. You think the smoke then came a little further in front of Archy? A little to his left side. Which way was he facing? He was facing south down towards the guard house. With his face down towards the guard house? Yes, sir. You could see his features? Yes, sir. And this man you think was a little to the left front of him? Yes, sir. Whoever fired that pistol the smoke appeared there? Yes, sir. Was there not a wind blowing that day? I don't recollect. Do you recollect whether it was a clear day or bright one? I think it was a bright day. You don't recollect whether it was a windy day? I don't think it was a windy day. Did you hear any exclamation in the crowd immediately after the shooting; any outcry? No, sir, I heard nothing after that? Did you leave the window? I did leave the window for about five minutes, and I went back and stood there I reckon an hour. Did you have the window open all the while? Yes, sir, never closed it. Was the day cold? No, sir, it was not very cold; I had the window up all the day. The window was not up till you raised it? No, sir. It was too cold to have the windows open? No, sir, it was not open till I raised it. When did you first make your statement of this matter, Mrs. Davis? I said something about it the next morning to a negro woman that I had. I don't ask you what it was; so that was the first time you had ever spoken of it? Yes, sir. When was the next? The next time was about six weeks afterwards. Who was that to? It was to a colored woman. When did you first give in your statement to the Counsel in this case, Mr. Fuller, in connection with this business? I didn't think I would have to tell I was summoned here. Havn't you ever given it to him before coming on the stand? Yes, sir. Was that since you have been here? Yes, sir. The first time you ever gave him a narrative of this transaction? Yes, sir. You say you knew Capt. Tolar very well? Yes, sir. Known him how long? About two years. Was he a frequent visitor at your house? No, sir, he never visited at our house at all. How many times do you suppose

you had seen him in these two years? He came to our house first on business, and I saw him on the streets a good deal from the window; I never spoke to him. And it was not a personal acquaintance then at all? No, sir. You only know him by sight? Yes, sir. Do you suppose you had seen him a dozen times in these two years? Yes, sir. Fifty? No, sir. You have seen him passing the street? Yes, sir, I had seen him a good deal at Mr. Taylor's store, across the way.

Re-direct examination by the Counsel for the accused:

Mrs. Davis, do you know whether Capt. Tolar had done business down the street, below your husband's office? I don't know, sir. He was passing there quite often? He was at the corner of Philliman's Taylor's store, right often. That is on the corner just opposite? Yes, sir. By seeing him in that way your knowledge of him was gained? Yes, sir. With regard to the position from which the smoke arose; you say it was about to the left of Beebee? Yes, sir. Did you say it was to the front of his left or just to his left? Just to his left, I think.

G. W. HOLLINGSWORTH, a witness for the defence, having been first duly sworn, testified as follows:

Examined by the Counsel for the accused.

What is your name? G. W. Hollingsworth. What does G. stand for? George. So that your name is George Washington Hollingsworth? Yes, sir. What is your age? Seventeen. What is your father's name? Isaac. How long have you been living in Fayetteville? Seven years. Where is your fathers place of business? On Person street, No. 51. Below the market house? Yes, sir. How far from the market house? About one hundred and twenty-six yards. From the nearest portion of the market house to your father's place of business? Yes, sir. Have you measured it? It was stepped off, one hundred and twenty-six steps. Were you in Fayetteville on the day that Archy Beebee was killed? Yes, sir. At the time he was killed where were you? I was at the store? What store? My father's store. How long had you been there before he was killed? I had been there about ten minutes. Where had you been before that time? I had been hunting. Had you been up to the market house that day? No, sir, I hadn't. How long after he was killed was it before they went to the market house? before you went down there at all? About ten or fifteen minutes. Will you swear you didn't go to the market house that day until ten or fifteen minutes after Archy Beebee was killed? Yes, sir. You say at the time he was killed, you were sitting or standing, which? I was sitting down on a stool chair; the back of the chair was broken. Any body with you? No, sir, there was not. Did you have any pistol that day, when you went to the market house? No, sir. You hadn't a pistol that day? No, sir. Neither at the time Archy was killed, before he was killed, nor at any time afterwards? No, sir. Did you holler out. " hurrah for Capt. Tolar "? No, sir, I didn t, Do you swear you didn't? Yes, sir.

Cross-examination by the Counsel for the prosecution.

Mr. Hollingsworth, you had been hunting that day? Yes, sir. Who was with you? Mr. Porter's son Willie. The same young man who testified here? Did you meet Monk Julia while you were not hunting? Yes, sir, we did. Where did the meeting take place? In Cambleton. It was down in Cambleton? Yes, sir. Did you hear talk about this attempt to ravish this young lady? I heard him say that there was an assault made; he told me he had heard that Jim Jones' dray driver had made an attempt upon a young lady there, Miss Massey. Was that all he said? That is all he said about it; he talked some more about it, but didn't say any thing more than that; he just told me that was all he knowed about it; I asked him if it was a mulatto fellow, and he said " no, it was a black fellow." What were you doing down to Campbellton, hunting? Yes, sir. Did you have a gun? I did. Did Willie Porter have a gun? He did. Did Monk shoot your gun? I let him shoot it once or twice. Did he shoot Willie Porter's gun? I disremember whether he shot Willie's or not. Were you about there with him some time? He stayed with us half an hour or so. Were you and Willie together all the time? No, sir. Monk was not with you, nor with him all the time? No, sir. He was first with one and then with the other? We were together right smart while when he first came there. Do I understand you to say that Monk was first with you when Willie Porter was not there, and sometimes with Willie Porter when you were not there? Yes, sir, me and Dave Jones; he was down there too. You were just shooting about there? Yes, sir. Where did Monk go when he left you? He went on up towards the upper end of the field, up that way somewheres. You didn't see what became of him? No, sir. He just went away? Yes, sir. You didn't hear him say anything about its going hard with Archy, if he was found guilty? I don't remember. Did he tell you he had been caught? Yes, sir, he told me had been caught. He told you, besides telling you that this attempt had been made upon the young lady, that the man had been caught? Yes, sir. Did he tell you when his examination was going to take place? No, sir, he didn't know any thing about that. Do you say he didn't know anything about it? He didn't tell me anything about it, was what I meant to say. When you went back home, did Willie Porter go along with you? Me and Willie left Campbellton, and went over in Mr. Curtis's field a while and then came on back home, and divided the birds; I gave him half and I took half, then we left home. Do you mean by home your father's store? No, sir. Your father don't live at his store? No, sir, the store is in Person street, and we live in Dick street. That was down at the residence in Dick street that you divided the birds? Yes, sir. Did you leave your gun there? Yes, sir. What did Willie do with his gun? He carried it around to Mr. John Overby's store, and he left the gun and birds there; me and him went on as far as to my brother's store. How far is that from the market house? It is about the same distance. One store is opposite the other, and they are on the same street? Yes, sir. What happened then? Pa blew his whistle for me and I went on over to the store, and he told me not to go up to the market house; if I did he would whip me. He forbade you to go to the market house? Yes, sir. When you last saw Willie was he going on towards the market house? He was. Did you see him go into the crowd? I didn't watch him all the way there. How near was he to the market house when you saw him last? About the Cape Fear Bank; about seventy five yards or eighty yards I suppose. How far is your father's store from the market house? About one hundred and twenty six yards. Willie was about seventy five yards from the market house. Yes, sir; may be more. .Still moving down there? Yes, sir. And you remained at your fathers store, and didn't go to the market house till after the killing? I didn't go up to the market house till after Beebee was shot. You are certain of that? I am. You have no sort of doubt about it. There ain't no doubt about it. Do you remember it

distinctly? Yes, sir. Do you remember every day as distinctly as that; can you tell what you were doing at any time? I suppose as far back as twelve years I can very well, not further back. Where were you yesterday at twelve o'clock? I was lying on my bed down here to the Hotel, at the Parker house. Where were you the first day of this month at twelve o'clock? I was down in the country, sir. Doing what? I was down on the river bank, if I am not mistaken. Can you speak with as much certainty about it as you speak of where you were on the day Archy Beebee was killed? do you swear as positively that you were on the river bank as you do that you were at the store that day? No, I won't swear that I was down there, but I think I was. But you are positively certain where you were on the day Archy Beebee was killed? Yes, sir. When you were first asked about it were you as certain as you are now, or did you have to think about it? I knowed I was at the store. You remember it then? Yes, sir. So you remembered it as well at first as you do now, I don't doubt you at all, but I merely want to know whether it was a refreshed recollection or whether you remembered it at first as well as you did afterwards, you have no doubt or never have had. that you were at the store when Archy was killed? No, sir. You remember the day he was killed and it made an impression on you? Slightly. Is it a general thing to have a man killed in the streets of Fayetteville? No, sir. Isn't it an unusual, didn't it strike you as an unusual, event so that you remembered where you were? Yes, sir. You remember now very distinctly that your father would not allow you to go up there the day it happened so that you were not in the crowd when the shooting took place, and therefore you could not have made the exclamation that " Capt Tolar killed him "? No, sir.

The Counsel for the accused asked if the witnesses from Fort Macon would arrive before day after tomorrow.

The Judge Advocate said they were expected this evening at half past three o'clock.

The Counsel for the accused said he had no witnesses to be examined whose examination would not consume an hour or two at least; whereupon on motion the Commission adjourned to meet on Tuesday the 20th, inst. at 11 o'clock, A. M:

RALEIGH, N. C. Aug. 20, 1867 11 A. M.

The Commission met pursuant to adjournment. Present, all the members of the Commission, the Judge Advocate, the Counsel for the prosecution, all the accused and their Counsel.

The reading of the testimony, taken yesterday, was waived, there being no objection thereto.

Yesterday's proceedings were read and approved.

The Counsel for the defence said; " I am informed by the Judge Advocate that those witnesses from Fort Macon have not yet arrived. There are two witnesses for the defence in the city, but to introduce them, at this time, would interfere, very seriously, with the order that has been determined upon, by the counsel for the defence."

The Judge Advocate said:

"I will state to the Commission that, on the sixteenth day of this month, I addressed a letter to Brevt. Lieut. Col. Charles B. Gaskill, commanding Fort Macon, requesting him to forward the two prisoners, who have been subpœnaed as witnesses for the defence—that they might arrive here yesterday afternoon, at the latest. The fault of their non-arrival is that of Colonel Gaskill, and not of the Judge Advocate."

The Court suggested that the letter be repeated.

The Judge Advocate informed the Commission that it had been repeated.

The Counsel for the accused asked when the first batch of witnesses would arrive from Fayetteville.

The Judge Advocate stated that they were due here to-morrow at nine o'clock, but he could not say whether they would arrive at that time or not.

The Counsel for the accused said they would be ready to proceed with the examination after the arrival of the witnesses from Fayetteville, even if the Fort Macon witnesses do not arrive, to-morrow; and the defense therefore asked for an adjournment until to-morrow.

The Judge Advocate said : "I will state to the Commission that I have received authority from the General Commanding the second military district, to employ an additional phonographer, with a view of making the sessions of the Commission continue a greater number of hours per day, and to enable the Commission to take a greater amount of testimony. I request the authority of the Commission to employ the phonographer whose employment has been approved by the General commanding the second military district, and of an additional clerk; the phonographer to be employed at a salary not to exceed ten dollars ($10,00) per day and the clerk to be employed at a salary not to exceed five dollars ($5,00) per day."

The request of the Judge Advocate was granted by the Commission; and the phonographer and clerk will be employed from and after this date.

On motion, the Commission adjourned, to meet on Wednesday, the 2nd inst., at 11 A. M.

RALEIGH, N. C., Aug. 21, 1867. 11 A. M.

The Commission met pursuant to adjournment.

Present, all the members of the Commission, the Judge Advocate, the Counsel for the prosecution, all the accused and their Counsel.

Yesterday's proceedings were read and approved.

RALPH B. LUTTERLOH, a witness for the defense, having been first duly sworn, testified as follows:

Examined by the Counsel for the accused.

What is your name? Ralph Buxton Lutterloh. Where do you reside? Fayetteville, Cumberland county. How long have you been living there? I was born there about eighteen years ago. Have you resided there all your life? Yes, sir. Where have you been for the past three weeks? Fort Macon. When were you subpœnaed for a witness in this cause? I don't exactly remember the time ; it was about the twenty-fourth or twenty-fifth of July. Was it before or after your arrest for complicity in this affair? It was before. Were you in Fayetteville the day Archy Beebee was killed? I was, sir. Were you at the market house in Fayetteville on that day? Yes, sir. At what time did you go to the market house? I suppose it was half after three. In the afternoon? Yes, sir. From what place did you go to the market house? From my store. Where is your store? It is nearly at the foot of Hay Mount. In what town? Fayetteville. On what street? Hay street. How far from the market house? About half a mile. Who went

with you to the market house that day? Edward P. Powers. Where is his place of business? On Hay street, near the foot of Hay Mount. How far from your place of business? It is the next door. At what hour in the day did you arrive at the market house? About half past three. What portion of the market house did you enter? Entered in the western arch. The main arch in the west? Yes, sir. Where was Archy Beebee at the time you got to the market house? He was up stairs. Then you hadn't got there when he was carried up? No, sir. At what portion of the market house did you take your station when you went there? It was nearly at the eastern arch. How far from the eastern arch? I suppose it was ten feet. Was it nearer to the centre, the bell rope, or nearer the outer edge of the eastern arch? It was about the centre of the market house; about the centre of the eastern arch. In the centre of the passage that runs through the market? Yes, sir. Who was in company with you there at that time? There was a crowd around there ; I remember Mr. Ed. Powers, Mr. Leggett and Capt. Tolar. Did you four, that you have mentioned, have any conversation together before the prisoner Archy Beebee was brought down? Yes, sir, we were talking. Did you make or did you not make, any arrangement or any combination, or any agreement to kill that man when he was brought down stairs, or to do him any harm? No, sir; we didn't. Was there any conversation between you upon that subject ; the subject of killing or doing that man any harm, when he was brought down stairs? No. sir. How was the conversation that day between you four, carried on at that place? They were talking about the affair. Did you converse about it loudly, or in an ordinary tone, or in whispers? In an ordinary tone. And you were speaking about the affair? Yes, sir. How long had you been at that place before the prisoner was brought down stairs? I suppose it was about twenty minutes. Did you four, that you have named, all maintain your position just there until the prisoner was brought down stairs? Yes, sir, I think we were standing about the same place. Did any of you go outside of the market house from the time you first got there, until the prisoner was brought down stairs, any of you four men? I can't say that, I didn't keep watch of them ; I didn't miss them—they may have stepped out but I didn't notice it. Did you see Miss Massey and Mrs. Massey when they came down these steps? Yes, sir. Where was your position at the time they came down the steps? I was about the same place. Who were with you at the time? Mr. Tolar, Mr. Leggett and Ed. Powers—there was a crowd all around us. Who came down those steps with Miss Massey and her mother; any one? I think Mr. Bond. The The town Constable? Yes, sir. Where did they go after they came down the steps? They went out and got in the carriage. Where was the carriage standing, into which they got? At the eastern part of the market house, about ten feet from the pavement. Opposite what portion of the market house? The eastern arch. The main eastern arch? Yes, sir. And about ten feet off from the pavement you think? Yes, sir. Who went to the carriage with Miss Massey and her mother, and Mr. Bond; any one else? I saw no one else. Who went to the carriage during the time it was standing there and after these ladies had gone to the carriage? I never noticed any body. Did any body go there from the crowd, of which you formed a part? I didn't see any one go there. Did you go? No sir. Did Ed. Powers? No, sir. Did Capt. Tolar go? I didn't see him go, sir. You saw nobody go from the crowd? No. sir. Did you notice the carriage with any particularity? No, sir. Do you know who were at the carriage, at the time it was standing there? There was a driver there that I noticed. Who was that driver? I don't know, sir. Was he a white man or a colored man? A colored man. Do you remember any persons who were at the carriage or about the carriage during the time it was standing there? No, sir. How long after the ladies got into the carriage before it drove off? I think it was a few minutes. What do you mean by a few minutes? Five minutes. How long was it after the carriage drove off before the prisoner, Beebee was brought down stairs? I reckon it was about five or ten minutes. Did you see him when he was brought down stairs? Yes, sir. Where were you standing when he was brought down stairs? I was standing in the crowd, close to a bench? What bench? The bench next to the main eastern arch, there was a sort of stand there between that and the steps. Which bench do you mean, the one that runs along the eastern wall of the market house or the one that runs perpendicular to that and up the aisle of the market house? It runs up the aisle, sir. Do you know whose bench that is? No, sir. Do you know who keeps that stall there? No, sir. How far were you standing off from that bench? I think I was right at it. Where were these other persons that you mention: Ed. Powers, Mr. Leggett, and Captain Tolar, at the time the prisoner was brought down stairs? I think they were near me, I was noticing the prisoner. Did you see the prisoner when he was first brought out of the door or the landing of the stair steps? Yes, sir. Do you remember who was with the prisoner—of the officers at that time? The policemen were with him and Mr. Wemyss; I don't remember seeing Sheriff Hardie with him at the time. You remember seeing Mr. Wemyss and some officers? Yes, sir. At the time the prisoner was brought there, and from that time until he reached the floor of the market house, what occurred to attract your attention or to attract the attention of any of the by-standers? I didn't see any thing, sir. Did you notice any one jump on the bench—that bench, when the prisoner appeared? No, sir. Did any one jump on the bench? I didn't see any one, sir. Do you know John John Maultsby? Yes, sir. Did you see John Maultsby at that time? No, sir. Did you hear any exclamation from any person in the crowd or on the bench at the time the prisoner appeared there? No, sir. Did you hear nobody cry out "shoot him; here he comes; watch out boys," or something of that sort? No, sir. Did anything of that sort occur there at that time? Not as I know of, sir. That brings us with the prisoner down on the floor; what occurred then, sir, to attract your attention? Well, sir, nothing occurred to attract my attention until he went to pass through the main eastern arch. Where were you standing, sir, at the time they passed you going out of the main eastern arch? I was standing there by the bench. Who were near you, who were with you at that time? I think Mr. Ed. Powers, Capt. Tolar and Mr. Leggett. Do you know where Sam Hall was at that time? No, sir, I don't. Do you know where John Maultsby was at that time? No, sir. Or Sykes? I never saw Sykes. You knew where none of them were except these four you have spoken of? No, sir. Did the party in charge of the prisoner pass you on the right or left hand? On the right. Which way were you looking? I was

looking at the prisoner; I was standing sort of with my back to them in the crowd there, and they passed nearly in front of me, a little to my right. Did you shift your position at all, until the prisoner was shot? Yes, sir. How far had they got with the prisoner at the time you shifted your position, as he passed out of the main eastern arch? I think I moved on out with the crowd on the pavement. When you moved out on the pavement where did you take your stand? I took it out about the edge of the pavement; I suppose it was about the middle of the main eastern arch. Who moved out with you? I don't remember, I think the crowd moved out; I think we all moved together. You think yourself, and Leggett, and Tolar moved out together? Yes, sir. What occurred after you got there? I saw some excitement in the crowd. Just describe it? It looked like they were pushing on after the prisoner, and the prisoner seemed to be trying to get out of the hands of the police. In the pushing on towards the prisoner did you notice Tolar, Ed. Powers or Leggett? No, sir. Were they with that crowd that were pushing on? No, sir. Well, sir, what was done with the crowd that was pushing on, any thing or nothing? While the prisoner was trying to get away, I saw Monk trying to get to him. I think I saw Mr. Nixon get hold of him, and the prisoner seemed to be trying to get away from the police at that time, and I heard the report of a pistol. We haven't got that far yet, and you say the prisoner made efforts as if he was trying to get away? Yes, sir. And then you saw Monk make at him with the knife? Yes, sir. Where was Monk? Monk was a good piece off from the pavement there out in the crowd on the eastern side of the market house. Was he to your right or left? I was looking right straight at him, he was in front of me. Diagram of market house at Fayetteville exhibited to the witness. Point out, if you please on this diagram, where you were standing, as near as you can, at the time Beebee was shot, first point out where Beebee was when he was shot? Here, just opposite the southern edge of the southern arch. Was he near the market house, near the center of the pavement, or near the edge of the pavement? About the center of the pavement. and about the southern portion of the southern arch, or the eastern side? Yes, sir. Now, where were you standing? I was standing about nearly the center of the main eastern, arch. What part of the pavement? I think I was about the edge of the pavement. Now where was Tolar standing? I didn't see Tolar at that time. Where was Ed. Powers standing? I can't describe where he was standing, I looked around once or twice and saw him near me. Did you see Tolar near you when you looked around? No, sir. Where was Leggett standing? I can't say that. Was he standing near you? I never noticed, sir; I didn't notice him after I took my position; I noticed him when he was going through the arch. Well, sir, did you see the prisoner when he was shot? Yes, sir. Did you see who shot him? No, sir. Did you see the smoke of the pistol? No, sir, I never saw the smoke. Did you see the flash of the pistol? No, sir. Did you hear the report of the pistol? Yes, sir. Well, sir, from where you were standing, from the report, where was the person standing who shot him? I think the person who shot him was rather to my rear and left. That would bring him off the pavement? Yes, sir. Which way were you looking? Right at the prisoner. How far do you think the person was from the prisoner who shot him? I think some three or four feet, I didn't notice particularly how far he was. Your idea of it is gathered entirely from the report and sound of weapons in the hands of any body at the time of the shooting? Yes, sir, just as I heard the report I saw a pistol. In whose hands was it? Sam. Phillips. What sort of a pistol was it, a large pistol or a small one? A large pistol. In what position did he have the pistol? About so, (down by his right leg, in his right hand.) Had you seen a pistol in the hands of any one before that time? No, sir. At the time you saw the pistol in the hands of Phillips, how long was it after the shooting? It was just as soon as I could look around. What attracted your attention to that direction? The report of the pistol. And being attracted by the report of the pistol, you looked around in that direction and saw Sam Phillips with a pistol in his hands in that way? Yes, sir. And that was the only pistol you saw? Yes, sir. Was Phillips far from the point where the report of the pistol appeared to you to be? He seemed to be right about in the place from where the report of the pistol came. When you heard the report of the pistol, you turned around and saw Phillips with a pistol down by his right side? Yes, sir. What became of you then, sir? I noticed the prisoner lying there and I walked off. Did you hear Sam Phillips say anything at that time? No, sir. What became of Phillips? I never saw him any more after that, sir. How long did you remain there in that position? It was about two or three minutes. Did Phillips leave you, or did you leave him? I never noticed him, when I left I don't know whether he was standing there or not. Did you see Capt. Tolar at the time the pistol was fired? No, sir. Was there more than one pistol shot fired that day? No, sir. What became of you, Mr. Lutterloh, after the negro was killed? I went up town, up to my store. You say you were on the pavement at the time the pistol shot was fired? Yes, sir. How far were you off from the prisoner? I was some three feet. And the man who fired you say you think he was a little to your rear and left, and off the pavement about three feet? I said the report of the pistol was about three feet from me. Were there any persons between you and the prisoner? Yes, sir. How many, sir? I didn't notice how many; there was some there. Were there any persons between the prisoner and the point where you heard the report of the pistol? Yes, sir. How many, sir? I can't say that. Did you know any of them? No, sir. Did you know whether they were white or black? No, sir. Is there anything else that you know about this matter? No, sir. I want to understand from you where Tolar was at the time you last saw him? He was under the market house about ten feet from the main eastern arch. Then you didn't see him at all after you went out upon the pavement? No, sir.

Cross-examination, by the Counsel for the prosecution.

Mr. Lutterloh, are you related to Miss Elvira Massey? No, sir. No family connection? No, sir. What day, and what hour of the day did you first hear that this negro had attempted to commit a rape? Early in the morning. Of Monday? Yes, sir. The day he was killed? Yes, sir. You had heard nothing of it on the Sunday previous? No, sir. Who told you that? I don't remember, sir. Where

were you when you heard it? I think I was up about the store, sir. When you saw Capt. Tolar at the market house, when you got down there that day, was that the first time you had seen him that day? Yes, sir. You and Ed. Powers went down together? Yes, sir. Had Ed. Powers told you of this attempt that had been made upon this young lady? No, sir. I don't think he did. Can you recollect who it was? No, sir. Did you hear it from several sources? Yes, sir. Did you know at that time that any attempt was going to be made to punish this negro by lynch law? No, sir. Did you hear nothing of this sort? No, sir. From any quarter? No, sir. Were you at your store all day, Mr. Lutterloh from the time you first heard of this thing early in the morning, until the time you went to the market house? I don't know that I was at the store all day; I went to dinner about one o'clock. Did you have any conversation with any person between the time you first heard of this event—I speak of the man Beebee having attempted to ravish Miss Massey; did you speak to no one upon that fact between the first time you heard of it, till the time you went down to the market house? I was in crowds and I heard them speak something about it. You heard it spoken of a great deal did you? No, sir. How many times did you hear it spoken of between early in the morning, and three or four o'clock that day? I must have heard it some two or three times. Do you remember any person spoke to you about it? No, sir. And in that conversation there was nothing like a threat of violence? No, sir. And you swear in the presence of Almighty God, that you know of no combination that was made for that purpose? Yes, sir. When you went down to the market house, Mr. Powers went with you? Yes, sir. Was that by agreement, or by accident? He came out of his store, and I was standing in my store door, and he asked me to walk down and hear the trial. Did you have any weapon on at that time? No, sir, none at all. Do you know whether Ed. Powers had any weapons on at that time? I don't know for certain; I didn't see any about him. Did you hear him say he had one? No, sir. Have you any reason for knowing that he had a weapon on at that time, when he left his store? I am pretty certain he didn't have one. Why is that, sir? I know all about him, and I know he is never seen with a weapon? Your conclusion is from your general knowledge of the man? Yes, sir. You didn't see any? No, sir. You don't know that he had one? No, sir. And you didn't have any weapon? No, sir. You went down to the market house together? Yes, sir. When you got there, did you find Mr. Leggett, and Mr. Tolar there already? I think they were there about the time we got there. Was Mr. Leggett there when you got there? I think he was, at the time or pretty soon after. Could you speak with certainty? No, sir. You don't know whether he was there when you went up, or whether he came afterwards? I think we got there nearly at the same time. Are you certain that Capt. Tolar was there when you got there? Yes, sir, I think so. And your impression is, Leggett came about the time you did? Yes, sir. You then took your station about ten feet from the center of the main arch on the eastern side? Yes, sir. Fronting which way? Fronting east. Were you facing Mr. Tolar as you stood in the group, or were you all facing the same way? We were facing each other, standing around there in a circle. What was the size of the crowd when you got there inside of the market house, I speak of? I think there must have been twenty or twenty-five people. Besides you four in the group? Yes, sir. Didn't I understand you to say there was a crowd -

around there, in giving in your testimony in chief? Yes, sir. Was that what you meant by the crowd; about twenty or twenty-five people besides yourselves? Yes, sir. There was no crowd large enough to fill the whole market house? No, sir. No crowd large enough to make an impression upon you as you stood there? No, sir. Who did you see in the market house besides these other gentlemen you have named, at that time, when Archy was up stairs in the twenty minutes before he came down; did you see Tom Powers there that time? I don't know him. Did you see Monk Julia there at that time? I didn't see him under the market house. Do you know any person who was there? I think Mr. Nixon was there, and Sam Hall I saw him under the market house. Where was Sam Hall when you saw him? About the center of the market house. Where the bell rope hangs? Yes, sir. Did you see Henry Sykes there conversing with Sam Hall? No, sir. Did you see John Maultsby then conversing with Sam Hall? No, sir. You don't remember any one except those three gentlemen you first named and Sam Hall and Mr. Nixon? That is all I remember. Did you see Sam Phillips there at that time? No, sir. Did I understand you to say you could not tell any other persons there that you saw? I don't remember any one else. Was there any crowd outside of the market house, besides this crowd that was inside? Yes, sir. How many persons do you suppose were around and about the market house? I have no idea, sir, I never took particular notice; I noticed some persons standing out there. Were they standing at the eastern end? Yes, sir. Were there as many outside as there were inside of the market house? Yes, sir, I reckon there were more. You suppose the crowd to have been forty or fifty people inside and outside of the market house? Yes, sir. When did you first see that carriage standing there, in front of the east end, about ten feet from the pavement? I noticed it when I first got there. Was that about the position it first occupied when you first saw it? Yes, sir. You saw Miss Massey and her mother when they first came down stairs? Yes, sir. Mr. Bond came down with them? Yes, sir. How long had you been there, when they came down? I was there about fifteen minutes I guess, sir. Up to the time that she came down had you seen any weapons in the hands of any one in that crowd? No, sir. Did you see any belt that might have borne any weapon, about any man's person? No sir. No weapons, either knives pistols or clubs? No, sir. But when these ladies came down you say Mr. Bond came with them? Yes sir. He went to the carriage with them? Yes, sir. Did you still retain your same position about the center of the market house? Yes, sir. Do you remember that when you first went to the market house, you didn't go right to the center, but you went a little to your left when you come in the west end, and when the ladies came down you moved towards them, changing your position to about the center, or do you think you were standing about the same place all the time? I think we were in the same place all the time. Until the ladies came down stairs? Yes, sir. Did you notice them pass to the carriage? Yes, sir. You didn't know Tom Powers? I know him now. You didn't know him at that time? No, sir. Didn't you know him when you saw him? No, sir. When these ladies passed out to the carriage, did you look at them as they passed? Yes, sir. At that time could you see the rest of these gentlemen who were with you standing there previously, or was your attention distracted by the carriage? I was noticing the ladies get into the

carriage. Did you see any one go to the carriage except Bond? No, sir. Did you see no one speak to Bond as he was standing near the carriage or coming from it? No sir. Did you see what became of Bond after he went to the carriage? No, sir. Do you know whether he went up stairs or remained near the carriage? The carriage drove off and I never noticed which way he went. Your impression is no one went to the carriage to speak to the ladies? Yes, sir. Were you looking at the carriage pretty much all the while it was standing there? Not all the while. How long did it stand there after the ladies got to it? About five minutes. Were you looking at the carriage when it drove off, or all the time from when the ladies first went there until it drove off? I noticed it when the ladies got in it, and when they drove off. But the interval of time between the time they first got there and the time they drove off you were not looking at it? No, sir. Did you see Mr. Tolar at the time that carriage was standing there, and you were looking at it? Yes, sir. Mr. Tolar was there near you? Yes, sir. Did you say he didn't move away and go to the carriage? If he did I didn't see him. Did you see Mr. Phil. Taylor go to the carriage? No, sir. Did you see Mr. Bob. Mitchell go to the carriage? No, sir. Did you see Mr. John Maultsby go to the carriage? No, sir. You say you didn't know Tom. Powers, but you saw no man at all go to that carriage except Bond? No one except Bond. And if Mr. Tolar went there you didn't know it? No, sir. Now, sir, after these ladies came down, did you notice any peculiarity about the lady; did she have her veil up? I noticed she was weeping. Had her handkerchief to her face? Yes, sir. Was her weeping noisy or quiet sobbing, as she passed through the crowd? It was not very noisy. Was her mother weeping also? I never noticed her mother. Did you see any marks of violence upon the young lady at the time? No, sir, I heard some person standing by me say "see how she is bruised." Who was that person? I can't say. Did you see any bruises? No, sir. You heard that remark from many voices or from one? I only remember it from one voice. You saw no signs of the bruises? No, sir. You saw no blood nor marks of violence? No, sir. Her face was concealed with the handkerchief? Yes, sir. And she went crying to the carriage? Yes, sir. Did you notice any outbreak in the crowd as she passed, any cries or threats of violence? No, sir. That crowd was very quiet was it? They were talking there. There was no exhibition of temper? No, sir. No exhibition of violence, no appearance of a mob or riot? None that I noticed of. And when the ladies passed through, you saw no disturbance either? No, sir. You did not, as I understand you, apprehend any violent outbreak at that time? No, sir. You saw no reason to apprehend it? No, sir. Now, when the prisoner started down stairs did you see him on the steps? I saw him about the bottom steps. Could you, from the position you occupied, see the door that opens at the top of the steps that he came out of at the top of the last flight? Yes, sir, I think I saw him about that time. Did you see him when he came out of the door? Yes, sir. How near were you to him while he was on the steps; how near were you to the steps; you were standing with your right side towards the steps? Yes, sir. And by glancing around you could see the steps distinctly? Yes, sir. How far were the steps from your right as you stood there? Twelve or fifteen feet I should think, sir. How wide do you think the market house is? I should think it was about forty feet. Then you were a little nearer to the right hand wall as you faced the east than you were to the left hand at that time? I was about fifteen feet from the steps. That would bring you about fifteen or sixteen feet from the wall, that is on your right as you looked east? Do you mean the southern wall? Yes, sir, how far that on your right do you suppose as you stood? I suppose it was about nine or ten feet. The steps were nearer to you than the southern wall? No, sir. Then you were further back inside of the market house; you were further west than where the door was that opens at the top of the stair steps? No sir. Do you think you were farther from the steps than you were from the south wall of the market house? Yes, sir. Weren't they between you and the south wall of the market house? No, sir. Where were they relatively to you, to your right and front, you were facing east? Not at that time the prisoner came down; I was noticing the prisoner. You turned towards the steps as he came down? Yes, sir. How far were you from those steps? About twelve feet. And you think you were nearer the south wall of the market house? Yes, sir. By a direct line from you to the south wall, would you be nearer to the wall than the steps? I should think I would be nearer to the steps. Then you were in the rear of the steps, were you west of the steps? No, sir, I was somewhat north-east. North-east of the steps? Yes, sir, if anything.

(Witness is shown a diagram of the market house.)

Weren't these steps between you and the south wall? No, sir. Are these steps ten feet from the small arch, that is, from the bottom of the steps would it be about ten feet? Yes, sir. As you were standing there at the moment you saw Archy land at the bottom of the steps, did you see these gentlemen with you who had been with you before; I mean Captain Tolar, Mr. Leggett and Ed. Powers? I think they were standing around me; I was noticing the prisoner. Then you can't speak with absolute certainty about them, except from the fact that you saw them there shortly before? No, sir. From the time he reached the bottom of the steps to the time he got into the main arch and turned out, was there any noise in that crowd? No, sir. No outcry? None that I heard of. No disturbance of any kind? No, sir. Didn't you see any rush made at the prisoner? Not until he got out of the market house; until he got outside of the arch; I never saw any till he got outside on the pavement. While he was inside of the market house, and while he was turning through the main arch, you didn't see any assault made on him? No, sir, not as I saw. You heard no outcry? No, sir. You saw no attempt to make an assault? No, sir. You saw no grabbing at him? No, sir. You didn't see anything upon the part of the officers, the Sheriff, and the others, like an attempt to keep the crowd off of him? No, sir, I never noticed that. Did you notice how Archy was

dressed that day? No, sir. Did you notice whether he had any hat on or not? I never noticed it. Did you notice whether he was bare-headed or not? No, sir. But you heard no noise, saw no disturbance, or anything like a rush or assault upon him, while he was inside of the market house, and until he had passed through the arch and got on the pavement out side? No, sir. When he got on the pavement, out side, immediately was it, then, that the first rush was made at him? The crowd seemed to be pushing out there towards him. What do you mean by pushing? The crowd seemed to be moving that way. Do you mean the crowd seemed to be pushing towards him? Yes, sir, they seemed to be closing up on him, as he went out the people from under the market house went out there. How many were there then? I never noticed. Had the crowd grown any? Yes, sir. Do you think it had grown considerably? Yes, sir. Were there none out side as well as inside at the time Archy passed out of the arch on the pavement in front? Yes, sir. What is your best estimate of the number of persons who were there at the time Archy passed out of the arch and got on the pavement? I should judge about one hundred and fifty people; say one hundrd and fifty people, or two hundred. Now, sir, had you moved out of the market house until the time Archy passed out of the arch? Yes, sir. Was he through the arch when you moved or was he in the arch? I think he was just passing out under the arch. Just as he was passing through, you moved towards the arch to get out. Yes, sir. You were standing near Becky Ben's bench until that? I don't know whose bench it was. You were standing near the bench that was on your right? Yes, sir. Just as he passed out of the arch you moved to get out; did you see Tolar at the time you started to go out? No, sir. When was the last time you had seen him up to that; had you seen him since the negro Archy had got to the foot of the stairs? No, sir, I remember seeing him about the time Miss Massey came down. Is that the last time you remember seeing him? Yes, sir. When you moved out who moved along with you, the whole crowd? Yes, sir. The crowd seemed to be moving out very quietly or did they rush out? I didn't see any rushing, whatever. They moved out in an orderly manner? Yes, sir. When you moved out did Ed. Powers and Mr. Leggett move along with you; you saw them after Archy got to the foot of the stairs? Yes, sir. Mr. Tolar you lost sight of. Yes, sir. Were these other gentlemen near you when you moved out of the arch on the pavement? Yes, sir. Did those two gertlemen go with you; can you speak confidently about that? Yes, sir. You stood together on the pavement? Yes, sir, we were around right together. Now, sir, was there any crowd behind you? Yes, sir. Was the crowd large enough to stand behind you, in front of you, and on each side of you? Yes, sir. Was the crowd in commotion or was it perfectly still? When the prisoner was outside it seemed to me to be in commotion. The crowd was in a stir? Yes, sir. Were they pressing on the prisoner Beebee? Yes, sir. Were they pressing on with violence? No, sir. Did you see see the Sheriff try to resist the pressure—you know Hardie don't you? Yes, sir. Didn't you see him resist the pressure of the crowd? No, sir. I am speaking now of just after the negro passed out of the arch on the pavement; you didn't see any resistance on the part of the Sheriff? No, sir. Did you see Wemyss there? Yes, sir. Did you see him or any of the police resist the crowd? He told them to keep back; I saw the police. Did you hear them say "keep back?" Yes, sir. Did you hear any other exclamations in that crowd? No, sir. Mr. Lutterloh, did you hear no exclamations in that crowd? I heard the police tell the people to get back. Didn't you hear the cry "kill him, kill him?" No, sir. Didn't you hear the cry "he will get away"? None but the police. Did you hear the police cry "he will get away"? Yes, sir, telling the people to stand back. Which one? I think there was several of them; Mr. Faircloth was one 'You think the police cried "he will get away," you heard that in an excited quick tone, such as a man would use on such an occasion? Yes, sir. You then did hear them tell the crowd to keep back, and you heard the exclamation, "he will get away," which you attributed to the police? Yes, sir. You didn't hear any remark "kill him" from any quarter at that time? No, sir. At the time these policemen were saying "he will get away," was it at the same time that they said that they were telling the crowd to keep back. There were several of them speaking; some of them were telling them to stand back, and others were telling them to go away. But I mean was there any exclamation in the crowd that the negro man Archy would get away? No, sir. You heard nothing of that sort? No, sir. You think the police were saying to the crowd "get away"? Yes, sir. Did they seem to be in earnest about it? Yes, sir. Did they exert themselves to keep the crowd back? Yes, sir. Who did you see in that crowd? I never noticed one of them. Couldn't you recognize a soul there that you saw? No one between me and the police. You saw no one between you and the police that you recognized? No, sir. Were they strangers to you? No, sir, their backs were towards me The police had their faces towards you? Some had and some hadn't. You recognized the police, but the men who were nearer to you, and many of them neighbors and people in town, you couldn't tell who they were? I never noticed none of them. I suppose there were fifteen or twenty people between you and the police? Yes, sir. Up to that time had you seen any weapons in the hands of any one? No, sir. Had you heard any one say they had a weapon, in the crowd. No, sir. Did you see any marks of weapons in any shape or way? No, sir. Do you know that any one had weapons in that crowd? No, sir. Have you any reason for knowing? No, sir. You neither heard of it nor saw signs of it, and have no reason for knowing that any one in that crowd had a weapon that day? No, sir. You don't mean to say you had no reason for knowing Mr. Phillips had a weapon? You mean about the weapons up to the time, I saw the struggle? I ask you if you have any reason for knowing that no persons had weapons up to the time that the negro was shot? No, sir. You saw Philips with a pistol; wasn't that a pretty strong ground for knowing that he had one at that time? I didn't see him have one at that time. You saw no belts nor you saw no protuberances about any man's person? No, sir. And the only man you saw with a pistol afterwards was Phillips? Yes, sir. Did I understand you to say upon your examination in chief, the prisoner seemed to be trying to get away? Yes, sir. What did he do? He seemed to be struggling to get away. How did he struggle, did he knock any one down? No, sir, he was just trying to pull away. Which way did he pull? He seemed to be jumping hard, I never noticed which way. Was that jumping about

taking place when the crowd was pressing on. Yes, sir. And you concluded he was trying to get away? Yes, sir. Did'nt you cry out that he would get away? No, sir. Did any one around you cry out he would get away? I never heard any one. Didn't you see him fall in his efforts to get away? Not in his efforts to get away. Didn't you see him fall before he was shot? No, sir, I never noticed it. His back was towards you was it? Part of the time it was and part of the time he wasn't. Was your face towards him until after he got out on the pavement? Yes, sir, I saw his face once. So he turned about at some time, and his face was towards the north? Yes, sir. What time was that, directly after he got outside? Yes, sir. What was he doing then? He seemed to be struggling to get away. Was the crowd pressing on him at that time, was it all one simultaneous thing, this pressure of the crowd and the struggle of the police keeping them back, and the negroes efforts to get away? No, sir, some of the crowd seemed to be pushing on him. Was it at the same time that some of the crowd seemed to be pushing on him that the police seemed to be trying to keep them back? Yes, sir. All these things occurred about the same time? Yes, sir. How long a time do you think elapsed between the time the negro got outside of the arch and the time he fell, being shot? I suppose it was five minutes. You think the struggle for his life lasted for five minutes between the corner of the arch and the corner of the pavement? Yes, sir. How many steps would it take to pass from the corner he went around to the point when he fell? It was about two steps. You think he didn't go more than two steps, and he was five minutes going those two steps? He seemed to stop there in one place. Was that just after he got outside? Yes, sir, about the time he was at the corner, the southern corner of the arch. You mean just before he was shot? Yes, sir. At the very point he was shot? Yes, sir, he was about the point he was shot. So that was where you noticed the stoppage? Yes, sir. Did you notice no stoppage between the time he got outside of the arch and the time he reached the point where he was stopped? No, sir. When he turned out of the arch he went about two steps and halted? Yes, sir. And there he remained, for the rest of the time that made up those five minutes that elapsed from the time he left the arch until he was stopped. Yes, sir, he was fooling around there, he was not standing in one particular place. This struggle with the police, did it take place at the mouth of the arch or the point where the negro was shot? I think it was about the time he got to the corner where he was shot. You think the rush was not made on him until then? No, sir. You don't think there was any rush made on him just after he got outside of the arch? Well, the crowd seemed to be pushing up there—I never noticed any great rush. You spoke just now of several persons having been engaged in the rush on him, and the police keeping them back, ot the negro's attempt to get away, all happening at one moment as if it was one event, now did that take place at the arch, or did it take place further down towards the corner where the negro was shot? Further down towards the corner. You saw no obstruction to his movements from the time he got out of the arch until he got about the point where he was shot? Yes, sir, just before he got to that point. And you think it was five minutes between the time he got out of the arch until the time he was shot? I think it was about that time. Think again, do you think it was as long as that? I could not say for certain; I said it was about five minutes. I know you said it was, and I know it is very difficult to estimate time on such occasions; I want you to think over what occurred in that brief space of time and see if you are correct? I would say three minutes any how. Did it happen almost as quickly as it could have been done, or was there some delay; you think about three minutes would cover the whole space? Yes, sir. You say you didn't see Archy come down to the ground at all until he was finally shot? I never noticed it. Did you see Sam, Phillips at all before Archy was shot? No, sir. I understand after you got outside of the market house you didn't see Tolar, but Mr. Leggett and Ed. Powers were near you? Yes, sir. Were they behind you or before you? I think we were standing nearly in a line; Were you in the middle, between the other two, or were you on the right or left of that line? I could not tell that, sir. You don't pretend to locate with perfect accuracy, but you have an abiding impression that you were all standing there pretty close together? Yes, sir. Who did you say was standing nearest to you before the pistol was fired; did you notice any one else? No, sir. Had you seen John Maultsby that day up to that time? Not to notice him. Did you see Henry Sykes that day up to that time? No, sir. You say you had seen Sam. Hall? Yes, sir. You saw him inside of the market house? Yes, sir. Did you see him outside in the crowd afterwards? No, sir. How far were you from the prisoner when the pistol shot was fired? I suppose I was about three feet. How far do you think the person was who shot, by the sound? About three feet, or perhaps four or five. Was the noise of the pistol behind you? It was rather to the left and rear. You think that Archy was about three feet from you when he was shot? Yes, sir. And he was a little further from this man who fired the pistol? Yes, sir. That man was on the left and a little to your rear? Yes, sir. You were standing on the pavement were you? I was standing on the edge of the pavement. And the man who fired the pistol must have been off the pavement? Yes, sir. What distance do you estimate as three feet; point out some object about three feet from you?

(Witness points out an object which measures five feet.)

Archy was nearer to you than that when he was shot? Yes, sir, he was some nearer. And you think he was standing on the pavement opposite the south-east corner of the market house, and opposite the south edge of the small arch? Yes, sir. You say after the firing of that pistol you didn't see Mr. Tolar? No, sir. Did you see Mr. Leggett? I don't remember seeing him, sir. You heard the report of the pistol distinctly, then; was it near enough for you see any blaze or light? I didn't notice the blaze, You didn't notice any smoke from it? No, sir. You turned instantly in that direction as soon as the negro dropped and looked around, and saw Sam Phillips standing about in the position that the man would have been who fired the pistol? Yes, sir. He had a large pistol in his right hand down by his right side? Yes, sir. Did he have it up rubbing it or taking the cap off, or anything of that sort? No, sir. Did he look very much alarmed? I didn't notice anything like that. Did you see any one else with a pistol? No, sir. No one passed a pistol to you at that time, or shortly afterwards? saw'o, sir. When that pistol just fired, or shortly see . didn't you hear any exclamation in reference as to who did it? I heard some boys say Tolar did it." Directly after it was done? How long after? I suppose it was some ree minutes afterwards; as soon as he 'd up and looked at him, and walked on

and stopped around at the southern end of the market house. Who were those boys? I didn't notice them. Did you see Geo. Hollingsworth there? No, sir. You know him? I might know him if I was to see him. You don't remember him particularly? No, sir. About these exclamations; how many of those boys were there that made the exclamation "Capt. Tolar shot him." I heard it once or twice; I don't know whether it was one boy or two. Was that at the point where the negro was shot? It was in the crowd somewhere, I didn't notice. The person was not standing right by you; he was not standing near enough for you to see who it was? No, sir. Did you hear anybody exclaim that any one else had done it in crowd? They laid it upon some one who I knew it was impossible for him to have done it; Mr. Williamson, who has got no hands; some one was hollering out it was him. There was a joke made right straight away, that it was no-armed Williamson who did it, that they saw his finger on the trigger? Yes, sir. That was directly after this tragedy was enacted? No, sir. I am talking about then and there; the only exclamation you heard in the crowd just after it happened within two or three minutes, was that Captain Tolar had done it? Yes, sir. You didn't hear any other exclamation then? No, sir. Were those boys in front of you or behind you, who made that exclamation? I think they were behind me. Were they on your right or your left behind you? I never looked around there at all at them; I could not say which. You spoke of the direction the pistol was from the sound; I thought you could not tell from the sound of the voice? No, sir, I could not say which way they were. Have you ever heard Capt. Tolar say since this event took place, that he had a pistol that day? No, sir. About this movement of Monk Julia, that you spoke of, I think you saw him at one time trying to make at the prisoner Beebee with a knife; when was that before he was shot? Yes, sir. Just before he was shot? Yes, sir. How close was he to him? Ten or fifteen feet from him. Appearing to make his way through the crowd? Yes, sir. Did he have a knife in his hand? I never saw a knife. I didn't hear you say he had a knife in his hand, but in the examination in chief the Counsel used the expression "with a knife;" and you replied "Yes, sir," you say now he didn't have a knife? I don't remember seeing one. This man was just trying to make his way through the crowd? Yes, sir. Did you see him strike at all? No, sir. Did you see his hands? No, sir, I might have seen his hands; I didn't notice them particularly. Did you see who the man was who had hold of him? I think it was Mr. Nixon. Didn't you see anybody else near about that negro at the time he was killed besides Monk and Nixon, in the ten feet that was between them and the prisoner; didn't you see andybody that you knew? I never noticed a soul. Have you tried to bring your best recollection to bear upon this subject? Yes, sir. Is that the only time you saw Monk that day? Yes, sir, that was the first time I had seen him that day. Was it the last time? It is the last time I remember seeing him.

Question by the Commission:

In what direction was the negro's face turned at the moment the negro was shot? I can't say, sir, which way; I never noticed particularly which way his face was. Was he facing towards you? He must have been facing rather south. We don't want to know what he must have been, we want to know what way he was facing? I think he was facing rather eastward or south-eastward. That would be facing towards Mr. Davis' store? Yes, sir. You think he was facing towards Mr.

Davis' store? Yes, sir. At the time Beebee was shot what was the position Sheriff Hardie had with reference to Beebee? Well, I don't remember, sir, I remember just as I saw B-ebee fall I saw Sheriff Hardie standing there feeling his hair; I thought he was shot first; I don't remember what position he had when he was shot.

EDWARD P. POWERS, a witness for the defence, having been first duly sworn testified as follows.

Examined by the Counsel for the accused.

What is your name? Edward P. Powers. Where do you reside? Fayetteville. How long have you been residing in Fayetteville? I was born and raised there. What is your business in Fayetteville? Merchant. Where is your place of business? Near the foot of Hay Mount. How far from the market house? Half a mile. How far is your place of business from Ralph Lutterloh's? We are joining doors. Is his to the east or west of your place? West. Immediately west? Yes, sir. Were you in Fayetteville the day Archy Beebee was killed? Yes, sir. Did you go to the market house that day? Yes, sir. At what hour did you go to the market house? About half past three. In the afternoon? Yes, sir. Who went with you to the market house? Ralph Lutterloh. On which side did you go to the market house, upon the eastern, the northern or the southern side? The Northern if I remember right. What portion of the market house did you enter, upon first getting there? The large west arch. Who went into that large western arch with you sir? A short distance from the arch I got up with Capt. Tolar. He had been absent in Bladen county, I hadn't seen him for perhaps a week or ten days. That was I suppose about four o'clock, and I went up and spoke to him. Where was Tolar when you first saw him? He was near Mr. Hinsdale's store. Is that on the northern or southern side of the street? On the southern side. Tolar had been absent for a week or ten days, down in another county, and you went up to him and spoke to him, just an ordinary salutation? A salutation, and I had just an ordinary conversation with him. Then you and Tolar moved into the market house. where was Lutterloh, did he go in at the same time? I didn't notice particularly, he might have entered the arch before we did, we were together under there. What part of the market house did you go in when you first went in? I was standing near Becky Ben's stall. Who was standing near you? If I remember Capt, Tolar was standing there, Ralph B. Lutterloh, Leggett, that was about all the party that was standing up there. Where was Archy Beebee, at the time you took your position there? He was up in the court room over the market. How long were you there before Beebee was brought down stairs? It was perhaps a half hour. During that half hour, between the time you first got there, and the time Beebee was brought down, was your position the same, or was it shifted? About the same. Did you see anything of Leggett there? Yes, sir, I saw Leggett there. Did Leggett get there before or after you? I can't tell that, I don't know. During the time you were standing there, the half hour while Beebee was up stairs, were these persons you have named, yourself and Leggett, and Tolar and Lutterloh, were you together, or were you separated? We were near together. And near that point? Yes, sir. Were you the only persons around that place? There was a good many others, How many persons do you think there were under the market house at the time you first got there? I should judge there was fifty or sixty. Under the market house? Yes, sir. And you say yon four stood there pretty near together—shifted your position as men will shift their positions who are conversing? Yes, sir, What was the nature of the conversation, or did any conversation occur between you four, while you were standing there? It was mostly an ordinary conversation—this subject was brought up. What subject? The attempt to commit a rape on this young lady. Well sir, during the time that you were standing and talking upon that subject, and upon other subjects, were there any threats of violence made, by any of that party, or anybody in your hearing? I heard some one to my rear speak, and he said the man ought to be killed—he deserved death. Who was that person? I can't tell. Was that assented to by anybody else in the crowd? Several spoke of the matter, some said it is true he deserved it, but the law ought to take its course, I remember Nixon and myself were speaking of it, we both made the same remark, he perhaps deserved it but not while he was in the hands of the law. So that remark was made by some one in the rear, and instead of assenting to it, other voices, yours among the number said—that he might deserve it, but it was in the hands of the law, and the law ought to take its course? Yes, sir. How was the conversation you have spoken of, carried on between you and Tolar, and Leggett and Lutterloh, in whispers or in an ordinary tone of voice or in a loud tone? Every word I used there was in an ordinary tone of voice, about as loud as I am talking now. About the others, Tolar and Leggett and Lutterloh? If either one of them whispered, I didn't hear it. Did either of them whisper to you? No, sir. Did either one of them whisper another? Not that I seen, sir. Were they there in your view all the time? They were, particularly Tolar and Lutterloh—I didn't see Mr. Leggett the whole time. Mr. Powers, was there any agreement, or any combination made between any of these parties at that time to kill this boy or to do him any harm? There were none on my part, I am certain, and none on Capt. Tolar's, he hadn't been about the market house until that evening. You know he had been out of town? Yes, sir. For the period you had spoken of? Yes, sir, because invariably when he was not absent and in town he came to our store and his uncle's store and we were generally conversing together. How long did you say you were there before the negro came down. About a half hour. Did you see Mrs. Massey and her daughter comedown the steps? I did, sir. How long was that before the prisoner Beebee came down? A very few minutes. Who accompanied them, any one? Mr. Bond accompanied them to the carriage, if I am not mistaken, Where was the carriage? It was in front of the eastern arch, the main arch. Mr. Bond went with them to the carriage? Yes, sir. How long did the carriage remain there, after the ladies got into it? It didn't remain long, I could not tell what length of time exactly, not long though several gentlemen went up and spoke to the ladies. Who were they that went up and spoke to the ladies? I remember Mr. Phil. Taylor, and Mr. Robert Mitchell, and I think an uncle of the young lady, Mr. Powers, then. Tom Powers? Yes, sir. Anybody else? Mr. Bond was speaking to them. He accompanied them there? Yes, sir, that is all I can remember. Did Capt. Tolar go to the carriage? If he did, I don't remember it; I didn't see him. Those were the only persons you saw go to the carriage? If I saw others, I don't remember. Are you any kin to Tom Powers? No, sir, not that I know of. Are you related at all to Miss Elvira Massey? No, sir. And these I understand you to say were the only persons you saw go to the carriage? All I can remember now. Do you know who was driving the carriage? I don't remember that, sir. Do you remember whether it was a white man or colored man? I could not say with any certainty. How long after the carriage drove off was it before Beebee was brought down stairs? It was not many minutes. Did you see Beebee and the party which had him in charge, at the time they first came down to the door, upon the landing of the stairs of the market house? Yes, sir. Where were you standing just at that moment? I was standing at Becky's stall, or near it, on the outside of her counter. Were these same parties that you have named near you and around you at that time? I would state there was another that I didn't mention, just now, John W. Maultsby. So that at the time the boy was brought down, there was standing in that group, Ralph Lutterloh, Capt. Tolar, Leggett, John Maultsby and yourself? Yes, sir. What John Maultsby? John W. Maultsby. The man in Fort Macon? Yes, sir; he made a remark that I heard at the same time? What was it? I heard him say that he went there for the purpose of trying to get bail for the boy, and that if Archy was innocent he ought not to suffer, that if he was guilty he would drop the matter, and have nothing to do with him. You say John Maultsby was standing there? Yes, sir. At the very time the boy came down the steps? Yes, sir, about that time, I don't remember seeing him right exactly at that time, but I remember seeing him after the boy was down, but I know he was in the crowd, for I heard his voice. At the time the boy was brought to the head of the stairs, did you hear any remark made by any person in the crowd—I want to confine you to the times—I ask you, now at the time the boy was brought to the head of the stairs, and you first saw him, did you hear anybody in the crowd make any remark? There were some remarks made to my rear, "there is the rascal," or something like that. Did you see anybody get upon that bench that was running there in front of Becky Ben's stall? Not at that time. Did you see John Maultsby get upon that bench? No, sir. Did you hear Maultsby make any remark at the time? No, sir, I did not. Did you see Maultsby at that time? I did not. You know him well? I know him very well. Did you see him in the crowd afterwards? Yes, sir. You didn't see him at that time? No, sir. Was that bench which runs in front of Becky Ben's stable, in your line of view as you were looking from the position you were, to the boy at the head of the stairs? Yes, sir. Directly in your line of view? Yes, sir. I ask you if anybody at that time jumped upon that bench and made any remark at all? I seen no one jump on there. There was some standing on there. Did any person who was standing on that bench make any remark at the time? No, sir. Was John Maultsby standing on that bench at that time? I don't know as he was—I didn't see him—it was in my line and I would have noticed him, I was well acquainted with him. And you did not see him standing there? No, sir. Do you remember anybody that you did see standing there upon that bench? I could not call any names that were standing there. Then they came down the steps; did anything occur that

attracted your attention in any way between the time you first saw Beebee and his reaching the floor of the market house? No, sir. Nothing occurred at all? No, sir. Who were with him at that time, of the party who had him in charge? Mr. Wemyss had him by the thumb—with a string around his thumb, and Mr. Faircloth had hold of the other arm, and Mr. Hardie, if I remember right, was in front of him. And so they came down the stairs? Yes, sir. Did anything occur to attract your attention before he got to the outside of the market house? No, sir. Did you keep that position until the boy got outside of the market house? Nearly that same position until he got out of the arch. Which arch do you mean? The eastern arch. The main eastern arch? Yes, sir. Did you shift your position then? Yes, sir. Where did you move then? I moved in front of the arch. Who moved out with you? Capt. Tolar moved out there, and Mr. Lutterloh, and Mr. Leggett, and Sam Phillips was standing there. Where was he standing? Outside, on the pavement. He didn't move out with you? No, sir. So the party that moved out with you were yourself, Mr. Lutterloh, Capt. Tolar and Leggett? Yes, sir. At the time you got out on the pavement, where was Beebee and the party having him in charge? When I first noticed him after coming out of the arch, he was near the place where he was shot. When you went out on the pavement where did you take positions, yourself and the party? Capt. Tolar and myself were about the center of the pavement. Were you near the north or center of the southern portion of the main arch, or where were you? Near the center. Nearly opposite the center of the main arch? Yes, sir. That was your position? Yes, sir. And Tolar, you say, was closely by you? Yes, sir. Did you notice Lutterloh and Leggett there? I noticed them there. They were about there, too? Yes, sir. What occurred after you got there? The first thing that attracted my attention was the attempt of Beebee to get away. Where was that made, at about the point he was killed? Near that point, not quite. Near about the point where he was killed? Almost there. Just describe the attempt if you please, that he made to get away. He attempted to jerk away from the officers, as I thought; he was pulled down, and what attracted my attention was somebody spoke at the time in the crowd, I could not tell who it was; they believed that the negroes would attempt to rescue him; I noticed several bad characters there amongst them, they didn't appear to take any part in it however. That remark was made in the crowd by some one? Yes, sir. You don't know who? No, sir. You said the negro had sunk down then? Yes, sir. How long was it before he got up again? Not long; it was not a minute. When he got up, Mr. Powers, who were with him, who of the guard party did you notice with him? The same party was with him, Mr. Wemyss and Faircloth, and Hardie; I think Mr. Hardie had changed his position some. Where was he then? I think he was to his rear, on one hand or the other, with his hand on him? Could you tell which hand? No, sir. Wemyss was on one side, and Faircloth on the other, and you think Hardie was to his rear, with his hand on him? Yes, sir. How long was it after he got up before he was shot? A very short space of time, sir. Almost as soon as he got up, he was shot. Yes, sir. Do you know who shot him? I could not swear positively who shot him, the crowd was so great. What was your impression?

Counsel for the prosecution objected to the question.

What did you see of the shooting? There was

a crowd of persons between Capt. Tolar and myself and Beebee, and I looked over; what attracted my attention was his struggle; and I kept my eyes on him, and was looking at him the whole time, and I seen a pistol barrel lowered down. Where was that? It was to the left, from the outside of the pavement, to my left. Your left and front, or left and rear? Left and front. Did you see the hand that held it? Not at the time it was fired. Was that the pistol which was fired? Yes, sir, it was the same. Where you saw the pistol and saw the smoke, how far was that from where you were standing? I thought at first it was seven feet, but since then I have been at the market house, and I find it was about eleven feet, I stepped it. From where you were? Yes, sir. Where was Capt. Tolar at that moment? Capt. Tolar was by my side, sir. Close by your side? As close as two persons could stand in a crowd. Did Capt. Tolar shoot that pistol? No, sir. Was there more than one pistol shot that day? There was but one pistol fired. Are you certain, sir, it was not Capt. Tolar that fired? I am certain as I could possibly be; I don't see how it was possible for him to have fired the pistol without my seeing him. Have you any doubt about the matter, Mr. Powers? I have no doubt but what it was somebody else, who fired it. How far was that pistol that was fired there off from the pavement? The barrel was near the man's head. How far was it from the head of the man Beebee, the pistol barrel? I suppose may be it was about two feet. Did you say you were looking there at the time; you saw the barrel, and heard the report? Yes, sir. You saw the flash? Yes, sir. And you saw the smoke? Yes, sir. And it was that pistol-shot that killed the man Archy Beebee? I have no doubt of that. And that was not Capt. Tolar? No, sir. Did Capt. Tolar have any pistol out on that occasion? No, sir. Did he have one upon him? Yes, sir, he habitually wore a pistol. Do you know he had it that day? Yes, sir. Did you see it that day? Yes, sir, the circumstance under which I saw it, after the pistol was fired the crowd rushed back, Dr. McDuffie was sent for, I think, and they hollowed for the crowd to stand back so that the man could get air; and the crowd knocked against us, I stepped back then; I think I stepped back before Capt. Tolar did; they knocked his shawl off, and I seen the pistol on him, in a holster. On which side? It was to the rear of him, I can't remember which side. Secured by a belt? Yes, sir. And when the crowd pressed back, you saw Tolar's pistol in the holster? Yes, sir. How long was that after the firing occurred? A very short space of time. Did you see anybody near the place where you saw the flash and the smoke, have a pistol? There were two or thee pistols drawn in the crowd, perhaps as many as four of them, and I was excited at the time, as soon as the pistol fired; I didn't know what it was, I was afraid Sheriff Hardie had been killed, that was what frightened me; Mr. Phillips—What Phillips? Sam. Where was he standing? To the left or the outside of the pavement. How far was he from the place where you saw the pistol, and saw the smoke, and saw the flash? Directly after it was done I seen him step back on a line with me nearly. How long was it after he had stepped back that you saw him have a pistol? He had it in his hands as he stepped

back, and made a remark to me, says he "Powers, you had better examine and see if my pistol is loaded," says I "all right," and he did not show it to me. What did he do with the pistol? He put it behind him when he made that remark to me. Did he make any motion with the pistol? He had it in both hands, says he "Powers, you had better see if my pistol is loaded." And you replied to him "all right?'" I started to look at it. What did I understand you to do when you made your remark "all right," did you make any motion towards taking the pistol? I turned around to him to look at the pistol. What did he do with it? He put it behind him immediately. Under his coat or outside? Under his coat, sir. You made that remark, turned around to him as if to take it, and he put it in his coat behind him? Yes, sir, with both hands. Did he make any other effort to show it to you, either at that time or any other time? No, sir, some time afterwards, it was a short time, but under these circumstances it would be some time, a minute would be a long time, he offered it to some one else. How long a time was that? I suppose a minute afterwards or more. Who was that other person, do you know? I can't remember; I don't remember who it was for I didn't pay any attention to it; I heard him make the remark "it was a large pistol." Did you see anything of Capt. Tolar after the firing of the pistol? Yes, sir. What became of him? He stood about the market there a little while. Where did he go? I don't remember where he went then. What became of you, sir? I came on up town. You say you didn't notice whether the other person examined the pistol, when he offered to show it the second time? No, sir, if they did I didn't see it; I was summoned as a witness very hurriedly and I could remember nothing about these details; but since then I went to the market house, and just pictured to myself as every person stood that I could remember; I was advised to go the market house, and just picture to my self as every person stood, so that I could give in my evidence correctly; then I remembered while I was standing there a number of persons that I could not remember that day. Mr. Powers, have you been arrested about this matter? I received a summons to appear as a witness; I was told, however, I would be arrested; when I got to Wilmington I then reported to General Avery's head-quarters, and General Avery turned me over to the officer of the day. So you were subpœnaed as a witness and were arrested as you got here? Yes, sir, I knew I was going to be arrested in Wilmington, I then reported in Raleigh and stayed there two days, and have been in Fort Macon since.

Cross Examination, by the Counsel for the prosecution.

What is your father's name? J. W. Powers. When was the first time that you had heard of the attempt of Archy Beebee to ravish Miss Massey? I heard it the evening that he attempted it. You heard it on the Sunday evening before he was killed? Yes, sir. What time in the evening? It was late in the evening. After tea? It was late in the afternoon I mean. Was it tea time, or after? About early tea time. Who told you of it at that time? I don't remember sir, so many parties were speaking of it. You heard a great deal of it that evening? Yes, sir. From a great many quarters? Yes, sir. Can't you remember any one who mentioned it to you? I can't bring to my mind any particular person. You have tried to refresh your memory? Yes, sir. According to the same rules of memory, and it is an act of memory, by picturing to yourself where you were at the time that this information was given to you, I should think you could tell. I think Sam Hall spoke to me on that subject that afternoon. Any one else that you can recollect? Joseph Avery. The way I come to think of it now, I was sitting in front of the hotel, and I heard it, and I remember now that Hall and Avery were talking about it. You heard them speaking of it? Yes, sir. Can you recall any other persons, whether they were speaking to you or not, that was the first you had heard of it, you heard Sam Hall and Joseph Avery? I may have heard others speaking of it before, but I don't recollect now. Did they speak to you, either one of them? The crowd was talking about it. Were they all in the same crowd? Yes, sir. Who else was present beside yourself and Mr. Avery and Mr. Hall? I think Mr. Reuben Jones was there. A large crowd there? Yes, sir, usually is, every Sunday evening, a large crowd in front of the hotel. Do you know John Jackson? You mean John D. Jackson. A man that has a still across the river? I don't remember seeing him. You say there was a considerable crowd there? A dozen or so of men. Did you and Sam Hall make any agreement, that you would go down to the market house to the trial the next day? No, sir. You had no agreement then that you would attend? I didn't intend to go to the trial at all. I had been busy that day at the store. I am talking about that Sunday evening, when it was first mentioned? No, sir, there was no agreement. You had nothing to do with the capture of Archy Beebee? No, sir. Who did form the posse that went for him? I think Faircloth was one of the party; he was the one that spoke to me about the details of the capture. You were not along? No, sir. You knew nothing about that; and you made no agreement to go down the next day? No, sir, none in the world. Did you have a weapon on that Sunday evening? No, sir, I never wear a weapon, unless I am on guard. In summer and winter, I wear an open coat, like the one I wear now. Did you hear persons, after this first time, speak of this affair of Beebee, from any quarter? It was universally talked of, all over town. And feelings of indignation expressed? Yes, sir. You heard no threats from any quarter, and you positively swear that you didn't know of any agreement, understanding or combination, upon the part of any men to punish the negro? I do positively swear to that. You never heard any such a thing, and you never anticipated any such a thing, when you went to the market that day? No, sir. Not only you didn't know of such an agreement, but you didn't even expect it to take place? I didn't expect it to take place? What time of day did you leave your place of business to go down to the market house? Between three and four. Is your father in the same business with you?

Yes, sir, he stays with me. You keep the same store? Yes, sir. Is he a partner in the concern? No, sir. Is the store yours; or his? Mine. Didn't your father request you not to go to the market house that day? He said he would not go up there to the trial, there would be a big crowd, and he was afraid there would be some difficulty. I told him I was just going down to hear the trial. Didn't he urge you not to go? I don't remember his urging me. He advised you to keep away? He made a remark at the time, he believed there would be an attempt by the blacks to take that boy away from the officers. He didn't want you to be in any row? He was afraid there would be a disturbance between the races. He didn't want you to go, but you insisted? I told him I would go down, and he said "all right." Did you stop for Lutterloh? We were standing together out on the pavement, the stores join. How did you get together? I proposed to Lutterloh to take a walk down, and hear the trial. Was that after the conversation with your father, or before? We had the conversation after I asked Ralph. Did you see any unusual stir in the street, going down Hay street? No, sir. Not more of a crowd than usual? Only at the Market House. Down the street it was just as quiet as usual? Yes, sir. Nothing to excite apprehension at all? No, sir. When you got to the market you saw Capt. Tolar before you went in? Yes, sir. Standing near Hinsdale's corner? Yes, sir. Were you coming down on the same side of the way as Hinsdales'? No, sir Did you cross over towards Hinsdales'? Yes, sir, he was coming towards the market from one side, and myself from the other, and we met. How far were you from the arch, when you came together—the western arch? I suppose about twenty feet. Where was Lutterloh? He was at the edge of the Market, I think. Did you stop for Capt. Tolar to catch up with you? We just come together, and merely stopped long enough shake hands. Lutterloh went in before you then? I think he went under the western arch, a little before me and Capt. Tolar. Wasn't Tolar inside of the market house when Lutterloh went in there? I won't be positive about Lutterloh; I know we got there together. Didn't Lutterloh shake hands with Capt Tolar? I don't think he did. Don't he know him? He knows him, but is not very well acquainted with him. You don't remember Lutterloh shaking hands with him? I know their acquaintance is merely passing, Tolar and myself have been very intimate. Do you remember exactly what did become of Lutterloh, whether he went in before you did, or whether he was with you, when you and Capt Tolar went in? He was going down on the north side of the street, with me, and I left him to meet Capt. Tolar. I understood you to say it was right in your way. I said he came from one side, and I from the other, and we met about the middle of the street. And then Lutterloh went on straight ahead, the way he was going? Yes, sir. You did'nt see him again until he got to the market house? No, sir, I didn't see him go into the market house. And you don't know when he did go in? No, sir. How long had Capt. Tolar been away, sir, before that day, sir. I could not tell the exact number of days, I think it was over a week, I know I hadn't seen him in eight or nine days. You think he had been away to Bladen, or one of those adjoining counties; how did you know that? He told me. He told you he had been away for eight or nine days? I knew at the time he did go, or rather the next day. How did you find that out? He spoke to me on the subject. He told you he was going? I asked him, when we shook hands, and he told me, he had been down in Bladen. You swear he had been down in Bladen? I swear he told me he had been down in Bladen. You were not down in Bladen with him? Of course I can't swear positive whether he was there or not. And therefore you ought not to have attempted to swear at all; you don't know anything about it, but you undertake to make Capt. Tolar's statement the basis of a statement you make yourself? Yes, sir. You swear he was down there for nine or ten days? I know I hadn't see him; I don't know whether he was away or not; I knew he hadn't come into town, because I would have been certain to have seen him, for he invariably stopped at our store. He habitually stopped at your store when he came down, and you hadn't seen him there for eight or nine days, and that is the ground upon which you concluded that he was away? Yes, sir. You met him at the door of the market house and went into together? I didn't meet him at the door, where we come together, it was about twenty or thirty feet from the market house, almost in the center. You moved right on down and went in together? Yes, sir. When you got in did you find Mr. Leggett? I seen Leggett there after we had been in a while. How long had you been in before you saw him? No time scarcely at all. How long had you been in before you saw Lutterloh? A very short space of time. As we went in Capt. Tolar and myself were talking together in an ordinary conversation, and we walked together and stood there near Becky Ben's stall, and then I turned around and I seen Lutterloh standing by me. How did Leggett come up? He was in the crowd, I don't know which arch he come in at. You only know that you found him near you and Lutterloh? He may have come in behind Mr. Tolar and me. Did you see any weapon on Capt. Tolar at that time? Not at that time. You didn't know that he had any then? I didn't know. You said he habitually carries it? He does, but I didn't know he had one at that time. The only time you saw it was in the holster, after the shouting? Yes, sir. How did you know it was a pistol? I can see a pistol in the holster. What was the length of the holster? I could not say. You have seen it frequently? No, sir. Could as large a pistol as that have got into the holster? (Exhibiting the pistol introduced in the evidence of Samuel A. Phillips, as that which Phillips had in his possession on the day of the shooting.) Somewhere about that size, I could not say it was exactly as large as that, I could not see the stock in the holster. Do you think this pistol could have got in the holster you saw? I could not say, some of those pistols look alike, and the same holster won't fit them. I could not tell whether it was a large army size, or a large navy size. You never saw the pistol at all? I never had it in my hands. Did you never see it in his hands out of the holster? No, sir. You never saw the pistol at all, only a portion of it—you just saw he had one, and you saw the stock? Yes, sir. You don't know what sort of a pistol it was, how large? I don't know whether it was a large army or navy size; I thought it was one of the two. How did you get that opinion, from the size of the holster? Yes, sir. It was a large sized pistol? Tolerably large sized. What size do you call this one? I am not familiarly acquainted with pistols, but I know there is a difference in the size; I have seen the two at different times at arsenal, and have been told there was a difference in the size. If you saw one in a man's hand, you could not tell whether it was a army or navy pistol at a glance? Hardly, at a glance. Can you tell whether th's is

an army or navy? I could not tell positively. Could you tell if you saw one by itself? If I remember right, the navy pistol is smaller than the large army pistol. That is so, sir, but I want to know whether just seeing the pistol, as you say, and not seeing the two sizes together, could you tell one from the other without comparing them? As I told you before, I am very little acquainted with pistols, I never carry one at all. You could not form any idea whether Capt. Tolar's pistol was an army or a navy size? There is a pistol at home that I have never had on in my life, except when I am on guard, and I know it is a navy size; and it is about the size of that pistol. You think then a navy pistol is about this size? Yes, sir. When you were standing in the market house with Capt. Tolar. Lutterloh and Leggett, you saw this lady and her mother, Miss Massey and her mother come down the steps, did you? I did. Did you see John Maultsby about the time they came down the steps, or was it after that you saw John Maultsby? I seen John Maultsby in the crowd, I don't remember the exact time; I overheard him make that remark. Was that before the lady came down stairs? I can't remember exactly. You can't remember whether it was before the lady came down or afterwards? He made a remark about the man but I can't tell exactly the time. What were those remarks you heard Mr. Maultsby make, and who was he talking to? He was talking to the crowd; he appeared a little excited; the negro boy was a favorite of his; he had him employed, I think, a good deal, says he "if Archy is innocent I don't want him punished, want to see him bailed or something, but if he is guilty, I will have nothing more to do with him." What did you say about bailing? He said he wanted to go his bail, or to get bail for him. Did he tell you how it was that an innocent man required bail? No, sir. If he was innocent he was going his bail? He said if he was innocent he was going to stand by him, or go his bail, or do something for him. Didn't he use the expression "go bail?" He said he went there for that purpose, to stand his bail. But still he said if the court found him guilty he would not stand his bail; he would have nothing more to do with him? Yes, sir, I remember that part of it, that he went there first to stand his bail; that is the way I wanted my language to go down. I want it to go down as you said it, and not as you meant. I understand you to say now, that Mr. Maultsby said, in that conversation, that this negro, if he was innocent, he was his friend, and was going to stand his bail? mean in this way. He said he went there for the purpose of giving bail or trying to get bail. Then he said if Archy was innocent he was for him. I can't remember the exact words. But the impression left on your mind was he went there to stand his bail, if he never did it? That was my impression. You can't say exactly when you heard Maultsby making these remarks about the bailing, whether it was before, or after the ladies came down? No, I can't remember exactly. After the ladies came down, didn't you hear Maultsby say that he had found out that the court had decided against him up stairs? I saw him ask Mr. Bond was Archy guilty, or not guilty. Didn't he ask him that after you had heard him make this other statement? I could not say positively. You heard him either before or afterwards ask Mr. Bond if Archy was guilty? Yes, sir. Did you hear what Bond told him in reply? Mr. Bond told him that he was guilty I think. Where were they standing, when you heard that conversation? They were standing near Becky's stall. In the market house? Yes, sir. Was it before Bond had been to the carriage with the ladies, or after he came back? If I remember right, it was before the ladies came down, so I can't say for certain. Do you remember now exactly where they were standing? They were standing near Becky's stall. Now do you remember whether it was before or after the carriage had driven off? I can't remember whether the carriage was driven away or not. There were so many circumstances that I can't remember the exact time. I know it is difficult, but I thought your going back to the place—that perhaps you might recollect all the events—you can't recollect whether it was immediately before the carriage drove off or afterwards? I can't say. How often did you see Bond that day; perhaps we can get at it in that way? I seen Bond several times. While you were there the twenty minutes before Archy came down, did any one come down the steps, during that time, before the ladies came down to go to the carriage, did Mr. Bond come before them. I think I seen Mr. Bond come down for some purpose or other; he was constable, and had to come down the steps for witnesses or something like that. You think you saw him come down? I think I did. Did you see anybody else? I don't remember seeing anybody else, only seeing a policeman come to the door. Do you think it was at that time, when Mr. Bond came down, that Maultsby asked the question? I could not say, sir. The next you saw come down the steps was this lady and her mother, and Bond was with them then? Yes, sir. Did he come out of the door with them? I think he came out before them. Was he on the steps outside of the door before the ladies came down, or did he seem to come from the room with them? I could not say positively, I knew he was in company with them. When these ladies came down, Mr. Bond went with them to the carriage? Yes, sir. You are certain of that? Yes, sir. They didn't stop in the crowd? No, sir. It could not have been at that time that Maultsby spoke to him? No, sir. Did you see Mr. Bond when he came back? I didn't notice him. Did you notice whether he came back from the carriage at all, and went up stairs again? I didn't notice it. Did you notice whether he went up in the Court from the carriage at all? I didn't notice it at all; there were so many there I could not tell. You saw certain persons go to the carriage and speak to the ladies—was Bond standing there at the time these persons went there? When Bob Mitchell was there I think Bond was standing there. Did you see Tom Powers there? I saw him go to the carriage. Did you see him have any conversation with the ladies? He said something to them, I could not say what. What became of him after he said this something; did you see him where he went? He came back to the market. Had you seen him in the market house before that day? Tom Powers was under the market house. When you first got there? I could not say that. Had you seen him there before the ladies came down? I could not say positively. Did you see where he joined the ladies, whether they called him to them or whether he joined them and walked out to the carriage with them? I think he walked out to the carriage behind them. And they had some conversation and he came back? Yes, sir. You said the carriage was there about five minutes after the ladies came down? A very short time, I could not say what time exactly. Were you looking at the carriage while the gentlemen were coming up? Yes, sir. Didn't Capt. Tolar go out and speak to the ladies? If he did, I didn't see him. You swear positively that he did not. I don't think he could have left my side at that time. Do you swear positively he did not do it to the best of your knowledge and belief and give your

reasons? To the best of my belief I don't think he went there. You think you saw him pretty much all the time the carriage was there, during that five minutes? He was near me after and before, I didn't keep my eyes on Capt. Tolar the whole time. You saw him shortly before and shortly afterwards? Yes, sir. And therefore you conclude that he was in the same place all the time? Yes, sir. But you don't swear positively he did not go to the carriage at all, you didn't see him? No, sir, to the best of my belief I would swear he didn't go. When Tom Powers came back where did he go? Underneath the market house. Did you see where he stood? I never noticed, I saw he was weeping, him and Mr. Mitchell were uncles of the girl. Mr Powers was weeping as he came back? Yes, sir, and before. He seemed to be a good deal overcome? Yes, sir, he was completely overcome. Did you see Monk about that time? Yes, sir. Did you see him have anything to say to Mr. Powers? I didn't see Monk have any conversation with Mr. Powers at all. Did you see them pretty near together? If they were I didn't notice it. Did you notice Henry Sykes sitting down by Powers? I never saw Henry Sykes the whole day. Did you see David Oliphant there that day? No, sir. The negro started to come down stairs five minutes after the carriage drove off? About that time. Now, all this time, from the first time you got there until this moment now that I am speaking of when the negro came down, or when he appeared at the head of the stairs, you and Capt. Tolar and Ralph Lutterloh had been standing together? Yes, sir, so far as Capt. Tolar and myself and Lutterloh were concerned, we were together, I am certain, all the time, and Leggett, he was very near us in the market. Was he standing in the same group? Yes, sir. Did Maultsby come up and have anything to say to you? No, sir. When the question was asked just now if after the negro Archy came out of the door, and was upon the steps, you saw any one jump up on Becky Ben's bench, you said not at that time, did you see them jump up there at any time? I never seen any one jump up on it. Did you see any one on it? There were several on it. How long had they been standing there before the negro came down? I could not tell; I noticed some one on the bench about the time he was brought down. And you can't name a single one of them? I can't, sir, for my eyes were on the negro. If Maultsby had been there you think you could have seen him? Yes, sir. But you can't name a single other soul you saw—you saw there —they were in your line of vision? Yes, sir. The crowd was mostly composed of your acquaintances and neighbors? I could not say that; there are a great many people in town I don't know. Do you think there were strangers on that bench? There might have been some of them that I was acquainted with—the whole of the bench was not full. But what I wanted to know is this, if you did not recognize any body there? I did not. Why is it, then, you think you would have known Maultsby? I think if he had seen me he would have spoken to me. And because he did not speak to you, you think he was not on the bench? I don't think he was. Now, as this negro came down stairs, I understand you did hear some exclamations behind you, of some sort, "there comes the rascal," or something to that amount? Yes, sir. How many voices did you hear that from? Perhaps a couple, or it might have been the same one. Did you hear any body say "rally boys?" No, sir, I never heard that expression. Did you hear any body say here he comes? Not that I remember, it may have been used; I think I heard the words used "here he is" but I never paid any attention to it. But you heard some exclamation of that sort, indcating that the negro was about to come down, or was there? Yes, sir. You can't pretend to use the exact words, simply "here comes the rascal," or "there he comes," or "here he is," or something of that sort? My eyes were on the police and the prisoner. And your attention was absorbed for the time being? Yes, sir. When this lady passed through the crowd just before that, how many do you suppose were in the crowd; you say there were about fifty in the market house when you got there, how many do you think there were there when she came down stairs? Fifty or sixty I would estimate the number, there was a larger crowd outside. On the east front of the market house? Yes, sir, east and south east. Around that corner? Yes, sir. There was a larger crowd outside of the market house, when the ladies came down, than there was inside of the market house? Yes, sir. Did the crowd grow less or greater from the time you first went to the market house, to the time he was killed? It was larger about the time he was killed, there were a great many colored people there then. There were more colored people you think than white? There was as many I should think. Was that the case, when you first got to the market house? I didn't notice then, outside particularly. Up to the time that Archy came down the steps, had you seen anybody with any weapon that day? No, sir, I dont think I seen any. Had you seen no one in that crowd with a belt, that looked as if he had a weapon, attached to it—no knife? I seen Monk with a knife—I seen no belt, What was Monk doing with a knife? He said if he was allowed he would fix him, or something to that amount. Who was he talking to? Nixon, as soon as Nixon took hold of him he stopped. Was that before the man came down stairs? No sir. I am talking about before the negro came down stairs, and you were standing underneath. No, sir I never seen any knife, And you never saw any weapon in the hands of any one, until after he came down? No, sir. See Tom Powers have a knife? No, sir. You didn't see what became of Tom Powers, after he came from the carriage? I didn't, Just before they were bringing the man down stairs you say you heard some voices behind you discussing the question, and some said he ought to be punished, and some men in the crowd said he deserved death, without a trial—but some of them said what? I said he may deserve death but while he was in the hands of the law it ought to take its course, and Jim Nixon he agreed with me, or rather spoke at the same time, whether he noticed my remark or not I could not say, Who was that used the other expression? I can't tell, it was in my rear. Did you turn around and speak back to them, to say you differed;with them, in the opinion? I addressed my conversation more to the crowd. Was Jim Nixon near you at that time? Yes, sir, because when he commenced talking I knew his voice, and I turned back. Then you did turn back towards where the voice came from? Yes, sir, but these other persons was in the crowd, and I did not see him. Did you recognize the first voice you heard? No, sir. Could you tell whose it was; didn't you think it was Sam Phillips? No, sir, I could not swear positively. Didn't you hear anybody say like that man that first spoke, was not there a difference of opinion expressed, or not, some saying one way and some another? Perhaps there was some who agreed with the man who spoke first—I didn't pay any attention. And you only heard yourself and Nixon reply to this man? Yes, sir. You know Tom Powers don't you? I know him very well. You say there is no relationship between you and him?

Not that I know of. You say Hardie came down in front of the negro? Yes, sir. You are certain about that? I am pretty certain about that? Did he come out of the door first, and get in front, or did he get in front of them after they had all got outside of the door? I noticed him in front, as he was coming out of the door. Didn't you see Hardie come out and shut the door, and walk down, two or three steps, and look around to see if everything was quiet? I couldn't say positive, sir. But you recollect seeing Hardie when he was coming;down, in front of the prisoner, and Wemyss was upon his right hand, and Faircloth on his left? Yes, sir. Were there any other police there beside Wemyss and Faircloth and Hardie? I could not say positive; I noticed Faircloth, I know him very well. You say nothing was done at all to the prisoner until he came down stairs? No, sir. And the only expression you heard was the one behind you? Yes, sir, "there comes the rascal." Did you hear that when he was on the steps? I could not say positive. You saw no assault made on him on the steps at all? No, sir. How many steps does it take to go from the foot of the steps to the arch where he turned out of? To the front of the arch? No, where did he go out of the arch, close to the side on his right? Yes, sir, I suppose it was about six or seven steps. During the time he was passing the six or seven steps, were you standing near Becky Ben's stall? Yes, sir. Was Tolar there? Yes, sir. You are certain? Yes, sir. You saw him then and there? Yes, sir. You saw Lutterloh then and there? Yes, sir. And Leggett? I seen Leggett about that time, I wont be positive whether I saw him at that moment or not. Did you see John Maultsby at that time? No, sir. Did you see Tom Powers at that time? Not at that time. Did you see Tom Powers between the time the negro got to the foot of the steps, and the time the negro got to the arch, and turned out? I seen Tom Powers as he got in the arch. You saw Tom Powers right at the arch by him? Yes, sir. Didn't you see Tom Powers grab at him? He made a motion at him. With which hand sir? I don't remember sir. He said "give him to me, he is my prisoner" and the Sheriff said 'go away Tom,' and Tom desisted. Did you see Monk then? Yes, sir. Did you see the Sheriff catch Tom Powers, by his wrist, and take him, and push him away, and force him back? No, sir. Did you see any knife in Mr. Power's hand at that time? No, sir. Did you see Tom Powers have any weapon that day, at any time? I did not sir. Did you see him have any pistol at that time? No, sir. You can't say which hand he used to grab him with? No, sir. Did he grasp at the prisoner just as he got into the arch? Yes, sir. Was Powers outside on the pavement? He was about the arch. Suppose the arch to be, here, on my right, wasn't he standing with his back right against the pillar? I can't say, I think though, probably he was inside. Did you see him make this grab? Yes, sir. And you heard Sheriff Hardie tell him to desist? Yes, sir. Didn't you hear him say "by God he is mine," didn't you hear strong expressions used by Tom Powers? I don't remember hearing any strong expressions. Didn't you hear Sheriff Hardie make use of a strong expression? No sir. Do you mean the Sheriff said "go way Tom," in a gentle tone? He always speaks emphatically, on all occasions, he speaks plainly. He is a very decided man. Was that the whole conversation you heard during that time? If anything happened before that I didn't know it. And you say that man immediately desisted when Sheriff Hardie spoke? He stepped back. Where did he step to? He stepped back out of the way, of the Sheriff. Where did stepping back throw him from the inside or outside? Inside. The Sheriff had not gone outside of the arch? No, 'sir, he was about under the arch. Don't you think the Sheriff had turned outside of the arch? I don't think he had. So he had to turn back to interrupt this man who was interrupting the prisoner? I don't think the Sheriff had got outside. Do you think he turned towards the man, Tom Powers, who was trying to grasp the prisoner? He sort of turned towards him. Then was Sheriff Hardie in front of Archy or behind him, when he turned towards Tom Powers at that time? Perhaps he may have turned towards him. Sheriff Hardie stood still until Archy passed in front of him, and there Sheriff Hardie kept behind him to protect him in the rear. I don't remember seeing Sheriff Hardie in the rear, at that time; don't you remember he came down in front of him, and when this assault was made on him he jerked back to stop the man who made the assault, and from that time he was in his rear; don't you remember that? I could not say distinctly, I just remember his telling the crowd to stand back a little and let the man alone. When did he say that? Just as he got outside of the arch? You say Tom Powers desisted from making this assault after the Sheriff spoke to him? Yes, sir. You didn't see him take hold of his wrist? No, sir. You didn't see the Sheriff grab as if he was grabbing at anything? No, sir. But you heard the Sheriff say, in emphatic tone, simply "Tom, go away from here and let him alone?" To the best of my belief that is all. And Tom immediately desisted and stepped back? Yes, sir. You didn't see anything of Monk at that time? I think it was about that time I saw Monk with a knife. Had the prisoner got outside of the market house before you saw Monk with a knife? No, sir. The prisoner was still in the market house between the foot of the steps and the arch? Yes, sir. And you saw Monk with a knife, was that about the time you saw Powers grabbing at him? It was not far from that time. Was it the same movement or not? No, sir. Was it a moment before or after? I can't remember about that. The things are in very close association in your mind? Tolerably close. What was Monk doing with that knife? When I seen him he had it in his hand; he said if he had the fellow in his power he would fix him. He was standing right still was he? He was there standing still or changing his position, he was not rearing. He was perfectly quiet? I don't say he was perfectly quiet. But he was not trying to get at him? No, sir. He was not pressing on him? No, sir. How was he holding the knife? I can't say. I want to know if he had it in his grasp? I can't say, he had it in his hand though. Was it an open knife? Yes, sir. What sort of a knife? A common knife, a common pocket knife. What do you call a common knife? The blade was about three inches. Did you see any more of Tom Powers after that; after he desisted and the sheriff told him to stop? I may have seen him afterwards, but I could not say positive. You don't know what became of him? No, sir. You moved on the pavement then? Yes, sir. Directly after the conversation between Hardie and Tom Powers? I moved out directly after the sheriff took the negro out. This happened just before Archy got to the arch? Yes, sir. And just after the sheriff got in the arch, he spoke to the people? Just after he got a little outside. Are the pavement of the market house and the pavement of the street the same level? Yes, sir. Had he stepped through the arch?

Yes, sir. Was it just after he stepped through the arch that he addressed the crowd? Yes, sir. What did he say? He just said very emphatically that the prisoner was in his possession, and he would protect him, or something of that sort. Was any one trying to got at the prisoner at that time? No, sir. What was the occasion of this speech? Because of the other attempt. You think this effort of Tom Powers induced him to speak to the crowd? I suppose he intended it as a warning to the people. Did you see any signs of the people making a rush at the negro at that time? No, sir. But the sheriff without any such signs told the crowd he was going to do his duty and the man was in his possession? Yes, sir; the only signs I seen was the colored people talking together in an excited manner. Didn't he speak to those colored men? No, sir, he spoke to the crowd; it was a general address to the crowd I judged. How near was the sheriff to the prisoner? When he spoke to the crowd he was very near him. Right at him? Yes, sir; I cant remember whether he was in front or rear. Were the policemen around the prisoner? The policemen were still at him. Did you see any policemen with clubs at that time? I won't say positive. Were you inside of the market house when the Sheriff made his little speech to the people? He made that after he got out. Where were you? I was about the centre of the arch at that time, and perhaps a little out. You were just moving out? Yes, sir. Was the whole crowd in motion? Yes, sir, and Capt. Tolar and myself stopped on the pavement, in the centre of the main arch, and the crowd rushed between us and the prisoner. When Sheriff Hardie made this speech to the people, was he right among the people—were they right up against him—or were they clearing out of the way; he had to get them out of the way to get along, didn't he? Yes, sir. When he made this speech, I want to know whether he had a clear space around him, between him and the crowd he was talking to? I could not say. Didn't you see him? Yes, sir, I saw him. Didn't you see the crowd? The crowd was all around. Warn't the crowd right up against him? I should judge they were. Were they not as near him as they could get? I don't know whether they were pressing right against him. Do you say they were not? I say I don't know whether they were or not. Were they close enough to press if they pleased? If they pleased they were. He was right in the midst of the crowd when he made this address? Yes, sir. You passed out and stood in the centre of the pavement? About opposite the centre arch, in the centre of the pavement. And Capt. Tolar was standing by you? Yes, sir. On your right or left? If I remember right he was on my right. Try and remember it rightly; you have been back to locate the positions? I was somewhat to his rear and I think to his left. A little to his rear and left then? Yes, sir. So he was to your front and right? Not much to my front. Now, what had become of Leggett at that time? Leggett was near us. How do you know? I know it because I seen him very near us, I think he was near me, perhaps he was little further to the rear, and perhaps a little further to my right, I heard his voice. His voice is peculiar. You don't remember seeing him? I noticed seeing him at different times in the crowd, but I could not say at that time. Where was Ralph Lutterloh at that time, when you got out side on the pavement, and took your station? Since I have been to the market house and took a view of where we stood, I think he was, a little to my left, and rather to my front. You think Capt. Tolar was a little to your right and front? Yes, sir. And Lutterloh a little to your left and front? Yes, sir. So that you stood, as it were, almost between the two? Yes, sir. And Leggett, you can't say where he was? No, sir, one circumstance made me remember where Lutterloh was, when Phillips stepped back he stepped back by Lutterloh. You remember where Lutterloh was standing then? Yes, sir, because I noticed Phillips as he stepped back. Well sir, after you got outside, how long was it before the negro was shot, could you have counted a hundred? No, sir. You don't think you could? No, sir, they walked on slow, and he tried to break loose and come down, and while he was down. Who was by him then? I could not see, because there was such a crowd between us. Didn't you see the sheriff knock him down, to prevent him from getting loose? No, sir. Didn't you see him catch him in the front of the comforter. I seen the policemen holding him, of course trying to keep him from getting away, and he went down. Didn't you see one of the policemen catch at the long comforter he had, in front? No, sir. Do you remember he had on a comforter that day? I don't remember now sir. You think he was jerked down? He went down, I don't know whether he was jerked down or not. You think he was trying to escape, and and the police threw him down to prevent him? He was trying to escape. And the police, in their struggle to hold him caused him to go down? Yes, sir. Now at the time he was trying to escape, was not some one trying to take his life that you saw? No, sir. You didn't see any body rushing upon him? No, sir. The crowd was perfectly quiet? It was not perfectly quiet, because they were moving. They were not pressing towards this man? They were not pressing on him that I saw. You swear positively they were not pressing on him, because you were there and could see him. I could not see him when he was down. When he went down I want to know what was done in the crowd that was around him, if there was nobody to get at him? I did not see him. You didn't see any pressure on him at all? No, sir. You didn't see the policemen use their clubs? No, sir. Didn't you hear the Sheriff tell the men to use their clubs? I remember hearing one policeman tell the men on his right to stand back out of the way, and if they didn't, he would use his club. Was that just before the negro fell? About the time the negro fell; it was near that time, but whether it was before or afterwards I could not say positively. But at the time you saw him try to escape, you don't think there was anything said? No, sir. You didn't see any danger from it? No, sir. He was not in any danger from the crowd? No, sir. You saw no clubs used? No sir. Did you hear a blow struck? No, sir. Did you see a knife fall out of a man's hand, and hear it clash on the pavement? No, sir. Did you see nobody pick up a knife that had fallen on the pavement? No, sir. Did you hear any exclamation of "kill him, kill him" that day, from any quarter? I heard some halloing. Where was the halloing? It was to my left, several voices, but my being back, I never made out what they were saying. What was to prevent you, you say it was a quiet crowd? My attention at that time was directed to the prisoner and the policemen, my whole mind was on that. Your whole mind being on that, you didn't see that there was any danger of an assault, and you didn't see them use their clubs at all? No, sir. You saw no pressure on the policeman? No, sir. You saw no necessity of their using their clubs? No, sir, only this one policeman, and I judged some of the crowd pressed against him. That is the only sign you saw of anything like an attempt to get at the negro? I didn't

think that was an attempt to get at the negro. You are certain there was not any attempt at the time he was trying to escape? Yes, sir. You didn't see anybody strike at him with a knife at that time? No, sir. When was this cry you heard, that you can't tell what the words were? was it before he attempted to escape or afterwards? I could not give the exact time. What was the exclamation you heard? Some persons hollowed out as near as I can remember, "fix him," or something like that. You can't swear what the exact words were? No, sir. Is that the only exclamation you heard, you swear you heard no one say kill him, kill him? I don't remember now of hearing the word, "kill him," I may have heard it, but I don't remember it now; the crowd was confused, men were talking every one was talking to somebody at the time and some word was used, it was either kill him, or something to that amount. Some expression of that effect was used, before he was shot? Yes, sir. Did you hear some one say "he will get away, kill him?" I heard the remarks that he was trying to get away? Didn't you hear several cry out that? Perhaps I did. You didn't see the assault made on him then, till the pistol was fired, except the one in the arch, when he was coming out? No, sir. Almost as soon as he straightened after he fell he was shot? In a very little time, was not it immediately? Yes, sir, you may say immediately. Now at that time you were standing at the point where you first stopped on the pavement, when you went out? Yes, sir, I didn't change my position at all, more than move a little. And the other gentlemen were standing there relatively, as you described them? Yes, sir, Tolar was to my right and front, to the best of my knowledge. You saw him there? Yes, sir, and Lutterloh was to my left and front, to the best of my knowledge. You are certain that they were in the same group with you, and Leggett also? Yes, sir. In this crowd you could not be certain what anybody said, at a little distance from you, but you know these gentlemen were near you? Yes sir. While you were standing in that position you saw a pistol, could you see Archy? When he was raising I seen him, his head and shoulders. And you saw a pistol protruding towards him? Yes, sir, There was perhaps fifteen or twenty heads between me and where the pistol was. What sort of a pistol was it? I only seen the barrel. How long was the barrel? I only saw a portion, about two or three inches. That was all you saw of that pistol? Yes, sir. What prevented you from seeing the rest? The crowd sir, the reason I seen it at the time it was shot there was a little opening, the persons seemed to move their heads. Did you see it before it fired? At the moment of my seeing it, it fired. Which end of the barrel was it you saw, the end towards the stock or the end towards the muzzle? The end towards the muzzle sir. Did you see the very muzzle? Yes, sir, I seen the end of the muzzle. About three inches of it? I would not say the exact distance. You didn't see the whole pistol, only the end of it? No, sir. How high was it elevated above the shoulders of the crowd? To the best of my knowledge it would be about the shoulders of the crowd, I should think, because the heads of the persons hid it from my view. Didn't you see more pistols in the crowd at that time? Yes, sir. Whose did you see? I went to the place and tried to bring my mind to where these pistols were, to see if I could possibly bring to my mind who it was that had them; I went to the market house and took my position as I was standing as near as I could; I knew I would be summoned as a witness, and as I stood there I took everything in view: things I could not remember on the inquest trial, because I was so hurried up there, and I was never inside of a Court House half a dozen times before in my life; and I went and stood as near as I could to where I was standing. What did you recollect when you went there about these pistols, you said upon the coroner's inquest you saw four pistols, where were they? They were scattered about in the crowd mostly in front of me. Who had them? The only person I can remember, I have tried my best to remember, but the only person that I can remember with a pistol that day in his hand, was Samuel A. Phillips. Is that one of the four you spoke of before the coroner's inquest? Yes, sir. You never told any thing about your seeing Mr. Phillips so closely connected with this matter before the coroner's inquest? No, sir, I went afterwards and brought to mind every person that was standing by me. But you remember you saw four pistols at that time, but you don't remember as I understand you, any thing about having seen Mr. Phillips in such close connection with the pistol? No, sir, until after the circumstance brought him to my mind. You were sworn upon that occasion? Yes, sir, and I said what I knew, to the best of my knowledge and belief. You were sworn to tell the whole truth that day, and you mentioned nothing about this matter about Phillips? No, sir, for I was bewildered at that time, I had never been a witness before. Your testimony at that time did not implicate Mr. Phillips in any shape, form or way? No, sir. Now, sir, when did you first give your testimony, afterwards to any body—stating what you were going to relate here, when did you tell Mr. Fuller? I said to him what I had seen. When, before you were summoned as a witness here at all? Yes, sir. Before Mr. Fuller. came up to attend the trial? He had been up here I think and came back. That was the first time you spoke to him about it? Yes, sir. Did you tell him, upon that first narration, upon your part, anything about Mr. Sam. Phillips, about your suspecting that he had something to do with this business? I think that was the first time I spoke to him about it. Didn't you know Sam. Phillips was on trial, and was one of Mr. Fuller's clients, when you spoke to Mr. Fuller? I will tell you what conversation. I don't want to know the conversation? I am not positive whether I mentioned Phillips' name in his office or not, I know I did not mention it to him yesterday, but I would not say positive whether I mentioned it to them or not, I only answered his questions. And you don't remember to have used Mr. Phillips' name at all? I remember distinctly using Mr. Phillips' name yesterday. I have no doubt you did, and that is the first time you recollect to have used it, in your examination with Mr. Fuller? I conversed with Mr. Fuller before on this case. But you never mentioned anything that attached special suspicion to Sam Phillips before yesterday? I just answered his questions. You didn't mention it before the coroner's inquest, you didn't mention it before you came up here, while Mr. Phillips was Mr. Fuller's client, and according to your best recollection yesterday was the first time you told him anything about Sam Phillips? Yes, sir. Did you think it was Sam Phillips all along? After I brought my mind to bear on the matter. Not very long afterwards, about the time I heard there was going to be a trial after Capt. Tolar was arrested, I went to the market house, I had been to the market house twice for that purpose. After Capt. Tolar was arrested you went there twice? Yes, sir. Did I understand you to say you were a very intimate friend of Capt. Tolar? Yes, sir. That he called at your place pretty much every day? Yes, sir. Now between the time that this thing

was committed, and the time Capt. Tolar was arrested, did you see Capt. Tolar at all; did he call like he used to call? Yes, sir, no change whatever. He just came about every day and had something to say? Yes, sir. This thing was talked about 'sometimes, I suppose? If it was it was a mere conversation, I can give the sum and substance of what we were talking about. I didn't call for the conversation? The only thing he said was, he had been accused of it. He never asked you to go to the market house and refresh your recollection? No, sir, the first time I went of my own accord. Who suggested it to you afterwards? Mr. McRae, a lawyer, came to me and said, "Ed. if I was in your place I would go to the market house and stand there, and bring in your mind everything that you saw, and refresh yourself." About Phillips, that came to my mind the first time I went there, and I kept it to myself because I was not sworn to tell it. The only conversation touching point blank, was the conversation Phillips had with me; Phillips came to my store one night about nine o'clock. I don't ask you Mr. Phillip's conversation, you recollected the first time about Phillips, how was it you recollected that? As I told you, when I came to think over this matter coolly a great many things were brought to my memory, the situations of some parties I was uncertain of, and I went to the market house for the purpose of refreshing myself. Did you go alone? Yes, sir, I did. You went there and recalled the events as you have related them here? Yes, sir. How long was that after the events occurred the first time, you went to the market house to refresh yourself? I could not state the exact time. Was it a week? Yes, sir, it was several weeks. It was not the day after, nor the week after? No, sir. After Capt. Tolar was arrested, wasn't it? Yes, sir. Certain? I don't remember what time he was arrested. Was it immediately after that? Yes, sir. Now you saw the pistol, or the barrel, to your left and front, just off the edge of the pavement—the man was off the pavement then, who fired? I am positive the portion of the pistol I seen was held by a man off the pavement. You say the pistol barrel appeared to be about two feet off from the head of Beebee? About that far, a short distance I said, I could not say positive. Very close to his head? Yes, sir. You could see Beebee's head and the end of the pistol barrel? Yes, sir. But you could not see back of that little piece of barrel? I was some distance back ot the man. You can tell how far the pistol barrel was from his head, you saw his head and the pistol barrel too? Yes, sir. Was there anything between his head and the pistol barrel in your view? Yes, sir. So you saw in the crowd for about two feet? Yes, sir. Back of that point towards where the butt of the pistol was, you could not see? I could see a crowd standing, and that was all. How far was the person from you who was holding the pistol judging from the position of the pistol? I should judge about eight feet, not quite eight. It was eight feet more or less? Yes, sir, I judge he was that distance where the pistol was, I don't know whether he was leaning over or standing erect; for that reason I can't say positive. Dropping a perpendicular from the point where you saw the pistol barrel, how far from you would it have struck? About eleven feet perhaps, somewhere near that. How far was Archy from you? Archy was near about that far, all I seen was the end of the barrel. Where was Lutterloh at the time you saw that piece of a pistol; did you see him at the time you saw the pistol? I didn't see him the time the pistol was fired. Did you see Mr. Tolar at the time you saw the pistol? Capt. Tolar was standing right by me. Was Mr. Lutterloh? He was standing near me, but I didn't see him at the time the pistol was fired. Did you see Capt. Tolar at the instant the pistol went off? Yes, sir. Who did you turn to look for first, or did you turn to look for either? I was little more to the rear of Capt. Tolar at that time not exactly to the rear side and side of him, but I was a little further back, and of course as my eyes glanced I remember having seen him, I remember seeing him more particularly because I was by him. I understand you to say Lutterloh was by you too; was anybody between you and Lutterloh? I don't think there was. You remember one man that was by you on one side, why not remember the man on the other side too; now I want to know if, immediately after the pistol fired, you noticed Lutterloh was there? I was looking in the direction of the pistol shot, and about that time Phillips had stepped back. I am asking you where Lutterloh was, as soon as you withdrew your eyes from the pistol? I could not give his exact position. Was he within your sight. He was directly afterwards. How do you mean directly afterwards, before you could have counted five? Not before I could have counted five. When was the first time you saw Lutterloh after the pistol was fired? I would not say positively, on my oath, what time it was; it was a very short time. I want you to say as near as you can come to it; you know whether something else transpired between the shooting of the pistol and your seeing him, don't you say Lutterloh was to your left, and front? He was directly afterwards, my eyes as I told you were not in that direction. But you saw Tolar directly afterwards didn't you? Yes, sir. Did you see Lutterloh as soon afterwards as you saw Tolar? No, sir. How much time was there between the time you saw Tolar, and the time you saw Lutterloh? I would not say what time, for I don't know. Did I understand you to say you saw him immediately, almost after the firing? Yes, sir, I don't say the exact time, but I could not help seeing him, he was standing near me. I simply want to know how long it was before you saw him? It was no time scarcely? Are you speaking of Tolar or Lutterloh? I was speaking of seeing Tolar. You saw Tolar immediately afterwards? Yes, sir. Now, when did you see Lutterloh? It was a short time afterwards. A short time is very indefinite. I don't care about venturing on a time. But you do venture to say you saw Tolar immediately? Yes, sir, I did. Now I want to know if it was immediately that you saw the other man. Not quite as soon as I saw Tolar, there was not much difference. One was immediately followed by seeing the other? I could not say his exact position at that time. Your impression is when you saw him he was to your left and front? Yes, sir. Was he between you and the point where you saw the pistol fired, I mean Lutterloh. No, sir. Was he nearer to the point than you were? He may have been nearer but he was not between me and that point. He was a little nearer the point where the pistol was fired, than you were, in your estimation? Yes, sir. Didn't the pistol fire from behind him? I could not say positively about that. Can't you say positively that it did not, from the the way you have been speaking? As I told you when, I first noticed Lutterloh, Phillips was just stepping back of him, and Phillips having a pistol in his hand drawed my attention to Lutterloh, when he passed him. When you first saw Lutterloh, Phillips was in front of Lutterloh? I should judge so for he was stepping back. He was in the very act of passing him? Yes, sir. Then this point you saw the pistol fire was near

the point you saw Phillips came from? Yes, sir. That point was in front of where you saw Lutterloh? I can't say that, for at the very instant the pistol fired, I didn't know the exact position of Lutterloh, Lutterloh himself may have changed his position five or six feet. But what I want to know, is, and I try to make myself comprehended, whether, when you did see Lutterloh, supposing him to have occupied the same position at the moment the pistol was fired; he was behind the point where the pistol fired, or before it; supposing Lutterloh was standing where you first saw him—was the pistol fired before his face or behind his back? I could not say positive to that, because Lutterloh may have shifted. And yet you say it was eight or eleven feet to your left and front, but you can't say whether it was in front of Lutterloh or behind him; I am not talking about when the pistol fired now; I want to know whether the position in which the pistol was fired was before or behind the position in which you saw Lutterloh afterwards? I should judge when I seen Lutterloh the pistol was fired in front of him, but he may have changed his position. You think he did change his position? I should judge so because nearly the whole crowd changed their position. I understand as soon as the pistol fired you turned sufficient to know that Tolar was on your right, you saw him? Yes, sir. And almost as quick as thought after that you saw Lutterloh? Not almost as quick as thought. Could you have counted ten? I could not say positive as to that. It was a while afterwards? Yes, sir. Was not Phillips further from you than Lutterloh at the time you saw him there? They were about together at that time. Wasn't Lutterloh between you and him as he stepped back? Rather, I don't know which one stepped back, him or Lutterloh. Do you know that Lutterloh did step back? I could not swear positive that he did. All I am trying to find out is—first, how long after the shooting of the pistol was it before you saw Lutterloh, and when you did see him, whether the spot you saw him in was in front of the point or spot where you saw the pistol fired? I will try to explain as nearly as I can, one remark that Lutterloh made to me afterwards made me believe that he had been frightened at something, and stepped back. "It sounded so in my ears, I thought it was shot over my shoulders, and it scared me," or something to that amount, and he saw he thought it was time to be getting away, for that reason I judged he was frightened, and stepped back. You still won't answer my question I ask you : when you did see Lutterloh, and you did see him, after the pistol was fired, as you say, I ask you at the time when you first saw him, after the pistol was fired, was the spot in which you saw him, with respect to you before or behind the spot where you saw the pistol go off; I think I have told you my meaning. As I told you just now, I could not say positive, it is a very delicate question, and I want to say as near correct on my oath as possible. You can't say? Not positive. Didn't you say positively that the pistol was fired from eight to twelve feet from you? Yes, sir. And I want to know whether the spot where you saw the pistol was nearer to you than where you saw Lutterloh afterwards? Lutterloh was nearer of course. The flash of the pistol was further off than the spot where you afterwards saw Lutterloh? Yes, sir. Which was the furthest to your front, the spot where you saw the flash of the pistol, or the spot where you first saw Lutterloh? The pistol was more directly in my front. And further from you? Yes, sir, what would change the distance to the eye, one was rather to my left and the other was nearer to my front. And you think Lutterloh was rather more to your left than the pistol. I rather think so. So the pistol man must have been to his right and front; that is your notion about it? I don't like to have a notion about this matter unless I was certain of it. I want you to be certain if you can? I told you just now I seen Lutterloh, and I told you just now that the pistol flash was nearly in front of me, and further off than Lutterloh. Then it must have been to the front of Lutterloh, if he was standing where you saw him? It may have been to his rear. It was not behind his back, either right or left, where he was standing at that time? I would not be positive about it. As you looked towards Lutterloh, you saw Phillips step back? I didn't look for Lutterloh when I looked around. As you saw Phillips you saw Lutterloh? About that time, it was a mere glance, what I was looking at was the pistol, and then Lutterloh making the remark afterwards. You didn't hear that remark on the spot? No, sir. Was it before Capt Tolar left that you heard Lutterloh make that remark? It was directly afterwards. How long afterwards? A few minutes. He said he thought he was shot? No, sir, he said he was frightened, the sound of it was just like the pistol was by his ear. Did he put his hand up to his ear as he described it. He pointed to his ear, when he was telling me about it. Which car did he point to? I don't remember that; these details I can't remember all of them. I should think you might hit upon one of them by accident; well, sir, when you did see Mr. Phillips, he was passing by Lutterloh stepping back? Yes, sir. Did he step back with his right foot, or left foot? He was making steps back, he got to the rear of Mr. Lutterloh. Was Lutterloh on his right or left, as he passed? To the best of my impression he was on Lutterloh's left. Was any body between you and Sam? If there was I don't remember; he spoke to me and said, "Ed, you had better look at my pistol, and see whether it was fired or not." Did he appear to be excited or not? He appeared to be excited some. He appeared to show some signs of excitement? Yes, sir. What, was he pale? Somewhat. Was his voice tremulous? Yes, sir. Could you see big drops of sweat on his face? I don't remember about that. You think he was pale and his voice tremulous? Yes, sir. Did the hand tremble that he had the pistol in? When he spoke to me, he had the pistol in both hands. Which way was the barrel pointed? When he showed it to me it was right in both hands, in front of him. As soon as you tried to take it, he put it back? Yes, sir. Did it strike you at the time it was singular, to ask you to look at the pistol, and put it up? I thought at that time he would not ask me to look at his pistol, unless all the loads were in it. Did it strike you as queer, that he took it away, and put it behind him? I thought during the excitement, he didn't know what he was doing. You thought that when you testified before the coroner's inquest? As I said, it made such a slight impression on my mind, the circumstance did not strike me then. I had no idea at the time that any barrel was shot, and I don't know now that there was. He may have thought that I didn't want to see it, by my not reaching my hand out. How long did he hold it there? Just a second. You moved towards him? Yes, sir, but I didn't reach my hand out. Before you moved back you say you saw him offer it to some body else? Yes, sir. After he put it under his coat he offered it again? Yes, sir, but he didn't move but a few steps. Who was that he offered it to? I think if I am not mistaken he spoke about it to a nephew of his? Kendricks? Yes

sir, but whether he examined the pistol or not I dont know, he didn't take it right then. That was right after the shooting was it? Yes, sir. It was all done in a few minutes? Yes, sir, any circumstance like that affair, a minute after seems a good deal. Your impression is it was Kendricks that he was showing the pistol to? He had his pistol in his hand some space of time before he showed it to Kendricks. How long a space of time, long enough to load it, was it not, secretly behind him? Yes, sir, if he could load it without taking it apart. It was long enough to reload one barrel? It was long enough for a man to slip in a cartridge and fix it all right? Yes, sir. But when you saw him after offering it to you, he put it under his coat behind, and the next you saw of him, he had it out before him. Do you say between these times was long enough to have loaded one barrel? Yes, sir, if he could have put the bullet in, without taking the cylinder out. He would have had time to have cocked it, taken off the old cap, put on another cap and put in a cartridge? Yes, sir, just as he put it behind Capt. Tolar made some remarks to me, and I turned. What was the remark? It was something in regard to Phillips pistol I think. He asked me what that was Phillips was asking about and at that time Mr. McDuffie or some of them was talking, and I said to Capt. Tolar, "hush and listen to what the Doctor says." Did Capt. Tolar go off after that? Capt. Tolar left, but I don't know exactly where he went. Do you remember when he left? I don't, exactly, after a while we separated, and I got with Mr. Hall and Lutterloh. Hall and Lutterloh and you got together? Yes, sir. When you were standing in this crowd, from first to last was any of the crowd behind you? There was very few behind me. When you came out on the market house and stood on the pavement, was any crowd behind you? There was some crowd come in afterwards from behind. I want to know, when the pistol fired, whether there was any particular crowd behind you? Yes, sir, a portion of the crowd. Were you in the crowd, or were you on the outside? I was not on the extreme outside edge, but very near it. The mass of the crowd was before you? Yes, sir, most of it. Didn't you hear anybody in the crowd shout out Capt. Tolar had killed him? I heard one remark that, I remember now, when Capt. Tolar fixed his shawl—some person had run against him, and pushed up his shawl; he stepped back to fix his shawl on, and that was the time I seen the pistol in his holster and some little black boy about seven years old, he said "there is a pistol, I bet that pistol killed him, I bet Capt Tolar killed him." That was all you heard of that sort? I noticed Simmons and Armstrong standing to my left, at that time Simmons was standing there quietly, but afterwards made some remark, after the prisoner was dead, Armstrong was standing talking, and as soon as the pistol fired Armstrong stepped closer. I remember him because he is a person if anyone sees him they will be apt to know him again. Was he standing near the point where you saw the pistol fired when you saw him? He was not standing right near it. How far off from that point was he standing when you saw him? I suppose he was standing as far as from here to that desk, (sixteen feet.) From the point where the pistol fired? No, sir, from where I was, How far from the point where the pistol was? About as far as from here to the desk where Mr. Fuller and Mr. Phillips are, (about twelve feet.) Was that little boy the only person you heard say, in the crowd that day, Capt. Tolar killed him? I heard John Armstrong and Sam Toomer afterwards say it.

Right then and there that was the only one? Yes, sir. Didn't you hear other persons cry out in the crowd that Capt. Tolar had killed him? Not at that time. What do you mean by that time? After the things had got sort of quiet, then I heard John Armstrong and Sam Toomer. I mean within three or four minutes after the pistol was shot, that boy was the only one? Yes sir, and he just saw the pistol, "there" says he "is a pistol" "that killed him," or something. Now sir, you say you did not, at any time that day see any one leap up upon that bench, and say "look out," or anything of that sort? If he did I don't bring it to my remembrance. You don't say nobody did do anything of that sort? No, sir. And I understand you to swear most positively, and that you have no doubt about it and never have had a doubt, that Capt. Tolar did not fire that pistol? I don't believe, on my oath, that Capt. Tolar killed that man. You saw him within one second of time, from the time the pistol went off? Yes, sir. And Capt. Tolar was immediately at your right hand you swear. He was to my right, and in front. You could put your hand on him? Yes, sir. And the pistol fired to your left and front? Rather to the left and front. Was not Lutterloh, at the time the pistol fired about three feet behind Archy Beebee, wasn't he way up in front of that crowd? I can't bring to my mind positively about the distances. Do you know where Mr. Lutterloh was, when the pistol fired at all; will you swear positive that he did not shoot the pistol? I would not swear positive that he did not. Do you say you swear positive that Tolar did not? On my oath I said I was standing by Capt. Tolar, and he didn't shoot the negro, because I know he could not have shot him without my seeing it. Then you swear positively he did not? I do swear to the best of my knowledge and belief he did not. Do you swear positively that Lutterloh did not shoot that pistol; can you speak as positively about him? That is a question I don't hardly know how to answer; the only reason I can swear about Tolar was because he was nearer to me. I understand you to say you saw Lutterloh just before and just after the firing? Yes, sir, and I know Lutterloh had no pistol about him that day. Was not it possible for Lutterloh to have got off that distance from you, in the crowd, and fired that pistol, and then got back to the same point he was before, without your seeing him; it seems to me you have an indisposition to tell me about Lutterloh? I have no indisposition to tell you about Lutterloh; it is not my purpose to show any indisposition, but I can't, on my oath, tell you the distance he was. If you will only tell me how long a time it was that you did not see him. I can form some idea? No time, hardly. Are you prepared to say he was not three feet from the man who shot the pistol? I am prepared to say that Lutterloh did not shoot him. Didn't he go up a heap closer to him than you were; was not he about three feet behind him, right close up among the very foremost of the crowd? If he was it was a very short time, and I didn't see him there. He was not standing there at all? No, sir, he was not; it must have been a rush up and back again very quickly; I want to be as plain as I can, sir: It is simply upon that point that it seems to me there is an avoidance to tell where Lutterloh was? As I told you, there was but a short time it was I did not see him. Was he within reach of your hand? He was near me, I could not touch him; the furthest off I seen Lutterloh was when Phillips was stepping back past him. How far was that, could you have stepped to him in one step? No, sir. Could you have stepped to him in two? I could have got there in two. You say you could not have touch-

ed him with your hand? After the firing was over I could not have touched him with my hands. Just before it took place could you? As I told you I could not say positive his exact position relative to me. Didn't I understand you to say Mr. Powers, from the time you got outside of the arch to the time that Beebee was shot, you could not have counted a hundred? Well, sir, I don't know whether I could have done it fast or not. I understood you to say you could not have counted a hundred from the time he went out of the arch to the time he was shot? Not in an ordinary tone I could not; I don't think I could. Now you went out of the arch just after he did? Yes, sir, to his rear, but there were some persons between me and him. You got out after he did, and therefore between the time you got out there and the time the pistol was fired, you could not have counted a hundred. I don't think I could in an ordinary tone. You saw Lutterloh, after you got out there? Yes, sir. It must have been while you could have counted one, two, three or four, or something like that; suppose you saw him after you counted five, and then just after the firing of the pistol; it must have been almost instantaneous, as I understand the thing? Yes, sir. And yet you are not prepared to swear that he didn't fire that pistol? I have not the least idea in the world he did it, I would like to swear that you did not do it positively. There are only two persons in the world, that you will swear did not do it, one is yourself, and the other Capt. Tolar? Yes, sir. Those two persons you will swear did not do it? I will swear that Capt. Tolar, to the best of my knowledge and belief, did not fire that pistol; he could not have done it without my seeing it. You swear you would have seen him if he had shot? I think I would have seen him. Now I understand you to say you didn't see Capt. Tolar fire the pistol? No, sir, I didn't see him fire. And you say he could not have fired the pistol without your seeing him, that your eyes were not off of him long enough for him to have fired the pistol without your seeing him? I don't think they were. Do you say positively? I say this, Capt. Tolar was standing a little in front of me, and I was looking at the pistol, and when that pistol fired Capt. Tolar could not have reached and fired the pistol. It was a physical impossibility? Yes, sir. Then you swear positively it is not so? As near as I can say. Can't you swear positively that you are sitting in that chair at this moment? Yes, sir. Are you as positive of one as the other? About, sir. Mr. Powers, this thing is certain, if that pistol was out to your left, eight or ten feet from you, and the instant after it fired you saw Mr. Tolar on your right, and standing where he had been before, it is a physical impossibility for him to have fired, and and you can swear as positively to that, as you can to anything that you saw with your own eyes? It is a physical impossibility from where I seen Lutterloh a moment afterwards. Then you can swear to that like you can to any other fact that is evidenced to you by your senses? Yes, sir. Then I understand you to swear positively that Tolar did not fire the pistol? I know it is a physical impossibility for him to have done it without my seeing it. Can't you swear I am not firing a pistol now? Yes, sir. Can't you swear to that as positively as you can that I am not firing a pistol? I can. Do you swear he did not fire that pistol? I do, that is the meaning I convey, sir, when I am put on my oath, I mean to convey the truth as near as I know to the best of my knowledge and belief. I want to ask you one question, do you believe or do you not that you are bound to tell the truth when you are sworn upon your oath? I do. Have you never heard a theory broached lately, that a man, before a Military Court, is under no obligation to observe his oath? No, sir, I know that I respect it as much I would in any Court, at least I respect an oath, I don't care where it is administered. And you feel bound to tell the truth here as well as in a civil court? Yes, sir. You have had no contrary doctrine preached to you by anybody? No, sir. Has any one ever told you that you can't be tried for perjury, in case you make a false statement? I know I can be tried for perjury before a Military Court as easily as I can before a civil court; if I was to go before a magistrate and take an oath, I would know I had to tell all the truth to the best of my knowledge and belief; but when it comes to want a man to swear that Mr. Lutterloh, or you or any other man did not kill the man, that is a word I don't like to bring out. I can't see why you should hesitate if you are sure he did not, as you say you are? I am sure, to the best of my knowledge and belief. What do you mean by the best of your knowledge and belief, a man must swear to what he sees, hears, smells, tastes or feels, and, if using those senses you are certain of a fact, you have a right to swear to it? I swear to tell the truth, and I tell that I seen that pistol at such a distance, and I swear at the time it was fired that Capt. Tolar was then at my side. You then qualify your fact by giving us your reasons for your opinions? Yes, sir. At the very instant the pistol was fired Capt. Tolar was standing by your side? Yes, sir, he could not have stepped without me seeing him.

Re-direct examination by the Counsel for the accused.

About this matter of Lutterloh, I understand you to say that you will not fix, and will not pretend to fix Lutterloh's position, at the time the pistol was fired, for the reason that at that time you did not see Lutterloh? At that time my eyes were on the pistol. And whether Lutterloh was close by where the pistol was fired, or whether he was close by you, or where he was at that time you don't know? I could not swear positive. But with regard to Lutterloh whether he fired the pistol, or whether some other of the hundred men who were in the crowd fired the pistol you don't know; and don't swear? No, sir. I understand you to say, and swear that you did not fire the pistol? Yes, sir. I understood you to swear in your direct examination that Capt. Tolar did not fire the pistol? I swear to the best of my knowledge and belief that he did not, that I know it was a physical impossibility for him to have fired it without my seeing it. That the matter could not have occurred without your seeing him, and that you did not see him, and therefore it did not occur?

Cross examination resumed, by the Counsel for the prosecution.

Did you have a pistol that day? I did not at any time that day.

Re-direct examination resumed by the Counsel for the accused.

I understood you to say in your cross examination, that you saw John Armstrong there, that day? I did. Did you see him before the pistol was fired, or after the pistol was fired? I noticed John Armstrong before and after. Did you see him before the pistol was fired? Yes, sir. Where was he then? He was near towards Ichabod Davis's store. How far was he from Capt. Tolar, from the center of the pavement? About as far as from that table to me, (about 16 feet.) How long was that before the pistol fired? I seen him there while the crowd was there, you know, a very short space of time before it was fired. Did

you see him directly after the pistol was fired? Yes, sir. Where was he then? I seen him step up nearer. Where did he step from? From towards Mr. Davis's store. Did he step up nearer to where you were? He stepped up towards where the negro was. How near did he come to Capt. Tolar? He come in about five feet of him. Nearer than that? If he did, I didn't know it. Did he make any remark to Tolar when he came up there? I never heard him make it, sir. Did Tolar turn off in the crowd or leave the crowd before you left, or did you leave together? My impression is Tolar left the crowd before I did. Up to the time of Tolar's leaving the crowd, did Armstrong make any remark to him? Not that I heard. You were there, close by him? We were pretty close for a while we did not stay together all the time, we stayed together a short time after the shooting.

Questioned by the Commission.

Are you a Mason, Mr. Powers? Yes, sir. Is Capt. Tolar a Mason? Yes, sir. In which direction was Beebee's face turned at the time he was shot? I could not say, I didn't see his face. What did you see? I saw the back of his head on one side. The part of his face that you saw, was that turned toward you? Yes, sir, of course if I saw it. The left side of the back of his head was turned towards you? I could not say positively, but I know it was one side. And you don't know which side. No, sir, I could not give it to you now, on my oath. Can you account for your having forgotten, at the time you were examined before the coroner's jury, all about Mr. Phillips having a pistol, about the conversation with Mr. Phillips, Mr. Phillips offering you the pistol? I have often thought since, how I come to forget it at that time, but I was unaccustomed to being a witness, and it bewildered me. Do you remember all the circumstances connected with that affair much clearer now than you did then? Yes, sir. Then a circumstance that took place six months ago you recollect better to day than you did the day it occurred? Some circumstances, I would. Do you not recollect, to day, six months after this occurred, all the circumstances connected with it, clearer than you did the very day? I remember it now. Do you remember it clearer than you did that day? Yes, sir, I do. Mr. Powers isn't that rather a singular fact, that your memory should be better a long time after an occurrence, than immediately afterwards? Recollect I have not just thought of this I have been thinking of it sometime. Will you forget all about this examination tomorrow, and to day six months recollect the whole of it? No, sir, but I may not be able to give it in the exact words.

Re-direct Examination, by the Counsel for the accused.

Before the coroner's inquest, were you asked any questions with regard to Mr. Phillips, about his connection with this affair? No, sir.

On motion the Commission adjourned to meet on Thursday, Aug. 27th, 1867, at 11, A. M.

RALEIGH, N. C., Aug. 22d, 1867, 11 A. M.

The Commission met pursuant to adjournment.

Present: All the members of the Commission, the Judge Advocate, the Counsel for the prosecution, all the accused and their Counsel.

The reading of the testimony taken yesterday was waived, there being no objections thereto.

Yesterday's proceedings were then read and approved.

Mr. EUGENE DAVIS having reported as one of the Recorders of the Commission, was duly sworn by the Judge Advocate, in the presence of the Commission, and in the presence of all the accused. HENDERSON LOCKAMY, a witness for the defence, having been first duly sworn, testified as follows: Examined by the Counsel for the accused. What is your name? Henderson Lockamy. Where do you reside? Fayetteville. What State? North Carolina. How long have you resided in Fayetteville? About twenty-seven years, ever since 1840. Were you in Fayetteville on the day Archy Beebee or Archy Warden was killed? Yes, sir. Were you at the market house that day? Yes, sir. At what time did you go to the market house? Well, sir, I was down about there most of the day; my business at that time was over the street, as I was buying timber for Mr. Slocum; I suppose I stopped there before the trial commenced or before Archy was carried out of the guard house. Did you see him carried up stairs? Yes, sir. Where were you standing; at what part of the market house; at the time he was carried up stairs? I was standing under the eastern end, in the main aisle, under the main arch. Under the main eastern arch? Under that end, not exactly at the arch but sort of opposite the stair steps. What was the size of the crowd under the market house at that time; or was there any crowd there? There was some there, I can't say, perhaps twenty-five. How long did you remain at the market house? I remained there until after the trial was over. How long was it from Archy's being carried up till the time the trial was over? I suppose three quarters of an hour or an hour. Did you remain in the same position all the time while he was up stairs? I didn't move much; I mought have moved about a little. During the time Archy was up stairs, was there anything unusual in the crowd which was assembled there; anything that attracted your attention? No, sir, nothing more than there was more persons around there than usual. Did you hear anything while there from any person whatsoever to kill Beebee, wrest him from the sheriff, or to do him any harm? Not that I recollect of. Did you see any whispering or any consultations between any persons there under the market house while he was up stairs? Not that I recollect of. Were you at the market house at the time Miss Elvira Massey and her mother went up? Yes, sir. Did you see them come there? Yes, sir, I seen them come. In what sort of conveyance did they come? Well, sir, it was a carryall, or something of that sort. Where did the carryall stop? In front of the eastern end about twenty or thirty feet from the pavement. Who accompanied them from the market house? Mr. Bond. The town constable? Yes, sir. How long do you think Miss Elvira Massey and her mother remained up in the market house? About three quarters of an hour, or something like that. Did you see them when they came down? Yes, sir. Where were you standing at the time these ladies came down? I was under the eastern end there, somewheres near it, I can't tell exactly the place, but it was somewheres under the eastern end near the same place where I was before. At the time they came down, did you then notice anything unusual in the appearance of the crowd? No, sir. How much larger was the crowd at that time; I mean the crowd under the market house, and outside of the market house; how much larger was it that day than it was when you first went there? It was a great deal larger at that time. Composed of white persons alone? Well, there mought have been some black ones around; I didn't notice any that I could call their names. Did you see Miss Massey and Mrs. Massey get into the carriage after they came down? Yes, sir, I seen them go to the carriage. Who escorted them to the carriage? Mr. Bond. Did he go down with them? Yes, sir. How long did the

carriage remain there after the ladies were helped in? A very few minutes, perhaps five, or hardly that much. Were you in a position where you could see the carriage at that time? Yes, sir, I was right down there at the eastern end. Did you see any persons go to the carriage while the ladies were in it? Yes, sir, there was some two or three. Do you know who they were? I know Mr. David Cashwell, Robert Mitchell and Mr. Taylor. Which Taylor? Phillimon Taylor. Did you see anybody else go to the carriage? Not that I recollect of. Did you see William J. Tolar at the market house at all that day? Yes, sir, I saw him there. Did you see him there at that time? I didn't see him there after Archy came down. I am speaking before that time when the ladies went to the carriage, did you see Tolar at that time? No, sir, I didn't see him at that time. Did Tolar go to the carriage? Not that I know of, I didn't see him. The carriage, then, you say drove off? Yes, sir. How long was it after the carriage drove off before Beebee, the deceased man, was brought down stairs? Well, sir, it was a very few minutes, perhaps five minutes, or not that much. Where were you standing; describe it as exactly as you can at the time Beebee was brought down stairs? I was standing on the end of one of them benches that is about there to set on, right on the eastern end of the bench. You mean you were standing on a bench which was on the eastern side of the aisle as you are looking towards the river? It was on the north-east side of the aisle, I was in the eastern end of the bench. How far did that throw you from the main central arch, the north east portion of that main central arch? It only throwed at that time three or four feet, I suppose. Which way were you facing? I was facing towards Archy at that time. Did you see him when he first appeared at the landing of the stairs? Yes, sir. You saw him there? Yes, sir. Can you tell who were with him, sir, at the time you first saw him there, who were in company with him? The Sheriff was with him. Sheriff Hardie? Yes, sir, and Mr. Faircloth and Mr. Wemyss. David Wemyss? Yes, sir, and there were two or three other policemen with him, Mr. McGuire and Mr. Hourrine. They were all with him? Yes, sir. Who came down the steps first in that party, Hardie, Faircloth, Wemyss or who? I can't say for certain who came down first. Did you notice anything that attracted your attention there in the man Beebee, or in the party with him, from the time of his first appearance on the landing until he reached the floor of the market house? No, sir. Did you at that time notice anything unusual in the crowd which was surrounding that place? No, sir, I didn't see anything unusual more than the crowd. Mr. Lockamy, did you know John Maultsby? Yes, sir. Young John Maultsby? Yes, sir. Did you see him there at all that time? No, sir, I didn't see him there at that time. The bench which runs in front of Becky Ben's stall, was that directly in your line of view from the place where you were standing looking up to the landing of the stairs, or was it not? I was standing on the bench opposite Becky Ben's. Was Becky Ben's bench in your line of view standing as you were on the eastern end of that bench opposite Becky Ben's bench, and looking up there at the landing of the stair steps? Yes, sir, it was right in my view. Did you see any person jump on that bench at that time? Not that I recollect of. Did you see John Maultsby jump upon that bench at that time? No, sir, I didn't see any person jump on it. Try to remember sir, whether you did or did not see John Maultsby jump upon that bench and cry out "watch out boys" or any thing to that effect? No, sir, I am satisfied I didn't see him; if I seen him I don't recollect any thing at all about it. What is your impression, that, that occurred, or it did not? My impression is, it did not occur. Then we bring Archy and the party with him to the foot of the stairs; were you still, maintaining that position, when he reached the floor of the market house? Yes, sir. What occurred then, after reaching the floor of the market house to attract your attention? Well sir; after they reached the floor of the market house, and came on out and turned the arch, or as they were turning the arch. Which arch? The south east arch on the southern side; the arch as you turn around to go down to the guard house. The arch you mean which opens towards the river? Yes, sir. That is the eastern arch; as Archy and the party with him went out that eastern arch, to go down towards the guard house, you then observed something that attracted your attention, what was it? Well sir; as they went to turn that arch, Mr. Powers. What Powers? Tom Powers, demanded the prisoner. What did he say? Well as well as I can recollect he took hold of him in the breast and said "I demand this prisoner." What reply was made to that if any? I believe that Sheriff Hardie asked the men to stand back, and at that time they all closed in and gathered around Archy, and Sheriff Hardie asked them to stand back. Did you see Capt. Tolar at that time? No, sir. You saw Tom Powers, you say at that time? Yes, sir. Did you see David Watkins otherwise called Monk Julia? Yes, sir, I saw him immediately after that. I am speaking of that time? At that time I had my eyes on Mr. Powers, I didn't see Monk. Did you see Ed Powers at that time? No, sir. Leggett? No, sir. Ralph Lutterloh? No, sir. Sam Hall? No, sir. Henry Sykes? No, sir. You saw none of them at that time? No, sir; none of them at that time. Well what occurred directly after that sir? Directly after that I saw Monk with a little knife in his hand make a pass or two. Where was the prisoner and the party with him at the time you saw Monk making the passes at him? They were trying to carry him to the guard house. They had cleared the arch? Yes, sir. How many steps do you think they had taken down the pavement at that time? Not over one or two, I can't say for certain. At that time you say you saw Monk make some passes at him with a knife? Yes, sir, one or two. How near was Monk to him at the time he was making those passes at him? I can't say for certain, perhaps two or three feet. Was he near enough to have reached him with a knife? I can't say for certain whether he was or not. A good many persons between you and the prisoner? Yes, sir. You can't say whether he had reached him with his knife or not? No, sir, but I don't think he did. What occurred after that? Directly after I can't say any thing that occurred, only as the crowd was sort of moving along a little. The crowd was in such commotion between you and the place that you could not see what occurred? No, sir, I could not recollect one from another at that time. Where was your position at that time? I had stopped off of the bench; I was out pretty much against the arch? Inside of the market house or out side of the market house? I was about the corner of the arch. Which corner, the north-east side of the aisle? About the north east corner. The north east corner of the main eastern arch? Yes, sir. Well sir, what was the next you saw? I don't know that I can say for certain by that time I suppose the pistol had fired. The next you saw was the firing of the pistol, how far had Beebee got down

in the pavement at the time the pistol had fired? Well sir, he had got some wheres nearly opposite the little arch there, a little below it. Below the center of the southern most arch of the eastern side, do you mean? Yes, sir. (Witness shows his position on the diagram as standing near the north east corner of the main eastern arch, and Beebee at the time he was shot at the south side of the small arch on the Eastern end of the market house.) Do you know whether Beebee was on the pavement or off at the time he was shot? He was on it I think sir; I couldn't see his feet. But you think he was on it? Yes, sir. Were there a good many persons between you and Beebee? Yes, sir. You didn't have a very distinct view of him? No, sir. Did you see any portion of him? I saw his head at the time after he started down. Now sir just state what occurred immediately before Beebee was shot, what did you see immediately before you heard the report of the pistol; looking at Beebee what did you see? I seen Beebee's head raise up. You lost sight of him before, and you saw his head raise up. Yes, sir. How long after you saw his head raise up, was it before the pistol shot was fired? I can't say, it was pretty much right away? You then lost sight of him, his head raised up, and pretty much right away the pistol shot was fired; at that time you say think Beebee was on the pavement? I think he was on, I can't say for certain, there was a good many people between me and him. Do you know who fired that pistol shot? No, sir, I can't say for certain. You don't know who fired it? No, sir. Did you see the smoke? I saw the smoke. Did you see the flash? I can't say for certain that I did. Did you hear the report? Yes, sir. You heard the report and saw the smoke? Yes, sir. Could you point out now upon that diagram the point at which the report was, and from which you saw the smoke rise? (Witness points on the diagram the point at which he saw the smoke rise as by the small tree opposite the south arch on the east end of the market house.) Was it on the pavement or off? Near the edge of it, I can't say whether he was on or off. How far was it from Beebee? It might have been four or five feet. You think it was about the distance of four or five feet. I think it was, I can't say for certain. You think it was either off the pavement or near the edge of the pavement, and about four or five feet from Beebee? Yes, sir. Was it to Beebee's front or to his rear? It was to his left and rear. Did you see any man at all who fired that pistol? No, sir, I didn't see any man fire it that I know of. Did you see any pistol then? I saw one pistol; it mought not have been the same one. Where did you see that pistol? It was at this same place. Where you heard the report and saw the smoke, you saw the pistol? It was very nigh the place. How long after the report of the pistol, and your seeing the smoke, was it that you saw this pistol that you speak of? It was immediately after I saw the smoke and heard the pistol. Could you have counted five? Perhaps. Who had that pistol? Samuel Phillips had that pistol. Well, sir, in what position did he have it, what was he doing with it at the time? At the time I saw it, it looked like he sort of raised it up just so. (Represents the pistol as in Phillips' right hand, his own bent within one foot of his breast, and directly in front of his breast, and from that position he placed it in his breast at his left side.) Did you see whether he put it under his coat or outside his coat, or where? I was too far off to tell that; I know he put it in his bosom, I don't know whether he put it in his pocket or not. Was there any other pistol fired that day at that time? Not that I heard, I didn't see any other pistol at all. What sort of a pistol was that you saw in the hands of Samuel A. Phillips? It was a repeater of some sort, I don't know the name of it; It was a repeater ten or twelve inches in length. It was a long repeater? Yes, sir. But you don't know what sort? No, sir. Did you see Capt. Tolar at that time? No, sir; I didn't see Mr. Tolar. Did you see Mr. Tolar any more that day? No, sir. Did you see Ed Powers or Ralph Lutterloh, Sam Hall or any of them any more that day? Yes, sir; I guess I saw some of them that evening: I know I saw Ed Powers up at his store. I mean at the market house or under the market house? I didn't see them there any more that evening that I recollect of. Mr. Lockamy, while you were there at the market house before the boy was brought down, were you mingling pretty freely with the crowd? No sir; I was not having much to say to them, that I remember, I mought have spoke to some person; I reckon I did, but I don't recollect who. You just were there as a silent spectator? Yes, sir; that was my position. Did you hear or did you know of any agreement or any arrangement or any combination by any persons to do any unlawful act there that day? No, sir; I didn't hear any thing of the sort.

Cross examination by the Counsel for the prosecution.

Mr. Lockamy what time did you rise the morning of the murder. Early in the morning. Did you go up to the market house right straight away? Not that I know of; I don't suppose I did. Don't you remember what you were doing in the early part of the day? Well, I was receiving staves and paying for them. How far from the market house? The place I received them at was some quarter of a mile or half a mile I suppose. When you first got up did you go to the place where you received staves, was that your first visit? Yes, sir. Did you go out before breakfast? I guess I did. Can't you tell? I can't tell for certain about that time, but I always went down to the shop before breakfast; I don't remember whether I went down before breakfast that morning or not, particularly. That is from a quarter to a half a mile from the market house? Between a quarter and a half a mile. You went home to breakfast? I live right at the shop; yes, sir, I went home to breakfast. Do you remember where you went after breakfast? No, sir. Where did you first hear that this negro man Beebee had attempted to ravish Miss Massey? I heard it Monday some time. Had you heard it when you got up in the morning? No, sir. Had you heard it when you went to breakfast? No, sir, I guess not. I don't want you to guess? I don't know that I did. When do you remember first hearing it? I can't say for certain what time of the day I heard it, but I heard it some time that day. Had you heard it before you went to the market house? No, sir, I don't reckon I had. What time did you go to the market house? Well, I was down there in the early part of the day; I was down there again afterwards. When did you first hear it; when you first went down to the market house or when you got down there to Archy's trial? Well, I think I heard it in the early part of the day; when I first started out. What time was that? before twelve o'clock? Yes, sir. Who told you of it? I don't recollect sir. Can't you recollect? I can recollect some person that told me; I don't recollect whether that was the first one or not. who was it? Mr. Jordan Branch, a brother in law of mine; he was the town constable that ar-

rested Archy. He told you of it; did you hear it from any other person? I suppose I did; I don't recollect the name of any other person that told me. You heard it before twelve o'clock that day? Yes, sir. Did you anticipate that there was going to be any difficulty with the populace? I didn't know that there was. Did you think there was? I didn't have any reason to think it. You didn't hear any person say any thing like that? I heard nothing of that sort. From no quarter? No, sir. Then I understood you to say you didn't expect any thing of that sort? I didn't expect that there was going to be any difficulty; I had no reason to expect it. When you went down to the market house and stopped there, what was your object in going? My object in going down the street was my business; it was in the street as much as any where else at that time. Was your business in the market house? Not particularly. Did you go to the market house for the purpose of attending to your business? No, sir. Why did you go to the market house? I went there because I was passing there. Didn't you go there because this trial was going on? I stopped there for that purpose. Your curiosity was excited about this trial, and you went there? Yes, sir, I was there before the excitement. How long were you there before Archy was brought up from the guard house? Very few minutes. What sort of a day was it, cold or warm? It was a tolerably cold day, I believe. Do you recollect whether the sun was shining or whether it was raining? I don't believe the sun was shining; I can't say for certain, it seems to me it was not shining. Your impression is it was cold: could you say whether it was a cloudy day? I think it was. At the time you got to the market house you think it was cloudy? I think it was cloudy late in the evening, about the time the trial came off, I can't recollect. Do you recollect whether it was a particularly still day, or whether the wind was blowing any? It was not blowing much, if any. Was it blowing at all? There might have been a little air stirring, but I don't recollect about it. You don't recollect whether it was windy or not? No, sir. I understand you, when first went in you went into the east end of the market house towards the east arch? No, sir, I don't recollect where I went in at. You don't know which arch you went in at? No, sir. Can't you tell now? I think I went in at the east end. That is your best impression? Yes, sir. As you went into the east end you say you went straight up through the aisle a little distance and stopped? Yes, sir. Did you stop to speak to any one? I don't recollect that I did. Don't you recollect any one that you spoke to that day? Not while I was there; I don't recollect the name of any person I spoke to. How many steps did you take inside of the eastern arch before you paused? I don't recollect. Did you go as far as the bell rope? I might, I don't recollect. I don't think I did at that time. I understood you to state distinctly you were in but a short distance into the eastern end upon your examination in chief? I only went in a short distance at that time. I am trying to get your position when you first in, you moved back, you say, a short distance and stopped? Yes, sir, I stopped I understood you in your examination in chief to say, at that place you remained from the time you first went there, till Archy came down. At or about that place. Where you took you station there you remained? Yes, sir, I think I stood some where close there. How far was that place that you first went to, and where you remained the greater portion of the time, or all the time; how far was that from the eastern arch; how many feet? Ten or twelve feet. Then I understand you to say you kept your position there abouts till Archy came downstairs? Yes, sir. It was then that you moved from that position and took your station on the bench was it? Yes, sir. All the time he was coming down, and until that time, you were standing about ten feet in from the main eastern arch? Yes, sir. Which way was your face turned towards the arch or towards Hay street, when you first went in? I can't say for certain. Did you stand looking towards the western end of the market house, didn't you have any acquaintances there, you had any conversation with? Yes, sir. Who were they; can't you remember one? I don't recollect the names now. You were standing there three quarters of an hour without speaking to some one of your acquaintances? I don't suppose I was, but I don't recollect any particular name that I spoke to. Can you recollect any general name that you spoke to? No, sir. You don't recollect a single individual that you spoke to during that three quarters of an hour, standing in that crowd of twenty five people, as you represent it? I don't recollect any name; I can't say for certain that I did. You can't recollect a single soul that you spoke to up to that time? No, sir. I understand you were standing in that same position when Miss Massey and her mother came down stairs with Mr. Bond? Yes, sir, I was some where there about when they came down. Up to that time you had noticed no disturbance in the crowd? No, sir. You heard no denunciation of this negro; nobody was talking about that thing? No, sir. The crowd was there but it was not talking about what Archy had done, didn't express its indignation any way? No, sir, not that I heard of. You heard nobody say even, that it was wrong or that he deserved punishment or expressed their horror or indignation in any way or shape? No person that I could recollect. Did you hear any person? Not that I recollect of. Did you hear any such thing without being able to name the person? I didn't hear anything, no, sir. The crowd was then a quiet crowd, it was not even talking about what was going to take place up stairs, or if it was, they were talking so low a tone that you didn't hear it? I didn't hear any of the plot that was made if there was any. I didn't say about any plot Mr Lockamy, I simply asked if the crowd which was gathered for the purpose of hearing something of the trial apparently, weren't talking about the subject matter of the trial? Not that I paid any attention to. You heard nothing of that sort? No, sir. Were there no persons in that crowd that you knew? There were some there that I knew. When you first went up I mean did it strike you there was a good many strangers in town? No, sir. You have been living there for twenty seven years, you know a great number of the population there, don't you, by sight? Yes, sir. When you first went there who were there that you knew. I saw Mr. Tolar under there, it mought not have been when I first went there, and Mr. Powers. Did you see Monk? Yes, sir, I seen him under there. When you first got there? It mought not have been when I first got there. Was it before these ladies came down stairs? I don't recollect, sir. Was it before Archy came down stairs, between the time you first went there and the time Archy came down stairs? I don't recollect, sir, when it was, after Archy came down stairs and went out on the pavement, I seen him then. Didn't you see him before? I don't recollect whether I saw him or not. Did you see Tolar and Tom Powers before? No, sir. I am speaking of the space of time that elapsed between the moment when you first got there and the moment when these ladies came

down stairs; during that time did you see anything of Ralph Lutterloh? I don't recollect that I did. Did you see him at the market house during that transaction? I don't recollect that I seen him there at the time. I understand you to say to the best of your recollection you didn't see Lutterloh at the market house from the time you first got there to the time Archy was killed? I don't recollect seeing him now. That is your best recollection, that you didn't see him? Yes, sir, I think it is. Did you see Mr. J. G. Leggett there? Yes, sir, I saw Mr. Leggett. What time was it you saw him? I saw Mr. Leggett during the trial; I suppose the trial was nearly over. Did you see Mr. E. P. Powers there at any time? I don't recollect that I did. Your best recollection is, that you didn't see him there at any time during that day? Yes, sir, I think I did see him under the market house while Archy was up stairs, I don't recollect what time it was; it was some time before Archy came down. Did you see John Maultsby there? No, sir, I hadn't seen him at that time. You hadn't seen him when Archy came down stairs? No, sir. From the time you first went there, to the time Archy came down stairs you hadn't seen John Maultsby? If I did I didn't notice him. Did you see Sam. Hall? I didn't notice him. I mean while Archy was up stairs? If I saw him I don't recollect it. Did you see Henry Sykes, the one-armed man? I don't recollect seeing him. You know him don't you? Yes, sir. I understand, however, that you do recollect seeing Tolar and Tom Powers, and Leggett, and Ed. P. Powers under the market house during the time Archy Beebee was up stairs undergoing his preliminary examination? Yes, sir, I seen them. Do you recollect seeing anybody else? I recollect seeing others, but I can't call their names. And your impression is that there were about twenty-five people under the market house when you got there? I don't know; I suppose there was about that at the time the trial was going on. When you saw Tolar, how long had you been at the market house? It was about the time I first got there. Where was he standing? At the time I saw him, he was standing something rather under the market house towards the middle. About the middle of the aisle? Somewhere near the center. Was he facing east or west? I can't say? Did you notice how he was dressed? He had on a shawl; I don't know what sort of pants and coat; but he had a grey shawl. Did you notice what kind of a hat he had on? He had on a black hat. Was it a crushed hat or a tall beaver hat? I don't recollect, I guess it was a soft hat. I don't want you to guess. I don't know what sort of a hat it was, but I think it was a black hat. Did he have his spectacles on? I didn't notice particularly. Was his face towards you or his back? I can't say for certain, I know I saw him there. How long did you keep him in your view, when was the time that you remember that you didn't see him? I don't suppose I kept him in my view but a very few minutes. So the last and only time you saw him was before Archy came down stairs? I don't know whether I saw him any more or not, I don't recollect that I did. Your best recollection is that you did not? I can't say that I saw him. Can't you say you didn't see him any more? I can say, if I did I don't recollect it. You say you don't recollect having seen him any more after you saw him when you first went up there, standing near the center of the market house? I don't recollect seeing him any more. Was Tom Powers standing near Tolar when you saw him and what time did you see him; when you first went up? I can't say, I don't think they were together when I saw them though.

Where do you think Tom Powers was standing when you first saw him that day? I saw him under the eastern end of the market house, I don't know whether he was standing there or going on. Before Archy came down? Yes, sir. Where was he standing? Near Becky Ben's stall, I can't say for certain where he was standing. You simply know he was there? Yes, sir. Where was Leggett when you first saw him? Leggett was somewhere along the eastern end there. Was he talking to Tom Powers? I didn't see him talking. Were they together? I don't think they were together. Were they apart? I didn't see them together is all I can recollect. Then you know they were apart? Yes, sir. You saw them both? Yes, sir. One on each side of the market house and the other on the other? I don't know that they were that way, but they were not close together. They were both in the east end of the market house? I guess they were. I beg that you won't tell me that you guess any more; I want to know whether you saw Leggett in the east end of the market house? Yes, sir. And you saw Tom Powers in the east end? Yes, sir. But you say they were not together, as I understand you? No, sir, they were not together when I saw them. You say they were apart? Yes, sir. How far apart? I can't say. Did you see E. P. Powers in the east end of the market house? I saw E. P. Powers under the market house there, I don't think he was as far down as the east end though. Was he standing near Tolar? Not that I recollect of. You didn't see him and Tolar and Lutterloh standing together? Not that I recollect of, sir. When you saw them they were not standing together? No, sir. Tolar was about the middle of the market house, and Tom Powers and Leggett were about the east end apart from one another, and E. P. Powers was further back than either one of those others? Yes, sir. When these ladies came down stairs Mr. Bond came with them? Yes, sir. Did you look at the ladies? Yes, sir. How many persons do you think there were in the market house when the ladies came down? I can't say sir. Was the crowd any larger than it was when you first went there? Yes, sir. Twice as large? I guess it was more than twice as large, I haven't much idea, a good deal larger though. Was the market house pretty full in the east end of it? Yes, sir. Entirely full? No, sir, not entirely. You estimated it to be about twenty five when you came there; now can't you give us your best estimate as to how many there were when these ladies came down stairs? Perhaps there were fifty, I can't say for certain for I was not paying much attention to it. You directed your attention to it enough to say very decidedly that there were about twenty five when you first went up there? Yes, sir. Were there about fifty when the ladies came down, can't you estimate one crowd as well as the other? I suppose there were fifty. Do you think there were more than fifty? I can't say. Do you think there were less than fifty? I can't say sir. Your best estimate of the crowd is about fifty? Yes, sir. Were there any persons on the east end of the market house, outside on the pavement? I think there were. How many do you estimate that crowd at? Well, sir, a good many, I can't say. As many as there were in the market house? I didn't notice them, I can't say, I knew there was right smart out there. Was the pavement covered? I can't say whether it was covered or not. Can't you give any idea as to the number, you can, no doubt, but will you give any idea? I didn't notice them. You say there were some persons there? Yes, sir, a good many, I can't say, A

good many; didn't you notice them distinctly? I didn't notice them particularly. You can't estimate that crowd at all? Not with any certainty, there might have been fifty. There might have been a thousand, what I want to know, is the best estimate of a man who was there. I didn't notice particular. You neither called them by name nor remember them, nor put it down on a piece of paper, but you saw the crowd and can give an estimate? I just saw them. You did'nt see them distinctly? No, sir. You saw these inside of the market house, better than you did the crowd outside? Yes, sir, Was any crowd outside on the pavement when you first came to the market house? I don't know that there was. Do you know that there was not? No, sir, I don't know that there was any there when I first came. Did you notice any crowd on the pavement when you first came? No, sir. The only crowd that you noticed when you first came was inside of the market house, about twenty-five people? Yes, sir. When the ladies came down stairs you noticed there was a crowd outside of the market house, and a crowd inside? Yes, sir. Were there any persons in the east end between you and the arch, or were they all further inside of the market house than you were? I guess there was some between me and the east arch. And the crowd out on the pavement was in front of you? I was not looking out that way particularly. You saw the carriage outside? Yes, sir. That was standing right in front of the eastern arch some twenty or thirty feet? Yes, sir. Were there any people between you and the carriage? Yes, sir. How many people? Eight or ten. Scattered immediately between you and the carriage? The crowd on the eastern end of the market I think was a little lower down than between me and the carriage. A little to your right? Yes, sir. So that the main part of the persons that were between you and the carriage were inside of the market house? Yes, sir. When those ladies went out you saw Bond go with them, and you saw David Cashwell, Phil. Taylor, and Robert Mitchell at the carriage, did any one else go there? Not that I recollect of. Do you recollect that any one else did go there? If they did I didn't see them. Did you look at the carriage from the time the ladies went to it, till they went off? I don't know that I had my eyes on them all the time. The carriage was standing there about five minutes after the ladies, went out. It might have been five or a little less. During that time you don't pretend to have had your eyes on it the whole time? I can't say that I was looking at it every moment. Who went to the carriage first, of these three gentlemen you have named, Cashwell, Taylor and Mitchell? I don't know for certain which went first. Did they go together? I don't believe they did. Didn't you see Tom Powers go to the carriage? I don't recollect that I did. Do you recollect that you didn't? If he went I don't recollect it; I didn't see him. You didn't see Capt. Tolar go to the carriage? No, sir. Did you see Bond come back from the carriage and go up stairs again? I saw him when he came from the carriage. What became of him? I can't say; I didn't notice. Did you say Maultsby spoke to Bond? No, sir. What were the ladies doing as they came down stairs, was one of them weeping? A little I think. Was she weeping loudly enough for you to hear it? No, sir; she looked like she had been crying. Did she have her handkerchief to her face? I think she had. Did she have a vail over her face? I can't say whether she had or not. Did you see any marks of violence about her person? I don' know that I did. You don't know; I don't know want my question answered in that way: I must have a direct answer? I can't say that I did. Why not say *no*? Well sir; I don't exactly know; I might have seen things that I don't recollect. Is your memory very bad? Yes, sir; I am not very good to recollect; that is unless I see it distinctly; if I do I recollect it. When these ladies drove off did you see what became of Mr. Mitchell or Phil. Taylor or David Cashwell? No, sir; I didn't notice them. You were still standing at the point you first stood when you went into the market house? About that point. You hadn't moved far from it? No, sir; I hadn't moved far from it. When the ladies drove off, Beebee started down stairs? Yes, sir. You say as Beebee started down stairs you went over and stood on the bench the east end of the bench which is on the north side of the market house, and you were fronting towards the steps as Beebee came down? Yes, sir. That in that position Becky Ben's bench was fully in your view? Yes, sir. Did you see anybody standing on that bench at all? No, sir. Do you say no one was standing on it? I can't say that there was; I didn't see any person on it. Did you see that it was vacant? I didn't notice the bench particularly, I saw the steps sir. You can't say that there was any body on it, and you can't say that there was not any body on it? I didn't see any body. Do you remember that you saw the bench at all? No, sir. It was within your view; if you had chosen to direct your attention to it, but you don't remember noticing that bench at that time? No, sir, I don't. So that you can't say whether any one was on it or was not? No, sir, I can't. There was a space of ground constituting the aisle between you and that bench of Becky Ben's wasn't there? Yes, sir. The width of the market house? Yes, sir. That was between you and Becky Ben's stall? Yes, sir. And you could see that portion of the ground as well as you could have seen the bench, couldn't you? Yes, sir. That was within your line of vision, wasn't it? Yes, sir. Now, sir, within that space any where, did you see Mr. Lutterloh and Mr. Leggett and Capt. Tolar and Mr. E. P. Powers standing there conversing together? No, sir. You saw nothing of that sort at that time? No, sir. Do you say they were not there? I didn't see them there sir. You didn't see them standing there; you didn't see any body on the bench, but you can't say that the bench was vacant, and you don't remember that these gentlemen were standing in the aisle at that time? No, sir. Do you remember they were standing there at all? I remember seeing them, but I don't remember seeing them together. I am speaking about the time when the ladies had driven off in the carriage you had changed your position and got on the east end of the bench, which is on the north side of the market house, and Archy was just starting down stairs, now at that time did you see any of these gentlemen that you have named, Tolar, or Leggett, or Lutterloh, or Ed. Powers? No, sir. Could you have seen them if they had been standing in that aisle and your attention had been directed to them? Yes, sir. Was no one standing in that aisle between you and Becky Ben's bench? Well, sir, I can't say, I guess there was, but I don't recollect now. I beg you won't guess, I must insist upon it that if you can't answer the question you will say so; you don't remember seeing these gentlemen standing there at all? No, sir. Either together or apart at that time? No, sir. Well, at that time, and just as Archy was coming down stairs, did you see Tom. Powers? Not just at the time he was coming down stairs. Who did you say came out of the door first at the landing as Archy was coming down? I can't say which came

out first. You simply remember that the group came down and Archy in the midst of it? Yes, sir. That in that group were Hardie and Faircloth, and Wemyss and McGuire, and a few others? Yes, sir, and Mr. Hornrine was one. You say nothing was done to Archy until he got to the foot of the stairs? No, sir. Up to this time that we have got Archy to the foot of the stairs in the market house, had you seen any weapons in any body's hand there? No, sir. Nor any knife? No, sir. Any pistol? No, sir. Any clubs? No, sir. No marks of any knife, pistol, about a man's person like a protuberance in his breast, or back, or side? No, sir. Did you see any belts? No, sir. You never saw a belt to which a pistol could be attached about any one that you remember? No, sir. You saw no holsters? No, sir. Nothing of that sort that indicated the presence of arms up to that time? No, sir. When Archy got to the foot of the stairs nothing was done to him still until just as he went to turn out of the arch, as I understand you? No, sir. You were looking there at the time, weren't you? Yes, sir, as well as I could. He was the chief object of your attention at that time? Yes, sir. And from the time he left the landing and got to the foot of the stairs and come to the arch and was in the act of turning out of it, you didn't see any thing done to him or said to him? No, sir. Didn't you hear the crowd say when they appeared on the stairs "there he is," "here he comes?" Not that I recollect of. You didn't hear any such expression as "there is the damned rascal." Not that I recollect of. You heard no expression of "rally boys?" No, sir. You heard no expression at all that you recollect? Not that I recollect of. Was the crowd perfectly still? They may have been moving about a little. But they were making no exclamation? No, sir. You heard no exclamation as "kill him," "shoot him," at that time? No, sir. He went to turn out of the arch and you say at that time Tom Powers grabbed him on the breast? Yes, sir. With which haud? I think it was his right hand. How was Powers standing, was he facing you? Powers was standing with his back south, I think. Are you pretty certain of that? Yes, sir. Was he standing right at the turn of the arch? Very nigh the turn. You think he grabbed with his right hand? I think so, sir. Have you any decided opinion about that? No, sir, I have not, I can't say which hand. Can't you now, by picturing the thing in your mind—it frequently helps a man—by just picturing in your mind, and placing the men, tell whether it was his left or right hand? I can't say which hand it was. Did you see any knife in Tom Powers' hand at that time, in either of his hands? No, sir. You saw him catch at the prisoner and say "I demand the prisoner?" Yes, sir. What happened then? The crowd closed up together. You said before that the crowd closed up; what do you mean by that? They gathered around him. Was it around Archy and Tom Powers? Yes, sir. Were any exclamations used? I didn't hear any thing else. You heard no word except Tom Powers demanding him? No, sir. When Tom Powers made this demand you say to the best of your recollection it was "I demand the prisoner?" Yes, sir. Did you hear nothing else? No, sir. Did you hear nothing like "by God I will have him, he is mine?" I can't say that I did, sir. You recollect hearing the words to the effect, "I demand the prisoner?" Yes, sir. And seeing the man grab at him?" Yes, sir. And that the crowd closed up? Yes, sir. Did they close up very quietly? I didn't hear any fuss particularly. I mean about the rapidity of the motion; did they move like they were going to a funeral when they closed up? I can't say. They moved close up around Archy and Mr. Powers? Yes, sir. Don't you think they closed up very quietly—there was no pressure? No, sir. You didn't see any thing like that? The crowd just closed up around him. Who was in that crowd? I can't say. Did you close up? No, sir, at that time I was on the bench. You didn't form any of that crowd that closed up? No, sir. Did the whole crowd that was within your view close up? No, sir, not all of them. Those that were nearest the prisoner closed up? I suppose so. Don't suppose, I want to know whether it was so or not? I can't say. Didn't you see? I can't say whether all that was nearest closed up or not. You say there were some who didn't close up? Yes, sir. And you say there was some who did? Yes, sir. Did the greater part of them close up or was it about half and half? I suppose so. These men that closed up did they come from a distance or were they those that were nearest the prisoner? I think they were those that were close to the prisoner. That was instantaneous with Powers making this demand and the sheriff's reply? Yes, sir. And then the sheriff said what? He said "stand back gentlemen," or "stand back men." Was that all; didn't he say the man was his prisoner, and he intended to keep him? I don't recollect that. Didn't he say he would protect the prisoner as long as he was in his hands? I didn't hear that. You heard him say "stand back gentlemen" in about the same tone of voice that you use now? It might have been louder; it was, I guess. A decided tone; did it indicate excitement? No, sir. Just in a calm voice "stand back gentlemen?" Yes, sir. Did he have any club? I can't say that he did. Did he make any motion with his hand when he said "stand back?" Yes, sir. Did he have his hand upon any one? I can't say that he had, sir. Didn't you see him grab Tom Powers' wrist when he attempted to seize this negro? No, sir. You saw nothing of the grabbing of the wrist? No, sir. When he said "stand back gentlemen," what did Tom Powers do? I only seen him for a moment, that I recollect of; I seen Mr. Powers when he demanded him, and after that I can't say. You don't know what became of him after that demand? No, sir. Was Sheriff Hardie speaking to him or the crowd when he told them to stand back? He said "stand back gentlemen." Was that his expression? Yes, sir. Was his face towards Powers or towards the outside of the arch? I can't say, sir. Beebee was between you and Powers was he when Powers made this grab? Yes, sir. Which side of the boy was Hardie, was he in front of him or behind him? I can't say. Do you know which way his face was turned; whether it was to the outside of the arch or in, when he addressed the crowd and said, "stand back gentlemen?" No, sir, I can't say. How long a delay did it occur? A momentary delay. Then they got Archy through the arch and he turned down with his face towards the guard house, did he? Yes, sir, they turned down that way, but I didn't see Archy at that time. Didn't you see him as he passed through the arch? I saw him then. He was going towards the guard house, wasn't he? Yes, sir. Wasn't his face that way when you last saw him as he turned out of the arch; I mean before he disappeared from your view? I can't say which way his face was turned? You saw him pass through the arch, however? Yes, sir. Did you see Tom Powers pass through the arch after him? It was just as he passed out that Tom demanded him. He was in the act of passing out as Tom demanded him? Yes, sir. When he did pass out, did Tom go out with the crowd? I can't say, sir. Were these other persons in the crowd who followed Tom that were further from Beebee? I can't say. Do you mean to say you can't tell whether there

was a single man in that crowd who was farther from Beebee than Tom Powers, I mean in the midst of that crowd that closed up, was Tom Powers in the midst of it, or was he on the outside edge? I guess he was in the midst of it. And then the crowd passed out? Yes, sir. And you can't pretend to say whether Powers passed out in the midst of it or not? No, sir. Where was it you saw Monk with this knife? He was a little in the crowd after they passed out. Did he pass out with the crowd? I didn't see him when he passed out, he was out when I saw him. And that was after Tom Powers made the grab? Yes, sir. How long? Well, sir, it was a very short time. Could you have counted ten? About that I reckon. What was Monk doing? He had a little old knife there. You noticed it was a small one? Yes, sir, something about six inches long. Handle and all? Yes, sir. What did he do with it? He made a pass or two, cutting towards Archy. Did he make one, or two, or three, or four? I think he made two. Which way was he cutting?

(Represents, had it grasped in his hand, the blade protruding beneath his little finger, and striking with a downward stroke.)

How close was he to Archy when he was striking that way? Perhaps three or four feet. Was he within reach of him? No, sir, he didn't strike him. I want to know whether he was in reach of him? I can't say, sir. You say he didn't strike him? Yes, sir, he didn't, I didn't see him strike him. Did the knife pass close to him? I can't say. How can you say it didn't strike him then, if you didn't see where it went? I can't say. You swear positively it didn't strike him? Yes, sir, I didn't see it strike him. Did you see where it did strike? It didn't strike anywheres. Did you see how far it was from Archy when he was striking? I can't say, sir. How do you know it didn't strike him? Because I know it didn't strike anything. If it didn't strike anything, you must have seen the knife at the moment it come down, and thus you can tell how far it was from Archy. No, sir, I can't say how far it was from Archy; I couldn't see because there was a good many around him. But you say it didn't strike him still? No, sir, I didn't see it strike him. You stated it didn't strike; I didn't ask you if you didn't see it? The licks I saw didn't strike him. You say you didn't see where the knife struck? It didn't strike anything. How do you know it didn't strike anything: did you see it at the moment it came down? Yes, sir. Now how far was the point where it came down from Archy? I can't say, sir. You mean you won't say? No, sir, I don't know; the crowd was so thick, and I was not paying much attention. You can't say whether it was three, or six, or twelve inches? No, sir. You won't swear it was not within three inches of him? I think it was more than that. Do you think it was more than six? I think it was twelve. You think it was twelve, you might just as well have given that in the first time. I could not say for certain. I know you couldn't say for certain; but you have to give your best opinion upon the matter; you think it was about twelve inches from him, and that it didn't strike him? Yes, sir. What became of Monk after this striking with the knife? I didn't see any more of him at that time. Did you see Archy when Monk was striking with the knife? Yes, sir, I saw Archy. Was it immediately after that, that Archy disappeared, that he went down as it were? Yes, sir. Did you see Archy trying to get away from the officers? No, sir, I didn't. But you saw this man strike at him with a knife, and immediately afterwards you saw him disappear from sight in the crowd? He went down pretty soon. I want to know how long? I can't say, sir. Was it immediately after the man struck with a knife? No, sir, they had got a little further down then. A little while after you saw Monk strike at him with a knife, you saw the man go down with the crowd—you don't know what had become of Monk in the meantime? No, sir, I didn't see Monk. Now this crowd which got close upon the prisoners, when Tom Powers made a demand for him, did it desist the from the prisoner after it got outside of the arch or did it still keep pressing on? They still kept pressing on. That crowd kept pressing on from the time they got close upon the prisoner when Tom Powers seized him till he was shot? Yes, sir. Did you hear any exclamation in that crowd about the time the negro went down; do you say immediately before he was shot that he went down? Yes, sir. Now at the he went down and between that time and the time he was shot, and between the time he left the arch and that time did you hear any exclamation in the crowd? No sir. Did you hear anybody say "kill him, kill him"? No, sir. Didn't you hear any body say "he will get away"? No, sir. Did you hear a knife clash in the crowd as it fell from a man's hand? No. sir. Did you hear knives struck by the policemen? No, sir. Did you hear Sheriff Hardie or any of the policemen say "men use your clubs"? No, sir. Did you see the policemen turn and flourish their clubs and keep off the crowd? No, sir. Did anything of that sort occur? Not that I seen. Where were you at that time? I was stepping off of the bench. When, after Mouk was using the knife or before? About the time Monk was using the knife. Did you go out by the north pillar of the east arch? Yes, sir. And you say you heard no sound, no exclamation, no shouting, either kill him, or shoot him, or he will get away; you heard no direction to the officers to use their clubs; you heard no noise of clubs striking; nothing clash upon the pavement, and saw no struggle between the police and the crowd? No, sir, I didn't see any clubs used. Did you see any struggle between the police and the crowd to keep the crowd back off of this man? No, sir, I was too far off to see any thing of that sort. Was there a continuous crowd the point where you were at the north arch of the market house up to the point where Beebee was? No, sir. Did the crowd fill the whole space? No, sir, it was a little vacant. How far did that vacancy extend in front of you, before you come to the edge of the crowd? I can't say, sir; it may have been six or seven feet, and it may have been ten. How wide do you think that arch is; the main arch, from the north pillar to the south pillar? I can't say; it is fifteen feet I reckon. Did this crowd begin south of the south pillar or north of it? I can't say sir, where it commenced; I know close at me there was an open space. Was there any body between you and the crowd further out to your left and rear? To my left I don't recollect sir. Was the pavement pretty empty? Rather to my left it was. You were standing looking at the negro and at this crowd and you say this crowd didn't reach to you within six or eight feet? No, sir, it didn't. That there was a vacant space on the pavement behind the crowd? Yes, sir. Was any body standing there? If there was, they were scattered. Did you notice any person; isn't it your impression that no person was standing there? I can't say, sir; I don't know—there was no crowd that attracted my attention. Don't you recollect Capt. Tolar was standing there in that vacant space at that time? No, sir; I don't recollect. Didn't you see Mr. Leggett there? No, sir. Mr. Lutterloh? No, sir. E. P. Pow-

ers? No, sir. And your impression is that there was a vacancy there, as I understand it, with very few people standing there? Very few. You think there were a few? I can't say whether there was any or not. You don't remember seeing any? No sir. But you have a distinct recollection of the point where the crowd ceased haven't you; the crowd was thick up to a certain place? Yes, sir, in front of me. You could pass to your left; it was in the same direction as you were looking towards the prisoner? Yes, sir. And you don't remember seeing Tolar, or Lutterloh, or Ed. Powers or John Maultsby at that time on the pavement behind the crowd? No, sir. Well, now, in this crowd that was pressing on to Archy just before he was killed, did you see any body that you knew? I don't recollect that I did, sir. Did you see anybody that you knew? Pressing on after Archy? Yes, sir. In that crowd that was pressing on after Archy, I can't recognize any person. Did you see anybody that you knew, I will have an answer and the Court will enforce it, did you see any one in that crowd that you knew? No, sir, I don't know that I did. You swear positively in the presence of God Almighty, that in that crowd of your neighbors that was pressing there at that time, you didn't see a single individual that you knew? None but Monk, sir. I understand you positively swear that you saw nobody but Monk in that crowd that you recognized, and Tom Powers just before it passed out of the arch? Not that I recollect the names of. Do you recollect the description of them without the names? No, sir. Do you recollect whether the crowd was composed of white men or black men, wasn't it almost entirely of white men? Yes, sir. Did you see any black men in it at all? I don't know that I did. You can't recognize a single acquaintance in that crowd? No, sir. How much space did they cover, about twenty feet square? Ten or twelve feet. There were enough in it and were standing closely pressed together to cover ten or twelve feet square, and you can't name one single individual? No, sir, I wasn't paying much attention to that, not enough to tell the names. Wasn't your attention very acutely excited at such a thing in the streets of Fayetteville? Yes, sir, but I wasn't trying to see any particular person, I was just looking on. Very well, you were looking on for the purpose of seeing what was going on weren't you? Yes, sir. And you heard nothing you say of any noise or exclamation, I suppose your eyes must have been very actively exerted, and now you say you saw nothing except that confused mass or crowd? I can't recollect any names, I saw the crowd move on at that time, sir. You say you can't name any one who you saw in that crowd? No, sir. You were still standing by that south pillar when the pistol went off? Yes, sir. Was the wind blowing? Not that I recollect of, sir. Was it still? I think it was tolerably calm. You say just before the pistol was fired, the negro raised his head up? Yes, sir. Did you see where Sheriff Hardie was standing as the negro raised his head up? No, sir. Was Sheriff Hardie with him in the crowd? I don't know, sir, I didn't see him at that time. Was Wemyss with him in that crowd? I don't know, sir. Was Faireloth with him in that crowd? I can't tell. Was McGuire with him? I didn't see him at that time. Then the solitary object that you saw was Beebee and Beebee's head just raise up? I saw that. You saw nothing else? I saw no other face. You did see Beebee and the smoke of the pistol? Yes, sir, I saw Beebee's head raise up. All other objects were lost to your view except these two? I don't recollect seeing any other face. While you were looking at Beebee the pistol was fired was it? No, sir. Were you looking at the point where the pistol fired? No, sir. Where were you looking? I can't say. Is it possible that there was a crowd in front of you say in the very act of taking the life of the prisoner, and your attention was not attracted to the scene at all? I can't say. Were you there, sir? Yes, sir, I was there, but as to the names of any that were in the crowd, I don't recollect. You say at the very moment when the pistol fired, you were not looking at the place where the smoke came from or the man fell? Not at that moment; as soon as the pistol fired, I looked in the direction of the sound. Which way did you draw your eyes from when you looked there? I can't say which way, I don't know, sir. You don't know whether you were looking north, south, east or west? No, sir. You saw the smoke of the pistol? Yes, sir. And directly after that you saw standing in the same spot, just near the smoke, Samuel A. Phillips with a pistol in his hand, which he was holding in front of him, and then returned to his left breast? It was nearly where the smoke was. How near? It was somewhere near the place. I want to know how near? I don't know, sir. Can't you say within six feet? Yes, sir, it was within a foot or two. Now you are much easier in coming at that estimate than you were before at any other? I want to answer them all as nigh as I can. Within about twelve inches of where you saw the smoke you saw Samuel Phillips standing with a pistol in his hand? As nigh as I can say. Who was standing close to Sam Phillips? I don't know, sir. You saw him? Yes, sir. You recognized no man in that crowd up to this time, but you saw Sam Phillips immediately after the pistol fired and you recognized him distinctly? Yes, sir. You recognized him with a pistol in his hand? Yes, sir. You saw him hold it up? He held it up for a moment. What was he doing with it—wasn't he taking the cap off? I didn't see him do it. Didn't you see some smoke come from the muzzle, or tube? No, sir. You didn't see him rubbing it with his thumbs to get the signs of smoke off? No, sir. He was just holding it up with one hand? Yes, sir. That was the first time you saw him that day? The first I recollect of. Was that the last time? No, sir. Where did you see him next? At his store in the evening. Was that the last you had seen of him at the market house? Yes, sir. Did you look at him at the time he had the pistol? Not more than a moment. And from that momentary glance you estimate the distance he was from the point where the pistol fired to have been about twelve inches; you concluded at that time, then and there, that Sam Phillips had fired it? At that moment I thought so. Where did you ever speak about it and to whom, knowing that this man had perpetrated a crime, a felony in the face of the day and before the law; to whom did you report it? I never reported it to any person. When did you first mention the fact that you knew it? I don't recollect, except to James Atkinson, two or three weeks ago. Had you heard that Sam Phillips had turned States evidence before you related this to James Atkinson? I heard. Answer me, had you heard it? I think I had. Don't you know you had? Yes, sir; I know I had. Why not answer directly? I heard about the same time that he hadn't turned State's evidence. After you had heard that Sam Phillips had turned State's evidence you went and told it to James Atkinson? Yes, sir. Did he ask you what you knew about this transaction? I don't know whether he asked me or not. Who told you that Sam Phillips had turned State's evidence, James Atkinson? No,

sir; he didn't tell me. When did you talk about it? I don't recollect. I want to know if that was the subject of conversation at that time? No, sir; I don't think it was. You say it was not? No, sir; it was not. Nor hadn't been immediately before that? No, sir. Now how long before you gave this information to Atkinson, did you know that Sam Phillips had turned State's evidence? I can't say for certain sir; a week or two. The first time you mentioned it was to James Atkinson two or three weeks ago? Yes, sir; about two weeks ago. When were you summoned? Monday. Are you a Mason, sir. No, sir. Do you know Capt. Tolar? I know him by sight sir. Is he an intimate acquaintance of yours? No, sir. Are you any connection of his? No, sir. Are you any relation of James Atkinson? Yes, sir. Well, sir; what is the relationship? We are brothers in law. Do you believe you are bound to tell the truth upon your oath here? That is what I want to do. You think it is perjury if you don't tell it? Yes, sir. You have no idea because it is a Military Commission that you are not to tell the truth? No, sir. You feel as much bound to tell the truth as if you were before an ordinary Civil Court? Indeed I do; I don't wish by any means to tell anything else. After this pistol fired at what place did you see Tolar in the crowd? any where? No, sir. How long did you stay after the pistol fired? I left immediately. I understand you to say the only time you saw Capt. Tolar that day was when you first went into the market house? A short time afterwards. When he was standing near the center of the market house? Yes, sir. You saw him at no other time? No other time that I know of. You can't tell who was near Phillips when he fired that pistol, you can't tell who was nearest Beebee in the crowd that was pressing on? No, sir; I can't tell; I was not paying attention. You saw the man who fired that pistol? No, sir, I didn't. And you never saw Capt. Tolar afterwards? No, sir. Did you see Lutterloh afterwards. I don't recollect that I did. Did you see him afterwards? I don't recollect sir. Did you see Leggett afterwards? Yes, sir. Where was he? He was down at our place. I mean on the ground before you went away? No, sir, I didn't see him. Did you see E. P. Powers afterwards or about the time the pistol fired? No, sir. Did you see Henry Sykes? No, sir. Sam. Hall? No, sir. John Maultsby? I saw John Maultsby after the pistol fired. Before you left the ground? No, sir, after I went away and come back. How long did you stay away when you went away? About half an hour. And come back and found John Maultsby? Yes sir. Just after the pistol fired didn't you hear any body in the crowd cry out who did it? No, sir. Didn't you hear anybody in the crowd say "Capt. Tolar killed him"? No sir. You heard no exclamation of that sort? No, sir. Didnt you see that the people expressed great indignation that a man should be killed, that way in the street? Not that I recollect of. You heard no expressions of surprise, indignation or even inquiry as to who had done it? Not that I recollect of. No name? No, sir. Did you see any effort to arrest the man who had done it? Yes, sir. What was it? They had a trial there. I mean straight away when the felony was committed there in the presence of the crowd, did you see anybody attempt to make an arrest, out of the whole crowd? No, sir, I didn't. Are you deaf? No, sir. You hear distinctly don't you? Yes, sir, Oh yes, sir.

Re-direct Examination, by the Counsel for the accused.

I understand you to say, sir, that just before

the pistol fired, the crowd was thick and dense between you and the negro man, Beebee? Yes, sir, it was thick between me and Beebee. And in motion? Yes, sir. And that though you saw many persons there, and perhaps persons whom you knew were strangers to you, that yet nothing having occurred up to that time to particularly excite your attention, you didn't charge your memory with it, and don't now remember their names; is that the statement I understand you to make? Yes, sir, that is it.

Counsel for the prosecution: I desire that the Counsel will please let him make his own statements.

Re-direct Examination resumed.

Just make it in your own language? After the prisoner was demanded, I don't recollect the names—I didn't pay attention enough to recollect the names of persons—of course there was men there that I would know, but I don't recollect their names.

Counsel for the accused: I think that is the the substance of the statement I made.

Counsel for the prosecution: I simply didn't want you to make a speech for him.

Re-direct Examination resumed:

What was your reason, or reasons for noticing and particularly charging your memory with the fact that Samuel Phillips was there? I seen him, I am very well acquainted with Mr. Phillips, and I saw him standing there, and I noticed the pistol. Then your only reason for noticing Phillips particularly and charging your memory with his being there was the fact of his having a pistol? Yes, sir, that was the cause of my noticing him particularly. Was there no other men except those you have named as having charged your memory with, Monk and Sam. Phillips, was there no other men in the crowd that you saw with weapons that day? No, sir, with the exception of Monk's knife and Sam Phillips' pistol. And I understand that your only reason for charging your memory with these two was the fact that they had weapons in their hands? Yes, sir, that is the only reason. You were asked just now, sir, if you had made this statement to James Atkinson before you heard that Phillips had turned State's evidence; I understand you to say (if I don't understand you correctly, correct me, sir,) that about the time you made this statement to Atkinson, that you had heard both ways; first, that Phillips had turned State's evidence, and then that he had not turned State's evidence? I was at Sam Phillips's house at a prayer meeting, when John Morgan told us positively that Calvin had been here, and Gen. Avery had told him positively that Phillips had turned State's evidence. So at the time you told this to Jim Atkinson, you had heard both ways, and you didn't know which way was true at that time—whether he had turned State's evidence or turned traitor, whether he had not done so? No, sir, I can't say for certain, I heard it both ways at that time.

Questioned by the Judge Advocate:

You had heard at that time that Samuel A. Phillips had been released from prison? Yes, sir. You knew at that time he had been released, did you not? I just knew it from what I had heard. You had heard it from those whom you believed? Yes, sir, of course.

SEBASTIAN AREY, jr., a witness for the defence, having been first duly sworn, testified as follows:

By the Counsel for the accused:

What is your name? Sebastian Arey. Your age? Fifteen years, on 20th next December. Where do you live? At Fayetteville. For how long? Ever since I was born. What have you been doing? Nothing but going to school; that is the last thing I have done. Were you at Fay-

etteville on the 11h of February last? Yes, sir. In the market house? Yes, sir. At what time do you get there on that day? Between three and four o'clock. What occurred on the 11th of February? I suppose there was a nigger killed there. What day of the week was it? I don't remember. You understood a negro was killed on that day, you were present at the market house, at what time did you arrive there? Between three and four o'clock. You went there from what point? From Maultsby and Russell's store, with Mr. John S. Maultsby's son, his name is William Maultsby. Where does he live? About the upper part of the town of Fayetteville, on Mumford street. How far from the market house? I suppose about half a mile. When you got there, was there anybody present at the market house? Yes, sir. How many? About twenty-five. In or outside? In and out together. Had Archy Beebee been carried up into the market house at that time? No. Where did you go first—what part of the market house? South-east corner. Where did you take your station? I went into the market house, and afterwards came out and sat on the bench? Where is the bench? It is in the small arch, at the east end of the market. At which side of the main arch? On the right hand side as you go out. You took a seat on a bench in that arch? Yes, sir. Did you get on that bench from the in or outside? From the outside. Were you sitting or standing there? Sitting down. Were you there when Archy Beebee was carried up there? No, I had gone to Mr. Draughon's corner. Where did you take your station then? I went back to the same corner of the market house. Did you sit down or staud up? Sat down for a quarter of an hour. In the arch? Yes, sir. In the same place as before? Yes, sir. Who did you see there that you recognized, Inside or outside? I don't exactly know who, but I saw Captain Bully there; I remember him because he was drunk. Do you notice here any parties whom you saw there? I don't remember. Neither Tolar, nor Tom Powers, nor Monk Julia? No. Could you see the place? I could see the steps. Leaning from the side you were on, or the opposite side? From the side I was on, I could not see any farther than the door. The door at the landing? Yes, sir. You took your station there for about fifteen minutes? Yes, sir. Did you leave there before Archie Beebee was brought down? Yes, Capt. Bully was there, and I went round to see what he had to say. Where did you go then? I staid right at the back of the arch until he was brought down. Were you there when he was brought down? Yes, when they brought him to the door. Where did you go then? Got upon the bench. As soon as you saw them bring him down, you took your station on the bench? Yes, sir. Did you see Miss Massey brought down? Yes, sir. Who was with her? Mr. Bond and her mother. Did you notice Miss Massey, what she was doing? She looked like crying. Had she a handkerchief to her face? Not that I know of. Did you see the carriage? Yes, sir. Where did it stop? Right in front of the east end of the market. How far from the main arch? Ten or twelve yards I guess. Did it stand there all the time, or was it moved after it was driven up? Didn't notice about that. Mr. Bond and Mrs. Massey went to the carriage with Miss Massey? Yes, sir. Did you see anybody else go there? No. Didn't you notice anybody else? I can't say for certain. How long did it remain after they went unto the carriage? I don't know, I wasn't noticing over there. You didn't notice when it was driven off you say? No. As I understand you then, as soon as you saw the negro brought to the door, you took your stand at the same place as before, on the bench in the small arch, at the eastern face of the market house? Yes, sir. Now tell us what you saw from the time that Archie first made his appearance, until he reached the arch? Well, the Sheriff came down before him with Faircloth and Wemyss, the policemen, the Sheriff came first. How was Wemyss standing as regards the prisoner? He had him by the thumb with a twitch. Which thumb was it? The right thumb. On which side was Wemyss standing? On the right of Beebee. Who else was with him? Faircloth. Was there nobody else? I think there was. Who? Maguire came along down behind. Were the others policemen? Yes, sir. Was any demonstration made as they came down the steps? No. As they reached the floor was there any demonstration made? No. What was the first demonstration you saw made towards the prisoner? I saw a crowd rush up towards the prisoner? Explain to the Court what your position was at the time. I was standing on the bench, leaning against the south part of the arch; was leaning against the bar at the south part of the bench. Inside or outside? Outside the bar. On which side did you have your head? Outside. Did the party, including the prisoner, turn to the right hand or to the left? The crowd rushed upon them. But what direction had they turned to? South, to the right hand. You mentioned some excitement, what was the nature of it? Looked as if they were trying to take him from the policemen. How many? I don't know. Did you see more than one excited? There was such a crowd I couldn't say whether there was more than one or not. What was the evidence, what did you see that made you think there were some trying to get hold of him? I heard a noise and saw a rush made towards him, and heard the sheriff tell them to hold back. Anything before that? No, sir. Not such a cry as "I demand the prisoner?" No, sir. What did the sheriff do? I heard him say "stand back gentlemen." Did they stand back or press on? Pressed on. What did they do? Nothing, at that time. How many? I can't tell. Was the crowd thick? Pretty thick, and kept coming up continually, How large a crowd was there then in front of the market house; how many do you think? I think there were over 50 outside and inside the market. How much over 50? I can't tell. You can't say you think there were as many as 60? I can't tell. The crowd was thick and you cannot tell how many were pressing upon the prisoner? I cannot. Did you see anybody with a hand raised or a weapon of any kind? I saw some one with a knife as I was coming out of the arch. Whose hand was it? I don't know. Did you see the man plainly? No, I just saw the hand with the knife in it. You only saw one hand with a knife; how many hands were presented towards the prisoner? I don't know. More than two? I don't know; can't say. Are you certain that you saw as many as two? I can't be certain. In what position was the hand you saw the knife in? He had it down to his side. What was he doing with it? He had it in his hand. The blade protruding from which side of the hand? The inside. Which hand? I don't know. How long a blade did the knife have? I don't know; two or three inches long I suppose. Was any effort made by the man that held the knife, to strike the prisoner? I never saw him any more; the crowd was all rushing in. Did you see any other weapon besides that knife? Not at that time. Mr. Arey, how came you to see the knife, without being able to see the face of the man that held the knife? He was in the crowd and I just seen it through the crowd, I didn't notice about his face. You were looking along the side of the market house at that time. Yes, sir. Were there many persons between you and the person who held the knife? About a dozen. Was your head higher, or on a level, or below the man who held the knife? I was standing on the bench. How high is it? About three feet from the pavement. You were standing up? Yes, sir. What's your height? About five feet and a half. You say you don't know what prevented you from seeing the hand that held the knife? I didn't look to see; the crowd was thick. That was the only weapon you saw at that time? Yes, sir. Were any cries being made just at that moment? That was about the time I heard the Sheriff cry out "stand back gentlemen." I saw the knife about that time. You heard no other cries after that? Not that I know of. Well, what occurred next? Well, the prisoner got to the edge of the little arch—the north edge—and the crowd kept rushing on; at last he got down on his all fours, and he got most up again when he fell again. How low down did he go at the first stumble? On his knees. He was then at the middle of the small arch? Yes sir; and when he stumbled his head was about even with the level of the arch. Who had hold of him at that time? Wemyss, Faircloth and the Sheriff. Where was the Sheriff? At his back. Did you notice at what time the Sheriff got back of the prisoner? No, at the time he got to the middle of the arch I noticed he was back. At the middle of the arch you say he stumbled again? He didn't stumble, but was about down. He had been down on his all fours and hadn't recovered himself. Where was Wemyss when he came on his all-fours? He had hold of him by the thumb. How close were you to him? I was on the bench. How close to Beebee? About three or four feet. How far was he from the wall of the market house? About three or four feet. Where was Wemyss then? On the right of the prisoner. And Faircloth; where was he? Didn't notice; he was on the far side of him from me. The Sheriff was behind at that time. Can you explain where, was he on the right or left at the time? I can't say. How close was he to him? He had hold of him. By the collar? Yes. By the back or front? About here as well as I can recollect. (Witness here placed his hand upon his coat collar at a point quite near the back of the neck.) Did you notice whether Beebee had on a hat or not? No; I didn't notice; I don't remember. Who else did you notice about the prisoner at that time? There was a big crowd around him. Did you notice anybody in particular? No, sir, I was just noticing the crowd and that was about all. Were there many in front of the prisoner at that time? No, but they were gathering in front of him. How many between where you were standing and the prisoner? I cannot tell. You were within about four feet from him? Yes, sir. And you cannot tell how many were between you? No. He had then fallen on his all-fours in the middle of the arch; what did you next notice? That Phillips had a pistol in his hand. Where was he standing? To the rear and left. How far from the prisoner? About seven feet. On or off the pavement? Somewhere about the edge; I could not see whether he was on or off. What was the position of the pistol where you first saw it? I saw him put his hand in his bosom, or under his coat. What did he do with the pistol after he took it out? I saw him with the pistol, and I got down from the bench, and in front of the arch where Phillips was. Did you see him cock it? Yes—no, I didn't see him cock it, but I saw it cocked. About how high was he holding it? About so high.

(Witness here placed his hand and arm in position to suit the words, bringing his hand to the height of the shoulder, and having it at a distance from the shoulder of about eight or ten inches—the same position, or nearly such, as would be taken by a person about to discharge a pistol.)

How was the pistol pointing, with reference to you at that moment? It was pretty much pointed towards me. Well, how was the prisoner to you and Phillips, between you, or on one side or the other? Near about between. And the pistol was pointing in your direction? It looked like it. What did you then do? I got off the bench. Jumped down? I sort o'jumped or swung down. Which way did you jump? Got in front of Beebee. Did you run or walk, or were you thrown there in getting down? Well, the crowd kind o'shoved and I just got there somehow; I was trying to get out of the crowd. Did you hear the pistol fired? Yes. Did you see it? Part of it. How much of it did you see? The muzzle of it. And you heard it? Yes, sir. Did you see any evidence of the discharge of the pistol; did you see the flash? I did, sir. And the smoke? Yes, sir. How far was the pistol from the place where you had seen Phillips? A little closer than when I first saw it. Was it closer or not to the prisoner? It was closer to him. What was the position of the prisoner at the time you saw the pistol in Phillips' hand? Well, he was then looking about south east. Was he erect, or down, or getting up when he shot at him? Just up. How was he when you jumped? Down on his hands and knees. Did you see him rise? Yes, sir. Where were you at the time? On the pavement. How far from him? Close enough to have touched him. How long after you got down from the bench did you see the pistol fire? About a minute or so. How many could you have counted, think you? Oh, I don't know. Can you say whether it was more or less than a minute? No, I can't come any nearer to it—but just before he was shot I heard some one holler out "shoot him." Did you see or hear who said "shoot him"? No. Did you recognise the voice or see the person? No. That was just before you got down from the bench? Yes, sir. Was anything else said at that moment? No. Not immediately before it? No, not that I know of. What were police Wemyss and Faircloth doing at that time? They had hold of him. Where was the prisoner at the time this holler of "shoot him" was heard? He was down. Did you, or did you not notice him making any efforts to get away? Well, it looked as if he was trying to get away on account of being scared of getting killed. Was that about the time some one said "shoot him"? Yes, sir. That was just before you got down from the bench? Yes, sir. And you had got how many steps from the bench when you heard the pistol fire? About two steps. In what direction did these steps take you, right or left? Straight forward. You were looking which way when you got down? To the east. Which way was your face after you got down? It was to the east. Did you go directly straight forward or a little to the right or left? To the right if anything. That took you in front of the prisoner, and within reach if you had held out yourarm? Yes. At that moment you heard the pistol fire? Yes, sir. How much nearer was it now than when you saw it on the bench? Not much nearer, not so much but that a man could have got up that close in the time. Had Beebee moved forward from the time you saw the pistol, or did he merely rise from where he was standing? He merely rose And the sheriff had him by the back of the neck? Yes. And the pistol was a little nearer than when

you saw him put up his hand? Yes, sir. How close was Phillips' hand to the prisoner; you say he was standing seven feet from him; but how far was his hand from his head? About four or five feet, And when you saw the smoke and heard the report the pistol was nearer than when you first saw it in his hand? It was nearer. Could you say how much? About two or three feet, I should think. What else did you see after that—what next occurred? The next thing I saw the nigger fall. Which way did he fall—with this head to the market house, or in the other direction? About towards the market house. How were his feet as he fell? East or somewhere in that direction. How far from the edge of the pavement? I can't say for certain, but my opinion is that one foot was off the pavement. The foot that was off the pavement was under the leg of the foot that was on, is that so? Yes, sir. Did you hear any cries after the shooting? I heard some one say "the damned rascal is dead," or something like that. Did you see who said it? No. Who was nearest to you when you had reached the position in which you were standing where the prisoner was shot? The only one I know was Jim Douglas. At which side of you? To my right side. How far from you? About right against me, about the edge of the pavement. Whither was he off or on? I didn't notice, can't tell. Did you hear any cries as to who shot him? No. Did you see Phillips after the shot? No. Did you see Captain Tolar at the time of the shooting? No. Did you see Tom Powers? No. Did you see Monk Julia? Yes. Where was he? To the south. In front or rear of the prisoner? To his face, after the fall. Are you acquainted with Tolar and Tom Powers? Yes, sir, I know Mr. Powers when I see him, but I didn't know his name. You had seen the man whom you say you know to be Tom Powers, but you were not acquainted with him at that time? Yes, sir. Were you acquainted with Captain Tolar at that time? Yes, sir. Did you see Captain Tolar after you saw Beebee come to the door of the stairs? I never saw him that day as I know of. Did you see Tom Powers that day? Not that I know of. Had you seen Monk on that day? I saw him in the market house. What was he doing? Walking along. What became of you after the prisoner fell? I started for home—went as far as the other part of the market house, and staid up there until it was about time for them to hold the jury, and then I left and went home. Did you stop on your way home? I don't remember. Did you see Phillips after the shooting? No. Did you look to see who shot him? No. Where did you look as the prisoner fell. At him. Are you a relation of any of the prisoners here? Mr. Tolar is some distant relative to me, but not close to me. What is it? About first or second cousin to mother. First or second? I don't know which. Are you related to any of the witnesses that have been examined? No, sir. Are you a relative to Squire Arey who has been examined? He is my grand father. Are you related to Lockamy? No. Are you related to any of the witnesses for the prosecution? No. To Kendricks? No. To Porter? No. Did you ever tell any body else about the matter before? I went home and when speaking about it I was told I had better not have any thing to say about it. When was that? The day it was done; I was told it didn't concern me, and I had better keep it all to my self. Who told you? I don't remember exactly, some people about there. Some of the folks at home? No, some neighbors, don't remember who they were. And you have not said any thing about it? No, I was told I might get myself into a scrape, or something of that kind, so I kept it to myself.

Cross examined by Counsel for prosecution. Did you say your mother was a first cousin or second of Capt. Tolar, you don't know which? I don't remember. Are you any relative of John Maultsby's? No, but I am of John Maultsby's uncle by marriage, but no relative to him. To old John? Yes, sir, he is my uncle by marriage, he married my mother's sister. Jno. Maultsby's wife is your aunt then? Yes. sir. Is young John Maultsby a son of your aunt? Yes, sir. Then John Maultsby is your first cousin? No, his uncle is only uncle by marriage, he married my aunt. Do you know John Maultsby under arrest at Fort Macon? Yes, sir. What kin is your mother to him? None at all. Do you know Henry Sykes; any kin to him? I know him but he is no relative of mine. Then the only relationship you know of is that your mother is cousin, first or second, to Maultsby? Yes, sir. What time of day was it when you went to the market house? Between three and four o'clock. You went before Archy was brought out of the guard house? I was going by there and heard about this thing; I wanted to see the nigger, so I stopped to hear the trial. You were going by you say and you thought you would stop; what induced you to stop, was there any crowd there? Yes, a right smart crowd. What caused you to stop at the market house? I wanted to see what nigger it was. From curiosity connected with this affair? Yes, sir. When you got there you found Archy hadn't come, so you moved down to Draughon's corner? Yes, and as they came I came behind them. And you took your station at the east front of the little south arch; you sat down there? Yes, sir. As Archy went up stairs? Yes, sir. Did you remain until he came down? No, I sat until Capt. Bully came up. Who is he? I don't know who he is, that's all I know of him. Did you get off on the outside? Yes, my legs were hanging outside. Now, this bench is about three feet from the ground, and up above that bench there is a bar, how high is that? I don't know. When you were standing on the bench could you reach it? Yes, even when setting down Did your head reach it when you were sitting down? I don't remember. Did it not inconvenience you when you were sitting down? Well, I was a sort of leaning over. That was not in your way? No, sir. You didn't go inside the market house did you, when Archy went up? No. You sat on the seat until Bully came along? Yes, I went up to the big arch and staid in it. Near the south end? Yes, sir. With your face to the south side of the arch? Yes, sir. Could you see the steps from there? Yes, if I looked. You remained there until Miss Massey came down stairs? Yes, sir. Did you see any one come down stairs before she did? No. Before Mr. Bond and herself came down the steps, didn't anybody come down? Don't remember. Before Mr. Bond came down with Miss Massey, didn't he come down alone? I don't recollect. During the time you were standing in the arch, before Archy came down, or before Mr. Bond came down, whom did you see in that crowd? I saw Alonzo Birket. Did you see Sam Phillips then? No. Did you see Tolar and Leggett and Lutterloh standing in the middle of the arch within a very feet of you? No. Did you see Lutterloh, Leggett, Tolar, or Powers standing within a few feet of the market house, in front of you? No. Don't you remember a single soul you saw? I saw Alonzo Burkett there and Capt. Bully. Was Bully standing in the arch with you? He was standing with his back to the south part of the arch; we were joking together; there were a number of boys of us together. Did that joking con-

tinue until the ladies came down stairs? Yes, sir. So that you were chiefly concerned in that jocose conversation? Yes, sir. Was the crowd perfectly still; were they not talking at all? I didn't notice any of them. Your attention was so much taken up with Capt. Bully that you did not notice the crowd much? You don't know how many people were there? No. And you don't now know anybody but Capt. Bully, Alonzo Birket, and some other boys? No, I saw others then that were not talking to Bully. Who? I saw Jonathan Hollingsworth. Did he have a weapon? He had a pistol buckled around his waist outside his coat. What became of him? I saw him about three several times. Did you see him there when the ladies came down? Yes, sir. Where was the last you saw of him? About the time the ladies came down. What was he saying or doing? He came up by the right hand side and went under the market house, but stopped about the middle of the market. To whom did he speak? I didn't notice. I understand you to say that from the time you went into the arch until the ladies came down stairs, you saw neither Lutterloh, nor Leggett, nor Powers, nor Sam Hall, nor anybody you knew, but Bully? I saw John Maultsby. Where was he standing? He was sort o' leaning on the bench. Was he speaking to anybody? Didn't notice that he did. Did you see Hollingsworth? No. Did you see Sykes or Hall? No. Nor Ed. Powers? No. Nor Leggett? No, sir, I did not know him anyway. Nor Lutterloh? No. Did you see Tom Powers there? No, the only way I know him is by his having had the small-pox; but I would have known him if I saw him in the crowd. These ladies came down and Mr. Bond with them Did you leave to move out of the arch to give them room to pass? I moved out. What became of Bully? I don't know. When you made way there, did you and Bully move off together. No. Where did you go? I went back to the bench. Still with your legs hanging outside? I was standing up, on the bench. When you first went up there you took your station on the bench; afterwards you left and went to the eastern arch trifling with Bully, and when the ladies came down stairs you stepped back to the arch and then staid at that arch? Yes, sir. Well, when you got up on the bench did you stand outside this bar or inside it? Outside. You turned your attention from the carriage then, and looked towards the steps? Yes. Did you see the ladies get into the carriage? I was watching to see Beebee come down. Did you hear it said in the crowd that he was coming? I heard something said about it but didn't know exactly. But didn't you go there because you heard some body say the prisoner was coming down? Yes. You heard he was shortly going to come down? Yes, sir. Did you hear it said when the ladies came down? Yes, sir. The carriage hadn't driven off before you started for the bench? No. How did you hear the prisoner was coming down? I dont know; but heard something about it. Did you hear a general buzz, people saying that he was coming down soon? Yes, sir. And you went and took your station in this place with your face inwards you were rather higher than the heads of the crowd? I was sir. Was there any body between you and the stairs? Becky Ben was. Was there any body between you and the steps of the stairs? if a person had to go down stairs, would he have come down against you? Not exactly, but very near me. Do you think the distance is twenty feet, from the foot of the landing to where you were? About fifteen or twenty. Was there any body in the place between you and the foot of the stairs? All that I remember was Becky

Ben. Did the steps land right in the middle of her stall? Yes, sir. Does she sit so that a man coming down stairs would tread upon her? No, she has a small place fixed with a kind of bench. You say there was a space of fifteen or twenty feet? Was there any one between you and her? I don't remember. Did you see Sam Phillips then? Not at present. You did'nt see a soul t iat you could recognise? No. Didn't you see Tom Powers? No. Did you see Capt. Tolar? No. Do you know him? Yes, sir. Did you see Monk Julia down there? Not at that time. I am speaking of the time you got to the bench with your face turned to the stairs; you say you didn't see Tolar? No. And you don't know Leggett, did you see Powers or Lutterloh? No. Nor Maultsby? I saw Maultsby leaning on the bench at Becky Ben's stand, inside the market. Was he speaking to any one? I don't remember. Was any one near him; I think so. Who? I don't know. Were there any other persons about or near him? I think there were, but I don't know whether they were speaking to him. Did you see any weapon about him then? No. You saw no one else but Maultsby that you recognized? No. Was Hollingsworth there then? No. Nor Sam Phillips? No. Nor anybody else? No, or if I ever did know I forgot. You have forgotten a good deal about it? I have, sir. You have never told it at all from the time it happened until very lately? I told it to some. To whom? I don't remember. Who did you tell it to? Well, I don't remember; it is two or three weeks ago; I told part of it to Ichabod Davis. Is he the first person to whom you remember having told it lately? Yes, sir. Did he come and ask you about it? No, he came to the field where they were playing base ball. Have you told it several times since then? No, I have not said much about it since then; I told him something about it and he said I had better keep it to myself. How much did you tell him? Not much, I don't recollect. You told him the particular part about Sam Phillips? Yes, sir. That was the first time in a long while that you had told it? Yes, sir. To whom have you spoken of it since? To no one, I was advised not to. You have not spoken of it to any one since speaking to Ichabod Davis about it? I have not that I can remember. You have not spoken to the Counsel in this case and told him what you were going to testify? No. They never asked you what you were going to testify on the stand? Mr. Fuller did. Did you tell your mother of it? Yes, sir. A full account of it the day it occurred? No. Did you tell her of it the day it occurred? I told her part of it. What Sam Phillips had done? A part of it; I don't remember what part. That Sam Phillips was standing with a cocked pistol in his hand? I don't remember. Upon your oath? Not that I can remember. Nor your father? No, sir. Then the first time you mentioned it, was to Davis? I told Pa. When? Just before I told Davis. How come you to tell him, did he ask you about it; or did you tell it to him of your own accord? Well, Ma knew that I knew something about it, and I suppose she told him—he asked me about it. Then the first ever said about the cocked pistol was to Davis? Yes, sir. Who were they, the day it happened that told you to hold your peace; was it your mother or father? No, sir, some of the neighbors. Can't you name some one? No. They had influence enough to keep you from naming it and yet you don't know who they were. I do not. You say you saw all that you have narrated on the day it happened and you know it now it now as well as you did then? Yes. Then you say the part you told your moth-

was, that Sam. Phillips was there with a loaded pistol? No. Your father then was the first to whom you mentioned it, you say, and that within the three or four weeks? Yes, sir. When you saw Archy coming down stairs you cannot tell anybody except Maultsby who was there. No, Do you remember whether Davis had been to Raleigh and gone back, or do you know? I think he had been here and gone back—I am not certain, but I think he had. Was it the last time he had gone back? After he had gone back the first time from Raleigh, I think. When you saw Archy coming down stairs who was in front of him? Sheriff Hardie—as well as I can recollect Sheriff Hardie came before Archy, and got near the foot of the steps before Archy came out of the door? Then he turned and looked around? I don't remember. Archy was about the door all this time, then you saw him come through? Yes. Was Wemyss on his right hand? Yes. And you say he had a twitch on his thumb? Yes. On his right thumb? Yes, sir. And you think Wemyss who held the twitch was on his right side also? Yes, sir. Where do you think Faircloth was? On his left, as well as I can recollect. In speaking just now of persons you had conversation with, did you mean you ever had any conversation with Tolar about it? No. You never told him anything you knew about it? No. Well, they came down stairs and nothing was done till they came to the foot? Nothing was done then. You were still looking at them; when did you turn about and look outside? When they got to the arch. You were looking inside until then? Yes, sir. You saw their movements from the time they got to the foot of the steps until they got to the arch? Yes, sir. When he got to the arch inside you turned about so that you could see him when he got outside? Yes. From the time he got to the foot of the steps inside to the time he got to the arch and was about to turn about, what happened? They then rushed on him, about the outer edge of the arch. You could see him from the outside? Yes, sir. Nothing was done inside? No. You didn't hear Tom Powers make a demand for him? No. No voice nor expression in the nature of a demand? No. No noise, disturbance or confusion whatever until he got to the arch? No. And yet you were looking inside from the time he got to the foot of the stairs until he got to the arch? Yes, sir. Did you recognise any body inside in the crowd from that time to the time he got to the arch? No. Was this bar in front of or behind you? Behind me. You were two or three feet above the level of the crowd? More than that. You could see the crowd well then? Yes, sir. Was it moving right at your feet? Not at that time. As Archy turned out of the arch there was a rush made for him? Yes. Was that a simultaneous rush of the whole crowd? Not at all, but some of them. Was it the greater portion of the crowd that was rushing? It looked to be about so, the whole crowd just about surrounded him. You used the expression rush on your first examination, do you mean to retract that? There was a rush around him. Did that come from the crowd behind or before, or did all get around him simultaneously? Sort o' from his left and front. The crowd didn't seem to come on him from the market house or behind him? When I first saw the crowd they were rushing, not before I looked around. Then when you did look round they were actually in the act of rushing? Yes, sir. The confusion was over then so you could not see it? Yes, sir. You are confident you saw that? Yes, sir. You are certain? I know I did. Any body there you knew? No. Is it possible that in the crowd you saw at that time you couldn't tell a single one of them? I might have at the time, but don't remember now? Do you swear, in presence of Almighty God, who knows your heart and conscience this day, and to whom all secrets are revealed, that with the best exertions of your memory you cannot say any one of those who were concerned in that rush that day. I do swear it. You have tried and you have failed. Yes, sir. Sheriff Hardie turned round and exclaimed "stand off gentlemen?" He was in the crowd and I didn't see him. You were standing about three feet higher? Yes, but I was not noticing him at the time, I was watching towards the nigger. Did you see him at that time? No, he made a sort o'stop in the arch. Now then this nigger, as I understand it, has got to the arch on the pavement, and turned to the right? He hadn't turned, but he was about ready to turn. At that time when he was about ready to turn, his face was due east; was your face turned to the east; you were not looking inside the market house? My attention was turned to some one on the bench. Which way were you looking inside or out? I don't know, when I looked round in front I seen the rush. Where you first got standing on the bench, what did you see; was the rush going on then? Yes. Was Archy outside on the pavement then? He was about even with the arch, about the outer edge. Did you see him when he turned to the right to go to the guard-house? Yes, sir. From that time did he ever get in front of you? Yes, he did. Before you jumped off the bench? Yes, sir. Was the crowd noisy from the time Archy commenced moving until he got close to you, or was it quiet? Most of them were saying something, but I couldn't understand. Was it noisy? You heard no one say he would get away? No. You heard one say "kill him?" I heard some one say that when he got about in front of me. Did Sheriff Hardie use his club? He never had a club. Did Wemyss use his? Not that I know of. Did you not hear him hit somebody that day, and a knife drop on the pavement? No. Then there was such a noise that you could not have heard the clash of a knife on the pavement, nor the blow of the club on a man's head. I might have heard it if it had been loud enough; there was fuss enough by the feet on the brick to prevent any hearing any such small noise as that. And the first exclamation was "kill him?" Yes, sir. Now, from the time Archy turned to the right and moved down the pavement until he got to you, did you recognize anybody at all? Not that I recollect now; the excitement for one thing would keep me from remembering—my attention was called to the negro. You can't say anybody who was in that crowd then? No. Have you not told anybody? Not that I can remember. Have you not told them that you knew some whom you were a little uncertain about, and they told you that because you were not certain you need not swear to it? No. Then you didn't know a single individual except the sheriff, his officers and the prisoner? No. Then you didn't hear any "kill him" until he got down there. Were you still standing on this bench until the prisoner was right up to you. Yes. This nigger had come down the pavement to opposite the center of that arch before you left your perch? Yes, sir. You recollect about that—he did get down the pavement directly opposite you before you left the perch? Yes, sir. Where did he fall—did he fall as soon as he got outside the big arch? Well, he had started on. Had he gone a step or more than that? More than that. He got near the arch before you saw him stumble? Yes, he recovered himself and then went down on his hands and knees. By the time he got down di-

rectly opposite you—you standing in this little arch you speak of? Yes, sir. Was he well down on his hands and knees when you jumped off the perch? Just rising. He was in the act of rising when you jumped? Yes, sir. While you were standing thus did you see Phillips with his pistol cocked? Yes. Was it full cocked? It looked to be. And now you who couldn't recognize a single one up to this time, say that you saw a pistol in a man's hand and that it was full-cocked? How far was Phillips from you: was he off the pavement? He was beyond the pavement. Phillips was in the crowd and off the pavement? Yes. And the crowd therefore spread on and farther than the pavement? Yes. How deep beyond Archy? About ten feet I should think; they were coming up in all directions. And in the midst of it you saw Sam Phillips distinctly with this pistol in his hand; did he cock it before he took it out, or after? The first I saw of it, 'twas cocked. When he put his hand in his breast, didn't you see him take it out; I ask you distinctly, did you see him take his hand out of his breast? I did not see him take it out. You saw him put his hand in his breast, you didn't see him take it out, but instantly afterwards you saw him with a cocked pistol in it; was that all in very quick succession? There was about a minute or half a minute's difference, somewhere's along there. Where was Archy at the moment you saw Phillips put his hand in his breast?. He was at the place where he was shot. Is that answer correct; you say he was in the spot where he was shot? Well, rather there or so near that the difference can't be noticed. You saw Phillips put his hand in his breast, you didn't see him pull it out, but you did see him with a pistol in his hand immediately afterwards? Yes, sir. Where was Archy at the time you saw Phillips with the pistol in his hand? On the pavement; he was down and just as he rose the pistol fired. If you will answer my questions, I will get at what I want without these long narratives; where was Archy when Phillips put his hand in his breast? About the south end of the arch near the south corner of the market house. Where was he when you saw Phillips with the pistol in his hand? About the same spot, he did not move at all; he might have moved a little, but not much. Was he down? Yes. Did you hear the holler "shoot him" before you saw Phillips put his hand in his breast? Yes, sir. Did you not say just now that you heard that cry of "shoot him" after you got down on the pavement? Yes, and I say so yet. Didn't you say you saw Phillips put his hand in his breast just after you heard the cry of "shoot him"? Well, ... I ask you distinctly, did you not say so; if you did, and that it was a mistake, correct yourself? If I did, I made a mistake. Very well; you say you saw him put his hand in, you didn't see him pull it out, but you afterwards saw him with a pistol in his hand: how long a time was there between these two events occurring, and where was Archy Beebee when the first event occurred, and where the second? He was down on the pavement. When? When Phillips was putting his hand in his bosom. Was he down on the pavement when Phillips had the pistol in his hand? It looked as if he was under the feet of the men. You were still standing there in the southern arch, on the east front when you saw Phillips put his hand in his breast; Archy was down during that whole transaction; then you jumped down? No, I saw him with the pistol drawn before I jumped down. You say it was cocked; was it ready to fire? Yes. Archy was down on the ground when you saw the pistol, was the pistol directed to him or not?

It was pointed in the direction he was. You saw the pistol cocked in Phillips' hand while you were standing in that small eastern arch of the market; at that moment Beebee was down on his hands and knees; now I ask you if that pistol was directed towards Beebee on his hands and knees at the time you say? It was as well as he could direct it at him when he wast down; Phillips had it directed up this way as if waiting for him to rise.

(The witness here raised his hand to the height of his shoulder, as if holding a pistol or presenting one.)

The pistol was pointed in his direction. Perhaps we don't mean the same thing by direction; when you first saw him, had he the barrel up? About on a level with his shoulder. At that time the negro was on the ground? He was rising. Then we come back to the original statement; when Phillips put his hand to his breast the negro was down, but when he had the pistol in his hand the negro was up? Yes, he was rising; about up. When you saw the muzzle of the pistol for the first time you say the negro was in the act of rising? How high was he up? About on his knees. While the negro was in that position you jumped off? Yes; and just as I lit on the ground, some one cried out "shoot him." Archy had come down right in front of you; was there not a crowd right in front of you? He had pushed between the crowd, I was trying to get out of the way. I want to know whether you got down in the midst of the crowd, or whether there was no crowd right at your feet? Well; there was space enough for me to get on the ground and about no more. Then you worked your way through this crowd, and after the cry of "shoot him" you worked your way round to his front? Yes; about a step or so. After you had taken that step you heard the pistol fire? Yes, sir. And it was in the position already gained in front that you heard the pistol fire? Yes, sir. Do you swear to that, without fear of being mistaken in any one of these particulars? I may have made some slight mistake; but it was in the direction of him. You saw that pistol and swear positively that it was at a full cock when you saw it? Well, if it was not a full cock, it must have been a very far back half-cock. What sort of pistol was it? A large pistol; like a navy pistol; a square barrel pistol. You saw the cock very distinctly? Yes, sir. Did you see the other parts as distinctly as the cock? It had a brass guard. That's about as much as I know. A brass guard, a square barrell, and then, it was cocked. Now sir, when you first mentioned this matter to Mr. Ichabod Davis did you tell him that the pistol had the brass guard? I dont remember, but I told him it was one of those big army pistols. Did you tell him it had a square barrel? I don't remember. Did you tell him it was cocked? I believe I did. When did you first know it had a brass guard? I saw it at the time. Do you remember now that it had a brass guard? Yes. Have you ever seen it since? No. Nor have had no description of it from any one? No. No body gave you any description of it? No, sir. What do you mean by "a square barrel pistol?" Well; some are round and some a kind o' square. Yes, hexagonal; when were you summoned? Last Monday. Have you talked with any one since you were here about this? No, sir. Did you know that the pistol that Phillips had, had been given to a man named Watson to be unloaded in the town of Fayetteville? I heard something about unloading, but didn't know anything about it. No body told you, neither the Counsel, nor any body else that it had a brass guard? No. You swear positively it was cocked?

Yes, sir. What sort of a day was it? As well as I can recollect it was a sort of cloudy day. Was the wind blowing, or was it still? I think it was a still evening, but cloudy. Was it cold or warm? Well, it was pleasant, I know it was so to me, I can't feel for others. One more question: you did not see Captain Tolar there at all that day? Not that I can remember. And you saw no weapons except those of which you have spoken? No, sir. Do you know of any body else who had a weapon there that day? No, sir, I don't. Neither from others telling you so nor from seeing? No, sir.

Re-direct examination by Counsel for accused.
Have you ever been a witness before this day? No, sir. Were you anxious to become a witness in this case? No, I didn't want to come. You say that during the time most of the matters you have been speaking of occurred that you were there, standing near the southern part of the main arch joking with Capt. Bully, and he was drunk? Yes, he was pretty well in for it. Yes, sir, and you were joking with him and thinking of that and attending more to it than to any thing else that occurred; and that although a great crowd might have been there at the time, you didn't notice that nor pay attention to any thing else? Yes, sir. Some time after that some of your neighbors told you not to have any thing to say about it, and from that day you didn't talk about it? No, sir. Shortly before Mr. Davis had the conversation with you, your father had a talk with you about it? Yes, sir. And you then told him in substance what you have told her to-day. Yes, sir. Shortly after Mr. Davis returned from Raleigh, and upon the ball field, asked you what you knew about Phillips' connection with this affair, and you told him what you've told here to-day. I didn't tell him so much, but I told him some of it. You were afterwards cautioned; who cautioned you, Major McRae, James McRae? Pa cautioned me about it, not McRae. You were summoned last Monday? Yes, sir. And before that you didn't know you would be a witness in the case? Well, Mr. McRae told pa that I would have to be. You came to Raleigh, had an interview with me, and told me what you know of the matter, and received the same caution to say nothing about it? Yes, sir. And what you have said about it you have seen; and here in the presence of Almighty God, well understanding the solemnities of an oath, you swear that what you have said is the truth? I do, sir.

[Counsel for accused: and there is no doubt of it.]

By Judge Advocate:
You recollect very clearly about that pistol—was that brass guard bright or dirty? It looked to be dark. Very dark? Yes, like old brass when it's been standing. How dark was it? Like an old door knob. When you were looking at that pistol, Mr. Arey, can you tell me whether there was a piece of steel or brass or any other metal passing over the cylinder? I didn't notice that sir. Oh, that was one of the little things you didn't notice—do you know a Colt's pistol, when you see it from any other pistol? I might know one of these big ones. Do you know a Remington pistol? No, sir. Did you particularly notice Mr. Phillips? Yes, sir. What sort of hat had he on; a black hat?

Counsel for the accused: I would like to ask if these are questions by the Court?

Judge Advocate: They are questions by the Judge Advocate, sir.

The Counsel for the accused then objected to any further question, as the witness had been examined and cross examined in the usual way.

Counsel for the prosecution: I understand the

rule to be as stated by my friend on the left, he introduces a witness, we cross examine him, and we have no right to enter into an examination again. At the same time it is not unusual, if a single question, or two, have been neglected to put them in this way.

The Commission: The form is that any member of the Court having a question to ask, passes it around upon a piece of paper. If any one objects to it, the sense of the Court is taken. If no ojection is made, it passess current as a question of the Court.

Counsel for the accused: I must state to the Court, that so far as these omitted questions are concerned, I am very sure the gentlemen managing the case for the prosecution will state that we have been exceedingly liberal, and they have been also. If, in this instance, I had been asked, I would have had no objection to offer, but when it is demanded as a matter of right, I must object. Besides, I think that, as a protection to a little boy, some limit should be had to the examination, for as the Court knows, he has already been examined with severity.

Counsel for prosecution: The question is in the decision of the Court.

Judge Advocate: I admit the objection and ask permission of the Commission to ask the witness the questions touching the dress of Samuel A. Phillips that I have already commenced to put to him.

Counsel for defence: We object.

The Commission: The matter cannot be discussed in open Court. We had better retire to consider it,

The Commission was then cleared for deliberation and after some time was so spent, was re-opened; when

The Judge Advocate announced that the Commission had decided that the objection of the Counsel for the defence is not sustained.

Mr. Arey, did you observe Samuel Phillips' coat when you saw the pistol? No, sir, I did not. Can you tell me what was the color of his coat? I cannot. Did he, or did he not have on an overcoat at that time. I don't remember. Can you tell the color of his pants? No, sir. You saw the pistol in his hand; did he have on gloves? I never saw him with any? Did he or did he not have gloves on? I never saw him with any. You saw him that day? Yes, sir. You saw his hand? I don't know that I saw his hand particularly; I saw the pistol in his hand. But you must have seen his hand if you saw the pistol in the hand? Well, his coat sleeve came down pretty well on his hand and I couldn't see. Was that coat a black coat? I don't remember. He had no gloves on? Not that I saw. Did you see his hand at all? I don't remember, his coat covered his hand; his overcoat came pretty well over his hand. Oh, did he have on an overcoat? Well, I can't be certain about that; I spoke a most too quick. Well, sir, did he or did he not have an overcoat? I can't say about that. Was it a:large coat? The sleeves were pretty big. Was the coat a large coat? I can't tell whether it was long coat or not.

At 3:30 P. M., on motion the Commission adjourned to meet on the 23rd instant, at 10 A. M.

Witness SEBASTIAN AREY, junior, on having the evidence read to him from the records, wishes to correct as follows:

To the question put here by Counsel for prosecution:

"Then the only relationship you know of is, that your mother is cousin, first or second, to Maultsby? (As on original record) "Yes, sir." Witness however wishes this answer corrected, so as to read: "not cousin, but sister-in-law."

RALEIGH, N. C., Aug. 2d, 1867, 10 A. M.

The Commission met pursuant to adjournment.

Present: All the members of the Commission, the Judge Advocate, the Counsel for the prosecution, all the accused, and their Counsel.

The reading of the testimony taken yesterday was waived, there being no objection thereto.

Yesterday's proceedings were then read and approved.

JOHN T. MULLINS, a witness for the defence, having been first duly sworn, testified as follows:

Examined by the Counsel for the accused:

What is your name? John T. Mullins. Where do you reside? In Fayetteville. Fayetteville, North Carolina? Yes, sir. How long have you been living in Fayetteville, North Carolina? I was born there and have lived there all my life. Were you in Fayetteville on the day that Archy Beebee was killed? I was, sir. Were you at the market house in Fayetteville that day? I was, sir. At what time did you go to the market house that day? I got to the market house just about the time that Archy Beebee and the guard with him got there; I was standing at Mr. Phil. Taylor's store on the north-east corner of the market square; I saw them as they were coming up from the guard house by Mr. Draughon's corner and I walked towards the market house and got there about the same time they did. How long did you remain at the market house? I remained there, sir, until Beebee was shot. To what point of the market house did you go? I went under the market house though the main aisle of the market house running east and west. At which arch did you enter the market house? The large central arch. About how many persons were there under the market house and around the market house at the time you got there? Well, sir, when I first got there the crowd was not large; I don't suppose there were more than fifteen or twenty persons out there; it continually increased in size. How long was it after you reached the market house before Archy Beebee was brought down stairs? From a half to three quarters of an hour as well as I can remember, sir. Did you leave your position, or did you remain about the same place during the time he was up stairs? I went to the market house for the purpose of haraing the trial and tried to obtain entrance, but it was announced that the trial would be strictly private; no one would be allowed up there except the relatives of the young lady and the Counsel for the prisoner. About what point did you remain, Mr. Mullins? I was at a bench ten or twelve feet from the steps that go up into the town hall, near Becky Ben's place where she sells cakes, &c. I was standing on that bench or sitting on that bench pretty much all the time. During the time that Archy was up stairs was there any thing occurring in the crowd that attracted your attention as being unusual? No, sir; I saw nothing unusual, the only thing that attracted my attention was there seemed to be a general disappointment on the part of the crowd, that they were not allowed to be present at the trial; a great many expressed themselves so, they seemed to be angry. Did you share in that feeling? I did, I thought the trial ought to be public; I thought it was due to the public that they should witness the trial. While you were there under the market house and before Beebee was brought down, did you see any thing of either of these three prisoners who set behind me? Yes, sir, I saw them all there Did you see any thing of Ed. Powers? Yes, sir, I saw Ed. Powers. Ralph Lutterloh? I don't remember seeing him whilst the prisoner was up stairs. That is the time to which I desire you to confine your remarks;

did you see any thing of John Maultsby? The first and only time I saw John Maultsby was when he was going to the carriage after the young lady and her mother had come down. Mr. Mullins, while the prisoner was up stairs what were these persons that you have named, these three men who are here upon trial, and Ed. Powers, and Leggett, and Maultsby, what were they doing? Tom Powers was standing on that bench by me a considerable time, I am sure of that, and Mr. Tolar was right behind me in the main aisle of the arch; I saw him standing there two or three times; I don't know how long he was standing there. Did you notice any conversation between these parties, or any of them? Only about the trial being secret; I heard a good deal of talk; I may have said something to Mr. Telar, I think I did; I recollect I said something to Mr. Nixon. Did you see any whispering between these parties or any of them? No, sir, all the talking I heard was in ordinary conversation. Did you see Mrs. Massey and her daughter, Miss Massey, at all that day? I saw them when the carriage drove off; the carriage was about thirty feet from the market house. Did you see them when they came down from the court room, up stairs? Yes, sir, I had got up and was standing on the bench facing the steps of the market house in front of Becky Ben's stall. Who came down with them? Mr. Bond. The town constable? Yes, sir. Where did they go, sir? When they came down stairs they went directly to the carriage. Where was the carriage standing at that time? In the middle of Person st, about opposite Mr. Ichabod Davis' store, and Mr. Phil. Taylor's store; Mr. Taylor's store is on one side of the street and Mr. Davis' on the other side of the street, and the carriage was about the centre of the st. Did Mr. Bond go with them to the carriage? He did. How long did the carriage remain there after the ladies got in? Well, sir, I think it was ten minutes at least. Was your attention attracted to the carriage during the time it was standing there? Yes, sir. Just tell if you please, who went to the carriage while it was standing there? I saw Mr. Phil. Taylor go to the carriage; I saw Mr. Robert Mitchell; I saw Mr. Cashwell go there. Mr. David Cashwell? I don't know what his name is beside Cashwell; the only Cashwell I know in Fayetteville. Who else did you see go there? I saw John Maultsby go there; that is the time I saw John Maultsby; when he was going to the carriage, and the only time I saw him. Did you see any body else go there? I don't remember any others; others might have gone. Did you see Tom Powers go there? I have no remembrance of him; he might have gone but I don't remember it now. Did you see Capt. Tolar go there? No, sir. How long was it after the carriage drove off before the prisoner Beebee was brought down stairs? Well, sir; it was almost immediately; not exceeding five minutes if that. Where were you standing at the time the prisoner Beebee was brought down stairs? I was standing on that bench. Just describe that bench if you please sir? It is a bench running east and west in the central aisle of the market, on the southern side of the large arch; Becky Ben has a large bench some three feet high probably, upon which her cakes and eatables are kept; this bench is a low bench in front of that, at which her customers sit to eat, about twelve feet from the stair steps. And it was upon that bench that you were standing at the time Beebee appeared on the steps? Yes, sir. Were there any other persons on that bench? Mr. Powers had been on there but whether he was on it at that time or not, I am unable to say; I was talking to him on that bench but can't say when he left it. At the time that Beebee appeared, to go down the steps

was John Maultsby on that bench? No, sir, there was no person on there. No person on it except yourself; the little bench you are speaking of? I don't remember any one being on it but Tom Powers and myself; I am sure John Maultsby was not on that bench. I understand you to say that Powers was upon the bench at the time the prisoner came down? I am not positive about that; I am sure he had been there. But whether he was at that time you can't say? No, sir. But you do say that John Maultsby was not on that bench at that time? He was not. Do you know John Maultsby well? I have known him since he was a little child. Do you know his voice? Well, yes, sir. Did you hear John Maultsby or anybody else at that time exclaim "watch out boys" or any thing like that? I heard several voices remark as he appeared at the door to come down the second flight of stairs "there they come." You heard several voices make that remark? Yes, sir. Where were those persons? About in different parts of the crowd. Were they upon that bench? No, sir, on the main floor of the market house. Several persons remarked as he appeared "there he comes"? There they come. Who came with Beebee down the stairs? Sheriff Hardie came down, he was in front—he was the first man I saw when the door opened, and Mr. Wemyss. Where was Wemyss? He was on the right hand side of the prisoner, and had a thumb screw, or twitch attached, with a string on the prisoner's thumb; Mr. McGuire and the other guard were immediately in the rear close to him. Well sir, what was the first thing that occurred after reaching the floor of the market, that attracted your attention? I saw nothing that attracted my attention; the crowd came down quietly? By the crowd, you mean the party attending the prisoner? Yes, sir, I heard or saw no disturbance then—I was standing on the end of this bench, furtherest from the arch, and I watched them as they went around the bench, and there was nothing occurred then at all, and I had on a blanket—it was a rather cool day, and I had been a little cool, and as they passed the end of the bench to go out of the arch, I turned and stepped off of the bench and my blanket fell off of my shoulders, and just at that time I heard some one say "I demand the prisoner," and then I heard the shuffling of feet, and the crowd had closed in on the boy. You say while you turned, the blanket had fallen off of your shoulders and while you were turning to pick it up, it was that you heard a remark made "I demand the prisoner"? Yes, sir. Where had the party with the prisoner got to at that time? Passed out of the central arch. Then you heard the remark "I demand the prisoner"? Yes, sir. Do you know who made that remark? No, sir, for their backs were all to me then. And because of your stepping from the bench and turning your back towards the crowd, you were not able to see the person who made it? No, sir, I heard Sheriff Hardie tell the men to stand back. Well, sir, what did you next notice? There was a little scuffle, and I heard Sheriff Hardie tell the guards "guards, use your clubs," and then I heard several licks passed. Where were you then? I was behind the crowd. Did you see the guard use their clubs? I didn't see the clubs, but I heard some licks passed. Then they passed out upon the pavement? Yes, sir. Near which side of that main eastern arch did the Sheriff and the party having the prisoner pass? On the southern side, the guard house was down Gillespie street? Yes, sir. Did you follow along out? Yes, sir, I did. What next occurred sir, that attracted your attention? I saw Monk there with a knife. How far had the prisoner and the party along with him got down the pavement before you saw Monk with a knife? About two steps. Where were you at that time? I was right immediately behind the crowd. Had you reached the pavement by that time? Yes, sir, by the central part of the arch I was then; Monk and the prisoner were about the center of the little arch, south of the central arch. You say you saw Monk with his knife? Yes, sir. What was he doing? He was cutting at the prisoner; I saw him make two or three licks in the direction of the prisoner. With a knife in his hand? Yes, sir, with a small knife. Did anything else occur there, sir? Monk didn't touch the negro; Wemyss, or some of them, beat Monk off, or he was got off any how, and I thought then that there would be no difficulty, you know, and the excitement had passed, and the guard would carry the prisoner to the guard house, and I turned then and was going off. Which way did you turn? I turned right around and was going down the street. Down Person st? Yes, sir. Then you were going down in the direction of Phil. Taylor's store, where you came from? Yes, sir, I had taken two steps, about. Did that carry you off of the pavement? No, sir, I was about the edge of the pavement; I was going right due north, and then I heard a moving of feet and I looked immediately and turned south towards the direction of the prisoner and the crowd, and he was struggling, making vigorous efforts to get away, I thought, and the crowd then rushed up close, I did, myself; I stepped back immediately towards the prisoner, then he went down and two of the guard fell with him, when he rose up by the aid of the guard; Mr. Wemyss was still on his right hand side, Mr. Faircloth on his left hand side, and Sheriff Hardie was sort of behind him, and had his hand on the back of his collar. Where was it that he was shot? Immediately then as soon as the prisoner got straightened up, the pistol fired. Just confine your testimony now to that point; where was the prisoner at the time he was shot? He was about the southern side of the small arch, near the southern corner of the market house. Was he nearer the wall of the market house, nearer the center of the pavement or nearer the edge of the pavement? He was nearer the center as well as I can remember, he was about the center at that time. Did you see anything of Tolar? Yes, sir, I had seen Tolar and Leggett as well as I can remember, and Ed. Powers and Lutterloh. You had seen them where? They were there in the crowd, they were more or less to my right and rear. Nearer the central arch than you were? They were to my left, I mean east of me. They were standing back of you? Yes, sir, I was about even with the southern side of the big arch, rather nearer the market house; Mr. Leggett and Ed. Powers, and Tolar were standing pretty much in the north-east direction from me. To your left and rear? Yes, sir. Well, sir, the pistol fired? Yes, sir. Did you see the pistol? I saw a pistol there; I saw but two weapons; I saw Monk's knife and I saw a pistol in the hands of Mr. Phillips. At what time did you see the pistol in the hands of Samuel A. Phillips? About the time the prisoner raised up. Where was Sam. Phillips at that time? He was standing about four or five feet from the prisoner. To his front? No, sir, to the left and rear of the prisoner. Was he on the pavement or off? I couldn't see his feet, he was near the edge of the pavement, I am sure of that from his position, it must have been very near the edge of the pavement, either on or off. You saw Sam. Phillips with a pistol and he was standing either off the edge of the pavement or very near the edge of the pavement, and some four or five

feet to the rear and left of the prisoner? Yes, sir. What was he doing with the pistol? I saw him draw the pistol, made me notice Sam. Phillips, I saw him take it out of his coat or vest on his left side. What was he doing with it? He pressed it immediately right through the crowd that was before him, then I could not see the pistol, but the pistol fired; I heard the report; I saw the smoke, and it was right in the direction I would have supposed that pistol to have been if I could have seen it. Then you heard the report of the pistol, you saw the smoke, and from the sound of the report and the spot you had seen the smoke it was right there where you had seen that pistol in the hands of Sam. Phillips? Yes, sir, I didn't see the pistol when it was fired. Well, sir, was there any other pistol beside that fired on that occasion? I heard but one pistol. Did you see where Captain Tolar was either at the time or shortly after that time? I don't think he changed his position; I know that I saw him there just before the pistol fired. What made you notice Tolar? I had on a blanket and he had on a shawl, and we two were the only persons that had any thing of that kind on that day that I saw. Do you know what became of Tolar after the pistol fired? I saw him leaning against the southern side of the market house; as soon as the pistol fired I threw a glance to see where the negro was shot, and I never noticed much about where any body was. Did you see any thing of Sam. Phillips after the firing of the pistol? I saw him when he had the pistol putting it back. You saw him recover the pistol directly after the firing? Yes, sir, he drew the pistol back and said "the negro is dead, and I didn't kill him," and he whirled the pistol a little in the air in front of his breast. What did he do with the pistol? He put it up again. Where did he put it? I am not clear about that. Did you see him after that? I don't remember seeing him after that time; I got up to where the negro was, and Dr. McDuffie come, and I don't remember seeing Sam. any more that day.

Cross examination, by the Counsel for the prosecution.

What is your business in Fayetteville, Mr. Mullins? Clerking, I am not clerking now. How long since you have been clerking? It has been nearly a year since I have had a permanent clerkship. What has been your occupation, in the meantime? I was accountant, posting up books. The last year, your business has been that of an accountant? Is that the only business you have followed, in the past year? Pretty much. What was your last permanent clerkship? My last permanent clerkship was at Rocktish saw mill, I was book keeper, and tended to the shipment of lumber. How long since you have been employed there? About ten months. How many times have you been employed as an accountant since? I don't remember how many times, not very many. Can't you remember who your employers were? Yes, sir, I know I have several times fixed up the accounts, and books of Mess. Clark and Burns. Any one else? I don't remember any one. Is there any one? No, sir. How much of your time did that take? Not long sir. Would a fortnight cover it all? Yes, sir. You had no occupation the rest of the time. No permanent occupation. What is the business that Clark and Burns are occupied in? They keep a bar room and a billiard table. Then the only occupation you have had for the last year has been posting their books and clearing up their accounts. Yes, sir, I have done other things in that time. Are you a married man? No, sir. Is that the only means of livelihood you have; these odd jobs you speak of? Yes, sir. Where is your place of residence in Fayetteville? A colored woman who used to belong to me cooks for me. Have you your room there? I don't sleep there. Where is your sleeping place? I sleep in different places. What, have you no habitual sleeping place? I sleep in different places sir. Do you mean to say you have no place that you habitually sleep at? I sleep when I get ready, at different places. You have no place that you occupy, no room for sleeping regularly? No, sir. Can you locate some of these different places that you speak of; where you sleep when you are ready? I sleep at different places sir. It is a very simple question, it seems to me, can you tell me where you most ordinarily sleep; will you tell me or not? I have told you that I have no particular place, where I sleep. Do you mean to say you sleep at one place, as much as another? In different places I sleep at. Do you ever sleep under the market house? I expect I have in my life time. Don't you know you have, in the course of this last year? I have not slept there in a year. Did you ever sleep in an omnibus, for a considerable length of time? When I was working at Rockfish, I used to sometimes. I want to know in the course of time you have had no employment, and had no source of income, where your place of sleeping was, and you won't tell me a single place where you sleep? Have you answered my question as fully as you intend to? I told you I had no particular place of sleeping at. Could you mention one place you have slept in, or are you one of those romantic gentlemen who have no abiding place? I have slept in that omnibus. You spoke of sleeping in that while you were employed at Rockfish? I never slept in it except when I come from Rockfish. Have you been employed at Rockfish during the last year? Yes, sir, it has not been a year since I left there. It has been ten months? Yes, sir. Have you never used that omnibus as a sleeping place during those last ten months? I don't think I have. Nor the market house? No, sir. Will you be good enough to tell me where you have slept? I slept at Mr. Monagan's tailor shop. Did you have a room there? I slept in there with James Hurn. I thought you said you had no regular place of sleeping? I don't, I sleep there sometimes. Where else? Sometimes I would sleep at other places. Can you give us some of the others? (Witness hesitates.) Do you decline to give any others? No, sir, I have no regular sleeping place. But you have irregular sleeping places; let us have some of them? Sometimes I sleep in Dr. McDuffie's office or shop. How often have you slept there, in the last eight months? I have slept there twenty or thirty times. Did you have a bed there? There is a settee there. When did you first give information that you knew anything of this transaction? It was four or five weeks ago. Whom to? I forget who. You don't forget? I do forget who I first told it to—I don't deny telling it; the first time I ever told it, I think was in the market house, one Sunday morning. To whom? I know that Mr. James Dodd was present there, and I think Mr. James Kendricks. You say it was Sunday morning, in the market house? Yes, sir. What Sunday do you know? Four or five weeks ago. Can you tell whether it was four, or five? About four weeks. Do you attend any place of worship on Sunday? Sometimes I do. Did you that Sunday? I did at night. Can't you remember from that what Sunday it was—how many Sundays ago? I can't tell. You don't know whether it was four or five Sundays? No, sir, Was it before this trial commenced? No, sir. Afterwards? Yes, sir. Was it after Mr. Dodd went back from here, when he had been summoned as a witness? I

could not say. You think it was four or five Sundays ago? I think it was, sir. Did any one ask you about it? They were all talking about the trial under there. When was the first time you told the Counsel about it? I never told him until I got to Raleigh on Sunday morning. Did'nt you tell Mr. James McRae in Fayettville, anything about it? Never in my life. Mr. Bartholomew Fuller? I never spoke to him upon the subject in my life. Is that the only time you have spoken of it? No, sir, I spoke of it several times, but not to the Counsel. Have you received any employment, or been put into any occupation since you first told this narrative? No, sir. Had no more to do than you had before? No, sir. You have no promise of any occupation? I have got a school that I expect to teach, as soon as the crops are in. When did you make an arrangement about this school? During the summer I have been making arrangements about it. Was it five or six weeks ago you commenced making arrangements about it. Yes, sir, a gentleman approached me and asked me if I would teach school. Who is that gentleman? Tom Nunnelly. Have you made any arrangements as to what pupils you are to get? No, sir. You have in contemplation some occupation in future? I always design doing that. Have'yon any promise of any reward, in any shape, for coming up here to give in your testimony? None whatever, no human being has ever made any promises to me. You have received no assistance pecuniary or otherwise, since you were connected with this case? No, sir. Have you purchased any clothing since this case was coming? Yes, sir. Who furnished the supplies? I bought this pair of shoes from Mr. Thompson's. Did you pay for them? No, sir. Are they the only things you have purchased, that you now wear? I bought this coat and pants. Who furnished you supplies for them? I bought them of Mr. Frank Thornton. Did you pay for them? No, sir. Did any one stand your security for them? No, sir. These good natured men let you have them on trust? Yes, sir. Have you any interest in the result of this trial? None in the world. You don't care how it terminates? I have no interest in it. You have no special enmity toward Sam. Phillips? None in the world. No special liking for Capt. Tolar? None in the world. How long have you known Capt. Tolar? Since the termination of the war—about two years. How many times did you ever see him before you saw him that day. I saw him a good many times, I have seen him at the market house—he had a store on Person street—I have been at his store. Do you know whether he was carrying on butchering, at the time the murder occured? I can't say. Did you see him there then; I mean before breakfast? No, sir, I never saw him that I remember, until the afternoon. Did you know that Capt. Tolar had stopped the business of butchering for a short time previous to this affair? It strikes me he had, but I don't remember. You went to the market house about the time the guard got there with Archy Beebee? Yes, sir. Archy went up-stairs, and you expected to go, but admittance was denied—the trial was private? Yes, sir. You then walked how far into the eastern arch, how many steps were you from the eastern entrance before you stopped? Twelve or fifteen feet. Then you were standing on the pavement? Yes, sir, I walked right in the main aisle to a bench. You entered the eastern arch, walked right up the aisle about twelve or fifteen feet, then you turned? I got right up on a bench. Did you get on the bench as soon as you went in? I think I got up there pretty soon after the prisoner came. How long is that bench, sir? An ordinary bench. Give an estimate. Six or eight feet I would say. Which end were you on? I was on the south end—the end that was furthest from the arch, I was nearer to that end than I was to the other. How far was the eastern end of that bench from the pillar of the market house, right in front? Well, sir, it was about four feet, or five feet. You were standing on that bench, a greater portion of the time, and sitting there, while Archy was up stairs? Yes, sir. And during that time you saw Tom Powers on the bench, do you remember when he left there? No, sir. While you were standing there during that time, did you notice who was in the market house? I noticed some persons. Did you see Capt. Tolar there at that time? I did, sir. And Tom Powers and Monk? Yes, sir, and Jim Nixon, I saw him and Sam Phillips, and Ed Powers. Did you see Sam Hall, Lutterloh or Maultsby about that time? I didn't see John Maultsby until I saw him go to the carriage. Did you see Sam Hall, while the negro was up stairs? No, sir. Did you see Sam Phillips in there? Yes, sir. Did you know after you saw Sam Phillips, was it just after you got to the market house? I don't remember about that. Did you see who was there all the time you were standing on that bench? I didn't see them. You saw him there, during the same portion of the time while the negro was up stairs? Yes, sir. Did you notice his dress at that time? No, sir. Did you notice that he had on a shawl? No, sir, I did not. Did you notice he didn't have on a shawl? I never noticed his dress. I thought you said you and Capt. Tolar were the only persons that had on shawls? We were the only ones that I saw. You saw Sam Phillips? If I did, I didn't notice his having on a shawl. Then you say he didn't have on a shawl? Not that I remember. You say it was a cold day? Yes, sir. Was it a windy day? I don't know whether it was very windy. Do you remember at all about that? I know it was cool, I know I felt very cool. You don't know whether it was cold or not? It was what I would call a cold day. Was it sunny or raining? It was not raining. Was it sunny or cloudy? I don't remember about the clouds, I think it was some cloudy. Do you know whether there was any wind blowing? Not that I remember, I don't remember about the wind. This was sometime in February? Yes, sir. You say the day was very cool, didn't Sam Phillips have some sort of wrapping on? If he did, I didn't notice it. Did you see any weapon about him when you first saw him; did you notice anything sticking out about his person? No, sir. Did you see Jonathan Hollingsworth there that day? No, sir, I don't remember seeing him. Did you see him there with a pistol strapped around his waist? No, sir. I think you told me you didn't see Sam Hall? Not then, I saw him afterwards. Henry Sykes, did you see him while the negro was up stairs? I saw him there one time, but I really forget whether it was while the negro was up stairs or not? Yes, sir. And the other two prisoners here, and E. P. Powers? Yes, sir. Did you see Leggett? Yes, sir. Did you see him about the time the negro was up stairs? Yes, I did. Now, sir, weren't Mr. Leggett and Lutterloh and E. P. Powers and Capt. Tolar standing together talking? When I saw Tolar he was standing behind me, in the aisle, down on the ground floor there, that was the first time I saw him. Is that the last time you saw him inside? I don't remember seeing him any where after that until I saw him outside. How far behind you was he? Four or five steps I suppose. And Mr. Powers and Mr. Leggett were standing near him? I can't say, what I know is I saw Mr. Nixon and

Mr. Phillips and Mr. Leggett, in and about the market. Can't you say you saw Lutterloh, and Ed Powers and Tolar talking together? I can't say that I remember. Do you say you didn't see them? No, sir, I won't, I might have seen them. And the only time you remember seeing Tolar he was standing behind you? Yes, sir. Where was Leggett, when you remember seeing him first? I don't remember where he was standing. Where was E. P. Powers? I don't remember where he was standing. Then you say you didn't see Lutterloh at that time? I saw Lutterloh, I didn't see Sam Hall. Was he standing with the others, or apart? I can't locate him. If they had been standing in the aisle within eight or ten feet of the east entrance, would they have been in your view? Yes, sir, but I suppose there were plenty of people that may have been there that I don't remember now. You were standing on that bench? Yes, sir, but I was facing south and these men were behind me, that is the reason I could not see them. They were on the other side of the market house? They were in the aisle, near the center of the aisle. How broad is the aisle? Twenty feet I reckon. You think that Tolar was standing in the aisle when you saw him? I know he was. Was he further from the eastern arch of the market house than you were, or closer to it? He was closer, I was further west than he was. He was standing closer to the eastern end of the market house than you were? Yes, sir. And he was behind you? Yes, sir. Was he behind you to your left, or right? He was behind me to the east. I thought you said he was north of you? Of course he was, you asked me which side he was on me, he was north east you may say. To your rear and left then? Yes, sir. You don't remember whether those other persons were standing with him or not? No, sir. Did you see any sign of any weapon about Capt. Tolar, that day? No, sir. Did you see no belt, or any mark of any weapon? No, sir. Did you see him with his hand in his breast? No, sir. When you saw him what was he doing, standing still? Yes, sir. Talking to no one? There were several around there, but I don't remember who they were, I talked to him myself one time. Did you get down from the bench and go over to him and talk to him? Yes, sir. Then you were not standing on that bench all the time? No, sir. Who were the nearest men standing about him, when you went to talk to him? I don't remember. Did you see Lutterloh there about Tolar, when you went there to speak to him? Not that I remember. Did you see J. G. Leggett there? I don't remember whether he was there when I spoke to him. See E. P. Powers? I saw him there, as to the exact point I could not say. Were they in conversation with Capt. Tolar? If they were I don't remember it. And when you went over to Capt. Tolar, if they were standing about Capt. Tolar, you don't remember it now? I don't know that I went there to Capt. Tolar. You told me you got down off the bench and went to him. I was sitting on the bench sometimes and sometimes standing. When you spoke to him didn't you move from the bench? No, sir, I think I talked right to him where I was, without going to him. Then part of the time you were sitting down with your face towards him? Yes, sir. During that time that you were sitting with your face towards him, did you see anything like a group of men standing there, that you remember, consisting of Lutterloh, Leggett, Powers and Tolar? No, sir. And you remained standing or sitting on that bench, until Miss Massey and her mother came down stairs? Yes, sir. You were looking directly at them as they came down? Yes, sir. Were you standing on that bench when they came down? Yes, sir. Was Tom Powers standing on that bench at that time? I don't know whether he was or not; I was looking at the persons coming down the steps. Do you remember whether it was before that or after, that you saw Tom Powers on the bench? I saw him before the ladies come down. You don't know whether he was there when the ladies come down or not? No, sir. You think the ladies were at the carriage about ten miuutes? Yes, sir. And during that time you saw Mr. Mitchell, Mr. Taylor, and Mr. Cashwell come up towards the carriage and John Maultsby? Others might have gone, but those are all I can remember. You don't remember seeing Tom Powers and Tolar go there? No, sir. Your attention was pretty fully directed to the carriage was it? Some of the time it was. You don't pretend you were looking at the carriage all the time? No, sir. It was in your sight all the time? Yes, sir. Did you see it through the main arch? Yes, sir. Did you see what became of Boud, when he turned away from the carriage to come back as the carriage drove off? I think he went up stairs. Did he come back before the carriage drove off, or after it drove off? He came from the carriage before it drove off and went back to the carriage again. I understand that Bond came down with the ladies and went with them to the carriage; then came back to the market house for some purpose? Yes, sir. Then did he go to the carriage again? I think he did. Did you notice where he came to when he came back the next time? I don't know where he went then. Did you see him in conversation with any of these persons who were standing at the carriage? I just simply saw him go to the carriage; I don't know whether he talked to anybody or not. Did you see him interchange any remarks with John Maultsby? I didn't see him speak to John Maultsby, sir. You remained in this same position until about five minutes after the carriage moved off? Yes, sir. When Archy came down stairs in the position you have named, Hardie in front, Wemyss on the right hand, Faircloth on his left, and certain other policemen behind him; up to that point you had noticed no disturbance in the crowd, except dissatisfaction at not being admitted to the trial? Yes, sir. Had seen no weapons in the hands of any one? No, sir. Did you see Sam Phillips in the market house as they were coming down stairs? I can't say about that right clearly; I don't know, sir; there was a good many people in the market house. How many do you suppose were there when Archy was coming down stairs? Seventy-five or a hundred. How many outside around the eastern end? Something more I should think. A hundred and fifty or two hundred people there altogether? Yes, sir. Was this crowd perfectly quiet? They were talking more or less. No outcries? I heard no outcry, only when they came down I heard several say "there they come," as the door opened as they got to the second flight of stairs. That was as he was on the stairs? Yes, sir. That was the announcement "there they come"? Yes, sir. Now was there no closing up of the crowd? Not then, there was not till they got out of the corner. Passing by the end of the bench you were standing on? Yes, sir, my shawl fell off and I stepped down, and then I heard some shuffling. Where was Archy when you jumped off the bench? He was at the end of the bench. Then your shawl fell and you jumped off the bench to get it? Yes, sir, and at that time I heard somebody say "I demand the prisoner." When you jumped down to get your blanket, did

you get up on the bench again? No, sir. You jumped down and formed part of the crowd? Yes, sir. How many feet, were you from the prisoner when you got to the ground? It was twelve or fifteen feet I should suppose—it may have been more or less. Now you think you were twelve or fifteen feet from him? Yes, sir. Didn't you say you thought that bench was about six feet long. Yes, sir. Then the distance between the bench and the wall was four or five feet? Yes, sir. And you were immediately at the end of the bench? I don't pretend to say the distance—I say it was ten or twelve feet I should suppose. Did he pass close to the end of the bench, or close to the wall—wasn't Wemyss on his right hand? Yes, sir. Didn't the other men pass through at the same time? Yes, sir. Hardie was in front, Wemyss on one side and he in the middle? Yes, sir. Then you say about the middle of that pass way you think was ten or twelve feet from you? Yes, sir. When you got down you heard this voice say "I demand the prisoner." Yes, sir. You swear positively to that? Yes, sir. Those identical words? Yes, sir, "I demand the prisoner" or something to that effect. Will you swear it was not "we demand the prisoner"? No, I would not swear it was "I" or "we." You can't speak to the words with such particularity as that? No, sir. Was it one voice or more than one? It was one voice. Do you know Tom Powers? Yes, sir. How long have you known him? I have known him for a good many years; ever since he was a little boy. You have known him well? Yes, sir. How often have you conversed with him in your life, a hundred times? I don't know about that sir—I don't believe I have conversed with him a hundred times. How often do you suppose you have seen him in the year before that thing occurred? I have seen him pretty frequently. You have heard him talk frequently? Yes, sir. Did you know his voice? No, sir: I could not have told from the voice. You could not have told from his voice if you had heard it in the crowd, whether it was his or not? No, sir. You can't pretend to say whose voice it was you heard, you have no idea? No, sir. You say at the time you heard this voice, you were down on the floor? Yes, sir. Did you immediately turn your face towards the eastern arch? Yes, sir. And you heard simultaneously with the demand for the prisoner, Hardie tell the crowd to "keep back gentlemen"? Yes, sir. When was it that you heard Hardie tell them to use their clubs? Soon after that. Could you have counted a hundred between the two, do you suppose? No, sir. It was a simultaneous transaction? It was not a minute or a minute and a half from that time to the killing, the whole thing, from the time he got to the foot of the steps until he was killed would not have occupied two minutes, I don't believe. When this demand was made, the whole crowd rushed in you say; you were in the crowd? I followed on after the crowd. When you got down to get this shawl of yours were there no persons further back in the market house than you? I could see they come from the western end of the market house. And there were some to your left and front? Yes sir. Any to your right inside of Becky's stall? Yes, sir. Did you see Tom. Powers in there? No, sir. Can't you remember some one you did see in there? I saw Sam. Phillips in there some time. Was it at the moment the demand was made for the prisoner? No, sir. Were you standing on the bench when you saw Sam. Phillips in there? I think I was talking to Sam. Phillips while I was on the bench about not letting the people go up to hear the trial. Was it while you were on the bench? Yes, sir. What I am trying to get at is, how the crowd was when you got down to get your blanket; my object is to find out what the amount of pressure was that was used, and from your being in the crowd you could tell; there were portions of that crowd who were behind you? Yes, sir. Pressing on your left and in your front? There were three or four people to the west of me, most of the crowd was to the east of the market, and between me and the eastern arch, and all along around them. Now, when this rush took place was it all in front of you, or did the persons behind, further back than you, come up and press in the direction of the prisoner and the crowd, as soon as the demand was made? Yes, sir. Did you see any person grab at the prisoner? No, sir, their backs were to me then. What is your height, sir. I don't know, I am a low man. You could not see over the top of the crowd? No, sir. After you heard this demand, and this rush was made, did you feel any pressure back, as if the rush had been repelled; were you conscious of any thing of that sort, being on the edge of the crowd; what I want to know is, if the crowd pressed on every moment after that demand until the prisoner was killed? There was a sort of stop right there; Hardie said "stand back gentlemen," and told the guard to use their clubs, and then I heard licks and blows passed. Had Beebee got outside of the arch? Yes, sir, he was going out of the arch; this demand for the prisoner was made while he was still inside of the arch, just as he was going outside of the arch. The two things happened so quickly he didn't change his position between the two? No, sir. When Hardie told them to use their clubs you say there was some reaction? Yes, sir, for a while they could not go with the prisoner. They were stopped for some little while and then the prisoner went on again? Yes, sir. How many steps had the prisoner taken from the arch? Ten or twelve feet from the point where the prisoner was when this demand was made. How many steps had he taken outside on the pavement before you got on the pavement; didn't you lose sight of the prisoner at all in changing your position to go out there? Yes, sir. He went out of your view for a minute? Yes, sir, he turned the arch quicker than I did. Did you pass out through the middle of the arch, or further south? About the center of the arch. How many steps had Beebee taken from the point where he went out of the arch when you got on the pavement? I don't think he had got more than two steps. You stood about the middle of the pavement when you first went out? Yes, sir. You walked out about the middle of the pavement and faced towards the prisoner? Yes, sir. Was there any crowd behind you then in that position; was the crowd large enough to stand to your rear? Yes, sir, there were men before me and behind me. Was it thick before you and behind you? Yes, sir. There were a good many of that crowd still behind you? Yes, sir. Did the crowd stand as far up as to the north-east corner of the market house? All up the pavement there were people; all around about there in the the street. I want to know if the crowd was thick about you when you were standing, and where the thick-pressed-together crowd began; how far from you in front? Right there at the right as they were coming out of the arch, the mass began. When you got inside and stood in the middle of the pavement opposite the centre of the main eastern arch with your face turned towards the prisoner, was there any space vacant between you and the crowd that was pressing on the prisoner? I don't think there was much space. Was there any, could you have stepped forward without striking against any

one? No, I could not have stepped a step without turning against some one. Would that some one have formed a part of this thick crowd? That some one would have touched some one that was touching some one else that would reach the crowd. Around the negro and the guard the crowd was thick? It was thicker than it was behind me. Now, there must have been some point where that thick-pressed together crowd became perceptibly thinner; I want to know whether you formed a part of the thick crowd or a part of the thin crowd. I was not right in the midst of the crowd that was pressing on the prisoner. How far was that crowd passing on the prisoner from you in front? Ten or twelve feet, I should say, as well as I can remember. Do you know how wide that central arch of the market house is? I think it is twenty feet; I think the market is about forty feet in front. And this thick crowd, you think was ten or twelve feet in front of you? Some of them was. Do you know where the nearest edge of it was towards you? I declare I can't tell where the edge was. I want to know whether the crowd was perceptibly thinner near you, whether you could perceive a difference? Yes, sir. You say it was perceptibly thinner as it neared you? Yes, sir, as it neared, it was perceptibly thinner. Where did you first notice Capt. Tolar after you had got out on that pavement, as soon as you got out? No, sir. Did you see him before the pistol fired? I saw him when Monk was cutting at him. That was after you got outside that you saw that? Yes, sir, I never saw any cutting at him inside. And you saw Captain Tolar after you saw that? Yes, sir. The prisoner fell down after Monk was cutting at him didn't he? Yes, sir, he had gone on further south. It was after Monk was pushed off and you saw Capt Tolar that you saw Monk? Yes, sir. Did you see him before you started to move north? That was the time I noticed him. He was standing with him or near him? There were four or five there, Mr. Leggett was there; Mr. Ed Powers and Mr. Ralph Lutterloh were standing near each other. Were they within speaking distance of one another, as if they formed the same group? Yes, sir. Was there any body intermixed between them? No, sir; they were closer to each other than any body else. Lutterloh was just as close to Tolar as Leggett was, wan't he? No, sir; Lutterloh was closer; he was in front of Tolar then. Which was the nearest to the market house, Lutterloh, Powers, Leggett or Tolar? Lutterloh, I think was. Which was the next nearest to the wall of the market house; I want to know the order in which they were standing? It strikes me that Powers—Leggett—I don't know which was the nearest. Was Tolar nearer to you than any of these? He was further off than any of those other gentlemen; he was to the left of them. I thought you said Lutterloh was nearer to the market house? I say that yet. Tolar was further towards the edge of the pavement? Yes, sir; that is what I meant, if I didn't say it. And Lutterloh was nearer to the wall of the market house than any of them? Yes, sir. And the other two, you don't remember what position they occupied? Rather between I think. Which was farthest north; was Tolar further back north than the others? I think he was. As you turned to go off you heard a noise that attracted your attention? I heard some scuffling; moving of feet. Did you hear any cry up to that time? No, sir. Any body say "kill him, kill him," "shoot him shoot him"? No, sir; nothing of that sort. Did you had seen no weapons at that time? None except that knife. Do you know that Capt. Tolar had a weapon on that day? No, sir. Did you see Ed

Powers with any? I saw no weapon except Phillip's pistol and Monk's knife. A person may answer that way and yet have seen any signs of weapons either a belt for holding a weapon, or the protruding garments under which a weapon was concealed. I don't mean to shirk it that way Mr. Haywood; I saw nothing in the world to make me believe any body had a weapon. Had the crowd moved in from the point where you last saw it, when you turned back? They had taken a step or two. As you turned, was Archy up or down? He was up; I saw him make two or three jerks, and then he fell. Did you see any body make an assault upon him at the time he fell? No, sir. Did you hear any blow of a club about the time he fell? No, sir. Did you hear any clash of a knife on the pavement just before the time he fell, struck out of some one's hand; when Monk was cutting at him you heard the clash of a knife in the pavement? Yes, sir. Did you hear a blow strike on some one's arm? I heard a blow strike. Did you hear any body complaining of his arm being broken or hurt? No, sir. You say at the time Monk was making these cuts you did hear a blow? Yes, sir. You heard no complaints? No, sir. At the time this negro fell it was that some body took off Monk as he was making the stroke? Yes, sir. The whole affair, from the time the negro left the entrance of the arch until he was shot, didn't occupy more than a minute or a minute and a half? Not exceeding two minutes. This turning about of yours, was done very quickly? Yes, sir. You took two or three steps? Yes, sir. That brought you nearer to Tolar when you turned to go north? Yes, sir. Did you pass these gentlemen as you passed north? They were all on my right. As you passed back, they were all east of you, still on your left? Yes, sir. You couldn't say how far they were from the point where you stepped when you came back to look again? No, sir. Did you notice them when you came back? No, sir, I was looking at the negro again. When was it that you saw Capt. Tolar? When I turned to go north, then I noticed him. When you turned to go south again, did you notice him again? I passed by him. You noticed him both times? Yes, sir. You didn't stop to speak to him? No, sir. You say you took but two or three steps and turned instantly; the whole transaction was within a minute or two? Yes, sir. Did you notice how Capt. Tolar was dressed then? I know he had on a shawl. When did you notice the fact that he had on a shawl? I noticed it under the market house. Did you notice it when you passed that second time? Yes, sir. Did you notice whether he had on spectacles? No, sir. Did you notice whether he had on a tall beaver hat? No, sir. Did you notice whether he had on any hat? I don't think he was bareheaded. You think he had on something? Yes, sir. Do you know whether he had on his shawl folded around him? I think he was standing that way, but I am not positive. This negro went down and just as he came up, you saw Phillips with a pistol? Yes, sir, as he raised. That was the first you had seen of Phillips, since the time you had seen him inside the market house? Yes, sir. Then you think you spoke with him in the market? I am confident of it. What was the subject of your conversation? It was about the privacy of the trial. And he you think was standing inside of Becky Ben's stall? Yes, sir. Then you didn't see him again until you saw him with this pistol in his hand? Not that I remember of. You say that the negro was up when you saw him with a pistol in his hand? Just in the act of rising. What did you say you saw him do with the pistol? I saw him

draw out the pistol. Didn't you say you saw him put his hand in and draw it out? Yes, sir. Didn't you see him put his hand in? No, sir, I saw the pistol come out. You saw the pistol in the act of coming out in his hand? Yes, sir. Was the negro up or down at that moment? He was just up. Did Phillips present the pistol instantly? Yes, sir, he poked it in so; (witness represents Phillips with a pistol holding it in his right hand presented towards Beebee.) Was it cocked, sir? I don't remember whether it was or not. Could you see the cock? I could see the whole pistol pretty much. Did you have any impression as to whether you saw it cocked or uncocked? I think it was cocked, I would not be positive about that. Did you see, notice or think at the time the pistol was cocked—are you conscious now that you noticed he had a cocked pistol? All that I am positive of is, that he had a pistol. Ain't you certainly positive of this that after he drew it he didn't stop to cock it, before he presented it? I didn't see him cock it. If it was cocked it was cocked before he drew it out of his breast? I didn't see him cock it. But that is the way it occurred? Yes, sir. There was no time to cock it between the time you saw him draw it, and the time you saw him present it? Not unless he cocked it while in motion. The presentation of the pistol was as soon as he drew it? Yes, sir. You say the pistol went out of your view when he presented it to fire? Yes, sir, I could not see the pistol, it was hid by the people that was between me and him. You could see Phillips? Yes, sir. Where did he cease to appear? I could see his body about half way of his arm, I should think. And then that part of the arm next the fire arm, and the whole went out of your sight? Yes, sir. You heard the report, did you see the smoke? Yes, sir. Where you supposed it was that the pistol disappeared? Yes, sir. Was there anybody between Phillips and the deceased, when he fired? Yes, sir. Did he fire over their shoulders? Sort of over their shoulders. It was nothing but their heads that kept you from seeing the arm? Yes, sir, the heads were close together; there were more people between me and the prisoner, than there was between Phillips and the prisoner. How far were you from the prisoner? I think it was about eight feet in his rear. To his left and rear? Yes, sir, I was nearer to the market house than he was. Phillips, you say, was within three or four, or five feet of him? Yes, sir. And this pistol was presented right in the direction of the negro's head? Yes, sir. And you say there were how many people between Phillips and the deceased? I don't know how many. Was there any body? There was people between him and the prisoner. This pistol was high enough to be fired over the shoulders and yet it was not visible to you? I didn't see the pistol when it was fired. After the pistol was fired, did you notice that Beebee fell? Yes, sir. Did you notice who was standing near Mr. Phillips? I don't remember that. Did you notice any body who was standing near him? No, sir. Did you notice what description of pistol it was? It looked to me like an ordinary repeater, about ten or eleven inches long, or twelve, something like that. Do you know the different varieties of pistols? No, sir. Do you know the difference between the "Colt's" and the "Remington" pistol. I could tell one from the other if I had them in my hands. Did you see that sufficiently to tell from your own judgment which it was? I think it was a Remington pistol. Did you think so at the time? I thought so at the time. Did you notice any thing peculiar about the pistol? No, sir. Did you notice it had a brass guard to it? No, sir. Didn't you notice it had an hexagonal barrel? Yes, sir, I noticed that it was not a round barrel, it was six or eight sided. Didn't you notice the fact that it didn't have a piece of steel over the top of the cylinder? I didn't notice that. Didn't you notice that it did have a piece of steel? No, sir. What made you think it was a Remington pistol; what was the mark that struck you? From its form and shape. Aint they very similar in shape? Not exactly. Where is the difference; why did you form a judgment that it was a Remington, more than a Colt's pistol; what was the difference? A Remington was larger than a Colt's pistol. That was the ground? Yes, sir. It was simply on that ground that you say it was a Remington? Yes, sir. You have never seen a Colt's pistol as large as a Remington? I don't know that I have. Do you know that you haven't? Yes, sir. You have never seen a Colt's pistol as large as a Remington you say? I have seen larger Colt's pistols than I have Remington; the large navy pistols. Then the size could not have been the reason why you knew it was a Remington pistol for you had seen larger ones; now what was the ground of your distinction; you say it was the size, but you say you have seen larger ones than that; you say you thought at the time it was a Remington pistol? Yes, sir. Well, I don't know what made you think it was a Remington? It was just my opinion. Then after Phillips fired this pistol did you see what he did? I don't know, sir, he put the pistol, I saw him holding it up, and he said "the negro is dead, but I didn't shoot him." You could see it when he held it up? He didn't hold it up a second; he drew his arm in and held it up in front of him. Was there any body close to him? Yes, sir. the whole crowd was right around him; not the whole crowd; the thickest part of the crowd was right there. Where the negro man was killed? Yes, sir. Wasn't he right in the midst of it; among the very foremost ones, close to the negro? Yes, sir. Had he stepped back when he shot the pistol? I don't think he had. He was right in the midst of the whole crowd, the thickest part of it? I don't know about its being the thickest part of it. Was it the thickest part of the crowd? I don't know that; he was right there in front or five feet from where the prisoner was. How many men could have laid their hands on him in that crowd do you suppose; how many could have touched him? Seven or eight, or more than that. There were seven or eight men then within reach of his hand when he made this exhibition of that pistol? Yes, sir, there was a crowd all around there. There was no cessation of the crowd between you and Phillips? People were all along there on the walk. There were a heap of people closer to Phillips than to you? Yes, sir. You hadn't got out of that crowd when he shot the pistol? He had just drawn his arm back. You saw his arm when it came back? Yes, sir. You saw that arm instantly after the explosion? Yes, sir. You saw the negro fall? Yes, sir. You saw all three of these things at the sametime? Yes, sir, all occurred pretty soon after one another, about the same time. You are certain the drawing back of the arm was after the firing of the pistol? Yes, sir. You swear to that positively? Yes, sir. You saw the man fall, the firing of the pistol and the withdrawal of the arm? Yes, sir. In this exhibition that occurred afterwards, did any one take it? Not that I saw, sir. Did you see what became of it? No, sir. Did you see what became of Phillips? No, sir, for I commenced then to go up to where the negro was to see him. When was the time you saw Capt. Tolar last before the pistol fired, was it when you passed him to go back? Yes, sir. Did you see Capt. Tolar again before

the pistol fired, between the time you got your stationary point when you saw Sam Phillips? I saw him when I turned to go north; and then I saw him when I turned to go south. Then you didn't see him again before the pistol fired? No, sir. You passed by him then and he was to your rear? Yes, sir. When you passed back that time, was Lutterloh as far from Archy Beebee when you passed him as Tolar was? No, sir, he was not as far. How much nearer? Not much, a foot or two. He was to the right and front of Tolar? He was to the west. That was on Tolar's right? Yes, sir. North-west from Tolar? Yes, sir. You are confident about this position? To the best of my knowledge that is the position. And he was the nearest to the market house of any of them, Lutterloh? Yes, sir. Did you see what became of Phillips after he shot the pistol there that day? No, sir, as soon as I could I worked my way up to the crowd; I moved up to the negro. Did you turn about and see this group of gentlemen that you spoke of before you went up to the negro, and after the firing of the pistol; I want to know whether between the time the pistol fired and the time you got up to the negro Beebee you saw Tolar? No, sir, I don't remember seeing him. Don't you know you didn't see him? I don't remember seeing him, I can't say that. Then you went up to the negro, what became of you then? I stood there until I saw him, and then I went off. Did you see Capt. Tolar after you saw Archy lying there dead? I saw him standing against the arch. Did you see him when he went away? No, sir, I didn't see him when I left the market house. Where did you spend that night? I forgot where I did. Do you remember where you went when you left the market house? No, sir. Do you remember where Capt. Tolar went when he left the market house? I don't know where I went nor where he went. You knew the day this occurred, all that you know now of this transaction? Yes, sir. Did you know a coroner's inquest was held? I did, sir. What was your reason for not giving your testimony? I was not summoned, and I did not feel it my duty to volunteer my information. Did you feel it your duty to volunteer your information here? I didn't volunteer it. You volunteered it so that it reached here. There is but few that has been about Fayetteville who hasn't reached here. The whole population has not been here? No, but a good many have. You didn't think it was your duty to volunteer your information? No, sir. And you never mentioned that thing until after the trial began? No, sir. Did you see what became of Sam Phillips? No, sir. I don't know when he left. What is the name of Mr. Lutterloh's father? Thos. L. Lutterloh. Have you received any pecuniary assistance from him in any shape or way since this transaction? I have never been to him, nor received any verbal or written correspondence with him whatever upon this or any other subject. I understand you to say positively that you have received no pecuniary assistance in any shape or way; no assistance of any sort from any one of these parties? None, sir. From Lutterloh, Leggett, Ed. Powers, nor their parents? No, sir. Nor from any other quarter whatsoever? No, sir, I have not. That your evidence here is the truth? So help me God, it is truth as far as I know. You have known about Phillips all this time; have you ever met since it occurred? I met him here. Have you met before you come up here, since this transaction? I have seen him in Fayetteville. Did you ever hear that Captain Tolar was arrested for this matter, sometime before the trial took place? Yes, sir. Charged with shooting this pistol? Yes, sir. Did you ever volunteer to the military authorities or anybody else to give your information? Not a word. You were aware all this time that an innocent man was arrested and you didn't think it was your duty to come forward and inform any one that you knew anything at all of this transaction? No, sir. What sort of a knife was that, that Monk had in his hand? It was a small knife. How many blades did it have? I did'nt see but one. How long a blade? About two and a half or three inches. You can speak with confidence that you did'nt see but one blade? I didn't see but one blade that was open. Did you see John Armstrong there that day? No, sir. Do you know him? Yes, sir. Did you see Robert Simmons? I saw Robert Simmons after the shooting. How long after? It was four or five minutes after him and Mr. Shepherd Maultsby had some words out in the street. Do you know Sam. Toomer? Yes, sir. Did you see him there? No, sir. Where did you say Beebee was standing at the exact time he was shot according to your best impression? Near the southern corner of the market house, about the center of the pavement. Was he further south than the south edge of the little arch there? Yes, sir. He was between the south edge and the corner? Yes, sir, if I would locate him, I would say opposite the southern corner of the market house. And you say the point from which this pistol came was where? It was to the east and rear. How far off? The person who fired it must have been off of the pavement, I could not see his feet. But he was right at the edge of the pavement? Yes, sir. A line dropped from his hand would have fallen on the pavement, wouldn't it? Yes, sir. Did you see the flash? Yes, sir. Saw the smoke? Yes, sir. How far was that point from Beebee's head; the point where you saw the flash and smoke? As well as I could see, it was about three feet; I could not be positive. You say Sam Phillips was the only person you saw with a pistol that day? Yes, sir. Did you hear any shouts of "kill him, kil! him, shoot him, shoot him," at any time that day? No, sir. Didn't somebody say just before Sam Phillips shot, "kill him"? No, sir. Nothing of the sort? No, sir. You heard no exclamations in the crowd that day? Not that I heard, according to my impression, at the time the pistol fired it was a perfect calm. Didn't you say in your examination in chief, that you saw Sam Phillips draw back his pistol, and put it up again? I said I saw him draw it back and it went out of my sight. You saw him elevate it for a moment, did you see whether it was cocked then or not; didn't you think it was cocked before? I don't know he didn't hold it long enough for me to tell. You had an impression that it was cocked when you saw it before he presented it? I said I didn't know whether it was cocked or not. But you said you had an impression that it was cocked? I said he might have cocked it as it was coming up but I didn't see it. You don't pretend to say whether it was cocked when you saw it.' No, sir Didn't you notice a brass guard underneath the pistol? No, sir. In levelling the pistol did he raise it and level it down, or reach out from his shoulder? Right from his shoulder I think it was. An instantaneous work? It was done monstrous quick. You say there was some persons standing in front of him? Yes, sir. Did they bend their heads? No, sir. It had to pass between some person's head and shoulder before he fired? Yes, sir. Did you know whether these persons were white or black? No, sir, I could not tell because their backs were towards me.

Re-direct examination by the Counsel for the accused.

Mr. Mullins, I understand you to say that after you got out on the pavement, just before the killing of the negro, that at some of the time you were standing there, you saw Tolar and Leggett, and E. P. Powers and Lutterloh? Yes, sir. But with regard to their exact positions that you will not undertake to give them? No, sir, I will not. That you saw them? I just saw them as I passed, I just noticed they were there. You could not undertake to give their positions? No, sir, my impression is that Lutterloh was nearest to the market. Whether Phillips shot this pistol or not you don't swear positively? No, sir, I could not. But you did see the pistol drawn by Phillips? Yes, sir. You did see the flash of the pistol and heard the report? Yes, sir. And it was just in the position where Phillips' pistol was? Yes, sir. That immediately after that you saw Phillips in the position you have described, recovering the pistol, and heard him say "the negro is dead, but I didn't shoot him," and the pistol then disappeared from you? Yes, sir. That was Sam Phillips and nobody else? Nobody else. No doubt about that? None in the world. You say that it was the only pistol which was fired there on that occasion? It was the only pistol I saw there that day, and I heard but the report of one pistol. Are you a rich man? Not very. Are you a poor man? Yes, sir. Something has been spoken about your past life and mode of life, I understand you to say sir, that you have no certain abiding place; that you sleep where you have an opportunity to sleep? Yes, sir. And that it is very difficult for you to provide bread? Yes, sir; I have no family; I am a single man and I live as economical as possible; I don't owe any body much; when I get any thing to do I do it, and when I don't I go without it. You have been in better circumstances than you are now, haven't you, and like many others you have fallen into poverty? Yes, sir. That you habitually employ yourself honestly when you can get anything to do? Yes, sir. When you can't you have to pinch? Yes, sir. And get on the best way you can? Yes, sir

Question by the Commission.

After Beebee was shot and up to the time that you last saw Tolar; I think you said you did see Tolar after he was shot, didn't you? Yes, sir; I saw him standing with his back against the market house. After Beebee was shot and up to the time you lost sight of Tolar, did you hear any exclamation in the crowd as to who had fired the pistol? No, sir, I didn't hear any body say who done it; I heard some one say after that, who shot him. How long? A half an hour after that. Are you a Mason? No, sir. I think you said you noticed the barrel of the pistol Phillips had was a square barrel? Yes, sir. Didn't you also say you didn't notice much about the pistol at all I didn't have it. But you say it was eight sided? I mean it was not a smooth round barrel. You said that Mr. Tolar had his shawl on? Yes, sir. Could you have seen Mr. Tolar put his hand in his breast if he had done so? He might have put it in there and I never have seen him, sir.

JAMES W. ATKINSON, a witness for the defence, having been first duly sworn, testified as follows:

Examined by the Counsel for the accused.

What is your name? J. W. Atkinson. What does the "J" stand for? James. Where do you reside? In Fayetteville. What State? North Carolina. What is your occupation? Painter. Were you in Fayetteville on the day Archy Beebee was killed? Yes. Were you in the market house on that day? I was. Stood, if you please, at what time you went to the market house that day? Well, I think about half-past two in the afternoon. From what place did you go to the market house? From Mr. McKethan's shop. Is that the place of your employment? Yes. Where was the negro man Beebee at the time you went to the market house? He had been brought out from the guard house. To what part of the market house did you first go? About the center. Did you see Beebee when he was brought from the guard house? I did. Who was in company with him, who had him in charge? Wemyss, Faircloth and McGuire. At what portion of the market house did that party enter? At the eastern arch. Where was the Court? Up stairs. When he was being carried up stairs what was your position? I cannot tell, it was under the market house. Did you remain in and about the market house during the whole time he was up stairs? No, I went down street to Mr. Clark's store. How long before Beebee was brought down, was it that you went to Clark's store? I don't understand you, sir. That's right, sir; whenever you don't understand, just say so; how long was it before Beebee was carried up stairs, that you went to Clark's store? About fifteen minutes. How long did you remain at Clark's? A very short time. Did you return to the market house? I did. How long after you left Clark's store? About half an hour. Where was you during that time? I walked up as far as the extreme south corner—Mr. Kyles. That is not the south corner? Well the north corner, then; I walked up there and then came back to the market house. Did you see Miss Massey and her daughter? I did. When they went up stairs? I think I did. When they came down stairs? I did. How large was the crowd assembled there under the market house and outside between the times that Miss Massey went up and came down stairs? Well I suppose there were about a hundred there. Within and without? Yes, sir. Who came down stairs with Miss Massey and her mother, any one? Nobody but Mr. Bond. Mr. Bond, the town constable? Yes, sir. Where were you when they came down stairs? Standing under the market, about seven feet from the large eastern arch. Standing upon the floor of the market house? Yes, sir. What became of Miss Massey and her mother, when they came down stairs? They went to the carriage, sir. Where was the carriage standing? About twenty feet from the edge of the pavement of the eastern arch. Who accompanied them to the carriage? Mr. Bond. Do you know if he helped them into the carriage or not? I don't know. I didn't look. Did you look at the carriage while it was there? I did. During the whole time? Well I didn't pay any very particular attention to the carriage. How long did it stand there after Mr. Bond helped the ladies in? Well I suppose five minutes. During that time that the carriage stood there, did you see any body go to it? I did. Who? Tom Powers. Where did he go from? From the market house. Where else? I saw Mr. Cashwell—Mr. David Cashwell. Where did he go from? I think he came from Taylor's store, but I'm not positive about that. Any body else? Not that I recollect. Well, up to that time, had you seen any thing of Captain Tolar? When I went to the north corner, and came down, I saw him standing about where he does his business. Did you see any body with him? I can't recollect—I can't say. Where did you see him next? Never saw him after that. And that was the first and only time you saw Captain Tolar that day; did you see him go to the carriage? No, sir. I did, not. Well sir, after

the ladies went to the carriage and after the carriage drove off, where was your position between that time and the time Beebee was brought down stairs? About the main arch, around in there; I can't recollect—I might have walked up the other side of the market house—I don't know exactly I was round there anyway. How long was it af ter the ladies came down, that Beebee was brought down? About ten minutes. Did you see Beebee when he first appeared upon the landing of the stairs coming down? Yes, sir. Where were you at that time? Standing about three feet from the corner of Becky Ben's bench, the inside bench. On the inside of her stall? No, on the out side. Were you nearer to the eastern wall, or where? Well, I was standing about the middle of the main aisle that runs from east to west through the market. And from that position you saw Beebee and the party having him in charge from the time they first appeared upon the landing of the stairs, how large do you think the crowd was at that time? Well, about one hundred and fifty I reckon, or two hundred. Composed of whites? Whites under the market, I didn't see any colored people at all under the market. Now was the crowd outside? I can't say. Who composed that party that accompanied Beebee down stairs? There was Sheriff Hardie. Where was he? I don't recollect where he was, as he came down until he got down the big arch and got out of the stall. You remember he was there? Yes. Who else? Mr. Wemyss. Who besides? I am not positive—I can't say. Anybody else; any other policeman? I don't know—if there were I can't recollect. Then from that position you could see everything that occurred, could you not? Pretty well. Do you know John Maultsby? I do. Had you seen him that day there? I had. Did you see him at that time? No, sir. At the time that you are speaking of Archy being upon the landing of the stairs, and you standing there near the main arch, could you distinctly see that bench that runs near Becky Ben's stall? No, sir, men were crowded round me. Do you know whether, at that time any one jumped on that bench or not? I dont. Did you hear any exclamation or outcry at that time such as "look out boys, here he comes," or any thing of that sort? No, sir, nothing of that sort reached my ears. You speak of having seen John Maultsby; where? Sitting on a bench on the right hand side of the market house as you go in at the eastern arch next to Mitchell's store. How long was that before the time that Archy appeared upon the landing? I suppose it was half an hour. Did you see him after that? No, sir. Did you see any thing of Tom Powers in the crowd at that time, or up to that time? I saw him once. Where was he? Under the market house. Can you tell about what place? About the center of the market house. When did you see him there? That was after the trial commenced; after Miss Massey and her mother went up stairs. Before they came down? Yes, sir. And between that time and the time that Archy appeared upon the landing you saw nothing of Tom. Powers that you remember of? I don't recollect seeing him any more. You spoke of John Maultsby's setting on the bench, who was with him? James Jones; I think James R. Jones is his name. Were they in conversation about this matter? Yes. Did you hear their conversation? Part of it. What was it sir? John said he came up to bail out Archy if he was not guilty, if he was innocent he wanted him not to be punished, but if he was guilty let him go. If Beebee was guilty he was to let him go, if not guilty he was to bail him out; are you positive about that? I am, sir. During the time you were standing there, and the time of Archy's coming down to the landing as you have described, did you see any thing of Monk? No, not up to that time. Nor of Sam. Hall? No. Of Powers? No. Did you see any thing of Leggett? Yes. Where? Under the market. Did any thing unusual occur between the time you first saw Beebee upon the landing and the time of his reaching the floor of the market house? Nothing at all. Any cries nor exclamations? No, sir. From nobody? Nobody. Did you notice any excitement in the crowd at all? Well, when the lady came down stairs I noticed that her neck had been scratched and bruised; every body noticed it and it created a sort of excitement. Did that excitement manifest itself by any threats of violence? No, but from the fact that they noticed her neck. Then we have got to the foot of the stairs and the floor of the market, did you still continue to hold that position? Yes, sir. I had my eyes on him. What first appeared then to draw your attention? When he got to the edge of the east arch then the crowd commenced to gather. When he got there how far was he from you? About five feet, I think. I can't be certain. What occurred there? Well, he was demanded. Who demanded him? Tom. Powers. Where was Powers standing? Right on the rear of him. So that Beebee had passed him? Yes. What did he say when he demanded him? He said "give him up to me." Well, sir, what reply, if any, was made to that? Then the crowd began to rush in. What next occurred? I heard Mr. Wemyss halloing to the crowd and to Monk to go away, and about that time I heard Sheriff Hardie crying out to the crowd to stand back. When did that occur; how far did the prisoner and the party in charge of him get at that time? About even with the small eastern arch, going down Gillespie street, on the eastern side. On the pavement? Yes. sir Where were you at that time, had you changed your position? I had moved as the crowd moved and was standing on the pavement outside, about the center I guess. Where did that throw you with regard to that eastern arch? I don't know, it threw me about three feet from under the eastern arch. Yes, but what corner of the main eastern arch? The southern corner and about three feet from the wall of the market house. Well sir at that time, how far were you from the prisoner Beebee? About five feet I reckon. What next occurred Mr. Atkinson, to attract your attention? I saw Monk cutting with a knife at Beebee. Where was Monk at the time he was doing that? In the crowd. What was he saying? Nothing at all, but he was cutting at him. That was the time Mr. Wemyss was halloing "go away Monk." Well, what next occured? The next thing was the shooting of Beebee. Did you see anything of a scuffle or an attempt to wrest him from the authorities; or did you see anything looking like an attempt to get away? From the way Monk was cutting at him, I suppose he was trying to keep him from doing it. Never mind suppositions. What did you see? Well, I saw him getting down, or shuffling about. What time was he shot? Just as he rose up. What point on the pavement or what point about the market house had he reached when he was shot? About the center, about the edge of the small eastern arch. Which edge, the upper or lower? The southern edge. What was his position? About two feet from the edge of the pavement. Where were you at the instant he was shot? Standing on the edge of the pavement, I had moved up my position. How far then from Beebee? About four feet. Were you directly to his rear? Yes, directly. Which way was Beebee looking at that time? Well, his head was turned in the direction of Mr. Whitehead's corner which made it about south west. His face was turned

in that direction? Yes, sir. Where were you looking? Right at him. Who was with him? Sheriff Hardie, Wemyss and other policemen whom I have forgotten. Do you remember where Sheriff Hardie was? To his right. And had his hand on his collar, was it to his right and front? To his side, about, as if I were to catch a man so: [placing his hand on the collar of his coat at the side.] Where was Wemyss? To his left and rear; I cannot tell very well how he was, he had hold of him, I know that. And Hardie had hold of him? Yes. Well then just as he got about straight the pistol was fired? Not quite straight about this position: [witness here sloped his body to an angle of about sixty degrees.] Was there more than one pistol fired that day? There was not. Was the person who fired that pistol off or on the pavement, what was his position with regard to Beebee, to his side, front, right, left, rear or where? A little to his rear and left. How far off from you was the man who fired that pistol? About five feet. What position did he occupy with regard to you? To my left and front. Did you see the pistol drawn? No, sir. Did you see it presented? Yes. Did you see it fired? I did. Who fired it? Samuel A. Phillips. He was standing where you have described him? Yes. You saw him present it. Yes. And you saw him fire it? Yes. And that was the only pistol fired on that occasion? Not a doubt of it. You have no doubt about it? Not at all. That Samuel A. Phillips shot the negro, and nobody else? Yes, sir, there's no doubt about that. What did he do after that? I turned off, he held the pistol up while you could count five, then he turned off. He presented the pistol, held it up, fired it, and returned it to his breast, and then you left? Yes. sir. He made no remark? None at all. And you saw the smoke, and the flash, and heard the report? Yes, sir. You saw the smoke from the muzzle of the pistol, and from that place only? Yes, sir. Do you know which way Phillips went after he fired that pistol? I do not. He then turned off you say? I don't know, I turned off. Where did you go then? I went down the street about my business. Did you see anything more of Captain Tolar that day? No, sir. Or of Phillips? No, I don't recollect. How long has it been, or when was it, that you first informed anybody under the Heavens that Samuel A. Phillips fired that pistol? You are the man, sir; I was up in my shop and heard Tolar was to be tried for it, and my conscience was disturbing me about it, and I heard that you were the counsel for the accused, and I went up to your office and told you of it. Where did you tell me of this? In the back room of your office. Did you find me sitting there? No, sir. Where did you find me sitting? In the front room at your window talking to Mr. Hollingsworth. Was it at your request that I went into the back room? Yes, sir. And you told me, then and there, knowing that I was counsel for the accused? Yes, sir. And did you tell me that Tolar was an innocent man, and that Phillips shot the negro? I didn't tell you that Phillips shot him. What did you tell me? That it was a particular friend of Mr. Massey before the war, that fired that pistol; I have, however, told you since of it.

Cross-examined by Counsel for prosecution:
Mr. Atkinson, just after that pistol fired, did you hear anybody in the crowd inquire who had done it? No, sir. No exclamation nor cry at all? No, sir. You didn't hear anybody say that Captain Tolar had done it, had shot the negro, before you left? No, sir. Nothing of that sort; do you live with McKeethan? I work with him. Does Tom Powers work there too? He does. Did you ever tell him about this business? I

never did. Did you tell this to Mr. Fuller before Tom Powers was arrested? Yes, sir. Did you know that a coroner's inquest was going on the day after the negro was killed for the purpose of ascertaining who had killed the man? I knew that Mr. Blake had been summoned that evening there by Mr. Hardie, who was coroner for the jury. You didn't know that there was any trial by a coroner? Only what I heard. You never heard at the time that there was an examination going on by the proper authorities as to who had killed this negro? Oh! I heard that there was a trial. You did hear of it? I did. You didn't feel it your duty to give any information at that time? No, sir. And the first you communicated of the matter was to Mr. Fuller? Yes, sir. How long after the transaction, the man was murdered about the 11th February, and the communication to Mr. Fuller was about when? About 1st July I reckon, I don't recollect exactly. How long was it before you were summoned? I got my subpoena on 21st July to report here on the 25th. Was it before that, you told Mr. Fuller? Yes, sir. Before that? Yes. How long, can you remember, before? I guess about two weeks. Had Sam Phillips been arrested by the time you received your summons? He had been. Do you remember how long before? I am not positive, I can't recollect. Had you heard any thing of Sam Phillips turning State's evidence before that? Oh! no, I had got up here before he done it. You had got up here and been examined for the defense before Sam Phillips became State's evidence? Yes, sir. Did you expect to testify; knowing that Phillips was to be on trial, and the Counsel was aware of what your testimony would be, from what you had told him before? Yes, sir. Do you think you are bound by the oath you have taken before this Commission? I do. Do you believe it to be perjury to tell a falsehood here? Undoubtedly I do. You do not think that because this is a Military Court, it would not be perjury to tell a falsehood? No, sir. Have you ever told any such idea to any body? No, nothing of the kind ever crossed my mind. You never said anything of that character to one Reverend Mr. Pepper. No, sir, don't know him. Have you ever met, since you have been here, with a man who was Chaplain in some regiment in the United States army, and talked with him in anything like that way? No, sir, never. Have you, Mr. Atkinson, borrowed any money from Thomas Lutterloh since you have been here? I did, six dollars, which he offered to me himself. Has any body offered you any more money? Nobody. Have you drawn a draft on him for further supplies? I wrote him to send me some money, he told me if I wanted any to write him. And you have written him, you have drawn on him for fifty dollars, have you not? No, sir. Just simply wrote him a letter, didn't you ask Jim Nixon to assist you to draw a draft for fifty dollars on Mr. Lutterloh? It wasn't fifty dollars. What was the amount? Twenty five dollars. That draft was drawn? Yes. Did Mr. Lutterloh ever lend you any money before that, before this trial? No, sir. Have you had any offers of pecuniary assistance since this trial began? I don't understand what you mean. Has anybody in Fayetteville offered to lend you money since this trial commenced, have you had no offers of this kind? No, sir. Did you not state, in the presence of several persons, that you could have brought two hundred dollars or more up with you, when you went home last time? Don't recollect anything of the kind. And the only supplies you have had are those you drew from Mr. Lutterloh? Yes, but General Avery gave me some papers. Yes, yes, I don't mean

that, did Mr. Lutterloh owe anything to you ever? Not a cent. When you went to the market house the first day, you say Archy had been there? No, I went there before Archy got up there. How long had you been there before Archy got there? I suppose about some fifteen minutes. Were you standing facing the east arch, as he came up? No, outside on the pavement then. He passed you and went up stairs? Yes, sir. Then you came inside? Yes. And you remained, I believe about ten minutes? Yes, about that time. Did you see any persons there that you knew, any of the prisoners at the bar? No, sir, not at that time. Did you see Mr. Lutterloh or Mr. Leggett or E. P. Powers at that time? I saw Mr. Leggett, but not at that time. Did you see Sam Hall or Henry Sykes or John Maultsby at that time? No, not at that time. Did you see Sam Phillips then? I don't recollect. You say you staid there about fifteen minutes, were you still or walking round? Just walking round, I didn't seat myself anywhere. You then went to Mr. Clark's store, how far is that from the market house? About fifty yards. How long did you stop there? About fifteen minutes, I think. And then you returned? Yes, sir. What was your business at Clark's store? Well, I just walked down there, seeing as I knowed him. Did you walk alone? Yes, sir. Did you walk back alone? Yes. Did you meet any one at Clark's store? I don't recollect seeing anybody. What was your business at the market house that day? Well, I had been working pretty hard the fore part of the day. What was your object in leaving your work and going to the market house? Well, I went to dinner at one o'clock, came back, and made a remark to the men I was working with, that seeing as the trial was going on, I would go up and hear it. When did you first hear that an outrage had been attempted? About two o'clock. You didn't hear it Sunday morning? No. What sort of store does Clark keep—what does he sell? In the back end a bar room. Does he do in the front? Nothing, that I ever saw. Was it a grocery store? Not at that time. Was it just a drinking shop? Yes, only that. Did you take any thing to drink? No, sir. Had you anything to drink that day? I had not. When you went back you say you staid from twenty minutes to half an hour after Mrs. and Miss Massey came down? Yes, sir. Then you went to the northwest corner; oh! there are two northern corners, which is it you went to, the north-east or north-west? Well, the the one to the north, the extreme northern corner. Do you mean the northwest corner? Yes. At that time you saw Tolar? I saw him as he came through. You went in at which end? I didn't go in at the end coming up but walked right round it. But after you had been to Clark's, did you go on in at the east end of the market house? No, sir, I went right up to the side of the market house as you go in from the street, on the pavement. Which arch did you go in at? The western arch. And it was after you came in you saw Tolar? Yes. On your right as you moved towards the east? Yes, That is his usual place of business? Yes, sir. That is the first and last time you saw them that day? Yes, sir. Did you notice whether he had any weapon? No. Did you know that he had? No. Or that he was in the habit of wearing a weapon? No, sir. Did you ever see him wear one? Never. Ever hear him say he wore one? Never. Was he talking to some one or standing alone? He was talking to some one but I can't recollect who. Then you walked off to the east? Yes, sir. You then remained tolerably stationary until Miss Massey and her mother came down stairs? Yes sir. When Miss Massey and her mother came down stairs, how far were you from the eastern arch of the market house? I was standing about three feet from the corner. They had passed right in front of you; where were you standing? In the main aisle. How far from the eastern arch? About three steps or so. Eight or nine feet then? I don't know, it was not very far, I can't be positive; I don't recollect exactly the distance. Was it at the east end of Becky Ben's stall, in front of you or behind? In front. It reached further east than you? Yes. You were as far back as the west end of that bench? No, near the east end. When Miss and Mrs Massey came down stairs, and you saw Bond come down with them and go to the carriage? Yes, sir. You saw those persons pass out to the carriage, and I understood you to say that you saw Tom Powers and David Cashwell go up and speak to the ladies at the carriage? Yes, sir. Did you see what became of Bond after he left the carriage? No, I don't recollect. You didn't see him after he went bac⋅ to the house? No. You didn't see Tolar go into the carriage? No, I never saw him at all. Did you see Robert Mitchell go to the carriage? No, sir. Philemon Taylor? No. Or John Maultsby? No. The only persons you saw go to the carriage were David Cashwell and Tom Powers? Yes, except Mr. Bond. Did you see what became of Tom Powers after he came back? I don't recollect. Do you think he came back from the carriage? Yes, he did. The next time you remember seeing him however, he was within the market house; you don't remember seeing him come back, do you? No. Was that young lady weeping as she passe l from the court? Yes, sir, she had a handkerchief to her face. Was her veil over her face? No. Did she have a veil? I didn't s e any. She was using a handkerchief was she? Yes. Did she have Mr. Bond's arm? I don't recollect. Then you think she was moving along and weeping. where did you see the marks? Around her neck Around in front? Yes, she looked red and black. Did she have a cloak on? No, sir. Was it a cold day or warm; it was in February, did she have no cloak on? If she did have, I don't remember. You saw her neck you are quite sure? I am. Didn't she have a wrapper nor shawl on her neck at that season of the year? No, not that I recollect. You could see her neck? Yes. You say others saw her neck also, how do you know that? I don't know, I suppose they did, everybody was looking. Well, I thought you were going too far, did you hear any exclamation like "how horribly she's been treated," or anything of that sort, or do you simply conclude that others saw it because you did? I don't recollect anything about that, and I don't want to say anything unless I saw it myself. You didn't hear any body cry out that they had seen it? No, sir. No outcry, no expression of excitement? No, not at that time. I understood you to say that the excitement you saw occurred at that time? Well, everybody seemed to be— Well, sir, if there was no outcry you have no reason to suppose that because you saw it, others did also? Well the people were gathering round. But you have as I understand it, conveyed the impression clearly that when this lady's neck was seen, it was seen by the crowd and it created some excitement? Yes, but the excitement I mean is the crowd getting up round. Did you see any movement of the features, any pallor of the face, any setting of the lip? No, sir. Oh, the only marks of excitement consisted on the closing up of the crowd after these ladies had gone into the carriage; who was with them? Sheriff Hardie and Mr. Wemyss. Were there others whom you cannot name? I cannot speak certainly. But you remember that Hardie and

Wemyss were there; was there any interruption to Archy coming down stairs? None at all. As As he came down stairs did the crowd go there towards the steps; was there any rush or crowding towards the steps any nearer than before? No further than to where the ball comes round; about the steps. Was there any movements in the crowd that you perceived, or can testify to, as Archy came in sight? Well, when he came down they all gathered round him. They did when he got to the foot of the steps, but there was no movement until then? No. It stayed perfectly stationary until he got to the foot of the steps, you saw no disturbance? None at all. You were standing then within three or four feet of where Archie went out of the market house? I suppose that was it—I can't remember exactly. He passed full in your view as he went out? Yes. And you were within a few feet of him; were you within a few feet of him when Tom Powers grasped him? I can't tell exactly. Were you within a few feet of Archy when Powers laid his hand on him? Four or five feet. Were you nearer Archy than Powers? Nearer to Archy. Were you facing east? No, I had my face to the south. Your left hand was east and you were facing Archy, then he hadn't turned to go out of the arch? Oh yes, when he came down stairs I was looking at him—I cannot tell precisely the position I was standing in. But I want to know precisely the point he was at when Tom Powers grasped him? He was in the main eastern arch. Where were you at that time? To the left of Powers, two or three feet from him. How far were you from the arch; which way was your face? It was turned about half round. Yes, but I am talking about the place Archy was standing on, when Tom Powers laid his hand upon him? I have told you he was in the corner Where was Archy; was he inside the arch when Powers put his hand on him? He was just about even with the arch, going out. He was facing north? I cannot tell, the officers had him, he was moving round to the right. Now, how thick are the walls? About eighteen inches I think Had Archy turned in that way before he turned out that way? Yes he was standing about the edge of the arch at the time Tom Powers put his hand on him. Which hand did Powers grasp him with? With his left, I think. Did you see his right hand? No. You didn't see a knife in his right hand? No, no weapons at all. What did he say? He said "give him to me." Where were you standing? Well, to the left of them as I have told you before. Well, but I cannot understand you to save my soul; have you ever seen this plot of the market house; (showing a diagram to the witness)? No, never in my life. Archy was standing where? Just about where that shading is, (pointing to a spot on the diagram, representing the south edge of the main arch.) He was standing in the arch then? On the edge of it. Was the arch over his head? Well, he had just moved at the time; if it had been raining the rain would have come upon him. Where was Tom? Right behind him. Where were you? Outside the market house. You were outside the market house when Tom. Powers put his hand upon Beebee? Yes, sir. You were on the pavement and Tom. was outside the market house? Yes, he was just where I've told you. I understand you to say that Archy had just passed out of the arch, so that the rain would have dropped on him if it had fallen? Yes, sir. And that Tom. Powers was right behind him? He was a little to his left, I think, or so, I cannot be positive. Where from you, where from Archy? I was a little to the left. How far from Archy? About five or six feet. Was there any body between you and Archy? Yes, sir. Who? The policemen. Were you trying to get to Archy? No, sir. You had made no agreement with anybody? No, sir. You know nothing of such an agreement or combination for the killing of this negro? No, sir, I do not. Do you know that Sam Phillips or somebody else was concerned in such a combination? I don't; positively I do not. Then you were a little distance from the eastern end of the arch when this grab was made by Powers, and he said—what? 'Give him to me.'' Did he say it in a mild tone or decidedly? Decidedly. In a commanding tone? Yes. Now I want to know if you understood it a positive demand for that prisoner? I did. What was the sheriff's reply? The reply from the sheriff was "he is under me, sir.'' or something like that. Do you recollect Sheriff Hard e't ling Monk to go away? I don't recollect. Now, I want to know, before Sheriff Hardie had got rid of Powers, if Monk was upon him? Yes. These things occurred almost at one time, then? Yes sir. You saw Monk have a knife, and strike at him with it then and there? Yes sir. Did you see Monk strike him with t at knife more t an once? I don't know whether he struck him or not. Well, he struck any way, was it once or twice? Twice, I reckon. Was that the only time you saw Monk strike him, or strike at him, with a knife? That was the only time. Well, when was the next time you saw Monk? Well, after the shooting. Did you see Monk make any effort with the knife, except at that time, before he was shot? Not before he was shot. He hadn't got down as far as that little arch at that time then? No, sir, it was just as he got out of the market house. How long between the time that Archy got out of the arch and the time that he was killed? No time, I suppose a minute? Do you think it was a minute? I declare I don't know. Did things go on in very rapid succession? Yes, sir. Was there any stir? Only that the crowd around were trying to see. You heard no outcry in the crowd? No. You heard the sheriff telling them to hold back and telling the men to use their clubs? He might have done that, but I didn't hear; Mr. Wemyss was using his. Did you see a knife fall out of Monk's hand? No, sir. Or out of anybody's hand? No, you could not have heard the drop of a knife in such a place. Well, some people have different opinion about that. Well, I never heard it. Was there a great noise at the time? No, nothing to make a man notice, more than that you could not hear anything for the policemen were hollering at them to hold back. Did they seem to be exerting themselves to keep off the crowd? Yes, sir. Was the crowd pressing on them? I don't know, sir, I can't say whether they were doing that or not. You say you saw the police strike? I saw Mr. Wemyss several times knocking. Was he the only one? There might have been another, but I can't swear to anybody else. What was he doing it for? He was telling Monk to keep back. Did you see any other clubs used? I don't recollect. Did you see any pressure of the crowd at all towards the prisoner? No, they gathered round as if to see. You were in the crowd? I was standing there in the crowd. How—close to the prisoner all the time? I moved along as he did. You were right in the midst then, were you not? Yes, sir. Were you not hustled about a good deal? Well, I was moved round a little. Were you not inconvenienced? Not particularly. You didn't expect any violence then? No, sir, had no idea of it. Not at that time? No, sir. Then, after this thing occurred about the man Monk and the knife; Tom Powers was standing at the door of the large eastern arch as Beebee came out? I can't be positive; if he was not standing

there he was somewhere about there. Now do I under tand you to say that from the time Archy Beebee got to the foot of the steps, until he got outside the arch no demonstration was made? No, sir, just as he got out, Powers and Monk made at him, one after the other. Had Tom let go of him when Monk made at him? I don't know. Did you see Tom Powers put his hand on him? I saw him throw his hand that way—[Witness here threw his hand up and out from him as if reaching over a crowd.] Did you see it come back? No, sir. When Powers put his hand out that way did you see Sheriff Hardie seize him by the wrist? No, sir. You don't know whether that hand was on Archy or not, when Monk made his assault and came forward with the knife? I do not. Has Sheriff Hardie ceased speaking to the crowd when Monk made his assault? Why he was talking while he pistol was fired. Hardie was still talking? Yes. And while he was thus talking, it was that this man Monk was cutting? Yes. Then from the time they left the arch until they got down to the south corner of the little arch, you never saw any assault made up on Archy? I did not. I understand you to say distinctly that the only time you saw Monk cutting at this man, except after he was dead, was just after Tom Powers put his hand upon him, and that Archy was there just at the outside door? Yes, sir, he was, when Tom grabbed him, 'twas just like that [witness here gave a fillip of finger and thumb.] How far had Archy got from the little arch when Monk struck at him with the knife? From the little arch—from the big arch—I can't tell. Had he gone a step? I don't know. Had he gone two? I don't know exactly. It seems to me that you said Tom Powers had his hand on him immediately after he got outside the arch, and that Monk attacked him immediately after Tom Powers, had he time to take two or three steps from the time Powers left his hand off up til Monk put his hand on? He could have taken two or three very short steps. Then I understand you to say in your examination-in-chief that it was while Monk was making at him with the knife that the negro bent over? He was dodging, I can't tell precisely. It was just after Tom Powers made the attack upon him, Monk was pitching in with the knife, and before he raised himself fully up he was shot. And you say he must have taken two or three short steps? I wont be positive about that. Are you positive about this, that the negro was dodging about while the knife was being struck? Yes. And while he was straightening up from that position, that he was shot? Yes, sir. And you say he was not shot until he got at the south side of the little arch? Yes, sir. And about two feet from the edge of the pavement? Yes, sir. Did you see him fall down at all? I saw him fall when the pistol fired and Sheriff Hardie was with him. Did you see him before the pistol fired? No, sir. Did you say Wemyss on his left? Yes, sir, I never saw him fall exactly, never saw him on his hands and knees, I lost sight of him pretty well, but could see his head all the time. Did you ever lose sight of him at all, and you swear you never saw him on his hands and knees? I do sir. It is your opinion that he didn't go down on his hands and knees? It is. Did you see any of the officers fall with him? No, sir. Did you see them helping him up? I don't know, I suppose they were trying to keep him up. Well, when he reached this point you say Sam Phillips presented that pistol and fired? He had the pistol in his hand. Did you see him draw it? I never saw him draw it. Did you see him cock it? It was already cocked, I didn't see him draw it, nor cock it. Did you see him fire it? I did see him fire it. Did he have the pistol presented when your eye caught it? No, sir, it was after it fired. When you saw him first what was he doing with it? He had fired it and had brought it up. You didn't see Sam Phillips until the pistol fired; you didn't see him draw the pistol? No, sir Nor cock it? No. Nor present it? No. Did you see him fire the pistol? I did sir. Then you saw him in the very act of firing the pistol, for the first time, that was the first time you had seen him that day? Yes, sir. Did you see him flourish it round that way? No, sir. Did you hear him say "the negro is dead, but I have not done it?" No, sir. You saw the pistol in his hand from the time it fired until he put it back in his breast? I did. Did he make such a remark? Not that I heard. Were you looking at him? Yes. While he had the pistol in his hand he made no such remark? No, sir. And you swear it? I do. He did hold up the pistol? Yes, sir, while you'd say one, two, three, four, five probably. Did you see him take the cap off? No. Was any one between you and Sam Phillips when he fired? Yes, two or three. Were they white or colored? I can't tell. You saw him however distinctly; how much of him; from his head to his heels? No, about to here (pointing to his waist.) About to the middle of the body; about to his waist? Yes, sir. Did he put it in the arm of his coat? He put it down in that direction. [Witness here placed his hand across his body and under his coat as if placing something in its side pocket.]

He didn't put it into the arm of his overcoat? I am not positive, well he put it just as I tell you and he could not have put it in his coat sleeve, if he put it that way Did you say he had an overcoat and put in the sleeve of that overcoat? I am not positive about his having an over coat—I cant describe his clothes. But one thing you saw about him was the pistol? He might have had one on for all I know. Can you say what sort of hat he had on? No I cannot. Can you tell any thing on earth about him? No: but that he shot Archy Beebee. Do you know the color of his clothes or any part of them? No, I can't recollect. Nothing but that you actually did see him fire it, did he make use of any expression? No. Did you say that pistol was cocked when it was presented? Yes, I didn't notice the cock but I saw it fire. You saw the flash? Yes. You saw the smoke? Yes, sir. And heard the report? I did. And didn't take your eyes off him all that time? No. Did you see the negro fall? Yes. Did you go to the negro? No. He drew the pistol back when? After the nigger fell. You say, you saw the negro fall before you saw Sam Phillips draw back that pistol? As he drew up the pistol the nigger fell. Then you say, Sam Phillips returned the pistol and turned off? Yes, sir. You never saw Tolar before that day? I never did. When was the first time you saw him after that day? After he came back from the country. Did you tell him you knew anything about that? No sir. Have you any pecuniary interest in this trial? Not a bit. You have no enmity or ill will against Sam Phillips? Not a bit, sir—I have more dealings with him than with Tolar. Have you talked about this thing since you have been here? To nobody at all. None at all? Nobody but my counsel—I mean Mr. Fuller, the counsel for the accused. You have not talked with anybody else about this business? I was told not to do so. Yes, that's what I supposed; were you ever questioned or examined about this thing by any one? None but Mr. Fuller. You never volunteered any information to any United States Army man about this bus-

inces in any shape or way? No, sir. You say you have not talked about this matter. you haven't even said that you did not know anything about it? No, sir, I haven't talked to anybody about what I knew about it. Have you not said to an officer of the United States army, named Pepper in this city, since you came here, that you didn't know who shot the negro? No, sir. Nothing of that sort? No, I have been asked several times by people what I knew of it, and I have told them I didn't know anything of it, and didn't know whether he was the person or not, and that when I got on the stand, I would tell all I knew of it, and not till then. This man I speak of, speaks of a conversation of an hour or an hour and a half? I don't know anything about them. Have you not expressed to this officer that this Court had no right to try this offence? I never made use of such an expression, sir, I never thought of such a thing. And you now swear, knowing what the consequences may be to Sam Phillips and others in presence of Almighty God, who knows your heart and conscience this day, as none of us can know, that Sam Phillips fired that shot, and you are as confident of that as you are of your own existence? Yes. And you have no doubt of it, whatever? No. And never had since the time it occurred? No. Why didn't you speak of it before? Well, it was not my business. Was that your reason? Yes, sir. If you saw a murder committed in the streets of Fayetteville, do you think it is your business to say nothing about it? Well, but I did say something about it. Yes, but not for some months after it occurred? No, to nobody except my wife. Now do you think you'd seen it, it would be no part of your duty to give information of it? Well but I have. Yes, but you kept it for three or four months; I want to know, if you were the solitary witness of a murder in Fayetteville, would you conceal it? No, I would report it. Who did you not report this? Well, because I didn't have anything to do with it. Well, but you would have had nothing to do with it, if you went into the street and saw a man shoot another, was your reason because it was a white man that shot a negro? No. Did you not feel greatly outraged that a negro should attempt to commit rape on a young lady? I did, but the law should take its course. Do you mean to say this, that you saw a foul crime like murder committed in the streets of Fayetteville, and you didn't conceive it your duty to inform anybody about it? Well, I consider I did my duty when I went to Mr. Fuller: I am close confined to my works and have no time to spare for anything else. Was your conscience not disturbing you before? No, it all wore off, I had forgotten all about it. Until Mr. Tolar was arrested? Yes, sir, I heard so many people talking about it. Did you know that the civil authorities were investigating the matter? No. I understood you to say that you were summoned while Phillips was still on trial? I don't recollect positively about that. Well, didn't you get here before Phillips was discharged? Yes, sir. And you were summoned before you got here? Yes. You were a witness in this case at the very time Phillips was on trial for his life? He was released, I think, sir, the day I got here. Yes, you were summoned on the 21st to appear on the 25th? I got here on the 24th. Phillips was released after you got here? Yes, sir. At the time you were summoned as a witness on the trial for his life, you were expecting to testify exactly as you have done now? Yes, I did. Even though Phillips were on his trial? Yes, sir, the very same way.

By Counsel for accused:

Mr. Atkinson, you say the subpœna was served on you in this case on the 21st July? It was, I think, sir. Do you know when that subpœna was issued, sir? I have forgot, my memory's not good any how about it, I can't recollect, I think my subpœna was dated Raleigh, 21st, probably; I know I was ordered to report here on the 25th, and I got here on the 24th. Do you know if Phillips had left Fayetteville by the time the subpœna was served upon you? Yes, he had come away. You told your wife about it the day it occurred? That night I think, sir. And you kept it to yourself after that time because it was no business of yours you could see, until you had learned that I had been employed as Counsel for Capt. Tolar, and as Tolar's Counsel you gave me the statement which you have made here to-day? I did, sir, and you know that yourself. By the Commission: Did you see the pistol at the moment the trigger was pulled? Yes, he had it in his hand. Did you see the pistol before you heard the report? About that time. Before you heard the report? Yes, I seen it pointed and immediately it was pointed it fired. The question is, did you see it before you heard the report? Well, before I saw it I heard the report, the time I saw it the pistol fired The pistol had fired, or did fire? Did fire. You swear that the pistol was just in the act of being discharged when you saw it first? I mean at the very instant I saw it, it fired.

(The Commission: We don't think the question is answered, it must be yes or nay.)

The Court insists pon a positive answer to that question, Mr. Atkinson; did you see the pi tol before you heard the report? I saw the pistol immediately—as soon as I saw the pistol it fired. Then if I un'erstan' your answer you mean to say tha at the very moment you saw the pistol, as your eye glanced on the pistol it was discharged? Yes, sir. You saw too s ooke? Yes, sir. You h ard the rep rt? Yes, sir. And saw the flas ? Yes, sir. At the ve y moment? Y s, sir. Then you didn't see it until you h ard the report? Yes, sir

The Commissi n: You mu t answe the question, sir, was it before you h ard the report or n t? B fore I heard the report, sir.

Commissi n: Very well, sir.

What caused you to look at the pi t l at that moment? Because I seen it. What attracted your attention tow rds that pistol and that point at that moment? The firing, sir. But you have positively sworn that you saw the pistol oefore you bear the report? W ll, the pistol, sir, I saw it just as it fi ed. Do you m an you ere attracted or the pointing of the pis ol? It w s all very quick, sir. I am well ware of that w want to get a wh t it was that caused you to look at that pistol; did you see Mr. Phill ps before you saw the pistol? No, sir. I don't underst nd why you were attracted t look at the pistol? Because, sir, it was all done so qu k; it w s pointing at him. The quickness with which it was done was what attracted your attention? And the pistol of course.

The Commission: What was your answer? (to the reporter.) read the answer.

The testimony as to what att acted his attention to the pistol w s read from the records.

At 2 o'clock, P. M, on motion, the Commission adjourned to meet at 11 o'clock, on 24 h inst.

RALEIGH, N. C., Aug. 24, 1867, 11 A. M. The Commission met pursu nt to adjournment.

Present: All the members of the Commission, the Judge Advocate, the Counsel for the prosecution, all the accused, and their Counsel.

The reading of the testimony taken yesterday was waived, there being no objection thereto.

JAMES W ATKINSON, a witness for the defence, upon hearing his testimony read, made the following corrections:

To the question by the Counsel for the prosecution.

Have you not stated, in the presence of several persons, that you could have brought up two hundred dollars, or more when you went home the last time? (In the original record) Don't recollect anything of the kind.

Witness wishes to add here: "If I had been in want of two hundred dollars or more, I could have borrowed it, but certainly no body offered to lend it to me, and if I had borrowed it, I would have to pay it back."

To the question by the Counsel for the prosecution. "And the only supplies you have had, are those that you drew from Mr. Lutterloh?" (As in original record) "Yes; but General Avery gave me some papers to get money." Here the witness wishes to correct, so as to read— "Yes, but General Avery made out my account as witness in this case, on which I obtained money."

Yesterday's proceedings were then approved.

JAMES H. MYROVER, a witness for the defence, having been first duly sworn, testified as follows: Examined by the Counsel for the accused.

What is your name? James H. Myrover. Where do you reside? Fayetteville, North Carolina. How long have you resided in Fayetteville? Ever since my birth, about twenty-four years. What is your occupation? Editor. Were you in Fayetteville on the day Archy Beebee was killed? Yes, sir. Were you at the market house that day? Yes, sir. At what time did you go to the market house? Between two and three o'clock. In the afternoon? Yes, sir. For what purpose did you go to the market house? For the purpose of reporting the preliminary trial The preliminary trial of Archy Beebee? Yes, sir, I had understood there was to be a preliminary trial before a magistrate. Did you go into the court room? No, sir. Why did you not go up, sir. I was not permitted to do so, I attempted it. How long did you remain at the market house? I don't know exactly in time. Did you leave there before the man Beebee was killed? No, sir. You remained there un'il after the man Beebee was killed? Yes, sir. About what position in the market house did you occupy, while there? Well, I was first at the eastern portion of the market house, and then in the center, and southern portion. Near what part of the eastern portion? I was directly under the main eastern arch. That was when you first went there? Yes, sir. And then about the southern portion? Yes, sir And then near the center? Yes, sir. How much of a crowd was there under the market house, when you first got there? It was before the time of the trial; he had been removed from the guard house and I left the market house and went across the street; there was not much crowd there at the time. How large a crowd was there at the time Beebee went up stairs, during the time the trial was progressing? I should judge that there were a hundred persons there What was the size of the crowd, at or about the time of the shooting, larger or smaller? I don't know, sir. During the time you were there under the Market house and before Beebee was brought down, was the crowd in an excited, agitated state? It didn't appear to me so, sir. Did you mix freely among the crowd at that time? Yes sir. Was there anything occurring in the crowd that attracted your attention? No, sir. Do you know now, or did you know then, of any combination,.

or any agreement or any conspiracy, to kill the man Beebee, or do him any harm? I do Lot, and I did not. From what you saw of the appearance and the demeanor of the crowd, there on that occasion, was it indicated to you that there was any undue heat or excitement about those who were assembled? The crowd was interested in the trial, nothing further than that, that I noticed. During that time did you see any of the prisoners at the bar, either of these three men, behind me, Captain Tolar, Thomas Powers, or David Watkins otherwise called Monk. I saw two of them. Which two, did you see. Capt. Tolar and Monk Julia. Where, and at what time, did you see Capt. Tolar? I saw Capt. Tolar standing at the northern span of the eastern arch, nearly against it or against it, I am not positive which. What was he doing? He was doing nothing, standing there. How long was that before the man Beebee was brought down stairs? It was some time, it was before Miss Massey was brought up as well as I can recollect. And after that you don't remember to have seen him at all? No, sir. At that time, did you see Tom Powers? No, sir. Monk? Not at that time. Ed. Powers? Not when I saw Tolar, J. G. Leggett? No, sir. Ralph B. Lutterloh? I didn't see him at all. sir, until after the killing. Sam Hall? Not at that time. You saw then nobody at that time, except Capt. Tolar? No, sir. And he was standing alone? He was standing at the arch—there were persons near him, but there was not any one in direct contact with him. Anybody in conversation with him? I spoke to him, sir. What was his manner and appearance there at that time? I noticed nothing unusual. They seemed calm and collected? Yes, sir. You say you saw Monk? Yes, sir. Where, and at what time did you see him. After that I passed through the market, and went there on the southern side and spoke to Dr. McDuffie, and Sheriff Hardie, and I then saw Monk standing on the pavement, I asked also of Major McRae, who was there, I asked him who he was, he told me that was Monk. Where was Monk at that time? He was on the pavement pointing South. Near the large arch? Yes, sir. How long was that before Beebee was brought down? I can't tell, sir. What was he doing? He was doing nothing—he was walking up and down the pavement, Dr. McDuffie nodded to him, and spoke to him. Was that the only remark that was addressed to him? I didn't hear the remark, but they were not in regular conversation. Did you see him in conversation with anybody? No, sir. Was there anything excited, or unusual about his appearance, or manner? I didn't notice it, sir. Did you see E. P. Powers there, at all? Yes, s r. When did you see him first? I saw him at the time that I was in conversation with Sam Hall. When was that, Mr. Myrover? That was between the time Miss Massey went up stairs and the prisoner was brought down. Where did he go? He passed away from us. Anybody with him? No, sir. In conversation with anybody? No, sir. What was his manner, excited? No, sir, he was walking down towards the eastern part of the market. What was he doing, sir? He was doing nothing, sir. Was he stationary, or was he moving when you saw him? He was moving. Did you see anything of Ralph Lutterloh? I didn't see him, sir, until after the killing. Did you see anything of Mr. J. G. Leggett? I saw him before I left the eastern see Leggett? I saw that was he doing? It part of the market. Was he standing still? was doing nothing, sir with any one? He Yes, sir. In conversation one else? A genwas conversing with me. tleman introduced him to me. That was your

first acquaintance with him? Yes, sir. What was his manner, excited? No, sir. Calm? Yes, sir. Did you see anything of John Maultsby? No, sir. Did you see anything of Henry Sykes? No, sir. Did you see anything of Sam Hall? Yes, sir. Just state, if you please, when you first saw him, how long you were with him, and when you parted? I saw him first, inside of the market house. About what point? About a stall which goes by the name of Tom Drake's stall I think. Near which corner of the market is that? It is on the southern side of the market. Southern and western, southern and eastern, or where? It is further west than east; it is the next stall to the last western stall on the southern side. Is it above the bell rope further towards the west? Yes, sir. There you first saw him? Yes, sir. Did he go to you, or did you go to him? He came to me, sir. Where did he come from Mr. Myrover, do you know? I don't recollect. What time was it that Hall came and joined you? Some short time before the prisoner was brought from the hall alone. Was it after Mrs. Massey and her daughter came down? I don't know, sir; I didn't see them come down. How long do you think it was before Beebee was brought down? I suppose it was at least five minutes. How long did Hall remain with you? He remained with me until the negro was shot, after the killing we parted, and I went down and looked at his body. So Hall remained with you until after the negro was shot? Yes, sir. About what position did you and Hall occupy, until you separated, which you say was about five minutes from the time you got together; about what point in the market house? We were standing right together, and I had my foot on a bench in front of Tom Drake's stall. And Hall was standing next to you? Yes, sir. Was that west or east of the bell rope? It was to the west of the bell rope. And you swear that Hall was there with you, for at least five minutes before the shooting occurred, until the shooting occurred? Yes, sir. He didn't leave your presence at all, during that position? Not until after the negro was shot. Have you any doubt about that Mr. Myrover? None in the world. Well, sir, after that, what became of Hall? I don't know, sir, he may have gone down through the market, I didn't go with him, I went out through the southern arch, and went around and looked at the boy, who was then dead. You separated from Hall there? Yes, sir. What became of him after that time you don't know? I don't know, sir.

Cross-examination by the Counsel for the prosecution

Where were you standing when Archy came down stairs? I was standing with my foot on the bench at Tom Drake's stall. That is west of the bell rell rope? Yes, sir. You didn't move out with the crowd? No, sir. You say Mr. Hall was with you, and he didn't move out? No, sir. Did you see Archy when you came down stairs? I could see him as he passed down the steps. Could you see who was with him, sir? Yes, sir. Who was with him? The guard. Do you remember who the guard consisted of? No, sir, I remember one of them. Who was that? Faircloth. Did you see Wemyss there, that you remember? I don't recollect. Do you remember seeing Hardie there? Yes, sir. Do you remember seeing Hornrinde and McGuire there, when they came down stairs? No, sir. Did you see any attempted violence of the crowd, while he was coming down stairs, I mean before he reached the foot of the stairs? No, sir. Did you see any attempted violence made by any person while he was still in the market house passing from the foot of the steps to go outside of the market house? Before he got out of the market house he passed out of my sight. Is there a pillar in the middle of the market house? Yes, sir. You could see him at the bottom of the stairs, and you could see him as he passed out of the arch? No, sir. He went out of your sight for a moment, then? Yes, sir. Did you see any disturbance in the crowd just as he got to the arch, or about the time he would have got there? I saw a crowd rush up, and a woman run from it up towards me, a black woman. That was just after you saw him moving out of your sight? Yes, sir. Did you see any thing of Tom Powers there that day? No, sir. Did you see any thing of Monk there that day? Yes, sir, not after I saw him at the southern side of the market house, near the center. Did you hear any demand made for the prisoner? No, sir. Did you hear any thing like a demand? I heard voices, and voices speaking, but I could not distinguish. Did you hear any cry, just before the shooting, of shoot him, shoot him, kill him, kill him? No, sir. Did you hear any cry of he'll get away? No, sir. Did you hear any cry, or any expression in the crowd that day? I only heard one expression, that I could distinguish, from the negro woman who was coming towards me. What was the expression? She said they were going to kill that man. That was at the very moment the crowd rushed up, as he was passing through the arch? As he was passing through the main arch the crowd was rushing into the main arch—the main eastern arch, I said they were rushing into the main eastern arch—they were rushing that way. You saw the motion of the crowd outside pressing towards the main eastern arch? Yes, sir. Did you see any motion of the crowd inside? A portion of the crowd that was inside was rushing towards the main eastern arch. So far as you could see? Yes, sir. You are perfectly confident and have remembered it from that time to this, that you were in conversation with Sam Hall at the time this tumult occurred? Yes, sir. How long were you standing in the eastern end of the market house, when you first went in, after Archy went up stairs? I remained there until Miss Massey was carried up stairs. Did Miss Massey go up stairs after Archy? Yes, sir. Are you confident of that? That was my impression, because he was carried from the guard house, and I followed him, and I saw Miss Massey come up afterwards—I may have lost sight of Archy. And you moved away from there immediately after she went up? Not immediately. How long did you remain there? Ten or fifteen minutes—not that long I guess. At the time you were standing there, I understand you to say that Captain Tolar was standing against the northern extremity of the eastern arch? Yes, sir. You didn't see him move away from there? I moved away first. You left him standing there when you moved? Yes, sir. Did you see who was in conversation with him, or standing about him at that time? There was none, sir. Have you disclosed every thing you know of this transaction? As far as I can remember, I have.

Questioned by the Commission:

The Court understands you to say that you had never seen Monk, before that day? I mean to know him. And that you asked at that time who he was. Yes, sir. You also stated that there was nothing unusual in his actions? Yes, sir. Now, if you had never seen Monk before, how do you know there was nothing unusual in his actions. His appearance is very peculiar it seems to me. His appearance then was unusual? No, sir, I mean his personal appearance was such as to attract one's attention. What the Court wanted to get at, is, how you are able to state that there

was nothing unusual in his actions, at that time, if you had never seen Monk? Taking the whole personal appearance of the man to be his actions, there may have been something unusual in his actions—I was struck at the man's appearance, and asked who he was.

MATTHEW MORGAN, a witness for the defence was duly sworn.

The Counsel for the accused tendered the witness to the prosecution.

The Counsel for the prosecution declined to examine him.

The Counsel for the accused said?

"I will state to the Commission that we have another witness in attendance to day who arrived yesterday, but his testimony is dependent upon other testimony, which must necessarily come in before it; we have two witnesses who arrived here this morning but they are so much jaded, by the long stage route of last night, that unless the Court shall request it, we prefer not to introduce them to day. Three witnesses are all we have in the city."

The Judge Advocate said:

"As far as the prosecution is concerned we prefer going on."

On motion the Commission adjourned, to meet on Monday Aug. 26, at 10, A. M.

RALEIGH, N. C., Aug. 26, 1867, 10 A. M.

The Commission met pursuant to adjournment. Present: All the members of the Commission, the Judge Advocate, the Counsel for the prosecution, all the accused and their Counsel.

The reading of the testimony taken on Saturday, the 24th instant, was waived, there being no objection thereto.

Saturday's proceedings were then read and approved.

The Judge Advocate stated that Matthew Morgan, a witness for the defence, had made application to him for his certificate of attendance, which he had declined to give, without the orders of the Commission.

The Counsel for the accused said:

"May it please the Court: I understand that the Court here is bound by the rules of practice, which govern in the State courts, and which govern in the courts of the United States. Having been informed by the Judge Advocate that the subject would be laid before the Court this morning, I have looked somewhat into the authority, and in the different States, as well as in the State of North Carolina, if there is one point in practice that is well settled, that is settled beyond all cavil, it is that a witness who has been tendered, is entitled to his certificate of attendance, and entitled to his costs. I would be frank to the Court, and state to them, that while I do not find an authority directly enunciating that doctrine, that I found it laid down in all the books, as so well a settled practice of evidence, that they merely referred to it in going on. The Supreme Court of North Carolina, in a case which was decided in 1859, reported in 6 Jones, alluded to it in this way that no witness can have his costs unless he be examined or called and tendered. Allusion is made to it in that way. I say it, sir, and if the Counsel for the prosecution were here, who is familiar with the practice, I would challenge denial, that this is one of the best settled points of practice in North Carolina. I have to state further that it is the practice of this Court, and for that I cite the authority of the Judge Advocate himself. A witness for the prosecution, I forget his name, Jones or Hall, a black man, that the Court will perhaps remember, was called, having been duly subpœnaed, was sworn, his name was asked, his testimony was not taken at all of any matter pertinent to this issue; he was tendered by the Judge Advocate to the Counsel for the accused, was declined precisely as in this case, and I am informed—the Judge Advocate can state differently if such be not the fact—that there was no question at all made with regard to giving him a certificate of attendance.

I will state to the Court further, that if there can be any question in the minds of the Court as to the general practice, and as to the practice of the Judge Advocate in this case, settling the law here most clearly, it can be made to appear to the Court that this man Matthew Morgan was summoned as a material witness, for the purpose of giving testimony very material to the issue before the Court; that he was not examined by the defence because the defence did not choose to examine him, not because of the immateriality of his testimony, but simply because the defence did not choose to examine him; some little tactics being allowed, as well in the conduct of cases as in the conduct of matters upon the field."

The Commission was cleared for deliberation, and after sometime so spent, the doors were reopened, and the Judge Advocate said, "The Commission decides that they will not order the witness Matthew Morgan to be paid, unless they can be first satisfied that Matthew Morgan knows something material to the case. They therefore will permit the Counsel for the accused, if they see proper, to call the witness into Court and examine him. Should the Counsel for the accused decline so to do, the Commission decides to examine the witness themselves, that they may ascertain whether or not he does know anything material to the case."

The Counsel for the accused, "I have no objection, I do not wish to say a word against the ruling of the Court; I merely desire to suggest to the Court, not by way of influencing their ruling at all, that in some States where the practice is perhaps different from what it is in North Carolina—I believe the furthest that it has ever gone is that, if there be a question as to the materiality of the witness, the party examining him shall be required to make an affidavit of the materiality. Although Matthew Morgan is a material witness, we have good reasons, which may suggest themselves to the Court, and certainly suggest themselves to the gentlemen of the Court, as to those who are conducting the prosecution in this case, and we decline, as we did the other day, to examine the witness; but we suggest to the Court, to the Judge Advocate, and the Counsel for the prosecution assisting, very respectfully, if the Court doubts the materiality, that it will be conforming to the practice of some States to require an affidavit only as to the materiality."

The Commission informed the Counsel for the accused that their remarks had been considered, but as they declined to examine the witness, the Commission would examine him.

The Judge Advocate announced that Matthew Morgan was not at present in attendance, but had been sent for.

The Commission suggested that another witness be called—whereupon

JAMES H. JONES, a witness for the defence was duly sworn, and testified as follows:

Examined by the Counsel for the accused.

What is your name? James H. Jones. Where do you reside? Fayetteville. Fayetteville, N. C? Yes, sir. How long have you resided there? Twenty-six years. Were you in Fayetteville on the day Archy Beebee or Archy Warden was killed? I was, sir. Did you know Archy Beebee? I did, sir, he was working for me at the time. In what business was he engaged? Driving a dray for me. In whose employment had he been before he was in your employment? John Maultsby's or his father's, both together I suppose. How long had it been since he quit working for Maultsby and came into your service? I really don't know, some two months I suppose. Had you heard before the killing had occurred, that Beebee was charged with an attempted violence upon the person of Miss Massey? I heard it that morning before I got out of bed. Who informed you? John Maultsby, he brought me my smoke-house key, and stable key, that Beebee had in his pocket, and informed me that he was arrested. Charged with a certain outrage? Yes, sir. When did you next hear about it? I heard it in going up to my work. Did you take any steps to defend Beebee or have him defended? That morning, in going up I saw Mr. Bond, the town Constable at the market house, and told him—— I don't desire the conversation—did you make any arrangement for a defence of Beebee, upon that charge? In what way do you mean. I mean in offering to procure the services of Counsel, or in any other way? I did, sir. Did any body join you in that arrangement, that you proposed to make? John Maultsby did. Were those arrangements perfected, or were they suggested arrangements? We were talking about it ourselves, and we never spoke to any person, because in a very few minutes after we were talking about it, the boy was killed. Before that time, did you see Dennis Hogans, or any other relative of the deceased man, with reference to that matter? I met Dennis that morning and told him to go to the trial and meet me there, but before the trial, to go and get you to appear there for the boy. He told me he didn't have the money, and I told him I would see that you were satisfied. Were you at the market house at the time Archy Beebee was killed? I was, sir. What time did you go there? I left my work about five minutes before four. Where do you work, sir? M. A. Baker's. Where is that, sir? Opposite the wagon weights. What street? Fayetteville street, sir, I think it is. This is Fayetteville street here? I know I didn't know the names of the streets. How far is that from the market house? I guess it is about a quarter of a mile. You left your work and went down to the market house? I did. Entering the market house from which side? From the west side. What was your object and purpose in going to the market house that day? For the purpose of giving bail for the boy, if they would take it. When you got there, where was Beebee? He was up stairs, I reckon, sir, I am not positive about it, I think he was up stairs. Where was Miss Elvira Massey and her mother, at the time you got there? She was in the carriage, I guess sir. Don't guess? I didn't see them at all. Did you see the carriage? I saw the carriage, it drove off in almost half a minute after I got there. Then you went into the western end of the market house, and which way did you go? Right straight out, through the eastern arch. Where did you stop first? On the pavement outside. On the outside of the eastern arch? Yes, sir. At that time did you see anything of John Maultsby? I saw John Maultsby. Where was he? He was standing close to the carriage. Who else did you see at the carriage besides John Maultsby? I saw Israel Bond, Robert Mitchell, and I think they are the only ones I noticed. Did you see William J. Tolar? I saw Captain Tolar. Where was he? He was under the market house, when I passed through. At what point under the market house? He was to my right as I passed through. Was he near the western, the eastern, the southern or northern arch? Under the market house under the main arch, under the cover of the market house, further to the northern side, I think, than to the southern. Who was standing near him? There was Mr. Leggett, Edward Powers, and Mr. Lutterloh, I did not notice any more. They were standing there near together? Yes, sir. Were there other persons close around them? Yes, sir. What were they doing? Standing there talking? How were they talking? I don't know the conversation, I heard some person remark, that the boy ought to be killed. Do you mean you heard some of this party remark that? I don't know who it was, I never noticed. You don't know who made this remark? No, sir. Did you see Capt. Tolar at the carriage? I did not. Or near the carriage? No, sir. You saw Maultsby there, with the others you have named? Yes, sir. Did you go near the carriage? I did not, sir, I didn't go off the pavement. Well, sir, what became of Maultsby when the carriage left? He walked up to me and told me that Beebee was found guilty. Where did you walk to? We walked around on the south side of the market house Inside of the market house or outside? Outside. Upon the pavement? Yes, sir, near the south west corner. You there had some conversation? Yes, sir. With regard to Beebee? Yes, sir. I don't care for you to state what that was; had Beebee then been brought down stairs? No, sir. Where were you, and where was Maultsby, at the time Beebee was brought down stairs? Well, at the first time Beebee came into our view me and Maultsby walked down towards the south east corner of the market. Outside or inside? Outside and looked through the arch. Through which arch? Through the corner of the arch on the south side. When you got there and looked through the arch where was Beebee? Beebee was on the outside, on the pavement. Beebee had got out of the market house? Yes, sir. You say, then, while Beebee was up stairs John Maultsby and yourself were outside of the market, near the western corner? Yes, sir. That you, together, yourself and John Maultsby, about the time you thought Beebee was being brought down, walked down on the outside of the market, on the pavement, to the south of the market, and when near the small southern arch, nearer the east front, that then Beebee had come down from the market and had got out on the pavement? Yes, sir. And Maultsby was at that time with you out there. Yes, sir, he was with me at that time. Did you see any rush made upon Beebee at all, either at that time or any other time? I saw the crowd was pretty close in advance. How far had you and Maultsby got before the pistol shot was fired which took Beebee's life? We were at the corner of the market house? Which corner? The south east corner. Yourself and Maultsby? At the time the pistol shot fired I don't know whether Maultsby was with me at that time. Was Maultsby engaged at all in that rush which was made upon Beebee? He was not. Where were you at the time the pistol shot was fired? Standing against the corner of the market house, on the outside, on the south side, against the south east corner rather. Do you know who shot the pistol? I do not. Did you see Beebee fall? I did not, sir. And I understand you to swear positively and distinctly that up to the time that Beebee had got out upon the pavement, and a very short time before the pistol shot was fired that Maultsby was with you there upon the southern pavement, outside of the market house? He was with me up to the time that Beebee was brought out on the pavement; I suppose he walked some seven or eight feet before he was shot, I can't say whether Maultsby was with me then or not; only when the boy was brought out on the pavement, he was

with me up to that time. Mr. Jones, I understand you are related to John Maultsby? I am. What is the degree of relationship? He is my first cousin. I am also told you are connected somewhat with the prisoner David Watkins? I am, sir. What is that connection? He is a brother-in-law of mine. You married his sister? I did, sir.

Cross-examination by the Counsel for the prosecution:

I understood you, Mr. Jones, that Beebee was in your employment at the time he was killed? He was. I understand you went to the market house for the purpose of giving bail for him? I did, sir. Was there any understanding between you and Mr. Maultsby that you were both to go his bail? No, sir. You found Maultsby at the market house when you got there? I did. Why didn't you go up stairs where the trial was going on? I understood they would not let any person go up. Did you attempt to go up? I did not. How did you expect to give bail down stairs without going before the magistrate? I saw the crowd there, and I expected that they would not allow the crowd to go up. You didn't apply to go up at all? No, sir. Those who were connected with the case were admitted weren't they, the witnesses and other persons connected with the case? I don't know whether they were or not. You didn't know that the trial went on up there? No, sir, I did not. So you knew as well that the witnesses were admitted to the trial as you did that the trial went on? I would suppose that they would be, I did not attempt to go up. You went there for the purpose of standing his bail? I did, when a man is convicted and sent to jail, a man can give bail for him as well then as before he is sent to jail. You expected to give bail for him after he was in jail? Yes, sir. What did you go to the market house then for? I went down to see if they would take bail after the trial. If you went to the market for the purpose of giving bail, I don't see why you didn't go up stairs and offer yourself as bail, and if you went down intending to stand his bail, after he was brought out, I don't see why you went to the market house at all? I understood the trial was to be at four o'clock; I went down there a few minutes before four, and the trial was over. He was coming down when you got there? No, sir, he was not coming down. He hadn't come out of the room where the trial was going on up stairs? No, sir. And you made no attempt to go up? No, sir. You didn't notify any officer that you had come there for bail, and therefore desired to go through the crowd? No more than I told to Mr. Bond that morning that I wanted to give bail. I understood you to say there was no understanding between you and Maultsby to that effect? No, sir, not before he got to the market. You say when you came to the market you came down Hay street? I came down the main street. You entered at the western arch of the market house? I did, sir. You passed through to the eastern right straight? Yes, sir. At that time Archy had come down stairs? No, sir. In passing there you remember Capt. Tolar and Lutterloh and Leggett, and E. P. Powers together? Yes, sir. They were standing in the east end of the market together? Yes, sir. Who do you remember seeing us pass? I saw a good many others, but I didn't notice who they were, You remember distinctly of seeing them? Yes, sir. And remember no other persons? No, sir, I remember no other person. Have you ever heard them say since they were standing there at the time? No, sir. Have you read any of the testimony in which it was told that they were standing out there? I don't know that I have. Your recollection now of where those four men were standing together is predicated upon what you remember of it at the time? Yes, sir. And you state distinctly that you passed from the market house and with the exception of stating the fact that those four men were standing together, you cannot state a single other while you were in that market house, of any other group that was standing together, in like manner? No, sir. There must have been some peculiarity about that group that distinguished them from the others? I rubbed right by them, There was sufficient in that group to attract your attention to them, whereas you saw no other group in the market house; how many other persons were in the market house do you suppose? I don't know how many persons, probably fifty or sixty. Did you pass through and go out on the pavement on the east end? Yes, sir. When you got to the east end, the carriage, you say, was in the act of driving off? Yes, sir. And Maultsby was standing near it? Yes, sir. Was Bond at the carriage? Bond was somewhere close about the carriage. Was Maultsby closer to Bond, or the carriage? I don't remember, sir. Were they both in your view at the same time, Maultsby and Bond? Yes, sir. You say that as the carriage drove off Maultsby turned back and joined you? Yes, sir. You then walked around to the southern side of the market house? Yes, sir. Did I understand that when you got to the south east corner of the market house, you walked on up to the west end, on the pavement? Yes, sir. You walked up there in conversation with Maultsby? Yes, sir. And you say that from the time that Maultsby went to the carriage, or came from the carriage, until the time you came back to the little arch, and looked in and saw Archy come down stairs, and saw Archy come out of the arch, Maultsby was not out of your presence? He was not, sir. As to what became of him after that you don't know? No, sir. Why was it you lost sight of him then? When the cry was given to shoot the boy, I was looking out for myself, I didn't look out for any one else. You say that Maultsby was not engaged in the rush? He was not. There was a rush was there? I guess there was. I wan't to know whether there was a rush for him to be in? I could not see, from where I was. Then how could you see he was not in it; if there was no rush what do you mean by answering the question that he was engaged in a rush? I saw that the crowd, when he came out of the market house was pretty close in advance of him; the cries was given to kill the boy Beebee, Maultsby was with me up to that time. Did you see any rush? I did not, sir. Then you can't say that John Maultsby was not engaged in the rush, if there was a rush. He may have been or may not have been, I didn't see the rush. It there was a rush there you didn't see it? I did not. But you have already sworn that Maultsby was not engaged in it; you don't know anything at all about where Maultsby was, after the prisoner passed out? No, sir. You say when you came back from the west corner, along the southern side of the market house, and you stopped at the arch on the south front? I did, sir. Was it looking through there that you saw Archy coming down? He was down. Down stairs and passing out of the eastern arch? Yes, sir. Was he in the very act of passing through the large arch, when you saw him? Yes, sir, coming out. Just coming out? Yes, sir. Was there no attempt made to seize him there at that time? Not at that time. Did you see Tom Powers, then? I didn't see him that day. Did you see at the time that Archy passed out of the arch, or just after he got on the pavement in front of the

market house, anybody make a demand, and could you hear anybody say "he is my prisoner?" No, sir. Any words similar to that? No, sir. Anything in the nature of a demand or request that the prisoner should be given up from any quarter? No, sir. You are not deaf? No, sir. Could you have heard a noise in ordinary conversation, from the place where you were, supposing the voice to be uttered at the eastern arch? I don't know that I could, there was so much tramping. You think the voice would have been drowned? Yes, sir. Was the tramping the only noise? There was a good deal of talking. In a loud tone of voice? Tolerable. An excited tone? No, sir. You heard nothing like demanding the prisoner? I did not. You heard nothing like the sheriff ordering the policemen to use their clubs? No, sir. You didn't hear the sheriff tell Monk or Tom Powers to go away? No, sir. Or use any other expression in the way of forbidding the crowd to press upon them. No, sir. You heard nothing of that sort? No, sir. And you say you didn't see Tom Powers that day? I didn't see Tom Powers that day as I remember of. Have you tried to remember? I have. You have no recollection of having seen Tom Powers that day? No, sir. When you were looking through this little arch, did you see what had become of the group that had attracted your attention so particularly, in the market house, when you passed through; I mean the group consisting of Tolar, Legget, Lutterloh and E. P. Powers—did you see what had become of that group? No, sir, I didn't see them any more, after I passed them. You saw none of these men in the crowd anywhere, after that? I didn't notice them at all. Did you see any one with weapons on that day? No, sir. Didn't John Maultsby have a weapon on that day? Not that I know of. Did you hear him say he had one? No, sir. Did you see any signs of any? No, sir. Did you hear any of these prisoners at the bar say they had a weapon on that day? I never have. Did you see any one with a weapon that day at the market house, at or about the time of the killing? I did not, sir. Did you leave the market house before the pistol was shot? No, sir. You were standing still at that little arch, on the south face, near the south east corner when the pistol fired? Yes, sir. Could you see the smoke from the point where you stood? I did not, sir. You heard the report, only? I heard the report. You could not see the flash and the smoke? No, sir. Did you hear any exclamations in the crowd, immediately after the firing? I did. What was it? I heard some person remark that Capt. Tolar shot him. Did you hear it from more voices than one? I did, sir, several voices. You heard it distinctly? I did. It was immediately after the shooting was it? Yes, sir. Did you hear any exclamation immediately before the shooting? I did, sir. Did you hear any such cries as kill him? I heard the cries of kill him. Did you hear any such cry as "shoot him," or was it "kill him?" it might have been both. That was immediately before the shooting? Yes, sir. And immediately afterwards you heard several persons in the crowd say, loud enough to be heard, "Capt. Tolar killed him?" Yes, sir, it was cried out there. Did you see Capt. Tolar? I did not, I saw him after the shooting. How long after, before he left the ground? No, sir, I left there soon after the shooting, and went on back to my work. Did you hear any such expression "as he'll get away?" No, sir. When was the next time you saw Maultsby, after the shooting? I don't know whether I saw him that day or the next. You didn't see him immediately after the shooting? James Nixon brought Watkins out of the crowd, he had hold of him soon after he shot; and I went up to Watkins, and grabbed hold of him and told him to behave himself, Nixon shoved me off, and Maultsby came up at the time, he said, go away, I can manage him. Nixon said so? Yes, sir. What was Monk doing? He was rearing and raging. What was he saying? I don't remember, he was cursing and swearing; I don't know that he was cursing anybody in particular. Did he have any weapon? I don't know that he did. You saw no weapon? No, sir. About that time you say you saw Maultsby? Yes, sir. And the last time you remember seeing him before the shooting was just as Archy was clearing the arch? Yes, sir. Where were you standing when you saw him that last time? On the south-east corner. Still at the same spot? Yes, sir. Did Maultsby come up? I reckon he did. Did he appear to be in motion or was he stationary when you saw him. He walked up, I stepped a few steps myself, towards Watkins. Was it immediately after the shooting that Monk was rearing about there? Some half a minute or minute probably. Was it after you had heard these cries of "Capt. Tolar shot him?" First, I saw Watkins, I think then after I saw him I walked around the crowd, and I heard the cries of "Capt. Tolar shot him." You don't suppose the whole thing was a minute after the shooting, as I understand you? No, sir. It was all very quick? Yes, sir. Did you and Maultsby leave then? We did not, he parted from me. Maultsby is your first cousin? He is, sir. Is there any great intimacy between you and Maultsby, or is it the ordinary cousinly kindness? That is all. You married Monk's sister? I did, sir. What is Monk's real name? William David Watkins, or David William Watkins, I am not certain about it. You say as you passed through the market house you heard from some quarter when you first got there, that the boy ought to be killed? Was it from a single voice, or from several voices? It was from one or two. Was it the same from both? Yes, sir. Was it near the group of Leggett and Lutterloh, etc. Yes, sir. About the time you were passing there? Yes, sir. I wish you to describe as well as you can, the nature of the movement of the crowd as Archy passed out of the main arch, whether there was any movement towards him by the crowd or not? They were advancing pretty closely on him. You heard no cries at that time? No, sir. You simply noticed that they were close on him, sir, and after the crowd got out there were cries of "kill him?" Yes, sir. I understand you to say you saw saw no one with any weapon there that day? I did not, sir. That you have no reason for knowing that there was any weapon there? No, sir. Do you know whether John Maultsby has any pistol? I do not, sir. Do you know whether Capt. Tolar habitually wears a pistol or did at that time? I am not very well acquainted with Capt. Tolar. That is not an answer to my question. I don't know, sir.

Re-direct examination by the Counsel for the accused:

Mr. Jones, I think I understood you to convey this idea, in your testimony at first that up to the time that Beebee had cleared the arch, and got upon the pavement that whether a rush was made at him you don't know but if a rush was made, you do know that Maultsby was not a party to it? At the time Beebee came out of the arch Maultsby was with me. And if any such rush was made up to that time, you know that Maultsby was not engaged in it. He was not engaged up to the time that Beebee came out, but after that I don't

know. And it was about that time you first heard the cries of kill him? After the crowd got outside. Then up to the time the crowd got outside, and Beebee got outside, and the cries of "kill him," were heard by you, Maultsby was not a party to any rush, or any advance upon him which may have been made. Maultsby was with me up to the time that Beebee passed out of the main arch, was coming out of the main arch, the crowd was advancing on him then; is all I know about Maultsby. Maultsby was not in that crowd that was advancing on him? Not at that time he was not. You say after the pistol shot was fired, you then passed around the crowd. Yes, sir. Which side of the crowd did you pass around? On the south side, or the south east side? Where did you go then? I went into the crowd far enough to see Beebee. You passed from the southern corner around the South eastern part of crowd, then into the crowd, until you got where you could see Beebee? Yes, sir. When was it you heard those cries of Capt. Tolar had shot him, where did you get before you heard the cry first? I was coming around the crowd. Had you penetrated the crowd upon that eastern front before you heard that Capt. Tolar shot him, do you recollect whether you were on the Southern south eastern, or eastern part of the crowd? I was on southeast part? At that time I understand you to say you didn't see Tolar? At that time I did not. You don't know whether Tolar was there or not? No, sir, not at that time. Where did these voices proceed from what part of the crowd? I really don't know, it was in amongst the crowd some where. And it was after you had walked from the south eastern corner, off of the pavement and you were on the south east side of the crowd, that you first heard the cries? I had walked some six or eight steps. How long was it, I don't expect you to answer with perfect accuracy, how long was it after you heard the report of the pistol, before you heard the first cry that Capt. Tolar has shot him? A minute or so. How was that first cry, do you remember, was it a loud cry, or was it in an ordinary tone of voice? Some one sung out Capt. Tolar was the man that shot. That you say was a minute or a minute and a half after the shooting.

The Counsel for the prosecution said he didn't say anthing about a minute and a half.

The Counsel for the accused said he said a minute or so, which would include two minutes, and he put it at a minute and a half at the smallest.

Re-direct examination resumed:

What did you mean when you said a minute or so? I was not exactly positive; it may have been more than a minute, a second or two more, or it may have been less. You saw no weapons there in the hands of anybody? I did not. You have no reason to know that any person had one? No, sir. You had no weapons yourself? No, sir. Mr. Jones, did I understand you to say that at the time of the shooting, you were standing against the wall? At the time the pistol fired I was. Which way were you facing? I don't exactly know. Did you move from your position against the wall immediately, upon the crack of the pistol, or did you stand there after a little while, to see what the result of the pistol shot had been? Very quick after the pistol fired, Watkins was brought out of the crowd by Nixon; then I advanced towards Watkins, and Nixon shoved me off, then I walked around the crowd, and the cries was given. Then you waited there at your place at the market house until Watkins was brought out? Yes, sir. And until you had gone up there, and told him to be quiet? Yes, sir. And until after Nixon had made the reply that he could take care of him? Yes, sir.

And after that occurred, then you commenced walking around the crowd? Yes, sir. And it was after you had commenced walking around the crowd, that you then first heard the exclamation Tolar shot him? Yes, sir. Now you say, when you first passed through the market house, in going down that portion of the pavement which was near where John Maultsby was, and where the carriage was, that in that group of Leggett, Lutterloh, &c., that you there heard some one say he ought to be killed? Yes, sir. On which side of that group did you pass coming east, did you pass them on your left, or did you leave them to your right? I think they were on my right, I am not positive about it. Do you know whether that exclamation that he ought to be killed, proceeded from the group, or somebody at the front, or somebody at the right or rear? It was in amongst the crowd there. Did I understand you to mean in reply to the question which was asked upon the cross-examination, that those men Leggett, Lutterloh and E. P. Powers and Tolar, were standing off as a distinct party, entirely separate from the balance of the crowd? They were standing about two steps from the main part of the crowd. And all around them was the main body of the crowd? Off a little; about two steps. How many persons were around there Mr. Jones? There was some fifty or sixty I suppose. Do you know whether that exclamation, that he ought to be killed, arose from the group, or whether it arose from those fifty or sixty persons? I can't say, wherever it came from, it was close to me as I passed the crowd.

Questioned by the Commission.

Did you see Mr. Samuel A. Phillips, at the moment the pistol was fired? I did not, sir.

The Commission here took a recess of five minutes, after which—

MATTHEW MORGAN was called, who, having been duly sworn, on Saturday the 24th instant, testified as follows:

Examined by the Commission.

Were you at the market house in Fayetteville, on the day, and at the time one Archy Beebee, or Archy Warden was killed? I was, sir. State on what day, and at what hour of the day the killing of Archy Beebee occurred? It was about four o'clock I think, in the afternoon of the eleventh of February. Did you see William J. Tolar there that day? Yes, sir. Did he have any weapon? He did, sir. Describe the weapon that he had? A pistol. What sort of a pistol? What I call a navy pistol; I don't know the kind myself. A revolving pistol? Yes, sir, as nigh as I could see. How long was it before the killing of Beebee, that you saw Tolar for the first time, with a pistol; one minute? More than a minute, I suppose about five or ten minutes. You saw him with a pistol five minutes before Beebee was killed? Yes, sir, I reckon about five. Did you see him during the whole time—during those five minutes? Yes, sir. What was he doing with the pistol? What attracted my attention, he had it like he was going to shoot, and I watched him to see whether he did or not. Was it cocked? If it was I didn't see it. Was it presented? He had it in his hands so (represents holding up the pistol with the breech in his right hand, the muzzle in his left, in front of him.) Was it presented towards Beebee? In that direction. Where were you standing at the time you first saw Tolar with a pistol? I was standing at the north side of the arch. The north side of what arch? The main arch, on the east side. On the pavement or inside of the market house? On the pavement. Were you stand there at the last time you saw him with it? Yes,

sir. State your position with reference to Tolar, where was Tolar? He was a little to my left, sort of in front. In front and to your left? Not exactly in front, and he was not behind. How far was he to your front? I suppose about three feet, in a straight line. How far to your left? Just right on my left side. Could you have reached him? No, sir. Was he on the pavement? Yes, sir. Where was Beebee? Beebee was near about the little arch. Directly in front of you? He was not exactly in front of me, you may say he was in front, because I was looking right towards him. Was he on the outside of the pavement or next to the market house? He was about near the middle of the pavement. And you were standing on the edge, next to the market house? Yes, sir. Was he directly in front of Tolar? I think he was a little more to the right. Was Tolar on the pavement or off? I think, sir, he was on the pavement, I am certain he was, right along the edge, somewhere. Where was Tolar standing when you first saw him with a pistol? He was standing right to my left. Was he standing in the same place when you last saw him with a pistol? Yes, sir. Was Tolar standing still all the time you saw him? He just sort of moved a little, not giving backwards or forwards. Moving his body, do you mean, without moving his feet? Yes, sir. Did he move his feet all? His body was working, that was all I noticed. Did Tolar fire the pistol he had? He did not, sir. At any time while you were looking at him? No, sir. What did he do with the pistol when you last saw him; what was he doing with it? He had it in his hand. Was that before Beebee was shot? Yes, sir. Did you see him with the pistol after Beebee was shot? I don't recollect whether I did or not; after he was shot they all crowded up around, and I hadn't my eyes off of the man. Do you know where the pistol is now that Tolar had on that day? No, sir. Have you at any time heard Tolar or either of the other prisoners now on trial or arrested for trial say where the pistol can be found? No, sir. Did you see Archy Beebee at the time he was killed? Yes, sir, I saw him when he fell. You saw him at the very moment he fell? Yes, sir, I think I saw him at the moment he fell. Were you looking at him? I was looking at Tolar till the pistol fired, and then I looked to Beebee. What attracted your attention to Beebee after the pistol fired? I heard the pistol and then I heard some of them say "he has killed him." What was his position at the moment he fell with reference to the market house? It was sort of rearing like he was trying to get away. Where was he? He was at the corner of the little arch. Near the south side of the little arch? Yes, sir. Was there more than one pistol fired at or about the time that Archy Beebee was killed? No, sir, only one that I heard. Did you see any other person beside Tolar with a pistol in that crowd before Beebee was killed? No, sir. Did you see any other person or persons with a pistol or pistols at the time Beebee was killed? No, sir, not until after he was killed? Did you see any other pistol on the ground there where Beebee was killed immediately after the pistol was fired that day? I did, sir. In whose hands was that pistol? Mr. Phillips. Where was Phillips at that time? He was standing out, sort of going towards his store. How long was that after Beebee was killed? It was some two or three minutes. Had he the pistol in his hand? Yes, sir. Which hand? In his right hand, I think. What sort of a pistol was it? It was one of those large, long pistols, like they have in the army. The same sort of a pistol you saw in Tolar's hands? I don't think it was. Was it the same size? If any thing

It might have been a little bigger than Tolar's. When did you first think it was a little bigger? The reason I thought so was because you showed me one and it was about the same sized pistol. Wasn't the pistol Tolar had the same sort too? I think his looked like it had silver around the edges. What was Phillips doing with that pistol when you saw him? He was not doing anything only he had it in his hand going towards his store, he didn't go far before he put it away. How far was he from you when you saw him put that pistol up? Not very far. How far? I could not say exactly. Was he twenty feet? No, sir. Was he ten feet? Something like ten feet, I reckon. Describe his position? I don't think I could. Why not? Because his face was down towards the store. His face was towards the store? Yes, sir. He was on what street? On Hay street.

Thomas A. Hendricks, a witness for the defence, having been first duly sworn, testified as follows:

By Counsel for accused:

Mr. Hendricks, where do you reside? In Fayetteville, sir. State of North Carolina? Yes, sir. How long have you been residing in Fayetteville? Ever since the latter part of 1845. What is your business? Manufacturer. Were you in Fayetteville on the day Archy Beebee was killed? Yes, sir. Were you at the market house on that day? No, sir. Were you a member of a coroner's inquest that sat upon the body of Archy Beebee to ascertain the manner in which he came to his death. Yes, sir. At what time did it commence? In the afternoon. On the day he was killed? Yes, sir. Did they make up their verdict on that day? No, sir, the third day. They made up their verdict on the third day—you met in the afternoon you say? Yes, sir. And when did you adjourn; when was your first adjournment? That evening. To meet when? To meet at ten o'clock next day. Did you meet then? Yes, sir. How long did you remain in session? Until dinner recess. Do you know what hour? I think between one and two. To meet again when? At three I think? And you met? Yes, sir. And when did you make up your verdict? We signed it on the third day. Now I desire sir, to confine your attention to the second day. The second day, sir, very well. Was Sam Phillips a member of that coroner's inquest? Counsel for prosecution: Stop. Counsel for accused: What we propose to prove is matter of fact, whether Sam Phillips was acting, not whether he was sworn, but whether he was there that day acting as a member of the coroner's inquest.

Counsel for prosecution: And we say in reply that it makes no difference. There is a record in existence relating to this matter, and the rule of law is, that the best evidence must be produced. The record that exists, of the proceedings of that jury, is the best evidence, and if the defence want the evidence, they ought to produce that paper. They cannot introduce secondary evidence in the shape of parole testimony so long as that record, showing the proceedings of the jury exists.

Counsel for accused: We are not aware of any principle of law, such as that laid down by Colonel Haywood. We insist that a matter of fact may be proven as fact; but when a paper is spoken of, the rule of law is, that the contents of that paper cannot be proved except by the introduction of the paper itself. That is the best evidence of what is in the paper, and the law respects nothing outside of that evidence. There is nothing clearer than that. The fact that Mr. Phillips was there that day cannot be produced in

evidence? That there was an inquest that day, or that he was not there is not admissible? Suppose he had not been there, I suppose this witness may tell he was not there; and if there was an inquest, or something in the nature of an inquest, it is a substantial fact, and no paper is necessary. To prove that fact, the paper is not the best evidence—it is not the best evidence of the fact. Of the contents of that paper it is the best evidence.

That a deed exists,—as that lands have been sold for instance,—(not that the deed was executed) can be proved; but the contents of that deed, the purport of that deed, can only be proved by the introduction of the deed itself. But in any other point of view it strikes me that this testimony is clearly admissible. Mr. Phillips himself has been introduced about this matter; he himself has testified about it; we asked him specific questions about this matter; put him on his guard that we were going to contradict him about this matter. We put him on his guard that he was going to be contradicted. We put to him certain specific questions which he answered. The Counsel for the prosecution asked him questions, and we put him on his guard about these questions; and now, we propose by this witness, to prove that he did not make correct answers to these questions. In either aspect of the case this testimony is admissible.

Counsel for prosecution: No amount of sophistry can get over this fact—that if Phillips was a member of that coroner's jury, the records are the best evidence of the fact, and according to the rule of law the best evidence mu t be produced. No secondary evidence will be admitted. I object to any thing of the sort.

The Commission: The Court will retire to consider the question.

The Commission was then cleared for deliberation, and, after some time so spent, was re-opened; when

The Judge Advocate stated that the Commission sustains the objection of the Counsel for the prosecution.

By Counsel for accused:

Mr. Hendricks, on the day that you have already spoken of at the store of Samuel A. Phillips in the town of Fayetteville, did you have any conversation with Samuel A. Phillips in relation to this matter? Yes, sir. Well, sir, just give the Court that conversation.

Counsel for prosecution: I object to it, sir.

Counsel for accused: Do you object to that?

Counsel for prosecution: Yes, sir.

Counsel for accused: Well, sir, let us have the grounds for your objection.

Counsel for prosecution: The declarations of Mr Phillips are proposed to be given in evidence; in the first place that is what I object to.

Counsel for accused: Can't we impeach him as a witness?

Counsel for prosecution: You can't impeach him in that way.

Counsel for accused: We think we can.

Counsel for prosecution: Very well; I understand, I think, what the gentlemen are aiming at, and, if the Court pleases, it may be as well to state our position upon it. Upon the examination of Mr. Phillips, the cross examination in this case, if the Court will remember, he was asked if, at a certain time mentioned, he had not in a conversation with this witness used certain expressions with respect to the proceedings before the coroner's inquest. I contend that according to the rules of law, that question, having been asked by the defence and answered by Phillips, they are bound by his answer, and ought not to be permitted now to introduce evidence, for the purpose of contradicting him. The rule of law is, that if Counsel has cross-examined a witness as to a collateral fact which is not immediately material to the issue, he is bound by the witness' answer, and cannot raise a collateral issue here by introducing other evidence to prove the existence or non-existence of the fact. Now, mark me,—if, in the cross-examination, Phillips had been questioned as to whether he had made different statements with regard to the main issue, stating time, place and circumstance,—or if he had not made certain particular statements, giving time, place and circumstance, and he had replied thereto, then evidence might be introduced for the purpose of contradicting him. The rule of law is, when, with regard to a collateral question, such as this one was, an inquiry is made of the witness on cross-examination, the Counsel asking the question is bound by his answer, and cannot introduce testimony for the purpose of contradicting him. The rule is evidently one of convenience; for, if Phillips could be examined as to a collateral conversation with regard to something else, to wit: the coroner's inquest, and then evidence could be introduced to contradict him, of course Phillips would have to be allowed an opportunity of rebutting, and there would never be an end to this thing. Here is what is stated in Greenleaf, p. 496, § 409. "In Cross-examinations, however, the rule is not [applied with the same strictness as in examinations-in-chief; but, on the contrary great latitude of interrogation is sometimes permitted by the Judge, in the exercise of his discretion, where, from the temper and conduct of the witness or other circumstances, such course seems essential to the discovery of the truth, or where the cross-examiner will undertake to show the relevancy of the question afterwards by other evidence. On this head it is difficult to lay down any precise rule. But it is a well established rule, that a witness cannot be examined as to any fact which is collateral and irrelevant to the issue merely for the purpose of contradicting him by other evidence, if he should deny it, thereby to discredit his testimony. And, if a question is put to a witness, which is collateral or irrelevant to the issue, his answer can not be contradicted by the party who asked the question, but is conclusive against him." Now if the Court pleases, the present case is this—the Counsel for the defense asked an irrelevant, collateral question of one of our witnesses,—what was this?—whether he had not at a certain place, at a certain time, in a conversation with Hendricks, stated something in regard to the Coroner's inquest; whether he had'nt made a certain statement in regard to the inquest, and he answered it,—it was a collateral and irrelevant question, and we insist upon it, that according to the rule laid down, the Counsel for the defense can't go on here with evidence of a collateral character which we in return will have to rebut by collateral evidence. Here is a case cited by Greenleaf, (p. 499, § 443, n. 7,) where it is stated, "thus, if he," (the witness) "is asked whether he has not said to "A", that a bribe had been offered to him by the party by whom he was called, and he denies having so said, evidence is not admissible to prove that he did so state to A." In another case, Greenleaf, (same page, section and note as last quotation,) states,— "when a witness was asked, on cross-examination, and for the sole purpose of affecting his credit, whether he had not made false representations of the adverse party's responsibility, his negative answer was held conclusive against the party cross examining." The mass of cases that might be cited on the point is enormous,

and the only nicety is, *when is a question collateral?* That is the only point. Now the rule confines relevancy to such question as these—if any question had been asked Phillips, with regard to previous statements about this trial, and he had said he had not made such statements, then evidence could be introduced for the purpose of contradicting him. If he had been asked whether he had been bribed, and he had said "No," evidence could be introduced to show that he was bribed. But when a collateral question is asked with regard to a conversation about a *collateral* matter, as in the case we have referred to,—where a man was asked if he had not stated that "A." had offered him a bribe, and he said not,—the answer is final. The rules of evidence are very plain; the first is, that the testimony must be relevant to the issue. The defence in cross-examination may ask collateral questions, with the view of showing that the witness' evidence is not to be relied upon. But there is a limit even to that; and when the defence asks an independent, collateral, irrelevant question with regard to something else, and the response of the witness is given on that point, it must be final, otherwise there would be no end to the trial. Of course matters of this kind are always more or less points in the discretion of the Court; but it must be apparent to the Court that what Mr. Phillips said, with regard to the conduct of the coroner's inquest, can have no bearing on the question whether Tolar and these persons charged with this crime, committed it. The Court will remember the question to Mr. Phillips,—the question was, whether he hadn't at a certain time and place, called upon Hendricks, and made a certain statement with regard to the proceedings before the inquest.

Counsel for accused: If the Court please :—I always dislike, very much indeed, to have to make any objection to testimony brought forward on the prosecution in Courts-martial or Military Commissions: and I always dislike very much to have these objections made to questions which I ask.

Counsel for prosecution: If the Court please,—I would prefer that the witness should withdraw for the moment.

Counsel for accused: I have no objection. Witness then withdrew.

Counsel for accused continues: As the Counsel has well remarked in his conclusion, these are matters always more or less addressed to the discretion of the Court. I am rather surprised, I must say, that such objections as these are being taken to testimony at this stage of the proceedings. All that we ask, all that we desire, is, that this matter may be fairly and impartially investigated. If these are the guilty men, and if the proof shall demonstrate it, let them be convicted, and let them suffer; but in God's name, if they be not the guilty men, why shut the door to the inquiry as to who are the guilty parties? There are some questions which appear to be collateral to the issue, but which are not collateral, and are directly pertinent. I admit the general rule of evidence, as stated by the Counsel, that if we shall cull out fairly collateral matter, we are bound by the answer of the witness, and we cannot contradict it. But is this collateral? Why if the Court will indulge me, just look at the nature of the defence. We come here, and we say that these men did not kill him, and that another man did. Is it not pertinent to the issue, to prove by any means that we can, that Samuel A. Phillips was the party who killed this man? Most clearly it is. Is it collateral to the issue that we shall show that Samuel A. Phillips had a pistol in his hand there that day, and that he discharged that pistol towards the head of Beebee, and then and there killed and murdered the man? Most certainly it is not collateral. What is the object with regard to the declaration of Phillips? It is to prove the same fact that we have attempted to prove by the declaration of witnesses from that stand. We asked Samuel A. Phillips a question as to whether he had not by his manner, conversation and declarations shown that he had killed this man Beebee? He says "no." Is that collateral? Then it is equally collateral, all the proof we have brought forward, to show the pistol in Phillips' hand, and to show the pulling of the trigger by Phillips. Suppose it appears now that, on the day after the killing, Phillips was nervous, that Phillips was uneasy, that Phillips was trying to suppress testimony, that he was making appeals to men not to examine testimony if they were friends of his, does it not tend directly to the establishment of the defence in this case? does it not tend directly to prove the fact that he was concerned in that killing? that he was the man that did it? Why, sir, to my mind it is perfectly irresistible. One is proof of facts, another of declarations, and if you exclude the declarations, to be consistent, the facts should be excluded; and the only testimony that could be offered then, that this Court could consider, would be as to the fact that Capt. Tolar did the shooting, and that would entirely exclude any evidence as to whether any other man did shoot him. Now, I confess that the distinction is nice sometimes, and one that a Court may not, in many cases, be able to see clearly at once. But it is a question involving the life or death of these men, and I hope and believe that the Court will consider this question well and thoroughly before they sustain the objection raised by the Judge Advocate. I must beg leave again to call the attention of the Court to the fact that one of the manifestations of our case is that Phillips killed Beebee, and any evidence that tends to establish that defence is directly pertinent to the issue, and is not at all collateral thereto. This is what we expect to prove by this witness; while the matter was fresh, while the affair was undergoing investigation, Phillips by his manner and by his conversation indicated as clearly as manner and conversation can indicate, that he was the guilty man, and that he desired to avoid the inquiry by the suppression of testimony.

The point will be found referred to in the reports of the Supreme Court of this State. The case is given in "North Carolina reports, vol. 2, p. 346." The judge who delivered the decision is one very well known to every member of this Court, the Hon. William Gaston. In that case, the general rule, as laid down by Col. Haywood, the Court admits. I will read all that is said on that point: (p. 352 N. C. Reports, vol. 2, Iredell,) "It is objected on the part of appellant that the Court below erred, in rejecting proper evidence, which was offered in his behalf. The case states that on the cross examination of Jacob Cluck and Daniel Cluck, witnesses examined on the part of the State to prove the first marriage of the defendant they were asked whether the prosecutor had not paid them for coming to the State as witnesses, to which question they replied that he had not, and that afterwards the prisoner called a witness, and proposed to ask him whether the said Jacob and Daniel Cluck had not told him that the prosecutor had paid them for coming to this State as witnesses. This question was objected to, and the Court sustained the objection. The case doesn't set forth for what purpose the question was asked, or on what ground it was overruled. If it was a proper question for any legitimate purpose, the refusal of the Court to let it

be proposed was error. It cannot be contended that" * * * * * * *

Counsel for prosecution:

Before you get through let me state that perhaps the defence does not understand my position. If Mr. Phillips had been asked "have you not upon some former occasion, stating time and place, said that Tolar didn't do this thing, and Phillips had replied " No,"—then evidence could have been introduced, to contradict him because it was pertinent to this issue. The case of Patterson I remember very well. The witness was asked whether he hadn't stated that a certain man had given him money to come from Georgia here to testify in a certain case of bigamy. The evidence to contradict the collateral questions in that case was not allowed. But the point I want to get at is this, if the question had been put to him whether he had not made different statements about the guilt of these parties, and the time and place named to him, and he had said he had not, then he could have been contradicted; but when the question is collateral it is treated differently. As it is law, I may as well state here, that if Phillips had gone through the streets of Fayetteville, and declared that he was the party guilty of shooting Beebee, it could not have been introduced as evidence, for the purpose of acquitting these parties.

Counsel for accused : Yes, but it could have been introduced in order to contradict him, that is the point. Hear Counsel read from some book, about impeaching the credit of witnesses.

"It is well settled that the credit of a witness may be impeached by proof that he has made representations inconsistent with his present testimony, and whenever these representations respect the subject matter in regard to which he has been examined, it never has been usual with us to inquire of the witness, before offering the disparaging testimony whether he has or has not made such representations." And the Court goes so far as to say that if a witness had made representation or statements inconsistent with those made on the stand in regard to a transaction, we were not even able to ask him whether he had made these statements. Now with respect to the collateral matters, we'll read on : " Of late, however, it is understood that this rule does not apply in all its vigor, when the cross examination is as to matters which, although collateral, tend to show the temper, disposition, or conduct of the witness in relation to the cause or the parties. His answers are not to be deemed conclusive, and may be contradicted by the interrogator . . . ." We put Phillips on his guard about the matter—we as much as intimated to him that we were going to contradict him about it; we put him fully on his guard, and therefore we have the right to show that he made representations here—that he made statements here—inconsistent with statements and representations which he made elsewhere; and about these representations and statements, we particularly and pointedly put questions, so that he might not be taken unawares by the evidence of the witnesses we were going to call in regard to that matter. Here in the case of Patterson, what Colonel Haywood says is correct, in part. These witnesses were asked whether they hadn't been paid to come there, and they stated they had not . . .

Counsel for the prosecution: Whether they had not stated they had been paid.

Counsel for accused: No, sir, that is not the point: I will read the given case again:

"The case states that on the cross examination of Jacob Cluck and Daniel Cluck, witnesses examined on the part of the State to prove the first marriage of the defendant, they were asked whether the prosecutor had not paid them for coming to this State as witnesses; to which question they replied that he had not."

Counsel for prosecution: Although the analogy is not strong, still there is a vast difference in the Courts of the different States.

Counsel for accused: It appears to me wonderful that it should be desired to strain the evidence as against men who are put upon trial for their lives. It is admitted now by the Counsel for the prosecution that the modern practice as laid down by Judge Gaston is against him.

Counsel for prosecution: I have admitted no such thing—I have never said so—and I object on the part of the government, to the statement that anything is being strained by the prosecution. Nothing has been strained—the prosecution has been conducted with the greatest leniency, and I am sure the defence has no reason to complain. Any such assertions as these I think it my duty to contradict promptly and emphatically. Nothing is strained. I lay down what I conceive to be the law, and in the best interests of justice, that a collateral, irrelevant question was asked in the cross examination of a witness and that the interrogator must be bound by the answer; and the rules of evidence are in no respect controlled or strained by the fact that men are on trial for their lives. * * * But as to my admitting that the law is now such as the Council states, the gentleman is totally and entirely mistaken; he misapprehended my statement: it was in an undertone, and not fully stated at all.

Counsel for accused: If I have misunderstood, I am willing to be corrected. We insist, however, that the rule is plain. Any other construction of the rule would put it out of the power of these men, who are on trial for their lives, to show what we regard as exceedingly material for the defence to lay down. This is the law as laid down by one of the greatest lawyers in the land;—one described by Mr. Webster as the greatest lawyer in the Congress of 1812, and one of the greatest judges in this or any other State.

Counsel for prosecution: Well, I object still; it now lies with the Court.

The Commission: We will retire to consider it.

The Commission was then cleared for deliberation, and after some time so spent, was re-opened, when

The Judge Advocate stated that the objection of the Counsel for the prosecution was sustained by the Commission.

The witness was now recalled and resumed his position upon the stand.

Judge Advocate: "I will state in presence of the witness that the objection to the question has been sustained."

Counsel for accused: I understand, may it please the Court, that the record is made up under the direction of the Court, and I would like to put the question in such a shape upon the record that it cannot be misunderstood. The question we desire to have inserted in the record is this: "In that conversation did or did not Samuel A. Phillips say to you, 'Mr. Hendricks, if you are a friend of mine, you will not examine the witnesses closely,' or words to that effect."

Counsel for prosecution: I object. If the witness were about to answer the question, it should certainly not be offered in such shape as to suggest the exact words of the answer. I think the question is an improper one. It seems to me that a question might be framed, of not so leading a character as for instance, ask the witness if he did not at the time and place and under the circumstances, mentioned in

Phillips examination, have a conversation with him, the subject matter being this coroner's inquest. If he says "yes" then the question might be put, "what was that conversation?" we would object to it even then, however, and do object to it in its present form.

Counsel for accused: The Court will perceive that all we desire is to get upon the record, the fact that we asked this witness a question to contradict a question that was asked of Phillips, and by him, (Phillips,) answered " nay." That this question was objected to, and ruled out by the Court. We wish to get upon the record, the fact that a question was ruled out, which would contradict a statement about which we had put Phillips on his guard.

Counsel for prosecution: I object again, so long as it has what he is expected to answer right on the face of it.

Counsel for accused: I think that the record should show that the question is more closely confined than as to a general conversation, or the substance of a general conversation, and to be directly in answer to a question which was asked Phillips, and by Phillips answered in the negative. I think that the reviewing officer should be able to see at a glance, the question that the defense wished to introduce, and the objection that was offered to it by the prosecution. The question was: "In that conversation did or did not Samuel A. Phillips say to you, 'Mr. Hendricks if you are a friend of mine you will not examine the witness closely,' or words to that effect."

Counsel for prosecution: We object to the question as being a leading question.

Judge Advocate: We object not merely to its being answered, but we object to the question as being a leading question, and an improper one.

Counsel for accused: Very well, sir, that is all we wished to say.

At 1.35, p. m., on motion, the Commission adjourned to meet on 27th, at 10 a. m.

RALEIGH, N. C., Aug. 27, 1867, 10 A. M.

The Commission met pursuant to adjournment.

Present: All the members of the Commission, the Judge Advocate, the Counsel for the prosecution, all the accused, and their Counsel.

The reading of the testimony taken yesterday was waived, there being no objection thereto.

Yesterday's proceedings were then read and approved.

WASHINGTON FAIRCLOTH, a witness for the defence having been first duly sworn, testified as follows:

Examined by the Counsel for the accused.

What is your name? Washington Faircloth. What is your age? Going on eighteen years old. Where do you live? I live in Fayetteville. Fayetteville, N. C.? Yes, sir. How long have you been living there? All my life. Were you in Fayetteville on the day Archy Beebee was killed? Yes, sir. Were you at the market house on that day? Yes, sir. At what time of the day did you go to the market house? About three o'clock I think. Was that before Beebee was carried up stairs? Yes, sir. Did you see him carried upstairs? Yes, sir. You saw him as he was carried up-stairs? Yes, sir. Where were you at that time? Out of the market house standing right under the edge of the market house. Which edge? By Becky Ben's stall. How long did you remain there? I remained there about five minutes. Where did you go from there? I went to Mr. Moore's store. Where is Mr. Moore's store? About four doors from the market. How long did you remain there at Mr.

Moore's store? Five minutes. Did you then return to the market house? Yes, sir. Where did you take your position, when you returned to the market house? At different places about the market house. Did you leave the market house any more until Beebee was brought down stairs? No, sir. Did you see Miss Massey and her mother go up stairs? Yes, sir. Did you see them come down stairs? Yes, sir. Where were you standing at the time Miss Massey and her daughter came down stairs? I was standing right at the edge of the market house. At which edge of the market house? The south edge. At which do you mean, the south edge? I mean where Beebee come down there. Get the places in your mind; towards the river from the market house is east; down towards the guard house is south; now which side were you standing on? The eastern side. Then you were standing on the eastern side of the market house? Yes, sir. Were you on the pavement, or off, or under the market house? I was just about the edge of it, and as she came down I walked to the edge of the pavement. Where did the ladies go when they came down? They went right down front st. Did they walk down? They rode down. Where was the carriage standing? Right in front of the market, about twenty feet from the pavement I reckon. Did you see them go out to the carriage? Yes, sir. Who went out with them? Mr. Bond; I don't recollect any person else. How long did the carriage remain there, after Mr. Bond and the ladies went out? About five or ten minutes I reckon. Who did you see go to the carriage during the time it was standing there? I didn't notice any more who went there. Was there any other person that you remember as being at the carriage at all except Mr. Bond? I don't think there was, I didn't notice particularly; I just noticed Miss Massey go to the carriage. How long was it after the carriage drove off before Beebee was brought down stairs? Just as the carriage turned to drive off he was coming down stairs. Now, where were you standing at the time Beebee made his appearance upon the landing of the stairs, coming down the steps? On the edge of the pavement. On which edge? The eastern edge. Opposite what arch, if any, of the market house? I was not opposite any arch; I was opposite the wall. Could you see Beebee? Yes, sir. When he was on the stair steps? Yes, sir. Which arch did you look through to see him? I looked through the one near the corner. The small arch on the eastern face down towards the south Gillespie street? Yes, sir. Did you see Beebee when he got upon the landing of the stairs? No, sir, I didn't see him when he stepped off the steps. I mean when he first came down and turned the corner coming down the steps, at that door at the market house, did you see him there? Yes, sir, just as he was coming out of the door. Who were with him at that time? Faircloth and Wemyss and Sheriff Hardie. Who is Faircloth? My father. Did you notice anything unusual in the crowd at that time? No, sir. Did you see Beebee from the time he reached the landing until he got down to the foot of the stairs? No. You didn't see him when he reached the foot of the stairs? No sir. Did you see him between the foot of the stairs and the eastern arch, as he turned out upon the pavement? No, sir, I didn't see him any more until he turned the corner. So you saw him upon the landing as he come down stairs, but you didn't see him after he had reached the foot of the stairs, and didn't see him any more until after they had turned out of the arch to go to the guard house? No, sir. Now at the time they turned to go to the guard

house when you caught sight of them again, where were you? Standing on the edge of the pavement. Where were you then with reference to the main eastern arch, were you opposite it towards the south, or towards the north of it, or where? I was right in front of it. And that was when Beebee turned down to go to the guard house? Yes, sir. Were you on the pavement or off? On the edge of the pavement. Well sir, what occurred at that place? Well, I seen the crowd rush at Beebee—I don't know who they were, and he went on about three foot further, and made some terrible efforts to get loose, and some body said "shoot the damned son of a bitch," and I seen Mr. Phillips draw out a pistol, and he cocked it as he brought it up and he held it so, (witness represents Phillips with a pistol presented, wavering in his hand,) and he sort of steadied it, and then I turned my head, and I seen John Armstrong about ten feet in front of me, towards Davis' tin shop; and he fired it, and the smoke was all in my face and his face, then I walked around and saw Monk Julia trying to get at him to cut him with a knife, and he was prevented by Mr. Nixon. He went down the pavement some distance, and you say he made struggles as if to get loose? Yes, sir. And directly after he fell and went down, and as he raised up, the pistol fired? Yes, sir. Now at the time he was fired upon, where was he? He was right even with the corner of the market, about a foot and a half of being even with it. Was he nearer the market house, nearer the center of the pavement, or nearer the edge? Nearer the edge I reckon, he was about three feet on the pavement. Now Mr. Faircloth, just at that time when Beebee had raised straight and when the pistol shot was fired, where were you standing? On the edge of the pavement. At what place? Right in front of the wall that separates the two arches; the little one and the big one. You say that you saw Sam Phillips? Yes, sir. And that he had a pistol? I seen him when he drew his pistol. How far were you off from Phillips? I was about two foot. Could you have touched him? Yes, sir. Were you to Phillips' right or to his left? To his left. You were to Phillips' left? Yes, sir. Were you directly to his left or to his left and rear, or to his left and front? To his left and rear. Was he on the pavement or off the pavement? He was on the pavement. Was he nearer the wall of the market, or nearer the center of the pavement, or nearer the outer edge of the pavement. Nearer the outer edge of the pavement; about three feet on the pavement. You say you saw him draw a pistol? Yes, sir. Where did he draw it from? From his left side. Did he cock it? He cocked it as he brought it up. And you saw him present it at Beebee? I saw him doing so, and he sort of steadied it, and I turned my head. So you saw him draw it from his left side, cock it as he drew it up, and saw him move it about so (representing); you saw him present it at Archy Beebee? I reckon he presented it at Archy Beebee. Was it in that direction? Yes, sir. That then you turned your head and looked off? Yes, sir. And at that instant the pistol fired? Yes, sir. That you heard the report? Yes, sir. That you saw the smoke; now where did that smoke arise from? From about where Phillips was standing, it went in my face and his face. Just at the point where Phillips was standing? Yes, sir. And the report, where did that sound from? It was a little to my right. To where Phillips was standing and there was the sound of the report, and there you saw the smoke of the pistol? Yes, sir. Right there? Yes, sir. Well, sir, what occurred after that time, did you see what Phillips did the with the pistol? He put it in his breast coat pocket, or in his vest, I don't know which. And returned it? Yes, sir. Which side did he return it to? To his left side. What became of you then, Mr. Faircloth? I went around to see if Beebee was hit, and I saw Monk Julia there trying to cut him with a knife, prevented by Mr. Nixon. Did you see any more of Phillips? No, sir, I don't recollect seeing him. Had you seen Capt. Tolar that day? Yes, sir. Where had you first seen him? At the market. What part of the market? He was standing about three feet from the market. Inside or outside? Outside. When you first saw him? Yes, sir. On the pavement or off the pavement? On the pavement. On the eastern side or on the western side, or southern or northern side? The eastern side. How long was that before Beebee was shot, that you saw him there? As Beebee was coming through the market from the stair steps. Did you see him any more after that? Yes, sir, I seen him standing there against the market. Did you see anything of Tom Powers there? Not that I recollect. Did you see anything of Ralph Lutterloh there? No, sir, I didn't see him. You don't remember to have seen him? No, sir. Do you remember to have seen Ed. Powers? No, sir, I don't remember to have seen him. Do you remember to have seen Mr. Leggett? No, sir. Or Sam Hall? No, sir. And your attention was directed to Phillips from the fact that you saw him draw a pistol and cock the pistol? Yes, sir. Do you know Phillips well? I know him well. How long have you known him? I have known him ever since I was big enough to know any body. Mr. Faircloth, have you any doubt about that matter? No sir. Have you no doubt about seeing Sam. Phillips draw that pistol and cock it? I am as certain I seen him do it, as I am sitting in this chair. And you say that all you have sworn to here to-day is the truth and nothing but the truth? Yes, sir. And about the matter you have sworn to there is no room for mistake? I don't understand you. Is there any room for your being mistaken about the facts you have sworn to here to-day? No, sir. How long did you remain there after the shooting? I remained there half an hour, I reckon. After the shooting? Yes, sir. Well, now, before the shooting did you hear any exclamations in the crowd, "kill him," "shoot him," or anything of that kind? Only I heard them, as he was making these efforts to get loose, I heard some body say, "shoot the damned son ot a bitch." Do you know who that was? No, sir. After the shooting occurred, did you, while you were there, at any time hear any body say who had shot him? I heard John Armstrong running around and say Capt. Tolar shot him. How long was that after the shooting occurred? About ten or fifteen minutes. Where did I understand you to say John Armstrong was at the time the shooting occurred? About ten feet in front of me, towards Davis's store. Immediately to your front, or to your front and right, or front and left? In front of me, as I turned my head. About ten feet in front of you towards Davis' tin shop, at that time you saw John Armstrong? Yes, sir. Do you know him well? Yes, sir. There is no doubt that he was there? Yes, sir. He was the man that attracted your attention away from Phillips at the time Phillips was firing? He was the only man I recollect seeing that I know. How came you to notice John Armstrong at that time? I knew him, and he was the only man I seen that way I knew, when I turned my head. How long had you known John Armstrong? I had known him three or four years. How did you come to turn

your head in that direction? Because Phillips drew the pistol; I always turn my head when any body shoots, and I turned my head then. When Phillips drew the pistol, fearing there was going to be shooting, you turned your head off from it? Yes, sir. And when you turned your head off, you saw Armstrong there, and noticed him because he was the only acquaintance of yours that was in the direction you were looking; do you know anything else about this matter, sir? No, sir. Are you related to Capt. Tolar? No, sir. To Tom. Powers? No, sir. To David Watkins? No, sir. To Ed. Powers? No, sir. To Ralph Lutterloh? No, sir. To Sam. Hall? No, sir. To John Maultsby? No, sir. To J. G. Leggett? No, sir. Are you related to any of the witnesses that you know, who have been summoned, or who have been brought here? Not that I know of. Have you ever told this matter to any one before coming up to Raleigh? Yes, sir. To whom did you tell it? James McRae in Fayetteville. When did you tell it to him? About two weeks ago. Under what circumstances did you tell it to Mr. McRae; did you go to him? No, sir, he came to me and asked me what I knew about it. And that was the first time you had ever told it? Yes, sir. Why didn't you ever tell before that time? Nobody never asked me. And you had never told it to any body before that time? No, sir. And you told James McRae because he came to you and asked you? Yes, sir. Did you know up to that time whether Mr. McRae was with the defence in this case? No, sir. Was that before the time or after the time that you understood, if you heard it at all, that Sam Phillips had turned State's evidence? It was about the time.

Cross examination by the Counsel for the prosecution:

How long was it before you were summoned to attend as a witness here that you informed Mr. James McRae of what the substance of your testimony would be? About two weeks. Before you were summoned? Yes, sir. I thought you said it was about two weeks before this day in your examination in chief; I understood you to say, when the Counsel for the defence was examining you, that it was about two weeks ago that you made this statement to Mr. McRae? Yes, sir, it was about two weeks. Now, I understand you to say to me, it was two weeks from the time you were summoned, which do you mean? I mean from the time I said at first. How many days since you were summoned? I was summoned Saturday. And you think it is not more than two weeks ago that you spoke of this matter first to Mr. McRae? No, sir. Had you heard at the time you made this communication to Mr. McRae that Sam. Phillips had turned State's evidence? I think I did. Don't you know you did? No, sir, I am not certain whether I did or not. You don't know which happened first, your communication to McRae or your hearing that Sam. Phillips had turned State's evidence? I think I heard he had turned State's evidence before. Don't you know you heard it first? I would not swear I did. Your best impression is, you did hear Sam. Phillips turned State's evidence first? Yes, sir. You never told this matter before you told it to McRae? No, sir. Did you go to him, or did he come to you? He come to me. Where were you? I was up town, about Mr. Lutterloh's store. Do you keep store there? No, sir. Which Lutterloh? Thomas Lutterloh. The father of the young man under arrest? Yes, sir. Have you any occupation in Fayetteville? No, sir, I light gas lights for my father sometimes; he is Captain of the police. You have no regular occupation? No, sir. It was at Lutterloh's store that McRae first approached you about this matter? About there, not right at his store. How far from it? It may have been twenty-five or thirty yards from his store, I was about the corner there somewhere. Had you been to Lutterloh's store that morning? Yes, sir. Was it in the morning or afternoon? It was in the afternoon. Had you been at Lutterloh's store that day? I had been about there. Had you been in the store? Not that I know of. Had you been lounging about there all day. Yes, sir, I live not far from his store Had you had any conversation with Thomas Lutterloh about this business? No, sir. You didn't speak a word about it? No, sir. No body told you Mr. McRae was going and see you? No, sir. No body told you to tell McRae what you knew about it? No, sir. Your father didn't tell you? No, sir, he didn't know I knew it, I reckon. You never told him nor your mother, nor any member of the family? No, sir. Until you met this man McRae? No, sir. That was after Sam Phillips had turned State's evidence? Yes, sir. You thought it was a very shabby proceeding on his part, didn't you? I don't know nothing about it. Haven't you any opinion about it? Not much. Give us what you have? I think it was a shabby trick. You have heard a good deal of that sort, haven't you? No, sir. Haven't you heard it said, at all? I have heard it said, but I haven't heard it said by a good many. You have heard it said by a very few? Yes, sir. Did you ever hear your father say so? No, sir, I hardly ever see my father in the day time. You may have heard him say it at night? I never heard him at night. You say you are almost eighteen years old? About eighteen. You were in Fayetteville the day this thing took place? Yes, sir. You went to the market house about three o'clock? Yes, sir, or may be a little later later or earlier. When you got there Archy was there, was he? No, sir. Where was he? He was at the guard house. Did you stay there until Archy was brought up from the guard house? I went to Mr. Moore's store, and a few minutes after I got back, I saw him come from the guard house. What does Mr. Moore keep for sale? He keeps whisky and tobacco, he did then. Did you go to take some? No, sir. You didn't take a drink that day? No, sir, and no other day. You never take anything? Not now, I used to take a little. What did you go to Mr. Moore's store for? I went down there to sit down and rest. You came back, and when you got back Archy Beebee was brought from the guard house. They were bringing him from the guard house, a few minutes after I got back. Where did you go when you got back? I went under the edge of the market. And stood by Becky Ben's stall? Yes, sir. And you saw Archy as he came to the market house? Yes, sir. Where were you standing? He had got to the market house when I went under the market house. Then you saw him from the pavement, and after you had got in the market house, he passed in and went up stairs? Yes, sir. Who was with him? Faircloth, Wemyss and Hardie. Any one else? I think Hornrinde was there; I don't know whether he went up stairs or not. Did you see any one else along with him that did not go up stairs? I seen Mr. Massey there, but I don't think they let him go up stairs. I mean any one in charge of the prisoner? I seen Mr. Bond. Then you saw Faircloth, Wemyss, Hardie, Bond, and may be Hornrinde? I think Hornrinde was there. Did they all go up stairs? I don't think they did. Which ones went up? Mr. Wemyss went up stairs, I think, and Mr. Hardie, and Faircloth, stopped at the door. Didn't Bond go up stairs? I don't know whether he went up stairs or not. After Archy had got up stairs, did you see the ladies come? They came before Archy I think. Are you certain about that? I am not certain about which went up first, I don't know exactly, I think they went up first though. You think the ladies had gone up stairs before Archy came? Yes, sir. Did you see the carriage when it came with them in it? No, sir. You didn't see that? No, sir. Did you see them get out of the carriage? No, sir, I did not. Did you see them on the pavement, coming towards the market house? No, sir, I seen them go up stairs, I didn't notice for the carriage. Did you see them on the pavement coming from the carriage? I seen them on the pavement, I don't know whether they were coming from the carriage or not. That was the first you saw of them? Yes, sir. You saw them pass through the market house, and go up stairs? Yes, sir. You don't know whether that was before or after Archy went up? I can't say for certain. Was it about the same time? About the same time. Try and recollect whether it was before or after. I think it was a little before. Did you stand by Becky Ben's stall when the ladies were going up stairs? Yes, sir. Until Archy had got up stairs? No, sir, I didn't stand there until he got up stairs, I stood there until he got to the foot of the stair steps. You were standing at Becky Ben's stall when the ladies went up? Yes, sir. You remember that with certainty? Yes, sir. And yon left Becky Ben's stall when Archy went up? Yes, sir. When you left Becky Ben's stall where did you go? I sat down there by Mr. Mitchell's stall. Where is Mr. Mitchell's stall? About the center of the market house. Which side, the north or south side? The north side. On the side opposite to Becky Ben's? Yes, sir. You sat down there for a while? Yes, sir. How long did you stay there? Half an hour I reckon. Where did you go when you left that point? I went to the edge of the pavement. Which arch did you go out of the market house? The eastern arch. While you were sitting at Mr. Mitchell's stall, about that half an hour, did you see any body in the crowd that you knew? The crowd was not about Mr. Mitchell's stall. Couldn't you see the crowd from Mitchell's stall? I didn't notice. What were you noticing? I was not noticing anything in particular. There was no crowd in the market house, was there? There was a crowd on the edge of the pavement, and under the edge of the market house. Under the eastern edge of the market house? Yes, sir. Couldn't you see them? I could have seen them if I had looked. Didn't you pass through them to go to the point where you were sitting, at Mr. Mitchell's stall? Yes, sir. Were you not pretty close to them then? Yes, sir. Didn't you see any body in that crowd that you knew? I didn't look to see. Did you shut your eyes? No, sir, I didn't look up in their faces. You can't say a soul that was in it at that time? No, sir. You swear it? No, sir, I would not swear there was no body there I did not know. You swear you can't name a person in that crowd, at that time? Becky Ben was in the crowd. But you did not see her out in the crowd, she was standing in her stall? Yes, sir. Who else was in the crowd—I am speaking of men? I didn't know any men, that I saw in the crowd at that time. You swear to the best of your recollection, you can't recollect a single man who was near you in that crowd? Yes, sir. When you left Mitchell's stall, you went through the crowd? Yes, sir. I went to the edge of the pavement. Didn't you see any body, as you passed there, that you recognized? Yes, sir. I seen Joe, Conner, and Alex. Faircloth, and several others. Let's have the several others? I seen Mr. Samuel Phillips. That was the first time you saw him that day? Yes, sir. Did you see him have a pistol then? No, sir. Where was he standing then? About the front of the big arch, about the middle of the pavement. Opposite the centre of it? About the middle of it. Well, sir, who else did you see besides Mr. Phillips—did you see Capt. Tolar? Not at that time, sir. Did you see Tom Powers? Not that I recollect of. Do you know him? Yes, sir. Did you see him under the market house at all, during the time we have been speaking of, the half hour you were sitting at Mitchell's stall, and the time you were standing at Becky Ben's stall? No, sir. Did you see Monk Julia? Yes, sir. You didn't see Captain Tolar at that time? No, sir. Not while you were standing at Becky Ben's stall, nor while you were sitting at Mitchell's stall, nor while you were passing through the crowd? No, sir. T. P. Powers? No, sir. You know him? Yes, sir. Did you see J. G. Leggett? No, sir. Do you know him? Yes, sir. Do you know Lutterloh? Yes, sir. Know them well when you see them? Yes, sir. Did you see John Maultsby? Yes, sir, I seen him. Where was he? He was standing under the market house. That is a big place, can't you tell me a little nearer than that? I can't tell you exactly. Was he in the crowd, or out of it? He was talking to some, I don't know who they were. They were strangers to you I suppose? I didn't look to see whether they were strangers or not, I passed on. You saw Maultsby? Yes, sir. You didn't look at the other men to see whether they were strangers or not? No, sir. Did you see Henry Sykes? I don't think I did. Did you see Sam Hall? No, sir. You saw Sam Phillips though? Yes; sir. How came you to see him? I don't know, sir, I seen him like I come to see John Maultsby, I reckon. How was it you missed seeing so many others? I seen others at that time, but I knew them well. Didn't you know Captain Tolar well? I didn't see him at that time. Did you know him well? Yes, sir. Do you know Thomas Powers well? I know him when I see him. Do you know him as well as you know Maultsby? No, sir. Do you know him as well as you do Sam Phillips? No, sir. Did you know Ed. Powers well? Yes, sir. Do you know him as well as you do Maultsby? Yes, sir. Do you know Leggett well? I know him when I see him? Do you know Lutterloh well? Yes, sir. As well as you do Maultsby and Sam Phillips? Yes, sir. You saw none of them? Not at that time. The only ones was you can speak of having seen are the two you first named; who were they? Joe Conner and Alex. Faircloth. And Maultsby and Sam Phillips? Yes, sir. Were Maultsby and Sam Phillips standing together? No, sir. They were standing apart. Yes, sir. You saw where Sam Phillips was, now why can't you tell me where Maultsby was? He was under the market house somewhere, about some of them stalls. About which stall? I don't know whose stall; there where old Mr. Leonard used to have his office. The east end of the market house? About the middle. How much of a crowd was there when you passed out of the market house, to go to the edge of the pavement? About a hundred, I reckon. Inside and out? Yes, sir. Were they all about the eastern end of the market? Yes, sir. Was a greater part of the crowd inside of the market or outside? A greater part about the stair steps I think. Any of them inside of Becky Ben's stall? Yes, sir. About the stair steps? Yes, sir. How many do you think were inside of the market house every

where? About twenty five, I reckon. How many of these were inside of Becky Ben's stall? Nearly all of them were inside of the stall, by the stair steps—the stall is right at the stair steps. You say nearly all of them were inside of that stall? They were there behind the stair steps, they were not in the stall. You said they were inside of the stall. They were around in behind the stall. Aint that inside of the stall? Yes, sir, I suppose so. Nearly all of them were between her stall and the stair steps, behind the stall? Yes, sir. Then there were very few or none standing in the aisle, that you had passed through? Yes, sir. How many were standing in the aisle that you passed through? I don't know, sir, there was right smart there. As many as there were behind the stall? I suppose there were. I thought you said the greater portion of those under the market were behind the stall? They were. Now you say there were as many outside of the stall, standing in the aisle? I mean outside standing right there by the arch, I don't mean under the market house. What I am talking about, is the persons under the market house and who were not inside of Becky Ben's stall, were there any such persons? I don't understand you. I will volunteer that there is not another person in the sound of my voice, that don't, you have just said the crowd consisted of persons who were outside of the market house, and of persons who were inside under the market house, didn't you? Yes, sir. You have told me that, of the persons who were under the market house, the major, or greater portion were behind or within Becky Ben's stall, and around the foot of the steps? Yes, sir. Now I ask you, of the persons who were under the market house, how many outside Becky Ben's stall, standing about the aisle, at the eastern end of the market house, under the cover of the roof. About fifteen or twenty, I reckon. Did you notice anybody who was inside of Becky Ben's stall, so you can name who they were? No, sir. Did you notice any one of the fifteen or twenty, who were standing in the aisle, as you passed through, so that you can name who they were? No, sir. You did notice Sam. Phillips outside? Yes, sir. Did you see Capt. Tolar in the crowd of fifteen or twenty in the aisle? No, sir. Did you see E. P. Powers? No, sir. Did you see Lutterloh? No sir. Did you see Leggett? No, sir. Now sir, how long was it, after you passed out through the market house, and went to the edge of the pavement, before Miss Massey and her mother came down stairs? It was about ten minutes I reckon. You had gone outside of the market house then before they came down? Yes, sir. Didn't you swear, upon your examination-in-chief, that when the ladies came down stairs you then walked to the edge of the pavement, along with them? I said I was standing at the edge of the pavement as they went to the carriage. You say now you didn't swear in your examination-in-chief that you moved to the edge of the pavement when these ladies came down? No, sir. You say now you were standing there before? No, sir. I did not. Did not what? Didn't say I was standing near there before they came down. Haven't you told me you were standing at the edge of the pavement, ten minutes before the ladies came down stairs? I don't think I did, if I did I made a mistake. I asked you after you moved from the market house, and went to the edge of the pavement, how long you had been standing there before the ladies came down stairs, and you said about ten minutes, Is that so or not? It ain't so, sir. How long had you been standing at the edge of the pavement before the ladies came down? I hadn't been standing there any. Then you were under the market house when the ladies came down stairs, were you? Yes, sir. Where were you? About Mitchell's stall. You stood at Mitchell's stall then until the ladies came down, you swear now? Until they came to the foot of the steps. And you then left Mitchell's stall, and passed through the crowd, and went to the edge of the pavement? Yes, sir. You went out to the edge of the pavement at the same time the ladies went to the carriage? I was a little behind them. Could you see the carriage? Yes, sir. Were you looking at it? I was looking at it at the time they went to it. Did you look right straight away from it afterwards? I didn't look right straight away, I turned my head, and I was looking in no way in particular. Which way was your face turned when you were looking at the carriage? Turned east. Which way was your face turned when you looked away from the carriage? Turned south. You were looking then down towards the guard house? Yes, sir. With your right towards the market house, and your left to the carriage? Yes, sir. What part of the edge of the pavement were you standing on, opposite what part of the market house? Front of the wall that separates the two arches. Which arches? The little one and the big one. There are two little arches, which little one? The south-east corner. You were standing opposite the wall, then, between the big arch and the little arch, the little arch nearest south? Yes, sir. And looking south? Yes, sir. Did you stand there until Archy Beebee came down stairs? Yes, sir. Were you standing there when you saw Archy first? I was standing there when I seen him come out of the door up stairs. Now, sir, when these ladies went to the carriage you were standing in the same position that you remained in until Archy came down, or came out of the door on the stairs? Yes, sir. Did you see nobody go to the carriage besides Bond? I didn't notice it. I didn't ask you whether you noticed it, I asked you if you saw it? I seen some, but I didn't know who they were. You can't swear who any of them were? No, sir, none but Mr. Bond. Some did go up to the carriage? Yes, sir. Did several go there? I don't know whether there were several or not; I should say there were as many as four went. You can't say who they were, although you can tell the number? There may have been five, I would not say for certain how many there were. There were four, or five or six, along there somewhere. Yes, sir. Your best estimate is about four, but you can't tell any of them except Bond? No, sir. After you were outside of the market house, and got your station there, on the edge of the pavement, while the carriage was standing, and just before Beebee hove in sight on these stairs, did you see Sam Phillips? He came there while I was standing there. He came where? About two foot from me. About two feet in front of you? Yes, sir. That was before Archy appeared on the stairs? No, sir. That is what I asked you; I understood you to say, you saw Samuel Phillips when you passed out of the market house? I did. You then took your station on the edge of the pavement opposite the pillar which is between the main arch and the litte arch, nearest south on the east front of the market house? Yes, sir. Now I ask you, while you were in that position, on the edge of the pavement; did you see Sam Phillips again before you saw Archy Beebee on the stairs? No, sir. Then you lost sight of him as you passed through the crowd? I didn't notice him any more. Now I ask you, while standing there in that spot, and before A. Beebee come in sight, if you can't name anybody you saw in that crowd? Yes,

sir, I can. Who? I saw Mr. Tolar there, while I was standing near the edge of the pavement. Before Archy was on the steps? While he was on the steps, I am talking about before you got there as the ladies went to the carriage didn't you? Yes, sir. Do you mean to say Archy Beebee came down stairs at the same time the ladies did? No, sir. How long afterwards? Ten minutes, I reckon. Then you were standing at this place on the pavement about ten minutes? Yes, sir. Now during that ten minutes, who did you see, before you saw Archy Beebee come down the stairs; or standing on the stairs? I don't recollect seeing any person but Mr. Tolar. Did you see Capt. Tolar then. Yes, sir. You saw Capt. Tolar before you saw Beebee on the steps? Yes, sir. You swear that? As he was on the steps. I asked you before he was on the stairs. No, sir. You didn't see him before? No, sir. I ask you again who you did see, during the ten minutes, you were standing there, stationary in the crowd, before Archy Beebee appeared on the steps? I dont know anybody. You can't name a soul you knew? No, sir. And you swear you can't name a soul? I don't think I can name any person at that time. Now you say you saw Tolar when Archy appeared in the door of the stairs? Yes, sir. You lost sight of Archy when he got to the bottom of the steps? Yes, sir. And didn't see him again until he came outside of the arch? No, sir. But you did see Tolar while Archy was up-stairs, coming down the steps, while he was coming out of the door? Yes, sir. Now, where was Tolar standing then? He was about three feet from the wall of the market. On the pavement? Yes, sir. Was he out side of the market house? Yes, sir. He was outside, on the pavement about three feet from the wall of the market house? I would not swear exactly where he was standing. You swear he was standing outside of the market house? Yes, sir. At the time Archy Beebee was on the stairs? Yes, sir. You swear to that? Yes, sir. Did you see Tolar when he came there? No, sir. But you did see Tolar while Archy was on the stairs? Yes, sir. Did you see who was near him? No, sir. Did you see Leggett near him? I didn't notice; I was looking at Beebee at that time. But you saw Capt. Tolar? Yes, sir, he was a large man. And he was standing about three feet from the market house? On the pavement in front of the wall that separates the two arches, you say? Which two arches? The big one and the little one. There are two little ones? On the south-east corner. He was standing between you and the market house then? Yes, sir. Tolar was standing then outside of the market house, between you and the wall of the market house? Yes, sir. About three feet from the market house, and you were on the edge of the pavement? Yes, sir. At the time the negro was on the steps? Yes, sir, he was coming down the steps. Now at that time did you see Lutterloh with Tolar? No, sir. Did you see Leggett at or near him? No, sir, I didn't see him. Did you see E. P. Powers at or near him? No, sir. Did you see Tom Powers or Monk at that time? No, sir, I didn't see either one of them at that time. Then your attention was directed to the man on the steps coming down? Yes, sir. Could you see the men who were inside of Becky Ben's stall from where you were standing? I could see them move, I could not see their faces, I could see their hats. But you could see this man, he being elevated as he came down? Yes, sir. You saw him through the little arch? Yes, sir. Now, when he came down you lost sight of him? Yes, sir. While he was coming down the steps, did you see anybody attempt to get at him? No, sir?

You saw nothing of that sort? No, sir. Did you hear anybody cry out that he was coming? I heard some one say there he comes. How many did you hear say that? Four or five I reckon. Were the voices you heard inside of the market house or outside? I could not say whether they were inside or outside, I didn't see them. Didn't you *hear* them? Yes, sir. You could not, from hearing, say where the voice was? No, sir. Did you ever see a voice? No, sir. You heard the voices? Yes, sir. You can't tell from the sound where they were, whether they were inside or out? No, sir. Then you lost sight of this man until he reached the arch, and turned round the corner, were you still in the same position? Yes, sir. Where was Tolar, had he gone? I don't think he had. You think he was still standing there? Yes, sir. When Archy Beebee turned to come out of the market house, did you see any one attempt to grab him? A rush was made at him, but I don't know who made it, as he got right around. Where did the rush come from, inside of the market house? From the inside of the market house, and outside too. Everybody in the crowd rushed at him? No, sir, not everybody in the crowd. Did the majority of the crowd rush at him? Yes, sir. They rushed right towards him? Yes, sir. Did you see anybody grab at him? No, sir. You swear you did not? No, sir, not at that time. Did you see any one attempt to catch hold of him? Not that I saw. Did you hear any one say give him to me? No, sir. Did you hear any one demand the prisoner, in any shape or way? No, sir. Did you hear the sheriff tell them to keep off men? Yes, sir. But you heard no demand for the prisoner, saw no grab at him? No, sir. How many persons were there between you and the prisoner, at the time you spoke of, when this rush was made? About eight or ten, I reckon. How many persons were there between you and Tolar? I didn't see Tolar just at that time. You lost sight of him? I lost sight of him as the rush was made. How many were there between you and Tolar the last time you saw him, just as the rush was made? About four or five. Then you lost sight of him in that rush? I was looking at Beebee. Is that the last time you saw him until Archy Beebee was killed? No, sir. You say at the time this rush was made you saw no demand for the prisoner made by anybody, but you heard the sheriff tell them to keep back. I heard some say keep off, I don't know whether it was the sheriff or police. Didn't you recognize the voice? No, sir. Do you know sheriff Hardie? Yes, sir. Was it his voice? I could not tell you, there were so many voices. Did you know Wemyss? Yes, sir. Was it his voice? I don't know, sir, I would not swear whose voice it was. Do you know your father's voice? Yes, sir. Was it his voice? I don't think it was. That was just as Archy come out of the arch, just as he turned to go to the guard house? He just put his foot on the pavement. Then the rush was made? Yes, sir. And then you lost sight of Tolar? Yes, sir. And you heard this exclamation in the crowd, you don't know who it was made it; and that is the only exclamation you heard? Yes, sir. What happened next? Beebee passed on two or three steps, or maybe further. Did you stand still? Yes, sir. Did you follow him with your eyes and body turning as he moved? I turned my body and eyes, and maybe my feet. You kept your eyes toward him as he moved, did you? Yes, sir. He moved two or three steps you say? Maybe further. Well now, this rush that you speak of, was it continued? No, sir. It stopped? Yes, sir. Was it repeated? I did not see it re-

peated? Didn't you hear or see it repeated? No, sir. Then when the Sheriff said stand back, the men did stand back? I think they did, they stopped anyhow. Then Beebee moved on without any body harrassing his movements? Yes, sir, I think he did. Did he walk toward the guard house? Yes, sir. Did he walk smoothly and quietly along that distance? No, sir, he made some terrible efforts to get loose. Were those efforts made at the end of those three or four steps, or while he was making them? Just as he stopped, he was shot as he was making those efforts just as he raised up. You say the rush was made on him, and he was about a foot outside of the market house? Yes, sir. Then he took some four or five steps? I reckon; may be more and may be less, and he may have gone three, and he may have gone six. Was he making those efforts while he was making those steps, or after the steps were made? After the steps were passed. After he had taken three or four steps, he made those efforts to escape? Yes, sir. Now while he was taking those three or four steps, I want to know whether anybody was trying to get at him? Not that I seen at that time. The pressure upon him had stopped? Yes, sir. He went along smoothly and quietly? Yes, sir. Then the next thing you noticed were these terrible efforts to escape? Yes, sir. You were still keeping the same position? I don't think I had moved a foot out of the position I was in at first. You were just following him with your eyes, and watching him in your same position? Yes, sir. At the end of these three or four steps he made a violent effort to escape? Yes, sir. What did he do, sir? He tried to get loose. What was he doing? He tried to jerk loose from the police. What did he jerk with? With his hands and feet. And whole body did he? Yes, sir. Did you see anybody try to get at him; about the time he was trying to escape? No, sir. You didn't see anybody strike at him with a knife? No, sir. How many men were between you and him at that time? Six or seven, I reckon. The crowd was all over that part of the pavement was it? Yes, sir. They were not pressing on him however? No, sir. You could see him distinctly. Yes, sir. Six or seven people were scattered between you and him, a pretty closely packed crowd you didn't see anybody strike at him with a knife however? No, sir. You didn't see Monk with a knife trying to get at him then? No, sir. You didn't hear anybody strike; any one of the police strike a dead blow as though upon a man's arm with a club? No, sir. You didn't hear any knife fall and clash upon the pavement? There was too much fuss to hear a knife fall? What was making the noise? People scrambling about, Beebee trying to get loose, and the police trying to hold him. Did they shout? No, sir. It was their feet that you heard? Yes, sir. You heard no exclamations at all, no cry of shoot him, before the cry you spoke of, when they said "shoot the damned son of a bitch," after he made the attempt to escape? Not before that time. Nor of kill him? No, sir. Nor any exclamation of rage at all? No, sir, not at that time. Now, sir, when you heard this cry of shoot him, that was just after he had attempted to escape, and had fallen down? Yes, sir, he fell down. When was the cry made, while he was down, or while he was raised? While he was trying to get loose. Before he fell? Yes, sir. What was the cry? "Shoot the damned son of a bitch." That was Phillips was it? I don't know who it was. Did you see Phillips at the time you heard the cry? He was standing by me at that time. At the time you heard that cry? Yes, sir. That was before the negro fell down? While he was trying to get loose. That was before he fell down? Yes, sir. Before the negro fell down, when you heard this cry, Phillips was standing by you? Yes, sir, a little in front of me. You were standing with your face towards Beebee's, were you? Yes, sir, on the edge of the pavement. And Phillips was standing by you a little to your front? Yes, sir. Now was it to your front and right, or front and left? Front and right. After this cry was made how long was it before the pistol shot? He drew the pistol just as the cry was made. How far was Phillips from you, could you have touched him? Yes, sir. Was he stationary or moving? He was standing still at that time. Now you saw Phillips draw the pistol just after the cry was made to kill the damned son of a bitch? Yes, sir. And it was while Archy was still struggling before he fell down? Yes, sir, while he was struggling and trying to get loose. He fell down after he was struggling? Yes, sir. Wasn't it the struggle that threw him down? Yes, sir. It was before he fell down you saw him draw the pistol? Yes, sir. He drew it from the left side you say? Yes, sir. And cocked it as soon as he drew it? He cocked it as he drawed it up. As soon as he drew it? No, sir. He didn't bring it up as soon as he drawed it? He drawed it right out and brought it up and cocked it as he drawed it. How long after he brought it up did he fire? He was sort of steadying it, and I turned my head and the pistol fired. Could you have counted five from the time you saw him draw the pistol to the time it fired? I think I could. Could you have counted ten? I didn't think I could. You saw him cock it? Yes, sir. As he brought it up? Yes, sir. He drew it from his left side, and presented it; it sort of wavered, and while it was wavering you turned your head off? Yes, sir. How many men were between you and Phillips? There was not any. You were the next person to him, and he was to your right and front, on the pavement? Yes, sir. How far was Archy Beebee from him? About six or seven foot I reckon. Did you see Archy fall down? I saw him while he was struggling, I don't know whether he fell or not. You saw when he went down? Yes, sir. Did you see when he got up? I didn't see him as he rose, when the pistol was held up I turned off my head. Did you see him rise at all? I seen him rise nearly up, he was assisted by somebody by catching him back of the collar. Who was assisting him up? I don't know, sir, his back was to me. Don't you know Sheriff Hardie by his back? I don't think I would in that crowd. Can't you tell anybody who helped him up? The police may have helped him up for what I know. And you turned off your head as you saw him rise? Yes, sir. Is that so or not? That is so, sir. At the same moment you saw him rise, Phillips had this pistol presented towards him? Yes, sir. You saw Phillips draw the pistol while he was struggling, and before he fell down, you saw him cock and present it straightway, and keep it wavering, and as the man rose he steadied it and you turned your eyes away? Yes, sir. Now sir, which way did you turn your eyes, to the left or right? To the right. And looked right down the street? Yes, sir. You say as you turned your eyes, you saw John Armstrong? Yes, sir. In the direction of Davis' tin store. Yes, sir, a little to my right towards Davis' tin shop. You turned your eyes to the left? Yes, sir. You were standing on the edge of the pavement, with your face towards. As Archy, when you turned your face to the left? Yes, sir. And you saw John Armstrong between you and Davis' store? Yes, sir. When you were standing on

the pavement, with your face towards Beebee; could you not see Davis' store? I was not looking at Davis' store then. Couldn't you see it, with your face towards Beebee? I reckon I could have seen it—one side of it. Were you not right in front of it; couldn't you have seen it plainly? No, sir. But by turning your head over your left shoulder you saw Davis' store very plainly? I saw the front part of it. You heard the pistol fire, and the smoke came right back on you and Armstrong? Armstrong was ten feet from me. Was he in front of you, or to the left of you? Front and right. And you, when you turned your head over your left shoulder saw it distinctly? I didn't turn my head over the left shoulder, I turned it just so (turns it to his left, but not over his left shoulder.) And you saw John Armstrong ten feet to your front and right? Yes, sir, (points to the left.) Do you call that your right? When I turned, I would. It was in the direction of Davis' store that you saw him? Not exactly in the direction of Davis' store, a little to the right. It was not right between you and Davis's store, it was further to the right? Yes, sir. How far was Archy in front of you? About seven feet. Did you see Armstrong in the same line you saw Archy? No, sir, I didn't. Was he further to the right than Archy? He was to my left, when I was looking at Archy. Did you see him while you were in the act of turning, or after you had got your head turned? While I was turning. Did you look at him? Not any time. Then you just saw him as you glanced your eyes around? Yes, sir. And you saw that one man in the crowd, and didn't distinguish any others; and you swear that just in casting your eyes away for the purpose of avoiding the immediate presence of the shot, you saw Armstrong, to your right and front, and almost ten feet off? Yes, sir. You didn't identify any one else at that time? The most that were standing there were colored, and I did not know them. You saw enough to see that? Yes, sir. You heard the pistol fire? Yes, sir. Did you look back to see who fired it? Yes, sir, I turned my head when the pistol fired. Your face was towards Beebee before you turned it to the left; I understand you didn't change your position—that you didn't change your feet? I said I didn't think I changed a foot from any position. Did you turn your body? Yes, sir. That was the way you got Armstrong on your right and front? Yes, sir. It was after you had changed your position that he was on your right and front? I turned around, I didn't go away from where I was standing. Didn't you say you turned your head over your shoulder? I turned my body, too. After you got in that position it was that Armstrong was to your right and front? Yes, sir. As soon as the pistol fired you turned about? Yes, sir. Between the time you last saw Tolar, did you see him again before the pistol fired? Yes, sir. Where did you see him again? Standing in front of the pillar that separates the two arches. The same pillar that you were speaking of before? Yes, sir. You saw him standing there? Yes, sir. Before the firing? Yes, sir. How far was he from you? About four feet. How far was he from the pistol? About a foot and a half. Was that just before the firing? Yes, sir. You swear then Tolar was standing near that pillar after the rush was made on Archy Beebee, and just before the firing? Yes, sir. Did you see him before you saw Phillips draw the pistol or after you saw him draw it, or at the same time? At the same time. You saw Tolar at the very same time you saw Phillips draw the pistol? Yes, sir, I was looking at Phillips when he drew the pistol, and of course I saw Tolar as he was standing on the other side of him. He was right close to him was he? About two feet. He was about five feet from you, you say? Yes, sir. And how far from the edge of the market house? About three feet, I reckon. And about two from Phillips? Yes, sir. Was Phillips a little to your right and front, and a little to Tolar's left and front? I think he was, I don't know. Did you see Tolar? Yes, sir. How did he stand with regard to him? He stood even with Tolar. They were about in the same line? Yes, sir. They were both to your right and front, and about two feet apart? Yes, sir. What was Tolar doing? He was not doing any thing. Standing there perfectly still? Yes, sir. Did he have his arms folded on his heart? I didn't notice, his arms were hanging down, I reckon. Could you see them? I could see them as far as the elbow. You didn't see him have on a shawl then? Yes, sir. Did he have his arms outside of the shawl? No, sir. Could you tell where his arms were hanging? I could judge by his shawl. This shawl was not fastened up at his throat? I don't know whether it was fastened or not. You say you could see his arms and that they were hanging by his side? Yes, sir, I seen about to his elbows. And from that you came to the conclusion that his arms were hanging by his side? Yes, sir. If the shawl had been pinned up close to the throat you could not have seen his arms; you saw his arms through the shawl, did you? No, sir. Did you see them inside of the shawl? I would judge by his shawl. He did have on a shawl? Yes, sir. Did he have on his spectacles? I don't know whether he did or not. Did he have on a hat that you can describe? Yes, sir, I guess I can. What sort of a hat was it? A tall, black wool hat. And you say you saw part of his arms, and from that you concluded his arms were hanging by his side, just before the pistol fired? I reckon they were. Was there any body between him and Phillips? Not that I know of. Didn't you see them distinctly—both? Yes, sir. Didn't you see anybody between them? No, sir. Who was furthest from Archy Beebee, Tolar or Phillips? I don't know about that; they were both the same distance, I reckon. Was he right in front of both of them? Mr. Tolar was sort of in front of Beebee, and Phillips to his left. Phillips was more to the left of Beebee? Yes sir. He was further towards the side where the shot entered? He was to the rear and left; I don't know where the shot entered. And Tolar was about square behind? Yes, sir. You didn't see any body between them? No, sir. And you saw Tolar you say, at the time Phillips drew the pistol? did you see him when Phillips cocked the pistol? I don't know that I seen him at the time he cocked it. You know you saw him when Phillips drew it? Yes, sir. You don't know whether you saw him when he cocked it or not? I don't know for certain. Did you see him when you saw Phillips present it? Yes, sir, I think I did. And then while it was wavering and uncertain you turned away? When he steadied it I turned away. How was Mr. Phillips dressed that day? I could not describe his dress, he had on a black coat I thought. Did he have on a shawl? No, sir, he didn't. Did he have on an over coat? No, sir, I don't think he had on an over coat. 'Aint you certain? I am rather certain he hadn't. He had on a black coat? Yes, sir, I think it was a black coat. Where did he draw this pistol from? From his left side; I don't know whether he run it down under his coat or not. What sort of a pistol was it? A pretty large pistol. Didn't he draw that pistol out of his sleeve? I don't know where he drew it from. Couldn't he have

drawn it from his sleeve from the way you saw him put his hand? I don't know where he drew it from. He might have drawn it out of his boot? He didn't draw it out of his boot; he drew it from under his coat some where. He drew it between his knee and his shoulder? Yes, sir, he did. Can you tell the nearest point between those two, whether it was about his arm or waist or about lower down? I think he drew it about his left vest pocket. When you saw this pistol presented and heard it fired, and turned about did you see Tolar when you turned back? No, sir, not at that time. He was gone was he? I didn't look. You had seen him before you turned your head, had you? Yes, sir. Was that the last time you saw him before the pistol fired? Yes, sir. The last time you saw him before the pistol fired was when Phillips drew his pistol? Yes, sir. You didn't see it after he cocked and presented it? No, sir. But at the time you saw Tolar he was standing perfectly still with his arms apparently by his side? Yes, sir. And his face towards the prisoner? Yes, sir. If he had a weapon in his hand could you have seen it? No, sir, I could not. Could Tolar have drawn a weapon and presented it without your seeing it? Not if he had drew it up high. Could he have drawn a weapon without your seeing it? He may have drawn it, but could not presented it, he could not have drawn it up even with his eye. Do you swear that Tolar drew no pistol at the same time Phillips drew his? No, sir, I didn't see him draw it. You say it might have been and you not have seen it? Yes, sir, it might have happened and I not seen it. You say nothing for certain about that, but you can't say it didn't occur? No, sir. These two men were standing side by side when you saw Phillips draw his pistol? They were not touching—they were apart two feet from one another. On the same level and about the same distance from the deceased? Yes, sir. When you turned back you say you didn't see Tolar? I didn't see him after I saw Phillips draw the pistol. When you turned back after you heard the pistol fired, did you see Tolar? No, sir. Did you see Phillips? Yes, sir. Did you see his pistol? Yes, sir. What was he doing with it? He was putting it in his pocket or vest. Did you see him draw it back and flourish it? No, sir. Did you hear him say any thing? Not that I recollect of. Think, sir, didn't you hear him say "that negro is killed, but I didn't kill him"? No, sir. If he had said that you would not have heard it? I was close enough to him to have heard it if he had said it. Just after the pistol fired did it create a silence in the crowd? Yes, sir. Then just after the pistol fired, you turned towards Phillips, and you didn't see him draw his pistol back, and hold it up so, (flourishing)? No, sir. You didn't hear him say "the negro is dead but I didn't kill him," do you swear you didn't hear that? I will swear I didn't hear him say it. Was there any body between you and him? No, sir. You could hear any ordinary tone of voice, and there was a great silence just after the pistol fired? It was very quiet. You turned immediately after the pistol fired? Yes, sir. And you saw Phillips there and he was in the crowd returning his pistol? Yes, sir. You didn't hear any such cry as "the negro is dead, but I didn't kill him"? No, sir. You heard him make no remark? No, sir. You swear positively there was no remark made there, that you heard by Phillips? No, sir. Were you alarmed, sir? No, sir. You were cool and self-possessed; you remember what occurred? Yes, sir. You were not frightened? No, sir. You were as cool and self-possessed as you are now? Yes, sir. What became of Phillips after you saw him return that pistol?

I don't know, sir, I walked on around to see if Beebee was shot. Did you leave Phillips standing where he was before? Yes, sir. Standing still? He was putting his pistol in. Did he draw his hand out after he put it up? I didn't see it. At that time you didn't see Tolar? No, sir. Which way did you move off? I walked off the pavement and walked around the crowd and went to Beebee. How did you get to Beebee? I went around the crowd. The crowd was all around him? There was not many in front of him when he was shot. You went around in front of him did you? Yes, sir. How long did you stay in that crowd? About half an hour I reckon. Did you go right up to Archy, where he was shot when you got in the crowd? I went as near as the police would let me. How close was that? About three feet. Did you see Phillips after that; I mean after you left the position you stood where Phillips had fired the pistol? No, sir, I didn't. Did you see him at all that day? Not that I remember. Did you see Tolar after you got around in front of Archy? I seen him in a few minutes after that. Where was he standing then? He was standing where he was when I first saw him by the pillar of the market. Was that the place where you first saw him that day? No, sir. You mean at the place where you last saw him then? Yes, sir. Was his back towards the pillar? Yes, sir, I think it was. Did you see Tolar with any weapon that day? No, sir. Do you know that he had any weapon that day? No, sir. Have you any reason for knowing he had any weapon that day? I know I didn't see him have any. Have you heard him say he had none? No, sir. Do you know anybody who knows whether he had one? I don't know who knows he had one. Did any one ever tell you? No, sir. You saw no signs of a weapon on him? No, sir. Did you ever see him wearing a weapon? I don't think I did. What sort of a pistol was that you saw Phillips fire? I didn't see him fire, I turned my head. What sort of a pistol was it you saw him draw and cock and present? It was a large pistol; it looked like a Navy pistol. Did you notice anything peculiar about it? No, sir. You saw it while he was drawing it and presenting it; could you have counted five or six or seven while you were looking at it? May be more, and may be not that much. Did you see it when you turned your head back to look after the pistol was fired? He was putting it away. Then you did see it after you turned your head back? Yes, sir, I seen him put it up. You saw it before it was put up? Yes, sir. In what position did he have it? He had it carrying it down to put in his pocket. Was it part in and part out? The muzzle of it was just about his coat. It was a large pistol, about the navy size? Yes, sir. You can't speak with absolute certainty about that? No, sir. What became of Tolar after you saw him standing against the market house after the shooting took place, when you went around in front of Archy, was he standing where you last saw him? Yes, sir. Didn't you hear anybody cry out in the crowd who it was that shot him? I heard John Armstrong say that. While Tolar was standing against the pillar of the market house? I think so. What did you hear him say? He said "Tolar shot him," "Tolar shot him." While Tolar was standing there? Yes, sir. What did Tolar do? I don't know that he done anything, I didn't notice him. You say that it was while Tolar was still standing there that you heard John Armstrong make that remark, and you didn't see Tolar do anything? No, sir. Was that the only person you heard say "Tolar shot him"? The only one. How many times did he say it? Two or three. How near was he to the

deceased man when he said it? About twelve feet I reckon. Which way was he standing from you, and from him, and from Tolar, was he on the pavement? No, sir. Was he toward Davis' store? Yes, sir, near the edge of the pavement. Opposite what part of the market house? The south-east corner of the market house. Down towards Davis' store, near the edge of the pavement? Yes, sir. Just on the south-east edge of the pavement was this man using the exclamation that "Tolar shot him"? Yes, sir. How many times? Two or three. Was it four or five? I don't know. Do you swear you didn't heard it five times? I won't swear, he may have said it six. When you say one or two you don't mean one or two? I mean what I say. You say you won't swear it was six times? I won't. Will you swear it was more than one? Yes, sir. Will you swear it was more than two? Yes, sir. Will you swear it was more than three? No, sir. You think it was about three times? Yes, sir. You might as well have told that at first? I said it was about three. Your impression is, it was three times in a loud enough tone for the crowd to hear it? They might have heard it, if they wanted to hear it. Was it as loud as I am talking to you now? I reckon it was. You didn't see Phillips fire the pistol? I turned my head as he raised the pistol. What was your reason for turning your head? I didn't want to stand there; I might get a cap or something in my eyes. Was that your reason, because you were afraid of getting a cap in your eye? Yes, sir, or being burned with the powder. You were close enough to render it dangerous, that a cap might fly into your eye or the powder burn you? Yes, sir. You were behind him, you say, a little to his rear? Yes, sir. And it was the fear that it might hurt you, that made you turn your eyes away? Yes, sir. Did you ever fire a gun? Yes, sir. Have you ever been out hunting? Yes, sir. Fired a gun frequently? Yes, sir. Do you turn your eyes away from where you shoot? No, sir. Do you ever shoot them? I shot one. Did you ever fire a pistol? Yes, sir. Did you shut both eyes when you fired that? No, sir, Do you shut both eyes when anybody else fires a gun? I turn them away, I don't shoot them, I don't want my eyes to get put out. You think there is danger of putting your eyes out? Yes, sir. And you always do that? Not when I shoot myself. When anybody else fires, you turn away, and you did that day for the same reason? Yes, sir. Did you see anybody else there with a weapon, that day? No, sir, I seen Monk have a knife. What was he doing with it? He was trying to get to Beebee, he was wanting to cut his throat. How do you know? He said "let me cut his damned throat." Did he have a knife then? Yes, sir? Didn't you see him strike at the man with a knife before? No, sir. Didn't you see Tom Powers there that day, at all? Not that I remember. Did you see Ed. Powers there that day at all? No, sir. Either before the pistol fired or afterwards? No, sir. Did you see Lutterloh there that day, at all? No, sir. Leggett? No, sir. Sam Hall? No, sir. Did you see Maultsby after the first time you have described? No, sir, I didn't see him but once. Did you see Jonathan Hollingsworth? No, sir, I don't know that I know him. Do you know George Hollingsworth? Yes, sir. Did you see him there? No, sir. Do you know Jas. Kendricks? Yes, sir. Did you see him there? No, sir. Who did you see after the shooting? I told you all I seen. Didn't you see any body after the shooting? I seen plenty of them. Who were they? The police and Bond and Faircloth and Wemyss. They are the very ones I don't want to know? They are the very ones I know.

Didn't you know any others you saw? No, sir. You saw no weapon there that day except the knife that Monk had and the pistol that Sam. Phillips had? That is all I seen. You saw nobody with a pistol at all but Phillips? No, sir. At no time while you were there did you hear any body say any thing about going to kill Archy Beebee? No, sir. Didn't you hear Phillips say something about it? No, sir. Didn't you hear Phillips make some threats that he was going to do it? No, sir. Were there any persons standing further from Beebee than you were at the time this shot was made? Yes, sir. You were right in the main crowd; the crowd was behind you as well as before you? Yes, sir. Was the crowd pressing pretty close? Not at the time the pistol fired, it was pressing pretty close when he turned the corner. After that the pressure ceased? Yes, sir. You were right in the midst of the crowd? Yes, sir, it was all around me. And so it was with regard to Tolar and Phillips? Yes, sir, it was all around them, but it wasn't quite as thick around them. It was around them though? Yes, sir. Could you tell me a soul who was among those persons who were nearest to Phillips and Tolar? I can't. Don't you remember recognizing ary body there? Only what I have told you. Then the first time you made this disclosure was about two weeks ago? It might have been two or more. How much more? It might have been less than two weeks, I don't know how long it was. Have you ever told it to any body else since? Yes, sir, I told it to Mr. Cashwell and Mr. Fuller. Any body else? I told my father. Any body else? No, sir. Do you know there was a coroner's inquest to enquire who committed this murder at the time it occurred? No, sir. You didn't know that? No, sir. You stayed at the market house about half an hour after Beebee was killed? I reckon half an hour. Where did you go then? I went home. Where had you been the previous part of that day? I had been about home, and about Mr. Lutterloh's corner. Did you hear about anybody's intention going there to kill Beebee? No, sir. Where did you first hear that Beebee had attempted to ravish Miss Massey? In the morning when my father came home off duty. What time in the morning? Before sun up. Did you go out before breakfast? Yes, sir. Where did you go? I went out in the street. Can't you tell me where you went? I don't know that I could now. Try? I went down the street. There are a good many streets? There ain't many about there. There ain't many streets about Fayetteville? No, sir. There are so many that I insist upon having a direct answer to that question? I went down Hay street to the market and back. Do you live on Hay street? No, sir. When you went out in the morning before breakfast on the day Archy Beebee was killed where did you go? I went down to the market and back and stood around Mr. Lutterloh's. Where did you go then? I came home and got breakfast. Where did you go after breakfast? I went down to the corner. Didn't you hear any body talking about this thing? I heard them say he had made a rape on Miss Massey; I didn't hear them say any thing about killing him. They said it was all right didn't they? I didn't hear them say whether it was right or wrong. Neither expressed their approbation nor disapprobation of it; just mentioned it as a fact? Yes, sir.

Re-direct Examination by the Counsel for the accused:

You have spoken of it as being a long time, in describing things as they occurred around there; how long a time was it after you first saw the negro Beebee turning the corner of the arch, to the time he was killed? I don't know, sir, I could not say about that. Was it a short time or a long time? It was a short time I should think; I reckon it was pretty short with him. How many do you think you could have counted between the time Beebee turned the arch to go down towards the guard house and the time he was shot? I don't know sir; I could not say for certain about that. Could you have counted fifty? I don't know, I might and might not have counted fifty—I might not have counted twenty and I might have counted a hundred. You think you could have counted between twenty and a hundred. I didn't say how many I could have counted. Matters were passing there in rapid succession one after another, no pause at all? There was no pause there then? What was the matter, now that most attracted your attention there, during that time? I went there to see Beebee tried. Between the time that Beebee appeared upon the steps to go down and the time he was shot, what was the principle thing that attracted your attention; what was the principal thing you took notice of? Beebee. And the matters which were occurring around there that you have spoken of were matters which didn't attract your attention so much because you were looking at Beebee to see what became of him? Yes, sir. I understand you to say that the time the pistol shot fired you turned to look down the street towards the east? Yes, sir. And that having turned you saw John Armstrong to your right and to your front. Yes sir. Over in a line with Ichabod Davis' corner? Yes, sir. And that is what you mean by his being to your right and front? Yes, sir. Not that he was to your right and front when you were facing towards Beebee? No, sir. But that he was to your right and front when you turned to look from the pistol? Yes, sir. And he was ten or twelve feet off from you, you say? Yes, sir. With regard to the positions of the parties, Tolar, &c, that you have spoken of, you say that Tolar was you think, rather to your rear, or to your front? To my front. To your right or left? To my right. That what Tolar did you didn't see very distinctly; whether he had a pistol or not, you will not undertake to swear? No, sir. That your attention was drawn to Sam. Phillips who took the pistol from his left side, cocked it, as he raised it, and moved it about as if to get a position to fire, and then before the firing occurred you turned your eyes down to the East. Yes, sir. What Tolar was doing in the mean time you don't undertake to say? I don't know. That whether Phillips fired the pistol or whether he didn't, you don't swear directly? I would not swear who shot it. But you heard the report and immediately turned your eyes back, and there you saw the smoke rising from where Phillips had his pistol? Yes, sir. And you saw Phillips return the pistol to his left side? Yes, sir. And though you say things might have occurred around there that didn't attract your notice, you swear that there is no mistake about it—that you did see that? Yes, sir, I saw that and it is so. That is so? It is that.

Questioned by the Commission:

Are you a judge of time? No, sir, I aint. You stated in your examination in chief, that it was ten or fifteen minutes after the pistol was fired before you heard any one say who had done the shooting? Yes, sir, it was about that. Do you swear positively that no one cried out "Tolar shot," or "Tolar shot him" immediately after the shooting? Not that I heard of, sir. You do swear then, that it was as long as ten or fifteen minutes? It might have been shorter or longer. Was it shorter or longer? I could not swear exactly. Was it ten minutes? I reckon it was ten.

Was it twelve? No, sir. Then it was between ten and twelve minutes from the pistol firing, before you heard John Armstrong make that remark which you have sworn you heard him? Yes, sir. And Tolar was then standing against the end of the market house? Yes, sir, near the wall. On the outside? Yes, sir. On the pavement? Yes, sir.

The Court here took a recess of five minutes.

DAVID CASHWELL, a witness for the defence, having been first duly sworn, testified as follows:

By Counsel for accused:

Where do you reside Mr. Cashwell? In Fayetteville, sir. What is your first name? David. How long have you resided there? Since seventeenth of January, 1863. What age are you? A little over fifty. Were you in Fayetteville on the day Archy Beebee was killed? Yes, sir. Were you at the market house at the time of the killing? Yes, sir. What time of the day did the killing occur? I can't say positively, it was in the afternoon. How long after dinner, about what time of the day, to the best of your recollection, did you go to the market house? I think between three and four o'clock. For what purpose? With the intention, sir, of witnessing the trial. Did you hear the trial? When I arrived there and started to go up stairs, I was told by some parties—I don't recollect who, now—that the trial was being conducted privately, and that spectators were not admitted,—that the doors were closed. Then I kept on through the market house and over to Mr. Taylor's store, on the corner. At which arch had you entered? I think by the southern. How long did you remain at Mr. Taylor's store? I don't recollect; I didn't note the time, it was not a great while, though; it might have been fifteen or twenty minutes. Well, sir, did you return to the market house? Yes, sir, I did, but not until after the ladies had been conducted down stairs, and had driven off in the carriage. Did you see the carriage at the time it came up? Yes. Did you see Mr. Bond escort the ladies to the carriage? Yes, sir. Did you see anybody else go to the carriage? I don't recollect anybody but him, at that time. Did you see anybody subsequently? None, except Mr. Bond, when he came up he ordered the carriage to go away. Did you visit the carriage? Yes, sir. Who else visited the carriage. Who else—Mr. Taylor? Did he go in company with you, or alone? In company with me. Did you see anybody else there? I don't recollect that I did. Did you see Robert Mitchell there? No, sir. Did you see Captain Tolar there? No, sir. Did he visit the carriage? If he did I didn't see him. Were you looking at it all the time? I was from the time the ladies entered it until the carriage drove away. Did Maultsby go to the carriage? I did not see him. Do you know him? Very well, sir. Are you acquainted with Tolar? Very well. You say you don't remember Mr. Mitchell's going there? No, sir. When the carriage drove off where did you go? When it drove off, of course it left me there in the middle of the street, about half way between Taylor's store and the market house; then I passed up towards the market-house and through the crowd, under the eastern arch of the market-house; inside, and under the market house. You say you passed through the crowd, how large a crowd was there? Not a very large crowd; the most that were there, that is, excepting negroe. —there were a good many negroes on the outside, and down a little in front of the arch and inclining towards the south-east corner. Yes, sir, would that be on the left or right as you entered the arch from Taylor's? On the left, most of them. Were they white or colored people? Most of them were

colored I think. Were there many persons under the market house at that time? The most that I noticed as being under, or about the market house, seemed to be collected just about under the arch. How many white persons did you estimate? I did not think of it at the time and made no estimate. But to the best of your impression now, how many were there? Well, sir, I can't say; there might have been fifty, or there might have been less, or there might have been rather more; I can't say. You passed through the crowd, did you see Capt. Tolar in that crowd? As I passed in I saw him. Where was he? He was to my right as I passed in and through the crowd. How far from the arch by which you entered? I think he was standing very nearly immediately under the arch, that is my impression. As you passed through the arch, was he to your right or left? To my right, I think, just to my right; I think I passed near enough to him to have touched him. Was any one standing near him at the time that you recollect? My impression is—I can't say about that. Was there a crowd round him: were there many persons near him? No, sir, I don't think there were many persons immediately near him; I think the body of the crowd was rather to my left as I entered. Were there many persons near Capt. Tolar at the time you entered the arch? There might have been one or two, or three, I didn't notice particularly. Was your attention attracted particularly towards him? Not at all. Was your attention attracted particularly by anything that occurred in the crowd as you entered? Not at all; I passed through the crowd, and just as I had about passed the crowd, some persons said, "there he is now," that was the negro. I halted and saw the negro coming down with the sheriff. Describe, as well as you can, the order in which the party was; first, though I would have you describe your own position at the time when they appeared upon the stair-steps? I think I was standing inside the arch, about ten feet from the end of the arch, near the middle aisle, as nearly as I can recollect. Well? When there I saw the Sheriff bringing Beebee down the steps: and I think I remained in that position until he was carried round, and perhaps until he was shot. You think you retained that position from the time you heard the cry of "there he comes now" until he was shot; was the sheriff before, behind, or one side of him? As well as I recollect he was on his right side. Did you notice any one else with the prisoner at that time? I think Mr. Wemyss was with him. Any one else? I don't recollect. You remember nobody else? I could not say now whether anybody else was with him. You were still in motion at the time you were attracted by the cry of "there he is now," or had you stopped? I can't say whether I was in motion particularly, or had partially turned round. How long after you entered the main arch before you heard that expression? I think a very short time. How many seconds or minutes? I couldn't say, I don't think it was minutes; don't think it was more than a minute, that is my impression. Did you see any demonstration made towards the prisoner as he descended the stair-steps? No, sir. Was there any thing of that kind? Not that I am aware of. Did you see any demonstration made upon him as he reached the market floor, about the time he had turned out of the aisle? Just about the time he was approaching very near the arch, and perhaps turning, I saw some demonstrations then made towards him. Tell the Court the character of these demonstrations. A crowd seemed to gather immediately in front of him, as he was being brought down, and several persons, as well as I can recollect, seemed to take hold of him. You saw several; how many, to the best of your recollection? I can't say, sir, it was done very quickly. How many hands did you see raised? I don't think I saw many, perhaps one or two, perhaps two. Were they the hands of the same person or of different persons? I could not say, I think they were the hands of different persons, however. Did these hands have weapons in them of any sort? I can't say that they had. Did you hear any cries at that time? Yes, a kind of confused noise, could not say that I heard any thing said distinctly. You heard no voice raised above the hum of the crowd? Some of the crowd were making some noise of course, but whether they were making demands for him or not I couldn't exactly understand, but what occurred made the impression on my mind, at the time, that they were demanding him from the sheriff. Did you hear any such demand made in distinct terms? I don't recollect that I did. From which direction were the crowd pressing upon the prisoner? It was the crowd that seemed to be immediately inside the arch, and filling up the way by which he had passed out. Northern or southern portion of the arch? The southern portion. Would he pass to the left or right of that crowd as he passed out of the arch? Who? The prisoner? He would have had to pass immediately through that crowd that I speak of now. Did you recognise the persons who were making the demonstrations? I did not. Did you see Tolar at that time? No, sir. Did you see Tom. Powers at that time? Not that I recollect. Are you acquainted with Tom. Powers? No, sir, I didn't know him. Have you become acquainted with him since that time? No. Did you see this man, the middle of these three, (pointing to Tom. Powers?) I might have seen him; I don't recollect, sir, at all. Are you acquainted with Monk? No, sir, never saw him before that day to know who he was; I think I saw him there that day, however. At what time, with reference to the death of the prisoner, did you see him? It was previous to the death of the negro that I saw him. At what time? As I passed through the market house first, when my intention was to go up and see the trial. What was he doing then? He was talking with some persons there; I don't know what he was talking about. Did you see him in the crowd that were making the demonstrations towards the prisoner. I think he was in the crowd that was rather blocking up the way by which the sheriff had to pass out; I wouldn't like to swear positively that this was the case; the reason that impression is on my mind is that it was about there I saw him when I did see him; I wouldn't like to state that I saw him there at that time. Did you see any weapons? No, sir. No weapons up to that time? No, sir. In the possession of any body? No. What attracted your attention next? After they passed the arch? Yes? My attention was next attracted by the report of a pistol. Could you see the deceased at the time the pistol fired? No, sir. Do you know where he was, of your own knowledge, at the time the pistol was fired? I know where he fell, sir, and where; he was lying when he was dead. You do not know of your own knowledge where he was standing at the time the pistol was fired? No, sir. Well, sir, did you see either of the prisoners after the firing and under what circumstances. I saw Capt. Tolar I may say immediately after the report of the pistol, I don't think it could exceeded two seconds. What attracted your attention towards Capt. Tolar, and where was he? When I heard the report of the pistol, my eyes were turned in that direction, I saw Capt. Tolar

in front of the arch then. Well, sir, where was he; how far from the arch, and in what position with reference to the center of the arch? My impression is that he was nearly opposite the center of the arch. With regard to the pavement where was he standing? Near the center. Near the center of the arch, and on the pavement? Yes, that is my impression. As you stopped in the middle aisle running from east to west and looked back you saw smoke, drifted by the southern wind, pass the arch, and within two seconds you also saw Capt. Tolar? Yes, sir, I think within two seconds. Opposite the center of the arch and about the center of the pavement? Yes, I think so. How far from Archy should you judge at the time you saw him? Well, since my subpœna as a witness here, I went to the place and got Mr. Wemyss to point out the exact spot where the negro lay after he was dead; and from that spot, designated by Mr. Wemyss—and it agrees with my own recollection of the spot—I think it must have been at least ten feet. What was his attitude at the time? Well, I only saw him for an instant, and it would be hard to describe; I think he was in motion, and that his motion was this:

(Making a half wheel forward and to the left.)

Did he turn his face from towards the deceased, or from an opposite direction? From an opposite direction I thought, as if he were turning his face inwards towards the market house and rather towards the scene of action; he seemed as though he had made the motion when I saw him. And that motion would have carried his face how? In front of me and rather to my right. Would it carry his face towards the spot where the prisoner was lying, or in another direction? Not exactly that spot, but rather in a direction between where I was and the position the prisoner was in, at the time he was shot. As he turned would his eyes, if directly before him, have looked to the right or left side of the arch, as he went out?—as I understand you, he was standing at the southern side of the pavement? He was not standing at the time I saw him—I mean his position was not stationary, I have tried to explain that when I saw him, and at the instant I did see him his motion seemed to be this:—[Describing again a half-wheel, forward and to the left.] Which way was his face directed at the movement he commenced making this half-wheel? You must excuse me, I cannot explain it better than by making the motion myself.

By Judge Advocate: Was it to the north, south, or east or to the north and west, or south and west, or in what direction? Just the moment I saw him, the motion he made seemed to be this:—(standing up and describing a half-wheel forward and to the left, as before.) If he had stopped, his face would have been south-west.

Judge Advocate: Looking towards Mr. Hinsdale's corner? Yes, sir.

By Counsel for accused: Which way was his face directed when you saw him, at the moment you first saw him? At the very instant I saw him his face was fronting west, and he turned it round to the south-west; the motion, when completed, would bring his face about looking towards the south-west. Then, if I understand it aright from your description of it, he moved, as you saw him, or was moving about forty-five degrees? Yes, sir. And that brought his face towards the south-west and towards Mr. Hinsdale's corner? Yes, sir. Could he have seen the spot where the deceased fell, with his eyes directed as they were at the time he stopped? I can't say about that, because his face was not fronting the spot where the deceased fell, at the instant I saw him. What was the height of the smoke as it drifted past the arch? I think the height of a tall man's head. Did you see that before or after you saw Capt. Tolar? Immediately before. You saw Capt. Tolar about two seconds after; how was he dressed? I could not say, I never notice a gentleman's dress. Did you notice any thing he held at the time? My impression at the time, sir, was that he had something in his left hand. Do you know what it was? I do not; however, you must understand me, Mr. Battle, that I only saw him for a second, and even if my attention had been directed to him at the time, I don't suppose my view of him could have continued any longer than that, because you see the crowd was pressing in. Were there any persons to his left as you were looking at him—that is, to what would have been his rear, looking towards the place where prisoner fell; or was he alone at that time? No, sir, there were persons all about him. Were they mostly to your right or left, looking towards him? To my right. What attracted your attention to Captain Tolar particularly? I can't say. Was it an accident or what? I suppose it must have been an accident. I simply recollect having seen him at the instant. Was there anything particular in his manner in the character of the movement that attracted you, or was it simply an accident? I suppose simply an accident. Had you heard any thing in the crowd as you passed through, that led you to expect the killing of Archy Beebee? Not at all, ... Now, however, this thing I will say that I did hear some party say, either in that crowd or some where else, I don't recollect who or where, that he deserved to be killed. You did? Yes, sir, I heard it said, but cannot say who did say it, for I don't recollect. Was it Captain Tolar? No, sir. Was it either one of these defendants, (pointing to the accused)? I don't think it was, I can't say. Are you at all related to either of the defendants? Not at all. Are you a particular friend to either of the defendants? I hope I am a friend to them all. I mean, have you more than an ordinary friendship for either of the defendants? My friendship for Captain Tolar has always been of a very strong character. Is there any peculiar tie between you and Captain Tolar? Yes, sir. What is it? We are both members of the same church, but whether we belong to the same organization or not I can't say. Are you a frequent visitor at his house and he at yours? No, sir, I may say however that I have known him for many years, and from his integrity as a gentleman and a christian I have formed a very strong opinion of him; I never visited his house except on one occasion, and that was in a case of affliction, and he never visited mine in his life. There is no particular intimacy then between you? No, sir. Did you see Sam Phillips on the day Archy Beebee was killed? I think I saw him in the crowd. Did anything attract your attention to him? No, sir. And you think you saw him there? I think I did.

Cross examined by the Counsel for the prosecution:

I understand you to say that you were standing at Mr. Taylor's store at the time the ladies got into the carriage? Yes, sir. At the time they got into the carriage you went forward with Mr. Taylor to speak to them, to show them respect and consideration? Yes, sir—now let me explain some, at the time they were brought down to the carriage, and handed in by the town officer, Mr. Boud, and as soon as they were seated in the carriage, the mother of the young lady took her seat in the carriage, next to Mr. Taylor's store. When they were fairly seated in the carriage, Mrs. Massey looked towards us very imploringly as I

thought, and I took it as a signal that she wanted to speak to us. I mentioned this to Mr. Taylor and we moved towards the carriage. I ought to explain as I go, that she and her daughters are members of the same church as I am. Well, when I got to the carriage, Mrs. Massey says to me: "Brother Cashwell, my troubles are more than I can bear—brother pray for me." While she was speaking, the town officer, Mr. Bond stepped up on the other side of the carriage and told the driver to drive off. I understood you to say you didn't see Robert Mitchell while you were there? No, sir. Nor Tom Powers? No. Nor Captain Tolar? No, sir, Mr. Bond was the only one you saw besides yourself? Yes, sir. Immediately after the carriage went away you went through the crowd? Yes, sir. Have you a distinct recollection that it was a windy day; you say there was a fresh southerly breeze? I cannot say there was a fresh southerly breeze; the smoke of the pistol wafted from the south and passed the pillar. There was breeze enough to carry the smoke of the pistol off as soon as it was fired? Yes, sir. I understand you to say, Mr. Cashwell—I shall trouble you with very few questions—that you were standing under the market house when Archy came down stairs in charge of the officer, and you were standing there from the time he passed through the arch until he was shot? Yes, sir. Just as he got from the arch and was passing through, there was a demonstration of assault, you don't know by whom? No, sir. You think there were efforts made to seize him? Yes, sir. And you saw two hands lifted in the position you described? Yes, sir. Did you hear any expressions that you can speak of? No, sir. Could you remember any, if they were repeated to you? I don't think I could; my impression was that there was a demand made for him. How many minutes do you suppose between this time of the demand and the shooting of the pistol? A very short time, because they were hurrying him along as fast as they could, and they only went, from the point where they turned the arch, a few paces, where he was shot. I want your best estimate of the time, do you suppose it was a full minute? I don't think it could have exceeded a full minute. From the time he passed the arch until he was shot? Yes, sir. Just before you heard the pistol fire, did you hear any exclamations at all? No, sir, none more than a murmuring noise. No cry of "kill him, shoot him," or anything like that? No, sir. The next thing that attracted your attention was the firing of the pistol? Yes. You had seen Capt. Tolar before that time? Yes, sir, when I came from the carriage and entered under the arch of the market house, I think he was just to my right, and probably near enough for our clothes to have brushed. Very near the center of the eastern arch? Yes, sir, that is my impression. This crowd, at the time of the apparent demonstration were surrounding the prisoner, was it about the same spot? It was to the southward of where I saw him. Were the limits of the crowd large enough to extend it up to the center of the arch; was the crowd large enough to spread itself that far from the southern edge of the arch up to the center? I think the crowd would have filled that space. And it extended outside and extended in, as I understand? Yes, and up towards the center of the arch. It took naturally a somewhat circular form? Yes, sir. You didn't see Captain Tolar at that time? No, sir. Not from the time you passed him until the pistol had fired, and you saw him again on the pavement? No, sir. Within two seconds of the time you heard this report, you saw Capt. Tolar, as you have described him? Yes. The motion was just about finished, was it? Yes. Your impression was that it was just the motion of a man who had moved in a particular direction and had stopped, who had just checked his movement. Well, you see I can't tell; I did not intend convey that impression, I simply want to state what I saw. His body was in motion when you saw him? Yes. And it came to a stop at the completion of the motion? I can't say that it ever stopped there, it was but a momentary glance. And you didn't see him again? No. Did you leave the crowd? Yes, sir, and after awhile I went back on the other side of the market house, I saw the negro as he was lying there dead. You saw no one with any weapons that day? If I did, I don't recollect; I couldn't state distinctly that I did. This time you saw Captain Tolar, it couldn't have exceeded two minutes from the firing of the pistol? I think not. And the point you saw him at, was about ten feet from where the nigger lay, or where you had the position pointed out to you? Yes, sir. You say your friendship is very strong for Captain Tolar, you have a high appreciation of him as a man of merit? Yes, sir. Are you a Mason? Yes, sir, and let me say, here, Mr. Haywood, that my Masonic obligation does not oblige me to to testify falsely, either in favor or against any man. I so understand, sir, I shan't trouble you any longer.

At 1:40 P. M., on motion the Commission adjourned to meet on the 28th inst., at 11 A. M.

RALEIGH, N. C., Aug. 28, 1867, 10 A. M.
The Commission met pursuant to adjournment.

Present: All the members of the Commission, the Judge Advocate, the Counsel for the prosecution, all the accused and their Counsel.

The reading of the testimony taken yesterday was waived, there being no objection thereto.

Yesterday's proceedings were then read and approved.

DUNCAN J MCALISTER, a witness for the defence having been first duly sworn, testified as follows:

The Counsel for the accused stated that this witness was merely a character witness, but owing to the irregularity of the arrival of the witnesses for the defence, and as Mr. McAlister was in town, they would introduce him at this stage of the trial, although his evidence properly came at the close of the defence.

Examined by the Counsel for the accused.

What is your name? Duncan J. McAlister. What is your occupation? Farming, sir. Where do you reside? Eleven miles north-east of Fayetteville, in Cumberland county. Do you know John Armstrong, a freedman? Yes, sir. How long have you known him? Since he was a small boy. Who did he formerly belong to? Mistress Jeanett Armstrong. How far did he reside from you? As long as he remained her property, until he was nearly grown, about a mile. Do you know of the general character of John Armstrong for truth? I know what his neighbors think of it. That is it, sir, that makes general character; what is that character for truth? It is not good, sir. How long have you known that general character for truth? As long as before he was grown. How long has his character been, as you say, not good for truth? As long as about the time he was grown.

Cross examination by the Counsel for the prosecution:

You say, Mr. McAlister, that you have known this boy Armstrong from the time he was born? Since he was a little boy. How old is he? I suppose between thirty-five and forty years of age.

Who did you say he belonged to? Mrs. Jeanett Armstrong. How far does she reside from Fayetteville? About 13 miles. Is her plantation joining yours? No, sir. Were you exactly in the same neighborhood? About a mile. In the same direction from Fayetteville? Yes, sir. Is she living or dead? She is dead. When did she die? I think she died about twenty years ago. Has John been living in that neighborhood since she died? After her death he moved to her son's about four miles west of there. Have you known him since he moved to the son's? Yes, sir. How long did he live there at the son's? Until they were emancipated. What is that son's name? F. C. Armstrong. You say during the whole time you have known him, or since he has grown to manhood, his character has been bad for truth? Yes, sir. Did you ever hear his character for truth called in question? Yes, sir, frequently. By whom? By the neighbors. Name some of them if you please, sir. Neill S. Stewart, P. B. Murphy, George McCoy, A. E. McCoy. Any others? William Murphy. Can't you recollect any others that you have heard speak of him in this respect? Geo. S. Gainey. You can name as many as you can remember that you have heard speak of it. John Pemberton, William McPhail, B. W. McAlister; I don't know that I recollect any others in particular. I understood you to say you have heard all these gentlemen express their opinion with regard to this man Armstrong's character for truth? Yes, sir. Did you hear them express their opinions at the same time or at different times? Different times. When was it that you heard Neill Stewart speak of his character for truth? That was during the last year. How long ago, sir? I should suppose some six months; I dont recollect it exactly. Was it since the killing of Archy Beebee? No, sir, I think it was before. What did he say? He spoke of him as having sworn to things, how impressed upon the administrator of F. C Armstrong's estate had been, the false statement he had made, he was speaking of his producing an account against his former master F. C. Armstrong. And said in that connection that he had sworn to a lie about it? Yes, sir, he had spoken about his general character, how hard it was that the estate should be defrauded by him. Is F. C. Armstrong dead sir? Yes, sir. Did he die before this man Armstrong was emancipated? No, sir, his son died first, he was the lawful owner of the negro, I think. He was living at the time he was emancipated, with F. C. Armstrong? Yes, sir. He died since the war was ended? Yes, sir. He lived with his son for a while, did he? Yes, sir. Whose estate was it in connection with that Neill Stewart was speaking? F. C. Armstrong's estate. That was since his emancipation? Yes, sir. Was Neill Stewart the administrator of the estate? No, sir. What connection did he have with it? He was an heir. He was next of kin? Yes, sir. He said the boy Armstrong had raised an unfair account against the estate, which diminished the share coming to the next of kin. Yes, sir. When did D. B. Murphy speak of it? It was before and since the emancipation. You heard him speak of it twice? I don't know how many times. At least twice? Yes, sir. The first time what was the nature of the conversation? It was about stealing cattle or killing cattle in the woods, and laying it on others. What was said substantially; I don't expect you to remember every word he said? He said they could prove anything by this John Armstrong; there was no use to prosecute them, that they could prove by John Armstrong any thing they wanted to. That was before the emancipation? Yes, sir. How long before? Sometime; it was during the war. Who was accused of stealing cattle? Armstrong's negroes. And you heard Murphy say that there was no use in prosecuting them, that John Armstrong would swear to anything? Yes, sir. Was he a witness in the business? I don't know that they took out any process against them, but he said he would be made a witness. Whose cattle was it that were missing, or had been injured? I don't recollect at that time whose they were, it was so often the case. Were they any cattle of Mr. Murphy's? I rather think they were McPhail's. Had he lost any cattle about that time? I don't think he had. You say you heard him talking of him again, since his emancipation? Yes, sir. What was that? That was regarding a mule. What regarding it? When Sherman's army passed through, his stock of horses and mules was taken off. Murphy's stock? Yes, sir. And he was informed where one of them was; and he got it back; he applied to the commander of the post in Fayetteville, and he got the mule back, and Armstrong volunteered his services to swear that it wasn't Murphy's mule. Who did he volunteer his services to? The negro that had him in his possession. Murphy told you that or did you know that? Murphy told me that. What did he say of him in that connection? He spoke of it. It was no doubt his mule? Yes, sir, they gave it up to him, he proved it by a good many persons, and the commander gave it up to him. Is that about all you have heard Murphy say of him? They are the only circumstances that I can recollect of. When did George McCoy speak of this man's character? Well, I heard him speak of him frequently, George McCoy acted as Deputy Sheriff in that county for a long while. Did Mr. Murphy live in the same neighborhood with Armstrong. Yes, sir. Did Stewart live in the same neighborhood? He lives some thirteen miles off, but he was frequently at his father-in-law's. He was a son in law of F. C. Armstrong? Yes, sir. George McCoy, did he live in that neighborhood? Yes, sir, all the balance live immediately in that neighborhood except John Pemberton. When did you hear Geo. McCoy speak of him? He was acting as an officer; I don't recollect any specific time; whenever he had any precept against the people in that neighborhood for misdemeanors, and the name of Armstrong would be brought up, he would speak of it as unworthy of credit. You say he was Deputy Sheriff some time? Yes, sir. That was before the murder of Beebee or since? That was before. You have never heard him speak of him since? No, sir. A. E. McCoy, where was it you heard him speak of him? It was during the same time mostly during the war—people in that neighborhood suffered a great deal—there was a great deal of stock in this section and there was always more or less complaint about its being killed. What did McCoy have to say about John? He represented him as being, he thought, the ringleader of the gang that was destroying the stock. Did he say anything about his truth? Yes, sir, that he believed he would swear to any thing. When was it you heard William Murphy speak of him? That was since this took place, I don't know how long it has been since the thing occurred, it hasn't been a great while. Since the 11th of February last? Yes, sir. I don't want to hear it then; have you heard John S. Gainey speak of him? Yes, sir, frequently. Was that before this murder, or since? I have not heard him since. What did he have to say? He said he was not to be believed on oath. What was the conversation about? In every instance I have mentioned, it was about the loss of stock. That was during the war? Yes, sir, and some since the war, but principally during the war.

As I understand, in connection with the loss of stock in that neighborhood? Yes, sir. These men spoke of John Armstrong as being ready to testify for any body? Yes, sir, since the war some of them have spoken of him in the same capacity. John Pemberton, where does he live? In Fayetteville, sir. You say you have heard him speak of Armstrong? Yes, sir. When? That was since this trial commenced. I don't want that—did you ever hear him speak of him before this trial? No, sir. William J. McPhail, when did you ever hear him speak of it? It was previous to the trial. Was it previous to the death of Beebee? Yes, sir, and I might have heard him speak of him since. I want what he said before? The conversation I have had with him was previous to this trial; I don't recollect the time Beebee was killed, I think it was before Beebee was killed, yes, sir, it was; the last time I heard him speak of it was during the trial of that mule of Murphy's. Did John swear in that trial? I don't know, sir, whether he did or not; they took witnesses there to prove before the Commander of the post his character, but what was done, I don't know. Did you hear McPhail say he had sworn falsely on that trial? I heard him say he proffered to do it. You didn't hear him say he had done it? No, sir. And he then spoke of his character as being bad for truth? Yes, sir. When did you hear W. B. McAlister speak of it? That was about the time of Murphy's mule; that brought more of them together than at any one time I recollect. Were those men speaking about the same time, Murphy and McPhail and McAlister? Yes, sir. It was in the same conversation? Not exactly, they were not all there; I don't recollect which ones it was, just about that time. Now, sir, I understand you; in one instance you heard Neill Stewart say he had sworn to a lie? Yes, sir. About raising an account against an estate in which he was interested? Yes, sir, if I said he had sworn to it—I would not be positive to his having sworn to it, he made out the account and proffered to do it or did do i', I won't say which, at any rate he got the account. I want to know if any of these men said they had known him to swear to a lie? I wouldn't say that I did hear either one of them say he had sworn to a lie. You say they spoke of him as having the reputation of a lying witness in matters in which he was interested, and that they spoke of his character for truth as being bad? Yes, sir. These speeches about his character occurred before he was emancipated? Yes, sir. You were not in Fayetteville the day Archy Beebee was killed? No, sir, I was not there. How came you to be a witness in this case? I don't know, sir, unless it was that I am acting magistrate in the district in which Armstrong used to live. Are you now a magistrate? Yes, sir. You don't know at whose suggestion you are summoned? No, sir. It was not your own? No, sir.

Re-direct examination by the Counsel for the accused:

I understand you to say the boy's character you have heard canvassed and talked about a good deal in the neighborhood? Yes, sir. And that the persons you have heard talking about it, both before and since this killing, all give him a bad character for truth? They do, sir. You spoke of Mr. George McCoy as having been a deputy sheriff in that neighborhood; you also spoke of having heard McPhail speak of his character, was Mr. Phail an officer in his county? He has acted as an officer, and he is justice of the peace. Are all these persons that you have named, together with other persons that you haven't named, say declare his character for truth to be bad? Yes, sir. I will ask you the question, sir, whether you have ever heard a single one of the neighbors around there, who knew him say that his character was good? No, sir, I never heard any one say it. And that in consequence of cattle stealing, and other things that you have heard of in which he has either been or proffered to be a witness, that his character has been questioned a great deal? Yes, sir. And that his general character for truth is very bad? Yes, sir.

Question by the Commission:

Mr. McAlister, you spoke of Armstrong's having committed some depredation: stealing cattle and so on, why was he not arrested? I say it was committed in that neighborhood, and it was supposed that he was concerned. Didn't you say that these parties said he was concerned? I said they thought him to be. If they believed him to be why was he not arrested? They never could get the proof, that was one reason what brought out so much about it. Was it expected that Armstrong would swear falsely in his own case? They thought he would swear falsely for any person. If Armstrong had been arrested would he have been a witness in his own case? No, sir. Was it a common thing in your neighborhood to allow such depredations as these you have spoken of, stealing cattle and so on, to go on without making any effort to arrest the parties committing those depredations? It was not, but they never proved successful in that neighborhood. Do you know any thing of John Armstrong's acts of your own personal knowledge? No, sir, I don't; let me correct myself in one instance: he came to me, speaking of what Neill Stewart said about him, he came to me to know from me, to get some advice if he could not make his master discount something for waiting on him after the emancipation; he told me he had bought some cattle or hogs, I forget which, from him and he was to pay a certain amount in greenbacks, or a certain amount in specie; he had waited on him and had tendered him a certain amount in greenbacks, and he did not have the specie, and he wanted to know if he could not make him take it; that went somewhat to confirm my opinion in what Neill Stewart told me that he had brought out this account against the estate. This conversation you had with him tended to make you believe what Neill Stewart told you about his character for truth? Yes, sir. During the war did you know whether there were any deserters from the rebel army living in your neighborhood in the woods? I know there were. Do you know whether those men ever did such things as steal cattle or hogs? I know that they did; I have a good reason to believe they did. Would you believe the testimony of a negro in any way, on any important occasion? Of this negro. Of any negro? Yes, sir, I know some negroes that I would believe as quick as most white men. Would you believe the testimony of negroes ordinarily—give it the same belief that you would to the testimony of white witnesses? No, sir.

The Judge Advocate:

If the Court please:—I have to lay before the Commission an affidavit, made on yesterday, by William J. Tolar, one of the defendants in this cause, asking that a man, by the name of Griffin Chance residing in Fayetteville, be summoned in this case.

The affidavit states that he expects to prove by said Chance that he William J. Tolar, did not fire the pistol shot which killed Archy Beebee.

I will state to the Commission that this man Griffin Chance was summoned by the prosecution upon having been informed that he knew something material to this cause, and upon examination

he knew nothing material to it, and he was discharged. If the Court orders him to be summoned, it will be done of course. I think it necessary to tell the court that there have been already thirty-five witnesses summoned on behalf of the defence.

The Commission asked if there had been any communication with Griffin Chance since that examination.

The Judge Advocate said there had been none on the part of the prosecution.

The Counsel for the accused:

I have to state that the information we have is such as is set forth in the affidavit. I understood the Court rule, not long since, that no other witness would be summoned for the defence, unless an affidavit was made that their testimony was material, and unless it was shown to the Court, in an affidavit what it was expected to prove, with the affidavit. That affidavit has been made, and I suggest that the only answer that can be made to the affidavit, is by a counter affidavit.

The statement the Judge Advocate has made, and I know very well he does not intend it—in the presence of the Court, is well calculated to prejudice the minds of the Court, against the witness, when he comes in. Mr. Tolar has sworn to that affidavit. He has that information, and he has that belief.

The Judge Advocate:

I was compelled to make this statement, in reference to this fact, as the Court did not at all understand the fact, in reference to the list of witnesses they ordered summoned. At the time they made the ruling you spoke of, they understood that list of witnesses to contain the names of all the witnesses summoned for the defence in the case from first to last, whereas, in fact, it contained but a little more than one-half.

The matter is entirely in the discretion of the Court. I lay it before the Court for them to decide.

The Commission was cleared for deliberation, and after some time so spent, the doors were reopened, and the Judge Advocate made the following announcement:

The Commission orders that the witness Griffin Chance, be summoned.

The Counsel for the accused:

In order to set this matter at rest, I desire to make a statement to the Court, that the testimony for the defence depends in a very great measure upon what testimony is brought out for the prosecution; and until the prosecution was closed it was impossible, utterly impossible for us to know what witnesses it was necessary for us to summon, to meet the case made by the prosecution. Therefore, at the time I handed the list of eighteen witnesses to the Judge Advocate, it was a week before the case closed, for the prosecution—it was impossible for me to know what witness I required, or whether I required more witnesses or not.

I will state to the Court that I am just as much averse to bringing witnesses here to testify to nothing material, as any member of the Court, or the Judge Advocate, I want to make no unnecessary expense about this matter, and we only ask to have the witnesses summoned which we believe to be material; and if they are not summoned we will have to bring them here ourselves and pay them out of a very scanty purse.

GURDON S. DEMMING, a witness for the defence, having been first duly sworn, testified as follows:

Examined by the Counsel for the accused:

What is your name? Gurdon S. Demming Where do you reside? In Fayetteville, N. C. How long have you resided in Fayetteville? It is always considered my home; I have been there for the past fifteen years now; I was away some ten or twelve years before that, most of the time, I have been back for the last fifteen years. Where is your place of business, Mr. Demming, in Fayetteville? At Mr. Davis'. Which Davis? I. B. Davis, the tinner. Where is that situated, what part of Fayetteville? On the south-east corner of Market Square. Were you in Fayetteville on the day Archy Beebee was killed? I was, sir. Where were you at the time Archy Beebee was killed? I was in Mr. Davis' shop, sir, the second story. Did you see Archy Beebee when he was carried up from the guard house to the market house? I did, sir. Did you go to the market house while Beebee was up stairs? I did, sir. Did you go up stairs? No, sir. How long after Beebee was carried up stairs before you went to the market house? I don't know that I could state. Was it a short time? I don't think it was more than three quarters of an hour, I don't recollect very distinctly about the time, I was busy myself. Did you go up stairs where this trial was going on? No, sir. How long did you remain at the market house? Only a few moments, the doors were closed and I went back to my business. In what business were you engaged at that time? Packing furs. In the second story of I. B. Davis' tin shop? Yes, sir. Were you engaged in your business in the front or the rear of the shop? In the front part. Were you near a window or door, or any opening? There were two windows within ten or twelve feet of me. Which way did those windows look, Mr. Demming? Towards the west and north. Did you see Archy Beebee when he was brought down from up stairs? I didn't see him, sir, until he was recovering from the fall which he had there. What fall? He fell down I suppose, he was getting up when my attention was first called to him. Where was he at that time? He was near the center of the market house, sir. On the pavement, or off the pavement? On the pavement. Near what corner? The south-east corner. You saw him just as he was recovering himself from the fall? Yes, sir; it looked like he was recovering when I first noticed him. You then saw him out of the window? Yes, sir. Was the window raised? Yes, sir, it was hoisted. Were you standing in the window? I was not, I was standing a few feet back. Were you looking at Archy Beebee at the time he recovered himself? Hearing a little disturbance I just stepped a few steps toward the window, and looked out. Just state what that disturbance was that attracted your attention. There was a little noise, some talk, &c.; just loud enough to attract my attention that way at that time. And you then looked out of the window? Yes, sir. And you saw Archy Beebee, as it were, just recovering himself from what appeared to you to have been a fall? Yes, sir. What occurred after that time? Well, sir, about the time he got straightened up, the pistol went off, and he fell, I don't think he had hardly got his position for more than a second before the pistol went off. Was there more than one pistol shot fired there on that occasion? I could not distinguish more than one from the report. Did you see that pistol? I did, sir. Did you see the hand that held that pistol? I could not say whose hand held it. Did you see any hand holding it? I don't know that I could say positively that I saw the hand that held the pistol. Did you see the pistol which was fired? Yes, sir. Did you see the flash? Yes, sir, I saw the smoke. And heard the report? Yes, sir. Well, sir, at the time you saw that pistol fired, where was Beebee standing? He was standing near the south-east corner of the market. On the pavement or off? He was on the

pavement, sir. Was he nearer to the market house, nearer to the center or nearer the outer edge of the pavement? I should think he was about midway as near as I could judge. In which direction was his face? I don't know that I can say positively, about that time he made a remark as well as I recollect to some one, "quit pulling me," or "let me loose," or something of that kind; I think his face was turned a little one way or the other, and I could not say which way, whether it was towards Sheriff Hardie, or towards the crowd, which appeared to be rather behind him, and to the left. At that time you think his face was turning a little from the straight-forward from the way he was marching? Yes, sir. But whether it was turned to his right or left, you do not know? No, sir. Where was the pistol which you saw, and which fired upon him? It looked to me about two feet and a half from his head, rather on his left and to his rear. You mean the muzzle of the pistol was fired that near? Yes, sir. Did you see any thing of a crowd around him at that time? Yes, sir, there was something of a crowd there. Which way was the heaviest, thickest portion of the crowd? Behind him, rather. Directly behind him? Rather behind him, there was a good many standing near the edge of the pavement. It was behind him, on the pavement, back towards the main eastern arch? Yes, sir. How thick was the crowd in that direction? They seemed to be pretty compact, I could not say how many persons were in it. Were they still or were they in motion? In motion, sir. It was a compact crowd in motion? Yes, sir. Standing there how near Beebee? So far as I could see and if my recollection serves me it was some ten feet from Beebee to the arch, and it appeared to be mostly between him and the arch. The crowd was standing back, you say, some ten feet upon the pavement. Yes, sir. How near to Beebee did the crowd come up? They appeared to be very close to him. How close? I think there were some as close as two or three feet to the rear of Beebee, ten feet back there was a dense crowd in motion. So the pistol fired very near the inner line of the crowd—nearest to Beebee, or was it fired from some other portion of the crowd? It looked to me like the pistol was almost two feet and a half from his head, the muzzle of the pistol. Was that distance as near as the crowd were, on that side of him to the man? I think the policemen were keeping the crowd back, some one of then raised his club about the time the pistol fired, which probably kept them back. Mr. Demming, who fired that pistol? I can't say, sir, who did it. You can't say who fired it? No, sir. Did you see the hand? I saw the pistol, but I don't know know that I could say that I saw the hand, I think, as near as my recollection serves me, I just got a glance, and I noticed the barrel of the pistol. And you say you swear you can't say who it was that fired? I can't say who fired it. Did you see any thing of Capt. Tolar there that day? I saw him there that day. What time did you see him there? It was some moments after the pistol was fired, I went down stairs, and went where the man Beebee was laying, I saw Capt. Tolar after that. Where was he? He was standing under the arch of the market house, some eight or ten feet probably under the porch like. When you went down stairs did you go out of the front door? I went out of the side door, the first door next to the stairs. Which way does that door open? It open upon the west side of the building, the stairs come right down to the door—I got out of that as quick as I could after the pistol was fired. Did you see anything of I. B. Davis about there that day? I did sir. When did you see him, and where did you see him? I saw him as I went down stairs. Where was he? He stood on the walk between the corner of his store and the market, probably about one third of the distance between the market and the corner of his store. He was standing there a few moments after the pistol fired, when you came down stairs? Yes, sir. And you passed him there? Yes, sir, How long did you remain in the crowd? Not exceeding half a minute. Where did you go then? I just stepped to the center of the street like, and went back to my business in a few moments. Did you pass Mr. Davis there when you returned? I think I did sir. You think you passed him standing about the same place. I think he remained in the same place when I went back. Did you see Capt. Tolar at all, before the pistol shot fired, during the entire day? I don't know that I saw him previous to the firing of the pistol. Did you see Sam Phillips that day? I did sir. Where did you see him? I might have seen him there during the day a half a dozen times, but I don't have any recollection of seeing him until after the pistol fired in the crowd. Where was he in the crowd, what point? When I first saw him I think about ten or twelve feet from where Beebee was lying. Did you see any body that you could recognize, with any weapon that day? I don't know that I saw any person have a weapon that day, I don't recollect seeing any. Was the pistol which you saw fired, the only weapon you saw there that day? As near as I can recollect, it was the only weapon I saw at all. Mr. Demming, do you know whether Robert M. Orrel was Captain of the local police, in July, 1865? I think he was, sir. Do you know whether he was or not.

The Counsel for the prosecution objected.

If the Court pleases—If Captain Orrell held a commission or appointment under the military authorities, there must be some written evidence of it in existence somewhere. It wont do to prove it by bare hearsay, or by the fact that he was acting as an officer.

The Commission said the same questions were allowed in a former examination.

The Counsel for the accused:

We cannot speak as to whether he was rightfully an officer or not. I think in the State of North Carolina we have had it decided often that you may prove the fact that a man is acting as an officer—either a judge, a justice of the peace, a sheriff, or a constable or any officer. The judge, the justice of the peace are certainly officers with commissions. There is a record of the election of the sheriff and his bond is recorded; there is a record of the appointment of the constable and his bond is filed of record. There is nothing more common, in the practice of North Carolina than to prove the fact that a particular officer was acting as such at the time. Indeed, sir, it occurs to me now, where there is a charge of bigamy, a criminal charge, which, in former times, went to a man's life, it was sufficient, amply sufficient, to show that the person who solemnized the rights of matrimony, was acting as a justice of the peace, no proof of his commission was ever required, nor was it ever suggested, or was it ever required that his commission should be produced. All that we desire to do, in this case, is to prove by the witness as a fact that Robert M. Orrell was at that time acting as captain of the local police. We think it is clearly admissible.

Counsel for the prosecution:

I object to it on another ground also, that the testimony is not at all relevant. It cannot have any possible bearing in this case whether Orrell was an acting officer or not. And besides, the gen-

tleman does not state the whole legal position. There are certain cases, where to prove that a man was acting as an officer is sufficient, while in other cases it is necessary to prove the fact of his appointment. I shall not attempt to draw the line between the two, not being prepared to do so to my satisfaction—and regarding as unnecessary to do so—at present. But the analogy of the judge, governor, &c., adduced by brother Fuller, is no analogy at all. The only object for which this evidence can be offered, is to justify Mr. Orrell in a certain course of conduct that he pursued towards a negro man; and what it can have to do with this case I can't see. When a man attempts to justify himself, on the ground that he is an officer, that is one of the cases in which he is bound to show his commission.

The Counsel for the accused:

May it please the Court. The Counsel for the prosecution, we apprehend, has not stated the object of this examination correctly. He will very well remember that he attacked Mr. Davis' testimony very much at length, upon this point, as to whether Orrell acted as an officer of the police, or as to whether he was acting as a magistrate. He questioned him very closely upon that, he attacked his credit upon that. Mr. Davis informed the gentleman, upon his cross examination, that he had an order some where, under which he acted, in tying up a certain witness, who had been summoned for the prosecution, by the thumbs—one John Shaw, if I recollect the name rightly. Mr. Haywood challenged him to produce such an order, and he intimated very plainly to the witness, that he did not believe such an order ever existed. He warranted he could have it produced and brought here, if Mr. Davis would tell him that it was at his house. We now offer to prove in vindication of the character of this witness of ours, who was attacked in this way, that there was such an order, purporting to come from a man who was filling the position of Captain of local police; whether he was rightfully so or not is a different question, but as far as the credit of this witness is concerned, all that we are interested in is to show that Mr. Orrell was acting in this capacity, and that this paper was issued, under which Mr. Davis inflicted this punishment. We now ask Mr. Demming the witness on the stand, whether Mr. Orrell was acting in that capacity; we then offer to prove the handwriting of Mr. Orrell, and to show that we have the order, the production of which was challenged by the Counsel for the prosecution; and it seems to me, in common fairness to the witness, whose credit is attacked, and according to the practice in every court, as far as my experience goes, we should be allowed to show these facts, in vindication of the character of the witness introduced. He is squarely attacked, fairely attacked by the Counsel for the prosecution, and we here offer to show that, in that matter, in which the Counsel may have thought he was entirely right, the witness was right, and the Counsel for the prosecution wrong.

The Commission was cleared for deliberation, and after some time so spent the door was reopened, and the Judge Advocate said:

The Commission sustains the objection of the Counsel for the prosecution, to the question. The Commission does not understand that the character of witness I. B. Davis was impeached, on this point.

Direct examination resumed by the Counsel for the accused.

Mr. Demming, are you acquainted with the handwriting of Robert M. Orrell? I am sir. Look at that paper, and tell whether that is the handwriting of Robert M. Orrell? I should say it was. Is it altogether in his hand-writing sir? Some of it is signed by him? I would say that is his signature.

The Counsel for the accused:

May it please the Court:—I propose to read an order, directed to Ichabod B. Davis, signed by Robert M. Orrell, dated July 20, '65 commanding I. B. Davis to tie up by the thumbs, Stewart McIntyre, and John Shaw, for sheep stealing. I propose sir, having proved the handwriting, to read an order to that purport to the Court.

Counsel for the prosecution.

For what purpose is it introduced?

The Counsel for the accused:

For the purpose of corroborating Ichabod B. Davis.

The Counsel for the prosecution:

Now, If the Court please:—It is palpable an instance has arisen to show to the Court how dangerous it is to depart, in the least degree, from the strict rules of evidence.

It is proposed by the Counsel for the defence, to introduce that written paper to corroborate one of their witnesses. The history of this case will show, that one John Shaw, a witness for the prosecution, while on the stand, was asked whether he had not been tied up by the thumbs, by order of Capt. Orrell, or somebody else, for sheep stealing, or some other offence. What his reply was I don't remember, nor is it material. I think the witness partially denied, and partially admitted it. He was a witness for the prosecution; he was asked—on the cross examination with a view to discrediting him—if he hadn't been subjected to that punishment for that particular offence? He answered—whether he confessed or denied, is not material. Then the thing was at an end. The defence asked him that collateral question upon the cross examination; his answer was final, and they can not introduce other testimony to show that he said falsely with regard to it, or that he said truly with regard to it. A witness for the defence is introduced here by the name of Davis, and is asked certain questions, and among them whether he inflicted this punishment upon the negro man Shaw. We ought to have objected then and there to Davis' testifying on this subject at all, because Shaw's answer was final upon that point, and Davis's evidence was only relevant, if relevant in the most remote degree, for the purpose of showing that Shaw had lied in his reply, to the Court. Now, it is proposed to go a step further still, not simply to show that the witness has lied, but to show that the witness who was introduced for the purpose of showing that Shaw had made a false statement of the fact—was speaking the truth. All this grows out of departing from the strict rules of evidence.

When a question of the character that the Counsel addressed to Shaw, is propounded, the rules are plain—a witness's *general character* for truth may be impugned by *general evidence;* you cannot ask for specific instances of misconduct. That is the rule. In examining as to general character they could introduce a witness here who could speak as to the general character of one of our witnesses, but he could not give evidence as to specific acts of misconduct, because a man does not come prepared to defend himself from all specific acts of misconduct, which may be alleged against him; but when the witness is on the stand himself, he can be impeached by showing specific acts of misconduct, by his own admissions on the stand. A witness may be impeached by showing that his general character is bad, but the impeaching witness is confined to general facts, he cannot give specific acts. While a witness

impeached is on the stand he may be cross-examined as to these specific acts; why? because the same objections do not apply to his response given to them, which would apply to the evidence of another witness on the same points, to wit, that it would branch out into innumerable collateral issues. Why, again? because by a rule of law the impeached witness' answer is final. Shaw was introduced here and examined, and upon the cross examination said, either he had been hung up by the thumbs, or he had not, by an order from Mr. Orrel. I say his answer to that question was final. Although that was the case, we allowed the defence to examine their witness, and ourselves extended the examination somewhat, to show what did actually happen with respect to Orrel and Shaw. That was wrong; and now they propose to go a step farther, and confirm that witness by introducing independent evidence to show that Orre! had the power to give that order. Now if the Court will pardon me for a moment; and I think we actually gain time by making these matters clear at first—upon impeaching a witness, Mr. Starkie says, page 207: "The credit of a witness may be impeached, either by cross examination, subject to the rules already mentioned or by general evidence affecting his credit, or by evidence that he has before done or said that which is inconsistent with his evidence on the trial; or lastly by contrary evidence as to the facts themselves. It is perfectly well settled that the credit of a witness can be impeached by general evidence only, and not by particular facts, not relevant to the issue, for this would cause the inquiry, which ought to be simple, and continued to the matters in issue, to branch out into an indefinite number of issues. The characters, not only of the witnesses in the principal cause, but of every one of the impeaching collateral witnesses might be impeached by separate charges and loaded with such an accumulated burthen of collateral proof that the administration of justice would become impracticable. Besides this, no man could come prepared to defend himself against charges which might thus be brought against him without previous notice; and though every man may be supposed to be capable of defending his general character, he cannot be prepared to defend himself against particular charges, of which he has no previous notice. Questions put to a witness himself upon cross examination are not, it may be observed, open to this objection since his *answer is conclusive* as to all collateral matters."

Here we have the collateral issue, as to whether Shaw had been tied up by the thumbs for sheep-stealing or any other offence. Shaw was asked the question upon cross examination, and he said either that 'he had been or that he had not been; his answer being given it was final, and evidence cannot be adduced here to contradict him—ought not have been introduced in the case of Davis, but cannot certainly be introduced for the purpose of sustaining Davis.

I do trust that the gentlemen will not insist upon raising questions of this kind to consume valuable time unnecessarily.

The Counsel for the accused:

I have no disposition to consume the time. I leave the matter entirely with the Court.

On the re-opening of the Court the Judge Advocate declared that the Commission sustains the objection of the Counsel for the prosecution.

Counsel for accused: Take the witness, sir.

Cross examined by Counsel for prosecution:

We have been discussing matters so far removed from your testimony, Mr. Demming, that I shall refresh your memory with what you have said.

You say you have been living in Fayetteville for fifteen or sixteen years? Yes, sir. That you were there on the day Archy Beebee was killed, and in the second story of Ichabod B. Davis' store, and packing furs? Yes, sir. Did you say there were two windows in the room you were in; is it a large room? More than two; it is a room of 20 by 30 feet. You spoke of windows to the north and west, do you mean one on the north front and the other on the west front of the house? Yes, sir. These windows were up? Yes, sir. Was it a cold day or not? I don't remember. You went to the market house while Beebee was up stairs? Yes, sir. For the purpose of hearing the trial? Yes, sir. And when you found you couldn't be admitted you returned home? Yes, sir. When you passed over to the market house that time how many persons constituted the crowd do you suppose; I mean taking those on the inside and outside on the east end? I noticed very little about it, sir. But we want your best estimate? Well, about probably twenty-five or thirty. Inside and out? Yes. Were the greater portion underneath the market house or outside? About an equal division. Did you see any one in the crowd that you recognized? I don't know that I can recollect any one particularly. Have you endeavored to refresh your memory? Not much. Well, you try and remember? I don't think I can. Neither when you passed going through the market nor when you passed coming back; you went inside, I suppose? No, I did not. Did not you go to the arch? No, I didn't go to that side at all. Where did you go? Well, the arch is on the end; it was to the side I went. You went on the south of the market house; then you didn't go inside? No, sir. You didn't pass through the crowd at all then? No, sir, I saw they wouldn't let my body up and I went back to my business. How long after you got back was your attention called by the noise? I don't know exactly. You must estimate whenever you can't speak positively? It was probably three quarters of an hour, more or less. After you returned? Yes, sir. You went to the market house shortly after Archy was carriage there? Yes, sir. And three-quarters of an hour after you returned from there the killing occurred? Yes, that was about it. Were both windows open? Yes, sir. What was the noise? Well, loud talking, and-so-forth. Did you hear any such cry as "kill him," "shoot him," or any thing of that kind? I don't know that I did—I dont think I did. There was some noise however that attracted your attention? Yes, sir, the first thing that attracted my attention was the ladies going to the carriage. How far was the point where you were working, from these two windows? About six or eight feet probably. Your attention was first attracted by Mrs. and Miss Massey going to the carriage? Yes, sir. Was there any noise particularly at that time? No, not much. Can you remember what attracted your attention? No, sir, I don't know, but when they went off I went back counting my furs. Did you go up to the window when they went into the carriage? I think so. To the north window or the west? To the North. You could see any body go to the carriage then? Yes sir. Do you remember who it was that went? I was not paying particular attention—I don't remember over half a dozen perhaps. Well sir, who were they? There was Mr. Bond and Mr. Taylor. Any body else? Yes, Mr. Cashwell, and perhaps Mr. Tom Powers. They went to the carriage? Yes, sir. Did you see Robert Mitchell? I think I did. Did you say you saw Tom Powers? I think so. Did you see Tolar go to the carriage? I did not, sir, that I recollect. Did you see anything of John Maultsby at or near the carriage? I think I did. You know him,

don't you? Very well, sir. You have mentioned all the persons you recollect seeing go to the carriage. I think I have sir. When the carriage drove off you went back to your work and some few moments elapsed before you heard the noise. Yes, sir. Did you go back to the window? I don't think I went to the window at all sir. Did you look from the point where you were at work? Yes, I think so, some five or six feet from the window. Was it the west window you were looking out from? Yes, sir. And when you saw Archy recovering from his fall you were looking out the west window also, were you? Yes, sir. Did the stairs pass right along by the window? No, sir, back of the window rather. In passing down stairs, did you pass the window on your right or left? The head of the stairs is some six or eight feet from the window probably. You can get to that window without going on the stairs? Yes, sir, the stairs rather run down under the window. Is there any rail at the head of the stairs? I don't think so. You were standing some four or five feet from that window, at any rate? Yes, sir, I think so. You saw Archy in the act of recovering apparently from a fall? That's what he appeared to be doing. Did you hear any exclamations in the crowd then? I don't recollect that I did. Never before the pistol shot? Only what he said himself. What was that? He said "don't kill me," or "let me go," or something like that. You didn't hear any one say "shoot the damn son of a bitch?" No, I don't think I did. Did you see any police, there? I saw Mr. Faircloth and Mr. McGuire. Did you see Wemyss? Yes, sir. Did you see them have any clubs? Mr. Faircloth had. Did you see him use it? Yes, sir. Were they facing the crowd? No, sir, I think he rather stood with his back to the crowd—his side was towards the market, I think. His back was towards the north, then? Yes, rather so. Did they seem to be resisting the crowd? Well, they appeared to be trying to keep between the crowd and the prisoner. That was the impression you got from that view? Yes, sir. Did you see any one making any assault on the prisoner before he was shot? I did not. Did you see no weapon at all? No, sir, I don't think I saw any weapon at all, except the pistol. You say it seemed to be two and a half feet to the left and rear of him? I should think a little to the left and rear, as nearly as I can recollect. You say you didn't see the hand that held the pistol? No, sir. Nor you didn't see the man to whom the hand belonged? No, sir, I think there was some obstruction to the view at the time. Did you see Captain Tolar at that moment? No, sir, Had you seen him by that time, that day? No, sir. When the pistol fired and the negro fell, did you see what became of the pistol? No, sir. Then you went down stairs, didn't you? Yes, sir. You saw Davis standing on the pavement? He was on the causeway, between the pavement and the market house, about six feet, as nearly as I can recollect from the corner of the pavement at his store. At what did you estimate the distance between the corner of the pavement at Davis' store, and the corner of the pavement at the market house? I think about thirty or forty feet. You think he had passed over five or six feet of that distance? Well, the distance between the store—. I am not talking about the distance between the store, but about the distance between the two pavements? Oh yes; about five or six feet from the corner of his pavement. Was his face towards the crowd? I could not say as to that, he was talking to some one at the time. Do you know who with? I do not. Do you think he was standing there as you passed back? I think he was.

You went into the crowd, did you not? No, sir, but within a few feet of where Archy was lying. Did not you go into the crowd at all? No, sir. Did you notice any body in the crowd that you knew at that time? Well, I merely went to see if he was shot, and didn't stop more than a few minutes and can't tell. Did you see Wemyss, or Sheriff Hardle there, or Faircloth, Maguire or Bond? Yes, they were close by the boy who was shot. Did you see any body that was not an officer? Well I presume I saw persons there but I cannot recollect now any that I knew beside these I have mentioned. Did you see Tolar there? I saw him and some others back under the market. How long did you stay there? A few minutes. I couldn't say exactly—don't think it exceeded two. You just went to the edge of the pavement looked and came back? Yes, sir, and I went towards the arch at the end of the market house. Towards the edge of the eastern arch? Yes, sir. Did you get opposite that? I did, sir. And when you got opposite that you saw Captain Tolar? Yes, sir. Where was he standing? About ten feet from the end underneath the market house. Was he facing you? I could not say, he was talking to some one at the time. Do you know to whom? No, sir. Did you notice anything peculiar in his appearance at the time? No, sir. Did you see any weapons at all, or any marks of weapons? I did not, sir. Had he a shawl or anything of that sort on? I think he had one on, sir? How did he have it? I think thrown over his shoulder, or over his arm. During that same time did you see Sam Phillips? About the same time, sir. Where was he? Outside the market house and ten or twelve feet from where the prisoner was shot. Was he on or off the pavement? Off at the time. In which direction, down Person street? Yes, sir. About east from where the negro fell? Well, it was in an easterly direction from the market; I think he stood between the boy that was shot and the middle of the street rather,—I think some ten or twelve feet probably from Beebee. Did you see him have any weapon, sir? I did not, sir. What was he doing? He was standing there talking to some person. Then you turned and went back? Yes, sir. When you passed, or went into the crowd, did you hear any one say who had shot the pistol? Heard some inquiry. Did you hear any answer? Yes, sir. Who was the person named as having shot the man? Capt. Tolar. How many times do you hear that? I don't know that I heard it more than once. Did you know the voice of the person? Yes, sir. Who was he? He goes by the name of Beckton. A negro man? Yes, sir. Are you sure about what you say about that? Yes, sir. Was the voice near enough to you to be heard? Yes, sir. How far were you from him? About five or six feet. Was he talking as loud as I am now? I think so. You say Tolar, when you saw him, was about twenty or thirty feet from the place where you heard the man state that it was Tolar who shot him? I should think that was about the distance, sir. Then you turned and went back up stairs, and that is all you know of it? Yes, sir. Have you any reason for knowing, sir, either from information or from your own knowledge, of any combination or agreement or understanding between any parties to take the man out of the hands of the authorities? I never knew of any thing of the kind sir. Did you ever see Capt Tolar wear a pistol? I don't know that I could say I ever did. Do you know whether he owns a pistol? I do not sir. You are a Mason sir, are you not? No, sir. You are not a Mason? No, sir.

Re-direct examination by Counsel for accused: Mr Denning I understand you to say that when you came down stairs you found Mr. Davis a step or two off from the pavement? Yes, sir, about six feet I think. And when you returned you think he was about the same place? Yes, sir. He was just at the corner of his pavement? Yes, some few feet beyond. You say that after the man was shot you heard a colored man named Becton say who shot him—how long after the man was shot did you hear Beckton say that? I don't think it exceeded a minute, or a few minutes at most. You say that at that time Captain Tolar was thirty feet off from Beckton? Yes, I should think at least twenty or thirty feet. Could Tolar from where he was, hear Beckton's reply to the question asked him, in the tone of voice in which it was spoken?

Counsel for prosecution:

I object to that. He can state the tone of the voice, and the position of the parties, as well as the amount of noise created by the buzzing and movements of the crowd, and it then remains for the Court to determine whether Tolar heard Beckton's declaration or not.

Counsel for accused:

We ask the Counsel for the prosecution as to whether he does not consider the testimony, as to what Beckton said, hearsay evidence—unless it has first been shown that Beckton was in the presence of Captain Tolar at the time the remark was made. It is the duty of any party who offers a declaration as against parties who are accused, to prove that the person making the declaration was in the presence of the party against whom the declaration is offered as evidence.

Counsel for prosecution:

A declaration of a third party made in the defendent's presence can be heard in evidence against even a drunken man; it is for the Court and jury to determine whether he was in a condition to hear the remarks and did not contradict them.

Counsel for accused:

May it please the Court—The remark made by another is not admissible in evidence as against a prisoner unless it is shown that the remark was made in the presence of the accused and not contradicted by him. We have not sought to exclude any testimony calculated to elucidate the questions at issue by any such objections as those offered by the Counsel for the prosecution. We might have objected to the declarations of Beckton at the time they were called for by the Counsel for the prosecution. We didn't think proper to do so, and we now desire to show that they are inadmissible as testimony by proving that the remark by Becton in the presence of the witness was not made in the presence of Capt. Tolar.

Counsel for the prosecution:

I am stricken with amazement to hear the gentleman take such a position. The fact that Tolar is shown to have been in the presence of Beckton at the time his declaration was made is prima facia evidence that Tolar heard his remarks, and there can be no possible objection to introducing the declaration. If it was a case before a civil Court the judge would admit the testimony and leave it to the jury to say whether the party accused had heard the remark or not. The fact is plain, that Tolar was there,—and it is possible he might have heard it—just as in the case of a drunken man, to which reference has been made. We do not know whether he Tolar heard it or not. We have a very decided opinion on that point, and we presume the Court has a shrewd suspicion that he did; this opinion is derive not only from that which this witness deposes to, but from the evidence of several others. But that this evidence should be objected to, on the ground that there is any thing in the least irregular in its introduction, would have strick en me with amazement, if it were not that I am learning daily, how far the zeal of the Counsel will carry them. The remark of Beckton has already been brought out in evidence, and if there was any objection it should have been offered at the proper time. If I did wrong, the time to complain of it was when this remark of Beckton's was first called for; but the Counsel proposes now to ask *the opinion* of this witness as to whether Tolar heard it or not. They can ask where Tolar was standing, where Beckton was standing, and in what position the witness was. They can ask with regard to the tone of voice in which this remark was made, and with regard to the hum caused by the talking and movement of the crowd, and then it is for the Court to say whether the remark was made in the presence of Tolar or not;—whether he heard it or not.

Counsel for the accused:

The difference between the Counsel for the prosecution and the Counsel for the defence is not a difference in a matter of law, but as to a matter of fact. The whole thing rests upon the construction to be placed upon the word "presence."

Now may it please the Court it is proved by this witness that Captain Tolar was six or eight feet inside and under the market house, and thirty feet distant from Beckton. That there was a large crowd between Beckton and Tolar, and that the remark by Beckton, as to who shot the man, was made in an ordinary tone of voice. We think therefore that it cannot be fairly contended that Beckton was in the presence of Tolar at the time he made the remark, and Tolar is in no sense bound by it. To illustrate, it could not be said that I am in the presence of a man who is talking in an ordinary tone, to another man in the passage outside this hall. It seems to us a very strange construction of the word presence. We think that Captain Tolar was not in the presence, actual or constructive, of Beckton when the remark was made, which is now offered in evidence against him.

Counsel for the prosecution:

I would like to know what practical question is before the Court. Does the Counsel move to strike out that question.

Counsel for the accused:

We say we have a right to examine this witness as to his opinion upon the point whether Captain Tolar could—taking into consideration all the circumstances—have heard the remark made by Beckton,

Counsel for the prosecution:

And I say, No.

Counsel for the accused:

Well, since the question is objected to, we'll withdraw it and put it in another form.

Judge Advocate:

Do you withdraw the question?

Counsel for the accused:

Yes, sir.

Re-direct examination resumed:

Mr. Demming, you say at the time this remark was made by Beckton, Tolar was standing about thirty or forty feet off? Yes, sir, I should judge so. And ten feet under the market house? Six or eight feet I think, somewhere along there. And Beckton was standing out in the open air? Yes, sir, in the street. Was he standing due east from the center of the arch? Pretty much east from the arch. Were there any persons between Beckton and Tolar? Yes, sir. How many? Well, I dont know. Were there a good many?

Yes, there was a crowd. Was it quiet or talking? They were talking sir, more or less excited I suppose. Was that crowd speaking in a loud tone of voice? Well, they were talking in rather an unnatural tone of voice. I understand you to say that Becton made that remark in an ordinary tone of voice? Yes, sir, the man that asked him stood near him. Was the crowd between Beckton and Tolar talking louder than Beckton? Sir? The question I asked, is, was the conversation which was going on in the crowd, which was between Beckton and Tolar, as loud, or louder, than the tone of voice in which Beckton said Tolar had done it? I should think there was very little difference. Very little difference between the way the crowd was talking and the way Beckton was? Yes, sir, I should think very little. How far did the crowd extend from the market house at that time, taking a direct line from where Tolar was standing? Partly on the pavement and partly off. That noise and that talking in the crowd between Beckton and Tolar, did it seem to be general talking or was it confined to certain portions of the crowd? It seemed to be a general talking all around. And in as loud a tone of voice as Beckton? I shouldn't think there would be much difference. I believe you said, sir, you saw nobody with a weapon? I don't recollect seeing anybody with one. Mr. Deming, you have said something about seeing Phillips, did you see him in the crowd at the time the man was shot, or after? It was after the man was shot.

Questions by the Commission:

How far were you from Beckton at the time Beckton made this remark? Well, sir, I should suppose, perhaps in the neighborhood of five or six feet. Where were you standing? I was passing him at the time. At what point from the market house? Towards Davis' shop. Were you between him and the market house, or between him and Davis' corner. Between him and the market house, I think as nearly as I can now recollect.

Judge Advocate:

That will do Mr. Deming.

The Counsel for accused, on being asked who the next witness was, said:—I shall have to announce to the Court that we are not ready just now to examine any other witness. We have two witnesses here who came, I suppose, this morning, and I have never had any conversation with them at all; in fact I didn't see them until I passed up to the Court this morning at 11 o'clock.

Judge Advocate:

I wish to enter my protest against this continual delay on the part of the Counsel for the defence.

The Commission:

At what time did they arrive? Were they here last night?

Counsel for defence:

No, sir, they got here this morning at nine o'clock; I would like to say, by way of setting the Counsel for the prosecution right, that we are not aware of having delayed the Court in the defence at all.

Judge Advocate:

Whether on the part of the Counsel or the witnesses the delay has been on the part of the defence.

Counsel for defence:

The witnesses who were examined yesterday were summoned on Saturday evening. It is certainly not our fault; we can't bring witnesses here; and I think every day that witnesses have come here, we have examined either upon the day they have come, or certainly the next day after.

Judge Advocate:
The difficulty is, may it please the Court, that some four or five witnesses are summoned to be here to-morrow, and we shall have a congregation of witnesses here waiting to be examined. There are three here now, and yet they are not prepared to go on with the examination of them. To-morrow there will be five more, or ought to be; they have been summoned a long time since—as long ago as last Thursday or Friday, and some of them should have been here before now.

Counsel for accused:
Well, sir, when the witnesses come, just as soon as I have an opportunity of talking to them I will put them on the stand until the Court wishes to stop. I do not desire, and I do not intend, to be put in the wrong about this matter. I have never had here yet, since this defence has commenced, over three or four witnesses at a time; whereas the prosecution had these benches almost full of witnesses, as many as ten or a dozen at a time.

Judge Advocate:
I must beg leave to correct the Counsel; he has had as many as seven, at any rate, many of whom remained here several weeks.

Counsel for defence:
Since the defence commenced?

Judge Advocate:
We are not talking about "since the defence commenced" sir.

Counsel for defense:
That is what I said sir.

Judge Advocate:
I didn't so understand it, sir. It is for the Court to say whether any more witnesses shall be examined to-day.

The defence not being ready to examine the witnesses who were present, the Commission concluded to adjourn, and,

On motion, at 1:45 P. M. the Commission was adjourned until 10, o'clock to morrow, 29th inst.

RALEIGH, N. C., Aug. 29, 1867, 10 A. M.

The Commission met pursuant to adjournment.

Present: All the members of the Commission, the Judge Advocate, the Counsel for the prosecution, all the accused and their Counsel.

The reading of the testimony taken yesterday was waived, there being no objection thereto.

Yesterday's proceedings were then read.

On motion that part of the record having reference to the hour of adjournment, was stricken out.

Yesterday's proceedings were then approved.

WILLIAM J. McPHAIL, a witness for the defence having been first duly sworn, testified as follows:

Examination by the Counsel for the accused:
What is your name? William J. McPhail. Where do you reside? In Cumberland county, ten miles east of Fayetteville. What is your occupation? I am a farmer, sir. Are you acquainted with John Armstrong? Yes, sir. How long have you known him? I have known him from a small boy. To whom did he formerly belong? He first belonged to Jeanett Armstrong, from her he passed to F. C. Armstrong. Is Jeanett Armstrong living or dead? She is dead, sir. Farquard C. Armstrong, is he living? He is dead. How far did John Armstrong live from you, at the time he belonged to Farquard? Three miles when he belonged to Jeanett, four miles when he belonged to Farquard. Do you know the general character of John Armstrong for truth? Yes, sir. What is that character? It is bad, for truth.

Cross examination by the Counsel for the prosecution:
Where did you say you lived Mr. McPhail? In Cumberland county, ten miles east of Fayetteville. How near do you live to Duncan J. McAlister? Two miles. In the same neighborhood? Yes, sir. Are you related to any of these parties on trial? No, sir. Are you related to any of the witnesses in this cause? None that I know, sir. Are you related to any of the parties who have been arrested for this offence? No, sir. You have no interest or bias whatever in this cause? None in the world, sir. How old is John Armstrong? Well, sir, I could not tell exactly his age, I think he is some thirty years old, or more. Nearer forty or thirty? I suppose between thirty and thirty-five, I think I am some older, and I am thirty-eight. How long have you known him? Since he was a boy. He lived in the same neighborhood that you did when he was a boy? Yes, sir. How long has his character been bad for truth? Since he was about grown, sir. He established his character before manhood? When he was about a man, sir, I began to be acquainted with his character. Who have you heard speak of his general character? I heard Joel Williams speak of his character. Does he live in that neighborhood? He is dead now; he did live in that neighborhood. What did he say about him? He said his character for truth was bad. What brought it up? He had a wife on his plantation, and he used to speak about his having been at a loss to know how to get rid of John's coming to his plantation; he said he was bad for truth and honesty. Did he say any thing about his truth as well as his honesty? Yes, sir. Well, sir, who else did you hear speak of? J. M. Williams. Is he a son of Joel? Yes, sir. Lives at the same place? Yes, sir. All these statements were made by these men before this man Beebee was murdered? Yes, sir. How long ago was it you heard J. M. Williams speak of him? I heard him speak of him since he was free and before. What did he say of him before. Well, sir, he said he was a bad character, and he didn't want him to be coming to his plantation. Did he say any thing about his truth? Yes, sir. How did his truth come in question? Well, sir, it was in connection with some hogs that were stolen on his plantation. Did he say Armstrong had stolen them? He spoke of John having said something in regard to them and he did not know whether it was so or not; he didn't have any confidence in him. John Armstrong had said something about this matter? Yes, sir. Did he give in his testimony? No, sir, there was no trial. Is that the only time you heard him speak of him before he was free? Yes, sir, I don't think I ever heard him speak of his truth since he was free. Who else have you heard speak of him for truth? I have heard William B. McAllister. Who else? John Holmes. Do these men all live in the neighborhood that John did? Yes, sir. Any one else? Louis Williams, a freedman, Frank Williams a freedman, and Jacob Avery, a freedman. When was that? In the spring of '66 I think. Do you remember any others? Yes, sir, Daniel B. Murphy; Sam Allen, a freedman of color. When was that sir? Some time in the spring of 1866, I think. Did he speak of his truth? Yes, sir. How did his truth come in question, in the spring of 1866—did Sam Allen's and Frank Williams' and Jacob Avery's? No, sir, it was a different matter. How was it with Sam Allen, what was the matter that brought up his truth? In Murphy's case, about a mule. Did he swear in that case? Yes, sir. His affidavit was taken? Yes, sir, taken by Major Lawrence, I was present. These men said they would not

believe him? Sam Allen said he swore to what was not so. Did he then go on and speak of his character? Yes, sir. Was Sam Allen a witness in the case? No, sir. Whose mule was it Murphy's? Yes, sir, the mule was in dispute between Murphy and Smith. Was it in connection with this matter that you heard Murphy speak of his character? Yes, sir. Between Murphy and Smith? Yes, sir. Do you recollect any others that you have heard speak of him? No, sir, I think that that is the most I have heard speak of him. You know nothing whatever in this case? No, sir. You were not in Fayetteville the day it took place? No, sir. When were you summoned as a witness? I was summoned the 24th, sir. Do you know how you came to be summoned? No, sir. You had nothing to do with procuring your summons? No, sir.

Re-direct examination, by the Counsel for the accused.

Mr. McPhail, you say you heard one of these parties speak of him, the remarks being brought out by some trial, which occurred between John Armstrong, and D. B. Murphy, about a mule? The trial was between Smith and Murphy. Did Armstrong have any interest in the matter; was he interested in the mule? I don't think he was sir, he was a voluntary witness. You say his affidavit was taken before Major Lawrence? Yes, sir. Who was Major Lawrence? He was in command of the Freedman's Bureau in Fayetteville. It was a bureau trial? Yes, sir. In connection with this affidavit, you heard these freedmen that you have mentioned, speak not only of what he had sworn to in that connection, but you heard them, speak of his general character for truth? Yes, sir. And these persons that you have named, are neighbors of Armstrong, and have known him long, and you have heard them call his character for truth in question often and they all said it was bad? Yes, sir. I will ask you sir, if you have ever heard a man in that neighborhood, speak of his character for truth, and say it was anything else but bad? No, sir. And his character in the neighborhood has been canvassed a good deal, before he was emancipated, and since he was emancipated? Yes, sir.

A. E. McKay, a witness for the defence, having been first duly sworn, testified as follows:

Examined by the Counsel for the accused:.

What is your name? Alexander Erskine McKay. Where do you reside? I reside within five miles of Fayetteville, this side. In the county of Cumberland? Yes, sir. Are you acquainted with John Armstrong, a freedman? I am. How long have you known him? I have known him since 1860. About what is his age? Well sir, I think he is about thirty or thirty five, to guess, I have no idea except from his looks. Do you know to whom he formerly belonged? I know by reputation sir, not by rights. Do you know with whom he formerly lived? Yes, sir, he was a divided property, as I understand—he was left by the grand mother of Canlepon Armstrong's children to them. How far did you live from him? I lived about two miles from him—two or three. Do you know the general character of John Armstrong for truth? I do sir. What is his character for truth? It is bad.

Cross examination, by the Counsel for prosecution.

How far did you live from Fayetteville? I live now about five miles from Fayetteville sir, perhaps. How long have you been living there? I have been living where I live only this year. Before that, where did you live? I lived about a mile higher up, nearer to where we were speaking of this man living. What is your occupation? Farming. How far was the place that John Arm-

strong lived, from the plantation where you lived, at the time you learned his general character? I was living then within two miles of him, farming in a mile of him—the plantations joined, in 1860–'61. What do you mean by a man's general character? I would make it what the neighbors generally say about him. That is correct sir; do you mean to say the neighbors of John, generally say that his character is bad for truth? They do. How many persons have you heard speak of it? I could not tell. Have you heard many? All that I have ever heard speak of him. You may not have heard but one? I have heard dozens speak of him. Did they speak of his character in other respects than for truth? Yes, sir, for honesty. Any thing else? He is pretty hard to drink, that is the report. He is a drinking man, aint honest and lies? That is the report. Any other crime laid to his charge? I don't recollect of hearing any.

Dilly Stewart, a witness for the defence, having been first duly sworn testified as follows:

Examined by the Counsel for the accused.

What is your name? My right name is Delia, they always call me Dilly. Dilly what? Dilly Stewart. Where do you live? In Fayetteville. Do you live in the town? I live in the edge of the town, between the toll house and town. How long have you been living in and about Fayetteville? About thirty years I reckon, I got there the year after the big fire. Did you know Archy Beebee, or Archy Warden? Yes, sir, I have known him ever since he was two days old, he was two days old when I called to see him and his mother. Were you at the market house in Fayetteville on the day Archy was killed? Yes, sir. What were you doing at the market house, why did you go? I went dar for a witness in the case of that girl. You went there as a witness in the case of Archy and Miss Massey? Yes, sir. Did you go up stairs where they were examining him? Yes, sir. What time did you come down stairs before Archy was brought down, or afterwards? I come down before Archy come down. How long before Archy was brought down? I think it was about a quarter of an hour. When you came down stairs where did you go? I stopped at Becky Ben's table where she keeps. Inside of her stall? Yes, sir, between the stove and the bench. Just tell where the stove is. As you come up the steps the stove is on the right hand there. What did you stop at the stove for? To warm my feet, it was pretty cold. You saw the crowd I suppose under the market house? Yes, sir. You stood there until after Archy was brought down? Yes, sir. Were you sitting there when Archy first appeared on the steps? When he come down I was sitting there. Did you see him when they first brought him to the head of the stairs, the landing of the stairs? I was there when he first started; as he come down the man that kept the door, I torget his name, but he kept the door, and when he come down I says to Morgan let us go home, because it was cold. Never mind what you said, you stayed there until he was brought down? Yes, sir. Did you stay there until he was shot? Yes, sir. Now at the time he first made his appearance on the stair steps, did you notice anything unusual in the crowd? No, sir, there was nobody on the steps at all, but the four men, one was Mr. Wemyss, tother was Sheriff Hardie, and I don't know who the other two men was. At the time Archy first made his appearance at the landing did anybody jump on that bench which runs close along there where you were, and say anything? No, sir, it was all mighty calm. From the time Archy first got to the landing until he got to the floor of the market house, did any one jump on that bench, and make use of any exclamation? No, sir. Did anybody jump on that bench and say "watch out, boys, here he comes"? No, sir. You swear nothing of that sort occurred? I never heard a thing of it. Do you know John Maultsby? No, sir. Do you know Capt. Tolar? I never seed him in my life before I seed him yesterday. Do you know Tom Powers? No, sir. Do you know David Watkins; otherwise called Monk? I never seed the Monk before I seed him yesterday. Do you know Ed Powers? No, sir. Do you know J. G. Leggett? Yes, sir, I know him. Did you see him there that day? No, sir, I disremember whether I seed him there or not. Do you know Sam Hall? No, sir. Do you know Ralph Lutterloh? I know his father, but I don't know him. Do you know Henry E. Sykes, the one-armed man? Yes, sir, I knowed him. Did you see him there that day? I never noticed. Do you know Sam Phillips? Yes, sir. Did you see Sam Phillips there that day? No, sir, I never seed him. So you came down and took your seat there by that stove inside of Becky Ben's stall? Yes, sir. Which way was your face fronting as he came down the steps? My face was towards the stove and when he got to the back post and went to wheel around, there was two small white men headed him up, and they says "hold him," and I says " dear God, is Archy having the assurance to run," "I would not run to save my life, I would have stood my post until the last drop of blood." Right off to the left there a man hollered "kill the God damned son of a bitch, shoot him," and the pistol went off there, and all of them that was there was white, I didn't see any colored men on the white side. Which way was your face at the time Archy came down? Right to the steps as he come down. I understood you to swear that nobody jumped upon that bench? Nobody didn't jump up on the top of the bench. There was no such expression used as "watch out, boys, here he comes"? If there was I never heard it. You never heard everything that occurred about there at the time, did you? It was all mighty calm, I didn't hear anything; it was most like a funeral, every thing was so calm. And if any such expression as that had been used upon that bench, you would have heard it? I would have heard it. That is all you know about this matter? Yes, sir. How long did you stay there, after Archy was shot? I reckon I didn't stay there a quarter. About ten minutes? I reckon about ten minutes. During the time you were there at the market house, did you hear anybody cry out in the crowd who had shot him? No, sir, I never heard who it was at all, until after I got over the bridge. You need not tell what you heard after you got over the bridge? I never heard nobody say who shot, not how he come to be shot. Before you left the market house, did you hear anybody say they knew who shot him, or anything of that sort?. No, sir. Can you hear well? Not exactly. Can you hear me? Yes, sir. You can hear well enough to hear what I am saying? Yes, sir.

Cross examination, by the Counsel for the prosecution :

Aunt Dilly, you came down stairs about fifteen minutes before Archy came down? Yes, sir. You were sitting down by the stove, inside of Becky Ben's stall? Yes, sir. With your face towards the stove? Yes, sir. Did you say it was a cold day? Yes, sir, it was mighty cold. Was there any wind? The wind was blowing very much. While you were sitting there warming, Archy came down? Yes, sir, and Mr. Wemyss and the sheriff, and I don't know the tother two,

men. You didn't see anything done to him, as he came down stairs? No, sir. Before Archy started down, did you see anybody standing on Becky Ben's bench? No, sir. And when he came down the first thing you heard of any disturbance was just as he was turning out of the arch? Yes, sir, I heard some one say "hold him, hold him, hold him." Was that said several times? Yes, sir, I saw two men seem to be heading him up, and I says—. Never mind what you said? I thought he was going to run, and some one said, shoot the nigger, God damn him. When you sat down there, which one of your sides was turned towards the point where this man Archy was—your left side? Yes, sir. You were looking over your left shoulder to see what was going on? Yes, sir. Did you hear the sheriff tell the men to keep off? No, sir. A good many times some one said hold him? Yes, sir. You say you don't hear very well? No, sir. Have you always been a little deaf? No, sir, I took it to be from working so much over a hot iron. It is only as you have grown older that you have grown a little deaf? Yes, sir. Now this person that cried "shoot him," how long was that after this crowd interrupted him in passing out of the arch? It was not more than a minute or so. You didn't see who fired the pistol? No, sir, there was so many there, it looked to me there was two or three hundred. Did you see any body with any pistol there that day? No, sir, I never seed a knife, nor a pistol. You saw no weapon at all? No, sir.

WILEY WRIGHT, a witness for the defence, having been first duly sworn testified as follows:

Examination by the Counsel for the prosecution.

What is your name? Wiley Smith. Do you ever pass by any other name than Wiley Smith? Yes, sir, Wiley Wright. Where do you live? I live at Mr. Wm. B. Wrights, about three miles from Fayetteville. Where does Miss Eliza live or where did she live at the time it was stated that this outrage was committed on her? She lived down below town. Who was she staying with? With Mr. Wright. Do you know Archy Beebee or Archy Warden? Yes, sir. Were you in Fayetteville on the day he was killed? Yes, sir. Did you go to the market house? Yes, sir. Who did you go with? I went with the ladies . mother. With Miss Massey? Yes, sir. How did you go with her? I drove her in the carriage sir. What sort of a carriage was that? A one horse carriage. What seat were you on? The front seat sir. What seat did she occupy? The back seat. Was there any division, either of a curtain or any thing else between the front and back seats? No, sir. How far was it from the front seat upon which you sat to the back seat of the carriage? It was not more than a foot. And an open space? Yes, sir. Then you drove Miss Massey? Yes, sir. You didn't drive Miss Massey, the young lady? No, sir, I didn't drive her to the market house. When you got to the market house which side did you stop the carriage on? On the east side. How far from the pavement? Well sir, about ten feet I reckon. Did any body go to the carriage when you drove up first? No person, only Mr. Bond. The town constable? Yes, sir. What did he do? He taken the ladies out. Was there more than one lady in the carriage at that time? No, sir, there was not but the one lady in there, the mother the one I drove. How did the young lady go there? Mr. Bond he drove her down in a buggy, and he helped her out of the buggy. Mr. Bond took the young lady down out of his buggy, and took Mrs. Massey out of your carry all, and went off? Yes, sir. Where did he go? Up in the market house.

Was Archy Beebee up stairs at that time, or was he brought out afterwards? He was brought out afterwards. Where were you at the time he was brought down? I was down on Dick St., we went there first, we didn't go straight to the market house, before they got ready for the trial, when they got ready for the trial, Mr. Vann came after me to go up to the market house. Let me understand you; you drove up there first before Archy Beebee was carried up stairs? I was not there, I never seed him yet; I don't know whether they carried him up stairs first or afterwards. What I want to get at is, what became of you after Mr. Bond helped the ladies out of the carriage? Then I got out of my carriage and went around the market house. You left your carriage standing there? Yes, sir. In charge of any body? No, sir. Which side of the market house did you go? I went on the south side. Did you remain there until the ladies came down stairs? No, sir, I didn't remain there all the time, I walked about under the market house and around the market house. Passing through the crowd that was there? Yes, sir. How large a crowd? It was a pretty smart crowd. Where was the crowd, under the market house? Yes, sir, and most on the side where my carriage was. On the east side? Yes, sir. Do you know Capt. Tolar? No, sir, I don't know him. You don't know whether you saw him there that day or not? No, sir. You didn't see that gentleman, (pointing to Captain Tolar?) If I did I didn't know him. Do you know Tom Powers? No, sir. Look at that gentleman, (pointing to Powers,) and see whether you remember to have seen him there? No, sir. I don't remember to have seen him there. Do you know David Watkins, otherwise called Monk? No, sir. Look at that gentleman (pointing to Watkins) and see if you remember to have seen him? I didn't see him that I remember of. Do you know Ed. Powers? Yes, sir. Do you remember to have seen him there that day? No, sir. Do you know Sam. Hall? No, sir. Do you know J. G. Leggett? No, sir. Do you know John Maultsby? No, sir. Do you know Sykes, the one armed man: Henry Sykes? No, sir, I don't know him. Do you know Sam. Phillips, who used to be constable? Yes, sir. Did you see him there? No, sir, I didn't see him. You were on the south side under the market house, and around the market house from the time the ladies went up stairs until they came down stairs? Yes, sir. Passing in though and around the crowd? Yes, sir. There was a very smart crowd? Yes, sir. Was there any excitement about the crowd that attracted your attention? If there was, I didn't see it. Did you hear any threats, any thing that was to be done to Archy Beebee? No, sir. Did you see any whispering in the crowd? No, sir. Where were you at the time Miss Massey and her mother were brought down stairs? I was under the market house then. Did you see them when they passed out and went to the carriage? No, sir, when I was called to the carriage they were at it. You saw them before they got up in the carriage? Yes, sir. Who called to your carriage? Mr. Bond. Did you go straight to your carriage? Yes, sir. What did you do when you got to your carriage; did you get up to your seat? Yes, sir, I got right up to my seat. Now while from the time that the ladies got into the carriage—you saw them when they got into the carriage? Yes, sir. To the time they drove off, who went to the carriage? I don't know, but one, gentlemen. Who was that? Mr. Taylor. Philimon Taylor? Yes, sir. How many other men were there that went to the carriage? Only one besides him. You didn't know him? No,

sir, I didn't know him. I ask you if this man here (pointing to Tolar) went to the carriage? No, sir, he didn't go to the carriage. Did this man here (pointing to Powers) go to the carriage? If he did, I didn't see him. Was there any whispering at the carriage between Miss Massey and Mrs. Massey, or either of them, with any man or with any men there? Mr. Taylor, he stepped to the carriage, and he didn't make out whatever it was he had to say, Mr. Bond ordered me to drive off. With that man that you didn't know who went to the carriage, was there any whispering? No, sir. Was there any conversation carried on between these ladies and any body at that carriage that you didn't hear? No, sir, none at all. Then you drove off? Yes, sir. You say before Mr. Taylor finished his sentence, that Mr. Bond directed that the carriage should be driven off. Yes, sir. Which way did you drive? I went down on Dick street east from the market house; I went down about a hundred and fifty or two hundred yards, and turned to the right down Dick street. Did you go back to the market house any more that day? Yes, sir. What time did you go back to the market house? In about twenty-five minutes. Where was Beebee at that time? Well, sir, they hadn't brought him down when I left. Where did you stop there? I went around with the ladies, and started with them home, the horse stopped and would not go, and they got out and I turned back. Where did you go then? I come up to the market house. That was in the twenty-five minutes you were speaking of? Yes, sir. You came back to the market house? Yes, sir. Were you there when Archy was brought down? No, sir. You were not there when he was brought down? No, sir. Where did you go? I went with the ladies, started with them home. Did you carry them home? No, sir. How far did you get? I reckon about half a mile. Let me see if I can't understand you; the carriage turned off and you went with the ladies down Dick street? Yes, sir. And then you came back up to the market house? No, sir, I didn't bring them back; they got out when the horse stopped and wouldn't pull. Where did the horse stop; on Dick street? Yes, sir, way down on Dick street about a half a mile. Then the ladies got out? Yes, sir. Where did you go with the carriage? I come right back to the market house. And you think it was about twenty-five minutes from the time you left with the ladies? Yes, sir. When you got back to the market house where did you go? I stopped there a little. How long did you stay that second time? I reckon I stayed there a quarter of an hour. Before you left there? Yes, sir. And left before Beebee was brought down? Yes, sir. I mean this last time? He was dead when I got back to the market house. How long after he was dead? I don't know how long he had been dead. Did you look at him? Yes, sir. You saw he was dead? Yes, sir. Who was about him at the time you looked at him? There was a good many about there. Did you hear the pistol fired? No, sir. Is that all you know about the matter? Yes, sir, all I know, sir.

Cross examination by the Counsel for the prosecution:

Did you drive the ladies to the market house that morning, the morning of the day Archy Beebee was killed? I drove her mother. Did you drive them there twice that day or only once? Only once. Was that after dinner? Yes, sir. You drove Mrs. Massey in the rockaway, and Mr. Bond drove Miss Massey in his buggy? Yes, sir. Did you drive at the same time? Yes, sir. Which was behind? I was behind. After Mr. Bond helped out the ladies, and went up stairs, what became of Mr. Bond's buggy? It stayed there. And your carriage stayed there too? Yes, sir. You left them there? Yes, sir. Any body in charge of Mr. Bond's buggy? No, sir. Was his buggy in front of your carriage? Yes, sir. You went around to the south side of the market house and stayed about there, and the first you knew Bond told you that the ladies were about to get into the carriage? Yes, sir. You went back, did both of the ladies get into your carriage then? Yes, sir. What became of Bond's buggy, was it still standing there? Yes, sir. Was it standing there when you drove off? Yes, sir. How long after you got back to the carriage, after the ladies got in before you drove off? I drove off as soon as I could get on my seat.

PHILIMON TAYLOR, a witness for the defence having been first duly sworn, testified as follows:

By Counsel for the accused:

Mr. Taylor, where do you reside? In Fayetteville. Fayetteville North Carolina? Yes, sir. What is your business? A merchant. Where is your place of business? On market square, sir. Which corner. The north east. Were you in Fayetteville on the day Archy Beebee or Archy Warden was killed? I was. Where were you? When he was killed, I was standing in my store door. Before that time? Well, I was out a little from the store towards the market house. Did you see him when he was carried up stairs? No, sir. Did you see Mrs. Massey and her daughter when they came to the market. I didn't see them until they returned from the trial. Where were you when Mrs. Massey and her daughter came down stairs. I was standing in my front door. Your front door looks which way? It faces the market. Where did you first see Mrs. Massey and her daughter? As they were coming down from trial—I saw them as they were being taken into the carriage? Did you look at them at the time particularly. Well, not more so than usual? Who was with them? Mr. Bond. Any body else at that time? I didn't see any other persons with the ladies. Were there any persons near them? There were quite a number standing round the market square. Did anybody seem to be in their company, except Mr. Bond? That was all that seemed to be in charge of the ladies. Did you go to the carriage? I did. How long after they got into the carriage, did you go there? About when they were seated. Who accompanied you? Mr. David Cashwell was in my store, and he said he thought he saw some sign made, and that we had better go and speak to them. He thought they wanted to speak to us. Were you looking at the time they went in? Yes, sir. You went up to the carriage? Yes, sir. Who did you find when you got there? No person that I recollect, except Thomas Powers, who was standing, I think about two or three feet from the side where his sister, Mrs. Massey, was sitting. Who else? I saw no other person in connection with the carriage. Did you remain there at the carriage until it was driven off? I did. Did Tom Powers have any conversation at all with the ladies? I didn't see him speak to the ladies or any other person. From the time the ladies got into the carriage until it drove off, did Captain William J. Tolar go there at all? I didn't see him. Well, sir, can you state as a fact, you say you saw it from that time,—can you state as a fact whether he went there or not? I don't think he went there; I didn't see him, and I think if he had been there I should have seen him. Who else went to the carriage? Mr. John Maultsby went up, I think in company with Bond; I saw Maultsby in the rear of the carriage, some five or six feet I think from where Powers was standing.

Did Maultsby have any conversation with the ladies? He didn't speak to them. You were at the carriage when he came up? Yes, sir. At which side of the carriage did he come up? Rather in the rear of the carriage from towards Davis' store. Which side of the carriage were you on, Mr. Taylor? The next side to the store. How was the horse's head facing? About something like north; that brought the ladies near facing in my store door. Was there any whispered conversation at that carriage? There was none while I was there, and I saw none. Who spoke to the ladies while you were at the carriage? No body that I recollect of, except Mr. Cashwell. How long a time elapsed between the ladies getting into the carriage and your arrival at it? Well, but a second or so. How far was it from the place you were standing at, to the carriage? Not as far as that center column (pointing to a column of the Court room, supporting the gallery, and about forty feet from the witness stand.) Was it forty feet? Well, about forty, or perhaps thirty-five. Was the view from where you were to the carriage obstructed at all, or was it unobstructed? It was perfectly open, sir. You had a perfectly open view from the time of the ladies coming to the carriage until you went to the carriage? Yes, sir. You saw nobody go with them except Mr. Bond, and no Lody go there at all after your arrival? There was no body there when I got there except Tom Powers, he was standing in the rear of the carriage. Was he speaking to any body? No, sir. What was he doing? Nothing at all, he was standing within two or three feet of the carriage towards the market house. And after you got there, you swear, there was no conversation between the ladies and any one except Mr. Cashwell? That was all that I heard or saw, and there was nothing else while I was at the carriage. So that Powers and Maultsby and Bond were all in the rear? Yes, sir. How much space was there between them? Do you mean between Powers and Maultsby. Yes? The position Powers had was I think about opposite the centre of the carriage, and Maultsby was to the left. How far to the left? About five or six feet. Where was Bond? About on the side where I was. Did you see any conversation or hear any between Bond and Maultsby, or Maultsby and Powers or between any of the three at that time? Not a word. Then they were not together, but separated? Yes, they were all separated when I saw them, I think that Maultsby and Bond were walking, Maultsby stopped on the rear of the carriage, and Bond went forward and told the boy to drive away. Do you know where Bond came from? I do not, I think he came from over the opposite side of the street. Who helped the ladies into the carriage? I think Mr. Bond. Do you know what became of him afterwards? No. Where did you say he came from when he came back? From Davis' corner I think. How long a time elapsed between the time the ladies went into the carriage and the carriage driving off? I don't think it exceeded a minute. You say Bond came from over towards Davis' corner? Yes, or, he might have been standing by the carriage. He came round the carriage and told the boy to drive off. Do you know where Tom Powers came from? I don't, he was standing at the carriage when I went up to it. Did he alter his position at all sir? I did not see any change in his position. Did you notice Tom Powers before you left your store go to the carriage? No, Sir, I didn't see him until I got to the carriage, he was standing some two or three feet from the side of the carriage. Which way did the carriage drive? Down Person street. And then became lost to your view? I saw no more of it. What became of you? I went back to my store. You say you think the carriage drove down Person street? Yes, sir. And then you think it went down Dick street? Well, sir, I only saw it turn down Person street. When you left the carriage Mr. Taylor and returned to your store what part of your store did you go to? I staid in the front door; about that time the prisoner was being brought down. So you took your stand in the front door, looking towards the market house? Yes. Did you have a clear view of all the eastern portion of the market house from your door? Yes, sir, it was all open. When you stood in your door were you on a level with the pavement, or above it, or below? Elevated above it—the door is about six inches above the pavement. Could you see the stair steps, and did you see the man Beebee when he came down stairs? I could see the stair-steps. You saw him come down stairs? Well, of course I saw the officers coming down stairs, but I didn't know him from any other colored man. Did anything unusual occur between the time you saw Beebee on the landing of the stairs and the time of his reaching the pavement outside the eastern arch? Not that I saw. Now, Mr. Taylor, having got Beebee to the outer edge of the eastern arch, on the pavement, tell the court what you saw. Well, about the time he cleared the east end of the market house, and turned to the right to go down Gillespie street, I saw commotion in the crowd. What was the nature of that commotion? Well, some persons in the rear seemed to be pressing up, and some were coming up on the other side, it seems about the time they got near the eastern corner, the crowd got in front of them, and brought a sort of halt there. The first commotion I saw I supposed was caused by some struggle or falling or something among the officers and the prisoners; after they got to the eastern corner of the market house, there was something like a halt made; there was more or less commotion in the crowd until the pistol was fired. What was the size of the crowd as nearly as you could judge of it? Up to that time I don't think there were more than fifty persons. Of all colors? I think so. Was it a scattered crowd or closely compact? Closely compact; I could not tell one man's head from another. There they got with the prisoner down about the south-east corner of the market house? Yes, sir, near the south side of the small arch. Well, sir, what occurred there? Well, there was a pistol fired. Did you see the flash? Yes, sir. Did you hear the report? Yes, sir. And saw the smoke? Yes, sir. Do you know who shot it? I do not. From what point was the pistol fired? Well, I am not positive whether the pistol was fired on the pavement or the market house, or just off the edge. You think it was near the edge? I should think so. How far from Beebee? It was very close. How close do you think? I think within two feet of him. What was the condition of the crowd at the time the pistol fired? There was some moving about, up to that time. Was the crowd dense towards the prisoner or around him? Pretty dense around him. Which way lay the densest portion of it. In his rear, extending back up to the pavement. As he came out the large arch, the crowd that was in the rear seemed to follow. Extending in the rear of the prisoner the crowd was close and dense? That is my notion of it sir. How was the crowd to the east of the prisoner;—say to his left hand and to his rear and left? Well they extended out into the street, some distance off the pavement. Say towards his rear and left and rear—there was where the crowd was pressing and thick? Yes,

that was my view of it. Was the pistol shot fired from the deceased man's rear, right and rear, to his left and rear, or to his right and front, or left and front, or where? Well, I think the pistol was a little to the rear, of the prisoner, and, I thought somewhat to his right. You say you don't know who shot the pistol. I do not sir. Did you see Captain Tolar at that time? I did not? Had you seen him at all during that day? I think I saw him either after dinner or before: but I can't tell whether before or after. Where did you see him? About the market, about the south side. At the time the pistol shot fired, if you saw Tolar you did not recognize him? No, sir, I don't know that I recognized any body at all in the crowd. How far, measuring straight back was it from the point you saw the pistol fired, to the center of the main eastern arch? I should think ten or twelve feet. Now, observing the crowd as you did that day, how long would it have taken a man to have gone from the front where the pistol shot was fired, straight back through the crowd to the middle of the main eastern arch?

Counsel for the prosecution:
Do you think this a proper question?

Counsel for the accused:
I think it is. I am not asking him for his opinion—he can say that he does or does not know, as the fact may be.

Counsel for the prosecution:
He can state the distances, and the density of the crowd.

Counsel for the accused:
He has, and I ask him, taking these into consideration, how long it would have taken a man to have passed from one point to the other.

Counsel for the prosecution:
That is a matter of opinion—he can give all the facts, and the positions; but I object to your question, as involving a mere matter of opinion.

Counsel for accused.
Well, if you object, we will not press it,
Examination resumed.

How many persons would you estimate, as being between the point you have named—ten feet off from the prisoner, and immediately in his rear—to the point where the pistol was fired? Well, I couldn't really swear how many there were. We do not expect you sir, to swear the exact number—estimate it? Well about twenty or thirty persons, I suppose. Were they standing thick? About as thick as they could stand, I think. And about to his left and rear? Yes, they were pressed in as closely as they could come, one to another. How long did you stay at your store after the pistol shot was fired? For some time—I went up town in the evening. Did the crowd increase after the shooting? Yes, sir, nearly doubled—hearing the shot probably induced people to flock there, from about almost every direction. Was the crowd calmer after the pistol fired, or more boisterous? Well, everything seemed to be quieted by the crack of the pistol. Before that time, sir, was the crowd in confusion? To a greater or less extent; they seemed to be anxious to change position, and I suppose one person was shoving another. Did you hear any exclamations or cries proceeding from the crowd? The only thing that attracted my attention to the crowd, I think, was, that about the time the prisoner and officers were passing the eastern arch, I thought I heard something said, and, as well as I can recollect I think it was "halt"! Do you know whether it was "halt,"? or "halt him"? I don't think I heard "him." How long was that before the pistol was fired? A very short time. Directly after the pistol was fired, did you hear any exclamations as to who had shot him? I heard nothing at all on that subject. No voice at all about the shooting? No. Did you see anything either before you went to the carriage, while at it or after you returned from it which led you to think that any injury was to be done to him? No, sir, I heard nothing and saw no movements indicating anything of the kind. Do you know of any agreement or compact between any persons at all to do the prisoner any harm? I do not. Did you hear anybody cry out immediately after the shooting that Capt. Tolar shot him, or that Tolar had killed him? No, sir. Did you hear any hurrahs for Capt. Tolar, any cry of "hurrah! hurrah! for Capt. Tolar." Nothing of the sort; the crowd was all still; everything seemed by the crack of the pistol to be brought to a perfect peace. And how long did it remain in that state of quietude? Until the crowd began to disperse. How many minutes? A few minutes, until the Mayor came round and told the people to disperse. But how long did that quiet remain? It was not broken at all; I saw no demonstrations. You were standing there looking at the crowd, and hearing what you could hear, and you heard nobody cry, "hurrah for Capt. Tolar!" nor anything of that kind? I heard nothing of the kind, sir. Is your hearing good? Well, it is tolerable good; I don't know that it's as good as that of some men. Is it as good as the average? I think it is. How far off was your door from the point at which the pistol was fired? From my door to the south east corner of the market is about ninety feet, I think. About thirty steps? Not more than that; I don't think it is; I have not stepped, but ——. Never mind about that, sir, your impression will do; are you related, Mr. Taylor, by blood or marriage, to Captain Tolar? No, sir. What are your church relations? Well, he is a member of the same denomination that I am, but we do not worship at the same place. You are both members of the Baptist persuasion, but you do not worship at the same Church? Yes, sir, exactly, Is there any intimacy between you? There has always been good feeling, I have known him personally since the breaking up of the war, before then I was not personally acquainted with him. But you have always been on good terms? Yes, sir, always. Is there any intimacy between yourself and Thomas Powers? None at all, more than the two are friendly when we meet; I have known him from his childhood. Between yourself and David Watkins, (Monk?) None at all. Ed. Powers? None, sir. Sam. Hall? None. J. G. Leggett? No. John Maultsby? None. H. E. Sykes? None, sir.

Cross examined by the Counsel for prosecution: Mr. Taylor, do you know whether there is any relationship between Capt. Tolar and Miss Elvira Massey? I do not, sir, if there is any it is very distant; I do not know that there is any, sir. Very well, sir; now suppose you were standing square in your store door, to which point of the compass would your face be turned—north, south, east or west? If standing in the door on Person street, south, if in the other door, west. There are two doors then; one, as I understand it, faces west and the other south? Yes, sir. The one facing west opens on market square and the one facing south on Person street? Yes, sir. Your store is directly opposite to that of Ichabod B. Davis? Immediately opposite. What is the width of the street? At that point? Yes, sir? I think ninety feet, or less; it is ninety feet from pavement to pavement; I am not positive about it, any way, but I think the streets are called —— ; I think Person street is a hundred feet; if so it would not be more than eighty feet from pavement to pavement. But from door to door?

About a hundred feet, I think. When you saw the ladies come into the carriage which door were you in? The south one. Opening on Person street? Yes, sir. How were the heads of the horses turned? To the north. If the carriage had been driven straight ahead as the horses heads ——? Counsel for accused: There was but one horse. Counsel for prosecution. Well, one horse, then,—if the carriage had been driven straight ahead as the horse's head was would it have passed to the west of your store? It would have passed to the north. Well, it would have been west, but going north? Yes, sir. Did you see two carriages drive up there? No. Did Miss Massey and her mother come in the same carriage? I don't know how they came. Did you see any other carriage standing there besides the carriage they went away in? I did not. You did not see them get out? I did not. When did you first see the carriage, when the ladies were out of it, or when they went in? I didn't see it until they went in. And you didn't notice any other carriage there? No, sir, not that I recollect. Was there any buggy or waggon? There might have been wagons in the street, I didn't notice. Did you see any buggy near the carriage, back or front, or immediately near? No, sir. You saw the ladies in the act of getting into the carriage? Yes, sir, just as they were about taking seats. Did you see Mr. Bond at that time? I think he was waiting on them. It was on the side of the carriage next the market house. You were then in your store? Yes, sir. Was Mr. Cashwell standing in the door also? Yes, sir, I think we were both in the door. You think he was standing in the west door, and you probably in the south? Yes, sir. And Mr. Cashwell mentioned to you that he thought the ladies intimated that they wished to speak to either or both of you? Yes, sir. When he made this intimation to you, did you turn to speak to him, or did he come to you? We stepped immediately to the carriage. Did both of you go by the same door. I think we ——. Counsel for prosecution. I want to know, if it is possible, by calling your attention to these minute details, whether it was possible for you to have lost sight of that carriage after you first saw it. Now, in that conversation that took place how were your faces turned? I expect his face was turned to me at that time Don't you think your face was turned to him? I don't know, I can't say. You can't say whether you lost sight of that carriage at that moment or not? Well, if I did it was but for a moment. You don't know whether he went out by the same door as you? I think so. After Mr. Bond helped the ladies into the carriage what became of him? I don't know. Did you notice that he had disappeared at all? No. You can't tell whether he staid still at the carriage or left there? He certainly was not there when I got there, but very soon after I got to the carriage he came up in the rear. You saw him when he was assisting the ladies in, and when you went towards the carriage you have no recollection of seeing him there? No, sir. Was the carriage standing right square in front of the main arch of the market house? Further north. How far? About opposite the north-east corner of the market-house, I think. Well, when you got to the carriage, you say almost immediately was it that you saw Mr. Bond and Mr. Maultsby—was it just after you got to the catriage? Well, I saw Maultsby directly after I got to the carriage, or rather I saw him in the rear of the carriage; and Mr. Bond came round to the side I was, and told the boy to drive away. Mr. Bond came from the rear to the right side of the carriage? Yes, sir, to the east side. Did you see where he came from except that he came from the rear of the carriage? Well, he came from the street south of the carriage,—in the rear. How many steps did you see him before he came up to the carriage? Well, I suppose enough to walk round the carriage. You don't know where he came from, to where you first saw him? No. I understand you to say in your examination-in-chief that you saw Maultsby and Bond about the same time; is it not' your impression also that you saw them together, or close together? Well, within two or three feet of each other. Within conversing distance? Yes, sir. Was Maultsby nearer the market house than you were? Yes, he was to the rear and south of the carriage door. Was he directly in the rear, square in the rear of the carriage? Yes, sir, south, when I saw him. You didn't see where he came from? No, sir. Did you see any conversation between him and Bond? No, sir. Nor hear any? No, sir. When you went up to the carriage you found Tom Powers, did you see his position? Yes, sir, two or three feet from the carriage on the side next the market house; that is my impression. Oh, yes, I understand very well that the distances have not been measured, and all I want is to ascertain how the scene was pictured on your mental consciousness; I want to know whether he was behind the carriage or on the west side of it. Who, Tom Powers? Yes. He was standing about amid-ship of the carriage, about where the door was open, about two or three feet of the carriage, between that and the market house. You didn't hear any conversation between him and his sister, Mrs. Massey? No, sir. You didn't see him until he got to the carriage I understand? No, sir. Did you see him when he got to that point? Yes, sir. Do you know where he came from to arrive at that point? No, sir. When did you see him, when he arrived—Oh! he was there when you saw him? Yes, sir. No conversation took place with the ladies you say, that you could hear, nor any at all while you were there yourself, except what Mr. Cashwell had? That is all. And you saw him from the time the ladies got into the carriage until it drove off—how long? Don't think it was more than a minute. Then you turned back? Yes, sir, I went back to my store. Do you know what became of Tom Powers? No, the crowd was rather promiscuous about the store. Did the crowd go back as far as the carriage? It didn't lack much of it that is, it was not dense there, you know, but there were some people about there. How far was that carriage from the market house? Well, I should think it was ——. Say from the edge of the pavement? About forty feet.

Counsel for accused:
Which pavement?

Counsel for prosecution:
I am speaking of the pavement in front of the market house. You understand, Mr. Taylor, that is the one I am speaking of? Witness, yes, sir. You think it was forty or fifty feet? That is my impression, sir, though I have never measured the ground. Oh, yes, we understand that,—did you see whether Tom Powers went back to the market house, or staid stationary, after the carriage drove off? I don't know. Did you see what became of Mr. Bond? No, sir. Nor of Maultsby? No, sir, I don't know what direction they took when the carriage drove off; I went immediately back to my store. You didn't see Capt. Tolar at the carriage? No, sir. Nor

in the crowd anywhere while you were at the carriage? No, sir. And the only time you saw him that day up to the point of time when the carriage drove off, occurred to your best recollection, was before that time? Yes, sir, it was either before dinner or soon after I came from dinner. Was the crowd there when you came from dinner? There was a crowd there, a sort of mixed crowd, blacks and whites. You saw him at the south side? Yes, sir. Were you passing on the same side of the street? I was crossing Gillespie street through the market square to my store, and I think I recognised Captain Tolar standing about the market house. And you never saw him in the crowd after that up to the time the carriage drove away? I never saw him any more until the latter part of that day. In the evening I was up street on business, and while I was coming down on one side of Hay street I saw Captain Tolar walking up on the other, the south side. That is the only time you saw him after the time you have described? Yes, sir. When you went back to your store, did you stand in your south door or the west one? The south one. Did Mr. Cashwell come back with you? He went into the crowd. I can't say where he went. The south door where you stood when you went back opens on Person street? Yes, sir. And you staid there until Archie came down stairs? Yes. How long from the time the carriage drove away ugtil Archy made his appearance? It was not long. How many minutes? Well, I dont know that I could say. Can't you estimate? 'Twas but a very short time, any way, I dont think I could say the time any way near. Directly the carriage drove away I walked back into the store, and soon after that I heard the movement of feet in the upper part of the market. That drew the attention of the people around who had not heard of it before; then I noticed they came down stairs; when they got to the pavement the crowd was so much around the prisoner and the officers that I couldn't tell one man from another. And you recognized no one? I think I saw officer Wemyss and I am satisfied I recognized Sheriff Hardie. Is your eye-sight at all impaired? It is as good at that distance as anybody's of my age; 'tis not so good as some people's, when close to a thing, except I use glasses. The first assault you saw made on the prisoner was just as he got out of the arch? I saw no assault, but a commotion in the crowd. Was it a close pressing on him; was that the nature of the commotion? Yes, sir. Did you hear any exclamations about that time, the time you heard the word "halt"? No, sir. Did you hear Sheriff Hardie's voice at all? No, sir. You didn't hear him use any such expression as "stand back, gentlemen," or "stand back, men, he is my prisoner," or anything of that sort? No, sir. Did you see the police have any clubs? I saw officer Wemyss with a club after the killing. Yes, but I mean the time of the first pressure? No, sir. Was the day cold or not, sir? Well, it might have been a raw day, what we call a raw day. What you call a bleak raw day? Well, I can't say exactly. Do you remember whether it was bright or cloudy? I can't say, sir. You don't remember whether there was a wind or not? Well, it is likely there was some wind blowing that day. Have you any recollection? I can't say positively. Did you notice whether the pistol was fired, whether the smoke remained stationary; or, did the wind move it? Well, I didn't observe particularly about the smoke or wind. You saw the flash? Yes, sir. And heard the report? Yes, sir. Well, you know, sometimes on a damp heavy day smoke remains in the spot where it is produced; you can't say, in this instance whether it was stationary, or whether it was drifted away by the wind? No, sir, I paid no attention. Did you, at any time that day, see any man in that crowd with any description of weapon? No, sir, I was not in the crowd at all. You were near the edge of it when you went to the carriage? Yes, sir. You saw no weapons then nor afterwards in the hands of any one? No sir, I did not? Did I understand you to say that a very solemn stillness fell over the crowd, after the firing of the pistol? That was my impression, sir. That was a noticeable stillness? That was my notion of it, sir. And the same state of partial excitement that you noticed at first, was not got up again until the crowd was dispersed? No, sir. You heard no body cry out in the crowd that Captain Tolar had shot him? No, sir. Did you notice Tom Powers at any other time that day except the time at the carriage? I can't say, I might have, my impression is I did see him that forenoon. Is your impression decided enough to speak, certainly? I don't know that I would speak of it as a certainty. You didn't see him after this firing, at all? No, sir, I have no recollection of seeing Powers after I saw him at the carriage. You say while you were at the carriage you heard no conversation and saw none between Tom Powers and Mrs. Massey? No, sir.

Counsel for the prosecution:
We have finished with the witness gentlemen.

Counsel for the accused:
We have no further questions to ask, sir. Oh, one question more, Mr. Taylor, with regard to these doors, one looking west and the other south, how far are they apart? You can step from one into the other, they are both corner doors. How far from the corner? Well, there is nothing but the corner of the building between the two doors. About how thick is the corner? Well I think it is two brick thick in the first story. How far are the doors from the extreme outer angle of the building? About two and a half feet each. And you can step from one door into the other? Well it might be a step and a half.

Counsel:
That will do, sir.
At one o'clock, P. M., on motion, the Commissioned adjourned, to meet on 30th inst., at ten, A. M.

RALEIGH, N. C., Aug. 30, 1867, 10 A. M.
The Commission met pursuant to adjournment.
Present: All the members of the Commission, the Judge Advocate, the Counsel for the prosecution, all the accused and their Counsel.

The reading of the testimony taken on Saturday, the 24th instant, was waived, there being no objection thereto.

Yesterdays proceedings were then read and approved.

The Counsel for the defence said, there is only one witness, who came this morning, Sergeant Kenstler.

Dr. Kirk did not arrive, Sergeant Kenstler informed me, and I suppose the Judge Advocate has the same information, that Colonel Cogswell, in consequence of sickness among the Garrison of Fayetteville, could not spare Surgeon Kirk at the present time. We will not be prepared to examine Sergeant Kenstler until the testimony of Dr. Kirk is taken, unless we can agree with the Judge Advocate and the Counsel for the prosecution, in regard to one or two matters, and I would suggest that Sergeant Kenstler be called, and we retire with the Judge Advocate and the Counsel for the prosecution, and see if we can agree upon these points.

The Judge Advocate stated on the part of the prosecution that they had no objection to conferring with the Counsel for the defence in this matter.

The Judge Advocate, the Counsel for the prosecution, the Counsel for the defence, and Sergeant Kenstler retired for the purpose of holding a consultation.

At the close of the consultation, the Counsel for the defence said:
I will state to the Court that the consultation which has been had with the Counsel for the prosecution, and the Judge Advocate has resulted in nothing, so far as dispensing with Surgeon Kirk's testimony is concerned. We propose, however, to introduce Sergeant Kenstler, in order that he may return to his post, but we shall be compelled to ask for the attendance of Surgeon Kirk.

The Counsel for the prosecution:
I will say to the Counsel and the Court now, that it will be absolutely necessary for us to introduce Sergeant Kenstler when the case for the defence is closed, and it seems to me, if it would answer the purposes of the defence that they might as well examine him then, and thus save time.

Counsel for the defence:
We prefer to introduce him now.

FRANCIS KENSTLER, a witness for the defence having been first duly sworn testified as follows:
Examined by the Counsel for the accused.
What is your name? Francis Kenstler. What is your rank in the service? First Sergeant, Co. K, 8th Infantry. At what point are you stationed? Fayetteville, N. C. Do you know whether the body of Archy Beebee has been exhumed at any time since his burial? I was ordered one day to go out and take up the body, with Dr. Kirk. You were ordered by whom? By Lt. Conner. The commander of your company? Yes, sir, at that time. Who constituted the resurrection party? I did sir, I was in charge of them. Who else were in the company? Two privates of one company, and Dr. Kirk. Any other persons black or white? There was some colored persons there, at the time we got there. Who were they? I didn't know them. By whose direction did they go there? I don't know sir. At what time was it that you exhumed this body? I don't know the date. How long has it been, weeks or months? It has been two weeks since, the time I came down here last. Well, sir, was the body taken up in your presence? The body could not have been taken up; we raised the lid of the coffin. Did you dig down to the coffin? Yes, sir. Did you find it coffined? Yes, sir. Did you open the coffin? Yes, sir. Removing the lid? Yes, sir. Did you take out the body? No, sir, we could not take out the body. Why didn't you take it out? We could not do it, the smell was too disagreeable. Did you remove the head? Yes, sir. How was the head removed? We cut it off, with an ax part of it, the other part with a knife. Cut it as it was lying in the grave? Yes, sir. Who ordered that operation, who cut off the head? One of the company and a colored man. What did you do with the head after you had taken it off? We took it aside, and I laid it on the ground, and sawed the skull off. You sawed the skull off, and searched for the bullet just there, near the grave? Yes, sir. Who made the search, Surgeon Kirk? Yes, sir, Surgeon Kirk. Who is Surgeon Kirk, sir? Assistant Surgeon of the post of Fayetteville. How did he open the head? He sawed the skull off. How did he saw the skull off? Right across below where the bullet went in. It was sawed straight across? Yes, sir. Did you see the hole in the skull where the bullet entered? I did, sir. Could you tell the precise point where

the bullet entered? I could not tell exactly. The ear was not on the skull, was it? It was there, the bullet entered about an inch and a half from the left ear, back of the left ear. Was the hair on the head? The hair come off as soon as we took the head out. Do you know whether the bullet entered below the hair or in the hair? There was not any hair there at the time we took the skull off. Was the bullet found in the head? Yes, sir. Do you know what part of the head the bullet was found in? In the brain. Do you know which way the bullet ranged? I could not tell that, sir. Do you know whether the bullet had struck the opposite side of the skull? I could not tell that, sir. Where was the bullet found by Dr. Kirk? In the brain. Was the brain in the skull at the time it was found? It was outside, lying on the ground, after the skull was taken off. What was the state of the brain; was it decomposed or was it pulsy and solid? It had the same color as the bullet—a lead color. After the brains fell upon the ground in a mass, by examination of the brain the bullet was found there? Yes, sir. What was done with that bullet? It was given in my care. By whom? By Dr. Kirk. What did you do with that bullet? I have kept the bullet, and brought it down here. How long did you keep the bullet before you brought it here? I kept the bullet about two days. And you then brought it here? Yes, sir. Did you bring it under orders? I brought it here under orders. Under whose orders? General Avery's. Then under the orders of General Avery, the Judge Advocate of this Court, you brought the bullet to the city of Raleigh? Yes, sir. What did you do with the bullet? I showed the bullet to General Avery and he returned it to me again? Where is that bullet now? I just now gave it to General Avery, when I stepped in here. Did you keep the bullet in your possession until just a little while ago? Yes, sir. When you brought it up here, you didn't leave it here? No, sir, I took it with me again. Since you have come into the Court this morning you have delivered it to General Avery? Yes, sir. Would you recognize that bullet if you were to see it again? I would recognize the bullet, sir. General Avery will you be kind enough to furnish the bullet?

The Judge Advocate:

I will not, sir.

The Counsel for the accused:

I understand the Judge Advocate refuses to furnish the bullet, which we insist is not only material, but is natural evidence, and we ask the Court to order the production of that bullet as a part of the evidence for the defence, which is in the hands of the prosecution. It is requested but he declines to furnish it.

Counsel for the prosecution:

I have to say on behalf of the prosecution, that we have this bullet in our possession, and it shall be produced before the close of the trial; but for reasons that will be evident, as I think, to the Court, and are very weighty with those engaged in the prosecution, we feel bound, in justice to the government, to decline to produce it now. This Court must have observed—without entering into a discussion now, to decide where the falsehood lies—that there has been much wilful and corrupt perjury on the part of some one during the progress of this trial. It is impossible, by any rule of law or of common sense, to reconcile the whole of this testimony: some one has lied before God and this Court, wilfully and corruptly. We do not desire, nor intend as yet, to enter into any discussion to show where that falsehood is to be found—this is not the time for it; but in a trial where it is evident to the Court that there has been perjury, every precau-

tion must necessarily be taken upon the part of the Government to prevent that perjury from being increased, and further than that—in the interest of truth—to arrive at the truth. We have no objection to stating our reasons for keeping back this bullet. Whether Capt. Tolar *fired* the pistol or not which killed Archy Beebee, according to his own showing, he was armed with a pistol that day. It is not in our power to produce it; we cannot compel him to produce it, the law giving a man liberty to refuse to testify against himself; but *he* can produce it. In a case into which so much falsehood has already crept, we are not willing to produce that bullet, unless he will *first* produce his pistol. The Court will see the reason,—if testimony has already been suborned, or even if it has not been suborned, and we produce this bullet, and show its size, quality and description, nothing is easier than to suborn witnesses, to prove that Capt. Tolar wore upon the day of the killing a pistol which the bullet will not fit. There is our reason for refusing to produce the bullet, plainly stated. If Capt. Tolar will produce and prove the pistol that he had on that day, the bullet shall not be kept back a moment; but if we produce the bullet, it will leave it in his power to produce any pistol that he pleases, and of course he may produce one that the bullet will not fit. We must therefore decline now to show the bullet. We think a reverence for truth demands that the bullet, being in the charge of the Government, who can have no interest to persecute or oppress any body, should not be given up. We here pledge ourselves on behalf of the Government, before the close of the trial, to produce this bullet. We think the defence has no right to *demand* its production at this time. The simple and solitary object of keeping it back is to prevent perjury, falsehood, and the misleading of the Court. If any pistol had been offered—in evidence by Tolar as the one he wore that day—this objection would not be so strong. But by producing the bullet now, we leave it in Capt. Tolar's power hereafter to offer in evidence a pistol of a size that the bullet will not fit. In a case where the Court must see there has already been a quantity of wilful and corrupt perjury upon the part of one side or the other, we think that justice to the Government, a reverence for truth, fairness to the different witnesses, white and black, who have been examined here—all demand of the Court that they should indulge the Counsel for the prosecution, so far as to permit them to retain that bullet until they see proper to introduce it. God knows that the Government thirsts for no man's blood. God knows that we have conducted this prosecution with a view to condemn no man to death, unless he be found guilty of crime—but that we have conducted it solely in the interests of justice and with a desire simply to arrive at the truth. Truth and justice require that the bullet should be kept back, and I think the Court will see the propriety of this course.

The Counsel for the accused:

May it please the Court—I shall not gainsay for one moment what the Counsel for the prosecution has said. There has been committed in this Court wilful, corrupt and God-defying perjury, and there is no other word for it.

There is no chance to reconcile the testimony in this case, and we have expected to show from the beginning, and we expect to show now, where that perjury lies, in part, by this very evidence, which the government seems disposed to withhold. We have relied upon it, and we rely upon it still. To be sure we have produced no pistol but the prosecution has put a pistol in our hands, and they are bound by it. Their witness, Samuel

A. Phillips, has come here upon the stand and wilfully, solemnly and deliberately sworn that the pistol which Tolar had on that occasion was a repeater, some two inches shorter than the pistol which the prosecution has produced.

We expect to produce no pistol here, and we will produce no pistol here as that which Tolar had that day; and we will not produce it for two reasons; first, that the defendant Tolar has not shown that he was there armed that day. He has not shown that he had any pistol in his hands that day. It has been shown by one of the witnesses that he had a pistol upon his person, but not one of the witnesses that he has examined, and not one of the witnesses that he will examine has proved, or will prove, that he had a pistol in his hands. Again, if we should produce the pistol which he had there that day upon his person, the Court knows, and the Court sees, that it is utterly impossible for us to identify that pistol as the pistol which he had. The Court sees, from the course of the prosecution, that they have endeavored to show that Tolar shot this man, and he shot him with a pistol other than his own; a pistol which was handed to him by some one else. The Court, therefore, knows it must be aware of the fact that it is impossible for us to introduce, and for us to identify any pistol that Tolar might have had upon that day; but there is evidence, as I said before, and evidence by which the prosecution is bound, and thoroughly bound, showing the size of the pistol which Tolar had. Now, I state to the Court here, and I state it in the presence of God, that it that ball is produced, I shall show, by weight, and by measurement, that it fit the pistol of Samuel A. Phillips, and that it was too large to have fitted any pistol which has been put into the hands of Capt. Tolar whatever.

Yes, there is perjury, and I call for that bullet that I may sift that perjury. I stand for truth, and for nothing but truth. If these men are guilty let them die; but, in the name of heaven, and in the name of fairness, if they be not guilty, and if there be any evidence which tends even to show the fact, I call upon that government which "thirsts not for blood;" I call upon these gentlemen who are laboring in the "interests of truth;" I demand it of them, in the name of humanity, that that bullet shall now be produced, and if they decline to do it, I call upon this Court to order its production. But, says the Counsel for the prosecution, the bullet shall be produced. When shall it be produced? When the defence has closed its case? Why, sir, I will stand here, at the sacrifice of every thing, until the day of my death before I will ever consent to close the defence, until the bullet is produced. We trace it into the possession of the Judge Advocate. That evidence is as much our evidence as it is evidence for the prosecution. It is material evidence for the prosecution. It is natural evidence. They have got no right to withhold it, and I call upon this Court, most respectfully and earnestly, as they intend, as I know they do intend, to give these accused men a fair trial. I call upon the Court to bring forward that evidence, and that evidence which will determine where the perjury lies in this case.

The Counsel for the prosecution:

I will only say to the Court, in reply, that the gentleman's remarks—a great many of them,—would be very applicable, and of great force, if it were not for the fact that the prosecution, stand here pledged, in good time, to produce the pistol bullet; but they all fall to the ground—it appears to me, when the Court knows, that in good time, the bullet will be produced, and is only held in the hands of the prosecution, because we are desirous to prevent perjury, as we have before said.

There is very strong evidence, on the part of the prosecution, that Captain Tolar had a pistol in his hand that day, and it has been shown, on the part of the defence, that he had one about his person. I think the court sees clearly our position. We simply deny this bullet to prevent perjury; but in good time it shall be before the Court, and they shall see it. We will not only produce it, but we will produce it in the hands of the very witness whom the defence has introduced—under the same circumstances that they wished to have it presented now; and it can be nothing but a captious objection upon the part of the defence; the pertinacity with which they insist upon having this bullet now.

The gentleman's threat as to how long he will stay here before he will close his case is a matter that has no weight whatever, with me, and I presume noneat ell with the Court. That is a matter about which the ruling of the Court may raise hereafter.

The Counsel for the accused:
One word, may it please the Court.

The Counsel for the prosecution objected:
I understand this is a case in which we are entitled to the opening and reply,—we being the party to show cause why the bullet shall not be produced.

The Counsel for the defence:
It is a proceeding on our part entirely, and we are entitled to the opening and reply.

The Counsel for the prosecution:
I insist upon it, that the ruling is to the contrary, in a matter of this sort.

The Counsel for the accused:
What is the rule then?

The Counsel for the prosecution:
The rule of practice is this—that upon a bare motion the rule is as the Counsel states it—but in a case where a party shows cause why evidence should not be produced, or where he shows cause upon any other rule served, he has the opening and reply. Blount vs. Greenwood, 1 Cow. 20.

The Counsel for the accused:
It is a motion for a rule.

The Counsel for the prosecution:
We consent that the Court shall grant the rule upon us, to show cause, why we should not produce the bullet.

The Counsel for the defence:
We propose to argue the question. The gentleman assents to the court giving a rule, and now the question comes upon that ground.

The Counsel for the prosecution:
I insisted upon it that we had the right to open and reply.

The Counsel for the defence thought he was entitled to the floor.

The Counsel for the prosecution:
I understand this as a bit of professional tactics, if the Court pleases. Upon a motion for a rule no discussion would be likely to arise—it would be an ex parte application to the Court and ordinarily granted as of course. The rule would be served upon us, and no discussion would arise, until we were called upon to show cause why the rule should not be made absolute—in which discussion—we, as the party showing cause, would be entitled to the opening and closing remarks. That is the ordinary way in which these questions ought to be conducted; in our loose practice in this State undoubtedly the motion for a rule—and the cause shown why a rule should not be made absolute, are often heard together.

I do not desire to continue this discussion, but I do insist upon it, that the matter has been fairly discussed, that we have a right to close, and if the Counsel insists upon addressing the Court being the second on the same side, I shall feel compelled to reply.

The Counsel for the accused :

I only wish to say to the Court, that they may bring down a cart load of English books and they will find that the man who moves for a rule, always has the reply—that is the rule of practice that may be found in every book. Talk about the "loose laws of practice in North Carolina," I appeal to the English practice, I appeal to any practice, and it will be found, as I said, that the person moving for a rule obtains the rule—the question before being as to whether it should be discharged or not—is entitled to the opening and the conclusion. Suppose it is a motion, what is the good sense of it? Why, the man that wants the Court to act shall, in the first place, suggest to the Court why they shall act—then counter arguments being produced on the other side, the person who wishes the Court to act shall have the right to reply, whether it be by motion, or any other thing, if he wish to put the Court into action. I have a right, first to move for it, to suggest reasons for it, and then after the gentleman has responded to that, I have a right to reply to it. That is the good sense of the rule, no matter what he called it—a motion or a rule. We here move that a piece of evidence, that we think important to us, shall be introduced.

The gentleman talks about tactics. He represents the United States here, as engaged in a pitiful game of push pin, concerning the life and death of a man, as to whether one bullet, that we think important to us, and to our defence, shall be introduced, and upon a suggested ground that we have been guilty of perjury. He suggests it here, before this matter is decided, when the question is as to how we shall make up a defence here, what is the amount of our evidence, and the evidence we shall introduce, to defend our lives with. He suggests that we have been guilty of perjury—there has been such an amount of perjury here, that it would be unsafe to allow us to introduce other evidence, in behalf of our lives. When was such a reason ever heard, in a Court of Justice?

I do not agree with Colonel Haywood, and my friend Mr. Fuller, as to the amount of perjury that has been committed. There has been a great deal of false swearing, but with regard to wilful and corrupt perjury, I take issue with them as to the amount that has been done here; but whether so or not, the question has to be decided—do not maim our evidence, do not maim our defence, upon any suggestion, that you may reconsider hereafter, and think unfounded; we have got enough to stand up against here, any way; we have the whole influence of the United States Government, against us. It is a government, I have no doubt, that don't seek the blood of any person. Still an humble individual who has to contend for the right, against the United States, has to contend against a great weight, as it were, but I don't believe it is the disposition of that government, or of any officer in the employment of it, to maim the defence, upon any such suggestion as has been made by the Counsel for the government. He says this bullet will be introduced all in good time. Good time for whom? Good time for the government, or good time for the prisoner? because there is at present going on here a genuine contest, not a tame contest, but a contest about life, and the government is ably represented and the prisoner has his representatives here, and in that contest we desire to introduce evidence, during the time allotted for the introduction of evidence, and it is important that we should be allowed to introduce such evidence as we consider material, and not be prevented from

so doing because there has been so much perjury that they are afraid to let us have a bullet, although it may be material to us, because there has been so much perjury committed here. They won't say upon which side it has been committed, but there has been so much perjury committed somewhere, that they will not allow us to have a bullet. Suppose the perjury has been committed upon the side of the government, why should they keep the bullet? Give us fair play, let us have the benefit of any testimony that we think important, and let the Court consider it; and if we are guilty we submit, but we cannot submit voluntarily. Whatever we may do, when ordered by the Court, and we will obey all its commands, we cannot submit to close our case until we have got in all the testimony that we think important for our prisoners, and we would be false to our profession if we were to do so. I don't think it has ever occurred yet, in any court, that a prisoner has been refused to be allowed to introduce testimony that was obtained on the ground that it was best for the Government that it be not produced by him, that it will be produced in good time by the Government. They do not deny that the testimony is material, they do not deny that it is material to us, and the only reason they can give why we should not introduce it is the very poor suggestion that perjury has been committed here, on which side they won't pretend to say, although they act upon the supposition that it has been committed by us. I think the prisoners are entitled to all the evidence we think substantial. I think that is the rule that a prisoner be allowed to introduce all testimony that he thinks is substantial; and if one of his witnesses, or two of his witnesses, may have committed perjury, that is no reason why he should not introduce another witness who may not commit perjury, and especially such a witness as this that cannot commit perjury.

The objections made by my friend Haywood to our introduction of this pistol have been answered. We would be very glad to introduce it, if we could identify it. How could we identify it? Unless some witness for the prosecution has committed perjury, that pistol was shot by Tolar and was passed out into the crowd. I say unless some witness for the government has committed perjury, the pistol Tolar shot is not known to be his pistol at all. Suppose it were his pistol, how could we prove it? Suppose he introduced a pistol here that proved contrary to the theory of that government, that it could not have carried this bullet, would not that be an additional evidence that he committed perjury. Suppose, we say, that the pistol we introduce here is a pistol that would not carry this ball, would not we be doubly damned as perjured and guilty, some of us perhaps, nobody knows who, of subornation of perjury? We think—of course we have no personal knowledge of it—that the pistol the prisoner had on that day would not have carried that bullet. That is our impression, that is our belief; but we are totally at sea for evidence by which to identify that pistol. Say the pistol is at Mr. Tolar's house—it was proved by Mr. Ed Powers that he hadn't really carried a pistol. Suppose we produce a pistol from his house, what evidence would that be to the Court that it was the pistol he had on that day? What is the evidence resorted to to identify this bullet? It has been sealed up from that time in a manner to identify it from all doubt. How can the pistol be identified by any analogous manner? If the pistol carries the ball, the government will admit it to be the pistol; if it would not carry that ball, then I suppose a subornation of perjury would be laid to our charge, and we would be held to the minutest evidence of identity; and it is impossible for us to supply it. I say it would be impossible that we should be able to introduce all those tests of identity which it would be required upon this head.

It is not for the court, it seems to me, at this stage of the trial, to decide whether or not this testimony is important for us, we must make out our testimony at our own responsibility, and under a very grave responsibility indeed; and the government desires that we should make it out fully; and I have no doubt that the gentlemen who compose this court desire if these men are innocent, that they should go away untouched; and they desire that we shall have the benefit of whatever testimony that we think important to their cause. It is not to be left with the gentlemen who represent the government to say, when we shall or shall not introduce testimony, and it is not for them to introduce important testimony when we have closed our case.

I think the Court will not be satisfied hereafter, upon reconsidering this matter, if it seemed to them they had made a mistake in refusing us permission to introduce certain testimony, that we desire to because of the general impression, which may impress their bosoms that there has been perjury committed, in the course of the defence.

This case has not yet been argued, and the Court has not made up any opinion about it, if the course of trial is as it usually is in civil tribunals, when the Judge warns the jury that they are not to make up any opinion of the case until its final close; I take it therefore, that the Court is as untouched with this testimony as it is possible for them to be, until we have closed our case and the government has closed its case; and that they will not maim our defence. They will do nothing I say to injure the defence of these parties upon a suggestion coming from the government, that there has been a wholesale amount of perjury committed here.

The Counsel for the prosecution:
If the Court please:—
The Counsel for the accused:
I will object now myself.
The Counsel for the prosecution:
I submit it to the Court,—whether they will hear me or not. I insist upon it that on a rule to show cause why we should not produce this bullet—the party that shows cause has a right both to open and close; and we are the party who are called on to show cause. Blount vs. Greenwood, 1 Cow. 20.
The Counsel for the accused:
It is a simple question of the introduction of testimony.
The Counsel for the prosecution:
It is for the Court to decide.
The Commission was cleared for deliberation and after some time so spent, the doors were reopened and the Judge Advocate said:
The Commission decides that this motion by the prisoner's Counsel, is in the nature of a rule to show cause, served on the prosecution and that as the argument was opened by Mr. Haywood he has the right to close to it.
Counsel for Prosecution:
I would say to the Court, that the Counsel for the defence, having stated their inability—or at least their unwillingness—to introduce any pistol in evidence as the one which was in the hands of Capt. Tolar, on the day of the killing, the point before us assumes a different aspect from that which it presented on the opening of the debate. In recurring, however, to that subject it occurs to me to say, that not only is it in evi-

dence by E. P. Powers a witness for the defence, that Tolar had a weapon on his person that day, but the witness Morgan who was introduced for the defence and afterwards examined by the Court, expressly swore that Tolar had a pistol in his hand. Not only then did he have a pistol on him, but he had it in his hand, by the showing of their own witnesses, by whose evidence the prisoners are bound.

The great object that we are aiming at is truth; justice to witnesses, reverence for truth, and the arriving at a just and legal conclusion in this cause are our guides. Now, I say justice to witnesses, a due reverence for truth, and the arriving at a just and legal conclusion, all demand that the government should be allowed to produce this evidence in its own good time. The gentleman has eloquently exclaimed here,— "In good time—for whom? Not for them, for they want it now—but that we mean in good time for the government." Why, if it please the Court, we have no interest in the conviction of these men if they be innocent,—the government has no interest whatever in their conviction, if they are innocent men. We say it will be produced all in good time for the purpose of ascertaining the truth,—all in good time for those who wish to arrive at truth,—all in good time for those who wish to do justice in this cause—all in good time to give the Court the information that is essential to their arriving at a just and legal decision. Now, I confess that my ingenuity, and I presume that of the Court, has been taxed to the uttermost, to ascertain what possible difference it can make, if this testimony be ultimately introduced, whether it be offered now, or after the prisoners have closed their testimony; and we think there is good reason why it should not be produced now. I have not suggested who the perjured persons are to the court, nor have I attempted, as I think one of the Counsel for the defense did, to state where the perjury lies. But there has been perjury; and whether for the government or the defense this Court are not interested, to protect one set of perjurers nor another; but they are interested in arriving at the truth and doing impartial justice—and in coming to a just and legal decision in this case. The best way to effect these ends is to retain this testimony in the hands of the government officers, who cannot possibly, in decency, be presumed to desire the conviction of these men, unless they be the guilty parties.

Now, almost all, if the Court please, that has been said by the Counsel for the defence, for the purpose of inducing the Court to compel the Judge Advocate to produce that bullet, is of no weight, for when the Court thinks fit, ultimately, it can be and will be produced. It is kept back on the part of the prosecution only to prevent more falsehood,—to prevent even an attempt at falsehood. It is held back, with the pledge on the part of the government, that it will be produced in good time. Now, I take it that this Court will not compel those prosecuting on behalf of the government to show evidence which they think is improper at this time, when they profess themselves willing to produce it hereafter, and in the hands of the very witness whom the defence now have on the stand. I cannot, for the life of me, see what injustice can follow this course. The gentlemen think they want all the help they can get for the purpose of rescuing these men from the hands of the government. Undoubtedly it is true that they do need all the help they can get, and it is the duty of the government to see to it that the persons conducting the case on its behalf do produce at some time, this testimony.

But if the Court is sure that this testimony will be here when necessary, what more can they ask? Neither the one gentleman nor the other have shown that either the cause of justice or their own cause,—which to my mind is not the cause of justice.—will be injured by the production of this testimony at a later date. Their whole argument is based upon the assumption that the government intends to keep back this testimony, an assumption entirely baseless.

Nor, if the Court please, is this any strategic movement nor any game of push-pin conducted by the Judge Advocate and myself on behalf of the government. It is a serious business, involving a man's life, and we do not intend to raise any of these collateral issues that are of trifling importance. We conceive it, however, to be of vital importance to keep back this testimony for the present. It is evidence that cannot lie, as witnesses can,—and we wish to bring it before the Court at such a time that it will be impossible for evidence to be subsequently introduced to make it lie. We have produced Phillips' pistol, sworn by him to be the pistol he had at the time; it is now before the Court. The bullet is in our possession, and cannot be changed, unless we are guilty of corruption ourselves. We therefore—even if we desired it, which is evident to suppose—cannot make it lie. But the production of the bullet, at this stage of the proceedings puts it in the power of the prisoners to show that they had no weapon to suit that bullet. Does not justice to the government, does not a reverence for truth require that we should hold it back? Do not the Court see that the defence cannot suffer any possible harm by keeping this testimony back, if it is ultimately brought before them? By the production of that testimony now, an inducement to perjury will be held out. We have the pistol that Phillips had : the government says that Phillips did not shoot the man and that Tolar did. If the bullet fits Phillips' pistol when produced, it must have its weight ; and it is impossible for us, by keeping it back to the latter part of this trial, to change the state of facts so far as Phillips is concerned. It seems to me that the Court in its sound discretion,—taking into consideration the circumstances of the case, ought not to compel the Judge Advocate and the prosecution to produce that bullet here before they see fit to do so. We submit to the Court that the prosecution should not be compelled to produce this testimony at this time,—it appearing upon the record that they have pledged themselves to produce it before the close of the trial.

The Commission was then cleared for deliberation, and after some time so spent was re-opened, when the Judge Advocate stated that the Commission declined to order the Judge Advocate to produce the bullet at this stage of the proceedings.

Examination resumed :

Counsel for accused :

Sergeant, how long did you have that bullet in your possession before you first brought it to the City of Raleigh? Two day sir. Did you show it to any one while in your possession? I showed it to no one man sir. What is his name? His name is Watson, he lives in Fayetteville. Have you seen him here to day? Yes, sir. Did he weigh that bullet? He requested me to show him the bullet, said he would like to weigh it. And he weighed it? Yes, sir. Did you ever deliver him but one bullet? Only one sir. And that was the identical bullet which came out of the skull of Archy Beebee? Yes sir. And no other? No other.

Cross examination, by Counsel for prosecution.

Sergeant, when was it you let Watson have this ball? The day we took the ball out of the man's head. Where? At our quarters. Did he have his scales along with him? Yes, sir. He took them out and weighed the bullet? Yes, sir. Did he tell you what it weighed? No, sir. Did he have any other bullets? I saw no other. After he weighed it he returned it to you, and then left? Yes, sir. It didn't go out of your hands until you delivered it to the Judge Advocate? No, sir. And afterwards delivered it at the bank, and took it from there? No, sir.

WALTER WATSON, a witness for the defence, having been first duly sworn, testified as follows :

Examined by the Counsel for the accused: What is your name? Walter Watson. Where do you reside? In Fayetteville. How long have you resided in Fayetteville? Five years last April. What is your age? Thirty-one years last September. What is your business? I am a gunsmith. How long have you been following the business of a gunsmith? I was apprenticed when I was eleven years of age. Did you serve a regular apprenticeship? Yes, sir, seven years. Where? In the city of London. Have you been following the business ever since your apprenticeship was concluded? Yes, sir. Have you had any other business? No, sir, only the business connected with gun making. Are you familiar with small arms? Yes, sir. Are you familiar with repeating pistols? Yes, sir. Did you ever see a pistol in the hands of Calvin W. McKay, a brother-in-law of Sam A. Phillips? I did. When did you see that pistol? I believe it was this day, three weeks. What kind of a pistol was that? It was an army Remington pistol. Do you think you would know that pistol, or one of the same patent, if you were to see it again? Yes, sir.

The Judge Advocate hands witness a pistol. Witness, I believe that is the pistol; it is a pistol like that anyhow, the same size and calibre. What is the calibre of that pistol? Forty-four one hundredths of an inch in calibre. When you saw that pistol at the time you have described, was it charged? It was charged, there were five charges in it. It was not fully charged; one of the chambers of the cylinder was not charged, and five were? Yes, sir. Did McKay bring that pistol to you? Yes, sir. For what purpose? To unload it. Did you unload it? I did, sir. How was that pistol charged at the time McKay brought it to you? Three chambers were loaded with buckshot and patching, and two with the regular bullets. How many buckshot were in each chamber? One buckshot with patching around it, and two chambers loaded with regular bullets. And one chamber empty? Yes, sir. How many pieces of patching were around those buckshot? I don't know, I didn't count them. Could you produce those charges or any of them? I can produce two of them. What has become of the others? I fired them off. Well, sir, produce those two, if you please?

Witness produces the charges.

Those are the two buckshot charges which were contained in the pistol? Yes, sir. And this is the patching that was around it? Yes, sir. Just as you withdrew the loads from the pistol—you say that the other three charges that were in the pistol, you discharged? Yes, sir. One of those was a buckshot charge. Yes, sir. Why did you fire them off instead of withdrawing them as you withdrew these? Because it would be a difficult matter to withdraw the bullets in a hurry, he wanted me to fire them all I wouldn't do it because they were loaded wrong. Were those loads freshly put into that pistol? No, sir. How long, in your opinion, had those loads been in the pistol? I can't say sir, the pistol was rusty, and the chambers of the cylinder were rusted, and the caps wouldn't explode; I had to cut them off they were rusted so; the detonating powder, under the cap got rusted, I suppose, and I had to put on new caps before it would explode. Were the caps upon the nipples of all the chambers of the pistol? Yes, sir, Was there a cap upon the chamber which had no load in it? Yes, sir. Had that cap ever been exploded? Yes, sir. Was it an old cap or a new one? An old one, made in the shape of a military cap; what we commonly call a "pistol hat" cap. Were these caps not exploded? No, sir, they were some of what we call the "G. D." cap, and the others were the hat caps. So you found these chambers charged with old charges, judging from the rust which was around the chamber and around the cap; you found on the discharged chamber, a cap which had been exploded and you found all the caps were corroded, and they would not explode the powder? No, sir, they would not explode, the powder in the tube got damp, and it corroded; and the caps exploded but wouldn't explode the powder, that is how I found out that the cap on the exploded chamber had been exploded, because the other five exploded, but would not explode the powder. What was the charge of powder in these different chambers in that cylinder judging from the report of those barrels or chambers that you fired; and from the powder that you took out after the withdrawal of those too charges you have produced? The charge was very small, because I could scarcely see the balls in the pistol; I could not tell until I looked at it very minutely, what kind of balls they were, or what kind of leads. So the charges were small and insufficient? Yes, sir. They were not the regular charge? No, sir. Are you acquainted very particularly with the range of pistols? Yes, sir. Are you acquainted with the range of such a pistol as you saw just now? Yes sir, up from a short distance to a hundred and fifty yards; I have never tried them over that, because I have never had the range. Are you acquainted with the range of Colt's pistol? Yes, sir. How many forms of the Remington pistols do you know of? The army size, the navy size, the pocket pistol—let me see, I know of five Remington repeating pistols. Which is the largest? The army pistol; the one of forty-four one hundredths of an inch calibre. What is the caliber of a Colt's pistol? Thirty-six one hundreths of an inch. At the distance of from two feet to ten feet, or fifteen feet, we will say up to the distance of twenty feet, from the distance of one foot to twenty feet from the object, what would be the penetration of the bullet fired from the army Remington pistol, with a sufficient charge of powder? Well, sir, it would not gain its velocity under twenty feet. What would be the penetration of a pistol of that size, discharged at an inch board? It would go through an inch board, not through a very hard inch board through, at that distance. But through an inch board of ordinary hardness at the distance of one foot? Yes, sir, I don't think it would go through a green pine, or turpentine pine, as the call it, at that distance, I have never tried it because it would be dangerous to stand behind a pistol at one foot. What would be its penetration at two feet and a half? It would be the very same, as at one foot. And its penetration at ten feet? It would be about the same, because the pistol ball would not have gained any velocity from the force. So from one foot up to ten feet a bullet fired with a sufficient charge of powder, from a pistol of that size and that manufacture would go through an inch board of ordinary hardness—entirely through it? Yes, sir.

Then at a greater distance than ten feet wou'd the penetration be greater or less? Greater over ten feet. Then how would the penetration be affected at short distances with the charge of powder less than what you stated to be a sufficient charge? It would have less force. So while that would be the penetration with a sficient charge of powder, if there was less than a sufficient charge, how would it be? If there was not a charge of powder it would have less penetration. Did you ever see a bullet in the hands of Sergeant Kenstler who has been examined here to-day? I have. Where did you see it, and under what circumstances? Three weeks ago to-morrow night. Where did you see it? At the "Dobbin House," Fayetteville. Under what circumstances? I merely wanted to see the bullett. Well, sir, did you handle that bullet? I did. Did you weigh it sir? I didn't weigh it on Saturday night but I saw it again Sunday morning, and then I weighed it. You saw it first Saturday evening and you handled it, and you saw it next, on Sunday morning and you weighed it? Yes, sir. In what kind of scales did you weigh it, have you the scales with you? I have. Are they accurate? I believe they are, they have been tested. What was the weight of that bullet which was in the hands of Sergeant Kenstler? I believe it was two drams, two scruples less one peny weight. Could you tell sir, from any thing that was about that bullet—what was the condition of that bullet, was it flattened or battered, or in its original form? It was battered. Could you, from your knowledge of forms tell whether it had, originally been a conical ball or a round ball? I believe I could. Which had it been? A round ball. What was the caliber? Forty four, one hundredth of an inch. Would that ball have fitted that pistol which has been shown you to day? Yes, sir. Would it have fitted it as an air tight bullet? Yes, sir. Is it the class of bullet for a pistol of that size? Yes, sir. How does the weight of the bullet that Sergeant Kenstler showed you, compare with the weight of a bullet of that caliber, put in the scales, one on one side and one on the other? Well, there is a small difference between even new bullets of perhaps one two or three penny weight, the difference between the battered bullet with the matter about it, and the new bullet, was about one scruple less one penny weight. What did that foreign matter seem to be? Corruption. That bullet which Sergeant Kenstler showed you, weighed a little more than the new round bullet of that caliber? Yes, sir. And what did you say the difference in weight was? About one scruple less one penny weight.

Counsel for the prosecution.

Which was the lightest bullet? The new bullet. And this was heavier, by one scruple less one penny weight? Yes, sir.

Direct examination resumed:

Could you tell whether the foreign matter was sufficient to have accounted for that difference in weight? Yes, sir, I discovered a piece of sand in it, which looked like a small piece of flint stone. And that you say would account for the difference in weight? Yes, sir. Would the ball which Kenstler showed you be too much, or too small, or the exact size for Colt's navy repeater, or any other navy repeater? No, sir, it is much larger than the bullet of the navy repeater. Is there no 'repeating pistol made by any manufactory smaller in size than the pistol which has been shown you, carrying a bullet of the same weight as a Remington pistol? Do you mean the size of the calibre or pistol? I mean the size of the pistol? No, sir, not to my knowledge. An inch or two shorter? No, sir. Is there no repeating pistol manufactured that you have any knowledge of that is one or two inches shorter than the Remington repeating pistol which carries a bullet of the same calibre? No, sir. Did you ever see more than one bullet in Sergeant Kentler's hands? No, sir. And the only one you ever saw was the bullet which you have weighed and of which you speak here to-day? Yes, sir. Do you think you would know that pistol if you were to see it again? I believe I should if it has not been tampered with or altered in any way.

Cross examination by the Counsel for the prosecution:

You say you are familiar with the subject of fire arms scientifically? Yes, sir, I believe I am from my experience. You have been at the business from the time you were eleven years of age until now? Yes, sir. Did you put any mark upon that pistol that McKay left at your store? I did not. How came you to keep those charges from the pistol? Well, sir, I believe most every person in Fayetteville was interested in this trial, and I felt a little interest in it, and wanted to find out who had done it, that is the reason. Why didn't you keep them all? I should have drawn them all out, but that Mr. McKay was in too great a hurry, he wanted it at that moment. He didn't ask you to give him back the charges? No, sir. He stayed in your store there until you got through? Yes, sir, I asked him to leave the pistol, and told him I would do it in a hour or so. You wanted to preserve them all did you? Yes, sir, but he was in too great a hurry, and I only got a chance to take out two; I believe I should have fired them all off if the pistol had been loaded right, but it was not; the thought didn't come into my mind until I found that it was loaded wrong. Nobody suggested it to you? No, sir, when I went into the back yard to fire it off, I had to come back, as it was loaded wrong. What was the trouble? Sometimes the powder of one chamber will get into the others, and they will all go off together. You thought at first to shoot them all off, and the second thought was that you would preserve them, did anybody suggest it to you? No, sir, besides they were very much agitated when I asked them to leave it. Did he tell you why he didn't shoot it off himself? No, sir, but everybody mostly in the town brings their pistols to me to unload; but he repented of it afterwards that he didn't unload it himself. How old is that little son of Phillips', that manifested such agitation? I believe about fourteen years of age. How did they show their agitation—were they pale and trembling? Well, by their voices, and the answers they made me, and when I asked them to leave the pistol. They refused to leave it? Yes, sir. Did they say anything about being called upon to present the pistol here? No, sir, they whispered to me, and there was no occasion of it, there was nobody in the shop. One said (whispering) I want you to unload this pistol for me. Did they whisper in your right ear or left ear? I can't say—in fact they didn't whisper in my ear at all: I was sitting down at work, at the bench, at the time; they had it covered up in a paper in a basket, covered over with cloth. What sort of a basket was it? I call it a linen basket. Did it have a corner? I can't say exactly, but I distinctly saw the cloth, and he took the pistol out out of the cloth. You started out then to unload it and found that some of the bullets were too small, and you came back and said it was dangerous to fire off, as one barrel might endanger the others—and then it was that you noticed their trepidation? Well, I noticed it at first, but not particularly at the time, because I thought perhaps

the order of General Sickles might make people a little scared, I took out two loads and laid them down on the bench, it was not dangerous to fire off the one with patching, or because the other two bullets were tight. In the course of this investigation you noticed what sort of bullets they were—that they fitted exactly. Yes, sir. Could you tell whether they were conical or round bullets? I have tried to think of it lots of times, but I can't say for certain. Now that is very unfortunate, as you remember so much of the rest about it. You say the bullet in Kentsler's hands was round, but could not say if the others were, although you had given so much investigation. The bullets were so much down in the cylinder that it was a very hard matter. Didn't it strike you as you were so anxious about this case, that the bullets were the most important part about the load? I didn't know, sir. Have you any decided impression about the kind of bullets? I have not. What is the difference in weight between the conical bullet and the round bullet, which is the heavier? The conical. What is the difference now in a Remington pistol of this kind? It would take thirty-two of the elongated bullets to weigh a pound, and forty-eight of the round bullets. You have tried to refresh your memory, as to whether these bullets were round or conical, have you never expressed your opinion to any one? No, sir, in regard to the bullets I have never mentioned it to any one. Have you ever mentioned to any person that you could not tell whether they were round or conical? No, sir. Not to any human being alive, not even to the Counsel in this case? No, sir. The Counsel asked you how long that pistol had been loaded—can't you form any conception? It had been loaded for some time; I know by the rust, and by the powder in the tube getting damaged so that the detonating of the caps would not fire it. The only answer I could make would be that the pistol had been loaded for some time, it depends upon how the pistol had been kept, you can keep a pistol in a dry place, and perhaps fire it in a year. You can only say that it might have been loaded a month, two, three, or six months, but you can't say exactly, or give any opinion upon it? No, sir. It was not freshly loaded? No, sir. The changes you took out of this pistol were very small? Yes, sir. Are you certain you got the whole charge out? Yes, sir. I have a tool on the bench for that purpose. You preserved the powder? No, sir. It struck you it was of importance to preserve those bullets, but nothing struck you about preserving the powder, so the size of the bullets, and the quantity of powder, which were matters of very considerable importance, were matters of which you cannot speak; and you did not preserve them, except that you saw the load was a very small one—do you mean it was half a load? Well perhaps it was a little less or a little more than half. Did you notice, when you fired off the pistol, the chambers that had bullets in, whether they sounded as if they were faintly loaded? Yes, sir, the explosion was not very loud or clear. And both went off with about the same report? Yes, sir, except the one with patching on. Did that make more noise? No, sir, less, because of not being air tight. And there was a difference in the chambers that had the bullets in them, and the buckshot—the bullet one's made the loudest report, and the report of the one two was exceedingly similar? Yes, sir. What did you fire at, any object? I have a little target for the purpose. What became of them, did you notice whether they penetrated the wood? I did not go to see—the target is twenty-five yards from where I stood to fire off the pistol? Do you think it was far enough to get its impetus on? Yes, sir, about that distance. How did the bullets do with regard to your target? I didn't look at it. Is it possible to get those bullets? No, sir, it is not possible to get them because I have fired off so many hundreds, and there are so many hundreds of loads there that I could not tell one from another now. It seems to me that by giving only a part of the information to us you make us only the more muddled—you can't give us the bullets, nor any description, as to whether they were conical or round? I can't say for certain. You were speaking about the size of these different pistols, you say there is an army pistol that has a caliber of forty-four—what is the next size? Thirty-six. Is there not a Colt's repeater that is larger than the navy repeater? No, sir, the regulation of the army and navy both in England and America is forty-four and thirty-six. Yes, but you speak of Colt's navy pistol being thirty-six calibre? Yes, sir there is a caliber forty-four Colt's army pistol. So the caliber of the army pistol, whether Remington's or Colt's, is the same? Yes, sir. You were speaking just now that in firing a Remington, the bullet did not get its impetus, until twenty feet, or yards? About twenty feet. Is it the same with the Colt's pistol? Yes, sir, it depends upon how you hold it. So that a Colt's pistol presented very close to its object would not get its impetus on either? No, sir. You say it was three weeks ago, or will be three weeks to-morrow, when you saw this bullet in the hands of Kenstler? Yes, sir. You saw it at night? Yes, sir. How came you to see that bullet. I had a wish to see it. Didn't any body suggest it to you? No, sir. Who did you say that you informed that you had seen it? James McRae. Did he never speak to you before? No, sir. How soon did you tell him, after you seen it? The next day morning. It was on Saturday you saw it, and you told him about it on Sunday morning? As near as I can recollect I told him on Sunday morning. How late? About nine o'clock, when the post office was opened. At what time in the evening was it you saw the bullet? Saturday evening about eight o'clock. You saw it in the possession of Sergeant Kenstler? Yes, sir. At his barracks? Yes, sir. You went there and asked him to show it to you? Yes, sir. Did he produce it at once? Yes, sir. Did he tell you that there was some objection to show it? No, sir. Did he show an unwillingness to produce it? No, sir. You then took it in your hands? Yes, sir. And you swear that, that bullet was a round bullet? I don't think ——. But you swore in your examination in chief that it was a round bullet, and not a conical one, now I want to know whether that bullet was round, or conical? Well I think I can swear that it was a round bullet, and put up with the chances. Kenstler showed no unwillingness to show you the bullet? No, sir, Mr. Brandt accompanied me on his way home, and he spoke to Sergeant Kenstler, in German, and what he said I don't know. Who is Mr. Brandt? A gentleman in Fayetteville. What is he? A dry goods merchant, I was walking with Brandt, he is very well acquainted with Kenstler. Did Brandt go in with you to see Kenstler? Yes, sir. He had a few words of conversation? Yes, sir, I spoke to him, and Mr. Brandt did, and what Mr. Brandt said to him in German I don't, recollect, I don't think he said anything about the bullet though. Why? Because he is so disinterested about it. You believe he was perfectly disinterested, do you mean by a person being disinterested they don't care who did it? Yes, sir. Mr. Brandt spoke to Kenstler when you went in together?—Yes, sir, and Kenstler turned to me, and said, do you want to see that

bullet, and I said yes, I would very much like to see it, we walked up to his quarters and came back again. You went up to his quarters for the purpose of seeing it? Yes, sir. You were together first at the "Dobbin House," and you procured Mr. Brandt on account of being a German? No, sir, I did not particularly for that purpose, I was walking down with him, and told him I would like to see the bullet. How long had Brandt left your society and that of Kenstler before you went to Kenstler's quarters to see the bullet—did you leave Brandt at the "Dobbin House"? I went there and he was talking with the Germans. I want to know whether you and Brandt didn't go together to Kenstler's quarters? Yes, sir, we had to pass the "Dobbin's House." And then you and Brandt and Kenstler went up to the quarters? Yes, sir. You then took it in your hands? Yes, sir. And you returned it? Yes, sir, it was in a little round box. You noticed it had a good deal of matter on it, and a piece of sand? Yes, sir. You mean a large grain of sand? Yes, sir. While speaking of weights—is there not a difference of weight in different leads—is there not a great deal of uncertainty in weighing a lead bullet, according to the number of times the lead is melted. Yes, sir. That according to the number of times you melt it, it differs very much in weight? Lead and pewter, yes, sir, It is a very uncertain test, and calibre is a better test than weight? Yes, sir. As it is melted more and more frequently, it grows heavier and heavier? Yes, sir, the more you refine it, the more it is made heavier, because all the dross will be out of the lead then, and it will be nothing but pure metal. A bullet moulded in a hot mould and suddenly turned out into the cold, will be less? Yes, sir. What would be the difference between a bullet made in a cold mold and in a hot one? I can't say, but it will make a slight difference, perhaps a pennyweight or two in a bullet. You say your scales were apothecary's scales? Yes. Well, sir, you went to see Mr. McRae this morning and told him you had this interview with Kenstler—did you meet him at the post office? Yes, sir. He was the man who suggested to you to take the scales and weigh it? No, sir, I had done that already. You had done it before you saw McRae? Yes, sir. You saw him early? Between nine and ten—I believe it was just nine. What time did you go to Kenstler's? I think about 8 o'clock. Did any one suggest to you to weigh that bullet—who was it? Well, I am not sure whether Mr. Lauder did or not, I believe Mr. Lauder did though. When did the suggestion strike your mind that you had better weigh the bullet? After I had seen it. And you went about eight o'clock Sunday morning? Yes, sir. Was there any difficulty then about seeing it? He could not show it to me then on account of drilling his men or something of that kind; I went to Mr. Hyde's; he brought it down to Mr. Hyde's store. In the same building? Yes, sir. How much did you say it weighed? Two drachms, two scruples, less one pennyweight. Now, do you know what the ordinary weight is of a conical bullet used in a Colt's navy revolver? Between two drachms and a half scruple, and two drachms and one scruple. Now, how much would the round bullet in a Colt's navy weigh? I don't know exactly,—there are eighty-six round bullets to the pound. Now, can you tell me the ordinary weight of a round bullet in an army size; I suppose the round ball for Colt's army and Remington's army is the same size? Yes, sir. Now, what is the weight of a conical bullet used in an army revolver? Something over three drachms. Sir, let me see. How many of them to a pound? Thirty-one, sir. Then a pound divided by thirty three would give the result, eh? Well, they don't go by apothecary's weight in dividing these balls, they say sixteen ounces to the pound—apothecary's weight is twelve. When you speak of a certain number to the pound you mean to the pound avoirdupois? Well, sir, it is easily reckoned up. As I understand you, and put me right if I am wrong, one pound avoirdupois of lead ought to make thirty-three conical bullets for an army revolver, and the same amount of lead, avoirdupois, ought to make forty-four round bullets for the army revolver? Yes, sir. Now, how is it; one pound of lead will make eighty-six round bullets for the navy revolver, and how many conical? Fifty, I believe, conical for the navy, and eighty-six round. Fifty for the navy, is there that much difference? Yes, sir. You say one pound of lead will make ——? Well, sir, I believe it is fifty of the elongated and eighty-six round bullets for the navy pistol. Well, now, these weights that you were speaking of when you spoke of the bullet that was in Kenstler's possession, were not by avoirdupois at all, but by apothecary's weight? Yes, sir. So the comparison, according to these calculations, would not do at all? No, sir, there are four ounces in the pound difference. You never weighed them by avoirdupois scales? No, sir. And don't know what they weigh by that system? No, sir. Have you no method at all by which you can take the calibre by measurement? No, sir. Did you use any of these tests upon it? Not upon the battered bullet. I understand you to say that by apothecary's weight, this bullet you saw in the possession of Kenstler weighed two drachms, two scruples, less one penny-weight? Yes, sir. That was weighing it, however, with all this extraneous matter on it? Yes, sir. Did you not say that you weighed another bullet along with it? No, sir. I understood you to say that you weighed some other bullet afterwards to see what that weighed? Yes, sir. Where did you get it? Out of my shop. You took it out by chance? Yes, sir. To what sort of pistol did that belong? An army pistol—calibre forty-four. In these same apothecary's scales? Yes, sir. When you went to Kenstler's on Sunday morning, you carried both conical and round bullets of the army size with you? Yes, sir. Any of the navy size? No, sir. Did you weigh the round bullet of the army size in these same apothecary's scales? Yes, sir. What did that round calibre forty-four army size bullet weigh? It weighed less than the battered bullet did, about a scruple less one penny-weight. The round bullet calibre forty-four weighed less than the battered bullet by one scruple diminished by one penny weight? Yes, sir. What was the actual weight of the new bullet, calibre forty-four? Well, sir, about ——. I don't want you to say about, did you weigh it? Well, I didn't take any particular bullet; you can't get two bullets to weigh alike. Well, but I understand you to say that you weighed a round bullet, calibre forty-four, and took the difference? I did not take the difference, I haven't learnt all this by heart, I am only stating—. You say it is one scruple diminished by one penny-weight? Yes. The new round bullet weighed less than the battered one; what was the actual, positive weight of that new bullet,—you must have got the weight of each before you could tell the difference? Well, but there are no two bullets that will weigh alike. But you weighed one? Yes, sir. What did that weigh? I don't know exactly to a hair's breadth, but I know that they weighed what I have said; I don't speak positively, I just tell you what I think now. I thought that was by admeasurement and weight?

No, sir, I am not talking positively at all about it. Eh, but you were speaking with certainty of the weight of the battered bullet, were you not? Oh, yes. Did you take a note of it? No, kept it in my mind. You say the bullet you got from Kenstler to weigh—weighed two drachms, two scruples, less one penny-weight, is that from actual admeasurement? It is the exact weight. Of that battered bullet? Yes, sir. You weighed that on Sunday? Yes. Now, you weighed at the same time a round bullet, calibre forty-four, I want to know with the same exactness what that weighed? The new bullet weighed two drachms, one scruple, less a penny-weight, I believe, to the best of my recollection. Can't you speak of your own knowledge, did you weigh it in the same scales? I did. Can't you tell what it weighed exactly, or can you not? I believe—. I don't want belief; if you can't tell me correctly I don't want you to guess it; you say you did weigh a round one; you tell us the difference between that and the mashed bullet, and yet you can't tell us the exact weight of the round one? It weighed one scruple, less a pennyweight than the battered one. Now you see, here is the difficulty you got into: we have calculations by avoirdupois and you weighed by apothecary's scales; what a new round bullet weighed in these scales, that day, we want to know, if you can't tell, we would like for you to say so? I can't recollect, sir, for certain. Did you weigh a conical bullet, forty-four, that day? Yes. What did it weigh? I can't say; there was so much difference between the weights that I didn't notice. The conical was so much heavier? Yes, sir. Then it was decidedly heavier than the mashed bullet? Yes. So much so that you didn't think it worth while to note the difference? Yes, sir. Did you weigh a conical bullet, calibre thirty-six, that day? Yes, sir. Did that weigh more or less than the mashed bullet? Less. Was there a decided difference also? Yes, sir. Was it as great a difference as between the battered bullet and the round bullet, calibre forty-four? There is a difference of between two and three in the pound, between the conical bullet thirty-six and the round forty-four? Yes, sir, I see, so the round forty-four weighs very nearly the same as the conical thirty-six? Yes, sir. And your calculation was that the mashed bullet was a round forty-four? Yes sir. Now sir, I ask you one question and a solemn one, and one that you need not be ashamed to answer, but I want you to be direct in your answer, I ask you whether the whole thing was not conducted with a bias against the witness, Phillips, was not that your feeling in conducting this examination? It was sir.

Counsel—I thought so, sir, and I am glad to see you have the candor to say so.

Re-direct examination by Counsel for accused:

Mr. Watson, with regard to the bullets you weighed, the mashed bullet which was delivered to you by Sergeant Kenstler and the round bullet of about the same calibre, I think I understand you to say that you put one in one side of the scales and the other in the other side? Yes, sir. You didn't just put one into the scales and weigh it, and then another and weigh it, but made up the difference between the two by weights, was that the way of it? No, sir, I weighed the bullets with weights. The mashed one? Yes, sir. And the round one? Yes, sir, afterwards. Did you weigh one against the other? Yes, and I found a great difference. The difference you have stated? Yes. You have been asked whether McRae asked you for these charges and you said not. I did sir. Has any body since that time, applied to you for them? Yes, sir. Who? Mr. Phillips, accompanied by his brother-in-law John McRae. What evening was that? I think last Saturday week, but cannot speak positively. You refused to give them up? Yes, sir. I understand you to say that you, in common with other persons in Fayetteville took a great and deep interest in this matter? I did sir. And your examinations and investigations arose from the deep, absorbing interest you felt in the matter? Yes, sir. I understand you to say frankly and candidly that there is in your mind a prejudice against Phillips? There is, slightly, sir, I never spoke to him in my life until Saturday week, but I have heard of him and his character is such that I would not associate with him. You have a prejudice against him from what you heard of him? Yes, sir, I felt a pity, too, on account of his family, I never had any particular enmity towards him in my life, he called on me last Saturday evening and insulted me grossly. Under what feeling was it that you conducted this examination regarding these bullets? Well, a curiosity to find what sort of pistol it was that had shot the man. I thought you said, in reply to Mr. Haywood's question, that you conducted it under some bias towards or against Phillips? Well, I can't exactly describe my feelings about it, I had no particular enmity against Phillips but I wanted to know the truth myself, that's all. Well, whatever the feeling might have been that you had about him, did it bias your judgement, or your testimony here? Not at all sir. What is the difference in length between the navy repeater caliber thirty-six and the army repeater, such as has been shown to you? About the same length, sir, in Remington's and Colt's. I am speaking of Colt's ——.

Counsel for prosecution:
I don't think he understands your question.

Counsel for accused:
The question is, what is the difference in length between Colt's army repeater? I believe there is half an inch.

Judge Advocate:—In the barrel, or in the whole length? I never mentioned the barrel sir. Well then you mean ——. I mean from the "strike" of the barrel to the end of the muzzle? Counsel for accused:—What did you say is the difference? About half an inch. Is there any intimacy between yourself and Tolar? None at all. Tom Powers? No, sir. David Watkins? No, sir, I have never spoken to him, though I may have perhaps on the street. What is your acquaintance with Captain Tolar? I met him at Mr. Boon's store very often, and said good-morning and evening; and he has been to my shop getting some things in my way. So that your acquaintance is not intimate by any means? No, sir, very limited.

Counsel for prosecution:
I understood him to say he would recognize that mashed bullet?

Counsel for accused:
He did, sir.

Counsel for prosecution, to witness:
Did you put a mark on it? Yes, a slight one with finger and thumb—not a heavy mark, but enough to recognize it by.

Counsel for accused:
That is the very reason we want the bullet, sir: to identify it, that he might put it in the scales here in Court.

Counsel for prosecution:
The difficulty is, that he didn't keep the other bullets.

Counsel for accused:
We can find some of the same calibre—he has his scales here, (turning to witness) havn't you? Yes, sir. You have both round and conical bullets, 44? Yes, sir. And round and conical for a pistol of calibre 36? Yes, sir. And you have here the same weights and scales with which you weighed the bullet Sergeant Kenstler gave you? Yes, sir.

Questions by the Commission:
How did you know that Sergeant Kentsler had that bullet? I was informed by ——, well, I don't know whom, sir: there were some boys over in the graveyard when they dug it up: I don't know who told me; I first heard about the exhuming of the body and the extracting of the bullet, from some person coming into my shop. You can't recollect at all? I believe it was a young man named John Boon, who told me that the Sergeant who came up with the prisoners told him Sergeant Kentsler had the bullet. Are all navy revolvers of the same length? All Remington's are. Are Colt's? Yes, sir. Are the Remington's navy and the Colt's navy the same length? Well, I've never measured, but I believe they are—Oh! I think there is half an inch difference. Which do you think the longer of the two? I think Colt's is longer; I know that Colt's army is half an inch longer than Remington's.

Judge Advocate:
That will do, sir. I would now state to the Court that there are three witnesses yet under summons to appear for the defence. One of them, Owen Moore, was summoned on the 21st day of July.

Counsel for accused:
It has been suggested to me that perhaps he has removed his residence.

Judge Advocate:
Well, I have done everything that is in tho power of the Judge Advocate to procure this witness. I have sent the order of the Commission, issued sometime since, to Colonel Frank, for his arrest, but until this moment I have never heard a word in relation to him. One of their witnesses is Surgeon Kirke, to whom, although summoned, Colonel Cogswell refuses permission to leave. I will send a peremptory summons for him to-day. At the earliest, there will not be another witness here before Sunday morning, and I would therefore suggest that the Court adjourn till Monday.

Counsel for accused:
Would it not suit the Court as well to adjourn till Tuesday? I fear no witnesses will be here until Monday morning at earliest.

Judge Advocate:
I am very anxious to close this case as quickly as possible consistent with justice. If the witnesses do not come, we cannot proceed, that's all.

Counsel for prosecution:
If the Court will adjourn till Tuesday, I will have the witnesses here.

The Commission:
Do you think it probable we shall have any witnesses here on Monday?

Judge Advocate:
I think it highly probable that we shall.

At 2 P. M., on motion, the Commission adjourned to meet on Monday, 2nd September at 10 A. M.

RALEIGH, N. C., Sept. 2, 1867, 10 A. M.
Present: Col. J. V. Bomford, 8th Infantry; Bvt. Lieut. Col. Thos. P. Johnston, Capt. A. Q, M., U. S. V.; Capt. P. H. Remington, 8th Infantry; 2d Lieut. C. E. Hargous, 40th Infantry; 1st Lieut. R. Avery, Judge Advocate; the Counsel for the prosecution, all the accused and their Counsel.

Absent: 2d Lieut. Louis E. Granger, 40th Inft.

The Judge Advocate stated that there were no witnesses present to be examined, whereupon on motion the Commission adjourned to meet on Tuesday, Sept. 3rd, at 10 o'clock, A. M.

RALEIGH, N. C., Sept. 3rd, 1867, 10 A. M.

The Commission met pursuant to adjournment.

Present, all the members of the Commission, the Judge Advocate, the Counsel for the prosecution, all the accused, and their Counsel.

The reading of the testimony taken on Friday, August 30, was waived—there being no objection thereto.

The Counsel for the accused, said:

I will state to the Court, that I received a note from Mr. Watson, yesterday morning, before leaving for Fayetteville, in which he asked to say that he desired to make a correction in his testimony, at these points:—wherever he made use of the word "pennyweight" he intended "grain." The Court will recollect very well that when he spoke of the weight, he qualified by saying that he spoke of apothecary's weight, and it will be manifest to the Court, that he did mean grains, and did not mean pennyweights, because pennyweights is not one of the measures of apothecary's weight, at all. He desires that that correction may be made in his testimony.

The Counsel for the prosecution:

The prosecution objects to any alteration being made in the testimony of Walter Watson, at this late stage. He had an opportunity of correcting his testimony, it was read over to him. He has now returned home, and having made his calculations and seeing the absurdity of some of his responses, he desires to make the correction. It is opening the door too wide for fraud. That will be a matter for debate when his evidence, come up for correction. He has testified, using the expression pennyweight in every description. There is a difference of twenty-three grains between a pennyweight and a grain, and we object to his alteration of twenty-three grains in the weight of the bullet. We think his testimony ought to stand as it is, and go for what it is worth, with this explanation: we do not think his testimony ought to be changed, for he has had an opprtunity of conning it over.

Counsel for accused:

I will state to the Court, that while that is so—Mr. Watson had the opportunity of having his testimony read over to him—that he had a portion of it read over to him, and was so well satisfied with the accuracy of it, that he did not ask that the whole of it should be read over.

But what would be the effect of this. The Court declines to admit that correction to be made. Watson is recalled from Fayetteville here, and put upon the stand, and makes the correction in a supplemental examination. What is saved by it? It must be perfectly manifest to the Court that this man Watson is an intelligent man, and that he certainly understands the weights and measures, about which he spoke. He says to the Court now, that he did not mean penny-weights, and it would be absurd to suppose that he did mean penny-weights, if you give him credit for intelligence; and that he did mean grains, which was the next weight to the weight he gave—so many scruples, and so many grains. It is perfectly manifest to the Court, that it was a mere inadvertance, a mere incorrect expression on his part, and if the Court will allow the testimony to be corrected now it will be doing to the witness only justice. If the Court shall not allow the testimony to be correct it will make it necessary

to recall the witness Mr. Watson, and then in a supplemental examination he can correct it.

I hold, sir—and I think the Counsel will not gainsay it, that all Courts of justice, ot all sorts, sit for the purpose not of entrapping witnesses, but to get at testimony which is fair and satisfactory to themselves; that the witness states what he means, and if by inadvertance, anything goes down on the record, which the Court must see that he did not mean—the Courts will always permit a correction. It therefore seems to us, to narrow itself down to this, whether a correction, which the Court must necessarily see is a proper correction, shall be made now, or whether we shall be compelled to recall the witness, from the town of Fayetteville, and put him on the stand, that he may correct his testimony here.

The Commission was cleared for deliberation, and after sometime so spent the doors were re-opened, and the Judge Advocate announced that the Commission sustained the objection of the Counsel for the prosecution to the alteration of the testimony of witness, Walter Watson.

Friday's proceding were then read and approved. '

Yesterday's proceedings were read and approved.

LOUIS R. KIRK, a witness for the defence, having been first duly sworn, testified as follows:

Examined by the Counsel for the accused:—

What is your name? Louis R. Kirk. What is your rank? Assistant Surgeon. In what command? Post of Fayetteville. Did you exhume the body of a colored man, by the name of Areby Beebee, or Arehy Warden? I had a body exhumed, that was said to be the body of Arehy Beebee. Were you present at the time of the exhuming of the body? I was. When was it sir? The third of August, I think. What time in the day sir? About ten o'clock. Before noon? Yes, sir. Who were present, assisting at the exhuming of the body? I had a detail, and a couple of colored men came there to assist. Who were they? One of the soldier's names was Armstrong, I don't know the others, one of the colored men was Armstrong, he had been a witness on the trial here. Did you request him to be there present? No, sir, I had Sergeant Kenstler with me, and I took the two detailed men to do the work, I sent back for two more, but when they got there I think the body was exhumed. Did Armstrong assist in exhuming the body? Yes, sir. Was he ordered to be present, or was he a mere volunteer? I think he volunteered, sir, one of the soldiers ask him to relieve him after he got there, I don't know sir, which. You didn't request him to be present? No, I had a colored man with me to close the grave. Armstrong came there after you had reached the grave? Yes. And he either volunteered his services, or was requested by one of the soldiers detailed to assist? Yes. Did you take up the whole body? No. How much of the body did you take up. I just had the head taken up. At what point did you have it severed from the body? At the neck. What was the state of the head, at the time it was taken up? The tissues were very decomposed, sir, all came off, fell to pieces; the whole body was decomposed. Were the ears, or any portion of the ears, upon the head? I can't say for certain, I rather think they were; the tissues were all hanging around them; it made me sick, and I kept as far from it as I could. Was the hair upon the head, or had it come off? It had all come off. Where did you make an examination of the skull, there at the place? Yes, sir, close by the grave. What was the character of the ground around that place? It was sandy ground, with some thin growth of grass or weeds over it. Was the skull sawed open? Yes, sir. Which way was it sawed? The back part was sawed off, nearly from the top to the bottom. Where was the bullet found? It was in the mass of the brain, sir. Was the mass of the brain examined while in the skull? Part of it was drawn out; the part that the ball was in was drawn out. And then the examination was made in that mass, and the bullet was found in it? Yes. Have you that skull now? I have part of it. Have you the part which shows the hole where the bullet entered? Yes. Where is it? It is now in the hospital at Fayetteville. Did you make a careful examination of the skull on the day the body was exhumed? Yes. Have you examined it since that day? Yes. State, if you please where the ball entered? It entered in the main lambdoidal suture about half way from the occipital bone, to the projection in the back back of the head—half way from the orifice of the ear to the large protuberance on the back of the head. The orifice of the left or right ear? The left ear. Did it enter the walls of the skull, or did it enter the suture? Right in the suture. What is the thickness of the skull, at the point the ball entered? It is not over an eighth of an inch, about an eighth. Would penetration be effected by a ball more easily in the suture, where this entered, or in the wall of the skull? In this skull, more easily through the suture. Why do you say this skull—was there anything peculiar about this skull? The sutures in the skull were rather open; I don't know how they were at the time the man was shot; they are not as close as I have seen in skulls. So penetration would be effected in this skull at the point where that ball entered more easily than it would in an ordinary skull, or other skulls that you have examined? I think so, I think it is the thinnest skull I most ever seen. Are you accustomed to examining skulls of people? Not a great many. Are you accustomed to examining skulls of colored persons? Not especially. Have you had much experience, sir, in surgical operations, and anatomical examinations? Not a great many anatomical examinations. Have you examined many skulls before? Yes, I have seen quite a number. And you think this skull was thinner at this point than any other you have seen? I think I never saw one so thin. And you never saw one with such open sutures? I don't think I ever did. Did it enter directly in the suture, or at the junction of two sutures? Right in one of the sutures. How far off from the junction of the two sutures? Two inches and a half, I should think. What was the character of the hole that you found in the skull? The general character was round, it was ragged. Did you examine it from the inside and from the outside? Yes. What was the outside appearance—was that jagged? Yes, sir, ragged, somewhat. And the inside appearance, was there any depression or any elevation in the skull? The lower part was slightly depressed, and in the inside the bone was chipped out, as the bullet went through, it chipped out the inner table of the skull to a very slight extent. So there was a depression in the point of the skull nearer to the left ear? One part of the bone was depressed there. Is that depression invisible from the outside? Yes. And there is a chipping out of the skull on the inside? Yes, all around about the aperture. Could you tell, sir, the range of that ball—which direction it ranged? It was very nearly perpendicular to the skull; it may have been a very little from the front and down; may have gone up and backward a little. Your opinion is that the strike came from a point perpendicular to that portion of the skull? Yes, or very

nearly so. From what do you make up that opinion, sir, from the appearance of the aperture? Yes, sir. Did you examine the opposite wall of the side of the skull on the inside? I did not, except the piece that I have; I looked at it, the other sk. ll I did not. I mean the skull on the right hand side? I didn't examine it. You could not tell then whether the ball had passed through the brain, and passed to the wall of the skull upon the right, or whether it had not? No, sir. But you did find the ball in the mass of the brain? Yes, sir. How far is the brain from the skull at the point that that aperture was? The base of the brain is very nearly against that place; it went in, I think, about the base of the brain. How broad is the base of the brain? About four inches, I think. It is very nearly against the point where the bullet entered? Yes, sir. And the base of the brain, at that point, is about four inches in width? Yes, sir. The soft pulpy substance? Yes. After penetrating the skull, getting into the inside of the skull, is there any obstruction that the ball would meet with except the soft pulpy substance of the brain, until it reached the opposite side of the skull—a bullet striking as you say perpendicularly? No, sir, if it did not go downward, it would not meet any thing, there is nothing between the opposite sides in a horizontal course. I understood you to say that it went upwards a little? Yes, I don't think there would be any obstruction whatever, in the direction the bullet took. You were present at the very instant the bullet was taken from the brain? I was. Could you tell whether the bullet was lodged about the center of the brain; or whether it was nearer to one side or the other side of the brain? I could not give any idea at all, the brain was in a fluid state, decomposed entirely. What did you do with the ball? I gave it to Serg. Kenstler, Company K. 8th U. S. Infantry. What was the size of the hole made by the bullet; did you measure it? I did not. You can give neither diameter nor circumference? No, sir, merely a guess; that would be all. I don't want a guess ,if you have an opinion? I have no definite idea. Can you describe it by any portion of your person; or anything that you have about you? My front finger just about goes in it. How far? To the first joint, or nearly there. Is your front finger a little front finger or a large front finger? A small one I should think, sir. Can you say in inches, or the fractional part of an inch, about how large across that aperture was? I could not with any certainty I am not very good at measure. What is your height, Doctor? About five feet eight, five feet seven and a half, or something about there. What is your weight? About one hundred and twenty-eight, I think. You say you saw the ball, and you delivered it to Sergeant Kentsler? Yes. Did you examine the ball before you delivered it to Sergeant Kentsler? Yes, sir. What was its condition, sir? It was somewhat corroded, sir. What was its form? It was an irregular square—more square than any other form, to my observation—not a round ball. Was it very much battered? Yes, sir. Could you tell why it was so much battered, Doctor? I could not, sir. Was it so much battered that you could not tell what its original form was? Yes, sir. Would the entering into a skull at the point, and of the thickness you have described, batter a bullet so much as that bullet was battered? I am not familiar enough with projectiles to know whether it would or not. Have you ever seen that bullet since at all? I saw it once since I gave it to Sergeant Kentsler. Where did you see it? In my office at the hospital; it was the same day that I delivered it to Sergeant Kentsler; I think it was the same day, I won't be perfectly positive about that. Since that day you have never seen it? No, sir. Did you weigh that bullet? Yes, sir, I weighed it. How did you weigh it? In an apothecary's scales. Well, sir, what did you find to be the weight of it? My impression is, sir, exactly three drachms, one hundred and eighty grains. Are you certain of that, or is it only an impression? That is what I took it to be at the time; and the note I made of it is three drachms. Did you make a note of it at the time? I did. Exactly three drachms? Exactly three drachms. Did you weigh it with any other bullet? No, sir. Did you weigh any other ball at that time? None. Have you weighed any other ball since? Yes. What other ball have you weighed since that time?

Counsel for the prosecution:

Don't mention the weight if you please.

They were lead bullets that I got, that fitted either a Remington pistol, or a Colt's navy revolver. What kind of bullets were those, what shape? I think they were both conical. Who said that they fitted those pistols? A boy in a gun smiths, I don't know who he is. Do you know whether they fitted those pistols or not? One of them does, one of them fits a Colt's revolver, I believe it is, that I had in my room; I pay little attention to revolvers, but I think it is a Colt's, I am confident it is. What sized Colt's revolve? The largest size but one. And you tried one of the bullets which you weighed, conical in its form, in that pistol? Yes, sir. You spoke something of having weighed another conical ball? It was said to be the largest size of Colt's revolver, no, I think he told me that he didn't know the pattern of that ball, first he told me it was a Colt's and afterwards he told me it was not, it was some other pattern, he thought. Did you weigh any round bullets? No, sir. You weighed those two conical bullets, one of which you say, fits a Colt's repeater, next to the largest size, that you know? Yes, sir, it just about fits the barrel. Does it fit it exactly, or just about fit it? It goes in without much trouble. So a mustard seed would go in, does it fit it very tight? It might perhaps, if it was forced in with a ramrod, I stuck it in the muzzle a little piece, so that I could pull it out again. Did you notice the bullet for Colt's revolver particularly, do you know whether it is smaller near the base, or whether it has a place cut out for a string, to tie on a cartridge? This one I think had ridges on. How many ridges do you think it had? I don't know that, I am not positive that the small one has ridges on, the large one I know has two. I am speaking of the small one, the one that fits Colt's revolver, the second size? I am not positive that it has, it was not in a cartridge when I got it. And you are not certain whether those ridges are on it or not? No, sir, I am not certain. What did you find to be the weight?

The Counsel for the prosecution objected to the question.

The Counsel for the accused said:

We do not press it, I wanted simply to show that we were entirely fair about this matter, I have not the remotest idea of what his answer would be.

Direct examination resumed.

Did I understand you to say that the suture of the skull, in any skull is more easily pierced than the balance of it? As a person becomes older the suture becomes solid, and then I suppose they would be harder to pierce, they become almost obliterated, and the skull is thicker there, than at any other part, so that in that case the suture would be harder to pierce than the plain surface of the skull. So that, while you can't give an answer to the general question, as to whether the suture would be more easily penetrated than the walls of the skull where there is no suture, you give your former answer, that a suture of this skull was more easily penetrated than the balance of the skull? From the present condition of the skull, I can't tell what decomposition may have done for the skull?

Cross examination by the Counsel for the prosecution.

After this negro boy's head was out of the grave, you say the back of the head was sawed off? Yes. What portion was sawed off? About the crown of his head. There was no possibility of another bullet being thrust into his head, while you were there, without your seeing it? I was not there when the head was taken off, a shower came up, and I got into an ambulance, I told them when they had the head sawed off to call me. Were you there when the head was opened? I saw the head opened, I told them not to do anything until they called me. After the back of the skull was taken off in this way did the whole contents of the skull fall out on the ground? Very nearly all of them, I had them poured out. You had the whole head emptied before you examined for the bullet? I presume all of it was poured out. Is it possible for you to say with any certainty, whether that bullet had penetrated the whole brain, or whether it was in the substance of the brain at the time the brain came out? It appeared to be surrounded entirely by the brain, when I found it—I should think it was in the substance of the brain. Your impression is, from the place where you found the bullet, and its condition, that it was right in the substance of the brain? Yes, sir, some part of the substance. Have you any doubt about this being the very bullet that was in the man's brain that you took the head off of? Not in the least sir. You say John Armstrong was there; you don't know how he came there? He came there from curiosity I believe sir—there were a number of women and children there? Did he have anything to do with taking the head off? They told me he cut the head off—I was not there just at the time. Was he standing by, when the head was emptied and during the whole examination? Yes, sir. The tissues were in a great state of decomposition? All the tissues of the skull nearly were off. Can you tell me, as a matter of surgical knowledge, whether a conical bullet, or a round bullet makes the largest hole, in passing through the skull? A conical bullet does. It makes a hole larger than its circumference? Yes sir. How is it with a round bullet? It is not much larger if any. Was the hole round? It was not entirely round. Could you pronounce, from its condition, whether it was made by a conical or a round one? I should think by a conical bullet; that is my impression. You say that 'ole was slightly irregular, as if it were made with a conical bullet—could you insert your finger up to the first joint? I should think nearly up to the first joint, not quite perhaps.

(The witness designates about the point of his fore finger which he could insert in the aperture, which measures one and seven eighths inches in circumference.)

You spoke of this ball having entered through one of the sutures, in the back of the head? Yes. At what age, do the sutures in the back of the head usually close? Well sir I could not answer that question; there is a difference in different individuals. Is not there a general medium sir; that you could give, as a scientific man, or is it a matter of very great uncertainty? It is a matter of very great uncertainty with me at least; I don't know that I could say. You say the sutures of this skull appeared to be more open than is customary? Yes, sir. The younger the subject is, the more open the sutures, as a general rule? Yes, sir. And after a man reaches maturity, I suppose they close fully? Yes—thirty or thirty-five, along there somewhere. Is it a fact or not, that a body having been burried, subject to decomposition and the action of the atmosphere, that the sutures of the skull open more and more; or do they remain in the condition they were, when the person died? I don't know, I can hardly give an opinion on that; I don't think the decomposition would open them, unless there was some cartilaginous matter, the bony matter I don't think would open much. Did you examine any of the other sutures? None, except in the piece I sawed off, they all appeared to be started. As much as the one through which the bull entered? Very nearly as much. You spoke of the width of the brain at the base, which way did you mean to measure the width, across the head? Across the widest point; it is a matter of uncertainty with me, I don't recollect any recorded measurement, but I think the skull was about four inches wide across the base. You say you weighed this bullet, that came out of Archy Beebee's head? Yes. And it weighed one hundred and eighty grains? I believe the scales are accurate, I don't know whether the weights are accurate or not; I just used them and I never tested them, it weighed three drachms with the weights I had, precisely. You were asked, sir, about the penetration of lead, something about the wound it would make, and so on,—is there a difference or not in leads or is it not your experience such as has called your attention to that; I mean with regard to the degree of density of lead? That is something I never thought of. Did you never observe that some leads are softer than others? Perhaps I have; I have never noticed it in connection with bullets, though. Have you ever examined the question, whether a bullet loses any of its substance in passing through a substance like the back of a skull, have you ever seen any lead detached? I don't remember ever having seen any lead detached. In examination of wounds you have never noticed that any lead was left on the points of the jagged ends of the wound? No, sir. You have expressed the opinion, sir, that this wound was made with a conical ball—is that a decided opinion? Either a conical bullet or a slug, not by a simple round bullet, I don't think. Is that opinion a decided one? Yes, sir. I understand the bullet entered about an inch or two behind the left ear? Yes, sir, perhaps further than that; it was just about half way between the ear and the back of the head, and very nearly in a line. As I understand you, the portion of the skull nearest the ear, was pressed in? Yes, a very little. When you spoke of a perpendicular wound, did you mean one that was given plumb upon the spot? Yes, with the plane of the brain at the place of the wound. Did I understand you to say that you had any reason for thinking this bullet was ranged upward, and to the right? Nothing more than that depression, my idea of the range would be up towards the right temple. Can you give any d cided opinion upon that point, as to what the range of the bullet was? I could not tell anything from the brain at all. And it is only from the depression? That is all; and that depression was so slight, and if the bullet ranged any from the perpendicular it was very little. But if it was not exactly perpendicular, it ranged towards the right temple? Yes, sir. You say this man's skull was an exceedingly thin one? A very thin one, sir. Have you examined many wounds in the brain, sir, in the course of your

experience? I have seen considerable wounds in the brain, sir. Does the substance of the brain oppose much resistance to the passage of a bullet or not. Very little.

Re-direct examination by the Counsel for the accused:

You gave it as your opinion that the bullet which made that hole, was a conical bullet? Conical or a slug; not a round bullet, an oblong ball of some description, sir. What are your reasons? A round bullet generally makes a cleaner wound than an oblong one. Suppose the conical ball was to enter point on, the apex striking directly upon the skull, and going in in that way, would not that make a smooth cut, as smooth as a round bullet would? The base of almost all the conical balls is made jagged from the hindrance of the groove of the pistol barrel, and it tears more from that fact: a conical ball generally has a wind, and it strikes differently from a round ball; that is why it makes a rugged wound. Do you know much about that subject? That is the general impression, and that is the way we are taught in our works. I ask you whether it won't depend in a very great measure, upon the nature of the barrel; I ask you whether a conical ball, fired from a rifled barreled pistol would make any different wound from a round bullet fired from the same barrel? I think it would, sir. And you think a conical ball would produce a wound that was more jagged in appearance than the round bullet? Yes, sir. How would it be, sir, if that round bullet was pressed hard down and the face of it were battered with a ram rod in getting it down, would it not have the same jagged appearance that a conical ball would produce? It would make a more jagged appearance than if it were not battered. Is your experience in gun shot wounds in the skull sufficient to enable you to say whether that wound was produced by a conical bullet or by a round bullet, with its face flattened by the action of a ramrod upon it? My experience in wounds of the skull is not very extensive; I didn't see a great many of these, but i speak from my general knowledge of wounds; that all I have seen made by conical balls have been ragged and larger than those made by round balls. Can you give an opinion, as a medical man, as an expert, whether a wound in the skull would present a different appearance if made by a conical ball striking point on, or if made by a round ball, the face of which had been battered by the pressure of a ramrod? Well, from the nature of projectiles I said the conical ball made the largest wound. I am not speaking of the size of t e whole, sir; I am speaking now of the general nature of the aperture; would it be more jagged if produced by a conical ball than it would be if produced by a round ball, one that was battered in the way I stated? I think it would You were speaking just now of the scales in which you weighed the ball, you say you are certain the scales are correct? Yes, sir. And not so certain with regard to the weights? No, sir. Why are you not so certain with regard to the weights? I have never tested them, I have tested the scales. Are they old or new weights? I have not had them a year. Did you get them when they were new? Yes, sir, they were issued to me by the government. Have you used them a good deal? Yes, sir. Suppose that they had been entirely correct—these weights, when they were given to you, then would it be possible or would it not be that in weighing as much as three drachms those weights might not have lost by friction and by use one grain? I don't think it possible for them to have lost any perceptable weight. I think I understand you to say that you weighed that ball on the same day that it was extracted from the brain? I think it was that day. Was the ball entirely dry at that time, or did it have any moisture, or any portion of the substance of the brain adhering to it? It had some portion of the substance of the brain on it. Was it dry? I think it was, sir. Do you think it was entirely dry or partially dry? I think entirely dry. Had you taken any means to dry it? I had not. Did you weigh it before you got back to your office? No, sir, I weighed it after I came back. Do you know how it was carried by Sergeant Keustler from the grave? I think he put it in an old envelope. Did you go direct from the grave to your dispensary? No, sir. How long was it after the extracting of the ball from the mass of the brain before you weighed it? I can't tell, sir, it was some time though, an hour or two, perhaps several hours. Which do you think it was, an hour, or two or three or four hours? I can't say positively; I went from the grave to headquarters and reported to the Colonel and came back, and it was after that I weighed it; it was three or four hours, if I weighed it the same day. Your impression is you weighed it the same day? Yes, sir. And at the time you weighed it there were portions of the brain or the matter you found upon the ball on it? Yes, sir. In speaking about putting your front finger in the aperture up to the first joint, do you mean to have put it in that far, you would have to press the flesh around the opening? Without much pressure, I think without any pressure at all. That was with the skull naked—denuded of all its outer covering? Yes, sir. How far do you think you could have put your finger in it, directly after the shooting occurred, say that same day, when the skin was on the skull and the hair upon the skin? I could not give an idea, sir. Would you have been able to put your finger in that far on that day? The wound would have been a little less that day, I should think, because the tissues would have been contracted, and there would have been a little difficulty probably in getting it in that far.

Question by the Commission:
That ball which you tried in your revolver you say it just went into the muzzle; do you mean the muzzle of the barrel or one of the orifices in the cylinder? In the cylinder.

A. A. McKETHAN, a witness for the defense having been first duly sworn, testified as follows:

Examined by the Counsel for the accused:—
What is your name? A. A. McKethan. Where do you reside? Fayetteville. Fayetteville N. C.? Yes, sir. How long have you resided in Fayetteville? I have been regularly in business there, since 1832. What is your business? Carriage business sir. Are you acquainted with the general character of William J. Tolar? I am sir, I was acquainted, with him before the war and since that time. You are acquainted with his general character? Yes, sir. What is that character sir? It is good sir. Good as a peaceable, quiet, orderly citizen? Yes, sir, I have never heard anything against him sir. Are you acquainted with the general character of Thomas Powers? Yes, sir. How long have you known Tom Powers? I really don't exactly recollect sir, but I have known him as much as five or six years. What is his character, sir? Very good sir, he was an apprentice to me before the war, and, has since been working with me. His character, you say, is very good? Very good sir. Good as a peaceable, quiet, orderly citizen? Yes, sir. Are you acquainted with the general character of E. P. Powers for truth? I am sir. What is his character? Very good sir. Are you acquainted with the general character of Ralph B. Lutterloh, for truth? I am sir. What is that

character? Very good sir. Are you acquainted whith the general character of J. G. Leggett, for truth? I am not very much acquainted with Mr. Leggett, sir, he has not been a citizen of our place a great while, I know him when I see him in the street, I know him well enough to speak to him, but never have had any particular dealings with him, I have heard him spoken of very well. When you are asked the question whether you are acquainted with the general character or a person, it is not for you to give your own knowledge of his character, but your knowledge of his character as derived from the community in which he lives. With that explanation can you say whether you are acquainted with the general character for truth of J. G. Leggett? So far as I know about his character, it is good. Are you acquainted with the general character of Ichabod B. Davis, for truth? Yes, sir, very well. What is that character? Very good sir. Are you acquainted with the general character for truth of John T. Mullins? Yes, sir. What is that character? Well, sir, his character for truth is good. No question about it? I have never heard it questioned, sir. Are you acquainted with the general character for truth of James Atkinson? I am sir. What is that character? Good, sir, I would say Mr. Fuller, that he was apprenticed to me in 1860, he went off to war in 1861 and returned afterwards, and has been in my employ up to the time he came here as a witness. And you have known him well, and you know his general character for truth? Yes, sir. And you say, without any hesitation that that character is good for truth? I do sir. Are you acquainted with the general character for truth of Mrs. Lucy J. Davis, the wife of Dr. Davis the Dentist. I only know the lady well enough to speak of her, I can only say as to what I have heard others say of her. It is the knowledge of the character that you have from others that we asked you about? It is very good, sir. Are you acquainted with the general character for truth, of a young man by the name of Sebastian Arey, jr.? I know him very well from a boy. What is his character? It is very good, sir. Are you acquainted with the general character for truth of Washington Faircloth, son of Faircloth, the policeman in Fayetteville? I can't say that I know the young man, I know his father very well, but I don't know him. Are you acquainted with the general character for truth of Walter Watson? I am not well acquainted with him; I have never had any particular dealings with him; I have heard others speak of him. Are you acquainted with the general character for truth of Gurdon S. Demming? I am, sir. What is that character? Very good, sir. Are you acquainted with the general character for truth of James H. Myrover, Editor of the Fayetteville News? I am, sir. What is that character? Very good, sir. Are you acquainted with the general character of James A. Hendricks? Yes, sir. What is that character? It is tolerably fair, sir. Are you acquainted with the general character of Philimon Taylor for truth? I am, sir. What is that character? Very good indeed, sir. And of David Cashwell? I am, sir. What is that character? Very good, sir, indeed. Are you acquainted with the general character for truth of James R. Jones? I can't say that I am very well acquainted with him; I know the gentleman when I see him well enough to speak to him. You can't say you are acquainted with his general character? Not particularly, sir. Are you acquainted with the general character for truth of Dilly Stewart, or do you know her, a colored woman? I don't know her at all.

Cross examination by the Counsel for the prosecution:

Were you in Fayetteville on the day Archy Beebee was killed? I was sir. Were you at the market house? No, sir. Did you see anything of it? No, sir. Was Tom Powers working for you at that time? Yes, sir. Was James Atkinson working at your shop also? Yes, sir. Do you know whether they were at the market house on the day Archy Beebee was killed? I can't say of my own knowledge, sir. Were you at your place of business the day Archy was killed? I was, sir. Do you know whether they were absent? I know they were both absent. Do you remember what time they returned that day, or either of them? I am not certain whether they returned—I am satisfied of this; that both of them returned as lost time on that day. As I understand you, it is the custom of your shop, that when a man fails to do his work, he gives it in as lost time? Yes, sir. And both of these men rendered the whole of this day as lost time? Atkinson I think, only a part; but I think Powers gave in the whole day. What part did Atkinson give in as lost, morning or afternoon? I think he gave in as lost half a day. Do you remember the fact of their returning that day? I don't know that I seen Powers that day; I think I seen Atkinson that day. Did you see Powers with any weapons that day at any time? I did not sir. Do you know whether he is in the habit of carrying any? I don't know that he is. Did you see Atkinson with any weapon that day? No, sir, none at all sir. What do you mean by the general character of these persons that you have spoken of? I mean that I would believe them on oath as swearing to the truth, That is what you understand by general character for truth—that you would believe them? Yes, sir, and it is the general opinion of those who are acquainted with them. Then you mean by their general character that the people, generally who know them, speak well of them for truth? Yes, sir; I have never heard anything else of them at all. Haven't some of them no character at all, either for truth or against it? I believe they have all established a character some way or other, the greater portion of them have been raised there. Do you know that that lad Arcy has established a character for truth or falsehood, at this time in his life? Yes, sir, he was raised there from a child. Do you mean the neighbors generally have ever discussed his character for truth or falshood? I dont know as to that sir, if any citizen were asked they would say his character for truth was good. You say you knew his general character; you say you understand by general character, what the neighbors generally, say of him, not what they would say of him if they were asked; now I want to know who you have ever heard speak of Sebastian Arcy's character for truth? I don't know that I have ever heard any person particularly, for I have never heard it called in question. And that is what I mean by saying he may not have established any character for truth; you never heard his truth called in question; you never heard it said that he was a truthful boy or that he was the contrary? No, sir. But when you swear that you know a man's general character, you mean you know what the neighbors generally say of him, in the neighborhood where he lives—now about this man Leggett; when did he go to Fayetteville? I think he has been there as much as twelve months. Do you think you know his general character at all? I don't think I do, except what I have heard others say of him. Have you heard others speak of him. I have. Since he has been a witness here or before? Since. Did you ever hear them speak of him before? No, sir. He has not been in Fayetteville long enough to establish a general character

there, has he? I don't know, with the persons whom he has been familiarly acquainted with, he may have established a character. That would not be a general character? No, sir, I don't know that it would be. Now I wan't to know whether in the majority of these cases, you are giving your own opinion or the opinion of the community, that you have gathered? Well, sir, I am giving my opinion, coupled with the opinions of the community, so far as I know. Now I want to know who you have heard speak of the character of Leggett, before he testified in this cause? I never heard anybody speak of him before. And yet you said you knew his general character? Yes, sir. You said you never heard Sebastian Arcy's character called in question, one way or the other? No, sir. Did you ever hear Mrs. Davis' character called in question? No, sir, she stands fair as a respectable lady. I have no doubt about it, but there are a great many men who live and die without establishing a character; you say you know the general character of E. P. Powers for truth? Yes, sir. Who have you ever heard speak of it? I know that by business, I have been more or less engaged in business with his father. His general character is given upon your own opinion? From what I have seen of him and from what I have heard others speak of him. Who have you heard speak of him? I have heard John H. Cook speak of him. When was that? I can hardly tell you, the young man was raised there. Did you hear him speak of his truth? I have always heard him spoken of as a very reliable young man. Was his truth called in question at all? I don't know that it was. Did you ever hear John H. Cook say that he was a man whose character was good for truth? I have heard him speak of him in that way; that he was a reliable, truthful man. Did he say anything about his truthfulness? Yes, sir. What called it up, sir? Cook and Powers were once in partnership, and it arose probably from that. What brought on the conversation with regard to his truth? I believe it was about business matters. Who else have you heard speak of his character for truth, besides J. H. Cook? I don't know that I have heard any person else that I can name. Who have you ever heard speak of Ralph B. Lutterloh's character for truth? Nobody, sir, I know the young man well. I understand that your opinion of him is good—the only thing that you can give in as evidence is what the neighbors in the neighborhood where he lives, generally say of him; and when a man swears that he knows a general character of another person, he swears that he knows that; not his own opinion of him, but what the neighbors generally say of him; now, you said you knew Ichabod Davis's character for truth? Yes, sir. Who have you ever heard speak of his character for truth? I don't know any person particularly, for I have never heard him doubted. Did you ever hear it called in question one way or the other? I don't remember that I have heard anybody speak of his being a man of good character for truth; I have had a good deal of dealing with him myself. But that is not what others say of him—that is your own opinion of him; now John T. Mullins—I should say he has a character one way or the other—you say he has established a character for truth? Yes, sir. Who did you ever hear speak of him? He is a man of a peculiar turn, and not disposed to do much business, but I have always heard him spoken of by our citizens in general there, that he was a man for truth; that whatever he said, you might rely on as true, whatever other faults he might have. You have heard that said of him frequently? I have heard him spoken of several times. Was that before or after the murder of Archy Beebee? Before and since. I don't care about any thing that has been said since, but I want to know who you have ever heard speak of Mullins' character as good for truth before Archy Beebee was killed? I have heard Major John T. Leonard. When was that? I could not say, sir, the time; the reason of my speaking of him was because he was a special magistrate there. Any others that you can name? I don't know any others particularly. Have you ever heard any other person speak of his character for veracity? I don't know that I have particularly. Have you in general; I want to know what your opinion is with reference to general character; I want to know how general your observation has been; I understand you to say upon one occasion, you have heard Leonard speak of John T. Mullins' character for truth? Yes, sir. Have you ever heard any one else? I have heard a brother-in-law of his by the name of James Sundy; he is not alive now. Did he live in Fayetteville? Yes, sir. Who else? I don't know any person else. How long have you known James Atkinson? He came to me on the 22nd of February, 1860; I have known him since that time. How long did he remain with you before he went into the war as you said? He went into the war on the first of May, 1861. When did he return? In October, 1865. And he has been working with you ever since? Yes, sir. How old a man is James Atkinson? I suppose between twenty-three and twenty-five, he was seventeen years old when he came to me in 1860. You spoke of his character as being good for truth? Yes, sir. You say you know his general character? I think I do, as well as any man. No man may know it for aught I know, I want to know whether you say you know his general character, not what you think of him, but his general character? His general character about the shop among the men who have been there with him every day, is that of truth. Then the persons whom you have heard speak of him, are men about the shop in your employ? Yes, sir. Did you ever hear any one else speak of his character for truth? I don't think I have at all since this affair. Who did you hear speak of it before in the shop, Tom Powers? I don't know that I have ever heard Tom Powers, I have heard the painter that I have in my shop, named Michael Gary. And what did he say about him? He said he would believe him. Why was this man's character for truth discussed by Michael Gary that caused him to make that remark? It occurred at the time he went off in the war: I recollect hearing Mr. Gary speak of him for truth particularly, about that time, and it originated in this way: he was my foreman in the paint shop, and this man was an apprentice in the same shop, and he said he had every confidence and trust in him, in every way, I have heard him speak of him frequently, as saying what James Atkinson would say, he could rely on. Who else have you heard speak of him in the shop, besides Michael Gary? I have heard my oldest son speak of him. Who else? I don't know that I have heard any one else. I understand you to say that you have never heard any one outside, speak of this man's character one way or the other, before this affair occured? No, sir. And you say the general opinion is, that he is a very reliable man, so far as truthfulness is concerned among those who have worked with him in the shop? Yes, sir, I know it sir, as much as any man. You spoke of Thomas A. Hendrick's having a tolerable fair character for truth, what do you mean by that, that his truthfulness has been questioned? I only referred to transactions of business, there are some men that I would rely on more than

others. And he is one you would not rely upon? It would depend on circumstances. What sort of circumstances? I don't think he is altogether as reliable as some men I have mentioned. Don't you know he is a notorious liar? I know his character is not so good for truth as those I have spoken of. Don't you know that this young man Atkinson has established a character for vaporing, big talk, or big stories, I dont mean malicious lies? No, sir, he is a quick, shrewd, smart young man, as you find any where, and if there is anything to be seen he would see it as soon as any man in this hall. You say you have never heard any such statement from any quarter, about him, as being given to telling big stories? No, sir. You know nothing about this killing of Beebee? Nothing at all, I didn't even go to the market house.

Re-direct examination resumed by the Counsel for the accused:

I understand you to say that these men that you have spoken of are men that you have known long, men who have long resided in the community where you live, and that though you can't say that you have ever heard any one speak of their character for truth in particular, you have never, in the whole course of their lives, heard their character for truth called in question? I never have. And from that, and from the fact of their always having borne good reputations, that you unhesitatingly say that they are men whose character for truth is good? Yes, sir. You have never heard any man say that the character of Governor Worth, of this State, was good for truth have you? No, sir. But you think you are perfectly confident to say that his general reputation is that of a man of truth? That would be my statement, sir. When you speak of these men having good reputations for truth, I understand you to say that you speak of them from your own personal knowledge, and from the fact that they have always been in good repute among their neighbors and among their acquaintances, and that you have never heard any man call their character for truth into question? I have never heard the character of one of them brought into question. Are they considered reliable men in the community in which they live for truth? Yes, sir. Strictly reliable? Yes, sir. Now, with regard to what you have heard said since the killing, since the parties came up here and testified, I want that, sir; has the subject of James Atkinson's testimony been spoken of at Fayetteville? I have heard it spoken of by a great many persons. During the time you have heard it spoken of have you heard one man—one single man—doubt the correctness of his testimony in any one part? I have never heard one single one. On the contrary, sir, I ask you whether any man ——?

Counsel for the prosecution objected to the question.

Counsel for the defence asked upon what ground.

Counsel for the prosecution:

Upon the ground that you had the examination in chief; that I did not call out the statement in regard to it in the cross examination, and you have no right to examine as to new matter, apart from other reasons.

Counsel for the defence:

I shall not insist upon the question of you object.

Counsel for the prosecution:

I do object.

Re-direct examination resumed.

So you give the Court to understand that when you say that you know the character of this man for truth that your knowledge is gained in the manner you have stated, to-wit: from what you have known of the men themselves,—from you having lived in the same community with them, and from your having never heard any man doubt their veracity, or call their character for truth in question at all,—and that you have precisely the same knowledge of their general character for truth that you have of the general character for truth of other men in the State of North Carolina who are acknowledged to be men of undoubted veracity? Yes, sir.

ARCHIBALD McLEAN, a witness for the defence, having been first duly sworn, testified as follows: Direct examination by the Counsel for the accused:

What is your name, sir? Archibald McLean, sir. Where do you live? In Fayetteville. For how long? Some thirty years. In what public capacities have you acted there? I have been Clerk of the County Court, County Trustee, Cashier of the Bank, and Mayor of the town. For how long a period have you been Mayor? For eight or nine years. Are you acquainted with William J. Tolar? Yes, sir. Do you know his general character? I do. What is it? Good. Do you know the general character of Thomas Powers? Yes. How long have you known him? I suppose eight or ten years. What is his general character for truth? I never heard any thing against it. Are you acquainted with Ralph B. Lutterloh? Yes, sir. Do you know his general character for truth? I may say I do. What is it? Good. Are you acquainted with J. G. Leggett? No, sir, not to allow one to speak of his character. With Ichabod B. Davis? Yes. For how long? I suppose eight or ten years. Are you acquainted with his general character for truth? Yes, sir. What is it? Good, as far as I have any information. Are you acquainted with John Mullins? Yes, sir. How long have you known him? From a boy. Do you know his general character? Yes. What is that character? Good. With James Atkinson? Yes, sir, for a long period. Are you acquainted with his general character? Yes. What is it? Good. Do you know Sebastian S. Arey? Well I know him as a boy. Do you know whether he has established a character for truth? I know nothing to the contrary. Are you acquainted with his general character for truth? Well, I can't say I have any information about that; I know his father and his family very well. Are you acquainted with Washington Faircloth? Not much—he is a boy. Have you ever heard any thing against the character of either of these boys? No, sir, I believe they have the reputation of being orderly boys. Are you acquainted with Gordon S. Demming? Yes. How long have you known him? I suppose for twenty years. What is his general character for truth? Good. Are you acquainted with Philimon Taylor? Yes, sir. For how long? For twenty odd years. Do you know his general character for truth? Yes, sir. What is it? Good. With David Cashwell? Yes, sir. Do you know his general character for truth? I do. What is it? Good—exemplarily good. Are you acquainted with Mrs. Lucy J. Davis? Yes. For how long? Six or seven years—five or six I guess. Do you know her general character for truth? Yes, sir—I suppose I do. Well, sir, just say whether you do or do not? I do. What is that character? Good. Are you acquainted with Delia Stewart? Yes, sir. For how long have you known the old lady? I suppose ten years. Do you know her general character for truth. Yes, I might say so, I know nothing against her character. Do you know Henderson Lockamy? White? Yes, sir. I can't get him to my mind. He describes himself as a

spirit barrel cooper? I don't think I can call him to mind—I may know him if he were here before me, but I can't think to whom you allude. Are you acquainted with James H. Jones, son of Daius Jones? Yes. For how long? Well, I knew him as a boy, for a considerable time, but my attention was directed particularly to him in the commencement of 1861. Do you know his general character for truth? Yes, sir. What is it? Good, as far as I have ever known. Are you acquainted with Walter Watson? The gun smith? Yes, sir? An Englishman? Yes, sir? I am. How long? Since two or three years ago. Do you know his general character for truth? I never heard any thing against it. Well do you know his general character for truth? I suppose I do, I have seen the man—an industrious—I suppose I can say that his character for truth is good. Are you acquainted with Thom as A. Hendricks? The Factory man? Yes, sir? I am. How long? Six or seven years. Do you know his general character for truth? Yes, sir. What is it? I know nothing of its being any other than good.

Cross examination by Counsel for the prosecution:

Were you in Fayetteville the day Archy Beebee was killed? No, sir. You were not? No, sir. In giving the characters of those persons named to you, is it your own opinion you give? Yes, sir, and what I know of the reports around in regard to them. Is it the one that you yourself have of them, or is it that which is held by the community; when you say you know a man's general character, do you mean what the neighbors think of him? Yes. And in these cases, when you say you know a man's general character do you mean what the people in the neighborhood think of him? Yes, sir. Did you say you knew the general character of Thomas A. Hendricks? Yes, sir. And you said his character was good? Yes, sir. Did I understand you to say you never heard it called in question, for truth? Yes, sir. Who did you ever hear speak well of him, for truth? I don't remember. Did you ever hear any one speak of his character for truth at all, one way or the other? I don't know that his character was ever brought in question; he passes, as far as I know, for a man of truth. But don't you suppose a great many men live and die without any general character, without acquiring any? Yes, without the attention of a great many persons being called to them. Do you swear that all these persons whose general character you say you know, have a general character? Well, when I say a general character, I don't mean as a public officer, but, as far as the word will apply to a private citizen, I do, sir; I would say that the public conceded their character to be good. I understand that you mean their characters were never called in question? Well, that is one of the points. Do you mean to say that James Atkinson, for instance, has established a general character at his time of life? Yes, sir, I think he is pretty generally known. You think he has a general reputation? I think he has. How often have you heard his general reputation spoken of, before the murder of Archy Beebee? I cannot name a time. Did you never hear of any reputation with regard to him; I don't want your opinion, nor a history of his life, nor yet individual acts, but what did people generally say of him? Well, I have had him before me as witness while Mayor, have observed his conduct while an apprentice, and have heard the boys remark about his neat appearance and orderly manner frequently. Did you never see a liar with a clean shirt? Yes, lots of them. You say you heard them remark upon his neat appearance? I mean my attention was directed that way frequently; it was generally remarked that he was kind to his mother, a spirited and clever boy. Well, sir, I don't see that anything yet has been conceded with regard to his truth. I have never heard anybody speak of his general character for truth, but I have taken his testimony myself for truth: I never heard it assailed. Did you ever hear anybody say he was particularly truthful? When I have taken his testimony all hands conceded it. Did you ever hear any one speak of his character for truth at all? I can't say that I ever did. Did you ever hear anybody speak of the character for truth of E. P. Powers? Do you mean if I have heard ever, that he would or would not tell truth? I mean did you ever hear his character for truth discussed? I can't say positively that I have; but I consider he has a good character, generally, when he keeps good company, and when good young men associate with him; he seems to pass before the community as a truthful man. I understand you to say you never heard his character for truth discussed? I mean I never heard a man say directly that he would or would not tell the truth. Did you ever hear his character for truth discussed? I cannot say that I did. Did you ever hear Mr. Lutterloh's character for truth discussed? No, sir, I cannot say that I did. Then I understand you, generally, and without going through the entire list of names, that when you spoke of the general characters of the parties named to you, not that they have established one, but that you never heard anything against it? Yes, sir, I have no hesitation in saying that I never did. I understand that is what you mean by their reputation? Well I mean what the community concede to them. What do you mean by "concede"? Well letting them pass as good men; if a man occupies a good position in society, I take for granted that his character is good. With regard to any one of these men can you tell me a single one of them whose character for truth you have heard discussed? I can't say there is any one. Walter Watson—I understood you to give some indefinite answer about him; do you know his general character; what I mean is, have you ever heard any one speak of him? I can't say I have. When you say you know his general character, you mean you never heard any one speak of his character for truth? Yes, sir. You give your individual opinion of his character for his general character? Yes, sir. And you say you have known Watson for a year or two? I think over two years. And you don't know anything of his reputation in the community? Well, I never heard his character for truth actually discussed. Then I want to know if you pretend to say you know his general character? Well I have formed the opinion from what I have already stated that he is a man of truth; I never heard his reputation assailed, and all seem to pass him as a man of truth, and I take him to be such.

Re-direct examination by Counsel for accused: I understand you to say that you know a man's character for truth when you know the general estimation in which he is held by his neighbors and the community in which he lives? Yes, sir, Did you ever hear the character for truth of the leading citizens of Fayetteville discussed—such men, for instance, as Charles T. Haigh, or other leading citizens? No, sir. But you say you have a knowledge of their general character for truth? Yes, I would say it is good. And the same thing that would lead you to suppose their characters good, and to believe and declare them such, is the same thing that prompts you to day in the case of the parties whose names I gave you? Yes, sir. I understand you to say that with re-

gard to Atkinson, he has been a witness before you on one or two occasions, when you were Mayor? Yes, sir. Were there any persons there interested in contradicting him if his testimony was false? Yes, sir. And even then you never heard his character for truth called in question? No, sir. Is it usual, as far as your experience goes, to say anything about a man's character for truth at all, unless it be suspected of falsehood? It is not usual with us. And while you cannot give the name of any man who has ever said to you that the character of either of these gentlemen was good for truth, they pass in the community of Fayetteville as men good for truth, and you have yet to hear the first allegation against them? Yes, sir.

GRIFFIN CHANDLER, a witness for the defence, having been first duly sworn, testified as follows:

Direct examination by Counsel for accused: What is your name? Griffin Chandler, though I am called Griffin Chance very often. What is your business? Running on the river. In what capacity? Deck hand at present. Were you in Fayetteville on the day Archy Beebee was killed? I was. Were you at the market house that day? Yes. At what time did you go to the market house? I can't say exactly, there was up stairs when I got there. Was it in the forenoon or afternoon? I can't say, sir. Did you see Beebee go up stairs? No, sir. Did you see Mrs. Massey and her daughter coming down stairs. Yes, sir. Where were you standing? On the south side of the market, close to Becky Ben's bench on the southern pavement of the market house. How far were you from the small arch on the south east side? I don't understand exactly. Do you know the arrangement of the market house? Yes, sir. Do you know what is meant by an arch? Yes, one of these openings. Do you know how many arches on that side of the market house looking down Gillespie street? Yes, sir. Do you remember whether there are any small arches, one to the right and one to the left? You know where Becky Ben's stall is? Yes. Well? Well, sir, I was standing at the upper end of that. Could you see Miss Massey and her mother coming down stairs? Yes, sir. Did you see them when they went to the carriage and got in? Yes, sir. Did you look at the carriage while it was standing there, until it went away? Yes, sir. Do you remember who went to the carriage? When? Between the time they got in and the time the carriage was driven off? Well I can't be positive, and I won't say unless I know it. You were about the same place when Archy was brought down? Yes, sir. At the time he first appeared on the landing? Very near the same place, sir. Did you see him there? I saw him when he got down. When he reached the floor of the market house? Yes, sir. Did anything occur there to attract your attention, could you see him until he got up to the main eastern arch going out? Well there was a crowd, I could not. Did you see what occurred at that main eastern arch? No, sir. Now, put yourself back precisely as you were that day, standing there and recollect that Archy has just passed out of the main arch and his face is turned towards the guard house, where did you next see him? Well, when he turned that arch to go towards the market house, there was a great alarm. What was it? One said, "I demand the nigger," and some said, "kill him," but I don't know who it was. Did you see Archy at that time? Well, you see the brick work was a sort o' between him and me then. When did you next see him? Well, there was a kind of rush come towards him from down the street and I kept stepping back towards Mr. Hinsdale's corner, on the pavement, soon after that I could see them coming down the corner of the market, and I was sort 'o making my way towards Draughon's, to get behind them. I saw Mr. Phillips there Did you see Beebee at the time he was shot, or about there? Not when the pistol was fired, but I did when he fell. How far was he off from the corner of the market house at the time he fell? It looked to be four or five feet. I don't mean from the wall, but from the corner back toward's Draughon's, a line drawn straight out from the corner? It looked so to me. When the pistol shot was fired, and a little before, where were you standing? Off the pavement some, around towards Draughon's store. From the position you had there, could you see the people on the pavement? Some of them. And those off the pavement down Person street? A good many of them. You didn't see Archy at the very instant he was shot? No, sir. Directly afterwards? Yes, about the time he fell. Did you see him just before he was shot? Yes. How long before? I couldn't say exactly. Was he near the same point when he was shot? He was not far from it. Did you see who shot him? No, sir. Did you see any weapon in any one's hand at that time, or before? I saw one man with a pistol. Just when he was shot? Well, about that time, a little before. Who was the man? Phillips. What Phillips? Samuel Phillips. Where was he standing? A little more towards the Cape Fear Bank—I mean he was a little more on the side towards Davis' tin shop, than on the other. Was he off or on the pavement? I can't be positive, he was from it any way. Was he to Beebee's left, or right, or front, or where? He was this way like (left and front.) Did you think it was left and front, or left and rear? I don't understand exactly but he was so, (illustrating again left and front.) How far from Beebee? About as far as that gentleman there, (pointing to a gentleman about nine feet from him.) How long before the pistol was fired did you see him? I couldn't say, sir. Did Beebee take any steps at all down the pavement after the time you saw Phillips, and before he was shot? I can't say, sir. How long before Beebee was shot, say as nearly as you can. I don't exactly understand How long before he was shot was it that you saw Phillips with the pistol in his hand? A short time. Could you have counted five? Yes, sir. Could you have counted ten? I can't say, sir. You think you could certainly have counted five? I think so. What was Phillips doing with the pistol? He had it pointed that way and was working it so, (witness illustrates by holding his arm out at full length, and moving his hand up and down gently.) Was it pointed in the direction of Beebee? Well, it must been that way. And a short time after that you heard the pistol fire? Yes. How many persons were there between Beebee and Phillips at the time you saw the pistol in his hand? I can't say, there was a crowd, and when some one said "kill him!" I got scared, and— Did you see the smoke? I couldn't say, sir. Did you see the flash? I couldn't say that I did. Did you hear the report? I did, sir. From what point? I couldn't say, exactly. You swear that just before he was shot you saw Phillips with a pistol pointing it towards where Beebee was? Yes, sir. And directly afterwards you heard a pistol fire? Yes, sir. You didn't see the smoke nor the flash, and can't say where the report came from? No, sir. Did you see anything of Phillips after that time? No, sir, I saw Beebee lying on the ground, and then went straight to my work. Did you see a pistol in anybody's hand at any time that day, before you saw the pistol in Phillips' hand? No, sir, I hadn't been

there long. Had you seen Phillips before during that day? No, sir. So that all you know of the matter is contined to the short space of time in which you think you could have counted five, just before Beebee was shot? Yes, sir. Did you see what Phillips did with that pistol? No, sir. Did you notice whether it was cocked or not? No, sir. Were you ever subpœned as a witness in this case before? I came here once. Did you come on the subpœna? I don't know what you call it, they fetched me a piece of paper and told me I must come here and I did. Did any body ask you what you knew about it? Yes, sir. Who? That gentleman, (pointing to the Judge Advocate.) Did you tell him substantially the same thing that you have told here to-day? I think I told him, as near as I recollect, everything I knew. Did you tell him you saw Phillips with a pistol? I told him just what I have told here, and that's all I know about the thing.

Cross examination by the Counsel for the prosecution:

Who went to the carriage with these ladies; who helped them in ? Let me study a minute; it seems Mr. Powers went with them, didn't he? Well, I am asking you the question? Well, sir, I wont be positive, but it seems Mr. Powers did, that's all I know about it, so help my Almighty God. You say that when Archy got out of the arch and came out on the pavement the hullaballoo was made and you got scared? Yes, sir, there was such a to-do about it that I got scared. Had you seen Sam. Phillips before you were frightened, or was it after? I can't say sir, but they were so soon after each other—I can't say, sir, indeed which. I understand you were standing on the south of the market house, near the south-east corner? Yes, sir. On the pavement, with your back towards Mr. Hinsdale's store? Yes, sir. When you saw Sam. Phillips, where were you standing, on the pavement or off? I think a little off—if I was'nt off, I stepped off. Was he right straight in front of you? Well if he was not exactly so, he was a little to my left. You were on his right and front? Yes. Let that represent the east end of the market house, (diagram shown to witness) Hinsdale's store is right here, (pointing); Beebee was right here you say, (pointing.) Yes, sir. Where were you, looking east? Yes, sir. And you were standing up here, (pointing.) Yes, sir. How many feet from the corner, were you off the pavement? At the time I saw Phillips I stepped off. Now here is Beebee (pointing,) were you on his right? Yes, sir. Where was Phillips? He was standing about that direction, about here (pointing.) In front and left of Beebee and nearly opposite you? Yes. So that if you were looking due east you would see Phillips? Yes, sir. Which side of you was Phillips? A little more to my left. How much? About a foot, I would not say. Have you seen this diagram? No, sir. Where was Phillips standing? Here, towards Mr. Davis' (pointing.)

Re-direct examination by Counsel for accused.

You say Phillips was either on the edge of the pavement or off? Not far from it, I wouldn't positively say unless I knew it.

At 1 o'clock, P. M., on motion, the Commission adjourned until the 4th September, at 11 o'clock, A. M.

RALEIGH, N. C., Sept. 4, 1867, 11 A. M.
The Commission met pursuant to adjournment.
Present : All the members of the Commission, the Judge Advocate, the Counsel for the prosecution, all the accused and their Counsel.
The reading of the testimony taken on Yesterday, was waived, there being no objection thereto.

Yesterday's proceedings were then read and approved.

ISRAEL BOND, a witness for the defence, having been first duly sworn, testified as follows:

Examined by the Counsel for the accused.

What is your name? Israel C. Bond. Where do you reside? Fayetteville. How long have you resided there? Between four and five years sir. What is your business in Fayetteville? I am town constable. What was your business on the day Archy Beebee was killed? I was town constable, sir. Were you in Fayetteville on that day? I was sir. Did you assist in carrying Archy from the guard house to the market house? I did sir. Did you see Mrs. Massey and her daughter Elvira there that day? I did sir. Did you see them up into the market house? I did sir. Did you go up there with them? I did sir. During the time they were up there, did you come down from the market house at all? I did sir. For what purpose did you come down? To get a drink of water. At what time was that, how long before Mrs. Massey and her daughter came down stairs? I could not set any time, I have no idea that it exceeded fifteen or twenty minutes or half an hour any way. Where did you get your drink of water from? I disremember, sir, whether I got it under the market or at Mr. Davis' store, I can't be positive. How much of a crowd was there at the market house at the time you came down to get a drink of water? I could not say sir, there was a right smart gathering about there. Did you notice whether there was any crowd outside of the market house upon the eastern side? They appeared to be partly under the eastern end and in front, sir. And you can form no estimate of the crowd? I cannot, sir, for I didn't stop one minute at all, I immediately got my drink of water and went up stairs. Did you speak to anybody while you were there at that time? I think not, sir. Nobody spoke to you? Not that I can recollect. Did you notice anything unusual in the crowd? I did not, sir, most positively I did not. Did you see any persons in the crowd with weapons? No, sir, I did not. Then you went back up stairs, did you come down again before Miss Massey came down? No, sir. Did you escort Miss Massey and her daughter down? I did, sir. Where did you carry them? To the carriage, sir. Where was the carriage? It was directly in front of the main eastern arch as well as I can recollect. On the pavement or off the pavement? Off the pavement. How far off the pavement? I think ten or twelve feet, sir. Were there two horses to the carriage or only one? Only one, sir. Which way was the horse's head turned? North, I think. So that threw one side of the carriage parallel to the eastern point of the market house? Yes, sir. What sort of a carriage was that? It was a two-seated rockaway, sir. Did it have curtains? It did, sir. Were any curtains up? The front curtains on both sides were up. Were there two curtains on each side? There were two, and perhaps three—some carriages have three. How many curtains on each side were up there? One on each side. And that was the front curtain? Yes, sir. So there were left down on each side at least one back curtain and perhaps two? Yes, sir. The rear curtain was that down or up? It was down, most positively it was down. Did any person speak to the young lady or her mother between the time that you started with them from up stairs to the time you seated them in the carriage? No, sir. Which side of the carriage did they get in? On the eastern side sir. Which seat of the carriage did they occupy? The back sir. Which side of the seat did Mrs. Massey occupy? The right sir. And her daughter occupi-

ed the other side? Yes, sir. How long did you remain there at the side of the carriage; next to the market house after you had seated the ladies before you changed your position? One or two minutes I presume, it might have been longer. Who came up to the carriage while you were there, upon that side of the carriage next to the market house and before you changed your position? I think Mr. Tom Powers walked up there sir. Did he have any conversation with the ladies? He merely spoke to his sister and said "howdy Helen." Did he give her his hand? Yes, sir. Did he have any conversation with her? Not that I could see, sir. What became of Tom Powers after that? I don't know, sir. That was while you were on the side of the carriage next to the market house? Yes, sir. Did you change your position at all? I did, sir. Which way did you go then? I walked to the rear and right of the carriage, sir. That side of the carriage which was nearest down towards the bridge? Yes, sir. Did you see what became of Tom Powers after he had given his hand to his sister? I did not, sir. Did you notice whether he stood there, or moved away? I don't know, sir. How far to the rear of the carriage did you pass in going around it? As near as a person could pass. Did you meet any one at the rear of the carriage? No, sir. How far was Maultsby off from the rear of the carriage? About ten feet I presume. Did you have any conversation with him when you passed there to the rear of the carriage? No, sir. Did he have any conversation with you? No, sir. Not a word passed between you? Not that I can recollect of. When you got around the carriage, who did you see? I saw Mr. Cashwell and Mr. Taylor. Where were they? They were coming from the store, sir, and were very near the carriage. Did either of them speak to the ladies, or to either of the ladies? Both did, I think, sir. Which spoke first? I think Mr. Taylor. Did you hear what either said to the ladies? Mrs. Massey said to Mr. Cashwell, "Bro. Cashwell, my troubles are more than I can bear, will you pray for me"? Do you know whether he made any reply to that? I don't, sir. What became of the carriage, then? It was drove off, sir. Directly afterwards? Yes, sir. Before Mr. Cashwell was through speaking, or afterwards? It must have been afterwards: they had no conversation that I could hear. Did John Maultsby speak to the ladies at all while they were in the carriage? He did not, sir. And he didn't speak to you? I can't be positive about that. What is your impression with regard to it? That he did not. Did Capt. Tolar go to the carriage while it stood there? He did not, sir. Have you any doubt about that? I have no doubt under the sun. Did he go near the carriage? Not that I could see, if he had, I certainly would have seen him. But you say you are confident he did not go up to the carriage? I am, sir. And he had no conversation with the ladies? He did not, sir. Who else did you see at the carriage? That is all I can recollect. Do you remember to have seen Robert Mitchell at the carriage? He was not there, sir. Do you remember to have seen old Mrs. Massey? No, sir. Did the carriage drive off by your direction? It did, sir. Which way did it drive off? Down Person street. What became of you then? I immediately went up into the market house, sir. Why was it, Mr. Bond, that you told the driver of the carriage to move off? I have no idea, sir, in the world; the young lady was crying and I probably thought the sooner she got away the better it would be. Were you a friend of the young lady, a special friend? Not more than other young ladies; I have known the girl sometime; she was under my supervision at the Sabbath School there. And it was for that reason you were paying some little attention to her? Yes, sir. It was because you thought it would be disagreeable for her to be gazed at by the crowd that you ordered the carriage away? I think it was. You had no other reason? None in the world, sir. How long was it after you got back up stairs before Beebee was brought down? Not exceeding fifteen minutes. Did you have any conversation with any body when you passed from the carriage up stairs? Not a word. Did any body have any conversation with you? Not a word. You went up stairs and Beebee was brought down? Yes, sir. You came with the party down? Yes, sir. Where were you? I was in the rear. How far in the rear? I was four or five steps. Do you mean four or five of the market house steps? Yes, sir. Did you look upon the crowd when you got there at the landing? Not in particular, sir. Can you form an estimate of the size of the crowd at the time you got to the landing? I could not, sir. Did you notice any thing unusual in the appearance of the crowd, or any member of the crowd? Not at that time, sir. Did you hear any exclamation, from the crowd or any members of the crowd during that time between the time that you came to the foot of the landing of the stairs to the time of your reaching the floor of the market, did you hear any exclamations from any of the crowd? I did not sir. You heard no exclamation of "charge boys," "rally boys" "here he comes" or any thing of that sort? No, sir. How far was the prisoner in advance of you at the time you reached the floor of the market? About four or five feet. Did you maintain that distance, you and the prisoner? I think so sir, until we got out on the pavement. When did you first notice any thing that attracted your attention? When I was turning the main eastern arch myself sir. At that time could you see the prisoner? No, sir. What hid him from your view? The crowd I suppose. So the crowd interposed between you and the prisoner? Yes sir. Well, now how was it about the gathering of the crowd did they gather from under the market house or from the outside? The most of them appeared to be outside as well as I could see sir. And they gathered there? Yes, sir. What was the next thing you saw? There appeared to be a kind of gathering or closing in of the crowd. At that time did you hear any exclamations? I did not sir. Did you hear anybody demand the prisoner, or words to that effect? I did not sir. Did you hear the Sheriff order the police to use their clubs? No, sir. What was the next you saw? There appeared to be a rush or gathering in of the crowd I don't know how you would term it. I want you to term it, was it a rush or gathering in? The people seemed to be gathering in from all around. Was any body runing? I did not see any body sir. At that time you were still four or five feet from the prisoner and in his rear? As well as I can recollect sir. What occurred then? As I was turning the main arch I caught two or three men in my arms and shoved them off, some person or persons struck me about the hip and we all went down together. Who were those persons that you caught? I could not tell to save my life sir. Who was the person that struck you? I could not tell, it was to my rear, and about my hip. What did he strike you with? I judge with a knee or something of the sort, probably I might have been pushed. Was it a heavy blow? Not extraordinary; enough to push a person down. What occurred then? The pistol fired sir. Before you recovered? Yes, sir. Did

you see the flash? I did not sir. Did you see the smoke? I did not sir. Did you hear the report? I did sir. What was the character of that report? Not more than an ordinary pistol sir. Not an extraordinary loud report? No, sir, From the report of the pistol could you tell the place or about the place from which it was fired? Not exactly, I could not sir. Did you see Capt. Tolar there that day? My impression is that I did sir. When do you think you saw him? That is more than I am able to say I can't tell whither I saw him before or after the killing of Beebee? Did you see Tom Powers there at all, after you saw him at the carriage? I don't think I did sir. Did you see anything of David Watkins there that day? I think I saw him afterwards sir. After the firing? Yes, sir. Where was he and what was he doing? Mr. Nixon had him going off with him. At what place? Between the market house and Mr. Taylor's store,

Cross examination by the Counsel for the prosecution.

Did you drive Miss Massey in a buggy to the market house? I did not, sir. Was your buggy in front of the market house? It was not, sir. There was but one carriage, as I understand you, at the market house? But one. And the two ladies came in at the same carriage? Yes, sir. You didn't drive Miss Massey there that day? I did not, sir. There is no doubt about that? No, sir, most positively I did not. And you say the two ladies came in the same carriage? They did, sir. Who drove them? A negro boy. Do you know who it was? I forget his name. Is his name William Wright? I can't say. Had Archy been carried up stairs before the carriage got there with the ladies in it? He was, sir. You had been down to the guard house and had assisted in carrying him up stairs? I had, sir. How came you to assist in bringing out the prisoner? He was in my jurisdiction. It was a part of your regular duty? It was, sir. What was the reason of the number of police that were there that day, was it customary to bring a prisoner out of the guard house—the sheriff, deputy sheriff, yourself, Hornrinde, &c.? I am not able to say for the simple reason that I had not been in the office a great while. You have been in several months, now? Yes sir. Is that the customary way? Generally when there is a desperate character, I believe it is. Are they generally of a desperate character? That is more than I am able to say. I want to know how many times in your experience you have had that many officers to assist you in carrying a prisoner to a preliminary examination? I suppose on one or two occasions since that? Who was present at the guard house and assisted in bringing Archy up to the market house? There was Mr. Wemyss and Mr. Hornrinde, Mr. Faircloth, Mr. Brown, Mr. McGuire and myself. Was the Sheriff there? I think not, sir. Was he inside as you came on up—do you remember the Sheriff's making any movement or giving you any sign to bring the warrant? I do not, sir. Was the prisoner in your immediate custody? He was, until he was delivered at the market house. You came on up stairs with him at that time? Yes, sir. Was Hardie up stairs then? I think he was. You say the carriage, with the ladies in it, had not come up at that time? It had not. Did you return down stairs immediately? I did, sir What was your object in going down? I went after the ladies. Did you find the carriage at the door when you got down? No, sir. Where did you go? They were at Isaac Hollingsworth's house. You went to his house? Yes, sir. Did you get into the carriage? I did not. You walked back? I did, sir. How far is Isaac Hollingsworth's place from the market house? Nearly the distance of one block. The carriage was in your sight all the time? Yes, sir. And you followed the carriage up from Hollingsworth's and assisted the ladies out? Yes, sir. And assisted them up stairs? Yes, sir. You remained up stairs for a short time? Yes, sir. Was it fifteen minutes? I can't say exactly. You then came down to get a drink of water? Yes, sir. Was there no water up stairs; is it customary to keep the justices there without such accommodations as these? I don't know, it is none of my business. You wanted water and found none there? Yes, sir. You say you can't estimate the crowd at that time? No, sir. You got the water from where? From under the market house or at Davis', I don't know which, sir. You returned immediately and went up stairs? Yes, sir. During that time you say you had no conversation with any one—do you mean you recollect or are you confident you had none? I cannot be confident, but I am almost sure. You went hastily to get a drink of water and you returned hastily? Yes, sir. When the examination was over you came with Mrs. Massey and her daughter when they went to the carriage? Yes, sir. You came with them directly to the carriage? Directly, sir. Was Mrs. Massey veiled? I am not able to say. Did she use her handkerchief or did she look as if she was weeping? I am not positive. Do you know whether her face was covered as she passed through the crowd? I can't say. Your impression is that she was veiled? Yes, sir, she was weeping but I can't say whether she was using her handkerchief or not. You say this carriage was standing about ten feet from the market house, from the eastern arch of it? Yes, sir. From the pavement or arch? From the pavement sir. The width of the pavement is about eight feet? Yes, sir. Was it directly in front of the arch? I think it was, but wont be positive. Did you find any difficulty in making your way through the crowd? Not a bit. Was the crowd dense enough to obstruct your passage? Not at all. Did you notice the size of the crowd at that time? Not particularly. Did you notice particularly, did you notice whether it was larger or smaller than it was the last time you passed there? I don't think it was any larger. Up to the time you assisted the ladies into the carriage nobody had spoken to them or you? No, sir. You say as I understand you that the right and left curtains by the side of the front seat were up? Yes, sir. But the right and left curtains by the side of the back seats were down? Yes, sir. And the back curtain of the rockaway were down? Yes, sir. So that the back seat was all closed in? Yes, sir. Mrs. Massey seated herself on the right with her face north? Yes, sir. Was the boy who was driving the carriage at the carriage when you got up there? Yes, sir. Did you not have to send for him? No, sir. You found him there? Yes, sir. You say the first person who got up to speak to the ladies was Mr. Tom Powers? Yes, sir. He shook hands with his sister? Yes, sir. Was Mrs. Massey weeping also at that time? Yes, sir. Did you hear her reply to his salutation? No, sir. Was that the whole conversation that passed between them? I heard no other—if they said anything I certainly would have heard it? When you moved from that side of the carriage to the opposite, did you see Tom Powers still standing there? I don't recollect, I am not positive. You don't recollect seeing him go away? No, sir. Did you hear any conversation from Mrs. Massey, exhorting him to leave the crowd and not to get into difficulty? I

did not, sir. Did you hear anything of that sort; refresh yourself and think of it, can't you think of anything of that sort that was said in your hearing? I do not; at that time I walked round to the right, and probably she might have said it to him, but I did not hear it. You have no recollection of it? No, sir. You went round to the rear, and you say you noticed there Maultsby about eight or ten feet from the rear of the carriage? I think about that. Which way was he facing? North, looking towards the carriage, I presume. Did he speak to you? Not at that time. Had you seen him before that day? I think I had. He didn't salute you even in passing? Not that time. Was he talking to any one? Not that I saw. Was he detached from the crowd? It appeared so to me. You saw no one with him, and he was outside the limits of the crowd? Yes. I suppose the crowd was not standing out that far? Not near. He was alone? Yes, sir. Then Mr. Taylor and Mr. Cashwell came up? Yes, sir. Do you swear positively that Mitchell was not at that carriage while it was out there? I do, sir. After he went round to the right of the carriage, Mr. Cashwell came up and Mr. Taylor; and almost immediately after that he had some conversation with Mrs. Massey; then the carriage drove off under your directions? Yes, sir. Did you see Mr. Taylor speak to the ladies as well as Mr. Cashwell? I think so. What did he say? I don't know, he merely shook hands with them. Do you think he said anything? I cannot say, probably he might have said "how do you do?" but I don't recollect. Your impression is that he said nothing? Yes, sir. Have you any decided impression, way or the other? I have not. You heard Mrs. Massey tell Mr. Cashwell that her troubles were more than she could bear, and ask him to pray for her? Yes, sir. How long a time elapsed from the time you left the steps with the ladies until the time the carriage drove off? It might have been five minutes, probably not so long. Now what is your best estimate? I would say three minutes. After the carriage drove off, did you see what became of Mr. Cashwell? No, sir. Did you see what became of Taylor? I did not. Nor Tom Powers? No. Nor Maultsby? Nor Maultsby. But you swear positively that you did not encounter Maultsby on your way back to the market house, and he said not a word from the time you came to the foot of the stairs with the ladies until the time you came up stairs? I can't be positive, my impression is he did not. But you cannot speak with positiveness? No, sir. Do you remember his asking whether Miss Massey had identified the boy Archy? I don't, sir. Do you remember his asking you any such question as whether the justices had committed Archy? I do not, sir. Do you remember any such question being asked by any one? I do not, sir, Did you tell any one the result of the trial? I did not. Did you not tell any one whether Miss Massey had or had not identified this boy Archy as the person who had been guilty of an attempt to ravish her? I don't recollect. When you say you don't recollect do you mean that you did not, or that you have no recollection? It is my opinion that I did not, I can't be positive about it. After the examination was over and you came down stairs, did any one come down before you who was present at the examination? I am not able to say, sir. Do you remember who was in the room? I could not tell, although I could tell you probably a few of their names, I could not tell you all? You can't say for certain whether any one preceded you in coming down? I can't say. The whole of the party had not gone down? No, sir. Had the parties who had participated in the examination, gone down? No, sir. Had the Sheriff gone down? I think he had not. If any went down you don't recollect? I do not, sir. Was the whole guard there that went up with Archy, according to your best recollection? I think they were up stairs. You returned immediately up stairs? Yes, sir. Did you notice the absence of any one whom you had left up there? I did not, sir. Have you any idea whether any one had left there or not? I am not able to say realy sir. Were any of the Court gone, with whom you were associated? I think not sir. Were the justices still there that had participated in the trial? Yes, sir. The prisoner was there? Yes, sir. Did you notice whether the witnesses were there who had been examined? Mrs. Massey was not there at that time. Of course not—but I spoke of the other witnesses—if they were there—whether you noticed the absence of any one during the time you were absent? My impression is that the same company was there that I left there. Your impression is that you were the first, after the trial was over, who left the justice's room? With the ladies; yes, sir. And your impression is that you were not asked by the crowd, nor did you communicate what the result of the examination was? No, sir. And you impression is that you had no conversation with Maultsby upon the subject, but that you you can't be very positive? I can't be positive about it? You swear very positively that Captain Tolar was not at the carriage while the ladies were there, and before they drove off? Yes sir. Had you seen Capt. Tolar before at any time that day before the carriage drove off? I am not able to say whether I saw him before or afterwards—my impression is that I saw him but where, I can't say. Your impression is you saw him in the crowd some time that day? I can't say that, I am not able to say whether I had seen him in the forenoon or in the afternoon. I want to know whether your impression was that you saw him at all about the market house? I can't say positively whether I saw him there or where I saw him. You can't say whether it was about the time this man was on trial that you saw him? No, sir. But you had an impression you had seen him that day? Yes, sir. But you have a very distinct impression that you saw him at the carriage? I am quite positive about it sir. And you are certain that Mr. Mitchell did not go to the carriage? Yes, sir. You are as certain of one fact as you are of the other? Yes, sir. How long did you remain up stairs after you returned from the carriage before Archy came down? I should say ten minutes, I would not like to go under that, and I would not go over fifteen, Was there any thing else to be done before the justice of the peace when you returned? I think not. How was the time occupied, that ten or fifteen minutes you were up stairs in the market house after you returned? I might have been sitting there waiting for them to commit him, sir. The order for commitment hadn't been written out? The justice was writing it at the time, sir. When you went down with the negro you were four or five steps behind him? Four or five steps sir. Did I understand you to say it was four or five steps on the stair steps? That is before I got to the platform, sir. What do you call the platform? Where the door opens going up into the market house. The first landing you mean? Yes, sir. When you came down to the landing Archy was before you? He was in front of me. He went out of the door before you got to the landing? Yes, sir. As I understand you he was down four or five steps towards the floor of the market house before you started down the last flight of

steps? Yes, sir. When Archy went out do you remember how the group that surrounded him went out, who went out first, of the officers surrounding him when he appeared in view of those who were inside of the market house? I think Mr. Hornrinde and Mr. McGuire were in front of him, Mr. Wemyss on his right and Mr. Faircloth on his left. What became of Sheriff Hardie? My impression is, he was in front too at that time, but as soon as he got under the market house he was in the rear. Do you mean that Sheriff Hardie, when he got to the floor of the market house preceded the prisoner? He was there in front of Mr. Hornrinde or Mr. Maguire or in front of the prisoner, they were there in some way. Your impression is that Mr. Hardie went out in front of the prisoner? Yes, sir. Until he came to the floor of the market house? Yes, sir. Then you say he got behind him? I think he did, I am not positive. You covered the rear? Yes, sir. You say there was no demonstration made at all as he was coming down stairs? No, sir. Did you hear any one say "there he comes?" No, sir. No exclamations at all? I have no recollection. Did you notice the size of the crowd at that time? Not particularly. Was there any crowd there? Yes, considerable. How many men do you think? There might have been one hundred and fifty sir. Now when this man came down stairs, do you mean to say the crowd stood stock still? They were standing looking at him. Were they moving? That is more than I am able to say. You did not see any movement towards the prisoner and the crowd didn't appear as though they were attracted by the prisoner? My attention was attracted to him, I didn't notice the crowd. You didn't see the crowd? Of course I saw the crowd when I got on the landing. What I want to know is whether there was any movement in the crowd as the prisoner came in sight? I can't say. Did you not observe a natural curiosity manifested by the crowd? If I had been in the crowd I might have noticed it. You can't remember having observed it? I didn't notice particularly. You didn't know any man in the crowd? Not particularly. Did you observe any man in the crowd at all? I am not able to say sir. You said the negro boy got to the foot of the stairs outside the arch before you saw any disturbance? Yes, sir. Up to that time you had seen no rush made on him? I had not, sir. And no assault? No, sir, You had seen no weapons in the hand of any one? No, sir. No exclamation at all? Not any. Neither a demand for him nor orders of resistance upon the part of the Sheriff? No, sir. I understand you to say then that from the time Archy got to the foot of the steps until he got outside the eastern arch on the pavement his passage through the ten or twelve feet was just that of any other prisoner? It occured to me so. You then got to the eastern arch of the market house yourself? Yes, sir. Archy was taken outside? He was. Four or five feet in front of you? Yes. And when you got there you noticed some disturbance? Yes, I was turning the arch. Do you mean when you were turning out of the market house? Yes, I was turning out of the arch and turning in the direction he was going. You were standing right in the arch when the crowd passed through? Yes, sir. What was the disturbance? It appeared to be a gathering in, or a rush—you may term it as you like, the crowd was closing up. Was the whole crowd closing up? It appeared so to me. Was it then you got the push in the back? Just as I had shoved these men off. What was your object in shoving them off? I had no idea they had any business there crowding up, I don't know why I did it, I was excited. Which way was your face? I think down Person street. Which way were these men coming that you caught in your arms? They were pushing down south. Did you press them back? I did, sir. Was their resistance pretty strong? Tolerably, sir. About that time you got the thump on the hips? Yes, sir. It was in that gathering up that you got this thump? Yes, sir, when I was pushing these men off. That gathering up that you have been speaking of, was the same thing that occasioned you to press back these men, and the occasion of the thump you got that was strong enough to knock you down? Yes, sir. After this gathering up, when you were recovering yourself—the pistol fired? Yes, sir. How far did you fall when you fell? I disremember whether or not I reached the edge of the pavement; it shoved me some distance across the pavement. When you recovered you were standing near the edge of the pavement? Yes, sir. When you received the shove, you were standing in the arch? No, sir, I was at the edge of the arch in the act of turning the arch. I understand you to say that you were standing in the arch in the act of passing through? Yes, sir. How thick is the wall of the arch, then? About eighteen inches. When you were turning the arch—I want to know whether you mean turning out of the market house to go out of the arch, or turning out of the arch to go on to the pavement? When I was turning out of the arch to go on to the pavement. The shove sent you nearly across the pavement then? Yes, sir. You heard the pistol fire? I did. Do you remember what sort of a day it was? I think it was a little windy. Do you remember in what direction the wind was? I do not, sir. Do you remember whether it was a sunny day or cloudy? I am unable to say. Your impression is that it was a windy day? Yes, sir. You didn't see the smoke of the pistol? No, sir. Did not see any sign of it in the atmosphere? No, sir. Did you perceive the smell of sulphur? I didn't pay particular attention. But you did hear the report? I did, sir. Did you see the prisoner Beebee fall? No, sir. How far was he from you when he fell? He might have been six feet, probably eight. Which way was your face at the time you heard the pistol fire if you had been standing erect? East, sir. Can you tell whether the report of the pistol was on your right hand or left? On my right as well as I can recollect. You recovered yourself immediately after the pistol fired? The pistol fired before I recovered, I was in the act of recovering before the pistol fired. You recovered yourself immediately afterwards, and then you moved towards the prisoner; is that correct, sir? Yes, sir. Did you make any effort to arrest the person who fired the pistol? I did not, sir, I could not tell anything about it. Did you make any investigation? I did not, sir. You were an officer? Yes, sir. You saw a felony had been committed in your presence? I can't exactly say it was in my presence. You don't call that your presence? I didn't see it. You made no effort to apprehend the person who committed it? No, sir, he was in the hands of the sheriff, I had no jurisdiction whatever over him at that time. You put it on the ground that he was not your prisoner? He was not my prisoner. And you saw a felony committed then and there on that spot, and made no effort to apprehend the person who committed it? No, sir. Did you see any effort on the part of the other officers to arrest the party? I don't recollect. Was there any inquiry to see who committed it? I am unable to say, sir. You saw no effort made to apprehend him? No, sir. You made none? No, sir. What is the reason you made none, Mr. Bond? Because I didn't deem it my duty; he

was in the hands of the sheriff, and I supposed if he wanted any thing done he would have ordered it. You did not make the exertion you say because you did not think it your duty; I understand you to give that as your reason for not having attempted to seize the perpetrator of that act? I can't be positive, because I didn't know whether it was my duty or not. You think it was not? No, sir, I think it was not. You thought there were others superior to you in authority, and not having seen the man who shot, you thought it was not your duty to exert yourself to find out who it was? Yes, sir. And you swear that that was your view of your duty? Yes, sir, that was my view of it. You say just after this pistol fired, you saw Monk come up where the negro was that was shot? I saw Monk I suppose some four or five minutes after the shooting, he was going off with Mr. Nixon. Which way was he moving? East, sir. Moving down Person street? Yes, sir. How far from the point where the negro was shot? Nearly the width of the market house. The negro was lying there and Monk was going off with Nixon; was he exerting himself to get away? Not that I could perceive. Did you notice whether Monk had any weapon at that time? I did not, sir. Now, sir, I will ask you, at the time you passed through this crowd, early in the difficulty when you carried the prisoner up stairs—I will ask you who you saw in the market house that you recognized? I could not say a single man, for I paid no attention whatever. I ask you when you came down to get a drink of water, and passed through that crowd, and got your drink of water, and passed back again, who you saw in that crowd that you recognized? I am not able to say, sir, because I was on business or duty, or whatever you call it, and I didn't stop an instant. You then came down with Miss Massey and her mother and went to the carriage; in passing through the crowd to go to the carriage do you remember seeing any man whom you recognized before you saw Tom Powers at the carriage? Not particularly, sir. Do you remember seeing any person you recognized? Probably I might have recognized them at the time, but I cannot call them to recollection at this time. You went back then through that crowd up in to the market house again; did you see any one then that you recognized besides the few you saw about the carriage—Maultsby, Tom. Powers, Cashwell, and Taylor,—did you see any one else as you passed back through the crowd that you knew? Probably I might have seen them, but I don't know that I paid any attention. You passed through that crowd five times back and forth, and you cannot swear with absolute certainty as to any one who was in it? No, sir. You swear with absolute certainty that Mr. Tolar did not go to the carriage? I do, sir. Well, sir, is this all you know about it? As far as my knowledge leads me, sir, it is. You are still a constable are you not? Yes, sir. Where do you receive your appointment? From the municipal authorities of the town; a mayor and seven commissioners. They appoint the town constable? They do. And you hold your office under their appointment? Yes, sir. Are you familiar with the city ordinances? Not particularly, I suppose I am familiar with a good many of them. Don't you know it is against the laws of the city for a pistol to be fired in the public street? It is, sir, if you can find it out; it is very often done and you can't find out any thing about it. Is it not one of your duties as town constable to arrest a person who violates a city ordinance? It is if I can find them out. Now, I understand you to give as a reason for not arresting this fellow that you didn't think

It was your duty—because you thought it was the sheriff's duty more than yours; did the sheriff have any thing to do in regard to the violation of the town ordinances? It is his duty, if he knows any thing of it, to report it to me. If you are present and a town ordinance is violated do you consider it your duty or the sheriff's to arrest the party? I consider it my duty; if I had seen the party I should have to arrest him. Did you see any man at any time that day, while you were about the market house, with any weapon in his hand. I disremember, I can't be positive. Have you any decided impression? My impression is that I saw Monk with a knife. That is the only one you have any impression about? As far as I can recollect. I understood you to say that you at no time that day heard the sheriff exhort the crowd to keep back, or tell his officers to use their clubs? I did not, sir, there was a considerable crowd between him and me at the time. He was then six feet from you; did you hear any such expression as "shoot him," "shoot him," "kill him," "kill him?" I did not, sir. You heard no shout in the crowd that day at all? No, sir.

Re-direct examination by the Counsel for the accused:

Mr. Bond, is your recollection distinct upon this point, or do you only have an impression, that the boy who drove the carriage was sitting in the carriage when you carried the ladies to it? I am not positive about that whether he was standing at the horses head, or sitting in the carriage. You are not positive where he was? He was close by, but whether he was at the horse or in the carriage, I cannot say. Have you a distinct recollection whether you ordered him to get into the carriage or drive off, or whether you did not? I ordered him to drive off. I want to know whether your recollection is distinct or not to tell the boy—wherever he was to get into the carriage and drive off? I don't recollect telling him to get into the carriage. Have you a distinct recollection one way or the other whether you told him to get into the carrige and drive off or whether you did not? I am not positive.

Questions by the Commission:

Had you any reason, or do you know whether the sheriff had any reason to expect an attempt on the prisoner that day? I do not sir. You had heard of nothing of the kind? No, sir. Is it customary to have so many officers as were on duty at that time with that prisoner, to accompany prisoners from the guard house to the market house? I don't know as it is upon all occasions! Do you know any case in which there were so many as there were on that day? I have never seen any case in which were so many, since I have been in office. Do you know any case? I am not able to say, sir.

JAMES W. BROWN, a witness for the defence, having been first duly sworn testified as follows:

Examined by the Counsel for the accused.

What is your name? James W. Brown. Where do you reside? Fayetteville. How long have you lived there? Twelve or fifteen years, I believe sir. What has been your occupation for the last twelve months? I came there first driving a mail stage and I have been there ever since. What was your occupation in February last at the time Archy Beebee was killed? I was one of the police. Were you or were you not one of the police that went with him to the market house? Yes, sir. From what point did you go with him to the market house? I went first to the guard house and then to the market house. You were one of those that carried him up to the market house? Yes, sir. Did you go into the market house, were you up stairs? Yes, sir. Did you

go down at all after you went into the market house? No, sir. You remained up there until after the trial? Yes, sir. Was there a crowd about the market house at the time you went up there? There was not very many. Where was the crowd then generally? Some of them in the market house, standing around about there. Did you notice any thing particularly in the crowd at that time? No, sir. Did you go down in the immediate vicinity of the prisoner when you came down the steps? I went down right behind him. Who else was with him? The Sheriff was with him, and I forget who else, I think there was another one and Mr. Faircloth I believe met him on the stairs. Was Mr. Wemyss with him? I believe it was Mr. Wemyss. You went down in the rear? Yes, sir. How far in the rear of the prisoner were you? I was as nigh as this man here (three or four feet.) Did you remain behind him until after he had got out of the market house? Yes, sir. About the same distance? Yes, sir. Did you notice any peculiarity in the crowd as you first reached the landing? Not when I first got down I didn't. When did you first notice any disturbance in the crowd? Well when we were turning the market house. You mean as you went to turn out of the market house, or as the prisoner did? All of us. You didn't notice anything unusual, up to that time at all? No, sir. No excitement or any thing of that character? No, sir. Which way did you turn as you came out upon the pavement? We turned to the right. That would put your face in which direction? It would be pretty much west I believe. You don't know much about the points of the compass do you? No, sir, I don't. To your right though? Yes, sir. Tell the Court, what you observed then Mr. Brown? Well, sir, there was a considerable rush on to us. And you were in the same position relatively to the prisoner, about three feet or four feet behind him? Yes, sir. Go on and tell the Court every thing you observed? Then, it was not but a very few moments after that rush on us before I heard that pistol fired. Did you see the pistol? No, sir. Where were you at the moment the pistol fired? I was right up nearly pretty close to the negro, there was Mr. Wemyss and the Sheriff between me and the negro. You were next to the Sheriff, you say? Yes sir. Were you to the right and rear of the Sheriff or to the left and rear? Right behind him. Were you nearer to the wall of the market house than the sheriff? Me and the sheriff were about alike I believe. How far were you from the wall of the market house, at the moment the pistol fired? I was nearly right agin it. Could you have touched it with your elbow? Yes, sir. No body could have stood between you and the market house, at that time? No, sir. Where were you, Mr. Brown, with reference to that little arch on the right hand side of the big arch, as you come out? As we come down, we turned right around to go towards the guard house. Had you passed the little arch? Yes, sir. And about elbow reach of the market house on your right? Yes, sir. At the time the pistol fired? Yes, sir. You didn't see who fired the pistol? No, sir, I didn't. Had you seen any weapon? Yes, sir, I saw several knives. Do you know who had the knives? I could not tell to save my life. What was the position of the knives? They had them in their hands coming right at us, I tried to push some of them off, but I couldn't. You could not tell who they were? I could not to save my life, tell who they were. Did the pistol firing alarm you? It did. You didn't see who did it? No, sir. Where was it with reference to you? It was sort of to my left, sort of behind me. How far off from you was it? I could not tell, sir. Was it off, or on the pavement, do you think? I don't know, sir, I could not say exactly about it. How wide is the pavement at that place? It is some six feet, I reckon. You have no best recollection as to whether the man who fired the pistol, was on or off the pavement? No, sir. Did you see any pistol at all? No, sir. You hadn't seen a pistol until that time? No, sir. Did you see any afterwards? No, sir. What became of you after the firing of the pistol? As soon as they fired the pistol I turned right back. Immediately on the firing of the pistol? Yes, sir. Which way did you go? I went right back in the market house. The same direction you had come? Yes, sir. Did you go quickly? Yes, sir, I walked right straight back as quick as I could. When you got back under the arch, did you recognize anybody there? I recognized Mr. Tolar. Where was he standing? He was standing right under the edge of the market. On which side of the main eastern arch? It looked to me like he was in the middle of the market under the edge of the market. Was it on the outside or inside? On the inside, I think. What was his position, was he standing still or moving at that time? He was standing, I think his face was towards the stair steps, the way we came down. Now, as you come out of the middle arch, would he be on the left or right? On the left. Did you see any thing peculiar about him? No, sir. Any weapons in his hand? No, sir. Any weapons about him that you saw? No, sir. Are you well acquainted with Mr. Tolar? No, sir, not in particular. You know him when you see him? Yes, sir. How long have you known him? I don't know, sir. Are you pretty intimate with Mr. Tolar? No, sir? Did you see Tom Powers there that day? I could not say, I don't think I did. Did you see Monk? Yes, sir. Where was he? I saw him a little before this thing happened, I didn't see him at the time. Where was he when you saw him? I think he was under the market house. Had you seen Tolar before that time? No, sir. Can't you tell, Mr. Brown, how long it was between the time the pistol fired until you went back to the arch? I could not, sir, to save my life. Any more than a minute or two, could you have counted fifty? No, sir. Could you have counted twenty five? I reckon so. You don't think you could have counted fifty? I don't know, it was a very few minutes.

Cross examination by the Counsel for the prosecution:

Mr. Brown, how many people were at the market house, just after that pistol fired? I could not tell to save my life. Was it a big crowd? I reckon there must have been a hundred or two. You were right in the midst of it near the prisoner? Pretty nigh. When you went back as soon as the pistol fired, you had to go through the crowd to get back? Yes, sir, most of the crowd was east of the prisoner; they were rather to my left. You had to make your way through a part of the crowd? Yes, sir. At the point where you saw Tolar—was that outside of the crowd, or did the crowd reach as far as it? I think he was out of the crowd altogether. Was he standing entirely by himself? Pretty much. Who else did you see at that time? I could not tell to save my life—there were several, I don't believe there was anybody under the market house. Didn't you see Mr. Cashwell under there? No, sir, I didn't. And the only person that you saw was Tolar when you got back under the market house,—was he standing completely by himself? Yes, sir, he was standing there under the market house. Nobody else near him? There were a good many pretty close to him. How close—as

close as I am to you? I reckon so, (about eight feet.) Do you know E. P. Powers? Yes, sir. Did you see him there? No, sir. Do you know Ralph Lutterloh? Yes, sir. Didn't you see him there? I did not sir. Did you see J. G. Leggett there? I think I saw him. Where was he? I can't tell. Didn't he stand close to Tolar? I could not tell to save my life. You think you saw Leggett, as you made your way back to the arch after the firing? I don't know whether I saw him, after the thing was done or before. How came you to remember Tolar? He was standing up there as I went on by. There were others standing pretty close too about there, why didn't you notice them? I did notice them, I could not tell who they were. You didn't know them? No, sir, I don't know who they were. But you remember with accuracy, that Captain Tolar was standing there at that time? I do. Was he right under the arch, or right at the arch? A little more inside than out. Did he have a shawl on? Yes, sir. Do you remember what sort of a hat he had on? I do not. Did he have on spectacles? I don't know sir. He was standing perfectly still, looking up stairs? I don't know whether he was looking up stairs or not, he had his face that way. You didn't notice whether he had on spectacles? I did not. The pistol had just fired and just as soon as you could make your way back you found him looking in a different direction than where the negro was shot? Yes, sir. And that was immediately after the pistol was fired? Yes, sir. You don't think there was any body inside of the market house? Not to my recollection—there was some nigger women. When you went back into the market house, were you very badly scared? It frightened me a little. Didn't it frighten you excessively? Yes, sir, it did. Did you run when you went back through the crowd? No, sir. Could you run? I don't know that I could, I didn't try to run. You got back pretty swiftly? Yes sir. I understood you to say you were pretty thoroughly alarmed? Sort of frightened. I want to know the degree of your fright—were you very much frightened? I was not scared to death. But were you well scared? It frightened me a little. What was your reason for turning back? I didn't want to see. You, an officer, turned back, to get out of the row? Yes, sir, after the negro was killed. After you saw Tolar standing there where did you go? I went towards the market house, and then come right back. Did you come right back in the crowd? No, sir. Did you come through the market house? I went under the market house. Didn't you go away? No, sir. How long did you remain there? I went back to the negro after the doctor came. You went back hastily, saw Tolar underneath the market house and when the doctor came you went back where the negro was? Yes, sir. How long from the time you went, away from the negro until you went back? I don't know exactly how long, it was a good little while. Who told you to go down to the guard house and assist in bringing up that negro that day? The captain of the guard. Who is that? Mr. Faircloth. What time did he give these orders? I could not say, sir, to save my life. Was it the same day that you brought the negro up? They put him in over night. Did you assist in catching him? No, sir. Were you at the guard house when he was put in? Yes, sir. Did you receive your orders then or the next day? The next day. What time of the day, before dinner or after? It was after dinner. Just before you went there then? Yes, sir. Did any body else receive orders at the same time you did? I think there were two or three of us, I think Mr. Hornrindo and McGuire. And Faircloth was the man under whose orders you, McGuire and Hornrinde acted? Yes, sir. Who went with you at the time you took the negro up to undergo his examination? Myself and Faircloth, and George Hornrinde, and McGuire. Any one else? No, sir. Wasn't Bond there? I believe he was. Wasn't Wemyss there? Yes, sir. You ought to speak more particularly? Wemyss aint one of our men. Was Sheriff Hardie there? Yes, sir. Was he down at the guard house when you brought him out? No, sir. Were Bond and Wemyss at the guard house when you brought the negro out? I don't think they were. Where did you come up with them? At the market house, I think. Where did you see Hardie first? I think the first place I saw the sheriff was up stairs, I would not be certain. You went up stairs, did you? Yes, sir. Were you in the justice's room while the examination was going on? Yes, sir. Do you remember when Miss Massey and Mrs. Massey went down stairs that Mr. Bond went with them? Yes, sir. Had any body else come down stairs before Mr. Bond? No, sir, not that I know of. Did you see any body come down while Bond was down stairs? No, sir. Do you remember whether Bond came back after going with the ladies? I think he did, sir. Do you remember any body leaving the room during that time? No, sir. Did any body else leave the room? Not to my recollection. Bond and the ladies were the first persons that went down after the examination was completed? Yes, sir. Who guarded the door to prevent the crowd from going up? Mr. Faircloth. When Mr. Bond came back you all went down with the prisoner? Yes, sir. In going out of the door at the first landing who went out first of the guard that was along with the prisoner? I think Mr. Wemyss and Faircloth to my recollection, I was behind them. You didn't go out in front of the prisoner? No, sir. Do you remember whether Sheriff Hardie came out behind or in front? I think the sheriff had hold of him. As he went out of the door? Yes, sir. And that he passed down stairs, along side of him? Yes, sir, all the way. You were behind? Yes, sir. Who else was along with you covering the rear? Nobody that I know of. Wasn't Bond there? If he was, I didn't see him. Your say Wemyss and Faircloth and the sheriff were with the negro and yourself, and Wemyss had hold of him? Yes, sir. Which side was Wemyss on? On the left. On which side do you think Faircloth was? I think he was sort of before me, I would not be certain. Your best impression of it, is that Wemyss was on the left and that Hardie had hold of him on the other side ; and Faircloth was behind, and you came down behind, and you don't remember where Bond was? No, sir, I don't. While you were coming down stairs, did you see anybody do anything with the prisoner? No, sir. Did you see the crowd gather up to look at him? Not until he got down stairs. You didn't notice any man in the crowd whatever until you got down stairs, and passed out of the arch? No, sir. Were you alarmed then, sir? No, sir. You were not alarmed until the pistol fired? No, sir. Just as the prisoner and the whole group were turning the arch I understand you to say there was a rush made by the crowd? Yes, sir. Which way did the crowd rush from? It looked like it was coming all around. You were a part of the guard? Yes, sir. Did you have any weapon? No, sir. Did you have a club? No, sir. Did any of the guard have clubs? I don't think any one had, only Wemyss. Now when this pressure was made, did you make any effort to keep the crowd off from the prisoner. Yes, sir. Did you have to exert yourself pretty sharply? We did

that. Could you keep them back? No, sir. The pressure was so great that you, a part of the guard, had to give way? Yes, sir. Did you resist it? Yes, sir. And yet you had to give way? Yes, sir. Did you notice how the other part of the guard were engaged whether they were assisting you or not? I did not. You had as much as you could do to 'tend to yourself? Yes, sir, I did. Did you get any further than the arch? We got further than the arch. How did you get there; was the crowd pressing all that time? Yes, sir. And you exerted yourself all that time, to keep them off of Beebee? Yes, sir. Did you see Wemyss use his club? No, sir. Your attention was absorbed by what you had to do yourself? Yes, sir. Were you actively exerting yourself all that time to keep the crowd off? We did. You were, yourself? I did. During that time between the time that you came out of the arch and the time you got past the little arch I understand you to say you saw several knives? Yes, sir. How many do you think? I saw some three or four I think. Were they striking at the prisoner? They were not in reach of the prisoner. What were they doing with them? They were trying to cut him. Were those the only weapons you saw there? All I saw. Do you know Tom Powers? Yes, sir. Did you see him there that day? I don't recollect. Try to recollect? I don't recollect. Don't you remember his saying "I demand the prisoner?" No, sir. Or "Damn him, give him to me?" No, sir. Did you hear Sheriff Hardie say "use your clubs men?" I heard him tell the men to stand back. Was that just after you got outside of the arch? No, sir, I think, it was about the time the negro was shot. I understand you to say sir, that you had passed the little arch, before the negro was shot? Yes, sir. And you were standing about where your right elbow would touch the wall, and that Sheriff Hardie was next to you? Yes, sir. Was he pretty nearly in front of you or behind? He was in front of me. Was he right in front of you? Yes, sir. Was he close against the wall? About. The Sheriff was on the right hand of Archy then? Yes, sir. Between him and the wall? Yes, sir. Where was Wemyss? He was on the left. And you were immediately behind the Sheriff? Yes, sir. Did you have hold of the prisoner? No, sir. Did the Sheriff have hold of him? Yes, sir. Which hand? I don't know sir which one, I think it was the left hand though. Do you remember the prisoner falling? I remember his stumbling. Did he go down? Not quite sir. Do you remember seeing any body jump out of that little arch, as you passed by or just before you passed by? No, sir. Did you pass it? I was close up by the little arch. You saw no such thing as that? No, sir. And you say the sheriff was on the right hand of Beebee, and Wemyss was on the left? Yes, sir. The Sheriff was standing between Beebee and the market house, pretty much, and you were right behind him? Yes, sir. And you could touch the wall of the market house with your elbow? Yes, sir. And that was at the very time that Beebee was shot? Pretty much sir. As soon as you heard that pistol shot you made your way back and saw Tolar as you described? Yes, sir. Now sir, during the whole time, you were in that crowd from the time you came down stairs to the time the negro was shot, who else did you see that you knew besides Toler? I be dogged if I could tell. You must be more careful of the expressions you use—you say you can't tell? No, sir. And you say you distinctly recognized Tolar, and that was the only face you recognized that day? Yes, sir. That is the only man you recollect to have seen in that whole crowd, that you can remember this moment? I recollect a heap. Just let us have them? I can't tell to save my life. Could you tell some of them, that you saw in that crowd? I saw a good many. Just tell me some of them? I forget who they were. Did you see E. P. Powers? No, sir. At any time that day? No, sir. Did you see Tom Powers in that crowd at any time 'that day? No, sir. You think you did see Leggett? I think I saw him. Did you see Ralph Lutterloh? No, sir. Did you see Saml. Hall? No, sir. Did you see Henry Sykes, the one-armed man? No, sir. Did you see Sam Phillips? Yes, sir. I thought so. I saw him before this thing happened. Did you see him afterwards? I don't recollect. Did you see James Kendrick? No, sir. Did you see James Atkinson? Yes, sir. Where was he? I think he was about close to the market there. You were up stairs until Archie came down? Yes, sir. And it must have been after you came down stairs that you saw him? I saw him before I went up there. Did you see James Atkinson after you came down? I don't think I did. Did you see David Oliphant there that day? I believe I did. Where was that? I think it was before I went up stairs. Did you see anybody after you came down stairs? I reckon I saw them, I don't recollect them, I saw a good many people, but to tell you all, I could not to save my life. I want you to tell me one you saw, after you came down besides Capt. Tolar? I don't know, sir, who they were, I could not pretend to say. Did you see Sam Phillips after you came down? I don't recollect. Do you know John Armstrong, the negro? Yes, sir. Did you see him? Not that I recollect. Did you see Bob Simmons? I saw him before we went up stairs. Did you see him after you came down? Not that I recollect of. I understand you to say you recollect distinctly seeing Tolar, after you came down and after the firing, but from the time you got down stairs until after the firing took place you can't recollect a single other soul that you did see—is that so or not? I could not recollect them. I want a direct answer to that question—can you name a single other individual that you saw after you came down stairs, until after the pistol fired? No, sir. Not even though I name over numerous persons whom you know, and who were there, you can't recollect whether they were there or not? Not after we came down stairs. You think now, even if I were to call the names of persons that you saw, you could not recollect whether you saw them after you came down stairs? I don't believe I did. But you do recollect Capt. Tolar there? Yes, sir, I saw him I am pretty sure. What is your position there—one of the town guard? Yes, sir. Did you attempt to arrest the man who fired the pistol? I didn't see the man. He was pretty close to you, wasn't he? He was pretty close to me, I thought. You ran away instead of going towards him? No, sir. But you got away? Yes, sir. It never entered your head to arrest the man for a breach of the town ordinance, firing a pistol in the street? Not at that time. Did you see anybody else make an effort to arrest him? No, sir. Did you hear anybody.in the crowd just after the firing of the pistol, say who shot him? I never did. Was the crowd perfectly still? Yes, sir. After the pistol fired it was very still, wasn't it? Not very—it was sort of still. Then it commenced humming again, did it? No, sir, I believe not. Do you mean to say that a man fired a pistol there in the presence of one hundred and fifty or two hundred people, and there was no inquiry as to who did it? I never heard a word of it. And you say just after the pistol was fired the crowd was still, but not unusually still? No, sir. I

ask you then, wasn't the crowd unusually quiet from the time you first saw it until the man was shot? Yes, sir. It was more quiet than a crowd usually is? Not more than usual. I understand you to say it was unusually quiet? Not more than common. You say it was not uuusually boisterous or noisy? No, sir. Wasn't it unusually quiet? It was very quiet, I never saw any thing wrong about it. It was just about like an ordinary crowd, that was at the market house? Yes, sir. You saw no burst of excitement there? No, sir. You saw no men with their lips fixed, or their eyes flashing, or any pallor on their cheeks? No, sir. No appearance of excitement then? No, sir.

Re-direct examination by the Counsel for the accused:

Mr. Brown, how many policemen had clubs? No one had clubs. Did anybody have a club? Mr. Wemyss had a club. You say you were coming along by that little arch, as you turned out of the main arch in the direction of the guard house. the crowd was pressing on towards you and you didn't notice what the others did? No, sir. Were any of these knives in reach of you that you talk about? Yes, sir, two or three they could have reached me, that sort of alarmed me, it made me feel sort ot bad, I tell you. And the firing of the pistol, made you feel more? Yes, sir. And you got away as rapidly as you could? Yes, sir, I returned right off? You heard nothing said as to who did it? No, sir, I did not. How long have you been a policeman,Mr. Brown? About five years during the war and since.

Questions by the Commission:

You said that you turned to go towards the market house because you didn't want to see; what was it you didn't want to see? I didn't want to see the negro shot. Then you knew it was going to take place and you turned in order not to see? No, sir, I didn't know it was going to take place, I turned after the shooting. I don't think it is quite clear to the court then why you turned? I don't know myself hardly. You say it was because you didn't want to see, what was it you didn't want to see? I turned as soon as the negro was shot down, I saw him fall and I walked right back to the market house. Was he lying on the ground before you turned away? Some of the rest of the guard took hold of him at the time, I don't know whether he had got clear down on the ground or not.

On motion the Commission adjourned to meet on Thursday, Sept. 5th, at 11 o'clock, A. M.

The Commission met pursuant to adjournment.

Present: All the members of the Commission, the Judge Advocate, the Counsel for the prosecution, all the accused and their Counsel. The reading of the testimony taken yesterday was waived, there being no objection thereto.

Yesterday's proceedings were then read and approved.

SAMUEL D. CARROW, a witness for the defence, having been first duly sworn, testified as follows:

Examined by the Counsel for the accused. What is your name? Samuel D. Carrow. Where do you reside? I reside in Beaufort county. How long have you resided in the county of Beaufort? Forty odd years. Have you ever held any official position in the county? I have, sir. What, sir? I am colonel of militia; I have been magistrate; I have been trustee of the county, and chairman of the board of wardens, and I am now sheriff of the county. How long have you been sheriff of the county? Since 1865. What is your business at present in the city of Raleigh? To see the public treasurer on some business connected with the State, and to attend this convention, sir. You have not been subpœnaed as a witness in this cause? I have not, sir, I had not heard there was a trial going on. You are not acquainted with any of the parties? No, sir. Are you acquainted with Jordan G. Leggett? I have been, sir; he was born and raised in my county. How long have you known Jordan G. Leggett? Ever since he was a boy until six or seven years ago; since then I have seen him. But you had not that intimate knowledge of him that you had before? No, sir. Are you acquainted with the general character for truth of Jordan G. Leggett? I was up to the time he left Beaufort county. Are you acquainted with his general character for truth do you think? It was very good, I never heard it complained of; I never heard his veracity questioned; he done business in my town, and he was a very respectable farmer, raised in the county.

Cross-examination by the Counsel for the prosecution :

How old was Mr. Leggett about the time he left your part of the country? About thirty-five. He is forty now? Yes, sir.

HENRY SYKES, a witness for the defence, having been first duly sworn, testified as follows :

Examined by the Counsel for the accused.

What is your name? Henry E. Sykes. Where do you reside? In Fayetteville. Where did you come from this morning to this hall? I came from the Raleigh prison. What were you doing in the Raleigh prison? I was put there by the order of General Sickles. With what are you charged? I know not, sir. How long have you been confined in the prison at Raleigh? Nearly seven weeks.

The Counsel for the prosecution :

Do you think this pertinent to this issue?

The Counsel for the accused :

I am not examining on this as matter pertinent to this issue, but for the purpose of removing any prejudice that may exist from the fact that he is a prisoner.

Examination resumed :

Were you in Fayetteville the day Archy Beebee was killed? I was. Were you at the market house on that day? I was. At what time did you go to the market house? Between two and three o'clock, Three o'clock in the afternoon? Yes, sir. Was Archy Beebee up stairs? No, sir, they carried him up afterwards. Were you there when he was carried up stairs? I was. At what point in the market house were you when he went up stairs? I was under the eastern arch, the large eastern arch. Did you remain there until he was brought down stairs? Until the ladies came down stairs. In the same position? Not exactly, I walked back and forwards under the centre of the market house. Who do you mean by the ladies? Mrs. Massey and her daughter. Did you see them when they came down stairs? Yes, sir. Who was with them? Mr. Bond was with them. Where did they go? They went to the carriage. Where was the carriage? It was about thirty feet from the main eastern arch of the market house. On the pavement or off the pavement? Off the pavement. Did you see them when they helped in to the carriage by Mr. Bond? I did. Where were you then? At the end of the pillar of the main eastern arch. Did you remain there until the carriage drove off? Yes, sir. Were you looking at the carriage during the whole time it was there after they got in? The principle part of the time, sir. Who did you see go to the carriage? I saw Tom Powers go to the carriage; I saw Mr. Bond,

and Mr. Taylor, and Mr. Maultsby go to the carriage. Did you see anybody else? Not that I recollect, sir. Did you see Mr. Cashwell? No, sir, I did not, Did you see Robert Mitchell? No, sir, I did not. Did you see Thomas H. Massey? No, sir, I never saw him go there. Did Capt. Tolar go to the carriage? Not that I saw. Did you see Capt. Tolar about there at all up to that time? I saw him just before around at his usual stall, under the western corner of the market house. Did you see him at all at the time the carriage was standing out there with the ladies in it? No, sir, I did not. You were looking at the carriage, and you saw nothing of Capt. Tolar? No, sir. You didn't see him about there at that time? No, sir, I did not. You saw the carriage when it moved off? Yes, sir. How long was it after the carriage moved off before Beebee the prisoner was carried down stairs? About five minutes, sir. What was your position from the time the carriage moved off, until Beebee was brought down stairs? I was standing in front of the small eastern arch. Were you standing on the pavement or off the pavement? On the pavement. Were you nearer the wall of the market house or nearer the edge of the pavement? I was nearer the market house. How far were you from the wall of the market house? I was leaning against the bevel. Which closes the lower portion of the small arch? Yes, sir. Were you opposite the center of that arch, or nearer to the northern or southern portion? I think I was nearer to the southern portion of it sir. From your position did you have a view of the stair steps which lead into the hall above? I did. Did you see the prisoner Beebee when he first appeared upon the landing of the stairs? I did. From your position could you see the crowd which was under the market house, or the people who were under the market house? I could see a portion of them sir. Could you see those who were out of the market house on the eastern side? I was standing with my back to them. How many persons do you estimate as having seen it at that time under the market house? I suppose some twenty-five or thirty. Who did you see with Beebee as he first appeared upon the landing of the stairs? I saw Mr. Wemyss first and Mr. Bond. Which side was Wemyss on? On the right side of the prisoner sir. Did he have hold of him in any way? He had a string tied around his thumb, he had that in his left hand. You saw Mr. Bond? Yes, sir. Where was Mr. Bond? He came down in front. Who else did you see along with him? I saw Mr. Faircloth. Where was Faircloth? He was to his left hand. Did he have hold of him? He had hold of him on his left. Who else did you see along with him? I saw Sheriff Hardie. Where was Mr. Hardie, I am speaking now of the time when Beebee first made his appearance upon the landing of the stairs. I disremember whether he came in front of him or in the rear. You remember to have seen him? Yes, sir. What occurred if any thing between the time of Beebee first appearing upon the landing of the stairs and his reaching the floor of the market house at the foot of the stairs? Nothing at all sir. From your position did you have a view of that bevel which stands on the left, of what is called Becky Ben's stall coming down the steps? Yes, sir. That bevel would then be on your right? Yes, sir. Did you see any one jump up on that bench at the time Beebee appeared? No sir I didn't. Did you hear any exclamation from any person in the crowd at that time? No, sir. Do you remember to have heard any such cry as 'watch out boys,' 'here he comes,' 'rally boys,' or any thing to that effect? No, such words were spoken that I heard. Do you know John Maults by? I know him. Did you see him there that day up to that time? Yes, sir, I saw him when he went to the carriage. Did you see him at the time Beebee came down stairs? No, sir, I did not. You didn't see him jump upon that here! and make any exclamation such as I used? I did not. Can you swear whether he did or did not? I can swear that if he did I never heard him. So that nothing occured to attract your attention before the boy got down to the floor of the market? No, sir. What was the condition of the crowd under the market house at that time was it excited? No, sir, I saw no excitement. Who did you see in the crowd at that time that you recognized and can now name—I mean other than those who were accompanying the prisoner? It seems to me I saw Mr. Massey, the old gentlemen, and Mr. Mitchell come down stairs, I recollect seeing Mr. Nixon and Mr. Phillips. At that time? Yes, sir. they were under the market house. Mr. Mitchell and Mr. Massey followed the party down stairs? Yes, sir. Are you certain Mr. Sykes whether they came down before or after the prisoner? I am not confident, it appears to me I saw them come down afterwards. You say you saw Nixon, and you saw Phillips? Yes, sir. What Phillips? Samuel A. Phillips. Where did you see them? I saw them go from under the market house, out of the main eastern arch. Did you see how far they got out, whether they came out upon the pavement, or whether they stopped under the market house? I don't recollect. But you saw them coming out from back in the market house towards the main eastern arch? Yes, sir, as the prisoner was coming from the landing down to the floor of the market. What next occured after the prisoner reached the floor of the market? I did not see any thing to attract my attention until I reached the outer edge of the main eastern arch. From your position there on the pavement outside of that southern arch were the prisoner and the party with him visible to you all the time until they turned out upon the pavement? They were not, the pillar was between me and them. They were hidden from your view? Yes, sir. While they were so hidden from your view behind the pillar, did you notice or observe any assault, or any disturbance or violence, made, towards the prisoner? No. sir, I saw a good many walking up apparently towards the main eastern arch like as though they were going to look at him. Walking up from where? From out of the street. Did you notice any movement on the part of those inside under the market house at that time? No, sir. So that was the only thing which attracted your attention while the prisoner was hidden from your view, the seeing of a good many walking up from the out side of the market house? Yes, sir. Did you hear any demand made for the prisoner at that time? When they reached the outer part of the main eastern arch, I did. Was the prisoner visible to you? Yes, sir. You heard what? I heard some person demand him. What did he say? "I demand the boy." Who was that? I could not ascertain who it was, they crowded around at that time. Did you know his voice? No, sir, I did not. What reply was made to that if any? The Sheriff said "he is my prisoner," and asked him to stand back. Did you hear anything else? I heard a good many of the police ask the gentlemen to stand back; the police crowded and shoved everybody out of the way, as they went toward him. Did the police use their clubs at that time? They did not strike anybody that I saw; they flourished their clubs and asked them to stand back. What next occurred, Mr. Sykes, to attract your attention? As they were talking

to the men and telling them to stand back, they moved off the pavement, at the eastern side of the pavement. How far was that from the pillar, how nearly opposite was it to the pillar of the main arch of the market? They moved rather south in an angle from the main eastern arch nearly opposite the pillar when they got off the pavement. I moved then on the south side of the eastern pillar. You say that while you were standing at that small arch, and after the police had used their clubs, and flourished them around, that when the police started with the prisoner across the pavement, they moved rather to the south than a straight course diagonally across the pavement? Yes, sir. And that they got off the pavement with the prisoner? They did. That at that time, just about the time the police had got off the pavement with the prisoner, you changed your position, and got down to the south eastern corner of the market house? Yes, sir. Were you just at the corner, or were you upon the southern side? I moved on the southern side, the south eastern corner. Did you stand up against the wall? I leaned against the wall. Just at the corner? Yes, sir. What did you next observe? I next observed them moving down towards the corner of the pavement. Did they go back on the pavement, or did they continue off the pavement? They attempted to come on the pavement, and three of them fell down—Wemyss, Faircloth and the negro. What next? The prisoner attempted to rise from there, and as he rose the Sheriff caught him in the back of the collar with his right hand, and as the negro was nearly straight, I saw a pistol presented over the left shoulder of the sheriff near his ear. Now at the time the sheriff had his hand in his collar, where was the sheriff? He was standing at his rear. With his hand in the back of the collar? Yes, sir. Was the prisoner on the pavement or off the pavement? I think he was just on the edge of the pavement. How far was he at that time from you? About eight feet. Was he due east from you? Very nearly. Bringing him very nearly opposite the south-eastern corner of the market? Yes, sir. And near the edge of the pavement? Yes, sir. Just as he rose, what occurred? The pistol fired over the shoulder of the sheriff and he fell. Did you see the sheriff? I saw the pistol when it fired. Where was the man standing who fired the pistol? Right at the sheriff's back. Was he on the pavement or off the pavement? Off the pavement. How much of the pistol did you see? I saw the barrel back to the hammer. How far was the muzzle of the pistol from the deceased man, Beebee? Not over eighteen or twenty inches. Pointing to what part of his head? The back part of his head. Which way was the prisoner Beebee looking at the time? Nearly due west. In the direction of Hinsdale's corner? Yes, sir And you saw the pistol point over some man's shoulder? Over the Sheriff's shoulder. Which shoulder? The left shoulder. What sort of pistol was it? It looked to be a repeating pistol? Large or small? One of the largest kind of repeating pistols. Did you see the flash? Yes, sir. Did you see the smoke? Yes, sir, I did. Did you hear the report? Yes, sir, I did. Was there any other pistol fired that day? No, sir. Do you know who fired that pistol? I do not. Did you hear no exclamation in the crowd from any one about the time the pistol fired? I heard some voice ordering some person to give him up, or he would shoot him. Just at that time? Just before the pistol fired. Instantly before? Yes, sir. "Give him up, or I will shoot him?" Yes, sir. Whose voice was that? I took it to be Samuel A. Phillips. Do you know Phillips well? I do. How long have you known him? I have been intimately acquainted with him for the last two years? Do you know his voice well? Yes, sir. And you say you took that voice to be the voice of Samuel A. Phillips? Yes, sir. Have you any doubt about that? I have not, it was his voice to the best of my knowledge. And immediately afterwards the pistol fired from the point you have named? Yes, sir. Did you see any thing of Samuel A. Phillips after that time? I saw him some two or three seconds after, sir. Where was he then? He was between three or four feet to the rear, and to the left of where the pistol fired. Was he in motion or was he stationary? He was in motion. Which way was he moving? A little back. Was he backing off with his face turned? He was backing off with his face turned in the same direction? So you saw him with his face in the same direction two or three seconds afterwards and backing off? Yes, sir. And then he was three or four feet from where the pistol was fired? Yes, sir. Did he have anything in his hand? He had a pistol in his right hand. What sort of a pistol was that he he had in his right hand? A large repeating pistol. How did its size compare with the pistol you saw fired upon the negro? As well as I could see it was nearly or quite the same sized pistol. What was he doing with the pistol? He had it in his right hand and looked to be rubbing the barrel against his pants, opened the left breast of his coat and put the pistol into his pocket. You saw that? I saw it. Is there any doubt about your having seen that? Not a bit, sir. Did you see any thing of Capt. Tolar at that time? I did not. Where was the last time you saw Tolar that day? He was standing under the market house at his usual stall. That was the time you spoke of? Yes, sir, that was the first time and last time I remember seeing him that day. Did you see Mr. Powers at that time? No, sir. When had you seen Tom Powers? I saw him during the time the negro was up stairs. Did you see any thing of Monk at that time? I saw him just before the pistol fired. What was he doing? He was running around the crowd at that time trying to get into where the prisoner was. What did he have? A small knife in his hand. What was he saying? He wanted to get to where the man was to cut him with his knife? Did he cut him or did he get to him? No, sir. What prevented him? Mr. Wemyss struck him across the hand with his club. Did you see him any more after that time? I recollect seeing him after the prisoner was shot down. Then it was before the firing that Wemyss struck him with the club? Yes, sir. I understood you to say that none of the policemen struck with their clubs? That was during the time when they first came out on the pavement. You then confine your remarks to the time when they first came out on the pavement? Yes, sir. Did Monk drop the knife when he was struck? I don't know sir. Did you see Sam Hall that day? I did not. J. G. Leggett? I saw him after the prisoner was shot down, I saw him on the walk between the market house and Mr. Taylor's corner. What was he doing? He was standing looking to be picking his fingers, and talking to Major Byrnn, I think. Did you see any thing of John Maultsby except the time you spoke of having seen him at the rear of the carriage? No, sir. Ed Powers? I don't recollect seeing him that day at all. Ralph Lutterloh? No, sir. You said just now Mr. Sykes that you have no doubt but that voice you heard just before the pistol fired was the voice of Samuel A. Phillips? I have no doubt about it. Was that what you thought then? Yes, sir. Is it not an after consideration? No, sir. But at that time the sound of the voice satisfied you that

it was the voice of Samuel A. Phillips? Yes, sir. Is there any thing further that you know about this matter? Nothing particular that I know. Mr. Sykes were you alarmed on that occasion? No, sir. Not a bit excited? No, sir. Your nerves were steady? Yes, sir. Are you accustomed to scenes of danger? I have seen a good deal of it in my time. The firing of the pistol did not scare you? No, sir. Have you ever told this matter before this time? I told it to Mr. Haywood and General Avery. You told it to them substantially as you have told it here to day? I think I did. Have you ever told it to any body else? No, sir, only yourself. When did you tell it to me the first time? I told you day before yesterday. And before that you have never told me about it? No, sir. Had you ever mentioned this matter before your arrest one way or the other? Never did in my life.

Cross examination by the Counsel for the prosecution.

I understood you to swear just now that you didn't know upon what charge you are confined? No, sir, I have never heard of any charge at all. You say you reached the market house on the day Archy Beebee was killed, about two or three o'clock? Yes, sir. When was the time that you first heard of the attempt to ravish Miss Massey? About ten o'clock in the morning, first. Who told you? I think Jonathan Hollingsworth told me sir. Where was that? In my store I think. How far is your store from the market house? About a hundred yards at that time. What street is it on? Person street, on the right hand as you go from the market house? Did you hear it from any other quarters? I heard a good many talking about it, I disremember who they were. Did you hear them talking at your store, or about the street? About the street. Who did you hear speak of it? I disremember. Did you hear Tom Powers? I never saw him until I went to the market house. Captain Tolar? I never saw Capt. Tolar that day, to my knowledge. Monk? No, sir, I never saw him until I saw him at the market house. E. P. Powers? No, sir, I never saw him that day that I can recollect. Ralph Lutterloh? No, sir. Sam Hall? I never saw him that day that I recollect. Sam Phillips? I heard Sam Phillips speak of it that morning. Now between that and the time you went to the market house, in the evening, I understand you heard it from a great many quarters? Yes. sir. Where was Sam Phillips when you heard it from him? He was up to the market house that morning, about ten o'clock. Was Sam Phillips the first person you heard speak of it? No, sir, Jonathan Hollingsworth was the first? You think Sam Phillips spoke of it after that? Yes, sir. That was at the market house? Yes, sir, while we were attending the market. Did you go to the market house before breakfast or after? Market hours are between nine and ten, and sometimes as late as eleven. How long did you remain at the market house? I don't recollect, sometimes I stay longer and sometimes not so long. I want to know how late you stayed there that day? I suppose I stayed there until after ten. Did you return to your store from the market house? Yes, sir. Did you stay there until three o'clock? I went to my meals, victuals at noon, and then returned to the store and stayed there until three o'clock. You met some of these gentlemen who are on trial, and none of the men I have mentioned, only Mr. Leggett. No, sir. I ask you, if during that time, from anything you saw or heard and that came to your knowledge, you had any reason to apprehend or to believe that an attack was to be made on Archy Beebee that day? I never heard or thought of such a thing. You went there about three o'clock? Yes, sir. You went under the last arch, as I understand you? Yes, sir. Archy was up stairs then? No, sir, he was not. That was before Archy got there? Yes, sir. You saw him brought and carried up stairs? Yes, sir. You were standing in the eastern arch, as he was carried up? Yes, sir. How far from Archy? I suppose some six or seven feet. Did you see the ladies go up stairs? Yes, sir. Which went up stairs first, Archy or the ladies? The ladies went up first. Are you certain of that? I am not positive, but it is my impression. You have a decided impression they went up first? Yes, sir. Who went up stairs with Archy? Mr. Wemyss, Mr. Faircloth, and Mr. Bond. Had you seen the sheriff up to that time that day? Yes, sir, I think he went up stairs just before Beebee came. How long was Beebee up stairs before the ladies came down? I suppose some half or perhaps some three quarters of an hour. You were under the market house all that while? Yes, sir, walking back and forth under the market house. Were the stair steps in your sight all that time? No, sir. At the time the stair steps were in your right did you see anybody coming down from the room up stairs before the ladies came—did you see Israel Bond in the crowd at all during three quarters of an hour? I don't recollect that I did. You saw nobody come down stairs? No, sir. Were the stair steps within your view the greater portion of the time? I don't know whether they were the greater portion of the time or not. When you moved from the point about six or eight feet from the eastern arch under the market house where did you go to? I went to about the center of the market. Who were you speaking with there? I don't recollect any person particular. Did you see Sam Hall there? I did not. Don't you remember standing with Sam Hall near the bell rope? No, sir. Don't you remember standing there talking to any one? No, sir, I do not. The point you went to was somewhere near the bell rope? I passed under it several times. Were you moving backwards and forwards all the time? Yes, sir, pretty much. Is that the only place you went to under the market house during your walk? Yes, sir, from the eastern end of Beeky Ben's bench up to the bell rope. Did you walk up and down there until the ladies came down? Yes, sir. During the time you were walking up and down who did you see there in the crowd? I recollect seeing Tom Powers and James Nixon and Sam Phillips and a colored man, I can't recollect his name. Did you see Capt. Tolar at the time Beebee was up stairs? I saw him there at his stall. Which was in the south west corner? Yes, sir. Who was with him? I think there was a black man there with him that usually butchered about the stall there. Any one else? Not that I can recollect. How often did you see him between the time you got there and the time you came away? Only one time. What was he doing? He was looking towards me at the time. Did he have his spectacles on that day? Not that I recollect. Where was Tom Powers? He was sitting on a bench, I think one of Beeky Ben's benches, on a small bench near Becky Ben's stall. Did you see Captain Toler have any weapons that day? No, sir. Did you see any belt that he might have a weapon in? No, sir. Did you see any weapons about Tom Powers? No, sir. Was Powers conversing at that time? He was conversing with Mr. Nixon, I heard him. Did you hear what he was saying? I heard Mr. Nixon ask him, if he had any pistol and he said no, he had not; Nixon told him he ought to have one and he said he ought

not, and he said, why? Tom said he would rather the law would take its course. You don't know anything about Powers going off near that time somewhere outside of the market house? No, sir. Did you see David Oliphant at time? No, sir. Did you see him in the neighborhood of Tom Powers at any time? I don't recollect that I did. Your impression is that Tom Powers remained on that bench till the ladies came down? Yes, sir. Did you hear any other conversation that day? No, sir, I did not. Did you see anything of Ed Powers or Legget underneath the market house? I did not. Did you see anything of Ralph Lutterloh under the market house? No, sir. How close were you to the arch in promenading down to the eastern end? I might have walked under the arch sometimes. Did you pass up and down the middle of the aisle? Yes, sir. When you were passing up and down the aisle, didn't you see Tolar and Leggett and Lutterloh? No, sir. Who did you see? I don't recollect, I saw a great many persons, but I never paid any attention to them. Was there much of a crowd there? There didn't appear to be any thing extra. Was there any obstruction to your walking at all? Very little. Were the persons that were there scattered, about in crowds? Yes, sir. Now when the ladies came down stairs, which way was your face turned? When the door opened at the head of the stairs, I was at the main eastern arch and I turned around to look at them. You saw them coming down and Bond with them? Yes, sir. Was Miss Massey veiled? I disremember, I think she was though. Did she have a handkerchief to her face? I think she did. Did you see any part of her face? I saw the upper part, I do not think her face was covered. Did you see any mark about her face? Not about her face, I saw on her neck the marks as it looked of some person's fingers. Could see her neck? Yes, sir. Had she a shawl on? Yes, sir. Was it fastened by the neck? Yes, sir. Do you remember whether she had a collar on? I do not. Do you remember whether she had any wrapping about her throat? No, sir, sho had not. Her throat was bare, so that you could see distinctly the marks upon her throat? Yes, sir. Were they bloody? They looked very red. Any marks of blood? No, sir. What sort of a pistol was yours? A small Colt's repeater. What sized Colt's pistol? A six shooter. What was the size of the ball? I don't recollect, I never bought any balls for it in my life. Did you ever load it? No, sir, it was loaded. I ask you upon your oath when you loaded it? I never loaded it in my life; it was loaded when I bought it, or rather when I got it pawned to me; it remained in my hands two or three months; the pistol does not belong to me. Who did you get it from? I got it from a person I let have some money by the name of Mr. Hybert, he pawned it to me for five dollars, I only kept it some two months. How long had you had it at that day? Some two or three weeks. Why did you put it on that morning? I generally carried it in my pocket all the time. Which pocket? In my left hand breast pocket. It was in your pocket when you dressed that morning? It was in my overcoat pocket. Did you have on your overcoat? Yes, sir. Is that your usual place of keeping the pistol? Yes, sir. When you took off your coat at night, did you keep your pistol there? Yes, sir, it remained in my pocket. Did you have that pistol on the day before Archy was killed? Yes, sir. Understand you are upon your oath. I understand that. Did you have it on the day before that? Yes, sir. And the day before that? Yes, sir. You always wore it? Yes, sir, I always carried it in my overcoat pocket. Is this man Hybert a colored man? Yes, sir. Was the pistol capped when you got it? Yes, sir. Did you never fire it off at all? I never did in my life—I recall that; coming up on the steamboat from Wilmington on the first of May, I fired it. What sort of a report did it make? A tolerable loud report for a small pistol. Now, sir, I want to know the size of that pistol? I don't know exactly. Do you know the army size? I don't know the calibre. You know the size when you see it? Yes, sir. You know the navy size when you see it? Yes, sir. You have been in the army, you are toler. bly familiar with arms? Yes, sir. Do you know the next size to the navy size? I don't recollect what they call them. Was yours the next size? No, sir. It was about as large as the second size. Did you judge of its size from its length or the size of the ball? From the size and length; it carries a common buck shot. Did you try it? No, sir, I never tried it in my life. Who has that pistol now? Mr. Hybert has it. Who is Mr. Hybert? A black man that lives in Fayetteville. When did you give it to him? About the time General Sickles ordered that no man should carry arms, I asked him to redeem it and he did so. You saw this lady come down with the marks upon her neck? Yes, sir. And you were looking at her? No, sir. Did you wait until she got into the arch to move out? As she came out from between the pillars and the bench, I moved to the front of the small eastern arch. She went on towards the carriage? Yes, sir. You stood with your back to the arch did you, and your face towards the carriage? At that time I did, sir. Now at that time did you see any thing of Tolar? No, sir, I did not. Did you see any thing of Phillips? No, sir, I don't recollect seeing any thing of him at that time. Did you see any thing of Nixon? Not that I recollect at that time. Did I understand you to say you went out of the main eastern arch and went around to the southern arch and stood with your back directly looking at the carriage? Yes, sir. Did you look at that carriage in the same position until the carriage drove away? I don't recollect that I did. Was your face towards the carriage until it drove off? I imagine it was. I don't want you to imagine? My impression is that it was. And you say you saw Bond go to the carriage? Yes, sir. And Tom Powers, Maultsby, and Phil. Taylor? Yes, sir. Did you see Maultsby go to the carriage. I saw him go near to it. How near? I thought about eight or ten feet in the rear of it. Now, where did he come when he went to the carriage? From under the market house. That was the first time you saw him that day? Yes, sir. Did you see Jonathan Hollingsworth that day? No, sir, not at the market. When you saw Jonathan Hollingsworth in the morning did he have a pistol? I think he had on a belt but I don't recollect seeing a pistol. You didn't see him at the market house? No, sir, he was standing guarding the bridge. You saw Maultsby go within nine or ten feet of the rear of the carriage? Yes, sir. Did you see him at that point until the carriage drove off? I don't recollect? You just got a glance at him? Yes, sir. Was he still moving? He was moving? Towards the carriage or from it? I think he was moving towards the carriage. When you saw him he was not stationary? No, sir. Where was Bond at that time? He was standing at the carriage. Which side? The side next to the market house. Where was Tom Powers? I disremember whether he went around to the opposite side of the carriage or remained at the side where he was. Where was he at the time that Maultsby was coming up? He was about the back part of it. The closest you saw

Maultsby was nine or ten feet from the carriage? Yes, sir. Did you see Bond go around to the other side of the carriage? Not that I recollect. Where did Philimon Taylor come from? He come up on the opposite side. You didn't see Mr. Cashwell? No, sir. Nor Mr. Mitchell? No, sir. Nor T. H. Massey? No, sir. You didn't see them that day? Yes, sir. And the time you saw them was coming down the stairs behind Archy? Yes, sir, I think they were. Was Mr. Powers at the carriage so that he could talk to the persons inside when you saw him? I think he was near enough to talk with them. Was he talking to them? I think he was. Did you hear what he said? I did not. Did you see him turn off? I think I saw him when he returned to the market, I think he came back with Mr. Bond. Did you see Maultsby say any thing to Mr. Bond while they were about the carriage? Not that I recollect. Do you swear he didn't say any thing to Bond? Not that I heard. Did you notice him speak to any person at all—I want to know whether you swear he didn't speak to him? I can swear I didn't see him talk to him. Did you see how Maultsby came away from there? No, sir. Did you see where Tom Powers went to when he came away? He went back under the market house I think. You were still standing about this arch? Yes, sir Was your back to it still? Not at that time I turned around expecting to see the prisoner come down. Was the carriage in your view all the time he was standing there? Yes, sir. And your attention was centred on the carriage until it drove off? Yes, sir. You didn't see Mr. Tolar go there? No, sir. Did you see Mr. Tolar about that time at all? No, sir, I did not. When was it you turned your face to look towards the steps inside of the market house? After Mr. Bond returned to the market. Did Mr. Bond go up stairs? He did sir. Did you see what became of Tom Powers when you turned your face inside? I did not. Did you see him through that arch at all? Not that I recollect. You don't know whether he stopped, or went in? No, sir. And in looking through that arch you didn't see him? No, sir. Did you see any weapon about Mr. Powers then? I did not, sir. At any time that day? I did not. From the place where you stood you could see the steps very distinctly? Yes, sir. Was there any body between you and the steps? There were some little children standing on the bench. What aged children? Varying from eight to ten I suppose. How many did you see there? I saw one or two there. Were those the only persons you saw there between you and the steps? Yes, sir. Were you leaning on that bench? Yes, sir. If I understand, that little arch there is a place where men can sit down, and there is a bar across there, a little higher up? Yes, sir. Was your hand on that bar? Yes sir. and you were looking through there? Yes, sir. Did you stay there till Beebee turned the arch and came outside? I staied until Beebee was hid by the pillar, there was a good many men walked up there I backed further down towards the south eartern corner. You stood there until Beebee had got out on the pavement, and this little difficulty had occurred at the main eastern arch? Yes, sir. During the time you were looking in there was any body standing or sitting on that bench across the little arch? None except those children that I recollect. Were they sitting on it? I forget whether they were standing or sitting on it. Were they looking inside or outside? I disremember. Did they intercept your view? No, sir. How many of those children were there then? Only two that I can recollect. Do you recollect who they were? I do not. Were their backs towards you or their faces? I think they were sitting facing each other as near as I can recollect. Their feet were not hanging outside? No, sir, they were sitting on the bench with their feet on the top of the bench. Do you know Sebastian Arey? I am not acquainted with him, sir. These two little children of the ages of eight or ten, were the only persons you saw there that you recollect? Yes, sir. During the time you were standing there, was there anybody standing there of the age of fifteen or eighteen? Not that I recollect, sir. You were there from the time you spoke of, until Archy got out on the pavement looking inside? Yes, sir. And no one was sitting in that arch with their feet hanging outside towards the place where you were? I was not paying any attention to them. How wide is that arch? I suppose some ten feet, some eight or ten feet wide the small eastern arch. Did you think a person might have staid there with his feet hanging outside, and you not have seen them? I might not have paid any attention to them. Your attention was so absorbed by the prisoner, I suppose. Yes, sir. Did you see any such person or any person who was sitting on that bench? Not that I recollect. But you think it might have happened and you not have seen it? Yes, sir. Just before this crowd came down, did you see anybody on Becky Ben's bench? No, sir, not that I recollect of. Did you see anybody on there at all? Not that I recollect. Did you see any body jump up there before Archy Beebee came in sight and say "he is coming." No, sir. "Look out boys?" No, sir. Anything of that sort? No, sir. I ask you if a person could have jumped up on that bench without your seeing it? If they got up on it I would have been very apt to have seen it then. But you think a person might have sat there in the arch within a few feet of you, and you not have noticed it, but if a person had jumped up on the bench you would have noticed them? Yes, sir, for that would have been nearly right in front of me. You say that if anything of that had happened you would have seen it? I think so. But you didn't see any such a thing? No, sir. You didn't see anybody on that bench at all? If there was any there I can't recollect it, there were some persons standing about there, but I don't know whether they were standing on the bench or not. But you think if any one had jumped upon that bench, and said anything, you would have noticed it immediately? Yes, sir. You say presently Beebee started down stairs? Yes, sir. Now, sir, give us the position they came down if you please? Mr. Bond came in front of him I think. Is that a decided impression? Yes, sir. Have you any doubt about it? I have not. Who else came? Mr. Wemyss on his right side. Didn't the Sheriff come in front? I disremember. Didn't the Sheriff come in front of him and come down to the bottom of the stairs before they came out of the door? I don't recollect. Wasn't your attention centered on that door and the party? Yes, sir. Now just before the prisoner came out, didn't Sheriff Hardie come out first and come to the bottom of the stairs? I disremember. What is your opinion about it? My impression was that he came down behind him, as he came down stairs? And that Bond came down before him? Yes, sir. And that Wemyss came where? On his right side and Faircloth on his left. And behind were who? The Sheriff was right in his rear and Mr. McGuire and Mr. Brown. Now these other parties that you saw came out of that door, Mr. Mitchell and Mr. Massey? I think they came immediately after the police. Were they on the

steps at the same time the police and Archy were? I think they were at the curve of the steps as the others came down to the floor? Did you see what became of them? No, sir. You say nothing was done at the prisoner at all, no effort made to get at him? Not a bit. Didn't you see any impatience on the part of the crowd to get up and look at him? I saw some walking around to look at him. Didn't you see all moving up to see? I could not see all. How many did you see gather to look at the man? Some twenty-five or thirty perhaps. And you lost sight of him for a moment? Yes, sir, How many steps could you see him from the foot of the stair case towards towards the main eastern arch? I suppose it was some five steps. Could you see him all the time he was passing from there? Yes sir. And you only lost sight of him while he was passing the pillar—but an instant? Yes, sir. During that time he was passing towards the arch was there any thing done to him? No, sir. Any thing said? No, sir. You heard no exclamation? No, sir. No outcry. No. sir. Did you see Tom Powers then? No, sir. Did you see Monk then? No, sir. Did you see anybody that you recognized then? No, sir except the officers around the prisoner. Where was your pistol then? It was in my pocket. In your left side pocket? Yes, sir, in my left breast pocket. In your overcoat? Yes sir. On the outside or the inside? On the outside—I am mistaken, I think it was on the right, in the pocket inside. When the party turned out of the main eastern arch the prisoner and the officers with him you did hear and see something? As he entered the outer part of the main eastern arch. As he got on the pavement? Yes, sir. Your face was turned towards him? I had moved backwards. Had you moved backwards then? I had moved back towards the south eastern corner. While he was passing around the pillar? Yes, sir. Did you move with your face towards the south eastern corner? I walked backwards? And it was from that point at the south-eastern corner that you saw and heard what you are now about to relate? Yes, sir. What was it? I heard some person demand the boy. What did he say? He said "I demand this boy." Yes, sir. It was not "we demand this boy." It was not as far as I can recollect. What did the Sheriff say in reply? He said stand back he is my prisoner. Did he say it in the same tone you are using now? Not altogether. Was it an excited tone? Not the first demand, that was very quiet. You didn't hear any oaths accompanying it? No, sir. You didn't hear him say "damn him, give him to me"? No, sir. And the only demand you heard was this quiet and undemonstrative character? Yes, sir. And you heard the Sheriff reply it was what? "Stand back, he is my prisoner." I ask if the Sheriff didn't say, "Stand back, gentlemen"? I disremember whether he said that or not. Have you any decided impressions about that? I have not. You didn't see the person who demanded the prisoner? No, sir. Where did the voice appear to come from? It was near the Sheriff. Where was the Sheriff? At the outer part of the arch. Where was the voice, apparently behind Archy? No, sir, in front of him I think. How many persons were between you and the group in which the Sheriff and Archy were? I suppose there might have been some half a dozen? Were they nearer to you or nearer to the Sheriff? They were nearer to the Sheriff. Were they very close to the Sheriff? Yes, sir, Robert Simmons, I think, was between me and him for one. Was he in that group pressing up close to the Sheriff? Yes, sir. Wasn't Sam Phillips there? I don't recollect seeing him at that time. Don't you think John Armstrong was there? I recollect seeing John Armstrong just before he came down stairs, I don't recollect seeing him at that time. You saw Simmons to recognize him? Yes, sir. Did you recognize anybody else, any white one among those five or six that you saw? I did not recognize any one else at the time. You are acquainted more extensively among the white persons than among the colored persons of Fayetteville. I have no very great acquaintance among them. How long have you been living there? Only about two years. You saw a black man's face that you recognized, but you can speak of no white man's face? No, sir, not that I can recollect. Have you tried to recollect? I have, sir. I want to know if these five or six persons were scattered along there? I say there were some five or six standing with their backs between me and the Sheriff. I want to know if the crowd extended from the main eastern arch to the point where you were at the southern extremity of the market? Not entirely. There was a space between you and where the crowd began? Yes, sir. How wide was that space? About four or five feet. And from the point where that space ended up to the sheriff, was a crowd? Yes, sir. How large a crowd was there? Some fifty persons or more. Were they close up to the sheriff? Yes, sir. Were they pressing close? Yes, sir And that crowd was close enough to prevent you from seeing the man who made this demand? Yes, sir. Did you see which way the sheriff's face was turned? No, sir. You could only tell from his voice it was him? Yes, sir. Do you know Tom Powers? I know his face when I see him. Do you know his voice when you hear it? I might at the present time. Did you have any acquaintance with him at that time? Nothing any more than I knew him when I saw him. You were better acquainted with Sam. Phillips? Yes, sir, I did a good deal of business with him, was one reason, and he was near by. You remained then at this point until the pistol fired? Not exactly at the point where I was at that time. You were still on the eastern side of the pillar? Yes, sir. Was this all the disturbance that occurred, just the demand of the prisoner and the sheriff's telling them to stand back? The police whirled their clubs around them. How many clubs did you see? I saw some three or four clubs. Who had clubs? I saw Wemyss and Faircloth, and McGuire and Brown. Did they all have clubs? Yes, sir. Did you see more than one club? Yes, sir. Are you confident Brown had one? Yes, sir. Was there any noise in the crowd then? No particular noise. Was there a general noise? There was a general noise among the men talking. What were they saying? Some said "push up," "and crowd up there; some said "take him away," and others were squealing out to "stand back?" Who were calling out "stand back?" The police. Who were calling out to "push on?" Some of the men that were trying to get to him. Did you see any of them to name them? I didn't, that I recollect; I was looking for the prisoner. Did you lose sight of him entirely? At the first time I did until he got out on the pavement. When he got off the pavement what part of the market house was the boy opposite? The north side of the small arch. That was about the point where he came off the pavement? Yes, sir. How far do you think he got from the pavement? He didn't go over three feet from the pavement. You could then see him distinctly? Yes, sir. Did you then move around to the south end of the market? About that time. Was the crowd extending from you to the point where Archy was then? No, sir, they had moved

around. Around where? Nearer to the rear. In the street? Yes, sir. Was there any crowd on the pavement at all? Not that I recollect, I had moved where I could not see exactly on the pavement at that time. When you left the pavement, was it covered with people? There were some people there in front of the arch. The main portion of the crowd had worked its way off from the market? Yes, sir. Were there any in front of him at that time? No, sir. They were full in your view? Yes, sir. Did you see any one standing near to you at that time? I don't recollect that I did sir. Did you see James R. Jones? No, sir, not that I recollect of. Did you see any thing of Mr. Maultsby? Not at that time. You saw no one that you remember now? No, sir, except the police. What became of Bob Simmons? I don't know. You say in attempting to get upon the pavement again, Beebee stumbled and brought down Wemyss and Faircloth? Yes, sir. Did you see any one trying to strike at him with a knife at the time they fell? Yes, sir. Who was that? Mr. Watkins. Before they got back on the pavement? Yes, sir. Was he trying to strike about the time they fell? Yes, sir. Did Wemyss reach him with his club? Yes, sir. Where was Monk? A little to the front and right. He was nearer to the pavement than Wemyss? I think he was on the edge of the pavement. Where was Wemyss? He was on the right side of the boy. Where was Faircloth? On his left, That was at the time he fell? Yes, sir. And Wemyss you say struck the men who had a knife? Yes, sir. Did you hear whether the knife fell out of the man's hand? I did not. Did you hear any complaint he made from the blow? Not a bit. As the negro recovered from this stumble on the edge of the pavement which he made about the north edge of the small arch on the east side he was shot? Not at that place he went off the pavement then. He didn't go back right straight on the pavement? No, sir, he went around the small tree. And got further south? Yes, sir, nearly opposite the southern corner. He was off the pavement some moment or so? Yes, sir. He took a step or two off the pavement? Yes, sir, about two or three steps. Was this hubbub still going on? They appeared to be coming on to him. Did you see the police use their clubs at all? I saw no licks struck except the one that struck Monk. When they came back on the pavement, where did they come back on? Opposite the south eastern corner of the market. They were coming due west, Yes, sir, as they made the effort to come back on the pavement. At that time did Wemyss have his face to the west? Yes, sir. And Faircloth had his face to the west? Yes, sir. And Archy Beebee had his face to the west? Yes, sir. And they stumbled on the edge of the pavement or for some reason or other went down as they were coming back? Yes, sir. And that was at the very time that Monk had struck with a knife? Yes, sir. You saw the negro rise after he fell, did you? Yes, sir. Was there any person between you and the group that had fallen down? Not that I recollect. You were not eight feet from it? About six or seven feet. The width of the pavement? Yes, sir. You were standing against the market house? Yes, sir. So that your left elbow touched the market house? Yes, sir. Your face due east and theirs due west? Yes, sir. And you saw them raise after they stumbled? Yes sir. And in the act of raising you saw Sheriff Hardie catch the negro in the back of the collar? Yes, sir. With which hand? His right hand. You are certain it was his right hand? Yes, sir. And he was standing to the left of Beebee then?

Yes. About half covering his rear? Yes. sir. And he caught him in the back of the collar with his right hand? Yes, sir. And Sheriff Hardie's face was to the east? His face was nearly south his face was turned to the negro. Was the negro's face on a way and the Sheriff's another? No, sir, he was looking at the negro. I thought you said when he went down that his face was to the west? Yes, sir. When the Sheriff helped him up was not the Sheriff's face to the west? I suppose it was his face was turned towards the negro. You saw his face? Yes, sir. And you saw him help the negro up? Yes, sir, well he only took hold of him as he rose. Sheriff Hardie's face was towards you then? Yes, sir. Towards the west? Yes, sir. And this group rose up facing towards the west they came up right in the rear of Sheriff Hardie? Yes, sir. Did they change that direction to go to the guard house before the pistol was fired? No, sir. The pistol was fired as the negro recovered himself? Yes, sir. That pistol came over the Sheriff's left shoulder? Yes, sir. You could see the muzzle over his left shoulder? Yes, sir. You saw the pistol barrel from the muzzle to the hammer? Yes, sir. And you saw the direction in which it was pointed? It was pointed towards the negro. And you saw the direction, extending back and forth? Nearly west. Was it nearly to the south of west? Yes, sir. It came over the Sheriff's left soulder? Yes, sir. And was pointed a little to the south of west? Yes, sir. Could you see the hand that held it? No, sir. Let me see about these positions when the negro recovered from his fall himself and Faircloth and Wemyss rose with their faces to the west? Yes, sir. Hardie was standing behind and as he rose up put his right hand in the back of his collar and stood with his face to the west? Yes, sir. He was a little further to the left than the negro? He was a little to the right of the negro. You have sworn to the left up to this moment from first to last? I think you are mistaken. Did you make the same sort of mistake about catching him with his left hand instead of his right? He caught him with his left hand. The negro was down when he took hold of him? He took hold of him just as he was rising? He took hold with his right hand in the collar? Yes. sir. Now, sir, how was it, will you explain to me, that you could swear in your examination-in-chief, and up to this point, that he was on the left of him? I say he was on the right and rear of the prisoner. Have you not sworn in your previous testimony about two or three times, that he was on the left of the negro? No, sir. You stick to it now that he had his hand on his collar? He had. And was to the right? Yes, sir. A little to the right of the negro? Yes, sir. And this pistol came over his left shoulder? Yes, sir. And the pistol was fired behind the Sheriff apparently? Yes, sir. It was behind in a westerly direction? Yes, sir, a little south of the west. How close was it to the Sheriff's face? The muzzle of the pistol was right opposite his ear I think. Was it visible in front of him—could he have seen it? I don't think he could have seen it. You think it was fired by some one close behind him? Yes, sir. You saw no one there? No, sir, none that I recognized at all. Almost as soon as you saw this pistol, you heard the report and saw the flash? Yes, sir. And the negro went down? Yes, sir. Now, sir, when was it that you heard this exclamation that you recognized as the voice of Sam Phillips? Just a moment before the pistol fired. Did you see anybody there that you recognized then except the police? No, sir. Was that said in a loud clear voice? Yes, sir. Was that the only expression

that you heard at that time? Yes, sir. You heard Phillips as you are confident, as you have no doubt say, "If you don't give him up, I will shoot him"? Yes, sir. And then the pistol was fired? Yes, sir. How many people were closer to the Sheriff than you were? A good many, all the police were closer, and the man who fired the pistol was closer. I ask you if you ever stated that circumstance before in giving your testimony to the Judge Advocate and myself? I did not. I ask you in giving in your testimony to us you were not told that you might tell just as little and as much as you pleased, it was left to your own option? Yes, sir. I ask you further when you gave us your statement if you didn't profess to have stated all that you knew with regard to this transaction? All of any importance. But you stated nothing in regard to this transaction? No, sir, you asked me if Phillips didn't do it, or if I didn't think he did it, and I told you yes. Now, sir, you have made this statement without my calling it out, now, sir, as you have given a part of that conversation, perhaps you will benefit the Court by giving the whole of it? I told you my impression was Phillips did it; when the pistol fired and I told him so in his presence at his store, and that he said, "you are mistaken," and afterwards I heard other people say who fired it, and I said I might have been mistaken perhaps. Do you remember saying anything about Oliphant? Yes, sir. Do you remember saying anything about Oliphant having been present when you were speaking to Phillips and told him you thought it was he? Yes, sir. When did you first tell about having heard Phillips' voice? To Mr. Fuller day before yesterday the first time. And that impression has been upon your mind from the time it happened until now that you heard Phillips' voice distinctly say "give him to me, or I will shoot him"? Yes, sir. To whom was the remark addressed? I could not tell except to the police. You have no doubt that that was Phillips' voice now? No doubt. You are very familiar with his voice? Yes, sir. You saw him frequently? Yes, sir. And you thought it was his voice then? Yes, sir. And you think so now? Yes, sir. And immediately after that, you heard the pistol fired? Yes, sir. Did the pistol come from the place where you heard the voice? About the same place. Well, sir, how long was it after the pistol fired before you saw Phillips? I suppose some five or six seconds; it was not half a minute. It was within a half a minute? Yes, sir. Did you remain there stationary after the pistol fired? I remained there until the crowd was pushed off by the police so that I could see the body. And during the time you were standing there it was that you saw Phillips? Yes, sir. Where was he standing then? He was standing some three four feet to the left and rear of where the pistol fired. Do you mean to your left or his left? Of his left as he was facing towards me. That was the first sight you had of him after the flashing of the pistol and the falling of the man? Yes, sir. What was he doing? He had the pistol in his right hand rubbing it against his pants. Which side of his pants? The right side. When you just got sight of him was he rubbing it? Yes, sir. How many times did he rub it? Half a dozen times. Back and forth? Yes, sir. What did he do with it then? He put it in his left breast pocket? You saw him do that? Yes, sir. Had he an overcoat on? Yes, sir. You could see the pocket then? Yes, sir. And he put it in his left overcoat pocket? Yes, sir. Now, sir, I ask you just after the firing of that pistol if he didn't elevate it and look at it? Not that I saw. Didn't you hear him say, after the pistol fired "the negro is dead but I didn't kill him?'' No, sir, I heard a great many cry out "he is killed," "he is killed." Were you near enough to have heard Phillips if he had spoken in an ordinary tone of voice? Not with the wrangling that was going on at that time. Was there a crowd wrangling there? There was a great many crying out he was killed. Was that a general cry? Yes, sir. Now, you say it was after the firing of the pistol before you saw Sam. Phillips? Yes, sir. Do you say you could not have heard Phillips in his ordinary tone of voice? No, sir. But the first time you saw him he was four or five feet to the left, and rear of Beebee, and rubbing his pistol against his pants? Yes, sir. Did you see what become of him afterwards? No, sir, I did not remain there long, I saw the prisoner and then turned and went off to my store. Could you form a conception of where the man stood who fired that pistol from what you saw of the pistol? I suppose he was between three and five feet off from the pavement, sir. Directly in the rear of Beebee and the sheriff? I think he was a little to the left of Beebee; the pistol was as it struck him in the left side of the head. I want you to form the opinion from what you saw of the pistol? From what I saw of the pistol it would bear a little to the left of the negro. Was that pistol ranged towards the south west? Yes, sir. Do you know the points of the comp s.? Yes, sir, not very well, I know tolerably well, I know north, south, east and west. What color was that over coat that Phillips had on? A black one. Did you notice any thing peculiar in its make or construction so that you could recognize it again if it was produced? I never noticed any thing more than that it was a black napped over coat, coarse napped. Now, sir, standing where Beebee was, what point do you think is south west from there? Up Hay street would be west. South west would be a little to the left of Hay street? Yes, sir, from where they were standing I suppose it would fall about the point between Hinsdale's and Thompson's. And the man who held that pistol was to the left of Beebee? Yes, sir. And the sheriff was to the right of Beebee, holding him? Yes, sir, a little to his right and rear. And the pistol was fired over the Sheriff's shoulder? Yes, sir. It was hidden by his head so that you could not see the whole of it? I could not see the man's hand for the hair and neck of the Sheriff. I ask you just after that pistol was fired, if you did not hear persons cry out in that crowd, "Capt. Tolar killed him?" Not at that time. Didn't you hear several persons say Capt. Tolar shot him? No, sir. Didn't you hear any one say Phillips shot him? I didn't hear any one say was shot him. Didn't the people ask who shot him after the firing? I didn't hear any one ask while I was there. The only ones you heard were "he is shot, he is shot?" Yes, sir. No, sir. Did you hear any one say hurrah for Capt. Tolar? I did not. Did you hear any expression from any quarter after the shooting, indicating who had fired the pistol? I did not. Have you any enmity towards Samuel A. Phillips? I have not a bit, me and him are intimate friends. Have you any especially kind feelings towards Capt. Tolar? I have not. Do you know where the pistol is Captain Tolar had on his person the day t his shooting took place? I do not. Do you swear you do not? I swear I do not. Have you heard him say where it is? No, sir. Have you been in the jail with him? Yes, sir. Had access to him for several weeks? Yes, sir. You have never heard him say where that pistol is that he had on that day? No, sir. You say you saw that pistol just enough to pronounce the sort of pistol it was, from the muzzle down to

the hammer? Yes, sir. And your impression is that it was the largest size of revolving pistol? Yes, sir. You don't know whether it was a Colt or Remington? I could not say. Was that a Colt or Remington you saw in Phillips' hand afterward? I don't know the difference between them. Do you know any other persons at the market house that day who had weapons? I do not. So the only pistol you saw was the one in the hand of Sam Phillips? That and the one that was fired, if they are different ones. And Jonathan Hollingsworth, you didn't see him there that day? No, sir, I never saw him at the market house once that day.

Re-direct examination by the Counsel for the accused.

How long has it been since you were examined about this matter by Mr. Haywood and the Judge Advocate the first time? I don't recollect, it was about four days after I arrived here. Up to that time had you had access to Captain Tolar in jail? Not a bit sir, not up to that time, I was put in prison with him when I first came to Raleigh. Up to that time had you talked this matter over with Captain Tolar? Not a bit sir. How long was it before you were examined the second time by Mr. Haywood and the Judge Advocate? I don't recollect how long it was. Up to the time you were examined the second time by them had you had any conversation with Captain Tolar about it? I never had any conversation with him about it not more than I heard him speak of sending for his pistol. Never mind about that you had no conversation about the subject matter of your testimony with Captain Tolar? I didn't know that I would be called on to give in any testimony. When did you have any reason to expect that you would be called to the stand as a witness in this case? When you told me of it. Day before yesterday? Yes, sir. In the conversation that you had with me about it did I ask any questions, or did I tell you to go on and tell your own story? You just told me to go on and tell you what I knew about it. Mr. Sykes you say you think you didn't hear of this outrage which it was said Archy Beebee attempted to perpetrate upon the young lady until the day of the killing? I never heard of it until the day he was killed. Do you remember what day of the week it was he was killed? I do not. You don't remember whether it was Monday? It was on Monday, it was on Sunday, I understood he committed the depredation, I heard on Monday—it was done on Sunday evening just before dark. And you don't remember who it was that told you about it first? I think Jonathan Hollingsworth was the first that mentioned it to me. And after that you think Sam Phillips mentioned it to you? Yes, sir. Did I understand you to say in reply to the question asked you by Mr. Haywood that in the different interviews you have had with Mr. Haywood and the Judge Advocate, that you always gave to them as your decided impression from what you saw, that Phillips was the man who did the shooting? Yes, sir, at the time it was done. That was your impression at the time it was done? Yes, sir. Have you ever swerved or varied from that at all? No, sir. That afterwards, as you told them, you heard a good many persons say it was Captain Tolar did it, and for a time you thought you might have been mistaken? Yes, sir. I don't care about the conversation at all but you spoke just now in your cross examination about having had some conversation with Sam Phillips after the thing occurred in which you charged upon him that it was your impression that he did it? Yes, sir. When was that? It was some hour or an hour and a half after the negro was shot. Where was it? It was at his store door. Who was present there besides yourself and Phillips at the time you told him? David Oliphant. And you there told him an hour or an hour and a half after the shooting, that it was your impression and belief that he was the man who did it? Yes, sir.

The Counsel for the prosecution:
I shall have to return to that clause unless I do it now.

Counsel for the defence:
You can do it now.

Counsel for the prosecution:
Do I understand you to say, that you declared to Phillips that it was then at that time your impression and opinion that he did the shooting? I told him I thought it at the time the shooting was done that it was him done it. Did you say Mr. Phillips I thought when the shooting took place it was you that did it? Yes, sir. Did you express to him that you thought so still? Yes, sir, it was my impression that it was you was the word I spoke. You told him it was your impression when it happened as thus: "It was my impression Mr. Phillips when this thing happened that you did it," or did you say you thought so now? I said I thought so then but I may be mistaken, says he; you are mistaken and then—

The Counsel for the accused said he did not want to hear the conversation.

Counsel for the prosecution said he wanted the whole conversation.

Counsel for the accused objected to that portion of the conversation which was had by Oliphant; I didn't call for the conversation at all, I just told the witness I did not wish the conversation at all, it was first brought out by the Counsel for the prosecution; still we have no decided objection to all that Phillips said on that occasion exclusively, although it is not strictly admissable.

Counsel for the prosecution:
I wont insist upon pressing it.
What further did Phillips say? That was all the conversation we had about it. You told Mr. Phillips it was your impression and you swear it now, that it was your impression that he did it, at the time the shooting took place and I think so now? Yes, sir. And that was all you said except that you thought you might be mistaken? Yes, sir. What was the ground upon which you might have been mistaken as to who the man was that fired the pistol? That I saw no man fire the pistol at all, I could not tell who did it. That was the very night after it happened? Yes, sir. And you say David Oliphant was present then? Yes, sir. You have a distinct recollection of that? Yes, sir. Did David Oliphant go there with you? Yes, sir, he went there with me from near my store door.

Re-direct examination resumed by the Counsel for the accused:

Mr. Sykes, you say you have no ill feeling, no ill will towards Samuel Phillips? Not a bit sir. That your store door is not far from Phillips? No, sir. How far from it? The width of the street? You are on the south side, and he on the north side of Person street? Yes, sir. You say you are in the habit of trading with him? Yes, sir. Both in the grocery line; Phillips a little more largely than yourself? Yes, sir. How long have you known Mr. Phillips. I have known him personally some eight years. How long have you known Captain Tolar? I have known him nearly all my life sir. Have you ever had any particular dealing with Captain Tolar? No, sir, nothing, except I used to buy a piece of meat under the market house from him. I understand you to say your relations with Capt. Tolar are not of an intimate character

by any means, that you only know him as a passing acquaintance? I only know him as an acquaintance, we were raised near each other. Mr. Sykes, I wish you would, if you please, if you can, do it with your one hand, just stand on the stage and give to the Court, as near as you can the manner of the person who held that pistol and the manner in which the pistol was pointed at the time you saw it?

(Down by his right leg, rubbing the cylinder against his pants, opened his coat in the left side and dropped it into his pocket.) What did he do with his hand? He dropped it back. (Witness represents the position of Beebee and the Sheriff and the man who fired the pistol, Beebee to the front of the Sheriff and about a foot to his left, the Sheriff grasping him in the back of the coat collar with his right hand, the pistol pointing in the direction of Beebee's head, and within a few inches of the Sheriff's left ear.) As to Tom Powers, you say us to that day you bar ly knew him only when you saw him? I knew him only when I saw him.

Questioned by the Commission:
When you saw that pistol presented to Beebee, did you try to see who had that pistol? No, sir, it fired so quickly I could not see. After that pistol fired did you make any effort to see who fired it? No, sir. You had no curiosity to know who fired it? No, sir, I did not. You stated that you were with David Oliphant at the store of Mr. Phillips, and you told Mr. Phillips that it was your impression that he had fired that pistol? Yes, sir. What did David Oliphant say? He said the same as Phillips did, he said I was mistaken. What else did he say? He said it was Capt. Tolar did it. He said he saw Capt. Tolar fire the pistol? Yes, sir. Was that what he said? Yes, sir.

The Judge Advocate announced that there was no witness in the city to be examined to-day, whereupon

On motion the Commission adjourned to meet on Thursday, Sept. 6th, at 11 o'clock, A. M.

RALEIGH, N. C., Sept. 6th, 1867, 10 A. M.
The Commission met pursuant to adjournment.

Present: All the members of the Commission, the Judge Advocate, the Counsel for the prosecution, all the accused and their Counsel.

The reading of the testimony taken yesterday was waived, there being no objection thereto.

Yesterday's proceedings were then read and approved.

ISHAM BLAKE, a witness for the defence, having been first duly sworn, testified as follows:

Examined by the Counsel for the accused.
What is your name? Isham Blake. Where do you reside? In the town of Fayetteville. Fayetteville, N. C.? Yes, sir. How long have you been residing in the town of Fayetteville? Sixty-three years, sir. Were you in the town of Fayetteville on the day Archy Beebee was killed? Yes, sir, and the day after also. Were you at the market house on the day he was killed? I was, sir. At what time did you reach the market house? It was a short time after dinner, I don't recollect the precise time, I eat dinner generally at one o'clock. Were you there after Archy Beebee was killed? I was, sir. What do you know about the killing of Archy Beebee? Nothing in the world. Where were you at the time the killing occurred? I was under the market house, and saw there was likely to be a disturbance there, and I turned my back and went towards the middle of the market house. Which way were you fronting at the time he was killed? That is a

question I don't think I could answer; the fact is I was excited a good deal, and I turned as I saw there was going to be a disturbance. You were there after the killing? Yes, sir. Did you go to the body of Beebee after his death? I did, sir. In what capacity, if any, did you go? I went there to see the body in the first instance; he just gasped his last breath when I got up there, and the Sheriff remarked to me, "Mr. Blake, you must act as coroner to-day," and called upon two or three magistrates there and took me up stairs and qualified me. Did you act as coroner? Yes, sir. Did you summon a jury? I did, sir. Did that jury find a verdict? It did, sir. I don't ask you what that verdict was; on what day did the jury find a verdict, the day of the killing or the day subsequent? It was the second day, I think, sir, the verdict was signed in the evening, I think; it was the second, probably it may have been the third; I know we were two or three days engaged. Was there any dissent to the verdict? None that I heard, sir, every member, as soon as the verdict was agreed upon—it was late in the afternoon, and there was some gentlemen from the country, Mr. Hendricks and one or two others that were very anxious to go home, and I agreed to wait upon them the next day. Those that were in town signed the verdict that afternoon? All that I could see, sir. And there was no dissent? Not a dissenting voice that I heard of. Were you applied to by any member of the jury for instructions as to their duty?

Counsel for the prosecution:
I object to that, sir.

Counsel for the accused:
State your objections.

Counsel for the prosecution:
I can't see any relevancy at all.

Counsel for the accused:
It would be as well to bring the question up; I supposed of course it would be objected to.

The Court must see that this witness Isham Blake, the coroner on that occasion, had been summoned here mainly for the purpose of proving that Samuel A. Phillips, a member of the jury on that occasion, did not, as he has sworn, apply to Mr. Blake for instructions with regard to his duty on that point. I know that it will be replied by the Counsel for the prosecution, as upon the proposed examination of Thomas A. Hendricks, that this testimony is not admissible, and it is not admissible because it is not regarded to be a collateral fact, and that with regard to the evidence the defence is bound by the answer of Samuel A. Phillips. I know the former ruling of the Court, and I desire to put the matter fairly before the Court in order that they may consider it again, and that upon fuller argument, and fuller and more mature deliberation than they had before, that they may either confirm their former decision or that they may recede from it.

I know the nature of this Court too well, I think, and my experience with regard to this Court for the last six or seven weeks has satisfied me too fully and too thoroughly of their intention to do what is right, and alone what is right, that I trust I shall not be considered as pressing the matter beyond due bounds, because I ask the Court to reconsider one of its decisions.

I desire to state here distinctly before the Court that the object and the only object of this question and the answer thereto, is to discredit the witness Samuel A. Phillips.

It is not to effect the matter at issue at all but to show to the Court that the witness, Samuel A. Phillips, has sworn here deliberately to a fact which is not a fact, and which he knew to be not a fact, at the time he swore to it. Now I am well aware that it has been decided that the rule *Falsum in uno falsum in omnibus* has no application

in criminal cases. I am also aware of the fact that while, when a Court be satisfied that a witness has even sworn falsely and criminally in one fact, they are not at liberty to reject his testimony in another. That is a principle of law, and it is a principle which has its basis in human nature, that a witness who has sworn falsely in one respect about a matter of which he must be cognizant, about a matter concerning which he could not have been mistaken, that if he swears falsely thereto it ought to effect, and it does effect a witness's credibility, and it is for that purpose, not touching the competency—not going to any other extent—not touching the matter at issue directly—but it is for the purpose of effecting the credibility of the witness, Phillips, that this testimony is introduced.

The Court will remember the testimony of that witness.

The Court remembers that he came upon the stand, and at his own instance, and at the suggestion of the counsel for the prosecution, drawn out of him from that side and not from ours, that he gave as a reason for finding that verdict that the deceased came to his death by the hands of an unknown person, that he thought himself, that he was bound by that evidence which reached his hearing from the lips of witnesses and that being uncertain upon that point, he appealed to the coroner and that the coroner confirmed him in that. The Court will remember that he said that he appealed to Blake the coroner to know whether he could act upon any other testimony than that of the testimony, which was delivered from the witnesses from the stand; and that Blake told him he was bound to take the testimony of the witnesses that fell from their lips, and he could not act upon any other matter. Now suppose it shall appear from the testimony of Blake, that Phillips made no such application to him at all; that he has a distinct recollection of what occurred there, and that Phillips never approached him upon this subject; suppose it shall appear that he never told Phillips any such thing; in what attitude does it place the witness Phillips before the Court. It places him necessarily in the attitude of a man who has sworn falsely and who has manufactured reasons for his falsehood and nothing else. Why, sir, all Courts of justice, Military Commissions as well as the Courts of the law set for the investigation of truth, and every thing which tends to throw light upon doubtful testimony; at any rate it is proper for the Court to receive and it is improper for the Court to reject.

Now this doctrine about matters collateral to the issue, and matters tending directly to circumstances, s a nice point. The line as was admitted by the Counsel, is finely drawn and it is a difficult matter to say where the shunshine fades into the shadow, where the one is and the other is. The boundaries are not well defined, but I put it to this Court, upon their heads, upon their consciences and upon their common sense, is this not pertinent to the issue?

Isn't it pertinent to show the character of Samuel A. Phillips and directly upon that question of character, isn't it admissible to show that he has sworn here in a matter which has assigned as a reason for certain actions of his which was false and he must have known to be false?

This is all we have to say about the matter, sir. We offer testimony for the only purpose in the world of discrediting Samuel A. Phillips; we offer it for the purpose of affecting his credit before the Court.

Counsel for the prosecution:
I don't think it necessary, if the Court please, to reply in this matter. I submit it to the Court under the former argument upon the same point,

only suggesting this : that should the Court reverse its former opinion and decide the matter differently, now, there necessarily will be an error in the record, one way or another.

The Court was cleared for deliberation, and after some time so spent, the doors were reopened and the Judge Advocate announced that the Commission sustained the objection of the prosecution, to the witnesses answering the questions propounded by the defence.

Counsel for the defence:

For purposes of record of cause upon the same line, expecting some objections to be made, I will ask the witness another question : Mr. Blake, did Samuel A. Phillips, a member of the coroner's jury, ask you on that day if all the jury was bound to find upon the testimony which was given in by the witnesses upon the stand, or if they were allowed to find upon what they knew of the matter themselves.

Counsel for the prosecution :

We object to that for the same reason.

The Court was cleared for deliberation, and after some time so spent, the doors were reopened and the Judge Advocate announced that the Commission sustained the objection of the prosecution, for the reasons set forth.

Direct examination continued :

Mr. Blake are you acquainted with the general character for truth, of James W. Brown ? I have known him some time. Are you acquainted with his general character for truth ? I believe he is a man of good character. Are you acquainted with the character of James W. Brown, answer the question, yes or no. Well, I believe it is generally good. Mr. Blake, I mean by general character for truth, what is said by those who know him, and those who live around him ? His character is said to be good, sir. When the question I ask you, is, are you acquainted, yes or no, with the general character of James W. Brown, for truth ? Personally, I can't say, I have never had intercourse with the man, only what I have heard. I don't want you to speak of your own knowledge of the man's character, I want you to answer the question, whether you are acquainted or whether you are not acquainted with his general reputation in the community for truth ? That is what others say of him, I think I can answer the question and say, I am. What is that character ? It is good for truth. That is what I asked for; are you acquainted with the general character for truth of Israel C. Bond ? I think I am, sir. What is that character ? Good, sir. Are you acquainted with the general character for truth, of Henry E. Sykes ? I am not, sir.

Cross examination by the Counsel for the prosecution :

Mr. Blake you went to the market house the day that Archy Beebee was killed just after your dinner ? I did sir. You went underneath the market house ? Yes, sir. Which end did you enter at ? The western arch ? Did you take a seat or were you moving about ? Just walking about. Were you inside of the market house when Archy Beebee was carried up stairs ? No, Did you go there after he was carried up ? Yes, sir. Were you in the market house when Miss Massey and Mrs. Massey came down stairs ? I think I was, I think they came down just about the time I got there, I saw some ladies go off, but I didn't put myself to any trouble to find out anything about it, I had heard they were going to be there, and I thought it was them. How long were you there altogether, fifteen or twenty minutes previous to the homicide ? Well I presume sir, it was probably between twenty or thirty minutes. Did you see any body in that crowd during these fifteen or twenty minutes that you recognized? Mr. Leggett, Mr. Nixon, Monk Ju-

lia, I don't think I recollect any person else. Did you see Ralph Lutterloh ? I saw him after. Did you see him before Archy came down ? No, sir. Did you see E. P. Powers there ? Yes, sir. Did you see Sam Hall any where about there ? No, sir. Do you know Henry Sykes, the one armed man ? I know him. Did you see him there ? I did not, sir to my recollection. Did you see Sam Phillips there ? I can't say that I did, sir. Can you tell me where Tolar was and what he was doing when you saw him ? He was standing about the eastern arch conversing with Mr. Leggett when I walked up. Any one else ? I think Mr. Powers was standing on the opposite side. Were they right at the arch or further under the market house ? They were further in the market than under the market near Becky Ben's bench. I ask the question if the prisoner was up stairs all this time ? Yes, sir, I started to go up but was prevented I then immediately came down and walked back in the market house. Do you know about what part of the market house you were when this disturbance first began that caused your anxiety ? Well sir I was in the eastern part of it, not far from the arch. Did you see the prisoner Beebee at all ? I saw him when he was brought down by Mr. Hardie sir. Did you see who was with him ? Mr. Hardie I think was with him and Mr. Wemyss and Mr. Faircloth, I recollect those gentlemen. Did you see Brown there ? I think he was too. Did you see Israel Bond there with him ? Yes, sir, I think he came down either immediately before or after the prisoner. Do you remember when Sheriff Hardie came down ? I think he came down in front as well as I recollect. Do you remember the relative positions of those different men about the prisoner while they were coming down the steps. I think Mr. Wemyss had him by a string around one of his thumbs. Do you remember on which side he was ? No, sir. What was the first appearance of violence that you saw, sir ? The first appearance of violence that I saw, sir, was a pushing of the crowd. Where was Archy at that time ? The Sheriff stopped him just about the time he got down to the foot of the steps. That was the first time you saw any appearance of violence, there was nothing on the step ? No, sir. Was there a rush towards him by the crowd when he got to the foot of the steps? I saw some men pushing forward. Rapidly ? No, sir. Was that what caused your anxiety ? It excited me as soon as I heard this commotion, and I left. You left on account of the commotion ? Yes, sir, I didn't wish to know anything about it. Your apprehensions were excited that something was in the wind ? Yes, sir. Did you leave ? I went into the upper part of the market. Did you see who any of these men were ? No, sir, I didn't know a single man that was there. How many men do you suppose were in the market house according to your best estimate ? I suppose there was a crowd of some fifty to a hundred in the market and around it. Was that a general rush up of the whole crowd, or only a few individuals ? I could not say positively because as soon as I saw the indications, I wanted to get out of there, and I moved my position. Did you hear any noise, any expression from any quarter ? I think I heard some one say "there he comes." Did you hear any one say. "I demand the prisoner" ? I can't say that I did. Have you any impression about that ? Well, sir, impressions are so easily formed in cases of excitement of that kind, I do not think that I would be safe in saying that I heard any expression of that kind. Did that movement of these few men produce that impression on your mind ? It produced this much when these men were coming down, I knew there was so large a crowd gathered there,

there must be something on hand. Were there any signs of excitement in the crowd? I didn't see any, only as I told you when they came down. Did you hear any such expressions after the negro got down to the foot of the stairs, and before he passed out of the arch as "damn him, give him to me"? No, sir. Did you hear Sheriff Hardie say "stand back, gentlemen"? I think when he first came down the steps, he remarked "stand back, gentlemen, he is in my custody and I shall defend him," I think I heard that remark. Was that the only exclamation you heard from that crowd, did you hear any such cries as "shoot him," "shoot him," "kill him," "kill him," "give him up," "pitch in," and so on? If there was any such exclamations as that, it must have been after he was out of the market house. You heard the pistol fired? Yes, sir. Was it a very faint explosion? I didn't think it was a very faint one, it was about as usual. Did you observe what sort of a day that was, whether cold or warm? I didn't take notice. Can you say whether the sun was shining, or it was a cloudy day—perhaps some recollection of your dress will cause you to remember? I can't recollect at present. Do you remember whether there was any wind blowing on that day? No, sir. After the pistol fired which way did you turn? I immediately came back. Which end? Out of the eastern end. You were at the western end? Yes, sir. Did you turn immediately? Yes, sir. Did you see Capt. Tolar when you got down to the eastern end? No, sir, I didn't see Capt. Tolar from the time the prisoner went out that I recollect. Did you see James W. Brown? I don't think I did. Did you see Mr. Cashwell? No, sir. You went to the spot where the negro was? Yes, sir. Was the market empty as you passed through it? No, sir. Were there any persons there beside these women that sell cakes? I can't recollect exactly for I was excited, and I moved out, my object was to see whether the negro was killed or not, and what had happened after I heard the pistol. You remember this, that you saw no one you can speak of, in passing through there, that you can't tell whether any one was in the market house or not? There were people in the market house but I can't tell who they were? Was it the same crowd that was in it when you saw Archy come down? I can't say, sir. Was it as large a crowd? No, sir. Now, Mr. Blake, you passed right through the main aisle of the market house? Yes, sir. Was your passage obstructed at all? No, sir, I don't think the crowd was large enough to obstruct my passage. Do you remember seeing any body in the market house? No one that I recognized. Did you stop in the arch or pass through it? I passed through. Did you notice any body in the crowd that you recognized besides the officers who were about the deceased man? No, sir, I don't recollect now of any particular person. Have you a son who was in that crowd that day? If he was I don't know it, I didn't see him. Have you a son who is grown to manhood? Yes, sir, four of them. Are they all living in Fayetteville? No, sir, Henry, Frederick and Joseph live in Fayetteville. Did you see any of them there that day? I didn't see one of them there. You are not the regular coroner, as I understand you? No, sir. You were appointed for the special occasion? Yes, sir, I have frequently served in that capacity. Who was the coroner? We have no coroner for the county. Was there none at that time? No, sir, I don't think there has been a coroner there for twenty years, no regular coroner. As you passed through that crowd immediately after this shooting did you hear any exclamations of who had done it? I did not, sir. You had to pass through the crowd to get back did you? Yes,

sir. In passing through that crowd did you hear any one enquire who had done it? No, sir. Was the crowd noisy or still? You know what the confusion would generally be in a case of that kind. There are various degrees of confusion on such an occasion as that; my impression is that after the first discharge there would be an immediate stillness for a moment or two, but I want to know whether there was an immediate stillness? Every person in the crowd appeared to be pushing to get to where the boy lay; there was a general push to get to where he was. You heard no conversation? I did not, sir. There was some noise? Yes, sir. Did you hear any conversation at all? No, sir. Did you hear any body ask who had done it? No, sir. Did you ask yourself? No, sir, immediately on going up I was asked by Sheriff Hardie to act as coroner. Didn't you ask him who fired the pistol? I did not that I recollect. A man shot there and you came right back in the crowd and didn't ask who did it? No, sir. Did you know who did it? No, sir, I did not, nor do I know now. And you heard no one ask? No, sir. And you heard no one state who did it? No, sir.

Re-direct examination by the Counsel for the accused:

Mr. Blake, you say that you saw some pushing up of the crowd—was that pushing up of the crowd when Beebee came down stairs greater than the pushing up of the crowd after he was dead? I think it was greater after he was dead. You say you heard nobody say who had killed him? I did not, sir. And that you passed through the crowd? Yes, sir. Passed from the eastern arch down the pavement? I came right out of the eastern arch and off the pavement—the pavement was so full I could not press my way through. How long after the shooting before you went out there? It could not have been more than a minute or two. Almost immediately after the shooting? Yes, sir, I think my face was westward when the pistol fired, and I think I wheeled around as soon as it fired, and came right out. You went around the crowd, where did you enter the crowd, from what point, the southward? No, sir, I entered the crowd from the north part, I just came out of the eastern arch and come down. You went around the crowd, I understand? Not exactly around it, I came through the crowd and I got off of the pavement and just made my way through the crowd. And where did you get on the pavement when you went up to see the body? Right at the corner of the market house, I think, where the deceased was. Did you experience any difficulty in passing through the crowd? When I went up stairs, I had. I am speaking of when you went out of the arch to go up and view the body? Yes, sir, there was some difficulty. And you say all that time you were passing through the crowd you heard no exclamation at all as to who had done the deed? I never heard a word that I recollect of. How long did you remain at the body? I don't think I was there more than a minute or two. When you started up from the body to go up stairs to be qualified as coroner, did you go through the crowd again? I don't think we did. Which way did you go out of it? I think I made my way through on the pavement. Which pavement? The pavement of the market house, just about where the body was laid out. There is a pavement running west, one south, one east, and one north—which one? I think I came towards the north and went up stairs, by this time the crowd was thinning off. During the time you were at the body or between the time that you left and went through the eastern arch of the market and up stairs, did you hear any body say who shot him? I did not, sir, the

whole time I never heard a man say who
had shot the boy at all. Mr. Blake, who summoned the witnesses to go before the coroner's
inquest? I summoned some; and some of the
policemen summoned some of them. Why were
more witnesses not summoned?
Counsel for the prosecution objected on the
ground that it was new matter.
Counsel for the accused.
We will not press the question at all.
Question by the Commission:
I believe you spoke of the character of Israel
Bond did you not? Yes, sir. Do you know
whether he is a member of any religious society,
or not? I do not sir. Is he or is he not a drinking man? I don't think he is, sir. You say you
saw Beebee as he came down stairs, just before
he made his appearance on the stairs, did you
hear any exclamation in the crowd something
like this "rally boys" or "look out boys"
"watch out boys" "here he comes" or any
thing to that effect? I did not. Did you hear
any such expression after he appeared on the
steps? I did not, sir. Did you hear any such
expression at any time? I did not sir.
The Counsel for the accused said there were no
more witnesses here to be examined, but one
witness had been sent from Fayetteville and he
supposed he would be here to-morrow.
The Judge Advocate said:
There seems to be a disposition upon the part
of witnesses to come when it best suits their convenience, without any reference to the summons
of the Court, and I suggest that some summary
means be taken to inform the witnesses in this
case and in the cases that shall come hereafter,
that the summons of this Court is not to be
lightly disregarded.
The Counsel for the accused:
In order that the Commission may understand
the matter, I think there is some fault in the
quartermaster's department. Mr. Blake informs
me he started here on Tuesday, that he went up
to get his transportation and the quartermaster
informed him that he could not give him transportation by the direct line but he would give
him transportation by the way of Wilmington,
and owing to a change of time in the schedule he
was delayed. Now it is altogether probable that
the other witnesses that have been summoned
have been started off in the same way and have
been delayed. I think that it is certainly not the
fault of the witnesses.
The Judge Advocate said:
There have been a great many cases in which the
fault has been entirely that of the witness and it
is only to such cases that I refer.
There being no more witnesses to examine, on
motion the Commission adjourned to meet on
Saturday, Sept. 7th, 1867, at 11 o'clock, A. M.

RALEIGH, N. C., Sept. 7th, 1867, 11 A. M.
The Commission met pursuant to adjournment.
Present, all the members of the Commission,
the Judge Advocate, the Counsel for the prosecution, all the accused, and their Counsel.
The reading of the testimony taken yesterday,
was waived—there being no objection thereto.
Yesterday's proceedings were then read and approved.
The Judge Advocate:
The witness referred to by the Counsel for the
defence, yesterday has not arrived. The Counsel
for the defence stated to me that he has received
a letter from his associate in Fayetteville, inform-
ing him that the witness is sick, and if I recollect
right he stated he could not come before Saturday
Now this is Saturday and the question is, what
Saturday is meant? In reply the Counsel for the
accused read the letter referred to, which stated

that the witness would leave Fayetteville on Sat-
urday morning.
The Judge Advocate:
I would like to know from the gentlemen if
this is their last witness.
Counsel for the accused:
We do intend to close the case for the defence
with the examination of these witnesses.
Judge Advocate:
Which witnesses?
Counsel for the accused:
Ahern and Owen Moore, such has been and
such is the intention of the Counsel for the defence.
Judge Advocate:
As the gentlemen have not yet been able to as-
certain or give us the precise residence of Owen
Moore and as every effort has been made by the
Judge Advocate to procure his attendance, I
shall object to any delay, waiting the arrival of
Owen Moore, after Monday. I wish to make this
statement now so that the Counsel on the other
side may definitely understand it.
Counsel for accused:
We are in hopes we shall be able to close for
the defence on Monday. We had hoped to close
to-day. These delays by non attendence of witnes-
ses are as hateful to us as they can be to the Court
or the Judge Advocate. I would ask when will the
case for the prosecution be closed?
Judge Advocate:
On Monday. We shall endeavor to close on the
same day that you do.
Counsel for the prosecution:
You don't, I suppose, expect to wait indefinite-
ly for Mr. Owen Moore?
Counsel for accused:
We do not, sir, expect to wait indefinitely for him.
Counsel for the prosecution:
If he is not here on Monday, we shall have to
insist on a close.
Counsel for accused:
I so understand it, sir.
There being no witnesses in attendance, on mo-
tion the Commission adjourned to meet on Mon-
day the 9th instant at 11 o'clock, A. M.

RALEIGH, N. C., Sept. 9, 1867, 11 A. M.
The Commission met pursuant to adjournment.
Present: All the members of the Commission,
the Judge Advocate, the Counsel for the prosecu-
tion, all the accused, and their Counsel.
Yesterday's proceedings were read and approved.
The Counsel for the accused said the witness
Ahern had not yet arrived.
The Judge Advocate:
I will state to the Commission that other witnesses summoned a week later than this one
Ahern have arrived in town. Witnesses starting
from Fayetteville on Saturday, arrived here yesterday (Sunday.) I move that the case for the
defence be closed without waiting the arrival of
the witness.
The Counsel for the accused:
All we have to say to it, sir, is that we are pretty well satisfied that the witness, Owen Moore,
has not been reached by a summons at all. The
testimony of witness Ahern is material, and we
regard it as very important. The prisoners are
not willing to have their case closed until his testimony is given in. I can give you no reason for
his absence unless it is that he is sick. Mr. Mc-
Rae wrote me on Saturday that Ahern was then
sick, and his sickness may be continued, and
that may be the cause of his absence. That is
the only suggestion we can make why he is not
here in obedience to the summons.
If the Court rules to close the case we have to
submit to it, but we regard the testimony of
Ahern as important—highly important. I would

like very much indeed to get it before the Court before we close.

The Judge Advocate:
On the part of the prosecution I will say that I am as anxious as the Counsel for the accused is that the testimony of the witness Ahern should be given in, but I am not willing that the time of this Court should be taken up in waiting from day to day for one witness, whose residence the Counsel have not been able to ascertain, and who is as easily reached perhaps as the man in the moon and for another witness who refuses to come—summoned by themselves, to prove something as they claim to be material to their case.

The Commission was then cleared for deliberation, and after some time so spent, the doors were reopened and the Judge Advocate said: The Commission does not sustain the motion of the Judge Advocate to close the defence. The Commission orders that the witness, Ahern, be immediately arrested and brought to Raleigh.

The Counsel for the accused said if the witness Ahern did not come to-morrow, they would be willing to close without him.

On motion the Commission adjourned to meet on Tuesday, Sept. 10th, at 11 o'clock, A. M.

RALEIGH, N. C., Sept. 10th, 11 A. M.
The Commission met pursuant to adjournment. Present: All the members of the Commission, the Judge Advocate, the Counsel for the prosecution, all the accused and their Counsel. The proceedings of yesterday were read and approved.

The Judge Advocate said:
The witness, Ahern, has not arrived, and I suppose will not arrive until he is brought here under arrest in accordance with the orders of the Commission issued yesterday.

The Counsel for the accused:
I will say to the Commission with regard to the witness, Ahern, that what we say we will stand up to. We announced to the Court yesterday that if the witness Ahern didn't come to-day, we would close without him, and if it be the Court's pleasure that we should do so, we are willing to make good our promise. I will lay before the Court what I have received this morning; I think that in justice to the witness, Ahern, it should be done. The Counsel then read a document of which the following is a copy:

FAYETTEVILLE, Sept. 6, 1867.
I hereby certify, on honor, that Mr. James Ahern has been under my treatment for more than a week, for rheumatism, and at present he is unable to bear the fatigue of a trip to Raleigh. It is probable that he can go up the first of next week.
(Signed)   W. C. McDUFFIE, M. D.

The Judge Advocate:
As the order has been issued for the production of this witness Ahern, before closing the Court, it would be as well probably to hear his testimony before closing. The Counsel stated yesterday that the witness was in his opinion necessary and material to his case, and if the Counsel for the accused does not wish to close without having his testimony, perhaps it would be as well to give them the benefit of it.

The Counsel for the accused:
We merely state to-day, sir, what we stated yesterday: if the Court wish, we are willing to stand by that.

The Court was then cleared for deliberation, and after sometime so spent, the doors were reopened, and the Judge Advocate announced that the Commission desired to be informed whether the Counsel for the accused wished to have the testimony of the witness, James Ahern. This without any reference to anything that has been said heretofore.

Counsel for accused:
I will state very frankly, that I have never seen this witness, but I have from Mr. McRae a letter in which he gives me at some length the testimony of Ahern. From this letter it appears that I can get along without it very well as main testimony, that Ahern will state no new points, but that his testimony will be corroborative of certain other witnesses upon certain material points. I don't know, sir, but what we may agree upon the testimony of Ahern.

The Judge Advocate:
Oh! no, we can't do that.

The Counsel for the accused:
Well, sir, it must be now apparent to the Court, that we are ourselves as anxious to close the case as any one can be.

The Judge Advocate:
Well, it is for the Counsel to decide. They can move either for a close or a continuance. It is entirely in the option of the Counsel for the defence.

The Counsel for accused:
We will just consider the matter for a minute. The Counsel for the accused then withdrew for a few minutes to consult upon the question and upon their return to the Court room announced that they were willing to close the case without the testimony of the man Ahern.

The Judge Advocate, I will now request the permission of the Commission to introduce the bullet heretofore spoken of in the evidence in this case, and to have it identified and weighed in the presence of the Court. If the Court has no objection this will now be done.

The Commission, we have no objection.

The Judge Advocate then suggested a recess of fifteen minutes as the witnesses were not yet in attendance.

The Commission then took a recess of a quarter of an hour, at the expiration of which time they proceeded to business.

CHARLES P. YOUNG, a witness for the prosecution having been first duly sworn testified as follows:
Examined by the Counsel for the prosecution.
Have you a package that was delivered to you by the Judge Advocate? Yes, sir. Will you produce it if you please?
(Witness produces the package.)
Who sealed that package? I did. Under whose direction? General Avery's. What is inclosed in it? A bullet. Has the bullet any inclosure about it? It was in a box within a broken envelope. Who broke the seal of the broken envelope. I broke the envelope. You tore off the edge of the envelope and opened it, and took out the bullet? Yes, sir. Is that the same bullet that you returned in there? Yes, sir. Just open the package if you please.
(Witness does so.)
That is the package that you enclosed when you sealed it up? Yes, sir.

FRANCIS KENSTLER, a witness for the prosecution having been first duly sworn testified as follows:
Examined by the Counsel for the prosecution.
Did you ever see that package before? Yes, sir. Was it sealed in your presence? Yes, sir. Do you recognize the impression of the seal? Yes, sir. Did you keep the seal? Yes, sir. What did you put in that package when you sealed it? A bullet was put in it. Just take that bullet out if you please?
(Witness does so.)
Where did that bullet come from originally? It come from the head of a man supposed to have been shot, by the name of Archy Beebee. That is the bullet that you brought from Fayetteville? Yes, sir. You saw it taken taken out of the head of Archy Beebee? Yes, sir. You have no doubt about its being the same bullet? No doubt at

all. The bullet that came out of Archy Bee-bee's head, was the one you sealed up in the package? Yes, sir. Did you put any mark on it? I did not, sir.

Cross examination by Counsel for the accused.

You say you saw that seal put upon the package? Yes, sir. And the seal you kept in your possession? Yes, sir. Where is the seal now? (Witness produces the seal.)

The Judge Advocate:

Has that seal ever left your possession from the time it was first given in your possession until now? No, sir.

WM. F. SMITH, a witness for the prosecution, having been first duly sworn, testified as follows:

Examined by the Counsel for the prosecution:

What is your name? William F. Smith. What is your occupation? Assistant Surgeon in the United States Army. Are you familiar with gun shot wounds? Yes, sir. Can you give any opinion as to whether a conical ball or round ball shot from a pistol of the same calibre, under the same circumstances identical, as to which one of these would make the larger wound in passing through the skull? In that case the conical ball would make a larger aperture. Would the aperture be regular or irregular in its form? Generally speaking a conical ball would make an irregular aperture. And make a larger one than a round ball from a pistol of the same calibre under the same circumstances identical? Yes, sir. But suppose you vary from these circumstances; that is diminish the load; increase the load; increase the distance, could you give any opinion in that case? There could be given no positive opinion in that case. The opinion is a very general one? Yes, sir. And subject to an imminence number of exceptions? Yes, sir. Supposing a bullet to have passed through the skull and entered the brain of a man to have killed him and to have remained in the brain for four or six months, is there a chemical substance in the brain that would act upon the bullet? Yes, sir, more than one. What are they? The principle ingredient would be sulphur which in the process of decomposition would give rise to sulphuretted hydrogen and would act on the bullet, also the phosphorous in the brain would give rise to phosphoretted hydrogen which would act in a very similar way. In acting upon the bullet would it diminish its weight? Yes, sir, it would be diffused through the whole brain after a time. Suppose the length of time were from February to July, in that length of time would it be diminished in weight perceptibly? Yes, sir. A portion of the substance of the bullet would be lost? Yes, sir. And the bullet would weigh less the instant when it was removed from the brain after that length of time than it would at the time it entered the brain? Yes, sir. Are you skillful in the use of the ordinary scales used in measuring medicine? Yes, sir. Will you weigh this bullet before the Court and pronounce what the weight is? I will do so.

Witness pronounces the weight of the bullet to be between 172 and 173 grains, nearer 172 grains, according to the scales used in the Court.

Cross examination by the Counsel for the accused:

Doctor Smith, in looking at that ball which has been shown you, and from what you have stated to be the action of chemical substances in the brain and head, could you give an opinion as to the probable diminution, upon a mass of lead of that size, lodged in the brain, say from the month of February to the month of July? I could not give you any thing but a mere opinion which would be only approximate in its results. If you have an opinion on the subject give it? I should judge that the bullet would lose in weight from five to ten grains, in that time, I judge that from the amount of sulphur and other decomposing influences in the brain. Would the effect of these chemical agencies cease as soon as the bullet was removed from the brain, or would it continue on? It would cease at once. As soon as the bullet was removed from the brain? Yes, sir. So it would not loose any of its weight after the time of its being extracted from the brain? No, sir. If there be thirty-three bullets to the pound avoirdupois weight, what would one of them weigh in grains, apothecary's weight, you can take your pencil, if you please, and figure it out?

The Counsel for the prosecution said he thought the Court could make its own calculations.

The Counsel for the accused said he only asked the Doctor in order that it might go down in the records in legal form. The calculations are made at two hundred and twelve grains and four thirty-thirds of a grain of thirty-three bullets to the pound, and one hundred and fifty-five and five-sixths grains of forty-eight balls to the pound.

Cross-examination resumed:

I believe you said you were familiar with gun shot wounds? Yes, sir. Could you state whether a bullet fired against the skull and penetrating the skull, would have lost any of its weight by friction in passing into the skull from the outer to the inner surface? Yes, sir, but the amount would be very small indeed. About what per centage could you say? I could not say, just enough to leave a mark and nothing more. It would leave a mark of lead upon the orifice? Yes, sir, and even this would only occur when it makes an almost perfectly clean cut. Supposing a bullet fired against the skull making almost a perfectly clean cut—then could you say what would be about the per centage of loss in weight of the bullet? No, sir, I could not say. But there is always some loss when it makes a clean cut? I could not say always, for I never made the subject one of special study, but I have frequently noticed slight marks of lead on gunshot wounds, not only in the skull but in other bones? The amount would be something like a mark of a lead pencil very trifling indeed. You could not undertake to say in a bullet of this size, how much in grains, or what per centage of any size? I could not. Suppose after the bullet has passed through one side of the skull, it should strike against the opposite wall of the skull, would there be any loss by that striking? It is possible there might be. Would the chemical substances in the brain act more rapidly upon a mass of lead round and smooth, or upon a mass of lead jagged and irregular as this which is here? It would act more rapidly on the irregular mass for the reason that the irregular ball would expose a greater surface? Then when you speak of the probable loss which would be produced by the action of those chemical substances that you speak of, did you speak with reference to a round bullet with a smooth surface, or with reference to a mass of lead, such as you have weighed in the scales to-day? The mass that I had in my mind was the one I had in my hand, and I only wish my answer to be taken in a very general way.

Re-direct examination by the Counsel for the accused.

You are accustomed to the use of these scales? Yes, sir. There are a good many of them which I suppose? Yes, sir. Are they ever made so imperfectly as to make a difference of ten, fifteen or twenty grains in weight? I have never seen any so imperfect as that, the very poorest kind ought not to make a difference of more than two grains. Is there a possibility of making an error of fifteen or twenty grains with any scales, in ordinary use by apothecaries? I never saw any such a difference, the scales would be useless where the error would be so great as that.

The Judge Advocate:—I propose to offer, in evidence, the Counsel for the accused not objecting, a circular issued by the "Colt's patent fire arm's manufacturing Company," setting forth the styles, sizes, calibers, weights of bullets, number of bullets to the pound, of the pistols and rifles, manufactured by them.

Also a circular issued by "Remington & Sons" manufacturers of fire arms, setting forth their styles of pistols, calibers, weights of bullets and number of bullets to the pound; to assist the Court, to a conclusion, in reference to the weights of different bullets.

The Government hereby closes the case for the prosecution.

The Counsel for the accused announced that they would be prepared to commence the argument to-morrow, whereupon on motion the Commission adjourned to meet on Wednesday September, 11th, at 10 o'clock A. M.

RALEIGH, N. C., Sept. 11th, 1867, 10 A. M.

The Commission met pursuant to adjournment. Present : all the members of the Commission, the Judge Advocate Counsel for the prosecution, all the accused and their Counsel.

The reading of the testimony taken yesterday, was waived, there being no objection thereto.

Yesterday's proceedings were then read and approved.

The Judge Advocated then addressed the Court as follows :

May it please the Court:—The murder here charged and specified, and the acts alleged to have been committed in pursuance thereof and with the intent laid, constitute a crime of the highest magnitude, whether the prisoners at the bar are guilty of this murder and the acts alleged to have been done, in pursuance thereof, is a question, the determination of which rests solely with this Court, and in passing upon which this Court are the sole judges of the law and the fact.

It is a matter of great moment to the people of the whole country, as well as to the people of this community and State, that the prisoners at your bar be lawfully tried and lawfully convicted or acquitted; the interests involved in the dread issue here joined, are, in my opinion, of the highest character, not only to the accused, but to the whole people.

The crime charged and specified upon your record, and proven by the testimony you have so patiently listened to for nearly two months, is not simply the crime of murdering a human being; but it is the crime of killing and murdering Archibald Beebee on the eleventh day of February, eighteen hundred and sixty-seven, while in the custody of the law officers of the county in which he was and had been for sometime living. It is murder aggravated by the fact that at that time Archibald Beebee was in the custody and under the protection of the law and its sworn officers. How inadequate that protection proved against the violence of the lawless men, then and there assembled and combined, defying the law and its officers, and determined upon compassing the death

of the young man Beebee—the evidence has already clearly disclosed.

I will not dwell on the shameless indifference to the commission of great crimes in their immediate presence, exhibited by more than a dozen of these same sworn officers of the law, or the shamelessness, with which they have testified before this honorable Court to their own turpitude.

To the charge and specification the defendants have pleaded, first : that this Court has no jurisdiction in the premises; and second, not guilty. As the Commission has already overruled the plea to the jurisdiction, I shall pass it by with but brief comment.

The civil courts, say the Counsel, are open in the County of Cumberland, where this crime was committed, and have jurisdiction in this case, which this Court has not. To this I answer that if the civil courts are open, it is but in form, that substantial justice cannot and could not have been obtained in the County of Cumberland, or any other county in this State, in this case. So strong is the feeling and prejudice in reference to this case in that County that many of the witnesses who have testified in this case, returned to their homes fearing that their lives are not safe from the vengeance of these conspirators, so completely unmasked by this voluminous testimony given before this honorable Court. Nor is this fear unnatural. No one who has followed the history of this case from the day on which this murder was committed and warning given that whoever dared to tell, should fare the same fate—should be murdered even as the man Beebee was murdered—who has seen a felony like this committed in the midst of a crowd of at least one hundred and fifty men, in the centre of a populous and busy town, and that for months no white man could be found who knew anything about it—it is not surprising, I say, that this fear should be felt by those who had given testimony in this case. The learned Counsel, who have so ably defended the prisoners at your bar, have not attempted to question or deny that this is a legally constituted Court—they content themselves with denying its jurisdiction in this particular case. A brief glance at the act of Congress entitled " an act to provide for the more efficient government of the rebel States," (passed over the President's veto March 2nd, 1867,) will speedily satisfy the gentlemen that their plea is baseless; that this Court, the members of which are officers of the army of the United States, and by the lawful order of the General commanding this Military District, are required to perform this duty, and that the General commanding lawfully made the order creating this Court, and authorized it as such Court to decide all questions of law and fact arising in the trial of this case, or any other he may see proper to send before it. I will read the preamble and first four sections of this bill:

"An Act to provide for the more efficient government of the rebel States, (passed over the President's veto, March 2d, 1867:)

WHEREAS, no legal State governments or adequate protection for life or property now exists in the rebel States of Virginia, North-Carolina, South-Carolina, Georgia, Alabama, Louisiana, Florida, Texas, Mississippi and Arkansas, and whereas,It is necessary that peace and good order should be enforced in said States until loyal and republican State governments can be legally established; therefore,

Be it enacted by the Senate and House of Representatives of the United States of America in Congress assembled, That said rebel States shall be divided into military districts, and made subject to the military authority of the United States, as hereinafter prescribed, and for that purpose Virginia shall constitute the first district; North-Carolina and South-Carolina the second district; Georgia, Alabama and Florida the third district; Mississippi and Arkansas the fourth district, and Louisiana and Texas the fifth district.

SEC. 2. *And be it further enacted*, That it shall be the duty of the President to assign to the command of each of said districts an officer of the army not below the rank of brigadier general, and to detail a sufficient military force to enable such officer to perform his duties and enforce his authority within the district to which he is assigned.

SEC. 3. *And be it further enacted*, That it shall be the duty of each officer assigned as aforesaid to protect all persons in their rights of person and property, to suppress insurrection, disorder, and violence, and to punish or cause to be punished all disturbers of the public peace and criminals; and to this end he may allow local civil tribunals to take jurisdiction of and try offenders, or when in his judgment it may be necessary for the trial of offenders, he shall have power to organize military commissions or tribunals for that purpose; and all interference under color of State authority with the exercise of military authority under this act shall be null and void.

SEC. 4. *And be it further enacted*, That all persons put under military arrest by virtue of this act shall be tried without unnecessary delay; and no cruel or unusual punishment shall be inflicted; and no sentence of any military commission or tribunal hereby authorized, affecting the life or liberty of any person, shall be executed until it is approved by the officer in command of the|district; and the laws and regulations for the government of the army shall not be affected by this act, except in so far as they may conflict with its provisions; *Provided*, That no sentence of death under the provisions of this act shall be carried into effect without the approval of the President."

But it is needless to discuss a question already ruled upon by the Court, and one upon which there can be so little doubt as to the justice and legality of your decisions.

I will briefly state what we conceive to be the question of law, and of fact upon which your verdict in this case, is to be made.

The questions of law, are two; First: What is the grade of this homicide, with reference to the person who discharged the pistol, the bullet from which pistol killed Archibald Beebee; was the shooting manslaughter or murder?

We contend that it was *murder*. Second: What with reference to the defendants, Powers and Watkins?—first, supposing them to have been co-conspirators with the person who actually discharged the pistol. Second: In the event that no conspiracy or combination is actually established; in either case we contend that their crime was murder.

To the first of these questions there can be but one answer, the crime is clearly that of murder, and I think that the same answer will be given to the second question; for if the combination be established it results that whatever was said or done by either of the parties thereto in the furtherance or execution of the common design, is the declaration or act of all the parties thereto; but even admitting the proof of combination defective, it will appear clearly to the minds of this honorable Court, that the fact that Powers and Watkins were engaged in and attempting to perform an unlawful act, even though they may not have contemplated (as we think the evidence has shown they did contemplate) the commission of this particular felony, yet if another comes into their assistance, and commits the felony, they are all alike guilty of the murder.

The questions of facts involved in this issue are first, did the accused, or any two of them conspire, confederate, or combine together in the commission of the murder as charged? Second—did the defendant Tolar, discharge the pistol which slew Archy Beebee? Third—did the accused or any of them in pursuance of such combination, or conspiracy, and with the intent alleged, commit either or all of the acts charged? Fourth—Did the defendants Watkins and Powers attack Archibald Beebee with the intent to kill him, or to do him serious bodily harm,—and did the defendant Tolar, without previous concert, come into their assistance and effect what they were contemplating, and attempting to do?

To the first question, I think there can be but one answer, for never was a conspiracy or combination more clearly proven, than in this case; nor is it possible to prove a conspiracy more clearly, unless one of the conspirators gives evidence against his fellow conspirators.

The second question is answered by the unqualified and direct testimony of witnesses, corroborated by nearly the same number, who although they did not see the defendant Tolar, in the very act of discharging the pistol, which killed Archy Beebee, did see acts which tend to show that the pistol was discharged by Wm. J. Tolar, and no one else.

The third and fourth questions, like the first and second, are answered in the affirmative by the evidence; and that so clearly as to leave no room for question or doubt.

ARGUMENT

OF

ED. GRAHAM HAYWOOD,

SPECIAL JUDGE ADVOCATE,

IN REPLY TO

The several arguments in defence of William J. Tolar, David Watkins and Thomas Powers, charged with the murder of Archibald Beebee, at Fayetteville, North-Carolina.

———◆———

MAY IT PLEASE THE COURT: As this most interesting and important cause has already occupied so much time—and as the patience of this Court, so courteously, and so laudably manifested, at every stage of this trial, must now be nearly exhausted,—I shall endeavor, in discharging the duty incumbent upon me, to consume as little more time as may be consistent with a clear exposition of the principles of law, necessary to be understood, in order that the Court may arrive at a just and legal decision.

The evidence in the case, however conflicting in its character, has been minutely and distinctly stated by the witnesses, and has been presented with a fullness of detail, and in accumulated masses, such as are not often to be obtained in the conduct of criminal prosecution; while the ingenious and able comments of the Counsel for the defence, upon the facts, and their eloquent and elaborate discussion, and illustration of legal principles involved—as seen from their point of view—give to me and to this Court the full and comforting assurance that the law is not likely to be administered with undue severity in reference to these defendants.

Of the many honorable duties which are assigned to the members of the legal profession, there are few higher and holier trusts, than that, committed to my brethren, who are engaged in this defence; with the lives, the liberties and the reputations of their clients committed into their hands—they stand for, lo! these many days, struggling in their behalf—battling with sleepless vigilance for their lives—bound alike in honor and by inclination to abate not one jot or tittle, of heart or hope till Death's pale flag flaunts on the ramparts. This Court I am sure cannot but admire the efforts of intellect and eloquence which have been made by the Counsel for the prisoners. In going—as they have gone—to the very verge of their professional rights—in endeavoring to fix the crime alleged in the charge and specification upon another citizen, who is comparatively innocent, they have, perhaps kept within the strict line of their professional duty, from which they were under no obligation to depart; but this Court will judge whether we will be equally within the line of our own duty, in sanctioning the charge of murder, which they have attempted to establish against the witness Phillips, and in sustaining their appeals in this behalf, which have been urged upon us, with all the exertions of strong minds forced into vigorous action by warm hearts

In them to make the attempt naturally grows out of their professional situation, but your position as a Court, and my position as representing the government in this prosecution, are wholly different.

We are now arriving at the conclusion of the first of a series of causes, which, from the novelty of the tribunal before which they are conducted, from the importance of their principles, from the interest felt, by at least, a portion of the community, in their results, and from the immense stake which the defendants have depending upon their decision, are almost without a precedent in the juridical history of this State.

In the very nature of things it was not to be expected but that such an investigation—involving in it so much of personal interest and of sectional prejudice—of political sentiments, and even of social feeling—should exhibit the vehement excitement, so painfully manifested by many of the witnesses throughout its progress. In none of these feelings do I myself—in none of these feelings I am sure does this court participate. Our duties are higher and holier. We are the chosen ministers of a great and powerful government, called upon to decide between that government and certain of her subjects, who are said to have forfeited their lives by a violation of the law. Our trust equally demands that the public law should be vindicated to the full extent that it has been infracted, and that no particle of the rights of the accused, guarantied by existing laws, should be compromised in order to accomplish that end. Our duty is to punish offenders, not to immolate victims; but it is also our duty to execute the public law, and not to search after excuses for its violation.

The task before us is one requiring no common effort; but cool heads and honest hearts have often achieved results much more difficult to be attained, and at the same time, these constituents of impartial justice are here this day imperatively demanded. Our chief difficulty arises from this, that we have here had given to us in evidence, versions of the unhappy events culminating in this homicide, coming from sources apparently equally trustworthy, seemingly irreconcilable with one another.

But before entering more fully into the consideration of the merits of this cause, the court, I am sure, will pardon me for a moment, under all the peculiar circumstances in which I am placed, while I speak of myself and of my connection with this prosecution; that I may say, once for all, that in the performance of the professional duty imposed upon me by my position here, the popular smile has for me no allurements, and the popular frown has no terrors. The breath of the people at the best is but air, and that not often wholesome. For what I have done in the prosecution of this cause—for what I shall do in its progress—I make no apologies; I have no apologies to make. I invoke no sympathy; I thank God I need it not; but I stand here to-day with the profound and proud conviction, that as a faithful, honest, and honorable member of the great profession to which I belong, and in the best interest, as I am well satisfied, of the common weal, I am daring to do what I believe to be my duty, amid trials and temptations, which, to say the least of it, are unusual in such cases, and which, I trust in God, for the sake of the public justice and virtue of the country, are not to become common; and I am willing to leave it to time and my manner of life to consign to oblivion the carpings of the envious and the calumnies of the malignant.

I am doing my professional part to administer the LAW, under the *only* government which *now* has the *power* to enforce any law, and to preserve any order in North Carolina.

The worst possible government is better than anarchy, and in times of such infinite difficulty that must be the best government, however little desirable in itself, which will most speedily restore peace and tranquility to the land, and stop the wounds, which contending parties are daily inflicting upon each other. Some one must be invested with power to enforce the law and preserve general order, and come what will in the future, peace and order and the restoration of law ought to be our first and most pressing objects. " *Interest rei publicae ut sit finis litium.*"

It may be easy to misrepresent these views; to call them abject; to say that they are prompted, if not by sordid hopes, at least by slavish minds: but in the performance of the duty with which I am charged in this case, I deem myself any thing but slavish to the prevailing temper of the day, and cannot perceive that I am subjecting myself to any just reproach ; our people ought to remember that the most uncompromising assertors of the duty of submission to the will of God, by yielding ready and cheerful obedience to the powers that be which are ordained of Him, have often proved, no less, the sturdiest champions of the rights of the people. There are some who know and feel, how just a pride, how true a glory—may spring from the very meekness of legitimate obedience.

And as for those, without this Court, who have been so good, as to criticise my conduct, because I do my professional part, to see to it, that felons shall not go " unwhipt of justice," and that criminals shall not escape the just terror of the law: and who—judging me by a standard of virtue, which scared consciences, and vicious practices have erected in their own bosoms— have assigned to me base and sordid, and unworthy motives for what I do ; *they* are entitled to my compassion and my contempt, and most richly are they rewarded with them both.

And now, I return to what I have said before, that we have comparatively few and easy legal problems to encounter, in coming to a finding in this case—and our chief difficulty arises from the fact, that we have had given to us, in evidence, versions of the unhappy events which culminated in this homicide, coming from sources, apparently equally trustworthy, seemingly irreconcilable with one another.

To those familiar with judicial investigations, there is no novelty, in the seeming inconsistency, and the apparently conflicting character of much of the evidence which has been adduced. We are perpetually observing, that witnesses, seemingly equally honest, describing transactions occurring in large tumultuous and highly excited assemblies, are in some of their statements, respecting even prominent facts, in direct collision. These discrepancies may arise from various causes, and do not necessarily, nor even probably, imply wilfull and corrupt perjury upon the part of any one. One man, from his immediate contiguity to the scene of the occurrences he describes, and from his attention being particularly directed to them—from his nervous organization being sound and cool in the midst of danger and excitement, and from the natural superiority of his perceptive faculties—from his imagination being healthy, and his having no particular personal interests, sympathy, or prejudice, in the subject matter of the investigation—may truly detail actual events of instantaneous occurrence, which another of equal integrity and, seemingly with the same means of knowledge, but, in reality less favorable circumstanced, declares he has not noticed, and which he may, even honestly, deny to have existed. The jurist familiar with the nature, and course of these disturbing influences, makes a just allowance for them ; and endeavors to reconcile such conflicting statements. *The law requires,* that those engaged in investigating facts, should reconcile *all* the apparently conflicting testimony, if it be reasonably possible, so to do, before imputing wilfull and corrupt perjury to any one, as an easier mode of solving the problem. Accordingly in cases of conflicting evidence, the *first* step in the progress of inquiry must naturally, and obviously be—to ascertain whether the *apparent* inconsistencies and incongruities which such evidence presents are *real*—whether the evidence cannot, without violence or constraint, *all* be reconciled. And in applying this principle, two well settled rules are to be observed.

First. It is to be noted that a great deal of the apparent discrepancy, observable in testimony, arises from omission ; from a fact or circumstance—which is indeed noticed at the time of its occurrence or existence by several witnesses,—being narrated in evidence only by one, or a few witnesses ; while some other fact or circumstance, omitted by the witness, or witnesses who stated the first fact or circumstance, is narrated in evidence by the deponents who omit the *first.* Now, *omission in reality creates* no *discrepancy,* and is, at all times, a very uncertain ground of objection to the veracity of a witness. We perceive it not only in the comparison of the evidence of different witnesses, but often even in the same witness, when compared with himself. There are a great many particulars, and some of them of importance, which an honest witness may set forth on one occasion of giving his testimony, and leave out entirely on a second occasion. It is never safe to conclude that evidence is hopelessly inconsistent and irreconcilable, because some witnesses have merely *failed* to state facts and circumstances, deposed to by others ; but such facts and circumstances—*cæteris paribus*—must be accepted as proved.

There is a marked illustration of this principle, to be gathered from a comparison of the several accounts of the different appearances of our Lord and Saviour, to his disciples, after his resurrection, contained in the New Testament, as narrated in Matthew, chap. xxvii, verses 16 to 20 inclusive—Mark, chap. xvi, verses 12 to 14 inclusive—Luke, chap. xxiv, verses 13 and 36—John, chap. xx, verses 19 to 29 inclusive, and chap. xxi, verse 1.

Thus, St. Matthew says, that while the eleven disciples were on a mountain in Galilee, where Jesus had appointed them, he appeared unto them ; and this is the only appearance of our Saviour, after his resurrection, which St. Matthew records. St. Mark speaks of our Saviour as having appeared unto two of them as they walked and went into the country, and of a second appearance unto the eleven, as they sat at meat, which last, is evidently not the same appearance mentioned by St. Matthew, as having occurred upon Mount Tabor, in Galilee. St. Luke also speaks in verse 13, chapter xxiv, of his appearance to two of the disciples on the day of his resurrection, as they were walking to the village called *Emmaus,* which was from Jerusalem, about three score furlongs ; he also states, in verse 33, that those two disciples rose up the same hour and returned to Jerusalem, and "found the eleven gathered together and them that were with them," and while they were narrating what had occurred "Jesus himself stood in the midst of them." St. John, at verse 19 of chap. xx, says : " Then the same day (the day of the resurrection) at evening, being the first day of the week, when the doors were shut where the disciples were assembled, for fear of the Jews, came Jesus and stood in the midst ;" and again at verse 26, the same narrator states that "after eight days again his disciples were within and Thomas with them, then came Jesus—the doors being shut—and stood in the midst." And in the first verse of chap. xxi, of this gospel, it is stated that "after these things Jesus showed himself again to the disciples of the sea of Tiberias." .

Now, here, if the Court please, are four honest men under the inspiration of the Holy Spirit—partially—at least—who severally undertake to narrate the evidence, to establish perhaps, the most important event, (the resurrection of Christ,) in the history of the most important man—who was at once man and God—who ever lived upon the face of the earth. The *fact* of His resurrection was the seal of His Commission—it was the crowning miracle of His life—it was the test of His divinity, for which the blaspheming Jews had asked, as He hung upon the Cross—when they bade Him come down from the Cross, and they would believe that He was the Son of God. And yet, if the Court will take the trouble to investigate the matters contained in the chapters to which I have called their attention—comparing the gospels of St. Matthew, St. Mark, St. Luke and St. John—they will find, that all the Evangelists give different accounts of the appearances of our Saviour after his resurrection, which accounts it is almost impossible to reconcile with one another; and this apparent variance can be accounted for, only upon the supposition of important omissions by one Evangelist or another.

The next rule under this sub-division is, that there is an important distinction between *positive* and *negative* testimony, and in cases where one is used for the purpose of repelling the other—unless the contrary manifestly appears—the presumption, in favor of human veracity shall operate to support the *affirmative* testimony. (1 Starkie on evidence p. 517.)

The application of this rule supposes that the positive may be reconciled with the negative without violence or constraint, and that the negative may be accounted for on the ground of either inattention, inadvertence, error, mistake, or defect of memory, in the person rendering it. If, for instance, two persons should remain in the same room for the same period of time, and one of them should swear, that during that time he heard a clock in the room strike the hour, and the other should swear, *he* did *not* hear the clock strike, it is very possible that the *fact* may be *true*, and yet each witness may *swear truly*. It is not only possible, but *probable*, that the latter witness, though in the same room, through inattention, might be unconscious of the fact, or, being conscious of it at the time, that the impression of it had afterwards faded from his memory. It follows therefore, as we have first stated—and by way of corollary to the last proposition—that *in such cases, unless the contrary manifestly appears, the presumption, in favor of human veracity, shall operate to support the affirmative testimony*.

But, if the different statements, upon examination, be found irreconcilable, it becomes an important duty, by careful investigation and comparison, to reject what is vicious; and, in so doing to distinguish between the misconceptions of an innocent witness, which cannot affect his general credibility, and wilful and corrupt misrepresentations which may destroy his credit altogether. The presumption of reason, as well as of law, in favor of innocence, will in the first instance, attribute a variance in testimony to innocent misconception, rather than to wilful and corrupt misrepresentation.

And it is here to be observed, that partial variances, in the testimony of different witnesses, on minute and collateral points—although they frequently afford the opposing advocate a topic for copious observation—are really of little importance, unless they be of too striking and prominent a nature to be ascribed to mere inadvertence, inattention, or defect of memory. It so rarely happens that witnesses of the same transaction perfectly and entirely agree on all points connected with it; that an entire and complete coincidence in every particular, so far from strengthening their credit, not unfrequently engenders a suspicion of practice and concert. (1 Starkie on Evidence, pages 468, 469.)

And admitting real inconsistencies and incongruities to exist in a mass of testimony—even upon important collateral points—I know of no more rash and unphilosophical conduct of the understanding, than to reject the substance of a narrative, by reason of some diversity in the circumstances with which it is related. The usual character of all human testimony, which is reliable, is *substantial truth* and *coincidence*, under *circumstantial variety.*

This is what the daily experience of courts of justice teaches. When accounts of a transaction come from the mouths of different witnesses, it is seldom, indeed, that it is not possible to pick out real inconsistencies between them. Numerous, and sometimes important, variations present themselves; not seldom, also, absolute and final contradictions; but neither the one nor the other is sufficient to shake the credibility of the main fact, or to fix upon the witnesses, who are otherwise unimpeached, the stigma of wilful and corrupt misrepresentation.

The real question in such cases must always be, whether the points of variance and discrepancy be of so striking and decisive a nature, as to render it impossible, or at least difficult, to attribute them to the ordinary sources of inattention, inadvertence, incapacity, mistake, error, or want of memory on the part of some one or more of the witnesses. As a just and satisfactory finding, on the case now in hand, depends much, if not entirely, upon a judicious sifting, and discriminating analysis, of the evidence adduced, I shall cite a few examples from written histories, touching upon the same scenes of action, to illustrate my meaning.

During the reign of the Emperor Caius Caligula at Rome, as cotemporary history tells us, he ordered the Jews to place his statue in their temple at Jerusalem. The Jewish nation sent an embassy from Alexandria to the Emperor, to protest against this sacrilege, and deprecate the execution of his order. Philo places the sending of this embassy in *harvest* ; Josephus in *seed time ;* both were cotemporary writers. Philo says it consisted of *five Jews at least ;* Josephus says it was composed of *Jews* and *Gentiles—three of each* But what reasonable man is led by this direct and positive inconsistency, to doubt, whether such an embassy was sent at all, or whether such an order was ever made by Caius ; or, finally, to reject the whole narrative of either author, because in this particular, one of them must have been mistaken.

Take an instance from English history—and it exhibits many examples of the same kind—say the execution of the Marquis of Argyle, in the reign of Charles the Second. Lord Clarendon, in his history of the rebellion, relates— that the Marquis was condemned to be *hanged,* that he *was accordingly hanged, on the very day of his condemnation* which was *Saturday.* On the contrary, Burnet, Woodrow, Heath and Echard, concur in stating—that he was condemned to be *beheaded,* that he *was beheaded,* not on the Saturday of his condemnation, but on the *Monday following.* Are we to reject the story of any one of these historians *in toto,* because in this instance, of the death of the Marquis of Argyle, one of them must be in error—and is skepticism to carry us so far, as to raise a question, because of these inconsistencies, and incongruities in the evidence, whether the Marquis of Argyle was executed at all ? Yet, this ought to be left in uncertainty, according to the principles upon which the Counsel for the defence in the case, have attacked the evidence for the prosecution. Take an instance from the New Testament again—I presume, that in this enlightened age, and in a christian country, it cannot be denied, that the birth, life, death and resurrection of our Lord Jesus Christ, are the most important events in the history of the world. I shall assume—and who can question it?—that the *doctrine of the atonement* is the very centre—the Omphalos—of the whole system of the Christian Religion; and the *fact of the crucifixion*, with all its surroundings, as evidencing that doctrine, is the most important event recorded in the Holy Gospels. It cannot be doubted, that the Evangelists, who give the history of this important event, were scrupulously exact, strictly conscientious, and fully aware of the magnitude of the event which they recorded, and of the high duty which was imposed upon them, of stating every circumstance connected with the crucifixion, with the most rigid adherance to truth. It may be unhesitatingly affirmed, that no form of attestation, however solemn, can be invented, which will impress upon a witness before our Courts, a more vivid sense of the obligation under which he lies, to tell the truth, the whole truth, and nothing but the truth, than that which was recognized by the Holy Evangelists, when they penned the Gospels, for the use and for the salvation of all mankind. Two of the Evangelists were eye-witnesses of the facts which they record; and all of them were familiar with the details, of those facts. That they were selected for the performance of this duty, in the early ages of the Christian church—when inspiration was direct, and miracles not usual—is the best evidence of their fitness and capacity for the task. We have, then, four capable men; to whom every opportunity has been afforded to know the truth; entirely conscientious; under the strongest possible inducement to tell the truth; with a full sense of their obligations, and of the importance of that truth; whose duty it has become to relate the most important event in the world's history, with circumstantial detail—that is to say, the crucifixion of Christ; for the benefit of all mankind; and yet, discrepancies, incongruities, and irreconcilable differences, of the same character as those which are exhibited in the evidence for the prosecution, adduced in this cause, and which have been urged by the Counsel for the defence, as a reason for discrediting the whole of a witnesses testimony, are to be found in the narratives of our Saviour's crucifixion, contained in the four Gospels of St. Matthew, St. Mark, St. Luke, and St. John. For example—take the time of the crucifixion; that is, to say, the hour of the day. It is given differently by the four Evangelists, as will be seen by reference to John xix. chapter, 14th verse, in which is placed, at the sixth hour, or twelve o'clock: Mark xv. chapter, 25th verse, in which it is said to have taken at the third hour, that is, nine o'clock. In Matthew xxvii. chapter, verses 37 to 45 inclusive;—it is not stated at what hour the crucifixion occurred, but the supernatural darkness connected and associated with it, is spoken of as having come upon the whole earth at the sixth hour, that is twelve o'clock; and according to the narrative the crucifixion must have taken place previous to that time. Luke xxiii. chapter, verses 33 to 44 inclusive, gives substantially the same account of this matter that St. Matthew does.

So, note in this case, that, the old man, Calvin Hunter, one of the witnesses for the prosecution, was in doubt whether the killing of Beebee occurred in the morning or in the afternoon. This uncertainty may not be used in the defense for the purpose of assailing his *integrity*, or showing that he has been *guilty of perjury;* but I am arguing to show that it ought not even to *diminish the weight* of his testimony as to the *main fact;* that such a circumstance as this, ought to have no weight whatever attached to it, as diminishing the credit of a witness because of any *incapacity* which it demonstrates; it cannot touch his *integrity*, for, as I have shown by various illustrations—including one from the Holy Evangelists themselves—variances of this character, will occur, as long as men have imperfect faculties, and these too, in important particulars.

So also with regard to the superscription which was written over our blessed Lord's head, when he was nailed to the cross. The Evangelists all differ from one another as to the precise wording of it. It was a striking circumstance connected with the crucifixion. It was evidently one which attracted attention; for it was written in three different languages, Hebrew, Greek, and Latin; and, we are told, the Jews requested of Pilate that its terms might be changed. It is then calculated to strike us with some astonishment, that the Evangelists differ in their accounts of so marked and prominent a circumstance connected with so great an event; and yet, a comparison of their different narratives will show, that the statement of the wording of this superscription, as given by each one of the Evangelists, differs from that given by each and all of the others. Saint Mathew says it was written "This is Jesus, the King of the Jews," (chap. xxvii verse 37). Saint Mark says it was, "The King of the Jews"(chap. xv verse 26). Saint Luke states that it was written, "This is the king of the Jews," (chap. xviii verse 38). And Saint John says it was written, "Jesus of Nazareth, the King of the Jews," (chap. xix verse 19).

Are we, on account of these and like discrepancies, to reject all of the Gospels, on the whole of any one of them; or to question whether there was any crucifixion of our Saviour at all; or whether any superscription was written over his head? We must do all these things if we follow the course of reasoning followed by the Counsel for the defence, to discredit Armstrong and some of the other witnesses for the prosecution. If *each* of the witnesses in this case, introduced on the part of the Government, in stating the words used by Tolar, or any of the other defendants at the time of the homicide, had stated them differently, the Counsel for the prisoners would—following their course of argument—have denounced the witnesses as perjured; or, if not perjured, they would, at least have insisted, that their memories were not to be relied on, as to the main fact of the shooting; but the existence of these minute inconsistencies, and actual conflicts upon collateral points is, in reality, the very best evidence, that there has been, on the part of the witnesses for the prosecution, no concert, or contrivance, or combination in preparing their testimony.

To recapitulate then; in weighing the testimony, the Court must reconcile all the evidence, if it be practicable and possible so to do, without violence or constraint; and—with this end in view—they must carefully consider, whether there is any *actual* inconsistency in the evidence—observing the rules with reference to *omissions*, and the rules which apply to *positive* and *negative* testimony, already laid down. Then, the Court, if it finds incongruities, must take another step, and ascertain where the inconsistencies are, and whether they arise from inadvertance, error or defect of memory on the part of some of the witnesses, or are to be attributed to wilful and corrupt misrepresentation. But even if the Court should find inconsistencies—if those inconsistencies arise on minute and collateral points, they can only be used for the purpose of attacking the witness's integrity, when *attributable to falsehood or prevarication on the part of the witness*, in whose evidence they arise, and ought not for the reasons already given—to be *of any weight* in determining the *ability* of the witness to state the fact with substantial

I come now to the *third head* of this branch of my subject. When the variances in the testimony of different witnesses are not of so prominent and striking a nature as to render it impossible, without violence and constraint, to ascribe them to mere inattention, inadvertence, incapacity, error, mistake, or defect of memory, the next step necessary is, to decide, *to what extent and in what particulars* the adverse evidence is irreconcilable, and then to determine what part of the testimony is to be rejected as *vicious*, and what part is to be accepted as constituting the true *res gestae*, upon which the tribunal is to act. In other words, the tribunal engaged in investigating the facts, must decide to what witnesses are to be attributed the inattention, inadvertence, incapacity, error, mistake or defect of memory, which causes the collision in the evidence; and in estimating the probability of mistake or error, as also in deciding on which side the mistake or error lies—a comparison must be made of the *means* and *opportunities* which the different witnesses had for making observation, supposing them to be equally honest; of the circumstances which were likely to excite their respective attentions; of their respective reasons and motives for attending, even supposing them to be honest; of the relative strength of their respective perceptive faculties; of their relative coolness in the midst of excitement and danger; of their respective intellectual abilities, including strength of memory and powers of recollection; and special regard should also be paid to the relative indifference of the conflicting witnesses to the point in question; and the number of the witnesses on each side, for even supposing them to be honest, it is more probable that one or a few should be mistaken than that many should be.

Now, I am about to broach a theory, which will somewhat startle my brethren on the other side, and which may, perhaps, on first view, also surprise the Court. It is this: presuming the uneducated colored persons who have testified in this cause, to be honest, I shall insist that it is probable they have given a more correct version of its *details of fact* than the better informed white witnesses have. I leave out of consideration altogether the relative opportunities of each set of witnesses for observation, and their respective reasons for attending to what transpired, and, for the nonce, assume these tests of credibility to be equal in white and black—educated and uneducated persons; and now—only regarding the relative strength of their respective perceptive faculties, and comparing their several and respective powers of recollection—and supposing them, as I have said, to be equally honest—my theory is, that the uneducated man has *quicker perception*, and *greater power of recalling physical ideas*, than the cultivated man. Men who are in the habit of reflecting a great deal neglect the cultivation of their perceptive faculties. Take an Indian—a savage—his perceptive faculties are keen and active to an extraordinary degree—and so ascend the scale of cultivation, and the acuteness of the perceptive faculties diminishes as you ascend. Now, all man's knowledge is derived from one of three sources; either through his senses, or *perceptive faculties*; or it is *intuitive*,—if it be admitted that we know anything by intuition; or it arises from reflecting on what is derived from the two other sources just named.

The perceptive faculties in the savage or in the brute beast are more acute than in the civilized man; for, the force which civilized man expends on reflection, the uncultivated man, and the mere animal, infuses into the perceptive faculties. So too the simplest *operations* of memory are more perfect in an uncultivated man, than in one of more culture and intelligence. I say the *simplest* operations—for there is no part of this complex machinery that we call MAN, more curious and manifold in its various manifestations than memory. The simplest operations of it, depending upon that law of mental association which, for want of a better name, we call *the law of contiguity*, are more perfect in uncultivated persons, than in those of cultivation and refinements. This may seem a digression, but I consider it important in this case—the more important—because these negroes have been attacked as natural liars; I consider it of importance that their testimony should have given to it the weight to which it is entitled, no more and no less. In urging these views, I do not wish to be understood as making myself their especial champion, or as claiming for them a general superiority to the more cultivated and more intellectual race; not at all. But, for the purpose of upholding justice and truth, it is important that their reliability in matters depending upon perception and recollection, should be established; and I say, that their memories, where this particular law of mental association which we call the law of *contiguity* applies, are stronger than those of cultivated men. The memory consists of two parts—*retention* and *recollection*. It is the theory of many celebrated metaphysicians, that we never, *absolutely, forget anything;* that there is a "store house of the mind"—as Lord Bacon calls it—which safely holds every idea that has ever, at any time, been the object of mental consciousness; and that every such idea, so held, is potentially liable to be recalled at any moment. We may set out with the proposition, then, that the retentive part of the memory, or the power of *retention*, is the same in all men, but the power of recollection varies greatly. This power of recollection depends upon certain laws. We have not gone very far in their investigation, but we call them *the laws of mental association, suggestion or reproduction;* and the simplest of these laws is what we call *the law of contiguity*. By this we mean, that whenever two objects of sense, or two ideas of any kind, have once been the subjects of mental consciousness at the same moment, or in quick succession to each other, each one of them ever after manifests a tendency to suggest or reproduce the other. As, for instance, if a man were driving along the road and talking to a friend sitting by him upon a particular subject, and he, at that moment, noticed a peculiarly built farm house, or any other striking object of sense, the probabilities are great, that if he, at another time, passes that farm house and observes it, the same idea will be again brought before his mind which was in it when he last saw it, and he will recollect, without effort, what he was saying to his friend. That is what we mean by the law of contiguity. We have a thousand illustrations of its operations in every-day life. You, gentlemen of the court, who are here for the purpose of administering civil law, and of endeavoring to do justice among petty disputants, have, in your daily experience, numberless instances of it—I do not doubt—as I have in my own office. Every lawyer has. A man will come to you who is without education, and in his efforts to present his difficulty to you, will mention a thousand circumstances that seem to have no sort of connection with the matter at issue. Why? Because the moment anything associated with the subject in which he is interested is mentioned by him, his mind is filled with everything that surrounded it at the time that he last saw it or considered it—when it was last the subject of his mental consciousness. He cannot from want of skill separate one part of the matter from the other, the important from the unimportant, the subject being recalled everything with which it was associated is recalled also. A striking illustration of this principle occurs in Shakespeare—the great master of human nature—of the mind, and of the heart. I allude to a scene in Henry IV, where Falstaff is about going off to the wars, and is arrested by Constable Fang for a debt due Mrs.

Quickly. It is somewhat ludicrous to be introduced on so sad an occasion as this is, but as it aptly illustrates my meaning I recur to it. Falstaff is arrested by Fang, to enforce a payment of his debt to Mrs. Quickly: he is advised to pay it; and he forthwith goes aside with Dame Quickly to make with her the best terms that he can. In asking the old lady " what he owes her?" she remembers that he owes her *himself*—having once promised to marry her; and no sooner has she recalled this promise of marriage, than she goes on, almost without volition, to narrate every event which occurred at the moment when this proposition was made. Here was a garrulous old woman, to whom this fact was recalled—" Falstaff once promised to marry me,"—and instantly, every circumstance that surrounded her at the time comes to her mind again You will better understand its application if I give you the passage. Sir John asks the Dame, " What is the gross sum that I owe thee?" whereto she replies, " Marry, if thou wert an honest man, thyself, and the money too. Thou didst swear to me—upon a parcel-gilt goblet—sitting in my Dolphin-chamber—at the round table, by a sea-coal fire—on Wednesday in Wheeson-week—when the prince broke thy head for liking his father to a singing man of Windsor—thou didst swear to me then, as I was washing thy wound, to marry me, and make me my lady thy wife. Canst thou deny it? Did not goodwife Keech, the butcher's wife, come in then—and call me gossip Quickly?—coming in to borrow a mess of vinegar—telling us she had a good dish of prawns—whereby thou didst desire to eat some—whereby I told thee they were ill for a green wound. And didst not thou, when she was gone down stairs, desire me to be no more so familiarity with such poor people, saying that ere long they should call me madam? And didst thou not kiss me, and bid me fetch thee thirty shillings? I put thee now to thy book-oath; deny it, if thou canst."

Now here is an illustration from the very greatest master of human nature. The very moment the idea of Falstaff's promise of marriage is recalled to her, every circumstance surrounding it, when it was first given to her, is immediately brought before her mind. This will give the Court a key to my meaning, when I say,—that—supposing these uneducated witnesses, white or black, to be honest—if any remarkable facts—such, for instance, as those given in evidence occurring at the Fayetteville market house—should happen in their presence—put one of these facts in their minds, and the whole train of circumstances will spring up in their memory, and be vividly pictured there. This will not be the case, to the same extent, in educated minds, whose powers of reflection are developed, and which are well stored with ideas ; because of the number of ideas which have, at different times been in them, and of their complex associations ; each idea having, at different times, been in contiguity with several others, no one idea has, with them, the same power of recalling others by the law of contiguity as it has with uneducated persons, whose ideas are few and simple. The laws of mental association—some of them—govern the operation of the memory in more educated persons; but this particular law of mental association—the simplest—the first fundamental law—the law of contiguity—by which one idea having once been associated in the mind with another, always manifests a tendency to recall it—this law of contiguity, is more accurate in its operations in persons of little education than in others.

Therefore, I say, that in considering the weight to be attached to the testimony of these negroes, or of any uneducated persons, some addition must be made because of the acuteness of their perceptive faculties, and of their great powers of recollecting material ideas. I have no doubt that the Court has been struck with the minuteness and detail of the testimony given by some of the witnesses in this cause, and perhaps, they may have considered it utterly impossible, for any one to speak with so much minuteness upon any matter not immediately in view ; but the Court must remember, that we were examining just the class of persons to whom old Dame Quickly belonged, and that, in them, the power of recalling events, depending on this law of contiguity, is developed to a degree, of which we of more training, can hardly conceive.

And now, may it please the Court, there is another thing to which I wish, in this connection, to call attention, and one which my brother, Battle, seemed to think of very little importance, and that is, the comparison of the number of witnesses on each side. I insist upon it that the comparative number of witnesses on each side is a very important test of truth. Not that we are to do as Irving's Dutch Governor did—in settling accounts—put one book in one side of the scale and the other book in the other, and decide by mere weight ; but supposing the witnesses to be honest, there is a stronger probability that one or a few should be mistaken than that a number should. It is more probable that ten persons should be mistaken than that twenty-five should be, even supposing them all to be honest. The force of the multiplicity of testimony, given by twenty-five men, is not simply the weight of the testimony of one witness, multiplied twenty-five times to arrive at the weight of the whole; but when you add the weight attached to the evidence of each witness—all together,—you must also add to the sum, the probability of the facts, deposed to by all, being true, arising from the improbability of so many being mistaken—or conspiring to commit perjury.— Thus as you multiply witnesses to a fact or set of facts, the weight of the testimony, seems to grow by a sort of geometrical progression, as you increase the number of witnesses. When two witnesses testify to the same fact, the probability of its truth is not necessarily *doubled ;* but an additional probability of its truth arises, from the improbability of two being mistaken about the same thing, or concurring in a lie; a probability which grows, and goes on, and on, increasing, until when you get a large number of witnesses to the same facts—the degree of proof is so overwhelming, that nothing can over-come it. *The admission of these principles* is the great argument, at last, upon which Christianity rests. The establishment of these principles furnished the only method in which Hume's argument against Christianity was ever successfully met. His argument was—that it is more probable that twelve men should lie, than that a miracle should be performed ; that it contradicts experience for a dead man to be brought to life, but does not contradict experience that twelve men should lie. And after moralists had exhausted themselves, and perhaps not conclusively answered the argument of Hume—for very few were just such skilful masters of fence as he,—mathematicians went to work, and calculated the degree of probability, arising from the concurrent testimony of so many witnesses ascertaining that, where a large number of witnesses concur in their statements, the weight, of the testimony of the whole depends upon a sort of geometrical progression— eventuating in a degree of probability that is overwhelming—thus meeting, at last, the argument against miracles, which had never been very successfully encountered by Paley—or any other of the Moralists. The only possible way of overturning the argument was by a mathematical demonstration of its fallaciousness—a demonstration which established the same principle which I am applying here ; that by increasing the number of witnesses to the same fact or set of facts—a degree of probability of their truth, amounting almost to mathematical or metaphysical certainty is attained; a probability which is to a great extent independant of the integrity and ability of the several witnesses; a probability resting upon the force of their *concurrent* testimony, and not upon the characters of the several witnesses; a probability which can only be overturned by establishing that not *one*, but all of the concurring witnesses are perjured—or mistaken; since the only way of accounting for the phenomenon of so many witnesses concurring in the same statement of fact, is, either to suppose the fact *true*, or that the witnesses *have all combined to* commit perjury.

I hope I have made myself understood by the Court upon these points. I am endeavoring, as clearly and as succinctly as I can, to lay down those rules of evidence, those regulations, which ought to control this Court in the investigation of facts: the first *leading* one being that they must reconcile all the evidence, if they can do so without violence or constraint; the second *leading* one being, that if they cannot reconcile it all, they must attribute the inconsistencies to inadvertence, incapacity, inattention, error, mistake, defect of memory, or some other human infirmity, if it be reasonably possible so to do; and so attributing them to mistake and the like, it is no ground for rejecting the whole of the testimony of a witness, that he has made some errors apparent to the Court; and indeed *that* is no ground for doubting the *main facts* of his testimony. And if going a step further, it becomes important to decide, to which ones of the witnesses these inadvertencies, errors, mistakes and the like, if they exist, are to be attributed, the Court must decide that; and in deciding it, these different questions which I have suggested come up, to wit: first their relative opportunities for observation; second, the respective character of the circumstances which attracted their attention; third, their several reasons for attending; fourth, the relative strength of their perceptive faculties; fifth, the relative strength of their intellectual powers, with their respective physical organization, and finally the prejudices of the several witnesses; and last of all, but not least, the number of witnesses on one side or the other.

If in the discussion of the testimony the Court shall come to the conclusion that collisions in the evidence *exist*, but *that they* are upon collateral and irrelevant and minute particulars, and that the *substance* of all the evidence can be reconciled, and the Court are satisfied, in addition to this, that these collisions can be attributed to inattention, inadvertence, incapacity, error, mistake or defect of memory, on the part of one witness or the other, one class of witnesses or the other, it is hardly necessary to trouble themselves to go further, and decide to which class these errors and the like are attributable. If the Court are satisfied that the whole of the substance of the testimony is reconcilable, and that the witnesses are honest, it cannot be necessary for them to go on, and decide upon these minute and collateral points, which of the witnesses were right, and which were wrong.

But at last we may come to a state of things—a precipitate that we cannot reduce any further. If we find a condition of things where the testimony of conflicting witnesses is irreconcilable, and the conflict is of such a character that it cannot be attributed to incapacity, inattention, error, mistake or defect of memory—it becomes our painful and difficult task to decide to which class of witnesses credit is due. That is unfortunately the state of mind to which, as I believe, the Court must arrive in this case—they will be called upon to decide to which class of witnesses credit is due.

And here, it is to be remarked, that the fact that a witness has sworn falsely, wilfully, and corruptly in one particular, goes, as was said by the

Counsel for the defence, to his *credibility* and not to his *competency* in other matters. It is a maxim of the *civil law*—"*falsum in uno, falsum in omnibus,*" a maxim which does not obtain in the common law ; where a man is detected in wilful and corrupt perjury as to one particular, you are not to throw all of his evidence aside, in cases of this character. At least such is the rule in our ordinary Criminal Courts, and I will presume that the same rules apply to this Military Court, although there may be reasons suggested for the contrary view. If then you discover that a witness has sworn deliberately and wilfully and corruptly false as to one particular, it goes simply to his credibility, and not to his competency ; you are still to consider and weigh the rest of his evidence in connection with all the circumstances, and decide to what weight you think it entitled. It is not *a rule of law* that the evidence of a witness who has made an intentional misstatement must be rejected altogether. The reasons for this are evident. The force of even direct testimony can never amount to absolute mathematical or metaphysical certainty. The force of direct testimony rests upon *a presumption of law* —that a disinterested witness who delivers his testimony under the sanction of an oath, and under the peril of temporal inflictions due to perjury will speak the truth. The effect of wilful and corrupt perjury in one particular is, *to repel this presumption of law*, since it manifestly appears, that the witness in question, is capable of perjury. But a tribunal engaged in the investigation of facts is still to weigh his testimony, and to give to it the degree of credit to which they may think, under the circumstances, is is entitled ; and it is obvious that wilful corruption in one particular, cannot be used to impeach the credit of the same witness, as to evidence given by him favorable to the adverse side. Say a witness for the defence, *gives in evidence some facts* favorable to the prosecution, and the Court come to a conclusion that he is wilfully and corruptly false in some one other particular— that is no reason for rejecting the portion of his testimony which is favorable to the prosecution. Such evidence is rather to be regarded as truth reluctantly admitted, and divulged only because it is not in the power of the corrupt witness to conceal it.

It is to be observed also in considering corrupt testimony, that the rejection of the whole of the testimony of a corrupt witness, which is favorable to the side introducing him, may not be the only consequence of his perjury. If there be reason to suspect, from the circumstances, that his perjury is the result of subornation, contrivance or concert, it affords a reasonable ground, in a doubtful case, for suspecting or even for rejecting the whole of the testimony adduced by the same party.

I beg that the court will pardon my tediousness, and will follow the course of my remarks.

I am endeavoring, before going into the examination of evidence, to lay down these different rules for sifting testimony, which ought to regulate this tribunal, so that they may apply them with ease in the investigation of the testimony. I know I am tedious. I regret that it is so. I know also that it is necessary to be tedious, in order that you may do, and that I may do— that we may *all* do our full duty to the government whose ministers we are, and to the prisoners whose lives are in our hands.

To go on then : if in coming to a decision the Court are satisfied that one witness or another, that one class of witnesses or the other, has been guilty of deliberate and wilful and corrupt misrepresentation, either upon a material point or upon a collateral and less material one, it becomes a matter of vital importance to discover where the perjury lies ; and, in tracing this out, there are a few general principles to be observed. The first one, in this investigation, is to consider the relative *integrity* of the witnesses, as it is gathered from their *general character;* as it is gathered from their *bias, interest,* prejudice or passion towards the cause; as it is gathered from their bearing on examination.

We are next to recur *in this connection—to the number of witnesses on both sides.* The Court will remember that in a former part of this address, *assuming the witnesses all to be honest,* I stated that the number of witnesses on each side was an important consideration, because it was more probable that one or a few *should be mistaken* than that many should be; but when we are satisfied that perjury has been committed on one side or the other, and the question arises whether one witness or many has sworn wilfully and corruptly false, the preponderating *number of witnesses* is entitled to immense weight, both as a rule of law and for reasons that are obvious—because it is more improbable that a number of witnesses should have conspired to commit a fraud, by direct perjury, than that a few should; because the difficulty of procuring a number of false witnesses is increased in proportion to the number; and because, finally, the risk of detection is increased in a far higher ratio, in proportion to the number of false witnesses.

The consistency of a witness's testimony with itself, and also its consistency with the testimony of other witnesses, is a strong and most important test, for deciding upon the integrity of witnesses. Where several witnesses gave testimony to the same transaction, and concur in their statement of a series of particular circumstances, and the order in which they occurred, such coincidences exclude all apprehension of mere chance or accident, and can be accounted for, by one only, of two suppositions; either the testimony is true, or the coincidences are the result of concert and conspiracy. If therefore the independency of the witnesses be proved, and the supposition of previous conspiracy be disproved, or rendered highly improbable, by establishing the integrity of *only a single one* of the concurring witnesses, to the same extent will the truth of their testimony, and the integrity of all the witnesses, be established. The consistency of a witness's evidence with admitted facts, is another test; and the consistency of the testimony of a witness with collateral circumstances is still another; and the last and perhaps one of the most important tests is the "*a priori,*" probability of the witness' story; by which I mean its confirmity or want of confirmity with general experience. A man easily credits a witness, who states that to have happened; which he himself has known to happen under similar circumstances; he may still believe, although he should not have had actual experience of similar facts; but where that is asserted, which is not only unapproved by common experience, but contrary to it, belief is slow and difficult.

I have thus endeavored to lay down for the guidance of the Court, the general rules and regulations, fixed by law, to govern the investigation of evidence. I have endeavored to state then as distinctly as I could, and to illustrate them from time to time—and have thus exhausted the first topic that I proposed to myself, for discussion. The immense mass of testimony we are compelled to sift, is my best apology, for the time thus consumed.

On motion, the Commission adjourned to meet on Saturday, September 14th, at 10 A. M.

The Commission met pursuant to adjournment.

Present: All the members of the Commission, the Judge Advocate, the Counsel for the prosecution, all the accused and their Counsel.

The reading of the addresses delivered yesterday was waived, there being no objection thereto.

Yesterday's proceedings were then read and approved.

Mr. Haywood continued his remarks as follows:

May it please the Court: Having, on yesterday, considered the rules of evidence prescribed by law for regulating a tribunal engaged in the investigation of facts, the next important question, to be decided by this Court is what law of homicide shall control them in the decision which they are called upon to make.

And here, I am unexpectedly met on the threshold, by the objection raised by my brother, Phillips, in opening this discussion on behalf of the defence—that this Court has no jurisdiction whatever, of the particular offence which they are engaged in trying. The Counsel for the defence, as represented by my brother Phillips, are prepared to admit, that, if the crime with which these defendants are charged, had been committed subsequent to the passage of what is called the first reconstruction act, the jurisdiction of this Court over the subject matter would be clear and incontrovertible.

But, they say, on account of the accidental circumstance that this homicide was perpetrated on the 11th of February, 1867, several days before the passage of the reconstruction acts, or any of them, those acts cannot have a retrospective operation, and include within their provisions, an offence which was committed previous to the passage of the first of the series of acts.

I desire to state the positions which were taken by the defence fairly and as forcibly as I am able, even as strongly as they were stated by the learned and able Counsel who addressed the Court in opening the defence.

I understood the admission to be full and frank, in the opening address for the prisoners,—for the purposes of this discussion, if for no other purpose,—that Congress had the power, which it claimed, to enact that crimes should be tried by courts, constituted as this Court is, if Congress saw fit so to do; but that as a matter of fact, the Congress had not so enacted. And that, the proper construction of the reconstruction acts, does not include, among cases which may be tried by Military Commission, an offence, committed previous to the passage of any of the series of acts.

I understood another position to be taken by the Counsel for the defence: that if the proper interpretation of the reconstruction acts does include this particular crime, committed on the 11th day of February, 1867, among those which may be tried by Military Commission, then the law so operating is an *ex post facto* law, or is in the nature of an *ex post facto* law, because—and I wish to state the reason correctly, and I think I apprehend it correctly—because, said Mr. Phillips, at the date when the offence was committed these defendants had a right to be tried by a jury of their peers, collected from the vicinage where the crime was perpetrated, and the effect of this law is, to deprive them of that right subsequently to the time when the offence was committed.

Now, if the Court pleases, I do not intend to enter *fully* into the discussion of this question of jurisdiction, for many reasons, and one or two of them I shall state to the Court. In the early stages of this cause, a plea to the jurisdiction of the Commission was filed by the Counsel for the defence. In its terms, it was broad enough to include the objection which is now taken to the jurisdiction of this Court; the plea was overruled by the Commission; and if the Court considered that plea at all, it is proper and natural to suppose that they considered *all* the objections their jurisdiction which arise in this case. And when in the progress of a cause a question of this character has once been raised and decided, I consider such decision a *final* decision of the point for all the purposes of the cause. Again, I understand from our declining to discuss that question of jurisdiction, when it was first mooted, and submitting its decision to this Court without argument, that it was considered both by the Court and all the Counsel prosecuting and defending—that such a question was so abstruse in its character, depending for its proper solution so entirely upon that peculiar technical knowledge, which none but men who are educated to the legal profession can be supposed or expected to have; that it was better that the point should be raised and discussed and finally decided in the review of this cause. Entertaining such views, I did not discuss this question when the plea was properly before the Court; nor do I think it necessary to discuss it fully now, for the same reasons. Moreover, when the plea to the jurisdiction was disposed of—overruled—I considered all the points raised by it decided, and therefore disposed of once for all.

But apart from all that, this is not an ordinary civil court; it is a Court of soldiers of the army of the United States; of officers who have superiors; of men who are subject to authority; to each of whom the superior officer says "go, and he goeth, come, and he cometh." The science of the organization of an army is obedience, and submission to superior authority; and when the superior authority under which this Court was constituted—I mean Gen. Sickles, who was then commander of this department, and who would have reviewed the decision of the Court, except that accidentally he has a successor—when he has once said that this case now before them is fit to be considered by this Court, and sends it here for trial. I think that the Court will have, and ought to have great hesitation in attempting to overrule a decision already made by him.

And here, I note, it has been suggested by the prisoners' Counsel that the terms of the order constituting this Court, are of such a character that they do not necessarily imply endorsement by the Commander of the District, of the propriety of this Court's investigating a case in which the crime was committed on the 11th of February, 1867. It is urged that this particular case is not nominally mentioned by General Sickles, in the order convening the Court. But the members of this Commission, familiar with the proceedings in such cases, know full well, that before any cause is brought before this Court, for trial, there is always an express order from Gen. Sickles directing it. So, although the particular order convening this Commission, may not contain the express direction that this identical cause, naming it, is to be tried before the Court; yet the knowledge which the Court officially has, that this identical case has, by other express orders from the Commanding General, been referred to them for their decision, indicates to them very plainly what the opinion of the Commanding officer of this District is, with reference to their jurisdiction of this crime, because of the time at which it was committed. It must also be apparent to the Court, that it is laborious, trifling, upon their part, to spend more time in the discussion of the consideration and decision of a question of this sort.

Therefore, upon the *merits* of this question of jurisdiction, I have only thus much to say: the two propositions upon which I understand my brother Phillips' argument to rest, are, in my opinion, false in reason, in logic, and in law. Far be it from me to cast any personal imputation upon the gentlemen engaged in the defence, and I beg they will not so understand me—it is sometimes difficult, if not impossible, in discussions, to avoid *appearing* to reflect upon Council when no such thing is in reality intended.

But I mean the two propositions—philosophically speaking—are false assumptions. His first proposition is, that the act of Congress of the second of March, 1867, commonly known as the first Reconstruction act, is *ex post facto* in its character and operations, if it takes away from these defendants *a method of trial* which was peculiarly their right at the time of the commission of the offence.

Now, if the Court pleases, such a law—a law *changing the method of prosecution* after the crime is committed—is not *ex post facto* in its character and operation. What constitutes an *ex post facto* law, has been long and well settled by the Supreme Court of the United States.

The use of these terms in the Constitution of the United States, has been well settled; and their full extension has been well settled ; and the distinction which we draw is, that where the new law provides that the crime already perpetrated shall be PUNISHED IN THE SAME WAY BUT BY A DIFFERENT METHOD OF PROSECUTION, it may be a retrospective but it is not an *ex post facto* law.

The celebrated and leading case upon this subject decided as early as the year 1798, is the case of Calder and wife, against Bull and wife, reported in third Dallas, Reports Supreme Court of the United States, page 386; and in that case Judge Chase pointed out the rules and distinctions upon this subject very perspicuously, in a few lines. " I will state what laws are considered *ex post facto* laws, within the words and the intent of the prohibition in the constitution. Every law that makes an action done before passing of the law, and which was innocent when done, criminal, and punishes such an action,"—that is an *ex post facto* law. If, for example, it were not criminal now, to retail spirits by the small measure without a license, and the legislature of the State, or the Congress of the United States should pass an act, to punish men who had done such a thing previous to the passage of the act, that would be an *ex post facto* law ; that would be making an act which was innocent when done, criminal, and punishing it.

The second sort of *ex post facto* law, is—" every law that aggravates a crime, and makes it greater than it was when committed." Crimes are divided into treason, felonies and misdemeanors. The lowest grade of crime is a misdemeanor. Next in grade stand felonies ; and, above all, stands the offence of treason, which is sometimes classed with felonies, but is, more properly speaking. *sui generis*. Now, if an act were a misdemeanor at the time of its commission, and by a law of Congress, or of a State legislature, were made a felony. a higher grade of offence—after its commission, such an act of Congress, or of the Legislature, would be an *ex post facto* law.

Third class—" every law that changes the punishment, and inflicts a greater punishment, than the law annexed to the crime when committed ;" as, for instance—suppose the offence of larceny to be punished with thirty-nine stripes—as I think it ought properly to be punished—with great respect for this Court—by the law in existence at the time of the fact committed, and, that a subsequent law were passed, making that past offence, punishable with forty, or fifty stripes ; such a law would be *ex post facto* in its character and operation ; because, it imposed a greater punishment upon the criminal act, that was its sanction, at the time of the commission of the fact.

Fourth class—" every law that alters the legal rules of evidence, and receives less, or different testimony, than the law required at the time of the commission of the offence, in order to convict the offender." For instance : the overt act of treason, must, under existing law, be proved, by two witnesses at least—so, perjury must be proved by two witnesses, or by one witness and confirmatory testimony—for the law conceives, that the oath of one man against the oath of another, makes a fair balance of testimony, and that it is not just, to convict any man of perjury, upon the evidence of a single other man. If, then, a law were passed, after the act of treason, or of perjury, committed, allowing a man to be convicted of treason, upon the unsupported evidence of a single witness, such a law would be *ex post facto* in its character and operation.

These are the classes of *ex post facto* laws; and the act of Congress under consideration is not within any of these classes.

This law simply *changes the tribunal* by which the offence is to be tried, without creating a new crime, without changing its grade, without adding any new degree of punishment, without allowing a conviction therefor upon less testimony than was requisite at the time of the commission of the act; and all laws subsequently enacted, which simply change the method of prosecuting an offence—an offence, which is admitted to have been a crime at the time of its commission—although they may be retrospective, are not *ex post factos.*

" But," says my brother Phillips, "admitting that these distinctions and rules just stated are those which generally obtain, yet where a man has *a right secured to him by the Constitution*, as the right of trial by jury, at the time of the commission of the offence, and a law, passed subsequent to the commission of the offence, deprives him of that particular constitutional right upon his trial, there I draw a new distinction. Such a law is an *ex post facto* law, and a fifth class must be added to the four already defined."

This distinction rests, I must be permitted to say, upon my brother Phillips' *ipse dixit* alone. No authority can be found to sustain it. The four classes of *ex post facto* laws are enumerated and defined here in this decision to which I have referred—in the volume which I hold in my hand—and this decision does not stand alone. It has been—since it was pronounced in 1798—*the* decision upon this subject in this country; and it has been repeated and endorsed over and over again, not only by the Supreme Court of the United States, but, probably, by every Court of Appeals, in every State of this Union, since the time it was first enunciated by Judge Chase: and yet, until this trial of these defendants here before this Court, in the year 1867, the subtle distinction which is attempted to be established by my brother Phillips, and for which no authority is adduced, was never drawn, and now, for the first time, it is suggested by brother Phillips, in this case, as a means by which he proposes to show that, if the act of Congress of the second of March, 1867, does actually intend that offences committed previous to its passage shall be punished under its provisions, by Military Commissions, such act of Congress is *ex post facto* in its character and operation, and is therefore unconstitutional and void.

It is enough for me to say that *here* is the authority laying down what particular characteristics make a law *ex post facto.* These definitions do not embrace this new class of *ex post facto* laws; and the bare *statement of the proposition* by my brother Phillips, whatever may be his legal attainments, without any *authority* to sustain it, without any reasoning to sustain it, has not, and ought not to have, so great weight with this Court as to induce them to refuse to take jurisdiction of a cause which is regularly constituted before them.

The next proposition laid down by the Counsel for the defence is—that at the time the offence charged was committed, these defendants could not have been tried by Military Commission therefor; but that they then had a right of trial by jury, *and by jury only.*

Now, assuming as the basis of this argument, only that which my brother Phillips assumes and admits—granting me that Congress has all the power of legislation which it claims—that the reconstruction acts and other acts in *pari materia* are constitutional—as the defence admits for the purposes of this argument—I assert, without fear of contradiction, that on the 11th of February, 1867, when the crime alleged in this charge and specification was committed, there *were* laws of Congress existing, directing that such offences as this is might be tried by Military Commission.

I allude especially to the act of Congress which extended the organization and the operations of the Freedman's Bureau. That act of Congress provides that where offences are committed by white persons against persons of color—freedmen—persons who have lately been elevated to the rights of free men—such offences may be tried and punished by Military Commission if the President sees fit so to direct. I invite attention to the fourteenth section, chapter two hundred, of the acts of 39th Congress, first session.

And I must be permitted to say, that I do not think the opening Counsel for the defence has acted with his usual candor in legal discussions, in extracting only a *part* of this section, and calling attention thereto, in his argument before this Court; for if he had gone on, and read the whole of this very section, to which he referred, instead of citing only a part of it, that provision would have appeared, to which I allude, in the words following:

"And whenever, in either of the said States or Districts, the ordinary course of judicial proceedings has been interrupted by the rebellion; and until the same shall be fully restored: and until such State * * * * shall be duly represented in the Congress of the United States, the President shall, through the Commissioner and the officers of the Bureau, and under such rules and regulations as the President, through the Secretary of War, shall prescribe, extend military protection and have military jurisdiction over all cases and questions concerning the free enjoyment of such immunities and rights &c."

It is a provision in this very act which was referred to by the Counsel for the defence: and in the very section of the act that was cited—which gives *military jurisdiction*, to preserve all the immunities and rights of, and to punish all offences committed, with reference to this particular class of persons. And it makes no difference, for the purpose of this argument, what the particular mode of the organization of *the Court* directed by that act was, for the very corner stone of the argument, built up by brother Phillips was, that at the time the offence alleged in the charge and specification was committed, these prisoners had a right to trial by jury, and could not under any act of Congress then in force, have been tried by military Commission, by a Court constituted under military authority as this one is.

It seems to me then, that the two assumptions made by the opening Counsel for the defence in his argument—the assumption first that the reconstruction acts are *ex post facto* laws, in a certain named event—and next,—that the particular offence charged in this case could have been tried only by a jury at the time of its commission,—having been overturned, the whole superstructure of the argument falls.

For the first reconstruction act declares in every letter, in every line, and in every section—especially when interpreted in the light of subsequent acts in *pari materia*—that the military commandant of this district when appointed, shall have the power to *sweep away* the State government altogether, and to substitute a military government with military officers in the executive, legislative and judicial offices of the State in its stead. And if such is the case,—and it cannot be controverted, for it is the leading principle which runs through all the reconstruction acts, and appears everywhere throughout them in burning letters, and if Congress had the power to establish these laws—which is admitted by the defence for the purposes of this argument—who can suppose, for a moment, that Congress intended these reconstruction acts, when the new military government was established, to operate as a general jail delivery? Who can suppose that Congress intended to leave all offences committed before the passage of the first reconstruction act in such a condition that no earthly power could try and punish them? Now look at it, if the Court please: here is an act, passed by the Congress of the United States, which gives the military commandant of the second district power to abolish the State government altogether, and substitute in its place some other government, if he sees fit. Gen. Sickles has not abolished the old State government *altogether*, but such government as now exists in North Carolina, is a government established by Gen. Sickles under the reconstruction acts—whose functionaries exercise the powers of government, because the commandant of the district *so wills it.* In *theory* the old government is entirely gone. Is it not most monstrous to conclude, that Congress, in passing such an act, intended, provided a man had committed an offence *before* the passage of that act, the new government should not have the power to punish him at all? Intended that, all criminals then in our jails were to go free, and all past crimes remain unwhipped of justice? Yet, such is the conclusion to which the argument for the defence necessarily leads. And I shall say no more upon this question of jurisdiction. I only introduced this passing notice of my brother Phillips' positions, for fear the Court might conclude that they were unanswerable—and that the prosecution concurred in them—for I had considered the question as decided already, for all the purposes of this case; and further because the question involved meets me at the very threshold of that part of my argument to which I am now addressing myself, and to which I now recur—that is—*what law of homicide shall control this Court, in the decisions which they are called upon to make?*—a general question—not only applying to this case, but applying also in many of its particulars to the different cases which may come before the Court.

May it please the Court:—The law of homicide is not universally the same in all the States. In many of the States of the Union the Common Law of England upon this subject—which constitutes the basis of all our law —has been altered by statutes, enacted by the local legislatures; and before coming to any conclusion *at all* in this case, the Court must decide upon the particular system of law which is to govern their decision.

It seems to me too plain for argument, for us to take any other ground than that the law of homicide as it existed in North Carolina at the time of the passage of the first reconstruction act, and at the time of the commission of the crime charged, is *the* law of homicide which governs the conduct of the Court. I invite the attention of the Court to the fact, that the offence with which these prisoners are charged, was committed before the passage of the first reconstruction act, and that principle of universal justice which requires that a man be tried by the law, and subjected to the penalties which existed at the time of the commission of the offence, applies to this case with peculiar emphasis. It is also to be noted, that in all the orders issued from the Headquarters of the Second Military District, it is *assumed* that all previous laws, existing under what are called the "provisional governments," continue in force, under the military government, *unless modified or repealed by orders*, issuing from the said headquarters.

A reference to General Orders, No. 1, Headquarters Second Military District, dated Columbia, South Carolina, March 21st, 1867, section III. will show the views of the late Commander of the District, upon the subject. He there says: "The civil governments now existing in North Carolina and in South Carolina are provisional only, and in all respects are subject to the paramount authority of the United States, at any time to abolish, modify, control, or supersede the same. *Local laws or municipal regulations, not inconsistent with the Constitution and laws of the United States, or the Proclamations of the President, or with such regulations as are, or may be prescribed in the orders of the Commanding General, are hereby* DECLARED TO BE IN FORCE; and in conformity therewith civil officers are hereby authorized to continue the exercise of their particular functions, and will be respected and obeyed by the inhabitants." It is evident from this section, that the Commander of the Second Military District intended, when Military Commissions were organized, under the Reconstruction Acts, for investigating crimes, that the local law, existing at the time of the passage of the acts, and continued in force by virtue of his orders, should regulate the degree and character of the crime, and the amount and nature of its sanction. Such being the case, it becomes my duty to lay down to the Court what particular ingredients constitute the crime of murder, according to the *lex loci* of the State of North Carolina; and I must beg that this Court will remember, until a suggestion is made by me to the contrary, that in what immediately follows from this point, my remarks are particularly addressed to the case of the defendant Tolar, and I propose to dispose of the law in its application to his case, before going on to the consideration of those particular and *peculiar* principles, which apply to that form of the offense, which is alleged against the other defendants.

The defendant Tolar is charged with the crime of MURDER. Now what particular constituents go to make up the crime of murder, according to the laws of North Carolina? In this State we have adhered to the exact definition of the common law, adopted by the English Jurists—upon this subject. And murder is defined as follows— *Whenever a person of sound memory and discretion, unlawfully kills any reasonable creature in being and in the peace of the commonwealth, with malice prepense or aforethought, either express or implied*, it is murder, (Wharton on Homicide p. 33: Wharton Criminal Law vol. I. sec. 930). The distinguishing feature of this definition, it will at once be perceived, is *malice*; and it is the only part of the definition, which lay-men can find the least difficulty in appreciating, or understanding. It is also to be observed, that the definition speaks of *malice aforethought, either express or implied*. There is no difficulty in understanding what the law means by malice aforethought, express; for the malice is *express when one person kills another, with a sedate, deliberate mind and formed design*. Malice is a passion of the mind, or heart; and, of course, its existence cannot be established by direct and positive evidence; the eye of God alone can see it; it is not cognizable by the senses. Its existence in the heart, must be determined by the actions of the criminal,—by the external manifestations which indicate its presence in the heart; and its ordinary proof, must of necessity, be circumstantial. Such acts, for instance, as lying in wait, antecedent menaces, former grudges and concerted schemes, to do the party injured some bodily harm; indicate the existence of malice in the heart, and all these indicate what the law means by *express malice,* or *malice aforethought, express.*

But what is meant in our definition by malace aforethought, *implied,* is very different from what would be intended, by an ordinary layman, when using the same expression. And the more proper mode of conveying the *technical meaning,* which the law attaches to these *technical terms,* would, perhaps, be, to alter the expression ; and instead of speaking of *malice aforethought, implied,* to call it MALICE IN A LEGAL SENSE ; for this term, at common law, is meant to include, not only special malevolence to the individual slain ; but a generally wicked, depraved, and malignant spirit, a heart regardless of social duty, and deliberately bent upon mischief. Some have been led into mistakes, by not well considering, what the passion of malice really is, *in its popular acceptation.* They have construed it to be a rancour of the mind, lodged in the person killing, *for some time* before the commission of the fact—which is a mistake—arising, from the not well distinguishing between *hatred* and *malice.* But even adopting its most correct popular signification, what is meant *in law* by malice aforethought implied, or malice in a legal sense, differs from what we mean when we speak of malice, in ordinary conversation. For all homicide is considered in law as *malicious,* however suddenly it may be committed, unless it be perpetrated, under such circumstances, as either *justify the act in law*—or *excuse it in law*—or *mitigate its character,* by reason of *accident,* or *the infirmities of human nature*— to a lower grade of felonious homicide, which we call *manslaughter.* And therefore, when questions of malice arise, in cases of homicide, the matter for consideration will be, *whether the act were done with or without just and legal cause or excuse ; whether it were committed under such circumstances of accident or of trial to human infirmity,* as would lower the grade of the offense, to what we call manslaughter. I therefore conceive, that it is advisable—first—and chiefly—in order that the Court may understand what we mean by malice aforethought implied—and also in order that this Court may see with what leniency the law regards the frailties and imperfections of human nature—and further yet, that the Commission may clearly and distinctly understand, what circumstances go to make up the crime of murder, to spend a short time, in a somewhat careful analysis of the law of homicide—to set down what circumstances the law regards as a justification for the killing of a human being ; what circumstances the law regards as an excuse for the killing of a human being : and what circumstances of accident, or of provocation, will prevail upon the law to reduce the degree of guilt from that which attaches to murder to that which attaches to manslaughter.

Homicide is divided into three kinds—first—justifiable homicide ; second—excusable homecide ; and third—felonious homecide—which, again, is sub divided into—first—manslaughter, and second murder.

And first of justifiable homicide. It is to be noted that the law attaches no shade of guilt whatever, or of blame, to justifiable homicide, and this is the only grade of homicide as to which this proposition can be predicated. This grade of homicide is of three kinds : First : Where the proper officer executes a criminal in strict conformity with his sentence ; for here it is evident the act is committed without any criminal intent—without any evil intention, or desire on the part of its perpetrator, to do wrong—without any inadvertance or negligence in the party killing. Second : Where an officer of justice, in the legal exercise of a particular duty, kills a person who resists or prevents him from executing it. A homicide committed under such circumstances, being for the advancement of public justice, receives the mendation, rather than the censure, of the law. Where an officer, in the due execution of his office kills a person who assaults and resists him—where a private person, or an officer, attempts to arrest a man, charged with felony, and is resisted, and in the endeavor to take him, kills him. If a felon flee from justice, and in the pursuit he should be killed, when he cannot otherwise be taken; if there be a riot or a rebellious assembly, and the officers or their assistants, dispersing the mob, kill some of them, when the riot cannot otherwise be suppressed; if prisoners in jail or going to jail, assault or resist the officers, while in the necessary discharge of their duty, and the officers or their aids, in repelling force by force, kill the party resisting.

Third. For the prevention of any atrocious crime attempted to be committed by force, such as murder, robbery, house-breaking in the night time, rape, mayhem, or any other act of felony against the person ; but in such cases the attempt must be not merely *suspected, but apparent* and the danger must be *imminent*, and the opposing force *necessary* to avoid the danger, or defeat the attempt. (See Wharton on Homicide, page 37, Greenleaf on Evidence, vol. 3, page 107, sec. 115, Wharton's Criminal Law, vol. 1, secs. 936-7-8.)

The second division of this subject relates to excusible homicide—and excusible homicide is of two kinds:

First. Where a man *doing* a *lawful act*, without any intention of hurt, by accident kills another; as for instance, where a man is hunting in a park and unintentionally kills a person concealed therein, or if a man be at work with a hatchet, and the head flies off, and kills a bystander. So if a parent is correcting his child or a master his apprentice or scholar, the bounds of moderation not being exceeded, either in the manner, the instrument or the quantity of punishment, and accidentally kills the child apprentice or scholar. If an officer is punishing a criminal within the like bounds of moderation, or within the limits of law, and in such case death ensues. This is commonly called homicide *per infortunium* or by misadventure.

Second. Homicide, *se defendo*, or in self-defence, which exists, when one is assaulted, upon a sudden affray, and in defence of his person, when certain and immediate suffering would be the consequence of waiting for the assistance of the law, and there was no other probable means of escape, he kills the assailant. To reduce homicide in self-defence, to this degree, it must be shown that the slayer was closely pressed by the other party, and retreated as far as he could conveniently or safely, with an honest intent to avoid the violence of the assault. [Wharton on Homicide, p. 36. Greenleaf on Evidence, vol. 3, p. 108, sec. 116. Wharton Crim. Law, vol. 1, sec. 934-5.]

The third division of this subject relates to felonious homicide which is of two kinds. First, Manslaughter—which is, the unlawful and felonious killing of another *without malice, either express or implied;* and second murder-of which more hereafter. And manslaughter, again, is also of two kinds ; first, *voluntary manslaughter,* which is the unlawful killing of another, without express malice, in an accidental quarrel, or in heat of passion, as where upon a sudden quarrel two persons engage in *mutual combat,* on equal terms, and one kills the other : So, if any person be assaulted, with circumstances of violence or gross indignity, and immediately, and in the heat of passion, kills his aggressor, in consequence thereof—it is manslaughter *upon legal provocation ;* Again, when a man discovers another *in the very act of adultory with his wife,* and *immediately* slays the adulterer, it is manslaughter upon legal provocation.

Second—Involuntary manslaughter, is where a man, *doing an unlawful act*, not *amounting to a felony*, by *accident kills another*. It differs from homicide excusable by misadventure, or *per infortunium*, in this, that misadventure always happens in the prosecution of a *lawful act*, but this species of manslaughter in the prosecution of an *unlawful act, not felonious*. It is also to be noted where an involuntary killing happens, in consequence of an unlawful act, it will be murder, *if the act* in the prosecution of which, it occurs, *be felonious*, or if in its *consequence*, it *naturally tends to bloodshed*, (Wharton on Homicide, p. 35 ; Wharton Criminal Law, vol. 1, sec. 931-2-3. Greenlief on Evidence, vol 3. sections 119 to 126, inclusive.)

The second sort of felonious homicide is murder. Now murder is as I have said before—where a person of sound memory and discretion unlawfully kills any reasonable creature in being, and in the peace of the commonwealth, with malice aforethought, either express or implied. And we are now prepared to show what is meant by malice aforethought, implied, or as we have before termed it, "Malice in a legal sense." For, as we have seen—by implications of the law—malice exists in every homicide, where the surrounding circumstances neither justify it, nor excuse it, nor mitigate its character to manslaughter, for any of the reasons set forth in the preceding analysis. From all which, we may deduce, the following corollaries for future use :

First, in every charge of murder—the fact of killing being proved against the party charged, malice is presumed, and to reduce the offence below that crime by circumstances of justification, of necessity, of excuse, of accident, or of trial to human infirmity, *the defendant must prove those circumstances or they must necessarily arise out of the evidence adduced against him*. Second, it may be assumed as a general rule that *all homicide is presumed to be malicious, where an instrument likely to cause death is used by its perpetrator*. Third, the facts of the killing—of his presence—and of his participation therein being proved, or admitted by the prisoner, every matter of justification, or excuse, or of mitigation, must be shown by *him ;* and it is incumbent on him to establish the matter of justification, excuse or mitigation, *beyond a reasonable doubt*.

State *vs.* Peter Johnson, 3 Jones, (N. C.) p. 266, N. B. 273.   State *vs.* Craton, 6 Ired. (N. C.) p. 164.   State *vs.* Starling, 6 Jones, (N. C.) p. 366. State *vs.* Ellick, Winst. L. & E. (N. C.) p. 69.

I have now clearly defined the limits of justifiable homicide, of excusable homicide, and of that species of felonious homicide called manslaughter, and have ascended, at least, to the highest grade of homicide, called murder. And I have addressed myself, with some prolixity, to the task, *principally* for the purpose of explaining what is meant in law by *malice ;* for every act of slaying a human being—all homicide—which is not either justifiable or excusable, or of the nature of manslaughter, as I have defined it, is, in law, malicious, and is murder. The law *implies* the malice, and that implied malice is what we mean by malice in a legal sense. When, therefore, we say, in defining murders, that murder is the unlawful slaying of a human being, in the peace of God, and of the State, of malice aforethought, either express or implied, we mean, by that part of the definition which speaks of malice aforethought, implied, or malice in a legal sense, that the homicide is committed under such circumstances that its perpetrator cannot show what, in law, is a justification, nor an excuse, nor a mitigation—by reason of accident, or human infirmity—of his crime : and there is no possible way of understandinging what we mean by malice aforethought, im-

plied, or malice in a legal sense, unless you first clearly comprehend what
is meant by justifiable homicide, excusable homicide, and manslaughter.
You must define all the latter before you can understand what is meant, in
law, by malice aforethought implied. You must define malice aforethought
implied, before you can take in the legal definition of murder; for all slaying is, in legal contemplation, accompanied with malice aforethought, unless
it evidently appears to be justifiable, or excusable, or mitigated, by reason
of circumstances of accident or of human infirmity, to a lower grade of
homicide than murder. The clear apprehension of these principles is important, because from them we draw the legal corollaries to which I have
referred—that the fact of the killing—of his presence thereat—and of his
participation therein—being proved, or admitted, against the person charged, to reduce his offence below the grade of murder, by circumstances of
duty, of necessity, of accident, or of human infirmity, he must *prove* those
circumstances, or they must necessarily arise out of the evidence adduced
against him. The principle enunciated is applicapble not only to the man
who actually commits the criminal fact, but to *all* the persons who were
present at its commission, aiding and abetting him therein.

If we prove that A actually shot the pistol which slew the deceased, and
that B and C were present, aiding and abetting him in the shooting, the
law calls it murder in *all;* and it is for the persons, who were present, apparently aiding and abetting, to show such circumstances of duty, of necessity, of accident, or of human infirmity, as shall either justify the act, or
excuse it, or reduce it to a lower grade of felonious homicide, which we call
manslaughter; or to show that their *apparent* aiding and abetting was
not real.

I repeat it—the application of this principle is not confined to what we
call *the principal in the first degree*—who is the actual perpetrator of the
criminal fact—but it embraces *all who are present apparently aiding and
abetting him;* and if we prove a killing by one man, and an actual presence
and an actual aiding and abetting, by two or three others, then the presumption of law arises that the killing was murder in all, until the defendants show the contrary,—and—as has been decided in North Carolina—until
they show the contrary *beyond a reasonable doubt.* State *vs.* Peter Johnson, 3 Jones, (N. C.) p. 266, N. B. 273.

If these defendants, Watkins and Powers, were present, aiding and abetting Tolar at the time the homicide is proved to have been committed, and
Tolar fired the pistol which slew Bebee, to reduce their offence to another
grade of homicide than murder, it is necessary for them to show, beyond a
reasonable doubt, the circumstances of duty, of necessity, of accident, or of
human infirmity which the law requires, to change the complexion of their
crime; or to show that their aiding and abetting was only apparent and
was not real.

But it was not my sole object, in thus, at length, considering the distinctions in homicide, to ascertain the meaning which the law attaches to the
word *malice*—to define the crime of *murder*—and to point out that some of
the same rules of law and evidence apply to persons charged as *aiders and
abettors,* which apply to those charged as principal felons in the first degree.
I had yet another, ulterior, object in view—I wished, by these means, to be
enabled to intelligibly illustrate a general principle of the law, for which we
shall have use further on in this argument, when we come more particularly
to consider the case made out against the prisoners Watkins and Powers,

who are charged to have been present aiding and abetting Tolar in the murder alleged.

That principle is—that where the criminal intent which contributes to the crime, is not commensurate with the criminal fact which constitutes its corpus, human law punishes the crime according to the guilt of the *act*, and not according to the guilt of the *intent*. This principal is very general, and to it there are no absolute exceptions, and but few limited ones. Every crime consists of a criminal intent, and a criminal act. However guilty the criminal intent may be, municipal law does not punish it, until it developes itself into either a criminal act, or, at least, an *attempt* to commit a criminal act. It is only the Divine law, which says that " the man who looketh on a woman to lust after her, hath committed adultery with her already in his heart," and threatens punishment accordingly. Yet, while so much is true, human governments are so far *vindictive*, that they never punish a criminal fact, unless it is accompanied with a criminal intent—however deleterious an act may be to society, governments, instituted for the preservation and protection of society, do not punish it, unless its perpetrator *deserves* punishment—in other words—unless he has some criminal will .or intent, which has contributed to the injury.

Laws are instituted for the preservation and protection of society, therefore they inflict no punishment on a criminal intent, until it takes a form which is deleterious to society, and developes itself into a criminal act; but however deleterious to society an act may be, as we have already stated, good laws do not prescribe a punishment for it, unless it is produced or accompanied by a criminal will or intent. The law punishes only when an *injury* has been done to society, and when moreover, the person doing that injury, is, to some extent, at least, deserving of punishment, for his guilty will.

This is what we mean when we say, every crime punishable by law consists of a criminal *intent*, and a criminal *act*. But the criminal intent is sometimes not co-extensive with the criminal fact—since a man sometimes fails to execute his *exact* purpose ; his criminal intent may develope itself into an action more or less criminal—that is more or less injurious to society than he intended. In such cases, if the will or intent be criminal at all, the law punishes the offender according to the guilt of the *fact*, and not according to the lesser or greater guilt of the *intent*.

Looking, then, closely into the doctrine of crime, we shall see, that the evil of the intent, and the evil of the act, added together, constitute the evil punished as crime; and, an act producing an unintended result, must, when evil, be measured either by the intent, or by the result. The legal measure is very generally by the latter, holding the person guilty of the thing done, where there is any kind of legal wrong in the intent, the same as though the thing actually done, were specifically intended.

Bishop on Crim. Law, vol. 1, sec. 411-412-414.

To apply these remarks to the subject of homicide—If A shoot at his own poultry, in a retired place where no one is likely to pass, without intention of bodily harm to any person, and using proper caution to prevent injury to others, and unfortunately happens to kill B, who is accidentally passing within range of his gun, it is excusable homicide only, though it resulted in the death of a man—for A had no criminal intent at all.

But if A wantonly, and without other evil intention, than merely to commit a civil trespass, shoot at the poultry of B—and by accident killeth B—or a stranger, the law calls it manslaughter—involuntary manslaughter, a felony —and punishes the second offence of the same character with death—because

A had some criminal intent—the intent to commit a trespass—and that intent has resulted in the death of a human being—the law measures the guilt of A's crime, by the *result* of his criminal intent, and not by the guilt of the intent itself, and would call his crime murder, but that the malice essential to the crime of murder, is *disproved* by the facts of the case,

Again: A shoots at the poultry of B, and by accident kills a man; it is collected, from the circumstances, that A's intention, in shooting, was to *steal*—the poultry; his crime will be murder—the *result* of A's criminal intent is the death of a human being—and the circumstances accompanying the act develop what the law calls *malice:* A's intent was to commit an inconsiderable theft—the measure of his criminal intent was so much and no more—but the measure of his legal guilt—is the result—*murder*—and the law punishes him accordingly.

(Kel. 107. 6. St. Tr. 222. Fosters Cr. L. 158. 1. Russell on Crimes 540.)

These examples might be multiplied *ad infinitum;* as, where a person gave medicine to a woman, to procure abortion; and where a person put skewers into the womb of a woman for the same purpose; by which acts in both cases, the women were killed, though it was evident the death of the women was not intended, the offences of both criminals were held, clearly, to be murder.

(1. Hale P. C. 429. Tinckler's case 1. East P. C. chap. 5, sec. 17, p. 230, and sec. 124, p. 354. 1. Russ. on Crim. 539.)

But, I refrain from fatiguing the Court, with furthur instances, and examples. I shall content myself, and it is enough for my purpose, to announce as a general and well established rule, derived from these principles: that if an action unlawful in itself, be done deliberately, and with intention of mischief or great bodily harm to particular individuals, or of mischief indiscriminately fall where it may, and death ensue against or beside the original intention of the party, it will be murder.—(Fist, C. S., 261. 1 Russ. on Cri. 538.)

And one more rule—equally general and equally well established, for which we shall have occasion, when we come to apply the law and facts of this case more particularly to Watkins and Powers—that where divers persons resolve generally to resist all opposers in the commission of any breach of the peace and to execute it, in such a manner, as naturally tends to raise tumults and affrays, they must, when they engage in such bold disturbances of the public peace, at their peril, abide the event of their actions—and, therefore, if in doing any of these acts, one of them happens to kill a man, they are all guilty of murder.

(1 Hale, P. C. p. 439, et. seq. 1 Hawk, P. C. chap. 31. sec. 51. 1 East. P. C. chap. 55, sec. 33, p. 257. 4 Bla. Com. p. 200. 1 Russ. on Crim. p. 541.)

May it please the Court: I have now laid down the rules, by which, a tribunal engaged in the investigation of facts, is to be governed, in analysing the evidence adduced, and in drawing legal deductions therefrom. I have also laid down what law of homicide it is, which is, to control this Court, in its decisions; and I have likewise made a careful analysis of the legal subdivisions of homicide, and ascertained what are the essential constituents of the crime called murder; we are, therefore, prepared, to proceed with the investigation of the facts of this case; and I conceive it will be of much assistance to the Court, to ascertain *at once* those points of the case, and those circumstances surrounding it, concerning which, the government, and the defence are agreed, and as to which there can be no reasonable possibility of dispute.

It appears, then, that on Sunday, the tenth day of February, in the present year, one Archy Beebee, a young man of color, was *accused of having attempted to commit a rape*, upon Miss Elvira Massey, in the county of Cumberland, near the town of Fayetteville. It no where appears, in evidence, and it is not proper, that it should appear, whether this charge was well or ill founded; but, in consequence of the charge, it is in evidence, that during the night of the same day Beebee was arrested, and in the afternoon of the ensuing day, at about three o'clock, he was carried to the town hall, in Fayetteville, by the local police, to undergo a preliminary examination, that it might be ascertained whether the proof of the offence charged, was sufficient to justify the magistrates, in committing him to prison to await his trial there for in due course of law. It is not proved, nor is it proper that it should have been proved, whether the committing magistrates came to a conclusion adverse or favorable to the accused, whether there was sufficient evidence to justify his committal or not; but there is a strong probability that the Justices had drawn conclusions unfavorable to Beebee, and had ordered his committal, arising from the fact, which is in evidence, that he left the town hall, still in the charge of the myrmidons of the law.

Some considerable crowd had assembled at, and near the market house in Fayetteville, (in the upper part of which was the town hall,) before Beebee went up for examination; and after he went up, and while this preliminary investigation was going on above stairs, a large, and seemingly, a quiet crowd—as to the number of which, there is a contrariety in the evidence, but which consisted, probably, of somewhere between one and two hundred persons—were assembled at and about, and within, the market house. The crowd was excluded from hearing the trial, by the magistrates, in tenderness to the feelings of the young lady and her friends. As Beebee descended the steps of the town hall, which terminated on the ground floor of the market house, in charge of the officers of the law, and before, or at the time when he passed out of the eastern arch, which forms the main entrance to the market house, on that side, he was assaulted, and efforts were made to take him out of the charge of the officers—for what purposes it does not absolutely and positively appear, except from the details following and by the event.

There can be no doubt as to some of the persons who were engaged in this assault. One of them was the prisoner at the bar, Thomas Powers, another was the prisoner David Watkins, otherwise called Monk Julia. The latter defendant was, without doubt, armed with a knife of no very formidable proportions. As to the other, Powers, there is some little contrariety in the testimony, whether he was armed with any weapon or not. One of the witnesses at least, has armed him both with a knife and a pistol: and I think the evidence with reference to his being armed with a knife, is sufficiently conclusive to justify me in stating *that* as one of the admitted facts of the case. But about this time Thomas Powers certainly attempted to seize Beebee, and made a verbal demand for him on the Sheriff.

From the time when the effort was first made to take Beebee from the hands of the officers, until the moment when he was shot, but a very short time elapsed. It could not have been upon a comparison of *all* the testimony, both for the prosecution and for the defence, more than a minute—at the uttermost two minutes—from the time Beebee crossed the threshold of the market house, to the moment when he lost his life. During that period of time, the assault, which had been initiated by Powers and Watkins or

Monk and others, and which consisted of verbal demands for the prisoner, made upon the Sheriff, conched in threatening language—of attempts to use their knives upon him—upon the part of the two whose names are specifically given, and of some others whose names are unknown, (for it appears that several knives were drawn, and brandished in the crowd during the rush, according to the evidence of so many witnesses) and also of a violent rush upon the part of many others, perhaps the greater part of the crowd, and an effort made by them to take him out of the hands of the officers, this assault thus initiated and continued, never ceased, but was extended by continuous and repeated pressure of the crowd, upon the officers who surrounded the prisoner, until the moment when he lost his life. During this rush or succession of assaults, the sheriff of the county exhorted the crowd to desist—ordered his assistants to use their clubs, and their clubs were used all in vain.

That Archy Beebee was killed then and there, is a point which does not admit of discussion. That he was killed by means of a leaden bullet, shot from a pistol, held in the hands of some one who was in that crowd, is another point, which is not open for discussion. That Tolar, as well as Powers and Watkins were in the crowd, at, and during the whole time of this transaction is also proven; and it is equally well established that Tolar was armed with a pistol on the occasion, and by several of the witnesses for the prosecution, and by one tendered by the prisoners, that he had the pistol out in his hand at or near the time of the killing. Such being the leading facts of the case, upon which both prosecution and defence must be agreed, it is plain, that, whoever, was the immediate instrument by whose hands, Beebee's life was destroyed, was guilty of no lower grade of homicide than the crime of murder, the legal definition of which offence I have endeavored to set out, in the preceding part of this argument.

The question, and one of the principal points of inquiry, it is according to the prisoners view of the case, here presents itself, although I think its importance has been greatly magnified and exaggerated by the defence—who shot the pistol the bullet from which slew Archy Beebee? In whose hands was it held? By whose volition was it directed, when Archibald Beebee was then and there shot to death.

And here I must pause—painfully pause—to direct the attention of the Court to the enormity of the crime that was committed, by whomsoever it was done—pause, because so much has been publicly said by the Counsel for the defence of a contrary character: pause, because this offence has been treated with so much levity, by the gentlemen who represent the prisoners; pause, because, as I conceive, it is the bounden duty of every prosecutor—representing, as he does the outraged justice of the government—not, simply, to endeavor to being felons to justice, but also, in performing that duty, when the occasion demands it, to inculcate sound principles of morality, and of policy—from the lofty station, in which his sacred duty places him—I say, I must pause, to consider the enormity of this offence if for no other reason—yet for this—that one of the Counsel for the prisoners, announced to this Court, and to the public, that the crime, which on that winter's day, stained a whole community with blood, "was murder, but it was as nigh akin to virtue, as murder ever grew to be." Aye—and also, because another counseller, in his address to this Court—at this very time—even now—when the waves of recent social strife—flecked with fragments of the wrecks of all of this life's precious things—are not yet sunk down into a calm political sea—declared, before what purports to be a Court of *justice,* that as he conceived, it was advisable, and proper, and desirable, and right,—that—when crimes of the nature of that charged against Beebee, were attempted—the public should understand, that the populace stood ready to redress them by mob violence—that when fathers went to their graves, they might know that he, and others who thought as he did—stood ready—if like evils should befall the orphans whom they left behind—not waiting for conviction—not waiting for discussion—not waiting for legal proof—to seize upon the victim, who was *accused* of an attempt to commit a rape, and suddenly to take away his life—that it was well to take their victim grossly—full of bread—"with all his crimes broad-blown, and flush as May"—and, unprepared, to send him to his last account. I have heard such principles enunciated, in the course of this discussion, as have filled me with horror; and, I intend here, as I have elsewhere—upon all occasions—under all circumstances—having entertained similar views even in the midst of revolution—to denounce mob-violence, in whatever shape it may be presented, or for whatever wrongs to the community, real or supposed, it may be called into action. Of all the creatures that God has made, there is not another one so terrible, as that many-headed monster—a mob. Of all the evil passions which have been evoked out of a corrupt and travailing creation, none are so wild—so fierce—so untamable—so foul, as those, which possess the hearts of an inflamed and brutal mob—even as the devils possessed the swine of Gadara, which "ran violently down a steep place into the sea, and perished in the waters." Upon the face of this accursed and troubled earth, there is no bear, robbed of her whelps, so deaf to reason—there is no hungry tiger of the desert so callous to pity—no hyena, battening on the horrid spoils of the church-yard, so obscenely foul—as a mad, unpitying vulgar mob. I will not, upon any occasion—especially when I am acting as the representative of the law—permit sentiments to pass unnoticed, and unrebuked, the tendency of which is to justify any man, or set of men, who, for any cause whatever, have taken the law into their own hands, and destroyed human life.

But at last, all the prisoners' Counsel have said upon this subject is from the purpose of this trial. It is hardly necessary for me to remind this Court of the fact, that the crime with which Archy Bebee was *charged* can have no weight whatever, in any point of view, with them in the decision at which they are to arrive. We are not engaged in investigating this case with a view to redressing the wrongs of Archy Bebee. He has gone to his place. The injury which has been done to society by this act of lawless violence is the immediate matter which is awaiting the sanction of the law. I am quite sure this method of discussion has had—I am equally sure that it will have—no effect; that it has thrown no appreciable weight into the scales of justice which are now poised in the hands of this Commission. Whether the deceased may have deserved the fate with which he was rewarded or not, is a question which, as I think, it is unnecessary to discuss. It will be in vain, I am sure it has been in vain, to attempt, by reason of Archy Bebee's alleged offence, to in any way control the decision of this Court. But so much denunciation has been heaped upon the head of the deceased that I am compelled to speak of his wrongs. It is fair and proper that I should submit to this Court that, *in the eyes of the law*, he was an innocent man, until he was pronounced guilty by a judicial tribunal, in which the law was administered according to the course of procedure prescribed by law. Until some legal tribunal had pronounced him guilty of the offence with which he was charged, he was as innocent, in the eyes of the law, as if he had never been charged. But admitting—*pro hac vice*—that the deceased was guilty of an attempt to ravish a defenceless girl—even that such a one should be cut off cruelly and suddenly, as Bebee was—no matter how redly he may have been stained with sin—no matter how deeply he may have been steeped in crimes—that the vilest felon should be thus cut off as he was—even " in the flowers of his sin—unhousel'd—disappointed—unan- nealed—no reckoning made, but sent to his account with all his imperfec- tions on his head,"—instead of checking crime, encourages it, by making its perpetrator the object of our commiseration and pity, rather than of our hatred, loathing and contempt.

Adopting, for the nonce, the views of the prisoners' Counsel—that the kill- ing of Beebee, under all the circumstances, was as mild a *murder* as is known to the law—regarding, for the present, the crime of these defendants, as a very trivial one—still, if it be the object of punishment to prevent crime, how much better, if Beebee were guilty, would it have been, to have left him to be degraded, and dishonored, and punished by the law, than by his sudden, cruel and remorseless murder—to have given a prominence to his *wrongs*, that overshadows his guilt, and makes him an object that now excites only our commiseration. I know not of what stuff the opposing Counsel, and the members of this Court are made, but for my own part I am not given overmuch to the melting mood—yet—guilty though that man may have been—there were moments, in the course of this trial, when I could with difficulty restrain the tears from springing to my eyes ; when the sad story of the cruel fate, and sudden, and untimely, death, of this young negro was told—when the Sheriff of Cumberland County stood upon that stand, calm, firm, immovable as Justice's self, and manfully did his painful duty, by testifying in this cause—when he imitated the last sough of the dead man's bursting heart, and told us how he breathed out his final sigh for life, leaning upon the breast of his jailor, the last minister of the law's most cruel vengeance, and closed his reproachful eyes upon the light of this world forever—I think it no shame to own, that my heart bled for him— for his wrongs—for his untimely fate. And from time to time, as the evi- dence in this cause was rendered, imagination pictured on her dim canvass— this young negro—lately enfranchised—with his heart and mind just open- ing to the consciousness of the great privileges, as he conceived, which had been so newly bestowed upon him, hoping now, for the future, to enjoy a new life—suddenly betrayed by his wild, hot, African blood, and the mad devil, Lust, into an attempt to commit the foulest crime known to society— as suddenly arrested with all the grossness of his sin yet in his heart—and, bound and helpless, carried into the midst of an angry, pitiless mob—assail- ed—struggling for his very life—springing like a wild deer in the forest, from the earth, to escape the knives of his assassins—striving—sobbing—sighing— begging—for his life, in his supreme agony—and there no soul to pity him— and I confess I have no patience with any such methods of administering *justice ;* I confess that with me, and, as I think, with the majority of men, the wild *justice,* thus administered, loses all good effect, is stripped of every shred of virtue—and shows itself in all its naked deformity, as cowardly and hideous assassination.

It is all radically wrong. If the laws are defective let them be changed by time, and proper exertion, but in God's name, let us not hear it proclaim- ed in a court of justice by counsel, learned in the law, high in position, of weight and authority in the community—that offences of the character of this one alleged to have been committed by the prisoners at the bar, are "as nigh akin to virtue as murder ever gets to be," that it is right and proper that the ravisher and the would-be ravisher, should understand, and that the public should know, that every honest hand is armed with the assassin's knife, and the mob stand ready, without investigation, to administer vengeance—not justice—for his foul offence.

But I beg of the Court, if at any time, in the zeal of advocacy, or in the heat, that necessarily arises in debate—I utter one word which is calculated to prejudice their minds, or to harden their hearts against the prisoners at the bar, to discard it in the name of God and justice, in coming to their finding. My desire and intention has been from the beginning of this case, my desire and intention is now—and I speak as in the sight of God—I have no personal or political interest in the event of this trial, and in all that I have done or shall do in this connection, my hands are clean—my heart pure—my conscience is unwounded—my desire and intention has been and is—only to assist this Court, in arriving at a just and legal decision—and if at any time I wander from that path by any heated expressions, or strained arguments, or erroneous statements of law, I beg that the Court, in their retirement, will correct my errors, and discard every sentiment, or thought which is calculated to inflame passion, or to excite prejudice against these unfortunate prisoners, and will consider the case even with tenderness towards the accused. I wish them to have a trial, which is strictly just, and leans towards mercy. There is one of them for whom in my heart of hearts I feel as deeply as I ever felt for a man in the like perilous situation. There are tender ties between one of the prisoners and myself, to which it is unnecessary and unbecoming for me to make further allusion here. But I have a duty to perform in this cause—and so help me God—I shall do it. I have no wish to take one step beyond it—but I do feel it to be my duty, and I shall feel it to be my duty, to speak in very plain terms of much that has been said by the Counsel for the prisoners, and of much that concerns this cause, and the prisoners themselves; and I shall speak out, and leave the consequences to fall where they may. I do feel it to be my duty to call a felon a felon : I do feel it to be my duty to the best of my ability to brush all the gloss and gilding off of crime, and to show it in its naked ugliness. I feel it to be my duty when an effort is made to make a hero of a very common place felon, and to dress him in a lion's skin, to the extent of my power, to strip off the lion's hide, and hang a calf skin on his recreant limbs. And when it is announced here, by learned and distinguished gentlemen, with a flourish of trumpets,—that if one of these prisoners goes from this dock to the gallows, for his crime, his name and his image will be enshrined in the hearts of the women of the land as the spotless martyr, who, in defence of feminine virtue, has lost his life—it is my duty to append as a part of the as yet unwritten history of this second Sir Launcelot du Lac—that having set his life upon a cast, in support of his mistaken principles, and in defiance of the law, he failed to stand the hazard of the die—that having had the *bravery* to commit the crime of murder, as the best means to protect the women of the land from the lewd assaults of their late negro lackeys, he failed to have the *courage* to own his offence and bear the consequencies of his act,—and that—oh, felon, like ! he attempted on his trial to thrust an innocent man into his place, and to leave another to suffer for this honorable crime, which he himself had committed. And if, in spite of all this, the prophecy of my brother Phillips shall be verified, and the women of the State select the prisoner Tolar as the hero martyr of their sex—I can but say the condition of the feminine mind of this community will be damnable, and need purging. I allude to these things, not to prejudice the Court—I entertain no fear of that—but it is a plain duty so to speak, roundly in the interest of public virtue and justice, and to show the absurdity of these attempts to make a Bayard out of a felon. For my convictions are strong as death of the guilt of these men, and I think, by the time that we get through with the case, this Court will fully concur with me. The Court, too, have heard the terms in which Phillips, a witness for the prosecution—has been spoken of by the prisoners' Counsel, but suppose—for the sake of argument—that Phillips is truly and entirely innocent—as I think the Court will come to the conclusion he is—and that these prisoners have suborned witnesses, or at least produced witnesses here who are endeavoring to prove that he is the guilty party— and Tolar innocent. Pray,—in what degree does the vileness of Phillips, as alleged by the prisoners' Counsel, differ from the vileness of those defendants, who introduced such evidence as proved,—if the Court shall agree with me that Phillips is to be believed?

"A man may see how this world goes, with no eyes—
Look with thine ears—see how yon justice rails
Upon yonder simple thief! Hark, in thine ear,
Change places, and—handy-dandy—which is the justice
And which is the thief?"

But, as I have before said, the injury which has been done to society, by this act of lawless violence, is the immediate matter which is awaiting the sanction of the law; and, in this connection, I have the right and it is my duty, especially when we consider the present political condition of this country, and of this State, to speak of the peculiar character of the offence which was committed that day in the most public part of the town of Fayetteville, in the presence of many of her citizens, and in the blaze of the noon-day sun. It indicated what, in my heart, I believe to be the prevailing and the pervading sin of this nation—a spirit of defiance to legitimate authority—of utter lawlessness and of insubordination; for not only was it an attempt, upon the part of those who were immediately concerned in this homicide, to administer mob-law upon one who, it was alleged, had been guilty of a very heinous offence—but it was an attempt, upon their part, to administer such law at a time when he was in the hands of the law, and especially and peculiarly under its protection. Its significancy went beyond this. On account of the peculiar relations which the State at that time sustained—and now sustains—towards the United States, a change in our own legislation had lately been effected, by which the punishment inflicted on a negro, for an attempted rape upon a white woman, had been diminished in its character and extent; for formerly if a man of color was charged with such an attempt, and found guilty, he was punished with death; but on account of the recent political revolution in the State, the local legislature had, not long before this crime is alleged to have been attempted, abolished the death penalty in such cases. I understand by their conduct that those who were engaged in the perpetration of the homicide now on trial, proposed, by that means, to enter their most solemn protest against any such changes in our legislation, or in the system of our laws; and, upon that issue, to stake their lives upon a cast, resolved to stand the hazard of the die. It is not necessary for me to dwell long upon this subject, in order to fix it in the minds of the Court, that crimes of this character, perpetrated under such circumstances as those which I have indicated, are amongst the more heinous offences of which one, who is a member of an organized political society, can be guilty. Such offences strike at the *very foundation of all law*. Nay, they sink deeper, and strive to cut up *even society*—which, in a logical sequence, is anterior to law—by the very roots; for man is so constituted that government is essential to society, and organized society is essential to the existence of human beings, even in the lowest state of civilization. For what shall we call a state of nature but the state in which men have ever been found—a state of society? And how is society capable of existing without government? and who has given man that complex nature, which is the last visible cause of both these results, but God himself? It is folly in us to resist the evidence of our senses, striving to found governments upon the false principles of selfishness alone, and of a state of warfare between all our species, when facts establish that if our race is a selfish it is also a social one; that our beneficent Father has not put us into the world with our hand against every man, and every man's hand against us; but that He delivers us into the hands of a *society*—of a society regulated by the dictates of wisdom and justice—of a society which gives alms to the indigent—defence to the weak—instruction to the ignorant—consolation to the despairing—support to the helpless—nurture to the aged—faith to the doubtful—and charity to the whole human race—which diffuses its beneficent exertions from acts of tenderness to the infant, when he first cries in his cradle, to acts of comfort and preparation to the dying man on his way to the tomb.

Now all of those crimes, which indicate a spirit of lawless insubordination tend to produce, and are intended and calculated to produce, and bring about, a state of anarchy and chaos. Our country has suffered too severely from, has been wounded too deeply by offences of this character. Courts to permit them to go unpunished. "Mercy but murders, pardoning for the those who kill."

I ask this Court—what is it, that gives force and stability to all governments. and induces peace, and tranquility throughout the land? what is it—but a reverence for authority, because it is authority, and a cheerful submission to the law, because it is law? It is this pervading sentiment inhabiting the hearts, and controling the acts of British subjects which has sustained the English monarchy while, all about it, other European governments, have tottered to their fall—until it stands in the midst of ruins. It is this sentiment which justified the great Commoner of England, in his impassioned burst of eloquence in commendation of Anglo Saxon liberty—when he declared, in a maxim of the law—that an English man's house was his castle. Said the illustrious Chatham: "In this country, the meanest peasant, within his cottage, may defy the power of the British crown. It may be frail—its doors may shake—its roof may shake—the wind may blow through it—the rain may enter it—the storm may enter it—but the King of England cannot enter. The Royal Majesty of Britain, surrounded with all his myrmidons of power, *dare not cross the threshold of that ruined tenement.*"

Nations have passed away—races of Kings have waxed old and perished—but these principles of liberty have endured—Stuarts and Tudors—Yorkists and Lancastrians—Plantagenets and Normans—Danes and Saxons—have died and been forgotten—they are all gone—sunk down—down—with the tumult that they made—and the rolling, and the trampling of ever new generations passes over them—and they hear them not any more again forever; but the principles of the British government—of the British constitution—still live; because her people acknowledge that they are founded in justice, they are planted in right. That justice which, emanating from the bosom of the Deity Himself, burns in a feeble spark, in the heart of every man that breathes—that right " whose throne is the bosom of God, whose is voice the

harmony of the world—which angels and men, and creatures, of what con
dition soever, must, with uniform consent, recognize and admire, as the pa·
rent, of their peace and joy." These principles yet endure ; yea, and they
shall endure.

> " When all that we know, or feel, or see,
> Shall pass like an unreal mystery,"
> "The cloud capped towers, the gorgeous palaces ;
> The solemn temples, the great globe itself ;
> Yea, all which it inherit, shall dissolve ;
> And like an unsubstantial pageant faded,
> Leave not a rack behind ; *we* are such stuff,
> As dreams are made of, and *our* little life,
> Is rounded by a sleep—"

But, there is that which existed before the world began, and which will
exist, when this earth, and all that it contains, shall have been burned into
ashes—Law—Truth—Right—Justice—they are eternal, and " GOD IS THEM."
But, it is not alone the spirit of lawlessness which this crime manifests,
that deserves the especial animadversion of the Court, but the ill chosen
time, which was selected, by its perpetrators, for the purpose of making this
manifestation of violence. Lawless violence at such a time as this, which
we live in, especially indicates, what, in the language of the law, is called, a
heart regardless of social duty, and fatally bent upon mischief. It indicates
that stubbornness of disposition—that deliberate determination to refuse to
be taught by the lessons of experience—the general adoption of which, upon
the part of her citizens, is the sure precursor of a nation's destruction.
The recent bloody war, which has brought upon this country, North and
South, so many woes, may--in my humble opinion—be traced to the same
spirit of insubordination, in both sections, North and South—peculiarly manifested by these prisoners, in the perpetration of their crime ; and if history
teaches anything--if any lesson of wisdom is to be gathered from the records
of the past--it is--that such evils as we have endured, are permitted to fall
upon a country, in order that her citizens may profit by the lesson which
they teach, and abandon the faults, which lead to such disasters.
I cannot but believe, that when a people have been subjected to heavy
misfortunes, which palpably result from a national fault, those who refuse to
be taught by past experience, and who, immediately after such experience,
persist in repeating that fault—even in a less degree, are peculiarly obnoxious
to the penalties of the law, and are amongst the worst enemies to society.
Lawlessness has been the curse of this nation ; and, as in other instances of
national sin, it has worked out its own punishment—woe be to the man !
woe be to the nation ! that refuses to be instructed by the teachings of the
Judge of the whole earth. For, I am not among those who have much faith in
frequent, direct visitation from the Most High : such visitations are possible, and undoubtedly *sometimes* occur ; but in controlling nations, as in all
other manifestations of His power, I cannot but believe, that, the God of all
the earth, *usually* works by general rules ; and permits national crimes to
effect their own cure, by showing mankind, the certain suffering, which is
their legitimate consequence. It is natural to attribute the sufferings
which overwhelm an afflicted country, to the immediate anger of God—to
his wrath, for the misdeeds of which that country has been guilty—but for
myself, I do not believe in such exhibitions of God's anger. When wars come,
and pestilence, and famine—when a general conflagration sweeps over the
land, or an earthquake sinks it—when the people of a land are worse than

decimated so that the living are hardly able to bury their dead—I cannot coincide with those, who attribute these things to the direct visitations of God I do not believe, that our God stalks darkly along the clouds, laying thousands low, with the arrows of death—and those thousands, the more ignorant—because men, who are not so ignorant, have displeased Him : nor, if in his wisdom he did so, can I conceive, but that He intends, by such means, to force a rebellious and stiff-necked generation to change their ways, and to do, for the future, that which His wisdom has shown to be good and right.

But—though I do not believe in exhibitions of God's anger,—I do believe in exhibitions of his mercy ; when men by their folly, and the shortness of their vision, have brought upon themselves penalties, which seem to be overwhelming—to which no end can be seen—which would be overwhelming, were no help coming to us but our own—then God raises His hand—not in anger, but in mercy—and by His wisdom does for us, that, for which our wisdom, had been insufficient.

But on no Christian basis, can I understand the justice, or acknowledge the propriety of any spurious mercy, extended by a nation, to those, who refuse to be taught, by reason, and by bitter experience, and who presume to combat the settled purposes of the Most High. If He be wise, would we change His wisdom. If He be merciful would we limit his mercy?

A mighty conflagration lays a great city in ashes, and very frightful are the flames, as they rush through the cabins of the poor ; and very frightful is the case of individuals who are ruined by the stroke. But—if this beneficent agency did not from time, disencumber our crowded places, we should ever be living in narrow alleys, with stinking gutters, and the supply of water at a minimum ; and wise men take the lesson to heart, and new cities rise up, in splendor, from the ashes, into which old cities had been consumed by fire.

There comes upon us some strange disease—and men pray God to stay His hand ; but the disease, when it has passed, has taught us lessons of cleanliness, which no master less stern, would have made acceptable. But mankind, if wise must accept the lesson, and obey its teachings. A famine strikes us ; and we again beg that His hand may be stayed ; beg as the Greeks were said to beg when they thought the anger of Phœbus was hot against them, because his priest had been dishonored—we so beg, thinking God's anger is hot against us. Lo! the famine passes away, and the land, which had been brought to the dust, by man's folly, is once more prosperous and happy, and blossoms as the rose; for men have accepted God's teachings, and abandoned the follies which lead to such fatal results. Very frightful are these violent remedies ; and very frightful has been the violent remedy, which was intended, in mercy, to bring us, as a nation, out of our misfortunes, and cure that terrible irreverence for authority—that excessive individuality, and self-sufficiency—that stubborn disregard of legitimate power—that fearful lawlessness—which has inflicted upon this nation an Iliad of woes. Can we not profit by the teachings of the book of books, for well doth it say, " Behold to *obey* is better than sacrifice, and to *hearken* than the fat of rams; for disobedience is as a sin of witchcraft, and stubborness is as iniquity and idolatry."

Entertaining such opinions—I have been astounded—I have been shocked at the levity, with which, the crime of these prisoners has been treated by the Counsel for the defence. To me, it seems frightful, at a time like the present, succeeding the recent social convulsions which have agitated this country, from its circumference to its center—to hear Counsel learned in the law—high in position—of weight and influence in society, lay down the propositions, and avow the principles, which have been uttered by the Counsel for the defence. I repeat it—the Counsel who opened this cause for the defence stated, that it was true—this was a case of murder, upon the part of some one, but it was as nigh akin to virtue as murder ever gets to be. The Counsel who succeeded him stated that, in his opinion, it was desirable—not only that the actual seducer, and the actual ravisher, but—that any man who was *charged* with having *attempted* to *ravish* a woman, should without further legal process, be punished by violence and mob law. I have stated before, that, in my opinion, the greatest woes of this country have sprung from this very spirit of lawlessness, which the Counsel for the defence seem willing to encourage and commend ; such sentiments, are objectionable at any time, but at a time like the present, there is a peculiar impropriety in their utterance in promiscuous crowds. Are the Counsel ignorant of the present disturbed times in which we live ? Have they failed to observe the spirit of the age, which has been evoked out of the abnormal and agitated state of the nation, which accompanied, and is immediately consequent upon a great and terrible social war ? Do our people intend to learn no lesson by their sad experience ? A subject so splendid as the short period of the late social war, so full of political, and military instruction—replete with such great and heroic actions—adorned by so many virtues and darkened by so many crimes, never yet fell to the lot of the historian. During the five years of its progress, this nation has gone through more than a hundred years of ordinary existence; and the annals of modern history will be searched in vain, for a parallel to that brief period of anxious effort and checkered achievement. In no former age were events of such magnitude crowded together, or interests so momentous at issue between contending parties. And are we to learn nothing from the past ? Pause for a moment to contemplate our situation.

North Carolina, with the rest of the States comprising the late Confederacy, is utterly ruined—thoroughly and entirely undone. I do not now urge this as a matter of complaint, or to induce despair—far from it. My object is to prevail upon our people—high and low, educated and uneducated, white and black, capitalists and laborers—to entirely realize the stern fact, as the first and most efficient step towards working out a remedy. The moneyed capital of the State has been destroyed—its labor demoralized—its cultivated lands have become waste places. It is nothing new in history—this sad picture. It is the old story—the old, old story—which has been mournfully repeating itself, from the time when Nimrod was a mighty hunter before the Lord, and went out and founded Babylon. It is but another version of " *vae victis ;*" it is but another instance, entered on the continually growing scroll of Clio to prove, that for unsuccessful revolutions, *the vanquished party must pay*—the men in groans and blood—the women and children in agony and tears. Seeing the horrors which lawlessness has brought upon us, may I not justly say, I am *horribly afraid* at hearing such sentiments advocated, as have been enunciated by the prisoners' counsel in the course of this trial.

For, now, that the immediate violence of war is over, we are at a more dangerous period of our national existence, than while it was in actual progress. This is what the great practical statesman of England meant, when he said, that "no revolution was so dangerous as a *restoration.*" For wars, even civil wars, are not productive of unmixed evil. There are sure to arise out of times of such fierce trial, and sharp suffering, examples of heroic virtue, of superhuman piety, and of noble self conquest and self-devotion, to set off the many moral and physical evils which a state of warfare drags in its bloody train. There is nothing supernatural in this. The magnitude of the effects produced arises entirely from the intensity of the feelings which are aroused; and the extremes of virtue and of vice which are exhibited, from the incitements to the former and the allurements to the latter which are presented. And—to those who measure human advancement by its approach to the standard of divine excellence—such examples of virtue—shining like good deeds in a naughty world—afford some compensation, for the sufferings which they themselves have undergone. But, when war is ended, these extraordinary incitements to virtue cease, while the evils of war do not end with the cessation of active hostilities. Perhaps the greatest danger to organized society occurs, when murder, rapine and open violence are at an end—when fire and sword are laid aside—and men's minds, being imbued with ideas incident to a time of storm and turbulence, they themselves are subject only to the milder influence and suasion of the principles of government, which obtain in times of peace. It is this season of trial, through which the United States, and the federal scheme of government which we have adopted, are now passing. And is this the time in which gentlemen of learning, of position, and of influence, should advocate a return to the principles of that "wild justice" of revenge—of which Lord Bacon speaks—as a substitute for the laws of the land?

Let me picture to these gentlemen who advocate a return to lawless violence, some of the fruits which it has borne. Let me sketch the scenes, or some of them, which have been so familiar to the gentlemen composing this Court, during the last five or six years—the thousands of valiant souls of heroes who have gone down into Hades; men who have not met death, in the due course of nature, and when supported by all the acts of comfort and preparation, which dying men desire, on their way to the tomb; but soldiers—who, face to face, have met and grappled with the last enemy—the pale monster, at whose approach the bravest of us shudder—amid the red glare of artillery, and the hurtling missiles of a battle; amid the charging of horsemen, and the fierce, hoarse shouts of soldiers; amid all the terrible agony, and pathos, and passion, of that fearful Aceldama, a field of battle.

It is true—no human power can give us back our dead. There is no Jesus now upon the earth, to stand at the open gates of Nain, to take by the hand the corpse carried out for burial, and already sinking into the infamy of corruption, and to give back into the arms of the mourning mothers of this land the only sons of those who are widows. There is no Divine Friend to visit our little village Bethanies throughout this sorrowing land—to weep at the sepulchres of our dead, and to restore Lazarus—bound hand and foot with grave'clothes—to the overflowing hearts of our Marthas and Marys. The fathers and the sons—the brothers and the lovers—who have been carried across our thresholds in their bloody shrouds, are laid to sleep, until the trumpet shall sound—and the dead shall be raised incorruptible—and the earth and the sea shall give up their dead—and we shall be changed. No earthly power can gather together the bleaching bones which now lie scattered over this continent, from Pennsylvania to Texas, knit them again into the manly forms they once made up, and infuse upon them the glorious glow of manly strength and youth they once sustained. No hand is there to rebuild the cheerful homesteads throughout this desolated land, where cluster all the happy memories and blooming hopes that lighted up our boyish days. No earthly power can cover with springing grass, and laughing corn, the naked fields, whose solitary garment now is but the purple gloom which hangs above the hillocks where our heroes sleep. No earthly gift can compensate us for the carking cares—the fierce and fiery anguish—the bitter brooding gloom—that have withered many a human heart to ashes during our late social struggle. No! we cannot bring back our dead—we cannot—*God cannot*—undo the past ; and they ! they have gone with the past. Some timid lads, that would have screamed at a scratch, met the King of Terrors with smiles and triumph ; and for them the grave was Jordan, and death but the iron gates to life everlasting ; and some were ripe Christians, and, like ripe corn, held their heads lower than when they were green—and the grave, it seemed to be ripening them—and lying wounded they waited for the end. Their bodies failed them more and more, until they could not even praise their Redeemer ; yet they lay and triumphed ; with hands put together in prayer—and eyes full of praise and joy unspeakable—they climbed fast to God ; and while they mounted in spirit their breath came at intervals unusually long ; and hard men and rough soldiers stood by and wept, to see Death conquer the body, and be conquered by the soul. And at last there came a breath unusually long—a breath like a sigh—and we waited—waited for another—waited—and waited in vain. They had calmly ceased to live. They had passed over the dark river, and rested under the trees—in the groves of Amaranth and the meadows of Asphodel. And we ! what can we do? All that is left us is the sad lesson which these gentlemen are advocating that we should unlearn. But shall I be recreant to these memories and to the lessons which they taught? I, who was the companion of the men who so suffered from the effects of this lawlessness, north and south—I their companion—and their brother-in-arms, who saw them enduring hunger—and thirst—and cold—and heat—and nakedness—and weariness—and at last, meeting the supreme moment of their fate, when life it self had become but an all-absorbing sense of throbbing, palpitating agony. God do so to me, and more also, if my lips are so dumb—if my heart is so cold—if I am so very a slave to momentary feeling and passion,—that I hesitate or waver to do my humble part to prevent the return of these horrors of the past.

The Court here took a recess of fifteen minutes, when Mr. Haywood went on as follows :

I am aware that I have said more than enough on this subject, and I now address myself to the discussion of some of the *facts* of this case. This Court is, in my opinion, quite as able to weigh the *testimony* in the cause as the Counsel, and I have not spent, and shall not spend, a great deal of time in its consideration ; but, may it please the Court, I shall inquire into this question of fact—among others—who fired the pistol shot which killed Archy Beebee? I think I can show to the Court, before I finish, that it is totally immaterial, to their decision in this case, whether Tolar fired that pistol or not ; that, even presuming it was fired by some one, who is not here *named* in the charge and specification, if the Court is satisfied that the pistol was fired by *some one* in the crowd at the market house, under the circumstances given in evidence, and that these prisoners were, at the time of the firing, acting, as the evidence shows them to have been, we have made out a case of murder against all of them ; and it is a murder sufficiently alleged, as to them, in the charge and specification now before the Court. Undue prominence has been given to this point, in the evidence, in our efforts to ascertain and identify the persons who fired the pistol; for whether the Court shall come to the conclusion that Phillips fired it, or that Tolar fired it, or that it was fired by some one to the Court unknown, if this Commission accept the rest of the evidence, offered by the prosecution, as proved—showing the relative position of the party who did fire—no matter who it was—with reference to Tolar, Powers and Watkins, and the manner in which they and all of them were engaged at the time of the firing—they were all guilty of murder, in the eyes of the law. But, chiefly in order to sustain the credit of one or two witnesses for the prosecution, who, as I think, are entitled to some consideration—partly because the Court may differ with me on the points of law just suggested and to be hereafter more fully stated—and partly, also, because the defence *has* given prominence to this point of fact, I shall enter at some length into the question—"who fired that pistol?"

One thing is apparent, at setting out, that seventeen men, white and black, have been produced here by the prosecution, and have sworn that Tolar fired it; that they saw him do it; and that there is no possibility that they could be mistaken about it. One man, and one only—James Atkinson—has been introduced for the defence, who swears, positively, that Phillips fired that pistol. Several other witnesses, offered by the prisoners—as Faircloth, Arey, Mullins and Sykes—have given in evidence *circumstances* which point directly towards Phillips as the man who fired the pistol shot ; but it is to be remembered, that it is admitted by the prosecution, and by Phillips himself, that he had a pistol in his hand, and was standing near Beebee, before, or at, or just after the moment when the deceased was slain ; and bearing this circumstance in mind, it is possible that the evidence of these four witnesses may be true, or that it may be a very slight exaggeration of the truth, and yet that Tolar may have fired the shot which slew Beebee, as the seventeen witnesses for the prosecution testified. As no one of the four witnesses named pretends to swear that Phillips actualled *fired* the pistol—indeed—as they all swear that they *did not see him* fire it—and so the act of firing, which is of so marked and striking a nature, did not fix their attention—it is even within the range of possibility, that *they* may have made innocent misrepresentations in their testimony on this point. But Atkinson swears positively that Phillips, while standing within a few feet of him, (the witness) fired the pistol, the bullet from which slew Beebee. If this be so, the firing must, necessarily, have attracted and absorbed his attention ; and if Atkinson has told an untruth, as to this matter, he has perjured himself. There is no possibility of accounting for his misrepresentations, on the ground of inadvertence, inattention, incapacity, error, mistake, defect of memory, or the like infirmity on his part. The same remarks, made upon Atkinson and his testimony, are also applicable to the seventeen witnesses for the prosecution, and their testimony—to each and all of them—who have sworn that Tolar fired the pistol. They told the truth, or they are perjured. There is no possibility of innocent mistake on their part. So the question fairly resolves itself into this: Did these seventeen perjure themselves, or did this one swear to a lie?

Suppose, may it please the Court, that a clock were set up in this room, and eighteen men were placed in this apartment, under the strictest injunctions to observe the clock, and note carefully, at what hour the hands pointed, when the clock first struck during their watch, and the number of strokes sounded. Suppose, at the end of two hours, the eighteen were called out, and examined, upon oath, touching the matters given them in charge ; and *seventeen* say, upon oath, that the clock first struck when the hands pointed to twelve o'clock, and that twelve strokes were sounded—and the eighteenth says, that it first struck when the hands pointed to one o'clock and that one stroke was sounded. They were put into the room, for the express purpose of noting these facts—their attention was especially directed to them—they all had equal opportunities for observation—they are all men of the ordinary general character for truth—they all knew they would be subsequently called upon to testify, as to the matter, under oath. Which would the Court believe—the seventeen—or the one? Which *ought* they to believe, according to the rules which regulate the force of human testimony? This is a practical illustration—and a *fair* illustration, of the question now before the Court. Is not the Court *bound*, according to the *rules of law*, which regulate the analysis and weighing of evidence, to come to the conclusion, that the seventeen have sworn to the truth, and that the one is perjured? Are not the probabilities overwhelmingly in favor of the truth of the seventeen, and the perjury of the one? Does not the presumption, in favor of the seventeen, amount, almost, to a certainty, because of the fact, that it is next to impossible to produce *seventeen* men, who can be induced to combine, in a wilful, and corrupt perjury? This point of fact—as to who fired the lethal weapon—fairly narrows itself down to a contest between the *seventeen* men and the *one*, as to who has committed the perjury. Perjury has certainly been committed—it lies at the door of the one, or the other. There is no room for inadvertence—inattention—incapacity—error—mistakes—or defect of memory—on the one side, or the other. The events given in evidence, by all, were of too marked and striking a character for *that*—the opportunities of all parties for observation were too good. The dilemma must be directly met, and solved—either Atkinson lied, or the seventeen witnesses for the prosecution did—defying God, and in the face of the country and of this Court. There is no option left with the Court; they must embrace one proposition or the other—there is no middle course.

One of the Counsel for the defence, has expressed his surprise, that so many men could be crowded together, within so small a space, as that which the witnesses for the prosecution must have occupied, if these witnesses held the relative positions towards the prisoner, Tolar, and the deceased, which they represent themselves to have held; and, at first blush, it does seem somewhat remarkable. But, if with a radius of five feet, a man describes a circle around himself as a centre, he will be astonished to find, how many persons can, be crowded into the space so enclosed. Most of the witnesses for the prosecution, who testified that Tolar fired the pistol, were within a circle, which a radius of five feet would describe, around the point, where they represent Tolar to have stood when the pistol was fired—at any rate, very little beyond that circle. There is room for a large number of persons within such a circle, with a circumference of about thirty feet; certainly quite room for seventeen men.

I ask the gentlemen of this Commission, with a view to fixing in their minds, the very great force of the evidence offered by the prosecution, on this particular question—the identity of the person who fired the pistol, the bullet from which caused Beebee's death—to locate in their mind's eye, or on a bit of paper before them, the positions of the witnesses for the prosecution, who have testified that Tolar fired the pistol, with reference to Tolar, as given in evidence by themselves. I think, I may safely assume, taking the whole evidence for the prosecution, and for the defence together—and if I am in error the Court will correct me—that Archy Beebee, at the moment when he was shot, stood just opposite the southern edge of the small arch, which is the south of the main arch, on the east face of the market house—and about two feet from the curb-stone of the pavement, with his face directed a little to the west of south. The man who fired the pistol —the discharge of which slew the deceased—whoever he was—stood—some four or five feet from him—about two or three feet off of the pavement, in the street, and to his left and rear. This is the best conclusion as to their relative positions, at which I have been enabled to arrive, after a careful comparison of all the testimony, both for the prosecution and for the defence; and it is the position assigned to Beebee, even by Atkinson, and also by Mullins—both of them witnesses for the defence. Now, here stands the man who fired the pistol, about three feet from the edge of the pavement, in the street, and to the left and rear of Beebee, not five feet from him ; and we have a host of witnesses for the prosecution, all around the perpetrator of the homicide—all of whom swear that Tolar is the criminal. Here is Matthew N. Leary, jr., whose character is unassailed, and unassailable, who says—he was standing to the right of the man who fired the pistol, and to his rear, about five feet. John Armstrong says—he was standing to the immediate left of Tolar, when he fired—nor do I think that Armstrong's testimony is open to all the assaults which have been made upon it ; it makes little difference as to a witness's credibility, in a particular instance, whether he is generally reliable or not, if his testimony is conformed in that instance, by witnesses who are entirely reliable. Armstrong says—he was immediate to the left of the man who fired the pistol, with his (the witness's) breast, almost against the murderer's left elbow. James Douglass, was standing in front of the man who fired the pistol, with his, (Douglass') back towards him, so that when this man fired, he put his left hand on Douglass' right shoulder, drew him out of the way, and fired past him. Between Leary and the man who fired his pistol, stood Lewis Smith. Square behind Armstrong—almost touching him—and within five feet or six feet of the man who fired the pistol, stood Henry Hagans ; a little further to the front than James Douglass, and to his left stood Robert Simmons ; and yet further to the front of the man who fired the pistol, than Douglass was. Still a little further to the front of him, stood Sam Toomer. Now, we have Leary just to the criminal's right and rear, about five feet off; Smith directly behind him ; Armstrong just to his left ; Douglass just to the front ; Hagan's just off here,— a little back of Armstrong ; Simmons just a little further to the front than Douglass—and Sam Toomer still a little further to the front. Now, immediately to the criminal's right, "square on his right," as he says, stood David Oliphant ; just a little to his rear and within three feet of him stood James Kendrick. At a little tree, on the edge of the pavement, a little further to the rear, stood William Porter ; Sam Phillips stood to the front and left, and within four or five feet of the man who fired the pistol—and note that I am stating all these positions with reference to the man who fired the pistol. Old Tom Jenkins stood off, at some distance, on the pavement, almost square in front of this man, and facing him. These witnesses were all around the man, who fired the pistol, and they occupied eight different points of the compass, and that too within a distance of five feet of him,— say, some few, within eight feet of him. Now, without going through the seventeen, let us select the witnesses located as above,—they were closest to him. If they did not see—if they had not opportunities of seeing what was done there at that time, and who it was that discharged the lethal weapon—it is impossible for witnesses to have any knowledge. They had every opportunity of seeing—there can be no doubt about that ; and there was a circumstance, I may say, many circumstances—to attract their attention. They might not have been looking at that man very particularly at first, but at the drawing of the pistol and the firing,—at so exciting a time,—the flash may be said to have burnt the fact and the memory of the fact, upon their minds. Their attention was at once centered, absorbed. It might not have been so absorbed if the pistol had not gone off—but the noise and flash, and discharge, attracted the senses of hearing, sight and smell,—each and all operating upon the subject matter before them,—within five feet of them. And if they swear falsely as to the man who fired that pistol, *they are perjured*, and there is no help for it. The Court must see that this is so.

I said early in this argument that the first rule of law, in investigating testimony was—that, if possible without violence or constraint, so to do, the Court must reconcile all of it. Can you reconcile the statements of these witnesses with that of Atkinson ? It is impossible. One set says Tolar fired the pistol, the other one, that Philips fired it. There is an irreconcilable difference ; you cannot account for it on the ground of omission. You cannot account for it on the ground that some of the evidence is positive, and some negative. They each and all swear to a positive fact, and both sets of witnesses cannot be correct.

The next step in the investigation, is as the law says—where you do find an actual collision in the testimony, such as there is in this case—that you must decide, whether, you can reasonably attribute that collision to inadvertance, inattention, incapacity, error, mistake, or defect of memory, upon the part of one witness or the other. Now, there is no room for any errors arising from these causes in the case in hand. The witnesses I have described, maintaining the relative positions just mentioned, towards the man who fired the shot, cannot be mistaken—cannot be in error, unless perjured. There is no reasonable hope to acount for the collision because of inattention, or of any other human *infirmity* merely. The pistol was fired, and of course attracted the attention of all who were near it—the discharge acted on *all* their senses. It is the same with respect to the witness, Atkinson, who testified that Phillips fired the pistol. Here was Atkinson standing on the edge of the pavement, directly behind Beebee—within five feet of the man who fired the pistol, as he says, and " Sam. Phillips," he swears, " fired it." "He saw him—there is no doubt about it." There is no possibility of either side being mistaken in such positive statements. Either the large number of witnesses for the prosecution, who have sworn that Tolar fired the pistol, have lied, or the witness Atkinson has lied. Surely the Court can come to no other conclusion. I shall consider presently the attempt made to bolster Atkinson with other witnesses, but I am now considering this collision which cannot be attributed to inattention, inadvertance, incapacity, error, mistake or defect of memory. It can only be ascribed to falsehood, wilful—deliberate—corrupt—damning—on one side or the other.

But, suppose the Court to come to the conclusion that there is a possibility of mistake upon one side or the other by which the inconsistency may be accounted for, upon which side ought they to conclude that the mistake lies ? It is not more probable that *one* man, having a position for observation in no way superior to that of several other men for seeing and hearing the firing of a pistol, should be mistaken as to who fired it, than that seventeen men should be, who are standing all about at *different* places in *several* directions, in *immediate propinquity* to the man who fired the pistol, and observing him from *several different points of new ?* But, if on the contrary, the Court say that *some one* has lied, I ask you, in the name of reason and common sense, whether you can conclude that these seventeen men lied, and the one man told the truth? Is it not more probable that James Atkinson told a lie—for into that it resolves itself—and swore to a lie—than that these seventeen witnesses for the prosecution did so. The firing of a pistol was one of those blazing, burning, facts, occurring in the midst of a crowd, accompanied with circumstances, which must have attracted every one's attention who was present. If these men differ, they do so in consequence of corrupt falsehood on one side or the other—there is no getting around or beyond that point.

But an effort is made by the defence to bolster up Atkinson's assertion by the testimony of Mullins, of Arey, of Faircloth, and of Sykes. These four witnesses say—they *almost* saw Phillips fire the pistol. If I had not thought that I had discovered perjury already on the part of Atkinson, I should have thought it *possible*—barely possible—that these four witnesses were speaking the truth—for their testimony is entirely reconcilable, with the fact, that Tolar shot the pistol—at last. For these witnesses bring us up to the point of time, immediately prior to the firing, and there drop off—they fail to see who did fire the pistol—on this point their testimony is negative evidence. There is nothing absolutely impossible in this. It is very possible for four or more men to see everything that occurs in a crowd up to the moment, when a pistol is fired, and yet to fail to see that. This failure of theirs to see more, might certainly be attributed to error, incapacity, or inattention, or something of that kind. But when four men, occupying *absolutely* and *relatively, different* positions towards the man who fired, and towards each other, are, by an *extraordinary concurrence of different accidents,* prevented, *just at the very crisis,* from observing *the most important fact of all*— why, I must be permitted to think that this extraordinary combination of events is due to the fact, that the state of things, of which they speak, did not exist— and that they have lied, partially at least. Just look at it a moment. Here is Mullins, who says he saw Phillips—he was close to him—a short distance behind the man who was shot: he saw Phillips present the pistol, and it was thrust immediately out of his (the witness's) sight: he did not see Phillips fire it: he did not see the pistol fire at all:—it disappeared in the crowd— although every other witness, who was looking, swears that he saw it plainly enough over the shoulders of the crowd. Then comes little Arey: he was standing in the small arch, on the east face of the market house, immediately by Beebee, or sitting on a bench there; he saw the pistol in the hands of Phillips pointed, thought it was aimed towards himself (the witness), and was unfortunately so afraid of being shot himself, that he jumped down and it was lost to his sight.

Faircloth had Phillips exactly at his right side, as he says, elbow to elbow. He saw him present the pistol, but turned round and would not look. He always had had a habit of turning himself away when he saw a pistol about to be fired!! FOR FEAR A PIECE OF THE CAP WOULD GET IN HIS EYE!!!!

Then comes Henry Sykes, for whom I felt very sorry while he was on the stand, and who really put everything in such a tangled condition, that I have never been able to unravel his meaning yet. He *hears* everything in the world, even to an exclamation from Phillips, " if you don't give him up I'll shoot him"—which no one else did hear—he sees Phillips to the right and rear of Sheriff Hardie—a pistol goes off, and, immediately afterwards, he sees Phillips with a pistol in his hand, which he was *rubbing.* But by another unfortunate accident in this long chapter, Sheriff Hardie puts his head in the way, just in the very nick of time, and Sykes did not see the pistol go off.

Here are four men, who see *all*, up to the very point of time when the pistol is about to be fired; they were all in different parts of the crowd—in different relative positions, towards the deceased, towards Phillips, and to each other—and not one of them saw the pistol fire. They all turned their eyes away, simultaneously, or closed them, at this most interesting epoch—and it is one of the most curious coincidences I have ever known.

Now I ask the Court, in the name of reason and of common sense again—when four witnesses come before you and testify as these have done—when they bring you up to the very point of the firing of a pistol which slew a man, and then break off, and see nothing more for a single instant, and immediately after return to their previous condition of bright-eyed vigilance—What do you think of them? Is not the Court forced to believe that they have lied? To believe—that either they *did see* the person who fired the pistol, and are unwilling to tell who it was—or that they *did not see* as much as that to which they have deposed? Is it not the most unnatural thing in creation, that such a curious concatenation of circumstances should arise? But that such things as these should happen, *is not absolutely impossible*—especially in an excited crowd—and if we had not set out with a knowledge of the direct collision—the irreconcilable difference—which exists, between Atkinson on one side and the seventeen witnesses for the prosecution, on the other, as to the agent who discharged the pistol—if we had no knowledge of *that* thing, we might deem it *possible*, that Mullins, Arey, Faircloth, and Sykes, had seen that to which they testified—or that any exaggeration of what they had seen, was attributable to mistake or innocent error; such a conclusion would be highly improbable, but still it would be possible. But when the known fact, that *one* witness for the defence has wilfully and corruptly perjured himself, is added to this choice and curious testimony—to which I have just been referring—on the same side,—human credulity cannot accept the four witnesses as honest. A suspicion at once attaches to all the evidence for the defence, and this Court, I am sure, will receive their whole testimony with many grains of allowance.

I am not presenting this case to the Court with any art—but naturally, and as it presents itself to me. I am not selecting isolated facts from the mass of evidence, and, of them, weaving a particular theory of the guilt of all these prisoners. And so reasoning, I am forced to the conclusion, that Atkinson lied, when he swore, that he saw Sam Phillips fire the pistol whose discharge killed Archy Beebee—that under some circumstances and conditions, we might be able to accept the evidence of the witnesses Mullins, Arey, Faircloth, and Sykes, as generally truthful, and the witnesses themselves as reasonably honest, but to an extent mistaken; but seeing that the defence had already offered a perjured witness, that the whole of the evidence of these four witnesses was built up with a view to sustaining that perjured witness, and that their statements present such glaring and striking improbabilities, we are compelled, to lose all confidence in them—to regard them as corrupt—and to view with suspicion all the testimony offered by defendants who have called such witnesses. And, in the rebound, our minds naturally and cheerfully accept the evidence of the seventeen witnesses offered by the prosecution, as true and credible—in which they testify, that William J. Tolar, one of the prisoners at the bar, was the immediate agent, who fired the pistol, the bullet from which slew Archy Beebee.

And how have the prisoners met this view of the case? They pounce upon *three* of the seventeen witnesses offered by the prosecution on this point, and denounce them as unworthy of credit. I speak of the witnesses, Shaw, Armstrong and Phillips. Shaw, they say was tied up, once on a time, by the thumbs, for cattle stealing. Armstrong's character for truth has been questioned, even declared notoriously bad by several witnesses, and withal he is a ginger-bread colored fellow, with a cock-eye; and Phillips is an informer—an accomplice—an approver—a man who has turned State's evidence, and is perjured besides, by his own admission.

But, I say, in reply, we can throw away the testimony of all these three witnesses we can admit, for argument's sake that it is worthless—and our case stands quite as impregnable without their evidence as with it. We only lose *three* of the *seventeen* witnesses, who prove the firing of the pistol by Tolar, and the other points material to this case, which were deposed to by those three witnesses, have been fully proved by other witnesses, who cannot be assailed successfully. I am consuming much time, and, as it is unnecessary, I do not care to occupy the Court with a defence of Shaw and Armstrong—let the Court take them for what they are worth. But I think, that Sam Phillips, who has been made the butt of the prisoners' unskilful archery, is entitled to a fair representation in the court. Phillips is spoken of, by the prisoner's Counsel—as one who has become State's evidence—this is not a fair statement of his position. He is declared purjured, by his own admissions—because he sat upon the coroner's inquest in Fayetteville, which viewed the body of Archy Beebee, knowing all that he has deposed to here, and suppressed what he knew, and failed to find a verdict according to his private personal knowledge, and *did* find, according to the evidence, that was adduced before the jury, that Beebee came to his death by the hands of some person unknown.

If the Court would consult the most learned men in the law, in this city, or in this State, or in this county, they would learn, what I now state to be law, that Phillips was *sworn* to find according to the evidence laid before the jury—and not according to his private information—that he would have been perjured had he acted on his own knowledge, without evidence offered. I will even go so far as this—that a man may, without committing perjury, sit upon a petit jury, while another man is on trial for his life, and find the prisoner guilty, if the evidence so establishes, although this juror knows that *he himself* committed the murder.

Counsel for the accused : If a man sitting upon a petit jury knows of any matter that is pertinent and material to the issue, it is not his bounden duty to make it known to the Court before sworn, to the end that he may be excused from the jury, and put upon the witness stand.

Mr. Haywood : I think it is his duty, undoubtedly, to challenge himself, under such circumstances ; but I *do not think he incurs the guilt of perjury* by failing to do so.

I am not holding the witness Phillips up as a model of heroic virtue. I have not put any lion's skin upon *him*. I do not think he exhibited any superhuman excellence by acting as he did ; but he did as the majority of men would have done under like circumstances ; and I believe, before God this day, that if Phillips *had* done his duty like a man, and stood forth and declared who fired that pistol, on the day of the inquest in Fayetteville, that he would have been himself hanged for the murder of Beebee, although he was not guilty of it. I believe that the public feeling in that town was of such a character that the same kind of evidence which has been introduced here would have been either collected or manufactured against him, and his performance of duty would have resulted in his own accusation, trial and conviction—perhaps before this very Commission. It is probable that his life was saved, either from this covert, or some more violent assault, by his failure to do his duty in this instance. I do not say he is a man who dares to do his duty under such risks as that; when a failure to do it involves him in only a very venial fault; but I *do* say that he has not the guilt of perjury upon his soul, because of that oath taken as one of the Coroner's inquest in Beebee's case. That a high-toned, strictly honorable man ought to have felt, and would have felt it to be his duty to speak out in such a dilemma, I am prepared to admit. That is quite another question. But there are very few men who—under all the circumstances of popular feeling—of personal danger, and of partial ignorance—which surrounded Phillips—in the absence of safe counsellors, would not have acted exactly as he did upon that occasion.

I am not saying but that he is in some sort blame worthy ; but I am saying that he is not *perjured*, because he said upon the finding of the coroner's jury, that the deceased came to his death by the hands of a person unknown.

Here is the oath which he took : "You solemnly swear, upon the Holy Evangelists of Almighty God, that you will well and truly inquire upon view and inspection of this dead body, how the deceased came to his death, and true presentment make, both of the means of death, and the person (if any) who caused the same, as it may appear according to your evidence."

It is the same oath that is taken by the petit juror, when he is trying a case on which a man's life is involved, so far as regards the evidence in which each is to act ; and it binds him to act upon nothing but the evidence which is laid before him ; if he acts on other information, he is perjured. The moral obligation, which rests upon every citizen, cognizant of a crime, to disclose it, is quite a different matter,—yet where so many were faulty, who would have expected this man Phillips to have exhibited superhuman excellence and virtue? But not only was he not guilty of perjury, but he does not stand before this Court, according to the ordinary acceptation of those terms, as State's evidence. A man who turns State's evidence is, properly speaking, one who is charged by the State to be guilty, and admitting himself to be guilty of complicity in the offence on trial, comes forward and exposes his accomplices. By the older system of practice in England, they were called *approvers*. One of several men, charged with a common crime, came forward, confessed and pleaded guilty, and then his sentence was suspended until his accomplices were tried ; and in case he convicted his confederates, by his evidence—he was let go free—and if he failed to convict them, he was hanged himself. Now, what I understand by a man's becoming State's evidence, is,—where one admits his own guilt, and either pleads guilty and puts himself entirely upon the mercy of the State ; or the State agrees to suspend further proceedings against him, and thereupon, in his own testimony, admitting his own guilt, along with the rest, he exposes and betrays others, his accomplices. Such a one is under strong temptation to perjure himself. But that is not the position occupied by the witness Phillips in this case. He is a man as to whose guilt the government is so doubtful, that they are unwilling to prosecute him—he at all times denying any complicity in the offences charged : that is what our *nolle prosequi* means. Under these circumstances he comes forward and gives his evidence in the cause, and, under oath, says he had nothing to do with this homicide whatever. His conduct and his evidence are not liable to the same suspicions, which attach, when one confessing his own guilt and complicity, yet exposes his fellows. If this position be the correct one, what fault, in the name of Heaven, are we to attribute to Phillips for coming in here to tell the truth, when the government demands it at his hands. He admits that he went to the scene of the homicide armed with his pistol; he asserts that his intention in so arming himself was to assist the Sheriff, if he needed help to protect himself or his prisoner. He made no efforts to conceal his pistol at the time, and since that time he has made no concealment of the fact that he was armed with a pistol. He produced his pistol here upon request, and he permitted it to go out of his possession, under circumstances, when several had access to it, even in the town of Fayetteville, where active enmity and hostility were already to his knowledge excited against him, because he chose to do his duty, by testifying in this case—and where it was watched from the time it left the hands of his brother-in-law until it was returned to his own keeping. If he had been guilty of complicity in the murder, he never would have permitted that pistol to have gone out of his own possession—that pistol, which his enemies have endeavored to torture into telling such fearful tales against him.

Just suppose, for the sake of argument—and there is strong evidence that it is true—that Phillips is entirely innocent of 'this homicide—and why should we suspect him of perjury? Why should we condemn him? What evil hath he done? Above all, of what have the prisoners a right to complain? He sat upon the Coroner's inquest; he knew the facts of this case; he had a friendship for Tolar; he did not wish to expose him; he was swayed by the prevailing popular sentiment and his personal fears, and he failed to do his whole duty to this extent—not being called upon to testify, he did not volunteer to disclose what he knew to the jury; he submitted to arrest; he said nothing; he disclosed nothing; he came up to this city in military custody; and finally, after a few days' imprisonment, under the pressure of the harshest circumstances of personal inconvenience and danger to his life, he did what he ought to have done at first—he disclosed to those in authority here what he had failed to disclose before the Coroner's jury, although he knew, at the time he made the disclosure, that such a course was fraught with danger to himself, and that efforts would be made, by Tolar's friends, to prove that he was the principal felon—"The very head and front of his offending—hath *this extent—no more.*"

This witness, Phillips, and John Armstrong seem to be particularly obnoxious to the Counsel for the prisoners. Upon their devoted heads the vials of the vicarious wrath of these defendants have been poured from first to last. The Counsel for the defence are fastidious. We cannot produce witnesses whose bearing is to their taste. We introduce Armstrong, and he is denounced as *too-willing* a witness—a witness whose feet are swift to shed blood! We introduce Phillips, *and he has retained his evidence too long!* The Counsel select two of our witnesses, who, as they conceive, are most hurtful to their cause—and one, as they say, has held back his evidence too long, and therefore he is not to be trusted. The other was too swift, and therefore he is not to be relied upon. Now I confess I was very much struck with the testimony of Mr. Phillips and his bearing on the stand. I thought, under the painful circumstances in which he was placed, he bore himself manfully—patiently—in every respect, well. I have no doubt that the story he told here was the true one. That is a question for the Court, however, upon which they no doubt will exercise their own judgment, and form their own opinion. But so far as my individual endorsement and opinion will go, I purposely and publicly say here, that I have no doubt of its truth.

But the Counsel for the defence—not being able to successfully encounter the evidence of the seventeen witnesses for the prosecution, who testified positively to the fact that Tolar fired the pistol which killed Beebee—either with their witness Atkinson *alone*, who swore that he saw Phillips fire that pistol, or with their witness Atkinson, as partially supported by the extraordinary testimony of their four other witnesses—Mullins, Arey, Faircloth and Sykes—who succeeded in seeing Phillips do everything else necessary to their case but fire the pistol—and being unable to overthrow the positive evidence of these *seventeen* witnesses, by ineffectual attempts to discredit *three* of them—Phillips, Armstrong and Shaw—have yet another gun in reserve. They propose to prove, *negatively, and by a sort of limited alibi*, that Tolar *did not shoot that pistol*, and that he was in the crowd at least ten or twelve feet from the point where the man stood, whoever he was, who did fire it.

The witnesses, upon whom the prisoners rely for this proof, are Mrs. Davis, Ichabod B. Davis, and Leggett, Lutterloh, and E. P. Powers, to whom must be added the witness Mullins, already noticed in this address in another connection. As to Mrs. Davis, the wife of a respectable dentist in Fayetteville, I have nothing to say. She is no doubt a very excellent and respectable lady, and intended to testify to the truth—*place aux dames*—but according to her own account her acquaintance with Tolar was very limited; she had not known him before socially; she gave but a momentary glance to the whole scene; she was at a considerable distance from it, in an upper story of a building, say forty or fifty yards distant; and allowing for the deception to which, according to the laws of perspective, the most accurate observer is subjected in such cases, her evidence, entirely admitting the uprightness of her intentions, cannot weigh, for an instant, against the evidence of the eight or ten witnesses for the prosecution, who profess to have occupied a position within five or six feet of the spot where Tolar stood at the time the pistol was fired.

But Mr. Davis— Ichabod, whose glory has departed—not the husband of the lady just named—but, like *the* Alexander whom St. Paul has made almost as notorious as Alexander the Great, *a coppersmith*—deserves to be mentioned at greater length. He testified, that he was standing at the north-western corner of the street pavement, directly opposite the south-eastern corner of the pavement which runs along the east front of the market house, and about fifty or sixty feet from the market house pavement, at the moment that Archy Beebee was shot, and for eight or ten minutes previous to that point of time; that he was at that same place while Beebee was up stairs in the town hall—when he descended the steps—when he passed along the market house pavement—and when the pistol was fired which caused his death; that from the first instant when he (witness) took his position as above, until Beebee was shot, and at the moment he was shot, which covered a space of time that was *certainly five, probably eight, and perhaps ten minutes* in length, he had his eyes intently fixed on Capt. Tolar; that he never lost sight of him (Tolar) for an instant; that his attention was attracted to Tolar by the fact that he (Tolar) was a very tall man, and was remaining motionless, while the rest of the crowd, which was in front of him, was in some commotion; that Tolar did not fire the pistol which slew Archy Beebee; that he cannot tell who did fire that pistol, not having seen the person who fired, nor his pistol; but that he heard the report of it, and saw the smoke of it; and that the report was heard, and the smoke was seen by him, at a point out in the street, east of the market house, off of the market house pavement, near the curbstone of said pavement, and a little to the right of the south east corner of the market house, while Tolar stood at that instant, and for at least five minutes previous thereto, directly opposite the centre of the main arch which forms the eastern entrance of the market house, in the middle of the pavement, at least ten or twelve feet from the point where the pistol was fired, and as many feet from the point where Archy Beebee fell. This is, I think, the substance of Davis' testimony, which covers just eight or ten minutes of time, outside of which he refused to know or to testify to anything—except that just after the firing Leggett passed him (witness) as he stood at the corner, and then again passed back by him with a Mr. Burns.

Now it may be that the Court can credit this testimony, but—as human credulity has its limits,—I do not think that they will. It has every mark of contrivance and practice about it, which testimony can have—and it bears a palpable and absurd lie upon its face. Who can believe, that any man, *in the midst of the excitement* which necessarily must have prevailed in the crowd that day, deliberately, *and for no other reasons than those given by Davis*—kept his eyes *intently fixed* upon another man, *for the space of from five to ten minutes*, when there was a mad mob, between the witness, and the object of his fixed attention, engaged in the very act of taking away a fellow creature's life? Leggett, the next witness introduced for the defence, testified that *he* was standing on the pavement by Tolar—in *front* of him—was taller than Tolar by two inches—and was perfectly still—at the time of the firing of the pistol. What then becomes of the absurd reason, with which Davis accounts for his fixed gaze at Tolar?

But the marks of artificial testimony, are seen in every part of this evidence; it is confined to exactly eight or ten minutes of time—it is bald and destitue of detailed circumstances—and then, one extraneous circumstance—the fact that Leggett passed and repassed the witness, just after the firing—is *voluntered*, to give the testimony a natural appearance; and it comes out later in the case, from Leggett himself, that this particular—*natural*—circumstance, relied upon by Davis to buoy up his testimony, was named to Leggett by Davis after he, (Davis,) had testified, as one of the points that he (Leggett) was to be sure and mention in giving in his evidence.

I can hardly suppose, that the Counsel for the prisoners, expect this Court to be so credulous as to accept this testimony as reliable. But "to make assurance doubly sure," Leggett, Lutterloh and Ed Powers, are introduced by the prisoners just after Davis, and each, and every, and all of them positively swear, that Tolar was in conversation with them, for twenty minutes, preceding the killing of Archy Beebee; that he was not in the position assigned to him by Davis *five*, *three*, nor *one* minute, preceding the appearance of Beebee out on the pavement, at the Eastern front of the market house; but that Tolar was under the market house with them, just at the moment, or just after Beebee moved out of the same arch—and that Beebee was killed about one minute after he passed the arch.

It is certain therefore, from the prisoners' own showing, by their own witnesses—either that Davis mistook some other person for Tolar—or that he has wilfully and corruptly perjured himself; either alternative will answer our purpose, but we are inclined to embrace the latter—having, as we think, already discovered the signs of corruption in other parts of the testimony for the defence—and also from the whole intrinsic character of Davis's testimony.

But, say the prisoners' Counsel, Davis, as well as Leggett, and Lutterloh, and Powers, concur in *this*—and the evidence of Mullins is to the same effect—that Tolar was standing in the spot assigned to him by Davis, at least twelve feet from the point where the pistol was fired, and as many feet from the point where Beebee fell—at the *very moment* when the pistol *was fired*. This is so *in a degree*. But can it be, that these prisoners introduce such witnesses here, as Leggett, Lutterloh, Ed. P. Powers—and I may add Sykes—and seriously expect this Court to give any weight to their testimony—all of them witnesses, as it appears in evidence, who are now under arrest, awaiting trial, for complicity in this very crime, which we are concerned at present in investigating—witnesses who might have been included in this very charge and specification, if we had known what we know now, at the time the charge was preferred, and who would then, by *a rule of law*, have been excluded from testifying—witnesses against whom, although they were not on trial, and the prosecution had no interest in making out proof against them, the case incidentally made by the rest of the evidence in the cause—exclusive of their own—was so strong that the Court is compelled to see their complicity—or, at least, to strongly suspect it? Why, the defence might as well expect the Court to call the prisoners from the dock, and hear their own affidavits of their innocence, and accept them as full proof of their guiltlessness. I do not believe the judgment of this Court will be one whit swayed by the evidence of Leggett, Lutterloh, Ed. Powers, and Sykes, wherein it was favorable to the prisoners, and themselves—they are all in the same boat—at least their boats are very close together—and must, in all human probability, sink or swim together. And it was a fearful position in which to put these young men—to thrust them upon the stand in this case. It was not our look out—we did not put them there—but, guilty or innocent, it was a fiery trial to their virtue, their honor, and their uprightness—a trial out of which poor, frail human nature, according to its ordinary constitution, could not pass unscathed.

Accordingly, as was to be expected, under the circumstances in which they were placed, Legget, Lutterloh, and Powers, agree in some general statement, most of which are damaging to them and the cause, which they espouse—but the instant we descend to details, they are as wide apart as in the nature of the case they can wander. It must be remembered that these witnesses have had free opportunities of intercourse, are men of intelligence, and alike feeling an interest in the result of this trial, must have conversed · with one another on the subject. It must also be remembered that they were present before, during, and at the time of the killing, and therefore can give an accurate account of such parts of the transaction as they desire shall go into evidence—and an *appearance of truth* to much of the rest of their testimony; making due allowances for these facts and conditions, their evidence is as wide apart on points as to which they could not prepare, as the strongest advocate of the perfection of the common law rules, of evidence and of detecting suspected witnesses, could desire.

I shall point out some of these discrepancies for the consideration of the Court—but before doing so, and as part of the process of so doing, I wish to remark upon some observations which fell from my brother Fuller. He seemed to think—as well as I understood him—that it was a *natural variance* in testimony and not at all *suspicious*—that different witnesses to the same facts, should locate the persons concerned in a transaction, at points far apart—say several feet apart—although the witnesses professed to have occupied the same relative position towards those persons—to have been looking at

them from the same point of view. To use a strong instance for an example—as in this case, that Lutterloh should swear, he was standing by Ed. Pow
ers, and Powers should swear he was standing by Lutterloh, at the time the
pistol fired—that both should testify they were facing in the same direction,
and that but one pistol fired, when Beebee was slain—and that Lutterloh
should testify, that pistol was fired from behind him where he could not see
it, very near his left ear, and E. P. Powers should testify, that pistol was fired eleven feet in front of him, where he could plainly see the smoke and flash,
nearly directly to his front and a little to his left. Now in those views of
my brother Fuller, I cannot concur; variances in statements and estimates
of time—variances in the statements and estimates of distances—are to be
expected; but in most instances where witnesses vary in the statement of
positive or relative positions or locations of things and persons, one witness
or the other, or both the witnesses are perjuring themselves.

I beg that the Court will understand me—one man may remember a part
of a scene—and another an entirely different part of the same scene, at which
they were both present; one man, during a commotion, may see or hear one
set of persons or things, and a second may see or hear a different set of persons or things; but if two men profess to have seen and heard the same set of
persons and things, at the same point of time—they will necessarily *locate*
those persons and things in the same *positive* and *relative localities* and *positions*, in narrating the scene, if the witnesses are honest; and especially is
this the case, when the two witnesses were professedly standing near together, looking at the scene from the same point of view. I shall not spend
time, in a metaphysical disquisition, to show *why* this is so. It is a simple
law of the mind on which every artificial system of memory rests. It is a
principle wonderfully illustrated, in this very case—out of two score witnesses,
or there-abouts, who have testified both for prosecution and defence in this
case, as to the positon on the pavement of Archy Beebee at the moment he
was shot—with very few and rare exceptions—you might cover the different
points assigned for the fall of the deceased, within a circle, whose radius does
not exceed twelve inches.

Now note what the four witnesses, Davis, Leggett, Lutterloh and Powers,
say of the position of Beebee, about the time he was shot. Davis says
" Beebee tell about the south-east corner of the building,"—Leggett says
" Beebee stood near the corner, near the outer eastern edge of the pavement,"—
Lutterloh says " Beebee was opposite the southern edge of the small arch,
about the centre of the pavement,"—and Powers locates him in about the same
way, at the same place.

Compare the statements of some of the other witnesses for the defence
with these statements and with one another. Atkinson says—" Beebee
stood about the center of the pavement, opposite the southern edge of the
small arch, about two feet from the outer edge of the pavement"—Mullins
says "Beebee was about the southern side of the small arch, near the southern corner of the market house, about the center of the pavement"—Faircloth says, "Bebee was opposite a point within eighteen inches of the corner
of the market house, near the edge of the pavement, about three feet on
the pavement."—Arey says " Beebee was opposite about the middle of the
small arch, when he stumbled—about four feet from the arch—and remained
about the same spot—until he was shot." I do not pretend to use the exact language of these witnesses, but I think I convey their exact meaning,
and the words are very nearly the same; and so I might go on with the statements of not only nearly all the witnesses for the defence, but with those of

the witnesses for the prosecution—which are to the same effect. But compare the statements of Davis, Leggett, Lutterloh and Powers—and also the statements of some of the other witnesses for the defence, fixing the point in space where the man stood—whoever he was—that fired the pistol, which killed Beebee, and notice the difference—you do not find the same coincidence. Davis and Sykes place the man beyond the corner of the east front of the market house, in the street, off of the pavement, to the right of the south-east corner of the market house, as you face east. Faircloth locates him in the middle of the pavement, opposite the pillar' which separates the main arch on the east front from the small southern arch, on the same front. Lutterloh testifies—that the man who fired the pistol was behind him and to his left, and that he, (witness) was facing to the south, and stood about the edge of the pavement, opposite the middle of the main arch, on the east front of the market house. Atkinson, Leggett, Powers, and Mullins, locate the firing of the pistol, at about the point indicated by the witnesses for the prosecution—nearly all of the seventeen referred to before—off of the pavement, and about five feet to the left and rear of the deceased. The point indicated by Davis and Sykes, is some twenty feet from that deposed to by Lutterloh—some ten or twelve feet from that which Faircloth gives in evidence—and some six or eight feet from the point to which Atkinson, Powers, Leggett and Mullins swear. Just after the pistol fired, several of these witnesses profess to have seen Phillips with a pistol in his hand—and to describe what he was doing with it. Powers says Phillips moved towards him just after the pistol was fired, which killed Beebee, holding a pistol in both hands and said—"Powers look at that pistol, and see that all the barrels are loaded," that he (witness) said "all right"—and turned to take the pistol, but Phillips put it behind him, under his coat, and moved away. Mullins says—that just after the pistol was fired, Phillips drew back a pistol, flourished it in the air, said " the negro is dead, but I didn't kill him"—and then returned the weapon to his left breast pocket. Atkinson swears most positively that he saw Phillips *fire the pistol which killed Archy Beebee*—draw it back—elevate it a moment and return it to his left breast pocket—but he swears as positively that he *did not* flourish it in the air, and did not say "the negro is dead but but I didn't kill him"—but was perfectly silent. Sykes says that Phillips had a pistol in his hand just after the firing, and he was rubbing it on the right side of the leg of his pantaloons—as if to remove the signs of a recent discharge.

Now, may it please the Court, how is it, that these witnesses for the defence concur so completely—so entirely agree with one another, when describing the locality in which Beebee stood, when he was slain, and differ so widely when deposing to the position from which the pistol was fired, which slew him—and in describing the movements of Phillips just after the firing? Is it not apparent, that their opportunities for observation of all of these particulars was the same—and that they concur in their statements as to the first particular of Beebee's locality, because they are swearing *to a fact which they have no interest to misrepresent ;* but in the last particulars, they are, either mistaken—some of them must be mistaken—or are corruptly swearing to matters which did not come under their observation, and which they have an interest to misrepresent ? If these witnesses really saw the man who fired the pistol, which killed Beebee, or really saw the flash and smoke of the pistol used, is it not certain, that their agreement would be as perfect in their statements of the particulars connected with this man, or this flash and smoke, as is their concurrence in their statements, with reference to the deceased, his locality and his movements?

But all these observations immediately preceding, and this tedious comparison of evidence, has been made by me, but as inducement to the main point out of which it grew—and that was, to show, how little credit is to be given to the evidence of Davis, Leggett, Lutterloh, and Powers, in their attempt to prove a limited *alibi* for Tolar. I have set out Davis testimony and have shown how completely his statement is contradicted by that of Leggett, Lutterloh, and Powers, in one particular—in-asmuch as Davis swears that Tolar was standing out side of the market house in the middle of the pavement for five or ten minutes at the *very time* when Leggett, Lutterloh and Powers, swear that Tolar was in *conversation with them* under the market house. It remains to compare the testimony of the three witnesses last named as to the position of Tolar, about the very instant when Beebee was shot—Lutterloh does not profess to have seen Tolar at that moment, but he undertakes to give us the positions of Powers and Leggett—who in their turn undertake to locate Tolar with reference to themselves. Lutterloh says, he (witness) stood—"about the edge of the pavement, opposite the centre of the main arch on the eastern front of the market house," and according to his best impression "he was facing south and Leggett and Powers, were facing in the same direction, in one line with him across the pavement." I do not pretend to give the witnesses exact words, to avoid prolixity—I endeavor to convey his exact meaning, as I apprehended it—and the same remarks are applicable to what I shall say of the evidence on this point of Leggett and Powers. According to Lutterloh's statement these three witnesses stood thus :

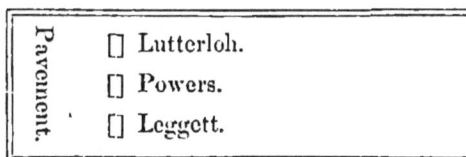

N   Pavement. [] Lutterloh.   S
       [] Powers.
       [] Leggett.

Leggett says—that—"he stood, together with Lutterloh, Powers and Tolar, all facing south, about the middle of the pavement, and opposite a point a little south of the center of the main arch ; that he himself was stationed a little to Tolar's left, and a little to his front, and nearer the middle of the pavement than Tolar—that Lutterloh was to his (witness's) right and front, and that Powers was also farther to his (witness's) right and front than Lutterloh :" according to Leggett's statement, Tolar and these three witnesses were located thus :

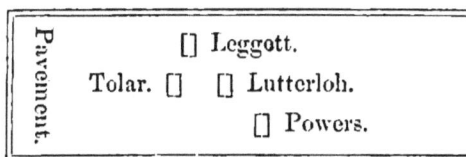

N   Pavement. [] Leggott.   S
      Tolar. [] [] Lutterloh.
       [] Powers.

Powers says, that—"he, with Capt. Tolar, stood about the middle of the pavement, nearly opposite the central point of the main arch—that Tolar was very near him, to his right and front, that Leggett was farther to Tolar's rear than he (witness) was, and to his (witness's) right, and that Lutterloh was to his (witness's) front and left, and near him"—according to Powers' statement Tolar and these three witnesses, were located thus :

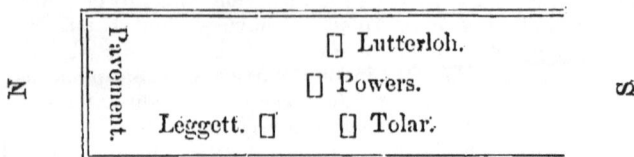

Now I beg the Court to note the diversity. The question is one of topography—one of location—the point is one to which the attention of these three witnesses was seriously and particularly drawn immediately after the act of killing was done, by the unsuccessful charge of homicide made against Tolar before the coroner's inquest; and if these three men were really standing with Tolar, as they describe themselves to have been, the very moment that memory recalls *that fact*, it will instinctively present it as it *actually was in all its particulars*, and their statements if truthful, must correspond with one another. To take a familiar illustration, let any gentlemen of this Court who has lately attended a dinner party, endeavor to recall the scene, and he will find he can at once locate the guests in their positions around the table with very little difficulty. It is said the principles of the art of improving the memory, were discovered in this identical way—and I give the story for what it is worth. Simonides, the Greek poet, was employed by Scopas, a rich Thessalian nobleman, to compose a song, in commemoration of a victory gained by him, at the Olympic Games. This was sung, at a banquet given in honor of the occasion ; but Scopas was so displeased, that part of it was occupied with the praises of Castor and Pollux, that he refused to pay the poet any more than half of the stipulated reward, as he had received but one half the praise, and he said that Simonides, might, if he pleased, apply to his friends the Tyndaridœ, for the rest. Shortly after this, and while he was yet at the feast, a message was brought to Simonides, that there were two young men at the gate, anxious to speak with him—when he went out, he found no one; but while he was searching for the two young men, the banqueting hall he had just left fell down, crushing to death Scopas and all who were with him. Their bodies were so mutilated that they could not be recognized, but Simonides, by calling to mind, the place which each one of them had occupied at the feast, was able to distinguish them ; and hence attention was first directed to the important aid afforded to the memory by the observations of positions and material objects.

And hence I confidently assume the position, that *if* Leggett, Lutterloh, and Powers *were* standing with Tolar at the moment when Beebee was shot, as they have testified they were, at the point on the pavement to which they testify—they would have little or no difficulty in locating themselves and Tolar—and they would necessarily agree in stating Tolar's position, and their several positions relatively to him ; and the fact that they do not thus agree, is *strong evidence*, that the state of things to which they swear never existed ; and either they have permitted their imaginations and their fears to mislead them—or they are corruptly false. The defence must embrace one alternative or the other and either is sufficient for our purpose.

May it please the Court : I have said all that I intend to say on the question of fact, "who fired the pistol, the bullet from which slew Archy Beebee?" and I think the Court will be satisfied, that the evidence of the seventeen witnesses for the prosecution, who have sworn *positively* that they saw and heard Tolar fire the pistol, is not *shaken*—either by the *positive* evidence of Atkinson that he saw and heard Samuel Phillips fire the pistol ;—or by the assaults made upon the credit of Shaw, Phillips and Armstrong, three of the several witnesses above referred to—by the prisoner's Counsel, and some of their witnesses—or by the *negative* evidence of Ichabod B. Davis, that Tolar did not fire that pistol—or by the attempted proof of a limited *alibi* of Tolar, by the witnesses, Leggett, Lutterloh, E. P. Powers, Mullins, and Ichabod B. Davis. And I beg the Court to observe, that in pressing this point, I have rested it upon the positive affirmative evidence of these seventeen witnesses for the prosecution alone ; and have not sought corroboration from incidental circumstances, from which I might have obtained aid.

For example—I have not used the conversation of Tolar with Daley, the sexton, who buried Beebee, during which Tolar paid the sexton, for digging the deceased man's grave; because I preferred to rely upon the force of the evidence of seventeen concurring witnesses, and because, of this circumstantial evidence, while it strongly tends to prove that Tolar was implicated in the killing, does not so strongly, nor necessarily indicate his hand as the one which fired the lethal shot. So I have not dwelt upon the pistol ball taken from Beebee's head, which being examined and weighed, does not naturally adapt itself to the pistol given in evidence, admitted to be the one in Phillips' hands on the occasion of the homicide ; because I fear, that at last this bullet throws very little light on the case—and even if it fit Tolar's pistol, might fit a hundred others. So the conversation detailed by James McNeel, in which Tolar said to Powers—"Tom, you grab him, and break the ice, and we'll put him through,"—and so of other declarations given in evidence as having been made by Tolar ; because the more direct tendency of this evidence is to show Tolar's complicity in a plot, to visit condign punishment on Archy Beebee, and not necessarily to prove that he was the immediate agent who slew Beebee. So the exclamations in the crowd, just after the homicide—"Capt. Tolar shot him!" "Tolar, Tolar, killed him"—and the like ; for all this is but *circumstantial*, and not *direct*, evidence that Tolar fired the pistol which slew Archy Beebee. And so on, I might multiply these attendant circumstances—of which I have made no use in arguing this question of fact ; for it was my intention to rest this point—and I do rest it—upon the force—the weight—which the Court *must give to the concurring testimony of seventeen men*, at least twelve of whom there has been no attempt to impeach by the prisoners. And so treating the point, it does seem to me that this Court are *forced* to the conclusion that the whole evidence overwhelmingly preponderates in favor of the hypothesis, that William J. Tolar fired the pistol, the bullet from which slew Archy Beebee. It Tolar did not fire it, may God help him, for circumstances are fearfully against him. And if he did fire it, according to the admissions of the Counsel for the prisoners—and the definition of murder, as hereinbefore given by me from many authorities—HE *at least is guilty of murder*.

May it please the Court : the Counsel for the defence have laid down two propositions, which they contend contain the law of this case : first, that, in order to find the prisoner Tolar guilty of murder under this charge and specification, we must show that he fired the pistol which killed Beebee ; second, in order to find the prisoners Powers and Watkins guilty, we must show that when Tolar fired this pistol, Powers and Watkins were present and were in a conspiracy, combination, or confederacy with Tolar to kill Beebee or to do him some great bodily harm, and that Tolar fired the pistol in the prosecution of the common unlawful design. I cannot assent to these propositions. I think there are views of this case, which I shall hereafter present, in which the Court will be compelled to convict Tolar of murder, though we utterly failed to make out that his hand directed the pistol which killed Beebee—points of view in which the identity of the person who fired the pistol which slew Beebee is a matter of no importance whatever. And I think there are also views of this case in which the Court would be in duty bound to convict Watkins and Powers of murder, though we failed to show that Tolar's hand directed the pistol which slew Beebee, in the prosecution of an unlawful design which was common to all three, and though we did not even offer evidence to establish, as an independent fact, any conspiracy, combination, or confederacy, between Tolar and the two other prisoners at the bar, to slay Beebee, or to do him some great bodily harm.

But I have met the defence upon their own ground on *one* point—and have shown that Tolar fired the pistol which killed Beebee; and before I am through with this address, I shall meet them upon their own ground, on *the other point also*—and shew as an independent fact, that there was a conspiracy, combination, and confederacy between Tolar, Powers and Watkins, to kill Beebee, or to do him some grevious bodily harm, in the prosecution of which common design, he was killed by Tolar—by evidence as cogent and conclusive as it is usually possible to offer on such a point. And then I shall ask the Court, according to the admissions of law of their own Counsel, to find these defendants *all* guilty of murder.

But I have now arrived at that point in this argument, where we are naturally, to consider, the law and facts of this case, applicable to the charge and specification, wherein their allegations apply to the defendants Powers and Watkins. Tolar is charged as the immediate actual apparent perpetrator of the homicide—in legal terms—*as principal in the first degree*; Powers and Watkins are charged as aiders and abettors of the felony, or in the language of the law—*as principals in the second degree.* There is no difference in the grade of the crime, or in the character of the guilt, of principals in the first, and principals in the second degree; but for many reasons, I think it well to clearly define the meaning of these legal terms.

A principal in the first degree, is one who is the actor, or actual perpetrator of the fact—a principal in the second degree, is, one who is present aiding and abetting in the commission of a felony.

(Foster's Crown, Cas. pp. 347, 349. Wharton on Hom. pp. 155, 157.)

Or to use the broader, and more clearly expressed definition of Bishop. In felony, a principal of the first degree, is one who does the act, either himself directly, or by means of an innocent agent—a principal of the second degree, is, one who is present, lending his countenance and encouragement, or otherwise aiding while another does it.

(Bish. on Crim. Law, vol. I, sec. 296.)

We have but little more to say of *principals in the first degree*—but to prove one to be a *principal in the second degree*, it must be proved—first—that he was *present* when the offence was committed; yet it is not necessary to show, that he was actually standing by, within sight or hearing of the fact. It is sufficient *if he was near enough to lend his assistance in any manner* to the commission of the offence. (2 Stark, on Ev. p. 7.) And *in general*, if a party be sufficiently near, to encourage the principal in the first degree with the expectation of immediate help or assistance in the execution of the felony he is *in point of law present.*

It must be shown secondly, that *he was aiding and abetting*—which terms seem to include every species of assistance, which one present can give another, either in act, or by his assent, or by his encouragement, or even by his readiness to further the unlawful purpose. For if any one comes for an unlawful purpose, *although he does no act*, he is a pricipal in the second degree. (Fost. Cr. Ca. p. 350. 1. Hale P. C. pp. 374,443. 2. Stark, on Ev. pp. 10, 11.)

And let the Court observe—that—the allegation that a defendant was *aiding and abetting in general* implies an *assent* to the principal act. And *this assent must be proved* by the prosecution—but the proof may be made in *two ways*—either by evidence of some act directly done in furtherance of the commission of the principal crime, which manifests the assent of the accused—as by evidence of his keeping watch, while others in his presence break open a house—or by evidence of a conspiracy, combination, confederacy, agreement, or understanding, between himself and the immediate criminal agent, in the prosecution of an illegal object, in the execution and furtherance of which the criminal fact was committed.

And I ask the Court also to note that this last proposition has the qualification that generally—not always—the allegation of aiding and abetting *implies an assent* to the principal fact; for there are cases known to the law where all that is implied by these terms is *an assent* upon the part of the defendant to some criminal fact, and not an assent to the particular specific criminal fact, in which the guilty assent resulted—according to a principle of the law we have already noticed while considering the general law of homicide, when speaking of the guilt of the *intent* and the guilt of the *fact*—and to which we shall have occasion to recur again. As in case murder were committed by B, in prosecution of an unlawful design—proof that A came to assist and carry that design into execution—though it were only a bare trespass—in other words evidence of his *assent to the trespass*—would be proof of his *aiding* and *abetting* the murder, on which to convict him as principal in the second degree. (Kel., 116 ; Fost. Dis., c. 3, sec. 8.)

Now a careful examination of these few legal propositions will plainly disclose to the Court, when it is incumbent upon the prosecution to make independent proof of a *conspiracy, combination, confederacy, agreement* or *understanding* between the felon, who is the immediate perpetrator of the criminal fact and those who are charged as principals in the second degree, before we can ask for a conviction of the latter, and when such proof is unnecessary. This examination will show that the law recognizes two kinds of presence, and two kinds of aiding and abetting—an *actual presence* and a *constructive presence*—an actual aiding and abetting, and a constructive aiding and abetting. To make a defendant guilty as a principal in the second degree, the prosecution must prove both his actual presence and his actual aiding and abetting; or his constructive presence and his actual aiding and abetting; or his actual presence and his constructive aiding and abetting ; or his constructive presence and his constructive aiding and abetting. When the prosecution is prepared to prove both an actual presence and an actual aiding and abetting, (and such is our case,) there is no necessity to prove the independant fact of conspiracy or combination; and it is only where there is a failure to prove either an actual presence, or an actual aiding and abetting—either one or the other—that it becomes necessary to prove a conspiracy or combination, or confederacy, as the means of establishing either the constructive presence or the constructive aiding and abetting.

(2 Stark on Ev., p. 12.   State vs. Simmons, 6 Jones, (N. C.) p. 21.   State vs. Morris, 3 Hawks, (N. C.) p. 388.)

A few examples will illustrate my meaning.   An *actual* presence is where one is standing by within *sight and hearing* of the criminal fact : an *actual* aiding and abetting, is where one does some act in *in direct furtherance of the commission of the criminal fact.*   Now suppose B commits a robbery or a murder, and A keeps watch or guard at some *convenient distance.*   A is not actually present, and to make out the proof of his *constructive presence,* you must establish some sort of combination, confederacy, agreement, or understanding between A and B—some connection between the two—before you are justified in convicting A.   Lord Dacre's case affords a notable instance, where there was conviction, though the *actual presence,* and the *actual aiding and abetting* were *both* wanting ; but the proof of combination supplied both.   Lord Dacre and others came to steal deer in the park of Mr. Pelham ; Rayden, one of the company, killed the keeper in the park— Lord Dacre and the rest of the company being in *other parts* of the park ; and it was held to be murder in them all, and they died for it.

(1 Hale, pp. 439, 443, 245.   Foster Crown Ca. p. 354.)

Now, here, to convict Lord Dacre and the rest of his company except Rayden, it was necessary to prove a constructive presence, and a constructive aiding and abetting at the place where Rayden slew the keeper ; and to make this proof, it was essential to establish a *combination* between Rayden, and Dacre, and the rest of his company—and this combination was established as the case shows—for it states that "Lord Dacre and the *others,* of whom Rayden was one, came to steal deer in the park of Mr. Pelham ;" they are all again mentioned as "Lord Dacre and the *rest* of the company."   So if A is actually present, standing by within sight and hearing, when a murder is committed by B, and takes no part in it, does no act in furtherance of the commission of the crime—and so much is given in evidence and no more— A cannot be convicted as a principal of the second degree, although there is an actual presence proved, because there is no proof of *his aiding and abetting,* either *actual* or *constructive.*   In such a case it is necessary for the prosecution to establish a conspiracy, combination or agreement between A and B to commit the murder, or at least to do some unlawful act before A can be found guilty, as principal in the second degree.   And in that event, if such proof be made, that A came for an unlawful purpose—although he does no act, he is a principal in the second degree.

(1 Hale, P. C. pp. 374, 443.)

While considering this branch of our subject, it may be well to state that there is a class of cases, in which it is important, not for the prosecution, but for the defence, to offer evidence and establish the fact of a *combination* in an unlawful object, between those who are charged as principals in the second degree and the immediate perpetrator of the criminal fact, as a ground for acquitting such as are charged as aiders and abettors.   It is a principle of law, that if a murder, or other felony, be committed by one of several engaged *in the prosecution* of an unlawful design, all who came to assist, and carry that design into execution, are guilty of the murder, or other felony, as principals in the second degree.   In such case, however, it is essential to prove that the murder, or other felony, was committed in the *prosecution of the specific unlawful design,* in which those, who are charged as principals in the second degree, were engaged.

(Kel. p. 116.   Foster, p. 351.   2 Stark on Ev. pp. 12, 13.)

For if the death, or other criminal fact, resulted from the particular malice of the individual who inflicted the blow, and who took the opportunity of revenging himself; or, if it resulted from the independent action of a part of the confederates, who had entered upon some *collateral, independent* illegal design, not contemplated by those who are charged as principals in the second degree, the others, who were assembled for a different purpose, will not be involved in his or their guilt.

(2 Stark on Ev. p. 13. Foster, p. 352. Kel. p. 111.)

Such being the law, cases will arise, wherein the prosecution, ignorant of the objects of the combination, will make *prima facie* proof of the *actual presence* of the prisoners at the fact, and of their actual or constructive aiding and abetting; when such aiding and abetting was not in fact *real*, but only *apparent*. And in order to show that it was *apparent* and not real, the prisoner must offer evidence—*proof*, tending to show, that the unlawful design for which they were assembled, and in which they were engaged, was independent and collateral to that specific design, in the prosecution of which one of their number committed a murder or other felony.

A few cases will illustrate this point. Three soldiers went together *to rob an orchard;* two got upon a pear-tree, and the third stood at the gate with a drawn sword in his hand. The owner's son coming by, collared the man at the gate and asked him what business he had there, and thereupon the soldier stabbed him. It was ruled by Holt to be murder in *him*, but that those on the tree were innocent.

(At. Sarum Law Assizes in 1697. Cited in Foster, p. 353.)

Here the unlawful combination was *to rob the orchard;* and the action of the soldier who killed the owner's son, was *independent* and *collateral* to the unlawful design, in which the two on the tree had combined with him; which fact saved their lives.

So in Plummer's case—the verdict stated, that Plummer and his accomplices, were assembled in order to transport wool of the growth of England to France, contrary to the statute; that an officer of the crown duly authorized for that purpose, met and opposed them, and that during the scuffle which ensued, a gun was discharged by one of the offenders, and John Harding, one of the same gang was killed. The question was whether Plummer and the rest of his party, were guilty of this murder. (Kel. p. 111.)

It was agreed by the Court: First, That had the King's officer or any of his assistants been killed by the shot, it would have been murder in all the gang. Second, That had it appeared that the shot was levelled at the officer or any of his assistants, this likewise would have amounted to murder in the whole gang, though an accomplice of their own happened to be killed—for the malice *egreditur personam;* but this fact not having been certainly found, the prisoner was discharged.

It is to be noticed, there was some evidence in this case, tending to show, that John Harding was purposely shot by one of the gang, because he was suspected of treachery.

Plummer was evidently acquitted, upon the ground that it appeared affirmatively that Harding was killed in the prosecution of some design, *which was independent of and collateral* to that specific unlawful design, of shipping wool to France, for which Plummer and his associates had assembled—and Sir Michael Foster remarks of this case—" I take it, that the point upon which the case turned was this—it did not appear from any of the facts found, that the gun was discharged *in prosecution of the purpose for which the party was assembled.* But had it been positively found, that the shot was levelled at the officer or any of his assistants, the Court, upon this finding, might, without incroaching on the province of the jury, have presumed it was discharged in prosecution of their original purpose." (Foster p. 352).

And now having ascertained the character of those cases in which, when a prisoner is charged as an aider and abettor, it is necessary for the prosecution to make *independent proof of a combination*, between the person so charged and the immediate agent of the criminal fact—it remains to inquire, whether the case made out by the prosecution in this trial against Powers and Watkins belongs to this class of cases. *Most clearly it does not.* We have made proof—so conclusive—that I do not understand the prisoners' Counsel even to question it—that within one or two minutes of the instant when the pistol was fired which killed Beebee, Powers and Watkins had made an assault upon him; Powers had with violent language endeavored to take the deceased from the officers in whose charge he then was, and both Powers and Watkins had endeavored to stab the deceased with their knives ; that Watkins, even after Beebee was slain, was still pressing on with his knife, expressing the desire and intention of cutting off his head ; that Powers was the first man in the crowd, who by his action in the premises incited the mob to press upon Beebee—and there is strong evidence—that from this imitation of his assault, until Beebee was slain, Powers, with his knife—armed with a pistol also, as one of the witnesses for the prosecution testified—formed part of the mad mob which continued to rush and press upon Beebee till he was slain. All these continued assaults, including the final one with the pistol which killed Beebee, transpired at the same moment of time—or at least in such quick succession, that it is almost impossible in narration to separate the one from the other—even Ed. P. Powers, a leading witness for the defence was compelled to admit, that Beebee was slain, within one minute from the time when he turned the entrance arch to go out of the market house. Beebee had not moved over twelve feet of ground—between the time when Powers, the prisoner at the bar, first attempted to seize him, and the time when he was shot with the pistol held—as we think we have proved—in the right hand of Tolar. Such being the facts, it does, to me, seem too plain for argument to the contrary—that the assaults made by Powers and Watkins with their knives, and their efforts to seize Beebee, " were acts done, in direct furtherance of the commission of the crime " of murder perpetrated by Tolar with the pistol upon Beebee, which acts manifest the assent " of these " two prisoners—Watkins and Powers—" to the principal criminal fact." In other words, we have made proof, of an *actual aiding and abetting*, in this felony, against Powers and Watkins—and without any further proof of combination between Tolar Watkins and Powers in an unlawful design, the *law presumes* the *assent* of these aiders and abettors to the principal criminal fact done by Tolar, unless these two defendants can plainly show, that this apparent actual aiding and abetting—was only apparent—and not real—or to vary the mode of expressing the same idea—unless these two defendants, can *plainly rebut* the presumption of their assent to the principal criminal fact, which the law raises from the *proof* of their apparent actual aiding and abetting therein.

Such is the *law* as I understand it ; and so far as my power and authority—as the legal adviser of this commission extends—such *I now charge* the *law* to be on these points.

But, may it please the Court, upon these points of law I am at issue with the Counsel for the defence, and have promised to meet them on their own ground—to take the law as *they* lay it down, and yet to show *all* their clients guilty—and I shall do it. The Counsel for the defence say—it is true that we have evidence here to convict Powers and Watkins of an assault upon Beebee—it may be—evidence to convict them of an assault upon Beebee, with the intent to kill him; but that if no person had done more than they did, Beebee would yet be living : and we can only convict them of, and for what *they themselves* did upon that occasion ; that they cannot be found guilty of murder because Tolar, or some one else, saw fit, at the time when they by chance were assaulting Beebee, to step forward and shoot him—unless we, the prosecution, establish as *an independent fact* in this case, that when Tolar, or some one else, fired the pistol, he was in combination, confederacy, agreement, conspiracy, or understanding of some sort with Watkins and Powers, to kill Beebee, or to do him some serious bodily harm, and Tolar—or whoever else it was—fired the pistol in the prosecution of the common design. I so understand the legal position of the Counsel for the defence—and I endeavor to state it fairly—and with the best of my poor ability—and my aim now is, although I consider it unnecessary for the success of the prosecution, to shew, that there is in this case *evidence*—cogent evidence—convincing evidence—conclusive proof, of a *combination* between Powers, and Watkins, and Tolar—or between Powers, Watkins, and *whoever it was*, who fired the pistol which slew Beebee, *to kill Beebee, or do him some great bodily harm.* I shall endeavor to shew that there is evidence here, which—if there were no *legal* objection to the prosecution of a conspiracy which has culminated in a felony—would justify a conviction of Watkins and Powers—and I may add Tolar—upon an indictment for a conspiracy to murder Beebee, or to do him some grievous bodily harm.

I was somewhat surprised to hear my brother Fuller say, while he was addressing the Court, that the *only* evidence of a combination to injure Beebee on the part of any one, which existed in this case, was the testimony of James McNeill—wherein he deposed, that he (witness) heard Tolar say to the prisoner, Powers, on or near the pavement, in front of the east end of the market house, as Powers was returning from the carriage, in which Mrs. and Miss Massey left the scene of the homicide—" When he comes down you grab him and break the ice—and we'll put him through,"—or as the witness first expressed himself—" When he comes down you grab him and break the ice—and that will be all you will have to do." That is *very direct* and positive evidence of a combination, between Powers and Tolar, it is true—but to me there seemed a good deal more evidence of the same character scattered throughout the testimony. But the strongest, weightiest, and most convincing evidence of a combination between Powers and Watkins, and the man who fired the pistol—is of a different character—and to me it seems conclusive unless it be repelled. The *strongest evidence* in this case, of a conspiracy—upon the part of Powers and Watkins and the man who fired the pistol—to kill Beebee or to do him some serious bodily harm, is found in the proof of the fact that they did combine in the act of assaulting him. It is proof of a stronger character than can usually be given upon a charge of conspiracy, and it is necessary for me to explain why this is so ; and also to elucidate more fully my meaning, which sounds like a truism.

A conspiracy, as an independent offence known to the law, is—a confederation of two or more persons to accomplish an illegal object—or to accomplish an indifferent object by illegal means.

(2 Whart, Am. Crim. L. Sec. 2291.)

The gist of the offence is the agreement or confederacy—and this is indictable, though the illegal object be in no degree prosecuted, or though the illegal means, be in no respect used. It is evident then, that in making proof of a conspiracy, which has not been at least partially prosecuted or carried into action, we can never have the evidence of the actual combination of the defendants in the execution of the illegal object to help us. But when the illegal object was to commit another misdemeanor, and is prosecuted to completion, the misdemeanor thus committed, is the offence generally prosecuted, and which finds its way into our Courts for trial, as being most deserving of punishment—and if the illegal object was to commit a felony, and is executed, the conspiracy as such cannot be indicted, because the conspiracy which is a misdemeanor, is merged in the felony; so that ordinarily, whether the object of the combination be to committ a felony, or to commit a misdemeanor, if it be actually prosecuted to completion—the offence which comes before the Courts for trial, is the felony or misdemeanor which there was a conspiracy to commit, and not the conspiracy itself. So that it is very rarely the case, that on trial of a *conspiracy*, we can produce such strong and convincing proof of its commission, as arises from establishing the fact, that the defendants did actually combine in the execution of the illegal object. But thus cogent proof we have, in our case—that Watkins and Powers, and Tolar—or whoever it was that fired the pistol—did, in fact, combine, in a simultaneous assault on Archy Beebee, during which, he lost his life—to establish a conspiracy, to kill Beebee or to do him serious bodily hurt, between Watkins and Powers, and the man who with his own hand slew the deceased.

Does the Court realize the force and weight of such evidence? Let me illustrate this point. The door of this hall stands open; suppose a man were to enter through it, holding in his hand a bond prepared for signature, and were to place it upon the table before the Court; and thereupon immediately, and without any apparent signal given by the man who had entered the hall, six persons here seated were to rise from their seats, approach the table and sign the bond thereon deposited, as sureties for the new-comer. The Court would have no evidence that these six men had agreed to sign the bond as sureties, except the fact that they had simultaneously congregated and executed it; yet how cogent—how conclusive—how overwhelming would be the proof, made by this fact, of a *previous agreement* between the new-comer and the six persons alluded to, and between the six persons among themselves, to sign the bond as sureties for the first. So the fact that Powers and Watkins were present at the scene of the homicide, and did actually assist Tolar to slay Beebee—supposing, for the sake of the analogy, that Tolar did shoot the fatal pistol, as I think we have already conclusively established he did do—is cogent, conclusive, overwhelming proof that the three had beforehand agreed to kill Beebee or to do him some grievous bodily harm. We need no stronger—it would be difficult to offer stronger—evidence of a *previous combination* between the prisoners to do an unlawful act.

But, say the Counsel for the prisoners, it is true the apparent, actual, simultaneous combination of the three in the criminal fact *would be* very strong evidence of a *previous agreement* between Watkins and Powers and Tolar to commit it, or some other act like it, except that our case is an exceptional one, and we can account for the fact of their simultaneous combination in action by another and more probable hypothesis than that of a previous agreement between the three to kill Beebee or to do him some serious bodily hurt. That Beebee had committed an offence—or at least was charged with having committed an offence—against the person of Miss Elvira Massey—an attempt to ravish her—of so heinous a character that it was well and naturally calculated to excite in *every* manly heart an irresistible impulse to redress her wrongs; that under the force of this impulse common to all of them—their souls being red with uncommon wrath—Watkins and Powers—and Tolar also, if he was a party to the killing—rushed upon Beebee to destroy him; and so we have, upon the face of this case, *a reason* for the simultaneous action of the three in the same direction, and it is not necessary for the Court to search for other reason, such as a *previous agreement* among them, to account for it. I am not using the words—I am endeavoring to convey the meaning and argument of the prisoner's Counsel.

I will myself supply an analogy—and I purposely select a homely one—to illustrate the position of the Counsel for the defence, according to my understanding of it. They say that their case is similar to the following one: Suppose we were all sitting around a fire, in a room where there was a handsome India matting on the floor, and a large spark were suddenly to fly out of the fire and fall on the matting in the midst of the circle. Say the Counsel for the defence by their reasoning, in such event, every man present—all simultaneously—would spring forward to put their feet upon the spark and extinguish it: and yet this simultaneous action would be no evidence of a previous agreement to do so—because the combination in action is accounted for by the natural impulse, which was common to all. And so, continue the Counsel—in our case, Watkins and Powers, and Tolar, if he took part, acted simultaneously in assailing Beebee from the sheer force of a *natural impulse* of our common humanity—and not from a previous agreement or understanding among them. The cases, however, are not really analogous, as I shall presently show—and the *law* does not permit this Court to regard the character of the offence committed by Beebee, or alleged to have been committed by him—*for any purpose*—of this trial. It would have been more proper to have tried this case, without permitting the nature of the offence alleged against Beebee to have come into evidence at all. Suppose in the trial of this cause, or one similar to it, before the Chief Justice of the United States, or any other Judge of established reputation, it had been gravely proposed by the Counsel for the defence to introduce evidence for the prisoners, which tended to show that the deceased man had a day or two before he was killed, committed a rape, or had attempted to commit one, or at least was accused of such an attempt. I could, and would straightway have objected to the introduction of such evidence, on the ground that it was impertinent, and irrelevant to the issue, and that it had no application to this case. The Judge would have said to the prisoner's Counsel, "unless you can show its relevancy and proper application, it must be excluded." I wish to know, if it can be possible that the Counsel for the defence suppose that they—with all their ability—even that brother Fuller, with all the *suaviter in modo* and *fortiter in re*, for which he is remarkable, could have brought any argument to bear on the Judge, to induce him to allow of the admission of this testimony in such a case as this one is?

Brother Fuller would have said: The prosecution, may it please the Court, rely upon the fact that there *was a combination* to kill Archy Beebee, between the person who shot him and the prisoners Powers and Watkins, as the ground of convicting the two prisoners last named of murder. The prosecution will insist that *this combination is *strongly evidenced, by proof of the fact, that Powers and Watkins made an assault upon Beebee with their knives, simultaneously with the assault which was made on him by Tolar with his pistol, when the latter slew the deceased. I propose to show that, *on the day before the homicide was committed*, Beebee committed a rape.

upon a respectable young white woman, who was a defenceless orphan—or
attempted to commit such a rape—or at least was accused of having attempted to commit the rape on the day previous; and the object of this evidence is to repel the conclusion of a combination between the three, drawn
from the fact of their simultaneous concurrence in the assault, since the enormity of Beebee's crime excited in all honorable men, within whose view he
came, an irresistible—or at least a natural—impulse to kill him, or do him
some serious bodily harm. The Judge would have replied: " The law says,
if a man detect another *in the very act* of attempting to ravish a woman, and
slay him to prevent the crime, the slayer shall be justified and commended,
provided the attempt was apparent, and the danger imminent, and the
amount of force used necessary to prevent the crime; because the human
impulse which impelled the slayer to kill was natural and laudable, and he
but saved the hangman a labor. If a man detect another *in the very act of
adultery* with the wife of his bosom, and at once slay him in the heat or
blood, yet shall he not be justified nor excused, but he is guilty of manslaughter—of the felonious slaying of the deceased; and if he allow the sun
to go down upon his wrath, and on the next day slay the adulterer, he is in
law a murderer: for the law so far regards the infirmities of human nature
as to palliate—not justify nor excuse—that impulse of passion which urges the
husband to slay an adulterer detected in the act, at the moment of detection;
but the law neither justifies, nor excuses, nor palliates, that impulse of passion which drives even the husband to slay even·the adulterer, when the
blood has had time to cool. The law, in no respect, and for no purpose, regards such an impulse of passion as this last *as natural*—as even an infirmity of our common nature. And shall the law—which does not regard even
the anger of the outraged husband against the destroyer of his peace, on the
day after his dishonor, as of any avail to mitigate his offence, nor allow
proof of the fact of his dishonor on the previous day to be received in evidence, for any purpose, on his trial for the adulterer's murder—permit the
evidence which you propose to introduce to be heard? It cannot be! If
the fact that Beebee had, on the previous day, ravished, or attempted to ravish, a respectable white girl, who was an unprotected orphan—or the fact
that he was accused of such an attempt on the day previous—*did excite* in
Powers and Watkins and Tolar an impulse to slay, or do great bodily harm
to Beebee, THE LAW says such impulse was neither pardonable nor natural,
but was diabolical—was a seduction and instigation of the devil—indicated
a heart regardless of social duty and fatally bent upon mischief—and THE
LAW FORBIDS BOTH COURTS AND JURIES to conclude, that any such impulse is
excited by any such cause, unless it be *clearly proved;* in which event it cannot help, but is fatal to the prisoner. *Cui bono*—then, should this evidence
of Beebee's crime, or the accusation against him, be heard? You propose to
introduce it to account for a *simultaneous concurrence* of several men in a
criminal fact, because, you say, this concurrence proceeded not from *previous
agreement*, but in fact from a common impulse which his crime excited in
the prisoners and in all other honorable men; but the law says, both as a
matter of fact and a matter of law, his crime excited no such impulse, and
therefore his crime cannot account for their concurrent action. The evidence offered is impertinent and irrelevant in every point of view, and must
be excluded." And such is undoubtedly the law.

It is only by accident—or rather—by some indulgence extended to the
prisoners by the prosecution—that the fact of the crime of which Beebee
was accused at the time of his death, has crept into the evidence in this

cause, and has become judicially known to the Court. If then, it was not proper evidence, to be heard by this Court *for any purpose*—how can the prisioners hope by means of it—to repel the strong presumptive proof of a combination among them in an unlawful design arising for the fact of their simultaneous concurrence in a criminal fact?

But, may it please the Court—if the evidence of the crime alleged against Beebee *could* be used, for the purpose proposed by the prisoner's Counsel, there is yet no analogy, between the case I have used for illustration, and the position taken by the Counsel for the defence. The true analogy is, between the case of the sureties who signed the bond—already suggested—and the case before us. I have suggested the illustration of the circle of gentlemen, the India matting and the spark of fire—because I wished to do *full justice* to the prisoners—and to bring the point raised by their Counsel, clearly and prominently—before the Court. Let us however, extend this illustration a little—suppose the party of gentlemen did not, when the spark first fell on the matting, *immediately* stamp it out, but walked about the room, in conversation with one another, and presently, simultaneously came back and put it out, we would then have a case more analogous to ours—would not the conclusion be irresistible, in such case, that they had, while so moving about in conversation, *consulted* on the matter, and *agreed to put it out*?

So, too, if, on the very day in which this crime of attempted rape was committed—which was alleged against Beebee—Tolar, Powers and Watkins had sought him out—rushed upon him—and then and there slain him—there would have been some sort of show of an analogy between their action, and that of the supposed circle of gentlemen. But when that day had passed by, and when Beebee had, but an hour before the assault, gone up into the market house, passing in the presence of these very men, who finally killed him, without being assaulted—and when these prisoners did not, driven by this natural impulse—spoken of by their Counsel—immediately leap upon him, and then and there take away his life—but within an hour afterwards, having in the mean time been moving about in conversation with one another—did simultaneously attack him, two, with knives and one with a pistol and slay him—*then*, their action is exactly analogous to that of the gentlemen, who, when the spark first flew out upon the matting, walked about the room in conversation together, and eventually, came back simultaneously and put it out—the analogy of the illustration holds good here. Such conduct indicates that the simultaneous concurrence in the assault by the three, was the *result* of an *agreement* to kill or do bodily harm to Beebee—that it was the result of an understanding—a combination to which Tolar, Watkins and Powers—and probably others—were parties.

It is admitted by the Counsel for the prisoners, that, if Tolar fired the pistol, he is guilty of murder; and if there was a combination between Tolar and Powers and Watkins to do grievous bodily harm to Beebee, in pursuance of which design the pistol was fired, then Powers and Watkins are also guilty of murder—and that the matter is sufficiently laid in the charge and specification. The presumptive *proof* of a combination among the three—arising from the established fact, that all three participated in a simultaneous, concurrent assault upon the deceased, at the moment when the pistol was fired which killed him, cannot—as I think I have shown—be *successfully* met, by the counter *allegation*—and we have nothing but the *allegation*—that their having *apparently united* in the *criminal fact is accounted for*, by a natural impulse of the human heart, which caused them *all* to leap simultaneously to its execution, without any previous agreement or understanding with one another.

As it seems to me, the Counsel for the defence have had a hard case. They *are* able; they *have been* indefatigable in the cause of their clients; but they were surrounded with difficulties at every point. There is hardly a path into which they turned on their road which did not lead them to destruction. My sympathies were often aroused, and the difficulties of the defence must have reached their climax, when Counsel were driven to assuming the position, that every man who attempted a rape deserved to be murdered by a mob—and that all men of generous instincts, warm hearts, and manly impulses, would naturally feel, an almost irresistible inclination, to murder the wretch, so soon as he came in their sight. This irresistible inclination is one which the *law* does not recognize, as I have already pointed out—it is an inclination which the *law* regards, as neither a justification, nor an excuse, nor a palliation of homicide. But the prisoners have put this proposition in the mouths of their Counsel, and it proves too much for their good. If the community in which Beebee was killed feel in that way—and many of its component parts, no doubt do; if the prisoners at the bar feel in that way; if they felt that this negro man after attempting what he did attempt—if the allegation against him be true—did not deserve any longer to live and merited death at the hands of every citizen; if that feeling produced so strong a passion in them, that Counsel representing them come *here*, and plead it, if not as an *excuse* for the act charged against them in the indictment, at least as strong and forceful evidence that the prisoners acted from impulse and passion—and not after deliberations, with designs—is it not a legitimate argument for me to urge, that they thus furnish us with an *a priori* probability, that they did agree beforehand to kill Beebee; as the means of more certainly and effectually doing that, which they all thought ought to be done, and felt a strong impulse—all of them—to do? According to the views of the Counsel for the defence, it is necessary for the prosecution to prove that there was a combination between Tolar and Watkins and Powers to kill the deceased or to do him serious bodily harm; we offer evidence that they all united simultaneously in an assault upon him, which was terminated by his death—as proof of a previous agreement or understanding among the three, that they would kill Beebee or do him some grievous bodily harm; and the Counsel for the defence say, it is highly probable that there was such an agreement or understanding—for every man of them thought Beebee deserved to die—ought to be murdered the moment he came within view of any man with the impulses of a man—felt a strong inclination and almost irresistable impulse to murder him—and to be certain that it was done and well done—what more probable than that they combined to do it? If the assumption of the Counsel proves any thing, it proves too much. But the Court ought not properly to know for what offence Beebee was arrested, and therefore arguments derived from his crime can have no legitimate application either for prosecution or for defence.

But, may it please the Court, there is some direct, and a great deal more circumstantial evidence of a combination to kill Beebee, or to do him serious bodily harm. I wish the Court, however, before proceeding farther, to disabuse their minds of the idea—if such idea they entertain—that a conspiracy must necessarily be as august in its dimensions and as long in its preparation as was the conspiracy of Cataline to assassinate the new consuls of Rome. Most persons, unaccustomed to legal language, think that the idea of a combination necessarily implies a great deal of forethought and pre-arrangement. It is true the allegation of combination does imply *some* degree of premeditation; but, though parties may have assembled for an entirely innocent purpose, yet if, upon a dispute or other cause for it arising, there is even a mute understanding of mutual assistance in a common design among several, there is in law a combination; so that it is not at all necessary to the establishing a combination between Tolar, Powers and Watkins—or to proving a confederacy or conspiracy between them, within the meaning of the law—to offer evidence that they *agreed* together the night before, or the morning before, or even a minute before they got to the market house, at the time when Beebee was killed, to make an assault on him. They may have combined after they got together at the scene of the homicide, and this would make a complete conspiracy. If there was an understanding or agreement between the prisoners at the bar, *one minute* after Bond got down stairs and announced the result of the trial—if there was even then an understanding or agreement as to what each man was to do, there was a complete conspiracy. If when Powers attempted to seize Beebee, he did so under a silent understanding, *that moment conveyed to him,* that he would receive aid, comfort, or even encouragement from Tolar and Watkins, there was just as complete a combination as if it had been entered into six weeks before hand in the most explicit terms.

Embracing these views, we set out with the fact, that Powers, Watkins and Tolar did combine *in action.* Powers and Watkins were cutting at Beebee with their knives within a minute after he made his appearance; Powers exclaiming " He's my prisoner!" " Damn him, give him to me!" and using many other like expressions. We *know* that the killing was *very* soon after the first assault—all the witnesses concur in this, and we know it not only from the positive, direct statements of the witnesses—but also from certain circumstantial facts that are embodied in the case. For instance—one of the witnesses for the defence, Isham Blake, says, he turned to go out of the market house, putting himself instantly in motion, as soon as he saw Beebee coming down the stairs of the market house, having some fear that there was to be a difficulty which he was unwilling to witness—and before he could get out of the market house, the man was shot. Robert Mitchell, a witness for the prosecution, left the market house before the negro had left the town hall above the market house: his store was but a hundred yards distant or thereabouts, and *before he reached it the man was shot.* It takes but a very short time to walk a hundred yards, at an ordinary pace. Therefore, from the time the first assault was made by Powers and Watkins to the time of the final assault with the pistol, there could not have elapsed a *minute*— Mitchell had not even got to his store before he heard the report of the pistol. So again, Carpenter, a witness for the prosecution, says, he arrived at the middle of the market house in passing through it; at that time the negro was on the stairs; the witness, without pausing, passed directly through the crowd present, and *before* he reached Davis's store, a distance not exceeding thirty yards, the *pistol was fired.* All these circumstances, as well as the statements of the witnesses, show that there must have been only an *exceedingly short interval of time* between the moment when Watkins and Powers were making the attempt to stab Beebee with their knives, and the instant when the pistol was fired by Tolar; the assault was continuous—and in fact we may say the assault of Powers and Watkins with their knives, and the assault of Tolar with his pistol, were made in the *same moment.* So, I conceive the actual combination in the criminal fact to be established. I have, therefore, endeavored to divest the minds of the Court of the idea, commonly entertained, that a conspiracy, or combination, must necessarily have been entered into some considerable time previous to the execution of the criminal design—and also to impress upon them, that *no further proof is necessary* to show a combination, when the object of the conspiracy is carried into action, and we can prove a general participation in the action—since *that* fact is the strongest possible circumstantial evidence of combination. And I am now prepared to enter upon the independent evidence of combination, scattered throughout the case—of which there is much—which implicates not only the prisoners at the bar, but several other persons, not now before the Court.

May it please the Court: it is seldom indeed that we are able to prove a conspiracy or combination, by positive, direct testimony. The Court ought not to expect such proof. The evidence in such cases must almost necessarily be circumstantial. It can be direct and positive only when one of the conspirators becomes a traitor to the unlawful combination and his associates. Unless this be done, it is impossible to prove a conspiracy by direct testimony.

I will read to the Court a quotation of some authority in connection with this subject. I read from the case of United States *vs.* Cole, 5th McLean's Reports, p. 513, N. B., p. 601:

"A conspiracy is rarely, if ever, proved by positive testimony. When a crime of high magnitude is about to be perpetrated by a number of individuals, they do not act openly, but covertly and secretly. The purpose formed is known only to those who enter it. Unless one of the original conspirators betray his companions and give evidence against them, their guilt can only be proved by circumstantial evidence. It is said by some writers on evidence that such circumstances are stronger than positive proof. A witness swearing positively may misapprehend facts, or swear falsely, but circumstances cannot lie. The common design is the essence of the charge, and this is made to appear where the defendant's *steadily pursue the same object, whether acting separately or together by common or different means*"—whether pursuing their object, one with a knife, another with a pistol, another with a club, or whether all with pistols—"all leading to the same unlawful result. And where *prima facie* evidence has been given of a conspiracy, the acts or confessions of one are evidence against all. This rule of evidence is founded upon the principles which apply to agencies and partnerships. And it is reasonable that, where a body of men assume the attribute of individuality, whether for commercial business or the commission of a crime, the association should be bound by the acts of one of its members in carrying out the design."

Says Stark. on Ev., vol. 2, Part IV, p. 401:

"Upon an indictment for a conspiracy, the evidence is either direct, of a meeting and consultation for the illegal purpose charged, or *more usually, from the very nature of the offence, is circumstantial. It is not necessary to prove any direct concert or even meeting of the conspirators.*"

Greenleaf says, 3 Greenlf. on Ev., sec. 93, p. 88:

"*The evidence in proof of a conspiracy will generally, from the nature of the case, be circumstantial.* The common design is the essence of the charge. *It is not necessary to prove that the defendants came together and actually agreed, in terms, to have that design and pursue it by common means.* If it be proved that the defendants pursued, by their acts, the same object, often by the same means, one performing one part and another another part of the scheme, so as to complete it, with a view to the attainment of the same object, the jury will be justified in the conclusion that they were engaged in a conspiracy to effect that object. Nor is it necessary to prove *that the conspiracy originated with the defendants, or that they met during the process of its concoction ; for every person entering into a conspiracy, or common design already formed, is deemed in law a party to all acts done by any of the other parties before or afterwards in furtherance of the common design.*"

The Court will see from all these authorities and many others, which might be produced—that we are not to be expected to adduce evidence here showing *when* and *where* and under what circumstances, Tolar, Powers and Watkins met and concocted this scheme or even to show that they ever met at all—we give the only evidence, of which, in its nature, the case admits. The law is reasonable. The common law is the very perfection of justice and of reason. It is not an artificial code—but it *grew up out of the necessities* of a brave and wise people jealous of their rights and liberties. This is the only kind of evidence, that can be had of a conspiracy or combination, unless one of the men who was party to the combination, himself comes forward, and admitting his own guilt—exposes his co-conspirators and gives us the details of the combination. And if, as we allege—and think we have proved—and shall hereafter *show*—there was a combination, to do Beebee harm, to which not only the prisoners at the bar, but also Leggett, Lutterloh, Powers and others were parties, we do not believe the oaths of any of these parties, with reference to the conspiracy will go for anything with this Court : or at any rate *very little* reliance will be placed on any statement they may make *to disprove its existence*. Leggett, Lutterloh and Powers, by their own admissions, connect themselves too closely with Tolar, to claim credence at our hands. I shall not take the trouble to analyze their testimony, in which they deposed they were not parties to any combination; *if they were parties* to a conspiracy to murder, I would not expect them to admit it, even when put to the crucial test of an oath ; and if I have satisfactory testimony that they were parties to such a combination—their oaths will not purge them in my estimation—any more than would the oaths of these prisoners at the bar, that they are not guilty of the offence, with which they are charged, convince me of their innocence.

I say thus much, by way of response, to the position taken by the defence—that they had negatively disproved any combination, by the testimony of Leggett, Lutterloh and Powers. But even accepting all which these three witnesses—Lutterloh, Leggett and E. P. Powers—deposed, as true—it only proves at most that *they*—these three—had no connection with the combination, and that they knew nothing of it. It does not even tend to disprove a combination to which Tolar, Powers and Watkins were parties. It is not necessary to our case—but I will also say, in reply to remarks which fell from the opposing Counsel, that there is strong evidence, that the witnesses Leggett, Lutterloh and Powers *were* parties to the criminal combination, as well as many more not named ; and upon this point my position is unchanged, and I stand just where I did, at the opening of the testimony in this cause.

At this point, the Court took a recess until eight thirty P. M.

The Commission met pursuant to adjournment.

Mr. Haywood continued as follows :

May it please the Court :—When the commission took a recess, at three o'clock to-day, I was endeavoring to demonstrate, from the evidence as an independent fact, that there was a combination, confederacy, or conspiracy, upon the part of these prisoners at the bar, and probably upon the part of others not now on trial, who were present upon the occasion of Archy Beebee's death, either to do him some great bodily harm, or to take away his life. I had insisted that it was not necessary to their conviction, according to my view of the law, to establish the fact of any conspiracy or combination. That if Powers and Watkins were actually present, and actually aiding and abetting in the homicide, when Tolar fired the pistol, there was no necessity whatever for establishing a conspiracy. For proof of a conspiracy was only necessary, when there was not an actual presence, or not an actual aiding and abetting, for the purpose of showing a constructive presence, or a constructive aiding and abetting; but as it had been admitted upon the part of the defence, if we showed that Tolar did fire the pistol which killed Archy Beebee; and further showed that there was a combination, a confederacy, or a conspiracy, between Tolar, and the defendants Powers and Watkins, to aid and abet him in what he did, then it was necessarily murder in all—I was going on to demonstrate, from the evidence, that there was a conspiracy; the first point I made, and the one from which I shall now begin my argument, was, that the strongest proof of conspiracy, was the fact that Powers and Watkins actually did combine with Tolar in the criminal fact, which position, I illustrated to the Court by one or two familiar analogies.

I now come to the other evidence of a combination—direct and positive, as well as circumstantial—and which, it is true, is almost altogether circumstantial, with which I was occupied when the Court adjourned. As I then showed the Court—from the principles—contained in McLean Reports, Starkie and Greenleaf, and other authorities—it is to be expected, that the evidence in such cases will be circumstantial. We are not prepared to prove—and if the Court should require so much of us, our case must fail—and most cases of a like character must break down—we are not prepared to prove that Tolar, Powers and Watkins actually met together, in a house, or at a particular spot in the night of the previous day, or in the earlier part of the same day when the homicide was perpetrated, and had, by express agreement, each with the other, in explicit terms undertaken to commit this murder. We could not be prepared with such proof as this, unless one of the criminals would turn State's evidence, and furnish us with the details of the nefarious scheme. But I do undertake to show, not from a single circumstance—as one of the Counsel for the defence alleged in his address—not from the single circumstance—to which James McNeill testified, that the defendant Tolar told Tom Powers, " Tom, as he comes down, you grab him and break the ice, and that is all you will have to do,"—but from a crowd— a host—of other circumstances, to which I shall now endeavor to direct the attention of the Court—that there was a combination among all the prisoners at the bar, the object of which was either to kill Beebee or to do him serious bodily harm.

There was something peculiar in the bearing of the crowd that day. It is evidenced at every turn in these proceedings. It is difficult to define what it was. It is difficult for the witnesses to testify to what constituted it; but every member of this Court, who has been in an excited crowd, knows that frequently, without the flourishing of deadly weapons—without noise—without expressions in the way of threats—without shouts—it may be gathered from the *general bearing of a crowd*—the expression of the face— the compression of the lip—the flashing of the eye, or the pallor of the countenance—the appearance of restlessness, or the appearance of determination or

of unnatural calm in a crowd—that some deed of violence is about to be enacted. There is a sort of electric current that passes through such a crowd—
an animal fluid, which communicates a knowledge of the impending fact to
those who come in contact therewith. It is intangible: it is almost impossible to lay the hand upon it—it is utterly impossible to express in words of
what it consists. From the actions of individuals in the crowd, within and
around the market house at Fayetteville on that day, the Court may see
that such a state of things existed there. Take Isham Blake, one of the witnesses for the defence. He was so conscious that something unusual and
terrible was about to occur, although, he says, he heard no threat, and saw
no violent outbreak, that he expressed himself here as having turned away
to leave the market house, to avoid seeing what was about to transpire.
Notice the exclamation of the negro woman, as mentioned by Myrover—another witness for the defence—as she came shrieking through the market
house, before the assault was made upon Beebee, crying out "they are going
to kill that poor boy." Notice the fact—that, after the deed of blood was
done, of those two hundred men, or thereabouts, who composed the crowd,
no voice—except a few of negroes and children—was heard inquiring "who
had perpetrated that act?"—no voice denouncing its perpetrator—no hand
was extended to seize the felon. It was unnatural. In the ordinary course
of things—as this Court well knows—if, in a crowd of one or two hundred
persons, a pistol were discharged which slew a man, every second man in
that crowd would be inquiring who fired it, except they all, or a very many
of them, had some *knowledge* of what was about to be done, or had at least
some *suspicion*, from the appearance of the crowd, of the deed which was
about to be enacted. Look also at the witness for the prosecution—James
McNeill. Hearing this injunction from Tolar to Powers—to which I have
already more than once alluded—*he turned and fled.* Why? There was
some cause for it. There was something in that crowd, as to which the witnesses cannot testify, so unintelligible to the senses that it is an essence for
which there is no name, and which pervaded that whole assemblage and indicated a consciousness of the coming deed.

Nor was this all on which we rely—there are proofs more tangible. John
Maultsby, says the witness Reynolds, an uneducated boy, who—although
from necessity introduced by the prosecution—evidently gave his testimony
with great reluctance, whenever it told with any force against the prisoners
at the bar—John Maultsby was in conversation with a red bearded man,
whose name the witness did not know, and Maultsby said, "If the man is
innocent I am his friend, but if he is guilty *I am in for* IT." There was
some doubt raised by the cross-examination, as to whether the expression
used by Maultsby was, "If he is guilty, *I* am in for it," or "*he* is in for
it." But an examination of the testimony, as recorded by the gentlemen,
who have with so much patience, fidelity, and accuracy, performed this part
of our painful duty, will show, that upon his examination in chief, Jesse
Reynold's expression was this: "If he is guilty, *I* am in for it, *as well as
the rest.*" What *it?* What *rest?* These expressions—this mode of expression used by Maultsby—indicate a consciousness, on his part at ved
of something about to take place to which he feared to give a name, and good
which *several besides himself* were concerned. Again; Nixon, according to
the testimony of Sykes—one of the witnesses for the defence—had a could
sation with Tom Powers, while Beebee was above stairs. Powers wBut
ting on a bench within the market house, near Becky Ben's stall, and after
told Powers, finding that he was unarmed, "he (Powers) *ought* not con-

pistol." What for, unless Nixon also knew of some event about to take place, in which arms would be needed by Miss Massey's nearest male relative living? What for, unless there was some communication going about that crowd—some understanding pervading it—that Beebee, the negro man who had attempted to ravish his (Powers') niece, was then and there to expiate his crime? But it will be insisted, this is *some evidence* that Tom Powers was no party to the combination, even if there was one—since he said "he did not have a pistol, and he wanted the law to take its course." It is probable that at the time when Powers made use of these remarks, his mind was in a state of indecision. He had not yet fully determined what he was to do—he was in that fearful interim "between the acting of a dreadful thing and the first motion." It is probable, when Nixon spoke to him, that he was debating with himself, whether he should take part in this combination to commit murder, even at the last moment. He *said* "he wanted the law to take its course." But *after this*, as we allege—although the proof is not positive whether it was after or before—David Oliphant, a witness for the prosecution, says that he saw Tom Powers leave the market house and its immediate neighborhood for a short time—say about fifteen minutes—and then return to his old seat on the bench within it. We naturally argue that his absence was caused by the previous suggestion, that he ought to be armed with a pistol, and he absented himself to provide one. Tom Powers left the market house again, when the ladies, Mrs. and Miss Massey, came down stairs, and went to the carriage—he moved to the carriage with them, or immediately after they did—and had a conversation with his sister, Mrs. Massey, in which conversation *she* advised him, "not to have anything to do with *it.*" What *it?* What was this deed without a name—to which neither Maultsby nor Mrs. Massey *dared* to give a name? Now, it is alleged by the Counsel for the prisoners—that there is a contradiction and a contrariety in the testimony here. That a number of their witnesses, and some of ours, have sworn, that *they did not see Tom Powers go to the carriage.* There can be no doubt about his having *gone there,* for witnesses—several of them on both sides—swear to it most positively; but, say the Counsel for the prisoners, McNeill stands *alone* in the statement that Mrs. Massey told Powers "he had better not have anything to do with it," and that thereupon Powers nodded his head, as if assenting. The Counsel misstates the matter—McNeill does not stand alone in his testimony of this conversation between Tom Powers and Mrs. Massey—David Oliphant confirms him—*he* heard the same expressions; and Mr. Mitchell, a friend and connection of the Massey family, so far as his testimony goes, confirms McNeill also—Mitchell had an impression that some such expressions were used by Mrs. Massey—he could not speak positively. But, if there was *no confirmation* at all—the character of McNeill, being unimpeached here, and he having sworn positively that he heard such an expression—all this negative testimony, upon the part of others, that such conversation did not occur, or that they didn't hear it, and the like, amounts to nothing—there is no real conflict. According to the rule of evidence to which I alluded, when speaking to the Court on the legal regulations, which control them in the investigation of testimony—one of the leading principles controlling the reconciliation of all the evidence is, that where positive testimony is opposed by negative testimony—the general rule, under ordinary circumstances, other things being equal, *positive is true and must prevail.* Why? Because when a man swears that it, and with circumstance, that he saw or heard a particular thing, happened, he must be swearing to a fact—to the truth—or he must be perjured. But when others swear they were present, or near about, and did not hear or see any such thing, or that it did not occur, to the best of their knowledge and belief, they may, through incapacity, or inattention, or inadvertence, or lack of memory, or error, or mistake, have failed to see, or hear, or notice—or may now be unable to recollect what really happened—and they may be mistaken or in error without being perjured. I take it therefore for a fact, and I think this Court will receive it for a fact, that Miss Massey said to Tom Powers, "don't have anything to do with *it*." I take it as another fact, and I think this Court will receive it as a fact—because an unimpeached witness—who has not been, and cannot be contradicted—has sworn to it, that as Tom Powers was passing back from the carriage to the market house, Tolar approached him, as James McNeill swears he did, and said to him what McNeill swears he said—Beebee having just left the town hall, and passed through the door at the head of the stairs—" when he comes down, you grab him, and break the ice, and *we'll* put him through." Now isn't the story natural? Doesn't the evidence of all the witnesses fit as if it were grooved and dove-tailed? Look at Tom Powers' whole course. He had been hesitating for hours before. He was hesitating when McNeill spoke to him, and asked him if Miss Massey was his niece. He had been with these ladies, his sister and niece, and had been advised to have nothing to do with it—the approaching tragedy. He was even more vacillating and uncertain than before, and Tolar, approaching him—perhaps mistrusting the softness of his disposition—saw his vacillation. Tolar, the leader, determined to strengthen his feeble knees—he told him his part in the approaching deed of blood was *but a small one*—only do that—only put your hand to the wheel, "and we'll put him through." The whole evidence fits like a glove. For only notice the different conduct of Powers *after this exhortation*. He seems to have changed his very nature. Finding he had but a small part to perform—finding that he was encouraged and supported by those gentlemen upon whom he relied, his whole course of conduct from that moment changed—no more vacillation—no more hesitation—no longer faltering and in doubt—he passed to the foot of the stairs, which Beebee was descending—he planted himself, knife in hand, near the point in the arch, over which the victim must pass—he was the first to lay his hand on the head of the doomed man, and to tell him to look his last upon the sun—leaving it to Tolar and the rest to fill the parts which they had promised to perform—and in another moment the curse of Cain was on him. James McNeill's testimony furnishes the only key by which we can account for the altered conduct of the defendant Powers; and evidence which hangs together as this does cannot be false—cannot be manufactured.

But there are other circumstances to which I pass on, tending to prove a combination, among the prisoners at the bar. Early in this trial Armstrong, a witness for the prosecution, testified, that Jno. Maultsby—just after going to the carriage in which Mrs. and Miss. Massey left the market house—returned therefrom to the market house, leaped upon a bench within the building, and said, " look-out boys," a moment or two before Beebee descended the stairs. There was no other witness who testified to that fact. It stood isolated and alone—unsupported and unconfirmed, as witness after witness for the prosecution was examined—it seemed singular that Maultsby could have done that act, and no one else have seen it, except Armstrong. But presently came Jesse Reynolds, another witness for the prosecution, after the evidence of many other deponents had intervened. Reynolds, not connected in any way with Armstrong, inclined to favor the defence—who could not himself, I am well satisfied, from his lack of intelligence, see the bearing of his testimony, nor the effect which it might have. Reynolds told us, that Maultsby, was also in a state of indecision, when he first saw him at the market house on the day of the homicide. The witness heard Maultsby say—" if the boy was innocent he was his friend, but if he was guilty he was in for it, as well as the rest." Then came other witnesses for the prosecution—Pickett among them—who testified to a fact of which he could not possibly see the bearing—that at some time, when Bond the town constable was in and about the Market house, to conduct Mrs and Miss Massey to the carriage, Maultsby, had a conversation with this constable—who had been present when the magistrates had Beebee before them—in which he satisfied himself, as to what the Court had determined to do with Beebee, and whether Miss Massey had identified the negro as the man who attempted to ravish her or not. Now note—that Maultsby had just before this conversation said—" if the boy was guilty *he was in for it ;*" as Bond went to the carriage with the ladies and returned, it is proved that Maultsby had a conversation with him, in which he learned that the Court above stairs thought Beebee guilty—and that Miss Massey had identified Beebee as *the* negro; what would the Court expect Maultsby to do, after that, but the exact thing which Armstrong says he did—announce to the conspirators, whom he knew, that he—Maultsby was *in for it as well as the rest* ; and this he did by leaping upon the bench and saying—" look-out boys "—as Beebee was about to descend. I find in all this, strong corroboration of Armstrong. And I find in all this testimony—pointing the same way—strong presumptive evidence of the fact, of some sort of combination, or understanding existing in that crowd, to which very many were parties.

In addition, let us now recall the testimony of the Sexton, Daley. My brother Battle, in addressing the Court, asks them, without rhyme or reason, to reject the whole of Daley's testimony, to strike it out, and disregard it. He says that the story Daley told, is so utterly improbable in itself; if true, it would prove his client to be so thoroughly a fool, that no man of reasonable judgment can conceive that Daley told the truth ; that the *a priori* improbability of his story is so great, its inconsistency with admitted facts is so patent that this Court ought to reject it *in toto*. Here then is a witness who swears positively that upon a certain day, certain events transpired—that a conversation was had between himself and Tolar. He is not contradicted. His character for truth is presumed to be good—for it is not attacked—and it is insisted by the defence that you ought to reject this man's testimony altogether, simply because his story is so utterly inconsistent with ordinary experience—assuming Captain Tolar to be a man of more than ordinary sense and judgment—that this Court cannot believe it. Now I undertake to advance the opinion, that when a tribunal engaged in the investigation of fact ventures to reject the positive evidence of an unassailed witness, on the ground of the *a priori* improbability of the tale that is told, the tale ought to be a very improbable one indeed—almost absolutely absurd—almost miraculous in its statements. But is Daley's story so very extraordinary—so very improbable? I trow not. Is it *at all* inconsistent with ordinary experience? Now take the facts as narrated by Daley and the surroundings. We are presuming, for the purpose of this argument at least, that Tolar shot Beebee. A coroner's inquest was held, the jury sat upon the case, it was the ordinary tribunal to decide in such cases, to what cause his death was to be attributed—and they did decide that Beebee came to his death by means of a bullet discharged from a pistol held in the hands of some person, to the jurors unknown. Tolar felt safe enough after this—he thought investigation was at an end. Why should he hesitate when several days were past—being a just and fair minded man—on meeting the negro in the street who had buried Beebee, to pay him for his labor. It is all perfectly natural—and has not a shadow of improbability about it. Daley told us that as he (witness) was crossing the street one day—about twelve days after the killing—he met Captain Tolar. Now, I say, at that time, Tolar thought he was entirely secure, he knew that the whole community in which he lived sympathized and felt with him and had no intention of annoying him—and he was bold enough to say to Daley, "Boy, what do I owe you, for burrying that boy the other day?"—and to pay him for the job. I was struck by the story and the manner of its telling, for Daley evidently disliked to tell it ; because he felt a little ashamed of himself, for having received the two dollars from Tolar, when he had already been paid by the sheriff for digging Beebee's grave—this fact he kept back from Tolar, till he had the money in hand, "but he did admit it at last," he said by way of exculpation—and he then described the bill, to us which Tolar paid him, as being split at one end. He says also, when he admitted to Tolar that he had been already paid, Tolar said it made no difference, or something to that effect, and they parted. Is not the whole story natural ? Is not it a natural enough *supposition* that Tolar might have acted just so, *if we have no evidence of it ;* but Daley swears most positively that it did occur, just as he narrates it ; and it is a *damning circumstance, to show that*—whether he fired the pistol or not—at least he was a party to some combination, in pursuance of which that negro Beebee was killed, and as a just man, he felt himself *to some extent responsible* for the expenses of his burial.

Nor does our evidence of a criminal combination end here. James Kindrick, a witness for the prosecution—than whom, during this tedious and extended trial, no man bore himself better and more becomingly on the witness stand, or gave in his testimony with more clearness and intelligence—James Kindrick testified—that, as Beebee came in sight descending the stairs, Tolar was standing in the main arch, on the east front of the market house, near the north end of the arch, and he (witness) heard him distinctly say to some one—witness could not say who it was—" I hope I won't have to shoot him, but if I do I'll make a good shot." Samuel A. Phillips also testified to having heard this same expression—though he could not say who uttered it—used by some one under the market house, when he (the witness) was outside.

And note, that when the assault was at first made on Beebee, *it was made, not with pistols, but with knives ;* and it was not until cries were heard in the crowd—that Beebee would get away—or was trying to get away—and after the first rush of the mob had apparently failed in effecting their purpose, that Tolar, or whoever it was who fired the pistol, stepped forward and discharged it, as the last resort. It is very evident, from the conduct of the mob, that the first aim was to kill Beebee with their knives ; and the pistol was not to be resorted to unless it became *necessary* to effectuate their purpose. Tolar expressed a wish, almost as the assault began, that the deed should be done without the use of his pistol ; the action of the mob coincided with this wish, and the conclusion is irresistible—whatever may be said of others—*that Tolar was in league, with the persons who made an assault with their knives,* to do bodily harm to Beebee.

I have not exhausted all the items of evidence pointing to a combination between Tolar, Watkins and Powers, and others, to take away Beebee's life; but I am satisfied I have cited enough evidence on this point.

Now, may it please the Court: any *one item* ALONE might not be conclusive; but take all these items just detailed in conjunction, and precede them with the admitted fact that Powers and Watkins were assailing Beebee with their knives—immediately before, if not at the very instant—when the pistol was fired by Tolar, or some one else in the crowd, which slew Beebee—and if we have not proved that there was a combination among many persons in that crowd, the object of which was to slay Beebee, or to do him great bodily harm, and to which Tolar and Powers and Watkins were consenting parties—then it is in vain, in future, to attempt to prove a combination or a conspiracy by circumstantial testimony. We can never count upon proving a combination without the assistance of informers and approvers; and as such testimony as theirs is not regarded as *perfectly* reliable, we may say that in future a conspiracy cannot be proved—the courts cannot have evidence weighty enough to establish one.

But it is said by the prisoners Counsel, it is absurd to conclude that Watkins, entered into a combination with these more respectable men; absurd from the respective characters of the men; absurd in the very nature of things—inconsistent, in other words, with ordinary experience. Does the Court think it is inconsistent with ordinary experience, for persons of greater respectability to select a man, such as the Counsel for the defence have admitted Watkins to be—as the instrument with which to do their dirty work or to carry out their plans of vengeance? Is not he the very type of the man, that would be selected, in any community, to make one of a general mob, associated for the purpose of taking away a man's life?

But Reynolds, the witness for the prosecution to whom I have already referred testified—that, as Powers was on his way back from the carriage at the time of which I have already spoken, Watkins had a conversation with Powers, and asked him—"what the ladies had said to him," and Powers replied that, the ladies said he had better let *it* alone. And thereupon Watkins said—"if it was his kin, as it was Powers', he would not let *it* alone;" which indicates, that, at that time Watkins was *part and parcel* of this same *arrangement* to take away Beebee's life—however inconsistent, it may be with ordinary experience for such men as Tolar and Powers, to combine in a criminal design with such a man as Watkins. But we contend it is not inconsistent with ordinary experience, that such a combination should exist.

And now—if it please the Court—I have said very nearly all that I intend to say, on the *facts* of this case. I have endeavored to demonstrate from the evidence—it is for this Court to decide how successfully—but *three* points of fact; 1st. That the prisoner Tolar fired the pistol the bullet from which slew Archy Beebee; 2nd. That at the time when Tolar fired the pistol, the prisoners Powers and Watkins were present—and *apparently* actually aiding and abetting him to kill Beebee; 3rd, That there was an agreement, a combination, or an understanding, entered into, *at some time*—previous to the act of killing—either to kill Beebee, or to do him some serious bodily harm, and that to this agreement, combination or understanding Tolar, Powers and Watkins were all consenting parties.

If I have established these three positions *of fact*, the government is entitled to a finding of guilty of murder, against all the prisoners, even according to the admissions of the Counsel for the prisoners. But there is a view of the case, to which I shall advert in closing my argument, in which, as I contend, it is entirely unnecessary to a conviction of any of the prisoners for murder, that I should establish the first point of fact that is—that Tola, fired the pistol, the bullet from which slew Beebee—provided I can satisfy the Court—*that some person in the crowd* fired the pistol the bullet from which slew Beebee—and that at the time when the pistol was fired by this person, not only Watkins and Powers, *but also Tolar*, were present *apparently* actually aiding and abetting in the homicide : or provided I can satisfy the Court, *that some person in the crowd* fired the pistol the bullet from which slew Beebee—and that there was any agreement, a combination or understanding entered into at some time previous to the act of killing, either to kill Beebee or to do him some serious bodily harm, and to this agreement, combination or understanding, the *person who* did *fire the pistol*, as well as *Tolar*, Watkins and Powers were consenting parties.

And I have been insisting all along—and do now insist—that there is *no view* which can be taken of this case, which renders it *necessary* for me to establish—a conspiracy—combination—agreement or understanding—to kill Beebee, or to do him bodily harm—to which Tolar, Watkins and Powers were consenting parties, *as an independent fact*—as a condition precedent to the conviction of all these defendents of murder. So that I have endeavored to demonstrate the fact that there was such a combination or understanding, not because it was *necessary* for my case—but because, if established, it was *decisive of the case*—and conclusively determined the guilt of all the defendants, of murder according to the law as stated by their own Counsel.

But as so much time—and breath—has since been expended in my efforts to establish the fact of a combination among these defendants—I believe it is best, to *shortly recur* to the position assumed by me in the earlier part of this argument, wherein I contended, that any proof of previous combination or understanding, was unnecessary to establish the guilt of the defendants Watkins and Powers, provided the Court was satisfied that they were both *actually present*, and both apparently actually aiding and abetting in the criminal fact—which presence and aiding and abetting were established by proof that they were both assaulting Beebee with their knives, at the very instant, or just before the moment when he was killed.

One point made, and fully presented, was—that if proof of a combination were a necessary part of our case, the best and strongest possible evidence of such previous agreement, was found in the fact that Powers, and Watkins did combine in the concurrent execution of the criminal fact, with the person who fired the pistol.

But I then contended, and do now insist, again, that no evidence of previous combination in a criminal design, is necessary in this case. And why do I say that proof of a combination against aiders and abetters is not necessary in cases like ours ? I say it for this reason—that proof of a combination is necessary only where the persons who are charged as aiders and abettors—or principals in the second degree—as Powers and Watkins are charged—either were not actually present, or were not apparently actually aiding and abetting in the execution of the criminal fact—in this case—the killing. We say that in this case there *was* certainly an actual presence and an apparent actual aiding and abetting, upon the part of Powers and Watkins, at the moment when Tolar—or whoever else it was—fired the pistol, which killed Beebee— and therefore it is not necessary for us to show any combination among them to prove either their presence, or their aiding and abetting.

Now if there had not been an actual presence, or there had not been an apparent actual aiding and abetting in the killing, the case would be different. Suppose, for example, we had proved that Watkins and Powers were half a block distant from the market house when the pistol was fired, standing, the one with a pistol and the other with a club in his hand, on the side walk of the street, along which Beebee would have to pass as he came back from the market house to the guard house, where he had been confined, and we had no other evidence against them. There would, in that event, have been no evidence of their actual presence at the homicide, and no proof of an apparent actual aiding and abetting therein. They would not have been apparently rendering any actual aid at the time of the commission of the act. The evidence would not be sufficient to justify their conviction. But suppose we added to this circumstantial evidence, which strongly indicated that they had previously combined and agreed together with the man who fired the pistol, to aid and assist him in doing great bodily harm to Beebee, or in killing him, we would make out a case justifying their conviction; and it would be necessary to prove the combination as part of our case; for if we prove a combination under such circumstances, then the *law* says that they were constructively present, and were constructively aiding and abetting in the criminal fact. In cases of that character, it is necessary to prove the combination, in order to prove a constructive presence, and a constructive aiding and abetting; but where the principal in the second degree was actually present, and apparently actually aiding and abetting, proof of previous agreement in the common design is not essential to conviction; and the proof of combination against principles in the second degree is only necessary for the purpose of supplying the want of proof of actual presence, and actual aiding and abetting, which is apparent.

Lord Dacre's case, to which I have already referred, as reported in Hale and other books of authority, was one in which it was necessary to show the criminal combination. Lord Dacre, and divers others, came to steal deer in the park of Mr. Pelham. Raydon, one of the company, killed the keeper in the park, Lord Dacre and the rest of the company being in other parts of the park, not *actually present*, and apparently *not actually aiding and abetting;* but they had gone together to do an unlawful act. It was ruled that it was murder in them all. and they died for it. Now, in that case the guilt of Lord Dacre and his companions could not have been established, without proving the previous unlawful combination to go and steal deer in the park. That was essential in order to make Lord Dacre an aider and abettor in the killing. It was necessary to prove the combination, because he was actually not present, and apparently not aiding and abetting in the criminal fact—to establish the constructive presence and the constructive aiding and abetting. But when the combination was proved, it supplied the place of the proof of presence and of an aiding and abetting, which was apparent—and, as Lord Hale says, " they died for it."

Pudsey's case as quoted in " Hale's Pleas of the Crown," Vol. 1, page 534, from Crompt. 34, illustrates the same principles " Pudsey and two others, viz: A and B assault C, to rob him on the highway, but C escapes by flight, and as they were assaulting him, A rides from Pudsey and B, and assaults D, out of the view of Pudsey and B, and takes from him a dagger by robbery, and comes back to Pudsey and B ; and for this Pudsey was indicted and convicted of robbery, though he assented not to the robbery of D, neither was it done in his view ; because they were all three assembled to commit a robbery, and this taking of the dagger was in the mean time."— 1 Hale P. C. 534.

Now in this case Pudsey was not actually present at the robbery of D, nor was he apparently aiding and abetting A therein ; and to prove his guilt, as an aider and abetter, it was absolutely necessary to prove a constructive presence at, and a constructive aiding and abetting in the robbery of D, and this proof was made—and it was necessary that it should be made—by evidence that all three—Pudsey, A and B, were in a combination to effect an illegal design—in other words, that "they were all three assembled to commit a robbery."

But where there is an actual presence at, and an actual aiding and abetting, which is apparent, in a criminal fact, no proof of conspiracy, confederation or combination is necessary to convict a man as an aider and abetter in the crime.

(2 Stark on Ev. p. 12. State *vs.* Simmons, 6 Jones (N. C.) p. 21. State *vs.* Morris 3 Hawks, (N. C.) p. 388.)

May it please the Court; there is yet another view *of the facts of this case*, which has been presented by the Counsel for the defence—which I do, not think it is possible for the court to take—which I may safely say, it is highly improbable the Court will take—but yet, on which, I conceive it to be my duty to state the law which arises, as I understand it to be ; since my brethren for the defence and myself differ "*toto cælo*," in the *conclusions of law*, which follow from this supposed state of facts. It may be also, that I have failed to satisfy the Court, upon some of the points, either of law or of fact, made by me in this extended address, which are essential to the conviction of the prisoners, and that it is necessary to state what the law is, taking the most favorable view for the prisoners possible of the evidence in this case—the view of the facts which is taken by the Counsel for the defence.

If the Court shall come to the conclusion, that there is *not sufficient evidence to establish previous combination*, to kill Beebee or to do him some serious bodily harm between *Powers and Watkins*, and Tolar—or whoever else it was who fired the pistol which killed Beebee—and that *as a matter of law* they cannot convict Powers and Watkins of murder *unless such combination is established :* if they shall come to the conclusion, that there is not sufficient evidence to establish—as against Watkins and Powers—a concurrent participation in the execution of the criminal fact—that is—the killing of Beebee—to justify the conviction of these two defendants for murder ; or that such concurrent participation in the execution of the criminal fact, if established, *is not proof* of previous unlawful combination on the part of these two prisoners, to kill Beebee or to do him serious bodily harm : if they shall come to the conclusion, that the man who shot Beebee, did that act, *without the knowledge or consent of Powers and Watkins :* I yet insist, *that the law pronounces Powers and Watkins guilty of murder*, if at the time the pistol was shot or immediately before, Powers and Watkins were assailing Beebee with their knives and endeavoring to take him out of the hands of the officers of the law—as the evidence shows that they were. The Counsel for the prisoners say the facts of this case are these—that Powers, who is a near relation of Miss Massey, and Watkins, who is a man of little character, but ready for any emergency in the way of disorder, were standing in the crowd, when Beebee passed in their sight, coming from the justices' room, where Miss Massey had recently identified him as the negro man who had attempted to violate her person the day previous : that Miss Massey herself had, but a few moments before, passed to the carriage, weeping, and with the wounds and bruises—marks of the violence of this brutal negro fiend—visible on her neck : that—exasperated at the sight of the ravisher so soon after they had seen his suffering victim—these two men, and perhaps others, in the press, impulsively, rushed, striking with their knives, upon

Beebee, and demanded of the officers of the law, that he should be surrendered to them: that this was done under the influence of natural passion—on the impulse of the moment—without concert—and without any previous understanding with, or expectation of assistance from, any person whatsoever—and that thereupon, Tolar—if the Court finds it was Tolar—Phillips—if the Court finds it was Phillips—or some other person to the Court unknown—if the Court so finds—*without the knowledge or consent of Powers and Watkins*, pressed forward into the crowd, drew his pistol, levelled it, fired, and killed Beebee. The Counsel insist, if these be the facts—that whoever fired the pistol is guilty of murder—but that *Powers and Watkins* are guilty only of *what they themselves did*, and that their offence, at the uttermost, was but an assault with the intent to kill. This I understand to be the position of the Counsel for the prisoners—and no one can possibly suggest a *more favorable view* of the *evidence*, for the prisoners, *than* this.

Now I undertake to say, that, assuming the facts to be exactly as stated above, even upon *that* state of facts, Powers and Watkins are guilty, not only of *what they themselves did*, but of what the man who fired the pistol did also—and that is murder—and upon this point I am not unfurnished with authority. The general rule, both of law and of reason, is, that whenever a man contributes to a particular result, brought about either by the sole volition of another, or by such volition added to his own, he is holden for the result, the same as if his own unaided hand had produced it; he whose act causes, in any way, directly or indirectly, the death of another, kills him within the meaning of the law. The proposition is thus laid down by Mr. Bishop in his work upon criminal law—" if a man is attempting to do a criminal thing, and another man, *without previous concert*, comes to his assistance and does it, the first is responsible for whatever results he himself intended, as though he were the sole perpetrator." (1 Bishop, Crim. Law, sec. 440.)

Or applying it to our case—if Powers and Watkins were, with their knives, attempting to kill Beebee, or to do him serious bodily harm, and Tolar *without previous concert*, came to their assistance and killed him, Powers and Watkins are responsible for the killing, as though they were the sole perpetrators.

Now the author from whom I have just quoted has been lightly spoken of by the Counsel for the prisoners—and it was asserted that this proposition of law rested upon that solitary authority—and could be found no where else; but I shall produce a host of authorities, English and American, establishing identically the same point, though mayhap not in the same words.

Wharton in his work on criminal law—and there is no higher American authority than Wharton—states the proposition thus: " He who attempts to strike with a deadly weapon, one who is at the same time struck by another with a deadly weapon, is joint principal in the offence." (1 Wharton, Am. Crim. Law, sec. 116.)

Is not that identically our case—were not Powers and Watkins attempting to strike Beebee with deadly weapons, at the time he was struck by Tolar with a deadly weapon, and killed?

Archbold and Hawkins enunciate the same doctrine in these terms: " If two are *fighting*, and a third come up and take the part of one of them, and kill the other, this will be *manslaughter* in the third party, and *murder or manslaughter* in the person whom he assisted, according as the fight was deliberated and premeditated, or on a sudden quarrel."

(Hawkins P. C. B. 1. chap. 31—sec's. 35, 56. Archbold's Criminal Law, p. 324.)

If the two had not *both been fighting*—it would have been *murder* in the *third party also ;* and it is apparent, that if the person assisted was engaged in a deliberate premeditated *fight* he was guilty of *murder*—*a fortiori*—he would have been guilty of *murder*, if there was *no fight* at all, *but he was assailing* a bound and helpless man, with a deadly weapon.

So again—" If several persons are present at the death of a man, they may be guilty of different degrees of homicide, as one of murder and another of manslaughter : for if there be no malice in the party striking but malice in an abettor, it will be murder in the latter, though only manslaughter in the former.

(I East, P. C. chap. 5, sec. 121, p. 350. 1 Russ. on Cri. p. 570.)

When Powers and Watkins attacked a bound and unarmed man with their knives, and endeavored to kill him, or to take him out of the hands of the officers of the law, for the purpose of killing him or doing him some serious bodily harm, there was malice in law—such malice as would have made them both guilty of murder, if by their proximate agency, Beebee had been even accidentally killed.

So again—" The master assaults with malice prepense, the servant takes part with the master, and kills the other, *it is murder in the master,* and manslaughter or murder in the servant, according as he was ignorant of the malice of the master or not."

(1 Hale, P. C., p. 445. 1 Russ. on Cri., p. 484. Rex vs. Salisbury Plow. p. 97.)

Is it not apparent that here the master is held responsible, not only for what he himself did, *but for that for which his servant did also ?*

There is a North Carolina case—not upon a trial of homicide, it is true—but the character of the *crime* cannot alter the principle—which enunciates this principle, and carries its operation further than the Court are required to carry it in this case, in order to find Powers and Watkins guilty of murder. This was an indictment against the defendant Morris and several others, for an assault and battery on one King, a constable, while in the execution of his office. On the part of the State, it was proved by several witnesses, that while King was conveying a prisoner to the jail of Mecklenburg, under a mittimus from a Justice of the Peace of that county, the defendant with several others came up to him and said—"the prisoner should not go to jail if money or security would save him." The defendant, and the officer in charge of his prisoner, at the request of the defendant, then went aside from the jail (at the door of which this conversation took place) followed by the other persons in company. When they had gone about ten paces, the defendant said—"the prisoner should not go to jail at all." This was repeated by others of the party, and *immediately several of them set upon the officer, attempted to rescue the prisoner,* and in the prosecution of this attempt the officer was assaulted and beaten.

It did not appear that *Morris himself assaulted or struck the officer,* but that *the observations* attributed to him above were made in a threatening manner. It was also in evidence, that when the officer was set upon. and the struggle was going on to rescue the prisoner, the defendant Morris *retired from the crowd,* and said, "boys, you had better take care what you are about, I will have nothing to do with this." The jury, under the instruction of his Honor below, found the defendant Morris " guilty"—whereupon he appealed to the Supreme Court of the State ; and his Honor, Chief Justice

Taylor, in giving the opinion of the Supreme Court of North Carolina, says: " It was distinctly decided by the Court (below) that the defendant (Morris) was guilty in point of law, upon the supposition of the jury's believing the witnesses for the State, although they should believe the defendant's witnesses. And upon looking into the case, it seems impossible to doubt as to the correctness of this opinion; for the defendant's witnesses testified, that when the officer was set upon, and the scuffle going on to rescue the party in custody, the defendant retired from the crowd and said, " boys, you had better take care what you are about, I will have nothing to do with it." The defendant had previously told the officer in a threatening and intimidating manner, that the prisoner, whom he had in custody, should not go to jail at all, and immediately several of the party set upon the officer and attempted a rescue, in the course of which the officer was assaulted and beaten—if the jury believed that the defendant (Morris) was an aider and abettor in the commencement, *he did not cease to be a co-trespasser because he was unwilling to go all lengths with his party*—the judgment must be affirmed."

(State *vs.* Morris, 3 Hawks, (N. C.) p. 388, N. B. p. 392.)

There is yet another authority upon this point, to which I invite the attention of the Court, and it seems to have been the identical case, upon which Mr. Bishop rests the legal proposition, which has given occasion for the animadversion of the Counsel for the prisoners. It is a case tried in Tennessee, and decided in the Supreme Court of that State, the opinion on having been delivered by Judge Green, one of the most eminent jurists of that commonwealth. The case is entitled " Beets *vs.* State," and I give the facts so far as they are referrible to the point under discussion. It was an indictment against the plaintiffs in error, for the murder of Samuel Rayle. It appeared in evidence, that all the parties were at a still-house drinking, and *James* Beets, one of the plaintiffs in error, and Rayle had angry words and were about to engage in a fight. *George* Beets, the other plaintiff in error, then came up, and interfered to prevent the fight, declaring, that they should not fight, but that if fighting was to be done, *he* would do it; whereupon Rayle struck him a blow, and a fight between them ensued, during which *George* Beets threw Rayle to the ground. *Joseph* Beets stood by and encouraged *George* in the fight, *and while it was progressing*, JAMES Beets returned to where the parties were engaged, and shot Rayle with a pistol, of which he died.

The court below charged the jury—that if *George* Beets *engaged in the fight in self-defence*, and while thus fighting *James* Beets shot Rayle, *without the knowledge or consent of* GEORGE, George would be guilty of no offence. But if *George* Beets *fought willingly*, so that he would be guilty of an affray, and while thus fighting *James* Beets shot Rayle, it would be manslaughter in *George, although* JAMES *shot without the knowledge or consent of George.* The plaintiffs in error, George and James Beets, were found ' guilty of manslaughter,' and they both appealed to the Supreme Court of Tennessee, upon the ground that the Judge below had misdirected the jury on points of law. Greene, Judge, in delivering the opinion of the Supreme Court, after stating the facts as above, said : " The first question is—whether the charge of the court is erroneous? It is certain that if *George* Beets *had himself* in the fight killed Rayle, it would be manslaughter. He was not fighting in self-defence, but was engaged willingly in the combat. The fact that Rayle gave the first blow does not affect the question, otherwise than to constitute a great provocation, which will reduce the killing to manslaughter. Archbold, bottom page 324. It is laid down in the same book, and also in 1st Hawkins, c. 31, sec. 35-56—that if, when *two are fighting*, a third comes up and takes the part of one of them, and kills the other, this will be manslaughter in the third party, and *murder or manslaughter in the person whom he assisted, according as the fight was deliberate and premeditated*, or upon a sudden quarrel.

(1 Russell on Crimes, 398; 1 Hale, 446.)

"The principle is this—if a party be engaged in an unlawful act, and another assist him and actually perpetrate the mischief, the first party shall be held responsible, as though he had been the sole perpetrator himself. If a man is fighting with another, *not intending to kill*, but by some unlucky blow death ensues, he is guilty of manslaughter. And why is this? Not because he intended to inflict death, but because he was engaged in an unlawful act, and the blow and the death were consequences of that act, and he must be responsible for it, as though he had designed the result. Upon the same principle it is that he is responsible to the same extent, though the fatal blow is struck by another, who assisted him without any concert on his part.

"The assistance is given because he is engaged in the unlawful act; and as he unlawfully creates the occasion for the interference and assistance of the third party, he must answer for the consequences as though he had been the sole actor. We are, therefore, of opinion that there is no error in the charge of the court below." * * * * *

(Beets *vs.* State, 1 Meigs (Tenn.) R., p. 106.)

Now in this case it is as plainly intimated as is possible, that if *George* Beets had been assaulting Rayle, under such circumstances, that if he himself, had, with his own hand, killed the deceased, it would have been murder, it would also have been murder on his part, although *James* Beets actually discharged the pistol which killed Rayle, without the knowledge or consent of *George*, and without any concert with him. Which last is our case, on the hypothesis of facts assumed for the purpose of this immediate argument.

I cite one more authority, but I shall not trouble the Court with it further than by citation. (King *vs.* State, 21 Ga. R., p. 220.)

I have not, up to this time, entered fully into the reasoning on which this legal position rests; but I have cited these many authorities—some more, and some less, directly applicable to the case in hand. It is true that some of these decisions are put by the courts, upon the point, that the concurrent apparent participation in the execution of a criminal fact was strong *prima facie* evidence against all the participators of a combination or concerted plan, which established the responsibility of all the participators for the criminal result, unless they could prove, that their apparent participation in the execution of the criminal fact was *only apparent* and not *real*—a point already made in this case; but others of these authorities, and most of them, lay down the naked position, in so many words, that if a man is making a felonious assault upon another, and a third party comes to the assistance of the first, and without his knowledge or consent, and without any concert with him, slays the assailed, the first assailant is guilty of murder; and either course of reasoning is sufficient for our purpose.

I think I may, therefore, safely say, I have made good my pledge of estab-tablishing—*by authority*—that if Watkins and Powers, under a sudden impulse of passion, aroused by a cause which the law does not regard as *a legal provocation*, were assailing Beebee with drawn knives, and endeavoring to take him from the officers of the law, and while they were so engaged Tolar,

Phillips, or any one else, without their knowledge and consent, and without any concert with them, came forward to their assistance and shot Beebee, Powers and Watkins are guilty of murder; and it makes no earthly difference in the grade of their crime whether they had a specific intent to kill Beebee, or only a general intent to do him serious bodily harm.

And not only do these *authorities* establish my position, but the *whole reason and analogy of the law* point in the same direction. Bishop states the general doctrine thus: "every act producing an unintended result, must, when evil, be measured either by the *intent* or by the *result.* The common law rule measures it substantially by *the latter*, holding the person guilty of the thing done. *where there is any kind of legal wrong in the intent*, the same as though it were specifically intended; not always however guilty of the crime in the same degree." (1. Bish. C. L. sec. 411.) "When we look more closely into this doctrine, we see, that the evil of the intent and the evil of the act, added together, constitute the evil punished as crime, the same rule applying here which prevails throughout the entire criminal law. And the only peculiarity of this doctrine is in its teaching, that the intent and the act, which constitute the sum, need not be the natural or usual accompaniments of each other, provided they did in fact accompany each other in the particular case. The consequence of which, is, that, whenever the intent is sufficient in turpitude, and an indictable result comes from it casually, an indictment will lie for this result. even in cases where, if the intent had accomplished its exact aim. the result would not have been indictable." (1. Bish. C. L. sec. 414.) "How intensely evil the intent must be, to infuse the bane of criminality into the unintended act is not easily stated in a word. Evidently there may be cases wherein, it is too minute in evil for the laws notice, the same as where the act is the true echo of the intent, and as where carelessness exists. So also, as, on the one hand, *the evil intended* is the measure of a man's *desert of punishment;* and on the other hand, *the injury done to society*, is the measure of its *interest to punish*; and punishment can only be inflicted when the two combine—it follows—that when the law has different degrees of the same offence, as in felonious homicide, which is divided into murder and manslaughter, the injury must be assigned to the higher or lower degree, *according as the intent was more or less intensely wrong.*"
(1. Bish. on Cr. L. sec. 417.)

So whenever the act, which whether intentionally or not, contributes to the death of human being, is an action unlawful in itself, and is done deliberately, and with intention of *mischief or great bodily harm to particular individuals,* or of mischief, indiscriminately fall where it may, and death ensue against or beside the original intention of the party doing the act, it will be murder.

(1. Russ. on Cr. p. 538.)

On this principle it is, if one intending to murder a particular individual, shoots at him, and by accident the charge lodges in another person whom it deprives of life, it is murder.

(Rex. *vs.* Plummer 12. Mod. pp. 627. 628.   Rex. *vs.* Jarvis 2. Moody and R. p. 40.)

Also where the intent is to do some *great bodily harm* to another, and accidentally death ensues, it will be murder—as, if A intended *only to hurt* B, in anger, or from preconceived *malice (in a legal sense)* and happen to kill him—it will be no excuse that A did not *intend* all the mischief which fol-

lowed. He beat B with an intention of doing him *some bodily harm* and is therefore answerable *for all the harm he did.*
(Fost. p. 259. 1. Russ. on Cr. p. 540.)

So, if one lays poison for another, and a *third* finding it takes it and dies—it is murder.
(Gore's. Case, 9. Co. 81. a. Rex. *vs.* Lewis 6. Car. & P., p. 161.)

So, if one attempting to steal poultry, discharges a gun to shoot the poultry, and thereby *accidently kill a human being*—it is murder.
(1. East. P. C. 225. Edin's Penal Law, 3rd. Ed., p. 227.)

So, if a jailor, *with no design against the life of his prisoner*, confines him, contrary to his will, in an unwholesome room, without allowing him the requisites necessary to cleanliness, whereby he contracts a distemper of which he dies—it is murder.
(Rex. *vs.* Huggins 2. Stra. p. 822. 2. Ld. Raym., p. 1574.)

So, if one with the *purpose of procuring an abortion*, does an act, which causes the child to be born so prematurely, as to be less capable of living, *and it dies from exposure to the external world*—it is murder.
(Reina *vs.* Wets., 2 Car. & K., p. 784.)

In all these instances, and others of like nature, the party causing the death is guilty—the same as if he had intended it—*of murder.*

In the instances above given, it may be said—and as to the most of them it is true—that the man who is by the law pronounced guilty of murder, is the immediate, proximate, direct agent who causes the death; but the law does not confine the guilt of murder to the man who, with an evil intent, by his *direct act* causes, the death of another, but as a general proposition, he whose act causes, in any way, directly or *indirectly*, the death of another, kills him within the meaning of the Law.

Hawkins puts the question " in what cases a man may be said to kill another"—and proceeds: " Not only he, who by wound or blow, or by poisoning, strangling or famishing &c., directly causes the death of another; but, also, in many cases, he who by wilfully and deliberately doing a thing, which apparently endangers anothers life, thereby occasions his death; shall be adjudged to kill him. And such was the case of him who carried his sick father, against his will, in a cold frosty season, from one town to another, by reason whereof he died. Such also was the case of the harlot, who being delivered of a child, left it in an orchard, covered only with leaves, in which condition it was struck by a kite, and died thereof. And in some cases, a man shall be said in the judgment of the law, to kill one, who is in truth actually killed, by another, or by himself; as, where one by duress of imprisonment compels a man, to accuse an innocent person, who on the evidence is condemned and executed ; or where one incites a madman to kill himself or another, &c. * * * * * Also, he who wilfully neglects to prevent a mischief, which he may and ought to provide against, is, as some have said, in judgment of law, the actual cause of the damage which ensues ; and therefore if a man have an ox or a horse, which he knows to be mischievous, by being used to gore or strike at those who come near them, and do not tie them up, but leave them to their liberty, and they afterwards kill a man, *according to some opinions*, the owner may be indicted, as having himself feloniously killed him—and this is agreeable to the Mosaical law. However it *is agreed by all*, such person is guilty of a very gross misdemeanor." [1 Hawk. P. C., p. 92, secs 4—8. (Cur-w's Ed.)]

And I may therefore safely state, as the general conclusion from the reason and analogy of the whole law of Homicide, that—whenever one man,

contributes by his act to the death of another, brought about either by the
sole volition of a third person, or by such volition added to his own, he is
held responsible for the result, the same, as if his own unaided hand had
produced it; and whenever the volition, of whatever kind, put forth by one
man, results in the death of another man, the former is to be charged with
having committed the homicide. And it is immaterial whether the action
be of the mind or of the body, whether it operates solely, or concurrently
with other things; whether it was consented to by the person on whom it
operated or not; whether it was a blow, or a drug, or an instrument, or other thing used to procure an abortion; or a command addressed to an inferior
under obligation to obey, or an unlawful confinement, or a leaving of a dependent person in a place of exposure, or a ball discharged from a gun;
whether it was accompanied with the acts of other persons concurring in
what was done, or operated alone; or was of any other nature whatsoever.

And whether Powers and Watkins, when they first made the assault upon
Archy Beebee, intended to kill him, or had no such specific intent, but simply intended to punish him severely—when their assault resulted, as a natural
consequence from all the surroundings, in Beebee's being shot by Tolar,
they are in law as responsible for that result as if it had been within their
original intention. And such is the law, not only according to the authorities, and according to the general reason and analogy of the law of homicide,
and the general reason and analogy of the criminal law in all its depart-
ments; *but such ought to be the law*, according to popular reason, and what
we call the common sense view of this question—as well. I put it to this
Court, as reasonable men—as laics, not learned in the law—knowing human
nature for what it is—who in that crowd were the most guilty men, and the
proximate agents who caused Beebee's death—if they were not Powers and
Watkins, who commenced the assault, and Tolar, who incited Powers to begin it—even if he did not fire the pistol? In every popular tumult the man
to " bell the cat " is the one most difficult to find, and the one without whose
agency the popular feeling would not culminate in open violence. It is so
from boyhood—we have all known school-boys, who were anxious to turn
out the master, and conspired for that purpose; and the difficulty always
was, and is, and, in such cases, always will be, to find the boy to strike the
first blow. The process of turning out is easy enough afterwards. *The man
to strike the first blow* is the man most difficult to find, and he is the man
who ought to be held most responsible for what follows. There are thousands of men who would shrink from *beginning* such deeds of blood as were
enacted at Fayetteville on that day, but who, the moment the first blow is
stricken, would rush into the conflict, and consummate the result towards
which popular feeling tends. And what could Powers and Watkins have
anticipated—reasoning from the view of this question presented by common
sense and popular reason—human beings, and especially the common humanity of Fayetteville, being constituted as is insisted by the Counsel for
the defence—what could these men have expected, when they commenced
the assault in that crowd, but that others would come to their assistance, and
slay Beebee; and if this is so, are not they, and their immediate inciter, the
most guilty parties in this homicide?

May it please the Court, there is one more matter to which I wish to invite the attention of the gentlemen composing this Commission, after which
I shall conclude what I have to say. I stated in opening the argument of
the facts of this case—and I have several times, as I proceeded, repeated the
statement—that undue importance had been attached, throughout the whole

of this trial, to the settlement of the *question of fact*—whether the prisoner Tolar did, or did not fire the pistol, the bullet from which slew Archy Beebee? I consider it a question of very little importance—and I say now, that it is entirely unnecessary to the conviction of any of the prisoners at the bar—even of Tolar himself—that this Court should be satisfied that *Tolar* fired the pistol, the bullet from which slew Archy Beebee.

As regards the prisoners Watkins and Powers—it must be apparent to the Court, that *the degree of their guilt* is the same, whether Tolar fired that pistol, or Phillips fired it, or it was fired by some person to the Court unknown. I think the Court will come to the conclusion that Tolar fired it—I do not see how it is possible for them to come to any other conclusion than, that, if Tolar did not fire it, then that Phillips undoubtedly did fire the pistol—but *this* is absolutely certain, that *some* one in the crowd at the market house in Fayetteville, on the 11th day of February, A. D. 1866, fired the pistol the bullet from which slew Archy Beebee.

If the Court shall find that Tolar fired the pistol—or that Phillips fired it—or that it was fired by some person to the Court unknown—it matters not which one of these conclusions this Court shall arrive it—any one will be sufficient—and shall find in addition either—that when the pistol was fired the prisoners at the bar Watkins and Powers, were present and apparently actually aiding and abetting the person who did fire it, in his felonious assault upon Beebee—or, that, when it was so fired, it was fired in pursuance of previous combination, the design of which was to kill Beebee, or do him serious bodily harm, and that Powers and Watkins, as well as the person who fired the pistol, were parties to that combination—that is, were present, and were constructively aiding and abetting in the commission of the homicide—or, that while Powers and Watkins were, with their knives, assaulting Beebee, and endeavoring to take him out of the hands of the officers of the law, this person, who fired the pistol without their knowledge or consent, and without any previous concert with them, came to their assistance and slew the deceased—in any one of these three contingencies, it matters not which, and it matters not who fired the pistol—Watkins and Powers are guilty of murder.

The only question, then, that can arise, in case the Court comes to the conclusion that Tolar did not fire the pistol—but that Phillips fired it—or that some person, not named in the charge and specification, fired it, will be—whether—since the charge and specification before them allege that *Tolar* fired the pistol, and that *Watkins* and *Powers* were present aiding and abetting him—the Court are at liberty under this particular form of charge and specification, to find the defendants Watkins and Powers guilty, when, as a matter of fact, it appears in evidence that Tolar did not fire the pistol, but some other person did, and Watkins and Powers were not aiding and abetting Tolar, but were aiding and abetting the other man who really fired the pistol. There is no difficulty, in deciding this question in favor of the prosecution upon the most overwhelming authority, but I reserve its discussion and consideration for the present.

So much for Watkins and Powers, upon the assumption that Tolar *did not* fire the pistol the bullet from which slew Archy Beebee. But as regards Tolar, himself, supposing he did not fire the pistol—how do we connect him with the homicide? Why, totally independent of the evidence of the seventeen witnesses for the prosecution, which establishes the fact that Tolar fired the pistol—there is *other evidence* to prove that he was a party to the homicide, almost, if not quite as strong and convincing, as that against Powers and Watkins. For note—some one in the crowd in which Tolar was, fired the lethal weapon—this is admitted on all sides; again—*Tolar was present* at the killing—this is also an admitted fact; he *was armed with a pistol*—so E. P. Powers one of his own witnesses swore; he had a pistol in his hand at the moment of the killing, so said Matthew Morgan, a witness introduced and accredited by him, and examined by the Court; he stood side by side with the man who fired the pistol, within from three to five feet of Beebee, and in his rear, at the very moment when he was shot from behind—so deposed Faircloth, a witness whom he himself put upon the stand. When in addition to this evidence furnished by himself, and which, unaided, strongly indicates that he was a consenting party to the killing—we have the evidence of McNeill, Kindrick, and Daley, the sexton, witnesses for the prosecution—which has been already called the attention of the Court—the first testifying, that he heard Tolar say to Powers, as the negro Beebee, appeared at the head of the stairs—" When he comes down you grab him and break the ice, and we will put him through "—the second testifying, that, which Beebee was descending the stairs, he heard Tolar say to some one, witness cannot say who—" he hoped he would not have to shoot—but if he did, it would be a good shot "—and the third testifying, that some twelve days after the homicide, Tolar, met the witness, asked what he owed him, (witness) for digging Beebee's grave, and paid him for it—when we have *all* this evidence—the conclusion is almost irresistable, that if Tolar did not act as the proximate agent in causing Beebee's death, he was at least present thereat, and a consenting party thereto. That he either actually aided and abetted in the homicide—or constructively aided and abetted therein—or was a party to the previous combination, in pursuance of which Beebee was slain—or was engaged with Powers and Watkins in their felonious assault upon Beebee, when the person who fired the pistol, without his knowledge and consent, and without concert with him, slew the deceased—or certainly, that he was the person present, who advised, encouraged, and incited Powers to begin that felonious assault. In any one of these events, Tolar is as clearly guilty of the murder of Beebee, as if he had fired the pistol the bullet from which slew Archy Beebee—and must be convicted by the Court, unless there be something in the form of the charge and specification here preferred, which, for the reasons already suggested, forbid his conviction, under this particular charge and specification.

Now this is the simplest view of the *facts* of this case possible, and the view which requires the *least proof* on the part of the prosecution; the Court *knows, as an admitted fact,* that *some one,* by means of a bullet, dicharged from a pistol, slew Archy Beebee at Fayetteville, on the eleventh day of February A. D. 1866. It is a fact which cannot be disputed, and will not be gainsayed, that these three prisoners at the bar were then and there present. I do not understand it to be disputed—and at least there is no ground on which to dispute the fact—that at or immediately before the moment of the homicide the prisoners Power and Watkins were actually engaged, with their knives, in an effort to strike the deceased, and take him out of the hands, of the officers of the law. And there is strong—cogent—conclusive evidence—which I need not here recapitulate, that the prisoner Tolar was assenting and contributing to the criminal acts—both of Powers and Watkins—and of the man whose hand slew Beebee. And I cannot for the life of me see, in view of these admitted facts, and of this proof—even admitting we *have not* proved that Tolar fired the pistol which slew Beebee—even admitting that the defence *have* proved that Phillips fired that pistol—even admitting we have *no proof, who* fired the pistol—I cannot for the life of me see, how this Court can avoid convicting these prisoners—and *all* of these prisoners—of the crime of murder—unless there be something in the form of the charge and specification, which forbids the conviction of some one—or more—or all of them—upon this view of the facts. And there is no objection to their conviction on this ground as I shall now proceed to show.

For an indictment against a man as principal of the first degree is sustained by proof of his being principal of the second degree; and, in the same manner, an indictment against him as principal in the second degree, is supported by proof that he is principal of the first degree. The law regards every one who is *present* in a legal sense, aiding and abetting in a legal sense, in a felony, as having committed the crime with his own hand—and hence, it makes no difference, in law, whether he is charged with having committed the act, or with being present aiding and abetting therein. And as—if A, B, C, and D, were jointly guilty of having each with his own hand committed a crime—an indictment would be good which charged A, B, and C, and omitted D, altogether—and A, B, and C, could be thereupon convicted, though it appeared in evidence that D, was a participant in their guilt—so an indictment is good, which charges A, with having committed the guilty fact and B, and C, with being present aiding and abetting therein, though it appear in evidence that D, a person not named in the indictment, committed the felony, and that A, B, and C, were all, only present and aiding and abetting him therein—and: A, B, and C, under such an indictment, may be lawfully convicted.

The Court will observe, on looking into the charge and specification now before them, that Tolar is charged with having fired the pistol, the bullet from which slew Archy Beebee; and that the prisoners Powers and Watkins, together with Phillips and McRae, are charged with being feloniously present aiding and abetting in the murder. We might with equal propriety have charged all the defendants named in the charge with having *fired the pistol*, the bullet from which slew the deceased. The legal effect and operation of the two forms of charge are the same. Now it is evident, to the humblest understanding, if we had selected the latter form of charge, it would have been no objection to convicting Tolar, Watkins and Powers, that we had proved Phillips *guilty* as well as the three others just named—or that we had failed in the proof against Phillips and McRae—or that it appeared in evidence, that other persons not named in the charge were participants in the crime, as well as the three prisoners at the bar.

Counsel for accused, (Mr. Fuller): Since McRae and Phillips are, to all intents and purposes, out of the indictment, I would like you to discuss before the Court whether, if they become satisfied that a person not now charged in the bill of indictment be guilty of the murder, they can convict these persons.

Counsel for prosecution, (Mr. Haywood): I will show the Court express authority upon the point I understand my brother Fuller to make—which is—whether the Court are at liberty to convict Tolar, Watkins and Powers, *under this charge and specification*, if they are satisfied that all three of the prisoners named were present, aiding and abetting in the felony, but that the immediate proximate act which caused death was the work of *some third person not named in the charge and specification ;* but I cannot assent to brother Fuller's proposition that "McRae and Phillips are, to *all* intents and purposes, out of the indictment."

It is true, *they themselves* are out of this trial—but their *names* remain in the charge and specification—and so far as they affect the prisoners now on trial, the allegations against McRae, and Phillips, originally set forth in the charge, &c., *remain in full force*, and are *as valid*, as if McRae and Phillips had never been released and were now on trial. If for *any reason*, it were essential to the validity of the *form* of this charge and specification, as against Tolar, Watkins and Powers, that they should contain an allegation, that, McRae and Phillips were or, that McRae was, or that Phillips was, feloniously present, aiding and abetting Tolar in Beebee's murder—the fact that the Government has seen fit to enter a *nol pros* as to McRae and Phillips, does not remove the allegation of their participation in the crime charged, from the form of the charge and specification—that allegation still remains in the charge and specification, as part of the allegations against the prisoners at the bar ; just as it might have been inserted, though McRae and Phillips had never been put upon trial at all, or though they had already been put upon trial and acquitted or convicted.

So, if this Court shall arrive at the conclusion that *Phillips fired the pistol* which killed Beebee, and I produce authorities to the effect—that on an indictment against A, B, C, and D, charging that A did the criminal act, and that B, C, and D, were feloniously present, aiding and abetting him therein— and proof that *D did the act*, and *A, B, and C, were feloniously present and aiding and abetting him*—there is no valid objection, on account of the form of indictment, to the conviction of A, B; and C—I shall have produced express authority, to justify this Court in convicting Tolar, Watkins and Powers under this charge and specification, if the Court believes that they were feloniously present, aiding, and abetting Phillips in the murder—even though the government has seen fit to enter a *nol pros* as to Phillips.

I have merely noted the suggestion of my brother Fuller—that the effect of the *nol pros* was to remove from the charge and specification the allegations against McRae and Phillips—in passing—to show my dissent therefrom ; and for fear that I may not satisfy the Court upon all the points of law which I make in this connection, and that *they* may think, there is some view of the law in this case, which renders it a matter of importance, that the charge and specification should contain an allegation, that Phillips was a participator in the criminal fact charged. But for myself, I think it entirely immaterial to a conviction of Tolar, Watkins and Powers under this charge, whether the charge contains an allegation of Phillips' participation or not—whether the effect of the *nol pros*, was to *strike out* of the charge and specification all the allegations against McRae and Tolar, for all purposes and intents, and for every purpose and intent, or not. For I shall contend, and proceed to produce authority to show, that, if the evidence satisfies this Court, that some person, not only, not now named—but some person who was never named in the charge and specification, fired the pistol, the bullet from which killed Archy Beebee, and that Tolar Powers and Watkins were feloniously present, aiding and abetting this person in the perpetration of the homicide— that then, they are bound to convict Tolar, Powers and Watkins of murder, under this charge and specification.

For where A and B are present, and A commits an offence in which B aids and assists him, the indictment may either allege the matter according to the fact, or charge them both as principals in the first degree ; for the act of one is the act of the other.

(Foster, pp. 351, 425. 2 Hale P. C., p. 344. 2 Hawkins P. C., c. 23, sec. 76. Young *vs.* Rex, 3 T. R., pp. 98, 105.)

And upon such an indictment, in either form, B who was present aiding and abetting may be *convicted, though A is acquitted.*

(Foster, p. 351. 2 Hale P. C., pp. 185, 292, 344, 345. 9 Co., p. 67. Rex *vs.* Taylor, 1 Leach, (4th Ed.) p. 360. 1 Hale P. C., pp. 437, 463. 2 Hawk. P. C., c. 46, sec. 195. Reg. *vs.* Wallis, 1 Salk., p. 334. Rex *vs.* Culkin, 5 Car. & P., p. 121.)

Again : if an indictment for murder charges that A gave the mortal stroke, and that B was present aiding and abetting, both A and B may be convicted, though it turn out that B struck the blow and that A was present aiding and abetting.

(Banson *vs.* Offley, 2 Show. p. 510. S. C., 3 Mod., p. 121. 2 Hale P. C., pp. 344, 345. Foster, p. 351. 1 Hale P. C., pp. 437, 463.)

Yet again : if an indictment for murder charges that A gave the mortal stroke, and that B was present aiding and abetting, both A and B may be convicted, though it turn out *that C, a person not named in the indictment, committed the act.*

(Rex *vs.* Plummer, J. Kel., p. 109. 1 Stark. Crim. Pl., (2d Ed.) pp. 81, 82. 1 Bishop Crim. L., sec. 596. 1 Chit. C. L., p. 260. Rex *vs.* Bortwick, 1 Doug., p. 207. 1 Bishop Crim. Pr., secs. 545, 546. State *vs.* Cockman, 2 Winst., (N. C.) p. 95. 1 East P. C., pp. 350, 351.)

And now, if it please the Court, I shall bring my remarks to a conclusion. I know I have been tedious ; to some extent, it was necessary that I should be so : the evidence has been voluminous—the trial has been a long one—and the whole case not without difficulty. I have endeavored throughout its entire progress, to be true to myself, faithful to the Government, honest with the Court, and just to the prisoners. It is for you, gentlemen of this Commission, to do the rest ; you are the judges of the law, and of the fact. It is a solemn moment for you ; it is a solemn moment for me ; it is a moment fraught with awful solemnity to these three prisoners at the bar—a moment which ought to call to all our minds that *great* day, when we must all appear before *the* judgment seat, to answer for the deeds done in the body, whether they be good, or whether they be evil. But for you, most of all, gentlemen of this Commission, is this moment awfully and intensely solemn—for you are this night invested with the highest powers that human government can entrust to mortal man. The issues of life and death are in your hands. I charge this Court *as law*—as law by which they are bound—as much bound as by the law of homicide or any other law—that if a doubt—an honest doubt—a reasonable doubt, as to the guilt of all, or any one of these prisoners at the bar—as to the proof—the full proof of any fact essential to their or any of their guilt—exist in the mind of this Court, they are bound to acquit that prisoner—or all of the prisoners if the doubt extends to all—and to give them the full benefit of the doubt. By this, I do not mean that this Court is to encourage a blind and visionary incredulity which refuses to be satisfied without the highest possible degree of proof, or the most minute particulars ; but I do mean—that the Court, before convicting, must be as fully satisfied of the guilt of each one of these defendants, as if one witness, well accredited, uncontradicted, and unimpeached, had positively sworn that he saw each one of them plant a dagger in Archy Beebee's heart. But if the Court are as well satisfied of the guilt of all these prisoners, as if their direct participation in the homicide were proved by a single well-accredited, uncontradicted and unimpeached witness—it is their duty to convict, and to leave the consequences with the higher authorities, and with God. I beg that this Court will weigh the evidence with caution ; and will consider it even with leniency towards the accused, and with a tenderness for their rights; and I am well satisfied, that this Court having so weighed and considered the evidence, calmly, and maturely—will give their decision according to the honest dictates of their own consciences.

As for my part in this prosecution—I may say in conclusion—that—on entering this, or any other Court of Justice for the performance of a professional duty—I know no friend but my client; I acknowledge no party affiliations; I recognise no social ties—no political bonds—and no personal obligations, outside of the limits of my oath, as an honest, honorable and faithful member of the legal profession; and I have no standard for the regulation of my conduct, but the laws of the land, as recognised and enforced by that Government in whose tribunal I am conducting my cause.

I commit the prisoners into the hands of the Court.

The Commission was then cleared for deliberation.

www.ingramcontent.com/pod-product-compliance
Lightning Source LLC
Chambersburg PA
CBHW032340280326
41935CB00008B/391